✔ **KT-524-006**

C015972141

Ben Box,
hris Wallace

Argentina is immense, intense and dramatic. Wherever you go, the contrasts are breathtaking. From the dry deserts of the north to the frozen landscapes of the south, you will never get bored in Argentina.

The capital, Buenos Aires, is reminiscent of a sophisticated, modern European city: life races past the grand baroque buildings at a dizzying speed, but step into a *milonga* and the mysterious rituals of the tango belong to a previous century.

In the north of the country the mighty Iguazú Falls thunder through lush jungle that is filled with electric-blue butterflies, while crumbling mission ruins lie undisturbed among the trees and vines. In the south, world-class ski resorts overlook dark, brooding lakes, and silent glaciers stretch endlessly before you, until they shatter with a roar into a milky, turquoise-blue lagoon.

And in between? Infinite space. Drive the desolate Ruta 40 through the lonely expanse of Patagonia and the only sign of life will be a couple of condors and a thousand prehistoric handprints on a cave wall. Yet throughout the country, from dusty Salta to wild Ushuaia, you'll find that the Argentine people are approachable, friendly and always welcoming.

PARAGUAY

Río Pilcomayo

Río Bermejo

4 Purmamarca
Jujuy
Santa Rosa
de Tastil
Salta

Mount
Llullaillaco
(6739m)

Cafayate

Ojos de
Salado
(6864m)

Bonete
(6759m)

Tucumán

Santiago
del Estero

Río Salado

Formosa

Puerto **7**
Iguazú

Río Alto Paraná

Resistencia

Posadas **6**

Corrientes

5

Mercedes

BRAZIL

Catamarca

La Rioja

Río Dulce

Laguna
Mar
Chiquito

Pacific
Ocean

Mercedario
(6770m)

Aconcagua
(6959m)

San Juan

2 Córdoba

Santa Fe
Paraná

Río Paraguay

Río Uruguay

URUGUAY

3

Tupungato
(6635m)

Mendoza

San Luis

Río Cuarto

Rosario

CHILE

San Rafael

BUENOS
AIRES

1

Río de
la Plata

La Plata

Chascomús

Tromen
(3978m)

Santa Rosa

Tandil

Pinamar

Río Neuquén

Neuquén

Río Colorado

Bahía
Blanca

Mar del Plata

Lanín
(3768m)

Río Limay

San Martín
de los Andes

Río Negro

Lago Nahuel
Huapí

Tronador
(3478m)

Bariloche
El Bolsón

Viedma

Puerto
Madryn

9

8 Esquel

Gaiman
Río Chubut

Trelew

Atlantic
Ocean

Lago
Buenos
Aires

Comodoro
Rivadavia

Perito
Moreno

Río Deseado

Puerto
Deseado

Lago San
Martín

11 El Chaltén

Fitz Roy
(3405m)

Lago Viedma

Puerto
San Julián

Lago Argentino

10 El Calafate

Falkland Islands/
Islas Malvinas

Río Gallegos

Puerto
Natales

Darwin

Punta
Arenas

Río Grande

Tierra del Fuego

CHILE

12

Ushuaia

N

200 km

200 miles

Baby elephant seal, Península Valdés

Don't miss...

See colour maps at end of book

Córdoba Cathedral

Itineraries for Argentina

ITINERARY ONE: One week
Buenos Aires and Iguazú

The essentials for any trip are the bright lights of Buenos Aires and the stunning Iguazú Falls. Buenos Aires is a great first port of call, whether you want to see the football, try tango or shop till you drop, and to get any sense of the city you need a minimum of three days. Then take an overnight bus (16 hours), or a more expensive but much quicker flight, to Iguazú Falls. These are the country's star attraction and should not be missed. Two days is sufficient to see both the Argentine and Brazilian sides of the falls, or better still allow two days to explore the larger Argentine park in more detail. Then, return to Buenos Aires in order to relax in the fantastic Hostelling International (HI) hostel in the delta river system just north of the city. Alternatively, if you've money to spare, spend the weekend at one of the grandiose *estancias* close to the capital, where you can ride horses, play sports, swim or just relax in the sun.

ITINERARY TWO: Two weeks
Mountains and glaciers

This itinerary is best suited to the warmer months (November to March); if you visit the glacier at other times take plenty of warm clothes! Start by enjoying fast-paced Buenos Aires in all its glory for three packed days and spend a couple of days at the Iguazú Falls. Then fly, via Buenos Aires, to El Calafate in Patagonia for breathtaking views of the southern ice field. Spend at least a day staring at the 60-m-high ice walls of the immense Perito Moreno Glacier from the wooden walkways on the peninsula, then catch the four-hour bus to El Chaltén to enjoy the relatively easy four-day hikes into the mountains. Otherwise, skip El Chaltén and head across the border to Puerto Natales in Chile. From there, hire your camping equipment and head off on the 'W' circuit of the spectacular Torres del Paine National Park. You could also visit the Parque Nacional Bernardo O'Higgins. Return to Buenos Aires for a night before your journey home.

Glaciers near El Calafate

Tango, Buenos Aires

Lighthouse, Beagle Channel

ITINERARY THREE: Two weeks
The northwest

An alternative itinerary heads northwest from Buenos Aires to Salta. The city's colonial splendour contrasts perfectly with the culture of the *puna*, where Pachamama festivities are a glimpse of another time. Hire a car here or catch a local bus to Quebrada de Humahuaca, a vast red gorge dotted with ancient rock formations in astounding colours, connecting a string of little villages, including Tilcara, Humahuaca and Purmamarca. Stay at the HI hostel in Tilcara for priceless views, or head to exclusive Purmamarca for a luxury resort. From

TRAVEL TIP

Your itinerary may be dictated by the weather and the seasons: the far south is most appealing from November to March, whereas the dusty northwest can be best enjoyed from May to October when the heat is bearable.

Salta you can also visit the timeless Valles Calchaquíes, where high-altitude wine is grown in dramatic rugged landscapes. Fly back to Buenos Aires and spend one last night drinking local wine and eating *dulce de leche* pancakes.

ITINERARY FOUR: One month
Land of contrast

A month is the ideal amount of time to spend in Argentina, giving you a feel for the country's extraordinary contrasts. Start in Buenos Aires, where you'll have time to explore chic Palermo Viejo and old San Telmo with its cobbled streets. You could also visit the delta river system just north of the city. Heading north, your trip to the Iguazú Falls should be combined with a visit to the Jesuit mission ruins hidden by the thick jungle, or time in a lodge in the Esteros del Iberá wetlands.

After Iguazú, fly south to El Calafate to experience the immensity of the Perito

Purmamarca

Cueva de las Manos

Moreno Glacier. From November to March head over to El Chaltén for a few days' hiking, or cross the border into Chile to trek in the Torres del Paine National Park. From El Calafate you have time to drive the lonely Ruta 40 north to Bariloche in Ernesto 'Che' Guevara's tyre tracks. Stop off at the Cueva de las Manos to see incredibly preserved prehistoric cave paintings in the middle of nowhere. Alternatively, fly south from El Calafate to Ushuaia to see the 'End of the World'. Tierra del Fuego offers the ultimate wilderness and, as you take a boat trip along the Beagle Channel, you'll feel like a true explorer. While you're here, stay at a local *estancia* or visit one of the world's most southerly ski fields.

From Ushuaia, take a flight to picturesque Bariloche, where you'll find chalet-style hotels, chocolate shops and a backdrop of peaks. The next few days should be spent exploring the Lake District on foot and by car: enjoy the serene lakeside setting of San Martín de Los Andes; discover quiet Villa Pehuenia, surrounded by monkey puzzle trees, or fish for giant trout at Junín de los Andes; head south to laid-back El Bolsón for superb hiking in the 2000-year-old forests of Los Alerces National Park or catch the Old Patagonian Express into the hills.

Moving on, head north by bus to Mendoza to visit the nearby vineyards and do a winery tour, before travelling to Córdoba to marvel at the colonial architecture and the restored Jesuit missions. Finally, make your way up to Salta in the northwest. This is another Argentina, of rich indigenous culture and ancient civilizations. Visit the Valles Calchaquíes and the Quebrada de Humahuaca, before heading back to Buenos Aires for your final night.

TRAVEL TIP
Make time in your itinerary to stay in an *estancia*, where you'll enjoy a real taste of Argentina.

Gaucho with his sheep, Patagonia

ix

Mendoza vineyards near Aconcagua

La Boca district, Buenos Aires

x

Contents

Contents

Footprint features

Essentials

Planning your trip

Best time to visit Argentina

Argentina is an appealing destination for warm, sunny holidays in the middle of the northern hemisphere winter. However, since the country covers such a vast area, there is somewhere to visit at any time of year. The southern hemisphere summer is from December to March, spring is from mid-September to November, autumn is from March to May and winter from June to August.

Before you look at when to go, start thinking about what you would like to see. Generally speaking, November to April is the best time for travelling to Mendoza, San Juan, Córdoba, Patagonia and Ushuaia. Trekking trails are open and national parks are at their prettiest. For the rest of the country, namely Salta, Jujuy, Tucumán, Corrientes and Iguazú Falls, May to October is best, as temperatures tend to be cooler and there is less rain. Exceptions are the marine reserve at Península Valdés, which has different seasons for different animals, and also the ski resorts, whose season runs from about June to mid-October, depending on the climate.

Buenos Aires city is wonderful any time of year but is at its best in spring and autumn, when the weather is sunny and mild. The city can be hot and humid in the height of summer, with temperatures over 40°C and humidity at 80%. If you come in summer, consider spending a night in the delta or on an *estancia* to cool down.

What to do in Argentina

Birdwatching

It comes as no surprise in a country so rich in untouched natural habitats that the birdlife is extraordinary and extremely varied. From the wealth of seabirds at Península Valdés to the colourful species in the subtropical rainforest near the Iguazú Falls, from the marshlands of Esteros del Iberá or the Chaco savannah to the Lake District and the mountainous interior of Tierra del Fuego, there are marvellous opportunities to spot birds. At least 980 of the 2926 species of bird registered in South America exist in Argentina, and many birdwatching hotspots have easy access. There are specialist tours led by

expert guides in most areas; see the travelling text for details.

All Patagonia, www.allpatagonia.com, runs birdwatching trips in Patagonia and Tierra del Fuego. In the northeast, contact Daniel Samay of **Explorador Expediciones**, www.rainforestvt.com.ar. An excellent British-based tour operator that can arrange birdwatching trips is **Select Latin America**, T020-7407 1478, www.selectlatinamerica.co.uk.

Climbing

The Andes offer great climbing opportunities. Among the most popular peaks are Aconcagua in Mendoza

Packing for Argentina

You'll be able to buy most things you're likely to need once you're in Argentina, and at cheaper prices than at home in most cases (except imported goods, which are prohibitively expensive). Scan all documents, your passport and flight ticket, and email them to yourself and a friend in case there's an emergency. Carry a photocopy of your passport at all times.

Rather than keeping your digital photos on a massive memory card, use an online cloud storage service to save them, such as Dropbox, Google Drive or One Drive.

Along with your usual clothes, camera and diary, consider bringing: a light waterproof jacket, comfortable walking shoes or boots, a lightweight fleece top, a smartish set of clothes (for the occasional night at a good hotel or restaurant), a money pouch (worn under your clothes, particularly in Buenos Aires), a padlock (if you're planning to stay in hostels), suncream, insect repellent, sunglasses, a torch/flashlight (useful for walking around remote, unlit villages at night) and a folding knife (handy for picnics, but remember not to carry it in hand luggage on the plane). Carry tissues for use in bus toilets. See page 10 for a list of trekking equipment.

province, Pissis in Catamarca, and Lanín and Tronador, reached from the Lake District. The northern part of Los Glaciares National Park, around El Chaltén, has some spectacular peaks with very difficult mountaineering. Climbing clubs can be found in Mendoza, Bariloche, Esquel, Junín de los Andes, Ushuaia and other cities, and in some places equipment can be hired. **Club Andino**, www.caba.org.ar.

Fishing

Argentina offers some of the world's finest fishing, in beautiful virgin landscape, and with good accommodation. In the Lake District, there's world-renowned fly fishing for trout (rainbow, brown and brook) and for chinook or landlocked salmon. The centre is around Junín de los Andes and Bariloche, in rivers Quilquihue,

Chimehuín, Collón-Curá, Meliquina and Caleufú, and lakes Traful, Gutiérrez, Mascardi, Cholila, Futalaufquén (in Los Alerces National Park), Falkner, Villarino; Huechulafquén, Paimún, Epulafquén, Tromen (all in Lanín National Park); and, in the far north, Quillén. In the Lake District, the season lasts usually from Nov to Apr.

In Tierra del Fuego, huge brown trout can be fished from Río Grande and Lago Fagnano, while over the border in Chilean Tierra del Fuego, Lago Blanco is fast becoming popular. In the northeast, *sorubim* and giant *pacu* can be fished at the confluence of rivers Paraná and Paraguay, as well as *dorado*, known for its challenging fight. The closed season in this area is Nov to Jan. On the Atlantic coast, San Blas is famous for shark fishing, for bacota shark and bull shark weighing up to 130 kg, while all along the coast, there's good sea fishing. Fishing can also be found in other parts of the country and is offered by many *estancias*. *Pejerrey*, *corvina* and *pescadilla* can be found in large quantities along the coast of Buenos Aires province, and many of the reservoirs of the Central Sierras, the West and Northwest are well stocked. All rivers are 'catch and release' and to fish anywhere in Argentina, you need a permit.

Fly Fishing Association of Argentina, T011-4773 0821, for fishing licences. In Patagonia, there's assistance from the **National Parks Administration**, T011-4311 8853/0303.

Horse riding

In a country that boasts the top 10 polo players in the world, the tradition of horse treks and horse riding is alive and strong. Offered all through the country, from Salta in the north to El Calafate in the south, horse-riding tours, or *cabalgatas*,

vary in length and in quality. Generally speaking, if you visit an *estancia* or working farm that offers horse riding you'll find healthy horses, huge expanses of land and the wind whistling through your hair. If you go with adventure tourism agencies, you may have an English-speaking guide more suited to beginners. Choose the best option to suit your level of experience. One of the most challenging and spectacular horse treks traces the path that General San Martín and his soldiers took across the Andes near San Juan. Reaching up to 4000 m, and scaling the cliff edge, the five-day ride uses donkeys due to the harsh terrain.

www.estanciasargentinas.com will help locate *estancias* that offer horse riding.

Skiing

The ski season runs from mid-Jun to mid-Oct, but dates vary between resorts. The country's best and deservedly most famous is Las Leñas, south of Mendoza, due to its long, varied and challenging pistes, its spectacular setting, superb accommodation, and also for having a dedicated snowboarding area. It's also the most expensive resort, so if you're looking for a cheaper option in the same area, consider Los Penitentes, a more modest but friendly resort. There's good skiing all along the Lake District, with the biggest centre at Cerro Catedral, near Bariloche. This is a huge resort with scope for cross-country skiing and snowboarding, and the advantages of a major town with excellent hotels and services. Nearby, the smaller but upmarket resorts of Cerro Bayo at Villa la Angostura and Cerro Chapelco at San Martín de los Andes have even more beautiful settings and cater for families. La Hoya, near Esquel, is much cheaper with a laid-back family feel. And at the

Tango

What was once the dance of immigrants from the Buenos Aires dockyards is now one of the most internationally recognizable aspects of Argentine culture. At the turn of the 19th century, the tango was seen as a dance practised by the lower classes in the streets and in brothels. And it wasn't until Argentine sailors brought it to Europe through French ports that it started to become acceptable in polite society in Buenos Aires. A little later, in 1913, Europe was officially in the grips of a tango craze. In London, the Waldorf Hotel introduced Tango Teas in the same vein as the French *Thés Dansants*, and Selfridges held a successful Tango Ball. In Paris, women's fashion was influenced by the dance, and shops sold tango stockings, tango hats and tango shoes. Even silent film star Rudolph Valentino danced it on-screen in 1921. Around this time, famous tango singer Carlos Gardel (whose name and face you'll see throughout Buenos Aires) toured South America as well as Paris, Barcelona, Madrid and New York. The so-called Golden Era for tango was from the 1930s to 1955 when a military coup ousted the president. From then onwards until the early 1980s, tango was in decline. It was ignored and even persecuted during the military dictatorship. Young people no longer wanted to dance it, and nearly two generations of Argentines grew up without learning it. However, after years of neglect, the Argentine people have re-embraced the dance at all levels. One more influence is fuelling this vibrant resurgence; the hundreds of tourists from around the world who arrive every year anxious to learn, practise and live the dance. A recent movement, which is causing a small sensation, is gay tango, known as Tango Queer. Several gay *milongas* have started up and there is a constant stream of dancers eager to learn the sexy steps. Each year in August, Buenos Aires hosts a tango festival, which boasts the best international and local dancers, free displays, classes and the sale of all things tango.

Useful websites

www.welcomeargentina.com/tango/lugares.html For an overview of tango shows available.
www.tangodata.gov.ar Fantastic government website listing *milongas*, classes and shows.
www.festivaldetango.gov.ar Everything you'll need to know about the annual Buenos Aires tango festival.
www.festivaltangoqueer.com.ar Official website for the Queer Tango Festival in Buenos Aires.
www.history-of-tango.com A comprehensive look at the history of the dance.
www.la2x4.gov.ar Website for tango radio station.

end of the world, in Ushuaia, there's great cross-country and downhill skiing at Cerro Castor. Details of all of these resorts are given in the text, together with websites.

www.welcomeargentina.com/ski and www.allaboutar.com/sports_skiing.htm are useful for general information on all resorts.

Six of the best treks

Aconcagua

Less than 200 km from Mendoza, Aconcagua National Park is home to the highest peak in the world outside the Himalaya. The mighty Aconcagua scrapes the sky at 6959 m and should only be attempted by experienced climbers with a guide. Allow at least eight days to acclimatize to the altitude before you attempt this trek, and speak to the park rangers about a permit. For more information, see www.aconcagua.mendoza.gov.ar.

Cerro Colorado

The Argentine Lake District links seven large beautiful lakes with camping grounds and trekking trails. Lush green vegetation, unspoilt geography and mirror-perfect lakes attract hordes of trekkers each year. The best thing to do is search out less crowded trekking areas. North of San Martín de los Andes, the trail to Cerro Colorado (1774 m), named for its bright red soil, is less travelled and therefore more attractive. The trek is intermediate, and takes about five to six hours return. More information can be found at www.parquesnacionales.gov.ar.

El Chaltén

Nestled in between jagged peaks and snow-laden valleys, El Chaltén is the perfect base for treks in the area. Follow the signs from the edge of town, and in less than 30 minutes you'll be all alone on a mountain pass overlooking deep blue lakes and fertile valleys. Return to your hostel and relax in one of the lively restaurants in town. The routes range from easy two-hour walks to challenging multi-day treks. A helpful website is www.elchalten.com.

La Cumbrecita

Located in the heart of Córdoba province, La Cumbrecita is a small

Trekking

The whole of the west of the country, along the mountains of the Andes, offers superb opportunities for trekking. The Lake District in summer is the most rewarding because there are so many spectacular landscapes to explore within easy reach of the centres of Bariloche, El Bolsón and San Martín de los Andes. The national parks here are well set up for walkers, with good information and basic maps available, and *refugios* and campsites that provide convenient accommodation on longer hikes. However, it's worth exploring the lesser-

known extremes of the lakes, at Pehuenia in the north, with wonderful walks among the araucaria trees, and at Parque Nacional Los Alerces, with trekking into the virgin forest. All these walks are described in detail in the relevant areas. The season for walking is Dec to Apr.

The mountainous region to the west of Mendoza, around Aconcagua, offers good and challenging trekking, as well as further north in the Cordón del Plata in San Juan, where oasis villages in the valley are good bases for several peaks around Mercedario. Altitude sickness (see Health, page 35) can be a problem in these areas, and you should allow town best accessed on foot. No cars or motorcycles are allowed into the village, and this simple rule creates a peaceful getaway. What you will see is lots of thirsty trekkers looking for some of the locally brewed beers. You can walk here from the German-style town of Villa General Belgrano and from some of the other little towns nearby as well. This is an easy to intermediate trek. The village's website has lots of useful information: www.lacumbrecita.gov.ar.

Perito Moreno National Park

If you are a lover of all things remote and inaccessible, head to the Perito Moreno National Park, just off the Ruta 40. Tours to the park are increasing, but it may be easiest to rent a car. The best trek to do is to Lago Burmeister, which is easy, relatively short and offers stunning views of the lake as well as the pristine surrounds. You will be the only person here. Camp by the lake and watch the shadows of the mountains dance in the moonlight. Check out www.losglaciares.com.

Sendero Chorro de los Loros

Only a short distance from Salta is El Rey National Park, located in a horseshoe-shaped valley, surrounded by the peaks of the Sierra del Piquete mountain range. Few people make it here due to its remote location, ensuring clean trails, more wildlife and the chance to be alone in the wild. There are eight trails, with the most interesting being the Sendero Chorro de los Loros, which takes you through the jungle for 10 km and brings you up close and personal with the local wildlife. This is an intermediate trek. See www.welcomeargentina.com/parques/elrey.html, for more details.

time in your schedule for adjustment. Further north, in Salta and Jujuy, there's a complete contrast of landscape. The *puna* to the west is dramatic desert, dropping to the arid and rocky mountainous landscape in the Quebrada de Humahuaca and, continuing east, there are cloudforests. It's possible to walk through all 3 zones in a single extended expedition, though you'd need to go with a guide. Throughout the area there are attractive villages to use as bases for day walks. In the northeast, there are a few good walks in the national park of the Iguazú Falls, and many more good places to walk in the provinces to the south. The centre of the country, in the sierras around Córdoba, are good for day walks, especially in the Traslasierra. In Patagonia, there are petrified forests and caves with pre-historic handprints to walk to, as well as the remoter reaches of Parque Nacional Perito Moreno. The most dramatic trekking is in the south of Patagonia, whether in the mountains around Cerro Fitz Roy or ice trekking on the glaciers themselves in Parque Nacional Los Glaciares. And near Ushuaia, there are unforgettable views from peaks in the Parque Nacional Tierra del Fuego, along the shores of the Beagle Channel and from wilder peaks in mountains behind the town.

These are the highlights, but wherever you go in Argentina, you can find somewhere to trek. The spaces are wide open and there really are no limits.

Shops in large towns in Argentina stock clothes and camping supplies, but the following are things to consider taking. **Clothing**: a warm hat (wool or man-made fibre), wicking thermal underwear, T-shirts/shirts, trousers (quick-drying and preferably windproof), warm (wool or fleece) jumper/jacket (preferably 2), gloves, waterproof jacket and overtrousers (preferably Gore-Tex), shorts, walking boots and socks, change of footwear or flip-flops. **Camping gear**: tent (capable of withstanding high winds), sleeping mat (closed cell, Karrimat, or inflatable, Thermarest), sleeping bag (3-season minimum), sleeping bag liner, stove and spare parts, fuel, matches and lighter, cooking and eating utensils, pan scrubber, survival bag. **Food**: take supplies for at least 2 days more than you plan to use; tea, coffee, sugar, dried milk, porridge, dried fruit, honey, soup, pasta, rice, soya (TVP), fresh fruit and vegetables, bread, cheese, crackers, biscuits, chocolate, salt, pepper, other herbs and spices, cooking oil. **Miscellaneous**: map and compass, torch and spare batteries, pen and notebook, Swiss army knife, sunglasses, sun cream, lip salve and insect repellent, first-aid kit, water bottle and towel.

Hikers have little to fear from the animal kingdom apart from insects, and robbery and assault are very rare. You are more of a threat to the environment than vice versa.

Note It's best not to go hiking alone, as hiking areas in Argentina are generally far less visited than those in Europe, and if you twist an ankle, it might be a long time before someone finds you. So try to join up with other people, and always register with *guardaparques* (rangers) before you set off.

Visit **www.parquesnacionales.gov.ar** for more detailed information.

Whitewater rafting

There are some good whitewater-rafting runs in Mendoza province, near the provincial capital and near San Rafael and Malargüe. In the Lake District there are possibilities in the Lanín, Nahuel Huapi and Los Alerces national parks.

Getting to Argentina

Air

Flights from Europe
There are flights to Buenos Aires from London, Amsterdam, Barcelona, Madrid, Frankfurt, Paris, Milan, Rome and Zurich with **Aerolíneas Argentinas** ① *Flighthouse, Fernhill Rd, Horley, Surrey, RH6 9SY, T0871-644 4453 or 0800-0969 747, www.aerolineas. com.ar*, and other European carriers. From Britain, only **British Airways** goes direct to Buenos Aires, and has been repeatedly recommended for comfort and service.

Flights from North America and Canada
Aerolíneas Argentinas and other South American and North American airlines fly from Miami, New York, Washington, Los Angeles, San Francisco, Atlanta, Dallas and Chicago. **Air Canada** and **LAN** fly from Toronto and Montreal.

Flights from Australasia and South Africa
Aerolíneas Argentinas, **LAN** and **Qantas** fly from Sydney (Australia), via Auckland (New Zealand) or Santiago (Chile), several times a week. **South African Airways** fly four times a week from Johannesburg, via Sao Paulo.

Flights from Latin America
Aerolíneas Argentinas and other carriers fly between Buenos Aires and all the South American capitals, plus Santa Cruz and Cochabamba in Bolivia and Guayaquil in Ecuador. Several flights between Buenos Aires, Rio de Janeiro and São Paulo stopover in Porto Alegre, Florianópolis and Curitiba. There are also flights from Belo Horizonte, Salvador, Recife and Fortaleza, Havana, Mexico City and Cancún.

General tips
Check your baggage allowance as airlines vary widely. The limit is usually between 20 and 32 kg per person for economy class, strictly enforced with high charges for excess baggage. You must check with your airline for its rules. For internal flights in Argentina, the baggage limit with **Aerolíneas Argentinas** is 15 kg, and they are extremely inflexible, also charging wildly for excess. This means you will either have to leave some things in your hotel in Buenos Aires, or consider limiting your baggage to 15 kg when you leave home.

Airport information
All flights from outside Argentina, apart from those from neighbouring countries, arrive at Ezeiza International Airport (officially known as Ministro Pistarini), situated 35 km southwest of Buenos Aires (for detailed information including transport to Buenos Aires, see page 51). All internal flights as well as some flights to or from neighbouring countries come to Jorge Newbery Airport, generally known as

Aeroparque, situated 4 km north of the centre of Buenos Aires on the bank of the Río de la Plata (see page 51 for details). Most provincial airports have a desk offering tourist information, banking facilities and a *confitería* (cafeteria) as well as car hire. There are usually minibus services into the city and taxis are available. For details of airport tax, see page 42.

Entry fee

In 2010 Argentina introduced entry fees for citizens of those countries that require Argentines to obtain a visa and pay an entry fee, namely Australia (US$100, valid one year), Canada (CAD$100, valid 10 years) and the US (US$160, valid 10 years). This fee is only payable by credit card online before arrival. You must print the receipt and present it to immigration wherever you enter the country. Go to www.migraciones. gov.ar or www.provinciapagos.com.ar for instructions.

Prices and discounts

Fares vary considerably from airline to airline, so it's worth checking with an agency for the best deal for when you want to travel. The cheap-seat allocation will sell out quickly in holiday periods. The busiest seasons for travelling to Argentina are 7 December to 15 January, Easter, and 1 July to 10 September, when you should book as far ahead as possible. There might be special offers available from February to May and September to November.

Road

There are many entry points from neighbouring countries, and with good long-distance bus services, this is a convenient way of entering Argentina if you're travelling around. The main routes are as follows: in the west from Santiago (Chile) to Mendoza; in the northwest from Villazón (Bolivia) to Jujuy and Salta; in the northeast from Asunción (Paraguay) to Resistencia, from Encarnación (Paraguay) to Posadas, and from Foz do Iguazú (Brazil) to Puerto Iguazú; in the Lake District by boat and bus from Puerto Montt (Chile) to Bariloche; in Patagonia by road from Puerto Natales (Chile) to El Calafate or by road and ferry crossings from Tierra del Fuego to Río Gallegos and El Calafate. There are also three road crossings from Uruguay via bridges over the Río Uruguay, as well several ferry crossings, the most important of which are from Montevideo and Colonia de Sacramento to Buenos Aires. For more information on border crossing, see the boxes in individual chapters.

Sea

It's possible to cruise to Argentina and there are some luxurious options available, as well as more basic freight travel options. Contact a specialist agency, such as Strand Travel in London, www.strandtravel.co.uk, or www.cruise-locators.com, who have information on all cruise lines.

Transport in Argentina

Air

Internal air services are run by **Aerolíneas Argentinas (AR)** ① *T0810-222 86527, www.aerolineas.com.ar,* **Austral** (part of AR), **LAN** ① *T0810-999 9526, within Chile T600-526 2000, www.lan.com,* and the army airline **LADE** (in Patagonia, Buenos Aires, Córdoba and Paraná) ① *T0810-810 5233, www.lade.com.ar;* its flights are booked up ahead of time. **Sol** ① *T0810-444 4765, www.sol.com.ar,* flies to cities in the centre of the country and, seasonally, to coastal destinations, the far south and Uruguay. **Andes** ① *T0810-777-26337, www.andesonline.com,* based in Salta, flies between Buenos Aires and Salta, Jujuy and Puerto Madryn.

All internal flights are fully booked way in advance for travel in December and January. Outside busy periods, it's usually possible to book internal flights with just a few days' notice, though note that flights to Ushuaia are always heavily booked. It's wise to leave some flexibility in your schedule to allow for bad weather, which may delay flights in the south, at El Calafate and Ushuaia. Meals are rarely served on internal flights, though you'll get a hot drink and a cake.

Airpasses
Airpasses allow you to pre-book between three to six internal flights at a discount, as long as your international flight is also with that company. Aerolíneas Argentinas has a Visite Argentina internal airpass which offers domestic flights at cheaper rates than those bought individually. Details can be found on www.aerolineas. com.ar: go to the 'Cheap flights' menu. You can buy from three to 12 coupons for a maximum of 90 days. Coupons cost from US$150 to US$220 each, depending on whether they're for north and central Argentina, or for Patagonia. It is unwise to set too tight a schedule because of delays caused by bad weather, or flight cancellations or postponements. LAN offers a multi-country airpass that includes Argentina; see www.lan.com. Airpasses are no longer the cheapest way of getting around, and can be very restricting since you have to book all dates when you book your international ticket. You'll probably find it easier to book internal flights separately. But check with the airlines directly, in case they have a promotion.

Road

Bus
This enormous country is connected by a network of efficient long-distance buses, which are by far the cheapest way of getting around, as well as being more environmentally friendly than plane travel. They are safe and comfortable, and long journeys are travelled overnight, which saves time, as long as you can sleep. There are three levels of service: *común*, which offers little comfort for overnight buses,

and with lots of stops (*intermedio*); *semi-cama*, with a slightly reclining seat; and *coche-cama*, where seats recline (some almost completely flat) and there are few stops. On *semi-cama* and *coche-cama* services videos will be shown (usually action movies, very loud, just as you're about to go to sleep), and meals will be provided. This might be anything from a *sandwich de miga* (very soft white bread with a slice of cheese and ham) to a full meal, with wine and a pudding. There will also be a toilet on board (of dubious cleanliness), and the bus will usually stop somewhere en route for toilets and food. The difference in price between the services is often small, and *coche-cama* is most definitely worth the extra for a good night's sleep. On long bus journeys it's a good idea to bring: water, both to drink and for brushing your teeth, as the water in the toilet usually runs out; tissues or toilet roll; toothbrush and toothpaste; fruit or snacks, and a sandwich. Whatever you do, avoid being downstairs as, although the larger seats are down there, they are right next to the toilet and the main door both of which are in constant use throughout the night. Ask the bus company to order you a vegetarian meal, if you want one, at least 24 hours before the scheduled departure.

Local buses are to be recommended too: since many Argentines rely on public transport, buses run to small villages and places in mountains, steppe or *puna*. Services are less frequent, but worth waiting for, to get off the beaten track and completely away from other tourists. Information on frequency and prices is given in the text where possible, but services may change, so it's worth ringing the bus terminal to check.

Bus companies may give a 20% discount if you show an international student card (or ISIC card), and this may also be available to teachers and university professors if they provide proof of employment. Note that discounts aren't usually available December to March. You can request the seat you want when you book; on old buses, seats at the back can be intolerably noisy with air conditioning (take a jumper in summer, since the air conditioning can be fierce). Make sure your seat number is on your ticket. Luggage is safely stored in a large hold at the back of the bus, and you'll be given a numbered ticket to reclaim it on arrival. It's always a good idea to lock your bags. *Maleteros* take the bags off the bus, and expect a small tip – 50 centavos or a peso is fine (many Argentines refuse to pay).

Bus company websites www.andesmar.com.ar and www.viabariloche.com.ar are useful for route planning across Argentina. Another great site to help you plan your journey is www.plataforma10.com. You can check bus prices and times, and can also book tickets for buses all over Argentina.

Car

You'll need a credit card to hire a car, since companies take a print of the card as their guarantee, instead of a deposit. You'll be required to show a drivers' licence (just the plastic bit of a British licence) and minimum age for renting is 25 (private arrangements may be possible). You must ensure that the renting agency gives you ownership papers of the vehicle, which have to be shown at police and military checks, and if you plan to take the car over a border into Chile or Bolivia, for example, you must let the hire company know, as they'll need to arrange special papers for

Responsible travel in South America

Since the early 1990s there has been a phenomenal growth in tourism that promotes and supports the conservation of natural environments and is also fair and equitable to local communities. While the authenticity of some ecotourism operators' claims needs to be interpreted with care, there are a great many whose aims and credentials are laudable and we try to highlight these in the book.

Try to balance the negative aspects of travel with positives by following these guidelines:

Cut your emissions Plan an itinerary that minimizes carbon emissions whenever possible. This might involve travelling by train, hiring a bike or booking a walking or canoeing tour. See below for details of carbon offset programmes. Visit www.seat61.com for worldwide train travel.

Check the small print Choose travel operators that abide by a responsible travel policy (it will usually be posted on their website). www.responsibletravel.com.

Visit local Try to use public transport, stay in locally owned accommodation, eat in local restaurants, buy local produce and local guides.

Waste Take biodegradable soap, shampoo and leave excess packaging, particularly plastics, at home. Find out if there are any charities or voluntary projects that you could include on your itinerary. For a list of projects that benefit from your support, see www.yourrucksack.com.

Learn the lingo Practise some local words. Respect local customs and dress codes and always ask permission before photographing people. Once you get home, remember to honour any promises you've made to send photographs.

Avoid the crowds Consider travelling out of season to relieve pressure on popular destinations, or visit a lesser-known alternative.

Take only photos Resist the temptation to buy souvenirs made from animals or plants. For more information, refer to CITES, the Convention on International Trade in Endangered Species (www.cites.org) and the Coalition Against Wildlife Trafficking (www.cawtglobal.org).

Use water wisely Water is a precious commodity in many countries. Treating your own water avoids the need to buy bottled water. If you don't carry water treatment equipment, support places that encourage the reuse of plastic bottles.

Don't interfere Avoid disturbing wildlife, damaging habitats or interfering with animals' natural behaviour. Leave plants and shells where you find them.

Code green for hikers and campers
- Take biodegradable soap, shampoo and toilet paper, long-lasting lithium batteries and plastic bags for packing out all rubbish.
- Use a water filter instead of buying bottled water.
- Keep to trails. Don't take short cuts, especially at high altitude where plants may take years to recover.
- If possible, use an existing campsite.

Driving in Argentina

Roads Only 29% of Argentina's roads are paved. Most main roads are rather narrow but roadside services are good. To avoid flying stones on gravel and dirt roads, don't follow trucks too closely, overtake with plenty of room, and pull over and slow down for oncoming vehicles. You'll find that most people won't use their indicator or brakes regularly, and the horn frequently. Most main roads have private tolls about every 100 km, US$0.20-1.50. Unprivatized secondary roads are generally poor. Internal checkpoints prevent food, vegetable and meat products from entering Patagonia, Mendoza, San Juan, Catamarca, Tucumán, Salta and Jujuy provinces.

Road safety All motorists are required to carry two warning triangles, a fire extinguisher, a tow rope or chain, and a first-aid kit. The handbrake must be fully operative and seat belts must be worn. Headlights must be on during the day in Buenos Aires province.

Documents Full car documentation must be carried (including an invoice for the most recently paid insurance premium) together with your international driving licence.

Organizations Automóvil Club Argentino (ACA), Avenida Libertador Gen San Martín 1850, Buenos Aires, T011-4808 4000 or T0800-888 9888, www.aca.org.ar, has a travel-documents service, car service facilities and road maps. Foreign automobile clubs with reciprocity with ACA are allowed to use facilities and discounts (with a membership card). ACA accommodation comprises: Motel, Hostería, Hotel and Unidad Turística, and they also organize campsites. All have meal facilities of some kind.

Car hire The minimum age for renting a car is usually 25, and a credit card is required. Prices range from US$50-100 a day, with the highest prices in Patagonia. In tourist centres such as Salta, Bariloche or Mendoza it may be easier and cheaper to hire a taxi for the day.

Fuel Petrol/gasoline (*nafta*) costs on average US$0.75 a litre and US$0.55 for diesel. Cars are being converted to *gas natural comprimido* (GNC), which costs around 25% cheaper than *nafta* but filling stations are further away.

you to show, and the car must have the number plate etched on its windows. The multinational car hire companies (**Hertz, Avis**) are represented all over Argentina, along with Brazilian company **Localiza**, who are very reliable. Local companies may be cheaper, but check the vehicles carefully. Details of car hire companies are given in the Transport sections throughout the book.

Security Car theft has become common in Buenos Aires, much less so in the rest of the country, but park the car in busy well-lit places, where possible throughout the country. Always remove all belongings and leave the empty glove compartment open when the car is unattended to reduce temptation. In tourist areas, street children will offer to guard your car, worth 50 centavos, or outside restaurant areas in cities, there may be a man guarding cars for a peso. It's worth paying, though doesn't guarantee anything.

Cycling

If you have the time, cycling offers you one of the most rewarding ways to explore Argentina. You can get to all of the out-of-the-way places and enjoy some exhilarating rides, especially in the Andes – anywhere between Salta to El Calafate, with some breathtaking and hair-raising rides in the Lake District in between. Travelling by bike gives you the chance to travel at your own pace and meet people who are not normally in contact with tourists. There's little traffic on the roads in much of the country, which are wide enough to let trucks pass with ease in most places. The challenges are the enormous distances, the fact that there are few places to stop for food and drink in much of the country, and the lack of shade.

Main roads are paved, apart from the famous Ruta 40 in its southern half, and many roads into rural areas, which are gravel. For these, a mountain bike is advisable. Bring a comprehensive tool kit and spares. Bike shops are few and far between, although there are excellent shops in the Lake District, for example. Consider hiring bikes here if you just want some gentle riding for a few days or so. It goes without saying that you'll need tough waterproof panniers and clothing.

Useful tips Wind, not hills, will be your biggest enemy when cycling in Argentina. Try to make the best use of the mornings when wind speeds are lowest. In parts of Patagonia there can be gusting winds of 80 kph around the clock at some times of year, whereas in other areas there can be none. Take care to avoid dehydration by drinking regularly, and carry the basic food staples (sugar, salt, dried milk, tea, coffee, porridge oats, raisins, dried soups, etc) and supplement these with whatever local foods can be found in the markets.

Always camp out of sight of a road. Remember that thieves are attracted to towns and cities, so when sightseeing, try to leave your bicycle with someone, such as a café owner. However, don't take unnecessary risks; always see that your bicycle is secure (most hotels will allow bikes to be kept in rooms). All over Argentina, the dogs are famous for barking at bikes and some can be vicious; carry a stick or some small stones to frighten them off. There's little traffic on most roads, but make yourself conspicuous by wearing bright clothing, and for protection, wear a helmet.

Train

The British built a fine network of railways all over the country, which gradually fell into decline through the second half of the 20th century and were dealt the final blow when control was handed over to the provinces in 1994. Few provinces had the resources to run trains and now the few tracks operating run freight trains only.

The only passenger services are within the area of Gran Buenos Aires, to Tigre with **Tren de la Costa**, T011-3220 6300, and a service from Buenos Aires Constitución station south through the Pampas to the coast: via Chascomús to Mar del Plata,

Necochea and Tandil, run by **Ferrobaires**, T0180-666 8736. There is only one long-distance train line, from Buenos Aires to Tucumán with **TUFESA**: long, uncomfortable and not recommended. The only other train services are the tourist **Tren a las Nubes**, www.trenalasnubes.com.ar, which runs from Salta up to San Antonio de los Cobres in the *puna*, and the narrow-gauge railway from Esquel in Patagonia, **La Trochita** (made famous by Paul Theroux as the *Old Patagonian Express*), www.patagoniaexpress.com/el_trochita.htm.

Maps

Several road maps are available, including those of the **ACA** (the most up to date), the **Firestone** road atlas and the **Automapa**, www.automapa.com.ar (regional maps, Michelin-style, high quality). The bigger cities in Argentina have just been added to Google Maps, so this will help with directions, though remember to ask a local as well, to make sure you are heading through a safe part of town.

Topographical maps are issued by the **Instituto Geográfico Militar** ① *Av Cabildo 381, Buenos Aires, T011-45765578 (1 block from Subte Ministro Carranza, Line D, or take bus 152), Mon-Fri 0800-1300, www.igm.gov.ar.* 1:500,000 sheets cost US$3 each there's better coverage on 1:100,000 and 1:250,000 sheets, but no city plans. walkers, the *Sendas y Bosques* (Walks and Forests) series are recommended. Th at 1:200,000 scale, laminated and easy to read, with good books containing F summaries, www.guiasendasybosques.com.ar.

- Before setting up camp, contact land-owners for area restrictions and permit requirements. Seek advice on sensitive areas. Always register with the appropriate authorities and advise friends or relatives of your itinerary and expected return date.
- Try to pitch your tent on non-vegetated areas, avoiding particularly sensitive habitats.
- Avoid disturbing wildlife or livestock, and avoid areas where access would cause unnecessary erosion.
- Avoid damaging historical, archaeo-logical and palaeontological sites.
- Do not dig trenches around your tent unless flash flooding is a real threat.
- For cooking use a camp stove. If you need to build a fire, use only fallen timber. Allow the fire to burn down to a fine ash. Aim to leave no trace of your fire. Be sure to observe any fire-use restrictions in place.
- If alternatives are not available, dig latrines at least 50 m from water sources, trails and camp sites. Cover the hole with natural materials and either burn or pack out your toilet paper.
- Wash clothing and cooking items well away from water sources and scatter grey water so that it filters through soil. Use biodegradable, phosphate-free soap.
- Pack out all rubbish and unused food, plus litter left by others.

Code green for ecological welfare
- Do not hire any mule or horse that is lame or has open sores from badly fitting tack.
- Avoid handling, feeding or riding on marine life or aquatic mammals.

This Handbook does not support the keeping of marine mammals (eg dolphins) in captivity.
- Choose resorts and lodges that treat sewage and support protected areas.
- Help conserve underwater and riverine environments by taking part in local clean-ups, or in diving areas collecting data for Project AWARE (www.projectaware.org).
- Choose dive operators that use mooring buoys or drift diving techniques, rather than anchors.
- Never touch coral. Practice buoyancy control skills and tuck away trailing equipment.

Offsetting carbon emissions
Carbon offsetting schemes allow you to offset greenhouse gas emissions by donating to various projects, from tree planting to renewable energy schemes. Although some conservation groups are concerned that carbon offsetting is being used as a smokescreen to delay the urgent action needed to cut emissions and develop alternative energy solutions, it remains an important way of counterbalancing your carbon footprint.

For every tonne of CO_2 you generate through a fossil fuel-burning activity such as flying, you pay for an equivalent tonne to be removed elsewhere through a 'green' initiative. There are numerous online carbon footprint calculators (such as www.carbon footprint.com). Alternatively, book with a travel operator that supports a carbon offset provider like TICOS (www.ticos.co.uk) or Reduce my Footprint (www.reducemyfootprint.travel).

Where to stay in Argentina

Hotels and guesthouses may display a star rating, but this doesn't necessarily match international standards. Many more expensive hotels charge different prices for *extranjeros* (non-Argentines) in US dollars, which is unavoidable since a passport is required as proof of residency. If you pay in cash (pesos) you may get a reduction. Room tax (VAT) is 21% and is not always included in the price (ask when you check in). All hotels will store luggage for a day, and most of the bigger hotels in cities have English-speaking staff. For upmarket chain hotels throughout Argentina contact N/A Town & Country Hotels, www.newage-hotels.com. For hostels, see **Hostelling International Argentina** ① *Florida 835, T011-4511-8723, www.hostels.org.ar, Mon-Fri 0900-1830*, which offers discounts to cardholders at their 66 hostels throughout Argentina, long-distance buses and backpacker tours. An HI card in Argentina costs US$16. For a complete listing of sleeping options, see www.welcomeargentina.com.

Hotels, hosterías, residenciales and hospedajes

The standard of accommodation in Argentina is generally good, and although prices have risen in the last two years, good hotels are generally very good value for visitors. You'll find that most cities and tourist towns list hotels and *hosterías* as separate: this is no reflection on quality or comfort, but simply on size: a *hostería* has fewer than 20 rooms. Both hotels and *hosterías* will have rooms with private bathrooms (usually showers rather than bath tubs, which you'll find only in the more expensive establishments). Prices often rise in high summer (January to February), at Easter and in July. During public holidays or high season you should always book ahead. A few of the more expensive hotels in Buenos Aires and major tourist centres such as Puerto Madryn, Bariloche and El Calafate charge foreigners higher prices than Argentines, which can be very frustrating, though there's little you can do about it. If you're given a price in US dollars, ask if there's a reduction if you pay in pesos and in cash. Most places now accept credit cards, but check before you come. It's worth booking your first few nights' accommodation before you arrive, and most hotels have an email address on their websites (provided in the Listings sections throughout the book) so that you can make contact before setting off.

Estancias

These are the large farms and cattle ranches found all over the country, many of them now open to tourists, which offer a marvellous insight into Argentine life. Gauchos still work the land on horseback in their traditional outfit of *bombachas* (baggy trousers, comfortable for spending hours in the saddle), *trensa* (a wide leather belt with silver clasps), a poncho (in the northwest), a *pañuelo* (neckerchief), a *boina* (beret) and, on the feet, *alpargatas* (simple cotton shoes). Most *estancias* are extremely comfortable places to stay and offer wonderful horse riding and other activities, such as birdwatching and walking. You'll certainly be treated to the traditional *asado*, meat cooked over an open fire, or most impressively, *asado al palo*, where the animal is speared on a cross-shaped stick and roasted

Price codes

Where to stay

$$$$ over US$150 $$$ US$66-150

$$ US$30-65 $ under US$30

Price of a double room in high season, including taxes.

Restaurants

$$$ over US$12 $$ US$7-12 $ US$6 and under

Prices for a two-course meal for one person, excluding drinks or service charge.

to perfection. There's a whole spectrum of *estancias* from a simple dwelling on the edge of a pristine lake in the Patagonian wilderness to a Loire-style chateau in the Pampas. They can seem pricey, but meals, drinks, transfers and activities are included, and it will certainly be the most memorable part of your stay. Some are accessible even to travellers on a budget, at least for a day visit. *Día de campo* (day on the farm) is offered by lots of *estancias*: a full day of horse riding, or a ride in a horse-drawn carriage, an *asado* lunch, and then often other farm activities, or time to relax in the peaceful grounds.

Though *estancias* are found throughout rural Argentina, they vary enormously in style and activities. In the province of Buenos Aires you will find *estancias* covering thousands of hectares of flat grassland with large herds of cattle and windpumps to extract water; horse riding will certainly be offered and perhaps cattle-mustering, at **Palantelén** for example. Some of the finest buildings are in this area, such as **Dos Talas** and **La Porteña**. In Patagonia there are giant sheep *estancias* overlooking glaciers, mountains and lakes, such as **Helsingfors**. There are *estancias* on Tierra del Fuego that are full of the history of the early pioneers who built them (**Viamonte** and **Harberton**), while on the mainland nearby, **Estancia Monte Dinero** has a colony of Magellanic penguins on its doorstep. There's more wildlife close at hand in the *estancias* on Península Valdés. And in Salta, there are colonial-style *fincas*, whose land includes jungly cloudforest with marvellous horse riding.

The most distinctive or representative *estancias* are mentioned in the text, but for more information see www.turismo.gov.ar (in English), the national tourist website with all *estancias* listed, and www.estanciasdesantacruz.com, a helpful agency which arranges *estancia* stays in Santa Cruz and the south, including transport. A useful book, *Turismo en Estancias y Hosterías*, is produced by **Tierra Buena**. You can, of course, contact *estancias* directly and reserve your stay, ideally with a couple of weeks' notice.

Cabañas

These are a great option if you have transport and there are at least two of you. They are self-catering cottages, cabins or apartments, usually in rural areas, and often in superb locations, such as the Lake District. They're tremendously popular among Argentine holidaymakers, who tend to travel in large groups of friends, or

Accommodation tips

Hotels

- Sometimes hotels offer cheaper deals through their websites: always check there first.
- Before you book have a look at where the hotel is located. Sometimes, such as in El Calafate, there are some fabulous hotels but they are quite a distance out of town and without a car you won't enjoy your stay quite so much.
- Note that most hotels, even the five-star hotels, do not provide tea- and coffee-making services, nor do they always have minibars.
- Two good websites for luxury hotels are www.tenriverstenlakes.com and www.designsuites.com (both in English).

Hostels

- Check the description in this guidebook, speak to other travellers or search websites like www.hostelz.com and www.tripadvisor.com, as some hostels look much better on their websites than in real life.
- In Patagonia most hostels either don't have cutlery in the kitchen or require a deposit to use it. Best to buy your own set and guard it with your life.
- In the North, the linen provided by some hostels can be old and thin. If you can, buy a pillow case and sleeping bag liner that can act as a set of sheets if need be. And don't forget the obvious things, such as a padlock, flip-flops for the shower and an indelible pen to mark your food in the kitchen.
- Some good websites for hostels are www.latinbackpackers.com, www.hostels.com, and www.hihostels.com (all in English).

of several families together, and as a result the best *cabañas* are well-equipped and comfortable. They can be very economical too, especially for groups of four or more, but are feasible even for two, with considerable reductions off-season. If you're travelling by public transport, *cabañas* are generally more difficult to get to, but ask the tourist office if there are any within walking or taxi distance. Throughout the Lake District, *cabañas* are plentiful and competitively priced.

Camping

Organized campsites are referred to in the text after the hotel listings for each town. Camping is very popular in Argentina (except in Buenos Aires) and there are many superbly situated sites, most with good services, whether municipal or private. There are many quieter, family orientated places, but if you want a livelier time, look for a campsite (often by the beaches) with younger people, where there's likely to be partying until the small hours. Camping is allowed at the side of major highways and in all national parks (except at Iguazú Falls), but in Patagonia strong winds can make camping very difficult. Wherever you camp, pack your rubbish and put out fires with earth and water. Fires are not allowed in many national parks because of the serious risk of forest fires. It's a good idea to carry insect repellent.

If taking a cooker, the most frequent recommendation is a multi-fuel stove that will burn unleaded petrol or, if that is not available, kerosene or white fuel. Alcohol-burning stoves are reliable but slow and you have to carry a lot of fuel. Fuel can usually be found at chemists/pharmacies. Gas cylinders and bottles are usually exchangeable, but if not can be recharged; specify whether you use butane or propane. Gas canisters are not always available. White gas (*bencina blanca*) is readily available in hardware shops (*ferreterías*).

Food and drink in Argentina

Asado and parrillas

Not for vegetarians! The great classic meal throughout the country is the *asado* – beef or lamb cooked expertly over an open fire. This ritual is far more than a barbecue, and with luck you'll be invited to sample an *asado* at a friend's home or *estancia* to see how it's done traditionally. *Al asador* is the way meat is cooked in the countryside, with a whole cow splayed out on a cross-shaped stick, stuck into the ground at an angle over the fire beneath. And in the *parrilla* restaurants, found all over Argentina, cuts of meat are grilled over an open fire in much the same way. You can order any cuts from the range as individual meals, but if you order *parrillada* (usually for two or more people), you'll be brought a selection from the following cuts: *achuras* – offal; *chorizos* – sausages including *morcilla* (British black pudding or blood sausage); *tira de asado* – ribs; *vacío* – flank; *bife ancho* – entrecote; *lomito* – sirloin; *bife de chorizo* – rump steak; *bife de lomo* – fillet steak. You can ask for '*cocido*' to have your meat well-done, '*a punto*' for medium, and '*jugoso*' for rare. Typical accompaniments are *papas fritas* (chips), salad and the spicy *chimichurri* sauce made from oil, chilli pepper, salt, garlic and vinegar.

Other typically Argentine meals → *See also menu reader, page 694.*

Other Argentine dishes to try include the *puchero*, a meat stew; *bife a caballo*, steak topped with a fried egg; *choripán*, a roll with a chorizo inside (similar to a hot dog, but better). *Puchero de gallina* is chicken, sausage, maize, potatoes and squash cooked together. *Milanesas*, breaded, boneless chicken or veal, are found everywhere and good value. Good snacks are *lomitos*, a juicy slice of steak in a sandwich; and *tostados*, delicate toasted cheese and tomato sandwiches, often made from the soft crustless *pan de miga*.

Italian influences

It might seem that when Argentines aren't eating meat, they're eating pizza. Italian immigration has left a fine legacy in thin crispy pizzas available from even the humblest pizza joint, adapted to the Argentine palate with some unusual toppings. *Palmitos* are tasty, slightly crunchy hearts of palm, usually tinned, and a popular Argentine delicacy, though they're in short supply and the whole plant has to be sacrificed for one heart. They're often accompanied on a pizza with the truly unspeakable *salsa golf*, a lurid mixture of tomato ketchup and mayonnaise. You'll probably prefer excellent provolone or roquefort cheeses on your pizza – both Argentine and delicious. Fresh pasta is widely available, bought ready to cook from dedicated shops. Raviolis are filled with ricotta, *verduras* (spinach), or *cuatro quesos* (four cheeses), and with a variety of sauces. These are a good option for vegetarians, who need not go hungry in this land of meat. Most restaurants have *pasta casero* – home-made pasta – and sauces without meat, such as *fileto* (tomato sauce) or pesto. *Ñoquis* (gnocchi), potato dumplings normally served with tomato sauce, are cheap and delicious (traditionally eaten on the 29th of the month).

Vegetarian

Vegetables in Argentina are cheap, of excellent quality, many of them organic, and available fresh in *verdulerías* (vegetable shops) all over towns. Look out for *acelga*, a large-leafed chard with a strong flavour, often used to fill pasta, or *tarta de verduras*, vegetable pies, which you can buy everywhere, fresh and very good. Butternut squash, *zapallo*, is used to good effect in *tartas* and in filled pasta. Salads are quite safe to eat in restaurants, and fresh, although not wildly imaginative. Only in remote areas in the northwest of the country should you be wary of salads, since the water here is not reliable. In most large towns there are vegetarian restaurants and, don't forget the wonderful vegetarian *empanadas* such as cheese and onion, spinach or mushroom (see below). Vegetarians must specify: '*No como carne, ni jamón, ni pollo*' ('I don't eat meat, or ham, or chicken'), since many Argentines think that vegetarians will eat chicken or ham, and will certainly not take it seriously that you want to avoid all meat products.

Regional specialities

The Argentine speciality *empanadas* are tasty small semicircular pastry pies traditionally filled with meat, but now widely available filled with cheese, *acelga* (chard) or corn. They originate in Salta and Tucumán, where you'll still find the best examples, but can be found all over the country as a starter in a *parrilla*, or ordered by the dozen to be delivered at home with drinks among friends.

Northwest Around Salta and Jujuy you'll find *humitas*, parcels of sweetcorn and onions, steamed in the corn husk, superb, and *tamales*, balls of cornflour filled with beef and onion, and similarly wrapped in corn husk leaves to be steamed. The other speciality of the region is *locro* – a thick stew made of maize, white beans, beef, sausages, pumpkin and herbs. Good fish is served in many areas of the country and along the east coast you'll always be offered *merluza* (hake), *lenguado* (sole), and often salmon as well.

Atlantic coast If you go to Puerto Madryn or the Atlantic coast near Mar del Plata, then seafood is a must: *arroz con mariscos* is similar to paella and absolutely delicious. There will often be *ostras* (oysters) and *centolla* (king crab) on the menu too.

Lake District The *trucha* (trout) is very good and is best served grilled, but as with all Argentine fish you'll be offered a bewildering range of sauces, such as roquefort, which rather drown the flavour. Also try the smoked trout and the wild boar. Berries are very good here in summer, with raspberries and strawberries abundant and flavoursome, particularly around El Bolsón. And in Puehuenia, you must try the pine nuts of the monkey puzzle trees: sacred food to the Mapuche people.

Northeast In the northeast, there are some superb river fish to try: *pacú* is a large, firm fleshed fish with lots of bones, but very tasty. The other great speciality is *surubí*, a kind of catfish, particularly good cooked delicately in banana leaves.

Desserts
Argentines have a sweet tooth, and are passionate about *dulce de leche* – milk and sugar evaporated to a pale, soft caramel, and found on all cakes, pastries, and even for breakfast. If you like this, you'll be delighted by *facturas* and other pastries, stuffed with *dulce de leche*, jams of various kinds, and sweet cream fillings. *Helado* (ice cream) is really excellent in Argentina, and for US$2 in any *heladería*, you'll get two flavours, from a huge range, piled up high on a tiny cone; an unmissable treat. Jauja (El Bolsón) and Persicco (Buenos Aires) are the best makes. Other popular desserts are *dulce de batata*, a hard, dense, sweet potato jam, so thick you can carve it; *dulce de membrillo* (quince preserve); *dulce de zapallo* (pumpkin in syrup). All are eaten with cheese. The most loved of all is *flan*, which is not a flan at all but crème caramel, often served on a pool of caramelized sugar, and *dulce de leche*. Every Argentine loves *alfajores*, soft maize-flour biscuits filled with *dulce de leche* or apricot jam, and then coated with chocolate, especially if they're the Havanna brand. Croissants (*media lunas*) come in two varieties: *de grasa* (savoury, made with beef fat) and *dulce* (sweet and fluffy). These will often be your only breakfast since Argentines are not keen on eating first thing in the morning (maybe because they've only just had dinner!), and only supply the huge buffet-style 'American Breakfast' in international hotels to please tourists.

Drink
The great Argentine drink, which you must try if invited, is *mate* (see box, page 26). A kind of green tea made from dried *yerba* leaves, drunk from a cup or seasoned gourd through a silver perforated straw, it is shared by a group of friends or work colleagues as a daily social ritual. The local **beers**, mainly lager-type, are excellent: Quilmes is the best seller, but look out for home-made beers from microbreweries in the lakes, especially around El Bolsón. **Spirits** are relatively cheap, other than those that are imported; there are cheap drinkable Argentine gins and whiskeys. Clericó is a white-wine **sangría** drunk in summer and you'll see lots of Argentine males drink the liquor *Fernet* with cola. It tastes like medicine but is very popular. It is best not to drink the **tap water**; in the main cities it's safe, but often heavily chlorinated. Never drink tap water in the northwest, where it is notoriously poor. Many Argentines mix soda water with their wine (even red wine) as a refreshing drink.

Wines Argentine wines are excellent and drinkable throughout the price range, which starts at US$1.50 or US$2 a bottle. Red grape varieties of Malbe, Merlot, Syrah, Cabernet Sauvignon, and the white Torrontés are particularly recommended; try brands Lurton, Norton, Bianchi, Trapiche or Etchart in any restaurant. Good

The *mate* ritual

Mate (pronounced *mattay*) is the essential Argentine drink. All over the country, whenever groups of Argentines get together, they share a *mate*. It's an essential part of your trip to Argentina that you give it a go, at least once. It's a bitter green tea made from the leaves of the *yerba mate* plant, *Ilex paraguaiensis*, and is mildly stimulating, less so than caffeine, and effective at ridding the body of toxins as well as being mildly laxative and diuretic. It was encouraged by the Jesuits as an alternative to alcohol, and grown in their plantations in the northeast of Argentina.

The *mate* container is traditionally made from a hollowed gourd, but can be made of wood or tin. There are also ornate varieties made to traditional gaucho patterns by the best silversmiths.

Dried *yerba* leaves are placed in the *mate* to just over half full, and then the whole container is shaken upside down using a hand to prevent spillage. This makes sure that any excess powder is removed from the leaves before drinking. Hot water is added to create the infusion, which is then sipped through the *bombilla*, a perforated metal straw. One person in the group acts as *cebador*, trickling fresh hot water into the *mate*, having the first sip (which is the most bitter) and passing it to each person in turn to sip. The water must be at 80-82°C (just as the kettle starts to 'sing') and generally *mate* is drunk *amargo* – without sugar. But add a little if it's your first time, as the drink is slightly bitter. When you've had enough, simply say *gracias* as you hand the *mate* back to the *cebador*, and you'll be missed out on the next round.

If you're invited to drink *mate* on your visit to Argentina, always accept, as it's rude not to, and then keep trying: it might take a few attempts before you actually like the stuff. To share a *mate* is to be part of a very special Argentine custom, and you'll delight your hosts by giving it a go.

---

sparkling wines include the *brut nature* of Navarro Correas, whose Los Arboles Cabernet Sauvignon is an excellent red wine, and Norton's Cosecha Especial. See Mendoza, page 190, and Salta, page 284, for more details.

Restaurants in Argentina

The siesta is observed nearly everywhere but Buenos Aires and some of the larger cities. At around 1700, many people go to a *confitería* for *merienda* – tea, sandwiches and cakes. Restaurants rarely open before 2100 and most people turn up at around 2230, often later. Dinner usually begins at 2200 or 2230; Argentines like to eat out, and usually bring babies and children along, however late it is. If you're invited to someone's house for dinner, don't expect to eat before 2300, so have a few *facturas* at 1700, the Argentine *merienda*, to keep you going.

If you're on a tight budget, ask for the *menú fijo* (set-price menu), usually good value, also try *tenedor libre* restaurants – eat all you want for a fixed price. Markets usually have cheap food. Food in supermarkets is cheap and good quality.

Entertainment in Argentina

Argentines, of whatever age, are generally extremely sociable and love to party. This means that even small towns have a selection of bars catering for varied tastes, plenty of live music and somewhere to dance, even if they are not the chic clubs you might be used to in Western urban cities. The point of going out here is to meet and chat rather than drink yourself under the table, and alcohol is consumed in moderation. Argentines are amazed at the quantities of alcohol that some tourists put away. If invited to an Argentine house party, a cake or *masitas* (a box of little pastries) will be just as much appreciated as a bottle of wine.

Dancing → *For further information, see Music, page 671.*

Argentines eat dinner at 2300, and then go for a drink at around 2400, so the dancing usually starts at around 0300, and goes on till 0600 or 0700. *Boliches* can mean anything from a bar with dancing, found in most country towns, to a disco on the outskirts, a taxi ride away from the centre. In Buenos Aires, there's a good range of clubs, playing the whole range from tango, salsa, and other Latin American dance music, to electronica. Elsewhere in Argentina nightclubs play a more conventional mixture of North American (lots of 80s classics) and Latin American pop with a bit of Argentine *rock nacional* thrown in, though you'll find a more varied scene in bigger cities like Córdoba, Rosario and Mendoza. **Tango** classes are popular all over the country, and especially in Buenos Aires, where *milongas* are incredibly trendy: a class followed by a few hours of dancing. Even if you're a complete novice, it's worth trying at least one class to get a feel for the steps; being whisked around the floor by an experienced dancer is quite a thrill even if you haven't a clue what to do with your legs.

Music → *For further information, see page 671.*

Live music is everywhere in Argentina, with bands playing Argentine cumbia as well as Latin American pop or jazz in bars even in small cities. The indigenous music is *folclore*, which varies widely throughout the country. Traditional gaucho music around the Pampas includes *payadores*: witty duels with guitars for two singers, much loved by Argentines, but bewildering if your Spanish is limited to menus and directions. The northwest has the country's most stirring *folclore*, where you should seek out *peñas* to see live bands playing fabulous *zambas* and *chacareras*. The rhythms are infectious, the singing passionate, and Argentine audiences can't resist joining in. Even tourist-oriented *peñas* can be atmospheric, but try to find out where the locals go, like **La Casona del Molino** in Salta. Most cities have *peñas*, and you'll often see some great bands at the gaucho **Day of Tradition** festivals (mid-November) throughout Argentina and at local town fiestas.

Festivals in Argentina

The main holiday period is January to March when all Argentine schoolchildren are on holiday and most families go away for a few weeks up to two months. All popular tourist destinations become extremely busy at this time, with foreign visitors adding to the crowds, particularly in Bariloche, El Calafate and Ushuaia. You should book transport and accommodation ahead. You'll find that most of Buenos Aires' residents leave town for the whole of January. The richest go to Punta del Este in Uruguay and the beaches in Brazil, everyone else heads to Mar del Plata and the rest of the coast. During Easter week, and the winter school holidays throughout July, hotels may also fill up fast, particularly in the ski resorts. No one works on the national holidays, and these are often long weekends, with a resulting surge of people to popular holiday places.

1 Jan New Year's Day (public holiday).
Mar/Apr Good Friday and **Easter** weekend (public holiday).
1 May Labour Day (public holiday).
25 May May Revolution of 1810 (public holiday).
10 Jun Malvinas Day (public holiday). Best not to announce it if you are British around this day.
20 Jun Flag Day (public holiday).
9 Jul Independence Day (public holiday).
17 Aug Anniversary of San Martín's death (public holiday).

12 Oct Columbus Day (public holiday).
10 Nov Día de la Tradición. There are gaucho parades throughout Argentina on the days leading up to this festival, with fabulous displays of horsemanship, gaucho games, enormous *asados* and traditional music. It's worth seeing the festivities in any small town.
25 Dec Christmas Day. Banks are closed and there are limited bus services on 25 and 31 Dec.
30 Dec (not 31 because so many offices in centre are closed). There is a ticker-tape tradition in downtown Buenos Aires.

Shopping in Argentina

Best buys
Argentine fashion and leather goods are good value; shoes, sunglasses and outdoor gear too are reasonably priced, and if you have a free afternoon in Buenos Aires, it might be worth considering buying your holiday clothes here when you arrive: head straight for Palermo Viejo.

Tax free shopping is relatively easy and it's worth following this simple procedure to get the IVA (VAT) returned to you at the airport as you leave the country: shop at places displaying the Global Refund TAX FREE sign. Before you pay, ask for the tax free refund form. The shop must fill this out for you as you pay. Keep this form, in the envelope they'll give you, together with your receipt. At the airport, after security, and before passport control, look out for the tax free kiosk. Hand them all your tax free envelopes, with the receipts, and they will give them the customs stamp. Then

Six of the best festivals

Empanada festival

Each September the *empanada* festival in Tucumán brings together the best *empanada* chefs in the country. There are cooking displays, music and, of course, the fiercely contested 'best *empanada*' competition. The region generally produces spicy *empanadas* with golden pastry. Don't eat for a week beforehand so you'll have room to fit in as many as you can. Book bus tickets and accommodation early, as this festival is popular with both tourists and locals.

Fiesta de la Tradición

To celebrate the culture and lifestyle of the Argentine gauchos, each November the population of San Antonio de Areco, a small town near Buenos Aires, swells as people arrive from far afield to attend the Fiesta de la Tradición. There are horse-riding displays, live music, stalls selling gaucho clothes and metal work, and gaucho-inspired artwork is on show. The festival concludes on 10 November with the Día de la Tradición, which pays homage to José Hernández who wrote the epic gaucho poem *Martín Fierro*.

Festival de la Luz

The Festival de la Luz (Festival of Light), each August and September in Buenos Aires, is a collaboration of more than 34 photography festivals around the world. All over the city, free exhibitions, events, conferences and workshops are held, and even the smallest of art galleries participate. It is a true celebration of the photographic arts. Look in newspapers for free events.

Fiesta Nacional de la Cereza

Situated just off the Ruta 40 in an oasis on the shores of Lago Buenos Aires, Los Antiguos is usually a sleepy country town. But come January and with the Fiesta Nacional de la Cereza (cherry festival), now nearing the ripe old age of 25, the hotels fill up, the streets crowd with cars, and people from all over Argentina come to enjoy the local produce. There are stalls selling local fruit, including cherries, and local crafts. Over the three days of the festival, the streets are never empty. Each night there are fireworks and at the end of the festival a Cherry Queen is chosen, attracting crowds of up to 30,000 people.

Oktoberfest

Attractive Villa General Belgrano in Córdoba keeps up the Oktoberfest tradition every year when the small German-style village turns into a mosh pit of beer lovers. Local beer halls fill up quickly and accommodation is really hard to find. Come for the party atmosphere and the mix of people. Don't come for a peaceful weekend away. The locally brewed beers are always a favourite.

Vendimia wine festival

The Vendimia wine festival in Mendoza lasts from January right through to the first weeks of March and involves huge flamboyant parades day and night, featuring floats carrying the 17 candidates for Harvest Queen. Some 200,000 people usually attend this event. The festival also promotes local growers and their products, as well as national musicians and artists. This festival has been celebrated for nearly 70 years and it attracts more and more people every year.

once you've gone through passport control, look for the Tax Free Refund Desk, also called Assist Card, where your stamped forms will be taken, and the tax will be refunded either in cash or to your credit card. Not all shops offer this service; the ones that do usually have a sign up. See www.globalrefund.com, for more information, or in Argentina call T011-43422413.

Argentine specialities

In Buenos Aires, leather is the best buy, with many shops selling fine leather jackets, coats and trousers, as well as beautifully made bags and shoes. With a mixture of Italian influenced design, and a flavour of the old gaucho leather-working traditions, there's a strong emerging Argentine style.

Handicrafts, *artesanía*, are available all over the country, but vary from region to region. Traditional gaucho handicrafts include woven or plaited leather belts of excellent quality, as well as key rings and other pieces made of silver. These are small and distinctive and make excellent gifts. Look out, too, for the traditional baggy gaucho trousers, *bombachas*, comfortable for days in the saddle, and ranging from cheap sturdy cotton to smart versions with elaborate tucks.

Take home a *mate*, the hollowed gourd, often decorated, and the silver *bombilla* that goes with it, for drinking the national drink (see box, page 26). In the northwest there are beautifully made woven items: brightly coloured rugs, or saddle mats, and the country's best ponchos. Look out for the hand-dyed and woven ponchos, instead of the mass-produced variety, available in smaller rural areas, or in the fine handicrafts market at Salta or Catamarca. There are the deep red Güemes versions or soft fine ponchos made of *vicuña* (a local cousin of the llama), usually in natural colours. In markets all over the northwest, you'll find llama wool jumpers, hats and socks, and brightly coloured woven bags, Bolivian influenced, but typical of the *puna* region. There are also fine carved wooden pieces. In the Lake District too, there's lots of woodwork, and weavings of a different kind, from the Mapuche peoples, with distinctive black and white patterns. Smoked fish and meat, and delicious home-made jams from *sauco* (elderberry) or *frambuesa* (raspberry) are among the local delicacies. In the northeast, there are Guaraní handicrafts such as bows and arrows. Argentina's national stone, the fleshy pink and marbled rhodochrosite, is mined in the northwest, but available all over Buenos Aires too, worked into fine jewellery, and less subtle paperweights and ashtrays.

Essentials A-Z

Accident and emergency

Police T101. **Medical** T107.

If robbed or attacked, call the tourist police, **Comisaría del Turista**, Av Corrientes 436, Buenos Aires, T011-4346 5748 (24 hrs) or T0800-999 5000 (English spoken), turista@policiafederal.gov.ar. Note that you will most likely not get your stolen goods back, but a police report is essential for your insurance claim.

Begging

There is increasingly more begging in larger cities, where you will be asked for 'una moneda' (some change). On trains and sometimes buses you'll see and hear people telling their stories and asking for help. Although not all Argentines give to beggars, they are universally polite and apologetic to them. So whether you decide to give or not, make sure you are just as polite as the Argentines in your conduct.

Children

Travel with children will most definitely bring you into closer contact with Argentine families and individuals, and you may find officials tend to be more amenable where children are concerned. Everyone will be delighted if your child knows a little Spanish.

Travelling with children in Argentina is potentially safe, easy and a great adventure. The country is full of wonders that children can enjoy, and Argentine people are extremely affectionate to children. There's a real feeling here that children are part of society, not to be

sent to be bed at 2000, and are often seen running around restaurants at 2300, or out with their parents in the evenings. This means that many family restaurants have play zones for kids with a climbing frame or soft play area, usually within sight of your table. And if you'd rather dine without your children, more expensive hotels provide a baby-sitter service. For more information see *Travel with Kids* by William Gray (Footprint).

Accommodation

Hotel accommodation in Argentina is good value for families; most places have rooms for 3, 4 or even 5 people, or 2 rooms with a connecting door. Many quite modest hotels have a suite, with 2 rooms and a bathroom, for families. If you're happy to be self-catering, look out for *cabañas* all over rural areas, like the Lake District, see page 21 for more information.

Food

Food is easy in Argentina, since most dishes aren't strongly seasoned, and easy meals like pasta, pizza and salads are of a high standard and available everywhere. The meat is lean and portions are huge, so that if you order a steak in a restaurant there will generally be enough for you and a child (or 2 hungry children). However, children's meals are offered at most restaurants, and many establishments have high chairs. Argentine children tend to drink fizzy drinks, but freshly squeezed orange juice is widely available, and it's best to order mineral water. If your children have special dietary needs, it's worth learning the Spanish to explain.

Transport

For most tourist attractions, there are cheaper prices for children. However, on all long-distance buses you pay a fare for each seat, and there are no half-fares if the children occupy a seat each. For shorter trips it is cheaper, if less comfortable, to seat small children on your knee. For long bus journeys, it's a good idea to bring water, fruit and biscuits, since the food provided may not be to your children's taste. There are toilets on all long-distance buses, and these are definitely improving, but they may not be clean or have water and toilet paper, so bring tissues. All bus stations have a *kiosko*, selling drinks, snacks and tissues. Bring games and perhaps music for them to listen to as the videos shown on most buses are generally action movies, not suitable for under 12s. On sightseeing tours you could try and bargain for a family rate – often children can go free. All civil airlines charge half for children under 12 but some military services don't have half-fares, or have younger age limits.

Customs and duty free

You can buy duty-free goods on arrival at Ezeiza Airport, though the shops are small and pricey, and you can also buy products on the boats to Uruguay.

No duties are charged on clothing, personal effects or toiletries. Cameras, laptops, binoculars, mp3 players and other things that a tourist normally carries are duty-free if they have been used and only 1 of each article is carried. This is also true of scientific and professional instruments for personal use. Travellers may only bring in new personal goods up to a value of US$300 (US$100 from neighbouring countries). The duty and tax payable amounts to 50%

of the item's cost. At the airport, make sure you have the baggage claim tag (usually stuck to your ticket or boarding card), as these are inspected at the exit from the customs inspection area. 2 litres of alcoholic drink, 400 cigarettes and 50 cigars are also allowed in duty-free. For tourists originating from neighbouring countries the quantities allowed are 1 litre of alcoholic drink, 200 cigarettes and 20 cigars.

If you have packages sent to Argentina, the green customs label should not be used unless the contents are of real value and you expect to pay duty. For such things as books or samples use the white label if available. A heavy tax is imposed on packages sent to Argentina by courier.

Global Refund

Some products give you the option to get the tax back on them, see page 42. The IVA (VAT) is usually 13.70% of the product's cost. For further information see **Global Blue Argentina**, Juan B Justo 637, 8th floor, T011-5238 1970, www.globalblue.com/customer-services/tax-free-shopping-in-argentina.

Disabled travellers

Facilities for the disabled in Argentina are sorely lacking. Wheelchair users won't find many ramps or even lowered curbs, although this is improving in Buenos Aires where the revamped BRT system is greatly improving bus travel for disabled travellers. Elsewhere, pavements tend to be shoddy and broken even in big cities. Only a few upmarket hotels have been fully adapted for wheelchair use, although many more modern hotels are fine for those with limited mobility. The best way to assess this is to ring or email the hotel in advance. Argentines generally go out of their way to help you, making up for poor facilities with kindness and generosity. Tourist sites aren't generally well adapted for disabled visitors, with limited access for the physically disabled, particularly at archaeological sites. However, many museums have ramps or lifts, and some offer special guided tours for the visually impaired, and signed tours for the hearing-impaired. Iguazú Falls has good access for wheelchair users or those with walking difficulties, along sturdy modern walkways with no steps, right up to the falls. Getting close to glacier Perito Moreno is not easy. Speaking Spanish is obviously a great help, and travelling with a companion is advisable.

Some travel companies specialize in holidays tailor-made for the individual's level of disability.

Books
You might like to read *Nothing Ventured* by Alison Walsh (Harper Collins), which gives personal accounts of worldwide journeys by disabled travellers, plus advice and listings.

Contacts
Other useful contacts include **Directions Unlimited**, New York, T914-241 1700; and **Mobility International USA**, T541-343 1284.

Websites
Disability Action Group, www. disabilityaction.org. Information on independent travel.
Global Access Disabled Network, www.globalaccessnews.com.
Royal Association for Disability and Rehabilitation, www.radar.org.uk.
Society for Accessible Travel and Hospitality, www.sath.org. Lots of advice on how to travel with specific disabilities.

Other useful sites include www. gimponthego.com and www.makoa. org/travel.htm.

Dress

Argentines of whatever class tend to dress neatly and take care to be clean and tidy so it's much appreciated if you do the same. Buying clothing locally can help you to look less like a tourist – clothes are cheap in Argentina in comparison with Western Europe and America.

Drugs

Users of drugs without medical prescription should be particularly careful, as Argentina imposes heavy penalties – up to 10 years' imprisonment – for even possession of such substances. The planting of drugs on travellers by traffickers or the police is not unknown. If offered drugs on the street, make no response at all and keep walking. Although the possession of cannabis has been decriminalized, it remains illegal to buy it, possess it or transport it.

Note that people who roll their own cigarettes are often suspected of carrying drugs and can be subjected to intensive searches. It is advisable to stick to commercial brands of cigarettes.

Electricity

220 volts AC (and 110 too in some hotels), 50 cycles. European Continental-type plugs in old buildings, Australian 3-pin flat-type in the new. Adaptors can be purchased locally for either type (ie from new 3-pin to old 2-pin and vice versa). Best to bring a universal adapter for British 3-pin plugs, as these are not available in Argentina.

Embassies and consulates

For all Argentine embassies and consulates abroad and for all foreign embassies and consulates in Argentina, see http://embassy.goabroad.com.

Gay and lesbian travellers

Argentina is fast becoming one of the most popular gay destinations in the world and there is enough happening in the capital to keep you busy for a few weeks. New gay hotels are opening, gay clubs are booming and there is a range of gay-orientated travel agencies to help you plan your stay, including **BA Gay Travel**, T011-4861 6086, www. bagaytravel.com. However, in the interior of the country, away from Buenos Aires, you might encounter homophobia; being openly demonstrative in public will certainly raise eyebrows everywhere apart from the hipper places in Buenos Aires. The tourist office produces a handy leaflet with a map showing gay friendly bars, pubs, saunas, health centres and wine bars, and change is gradually reaching government levels as well. Discrimination on the grounds of sexual orientation was banned in 1996, and in 2005 Argentina was the first South American country to legalize same-sex marriages.

Accommodation

There are plenty of gay-friendly hotels, see www.Gmaps360.com, for recommendations in Buenos Aires and Mar del Plata. For exclusively gay accommodation we recommend the **Axel Hotel** and **Lugar Gay de Buenos Aires**, both in the San Telmo area of Buenos Aires, see page 70.

Clubs

There are many gay-friendly and gay-exclusive clubs. See www.theronda. com.ar, for more details, and page 75 for listings.

Publications

The 2 best publications are bi-monthly: *Gmaps* (www.Gmaps360.com) and the *Ronda* (www.theronda.com.ar), both found in coffee shops, hotels and gyms around the city. *Gmaps* also produce a free **G-Card** which gives you discounts, free passes, and extra services in a range of places. Order one and have it sent to your hotel.

Useful websites

www.gaytravel.com Excellent site with information on gay travel.
www.nexo.org A useful site for gay information within Argentina (Spanish only).
www.purpleroofs.com/southamerica/ argentina.html For help in planning your trip.
www.thegayguide.com.ar For travel tips on bars in Buenos Aires.

Greetings

Argentines are extremely courteous and friendly people, and start every interaction, no matter how small, with a greeting. You'll be welcomed in shops and ticket offices too. Take the time to respond with a smile and a *Buenos días* or *Hola* in return. Argentines are sociable people, and haven't yet lost the art of passing the time of day – you'll be considered a bit abrupt if you don't too. As you leave, say *Chau* (bye) or *Hasta luego* (see you later). Strangers are generally treated with great kindness and generosity and your warmth in return will be greatly appreciated.

If you're introduced to new people or friends, you'll be kissed, once, on the right cheek as you say hello and goodbye. This sometimes goes for men to men too, if they're friends (although it's more of a touching of cheeks than a kiss). In a business or official context, Argentines tend to be formal and very polite.

Health

See your GP or travel clinic at least 6 weeks before departure for general advice on travel risks and vaccinations. Try phoning a specialist travel clinic if your own doctor is unfamiliar with health conditions in Argentina. Make sure you have sufficient medical travel insurance, get a dental check, know your own blood group and if you suffer a long-term condition such as diabetes or epilepsy, obtain a Medic Alert bracelet/necklace (www.medicalert.org.uk). If you wear glasses, take a copy of your prescription.

Vaccinations and anti-malarials
Vaccinations for hepatitis A, tetanus, typhoid and, following the 2009 outbreak, influenza A (H1N1) are commonly recommended for Argentina. Sometimes advised are vaccines for hepatitis B and rabies. The final decision, however, should be based on a consultation with your GP or travel clinic. You should also confirm your primary courses and boosters are up to date.

Malaria is a substantial risk in parts of north and northeastern Argentina. Specialist advice should be taken on the best anti-malarials to use.

Health risks
The most common cause of travellers' **diarrhoea** is from eating contaminated food. Be wary of salads (what were they washed in, who handled them), re-heated foods or food that has been left out in the sun having been cooked earlier in the day. There is a simple adage that says wash it, peel it, boil it or forget it. It is also standard advice to be careful with water and ice. Ask yourself where the water came from. If you have any doubts then boil it or filter it and treat it. Tap water in the major cities, especially in Buenos Aires, is in theory safe to drink but it may be advisable to err on the side of caution and drink only bottled or boiled water. Avoid having ice in drinks unless you trust that it is from a reliable source. There are many filter/treatment devices now available on the market. Swimming in sea or river water that has been contaminated by sewage can also be a cause; ask locally if it is safe. Diarrhoea may be also caused by viruses, bacteria (such as E-coli), protozoal (such as giardia), salmonella and cholera. It may be accompanied by vomiting or by severe abdominal pain. Any kind of diarrhoea responds well to the replacement of water and salts. Sachets of rehydration salts can be bought in most chemists and can be dissolved in boiled water. If the symptoms persist, consult a doctor.

Travelling in high altitudes can bring on **altitude sickness**. On reaching heights above 3000 m, the heart may start pounding and the traveller may experience shortness of breath. Smokers and those with underlying heart or lung disease are often hardest hit. Take it easy for the first few days, rest and drink plenty of water – you will feel better soon. It is essential to get acclimatized before undertaking long treks or arduous activities.

Mosquitoes are more of a nuisance than a serious hazard but some, of course, are carriers of serious diseases such as **malaria**, so it is sensible to avoid being bitten as much as possible. Sleep off the ground and use a mosquito net and some kind of insecticide. Mosquito coils release insecticide as they burn and are available in many shops, as are tablets of insecticide, which are placed on a heated mat plugged into a wall socket.

If you get sick

Contact your embassy or consulate for a list of doctors and dentists who speak your language, or at least some English. Doctors and health facilities in major cities are also listed in the Directory sections of this book. Good-quality healthcare is available in the larger centres of Argentina but it can be expensive, especially hospitalization. Make sure you have adequate insurance (see below).

Useful websites

www.bgtha.org British Global Travel Health Association.
www.cdc.gov US government site that gives excellent advice on travel health and details of disease outbreaks.
www.fco.gov.uk British Foreign and Commonwealth Office travel site has useful information on each country, people, climate and a list of UK embassies/consulates.
www.fitfortravel.scot.nhs.uk A-Z of vaccine/health advice for each country.

Insurance

Insurance is strongly recommended and policies are very reasonable. If you have financial restraints the most important aspect of any insurance policy is medical care and repatriation. Ideally you want to make sure you are covered for personal items too. Read the small print *before*

heading off so you are aware of what is covered and what is not, what is required to submit a claim and what to do in the event of an emergency.

Internet

The best way to keep in touch is undoubtedly by email. Telephone is expensive in Argentina so all Argentines have adapted rapidly to internet, with broadband widely available even in small towns, many of them also offering Skype. Most *locutorios* (phone centres) also have internet, and there are dedicated centres on almost every block in town. Prices vary.

Language

→ *See Footnotes, page 688, for a list of useful words and phrases, and page 694 for the menu reader.*
Your experience in Argentina will be completely transformed if you can learn even a little of the language before you arrive. Spanish is the first language, with a few variations and a distinctive pronunciation. In areas popular with tourists, you'll find some people speak English and perhaps French or Italian, but since much of the pleasure of Argentina is in getting off the beaten track, you'll often find yourself in situations where only Spanish is spoken. Argentines are welcoming and curious, and they're very likely to strike up conversation on a bus, shop or in a queue for the cinema. They're also incredibly hospitable and your attempts to speak Spanish will be enormously appreciated.

If you have a few weeks before you arrive, try and learn a few basic phrases, useful verbs and numbers. If you're reading this on the plane, it's not too late to get a grasp of basic introductions, food and directions.

Argentine Spanish sounds like no other. The main difference is that in words with 'll' and 'y', the sound is pronounced like a soft 'j' sound, as in 'beige'. The 'd' sound is usually omitted in words ending in 'd' or '-ado', and 's' sounds are often omitted altogether at the ends of words. And in the north and west of the country, you'll hear the normal rolled 'r' sound replaced by a hybrid 'r j' put together. Grammatically, the big change is that the Spanish '*tú*' is replaced by '*vos*' which is also used almost universally instead of '*usted*', unless you're speaking to someone much older or higher in status. In the conjunction of verbs, the accent is on the last syllable (eg *vos, tenés, podés*). In the north and northwest, though, the Spanish is more akin to that spoken in the rest of Latin America. In Buenos Aires, you might hear the odd word of *lunfardo*, Italian-oriented slang.

Language schools

Large cities all offer Spanish-language classes, see individual chapters for recommendations. If you would like to arrange your classes before you arrive, as well as your accommodation, try one of the following organizations:

Academia Buenos Aires, Hipólito Yrigoyen 571, 4th floor, Buenos Aires, T011-4345 5954, www.academia buenosaires.com. Spanish classes in Buenos Aires, Bariloche and Montevideo.
Amerispan, 1334 Walnut St, 6th floor, Philadelphia PA 19107, USA, T0800-879 6640, www.amerispan.com. North American company offering Spanish immersion programmes, educational tours, and volunteer and internship positions in Buenos Aires, Córdoba and Mendoza. Also programmes for younger people.
Expanish, Viamonte 927, 1st floor, T011-4322 0011, www.expanish.com. Buenos Aires-based agency that can organize packages including accommodation, excursions and classes in Buenos Aires, and Patagonia in Argentina, as well as in Peru, Ecuador and Chile. Highly recommended.
Spanish Abroad, 5112 N, 40th St, Suite 101, Phoenix, AZ 85018, T1-888-722 7623, www.spanishabroad.com. Spanish classes in Buenos Aires and Córdoba.

Media

Newspapers

The national daily papers are *La Nación*, a broadsheet, intelligent and well written (www.lanacion.com.ar); and *Clarín*, more accessible, also a broadsheet (www.clarin.com.ar). Both these papers have good websites and excellent Sunday papers with informative travel sections. Other daily national papers are *La Prensa*, *La Razón*, and the left wing *Página-12*, always refreshing for a different perspective. There's a daily paper in English, the *Buenos Aires Herald* (www.buenosairesherald.com), which gives a brief digest of world news, as well as Argentine news. Magazines you might like to look at include: *Noticias*, news and culture; *Gente*, a kind of *Hello!* for Argentina; *El Gráfico*, a good sports magazine; and particularly *Lugares*. This glossy monthly travel magazine has superb photography and is a very useful resource for travel tips and ideas of where to go, often with English translation at the back. Issues are themed; the northwest, the lakes, etc, and previous issues are often available from *kioskos* too. For information in English on what is going on around the country, see www.theargenaindependent.com.

Few foreign-language newspapers are available outside Buenos Aires, but to keep in touch with world news, websites of your own favourite newspaper are invaluable. Many hotels have cable TV in the rooms, but rarely have any English news channels.

Money

→ *US$1=Arg $8.41, £1=Arg $13.62, €1=Arg $10.89, AUS$1=Arg $7.8 (Sep 2014).*

Currency

The unit of currency is the Argentine peso (Arg $), divided into 100 centavos. Peso notes in circulation are 2, 5, 10, 20, 50 and 100. Coins in circulation are 5, 10, 25 and 50 centavos and 1 peso. Restrictions on Argentines buying

US dollars have created a free, or "blue", market rate for dollars (*mercado azul*). Before Jan 2014, when the official rate was devalued to AR$8=US$1, the advantages of using the blue market were significant; since the devaluation the gap between the 2 rates has narrowed a little, with the blue rate at AR$14=US$1 in Sep 2014. The blue market is not legally available to tourists, but there are ways round this and its use is common (2014). Ask a trusted local resident for advice on the safest places to change money. Use dollars in cash whenever possible; some establishments may accept them at near the blue rate (some may also take euros). Alternatively, find better rates at www.exchangeinargentina.com or by wiring US dollars from a US bank account via www.xoom.com, which allows transfers to its Argentine outlet, More Argentina (www.moreargentina.com.ar), at a rate close to the blue rate. **Note** The exchange rate changes on a daily basis and inflation is high, so prices fluctuate. Prices given in this edition are calculated at the official exchange rate at the time of research. Always pay the exact amount of a bill as small change is in short supply. Note that fake notes circulate, mostly AR$100, 20 and 10. Check that the green numbers showing the value of the note (on the left hand top corner) shimmer; that there is a watermark, and that there is a continuous line from the top of the note to the bottom about ¾ of the way along. US dollar bills are often scanned electronically for forgeries.

Cost of travelling

Argentina's economy has picked up since the 2001 economic crisis, but prices have risen steeply, particularly for hotels and tourist services. Nevertheless, you'll still find Argentina a very economical country to travel around.

You can find comfortable accommodation with a private bathroom and breakfast for around US$45-60 for 2 people, while a good dinner in the average restaurant will be around US$12-20 per person. Prices are much cheaper away from the main touristy areas: El Calafate, Ushuaia and Buenos Aires can be particularly pricey. For travellers on a budget, hostels usually cost US$12-20 per person in a shared dorm. Cheap breakfasts can be found in any ordinary café for around US$4-5, and there are cheap set lunches at many restaurants, costing around US$8, US$10 in Buenos Aires. Camping costs vary widely, but expect to pay no more than US$3-6 per tent – usually less. Long-distance bus travel on major routes is very cheap, and it's well worth splashing out an extra 20% for *coche-cama* service on overnight journeys.

Credit and debit cards

The easiest way to get cash while you're in Argentina is to use a credit card at an ATM (*cajero automático*). These can be found in every town or city (with the notable exception of El Chaltén in the south) and most accept all major cards, with **MasterCard** and **Visa** being the most widely accepted in small places. They are usually **Banelco** or **Link**, accepting international cards, but they dispense only pesos, impose withdrawal and daily limits and a charge per transaction (limits change, check on arrival). You will also have to add any commission imposed by your card's issuing company. Note that Argentine ATMs give you your cash and receipt

before the card is returned: don't walk away without the card. Most important to recognize, though, is that transactions at ATMs (known as *cajeros automáticos*), as at exchange houses (*casas de cambio*) and banks, are at the official rate. If you withdraw cash from the bank counter with a card and when making a purchase with a credit card, you will also have to show your passport. It's a good idea to carry cash to pay in cheaper shops, restaurants and hotels, and some places will give a discount for cash. **MasterCard** emergency number is T0800-555 0507 and **Visa** is T0800-32222

Traveller's cheques

There's little point in carrying traveller's cheques in Argentina since there are exchange facilities only in big towns, and commission is very high: usually 10%. A passport is essential and you may have to show proof of purchase, so transactions can take a long time. Traveller's cheques also attract thieves though you can of course arrange a refund.

Opening hours

Business hours Banks, government offices and businesses are usually open Mon-Fri 0800-1300 in summer, and Mon-Fri 1000-1500 in winter. Some businesses open again in the evening, 1700-2000. **Cafés and restaurants**: cafés are busy from 2400. Restaurants are open for lunch 1230-1500, dinner 2100-2400. **Nightclubs**: open at 2400, but usually only get busy around 0200. **Post offices**: often open *corrido* – don't close for lunch or siesta. **Shops**: in Buenos Aires most are open 0900-1800. Elsewhere, everything closes for siesta 1300-1700.

Police

Whereas Europeans and North Americans are accustomed to law enforcement on a systematic basis, enforcement in Argentina is more of a sporadic affair. Many people feel that the police are corrupt and unreliable due to incredibly low pay, and there are reports that they sometimes work with local thieves to turn a blind eye to muggings. In fact, they are usually courteous and will be helpful to tourists.

Post

Be aware that mail sent to Argentina may not arrive or may arrive late. Sending mail home is not a problem, it is cheap and efficient. Letters from Argentina take 10-14 days to get to Europe and the USA. Rates for letters up to 20 g to Europe and USA, up to 150 g. Post can be sent from the *correo* (post office) or from private postal service *Oca*, through any shop displaying the purple sign. The post service is reliable, but for assured delivery, register everything.

Small parcels of up to 2 kg can be sent from all post offices. Larger parcels must be sent from the town's main post office, where your parcel will be examined by customs to make sure that the contents are as stated on your customs form, and taken to *Encomiendas Internacionales* for posting. Any local *correo* can tell you where to go. Customs usually open in the morning only. Having parcels sent to Argentina incurs a customs tax, which depends on the value of the package, and all incoming packages are opened by customs. If when you are in Buenos Aires you are sent anything large or electronic, it will get stopped at Ezeiza International Airport Customs, you will then have to go

there, wade through paperwork for about 2 hrs and then possibly pay a duty tax. Try to avoid being sent anything really valuable. Poste restante is available in every town's main post office, fee US$5.

Safety

Relatively speaking, Buenos Aires is one of the safest cities in South America, and Argentina as a whole is an easy and safe place to travel, but that doesn't mean you need to drop your guard altogether. There are a few simple things you can do to avoid being a victim of crime.

Fake money

There is a big problem with fake notes in Argentina. The best way to tell if your money is not a fake is to look for the following 3 things: the green numbers showing the value of the note (on the top left-hand corner) should shine, or shimmer; if you hold the note up to the sky you should see a watermark; lastly there should be a continuous line from the top of the note to the bottom about ¾ of the way along (also when held up to the light). The most common fake notes are $100 pesos, $20 pesos and $10 pesos. Some taxi drivers reportedly circulate fakes late at night with drunk passengers, or you may be given them back in change in markets and fairs. Check the notes thoroughly before walking away. Try to break large notes in hostels/hotels or supermarkets to avoid being given a fake in change.

Places to avoid

In most towns the train and bus stations should be avoided late at night and early in the morning. If you arrive at that time, try to arrange for your hotel or hostel to pick you up. If you can, in Buenos Aires and when you are travelling, visit the bus station to buy your tickets the day before so you can find out where the platform is and where you need to go. Also watch your belongings being stowed in the boot of the bus, and keep the ticket you'll be given since you'll need it to claim your luggage on arrival.

Precautions

Some general tips are: don't walk along the street with your map or guidebook in hand – check where you are going beforehand and duck into shops to have a quick look at your map. In cafés make sure you have your handbag on your lap or your backpack strap around your ankles. Try not to wear clothes that stand out, and certainly don't wear expensive rings, watches or jewellery that shines. Remember that the people around you don't know that you bought that watch for US$10 second hand – to them it looks expensive. Always catch Radio Taxis ask at your hostel/hotel the best taxi company to use and their direct number. When in a taxi, if possible lock the doors, or ask the driver to.

And finally, just remember the golden rules: store your money and credit cards in small amounts in different places in your luggage; if carrying a wallet, keep it in a front rather than a back pocket; scan and email yourself copies of your passport, visas and insurance forms; and keep an eye on the news or newspapers to be aware of what is happening in the country that you are travelling in.

If you are the victim of a **sexual assault**, you are advised in the first instance to contact a doctor (this can be your home doctor if you prefer). You will need tests to determine whether you have contracted any sexually transmitted diseases; you may also need advice on post-coital contraception. You should also contact your embassy, where consular staff are very willing to help in cases of assault. For more advice see www.dailystrength.org and www.rapecrisis.org.uk.

Scams

Be aware of scams. There are 2 favoured scams in use. One is that someone will discreetly spill a liquid on you, then a 'helpful stranger' will draw your attention to it and offer to help you clean it off. Meanwhile someone else has raided your pockets or run off with your bags. If someone does point out something on your clothes, keep walking until you see a coffee shop and clean up there. The second scam involves someone driving past you on a motorbike, ripping your bag off your shoulders, and driving away off into the sunset. To avoid this, wear your bag with the strap over your head and one shoulder and keep your bag on the opposite side of your body to the street. If travelling with a laptop, don't use a computer bag. Buy a satchel or handbag big enough to carry it in.

Taxis

Always take Radio Taxis. Ask your hostel or hotel for a reputable company and call them whenever you need a taxi. They generally take only around 10 mins to come. Always lock the doors in the taxi as taxi doors have reportedly been opened at traffic intersections when the car is stationary.

Student travellers

If you're in full-time education, you're entitled to an International Student Identity Card (ISIC), www.isic.org, available from student travel offices and agencies. This gives you special prices on transport, cultural events and a variety of other concessions and services. All student cards must carry a photograph. Some hostel chains also give ISIC card discounts. See **Hostelling International**, www.hostels.org.ar.

Asatej, Paraguay 523, 2nd floor, Buenos Aires, T011-5218 6556, www.asatej.com. Helpful Argentine travel organization, which runs a Student Flight Centre, Florida 835, p 3, oficina 320, T011-4114 7600, Mon-Fri 1000-1900 (and 5 other branches in BA: Belgrano, Montserrat, Palermo, Recoleta, Caballito). Sells flights, including cheap 1-way flights, hires cars and arranges accommodation, and group and individual tours to places in Argentina. Information for all South America, noticeboard for travellers, ISIC cards sold (giving extensive discounts; Argentine ISIC guide available here), English and French spoken. Also runs **Red Argentino de Alojamiento Para Jovenes** (affiliated to HI) and the **Asatej Travel Store**, at the same office, selling wide range of travel goods.

TIJE, San Martín 640, p 6, Buenos Aires, T011-5272 8453, www.tije.com, and at STB (STA representative), Viamonte 577, p 3, Buenos Aires, T011-5217 2727, www.stb.com.ar. Cheap fares.

YMCA (Central), Reconquista 439, Buenos Aires, T011-4311 4785.

YWCA, Tucumán 844, Buenos Aires, T011-4322 1550.

Tax

Airport tax

By law airport taxes must be included in the price of your air ticket. When in transit from one international flight to another, you may be obliged to pass through immigration and customs, have your passport stamped. There is a 5% tax on the purchase of air tickets. There is now an entry fee for Argentina, see page 12.

VAT

21%; VAT is not levied on medicines, books and some foodstuffs.

Telephone → *Country code +54.*

Ringing: equal tones with long pauses. Engaged: equal tones with equal pauses.

Phoning in Argentina is made very easy by the abundance of *locutorios* – phone centres with private booths where you can talk for as long as you like, and pay afterwards, the price appearing on a small screen in your booth. There's no need for change or phonecards, and *locutorios* often have internet, photocopying and fax services.

An alternative to *locutorios* is to buy a phonecard and use it from your hostel or hotel. 2 good brands are **Argentina Global** and **Hable Mas**, available from *kioskos* and *locutorios* for 5 or 10 pesos. Dial the free 0800 number on the card, and a code (which you scratch the card to reveal), and you can phone anywhere in the world. Call from your hotel/hostel, as it only is the cost of a local call. These can sometimes be used in *locutorios* too, though the rates are higher, and sometimes from your hotel room, ask reception. Otherwise Skype, www.skype.com, is the cheapest way to keep in touch.

Time

GMT -3.

Tipping

10% in restaurants and cafés. Porters and ushers are usually tipped. Tipping isn't obligatory, but it is appreciated.

Tour operators

If the choices available in Argentina are overwhelming, and you have little time to spend, or if you're not keen on travelling alone, it's worth considering booking a package with a specialist tour operator. Whether you choose an adventurous expedition, or a more sedate trip; a bespoke journey just for you, or a group holiday, these companies work with agents on the ground who will book all your transport and accommodation, so that you can just enjoy the experience. UK and Australian travellers are advised to choose a tour operator from **LATA**, the Latin American Travel Association, www.lata.org, which is also a useful source of country information.

In the UK

Abercrombie and Kent, St Georges House, Ambrose St, Cheltenham, Gloucestershire, GL50 3LG, T0845-485 4736, www.abercrombiekent.co.uk. Upmarket tailor-made travel.
Andean Trails, 33 Sandport St, Leith, Edinburgh, EH6 6EP, T0131-467 7086, www.andeantrails.co.uk.
Audley Travel, New Mill, New Mill Lane, Witney, Oxfordshire, OX29 9SX, T01993- 838 000, www.audleytravel.com. High-quality tailor-made travel, including the Northwest, Lake District and Patagonia. Good on the ground knowledge. Recommended.
Cazenove and Loyd, Argon House, Argon Mews, Fulham Broadway, London, SW6 1BJ, T020-7384 2332, www.cazloyd.com.
Cox and Kings, 6th Floor, 30 Millbank, London, SW1P 4EE, T020-7873 5000, www.coxandkings.co.uk.
Discover the World, Arctic House, 8 Bolters Lane, Banstead, Surrey, SM7 2AR, T01737-214 250, www.discover-the-world.co.uk.
Dragoman, Camp Green, Debenham, Suffolk, IP14 6LA, T01728-862211, www.dragoman.co.uk.
Explore, Nelson House, 55 Victoria Rd, Farnborough, Hampshire, GU14 7PA, T0843-634 6070, www.explore.co.uk. Quality small-group trips, especially in Patagonia. Also offers family adventures, or with a focus on culture, wildlife or trekking.
Journey Latin America, 401 King St, London, W6 9NJ, T020-8747 8315, www.journeylatinamerica.co.uk. Deservedly well regarded, this excellent long-established company runs adventure tours, escorted groups and tailor-made tours to Argentina and other destinations in South America. Also cheap

flights and expert advice. Well organized and very professional. Recommended. **Last Frontiers**, The Mill, Quainton Rd, Waddesdon, Bucks, HP18 0LP, T01296-653000, www.lastfrontiers.com. Excellent company offering top-quality tailor-made trips all over Argentina, including superb wine tours, trips combining Iguazú and Salta, trips to the Esteros del Iberá, and horse riding in Patagonia and Córdoba. By far the best company for *estancia* stays; a real in-depth knowledge of Argentina. Highly recommended. **Select Latin America**, 3.51 Canterbury Court, 1-3 Brixton Rd, Kennington Park Business Centre, London, SW9 6DE, T020-7407 1478, www.selectlatinamerica.co.uk. Specializing in tailor-made and small-group tours with a cultural or natural history emphasis, this is a friendly small company with some good itineraries, including birdwatching in the Los Esteros del Iberá, Antarctica and the R40. **Steppes Travel**, Travel House, 51 Castle St, Cirencester, GL7 1QD, T0843 636 8323, www.steppestravel.co.uk. Tailor-made and group itineraries throughout Argentina and Latin America.

Specialist tour operators

There are many more specialized tour operators, offering specialist trips for birdwatching and horse riding. Below is just a selection.
Adventures Abroad, T0114-247 3400, www.adventures-abroad.com. Impressive company running superb and imaginative tours for small groups to Patagonia, Iguazú and Puerto Madryn, the glaciers and Ushuaia. Great itineraries.
Exodus, Grange Mills, Weir Rd, London SW12 0NE, T0845 805 5459, www.exodus.co.uk. Excellent, well-run trekking and climbing tours of Patagonia and Chile, including Torres del Paine, cycling in the

Lake District, Antarctica and a great tour following in Shackleton's footsteps.
Naturetrek, Cheriton Mill, Cheriton, Alresford, Hampshire, SO24 0NG, T01962-733051, www.naturetrek.co.uk. Small group birdwatching tours, fixed departure.
STA Travel, offices worldwide, www.sta travel.co.uk/.com. Cheap flights, and sell Dragoman's trip which includes Argentina.
Trailfinders, 194 Kensington High St, London, W8 7RG, T020-7938 3939, www.trailfinders.com. Reliable for cheap flights and tours.

In North America

Argentina For Less, 203 Valona Drive, Round Rock, TX 78681, USA, T1-877-661 6989, T+44-203-002 0571 (UK), www.argentinaforless.com. Progressive tourism company with a focus solely on Latin America. US-based but with local offices and operations.
ExpeditionTrips.com, 6553 California Av SW, Seattle, WA 98136, T1877-412 8527, www.expeditiontrips.com.
Worldwide Horseback Riding Adventures, PO Box 807, 10 Stalnaker St, Dubois, Wyoming 82513, toll free T0800-545 0019, www.ridingtours.com. US-based horse-riding company.

In South America

Navimag, Navimag Ferries SA, Angelmó 1735, Puerto Montt, Chile, T 0056-65-24 32 360, www.navimag.com.
Say Hueque, Thames 2062, Palermo, Buenos Aires, T+54 11-5258 8740, and Chile 557, San Telmo, Buenos Aires, T+54 11-5352 9321, www.sayhueque.com. Recommended Argentine travel agency offering good-value tours, with friendly English-speaking staff, aimed at independent travellers. Specialize in tours to Patagonia, Iguazú and Mendoza.

South America Adventure Travel, Global Encounters, JA Cabrera 4423/29, Buenos Aires, Argentina, T512-592 3877 (US or international), T877-275 4957 (US toll free), www.southamericaadventure. travel. With offices throughout South America, they specialize in quality, budget adventure tours.

Tourist information

There are tourist information offices in all provincial capitals, in major tourist destinations and many bus terminals/ airports in popular destinations. Infrastructure varies across the country, but they can usually give you a town map and sometimes a list of accommodation, as well as the tours, sights and festivals in the area. Staff in more popular tourist areas usually speak at least some English (and sometimes French, German, Italian) and are usually helpful. Opening hours are long – typically 0800-2000 in summer but may close at weekends. All bus terminals have an office (often signed *Informes*) with bus information.

Information
Administración de Parques Nacionales, Santa Fe 690, opposite Plaza San Martín, Buenos Aires, T011-4311 0303, Mon-Fri 1000-1700. Has leaflets on national parks.
Aves Argentinas/AOP (a BirdLife International partner), 25 de Mayo 749, p 2, Buenos Aires, T011-4312 8958. Information on birdwatching and specialist tours, good library open Wed and Fri 1500-2000 (closed Jan).

Tourist offices
Loads of information on Argentina is now available on the internet, much of it reasonably up-to-date and in English.

Most provinces in Argentina have their own website and it's useful to have a look before you travel for inspiration and information. Each province has a tourist office, **Casa de Provincia**, in Buenos Aires, Mon-Fri 1000-1630/1730. The following regional websites are also recommended:
Buenos Aires Province, Av Callao 237, T011-5300 9500, www.casaprov.gba.gov.ar, www.turismo.buenosaires.gob.ar (official site of city of Buenos Aires tourism).
Catamarca, Av Córdoba 2080, T011-4374 6891, www.cata.gov.ar.
Chaco, Av Callao 322, T011-4372 3045/5209, casa.del.chaco@ecomchaco.com.ar.
Chubut, Sarmiento 1172, T011-4382 2009, www.chubutpatagonia.gob.ar.
Córdoba, Av Callao 332, T011-4371 1668, casadecordoba@cba.gov.ar.
Corrientes, Maipú 271, T011-4394 7418, casadecorrientes@argentina.com.
Entre Ríos, Suipacha 844, T011-4328 5985, www.casadeentrerios.gob.ar.
Formosa, Hipólito Yrigoyen 1429, T011-4384 8443, www.casadeformosa.gov.ar.
Jujuy, Av Santa Fe 967, T011-4393 1295, see Facebook page.
La Pampa, Suipacha 346, T011-4326 0511, www.casa.lapampa.gov.ar.
La Rioja, Av Callao 745, T011-4816 7068, www.turismolarioja.gov.ar.
Mendoza, Av Callao 441, T011-4371 7301, http://casa.mendoza.gov.ar.
Misiones, Santa Fe 989, T011-4317 3700, www.turismo.misiones.gov.ar.
Neuquén, Maipú 48, T011-4343 2324, casanqn_turismoycultura@neuquen.gov.ar.
Río Negro, Tucumán 1916, T011-4371 7273, casarionegro@sion.com.
Salta, Av Roque Saenz Peña 933, T011-4326 2456, www.casadesalta.gov.ar.
San Juan, Sarmiento 1251, T011-4382 9241, sarmientna@ciudad.com.ar.
San Luis, Azcuénaga 1087, T011-5778 1621, cslsecretaria@sanluis.gov.ar.

Santa Cruz, 25 de Mayo 279, T011-4343 8478, www.casadesantacruz.gov.ar.
Santa Fe, 25 de Mayo 178, T011-4342 0408, delegacionsantafe@ciudad.com.ar.
Santiago del Estero, Florida 274, p 1, T011-4322 1389.
Tierra del Fuego, Esmeralda 783, T011-4328 7040, www.tierradelfuego.org.ar.
Tucumán, Suipacha 140, T011-4322 0564, casaenbsas@tucumanturismo.gov.ar.

For tourist information on **Patagonia**, see www.patagonia.com.ar or www.patagonia-argentina.com. For bookings for cheap accommodation and youth hostels, contact **Asatej**, see student travellers on page 42.

Websites

www.alojar.com.ar Accommodation search engine and tourist information in Spanish.
www.buenosairesherald.com *Buenos Aires Herald*, English-language daily.
www.expat-connection.com Expat group in Buenos Aires which organizes events.
www.getsouth.com A fantastic site filled with accommodation and tour recommendations, as well as discounts and travel advice. Highly recommended.
www.infobae.com An Argentine online newspaper, in Spanish.
www.mercotour.com Information on travel and other matters in Argentina, Uruguay, Chile and Brazil, in Spanish, English and Portuguese.
www.responsibletravel.org A great website for people interested in responsible travel (also see www.travelersphilanthropy.org).
www.streema.com Site that enables you to listen to radio stations all over the world.
www.tageblatt.com.ar *Argentinisches Tageblatt*, German-language weekly, very informative.

www.welcomeargentina.com Information for the whole country, in several languages.

Vaccinations

No vaccination certificates are required for entry. For further details, see Health, page 35.

Visas and immigration

Visas on entry
Passports are not required by citizens of neighbouring countries who hold identity cards issued by their own governments. Visas are not necessary for US citizens, British citizens, citizens of EU countries, nationals of Central American countries and nationals of some Caribbean countries (Jamaica), plus Australia, Canada, Hong Kong, Israel, Japan, Malaysia, New Zealand, Russia, Singapore, South Africa and Turkey. Visitors from these countries are given a tourist card on entry and may stay for 3 months. For visitors from all other countries, there are 3 types of visa: a tourist visa (multiple entry, valid for 3 months; onward ticket and proof of adequate funds must be provided; fees vary depending on the country of origin; can be extended by 90 days), a business visa and a transit visa.

Visa extensions and renewals
All visitors can renew their tourist visas for another 3 months by going in person to the **National Directorate of Migration**, Antártida Argentina 1365, Buenos Aires, T011-4317 0234, Mon-Fri 0800-1400, or to any other delegation of the Dirección Nacional de Migraciones (www.migraciones.gov.ar) and paying a fee of US\$35: ask for *Prórrogas de Permanencia*. No renewals are given after

the expiry date. Alternatively, for a 90-day extension of your stay in Argentina, just leave the country at any land border, and you'll get another 3-month tourist visa stamped in your passport on return. Alternatively, you can forego all the paperwork by paying a 400 peso fine at a border immigration post (queues are shorter than in Buenos Aires, but still allow 30 mins). The most popular way of renewing your visa from Buenos Aires is to spend the day in Uruguay, which is only 45 mins away by boat.

Advice and tips

All visitors are advised to carry their passports at all times, and it is illegal not to have identification handy. In practice, though, this is not advisable. Photocopy your passport twice, carry 1 copy, and scan your passport and email it to yourself for emergencies. You'll often be asked for your passport number, when checking into hotels and if paying by credit card, so learn it off by heart. The police like searching backpackers at border points: remain calm – this is a normal procedure. If you are staying in the country for several weeks, it may be worthwhile registering at your embassy or consulate. This will help if your passport is stolen as the process of replacing it is simplified and speeded up.

Weights and measures

The metric system is used in Argentina.

Women travellers

Single women might attract surprise – *¿Estás sola?* Are you travelling alone? – but this is rather because Argentines are such sociable people and love to travel in groups, than because it's dangerous.

Argentine men can't seem to help paying women attention, and you may hear the traditional *piropo* as you walk past: a compliment, usually fairly unimaginative, and nothing to cause offence. Just ignore it and walk on. Men are generally respectful of a woman travelling alone, and won't make improper suggestions, but just in case here are some tips: Wear a ring on your wedding finger, and carry a photograph of '*mi marido*', your 'husband'. By saying that your 'husband' is close at hand, you may dissuade an aspiring suitor. Argentine men are famously charming and persistent chatters up, so firmly discourage any unwanted contact and be aware of any signals that might be interpreted as encouragement. If politeness fails, don't feel bad about showing offence and leaving.

Do not walk alone around Buenos Aires in quiet areas or at night. When accepting a social invitation, make sure that someone knows the address you're going to and the time you left. And if you don't know your hosts well, a good ploy is to ask if you can bring a friend, even if you've no intention of doing so, to check the intentions of whoever's inviting you. Wherever you are, try to act with confidence, and walk as though you know where you are going, even if you don't. Someone who looks lost is more likely to attract unwanted attention. Do not disclose to strangers where you are staying. When you set out, err on the side of caution until your instincts have adjusted to the customs of a new culture. Always ask the hotel, the restaurant or your hosts to call you a **Radio Taxi** as these are usually much safer and regulated closely.

Book accommodation ahead so that when you arrive in a new town you can take a taxi straight to your hotel or hostel and avoid looking lost and vulnerable at bus stations. Many hotels or hostels are open 24 hrs, but if you arrive in the early morning, it's safest to wait in the bus station *confitería*, where there are usually people around, than to venture into the centre.

Women should be aware that tampons are quite hard to find in Argentina and it may be best to bring a supply. In most chemists and supermarkets tampons are generally held behind the counter and you'll need to ask for them (pronounced, roughly the same in Spanish, *tampón*). Tampons and towels must never be flushed, whether in a private home or hotel. Carry a supply of plastic bags in case bins aren't provided.

For more advice for women travellers see www.womenstravelclub.com and www.travellingwomen.blogspot.com.

Working in Argentina

Foreigners can't work in Argentina without a work permit which you'll only get with an official job (or if you are from New Zealand as you can apply for a 12-month working visa). At a time of high unemployment, it's hard to find work and you might consider it unfair to take work away from Argentines. The exception to this is teaching English, and it's possible to pick up work with a school, even if you don't have any qualifications. But you will be paid more if you have a TEFL certificate (Teaching English as a Foreign Language) and experience. Otherwise, private lessons are always an option, but they pay very poorly. Jobs in schools are advertised in the English-language newspaper, the *Buenos Aires Herald*; www.craigslist. com; the *South American Explorers* free newsletter, www.saexplorers.org; and in the schools themselves.

EBC, www.ebc-tefl-course.com, offer a comprehensive 4-week TEFL training course that is highly recommended. Most graduates walk away with a job already organized.

If you are intent on trying to obtain a work visa speak to **Immigration**, Antártida Argentina 1365, Buenos Aires, T011-4312 8663. A good level of Spanish is essential.

Contents

At a glance

◉ **Getting around** Cheap and frequent buses, trains and relatively affordable taxis. Some areas like Palermo, Recoleta and San Telmo are best on foot.

⏱ **Time required** At least 1 week to see the sights, go to a tango show and enjoy a day trip.

❀ **Weather** Dec-Mar can be quite hot and humid, May-Aug can be windy, cold and rainy.

✖ **When not to go** May-Aug when the winds can be ferocious, or Mar when the torrential rains can wash the streets away.

→ **Buenos Aires maps**
1 Buenos Aires orientation, page 50
2 Metro (Subte), page 52
3 Buenos Aires centre, page 54
4 Recoleta & Palermo, page 59
5 San Telmo, page 63

To Route 9, Route 8, Tigre
& San Antonio De Areco

VICENTE
LOPEZ

SAAVEDRA

GENERAL SAN
MARTIN

General Paz

BELGRANO

Río de la Plata

Aeroparque

Parque 3
de Febrero

Libertador

CHACARITA

PALERMO

Córdoba

Santa Fé

RECOLETA

Retiro Bus
Terminal

Plaza
San Martín

To Route 5 to Luján

PATERNAL

Callao

9 De Julia

Puerto
Madero

Reserva
Ecológica
Costanera
Sur

VILLA DEL
PARQUE

CABALLITO

Plaza
de Mayo

LINIERS

FLORES

SAN
TELMO

General Paz

MATADEROS

LA BOCA

BARRACAS

Río Riachuelo

AVELLANEDA

LANUS

To Route 2, La Plata & Mar del Plata

LOMAS DE
ZAMORA

To Route 2

To Ezeiza Airport

N

1 km
1 miles

★ **Don't miss ...**
1 Recoleta Cemetery, page 58.
2 Palermo Viejo, page 60.
3 San Telmo, page 62.
4 Tigre and the delta, page 64.
5 Café Tortoni, page 72.
6 Boca Juniors, page 79.

Buenos Aires

With its elegant architecture and fashion-conscious inhabitants, Buenos Aires is often seen as more European than South American. Among its fine boulevards, neat plazas, parks, museums and theatres, there are chic shops and superb restaurants. However, the enormous steaks and passionate tango are distinctly Argentine too and to understand the country, you have to know its capital. South and west of Buenos Aires the flat, fertile lands of the *pampa húmeda* stretch seemingly without end, the horizon broken only by a lonely windpump or a line of poplar trees. This is home to the gaucho, whose traditions of music and craftsmanship remain alive.

Arriving in Buenos Aires → *Phone code: 011. Population: Greater Buenos Aires 12.8 million; rest of the province 5.7 million (2010 census).*

Orientation

Buenos Aires has two **airports**, Ezeiza, for international and few domestic flights, and Aeroparque, for domestic flights, most services to Uruguay and some to Brazil and Chile. Ezeiza is 35 km southwest of the centre, while Aeroparque is 4 km north of the city centre on the riverside. All international and interprovincial buses use the Retiro **bus terminal** at Ramos Mejía y Antártida Argentina, which is next to the Retiro **railway station**.

The commercial heart of the city, from Retiro station and Plaza San Martín through Plaza de Mayo to San Telmo, east of Avenida 9 de Julio, can be explored on foot, but you'll probably want to take a couple of days to explore its museums, shops and markets. Many places of interest lie outside this zone, so you will need to use public transport. City **buses** (*colectivos*) are plentiful, see below for city guides, and the **metro**, or Subte, is fast and clean; see Transport, page 82, for fares. Yellow and black **taxis** can be hailed on the street, but if possible, book a radio or a *remise* taxi by phone. Again, see Transport for details. Street numbers start from the dock side rising from east to west, but north/south streets are numbered from Avenida Rivadavia, one block north of Avenida de Mayo rising in both directions. Avenida Roque Sáenz Peña and Avenida Julio A Roca are commonly referred to as Diagonal Norte and Diagonal Sur respectively. ▸▸ *See also Transport, page 82.*

Tourist information

National office ① *Av Santa Fe 883, T011-4312 2232 or T0800-555 0016, info@turismo. gov.ar, Mon-Fri 0900-1700,* maps and literature covering the whole country. There are kiosks at Aeroparque and Ezeiza airports, daily 0800-2000. **City information**

ⓘ www.turismo.buenosaires.gob.ar, in Spanish only. There are tourist kiosks open daily downtown at Plaza Roberto Arlt (Esmeralda y Rivadavia), in Recoleta (Avenida Quintana 596, junction with Ortiz), in Puerto Madero (Dock 4, T011-4315 4265), and at Retiro bus station (ground floor, T011-4313 0187).

Guided tours are organized by the city authorities, including a Pope Francis tour throughout the city and bike tours in Palermo parks, both on weekends and holidays only: free leaflet from city-run offices and other suggested circuits on city website.

Those overcharged or cheated can go to the **Defensoría del Turista** ⓘ *Defensa 1250 (San Telmo), T15-2017 6845, turistasantelmo@defensoria.org.ar, Mon-Fri 1000-1800, Sat-Sun and holidays 1100-1800.*

② Metro (Subte)

➡ **Buenos Aires maps**
1 Buenos Aires orientation, page 50
2 **Metro (Subte), page 52**
3 Buenos Aires centre, page 54
4 Recoleta & Palermo, page 59
5 San Telmo, page 63

A good guide to bus and subway routes is *Guía T*, available at newsstands. There is also the interactive map at http://mapa.buenosaires.gob.ar. Also handy is Auto Mapa's pocket-size *Plano* of the Federal Capital, US$8.50, or the more detailed *City Map* covering La Boca to Palermo, both available at newsstands, US$3.80; otherwise it is easy to get free maps of the centre from tourist kiosks and most hotels. The daily press has useful supplements, such as the Sunday tourism section in *La Nación* (www.lanacion.com.ar), *Sí* in *Clarín* (www.si.clarin.com) and the equivalent *No* of *Página 12* (www.pagina12.com.ar). The *Buenos Aires Herald* also has information on what's on at www.buenosairesherald.com. For entertainments, see www.agenda cultural.buenosaires.gob.ar, www.vuenosairez.com, www.wipe.com.ar and www. whatsupbuenosaires.com. Also very useful are www.gringoinbuenosaires.com and www.discoverbuenosaires.com. Blogs worth exploring include http://baexpats. com and www.goodmorningba.com.

Places in Buenos Aires → *For listings, see pages 67-87.*

The capital has been virtually rebuilt since the beginning of the 20th century and its oldest buildings mostly date from the early 1900s, with some elegant examples from the 1920s and 1930s. The centre has maintained the original layout since its foundation and so the streets are often narrow and mostly one way. Its original name, 'Santa María del Buen Ayre' was a recognition of the favourable winds which brought sailors across the ocean.

Around Plaza de Mayo

The heart of the city is the **Plaza de Mayo**. On the east side is the **Casa de Gobierno**. Called the *Casa Rosada* because it is pink, it contains the offices of the President of the Republic. It is notable for its statuary and the rich furnishing of its halls. The **Museo del Bicentenario** ① *Paseo Colón 100, T011-4344 3802, www.museobicentenario.gob. ar, Wed-Sun and holidays 1000-1800 Dec-Mar 1100-1900), free*, in the Fuerte de Buenos Aires and Aduana Taylor, covers the period 1810-2010 with historical exhibits and art exhibitions, permanent and temporary. **Antiguo Congreso Nacional** (Old Congress Hall, 1864-1905) ① *Balcarce 139, Thu, 1500-1700, closed Jan-Feb, free*, on the south of the Plaza, is a National Monument. The **Cathedral** ① *San Martín 27, T011-4331 2845, www.catedralbuenosaires.org.ar, Mon-Fri 0800-1900, Sat-Sun 0900-1930; guided visits to San Martín's Mausoleum and Crypt, religious artefacts, and Temple and Crypt; Mass is held daily, check times*, on the north of Plaza, stands on the site of the first **church** in Buenos Aires. The current structure dates from 1753-1822 (its portico built in 1827), but the 18th-century towers were never rebuilt. The imposing **tomb** (1880) of the Liberator, General José de San Martín (Monday-Saturday 0930-1300, 1500-1700, Sun 0900-1100, 1500-1900), is guarded by soldiers in fancy uniforms. A small exhibition to the left of the main nave displays items related to Pope Francis, former archbishop of Buenos Aires. **Museo del Cabildo y la Revolución de Mayo** ① *Bolívar 65, T011-4334 1782, www.cabildonacional.gob.ar, Wed-Fri 1030-1700, Sat-Sun and holidays 1130-1800, free*, is in the old Cabildo where the movement for Independence from

3 Buenos Aires centre

To Palermo Parks & Aeroparque

To Recoleta

→ **Buenos Aires maps**

1 Buenos Aires orientation,
  page 50
2 Metro (Subte), page 52
3 **Buenos Aires centre, page 54**
4 Recoleta & Palermo, page 59
5 San Telmo, page 63

200 metres
200 yards

Where to stay

1 06 Central *D3*
2 BA Stop *D2*
3 Bisonte Palace *B3*
4 Casa Calma *B3*
5 Castelar *E2*
6 Colón *C3*
7 Dolmen *B3*
8 Dorá *B3*
9 El Cóndor y el Aguila
  Hostel *D1*
10 El Conquistador *B3*
11 Faena Universe *C5*
12 Goya *C3*
14 Hispano *D3*
15 Hostel Suites Obelisco *D3*
16 Kilca Hostel &
  Backpacker *E1*
17 La Argentina *E3*
18 Limehouse *D2*
19 Marbella *E2*
20 Milhouse Hostel *E3*
21 Moreno *E4*
23 Panamericano &
  Tomo 1 restaurant *C3*
25 Plaza San Martín Suites *B3*
27 Portal del Sur *E3*
27 St Nicholas *D1*
28 V&S *C3*
29 Waldorf *B4*

Restaurants

1 Al paso y algo más *C4*
2 Cabaña Las Lilas *D5*
3 Café Tortoni *D3*
4 Clásica y Moderna *B1*
5 Confitería Ideal *D3*
6 Dadá *B4*
7 El Gato Negro *C1*
8 Fiká *E3*
9 Florida Garden *B4*

10 Gijón *E2*
11 Güerrín *D2*
12 Gianni's *B4/C4*
13 Las Cuartetas *D3*
14 Le Grill *D5*
15 Sam Bucherie *C4*
16 Sorrento *C4*
17 Tancat *B3*

Bars & clubs

18 Bahrein *B4*
19 Druid In *B4*
20 La Cigale *C4*

Museums

2 Museo de Armas *B3*
3 Museo de Arte
  Hispanoamericano
  Isaac Fernández
  Blanco *A3*
4 Museo de la Ciudad *E4*
5 Museo del Bicentenario *E5*
6 Museo del Cabildo
  y la Revolución
  de Mayo *E4*
7 Museo del Holocausto *B1*
8 Museo Etnográfico
  JB Ambrosetti *E4*
9 Museo Judío *C2*
10 Museo Nacional
  Ferroviario *A3*
11 Museo y Biblioteca
  Mitre *D4*

Spain was first planned. It's worth a visit for the paintings of old Buenos Aires, the documents and maps recording the May 1810 Revolution, and memorabilia of the 1806 British attack; also Jesuit art. In the patio is a café and restaurant and stalls selling handicrafts (Thursday-Friday 1100-1800). Also on the Plaza is the Palacio de Gobierno de la Ciudad (City Hall). Within a few blocks north of the Plaza are the main banks and business houses, such as the **Banco de la Nación**, opposite the Casa Rosada, with an impressively huge main hall and topped by a massive marble dome 50 m in diameter.

On the Plaza de Mayo, the **Mothers of the Plaza de Mayo** march in remembrance of their children who disappeared during the 'dirty war' of the 1970s (their addresses are H Yrigoyen 1584, T011-4383 0377, www.madres.org, and Piedras 153, T011-4343 1926, www.madresfundadoras.org.ar). The Mothers march anti-clockwise round the central monument every Thursday at 1530, with photos of their disappeared loved-ones pinned to their chests.

West of Plaza de Mayo

Running west from the Plaza, the Avenida de Mayo leads 1.5 km to the **Palacio del Congreso** (Congress Hall) ⓘ *Plaza del Congreso, Av Rivadavia 1864, T011-6310 7222 for guided visits, Mon, Tue, Thu, Fri 1000, 1200, 1600, 1800, www.congreso.gov. ar; passport essential.* This huge Greco-Roman building houses the seat of the legislature. Avenida de Mayo has several examples of fine architecture of the early 20th century, such as the sumptuous La Prensa building (No 575, free guided visits at weekends), the traditional **Café Tortoni** (No 825, www.cafetortoni.com.ar), or the eclectic **Palacio Barolo** (No 1370, www.pbarolo.com.ar), and many others of faded grandeur. Avenida de Mayo crosses **Avenida 9 de Julio**, one of the widest avenues in the world, which consists of three major carriageways with heavy traffic, separated in some parts by wide grass borders. Five blocks north of Avenida de Mayo the great **Plaza de la República**, with a 67-m obelisk commemorating the 400th anniversary of the city's founding, is at the junction of Avenida 9 de Julio with Avenidas Roque Sáenz Peña and Corrientes. **Teatro Colón** ⓘ *Cerrito 628, entrance for guided visits Tucumán 1171, T011-4378 7127, www.teatrocolon.org.ar,* is one of the world's great opera houses. The interior is resplendent with red plush and gilt; the stage is huge and salons, dressing rooms and banquet halls are equally sumptuous. Consult the website for details of performances, tickets and guided visits. Close by is the **Museo Judío** ⓘ *Libertad 769, T011-4123 0832, www.judaica.org.ar; for visits make an appointment with the rabbi (take identification),* which has religious objects relating to Jewish presence in Argentina in a 19th-century synagogue. Not far away is **Museo del Holocausto** (Shoah Museum) ⓘ *Montevideo 919, T011-4811 3588, www. museodelholocausto.org.ar, Mon-Thu 1100-1900, Fri 1100-1600, US$1.70 (ID required),* a permanent exhibition of pictures, personal and religious items with texts in Spanish on the Holocaust, antisemitism in Argentina and the lives of many Argentine Jews in the pre- and post-war periods. **La Chacarita** ⓘ *Guzmán 670, daily 0700-1700, take Subte Line B to the Federico Lacroze station.* This well known cemetery has the lovingly tended tomb of Carlos Gardel, the tango singer.

North of Plaza de Mayo

The city's traditional shopping centre, Calle Florida, is reserved for pedestrians, with clothes and souvenir shops, restaurants and the elegant **Galerías Pacífico** ⓘ *Florida entre Córdoba y Viamonte, www.galeriaspacifico.com.ar, guided visits from the fountain on lower ground floor, Mon-Fri, 1130, 1630,* a beautiful mall with fine murals and architecture, many exclusive shops and good food outlets. More shops are to be found on Avenida Santa Fe, which crosses Florida at Plaza San Martín. Avenida Corrientes, a street of theatres, bookshops, restaurants and cafés, and nearby Calle Lavalle (partly reserved for pedestrians), used to be the entertainment centre, but both are now regarded as faded. Recoleta, Palermo and Puerto Madero have become much more fashionable (see below). The **Basílica Nuestra Señora de La Merced** ⓘ *J D Perón y Reconquista 207, Mon-Fri 0800-1800,* founded 1604, rebuilt for the third time in the 18th century, has a beautiful interior with baroque and rococo features. In 1807 it was a command post against the invading British. **Museo y Biblioteca Mitre** ⓘ *San Martín 336, T011-4394 8240, www.museomitre.gov.ar, Mon-Fri 1300-1730, US$1.70,* preserves intact the household of President Bartolomé Mitre; has a coin and map collection and historical archives.

The **Plaza San Martín** has a monument to San Martín at the western corner of the main park and, at the north end, a memorial with an eternal flame to those who fell in the Falklands/Malvinas War of 1982. On the plaza is **Palacio San Martín** ⓘ *Arenales 761, T011-4819 8092, www.mrecic.gov.ar, Thu 1500 free tours in Spanish and English.* Built 1905-1909, it is three houses linked together, now the Foreign Ministry. It has collections of prehispanic and 20th-century art. On the opposite side of the plaza is the opulent **Palacio Paz** (Círculo Militar) ⓘ *Av Santa Fe 750, T011-4311 1071, www.circulomilitar.org, guided tours Wed-Fri 1100, 1500, Tue 1500, Sat 1100, US$7.50 (in English Wed 1530, US$9,20).* The Círculo Militar includes **Museo de Armas** ⓘ *Av Santa Fe 702, Tue-Fri 1300-1900, Sat 1400-1900, US$1.70,* which has all kinds of weaponry related to Argentine history, including the 1982 Falklands/Malvinas War, plus Oriental weapons.

Plaza Fuerza Aérea Argentina (formerly Plaza Británica) has the clock tower presented by British and Anglo-Argentine residents, while in the **Plaza Canadá** (in front of the Retiro Station) there is a Pacific Northwest Indian totem pole, donated by the Canadian government. Behind Retiro station is **Museo Nacional Ferroviario** ⓘ *Av del Libertador 405, T011-4318 3343, daily 1030-1800 (closed on holidays), free.* For railway fans: locomotives, machinery, documents of the Argentine system's history; the building is in very poor condition. In a warehouse beside is the workshop of the sculptor Carlos Regazzoni who recycles refuse material from railways.

The **Museo de Arte Hispanoamericano Isaac Fernández Blanco** ⓘ *Suipacha 1422 (3 blocks west of Retiro), T011-4327 0228, www.museos.buenosaires.gob.ar/mifb. htm, Tue-Fri, 1400-1900, Sat, Sun and holidays 1100-1900, Thu free, US$0.85,* is one of the city's best museums. It contains a fascinating collection of colonial art, especially paintings and silver, also temporary exhibitions of Latin American art, in a beautiful neocolonial mansion (Palacio Noel, 1920s) with Spanish gardens; weekend concerts.

Recoleta and Palermo

Nuestra Señora del Pilar, Junín 1898, is a jewel of colonial architecture dating from 1732 (renovated in later centuries), facing onto the public gardens of Recoleta. A fine wooden image of San Pedro de Alcántara, attributed to the famous 17th-century Spanish sculptor Alonso Cano, is preserved in a side chapel on the left, and there are stunning gold altars. Upstairs is an interesting museum of religious art. Next to it, the **Cemetery of the Recoleta** ① *entrance at Junín 1790, near Museo de Bellas Artes (see below), www.cementeriorecoleta.com.ar, 0700-1700, tours in Spanish and English are available (visitasguiadasrecoleta@buenosaires.gob.ar)*, is one of the sights of Buenos Aires. With its streets and alleys separating family mausoleums built in every imaginable architectural style, La Recoleta is often compared to a miniature city. Among the famous names from Argentine history is Evita Perón who lies in the Duarte family mausoleum: to find it from the entrance go to the first tree-filled plaza; turn left and where this avenue meets a main avenue (go just beyond the Turriaca tomb), turn right; then take the third passage on the left. On Saturday and Sunday there is a good craft market in the park on Plaza Francia outside the cemetery (1000-1800), with street artists and performers. Next to the cemetery, the **Centro Cultural Recoleta** ① *T011-4803 1040, www.centroculturalrecoleta.org, Tue-Fri 1400-2100, Sat, Sun, holidays 1200-2100*, specializes in contemporary local art.

The excellent **Museo de Bellas Artes** (National Gallery) ① *Av del Libertador 1473, T011-5288 9999, www.mnba.org.ar, Tue-Fri 1230-2030, Sat-Sun 0930-2030, free*, gives a taste of Argentine art, as well as having a fine collection of European works, particularly post-Impressionist. Superb Argentine 19th- and 20th-century paintings, sculpture and wooden carvings; also films, classical music concerts and art courses. **Biblioteca Nacional** (National Library) ① *Av del Libertador 1600 y Agüero 2502, T011-4808 6000, www.bn.gov.ar, Mon-Fri 0900-2100, Sat and Sun 1200-1900, closed Jan*, is housed in a modern building and contains an art gallery and periodical archives (only a fraction of the extensive stock can be seen); cultural events are held here too. Next to it is the **Museo del Libro y de la Lengua** ① *Av Las Heras 2555, T011-4808 0090, Tue-Sun 1400-1900, free*, whose exhibitions illustrate singularities of the Spanish (castellano) spoken in Argentina and the local publishing industry. The **Museo Nacional de Arte Decorativo** ① *Av del Libertador 1902, T011-4802 6606, www.mnad.org.ar, Tue-Sun 1400-1900 (closed Sun in Jan), US$1.70, Tue free, guided visits US$2.50 in Spanish, English and French, check times*, contains collections of painting, furniture, porcelain, crystal and sculpture exhibited in sumptuous halls, once a family residence.

Palermo Chico is a delightful residential area with several houses of once-wealthy families, dating from the early 20th century. The predominant French style of the district was broken in 1929 by the rationalist lines of the **Casa de la Cultura** ① *Rufino de Elizalde 2831, T011-4808 0553, www.fnartes.gov.ar, Tue-Sun 1500-2000 (Jan closed)*. The original residence of the writer Victoria Ocampo, this was a gathering place for artists and intellectuals and is now an attractive cultural centre with art exhibitions and occasional concerts.

The **Museo de Arte Popular José Hernández** ① *Av del Libertador 2373, T011-4803 2384, www.museohernandez.buenosaires.gob.ar, Wed-Fri 1300-1900, Sat-Sun*

4 Recoleta & Palermo

To ⑤ ⑨ ①, Palermo Metro Station & Las Cañitas

To Belgrano, Museo Histórico Sarmiento, Museo de Arte Español Enrique Larreta & Museo Casa de Yrurtia

To Museo de Artes Plásticas Eduardo Sívori

Planetarium

Colombia

Av Sarmiento

Plaza Italia

PALERMO

A Berro

Japanese Garden

Palermo Parks (Parque Tres de Febrero)

Botanical Gardens

Zoological Gardens

Rep de la India

Lafinur

Av del Libertador

Av Casares

Museo Evita

Gutierrez

Cabello

Cervino

E Segui

República Arabe Siria

200 metres

200 yards

Av Gral Las Heras

Ugarteche

Cavia

Av Pte J Alcorta

Paseo Alcorta Shopping Mall

S Ortiz

Av Scalabrini Ortiz

J Salguero

M Coronado

MALBA

Benti

Araoz

French

Paunero

S Martin de Tours

Alzani

J Alvarez

J Salguero

S Ruggeri

Bulnes

Carter

Av Ocampo

Museo de Motivos Populares Argentinos José Hernández

Bulnes

Av Cnel Diaz

Elizalde

Casa de la Cultura

Billinghurst

Pacheco de Melo

Peña

Museo de Arte Popular José Hernández

P Lucena

V López

Tagle

Austria

S de Bustamante

Bollini

Museo del Libro y de la Lengua

Biblioteca Nacional

Austria

Libres del Sur

Austria

French

Aguero

Gutierrez

Av Gral las Heras

Galileo

Coper

Guido

Gelly y Obes

Museo de Bellas Artes

Bibiloni

Juncal

Laprida

Anchorena

Barrientos

Cantilo

Av Alvear

Dr Agote

Av Pte Alcorta

Gonzalez

RECOLETA

Azcuenaga

Vicente López

Av Pueyrredon

Larrea

Peña

de Melo

Av Pueyrredon

Centro Cultural Recoleta

R M Ortiz

Schiaffino

Pte J E Uriburu

Junin

Recoleta Mall

Cemetery of the Recoleta

Nuestra Señora del Pilar

Ayacucho

Av Callao

Quintana

Av Alvear

Av Libertador

To Retiro Station & City Centre

Av Santa Fe

Marcelo T de Alvear

Rodriguez Peña

Montevideo

Patio Bullrich Shopping Centre

Plaza V López

Parera

Ayacucho

Riobamba

Juncal

Arenales

Rodriguez Peña

Paraguay

Av Callao

Plaza R Peña

Montevideo

Arenales

Pavon

Uruguay

Juncal

Arroyo

Cerrito

Libertad

M Callao

Where to stay

1 Alvear Palace
2 Art
3 Back in BA
4 Bo Bo
5 Casa Esmeralda
7 Hostal El Candil
8 Hostel Suites Palermo
9 Krista
10 Legado Mítico
11 Magnolia
12 Querido
13 Solar Soler

Restaurants

1 Arkakao
2 Bröet
3 Clásico y Moderna
4 Como e Casa
5 El Mirasol de la Recova
6 Juana M
7 La Madeleine
8 María de Bambi
9 Milion
11 Persicco
12 Rodi Bar
13 Sirop & El Foiie

Bars & clubs

15 Buller Brewing Company
16 Casa Bar
17 Notorious
18 The Shamrock

➡ Buenos Aires maps

1 Buenos Aires orientation, page 50
2 Metro (Subte), page 52
3 Buenos Aires centre, page 54
4 Recoleta & Palermo, page 59
5 San Telmo, page 63

To ③ ④ ⑨ ①②

To Plaza Cortázar & Palermo Soho Restaurants

To ⑦ ①②

To ①①

To Alto Palermo Shopping Mall

M Bulnes

To Aeroparque

To Aeroparque

To ⑤ To ⑥

and holidays 1000-2000, US$0.20, free Sun; see website for exhibitions, events and workshops, has a wide collection of Argentine folkloric art, with rooms dedicated to indigenous, colonial and gaucho artefacts; there's a handicraft shop and library. The **Museo de Arte Latinoamericano (MALBA)** ① *Av Figueroa Alcorta 3415, T011-4808 6500, www.malba.org.ar, Thu-Mon and holidays 1200-2000, US$5.50, students and seniors US$2.75 (Wed half price, students free, open till 2100); Tue closed*, one of the most important museums in the city, houses renowned Latin American artists' works: powerful, moving and highly recommended. It's not a vast collection, but representative of the best from the continent. It also has a good library, cinema (showing art house films as well as Argentine classics), seminars and a shop, as well as an elegant café, serving delicious food and cakes. Of the fine Palermo parks, the largest is **Parque Tres de Febrero**, famous for its extensive rose garden, Andalusian Patio, and the delightful **Jardín Japonés** (with café) ① *T011-4804 4922, www.jardinjapones.org.ar, daily 1000-1800, US$4, seniors free*. It is a charming place for a walk, delightful for children, and with a good café serving some Japanese dishes. Close by is the **Hipódromo Argentino** (Palermo racecourse) ① *T011-4778 2800, www.palermo.com.ar, races 10 days per month, free*. Opposite the parks are the Botanical and Zoological Gardens. At the entrance to the **Planetarium** ① *just off Belisario Roldán, in Palermo Park, T011-4771 6629, www.planetario. gov.ar, 3 presentations Tue-Fri, 5 at weekends, US$4.20; small museum*, are several large meteorites from Campo del Cielo. The **Museo de Artes Plásticas Eduardo Sívori** ① *Av Infanta Isabel 555 (Parque Tres de Febrero), T011-4774 9452, www.museosivori.org.ar, Tue-Fri 1200-2000, Sat-Sun and holidays 1000-2000 (1800 in winter), US$1.70, Wed free*, emphasises 19th- and 20th-century Argentine art, sculpture and tapestry. The **Botanical Gardens** ① *Santa Fe 3951, T011-4831 4527, www.jardinbotanico.buenosaires.gob.ar, entrance from Plaza Italia (take Subte, line D) or from C República Arabe Siria, Mon-Fri 0800-1800, Sat-Sun 0930-1800 (closes at 1900 in summer), free guided visits Sat-Sun and holidays 1030, 1500*, contain characteristic specimens of the world's vegetation. The trees native to the different provinces of Argentina are brought together in one section; see also the *yerba mate* section. One block beyond is **Museo Evita** ① *Lafinur 2988, T011-4807 0306, www. museoevita.org, Tue-Sun 1100-1900, US$3.50 for non-residents*. In a former women's shelter run by Fundación Eva Perón, the exhibition of dresses, paintings and other items is quite interesting though lacks the expected passion; there's also a library and a café-restaurant. Southwest of here, around Plaza Cortázar, is **Palermo Viejo**, the most atmospheric part of Palermo. It's a very seductive place, characterized by leafy, cobbled streets, bohemian houses and chic eateries and shops.

In Belgrano is the **Museo de Arte Español Enrique Larreta** ① *Juramento 2291, T011-4784 4040, Mon-Fri, 1300-1900, Sat-Sun 1000-2000, guided visits Sat-Sun 1600, 1800, US$0.35, Thu free*. The home of the writer Larreta, with paintings and religious art from the 14th to the 20th century, it also has a beautiful garden. See www.mibelgrano.com.ar/museos.htm for two other museums in this district: **Museo Histórico Sarmiento** ① *Juramento 2180, T011-4782 2354, www.museo sarmiento.gov.ar*, and **Museo Casa de Yrurtia** ① *O'Higgins 2390, T011-4781 0385*.

Jorge Luis Borges

More than any writer, Borges has most vividly captured the spirit of Buenos Aires. Born in the city in 1899, he was obsessed with the myths and realities of Argentina and its culture, and by the wealth of literature from world classics. His entirely original blend of these two different worlds has made him the most influential figure in Argentine literary culture, with a worldwide reputation. In 1914, Borges travelled with his family to live in Switzerland and Spain, where he added Latin, French and German to his already fluent English (he had an English grandmother). He started to write, and became involved with the *Ultraísmo* literary movement, which scorned the mannerism and opulence of *Modernismo* for a style that embraced shocking imagery and free verse, which Borges described as 'avoiding ornamental artefacts'. Borges became an active member of the literary avant garde when he returned to Buenos Aires in 1921, and in the following few years, he contributed regularly to literary magazines, publishing seven books of poetry and essays that established his lifelong obsessions: a view of life from the margins, and a fascination with authorship and individual consciousness.

From 1933, Borges was Literary Editor of the Newspaper *Crítica*, where he published his *Historia Universal de la Infamia* (A Universal History of Infamy) in 1935, establishing a style somewhere between the non-fictional essay and the fictional short story. In the late 1930s he published a series of significant essays and short stories collections, including *El Jardín de Senderos que se Bifurcan* (The Garden of Forking Paths), in 1931, with one of his most famous stories, *El Sur* (The South). In 1944 Borges published arguably the most important series of stories in the history of Latin American literature, the great *Ficciones* (Fictions), which overturned conventions of realism while exploring the nature of literature itself, together with philosophy and metaphysics. *El Aleph* followed in 1949, and his most important essays, *Otras Inquisiciones* (Other Inquisitions) in 1952. A masterful storyteller, Borges never wrote more than a few pages, and was never tempted by the novel form, insisting that more could be explored in a few elliptical, highly suggestive and poetic lines than in hundred of pages of dull realist prose.

The late 1940s brought him almost total blindness due to glaucoma, and a running dispute with the Perón regime. Borges' work was overlooked in Europe and the USA until the late 1960s, by which time he was completely blind, and wrote mainly poetry, a form that he could compose in his head. The worldwide popularity of his fiction led him to publish two further books of short stories later in life, *El Informe de Brodie* (Dr Brodie's Report, 1970), and *El Libro de Arena* (The Book of Sand, 1975). In his final years, he travelled the world with his companion María Kodama, whom he married. He died in Geneva, of liver cancer, in June 1986.

South of Plaza de Mayo

The church of **San Ignacio de Loyola**, begun 1664, is the oldest colonial building in Buenos Aires (renovated in the 18th and 19th centuries). It stands in a block of Jesuit origin, called the **Manzana de las Luces** (Enlightenment Square – Moreno, Alsina, Perú and Bolívar). Also in this block are the **Colegio Nacional de Buenos Aires** ① *Bolívar 263, T011-4331 0734*, formerly the site of the Jesuits' Colegio Máximo, the Procuraduría de las Misiones (today the **Mercado de las Luces**, a crafts market) and 18th-century **tunnels**. For centuries the whole block was the centre of intellectual activity, though little remains today but a small **cultural centre** ① *T011-4343 3260, www.manzanadelasluces.gov.ar, guided tours from Perú 272, Mon-Fri 1500, Sat and Sun 1500, 1630, 1800 in Spanish (in English by prior arrangement), arrive 15 mins before tour, US$2.50; the tours explore the tunnels and visit the buildings on C Perú*, with art courses, concerts, plays and film shows. The **Museo de la Ciudad** ① *Alsina 412, T011-4343 2123, Mon-Fri 1100-1900, Sat, Sun 1000-2000, US$0.20, free on Mon and Wed*, has a permanent exhibition covering social history and popular culture, and special exhibitions on daily life in Buenos Aires that are changed every two months. There's also a reference library open to the public.

Santo Domingo ① *Defensa y Belgrano, Mon-Fri 0900-1300, Sun 1000-1200*, was founded in 1751. During the British attack on Buenos Aires in 1806 some of Whitelocke's soldiers took refuge in the church. The local forces bombarded it, the British capitulated and their regimental colours were preserved in the church. General Belgrano is buried here. The church holds occasional concerts.

Museo Etnográfico JB Ambrosetti ① *Moreno 350, T011-4345 8196, see Facebook, Tue-Fri 1300-1900, Sat-Sun 1500-1900 (closed Jan), US$0.50, guided visits Sat-Sun 1600*. contains anthropological and ethnographic collections from Patagonian and Argentina's northwest cultures (the latter a rich collection displayed on the first floor). There's also a small international room with a magnificent Japanese Buddhist altar.

San Telmo and La Boca

One of the few places which still has late colonial and Rosista buildings (mostly renovated in the 20th century) is the *barrio* of **San Telmo**, south of Plaza de Mayo. It's an atmospheric place, with lots of cafés, antique shops and little art galleries. On Sundays, it has a great atmosphere, with an antiques market at the Plaza Dorrego (see page 79), free tango shows (1000-1800) and live music. The **Museo de Arte Moderno de Buenos Aires (MAMBA)** ① *Av San Juan 350, T011-4342 3001, Tue-Fri 1100-1900, Sat, Sun and holidays 1100-2000, US$0.85, Tue free*, has temporary art exhibitions from local and foreign artists. Next door is the **Museo de Arte Contemporáneo de Buenos Aires (MACBA)** ① *T011-5299 2010, www.macba.com.ar, Mon-Fri 1200-1900, Sat, Sun 1100-1930, US$3.50 (Wed US$1.70)*, focusing on geometric abstraction.

East of the Plaza de Mayo, behind the Casa Rosada, a broad avenue, Paseo Colón, runs south towards San Telmo and, as Avenida Almirante Brown, on to the old port district of **La Boca**, where the Riachuelo flows into the Plata. To get there, take a radio taxi from the centre or San Telmo; to return, call for a taxi from any café, US$7 one way. The much-photographed, brightly painted tin and wooden houses cover one block of the pedestrianized Caminito. As La Boca is the poorest and roughest area within central Buenos Aires, tourists are limited to this little street running from the Plaza La Vuelta de Rocha. You can also visit **Fundación Proa** ⓘ *Av Pedro de Mendoza 1929, T011-4104 1000, www.proa.org, Tue-Sun 1100-1900*, for varied art exhibitions, cultural events and for its café-restaurant with a view, and the **Museo de Bellas Artes Benito Quinquela Martín** ⓘ *Av Pedro de Mendoza 1835, T011-4301 1080, www.museoquinquela.gov.ar, Tue-Fri 1000-1800, Sat, Sun and holidays 1100-1800 (Tue-Sun 1100-1730 in summer), US$1.70*, with over 1000 works by Argentine artists, particularly Benito Quinquela Martín (1890-1977), who painted La Boca port life. It also houses sculptures and figureheads rescued from ships. Do not go anywhere else in La Boca and avoid it at night. The area is especially rowdy when the Boca Juniors football club is playing at home. At Boca

Buenos Aires maps
1 Buenos Aires orientation, page 50
2 Metro (Subte), page 52
3 Buenos Aires centre, page 54
4 Recoleta & Palermo, page 59
5 San Telmo, page 63

Where to stay
1 Art Factory
2 Axel
3 Circus
4 Garden House
5 Hostal de Granados
6 Hostel-Inn Buenos Aires
7 Kilca Hostel & Backpacker
8 La Casita de San Telmo
9 La Cayetana Historic House
10 Lola House
11 Lugar Gay de Buenos Aires
12 Mansión Dandi Royal
13 Ostinatto
14 Sabatico Travelers Hostel
16 Telmho

Restaurants
1 Brasserie Petanque
2 Británico
3 Dorrego
4 Dylan
5 Gran Parilla del Plata
6 La Brigada
7 La Poesía
8 Naturalisa Sabia
9 Nonna Bianca
10 Pride Café

Bars & clubs
11 Bar Seddon

Juniors stadium is **Museo de la Pasión Boquense** ① *Brandsen 805, T011-4362 1100, www.museoboquense.com, daily 1000-1800, US$9, guided tour of the stadium in Spanish or English, 1100-1700, plus ticket to the museum, US$12.*

Docks and Costanera Sur

Fragata Presidente Sarmiento ① *dock 3, Av Alicia Moreau de Justo 980, Puerto Madero, T011-4334 9386, daily 1000-1900, US$0.35,* was a naval training ship until 1961; now it's a museum. Nearby, in dock 4, is the **Corbeta Uruguay** ① *T011-4314 1090, daily 1000-1900, US$0.35, for both ships see www.ara.mil.ar,* the ship that rescued Otto Nordenskjold's Antarctic expedition in 1903. The **Puerto Madero** dock area has been renovated; the 19th-century warehouses are restaurants and bars, an attractive place for a stroll and popular nightspot. In dock 4 there is also **Colección Fortabat** ① *Olga Cossettini 141, T011-4310 6600, www.coleccionfortabat. org.ar, Tue-Sun 1200-2000, US$6,* which houses a great art collection. East of San Telmo on the far side of the docks, the Avenida Costanera runs as a long, spacious boulevard. A stretch of marshland reclaimed from the river forms the interesting **Costanera Sur Wildlife Reserve** ① *entrances at Av Tristán Achával Rodríguez 1550 (take Estados Unidos east from San Telmo) or next to the Buquebús ferry terminal (take Av Córdoba east), T011-4315 4129; for pedestrians and bikers only, Tue-Sun 0800-1800 (in summer, closes at 1900), free,* where over 150 bird species have been spotted over the past few years. Free guided tours at weekends and holidays 0930, 1600, from the administration next to the southern entrance, but much can be seen from the road before then (binoculars useful). Also free nocturnal visits every month on the Friday closest to the full moon (book Monday before, T011-4313 4275). To get there take colectivos 4, 130 or 152. It's half an hour walk from the entrance to the river shore and about three hours to walk the whole perimeter. In summer it's very hot with little shade. For details (particularly birdwatching) contact **Aves Argentinas/ AOP** (see page 87), or see www.reservacostanera.com.ar (English version).

Around Buenos Aires → *For listings, see pages 67-87.*

Tigre → *Population: 42,000 (Partido de Tigre –Tigre county – 376,000).*

This touristy little town, 32 km northwest of Buenos Aires, is a popular weekend destination lying on the lush jungly banks of the Río Luján, with a funfair and an excellent fruit and handicrafts market (Puerto de Frutos, Monday-Friday 1000-1800, Saturday, Sunday and holidays 1000-1900 with access from Calles Sarmiento or Perú). There are restaurants on the waterfront in Tigre across the Río Tigre from the railway line, along Lavalle and Paseo Victorica; cheaper places can be found on Italia and Cazón on the near side, or at the Puerto de Frutos. North of the town is the delta of the Río Paraná: innumerable canals and rivulets, with holiday homes and restaurants on the banks and a fruit-growing centre. The fishing is excellent and the peace is only disturbed by motor-boats at weekends. Regattas are held in November. Take a trip on one of the regular launch services (*lanchas colectivas*) which run to all parts of the delta, including taxi launches – watch prices for

Carlos Gardel

To this day there is still a lot of controversy about the origins of Argentina's favourite performer. Most people argue that Gardel, the legendary singer whose name is virtually synonymous with tango, was born in 1890 in Toulouse, France, to Berthe Gardés and an unknown father. To avoid social stigma, his mother decided to emigrate to the Abasto market area of Buenos Aires when her son was just two years old, and it was partly these humble beginnings that helped him to become an icon for poor *Porteños*.

Just as the exact origin of tango itself is something of a mystery, Gardel's formative years around the city are obscure, until around 1912 when he began his artistic career in earnest, performing as one half of the duo Gardel-Razzano. He began his recording career with Columbia with a recording of 15 traditional songs, but it was with his rendition of *Mi Noche Triste* (My Sorrowful Night) in 1917, that his mellifluous voice became known. As *tango-canción* became popular –

the song rather than just a musical accompaniment to the dance – Gardel's career took off, and by the early 1920s he was singing entirely within this new genre, and achieving success as far afield as Madrid.

Gardel became a solo artist in 1925 and with his charm and natural machismo was the very epitome of tango both in Argentina and, following his tours to Europe, around the world. Between 1933 and 1935, he was based in New York, starring in numerous Spanish-speaking films, and the English language *The Tango on Broadway* in 1934. On 24 June 1935, while on a tour of South America, his plane from Bogotá to Cali crashed into another on the ground while taking off. Gardel was killed instantly, he was only 45. Gardel had recorded some 900 songs during his relatively short career, and the brilliance of his voice, the way he represented the spirit of the Río de la Plata to his fans at home, and the untimely nature of his dramatic death ensured the endurance of his popularity.

these – from the wharf (Estación Fluvial). Tourist catamarans run daily services: one- to two-hour trips, US$13-17, from Lavalle 499 on Río Tigre, T011-4731 0261/63, www.tigreencatamaran.com.ar, and three to seven services daily, 1½-hour trips, US$15, from Puerto de Frutos, **Río Tur** (T011-4731 0280, www.rioturcatamaranes. com.ar). **Sturla** (Estación Fluvial, oficina 10, T011-4731 1300, www.sturlaviajes. com.ar) runs four one-hour trips a day, US$15 (includes a ride on **Bus Turístico**); they also have trips with lunch, night-time boat trips, full-day excursions from the centre of Buenos Aires, commuting services to Puerto Madero, and more. You can also hire kayaks, canoes or rowing boats, rent houses, or visit *recreos*, little resorts with swimming pools, tennis courts, bar and restaurant. **Bus Turístico** (T011-4731 1300, www.busturisticotigre.com.ar) runs one-hour tours, US$5, every hour on an open-top bus with 10 stops, starting 1040 at the railway station. **Tigre tourist office** ① *by the Estación Fluvial, Mitre 305, T0800-888 84473, www.tigre.gov.ar/turismo, also* *at Juncal 1600 and the Puerto de Frutos*, with a full list of houses to rent, activities, etc. **Centro de Guías de Tigre y Delta** ① *Estación Fluvial of 2, T011-4731 3555, www.guiastigreydelta.com.ar*, can organize guided walks and launch trips.

The **Museo Naval** ① *Paseo Victorica 602, T011-4749 0608, Tue-Fri 0830-1730, Sat-Sun and holidays 1030-1830, US$1.70 (voluntary fee)*, is worth a visit to see the displays on the Argentine navy. There are also relics of the 1982 Falklands/Malvinas War. The **Museo de Arte** ① *Paseo Victorica 972, T011-4512 4528, www.mat.gov.ar, Wed-Fri 0900-1900, Sat-Sun 1200-1900, US$2.50*, hosts a collection of Argentine figurative art in the former Tigre Club Casino, a beautiful belle époque building.

Museo del Mate ① *Lavalle 289, T011-4506 9594, www.elmuseodelmate.com, Wed-Sun 1100-1800 (1100-1900 in summer), US$2.50*, tells the history of *mate* and has an interesting collection of the associated paraphernalia.

Isla Martín García

This island in the Río de la Plata (Juan Díaz de Solís' landfall in 1516) used to be a military base. Now it is an ecological/historical centre and an ideal excursion from the capital, with many trails through the cane brakes, trees and rocky outcrops – interesting birds and flowers. Boat trips: four weekly from Tigre at 0900, returning 2000, three-hour journey, US$55 return including lunch, *asado* and guide; US$90 per person, including weekend overnight at inn, full board. Reservations only through **Cacciola** (address under Tigre, Transport, page 85), who also handle bookings for the inn and restaurant on the island. There is also a campsite.

For hotel and restaurant price codes and other relevant information, see pages 20-26.

⦿ Where to stay

Shop around for hotels offering discounts on multi-night stays. The tourist offices at Ezeiza and Aeroparque airports book rooms. A/c is a must in high summer. Finding hotels for Fri, Sat, Sun nights can be difficult and hostels can get very busy, resulting in pressure on staff. A bed in a hostel dorm costs US$10-20. The range of 'boutique' hotels and hostels is impressive, especially in Palermo and San Telmo. The same applies to restaurants, bars and clubs. There are far more than we can list here. There are fine examples of the **Four Seasons** (www.fourseasons.com/buenosaires), **Hilton** (www.hilton.com), **Hyatt** (www.buenosaires.park.hyatt.com), **Marriott** (www.marriott.com), **NH** (www.nh-hoteles.com), **Pestana** (www.pestana.com), **Sofitel** (www.sofitel.com) and **Unique Hotels** (www.uniquehotels.com.ar) chains. Hotels will store luggage, and most have English-speaking staff.

Centre *p53, map p54*
$$$$ Alvear Palace, Av Alvear 1891, T011-4808 2100, www.alvearpalace.com. The height of elegance, an impeccably preserved 1920s Recoleta palace, sumptuous marble foyer, with Louis XV-style chairs, and a charming orangery where you can take tea with superb patisseries. Antique-filled bedrooms. Recommended.
$$$$ Casa Calma, Suipacha 1015, T011-5199 2800, www.casacalmahotel.com. A relaxing haven in a downtown setting, homely yet luxurious, with a wellness centre and honesty bar.

$$$$ Faena Universe, Martha Salotti 445 (Puerto Madero), T011-4010 9000, www.faena.com. Set in a 100-year-old silo, renovated by Philippe Starck, this is not for all budgets or tastes. Eclectic decoration, staff trained to be perfect.
$$$$-$$$ Castelar, Av de Mayo 1152, T011-4383 5000, www.castelarhotel.com.ar. A wonderfully elegant 1920s hotel which retains all the original features in the grand entrance and bar. Cosy bedrooms, charming staff, and excellent value. Also a spa with Turkish baths and massage. Highly recommended.
$$$$-$$$ Dolmen, Suipacha 1079, T011-4315 7117, www.hoteldolmen.com.ar. Good location, smart spacious entrance lobby, with a calm relaxing atmosphere, good professional service, modern, comfortable well-designed rooms, small pool.
$$$$-$$$ El Conquistador, Suipacha 948, T011-4328 3012, www.elconquistador.com.ar. Stylish 1970s hotel, which retains the wood and chrome foyer, but has bright modern rooms, and a lovely light restaurant on the 10th floor with great views. Well situated, good value.
$$$$-$$$ Panamericano, Carlos Pellegrini 551, T011-4348 5000, www.panamericano.us. Very smart and modern hotel, with luxurious and tasteful rooms, covered rooftop pool, and superb restaurant, **Tomo 1**. Excellent service too. Also has properties in Bariloche (www.panamericanobariloche.com) and El Calafate (www.casalossauces.com).
$$$ Art, Azcuénaga 1268, T011-4821 6248, www.arthotel.com.ar. Charming boutique hotel on a quiet residential street, only a few blocks from Recoleta or Av Santa Fe, simply but warmly

decorated, good service, solarium, compact standard rooms.

$$$ Bisonte Palace, MT de Alvear 902, T011-4328 4751, www.hotelesbisonte. com. Charming, with calm entrance foyer, which remains gracious thanks to courteous staff. Plain but spacious rooms, ample breakfast, good location. Very good value.

$$$ Colón, Carlos Pellegrini 507, T011-4320 3500, www.exehotelcolon. com. Splendid location overlooking Av 9 de Julio and Teatro Colón, extremely good value. Charming bedrooms, comfortable, gym, great breakfasts, and perfect service. Highly recommended.

$$$ Dorá, Maipú 963, T011-4312 7391, www.dorahotel.com.ar. Charming and old-fashioned with comfortable rooms, good service, attractive lounge with paintings. Warmly recommended.

$$$ Goya, Suipacha 748, T011-4322 9269, www.goyahotel.com.ar. Welcoming and central, worth paying more for superior rooms, though all are comfortable. Good breakfast, English spoken.

$$$ Hispano, Av de Mayo 861, T011-4345 2020, www.hhispano.com.ar. Plain but comfortable rooms in this hotel which has been welcoming travellers since the 1950s, courtyard and small garden, central.

$$$ Marbella, Av de Mayo 1261, T011-4383 3573, www.hotelmarbella.com.ar. Modernized, and central, though quiet, multilingual. Recommended.

$$$ Moreno, Moreno 376, T011-6091 2000, www.morenobuenosaires.com. 150 m from the Plaza de Mayo, decorated in dark, rich tones, large rooms, good value, jacuzzi, gym and chic bar, winery and restaurant.

$$$ Plaza San Martín Suites, Suipacha 1092, T011-5093 7000, www. plazasanmartin.com.ar. Neat modern self-contained apartments right in the city centre, comfortable and attractively decorated, with lounge and little kitchen. Pet friendly, room service. Good value.

$$$ Waldorf, Paraguay 450, T011-4312 2071, www.waldorf-hotel.com. ar. Welcoming staff and a comfortable mixture of traditional and modern in this centrally located hotel. Good value, with a buffet breakfast, English spoken. Recommended.

$ La Argentina, Av de Mayo 860, T011-4342 0078. Cheap, central and rickety, but it stands the test of time. Amazing old building, bringing new meaning to the term 'high-ceilinged'; can be noisy if your room is near the 'slam-the-door-shut' elevator. Good, cheap and cheerful restaurant attached, doing very affordable *menú del día*. Recommended.

Youth hostels

$ pp 06 Central, Maipú 306, T011-5219 0052, www.06centralhostel.com. A few metres from the Obelisco and Av Corrientes, simple, spacious dorms, nicely decorated doubles (**$$**), cosy communal area.

$ pp BA Stop, Rivadavia 1194, T011-4382 7406, www.bastop.com. In a converted 1900s corner block, dorms, private rooms (**$$** double), large-screen TV, table tennis, bar, English spoken, safe, very helpful staff. Repeatedly recommended.

$ El Cóndor y el Aguila Hostel, Espinosa 1628, near junction Av San Martín and Av Juan B Justo, T011-4581 6663, www.el condoryelaguila.com.ar. 5 private rooms and 4 dorms. Terrace, laundry and internet access. Free transfer from Retiro and Aeroparque, and free tea and coffee.

$ pp Hostel Suites Obelisco, Av Corrientes 830, T011-4328 4040, www.hostelsuites.com. Elegant hostel built in a completely restored old building in the heart of the city.

Dorms, doubles and private apartments (**$$**), DVD room, laundry service. Free transfer from Ezeiza airport. HI discount.
$ pp **Limehouse Hostel**, Lima 11, T011-4383 4561, www.limehouse.com.ar. Dorms for up to 12 and doubles with and without bath (**$$**), popular, typical city hostel with bar, roof terrace, 'chilled', great if you like the party atmosphere, efficient staff. Recommended.
$ pp **Milhouse Hostel**, Hipólito Yrigoyen 959, T011-4345 9604, www.milhouse hostel.com. In 1890 house, lovely rooms (**$$$** in double) and dorms, comfortable, laundry, tango lessons, very popular so reconfirm bookings at all times.
$ pp **Portal del Sur**, Hipólito Yrigoyen 855, T011-4342 8788, www.portaldel surba.com.ar. Nice dorms and especially lovely doubles (**$$$**) and singles in a converted 19th-century building. Recommended for single travellers.
$ pp **St Nicholas**, B Mitre 1691, T011-4373 5920, www.snhostel.com. Beautifully converted old house, now a party hostel with spotless rooms, large roof terrace and a pub with daily live shows; also double rooms (**$$**).
$ pp **V&S**, Viamonte 887, T011-4322 0994, www.hostelclub.com. Central popular hostel (**$$$** in attractive double room, bath), café, tango classes, tours, warm atmosphere, welcoming. Recommended.

Palermo *p58, map p59*
$$$$ Legado Mítico, Gurruchaga 1848, T011-4833 1300, www.legadomitico.com. Stylish small hotel with 11 rooms named after Argentine cultural legends. They use local designs and products. Luxurious and recommended.
$$$$ Magnolia, Julián Alvarez 1746, T011-4867 4900, www.magnoliahotel boutique.com. Lovely boutique hotel in a quiet area. This refurbished early 20th-century house has attractively designed rooms opening onto the street or to inner courtyards and a perfect retreat on its rooftop terrace.
$$$$ Querido, Juan Ramírez de Velazco 934, T011-4854 6297, www. queridobuenosaires.com. Purpose-built, designed and cared for by a Brazilian-English couple. 7 rooms, 4 of which have balconies, for a comfortable stay in Villa Crespo area, a few blocks from Palermo Soho and from the subway.
$$$$-$$$ Bo Bo, Guatemala 4882, T011-4774 0505, www.bobohotel.com. On a leafy street, 15 rooms decorated in contemporary style, some with private balconies, excellent restaurant.
$$$$-$$$ Krista, Bonpland 1665, T011-4771 4697, www.kristahotel.com.ar. Intimate, hidden behind the plain façade of an elegant townhouse, well placed for restaurants. Good value, comfortable, individually designed spacious rooms, wheelchair access.
$$$ Solar Soler, Soler 5676, T011-4776 3065, www.solarsoler.com.ar. Welcoming B&B in Palermo Hollywood, excellent service. Recommended.

Youth hostels
$ pp **Back in BA**, El Salvador 5115, T011-4774 2859, www.backinba.com. Small hostel with dorms for up to 6 and private rooms (**$$**), lockers with charging points, patio, bar, information, tours and classes can be arranged, good Palermo Soho location.
$ pp **Casa Esmeralda**, Honduras 5765, T011-4772 2446, www.casaesmeralda. com.ar. Laid-back, dorms and doubles (**$$**), neat garden with hammocks. Offers basic comfort with great charm.
$ pp **Hostal El Candil**, Lerma 476, T011-4899 1547, www.hostalelcandil.com. Argentine/Italian-owned hostel with

shared rooms and doubles (**$$**), international atmosphere, quiet, comfortable, welcoming, rooftop terrace, tours arranged.

$ pp Hostel Suites Palermo, Charcas 4752, T011-4773 0806, www.suites palermo.com. A beautiful century-old residence with the original grandeur partially preserved and a quiet atmosphere. Comfortable renovated dorms and private rooms with bath (**$$** doubles), good service, small travel agency, free internet, Wi-Fi, cooking and laundry facilities, DVD room and breakfast included. Free transfer from Ezeiza airport. HI discount.

San Telmo and around *p62, map p63*
$$$$ Mansión Dandi Royal, Piedras 922, T011-4361 3537, www.hotelmansion dandiroyal.com. A wonderfully restored 1903 residence, small upmarket hotel with an elegant tango atmosphere, small pool, good value. Daily tango lessons and *milonga* every Fri at 2130.

$$$$-$$$ Axel Hotel, Venezuela 649, T011-4136 9393, www.axelhotels.com. Stunning gay hotel with 5 floors of stylishly designed rooms, each floor with a cosy living area, rooftop pool, gourmet restaurant. Recommended.

$$$$-$$$ La Cayetana Historic House, México 1330, T011-4383 2230, www.la cayetanahotel.com.ar. 11 suites in a beautifully restored 1820s house, each room individually designed, quiet, buffet breakfast, parking. Recommended.

$$$ La Casita de San Telmo, Cochabamba 286, T011-4307 5073, www.lacasitadesantelmo.com. 7 rooms in restored 1840s house, most open onto a garden with a beautiful fig tree, owners are tango fans; rooms rented by day, week or month.

$$$ Lola House, Castro Barros 1073, Boedo, T011-4932 2139, www.lolahouse. com.ar. Small boutique hotel in a nicely refurbished house, welcoming owners, comfortable, safe; 10 mins from centre on Subte E, also on bus routes.

$$$ Lugar Gay de Buenos Aires, Defensa 1120 (no sign), T011-4300 4747, www.lugargay.com.ar. A men-only gay B&B with 8 comfortable rooms, video room, jacuzzi, a stone's throw from Plaza Dorrego.

$$$ Telmho, Defensa 1086, T011-4116 5467, www.telmho-hotel.com.ar. Smart rooms overlooking Plaza Dorrego, huge beds, modern bathrooms, lovely roof garden, helpful staff.

Youth hostels
$ pp Art Factory, Piedras 545, T011-4343 1463, www.artfactoryba.com.ar. Large, early 1900s house converted into a hostel, informal atmosphere with individually designed and brightly painted private rooms (some with bath, **$$**), dorms, halfway between the centre and San Telmo.

$ pp Circus, Chacabuco 1020, T011-4300 4983, www.hostelcircus.com. Stylish rooms for 2 (**$$**) to 4 people, tastefully renovated building, small heated swimming pool, bar and restaurant.

$ pp Garden House, Av San Juan 1271, T011-4304 1824, www.gardenhouseba. com.ar. Small, welcoming independent hostel for those who don't want a party atmosphere; good barbecues on the terrace. Dorms and some doubles (**$$**). Recommended.

$ pp Hostal de Granados, Chile 374, T011-4362 5600, www.hostaldegranados. ar. Small, light, well-equipped rooms in an interesting building on a popular street, rooms for 2 (**$$**), dorms for 4 to 8, laundry.

$ pp Hostel-Inn Buenos Aires, Humberto Primo 820, T011-4300 7992, www.hibuenosaires.com. An old 2-storey mansion with dorms for up to 8 people and also private rooms (**$$**), activities, loud parties, individual lockers in every room. HI discount.

$ pp Kilca Hostel & Backpacker, México 1545, between Sáenz Peña and Virrey Cevallos, T011-4381 1966, www.kilcabackpacker.com. In a restored 19th-century house with attractive landscaped patios. A variety of rooms from dorms to doubles; all bathrooms shared, but 1 double with bath (**$$**).

$ pp Ostinatto, Chile 680, T011-4362 9639, www.ostinatto.com. Shared rooms, also has double rooms with and without bath (**$$**), and apartments for rent. Minimalist contemporary design in a 1920s building, very nice, promotes the arts, music, piano bar, movie room, tango lessons, arranges events, rooftop terrace.

$ pp Sabatico Travelers Hostel, México 1410, T011-4381 1138, www.sabaticohostel.com.ar. Dorms and double rooms with and without bath (**$$**), full range of services and information, rooftop barbecue, mini pool and bar. Good location.

Apartments/self-catering/homestays

B&T Argentina, T011-4876 5000, www.bytargentina.com. Accommodation in student residences and host families; also furnished flats.

Bahouse, www.bahouse.com.ar. Very good flats, by the week or month, all furnished and well located in San Telmo, Retiro, Recoleta, Belgrano, Palermo and the centre.

Casa 34, Nicaragua 6045, T011-4775 0207, www.casa34.com. Helpful, with a big range.

Tu Casa Argentina, Fitzroy 2179, T011-4773 5544, www.tucasargentina.com. Furnished flats by the day, week, month (from US$55 per day). Credit cards not accepted, deposit and rent payable in dollars. Efficient and helpful.

Tigre *p64*

$$$$ La Becasina, Arroyo Las Cañas (Delta islands second section), T011-4328 2687, www.labecasina.com. One of Argentina's most delightful places to stay, an hour by launch from Tigre, buried deep from the outside world, with 15 individual lodges on stilts in the water, connected by wooden walkways, all comforts and luxuries provided and tasteful decor, with intimate dining room, jacuzzi and pool amidst the trees. Full board, excellent food and service. Recommended.

$$$$ Villa Julia, Paseo Victorica 800, in Tigre itself, T011-4749 0642, www.villajulia.com.ar. A 1906 villa converted into a chic hotel, beautifully restored fittings, comfortable, good restaurant open to non-residents.

$$$ Los Pecanes, on Arroyo Felicaria, T011-4728 1932, www.hosterialospecanes.com. On a secluded island visited regularly by hummingbirds. Ana and Richard offer a few comfortable rooms and delicious food. Ideal base for boat excursions and birdwatching. Cheaper Mon-Fri.

$$$-$ Posada de 1860, Av Libertador 190, T011-4749 4034, www.tigrehostel.com.ar. A beautiful stylish villa with suites and an associated **Hostel Tigre** at No 137 (same phone and website) with dorms for up to 6 (**$ pp**), and private rooms (**$$$** double).

$$ TAMET, Río Carapachay Km 24, T011-4728 0055, www.tamet.com.ar. For a relaxing stay on an island with sandy beaches and quite comfortable premises, with breakfast, games and canoes. Also has camping.

⑦ Restaurants

Eating out in Buenos Aires is one of the city's great pleasures, with a huge variety of restaurants from the chic to the cheap. To try some of Argentina's excellent steak, choose from one of the many *parrillas*, where your huge slab of lean meat will be expertly cooked over a wood fire. If in doubt about where to eat, head for Puerto Madero, the revamped docks area, an attractive place to stroll along the waterfront before dinner. There are good places here, generally in stylish interiors, serving international as well as local cuisine, with good service if a little overpriced. Take a radio taxi to Palermo or Las Cañitas for a wide range of excellent restaurants all within strolling distance. For more information on the gastronomy of Buenos Aires see: www.guiaoleo. com.ar, restaurant guide in Spanish.

There is a growing interest in less conventional eating out, from secret, or *puerta cerrada*, restaurants, to local eateries off the normal restaurant circuit, exploring local markets and so on. 2 fantastic food-oriented blogs in English are: www.saltshaker.net, chef Dan Perlman who also runs a highly recommended private restaurant in his house, see website for details; and www. buenosairesfoodies.com. Another highly regarded closed-door option can be found at **The Argentine Experience**, http://theargentineexperience.com, while tours are run by **Parrilla Tour Buenos Aires**, http://parrillatour.com/.

Some restaurants are *tenedor libre*: eat as much as you like for a fixed price. Most cafés serve tea or coffee plus *facturas* (pastries) for breakfast.

Centre *p53, map p54*
$$$ Dadá, San Martín 941. A restaurant and bar with eclectic decoration. Good for gourmet lunches.
$$$ Sorrento, Av Corrientes 668 (just off Florida). Intimate, elegant atmosphere, one of the most traditional places in the centre for very good pastas and seafood.
$$$ Tancat, Paraguay 645. Delicious Spanish food, very popular at lunchtime.
$$$-$$ Gijón, Chile y San José. Very good-value *parrilla* at this popular *bodegón*, south of Congreso district.
$$ Al paso y algo más, San Martín 487. Open till 1630. Recommended choice for *choripan* and *churrasquito* sandwiches plus other meat dishes, cramped at lunchtime.
$$ Fikä, Hipólito Yrigoyen 782. Mon-Fri open till 1900, Sat closes at 1600. Popular at lunchtime with a varied menu, is also attractive for a coffee break or a drink.
$$ Gianni's, San Martín 430 and Reconquista 1028. The set menu with the meal-of-the-day makes an ideal lunch. Good risottos and salads. Slow service; open till 1700.
$$ Güerrín, Av Corrientes 1368. A Buenos Aires institution. Serves filling pizza and *faina* (chickpea polenta) which you eat standing up at a bar, or at tables, though you miss out on the colourful local life that way. For an extra service fee, upstairs room is less crowded or noisy.
$$ Las Cuartetas, Av Corrientes 838. A local institution open early to very late for fantastic pizza, can be busy and noisy as it's so popular.
$$ Sam Bucherie, 25 de Mayo 562. Open till 1800. The most imaginative sandwiches and salads downtown.

Cafés
Café Tortoni, Av de Mayo 825-9. This most famous Buenos Aires café has been the elegant haunt of artists and writers

for over 100 years, with marble columns, stained-glass ceilings, old leather chairs, and photographs of its famous clientele on the walls. Live tango. Packed with tourists, pricey, but still worth a visit.
Confitería Ideal, Suipacha 384. One of the most atmospheric cafés in the city. Wonderfully old-fashioned 1930s interior, serving good coffee and excellent cakes with good service. See Tango shows, page 76.
El Gato Negro, Av Corrientes 1669. A beautiful tearoom, serving a choice of coffees and teas, and good cakes. Delightfully scented from the wide range of spices on sale.
Florida Garden, Florida y Paraguay. Another well-known café, popular for lunch, and tea.

Ice cream

The Italian ice cream tradition has been marked for decades by '*heladerías*' such as **Cadore**, Av Corrientes 1695, or **El Vesuvio**, Av Corrientes 1181, the oldest of all.

North of Plaza de Mayo *p57, map p50*
3 blocks west of Plaza San Martín, under the flyover at the northern end of Av 9 de Julio, between Arroyo and Av del Libertador in La Recova, are several recommended restaurants.
$$$ El Mirasol de la Recova, Posadas 1032. Serves top-quality *parrilla* in an elegant atmosphere.
$$$ Juana M, Carlos Pellegrini 1535 (downstairs). Excellent choice, popular with locals for its good range of dishes, and its very good salad bar.

Recoleta *p58, map p59*
$$$ Rodi Bar, Vicente López 1900. Excellent *bife* and other dishes in this typical *bodegón*, welcoming and unpretentious.

$$$ Sirop & Folie, Pasaje del Correo, Vte Lopez 1661, T011-4813 5900. Delightful chic design, delicious French-inspired food, superb patisserie too. Highly recommended.
$$$-$$ La Madeleine, Av Santa Fe 1726. Bright and cheerful choice, quite good pastas.
$$$-$$ María de Bambi, Ayacucho 1821 (with a small branch at Arenales 920). Open till 2130, closed on Sun. This small, quiet place is probably the best value in the area, serving very good and simple meals, also *salón de té* and patisserie.

Tea rooms, café/bars and ice cream
Arkakao, Av Quintana 188. Great ice creams at this elegant tea room.
Bröet, Azcuénaga 1144, www.broet.com.ar. Austrian-owned artisanal bakery with traditionally made bread from around the world.
Clásica y Moderna, Av Callao 892, T011-4812 8707, www.clasicaymoderna.com. One of the city's most welcoming cafés, with a bookshop, great atmosphere, good breakfast through to drinks at night, daily live music and varied shows.
Como en casa, Av Quintana 2, Riobamba 1239, Laprida 1782 and at San Martín y Viamonte (former convent of Santa Catalina). Very popular in the afternoon for its varied and delicious cakes and fruit pies.
Freddo, and **Un'Altra Volta**, ice cream parlours, both with several branches in the city.
Milion, Paraná 1048. Stylish bar and café in an elegant mansion with marble stairs and a garden, good drinks, mixed clientèle. Recommended Fri after midnight.

Palermo *p58, map p59*
This area of Buenos Aires is very popular, with many chic restaurants and bars in

Palermo Viejo (referred to as 'Palermo Soho' for the area next to Plaza Cortázar and 'Palermo Hollywood' for the area beyond the railways and Av Juan B Justo) and the Las Cañitas district. It's a sprawling district, so you could take a taxi to one of these restaurants, and walk around before deciding where to eat. It's also a great place to stop for lunch, with cobbled streets, and 1900s buildings, now housing chic clothes shops. The Las Cañitas area is fashionable, with a wide range of interesting restaurants mostly along Báez, and most opening at around 2000, though only open for lunch at weekends:

$$$ Bio, Humboldt 2192, T011-4774 3880. Open daily. Delicious gourmet organic food, on a sunny corner.

$$$ Campobravo, Báez y Arévalo and Honduras y Fitz Roy. Stylish, minimalist, superb steaks and vegetables on the *parrilla*. Popular and recommended, can be noisy.

$$$ El Manto, Costa Rica 5801, T011-4774 2409. Genuine Armenian dishes, relaxed, good for a quiet evening.

$$$ El Preferido de Palermo, Borges y Guatemala, T011-4774 6585. Very popular *bodegón* serving both Argentine and Spanish-style dishes.

$$$ Janio, Malabia 1805, T011-4833 6540. Open for breakfast through to the early hours. One of Palermo's first restaurants, sophisticated Argentine cuisine in the evening.

$$$ La Cabrera, Cabrera 5127 and 5099. Superb *parrilla* and pasta, huge portions, with 2 branches; very popular. They offer a sparkling white wine while you wait.

$$$ Morelia, Baez 260 and Humboldt 2005. Cooks superb pizzas on the *parrilla*, and has a lovely roof terrace for summer.

$$$ Siamo nel forno, Costa Rica 5886. Excellent true Italian pizzas, recommended tiramisu.

$$$ Social Paraíso, Honduras 5182. Closed Sun evening and Mon. Simple delicious dishes in a relaxed chic atmosphere, with a lovely patio at the back. Good fish and tasty salads.

$$ Krishna, Malabia 1833. A small, intimate place serving Indian-flavoured vegetarian dishes.

Tea rooms, café/bars and ice cream
Palermo has good cafés opposite the park on Av del Libertador.
Cusic, El Salvador 6016, T011-4139 9173, www.cusic.com.ar. Closed Mon. For breakfast and lunches, breads, sandwiches, wraps, puddings.
Persicco, Honduras 4900, Salguero y Cabello, Av Santa Fe 3212, Maure y Migueletes, Tucumán y Reconquista (Centre) and Av Rivadavia 4933 (Caballito). The grandsons of **Freddo**'s founders also offer excellent ice cream.

San Telmo *p62, map p63*
$$$ Brasserie Petanque, Defensa y México. Very attractive, informal French restaurant offering a varied menu with very good, creative dishes. Excellent value for their set lunch menus.
$$$ Gran Parrilla del Plata, Chile 594, T011-4300 8858, www.parrilla delplata.com. Popular, good value *parrilla* on a historic corner.
$$$ La Brigada, Estados Unidos 465, T011-4361 5557. Excellent *parrilla*, serving Argentine cuisine and wines. Very popular, expensive. Always reserve.
$$$-$$ Naturaleza Sabia, Balcarce 958. Tasty vegetarian and vegan dishes in an attractive ambience.

Tea rooms, café/bars and ice cream
Británico, Brasil y Defensa 399. Open 24 hrs. A historic place with a good atmosphere at lunchtime.

Dorrego, Humberto Primo y Defensa. Bar/café with great atmosphere, seating on plaza outside, good for late-night coffee or drinks.
Dylan, Perú 1086. Very good ice cream.
La Poesía, Chile y Bolívar. Ideal for a coffee break on the sunny sidewalk.
Nonna Bianca, Estados Unidos 425. For ice cream in an internet café.
Pride Café, Balcarce y Giuffra. Wonderful sandwiches, juices, salads and brownies, with lots of magazines to read.

Puerto Madero (Docks) *p64*
$$$ Cabaña Las Lilas, Av Moreau de Justo 516, T011-4313 1336. Reputedly one of the finest *parrillas* in town, pricey and popular with foreigners and business people.
$$$ Le Grill, Av Moreau de Justo 876, T011-4331 0454. A gourmet touch at a sophisticated *parrilla* which includes dry-aged beef, pork and lamb on its menu.

⚘ Bars and clubs

Generally it is not worth going to clubs before 0230 at weekends. Dress is usually smart. Entry can be from US$10-15, sometimes including a drink. A good way to visit some of the best bars is to join a pub crawl, eg **The Buenos Aires Pub Crawl**, www.buenosairespubcrawl.com, whose daily crawls are a safe night out.

Bars
Buller Brewing Company, Roberto M Ortiz 1827, Recoleta, www.bullerpub. com. Brew pub which also serves international food.
Casa Bar, Rodríguez Peña 1150, Recoleta. Beers from around the world in a restored mansion, good place to watch international sports matches, also serves food.

La Cigale, 25 de Mayo 597, Centre, T011-4893 2332. Popular after office hours, good live music.
Mundo Bizarro, Serrano 1222. Famous for its weird films, cocktails, American-style food, electronic and pop music.
Seddon, Defensa y Chile. Traditional bar open till late with live music on Fri.
Sugar, Costa Rica 4619. Welcoming bar with cheap beer and drinks, happy hour nightly, shows international sports.

The corner of Reconquista and Marcelo T de Alvear in Retiro is the centre of the small 'Irish' pub district, overcrowded on St Patrick's Day, 17 Mar. **Druid In**, Reconquista 1040, Centre, is by far the most attractive choice there, open for lunch and with live music weekly. **The Shamrock**, Rodríguez Peña 1220, in Recoleta, is another Irish-run, popular bar, happy hour for ISIC holders.

Clubs
Bahrein, Lavalle 345, Centre, www. bahreinba.com. Funky and electronic.
L'Arc, Niceto Vega 5452, Palermo. Hosts The X Club weekly, with a cocktail bar and live bands.
Niceto Club, Niceto Vega 5510, Palermo, T011-4779 9396, www.nicetoclub.com. Early live shows and dancing afterwards. Club 69 weekly parties for house, electronic, hip hop and funk music.

Gay clubs Most gay clubs charge from US$10 entry. **Amerika**, Gascón 1040, Almagro, www.ameri-k.com.ar, Fri-Sun, attracting more than 2000 party-goers over 3 floors; **Bach Bar**, Cabrera 4390, www.bach-bar.com.ar, a friendly lesbian bar in Palermo Viejo, Wed-Sun; **Sitges**, Av Córdoba 4119, Palermo, T011-4861 3763, www.sitgesonline.com.ar, a gay and lesbian bar.

Jazz clubs Notorious, Av Callao 966, T011-4813 6888, www.notorious.com.ar. Live jazz at a music shop with bar and restaurant. **Thelonious**, Salguero 1884, www.thelonious.com.ar, T011-4829 1562, for live jazz and DJs; **Virasoro Bar**, Guatemala 4328, www.virasorobar.com.ar, T011-4831 8918, for live jazz in a 1920s art deco house.

Salsa clubs La Salsera, Yatay 961, T011-4866 1829, www.lasalsera.com, is highly regarded.

⊕ Entertainment

At carnival time, look for the **Programa Carnaval Porteño** (it's on Facebook).

Cinemas

The selection of films is excellent, ranging from new Hollywood releases to Argentine and world cinema; details are listed daily in main newspapers. Films are shown uncensored and most foreign films are subtitled. Tickets best booked early afternoon to ensure good seats (average price US$9, discount on Wed and for 1st show daily).

Independent foreign and national films are shown during the **Festival de Cine Independiente** (BAFICI), www.bafici. gov.ar, held every Apr.

Cultural events

Centro Cultural Borges, Galerías Pacífico, Viamonte y San Martín, p 1, T011-5555 5359, www.ccborges.org.ar. Art exhibitions, concerts, film shows and ballet; some student discounts. **Ciudad Cultural Konex**, Sarmiento 3131 (Abasto), T011-4864 3200, www. ciudadculturalkonex.org. A converted oil factory hosts this huge complex holding plays, live music shows, summer

film projections under the stars, modern ballet, puppet theatre and, occasionally, massive parties.

Usina del Arte, Caffarena y Av Pedro de Mendoza (La Boca), www.usinadel arte.org. Temporary art exhibitions, plays, live music, film shows at an impressive 1910s converted power station which also offers guided visits. **Villa Ocampo**, Elortondo 1811, Beccar, Partido de San Isidro, T011-4732 4988, www.villaocampo.org. Former residence of writer and founder of Revista Sur Victoria Ocampo, now owned by UNESCO, in northern suburbs, Thu-Sun and holidays 1230-1800, US$2.50 (weekends and holidays US$4) entry, open for visits, courses, exhibitions and meals at its café/restaurant.

See also the programmes of the **Alliance Française**, www.alianzafrancesa. org.ar, **British Arts Centre**, www.british artscentre.org.ar, **Goethe Institut**, www.goethe.de/ins/ar/bue/esindex. htm, and **Instituto Cultural Argentino Norteamericano**, www.icana.org.ar.

Tango shows

There are 2 ways to enjoy tango: you can watch the dancing at a tango show. Most pride themselves on very high standards and, although they are not cheap (show only US$50-90, show and dinner US$75-150), this is tango at its best. Most prices include drinks and hotel transfers. Or you can learn to dance at a class and try your steps at a *milonga* (tango club). The Tango page on www.turismo. buenosaires.gob.ar lists *tanguerías* for tango shows, classes and *milongas*.

See also the websites **www.tangocity. com** and **www.todotango.com**.

Every Aug there is a tango dancing competition, **Festival y Mundial de Baile**, open to both locals and foreigners.

Bar Sur, Estados Unidos 299, T011-4362 6086, www.bar-sur.com.ar. Open 2000-0200. Price with or without dinner. Good fun, public sometimes join the professional dancers.

El Querandí, Perú 302, T011-5199 1770, www.querandi.com.ar. Daily shows, with or without dinner, also open for lunch. Tango show restaurant, dating back to 1920s.

El Viejo Almacén, Independencia y Balcarce, T011-4307 7388, www.viejo almacen.com.ar. Daily, dinner from 2000, show 2200. Impressive dancing and singing. Recommended.

Esquina Carlos Gardel, Carlos Gardel 3200 y Anchorena, T011-4867 6363, www.esquinacarlosgardel.com.ar. Opposite the former Mercado del Abasto, this is the most popular venue in Gardel's own neighbourhood; dinner at 2030, show at 2230. Recommended.

Esquina Homero Manzi, Av San Juan 3601 (Subte Boedo), T011-4957 8488, www.esquinahomeromanzi.com.ar. Traditional show at 2200 with excellent musicians and dancers, dinner (2100) and show available, tango school. Recommended.

Piazzolla Tango, Florida 165 (basement), Galería Güemes, T011-4344 8201, www.piazzollatango.com. A beautifully restored belle époque hall hosts a smart tango show; dinner at 2045, show at 2215.

Milongas These are very popular with younger *Porteños*. You can take a class and get a feel for the music before the dancing starts a couple of hours later. Both tango and *milonga* (the music that contributed to the origins of tango and is more cheerful) are played. Cost is from US$8; even beginners are welcome.

Centro Cultural Torquato Tasso, Defensa 1575, T011-4307 6506, www.torquatotasso.com.ar. See web for programme and prices (daily lessons), English spoken.

Confitería Ideal, Suipacha 384, T011-4328 7750, www.confiteriaideal.com. Very atmospheric ballroom for daily *milongas* at this old central café. Most days dancing starts as early as 1500; lessons start 1230 on some days, 1530 on others (not on Sun). Also evening tango shows.

La Viruta (at Centro Armenio), Armenia 1366, Palermo Viejo, T011-4774 6357, www.lavirutatango.com. Very popular, classes every day except Mon, entry US$7 (check website for times), also salsa and rock dancing classes, with restaurant.

Theatre

About 20 commercial theatres play all year and there are many amateur theatres. The main theatre street is Av Corrientes.

Complejo Teatral de Buenos Aires, Corrientes 1530, T011-4371 0111/8, http://complejoteatral.gob.ar, is a group of 5 theatres with many cultural activities. Book seats for theatre, ballet and opera as early as possible. Tickets for most popular shows (including rock and pop concerts) are sold also through **Ticketek**, T011-5237 7200, www.ticketek.com.ar. See also www.alternativateatral.com and www.mundoteatral.com.ar. For live Argentine and Latin American bands, best venues are: **La Trastienda**, Balcarce 460, San Telmo, www.latrastienda.com, theatre/café with lots of live events, also serving meals and drinks from breakfast to dinner, great music; or **ND Teatro**, Paraguay 918, www.ndteatro.com.ar.

○ Shopping

The main, fashionable shopping streets are Florida and Santa Fe (from Av 9 de

Julio to Av Pueyrredón). Palermo is the best area for chic boutiques and well-known international fashion labels; head for C Honduras and C El Salvador, between Malabia and Serrano. C Defensa in San Telmo is known for its antique shops. It also has a few craft stalls around C Alsina, Fri 1000-1700. **Pasaje de la Defensa**, Defensa 1179, is a beautifully restored 1880s house containing small shops.

Bookshops
Buenos Aires is renowned for its bookshops and was UNESCO's World Book Capital in 2011. Many shops are along Florida, Av Corrientes (from Av 9 de Julio to Callao) or Av Santa Fe, and in shopping malls. Second-hand and discount bookshops are mostly along Av Corrientes and Av de Mayo. Rare books are sold in several specialized stores in the Microcentro (the area enclosed by Suipacha, Esmeralda, Tucumán and Paraguay). The main chains of bookshops, usually selling a small selection of foreign books are: **Cúspide**, **Distal**, **Kel** (imported books, mostly in English) and **Yenny-El Ateneo**, whose biggest store is on Av Santa Fe 1860, in an old theatre; there is café where the stage used to be.
Eterna Cadencia, Honduras 5574, T011-4774 4100, www.eternacadencia.com. Has an excellent selection and a good café.
Walrus Books, Estados Unidos 617, San Telmo, T011-4300 7135, www.walrus-books.com.ar. Sells second-hand books in English, including Latin American authors, good children's section.

Handicrafts
Arte y Esperanza, Balcarce 234 and Suipacha 892, www.arteyesperanza.com.ar. Crafts made by indigenous communities, sold by a Fair Trade organization.

Artesanías Argentinas, Montevideo 1386, www.artesaniasargentinas.org. Aboriginal crafts and other traditional items sold by a Fair Trade organization.
El Boyero, Florida 753 (Galerías Pacífico) and 953, T011-4312 3564, http://es.elboyero.com. High-quality silver, leather, woodwork and other typical Argentine handicrafts.
Martín Fierro, Santa Fe 992. Good handicrafts, stonework, etc. Recommended.
Plata Nativa, Galería del Sol, Florida 860, local 41, www.platanativa.com. For Latin American folk handicrafts and high-quality jewellery.
In Dec there is a **Feria Internacional de Artesanías**.

Leather goods
Several shops are concentrated along Florida next to Plaza San Martín and also in Suipacha (900 block).
Aida, Galería de la Flor, local 30, Florida 670. Quality, inexpensive leather products, can make a leather jacket to measure in the same day.
Casa López, MT de Alvear 640/658, www.casalopez.com.ar. The most traditional and finest leather shop, expensive but worth it.
Dalla Fontana, Reconquista 735, www.dalla-fontana.com.ar. Leather factory, fast, efficient and reasonably priced for made-to-measure clothes.
Galería del Caminante, Florida 844. Has a variety of good shops with leather goods, arts and crafts, souvenirs, etc.
Prüne, Florida 963 and in many shopping centres, www.prune.com.ar. Fashionable designs for women, many options in leather and not very expensive.

Markets and malls

Markets can be found in many of the city's parks and plazas, which hold weekend fairs. You will find they all sell pretty much the same sort of handicrafts. The following offer something different:

Feria de Mataderos, Lisandro de la Torre y Av de los Corrales, T011-4342 9629, www.feriademataderos.com.ar, subte E to end of line then taxi (US$7), or buses 55, 63, 80, 92, 103, 117, 126, 141, 155, 180. Sat from 1700 (Jan-Feb), Sun 1100-2000 (Mar-Dec). Long way but few tourists, fair of Argentine handicrafts and traditions, music and dance festivals, gaucho horsemanship skills; nearby **Museo Criollo de los Corrales**, Av de los Corrales 6436, T011-4687 1949, Sun 1200-1830, US$0.20.

Mercado de las Luces, Manzana de las Luces, Perú y Alsina. Mon-Fri 1030-1930, Sun 1400-1930. Handicrafts, second-hand books, plastic arts.

Parque Centenario, Av Díaz Vélez y L Marechal. Sat-Sun and holidays 1100-2000, local crafts, cheap handmade clothes, used items of all sorts.

Parque Rivadavia, Av Rivadavia 4900. Sun 0900-1300. Second-hand books, stamps, coins, records, tapes, CDs and magazines.

Plaza Dorrego, San Telmo. Sun 1000-1700. For souvenirs, antiques, etc, with free tango performances and live music, wonderfully atmospheric, and an array of 'antiques'.

Plaza Italia, Santa Fe y Uriarte (Palermo). Sat 1200-2000, Sun 1000-2000. Second-hand textbooks and magazines (daily), handicrafts market.

The city has many fine shopping malls, including **Abasto de Buenos Aires**, Av Corrientes 3247, T011-4959 3400, nearest Subte: Carlos Gardel, line B, in the city's impressive, art deco former fruit and vegetable market building, and **Patio Bullrich**, Av del Libertador 750 and Posadas 1245, T011-4814 7400, nearest Subte: 8 blocks from Plaza San Martín, line C, the most upmarket mall in the city.

⏻ What to do

Cricket

Asociación Argentina de Cricket, Juan María Gutiérrez 3829, T011-3974 9593, www.cricketargentina.com, for information. Cricket is played Sep-Apr.

Cycle hire and tours

La Bicicleta Naranja, Pasaje Giuffra 308, San Telmo and Nicaragua 4825, Palermo, T011-4362 1104, www.labicicletanaranja. com.ar. Bike hire and tours to all parts of the city, 3-4 hrs.

Lan&Kramer Bike Tours, San Martín 910 p 6, T011-4311 5199, www.biketours. com.ar. Daily at 0930 and 1400 next to the monument of San Martín (Plaza San Martín), 3½- to 4-hr cycle tours to the south or the north of the city; also to San Isidro and Tigre, 4½-5 hrs and full day tours, plus summer evening tours downtown; also, bike rental.

Urban biking, Maipú 971, T011-4314 2325, www.urbanbiking.com. 4½-hr tours either to the south or to the north of the centre, starting daily 0900 and 1400 from Av Santa Fe y Maipú; night city tours, 3½-4 hrs, full day tours to San Isidro and Tigre (including kayak in the Delta), or occasionally, to the Pampas. Also rents bikes.

Football and rugby

Football fans should see **Boca Juniors**, matches every other Sun at their stadium (La Bombonera, Brandsen 805, La Boca, www.bocajuniors.com.ar, tickets for non-members only through tour operators, or the museum – see the murals), or their arch-rivals, **River Plate**, Av Figueroa

Alcorta 7597, T011-4789 1200, www.cariverplate.com.ar. Football season Feb-Jun, and Aug-Dec, most matches on Sun. Buy tickets from stadiums, sports stores near the grounds, ticket agencies or hostels and hotels, which may arrange guide/transport (don't take a bus if travelling alone, phone a radio taxi; see also **Tangol**, page 81). Rugby season Apr-Oct/Nov. For more information, **Unión de Rugby de Buenos Aires**, www.urba.org.ar, or **Unión Argentina de Rugby**, T4898 8500, www.uar.com.ar.

Polo

The high handicap season is Sep-Dec, but it is played all year round. Argentina has the top polo players in the world. A visit to the national finals at Palermo in Nov and Dec is recommended. For information, **Asociación Argentina de Polo**, T011-4777 8005, www.aapolo.com.

Tour operators and travel agents

An excellent way of seeing Buenos Aires is on a 3-hr tour. Longer tours may include dinner and a tango show, or a boat trip in the Delta, or a gaucho fiesta at a ranch (great food and dancing). Bookable through most travel agents. See also **BA Free Tour**, www.bafreetour.com, www.buenosaireslocaltours.com and **City Walkers**, www.citywalkers.com.ar, for free walking tours. For another type of walking tour, see **BA Street Art**, http://buenosairesstreetart.com, and **Graffitimundo**, http://graffitimundo.com, who offer tours of the city's best graffiti, see websites for prices and times.
Anda, T011-3221 0833, www.andatravel.com.ar. Operator specializing in socially and environmentally responsible tourism in Buenos Aires and around the country, including volunteering opportunities.

Argentina Excepción, Costa Rica 5546, T011-4772 6620, www.argentina-excepcion.com. French/Argentine agency offering tailor-made, upper-end tours, fly-drives, themed trips and other services. Also has a Santiago branch, www.chile-excepcion.com.
BAT, Buenos Aires Tur, Lavalle 1444 of 10, T011-4371 2304, www.buenosairestur.com. City tours, twice daily; Tigre and Delta, daily, 5 hrs.
Buenos Aires Bus (Bus Turístico), www.buenosairesbus.com. Open yellow double-decker buses follow 2 routes every 10-20 mins covering main sights from La Boca to Núñez with multilingual recorded tours. 1-day (US$27) and 2-day (US$33) hop-on/hop-off tickets can be purchased online or onboard. Find bus stops on website or on map provided at city's tourist offices.
Buenos Aires Vision, Esmeralda 356, p 8, T011-4394 4682, www.buenosaires-vision.com.ar. City tours, Tigre and Delta, Tango (cheaper without dinner) and Fiesta Gaucha.
Cultour, T011-156-365 6892 (mob), www.cultour.com.ar. A highly recommended walking tour of the city, 3-4 hrs led by a group of Argentine history/tourism graduates. In English and Spanish.
Eternautas, Av Julio A Roca 584 p 7, T011-5031 9916, www.eternautas.com. Historical, cultural and artistic tours of the city and Pampas guided in English, French or Spanish by academics from the University of Buenos Aires, flexible.
Flyer Lufthansa City Center, Av Fondo De La Legua 425, San Isidro, T011-4512 8100, www.lcc-flyer.com. English, Dutch, German spoken, repeatedly recommended, especially for *estancias*, fishing, polo, motorhome rental.
Kallpa, Tucumán 861, p 2, T011-5278 8010, www.kallpatour.com. Tailor-made

tours to natural and cultural destinations throughout the country, with an emphasis on adventure, conservation and golf. **Mai10**, Av Córdoba 657, p 3, T011-4314 3390, www.mai10.com.ar. High-end, personalized tours for groups and individuals, covers the whole country, special interests include art, cuisine, *estancias*, photo safaris, fishing and many more.

Say Hueque, branches in Palermo at Thames 2062, T011-5258 8740, and in San Telmo at Chile 557, T011-5352 9321, www.sayhueque.com. Recommended travel agency offering good-value tours aimed at independent travellers, friendly English-speaking staff.

Tangol, Florida 971, PB local 31, Centro, and Defensa 831, San Telmo, T011-4363 6000, www.tangol.com. Friendly, independent agency specializing in football and tango, plus various other sports, such as polo and paragliding. Can arrange tours, plane and bus tickets, accommodation. English spoken. Discounts for students. Overland tours in Patagonia Oct-Apr.

⊖ Transport

Air

Ezeiza (officially Ministro Pistarini, T011-5480 6111, www.aa2000.com. ar), the international airport, is 35 km southwest of the centre (also handles some domestic flights). The airport has 3 terminals: 'A', 'B' and 'C'. There are duty free shops (expensive), ATM and exchange facilities at **Banco Nación** (terminal 'A') (only change the very minimum to get you into the city), a **Ministerio de Turismo** desk, and a post office (Mon-Fri 0900-1700, Sat 0900-1200). No hotels nearby, but there is an attractive B&B 5 mins away with transfer included: **$$$ Bernie's**, Estrada 186, Barrio Uno, T011-4480 0420, www. posadabernies.com, book in advance.

There is a **Devolución IVA/Tax Free** desk (return of VAT) for purchases over the value of AR$70 (ask for a Global Refund check plus the invoice from the shop when you buy). Hotel booking service at Tourist Information desk – helpful, but prices are higher if booked in this way.

Airport buses A display in immigration shows choices and prices of transport into the city. A good dual carriageway links with the General Paz highway which circles the city. The safest way between airport and city is by an airport bus service run every 30 mins by **Manuel Tienda León** (office in front of you as you arrive), company office and terminal at Av Madero 1299 y San Martín, behind Sheraton Hotel in Retiro (take a taxi from the terminal; do not walk outside), T011-4315 5115, www. tiendaleon.com.ar. The bus costs US$14 one way, pay by pesos, dollars, euros or credit card. **Manuel Tienda León** will also collect passengers from addresses

in centre for a small extra fee, book the previous day. Bus from Ezeiza to Aeroparque, 1½ hrs, US$14. Remise taxis for up to 4 passengers (**Manuel Tienda León**, **Taxi Ezeiza**, www.taxiezeiza.com. ar, and other counters at Ezeiza) charge US$50 airport to town, but less from city to airport. Radio taxis charge US$45 (make sure you pay for your taxi at the booth and then wait in the queue), see Taxi, page 84, for more details. On no account take an unmarked car at Ezeiza, no matter how attractive the fare may sound. Drivers are adept at separating you from far more money than you can possibly owe them. Always ask to see the taxi driver's licence. If you take an ordinary taxi the Policía de Seguridad Aeroportuaria on duty notes down the car's licence and time of departure.

Aeroparque (Jorge Newbery Airport), 4 km north of the centre, T011-5480 6111, www.aa2000.com.ar, handles all internal flights, and some flights to neighbouring countries. On the 1st floor there is a *patio de comidas* (food hall) and many shops. At the airport there is also tourist information, car rental, bus companies, ATM, public phones and luggage deposit (ask at information desk in sector B). **Manuel Tienda León** buses to Aeroparque (see above for address), more or less hourly; from Aeroparque, 0900-2330, 30-min journey, US$5. Local bus 45 run from outside the airport to the Retiro railway station. No 37 goes to **Palermo** and **Recoleta** and No 160 to **Palermo** and **Almagro**. If going to the airport, make sure it goes to Aeroparque by asking the driver. *Remise* taxis to **Ezeiza**, operated by **Manuel Tienda León**, US$50; to the city centre US$16. Taxi to centre US$8. **Manuel Tienda León** operates buses between Ezeiza and Aeroparque airports, US$14.

Bus

Local City buses are called *colectivos* and cover a very wide radius. They are clean, frequent, efficient and very fast. Colectivo fares are calculated in 3-km sections, US$0.50-0.60, but fares are cheaper if you have a pre-paid smart card called *Sube* (see www.xcolectivo.com.ar for details). If not using a smart card, have coins ready for ticket machine as drivers do not sell tickets, but may give change. The bus number is not always sufficient indication of destination, as each number may have a variety of routes, but bus stops display routes of buses stopping there and little plaques are displayed in the driver's window. A rapid transit system, **Metrobús**, incorporating existing bus routes, is being implemented, including along Av 9 de Julio. See www.omnilineas.com.ar for city guides listing bus routes.

Long distance Bus terminal for all international and interprovincial buses is at Ramos Mejía y Antártida Argentina (Subte Line C), behind Retiro station, T011-4310 0700, www.tebasa.com.ar. The terminal is on 3 floors.

Bus information is at the Ramos Mejía entrance on the middle floor. Ticket offices are on the upper floor, but there are hundreds of them so you'll need to consult the list of companies and their office numbers at the top of the escalator. They are organized by region and are colour coded. Buenos Aires city information desk is on the upper floor. It is advisable to go to the bus station the day before you travel to get to know where the platforms are so that when you are fully laden you know exactly where to go. At the basement and ground levels there are left-luggage lockers; tokens are sold in kiosks; for large baggage, there's a *guarda equipaje* on

the lower floor. For further details of bus services and fares, look under proposed destinations. There are no direct buses to either of the airports.

International buses International services are run by both local and foreign companies; heavily booked Dec-Mar (especially at weekends), when most fares rise sharply. To **Uruguay**: Do not buy Uruguayan bus tickets in Buenos Aires; wait till you get to Colonia or Montevideo. To **Montevideo**, **Bus de la Carrera**, **Cauvi** and Cóndor Estrella, US$51-59, 8 hrs; see Ferries, below.

Car

Driving in Buenos Aires is no problem, provided you have eyes in the back of your head and good nerves. Traffic fines are high and police look out for drivers without the correct papers. Car hire is cheaper if you arrange it when you arrive rather than from home. **Sixt**, Cerrito 1314, www.sixt.com.ar, and national rental agencies, such as **Dietrich**, Cerrito 1575, T0800-999 2999, www.localizadietrich.com. **Ruta Sur**, Av General Paz 1260, T011-5238 4071, www.rutasur.eu. Rents 4WDs and motorhomes.

Ferry

To **Montevideo** and **Colonia** from Terminal Dársena Norte, Av Antártida Argentina 821 (2 blocks from Av Córdoba y Alem). **Buquebus**, T011-4316 6500, www.buquebus.com (tickets from Terminal, Retiro bus station, from offices at Av Córdoba 867 and Posadas 1452, by phone or online): **1)** Direct to **Montevideo**, 1-4 a day, 3 hrs, from US$105 tourist class, one way, also carries vehicles and motorcycles.
2) To **Colonia**, services by 3 companies: **Buquebus**: minimum 5 crossings a day, from 1-3 hrs, US$53 tourist class one

way on slower vessel, US$72 tourist class on faster vessel, with bus connection to **Montevideo**. (**Buquebus** also offers flights to Uruguay and Brazil with onward connections, www.flybqb.com.uy.)
Colonia Express, www.coloniaexpress. com, makes 2-3 crossings a day between Buenos Aires and Colonia in a fast catamaran (no vehicles carried), 50 mins, prices range from US$18 to US$35 one way, depending on type of service and where bought. Office is at Av Córdoba 753, T011-4317 4100; Terminal Fluvial is at Av Pedro de Mendoza 330. You must go there by taxi, US$8 from Retiro. **Seacat**, www.seacatcolonia.com, 3 fast ferries to Colonia, 1 hr, US$42 one way, from the same terminal as Buquebus, with bus to Montevideo (US$40-52) and Punta del Este (US$58-66) on most crossings. Office: Av Córdoba 772, T011-4322 9555, phone sales: T011-4314 5100.

Metro (Subte)
7 lines link the outer parts of the city to the centre. **Line 'A'** runs under Av Rivadavia, from Plaza de Mayo to San Pedrito (Flores). **Line 'B'** from central Post Office, on Av L N Alem, under Av Corrientes to Federico Lacroze railway station at Chacarita, ending at Juan Manuel de Rosas (Villa Urquiza). **Line 'C'** links Plaza Constitución with the Retiro railway station, and provides connections with all the other lines but 'H'. **Line 'D'** runs from Plaza de Mayo (Catedral), under Av Roque Sáenz Peña (Diagonal Norte), Córdoba, Santa Fe and Palermo to Congreso de Tucumán (Belgrano). **Line 'E'** runs from Plaza de Mayo (Cabildo, on C Bolívar) through San Juan to Plaza de los Virreyes (connection to Line 'P' or Premetro train service to the southwest end of the city). **Line 'H'** runs from Corrientes, via Once to Hospitales

(Parque Patricios), under Av Jujuy and Av Almafuerte. Note that 3 stations, 9 de Julio (Line 'D'), Diagonal Norte (Line 'C') and Carlos Pellegrini (Line 'B') are linked by pedestrian tunnels. The fare is US$0.45, the same for any direct trip or combination between lines; magnetic cards (for 1, 2, 5, 10, or 30 journeys) must be bought at the station before boarding; only pesos accepted. Trains are operated by **Metrovías**, T0800-555 1616, www.metrovias.com.ar, and run Mon-Sat 0500-2220 (Sun 0800-2200). Line A, the oldest was built in 1913, the earliest in South America. Backpacks and luggage allowed. Free map (if available) from stations and tourist office.

Taxi
Taxis are painted yellow and black, and carry Taxi flags. Fares are shown in pesos. The meter starts at US$1.50 when the flag goes down; make sure it isn't running when you get in. A fixed rate of US$0.15 for every 200 m or 1-min wait is charged thereafter. The fare from 2200 to 0600 starts at US$1.80, plus US$0.18 for every 200 m or 1-min wait. A charge is sometimes made for each piece of hand baggage (ask first). About 10% tip expected. For security, take a *remise* or radio taxi booked by phone or at the company's office. Check that the driver's licence is displayed. Lock doors on the inside. The 2 airports and Retiro bus station are notorious for unlicensed taxi crime; use the airport buses and *remises* listed on page 82, and taxis from the official rank in the bus terminal which are registered with police and safe.

Radio taxis are managed by several different companies; extra fee US$0.90. Phone a radio taxi from your hotel (they can make recommendations), a phone box or *locutorio*, giving the address where you are, and you'll usually be collected within 10 mins. **City**, T011-4585 5544; **Porteño**, T011-4566 5777; **Premium**, T011-5238 0000; **Tiempo**, T011-4854 3838.

Remise taxis operate all over the city, run from an office and have no meter. The companies are identified by signs on the pavement. Fares are fixed and can be cheaper than regular taxis, verifiable by phoning the office, and items left in the car can easily be reclaimed. **Universal**, T011-4105 5555.

Train
There are 4 main terminals: **1) Retiro** (3 lines: **Mitre**, **Belgrano** and **San Martín** in separate buildings). The state of services changes all the time, owing largely to poor maintenance. The independent website, www.satelite ferroviario.com.ar, is a good source of information on all services. Urban and suburban services include: Mitre line (T0800-222 8736) to **Belgrano**, **Mitre** (connection to Tren de la Costa, see page 86), **Olivos**, **San Isidro**, and **Tigre** (see page 64); long-distance services to **Rosario Norte**, 7½ hrs, US$3-7; to **Tucumán** via Rosario, Mon and Fri, 0728 (return Wed 1552, Sat 1900), an extra weekly service is added in summer, 26½ hrs, US$50 sleeper (for 2, breakfast included), US$17 pullman, US$9 1st class, US$5 *turista* (run by **Ferrocentral**, T0800-1221 8736, www.ferrocentralsa.com.ar). To **Córdoba** via Rosario, Mon and Thu 2035 (return Wed and Sun 1439), 17 hrs, US$38 sleeper (for 2, breakfast included), US$11.50 pullman, US$6.50 1st class, US$4 *turista* (run by **Ferrocentral**). Belgrano line to northwestern suburbs, including Villa Rosa, run by **Ferrovías**, T0800-777 3377. San Martín line for services to Pilar and long-distance

services to Junín and Alberdi (see www. ferrobaires.gba.gov.ar).

2) Constitución, Roca line urban and suburban services to La Plata, Ezeiza, Ranelagh and Quilmes. Long-distance services (run by **Ferrobaires**, T011-4304 0028, www.ferrobaires.gba.gov.ar): **Bahía Blanca**, 5 a week 1945, 14 hrs, US$15-22. Also services to **Mar del Plata** (3 a week in early 2014, US$21-26) and Tandil.

3) Federico Lacroze, Urquiza line and Metro headquarters (run by **Metrovías**, T0800-555 1616, www.metrovias.com.ar). Suburban services: to General Lemos.

4) Once, Sarmiento line, urban and suburban services to Moreno and Luján. Long-distance services to Lincoln (run by **Ferrobaires**).

Tram
Old-fashioned street cars operate Mar-Nov on Sat and holidays 1600-1930 and Sun 1000-1300, 1600-1930 and Dec-Feb on Sat and holidays 1700-2030, Sun 1000-1300, 1700-2030, free, on a circular route along the streets of Caballito district, from C Emilio Mitre 500, Subte Primera Junta (Line A) or Emilio Mitre (Line E), no stops en route. Operated by **Asociación Amigos del Tranvía**, T011-4431 1073, www.tranvia.org.ar.

Tigre *p64*
Bus
From central **Buenos Aires**: take No 60 from Constitución: the 60 'bajo' is a little longer than the 60 'alto' but is better for sightseeing.

Ferry
To **Carmelo** (Uruguay) from Terminal Internacional, Lavalle 520, Tigre. **Cacciola**, T011-4749 0931, www.cacciolaviajes.com (in Buenos Aires at Florida 520, p 1, of 113, T4393 6100), 2 a day, 2½ hrs, US$42. To

Montevideo (bus from Carmelo), 5½ hrs, US$52. To **Nueva Palmira** (Uruguay) from Terminal Internacional. **Líneas Delta Argentino**, oficina 6 at Estación Fluvial, T011-4731 1236, www.lineasdelta.com.ar. Daily at 0730, 3 hrs, US$30, US$47 return. To **Carmelo** US$35, US$53 return, and **Colonia**, 4½ hrs from Tigre, US$45, US$63 return, both daily 0730. **Note** Argentine port taxes are generally included in the fares for Argentine departures.

Train

From **Buenos Aires**: Mitre line from Retiro. Alternatively **Tren de la Costa**, T011-3220 6300, US$3.35 one way from Maipú station (reached by Mitre line from Retiro) to Delta station (Tigre) every 30 mins. (Buses to Tren de la Costa are No 60 from Constitución, No 19 or 71 from Once, No 152 from centre.) Terminus, Estación Delta, has the huge funfair, El Parque de la Costa, and a casino.

⊕ Directory

Banks

ATMs are widespread for MasterCard or Visa. The financial district lies within a small area north of Plaza de Mayo, between Rivadavia, 25 de Mayo, Av Corrientes and Florida. In non-central areas find banks/ATMs along the main avenues. Banks open Mon-Fri 1000-1500. *Casas de cambio* include **Banco Piano**, San Martín 345, T011-4321 9200, www.banco piano.com.ar, changes all TCs (commission 2%). **Forex**, MT de Alvear 540, T4010 2000. Other South American currencies can only be exchanged in *casas de cambio*.

Embassies and consulates

For all foreign embassies and consulates in Buenos Aires, see http://embassy.goabroad.com.

Language schools

Academia Buenos Aires, Hipólito Yrigoyen 571, p 4, T011-4345 5954, www. academiabuenosaires.com. **All-Spanish**, Talcahuano 77 p 1, T011-4832 7794, www. all-spanish.com.ar. One-to-one classes. **Amauta Spanish School**, Federico Lacroze 2129, T011-4777 2130, www. amautaspanish.com. Spanish classes, one-to-one or small groups, centres in Buenos Aires, Bariloche and at an *estancia* in the Pampas. **Argentina I.L.E.E**, T011-4782 7173, www.argentinailee.com. Recommended by individuals and organizations alike, with a school in Bariloche. **Cedic**, Reconquista 715, p 11 E, T011-4312 1016, www.cedic.com.ar. Recommended. **Elebaires**, Av de Mayo 1370, of 10, p 3, T011-4383 7706, www. elebaires.com.ar. Small school with focused classes, also offers one-to-one lessons and excursions. Recommended. **Expanish**, Perón 698, T011-5252 3040, www.expanish.com. Well-organized courses which can include excursions, accommodation and Spanish lessons in sister schools in Peru and Chile. Highly recommended. **IBL (Argentina Spanish School)**, Florida 165, p 3, of 328, T011-4331 4250, www.ibl.com.ar. Group and one-to-one lessons, all levels, recommended. **Bue Spanish School**, Av Belgrano 1431, p 2, apt18, T011-4381 6347, www.buespanish.com.ar. Intensive and regular Spanish courses, culture programme, free materials. **Laboratorio de Idiomas (Universidad de Buenos Aires)**, 25 de Mayo 221 (also other branches), T011-4334 7512 or T4343 1196, www.idiomas.filo.uba.ar. Offers cheap, coherent courses, including summer intensive courses. For other schools teaching Spanish, and for private tutors look in *Buenos Aires Herald* in the classified advertisements. Enquire also at **Asatej** (see Useful addresses, below).

Medical services

Urgent medical service: for free municipal ambulance service to an emergency hospital department (day and night) **Casualty ward**, **Sala de guardia**, T107 or T011-4923 1051/58 (SAME). Inoculations: **Hospital Rivadavia**, Av Las Heras 2670, T011-4809 2000, Mon-Fri 0700-1200 (bus Nos 10, 37, 59, 60, 62, 92, 93 or 102 from Plaza Constitución), or **Dirección de Sanidad de Fronteras y Terminales de Transporte**, Ing Huergo 690, T011-4343 1190, Mon-Fri 1000-1500, bus No 20 from Retiro, no appointment required (yellow fever only; take passport). If not provided, buy the vaccines in **Laboratorio Biol**, Uriburu 153, T011-4953 7215, or in larger chemists. Many chemists have signs indicating that they give injections. Any hospital with an infectology department will give hepatitis A. **Centros Médicos Stamboulian**, 25 de Mayo 464, T011-4515 3000, Pacheco de Melo 2941, also in Belgrano, Villa Crespo, Villa Urquiza and Flores, www.stamboulian.com.ar. Private health advice for travellers and inoculations centre. Public hospitals: **Hospital Argerich**, Almte Brown esq Py y Margall 750, T011-4121 0700. **Hospital Juan A Fernández**, Cerviño y Bulnes, T011-4808 2600/2650, probably the best free medical attention in the city. **British Hospital**, Perdriel 74, T011-4309 6400, www.hospitalbritanico.org.ar. **German Hospital**, Av Pueyrredón 1640, between Beruti and Juncal, T011-4827 7000, www.hospitalaleman.com.ar. Both have first-aid centres (*centros asistenciales*) as do other main hospitals. Dental treatment: excellent dental treatment centre at **Croid**, Vuelta de Obligado 1551 (Belgrano), T011-4781 9037, www.croid.com.ar. **Dental Argentina**, Laprida 1621, p 2 B, T011-4828 0821, www.dental-argentina.com.ar.

Useful addresses

Migraciones: (Immigration), Antártida Argentina 1355, edif 4, T011-4317 0234, www.migraciones.gov.ar, 0800-1400. **Central Police Station**: Moreno 1550, Virrey Cevallos 362, T011-4346 5700 (emergency, T101 or 911 from any phone, free). **Aves Argentinas/AOP** (a BirdLife International partner), Matheu 1246, T011-4943 7216, www.avesargentinas.org.ar. For information on birdwatching and specialist tours, good library, open Mon-Fri 1030-1330, 1430-2030 (closed Jan). Student organizations: **Asatej**: Helpful Argentine Youth and Student Travel Organization, runs a Student Flight Centre, Florida 835, p 3, oficina 320, T011-4114 7528, www.asatej.com, Mon-Fri 1000-1900 (with many branches in BA and around the country). Booking for flights (student discounts) including cheap 1-way flights (long waiting lists), hotels and travel; information for all South America, notice board for travellers, ISIC cards sold (giving extensive discounts; Argentine ISIC guide available here), English and French spoken. Cheap fares also at **TIJE**, San Martín 601, T011-5272 8480 or branches at Av Santa Fe 898, T011-5272 8450, and elsewhere in the city, Argentina, Uruguay and Chile, www.tije.com. **YMCA**: (Central), Reconquista 439, T011-4311 4785, www.ymca.org.ar. **YWCA**: Humberto 1º 2360, T011-4941 3776, www.ywca.org.ar.

Contents

Footprint features

Buenos Aires province

At a glance

⊕ **Getting around** Local bus and some short-distance trains. Hiring a car is recommended for visiting *estancias* and exploring the coast.

🕐 **Time required** A long weekend is enough to visit one area.

☁ **Weather** The coastal areas can be pleasantly warm from Dec-Mar, but windy and cold the rest of the year. Inland, May-Aug is cold and can be unpleasant.

✖ **When not to go** The coast is popular with locals during Dec-Jan; you'll be lucky to find accommodation. May-Aug can be windy and cold but less crowded.

★ **Don't miss ...**
1 Gaucho towns: San Antonio de Areco and Chascomús, pages 95 and 101.
2 Estancias, page 96.
3 Mar del Plata, page 113.
4 Sierra de la Ventana, page 133.
5 Tandil, page 133.

The Pampas are the perfect antidote to the frenzied pace of Buenos Aires. These peaceful flatlands, stretching out in all directions towards dramatic mountains in the south and the unspoiled Atlantic coast to the east, are wonderful places for escape and relaxation within a few hours' drive of the capital.

Argentina's *estancias* (loosely translated as ranches) produce the superb beef that once made this country the breadbasket of the world, and staying in one is a quintessential part of Argentine life, complete with gauchos (cowboys) and *asados* (much more than a barbecue). Whether you choose a grand colonial mansion, or a simple working farm, you'll be welcomed as part of the family, and will gain a real insight into the culture, while enjoying the pleasure of life on the land. Ride your horse across the plains, and then tuck into a meal of succulent home-grown beef cooked on an open fire under the stars: an unforgettable experience. Gauchos are still very much part of Argentine rural life and you can enjoy their music and fine horsemanship in quaint Pampas towns such as San Antonio de Areco and Chascomús, virtually unchanged since the early 1900s.

The Atlantic beaches are a great way to cool down in the summer. Avoid the tawdry casinos of famous Mar del Plata and head instead for the chic resorts of Mar de los Pampas and Cariló, or escape to Pinamar where in summer you can party with the young *Porteños* of Buenos Aires.

Two of the oldest mountain ranges in the world pop up from the flat Pampas at Tandil and Sierra de la Ventana, attracting climbers, hikers and anyone looking for a relaxing weekend in beautiful countryside. For information on the region, see www.turismo.gba. gov.ar (in English).

The Pampas

The Pampas are home to one of the most enduring images of Argentina: the gaucho on horseback, roaming the plains. All over the Pampas there are quiet, unspoiled towns where gaucho culture is still very much alive. Two impeccably preserved gaucho towns very much worth visiting are San Antonio de Areco and Chascomús. The former is home to expert craftsmen, working silver and leather in the traditional gaucho way. Near here there are many of the finest and most historical *estancias*: two are recommended, El Ombú and La Bamba. Further southeast, Chascomús is similarly charming, a traditional cowboy town come to life, with pristine examples of 1870s architecture, a good museum of the Pampas and gauchos, and a lake for watersports in summer. There are fine *estancias* here too: friendly, relaxed La Fe, and best of all, Dos Talas, with its extraordinary history and beautiful grounds. Whether you stay the night or just visit for an afternoon to eat lunch and ride, you'll get an unforgettable taste of life on the land. The Pampas are also rich in wildlife, and on lakes and *lagunas* you're likely to spot Chilean flamingos and herons, maguari storks, white-faced ibis and black-necked swans. Ostrich-like greater rheas can also be seen in many parts. For more information, see www.turismolapampa.gov.ar (in Spanish).

Arriving in the Pampas

Getting around It's easy to get around the province with a network of buses to and from Buenos Aires, and between towns. Train lines operate to Mar del Plata, and to Chascomús and Tandil, stopping at many coastal towns on the way. Some services are a good budget option, if not very comfortable. You'll need to hire a car to reach the more remote *estancias*, and there are good, fast toll roads radiating out from the capital to Mar del Plata, via Chascomús, San Antonio de Areco and Lobos. Check out www.chascomus.com.ar, www.lobos.gov.ar, www.sanantoniodeareco. com/turismo, and www.turismo.gba.gov.ar; www.turismo.gov.ar also has links to all these small towns. ▶ *For further details, see Transport, page 106.*

Background

Travelling through these calm lands you wouldn't think they'd had such a violent past, but these are the rich fertile plains that justified conquering the indigenous people in the bloody 19th-century Campaign of the Desert (see box, page 100). Once the Spanish newcomers had gained control, their produce made Argentina the 'breadbasket of the world', and the sixth richest nation on Earth, exporting beef, lamb, wheat and wool when a growing Europe demanded cheap food and clothing. When you see these huge, perfect wheat fields, and superbly healthy Aberdeen Angus cattle roaming vast plains, you might wonder how a country with such riches can possibly have suffered an economic crisis. It's one of the great enigmas of Argentina. To get an idea of Argentina's former wealth, visit an *estancia* with history, like Dos Talas, and ask their owners what went wrong. Some blame Perón, and now the Kirchners, for taxing the farmers too harshly, or Menem for resorting to desperate measures to keep up with the US dollar by selling the nationalized industries. Farmers complain the government imposes impossible taxes for those who produce from the land. The fields of Buenos Aires province provide more than half of Argentina's cereal production, and over a third of her livestock, but many *estancia* owners have had to turn to tourism in order to maintain the homes built by their ancestors in more affluent times. Still, staying in an *estancia* is a rare privilege, to be wholeheartedly enjoyed.

Luján → *Phone code: 02323. Population: 65,000.*

This is a place of pilgrimage for devout Catholics throughout Argentina. In 1630 an image of the Virgin brought by ship from Brazil was being transported to its new owner in Santiago del Estero by ox cart, when the cart got stuck, despite strenuous efforts by men and oxen to move it. This was taken as a sign that the Virgin willed she should stay there. A chapel was built for the image, and around it grew Luján. The chapel has long since been superseded by an impressive neo-Gothic basilica and the Virgin now stands on the High Altar. Luján is a very popular spot at weekends, and there are huge pilgrimages on the last weekend of September (La Peregrinación Gaucho), the first weekend of October (Peregrinación Juvenil), 8 May (the saint's day) and 8 December (Inmaculada Concepción), when the town is completely packed.

Complejo Museográfico Provincial Enrique Udaondo ① *T02323-420245, www.ic.gba.gov.ar, Wed-Fri 1200-1800 (Nov-Mar), Wed-Fri 1100-1700, Sat, Sun 1000-*

Gaucho life

The gaucho is the cowboy of Argentina, found all over the country, and one of Argentina's most important cultural icons. Gauchos emerged as a distinct social group in the early 18th century. Brought over by the Spanish to tend cattle, they combined their Moorish roots with Argentine Criollo stock, adopting aspects of the indigenous peoples' lifestyle, but creating their own particular style and dress. The gaucho lived on horseback, dressing in a poncho, *bombachas* (baggy trousers) held up by a *tirador* (broad leather belt) and home-made boots with leather spurs. He was armed with a *facón* or large knife, and *boleadoras*, a lasso made from three stones tied with leather thongs, which when expertly thrown would wrap around the legs of animals to bring them swiftly to the ground. Gauchos roamed the Pampas, hunting the seemingly inexhaustible herds of wild cattle and horses in the long period before fencing protected private property. The gaucho's wild reputation derived from his resistance to government officials who tried to exert their control by the use of anti-vagrancy laws and military conscription. Much of the urban population of the time regarded the gaucho as a savage, on a par with the 'indians'.

The gaucho's lifestyle was doomed in the advent of railways, fencing and the redistribution of land that followed the massacre of indigenous peoples. Increasingly the term gaucho came to mean an *estancia* worker who made a living on horseback tending cattle. As the real gaucho disappeared from the Pampas, he became a major subject of Argentine folklore and literature, most famously in José Hernández' epic poem of 1872, *Martín Fierro*, and in Güiraldes' later novel *Don Segundo Sombra*. But you can still see gauchos in their traditional dress at work today in any *estancia*. Visit Mataderos, Chascomús, or San Antonio de Areco for displays of traditional gaucho horsemanship, music, silversmithing and leatherwork.

1800 (Apr-Oct), US$0.75, in the old Cabildo building, is one of the most interesting museums in the country. Exhibits illustrate its historical and political development. General Beresford, the commander of the British troops which seized Buenos Aires in 1806, was a prisoner here, as were Generals Mitre, Paz and Belgrano in later years. Next to it are museums devoted to transport and to motor vehicles. Behind the Cabildo is the river, with river walks, cruises and restaurants.

Some 20 km before Luján, near General Rodríguez, is **Eco Yoga Park** ① *T011-15-6507 0577, www.ecoyogapark.com.ar*, a spiritual centre and farm with volunteering opportunities, yoga, meditation, organic gardens and vegetarian food. See website for day and weekend packages. Take Luján bus (see Transport, below), get off at La Serenísima, then take taxi US$8-10.

San Antonio de Areco, 113 km northwest of Buenos Aires, is *the* original gaucho town and makes a perfect escape from the capital. Built in the late 19th century, much of its charm lies in the authenticity of its crumbling buildings surrounding an atmospheric plaza filled with palms and plane trees, and the streets lined with orange trees. The attractive *costanera* along the riverbank is a great place to swim and picnic. There are several *estancias* nearby, and the town itself has several historical *boliches* (combined bar and provisions stores), where you can lap up the atmosphere, listen to live music and meet locals. Gaucho traditions are on display in the many weekend activities, and the town's craftsmen produce wonderful silverwork, textiles and traditional worked leather handicrafts of the highest quality. Annual events include the *pato* games in January, a poncho parade in February and the **Fiesta Criolla** in March. Most important of all, however, is the **Day of Tradition**, in the second week of November (book accommodation in advance). For more information, see Festivals, page 106. The **tourist information centre** ① *Parque San Martín, Zerboni y Arellano, T02326-453165, www.sanantoniodeareco.com,* has friendly, helpful, English-speaking staff who can advise on gaucho activities in the town, as well as accommodation and transport. Other useful websites include www. pagosdeareco.com.ar and www.areco.mun.gba.gov.ar.

The **Museo Gauchesco Ricardo Güiraldes** ① *Camino Güiraldes, T02326-455839, www.museoguiraldes.com.ar,* is closed indefinitely after flooding. It is a replica of a typical *estancia* of the late 19th century and is dedicated to the life of the writer, who was a sophisticated member of Parisian literary circles and an Argentine nationalist who romanticized gaucho life. Güiraldes spent much of his early life on **Estancia La Porteña** ① *8 km from town, T011-15-5626 7347, www.laporteniadeareco.com,* which dates from 1823. It is a national historic monument and offers day visits and accommodation (see Where to stay). He settled there to write his best-known book, *Don Segundo Sombra* (1926), which was set in San Antonio. The *estancia* and sights in the town, such as the old bridge and the Pulpería La Blanqueada (at the entrance to the museum), became famous through its pages.

Superb gaucho silverwork is for sale at the workshop and **Centro Cultural y Museo Taller Draghi** ① *Lavalle 387, T02326-454219, www.draghiplaterosorfebres. com, Mon-Sat 0900-1300, 1530-2000, Sun 1000-1300, US$1.70 for a guided visit.* You can get a further idea of the life of the gauchos at the **Museo Las Lilas** ① *Moreno 279, T02326-456425, www.museolaslilas.org, Thu-Sun 1000-2000 (until 1800 in winter), US$3.75,* which houses a collection of paintings by famous Argentine artist Florencio Molina Campos, who dedicated his life to the display of the gaucho way of life. Excellent chocolates are made at **La Olla de Cobre** ① *Matheu 433, T02326-453105, www.laolladecobre.com.ar,* with a charming little café for drinking chocolate and trying the most amazing home-made *alfajores*. There is a large park, **Parque San Martín**, spanning the river to the north of the town near the tourist information centre. While you're here, you should visit one of the old traditional bars, or *pulperías*, many of which have been lovingly restored to recreate the 1900s

Estancias

Argentina's *estancias* vary enormously from ostentatious mansions to simple colonial-style ranches that still work as cattle farms. Many now open their doors to tourists as paying guests, enabling you to experience traditional Argentine rural life. There are two main types of *estancia*: those that function as rural hotels, and those where you're welcomed as a guest of the family. The latter are particularly recommended as a great way to meet Argentine people. You dine with the owners and they'll often tell you about their family's history and talk about life on the farm, turning a tourist experience into a meeting of friends. Some *estancias* offer splendid rooms filled with family antiques. Others are simple affairs where you'll stay in an old farmhouse, and the focus is on peace and quiet. They can be the perfect place to retreat and unwind for a few days or to try an activity such as horse riding or birdwatching. Whichever kind you choose, a good *estancia* will give you an unparalleled taste of traditional hospitality: welcoming strangers is one of the things Argentines do best.

Activities These depend on the *estancia*, but almost all provide horse riding, which is highly recommended even if you've no experience. Galloping across the plains on a *criollo* horse has to be one of the biggest thrills of visiting the country. If you're a beginner, let your hosts know beforehand so that they can arrange for you to ride an especially docile creature. The horse-shy might be offered a ride in a *sulky*, the traditional open horse-drawn carriage, more relaxing, but just as much fun. Cattle mustering, meanwhile, may sound daunting but is the best way to get into life on the *campo*. You'll help your hosts move cattle while sitting astride your trusty steed. Gauchos will be on hand to guide you and by the end of the day you'll be whooping and hollering with the best of them.

Access As *estancias* are inevitably located in the country you'll need to hire a car, although many will pick you up from the nearest town if you don't have one. If you're visiting for a few days ask your hosts to arrange a *remise* taxi; some *estancias* will arrange transfers on request. There are many *estancias* within easy access of Ezeiza International Airport in Buenos Aires, so it can be an ideal way to relax after a long flight at the start of your trip, or to spend your last couple of nights, allowing you to return home feeling refreshed and with vivid memories of Argentine hospitality.

Recommended *estancias* in Buenos Aires province include Dos Talas (pages 102 and 105), Casa de Campo La China (page 101) and Palantelén (page 110).

ambience and are brought to life by a genuine local clientele every night. Try La Vieja Sodería, on General Paz and Bolívar, or El Almacén de Ramos Generales Parrilla, at Zapiola 143. At Alsina 66 is the city museum, **Centro Cultural y Museo Usina Vieja**① *Tue-Sun 1100-1700, US$0.50*. There are ATMs on the plaza, and at the country club you can play golf or watch a polo match in restful surroundings; ask at the tourist office for directions.

Some of the province's finest *estancias* are within easy reach of San Antonio for day visits, offering an *asado* lunch, horse riding and other activities. One such place is **La Cinacina** ① *T02326-452045, www.lacinacina.com.ar*, which offers day visits to groups of 30 or more. For a list of those offering accommodation, see Where to stay, page 103.

La Plata → *For listings, see pages 103-106. Colour map 4, B6.*

The capital of Buenos Aires province is La Plata, a modern university city with a lively student population, and consequently good nightlife, with lots of restaurants and bars. There's no particular reason to visit as a tourist, but if you're passing through or on a day trip from Buenos Aires (only 60 minutes by bus), you'll appreciate the broad avenues, leafy plazas and elaborate public buildings. It's a young and vibrant place, where football and rugby are major passions. At the east of the city there's a beautiful park, **Paseo del Bosque**, popular at weekends with families for *asados*, with its famous science museum, the magnificent but slightly run-down **Museo de Ciencias Naturales**.

Arriving in La Plata → *Phone code 0221. Population 642,000.*
Getting there La Plata is 56 km southeast of Buenos Aires, 45 minutes by car. There are frequent trains, taking one hour 10 minutes. Buses to La Plata from Buenos Aires leave every 30 minutes and take about 1½ hours. They leave from the Retiro bus terminal day and night, and from Plaza Constitución (less recommended) daytime only. The terminal in La Plata is at Calle 42 entre 3 y 4, at Diagonal 74. Long-distance buses arrive here from all major cities.

Getting around The city is easy to get around, but note that the streets have numbers, rather than names, and diagonal streets cross the entire city, which can be very confusing. When you approach one of these crossroads with six choices, make sure you remember the number of the street you're on. There's an efficient network of buses all over the city, and taxis are safe, cheap and plentiful.

Tourist information The main tourist office is **Dirección de Turismo** ① *Diagonal 79 entre 5 y 56, Palacio Campodónico, T0221-422 9764, www.laplata.gov.ar, Mon-Fri 0900-1700*. There is also a small **tourist booth** ① *C 50 entre 6 y 7, T0221-427 1535, daily 1000-2000*, at Pasaje Dardo Rocha. The provincial tourism website is www.turismo.gba. gov.ar (in English). A helpful website for exploring *estancias*, stables and for visiting craftsmen in the Pampas is **Camino del Gaucho** ① *57 No 393, T0221-425 7482, www. caminodelgaucho.com.ar*. The English-speaking staff are extremely informative and will help you arrange your own itinerary.

Places in La Plata
The major public buildings are centred around two parallel north–south streets, 51 and 53, which run north from the Plaza Moreno to the Plaza San Martín,

Argentine steak

So how did Argentina come to be synonymous with great beef? Cattle certainly aren't indigenous to the Pampas. But after Juan de Garay's expedition in 1580 brought cattle from Paraguay, the animals roamed wild on the fertile plains, reproducing so quickly that by the time the Spanish returned in 1780, there were 40 million of them. But by then, local indigenous groups were making a roaring trade, driving herds of cattle through the Andean passes to sell in southern Chile. Gauchos, meanwhile, were hunting cattle with the use of *boleadoras* (a lasso with three stone balls), and slaughtering them by the thousand for their hides alone, sometimes leaving the meat to rot. When salting plants – *saladeros* – arrived in 1810, the hides were transported to Europe, together with tallow for candles. The meat was turned into *charqui*, cut into strips, dried and salted, and sold to feed slaves in Brazil and Cuba. It was only with the invention of refrigerated ships that Argentina's produce was exported to meet the growing demand for beef in an expanding Europe. Cattle farmers introduced new breeds to replace the scrawny Pampas cattle, and sowed alfalfa as richer fodder than Pampas grasses. Today Herefords and Aberdeen Angus are still bred for meat.

And why is Argentine beef so good? Because these cows are healthy! With such vast expanses of land to roam, the cattle burn off any fat, are well-toned and lean: the meat is even high in Omega 3. So head straight for the best *parrilla* in town, and, unless you're vegetarian, try a few different cuts. Better still, stay at an *estancia* to try home-reared beef cooked on the *asado*, the traditional way over an open wood fire. Delicious. A word of warning: learn some of the names for the parts of a cow so you don't end up eating hoof, intestines or glands. See the menu reader, page 694.

and from there to the Paseo del Bosque at the north of the city centre. On the west side of Plaza Moreno is the enormous brick neo-Gothic **cathedral** ① *daily Mon-Sat 0900-1830, Sun 0900-2100, www.catedraldelaplata.com*, built between 1885 and 1936, and inspired by Cologne and Amiens. It has a beautiful and inspiring interior, and is definitely worth a visit. Opposite is the large, white building of the **Muncipalidad** in German Renaissance style, with a striking clock tower. Plaza San Martín, six blocks east, is bounded by the **Legislature**, with its huge neoclassical façade and, opposite, the **Casa de Gobierno** is a mixture of French and Flemish Renaissance styles. On the north side of the plaza is the lovely **Pasaje Dardo Rocha**, designed as the main railway station in Italian Renaissance style. It now houses a tourist information office (see above) and the **Centro Cultural** ① *C 50 entre 6 y 7, T0221-427 1843, www.macla.laplata.gov.ar, Tue-Fri 1000-2000, Sat-Sun 1400-2100 (1600-2200 in summer), free*, with a gallery of contemporary Latin American art, a café and two theatres. East of the Municipalidad, **Teatro Argentino** has its own orchestra and ballet company. Nearby on streets 6 and

7 are the imposing **Universidad Nacional** and the **Banco Provincial**. The main shopping streets are 8 and 12. A good market selling handicrafts and local *artesanía* is in Plaza Italia at weekends.

If you do find yourself in La Plata at the weekend, or on a sunny evening, head straight for **Paseo del Bosque**, a pretty public park of woodlands and an artificial

La Plata

Where to stay 🛏
La Plata 1
La Plata Hostel 4

Restaurants 🍴
Cervecería Modelo 5
Confitería París 1
Don Quijote 2
El Chaparral Platense 4
La Aguada 6

Bars & clubs 🍸
Block 9
Ruta Bacalao 12
Wilkenny 13

300 metres
300 yards

The Conquest of the Desert

Until the 1870s, the Pampas, and indeed most of Argentina, was inhabited by indigenous tribes. After independence, President Rosas (see Background, page 652) launched the first attempt to claim territory in Buenos Aires province in his 1833 Campaign of the Desert. But in the 1870s, pressure grew for a campaign to defeat the indigenous people, since the withdrawal of Argentine troops to fight in the War of Triple Alliance had led to a series of increasingly audacious raids by *malones*, the indigenous armies. War minister Alsina planned a series of forts and ramparts to contain the indigenous peoples, and defend the territory won from them. But his successor General Julio Roca found these plans too defensive, and called for a war of extermination, aiming to make the whole of Patagonia available for settlement. Roca's Conquest of the Desert was launched in 1879, with 8000 troops in five divisions, one of them led by Roca himself. Five important indigenous chiefs were captured, along with 1300 warriors. A further 2300 were killed or wounded. Roca's view was that "it is a law of human nature that the Indian succumb to the impact of civilized man". He destroyed villages and forced the inhabitants to choose between exile in Chile, or life in a reservation. After the campaign, mountain passes to Chile were closed, and any remaining indigenous groups were cruelly forced onto reservations.

Although Roca claimed victory in the Conquest of the Desert as a personal triumph, he was aided by technological advances: the telegraph gave commanders intelligence reports to offset the indigenous peoples' knowledge of the terrain and enabled them to co-ordinate their efforts. Railways moved troops swiftly, and Remington repeating rifles enabled any one soldier to take on five indigenous people and murder them all.

Roca was hailed as a hero, elected president in 1880, and dominated Argentine politics until his death in 1904. The land he conquered was handed out mainly to Roca's friends, since the campaign had been funded by mortgaging plots in advance, with bonds worth 25,000 acres being bought by only 500 people. Argentina has yet to come to terms with this shameful part of its history. But you can see that most statues of Roca throughout the country have been defaced with red paint symbolizing the blood he spilt. There is no attempt made by the authorities to stop this. In Buenos Aires the statue of Roca is on the corner of Perú and Roca, and it is covered in graffiti which is neither removed nor cleaned, unlike other public monuments.

lake, where all the locals head for *asados* and picnics. Also here are the **Zoological Gardens,** with giraffes, elephants and pumas amongst others, an astronomical observatory and the Hipodromo, dating from the 1930s and one of the most important racecourses in the country. The **Museo de La Plata** ① *Av 122y 60, T0221-425 8252, www.fcnym. unlp.edu.ar, Tue-Sun and holiday Mon 1000-1800, closed 1 Jan,*

1 May, 24, 25, 31 Dec, US$1.20, is one of the most famous museums in Latin America. It is particularly outstanding on anthropology and archaeology, with a huge collection of pre-Columbian artefacts including pre-Incan ceramics from Peru and beautiful ceramics from the northwest of Argentina. It is slightly run-down and some exhibits need replacing, but the preserved animal and dinosaur sections are worth visiting. The **Parque Ecológico** ① *Camino Centenario y San Luis, Villa Elisa, T0221-473 2449, www.parquecologico.laplata.gov.ar, daily 0900-1930, free, getting there: take bus 273 D or 6*, is a good place for families, with native *tala* forest and plenty of birds.

Around La Plata → For listings, see pages 103-106.

Eight kilometres northwest of the city, the **República de los Niños** ① *Col General Belgrano and Calle 500, T0221-484 1409, www.republica.laplata.gov.ar, Mon-Fri 1000-1800, Sat-Sun 0900-1900, US$2, children free, parking US$1.25*, is Eva Perón's legacy and was built under the first Perón administration. It is a delightful children's village, with scaled-down castles, oriental palaces, boating lake, cafés and even a little train. It's a fun place for families to picnic.

This area of the country has some lovely rural accommodation. A delightful option close to La Plata is the **Casa de Campo La China** ① *T0221-421 2931, www.casadecampolachina.com.ar*, a charming 1930s adobe house set in eucalyptus woods, with beautifully furnished accommodation and far-reaching views. Stay with the charming English-speaking family, or visit for the day, ride horses and enjoy carriage rides.

Parque Costero Sur Reserve

Parque Costero Sur is a large nature reserve 110 km south of La Plata, and 160 km south of Buenos Aires – just two hours' drive away. Declared a UNESCO Biosphere Site in 1997, it extends along 70 km of the coastline of Bahía Samborombón and was created to protect a wide range of birds that come here to breed. There are several *estancias* inside the reserve.

Chascomús → For listings, see pages 103-106. Colour map 4, B6.

This quaint historical town, 126 km south of Buenos Aires, is worth visiting to enjoy the vibrant combination of gaucho culture and fine 19th-century architecture, creating an atmosphere of colonial refinement with a Wild West feel. Chascomús was founded in 1779, when a fort was built as protection against the indigenous tribes. In 1839, it was the site of the Battle of the Libres del Sur (the Free of the South), and its streets are full of well-preserved buildings dating from the mid-1800s, and lined with mature trees. Despite the strong historical significance, the town has a lively feel and its position along the eastern edge of the huge Laguna Chascomús gives it an attractive *costanera*, which comes to life in summer. The **tourist office** ① *Av Costanera España y Espigón de Pesca, T02241-430405,* *www.chascomus.com.ar*, and *www.chascomus.net*, *daily 0900-1900*, is four blocks from the main avenue, Las Astras. You can take a boat out on the *laguna*, or head to a couple of fine *estancias* nearby.

Places in Chascomús → *Phone code 02241. Population 40,000.*

Around the quiet Plaza Independencia are the fudge-coloured colonial-style **Palacio Municipal** and **Iglesia Catedral**. Southeast of the plaza is the extraordinary **Capilla de los Negros** (1862) ⓘ *Tue-Fri 0900-1500, Sat-Sun 1100-1700*, a small brick chapel with earth floor, built as a place of worship for African slaves who were bought by wealthy families in the early 1800s; it's an atmospheric place that still holds the slaves' offerings. A highly recommended museum for an insight into gaucho culture is the **Museo Pampeano** ⓘ *Av Lastra and Muñiz, T02241-430982, summer Tue-Fri 0800-1400, Sat-Sun 1000-1400, 1700-1900, winter Tue-Fri 0900-1500, Sat-Sun 1030-1630, US$0.50*, which has lots of information on gaucho traditions, fabulous maps of the Spanish conquest, furniture and all the evident wealth of the early pioneers.

To the south of the town lies the **Laguna Chascomús**, one of a chain of seven connected lakes; the *costanera* is a pleasant place to stroll, you can sail and windsurf in the summer, and there are frequent regattas. It's also an important breeding site for *pejerrey* fish, with amateur fishing competitions held from November to March. The delightful **Estancia La Fe** ⓘ *www.estancialafe.com.ar*, is nearby (see page 104).

Dolores → *For listings, see pages 103-106. Colour map 4, C6. Phone code 02245. Population 30,000.*

Dolores is a pretty, sleepy little town, 204 km south of Buenos Aires. Founded in 1818, it was the first town in independent Argentina, and its attractive old buildings would be perfect as a film set for a 19th-century drama. There's an interesting little museum, **Museo Libres del Sur** ⓘ *Parque Libres del Sur, daily 1000-1700*, with good displays on local history, in particular about the Campaign of the Desert and the subsequent revolt against Rosas. It also contains lots of gaucho silver, plaited leather *tableros*, branding irons and a huge cart from 1868. There's a charming plaza at the heart of the town, with a central obelisk and impressive classical-style church, the **Iglesia Nuestra Señora de Dolores**. In mid- to late February, the **Fiesta de la Guitarra** is held, with performances from internationally famous musicians, dancing and processions. This is a good time to visit, but book ahead. For further information, contact the **tourist office** ⓘ *T02245-441925, www.dolores.gov.ar*. The railway station is 15 minutes' walk from the centre.

Estancia Dos Talas

The main reason to visit Dolores is its proximity to one of the oldest and most beautiful *estancias* in the Pampas, **Dos Talas** ⓘ *10 km south of Dolores, 2 hrs' drive from Buenos Aires, T02245-443020, www.dostalas.com.ar*. The fabulously elegant house is set in grand parkland designed by Charles Thays, with a lovely chapel copied from Notre Dame de Passy and a fascinating history. Come for the day or, even better, stay. You'll be warmly welcomed by the owners, who are descendants of the *estancia*'s original owner, Pedro Luro. This beautifully decorated home is one of Argentina's really special places to stay.

◉ The Pampas listings

For hotel and restaurant price codes and other relevant information, see pages 20-26.

◉ Where to stay

San Antonio de Areco *p95*
Most hotels offer discounts Mon-Fri.
$$$ Antigua Casona, Segundo Sombra 495, T02325-15-416030, www.antigua casona.com. Charmingly restored 1897 house with 5 rooms opening onto a delightful patio and exuberant garden, relaxing and romantic. Bikes to borrow.
$$$ Paradores Draghi, Lavalle 387, T02326-455583, www.paradoresdraghi. com.ar. Traditional-style, comfortable rooms face a manicured lawn with a pool. Just metres away Draghi family has its silversmith workshop. Recommended.
$$$ Patio de Moreno, Moreno 251, T02326-455197, www.patiodemoreno. com. The top hotel in town is a stylish place with spacious, minimalist rooms, a large patio with a pool and great service.
$$ Hostal de Areco, Zapiola 25, T02326-456118, www.hostaldeareco.com.ar. Popular, with a warm welcome, good value.
$$ Los Abuelos, Zerboni y Zapiola T02326-456390. Very good, welcoming, small pool, plain but comfortable rooms, facing riverside park.

Estancias
Some of the province's finest *estancias* are within easy reach for day visits, offering horse riding, an *asado* lunch

and other activities. Stay overnight to really appreciate the peace and beauty of these historical places. Look online at: www.sanantoniodeareco.com/turismo/estancias/index.htm.
$$$$ El Ombú, T02326-492080, office T011-4737 0436, www.estanciaelombu. com. Fine house with magnificent terrace dating from 1890, comfortable rooms, horse riding, English-speaking owners; price includes full board and activities but not transfer. Recommended.
$$$$ La Bamba, T02326-454895, www. la-bamba.com.ar. Dating from 1830, in grand parkland, charming rooms, English-speaking owners who have lived here for generations, superb meals, price is for full board. Recommended.
$$$$ La Porteña, Ruta 8, Km 110, T011-15-5626 7347, www.laporteniadeareco. com. One of Argentina's most famous *estancias* was once host to writers Ricardo Güiraldes and Antoine de Saint Exupéry. Stunning traditional building built in 1822, with original features, large grounds with 150-year-old trees and working horses. There are 3 lovely houses where you can stay, including huge banquets of food (lots of meat), or you can spend a day here, enjoying the grounds.

Camping
Club River Plate, Camino de la Ribera, T02326-453590. The best of 3 sites in the park by the river. It's an attractive sports club offering shady sites with all facilities, a pool and sports of all kinds, US$6 per tent.

La Plata p99, map p99

$$$ La Plata Hotel, Av 51 No 783, T0221-422 9090, www.weblaplatahotel.com.ar. Modern, well furnished, comfortable, spacious rooms and nice bathrooms. Price includes dinner (drinks extra).

$ pp La Plata Hostel, C 50 No 1066, T0221-457 1424, www.laplata-hostel.com.ar. Well-organized, convenient hostel in a historic house, high ceilings, small garden, simple but comfortable dorms for 4 or 8.

Around La Plata p101
Estancias

$$$$ Casa de Campo La China, 60 km from La Plata on Ruta 11, T0221-421 2931, www.casadecampolachina.com.ar. A charming 1930s adobe house set in eucalyptus woods, with beautifully decorated spacious rooms off an open gallery, day visits (US$45) to ride horses, or in carriages, eat *asado*, or stay the night, guests of Cecilia and Marcelo, who speak perfect English. Delicious food, meals included in price. Highly recommended.

Chascomús p101

For a full list see www.chascomus.com.ar.
$$$ Chascomús, Av Lastra 367, T02241-422968, www.chascomus.com.ar (under 'hoteles'). The town's most comfortable hotel, atmospheric, welcoming, with stylish turn-of-the-century public rooms and lovely terrace.

$$$ La Posada, Costanera España 18, T02241-423503, www.chascomus.com.ar (under '*cabañas*'). On the *laguna*, delightful and comfortable *cabañas* with cooking facilities.

$$$ Roble Blanco, Mazzini 130, T02241-436235, www.robleblanco.com.ar. A very good choice in a refurbished 100-year-old house, modern comfortable rooms,

a large heated pool with attractive deck and welcoming common areas. Also has a spa. Recommended.

$$ Laguna, Libres del Sur y Maipú, T02241-426113, www.lgnhotel.com.ar. Old-fashioned, sleepy hotel by the station. Pleasant, quiet rooms.

Estancias

Estancias will collect you from Chascomús.
$$$$ Estancia La Fe, R2, Km 116, T02241-154 42222, www.estancialafe.com.ar. A charming and typical place to come for a few days to get a feel for life on the land. Activities include horse riding, riding in carriages and walking in the grounds. Simple, comfortable rooms, wide views from the grounds, great *asado*.

$$$$ Haras La Viviana, in Castelli, 65 km from Chascomús, T011-4702 9633, www.haraslaviviana.com.ar. Perfect for horse riding, since fine polo ponies are bred here. Tiny cabins in gardens by a huge *laguna* where you can kayak or fish, very peaceful, good service, wonderful welcome from lady novelist owner, fluent English spoken, also French, Italian, Portuguese.

$$$ La Horqueta, 3 km from Chascomús on Ruta 20, T011-4777 0150, www.la horqueta.com. Full board, mansion in lovely grounds with *laguna* for fishing, horse riding, bikes to borrow, English-speaking hosts, safe gardens especially good for children, plain food.

Camping

There are 7 sites all with good facilities: **Monte Corti** is closest, 2.2 km away at Costanera y Gonzáles Chávez, T0221-430767, but there are 5 on the far side of the *laguna*; **Mutual 6 de Septiembre**, 8 km away, T011-155 182 3836, has a pool.

Dolores p102
$$$$ Estancia Dos Talas, 10 km from Dolores, T02245-443020, www.dostalas. com.ar. One of the oldest *estancias*, you are truly the owners' guests here. The rooms and the service are impeccable, the food exquisite; stay for days, and completely relax. Pool, riding, English spoken. See also page 102.
$$ Hotel Plaza, Castelli 75, T02245-442362. Comfortable and welcoming old place on the plaza, all rooms with bath and TV, breakfast extra, good *confitería* downstairs. There's another good café next door.

Camping
Camping del Náutico, Lago Parque Náutico.

🍴 Restaurants

San Antonio de Areco p95
Many *parrillas* on the bank of the Río Areco.
$$ Almacén de Ramos Generales, Zapiola 143, T02326-456376 (best to book ahead). Perfect place, popular with locals, very atmospheric, superb meat, very good pastas and a long wine list.
$$ Café de las Artes, Bolívar 70, T02326-456398 (better book ahead). In a hidden spot, this cosy place serves delicious pastas with a large wine selection.
$$ La Costa, Zerboni y Belgrano (on the riverside park). A very good traditional *parrilla* with an attractive terrace.
$$ La Ochava de Cocota, Alsina y Alem. Relaxing, attractive, excellent service, superb *empanadas* and vegetable pies. It is also a café.
$ La Esquina de Merti, Arellano y Segundo Sombra. The ideal place for a beer on the main plaza. Go early to get a table outside.

La Plata p99, map p99
$$ Cervecería Modelo, C 54 y C5. Traditional German-style *cervecería*, with good menu and beer.
$$ Don Quijote, Plaza Paso. Delicious food in lovely surroundings, well known.
$$ El Chaparral Platense, C 60 y C 116 (Paseo del Bosque). Good *parrilla* in the park, great steaks.
$$ La Aguada, C 50 entre 7 y 8. The oldest restaurant in town, good for *minutas* (light meals), famous for its *papas fritas*.
Confitería París, C 7 y 48. The best croissants, and a lovely place for coffee.

Chascomús p101
$$ Colonial, Estados Unidos y Artigas. Great food, pastas and cakes are recommended.

Dolores p102
$$ Restaurant La Farola, Dolores 260. Welcoming, serves good pasta dishes.
$ Parrilla Don Pedro, Av del Valle and Crámer. Ignore the unimaginiative decor, order steak.
$ Pizzería Cristal, Buenos Aires 226. Pizzas.

🍸 Bars and clubs

San Antonio de Areco p95
Pulpería La Ganas, Vieytes and Pellegrini. An authentic, traditional old bar, full of ancient bottles. Live music at weekends.

La Plata p99, map p99
The following bars are popular and lively: **Block**, corner of Calles 122 and 50, and **Ruta Bacalao**, in Gonnet, a pleasant residential area to the north of the city. **Wilkenny**, Calle 50 corner of 11. Hugely popular, Irish-style pub.

🎭 Entertainment

La Plata *p99, map p99*
El Viejo Almacén, Calle 13 at 71.
Tango and tropical music.
Teatro Martín Fierro, Paseo del Bosque.
Free concerts during the summer.

🎉 Festivals

San Antonio de Areco *p95*
Nov Day of Tradition, www.
sanantoniodeareco.travel/. Traditional
parades, gaucho games, events on
horseback, music and dance.

⏰ What to do

All *estancias* offer horse riding. Other
operators can be contacted from the
hotels in the Pampas towns.

San Antonio de Areco *p95*
Country Club, R8, Km 11, T02326-453073.
Play golf or watch a polo match in restful
surroundings. Good food is also served.
Ask tourist office for directions.

🚌 Transport

Luján *p93*
Bus From **Buenos Aires** Bus 57
Empresa Atlántida, either from Plaza
Once, route O (the fastest), or from
Plaza Italia, routes C and D, US$3. To
San Antonio de Areco, several a day,
US$4.50, Empresa Argentina, 1 hr.

San Antonio de Areco *p95*
Bus From **Buenos Aires** (Retiro bus
terminal), 1½-2 hrs, US$8, every hour
with **Chevallier** or **Pullman General
Belgrano**. **Remise taxis Sol**, San
Martín y Alsina, T02326-455444.

La Plata *p99, map p99*
Bus
Terminal at Calle 42 entre 3 y 4, T0221-421
0992. To **Buenos Aires**, very frequent
during the day, hourly at night, **Costera
Metropolitana** and **Plaza**, 1 hr 10 mins
either to Retiro terminal or to Centro
(stops along Av 9 de Julio), US$1.80. To
Mar del Plata, US$41 with **El Rápido.**

Train
To/from **Buenos Aires** (Constitución),
frequent, US$1.15, 1 hr 20 mins.

Chascomús *p101*
Bus
Frequent service, several per day to
Buenos Aires (2 hrs, US$9), **La Plata**, **Mar
del Plata**, and daily to **Bahía Blanca** and
Villa Gesell; terminal T02241-422595.

Train
T02241-422220. **Ferrobaires**, www.
ferrobaires.gba.gov.ar, 3 trains per week
to **Buenos Aires** (Constitución) and to
Mar del Plata, passing **Dolores** en route,
erratic service.

Dolores *p102*
Bus
To **Buenos Aires**, 3 hrs, US$17, and to
La Plata, US$12, **El Rápido**, T02245-
441109, or T0800-333 1970.

Taxi
There is a stand at Belgrano and Rico,
1 block from plaza.

Train
Daily service to **Buenos Aires**, US$21-27.

Atlantic Coast

There are 500 km of beautiful beaches and some splendid resorts spread out along the great sweeping curve of coastline between La Plata and Bahía Blanca. Closest to Buenos Aires, there's a string of sleepy seaside towns known collectively as the Partido de la Costa, popular with older retired Argentines and better for sea-fishing than beachcombing. For more beautiful beaches, head further southwest to party town Pinamar, the jewel of the whole coast with its excellent hotels and fine restaurants. Its neighbour, smarter still, is chic Cariló, where the *balnearios* (swimming beaches) are exclusive and the *cabañas* luxurious. Nearby Villa Gesell is more of an ugly working town and best avoided. Nearby is a quieter resort becoming known for its natural beauty and complete peace: Mar de las Pampas, where you can find *cabañas* set in idyllic woodland right by to the sea.

Argentina's most famous resort, Mar del Plata was the very height of chic in the 1920s, but it's now a busy seaside city, with packed beaches and casinos – not the best place to relax but still interesting. To the west, two old-fashioned resorts are rather more appealing: Miramar is quiet and low-key, good for young families; and larger Necochea has an appealing woodland park along its coastline, with a vast area of unspoilt dunes, perfect for exploring on horseback. The southern stretch of beaches ends in the major port of Bahía Blanca, a useful transport hub if you're heading south, with an attractive town inland from the sea.

Arriving on the Atlantic Coast

Getting there All resorts on the coast are linked to each other and to Buenos Aires by frequent bus services. Trains to Mar del Plata also stop at many coastal towns. If you're combining beaches and *estancias*, it's best to hire a car. The main artery south is the fast, privately run toll road Route Provincial 2 (with US$2-3 tolls every 100 km), which runs from Buenos Aires to Mar del Plata, via Chascomús and Dolores, with another fast road branching off to Pinamar from Dolores: take Route 63 and then 56. Alternatively, head along the coast from La Plata on Route Provincial 11, also fast and with tolls, to San Clemente del Tuyú and then parallel to the coast to Mar del Plata. Route Provincial 88 links Mar del Plata and Necochea, further southwest. Remember to have small change for the tolls as they will not give change for large bills, and do not take credit cards. Mar del Plata also has a domestic airport with flights from Buenos Aires. ▸▸ *For further information see Transport, page 128.*

Best time to visit Avoid January if you can, when the whole coast is packed out with hordes of tourists from Buenos Aires. December and late February are ideal for hot weather and fewer crowds. Many resorts are very pleasant in spring and autumn, but out of season (and the season is from December to March) most resorts apart from busy Mar del Plata are ghost towns. The winter wind can be harsh, but if you want a quiet weekend away to read books and relax, then it can be a good time to travel, with good deals to be had at resorts.

Tourist information There are well-organized tourist information offices in all resorts with complete lists of places to stay. There's plenty of accommodation along the coast, so only a small selection is listed. There's a useful provincial website, www.gba.gov.ar (in Spanish) and each town also has its own website: **Partido de la Costa**, http://lacosta.tur.ar/; **Pinamar**, www.pinamar.gov.ar and www.pinamarturismo.com.ar; **Mar de las Pampas** and **Mar Azul**, www.mardelaspampas.com.ar; **Mar del Plata**, www.mardelplata.gov.ar and www.turismomardelplata.gov.ar; **Miramar**, www.miramarense.com.ar; **Necochea**, http://necochea.gov.ar and www.necocheanet.com.ar; **Bahía Blanca**, www.bahiablanca.gov.ar.

Partido de la Costa → *For listings, see pages 120-130.*

Heading south from Buenos Aires, San Clemente del Tuyú is the first of a string of 14 small seaside towns, known as Partido de la Costa, stretching down to Mar de Ajó. First built in the 1930s, they lost popularity when the more glamorous resorts were built further south. It's not the best part of the coast and can't be recommended as most of the resorts are slightly run-down with peeling 1950s seafront hotels and tacky attractions, though they're also rather cheaper than the more upmarket resorts. The beaches are crowded in January but absolutely deserted at other times and particularly forlorn in winter. However, there is an interesting nature reserve and excellent sea fishing. The Río de la Plata has gained international recognition as the widest freshwater river in the world, and here at its mouth you can fish for shark, *pejerrey* and *brótola* from piers or from boats. Fish can often be bought on the beach from local fishermen.

San Clemente del Tuyú → *Colour map 4, C6. Phone code 02252. Population 11,400.*
Some 320 km south of Buenos Aires, San Clemente's main attraction is **Mundo Marino** ① *Av Décima No 157, signposted from the main road into town, T02252-430300, www.mundomarino.com.ar, daily Jan-Feb 1000-2000, Mar, Jul, Dec daily 1000-1800, off season Sat-Sun only, US$25, children US$16.75.* This is the biggest sea life centre in South America, where you can watch performing seals, dolphins, whales and penguins go through their completely unnatural routines; it's fun for children. There's also a smaller, far less spectacular theme park, **Termas Marinas** ① *take the road to Faro San Antonio at the far south of Bahía Samborombón, T02252-423000, www.termasmarinas.com.ar, daily 1000-2000 in summer, closing earlier in winter, US$17.50, children US$12 (cheaper online),* where children can swim in thermal pools, identify birds and, for a small extra fee, ascend to the top of a historical lighthouse, which has impressive views.

Even more appealing is the unspoilt wildness of **Reserva Natural Punta Rasa** ① *2 km from San Clemente, take the road to Faro San Antonio and follow signs, free, managed by the Fundación Vida Silvestre, www.vidasilvestre.org.ar.* This is a private reserve protecting a special area at the southernmost point of the Bahía de Samborombón, where a long tongue of dense sand stretches into the bay where the Río de la Plata meets the sea. Vast numbers of migrating birds and a resident population of crabs and shellfish make this an interesting place to spend an afternoon. It's a great place for a walk, with a short, self-guided trail and a lighthouse to visit. It's also a world-famous sea-fishing site; the water around the peninsula can be up to 20 m deep, attracting large specimens of *corvina negra* (black sea bass) weighing over 20 kg. It's possible to drive along the 5-km peninsula but watch out for the tides. Information is available from *guardaparques* at the entrance and at the tip of the peninsula.

San Clemente has a busy fishing port, with yolk-yellow boats characteristic of the area, and the **Club Náutico**, at Tapera de López, offering all kinds of water sports. South of the centre, there's an attractive area of woodland, **Vivero Cosme Argerich** ① *T02252-421103, daily 0800-1900, free, guided visits offered,* a 37-ha park with woodlands, a plant nursery and sports centre. For further information on activities in the area, visit the **tourist office** ① *Calle 2 Sur and 63 Sur, San Clemente, T02252-430718, also at the bus terminal, T02252-423249, turismocentrosc@lacosta.gob.ar.*

Santa Teresita → *Phone code 02246. Population 13,000.*
From San Clemente, drive through Las Toninas and Costa Chica to reach Santa Teresita, where the biggest attraction is fishing, though there's also a good golf course, tennis and horse riding on offer. The **pier** is one of the largest on the coast and is lit for night fishing. ▸▸ *For further information, see What to do, page 127.*

There's a **motor museum** Museo del Automóvil Santa Teresita ① *Av 32, No 1550, between 15 and 16, daily 0930-2000 in summer, US$2, children US$1,* which has some stylish 1920s models and is fun for enthusiasts. The **tourist office** ① *Calle 3 and 42, T02246-420542, www.santateresita.com.ar,* can advise on accommodation.

Mar del Tuyú → *Phone code 02246. Population 6900.*
Approximately 20 km south of San Clemente del Tuyú, Mar del Tuyú is the administrative centre of Partido de las Costa. It's a tranquil place to visit in February, with a little more life than the other resorts nearby in winter. Boat trips are organized along the coast in summer, all the way to **Faro San Antonio**, where you can see whales basking at close proximity in August and September. Fishing is also a big attraction (see What to do, page 127). The **tourist office** ① *Municipalidad, Costanera 8001*, is helpful.

Mar de Ajó and around → *Colour map 4, C6. Phone code 02257. Population 13,800.*
Another quiet, old-fashioned resort, 40 km south of San Clemente del Tuyú, Mar de Ajó has a couple of natural attractions as well as motor racing, a shipwreck and a casino. The **Autódromo Regional** ① *follow signs from the access roundabout for Mar de Ajó*, holds important motor-racing championships every summer. You can dive or snorkel at the *Naufragio Margarita*, a large German ship, wrecked off the coast here in 1880, and one of the oldest in the region. Mar de Ajó has one of the largest fleets of small fishing boats on the coast, as well as the largest pier.

The most spectacular part of this area of coastline is **Altos Médanos**, a long stretch of high sand dunes that are, apparently, constantly changing shape. It's one of the wildest and most unspoilt areas of the coast, bordered along the shore by a wide flat beach, perfect for walking, horse riding or 4WD.

The best way to enjoy this area is by visiting one of the few *estancias* near the coast. **Estancia Palantelén** ① *15 km south of Mar de Ajó, T011-15-5342 4120 or T02257-420983, www.palantelen.com.ar*, is owned by descendants of a pioneering Pampas family, whose atmospheric old house has views of the sea and is beautifully furnished and lined with mahogany panels salvaged from a shipwreck. Walk onto the sands, birdwatch or gallop across the miles of beaches, either on horseback or in a *sulky* (open horse-drawn carriage). Spend a few days here and absorb the complete peace; you could even have private tango lessons on the terrace under the stars. All highly recommended.

Pinamar → *Colour map 4, C6. Phone code 02254. Population 20,600.*
The two most desirable resorts on the coast are right next to each other, with the quieter old-fashioned **Ostende** in between (see below). Both party-town Pinamar and forested Cariló are upmarket places to stay, attracting wealthy Argentines, and have far smarter hotels than elsewhere on the coast, not to mention fine restaurants and, in Pinamar, plenty of trendy beach bars and nightclubs. Pinamar is perfect for young people and families, with live bands playing at its beach clubs in the evenings in high season; these are also quiet and elegant places to dine on superb seafood.

Access to the beach is mostly by day membership to a *balneario* (beach club). You pay a fee of US$20-50 per family or group of friends per day, and then you can make use of all the *balneario's* facilities. You can rent a *carpa* – little wooden beach huts, built in tightly packed rows perpendicular to the sea, and furnished with tables and chairs to use when you retreat from the hot sun. Alternatively, you can rent a big beach umbrella and stake a claim on an area closer to the sea. Renting either will allow you to use the *balneario's* showers, toilets, restaurants and even beach games. Pinamar's *balnearios* range from exclusive, quiet places with superb restaurants, to party spots with loud music, beach parties and live bands at night. There is free public access to the beach between the *balnearios*, but it's worth visiting one for a day to enjoy beach life. Their restaurants are also open to those not renting *carpas*.

The town also has golf courses and tennis courts, and there are lots of hotels and smart restaurants along the main street, Avenida Bunge, running perpendicular to the sea. Explore the dunes at **Reserva Dunícola**, 13 km north, by horse or 4WD. The **tourist office** ① *Av Shaw 18, T02254-491680, www.pinamar. gov.ar, www.pinamarturismo.com.ar, English spoken*, is helpful and can arrange accommodation. During the peak month of January, Pinamar is packed with Argentines, accommodation is extremely hard to get and very expensive. Best to visit in December or February/March. During the rest of the year, especially in June/ July, the town virtually shuts down, and few hotels and restaurants are open. The **bus terminal** ① *Av Bunge and Intermédanos, T02254-403500*, is near the access road into town, a 20-minute walk to the beach, and the railway station is a few kilometres from town, but there are free bus transfers.

Cariló

Cariló is the most exclusive, and expensive, beach resort in Argentina, and you'll soon see why. There's a large and lovely area of mature woodland right on the beach, where luxury apart hotels and very chic *cabañas* are all tastefully concealed, so that its visitors have complete privacy – something that inevitably appeals to the many celebrities, sports stars and politicians who visit. The *balnearios* are neat and exclusive – Hemingway (T02254-487388) is *the* place to be seen for wealthy *Porteños*. Around the tiny centre, on Cerezo and Carpintero, there are good restaurants and chi-chi arcades with upmarket clothing shops where you can browse for top Argentine fashion labels among the usual international designers. You might find Cariló less friendly than Pinamar if you're in search of nightlife, since the emphasis is on exclusivity, but it's a good place for couples or for a quiet solo retreat. There is a **tourist office** ① *Boyero and Castaño, T02254-570773, www.carilo. com and www.parquecarilo.com (both in Spanish)*.

Around Pinamar and Cariló

In between Pinamar and Cariló is **Ostende**, a small town founded in 1908 but largely abandoned on the outbreak of the First World War. This is a wilder part of the coast and there are plenty of campsites. Inland, **General Madariaga** is a quaint 1900s town that is definitely worth visiting for the **Fiesta Nacional del Gaucho** on the second weekend in December, when there are processions, singing and dancing. From General Madariaga, fishing enthusiasts could visit the **Laguna Salada Grande**, the largest lake in the province with a nature reserve and excellent *pejerrey* fishing. The **tourist office** ① *Rivadavia No 1086, T02267-421058, www.ruta0.com/general-madariaga.htm*, can advise on where to stay.

Villa Gesell → *Colour map 4, C6. Phone code 02255. Population 24,000.*

In complete contrast to overdeveloped Mar del Plata and upmarket Pinamar, Villa Gesell, 22 km north, was planned by German inventor, Carlos Gesell, as an eco resort. He came to live here in 1931 with the aim of growing trees for wood on the barren sand dunes. His project then evolved into an ecological holiday retreat and the first guests were invited in the 1940s. He planned and built the town in harmony with nature, planting thousands of shady trees that would draw water to the surface and constructing roads around the sand dunes. Today, however, it bears no resemblance to his idea. It is crammed full of decaying 1970s holiday homes and apartment blocks, broken cars and tacky shops. Gesell would be aghast at the commercial feel of the main street, Avenida 3, which is filled with games arcades, fast-food shops and noisy cafés. It is best to avoid staying here, although it can be much cheaper than Pinamar only 10 minutes away.

The main **tourist office** ① *Paseo 107 entre 2 y 3, T02255-478042, www.gesell.gov. ar, daily 0800-0000*, is on the right-hand side of the road as you enter the town, *also in bus terminal and 3 other locations*. There's a good website with lots of accommodation and other information, www.gesell.gov.ar. The **bus terminal** ① *Av 3 and Paseo 140, information T02255-477253*, is at the southern end of town.

The **Reserva Forestal and Parque Cultural Pinar del Norte**, at the eastern end of Avenida 3, is where Carlos Gesell built his first house in the woods. It's now a museum, **Museo Casa Histórica** ① *T02255-468624, daily 1400-2100 in summer, Tue-Fri 1000-1600, Sat-Sun 1100-1700 in winter*, with inspiring biographical information (in English) and an interesting daily tour. Gesell's second house, **Chalet Don Carlos Gesell**, is now a cultural centre for exhibitions and concerts.

Mar de las Pampas and Mar Azul

Just 5 km south of Villa Gesell, two quiet resorts are developing: the pine forests and dirt-roads of **Mar de las Pampas** and the more commercial, less pretty **Mar Azul** are wilder and quieter than anywhere else on this coast and have some appealing accommodation in more natural surroundings. There are lots of *cabañas* for rent and an increasing number of hotels, but most people rent a house for the weekend; this is especially good if you are in a group. The beach here is broad and uncrowded, so although there is less to do than in Pinamar or Mar del Plata and no nightlife to speak of, you can completely relax and enjoy the sea in peace. It's a perfect retreat for writing or reflecting, or a cosy hideaway for couples, although in January you'll find traffic jams and queues at restaurants. Mar de las Pampas has a **tourist office** ① *Mercedes Sosa y El Lucero, T02255-452823, summer daily 0800-0000*. See also www.mardelaspampas.com.ar, for more information.

The oldest and most famous Argentine resort – built in 1874 – has lost much of its charm since its heyday in the 1930s but it is still an interesting place to stay. It's now a big city with plenty of entertainment, but unless you're a lover of crowds or casinos, there are better beaches elsewhere. There are some good bars and cafés along Güemes and Alem, near the cemetery, and superb fish restaurants by the port and on the pier. There are hundreds of hotels, all busy and overpriced even in low season (although prices double in January and February), as this is a popular conference city. Winter is the best time to visit if you want to see the town itself and the sea lion colony, although the wind is relentless.

Mar del Plata

Where to stay 💮	Restaurants 🍴	Manolo 1
Abra Marina 1	Selent 11	Pehuén 10
Costa Galana 6		Taberna Baska 11
Dos Reyes 5	Almacén El Condal 3	Tisiano 12
Los Troncos 9	El Viejo Pop 7	

Arriving in Mar del Plata → *Phone code 0223. Population 542,000.*

Getting there There are daily flights from Buenos Aires (several in summer) to **Camet Airport**, 10 km north of town, T0223-478 3990. In summer there are also LADE flights to towns in Patagonia. Regular buses (bus No 542, US$1, payable with a magnetic card) run from the airport into town, or it's US$10 in a *Remise* taxi.

The **bus terminal** and **railway station** are combined in a new terminal, the **Terminal Ferroautomotora** ⓘ *Av Luro y San Juan, T0223-561 3743, www.nueva terminalmardel.com.ar*, about 13 blocks northwest of the centre. Bus Nos 511, 512, 512B and 541 run to the centre. Bus No 511 continues to the lighthouse, south to the beaches and to the port, with buses running every 10 minutes or so (less frequently at night). Single trips cost US$0.40-0.60, depending on how far you travel. Some buses, including No 511, can only be used with a top-up card available from any kiosk. In general, buses are quick and comfortable.

Tourist information The city's **tourist office** ⓘ *Belgrano 2740, T0223-494 4140 (ext 130 or 131) or, more conveniently, next to Casino Central, on Blvd Marítimo 2270, T0223-495 1777, www.turismomardelplata.gov.ar, Mon-Sat 0800-2200, Sun 1000-1700*, is very helpful and can provide good leaflets on events, information on bus routes and lists of hotels and apartment/chalet letting agents, including family homes (when everywhere else is full). There are also tourist offices at the airport and the bus station. For what's on, see www.todomardelplata.com.

Best time to visit There are several festivals throughout the summer, with live music shows, parades and the coronation of all kinds of carnival queens. For more details, see Festivals, page 127. If you're coming for the beaches, January is best avoided because of overcrowding; December or late February are much more pleasant and it's still warm.

Places in Mar del Plata

The city centre is around **Playa Bristol**, where a broad promenade, the Rambla, runs past the fine casino (upper floor open to the public) and the new luxury refurbished **Gran Hotel Provincial**, both of which were designed by famous Argentine architect Bustillo, and date from the late 1930s. Six blocks north along San Martín is the Plaza San Martín, a good place for shopping, flanked by an attractive **cathedral**. Ten blocks southwest, at the end of Avenida Colón there are some impressive and attractive mansions dating from Mar del Plata's heyday, from mock-Tudor **Villa Blaquier** to **Villa Ortiz Basualdo** (1909), inspired by a Loire chateaux, now the **Museo Municipal de Arte** ⓘ *Av Colón 1189, T0223-486 1636, daily 1700-2200 in summer, Wed-Mon 1200-1700 in winter, US$1, including tour*, with rooms furnished in period style. The **Centro Cultural Victoria Ocampo** ⓘ *Matheu 1851, T0223-492 0569, daily in summer, closed Tue and mornings in winter; ring to check current opening times, US$1*, is in a beautiful 1900s wooden house in lovely gardens, where the famous author entertained illustrious literary figures. In summer, concerts are held in the grounds. Nearby is the **Villa Mitre** ⓘ *Lamadrid 3870, T0223-495 1200, Mon-Fri 0800-1800, Sat-Sun 1400-1800, US$1.25*, owned by a son of Bartolomé Mitre, with an eclectic collection of artefacts including old photos of the city. There's no shortage of entertainment in the city, with lots of theatres and cinemas, live music and the casino. See Entertainment, page 126.

Beaches and port area

There are several beaches along this stretch of coast, each with a different feel. Fashionable **Playa Grande** has the best hotels and shops, as well as the famous golf course, with private *balnearios* attracting wealthy *Porteños*, and a small area open to the public. **Playa La Perla** is packed in summer and far from relaxing, while **Playa Punta Mogotes**, further west, is by far the most appealing beach. However, a short bus ride (Nos 511 or 221) further south will take you to some other quieter beaches, including La Morocha and La Arena, where it is also possible to park the car on the beach close to the sea for a small fee. The **port area**, south of Playa Grande, is interesting when the old orange fishing boats come in, and this is the place to come at night, as there are many seafood restaurants gathered in one place; be selective as some are very touristy. A sea lion colony basks on rusting wrecks by the **Escollera Sur**, the southern breakwater that stretches out into the sea. Fishing for *pejerrey*, *corvina* and *pescadilla* is good all along the coast. Beyond the port are the **Punta Mogotes lighthouse**, built in 1891, and the **Bosque Peralta Ramos**, a 400-ha forest of eucalyptus and conifers, which is an excellent place to take a stroll. There's a tasty local restaurant, **El Descanso del Marino**, here too. If you want sea and sand, rather than bars and entertainment, the best beaches are further southwest of the city, along the road to Miramar. Here you'll find several fine broad beaches interrupted by high cliffs; all are easily reached by regular buses from the terminal.

Around Mar del Plata

Santa Clara del Mar is a low-key family resort 18 km north of Mar del Plata that has *balnearios* and a relaxed feel. Though it's far from chic, it's a welcoming place. For further information, contact the **tourist office** ① *T0223-460 2433, www.marchiquitadigital.com.ar*. Beyond, some 34 km northeast of Mar del Plata, is the **Mar Chiquita**, a lagoon joined to the sea by a narrow channel, with huge dunes in between, offering good beaches, sailing, fishing and boating, and rich bird life.

Balcarce, 68 km northwest and inland from Mar del Plata, is an attractive small town, with some splendid art deco buildings and a leafy central plaza. The main reason for visiting, though, is to see the famous **Museo Juan Manuel Fangio** ① *Dardo Rocha y Mitre, T02266-425540, www.museofangio.com, daily Jan-Mar 1000-1900, rest of year 1000-1700, closed Christmas-New Year, US$8, children US$5, seniors US$4*. Argentina's most beloved racing driver was born here, and the *municipalidad* on the plaza has been turned into a great museum, housing all his trophies and many of the racing cars he drove. Recommended for car enthusiasts. For further information, contact the **tourist office** ① *Calle 17 No 671, T02266-425758, www.sierrasdebalcarce.com.ar*.

The **Laguna La Brava**, 38 km away, at the foot of the Balcarce hills, offers *pejerrey* fishing and plentiful birdlife in lovely wooded surroundings. Visit **Estancia Laguna**

La Brava ① *R226, Km 36.5, T0223-4608062, www.lagunabrava.com/antcasco.htm*, for horse riding, trekking, mountain biking and water sports on the lake with fine views of Sierra Brava. ▸▸ *For further information on fishing, see What to do, page 127.*

Miramar → *Colour map 4, C6. Phone code 02291. Population 24,500.*

A delightful, low-key alternative to Mar del Plata, Miramar lies 47 km southwest along the coast road and is an old-fashioned little resort, known as the 'city of bicycles' and orientated towards families. It has a big leafy plaza at its centre, a good stretch of beach with soft sand, and a pleasant atmosphere. The most attractive area of the town is away from the high-rise buildings on the seafront, at the **Vivero Dunícola Florentino Ameghino**, a 502-ha forest park on the beach, with lots of walks, restaurants and picnic places for *asado* among the mature trees. There's also a small **Museo Municipal**, with displays of animal fossils and indigenous Querandí artefacts. Further east is the dense wood of the **Bosque Energético**, possessed of an allegedly magical magnetic energy, which attracts large twigs to hang from tree trunks and groups of meditators to sit in hopeful silence.

There are plenty of banks with ATMs around the plaza. The **tourist office** ① *Av Costanera y 21, T02291-420190, www.turismodemiramar.com.ar, Mon-Fri 0700-2100, Sat-Sun 0900-2100 in summer,* has helpful accommodation lists and maps. There are **bus terminals** ① *T02291-423359,* at Calle 34 and Avenida 23, and at Fortunato de la Plaza and Calle 19, and a few others. The **railway station** ① *T02291-420657,* is at Avenida 40 and Calle 15.

From here, you can easily visit **Mar del Sur**, 14 km south, a peaceful resort with good fishing in a lagoon and bathing on the beach among dunes and black rocks.

Necochea → *Colour map 4, C5. Phone code 02262. Population 65,000.*

One of the most surprising resorts on the whole Atlantic coast, Necochea, 100 km west of Miramar, is a well-established town, famous for its enormously long (74 km) beach. While the central area is built up and busy in summer months, further west is a spectacular expanse of sand with high dunes, perfect for exploring on foot, horseback or 4WD. There's also a huge forest park, a golf club and rafting on the river Quequén.

Arriving in Necochea There are several buses daily from Mar del Plata, Buenos Aires and Bahía Blanca to Necochea's **bus terminal** ① *Av 58 y Jesuita Cardiel, T02262-422470,* rather inconveniently northeast of the centre (3 km from the beach). Take local bus No 513 to the beach area, or a taxi for US$5. There's a good bus network all over the city. There is also a **train station** at the corner of streets 580 and 563 in Quequén, east of Necochea across the bridge (see below). There are a number of banks with ATMs and *locutorios* along the pedestrianized shopping street, Calle 83.

Tourist information There is a **tourist information office** ① *Av 79 y Av 2, T02262-438333, www.necochea.tur.ar, Apr-Nov daily 1000-1600, Dec-Mar 0800-2000,* on the seafront, which is useful for accommodation and entertainment.

Places in Necochea The town lies on the west bank of the Río Quequén and is in two parts, with its administrative centre 2 km inland from the seafront area. On the opposite bank of the river, Quequén (population 15,000) is mostly a residential area, with one of the most important grain-exporting ports in the country. The two towns are linked by three bridges; one of them, Puente Colgante, is a 270-m suspension bridge built in Cherbourg and opened here in 1929.

The **Parque Miguel Lillo** (named after the Argentine botanist) is a wonderful dense forest of over 500 ha with more than a million trees, open to the public for all kinds of activities. It starts three blocks west of Plaza San Martín, and stretches along the seafront. There are lovely walks, many campsites and picnic spots, a swan lake with paddle boats, an amphitheatre, lots of restaurants, a couple of tiny museums and places to practise various sports.

West of Necochea, there's a natural arch of rock at the **Cueva del Tigre**, and beyond it stretches a vast empty beach, separated from the land by sand dunes up to 100 m high, the **Médano Blanco**. This is an exhilarating area for walking or horse riding, and the dunes are popular for 4WD, riding and sand boarding. East of Quequén harbour there are equally tranquil beaches, particularly **Balneario La Virazón**, and a lighthouse built in 1921, with a good 18-hole golf course.

Around Necochea

You can go rafting on the **Río Quequén** and visit the **Cascadas de Quequén**, small waterfalls 13 km north. The forested **Parque Cura-Meucó** is 70 km north, on the river. There's also diving off the coast at **Parque Subacuático Kabryl**, just 1500 m from the coast. More information on diving is available at www.buceoprofundo. com.ar (in Spanish).

Bahía Blanca and around → *For listings, see pages 120-130. Colour map 4, C4.*

The province's most important port and a big naval base, Bahía Blanca is a busy city, and yet it's a relaxed and attractive place with some fine early 20th-century architecture around its large plaza. There's not much to attract tourists, but it's a useful stopping point on the route south, or a base for exploring the beautiful mountains 100 km north at Sierra de la Ventana. It's a city with the feel of a small town, where people are friendly and everyone knows everyone else.

Arriving in Bahía Blanca → *Phone code 0291. Population 275,000.*

Getting there There are several flights daily from Buenos Aires to **Airport Comandante Espora** ① *11 km northeast of town, T0291-486 0300, US$10 in a taxi*, and weekly flights with **LADE** to many places in Patagonia. There are buses from all over the country to the **bus terminal** ① *Estados Unidos and Brown 1700, 2 km east of the centre, T0291-481 9615, information Mon-Fri 0700-1300*. Buses 512 and 514 run to the centre, or it's US$5 in a taxi; there are no hotels nearby. There are trains from Buenos Aires; the **railway station** ① *Av General Cerri 750, T0291-452 9196*, is six blocks east of the plaza.

Getting around The city is pleasant to walk around, with a small centre and most things you'll need on streets Alsina or San Martín north/east of the plaza. There's a good network of local buses, taking *Urbana* cards rather than cash (available from shops and kiosks), which you'll need to catch if you want to get to the shopping mall 20 blocks north. Taxis are cheap and plentiful.

Tourist information The tourist office ① *Drago 1800, T0291-481 8944, information posts at Av Colón y Drago and bus terminal, www.bahiablanca.gov.ar, Mon-Fri 0700-1300,* is very helpful.

Background

Bahía Blanca was founded in 1828 as a fort, the Fortaleza Protectora Argentina, both to control cattle-rustling by the indigenous population and to protect the coast from Brazil, whose navy had landed in the area in 1827. Though the indigenous people of the area were defeated in the campaigns of Rosas, the fortress was attacked several times, notably by 3000 Calfucurá warriors in 1859. An important centre of European immigration, it became a major port with the building of the railways connecting it to grain-producing areas in the Pampas. The biggest industry now is a huge petrochemicals plant 8 km from town at the port.

Places in Bahía Blanca

Bahía Blanca is pleasant to walk around, with well-preserved architecture from the early 20th century. At the city's heart is the large **Plaza Rivadavia**, a broad, well-kept leafy space, with a striking sculpture. On the west side is the Italianate **Municipalidad** (1904), and to the south the impressive French-style **Banco de la Nación** (1927); it's worth popping in to see its perfectly preserved interior. Three blocks north is the classical **Teatro Municipalidad** (1922) ① *T0291-456 3973,* which hosts regular theatre, live music and dance. At the side of the theatre, the **Museo Histórico** ① *Dorrego 116, T0291-456 3117, mhistorico.bahiablanca.gov.ar, Tue-Fri 0800-1200, 1600-2000, Sat-Sun 1600-2000,* has interesting displays on the city's history.

To the northwest of the centre, along the attractive Avenida Além, the **Parque de Mayo** is filled with eucalyptus trees, children's play areas and bars. Nearby there's a golf course, sports centre and a long area for walking by the river through a sculpture park.

Not to be missed is the **Museo del Puerto** ① *7 km away at the port area Ingeniero White, Torres 4121, T0291-457 3006, Mon-Fri 0830-1230, Sat-Sun 1530-1930, free, bus No 500A or 504 from the plaza, or a taxi; US$5.* Set in a former customs building, this has entertaining and imaginative displays on immigrant life in the early 20th century, with witty photographs, evocative music and sound. And there's a great café in one of the exhibition spaces on Sundays. Highly recommended. The port also has a couple of fine fish restaurants in its red-light district; take a taxi.

Around Bahía Blanca

Bahía Blanca has both mountains and beach within an hour's drive. At **Pehuén-Có**, 84 km east, there's a long stretch of sandy beaches and dunes, all relatively empty and unspoilt (beware of jellyfish when the wind is in the south). It's signposted from the main road 24 km from Bahía Blanca. It has a wild and un-touristy feel, with a single hotel, several campsites well shaded by pine trees and a couple of places to eat.

There's a more established resort at **Monte Hermoso**, 106 km east, with good hotels and better organized campsites, but still retaining a quiet, family feel, and with wonderful beaches for bathing. Its claim to fame is that it's one of the few places where the sun rises and sets over the sea (here too, don't swim when the wind is in the south because of jellyfish – ask a local if in doubt). **Tourist office** ① *Faro Recalada y Pedro de Mendoza, T02921-481123, www.montehermoso.porinternet. com.ar.* To get there, **Combis Ariber** ① *T0291-452 2801,* run a door-to-door minibus service; they will collect you from anywhere in town.

Santa Rosa de la Pampa → *Colour map 4, C2. Phone code 02954. Population 102,000.*
Santa Rosa is the capital of La Pampa province. Founded in 1892, it's an important administrative centre 663 km from Buenos Aires, and though it's not a wildly exciting destination, it's a friendly place. There aren't really any tourist sights, though the **Teatro Español**, Lagos 44, dates from 1908, and 10 blocks west of the Plaza San Martín is **Laguna Don Tomás** and a park with sports facilities. There's a **tourist office** ① *Luro y Corrientes, T02954-436555, www.santarosa.gov.ar,* in the bus terminal, which is seven blocks east of Plaza San Martín.

The main reason to stop here is to visit the Parque Nacional Lihue Calel (see below). Closer however, is the **Parque Luro** ① *32 km south of Santa Rosa, T02954-15511894, www.parqueluro.gov.ar, reached by bus,* which covers over 6500 ha. This provincial park occupies the former estate of Pedro Luro, who created his own hunting grounds for aristocratic friends visiting from Europe, introducing red deer and wild boar to run wild in the park, with many species of bird. Luro's mansion, a French-style chateau, has been turned into a museum, and opposite is a **Centro de Interpretación Ecológico**, with displays on the flora and fauna of the Pampas.

Parque Nacional Lihue Calel
① *T02952-436595, www.lihuecalel.com.ar and www.parquesnacionales.gov.ar. There's a camping area and toilets at the administration centre.*
The Lihue Calel National Park is situated 240 km southwest of Santa Rosa and 120 km from General Acha, and is reached by paved Route 152. The name derives from the Mapuche for 'place of life', and you can understand why when you see its low vegetated hills rising out of rather arid desert. Its microclimate allows it to support a wide variety of plant species, including a number of unique species of cactus in its rocky terrain. Wildlife includes pumas, but you're more likely to spot *maras* (Patagonian hare), vizcachas, guanacos and rheas as well as a wide variety of birds. The area was home to various groups of indigenous people 2000 years ago; there are geometric cave paintings in the **Valle de las Pinturas** and the **Valle de Namuncurá**, seen on one of two self-guided trails through the park. The other trail, **El Huitru**, climbs the highest hill in the park and explores some of its amazing flora. The park is best visited in spring.

For hotel and restaurant price codes and other relevant information, see pages 20-26.

⊖ Where to stay

Since accommodation is plentiful all along the coast, only a small selection is listed here. All the resorts also have a wide selection of campsites; most are well-equipped and many have *cabañas* as well as tent sites. Most resorts have *balnearios*, private beaches, where you pay US$25-50 per day for family/group use of a sunshade or beach hut, showers, toilets and restaurants. Avoid Jan when the whole coast is packed out.

San Clemente del Tuyú *p109*
See www.portaldesanclemente.com for a complete list.
$$$-$$ Altair Hotel, Calle 3, 2283, T02252-421429, www.altairhotel.com.ar. A 3-star hotel with decent, simple rooms, some with balconies with sea views, in a modern block.
$$$-$$ Fontainebleau, Calle 3, 2294, T02252-421187, www.fontainebleau.com. ar. Dated but comfortable 4-star hotel on the coast, good value, with an elegant entrance and light airy rooms. There is a pool and a restaurant.
$$ Morales, Calle 1, 1856, T02252-430357, www.hotelmorales.com.ar. A welcoming option that also has a large pool and a restaurant. Rooms are plain but comfortable.
$$ Sun Shine, Av Talas del Tuyú 3025, T02252-430316, www.sunshinehotel. com.ar. The most recommendable of the cheaper places to stay.
$$ Sur, Calle 3, 2194, T02252-521137, hotelsur.wix.com/hotelsur. A central location with simple accommodation.

Campsites
Los Tres Pinos, T02252-430151, www.los3pinos.com.ar. Nice, well-organized campsite (US$10 per person) as well as basic wooden cabins (US$24 for up to 4 people). Good option for budget travellers.

Santa Teresita *p109*
See www.santateresita.com.ar for a complete list.
$$$-$$ Sorrento, Calle 37, 235, between Calles 2 and 3, T02246-420 0298, www.santateresita.com.ar/sorrento. Dated 3-star hotel with pleasant rooms, though somewhat on the kitsch side.
$$ Hostería Santa Teresita, Av Costanera 747, between Calles 34 and 35, T02246-420202, www.hosteriast.com.ar. A nicely maintained, simple, family chalet-type hotel by the sea.
$ Turista, Av 32, 464, T02246-526093, www.santateresita.com.ar/turista/. Rather basic, with simple rooms around a central courtyard, but clean and friendly.

Campsites
Estancia El Carmen, Calle 23 and Playa, T02246-420220, www.estanciaelcarmen. com.ar. A really excellent site on the beach, with grassy shaded areas and all facilities. Camping US$22.50 per tent for 2; *cabañas* for rent. Recommended.

Mar del Tuyú *p110*
There's little on offer in Mar del Tuyú itself, but Costa del Este next door has a couple of places, both comfortable; see www.mardeltuyu.com for a complete list.

Campsites
El Refugio, Calle 94 between 2 and 3, T02246-435195.

Mar de Ajó and around *p110*

This town has a couple of good places to stay, but there is better accommodation offered at San Bernardo, the next resort along; see www.sanbernardo.com.ar for a complete list.

$$$ Gran Playa Hotel, Costanera Sur 195, Mar de Ajó, T02257-420001, www.hotelgranplaya.com.ar. The best choice in town and also the oldest, still in the family of the original owners. A comfortable beach-front place. All rooms have bathrooms and sea views, some have jacuzzis too. Good buffet breakfast.

$$$-$$ Neptuno Plaza, Hernández 313, San Bernardo, T02257-461789, www.neptunoplaza.com.ar. A well-equipped 4-star place with good service.

$$ Hostería Mar de Ajó, Av Costanera Norte 205, Mar de Ajó, T02257-421030, www.hosteriamardeajo.com.ar. A modest but comfortable beachfront *hostería*.

Estancias

$$$$ Estancia Palantelén, 15 km south of Mar de Ajó, T011-15-5342 4120 or T02257-420 983, www.palantelen.com. ar/index.htm. The best place to stay for miles around. A delightful house close to the beach, where you can go horse riding and even learn tango. Highly recommended. See also page 110.

Camping

ACA, Avellaneda 147, www.aca.org.ar, T02257-420230.

Pinamar *p110*

There are plenty of hotels of a high standard in Pinamar; all 4-stars have a pool but some hotels are a long way from the beach. Book ahead in Jan and Feb. All those listed are recommended.

$$$$-$$$ Del Bosque, Av Bunge 1550 y Júpiter, T011-4394 9605,

www.hotel-delbosque.com. Very attractive, in woods, not on the beach, a smart 4-star with a wide range of rooms and seasonal prices, pool, tennis courts, nice restaurant, good service.

$$$ La Posada, Del Tuyú y Del Odiseo, T02254-482267, www.laposadapinamar. com.ar. Very comfortable, small, quiet, with spacious rooms, next to sea and town centre, pretty gardens where breakfast is served. An excellent choice.

$$$ Viejo Hotel Ostende, Biarritz y El Cairo, T02254-486081, www.hotel ostende.com.ar. Attractive, smallish hotel, open since 1913. Although it has been renovated, it retains some historic flavour in the old wing, comfortable in a simple way, excellent service. There's a pool and private *balneario*. Breakfast, dinner and a beach hut are all included. Open summer only.

Estancias

$$$ Estancia La Unión, Ruta 56, 45 km from Pinamar, outside Gral Madariaga, T02267-15-637983, estancialaunion@ telpin.com.ar. An early 19th-century *estancia* offering fine hospitality and excellent riding, including polo ponies; good birdwatching too. Swimming pool and other activities, good food, children welcome.

$$$ Rincón de Cobo, access on R91, 30 km north of Pinamar, T02257-15-638903, www.rincondecobo.com.ar. 3 secluded houses by the sea offering rustic comfort and the kind of service you'd expect in a hotel, with all the usual calm of the Pampas. It has its own airstrip in case you're tempted to fly here yourself.

Cariló *p111*

Most of the accommodation is in apart hotels and timeshares, see www.carilo.com for more options.

$$$$ Cariló Village, Carpintero and Divisadero, T02254-470244, www. carilovillage.com.ar. Well-designed, cottage-style, attractive but not luxurious rooms and apartments; there is a very good restaurant and a spa with 2 pools.
$$$$ Marcin, Laurel (on the oceanfront), T02254-570888, www.hotelmarcin. com.ar. Modern and large, very swish complex, right on the beach, with a spa and a restaurant.

Around Pinamar and Cariló *p111*
There are several well-equipped campsites (US$26 per day for 4 people in 2 tents) near the beach at Ostende, between Pinamar and Cariló; try www.campingostende.com.ar.

Villa Gesell *p112*
$$$ De la Plaza, Av 2 entre 103 y 104, T02255-468793, www.delaplazahotel. com. Small, spotless, with excellent service, open all year round. Rooms are plain but very comfortable, good value.
$$ Hostería Gran Chalet, Paseo 105 No 447 entre Av 4-5, T02255-462913, www.gesell.com.ar/granchalet. Warm welcome, comfortable large rooms, good breakfast. Recommended. Closed off season.
$ pp Hostel El Galeón, Av 5 No 834 (entre Paseos 108 y 109), T02255-453785, www.galeongesell.com.ar. Popular hostel, can accommodate from singles to groups of 8 but no dorms; some rooms have kitchen. DVDs, laundry service, cooking facilities, good communal areas, convenient.

Mar de las Pampas and Mar Azul *p112*
See www.mardelaspampas.com.ar for a complete list of accommodation.

$$$$ La Mansión del Bosque, Juez Repetto y R Peñaloza, T02255-479555, www.lamansiondelbosque.com.ar. Open all year round. Just 150 m away from the sea, this attractive large house is beautifully decorated in minimalist style and has extremely comfortable rooms. It's one of the area's more pricey options, but there's a great spa that attracts affluent, stressed young *Porteños* from Buenos Aires.
$$$$-$$$ Posada Piñen, Juan de Garay y R Payró, T02255-479974, www. posadapinen.com. A very comfortable *hostería*, with a wonderfully rustic atmosphere. Breakfasts are gorgeous and include delicious home-made pies.
$$$ Posada La Casona, Hudson entre Mercedes Sosa y JV González, T02255-479693, www.posadalacasona.com.ar. A really stylish, comfortable place with a great restaurant. Excellent value.

Apart hotels
There are many apart hotels in the woods; the following is recommended:
Village de las Pampas, Corvina y Mercedes Sosa, T02255-454244, www.villagedelaspampas.com.ar. Several apartments of different sizes, all very comfortable and attractively designed, and only a few metres from the sea.

Cabañas
There are many attractive, well-equipped *cabañas*, including **Arco Iris**, Victoria Ocampo between Los Alamos and Ombú, T02255-15-471 1197, www.arcoiris.rtu.com.ar.

Mar del Plata *p113, map p113*
Busy traffic makes it impossible to move along the coast in summer, so choose a hotel near your preferred beach.

$$$$ Costa Galana, Blvd Marítimo 5725, T0223-410 5000, www.hotelcostagalana. com. The best by far, a 5-star modern tower, all luxury facilities, at Playa Grande.
$$$ Dos Reyes, Av Colón 2129, T0223-491 0383, www.dosreyes.com.ar. Long-established but modernized town centre hotel with smart, well-equipped rooms. Guests have access to a *balneario*. Good value off season, big breakfast.
$$$-$$ Selent, Arenales 2347, T0223-494 0878, www.hotelselent.com.ar. Quiet with neat rooms, warm welcome, great value. Open all year. Recommended.
$$ Abra Marina, Alsina 2444, T0223-486 4646, http://users.copetel.com.ar/ abramarinacafehotel. A good budget choice open all year round, simple rooms, all services, café/bar, central.
$$ Los Troncos, Rodríguez Peña 1561, T0223-451 8882, www.hotellostroncos. com.ar. Small, chalet-style hotel in quiet residential area, handy for Güemes bars and restaurants, garden.

Apartment rental
Prices vary a lot, with higher rates in Jan, slightly lower in Feb and even lower in Dec and Mar. Prices rise again at Easter and over long weekends; cheap deals off season. The tourist office has a list of agents and a helpful section in English on their website, www.mardelplata.gov.ar. Try **Gonnet**, Corrientes 1987 (y Moreno), T0223-495 2171, www.gonnet.com.ar.

Camping
Many on the road south of the city, but far better sites at Villa Gesell.

Around Mar del Plata *p115*
$$$ Balcarce, Calle 16 646, Balcarce, T02266-422055, www.hotel-balcarce. com.ar. Next to the museum, on the main

plaza, the most comfortable option, with breakfast, spa.

Camping
Campsites are plentiful, and include:
Club de Pesca Balcarce, at Laguna La Brava, R226, Km 39.4, T0223-460 8029, www.clubdepescabalcarce.com. Well-organized site, with all facilities and good fishing.
Municipal, R55, Km 63.5, south of centre in Parque Cerro El Triunfo. Pools and good facilities, all kinds of sports too.

Miramar *p116*
Dozens of hotels and apartments between Av 26 and the sea. For a full list see http://turismodemiramar.com.
$$ Brisas del Mar, Calle 29, 557, T02291-420334, www.brisasdelmarhotel.com.ar. Family-run seafront hotel with neat rooms, cheery restaurant and attentive service; good value. Open in summer only.

Camping
There are lots of campsites, including:
$ pp El Durazno, R91, T02291-431984, 2 km from town. Good facilities, shops, restaurant and *cabañas*. Take bus 501 marked 'Playas'.

Necochea *p116*
Most hotels are in the seafront area just north of Av 2. There are at least 100 within 700 m of the beach. Many close off season, when you can bargain with those still open.
$$$ Hostería del Bosque, Calle 89, 350, T02262-420002, www.hosteria-delbosque.com.ar. 5 blocks from beach, quiet, comfortable, lovely atmosphere in this renovated former residence of an exiled Russian princess, great restaurant. Recommended.

$$$ Presidente, Calle 4, 4040, T02262-423800, www.presinec.com.ar. A large 4-star hotel recommended for excellent service, comfortable rooms and pool, price depends on room category and season, closed in winter.
$$ Bahía, Diagonal San Martín 731, T02262-423353, hotelbahia@ necocheanet.com.ar. Really kind owners, comfortable rooms, pool in neat gardens. Recommended.
$$ San Miguel, C 85 No 301, T02262-521433, www.hotel-sanmiguel.com.ar. Good service and value, comfortable, open all year.

Camping
The following are recommended:
Camping UATRE, Av 10 y 187, T02262-438278. The best site, a few kilometres west of town towards Médano Blanco, with great facilities, and beautifully situated *cabañas* too.
Río Quequén, Calle 22 y Ribera Río Quequén, T02262-428068, www.cabanias rioquequen.com.ar. Lovely area, cabins available. Sports facilities, pool, bar and cycle hire. Well-maintained in attractive setting on the river.

Bahía Blanca *p117*
$$$ Argos, España 149, T0291-455 0404, www.hotelargos.com. 3 blocks from plaza, 4-star business hotel, smart, Wi-Fi, good breakfast, restaurant.
$$ Bahía Blanca, Chiclana 251, T0291-455 3050, www.bahia-hotel.com.ar. Business hotel, good value, well-equipped comfortable rooms, bright bar and *confitería*. Recommended.
$$ Barne, H Yrigoyen 270, T0291-453 0294, www.hotelbarne.bvconline.com.ar. Family-run, low-key, good value, welcoming.
$ Hostel Bahía Blanca, Soler 701, T0291-452 6802, www. hostelbahiablanca.com.

Light, spacious dorms from US$12 and doubles with and without bath in this old building. Close to town, offers lots of travel advice.

Camping
Best to head for Pehuen Có or Monte Hermoso – both lovely beach places with plentiful campsites 1 hr away by bus; see below.

Around Bahía Blanca *p118*
$$ Petit Hotel, Av Argentina 244, Monte Hermoso, T0291-481818, www.petitfrentealmar.com.ar. Simple, modernized 1950s style, family-run, on the beach, restaurant, breakfast extra, cooking facilities. Recommended.

Camping
See http://campingpehuen-co.com.ar/. There are many sites around Monte Hermoso with good facilities.
Camping Americano, T0291-481149, www.campingamericano.com.ar, signposted from main road 5 km before town (bus or taxi from town). A lovely, sprawling, shady site by a quiet stretch of beach, with excellent facilities, hot showers, pool, electricity, restaurant, fireplaces, food shop and *locutorio*. US$10-$15 (depending on season) for 2 per day. Recommended.

Santa Rosa de la Pampa *p119*
See www.santarosa.gov.ar for a complete list.
$$$ Club de Campiña, R5, Km 604, T02954-456800, www.lacampina.com. A rather more appealing option than below if you have transport. Wonderful old building, cosy rooms with high ceilings, attractive gardens, pool, gym and spa.
$$$-$$ Calfucura, San Martín 695, T02954-433 303, www.hotelcalfucura.com.

A 4-star, business-oriented place with comfortable rooms. Pool, restaurants and a few apartments to rent.

Camping
There is a municipal site near the Laguna Don Tomás.

🍴 Restaurants

Mar de Ajó *p110*
If you're self-catering, buy fresh fish on the beach from the fishermen.
El Quincho ($), Francisco de las Carreras 800, and **Parrilla San Rafael ($)**, Av Libertador 817, are both recommended.

Pinamar *p110*
The restaurants listed here are the best options in town.
$$ Tante, De las Artes 35, T02254-482735, www.tante.com.ar. A small, elegant place – and one of the most expensive – serving a good variety of dishes. Often recommended. Fantastic hot chocolate.
$ Tulumei, Av Bunge 64. A nautical theme in the decor goes with the excellent fish served in this small and popular place.
$ Viejo Lobo, Av del Mar and Av Bunge, T02254-483218. On the beach. Good seafood and international menu.

Cariló *p111*
$$ Divisadero del Mar, Benteveo and the beach, T02254-572010. Wonderful location overlooking the beach. Try the Caribbean salad and the grilled salmon.
$$ El Totem, Av Divisadero and Cerezo, T02254-571936. Local favourite for pizzas and quick meals.

Mar de las Pampas and Mar Azul *p112*
$$ Marechiare, Julio Roca and Corvina, T02255-453061. Next to the sea, with an excellent range of fish and seafood dishes.
$$ Viejos Tiempos, Leoncio Paiva between Cruz del Sur y Peñaloza, T02255-479524. This is owned by local pioneers, who also serve some Mexican and German specialities together with more refined meals. Homely surroundings. This is *the* place to come for tea – worth a detour for the gorgeous cakes.

Mar del Plata *p113, map p113*
Two areas have become popular thanks to their smaller shops, bars and restaurants.

Around C Güemes
$$ Almacén El Condal, Alsina y Garay. Charming old street-corner bar, serving *picadas* and drinks, popular with young crowd.
$$ Tisiano, San Lorenzo 1332. Good pasta restaurant in leafy patio.

Around Alem
There are lots of pubs and bars next to the cemetery, including traditional favourites.
$$ Manolo, Rivadavia 2371 and on the coast at Blvd Marítimo 4961. Famous for *churros* and hot chocolate in the early hours, popular with post-party people.
$$ Pehuén, Bernardo de Irigoyen 3666. Very good and popular *parrilla*.

Centro Comercial Puerto
Many of the seafood restaurants at the port are brightly lit and not atmospheric.
$$ El Viejo Pop. The best place, ship design, candlelit, superb paella.
$$ Taberna Baska, 12 de Octubre 3301. Seafood and Basque country dishes, next to the port.

Miramar p116

Lots of restaurants along Calle 21 and at the *balnearios* on the seafront.

$ Cantina Italiana, Calle 19, 1460. As its name suggests, this is recommended for good pasta and seafood; also offers a delivery service.

$ El Pescador Romano, Calle 19, 1058. Excellent fish in a popular family restaurant.

$ Mickey, Calle 21 No 686. A lively long-established *confitería* serving cheap meals.

Necochea p116

There are some excellent seafood restaurants.

$$ Chimichurri, C 83 No 345, T02262-420642. Recommended for *parrilla*.

$$ Parrilla El Loco, Av 10 y 65, T02262-437094. A classic *parrilla*, deservedly popular for superb steaks.

$$ Sotavento, Av Costanera y Pinolandia. On the beach, varied menu, can get very busy but good value.

$ Pizzería Tempo, Calle 83 No 310, T02262-425100. A lively traditional place serving good pizzas.

Bahía Blanca p117

$$ Micho, Guillermo Torres 3875, T0291-457 0346. A superb chic fish restaurant at the port (take bus 500 or 501, but go there by taxi at night, as it's in an insalubrious area).

$$ Santino, Dorrego 38. Italian-influenced, quiet, sophisticated atmosphere, good value. Recommended.

$ El Mundo de la Pizza, Dorrego 55. Fabulous pizzas, lots of choice, the city's favourite.

$ For You, Belgrano 69. Good *tenedor libre*.

Cafés

Café del Angel, Paseo del Angel, entrances at O'Higgins 71 and Drago 63. Good-value lunches, friendly place.

Muñoz, O'Higgins y Drago. Sophisticated café, good for reading the papers.

Piazza, on the corner of the plaza at O'Higgins y Chiclana. Great coffee, buzzing atmosphere, good salads, and cakes too.

Around Bahía Blanca p118

$$ Marfil, Valle Encantado 91, Monte Hermoso. The smartest, delicious fish and pastas.

$ Pizza Jet, Valle Encantado e Int Majluf, Monte Hermoso. Hugely popular for all kinds of food, arrive before 2130 to get a table.

⊙ Bars and clubs

Mar del Plata p113, map p113

Many bars and nightclubs are on Alem or its surroundings and start at around 0200:

Bykein, Formosa 254; and **Mr Jones**, Alem 3738, www.mrjonesbar.com, are both for the trendy under-25 crowd, while **La Llorona**, on Olavarría, near Blvd Marítimo and the Torreón del Monje, is the place if you're not 25 anymore.

Bahía Blanca p117

Lots of discos on Fuerte Argentino (along the stream leading to the park) mainly catering for under 25s, including **Chocolate**, www.chocolatedisco.com.ar, and **Toovaks**. The best place for the over 25s is **La Barraca**.

⊙ Entertainment

Mar del Plata p113, map p113

On Wed there is a discount at all cinemas. Cinemas and shows are listed in the free leaflet *Guía de Actividades* from the city tourist office, www.turismomardelplata.gov.ar.

Casino Central, Blvd Marítimo Patricio Peralta Ramos 2100, Sun-Thu 1100-0230, Fri-Sat 1100-0330 (May-Nov) or 1600-0500 (Dec-Apr), free. There are others that operate nearby in summer.
Centro Cultural Osvaldo Soriano, 25 de Mayo 3102, T0223-499 7883. Daily screenings, music shows, plays or conferences, mostly free or for a small fee.

⊛ Festivals

Mar del Plata *p113, map p113*
Jan National Fishing Festival.
Nov International Film Festival, www.mardelplatafilmfest.com. This famous festival showcases new Argentine films and attracts some good premières from all over the world.
Dec Fiesta del Mar. One of the biggest festivals, it takes place mid-month.

⦿ Shopping

Bahía Blanca *p117*
There's a smart, modern shopping mall, **Bahía Blanca Plaza Shopping**, 2 km north of town on Sarmiento, with a cheap food hall, cinema (T0291-453 5844) and supermarket. There's also the supermarket, **Cooperativa**, on Donado and plenty of clothes and shoe shops on Alsina and San Martín within a couple of blocks of the plaza.

⦿ What to do

Mar del Tuyú *p110*
Fishing
Excellent fishing either from the pier or on a boat trip.
El Pescador II, Calle 2, between 67 and 68, T02246-430733. Organizes day trips to Laguna La Salada, as well as the usual sea excursions.

Tiburon II, Av 1 BIS No 7503 and Calle 75, T02246-434698, www.tiburon2.com.ar. 3-hr boat trips, leaving daily at 0700.

Villa Gesell *p112*
Horse riding
Tante Puppi, Alameda 205 E/calle 307 y 308, T02255-455533. Offers horse rides in the dunes daily on summer afternoons and also moonlit rides on the beach.

Mar del Plata *p113, map p113*
There are lots of tour operators at the port and in the town centre along the promenade where you can find information about city tours or tours to the surrounding areas.

Boat trips
Anamora, T0223-489 0310, www.cruceroanamora.com.ar. 1-hr boat trips along the city coast, several times daily in summer, Sat-Sun only in winter. Departs from from Dársena B, Muelle de Guardacostas in the port, US$19.

Cycling
Bicicletería Madrid, Hipólito Yrigoyen 2249, on Plaza Mitre, T0223-494 1932, hires bikes for 1 and 2 people.

Fishing
There is good fishing all year along the coast from the shore and off shore in hired boats. *Pejerrey* and *corvina* abound or you can charter a private launch for shark fishing. Offshore fishing is best in Nov and Dec, when *pescadilla* are plentiful; winter is ideal for *pejerrey*. Deep-sea fishing yields salmon and sea bass. Contact the tourist office for advice, T0223-495 1777, www.mardelplata.gov.ar.
Fishing licences are available from **Dirección de Fiscalización Pesquera,**

Mitre 2853, T0223-493 2528, and fishing gear shops.

Golf
Mar del Plata Golf Club, Aristóbulo del Valle 3940 (near Playa Grande), T0223-486 2221, www.mardelplatagolfclub.com.ar. This is a great course and deservedly famous, in a wonderful elevated position by the beach.

Tour operators
City tours leave from Plaza España and Plaza Colón. Tours also to Miramar and the sierras.

Around Mar del Plata *p115*
Fishing
Club de Pesca Balcarce, Villa Laguna Brava, T0223-460 8029, www.irapescar.com (in Spanish).

Necochea *p116*
Cycling
There are several options for bike hire in the park, Av Pinolandia between 2 and 10.

Fishing
There's splendid *pejerrey* fishing at Laguna Loma Danesa, near La Dulce (60 km northwest of Necochea), T02262-1550 6504. Tackle can be bought from **Gómez Pesca**, Av 59, 1168, T02262-427494.

Golf
Golf club, Armada Argentina and 575, Quequén, T02262-450684, www.necocheagolfclub.com.ar.

Bahía Blanca *p117*
Tour operators
ASATEJ, Zelarrayán 267, T0291-456 0666, www.asatej.com.ar.

✈ Transport

San Clemente del Tuyú *p109*
Bus
To **Mar del Plata** (and to resorts in between) services are frequent with **El Rápido** and **El Rápido Argentino**. To **Buenos Aires**, US$26-30, several companies.

Pinamar *p110*
Bus
For bus terminal information, see page 111. To **Buenos Aires**, US$39-43, 4-5 hrs, several companies.

Train
For information about the railway station, see page 111. To **Buenos Aires** (Constitución), check with **Ferrobaires** (www.ferrobaires.gba.gov.ar) to see if the Fri train to Pinamar (return Sun) is running.

Villa Gesell *p112*
Bus
For bus terminal information, see page 112. Direct to **Buenos Aires**, many companies, 5 hrs, US$41-46. To **Mar del Plata** see below.

Mar del Plata *p113, map p113*
Air
For airport information, see page 114. Several flights daily to **Buenos Aires**, and **LADE** to many Patagonian towns once or twice a week.

Airline offices Aerolíneas **Argentinas**, **Austral**, Moreno 2442, T0223-496 0101; **LADE**, Corrientes 1537, T0223 491 1484.

Bus
For bus terminal and local bus services information, see page 114.

Local El Rápido del Sud line 212 from Terminal goes south along the coast via **Miramar** up to **Mar del Sud**.

Long distance El Rápido (T0223-494 2507, www.el-rapido.com.ar) runs several services a day to most coastal towns: to **Villa Gesell**, 1½ hrs, US$10; to **Pinamar**, 2 hrs, US$12.50; to **Miramar**, 40 mins, US$2.50; to **Necochea**, US$11 (also **Río Paraná**, T0223-561 1907, and **Cóndor Estrella**, T0223-561 3999); to **Bahía Blanca**, 7 hrs, US$42. The same company also goes to **Balcarce**, 1½ hrs, US$5.75. To **Buenos Aires**, 5-6 hrs, US$41-54, many companies. To **Bariloche**, **Vía Bariloche** and **El Rápido Argentino**, 18-20 hrs, US$176. To all Patagonian towns along RN 3, ending at **Comodoro Rivadavia**, 23 hrs, US$130-170, with **Transportadora Patagónica**. To **Mendoza**, **Andesmar**, daily, 19-22 hrs, US$120-153.

Train
For information on the railway station, see page 114. Enquire beforehand if any trains are running to/from **Buenos Aires** (Constitución).

Around Mar del Plata *p115*
Bus
Frequent services to Balcarce from **Mar del Plata**, with **El Rápido**, address above.

Miramar *p116*
Bus
To **Buenos Aires**, 6½-7 hrs, US$49-60. To **Necochea**, **Cóndor Estrella**, 1½ hrs, US$3.50.

Train
To **Buenos Aires** (Constitución), via **Mar del Plata**, daily in summer, once a week off season, US$40.

Necochea *p116*
Bus
For bus terminal information, see page 116. To **Buenos Aires**, 6½-8½ hrs, US$54-60. To **Bahía Blanca**, US$20.

Bahía Blanca and around *p117*
Air
For airport information, see page 117. Daily flights to **Buenos Aires**. LADE (T0291-452 1063) has weekly flights to **Buenos Aires**, **Necochea**, **Mar del Plata** and Patagonian coastal towns. **Airline offices** Aerolíneas Argentinas, San Martín 298, T0291-4560561. **LADE**, Darregueira 21, T0291-4521063.

Bus
For local services and bus terminal information, see page 117.

Long distance
To **Buenos Aires** frequent, several companies, 8-10 hrs, US$74-80, shop around. Most comfortable by far is **Plusmar** suite bus (T0291-456 0616), with flat beds, US$91. To **Mar del Plata**, see above. To **Córdoba**, 13-15 hrs, US$89-105. To **Bariloche**, **El Valle**, **Vía Bariloche**, 11-13 hrs, US$110-125. To **Mendoza**, **Andesmar** (T0291-481 5462), 16 hrs, US$112-132. To **Puerto Madryn**, **Andesmar**, **Don Otto** (T0291-481 8585), **Cóndor Estrella** (T0291-481 4846, www.condorestrella.com.ar), 8½-10½ hrs, US$55-74. To **Tornquist**, US$6, **Cóndor Estrella**, 1 hr 20 mins; to **Sierra de la Ventana** (town) **Cóndor Estrella** and **Expreso Cabildo**, 2 hrs 20 mins, US$9. Also minibus to Tornquist with **Cerro**, T0291-494 1129. **Other bus companies**: Ceferino (T0291-481 9566), **Rápido del Sur** (T0291-481 3118).

Taxi
Taxi Universitario, T0291-452 0000, T0291-454 0000.

Train
For information on the railway station, see page 117.

To **Buenos Aires** 1 a day Mon-Fri at 1935 or 1945, 14 hrs, 3 classes, US$15-22.

Around Bahía Blanca p118
Bus From Monte Hermoso either to **Buenos Aires** or **Bahía Blanca** (US$7) with **Cóndor Estrella**. Several combis or minibuses also to **Bahía Blanca**. From Pehuén-Có to Bahía Blanca, with **La Patagonia** (T0291-4553215).

Santa Rosa de la Pampa p119
Bus
To **Buenos Aires**, 8 hrs, US$50-56; to **Neuquén**, 8 hrs, US$47-53, with **Andesmar** (T02954-432841), **El Valle** or **Vía Bariloche** (T02954-432694).

❶ Directory

Mar del Plata *p113, map p113*
Banks Many ATMs all around the central area, along Peatonal San Martín, at Santa Fe y Rivadavia and by the casino. **Immigration office** San Lorenzo 3449, T0223-475 5707, Mon-Fri 0800-1400. **Post office** Av Luro 2460, also international parcels office.

Bahía Blanca *p117*
Banks Many ATMs on plaza for all major cards. **Embassies and consulates** Chile, Belgrano 503, T0291-453 1516; Italy, Colón 446, T0291-454 5140; Spain, Drago 64, T0291-4522549. **Immigration office** Brown 963, T0291-456 1529, Mon-Fri 0900-1300. **Internet** Try places along Estomba and Zelarray and near plaza. **Laundry** Laverap, Av Colón 197; Las Heras, Las Heras 86. **Post office** Moreno 34.

Southern Sierras

The south of Buenos Aires province has two ranges of ancient mountains rising suddenly from the flat Pampas; both are easily accessible and offer great opportunities for a weekend escape. The Sierra de Tandil range, due south from Buenos Aires, is 340 km long and 2000 million years old – among the oldest in the world. The beautiful, curved hills of granite and basalt offer wonderful walking and riding, with the pleasant airy town of Tandil as a base. There are plenty of small hotels, though nearby *estancias* offer the best way to explore the hills.

Further west, the magnificent Sierra de la Ventana is the highest range of hills in the Pampas and so called because craggy Cerro de la Ventana has a natural hole near its summit. Located next to the Parque Provincial Ernesto Tornquist, it is within easy reach of Bahía Blanca for a day or weekend visit, and the attractive villages of Villa Ventana and Sierra de la Ventana nearby are appealing places to stay, with plenty of accommodation options. These mountains are not quite as old as those in Tandil but offer more demanding hikes in wilder terrain, with stunning views from their summits. There are daily buses and combis from Bahía Blanca, but you could break the journey at the quaint sleepy town of Tornquist.

Tornquist → *For listings, see pages 135-138. Colour map 4, C4. Phone code 0291. Population 6066.*

Tornquist, 70 km north of Bahía Blanca, is a pretty, sleepy, rural town that you will pass through if travelling to Sierra de la Ventana via Route 33. It has an attractive church on the large central plaza (which is more like a tidy park), a strangely green artificial lake, and a big children's play area. It's not a touristy place, but that's precisely its appeal, and it's a good starting point for excursions into the sierras. About 11 km east of town is the Tornquist family mansion (not open to tourism), built in a mixture of French styles. The town is named after Ernesto Tornquist (1842-1908), the son of a Buenos Aires merchant of Swedish origin. Under his leadership the family established an important industrial investment bank and Tornquist helped to establish the country's first sugar refinery, meat-packing plant and several chemical plants. There's a **tourist office** ⓘ *Plaza Ernesto Tornquist, 9 de Julio and Alem, T0291-494 0081, www.tornquist.gov.ar,* for information.

Parque Provincial Ernesto Tornquist → *For listings, see pages 135-138.*
Phone code 0291.

The sierras are accessed from the Parque Provincial Ernesto Tornquist which is 25 km east of Tornquist on Route 76. There are two main access points, one at the foot of Cerro Ventana and the other one, further east, at the foot of Cerro Bahía Blanca. It's US$1.25, $0.50 for children to enter the park. Other than the Campamento Base (see below), the nearest places for accommodation are the two towns of Sierra de la Ventana and Villa Ventana. ▸ *For transport to the park, see page 137.*

Cerro Ventana
To enter this section of the park, turn left after the massive ornate gates at the entrance to the Tornquist family home. There are showers, a food kiosk and an **information point** ① *Dec-Easter daily 0800-1700*, and *guardaparques* who you can ask for advice and register with for the longer walks. Nearby is the hospitable **Campamento Base** ① *T0291-156 495304, www.haciafuera.com.ar/campamentobase.htm*, with hot showers, dormitory accommodation and an attractive campsite. From this entrance, it's a three-hour walk, clearly marked, but with no shade, up **Cerro de la Ventana** (1136 m), which has fantastic views from the 'window' in the summit ridge. Register with *guardaparques* and set off no later than midday. Alternative hikes are a gentle stroll to **Garganta Olvidada** (one hour each way), where you can set off up to the **Piletones**, small pools (two hours each way), and **Garganta del Diablo** (six hours return), a wonderful narrow gorge with waterfalls. Guides are available for the walk to Garganta Olvidada, for a minimum of 10 people.

Cerro Bahía Blanca
The entrance to this section of the park is 4 km further east along Route 76. There's a car park and **interpretation centre** ① *T0291-491 0039, Dec-Easter 0800-1800*, with *guardaparques* who can advise on walks. From here you can go on a guided visit to **Cueva del Toro** (only with your own vehicle, four to five hours), natural caves and the **Cueva de las Pinturas Rupestres** which contains petroglyphs. There are also good walks, including up **Cerro Bahía Blanca** (two hours return), a gentle climb rewarded with panoramic views, highly recommended. There's lots of wildlife to spot, but you're most likely to see grey foxes, guanacos, wild horses and red deer.

Villa Ventana
Some 10 km beyond from the park's second entrance at Cerro Bahía Blanca is an attractive laid-back wooded settlement with weekend homes, *cabañas* for rent and a municipal campsite by the river with all facilities. There's an excellent tea shop, **Casa de Heidi**, and good food served in rustic surroundings at **Las Golondrinas**. The pretty village is the base for climbing **Cerro Tres Picos** (1239 m), to the south of the park, which is the highest peak in the province. The ruins of the **Hotel Club Casino** (1911) can still be seen; once the most luxurious hotel in Argentina, it burned down in 1983. There's a helpful **tourist office** ① *T0291-491 0001, www.sierradelaventana.org.ar*, at the entrance to the village.

Sierra de la Ventana → *Colour map 4, C4. Phone code 0291. Population 1800.*
Continuing east, the town of Sierra de la Ventana is a good base for exploring the hills, with a greater choice of hotels than Villa Ventana and wonderful open landscapes all around. There is an 18-hole golf course and good trout fishing in the Río Sauce Grande. There's also a wonderful tea shop, **La Angelita**, in the leafy lanes of Villa Arcadia (across the river), and several places on the river to bathe. The helpful **tourist information** ① *Av Roca 19, just before railway track, T0291-491 5303, www.sierradelaventana.org.ar*, has a complete list of all hotels, *cabañas* and campsites with availability and prices.

Tandil → *For listings, see pages 135-138. Colour map 4, C5. Phone code 0249. Population 101,000.*

Tandil is an attractive town, with a light breezy feel, and is a centre for outdoor activities, making it a good base for exploring the nearby sierras. There are a couple

Tandil

Where to stay 🛏
Ave Maria 6
Cabañas Brisas Serranas 2
Casa Chango 10
Chacra Bliss 11
El Solar de las Magnolias 12
Hermitage 3
Hostal de la Sierra
  del Tandil 5

Jazmines en la Sierra 7
Las Acacias 9
Plaza de las Carretas 4
Tanta Pacha Hostel 13

Restaurants 🍴
1905 11
El Molino 2
El Viejo Sauce 9

Epoca de Quesos 3
Parador del Sol 7
Taberna Pizuela 10

Bars & clubs 🍸
Antares 12
Liverpool 6

of marvellous *estancias* in the area and a clutch of restaurants, cafés and bars within the town.

Arriving in Tandil

The main **tourist information office** ⓘ *at the access to town (next to R226), Av Cte Espora 1120, T0249-432225, Mon-Sat 0800-2000, Sun 0900-1300,* is very well organized and has good brochures and urban maps. There are other offices in the **main plaza** ⓘ *near the corner of General Rodríguez NS Pinto, www.tandil.gov.ar,* and at the **bus terminal** ⓘ *Av Buzón 650, T0249-432092,* 12 blocks northeast of the centre. The **railway station** ⓘ *Av Machado and Colón, T0249-423002,* is 15 blocks north of the plaza.

Places in Tandil

On the south side of the main Plaza Independencia are the neoclassical **Municipalidad** (1923), the former **Banco Hipotecario Nacional** (1924) and the **Iglesia del Santísimo Sacramento** (1878), inspired (apparently) by the Sacre Coeur in Paris. Six blocks south of the plaza, up on a hill, is the **Parque Independencia**, with a granite entrance in Italianate style, built by the local Italian community to celebrate the town's centenary. Inside the park, the road winds up to a vantage point, where there's a Moorish-style **castle**, built by the Spanish community to mark the same event, with marvellous views over the surrounding sierras. At the base of the hill is an amphitheatre, where a famous community theatre event takes place during Easter week (book accommodation ahead). South of the park is the **Lago del Fuerte**, a popular place for water sports; bathing is possible at the Balneario del Sol in a complex of several swimming pools. For more information on the city, see www.tandil.com (in Spanish).

West of the plaza on the outskirts of town is **Cerro Calvario**, an easy walk leading to the **Capilla Santa Gemma** at the top. Further away, 5 km from town, **Cerro El Centinela** has a large, attractive, family-oriented tourist complex that includes a 1200-m cable car ride, a good restaurant (book your table in advance) and swimming pools.

It's easy to get out of the city to explore the hilly countryside on foot or by bike. Heading south past the lake, follow Avenida Don Bosco or one of the nearby tree-lined roads into the beautiful surroundings. Note that you should not enter any private land without permission. Instead, contact local tour operators who have arranged exclusive access with the land owners.

Six kilometres south is the 140-ha **Reserva Natural Sierra del Tigre**, with good views over Tandil from **Cerro Venado**. Wild foxes and guanacos can be seen occasionally, as well as llamas.

For hotel and restaurant price codes and other relevant information, see pages 20-26.

◉ **Where to stay**

Tornquist *p132*
$ La Casona, Rawson 232, T0291-494 0693, http://com-tur.com.ar/lacasona/. A renovated house with plain rooms.
$ San José, Güemes 138, T0291-494 0152, www.sanjose-hotel.com.ar. Small, central, with plain, faded rooms.

Villa Ventana *p132*
Lots of accommodation in *cabañas*; municipal campsite by river with all facilities. See www.sierralaventana.org.ar.
$$$ El Mirador, on RP 76 Km 226, T0291-494 1338, www.complejoelmirador.com.ar. Great location right at the foot of Cerro de la Ventana, comfortable rooms, some with tremendous views, very peaceful, good restaurant.
$$ San Hipólito, on RP 76 Km 230, T0291-15-642 8281, campoequino@celt.com.ar. Fully furnished, comfortable, small cabins on a large ranch, welcoming owners, Polito and his wife. Ideal for families with kids. Enjoyable horse rides in the hills.

Sierra de la Ventana *p133*
$$$ Cabañas La Caledonia, Los Robles y Ombúes in **Villa Arcadia**, a couple of blocks over the railway track, T0291-491 5268, www.lacaledonia.com.ar. Well-equipped, comfortable small cabins in pretty gardens with a pool. Price is for a cabin for up to 4 people.
$$$ Las Vertientes, RP 76, Km 221, signposted just west of the turning to Villa Ventana, T011-4773 6647, http://com-tur.com.ar/lasvertientes/. Very welcoming ranch with a house for rent (price is for 6 people; breakfast extra) in lovely relaxing surroundings, with horse riding, mountain biking, trekking, day visits.
$$ Alihuen, Tornquist y Balneario, T0291-491 5074, http://com-tur.com.ar/alihuen. A delightful old place near the river, dining room, garden, pool, good value.
Camping Yamila, access on C Tornquist, T0291-15-418 9266, www.campingyamila.8m.com. Camping and small cabins with bunks (**$**). Lovely shady site by river, hot showers, food shop.

Tandil *p133, map p133*
The real joy of Tandil lies in the beauty of its surroundings, best explored by staying in an *estancia*. Ask at the tourist offices for suggestions. Otherwise, there are some good options around town; see www.tandil.com for a complete list.
$$$$ Ave María, Paraje la Portena, T0249-442 2843, www.avemariatandil.com.ar. One of the most exquisite small hotels in the whole province, this may call itself a *hostería*, but the splendid Norman-style building set in beautiful gardens overlooking the rocky summits of the sierras is much more like an *estancia*. Charming owner Asunti encourages you to feel completely at home and ramble around the place as you please. There are only 8 rooms, all impeccably designed with everything you could possibly need, some with doors opening directly onto the gardens. The discreet staff speak perfect English. A great place to relax and swim in the pool or walk in the grounds, hills and woodland. Prices are half-board and discounts apply Mon-Thu. Highly recommended, not to be missed.

$$$$-$$$ Chacra Bliss, Paraje La Porteña, T011-15-3179 8000, www.chacrabliss.com.ar. Charmingly decorated rooms with simple but comfortable furniture, a welcoming pool and a long veranda that catches the afternoon sun. Very relaxing.

$$$$-$$$ Las Acacias, Av Brasil 642, T0249-442 3373, www.posadalasacacias.com.ar. *Hostería* in a restored 1890s dairy farm in the Golf Club area, with very comfortable rooms looking out on to large gardens with a splendid pool. Friendly owners, who speak English and Italian, and excellent staff help to create a welcoming and homely atmosphere for a delightful stay. Recommended.

$$$$-$$ Cabañas Brisas Serranas, Scavini y Los Corales, T0249-440 6110, www.brisasserranas.com.ar. Very comfortable and well-furnished *cabañas*, pool, lovely views and welcoming owners.

$$$$-$$ El Solar de las Magnolias, Ituzaingo 941, T0249-442 8618, www.solarmagnolias.com.ar. Apartment complex of lovely, roomy traditional single-storey buildings, with a mix of antique and modern furniture. Parking and breakfast included.

$$$ Hostal de la Sierra del Tandil, Av Avellaneda 931/41, T0249-442 2330, www.hostaldeltandil.com.ar. Spanish-style building, with boldly designed rooms with bath, appealing areas to sit, a good restaurant for residents only and a pool.

$$$-$$ Jazmines en la Sierra, Libertad 316, T0249-442 2873, www.jazminesenlasierra.com.ar. 6 attractive rooms with a colour theme, a lovely cottage garden and slightly less appealing common areas with fireplace.

$$$-$$ Plaza de las Carretas, Av Santamarina 728, T0249-444 7850. An early 20th-century family house, now a homely and quiet place to stay, with

good rooms with eclectic decor and a nice garden at the back.

$$$-$$ Hermitage, Av Avellaneda and Rondeau, T0249-442 3987, www.hermitagetandil.com.ar. Good value in this quiet, old-fashioned hotel next to the park. There are some smart modernized rooms, though these aren't very different to the standard ones, all very simple, but the service is welcoming.

Hostels

$ pp Casa Chango, 25 de Mayo 451, T0249-442 2260, www.casa-chango.com.ar. Bright, colourful hostel set in an old house with lovely communal areas. Central and friendly. Also room for camping.

$ pp Tanta Pacha Hostel, Dabidos 1263, T0249-15-439 0142, www.tantapacha.com. Lovely, spacious hostel set in an old country house in attractive grounds. Rustic wooden furniture, dorms only.

🍴 Restaurants

Tandil *p133, map p133*
Local produce here traditionally includes cheese and sausages, both excellent and served as part of the *picadas* (nibbles with drinks) offered in local bars and restaurants, or available to take away in several good delis in town, such as **Syquet**, General Rodríguez and Mitre, or **Epoca de Quesos**.

$$ 1905, Av Santamarina and San Martín. A minimalist setting in a charming old house that serves excellent, finely elaborate meals.

$ El Molino, Curupaytí 95. A small, simple place with a little windmill. It specializes in different cuts of meat cooked traditionally *al disco* – in an open pan on the fire.

$ El Viejo Sauce, Av Don Bosco and Suiza. Next to the Reserva Sierra del

Tigre, in attractive natural surroundings, this is an ideal stopover at tea time for its cakes and home-made jams.

$ Epoca de Quesos, San Martín and 14 de Julio, T0249-448750. An atmospheric 1860s house serving delicious local produce, wines, home-brewed beers and memorable *picadas* to share, which include a great range of cheeses, salami, sausages and traditional Pampas bread. Recommended.

$ Parador del Sol, Zarini s/n, T0249-435697. Located in the attractive *balneario* by Lago del Fuerte, serving great pastas and salads in a smart beach-style trattoria.

$ Taberna Pizuela, Paz and Pinto. Attractive old place serving a broad range of very good simple dishes, including pizzas – the speciality.

🎵 Bars and clubs

Tandil *p133, map p133*

Antares, 9 de Julio 758. A popular brewpub, lively in the late evening with excellent beers, good meals and live music every Mon.

Liverpool, 9 de Julio and San Martín. Pictures of the Beatles in this relaxed and friendly bar.

⊙ What to do

Sierra de la Ventana *p133*

Geotur, San Martín 193, Sierra de la Ventana, T0291-491 5355, www.com-tur. com.ar/geotur. Trekking, mountain-biking and horse-riding excursions. Also operate a minibus which leaves a few times a day along R76 from Sierra de la Ventana to Tornquist, dropping you off at the entrance to the park.

Tandil *p133, map p133*
Golf
Tandil Golf Club, Av Fleming s/n, www.tandilgolfclub.com.

Horse riding
Gabriel Barletta, Avellaneda 673, T0249-15-450 9609, cabalgatasbarletta@ yahoo.com.ar. Recommended rides with Gabriel, expert on native flora, who might end your tour with an informal acoustic guitar session.

Trekking
To find an approved guide who will take you to otherwise inaccessible land for trekking, see www.guiasdetandil.com.ar.
Eco de las Sierras, Maipú 714, www. ecodelasierras.com. Run by Lucrecia Ballesteros, a highly recommended guide who is young, friendly and knowledgeable. Day trips from US$24
Kumbre, Av Alvear 124, T0249-443 4313, www.kumbre.com. Trekking, mountain biking and some climbing guided by experienced Carlos Centineo.

⊖ Transport

Parque Provincial Ernesto Tornquist *p132*
Bus
La Estrella/El Cóndor has daily services connecting Tornquist and Sierra de la Ventana with Buenos Aires and **Bahía Blanca**. To **Bahía Blanca** also **Expreso Cabildo** and a few minibus companies. **Geotur**, San Martín 193, T0291-491 5355, operates a minibus a few times a day along RP 76 from Sierra de la Ventana to Tornquist, dropping off hikers at the entrance to the park.

Tandil *p159, map p158*

Bus

To **Buenos Aires**, 5-6 hrs, US$30, with **La Estrella/El Cóndor, Parque** and **Río Paraná**. **Río Paraná** also goes daily to **Bahía Blanca**, 6 hrs, US$27.50, and to **Mar del Plata**, 4 hrs, US$12.75.

Train

To **Buenos Aires**, 2 services a week, Tue and Fri, return Wed and Sun, 7 hrs, US$12.25-15.

Contents

Córdoba & Central Sierras

At a glance

◉ **Getting around** Short-distance minibuses are frequent and comfortable. A hire car is helpful if you want to see more in less time.

⟳ **Time required** Between 3 and 5 days allows you to visit some small towns and see Córdoba city.

☁ **Weather** The mountain air stops the summers from being too humid and the winters from being too windy.

✖ **When not to go** Jan is busy with family holidays, as is Easter, and during Oktoberfest it can be hard to find accommodation.

★ Don't miss ...
1 Córdoba city's Jesuit heritage, page 144.
2 The Jesuit *estancia* trail, page 151.
3 Estancia Los Potreros, page 157.
4 Paragliding in La Cumbre, page 162.
5 Villa General Belgrano, page 167.
6 Climb Cerro Champaquí, page 168.

Córdoba, Argentina's second biggest city, has an entirely different character from Buenos Aires. The sparky Cordobeses are known for their quick wit and warm welcome, and are understandably proud of their city's history. The Jesuits established the country's oldest university here in the 17th century, funded by the foundation of *estancias* in the Sierras Chicas. These magnificent *estancias* are the province's main tourist attraction, and the surrounding mountains can be enjoyably explored on horseback. North of here are the remote reaches of Cerro Colorado, where there are amazing displays of art in a bizarre rocky landscape.

South of the city in Alta Gracia is Che Guevara's childhood home, but don't miss the best Jesuit museum inside the spectacular *estancia* in the centre of town. Nearby, Villa General Belgrano remains a German stronghold, with chalet-style architecture and endless microbreweries and *apfelstrudel*.

Escape from the crowds to Córdoba's most stunning scenery, high along the Camino de las Altas Cumbres into the Valle de Traslasierra. Hike into the mountains and gaze at condors in flight at the Parque Nacional Quebrada del Condorito, where these majestic birds wheel above the dramatic peaks, teaching their young to fly.

To the southwest, the sleepy provincial capital of San Luis lies at the foot of its own magnificent sierra, which intrepid travellers can explore in Parque Nacional Sierra de las Quijadas, with its dramatic red sandstone canyon. At sleepy villages El Trapiche and Carolina you can even mine for gold.

Córdoba city

At the centre of an area of great natural beauty lies a modern city with a fascinating past. Córdoba is the capital of one of the country's most densely populated and wealthy provinces, with a lively student population and buzzing atmosphere. It lies on the Río Suquía, extending over a wide valley, with the sierras visible in the west. The city has been an important trade centre since the area was colonized in the 16th century, and it retains an unusually fine set of colonial buildings at its heart, the astonishing Manzana de los Jesuitas, complete with its temple still intact. Cordobeses are renowned throughout the country for their sharp sense of humour, defiant attitude and a lilting accent that other regions delight in imitating. However, along with their strong sense of civic pride, the locals' warm welcome makes Córdoba one of the most hospitable areas in the country.

> **Arriving in Córdoba city** → *Colour map 4, A2. Phone code 0351.*
> *Population 1.5 million. Altitude: 484 m.*

Getting there

There are frequent flights from Buenos Aires (two hours), Santiago de Chile and major northern Argentine cities to Córdoba's airport, Aeropuerto Internacional Ingeneiro Ambrosio Taravella, more commonly known as **Pajas Blancas** ① *T0351-475 0877*, 12 km northwest of centre. It has shops, post office, a good restaurant and a *casa de cambio* (Monday-Friday 1000-1500). The **airport** is best reached by taxi (US$12.50), as the bus service is unreliable.

Long-distance buses connect the city with almost everywhere in the country and arrive at the central **bus terminal** ① *Blvd Perón, T0351-434 1692, www. terminalcordoba.com*, eight blocks east of the main plaza. The terminal has restaurants, internet facilities, a supermarket, left-luggage lockers, a *remise* taxi desk, an ATM and a tourist office on the lower level, where the ticket offices are. To leave the terminal, go upstairs and cross the bridges towards the city centre. A taxi to Plaza San Martín costs US$4. Minibuses that travel to nearby towns stop at the main terminal and then stop at the **minibus terminal** on Boulevard Illia.

▶ See Transport, page 149.

Getting around

Most of the city's sights can easily be visited on foot within a day or so. There's a leafy pedestrian shopping area to the north of the Plaza San Martín, and the historical Manzana de los Jesuitas is two blocks southwest of here. Buses share the main roads with trolleybuses. Neither accept cash; instead you have to buy tokens (*cospeles*) or cards from kiosks (normal fare US$0.65). Ordinary yellow taxis are usually more convenient for short distances than green *remise* taxis, which are better value for longer journeys.

Córdoba

Where to stay 🛏
1 Aldea *A1*
2 Alex *B3*
3 Amerian Córdoba Park *B1*
4 Baluch Backpackers Hostel *A2*
5 Córdoba B&B *A1*
6 Córdoba Hostel *C2*
9 Palenque Hostel *B2*
11 Sussex *A2*
12 Tango Hostel *C1*
13 Windsor *B2*

Restaurants 🍴
1 Alfonsina *B2*
2 El Arrabal *C1*
3 Farro de Garrido *A1*
5 Juan Griego *A2*
8 Mandarina *A2*
9 Sol y Luna *A2, B1*
10 Sorocabana *A2*
11 Sushi Man *C1*

Best time to visit

Avoid the hot and stormy summer months from December to February, when daytime temperatures are around 30°C. The dry season is April to September, with clear skies and cooler, but still pleasantly warm, temperatures.

Tourist information

Agencia Córdoba Turismo ① *Cabildo viejo, Pasaje Santa Catalina, T0351-434 1200, www.cordoba.gov.ar and www.cordobaturismo.gov.ar, daily 0800-2000. Also at the bus terminal, T0351-433 1982, daily 0700-2100, and at the airport, T0351-434 8390, daily 0800-2000.* All have useful city maps and information on guided walks and cycle tours.

Background

Founded in 1573 by an expedition from Santiago del Estero led by Jerónimo Luis de Cabrera, Córdoba was the most important city in the country in colonial times. During the late 16th and 17th centuries, the Jesuit Order made the city their headquarters for the southern part of the continent and founded the first university in the country here, giving the city its nickname, 'La Doctora' (the Learned). In 1810, when Buenos Aires backed independence, the leading figures of Córdoba voted to remain loyal to Spain, and after independence the city was a stronghold of opposition to Buenos Aires. It has remained fiercely independent ever since, supporting many Radical party governments, and in May 1969 disturbances in the city ignited opposition to military rule throughout the country. Since the 1940s Córdoba has grown from a cultural, administrative and communications centre into a large industrial city, though more recently the recession has resulted in growing unemployment. However, the city has an upbeat feel and fabulous nightlife.

Places in Córdoba city → *For listings, see pages 146-149.*

Old City

Córdoba's centre comes as a pleasant surprise. Its most interesting buildings are grouped around a pedestrianized area, enabling you to gaze up at the magnificent architecture without being mown down by traffic. Most of the older buildings lie within a few blocks of the **Plaza San Martín**, which dates from 1577 when it was the site for the odd bullfight. Now it's a wide open space, with lots of cafés, a fine statue of San Martín, and jacaranda trees creating a mass of purple in late spring. On the west side, the former **Cabildo**, built in 1610, with characteristic arches and two interior patios, has a colourful history. It has served as a prison, courthouse and clandestine detention centre during the last military dictatorship. Next to it, the **cathedral** ① *T0351-422 3446, daily 0800-1300, 1630-2000*, is the oldest in Argentina, an extraordinary confection of 17th- and 18th-century styles from successive renovations. The marvellous neo-baroque interior has wooden doors from a Jesuit temple and statues of angels resembling the indigenous peoples, with a silver tabernacle and lavishly decorated ceiling.

Just south of the cathedral is the 16th-century **Carmelo Convent** and chapel of **Santa Teresa** ⓘ *Independencia 122, Mon-Sat, 0700-1430, 1730-1930*, whose rooms and beautiful patio form the **Museo de Arte Religioso Juan de Tejeda** ⓘ *Wed-Sat 0930-1230, US$0.75, guided visits also in English and French*. This houses one of the finest collections of religious art in the country and is not to be missed.

One block west, on the west side of pleasant Plaza del Fundador, is the convent and church of **Santa Catalina de Siena**. It was founded in 1613 but rebuilt in the late 19th century and contains a splendid collection of paintings from Peru as well as colonial Spanish tapestries and carpets. For more contemporary art, the **Museo Municipal de Bellas Artes** ⓘ *Av General Paz 33, T0351-433 1512, Tue-Sat 0900-2100, US$0.40*, has a permanent collection by celebrated Argentine artists in an early 20th-century French-style mansion.

The **Manzana Jesuítica (Jesuit Block)**, contained within the streets Avenida Vélez Sarsfield, Caseros, Duarte Quirós and Obispo Trejo, has been declared a World Heritage Site by UNESCO. The **Iglesia de la Compañía**, at the corner of Obispo Trejo and Caseros, was originally built between 1640 and 1676, and its curious vaulted ceiling is a ship's hull, created by a Jesuit trained in the Dutch shipyards. Behind the church, on Caseros, is the smaller, more beautiful **Capilla Doméstica**, a private 17th-century Jesuit chapel, accessible only on the guided tour (see below) and worth seeing for the indigenous painting on the altar. To the south is the main building of the **Universidad Nacional de Córdoba** ⓘ *T0351-433 2075, Tue-Sun 0900-1300, 1600-2000, US$2 by guided tour only (see below)*, originally the Jesuit Colegio Máximo. It now houses one of the most valuable libraries in the country, as well as the Colegio Nacional de Montserrat, the most traditional high school in the province. Guided visits in English to the church, chapel, university and school leave from Obispo Trejo 242 daily at 1000, 1100, 1700 and 1800.

Other fine examples of religious architecture are the **Iglesia de San Francisco**, Buenos Aires and Entre Ríos, on a leafy plaza, and the **Iglesia de San Roque** at Obispo Salguero 84. One block east of Plaza San Martín is the **Museo Histórico Provincial Marqués de Sobremonte** ⓘ *Rosario de Santa Fe 218, T0351-433 1661, Mon-Fri 0900-1400, US$1.50*, the only surviving colonial family residence in the city, dating from 1760. It has a labyrinth of patios and simply decorated rooms with texts in English and German. The **Basílica de La Merced** at 25 de Mayo 83 has a fine gilded wooden pulpit dating from the colonial period and beautifully carved wooden doors, with fine ceramic murals revealing Córdoba's history on the outside by the local artist Armando Sica.

Nueva Córdoba

Over the past few years Nueva Córdoba (south of the Plaza San Martín) has become the hippest part of town, due in part to the numbers of students that frequent the area (the university is a short walk from here). There are cute shops, cafés and lots of hostels, and, at night, the area is taken over by bars and clubs; head to Rondeau and Cañada, or Boulevard San Juan and Larrañaga, to be part of the action. There is an eclectic mix of building styles along Avenida Hipólito Yrigoyen. The **Paseo del Buen Pastor** ⓘ *Av Hipólito Yrigoyen 325, T0351-411 1312*, has a cultural centre at its heart with an **art gallery** ① *daily 1000-2100, free*, a book shop, three **cafés (Colores Santos, La Fontaine** and **Black Sheep**; all open from 0900) and a beautifully presented **chapel** ① *daily 0900-2000*. Next door the neo-Gothic **Iglesia de los Capuchinos** ① *T0351-468 1922 Tue-Fri 0900-1200, 1600-1945, Sat 0900-1200, Sun 1030-1200, 1930-2100*, displays the night skies for every month of the year.

Further up towards the park are two worthwhile art galleries. Set in an amazing turn-of-the-century palace, the **Museo Superior de Bellas Artes Evita-Palacio Ferreyra** ① *Av Hipólito Yrigoyen 511, T0351-434 3636, Tue-Sun 1000-2000, US$1.50, Wed free*, has 12 salons spread out over three floors and shows a range of Argentine and international artists. Opposite, in front of Plaza España, is the modern **Museo de Bellas Artes Emilio Caraffa** ① *Av Hipólito Yrigoyen 651, T0351-433 3412, www.museocaraffa.org.ar, Tue-Sun 1000-2000, US$1.50, Wed free (near 50% discount when buying tickets for both Bellas Artes and Museo Caraffa)*, which is dedicated to presenting the best of Cordobese visual arts.

Parque Sarmiento is the largest green area of the city, laid out by French architect Charles Thays in 1889 with small lakes, a neat rose garden and a **zoo** ① *T0351-421 7648, www.zoo-cordoba.com.ar, daily 1000-1730, US$6.25*, set among steep hills.

Other sights

The magnificent **Mitre railway station**, near the bus terminal, has a beautifully tiled *confitería*, still in use for Sunday evening tango shows (see Entertainment, page 148). The lively, crowded market, **Mercado de la Ciudad**, provides a taste of local urban culture.

ⓦ Córdoba city listings

For hotel and restaurant price codes and other relevant information, see pages 20-26.

ⓦ Where to stay

Córdoba city *p142, map p143*
$$$ Amerian Córdoba Park, Blvd San Juan 165, T0351-420 7000, www.amerian.com. Swish, modern hotel with marbled foyer and professional service. Comfortable, superb breakfast, convenient and reliable. Also has a business centre, gym, spa and pool.
$$$ Windsor, Buenos Aires 214, T0351-422 4012, www.windsortower.com. Small, smart, warm, large breakfast, sauna, gym,

pool. Excellent white tablecloth dining at the expensive Sibaris restaurant.
$$ Alex, Blvd Illia 742, T0351-421 4350, www.alexhotel.com.ar. Good value, modern, cosy despite a slightly off-putting exterior. All rooms include a *mate* kit, helpful staff, close to the bus station.
$$ Córdoba B&B, Tucumán 440, T0351-423 0973, www.cordobabyb.com.ar. Sparsely decorated but pleasant doubles and triples, central, parking, good value.
$$ Sussex, San Jerónimo 125, T0351-422 9070, www.hotelsussexcba.com.ar. Well kept, with family welcome, small pool, buffet breakfast.
$ pp Aldea, Santa Rosa 447, T0351-426 1312, www.aldeahostel.com. Nicely

designed and decorated, welcoming, terrace with sofas, games, dorm prices depend on number sharing, quite central.
$ pp Baluch Backpackers Hostel, San Martin 338, T0351-422 3977, www.baluchbackpackers.com. Inviting dorms for 4-6 (US$10.50-11.50) and nice doubles (US$32). Owned and run by backpackers, central, information and bus tickets, many services, organizes various activities.
$ pp Córdoba Hostel, Ituzaingó 1070, T0351-468 7359, www.cordobahostel.com.ar. In Nueva Córdoba district, small rooms (US$13-14 in dorms, US$44.50 in double), quite noisy, private lockers in rooms. Small discount for HI members.
$ pp Palenque Hostel, Av Gral Paz 371, T0351-423 7588, www.palenquehostel.com.ar. Lovely hostel in a 100-year-old building, spacious common areas, small dorms, doubles with TV.
$ pp Tango Hostel, Fructuoso Rivera 70, T0351-425 6023, http://tangohostel cordoba.com. Good hostel in Nueva Córdoba student district, clubs and bars all around, rooms for 2-5 (US$10.50-11.50, double US$32.50), library, free coffee/ *mate*, local trips arranged.

🍴 Restaurants

Córdoba *p142, map p143*
$$$-$$ Juan Griego, Obispo Trejo 104, T0351-15-573 9760, www.juangriego restobar.com, Mon-Fri 0800-1600. On the 7th floor of the Colegio de Escribanos with a view of the Manzana Jesuítica, this modern Argentine restaurant is unmissable. Open for breakfast and lunch.
$$ Faro de Garrido, Av Figueroa Alcorta 366, T0351-15-653 0247. Succulent grilled meats are the order of the day at this traditional, high-quality *parilla*. Great for lunch or dinner.

$$ Sushi Man, Independencia 1181, T0351-460 3586, www.sushimanweb.com. Those who have had their fill of meat and would like to order in can opt for this chain restaurant offering decent, if not spectacular, sushi options.
$$-$ Sol y Luna, Gral Paz 278, T0351-425 1189, www.solylunaonline.com.ar. Mon-Sat 1200-1530. Vegetarian with a change of menu daily, fresh food, lunchtime specials, good desserts. 2nd branch at Montevideo 66, Nuevo Córdoba, T0351-421 1863.
$ Alfonsina, Duarte Quirós 66j, T0351-427 2847. Daily 0800-0200. Rural style in an old house, simple meals, pizzas and *empanadas*, or breakfasts with home-made bread, piano and guitar music, popular.

Cafés
Mandarina, Obispo Trejo 171, T0351-426 4909. Central, welcoming, leafy, lots of great breakfasts, good for lunch and dinner. Highly recommended.
Sorocabana, San Jerónimo 91, T0351-422 7872. Daily 24 hrs. Great breakfasts, popular, good views of Plaza San Martín.

🍷 Bars and clubs

Córdoba *p142, map p143*
Córdoba has plenty of bars, *pubs* and *boliches* in to drink and dance the night away; see www.nochecordobacapital.com.ar. In **Nuevo Córdoba** head to calles Rondeau, Larrañaga and Cañada. Also try Calle Buenos Aires between Centro and Nuevo Córdoba for trendy nightspots and **El Abasto** district on the river (about 8 blocks north of Plaza San Martín) for several good, cheap places. Another popular nightlife area lies further northwest in **Chateau Carreras**.

⊕ Entertainment

Córdoba *p142, map p143*
See free listings in the local newspaper
La Voz del Interior (www.vos.com.ar),
and **www.cordoba.net**, for events.

Cinema
Many, including **Cineclub Municipal**,
Blvd San Juna 49, Teatro Córdoba, 27 de
Abril 275, both showing independent
and foreign-language films. The cinema
in **Shopping Patio Olmos** (see below)
shows new releases.

Music and dance
Cuarteto is a Cordobés music style with an
enthusiastic following; see www.kuarteto.
com for groups, news and shows. There
is a free **tango** show every Sat at 2100 in
Plaza San Martin and in Shopping Patio
Olmos on Sun at 2000. The restaurant
El Arrabal, Belgrano y Fructuoso Rivera,
www.elarrabalconcert.com.ar, offers
dinner and a tango show at 2330 Fri and
Sat; ask here about private lessons.

Theatre
Teatro del Libertador, Av Vélez Sarsfield
365, T0351-433 2323, is traditional and
sumptuous, with a rich history. There are
several other smaller theatres.

⊖ Shopping

Córdoba *p142, map p143*
The main shopping area is along the
pedestrian streets north of the plaza.
Shopping Patio Olmos, Av Vélez Sarsfield
and Blvd San Juan, is the city's best mall,
located in a wonderful old palace with
a stylish food area. There's a weekend
handicraft market at **Paseo de las Artes**,

Achával Rodríguez y Belgrano, Sat-Sun
1600-2100 (in summer 1700-2300), selling
ceramics, leather, wood and metalware.
At other times visit **Mundo Aborigen**,
Rivadavia 155, an NGO promoting
indigenous communities.

⊙ What to do

Córdoba city *p142, map p143*
City tours
The city tourist office (see Tourist
information, above) offers city tours on
foot or bike, as well as cheap guided visits
to the Jesuit *estancias* in Jesús María and
Alta Gracia. The **Municipality**, Rosario
de Santa Fé 39, T0351-434 1200, www2.
cordoba.gov.ar/turismo/visitas-guiadas,
also runs good daily tours of religious
buildings and of Córdoba Misteriosa;
most are free although a charge may be
made for an English-speaking guide.
Córdoba City Tour, T0351-15-537 8687,
www.cordoba.gov.ar, Thu-Tue 1100,
1400, 1630. The big red sightseeing bus
departs from outside the cathedral.

Provincial tours
The main destinations are in the Punilla,
Calamuchita and Traslasierra valleys and
all Jesuit-related places.
Explorando, T03543-645601, www.
explorandosierras.com.ar. Tours include
birdwatching, mountain biking, horse
riding and local excursions.
Itatí, 27 de Abril 220, T0351-422
5020. Good local company with
tours throughout the province.
Nativo, Independencia 174, T0351-424
5341, www.cordobanativoviajes.com.ar.
Huge range of tours, very professional
and reliable.

⊖ Transport

Córdoba *p142, map p143*
Air
AR/Austral runs a shuttle service several times a day between Córdoba's Pajas Blancas airport and **Buenos Aires** (2 hrs); **LAN** also flies to Buenos Aires. **Sol** flies to **Rosario** on weekdays, with a connection to **Punta del Este** in summer. Most other major Argentine cities are served, usually via Buenos Aires, and there are direct international flights to **Peru**, **Brazil** and **Chile**, and to other countries via Buenos Aires.

Bus
To **Buenos Aires**, several companies, 9-11 hrs, US$60 *común*, US$68-85 *coche-cama*). To **Salta,** 12 hrs, US$78-107 (*semi-cama* and *ejecutivo*). To **Mendoza**, 9-12 hrs, frequent, US$64-85 (*semi-cama* and *ejecutivo*). To **La Rioja**, 6-7 hrs, US$40-44. To **Catamarca**, 6 hrs, US$38-43. **TAC** and **Andesmar** have connecting services to several destinations in **Patagonia**. See towns below for buses to the **Sierras de Córdoba**.

⊕ Directory

Córdoba *p142, map p143*
Banks Open in the morning (0800-1300). There are many **Link** and **Banelco** ATMs; all accept international credit cards. **Consulates** Bolivia, Vélez Sarsfield 56, T0351-411 4489. **Chile**, Buenos Aires 1386, T0351-469 2010. Immigration office **Dirección Nacional de Migraciones**, Caseros 676, T0351-422 2740. **Language schools** Espanex, Av General Paz 55, p 18, T0351-421 8954, www.espanex.org. Large organization with schools in Bariloche and Buenos Aires too, can arrange accommodation. **Medical services** Hospital Córdoba, Libertad 2050, T0351-433 9022. **Hospital Clínicas**, Santa Rosa 1564, T0351-433 7014. For both, www.fcm.unc.edu.ar.

Northern Córdoba province

Stretching north from Córdoba city are two parallel chains of mountains known as the Sierras Chicas, with wonderfully wild landscapes to explore. There are two main routes north offering quite different pleasures.

Head up Route 9, named by the tourist board as the Camino de la Historia, to visit Jesús María and the Jesuit *estancias*, the cultural highlights of Córdoba province. Hiring a car is the best way to travel this route, as you can stop off at the more attractive villages in the hills and stay at rural *estancias* too, such as luxurious La Paz in Ascochinga; otherwise, the local minibuses are clean and efficient, and taxis are cheap. North of Jesús María birdwatchers should head east to Laguna Mar Chiquita, a lake the size of a small sea that attracts a plethora of migratory birds. Route 9, meanwhile, continues to the Reserva Natural Cerro Colorado, where there are extraordinary pre-hispanic paintings in red rocky landscapes. Or, you could follow the old Camino Real, now Route 60, northwest to quaint unspoiled villages and the remote Estancia San Pedro Viejo.

The alternative route north along the Punilla valley (Route 38) takes you through depressing built-up tourist towns, so keep going until you reach the pretty little mountain town of La Cumbre, which offers spectacular paragliding and golf. The region's most interesting rural landscapes lie to the east of Route 38 in the Sierras Chicas; explore the beautiful rolling mountains on horseback from the traditional rural *estancia*, Los Potreros, just an hour from Córdoba.

Camino de la Historia and the Jesuit estancias → For listings, see pages 159-164.

The real jewel in the crown of Córdoba province is the collection of fine 17th-century Jesuit *estancias* in the hilly, rural areas to the north of the provincial capital. Three of the oldest *estancias* – **Estancia Jesús María**, 40 km north of Córdoba, **Estancia Caroya,** nearby, and **Santa Catalina**, 20 km further northwest – lie close to what used to be the **Camino Real** (the 'royal road'), used by the Spanish to link Córdoba with Lima and the Alto Perú mines. Jesuit missionaries established huge, enterprising *estancias* in the countryside here in order to finance their educational and artistic work in Córdoba city. The elegant residences and beautiful chapels built for the priests still remain, complete with some wonderful art and walled gardens. You could visit all three Jesuit *estancias* in a day's drive from Córdoba, but part of the charm of exploring the sierras is to enjoy a night or two in the area's modern-day *estancias* – the kind where you're offered fine wine and horse riding, rather than religious instruction. For more information, visit www.sierraschicas.net and www.cordobaciudad.com/estanciasjesuiticas.

Jesús María → *Colour map 4, A3. Phone code 03525. Population 27,000.*

The sleepy town of Jesús María, its avenues lined with trees, is a good base for exploring two of Córdoba's oldest Jesuit *estancias*. It's typical of a number of towns that developed in the late 19th century, following a wave of immigration from Friuli in the north of Italy, starting with 60 families in 1878. There's a distinctly Italian influence to the food, with some superb salamis to be found in the cafés and shops. Jesús María itself has little to offer tourists, but during the first half of January it hosts the **Festival de Doma y Folclore**, a popular *folclore* music and gaucho event whose profits benefit local schools.

There are two **tourist offices**: one at the **bus station** ① *Belgrano 580, T03525-426113*, and one on the way into town on R9 ① *T03525-465700, www.jesusmaria. gov.ar*, which provide useful information. Ask for the leaflet *Caminos de las Estancias Jesuíticas*, which includes a handy map of the *estancias* in relation to Córdoba and some information on each *estancia* (in Spanish). From the main road into town, Estancia Jesús María and Estancia Caroya are clearly signposted.

Estancia Jesús María

① *1 km northeast of the centre of Jesús María, T03525-420126. Tue-Sun 1000-1300, 1400-1800 winter (1430-1900 summer), US$1.75.*

This is a well-conserved example of a Jesuit-built *estancia*, whose produce supported the schools in Córdoba. Argentina's first vineyards were created here and wine from Jesús María was reputed to have been the first American wine served to the Spanish royal family. The residence and church, built mainly in 1618, form three sides of a square enclosing a neat garden, with pleasing cloisters on two sides. The imposing façade of the church is in good condition, with tall, plaster-covered pillars contrasting with the stonework of the main building, but it's a sober affair compared with the opulent interior of the church and its finely decorated cupola.

In the adjoining **Museo Jesuítico**, beautiful Cuzco-style paintings, religious objects and a curious collection of plates are on display, together with early winemaking artefacts. There are no remains of the housing for slaves and indigenous workers, or of the cultivation areas, but, with its lovely pond underneath mature trees and a small graveyard to the left of the church, the whole place is very attractive and peaceful. Highly recommended for a few hours' visit.

You can get there by taxi, or it's an easy 15-minute walk from the Jesús María bus station: take Avenida Juan B Justo, north, turn left at Avenida Cleto Peña, cross the bridge over the river and follow a dirt road right about 300 m.

Estancia de Caroya

ⓘ *In the southern suburbs of Jesús María, T03525-426701. Tue-Fri 0900-1900, Sat-Sun 0900-1200. 1700-2000, US$2.*

Estancia de Caroya, dating from 1616, was the first of the Jesuit establishments to be built in the area and has an interesting history. It was acquired in 1661 by the Jesuit founder of the Colegio Convictorio de Montserrat (in Córdoba city). While its agricultural activities funded the college, it was also used as a holiday home for the students. Between 1814 and 1816, it was used as a weapons factory for the Army of the North fighting in the Wars of Independence, and then in 1878 the first Italian immigrants stayed here. A simpler construction than Jesús María, Estancia de Caroya consists of single-storey cloisters around a central patio, with access to kitchens, dining rooms and a simple stone chapel. The fascinating history is well presented in the displays here, including a room with artefacts from the Italian immigration. (Note that, although the tour is informative, your guide may not speak English.) Ruins of a dam and a mill can be seen in the surrounding gardens.

You can go by taxi or it's a 20-minute walk from the bus station: take Avenida Juan B Justo, south, and turn right at Avenida 28 de Julio. After 500 m, the gates of the *estancia* are on the left side of the road. Ask the staff at the *estancia* to call you a taxi to get back into town; they are very helpful.

Around Jesús María

Just south of Jesús María, **Colonia Caroya** was the heart of Italian immigration to the area, and you can taste delicious salami at any of the local restaurants. The long access road is beautifully lined by an uninterrupted avenue of mature sycamore trees, where you'll find **Bodegas La Caroyense** ⓘ *Av San Martín 2281, T03525-466270, www.lacaroyense-sa.com.ar, Mon-Fri 0700-1200, 1500-1900, Sat-Sun 1000-1800, free,* a winery offering guided visits.

Set picturesquely among hills, 22 km west of Route 9, the attractive village of **Villa Tulumba** has hardly changed since colonial times. It's worth visiting for the beautiful 17th-century baroque tabernacle in its church, crafted in the Jesuit missions.

Estancia Santa Catalina

ⓘ *70 km northwest of Jesús María, T0351-15-550 3752, www.santacatalina.info. Tue-Sun 1000-1300, 1500-1900 in summer, 1400-1800 in winter, US$1.25.*

This is the largest of the *estancias*, beautifully located in rolling fertile countryside northwest of Jesús María, and not to be missed. It is also the best preserved of all the *estancias* and the only one that remains in private hands, having the added advantage of being close to Ascochinga (see below), which has some good accommodation.

The house is still in use by the extended Díaz family as their weekend and summer home, but the church and all the outbuildings are open to the public. The guided tour (Spanish only) is included in the entrance price and provides lots of information on the way of life here, as well as allowing you to visit the seminary buildings and the second and third patios (not during January, February, July and Easter), which are rich in architectural detail.

Built in 1622, the church has the most wonderful baroque façade, with swooping curves and scrolls in white plaster, and twin bell towers. The beautifully maintained interior has a fabulous gold pulpit and retable, brought from Alto Perú, with religious figures made by indigenous craftsmen betraying certain anatomical details of their makers, such as their big knees and robust workmen's thighs. There are superb Cuzco-school paintings representing the Passion and, opposite the retable, an intriguing articulated sculpture of Jesus on the cross. This was used by the Jesuit priests as a teaching device to evangelize the indigenous peoples, and unlike most such figures, this Jesus has his eyes open: his arms could be lowered to enact scenes from his life, pre-crucifixion, and then raised, as he was mounted on the cross. A moving and fascinating figure.

The house has a beautiful central patio, where just three priests lived in spacious splendour, organizing a staff of 600 and a workforce of thousands of African slaves and local indigenous peoples. Santa Catalina was the most important of the *estancias* economically, with its 25,000 head of cattle and extensive agriculture. To the right of the church is a huge vegetable garden and, further out, a little brick building with six tiny rooms where novice priests were trained. The slaves' quarters were even more miserable and can be found on the road leading to the *estancia*, now converted into a restaurant. The servants for the main house were housed in the second patio, and in the third patio were wood and metal workshops. In the lovely surrounding parkland, you can see the *tajamar* – a reservoir used for the sophisticated watering system for crops.

Access to the *estancia* is along a 14-km dirt road branching off Route E66 to Ascochinga, 6 km west of Jesús María (signposted, 20 km in total). From Jesús María bus station, *remise* taxis make a return trip, including two hours' waiting time at the *estancia*. Good lunches are available at La Ranchería de Santa Catalina ① *T03525-424467*, a simple rustic restaurant on the right as you approach the *estancia*. It also has two small guest rooms with shared bathroom.

Ascochinga and Estancia La Paz

The upmarket little village of **Ascochinga**, 13 km west of Santa Catalina, is full of second homes for rich *Córdobes* and has a couple of shops, a part time *locutorio*, an ACA petrol station and plenty of accommodation options. A fabulously opulent place to stay is the historical **Estancia La Paz** ① *Ashcochinga, www.puebloestancialapaz. com*, which was owned by President Roca from 1872 until his death in 1914, and remains almost untouched. Just try not to think about him planning the massacre of the indigenous peoples in the Conquest of the Desert when he stayed here. Roca added the neoclassical Italianate touches to the building, and commissioned a splendid 100-ha park from Argentina's most famous landscape architect Charles Thays, whose work includes the parks at Palermo, Tucumán and Mendoza. There are grand bedrooms, with enormously high ceilings, coming directly off a long terrace with wonderful views across the huge ornamental lake where you can go rowing if the mood takes you. There are immense groves of exotic trees and blissful, private places to sit on the 1930s garden furniture and order tea from the impeccable staff. Old-fashioned opulence is combined with more modern luxuries such as an Olympic-sized pool, tennis courts, a spa with expert masseuse and a superb restaurant, making this a real treat. They also offer day-rates, if you don't have the time or the money to stay the night.

Asochinga to La Cumbre

From Asochinga a spectacular route heads over the mountains to **La Cumbre** (see page 158). The road courses through wonderful landscapes of rounded mountain ridges and deep valleys and is much loved by rally drivers and cyclists in training. This winding dirt road, full of hairpin bends, is probably best not attempted in the dark or in bad weather. Keep your speed below 40 kph, watch out for hares and perdis crossing the road, and allow at least two hours for the journey. The vegetation varies from lush subtropical woodlands to lush scrub on the summits, and there are consistently great views on a fine day.

Northeast of Córdoba → *Colour map 4, A3. Phone code 03563.*

From Route 9 north of Ascochinga you can head east to Argentina's largest inland sea, the **Laguna Mar Chiquita** ('Lagoon of the Small Sea'), set on the borders of the Pampas and the Chaco, 192 km northeast of Córdoba. The lake is very shallow (maximum depth 12 m) and has no outlet into any rivers, so its size varies (from 65 km by 80 km, to 30 km by 40 km) according to rainfall patterns. At times, the water is apparently so salty you can float in it.

A reserve, called the **Reserva Natural Bañados del Río Dulce y Laguna Mar Chiquita** ① *www.promarmarchiquita.com.ar*, has been created to protect the huge numbers of migratory birds that flock here in summer from the northern hemisphere. So far, over 300 species of bird have been spotted here, returning to different parts of the lagoon each year. There are also large resident populations of flamingos representing all three species extant in South America. It's the site of greatest biodiversity in the province, and is also popular for fishing *pejerrey* all year round. During the summer, human visitors flock here too, since the salty waters are used in the treatment of rheumatic ailments and skin diseases. It's a singular and spectacular landscape and, although you may feel it's not worth a big detour, if you're spending some time in the area, it would make a good relaxing day out. Park administration is in Miramar on the southern shore, the only settlement nearby, where there are a few hotels and campsites. There's a **tourist office** ① *Libertad 351, T03563-493777.*

If you're enjoying getting off the beaten track and want to see where the Camino Real leads, keep going northwest from Jesús María along Route 60 into the northernmost extreme of the province. In **Deán Funes** (118 km from Córdoba), you'll find a couple of decent hotels, plenty of places to eat and a **tourist information office** ① *Sáenz Peña 466, T03521-420020.*

From Deán Funes head east on provincial road 16 to find **San Piedro Viejo** ① *www.sanpedroviejo.com.ar.* This tiny hamlet has a beautiful little church, built in adobe with a squat square bell tower, and an *estancia*, where you can stay for a few nights to completely unwind and explore the rolling land on foot or horseback. This place has a history: it was an important staging post on the royal road between the Río de la Plata and Perú, and such illustrious figures as General San Martín and President Belgrano stayed in the building which is now a chic and rustic boutique hotel.

Reserva Cultural y Natural Cerro Colorado

① *www.cordobaturismo.gov.ar/CerroColorado.aspx. Guided tours daily 0800-1900, US$2.* Some 104 km north of Jesús María, reached by an unpaved road (12 km) that branches off Route 9 at Santa Elena (see Transport, page 163), is this provincial park covering 3000 ha of rocky hills and woodlands protecting some 35,000 rock paintings in around 200 sites, some of them underground. It's thought that they were painted by the indigenous Comechingones people sometime between the 10th century and the arrival of the Spanish roughly 600 years later. The strikingly bold paintings, in red, black and white, portray animals and plants, hunting scenes, magic rituals and dancing; even battles against the Spanish, mounted on horseback. There are lots of more enigmatic paintings with geometric patterns, open to wildly imaginative interpretations. The park can only be visited as part of a guided tour which lasts 1½ hours and is included in the entry. There are also two small museums: **Museo Arqueológico** ① *daily 0700-1300, 1400-2000, tours at 0830, 1030, 1600 and 1800,* at the foot of Cerro Intihuasi, has information on the site itself; **Museo Atahualpa and Yupanqui** ① *T0351-15-6685 3900, www.atahualpayupanqui. org.ar, daily 0900-1300, 1600-2000, US$2.50,* at the end of the winding road to Agua Escondida, also offers guided tours. The vegetation is interesting with lots of ancient algarrobo trees, molles and a rare *mato* forest in the park, where you can also spot small armadillos.

There's a hotel and a few *cabaña* complexes nearby in the sprawling villages at the foot of the Cerro, and plenty of handicrafts for sale. A useful website is www. cerrocolorado.infoturis.com.ar (in Spanish).

The Punilla Valley, situated between the Sierras Chicas to the east and the Sierra Grande to the west, was the first area of the sierras to become populated by weekend and summer visitors from the cities of Córdoba and Buenos Aires back in the 1920s. Sadly, these once-idyllic weekend retreats have now developed into one long string of built-up urban areas alongside Route 38: **Villa Carlos Paz**, **Cosquín**, **Valle Hermoso** and **La Falda**. There's no real reason to stop, unless you're keen to visit Cosquín's famous *folclore* music festival, which is held every year in January and attracts the country's best musicians and budding talent. The whole valley is unbearably busy during the Argentine holiday periods of January, February and Easter, when it is best avoided. Any time of the year, it is preferable to head straight for **La Cumbre** further north (see page 158), where there's a more civilized pace of life and plenty of appealing places to stay in this pretty hill-side town. A brief description of the main Punilla Valley towns is followed by a more complete description of La Cumbre. For further information, see www.lacumbre.gov.ar and www.alacumbre.com (both in Spanish).

Villa Carlos Paz and around → *Colour map 4, A2. Phone code 03541. Population 56,000.*

Ghastly Villa Carlos Paz, 35 km west of Córdoba, is a large and overpopulated resort, crammed with hotels and brimming with Argentine tourists in summer. There are lots of activities on offer and a chairlift runs from the Complejo Aerosilla to the summit of the Cerro de la Cruz, but your only reason to come here would be if everywhere else is full, or to use it as a base for the area's superb trekking. There are plenty of hotels, and some quieter places to bathe and hang out, such as the *balnearios* along Río San Antonio, and **Villa Las Jarillas**, 15 km south of town. See www.villacarlospaz.com and www.villacarlospaz.gov.ar (both in Spanish) for more information on the area. **Municipal tourist office** ① *Av San Martín 400, T03541-421624, www.villacarlospaz.gov.ar.*

Villa Carlos Paz is on the road to Traslasierra further west (see page 173), but if you're not going that far and are into hiking or climbing, it's worth heading for **Cerro Los Gigantes** (2374 m), 39 km west of Villa Carlos Paz, with its spectacular views and challenging walks. To get there, take the unpaved Route 28 via **Tanti** over the Pampa de San Luis towards **Salsacate**. Los Gigantes is signposted at Km 30, where you turn off left; here you'll find the nearest base for climbing the granite massif. By public transport, you'll need to get a local bus from Villa Carlos Paz to Tanti, and from there to Los Gigantes. Daily buses to Salsacate stop at Los Gigantes.

Cosquín and around → *Colour map 4, A2. Phone code 03541. Population 18,800.*

Cosquín, 20 km north of Carlos Paz, is not an attractive town, but its setting on the banks of the wide Río Cosquín gives it several *balnearios* (swimming areas), of which **Pan de Azúcar** is the quietest option. Cosquín is also known as the national *folclore* capital, and Argentina's most important *folclore* festival is held here in the last two weeks of January. The country's most famous bands and singers play every night on **Plaza Próspero Molina**, and there are plentiful food and handicrafts stalls. An increasingly popular rock festival (www.cosquinrock.net) is held here in early February, so accommodation is almost impossible to find between 10 January and 10 February. There is a **tourist office** ① *Av San Martín 590, Plaza Nacional del Folclore, T03541-454644, www.cosquinturismo.gob.ar,* and a bus terminal at Perón and Salta.

Sierras Chicas and Estancia Los Potreros

To really get into the wild, remote country that is the Sierras Chicas, you need to spend a few nights away from civilization, and the best way to do this is to stay at an *estancia* such as Estancia Los Potreros, an exclusive 2500-ha working cattle farm in the wild and scenic Córdoba hills. One of Argentina's finest riding *estancias*, it is situated in the middle of its own range of peaks, but is easily accessible, just an hour from Córdoba airport. It's own by a British family, Robin and Kevin Begg, who were brought up on this land and who breed fine horses and offer a wonderful mixture of real gaucho Argentine ranch culture and British hospitality in keeping with a time past. If you're not a rider, you can walk, birdwatch, swim or simply relax, and enjoy the peace and immense vistas. If you'd like to learn to ride, the Beggs are the most patient teachers and the horses are very tame, impeccably trained and sure-footed. There's a three-night minimum stay which allows you to get a feel for the place, with delicious food and wine all included; for those with more time, a riding tour of the sierras taking several days can be arranged. As well as enjoying spectacular scenery, a longer tour allows you to explore remote mountain villages with their tiny churches and schools, and stay at other mountain *estancias* in the region, gaining invaluable insights into the local culture and communities that you could never otherwise access. This is an unique way to experience the Sierras de Córdoba.

Estancia Los Potreros, Sierras Chicas, Casilla de Correo 64, 5111 Río Ceballos, T011-6091 2692/4313 1410, www.estancialospotreros.com. To get there, either take a bus to the nearest town, Río Ceballos, or the managers, Kevin and Louisa, will arrange a taxi from Córdoba city or airport (one hour).

La Falda and around → *Colour map 4, A2. Phone code 03548. Population 16,000.*
La Falda, 20 km north of Cosquín, is another seething and tawdry tourist town, once the destination of Argentina's wealthy and influential who all stayed at the magnificent Hotel Edén. The hotel is now sadly in ruins but the bar gives you a

flavour of its former grandeur, with an exhibition of old photographs. The town is known for its nightlife – bars and casinos abound – but it's really a place to avoid unless you want to use it as a base for hiking in the surrounding hills and Pampas. The **tourist office** is at ① *Av Edén 93, T03548-423007, www.turismolafalda.gob.ar*; the **bus terminal** ① *Av Buenos Aires y Chubut*, is a five-minute walk north of Avenida Edén.

The sierras to the east of La Falda are a good place for hiking. **Cerro La Banderita** (1350 m), which is also popular with paragliders, is a 1½-hour walk from the town centre and provides panoramic views of the valley: leave from the left side of Hotel Edén and take the street called Austria. Ask at tourist office for a map and directions. From La Falda you could also head out west to the Pampas: an 80-km rough, winding road goes to La Higuera, on the west side of the Cumbres de Gaspar. It crosses the vast **Pampa de Olaén**, a grass-covered plateau at 1100 m, where you'll find the tiny Capilla de Santa Bárbara (1750), 20 km from La Falda, and waterfalls Cascadas de Olaén, 2 km south of the chapel. There are more beautiful rivers and waterfalls at **Río Pintos** (26 km from La Falda) and **Characato** (36 km from La Falda). Jesuit **Estancia La Candelaria** lies further along this road, 53 km west of La Falda. This is a great area for cycling, but take water.

La Cumbre and around → *Colour map 4, A2. Phone code 03548. Population 7200.*

By far the most attractive town in this whole area, La Cumbre sits at the highest point of the Punilla Valley at 1141 m and is only 1½-hour's drive from Córdoba, if you head straight here without stopping on the way. It was founded by the British engineers and workers who built the railway here in 1900 and who have given the place its distinctive flavour, with trees lining the avenues in the attractive residential area to the east of town, where you'll find the best hotels. **Golf Club La Cumbre** ① *T03548-452283, www.lacumbregolf.com.ar, US$18-20 for a round,* to the southeast of town, was built 90 years ago and is beautifully landscaped with mature trees and a quaint Tudor-style clubhouse. Further east you'll find lots of craftsmen selling their wares. Unlike the rest of the valley, this friendly little town still feels authentic and the town centre bustles busily just before midday. There are some classy shops, as well as lots of places to eat and a couple of tea rooms selling superb cakes. For the more adventurous, there's excellent paragliding nearby in **Cuchi Corral** southwest of the town (see What to do, page 162). There are also plenty of places to walk in the mountains, with access from residential areas **Cruz Chica** and **Cruz Grande**, on the road to **Los Cocos**.

The **tourist office** ① *Av Caraffa 300, T03548-452966, daily from early morning until late in the evening*, is in the old train station, and many of the friendly staff speak English. They'll give you a very helpful map listing all the hotels and restaurants. See also www.alacumbre.com.ar and www.turismolacumbre.com.ar (both in Spanish). The **bus terminal** ① *Juan José Valle and Ruznak, T03548-452440*, is around the corner from the tourist office.

As a visitor to Argentina, you might not have noticed the national obsession with *alfajores*, the soft cakey biscuits made of a double layer of cornflour sponge, and sandwiched with *dulce de leche*. The chocolate-covered ones from **Havanna** *alfajores* shops in any town centre are particularly recommended. While you're in La Cumbre, you could visit the famous *alfajores* factory, **Estancia El Rosario** ① *R66,*

5 km east of town, T03548-451257, www.estanciaelrosario.com.ar, Mon-Fri 1000-1800, Sat-Sun 1000-1900, to see them being made and try a fine specimen or three. The factory has been operating since 1924 and was, for many years, a major tourist attraction. These days there are still free guided visits to the small factory where fruit preserves and other sweet delicacies are also made.

Located 11 km from La Cumbre is the **Centro de Rescate Rehabilitación y Conservación de Primates** (Center for Rescue, Rehabilitacion and Care of Primates) ① www.proyectocaraya.com, daily 0900-2030, US$16, where visitors can see a wide array of howler monkeys in their natural environment. Guided tours available. To get there, take a taxi from La Cumbre (US$16).

Head east from the golf course along Route 66 for the spectacular mountain crossing that leads to Ascochinga (for a route description, see page 154). North of La Cumbre, there are more hotels in the lovely leafy residential areas of Cruz Chica, Cruz Grande and Los Cocos. Further along this picturesque road are two popular places for families: **El Descanso**, with its well-designed garden and maze, and **Complejo Aerosilla** (www.aerosilla.com), with a chairlift to the nearby hills (US$3), an aquarium and toboggans.

Capilla del Monte and around → Colour map 4, A2. Phone code 03548. Population 8940.
Capilla del Monte is a quiet town which offers a base for good trekking and paragliding, and for exploring nearby rock formations at Agua de los Palos. The landscape is hilly and scrubby, with places rather reminiscent of the lunar landscapes in Ischigualasto – Valle de la Luna in San Juan (see box, page 230). The **tourist office** ① RN 38 y F Alcorta, daily 0830-2030, T482200, www.capilladelmonte.gov.ar, is at the end of the diagonal Buenos Aires. The town is overlooked by dramatic **Cerro Uritorco** (1979 m), which you can climb: head 3 km east of town and it's another 5 km to the summit, though be warned that this is a four-hour climb each way with no shade (US$2.50 entry).

UFO-spotters flock to the amazing landscape of **Quebrada de la Luna**, **Los Terrones** and **Parque Natural Ongamira**, where there are curious rock formations. Ask in the tourist office for more information and for a remise to take you there. The area is popular for 'mystical tourism' and holds an annual Festival Alienígena in February.

⊛ Northern Córdoba province listings

For hotel and restaurant price codes and other relevant information, see pages 20-26.

⊜ Where to stay

Jesús María p151
$$$ Hotel Jesús María, Calle Almafuerte 177, T03252-445888, www.hoteljesus maria.com.ar. Modern hotel with rooftop pool, small gym and spacious rooms.
$$$ La Cabaña del Tío Juan, R9, Km 755, T03525-420563, www.lacabana deltiojuan.com.ar. *Estancia*-style building with basic but appealing doubles, a small, slightly old-fashioned restaurant and a lovely pool in the gardens.

$$$-$$ Napoleón, Ameghino 211, T03525-401700, www.napoleononline. com.ar. Modern tower block with a/c and a rooftop pool.
$$ La Gringa II, Tucumán 658, T03525-425249, 1 block across the railway lines from the bus station. A/c, breakfast included.

Estancia Santa Catalina *p152*
$$ La Ranchería de Santa Catalina, 10 m before the entrance to the estancis, on the right-hand side, T03525-424467. Basic, but convenient for visiting the Jesuit *estancia*. 2 small rooms in the former slaves' quarters. Separate bathroom.

Ascochinga and Estancia La Paz *p153*
$$$$ Estancia La Paz, Route E66, Km 14, a few kilometres from Ascochinga, signposted, but ring for directions, T03525-499760, www.puebloestancialapaz.com. Opulence and splendour, presidential style, but this is a warmly welcoming luxury *estancia* with impeccable service and beautiful parkland. Offers golf, horse riding and a spa. Bilingual reception staff. Recommended.

Córdoba Norteña *p155*
$$$$ Estancia San Pedro Viejo, Ruta Provincial 18, San Pedro Norte, San Pedro Viejo, T0351-15-543 1797, www.sanpedroviejo.com.ar. A quaint, historical post house converted into a chic boutique hotel with 1-m-thick walls, old fireplaces, and ancient trees near a charming lake. 6 bedrooms decorated with antiques, some with jacuzzi. Price is for full board. Great food and wines, relaxing walks and horse riding in the nearby hills. A lovely retreat.

Reserva Cultural y Natural Cerro Colorado *p155*
There are several places to stay in the hamlets around the foot of the *cerro*, and you can also stay with local families if the hotel is full. The tourist office produces a helpful free leaflet, *El Chasqui de Cerro Colorado*, available in Córdoba city before you set off. A few to try (all $$) are **Cerro Colorado**, T03522-1564 8990, www.hotelcerrocolorado.com; **Complejo Argañaraz**, T0351-15-697 7193; and **La Italiana**, T0351-15-687 0445, www.cab-laitaliana.com.

Cosquín and around *p156*
$$$ La Puerta del Sol, Perón 820, T03541-452045, www.lapuertadelsolhotel.com.ar. **$$$$** in high season. A decent choice, pool, car hire, half board available.
$$ Siempreverde, Santa Fe 525, behind Plaza Molina, T03541-450093, http://hosteriasiempreverde.com. Spotless, welcoming and informative owner, some rooms small, comfortable, gorgeous garden.

La Falda and around *p157*
All 80 hotels are full in Dec-Feb.
$$$ L'Hirondelle, Av Edén 861, T03548-422825, www.lhirondellehostal.com. Lovely building, some rooms retain their original parquet floor and there's a large garden with a pool. Welcoming owners.
$$ La Asturiana, Av Edén 835, T03548-422923, hotellaasturiana@yahoo.com.ar. Simple, comfortable rooms, pool, superb breakfast.

La Cumbre and around *p158*
There are plenty of hotels, and *cabañas* here are high quality and in attractive settings, ideal for larger groups who want the flexibility of self-catering.

Cruz Chica is a lovely area to stay, but you'll need a car or taxi to get there.
$$ Hotel La Viña, Caraffa 48, T03548-451388, www.hotellavina.com.ar. Nice budget option, with cosy flowery rooms, a large pool and pleasant gardens.
$ pp Hostel La Cumbre, Av San Martín 282, T03548-451368, www.hostella cumbre.com. Dorms, rooms for up to 6 and doubles (**$$**). Family-owned, HI member, historic building with garden and pool, occasional *asados*, laundry, information and activities. Recommended.

Capilla del Monte and around *p159*
See www.capilladelmonte.gov.ar for more listings.
$$$ Montecassino, La Pampa 107, T03548-482572, www.hotelmonte cassino.com. Beautiful building from 1901, with lovely rooms, cable TV, jacuzzi and pool with stunning views.
$$ Petit Sierras, Pueyrredón y Salta, T03548-481667, www.cordobaserrana. com.ar/capilla/c petitsierras.htm. Renovated hotel with comfortable rooms. The owners run the restaurant *A Fuego Lento* (**$$**), at the access to town (discounts and free transport for guests).

🍽 Restaurants

Jesús María *p151*
$ Fertilia, signposted from Av San Martín 5200, Colonia Caroya, T03525-467031, www.fertilia.com.ar buses stop on the main road, from here it's a 15 min-walk along a dirt road to the farm. An unmissable treat. Welcoming farmers serve excellent quality salamis and ham accompanied by delicious local red wine.
$ Viejo Comedor, Tucumán 360, T03525-421601. Popular for cheap meals.

Reserva Cultural y Natural Cerro Colorado *p155*
$ Inti Huasi, in the visitor centre for *Córdoba Ambiente* agency. More of a café with food.

Cosquín and around *p156*
$$ La Encrucijada del Supaj-Ñuñú, on the way to the Cerro Pan de Azúcar, T03541-15-569864. Pleasant restaurant, tea house and brewery, serving meals, fondue, cakes or sandwiches at moderate prices.

La Falda and around *p157*
$ Pachamama, Av Edén 127. If you're tired of eating beef, there is a health food shop with a few neat tables at the back where you can have cheap organic vegetable pies, or wholemeal pizzas and *empanadas*.

La Cumbre and around *p158*
$$ La Casona del Toboso, Belgrano 349, T03548-451436. Also highly recommended for excellent food across a wide menu, including *parrilla*.
$ Dany Cheff, opposite the tourist office, Av Caraffa and Belgrano, T03548-451379. The best place for afternoon tea, serves delicious pastries and cakes, and there's a lively buzz mid-morning when locals flock there.

🎉 Festivals

Jesús María *p151*
Jan Festival de Doma y Folclore, www.festival.org.ar, entry US$5.50. Popular *folclore* music and gaucho event. The profits benefit local schools.

Cosquín and around *p156*
Jan Festival Nacional del Folclore, www.aquicosquin.org (in Spanish).

Cosquín's famous music festival attracts the country's best musicians and budding talent. In the last 2 weeks of Jan, the country's most famous bands and singers play every night on Plaza Próspero Molina.

Feb Cosquín Rock, www.festival.org. ar. Showcases national rock singers and groups, as well as international rock bands from Spanish-speaking countries.

○ What to do

La Falda and around *p157*
Tour operators
Turismo Talampaya, T03548-470412, turismotalampaya@yahoo.com.ar. Run by Teresa Pagni who guides 4WD full-day trips to the Pampa de Olaen and Jesuit *estancia* La Candelaria.

La Cumbre and around *p158*
Golf
Golf Club La Cumbre, Belgrano 1095, T03548-452284, www.lacumbregolf. com.ar. Follow Belgrano from the town centre, opposite the tourist office, to reach the corner of the golf course, then turn left onto Posadas. Very attractive 18-hole golf course, with caddies and coaching. Also putting green and Olympic-sized pool.

Horse riding
Chachito Silva, T03548-451703, Hires horses and offers ½-day, 1- and 2-day guided horse riding trips to the sierras and Candonga.
La Granja de los Gringos, R38, T03548-556389, www.cordobaserrana.com.ar/ lacumbre/cabalgatas.htm. Guided horseback rides by the hour, day or for multiple days.

Paragliding
The world-renowned paragliding site of **Cuchi Corral is** 9 km west of La Cumbre on an unpaved road; **Escuela de Parapentes**, Ruta 38, Km 65, T03548-403580, www.cordobaserrana.com.ar/ parapente.htm. Several local companies offer flights, which start at US$90 for your 1st flight, the *Vuelo Bautismo*, 20 mins, accompanied by a trained paragliding instructor in tandem.

Trekking
Escuela de Montaña y Escalada, T03548-451393, jorgemallory@ yahoo.com. Run by Jorge González, for parapenting, but also climbing and mountain trekking courses and excursions, eg to the Cascada de los 70 Pies in Cruz Grande. Equipment hire.

Tour operators
Estancia Puesto Viejo, T03548-15-566504, www.estanciapuestoviejo.com. Lots of outdoor activities (trekking, riding, parapenting, birdwatching), at a remote *estancia*, northwest of La Cumbre.

Capilla del Monte and around *p159*
Cycling
Claudio, Deán Funes 567. Mountain bike hire.

● Transport

Jesús María *p151*
Bus
To **Córdoba direct**, 1 hr, US$2, with **Ciudad de Córdoba, Colonia Tirolesa**, or minibus **Fono Bus** (US$2.50). To **Córdoba** via Ascochinga, 2½ hrs, US$2.50, **Ciudad de Córdoba**. To **Colonia Caroya**, US$1, with **Ciudad de Córdoba** or **Colonia Tirolesa**.

Northeast of Córdoba *p154*
Bus
Laguna Mar Chiquita to **Córdoba**, **Expreso Ciudad de San Francisco** (from **Miramar**), 3½ hrs, US$3; and **Transportes Morteros** (from **Balnearia**), 3 hrs, US$4.

Reserva Cultural y Natural Cerro Colorado *p155*
Bus
Ciudad de Córdoba, T0351-424 0048, go to **Córdoba** 3 times weekly, but check for current days, 3½ hrs, US$4. There are also combis to **Santa Elena** with **El Tatú**, T0351-423 6335, and **Río Seco**, T0351-424 5610.

Cosquín and around *p156*
Bus
Ciudad de Córdoba, La Calera, and TAC run frequent buses to **Córdoba**, 1-1½ hrs, US$4, and along the **Punilla Valley** to **La Falda**, US$2; to **La Cumbre** US$1.50; to **Capilla del Monte** US$2. Several minibuses do the same route.

Train
A tourist Tren de las Sierras runs 52 km between Cosquín and Rodríguez del Busto, via La Calera, 2 a day Mon-Fri, 3 a day Sat, Sun, 2¼ hrs, US$1.20. It is planned to extend the line from Córdoba to Cruz del Eje; see www.ferrocentralsa.com.ar.

La Falda and around *p157*
Bus
Chevallier, General Urquiza and Sierras de Córdoba go daily to **Buenos Aires** and to several other domestic destinations. **Ciudad de Córdoba** and **La Calera** run frequent buses to Córdoba,

US$5, and along the **Punilla Valley** to Cosquín, US$1.50; to **La Cumbre**, US$2; to **Capilla del Monte**, US$2. Several minibuses also travel the same route.

Remise taxis
Casa Blanca, 9 de Julio 541, T03548-422 912.

La Cumbre and around *p158*
Bus
Daily buses to **Buenos Aires** with **El Práctico**, T03548-451144, and **General Urquiza/Sierras de Córdoba**, T03548-452400, 11 hrs, US$55-75. To **Córdoba**, Ciudad de Córdoba, T03548-452442, and La Calera, T03548-452300.

Car hire
Reynas, 25 de Mayo 448, T03548-452107, gustavobecker2003@hotmail.com. Ask for a discount if you hire for several days. Bring credit card and passport.

Taxis
Auto Remis, López and Planes 321, T03548-451800, T0800-444 7040; Taxi Victoria, 25 de Mayo 260, T03548-452150.

Capilla del Monte and around *p159*
Bus
Daily buses to **Buenos Aires**, 12 hrs, US$55-65, and to **Córdoba**, US$4. **Ciudad de Córdoba** and **La Calera** and minibuses **El Serra** run services along the **Punilla valley**. Twice a day, **Ciudad de Córdoba** goes to **Traslasierra Valley** via Cruz del Eje.

Remise taxis
El Cerro, Pueyrredón 426, T03548-482300.

Southern Córdoba province: Calamuchita Valley

South of Córdoba, there's another fascinating and well-preserved Jesuit *estancia* in the unprepossessing town of Alta Gracia, which is the gateway to a picturesque hilly area between the high peaks of the Sierra Grande and Sierra de Comechingones. Fans of that great 20th-century icon Ernesto 'Che' Guevara will also want to visit his childhood home. Further south still, there's superb walking in the wooded countryside near the quaint Germanic town of Villa General Belgrano and, prettier still, the mountain town, La Cumbrecita. It's well worth spending two or three days combining the Jesuit heritage with some walking or relaxing in the hills to understand the essence of Córdoba's history and landscapes.

Alta Gracia → *For listings, see pages 170-172. Colour map 4, A2.*

Alta Gracia's great attraction is the wonderful 17th-century **Estancia Jesuítica Alta Gracia** (see below), whose church, residential buildings and small lake make a splendid hilltop centre to the town, around the scrappy Plaza Solares. The rather tawdry main commercial area spills down Belgrano, with everything you need, but no charm whatsoever. Head instead to the pretty residential area west of centre **El Alto**, where the most appealing restaurants are to be found. El Alto was built when the British came here to build the housing which the locals describe as typically 'British': two stories with corrugated-iron roofs. The rather grand **Hotel Sierras** (www.hojoar.com), stylishly built in 1907 as Argentina's first casino, was made popular by the rich upper classes who flocked to the area for the summer in the 1920s when Alta Gracia was in its heyday. It has been restored and now is a four-star hotel and casino. There's also an attractive golf course in this area, whose club has one of the town's best restaurants, open to non-members (see page 170). All this aristocratic pleasure might sound an unlikely environment for Ernesto 'Che' Guevara to have grown up in, but his family house can now be visited, see the **Museo Casa de Ernesto Che Guevara**, opposite.

Arriving in Alta Gracia → *Phone code 03547. Population 42,600.*
The **bus terminal** ① *T03547-428127*, is 10 blocks from the centre on the river at Butori and Perón 1977. The **tourist information** ① *El Molino y Av del Tajamar, T03547-428128, www.altagracia.gov.ar*, is at the base of the clock tower on the corner of the Jesuit reservoir, the *tajamar*. Staff don't speak much English but are helpful and will give you a map and a useful *Guía Turística*.

Estancia Jesuítica Alta Gracia and Museo Casa de Virrey Liniers

① Plaza Solares, Av Padre Viera 41, T03547-421303, www.museoliniers.org.ar. Summer Tue-Fri 0900-2000, Sat-Sun 0930-2030; winter Tue-Fri 0900-1300, 1500-1900, Sat-Sun 0930-1230, 1530-1830; 4 guided visits a day (8 per day Jan-Mar); phone in advance for English tours; closed 1 Jan, 1 May, 25 Dec. US$1.75, free Wed.

Part of the same development of Jesuit establishments as Jesús María and Santa Catalina (see pages 151 and 152), Alta Gracia is a fascinating testimony to the Jesuits' culture, and the entire *estancia* is now an excellent museum. If you visit only one Jesuit *estancia* in Córdoba, make it this one. There's added interest in the life of Viceroy Liniers, who owned the house from 1810. An excellent guided tour is included in the entry ticket, but ask in advance for an English-speaking guide. There are also informative laminated cards in several languages in each room.

Alta Gracia dates from 1643, when Córdoba was the capital of the Jesuit province of Paraguay, and this *estancia* – one of their most prosperous rural establishments – was built to fund the religious education of their young men in the Colegio Maximo in Córdoba city. The centre comprised a **Residence** (now a museum), the **Obraje** (industrial workshops), the **Ranchería** (where the slaves lived), the **Tajamar** (built by the Jesuits as a water reservoir), the **watermill** and the **church** (open only for Mass). This latter was started in 1659 and completed only in 1723. It has a splendid baroque façade and a grand cupola, which is the only part that has been renovated. The rest is all now sadly a little dilapidated, but it's the only Jesuit church that still functions today as the parish church.

The Jesuits built their ambitious project in two stages: first they lived in an adobe building while the main house was constructed of brick. This first building then became the *herrería* (smithy), where iron was smelted with the aid of bellows, and workers made all the tools they needed for construction. There are impressive locks, keys and nails on display, testimony to their fine metalworking skills. Just three Jesuit priests lived in the Residence, which was built on two floors around an enclosed patio; the lower floor was used only for storage. All the workers lived outside the *estancia*, but 310 African slaves lived on the premises in the Ranchería. They were of great importance to the Jesuits, as they were used as overseers in the ranches, and did carpentry, brickwork, and blacksmithing. In the Obraje, African women and girls learned to spin and knit. The Jesuits built canals to bring water here to the Tajamar, a large reservoir outside the *estancia*, which supplied them with the power to run a flour mill (*molino*), which was built in the wall of the reservoir; it's now ruined, but there is a good model upstairs in the Residence. There are also some original clay tiles on display here that were moulded on the thighs of the slaves.

Part of the Jesuits' evangelizing technique included using music, and their exquisite little organ can be seen here, made in the Guaraní missions further northeast. There are some fine paintings and sculptures on display, made by the local population under the supervision of the Jesuit priests – beautiful in their simplicity. Even the toilets are impressive, complete with running water to wash the waste away, half of it channelled to be used in the kitchen garden. All the wooden doors and windows are original, and the overall impression is of sophisticated organization and pleasing aesthetics. A couple of rooms are filled with 18th- and

19th-century original furniture from Liniers' family, less interesting, but evocative of the life of a Spanish Viceroy of the Río de la Plata from 1807 to 1809.

Museo Casa de Ernesto 'Che' Guevara

ⓘ *Avellaneda 501, T03547-428579. Summer daily 0900-2000, winter Mon 1400-1900, Tue-Sun 0900-1900, US$12 (US$7 for students). From the Sierras Hotel, go north along Vélez Sarsfield, which becomes Quintana, and turn left on to Avellaneda.*

Guevara's parents moved to Alta Gracia when the young revolutionary was four years' old, hoping that the dry climate here would help the boy's asthma. They lived in this pleasant middle-class neighbourhood for 12 years. Unfortunately, the museum inside his old family home is utterly disappointing and retains few relics of Guevara's upbringing. The biographical information is scant, the photographs are all photocopies and there is no intelligent thesis behind the displays. It's best to bring a biography with you, since the books on sale are in Spanish only. Cheap quality T-shirts are also on sale. For more information on 'Che', see box, page 342.

Among the limited details about his early years, you will learn that his mother educated him at home, and that asthma should have prevented him from being too athletic, but he played rugby and golf, was a keen cyclist and had a wide group of friends, among whom he was known as being fair-minded and kind to the poor. His motorcycle trips around Argentina in 1951-1952 and 1953-1956 are well documented in his own book *The Motorcycle Diaries*, which is recommended reading. There are two videos shown here, a 10-minute extract of a longer documentary, which is almost unintelligible, in Spanish with English subtitles, and a short introductory documentary, with interviews of some friends and teachers from his childhood and the family's former maid. The best photos are in the video room, unfortunately, so you'll have to scoot around them fast between screenings of the videos.

Other places in and around Alta Gracia

If you've time and energy for more museums, you might be interested in **Museo Manuel de Falla** ⓘ *Carlos Pellegrini 1001, T03547-429292, museomanueldefalla@ altagracia.gov.ar, Mon 1400-1830, Tue-Sun 0900-1830, US$2.50*, the charming home of the famous Spanish composer for the last four years of his life from 1942 to 1946. It's an attractive Spanish-style house with great views from its beautiful garden. There are concerts from April to November, and the **Festival de Falla** in November attracts some fine musicians.

There's an easy 5-km walk to **Los Paredones**, with the remains of a Jesuit mill in a rocky section of the river. To get there, follow Avenida Sarmiento to the west and cross the river, passing the bus station on your left. On the way is the **Gruta de Lourdes**, where, every 11 February, hundreds of pilgrims arrive on foot from Córdoba city. Nearby lies the **Laguna Azul**, a small lake surrounded by impressive cliffs. From Alta Gracia take Avenida Sarmiento, turn right at Vélez Sarsfield and left at Carlos Pellegrini until the end of the road, where you turn right and follow the road, passing Parque García Lorca on your left.

Some 21 km northwest of Alta Gracia is the **Observatorio Bosque Alegre** ⓘ *www. oac.uncor.edu, summer Tue-Sun 1100-1300, 1500-1900, winter Fri-Sun 1100-1300, 1500-*

1900, US$3.75, built in 1942 for astrophysics research. At 1250 m, it offers good views over Alta Gracia, Córdoba and the Sierra Grande. Visits are guided by astronomers.

Villa General Belgrano → *For listings, see pages 170-172. Colour map 4, A2.*
Phone code 03546. Population 6500.

Imagine a German theme park, Disneyland-style, with *bierkellers* and chocolate shops, carved wooden signposts and cute Alpine architecture, and you get an idea of what the centre of Villa General Belgrano is like. It's a pretty mountain town, with wooded avenues and wonderful views of the sierras beyond. It's a lovely place to spend a few days.

The town was founded in 1932 when two German immigrants bought land and sold it off through advertisements in the German newspapers, with the intention of starting a German colony. Its German character was boosted by the arrival of 155 sailors from the *Graf Spee* in 1939 (see box, page 169), many of whom later settled here. Plagues of locusts and heavy rainfall meant that the colony grew slowly at first, and so children from German schools in Buenos Aires were encouraged to come here for holidays, bringing the very first influx of tourists to the town. German is still spoken by older inhabitants, and the architecture along the main street, Avenida Julio Roca, is dominated by Swiss chalet-style buildings and German beer-houses. (Note that the street of Julio Roca changes its name to San Martín at the oval plaza, halfway along.) You can find genuine German smoked sausages and a wide variety of German breads, delicious Viennese cakes and locally brewed beer. You can even celebrate **Oktoberfest** ⓘ *www.elsitiodelavilla.com/oktoberfest*, when the town is packed with 12,000 tourists. This is not the best time of year to appreciate the town, but the **Viennese Pastry Festival** in Easter week and the **Alpine Chocolate Festival** during the July holidays are certainly worth a visit. Book accommodation in advance at these times.

The town makes a great centre for hikes in the nearby hills, with plenty of places to stay and good restaurants. The souvenir shops along the main street are crammed with Tirolean hats, beer mugs and *Graf Spee* memorabilia; however there are also fine chocolates for sale and a handicrafts market near the small oval plaza on Sundays and during the holidays.

Arriving in Villa General Belgrano
To reach Villa General Belgrano from Alta Gracia, take the new faster route via Portrero de Garay. The **tourist office** ⓘ *Av Roca 168, T03546-461215, or call T125 free from inside the town, www.vgb.org.ar, daily 0900-2100*, has friendly English- and German-speaking staff, who'll give you a great map, accommodation list and a free booklet with loads of tourist information. You can go to the top of the tower above the tourist office for amazing views of the surrounding hills. For more help with planning your visit, see www.elsitiodelavilla.com (in Spanish and German).

Walks around Villa General Belgrano
There are plenty of walks in and around the town itself; a map is available from the tourist office, ask for directions before setting off. Two rivers run through the town,

La Toma and El Sauce, and a lovely shaded area for walking has been created along their banks. You could also hike up the **Cerro de la Virgen** (one hour), the hill to the east of town. Start at Ojo de Agua, 200 m east of Avenida Julio Roca. Walk along Ojo del Agua, turn right onto the main road, Route 5, then left where signposted. It's a steep walk, but there are rewarding views. Alternatively, a lower and easier hike is up to **Cerro Mirador**, northeast of town. To get here, walk along Avenida las Magnolias, turn left on the main road and then right along Pozo Verde (one hour). From the top there are great views of the valley and the town.

La Cumbrecita and the sierra villages → For listings, see pages 170-172.
Phone code 03546.

To get right into the mountain scenery, head west from Villa General Belgrano via the tiny hamlet of **Los Reartes** with its old chapel to **La Cumbrecita**, a charming, Alpine-style village hidden away in the forested hills, where there are no cars permitted. Although crowded in summer, life here is very tranquil indeed and if you visit during spring or autumn to walk in the surrounding mountains, you'll probably have them all to yourself. It's an excellent centre for trekking or horse riding, with walks from half a day to three days, including to **Cerro Champaquí**, though this peak is better accessed from Villa Alpina (see below). There are short walks to a 14-m-high waterfall **La Cascada**, and to a small lake of crystalline water, **La Olla**, a natural pool with sandy beaches that is good for swimming. Longer walks or horse rides follow footpaths or 4WD vehicle tracks to the **Cerro Cristal**, the pools along **Río del Medio**, or for spectacular panoramic views, hike up **Cerro Wank** (1715 m), two hours return. A footpath leads south to another quaint village, Villa Alpina, but it's a six-hour walk (return) and you should take a guide. You can also go horse riding, try rappelling, or explore the area with 4WDs. Many summer visitors just come for the day, but there are plenty of places to stay and eat including *cabañas* for hire, and tasty food in chalet-style restaurants with lovely settings and great views.

Arriving in La Cumbrecita and the sierra villages
Regular minibuses go to Los Reartes, Villa Berna, La Cumbrecita, Villa Alpina, Santa Rosa and Yacanto de Calamuchita. There's a **tourist office in Cumbrecita** ① *T03546-481088*, where staff can advise on walking guides and where to get information on riding and other activities. For general information, see www.calamuchita.com, and www.lacumbrecita.gov.ar (in Spanish).

Villa Alpina and Cerro Champaquí
South of La Cumbrecita is another quaint mountain village, **Villa Alpina**, a small remote resort set in the forested upper valley of **Río de los Reartes**. On the map it looks close to La Cumbrecita, but there's no road connecting the two so the only direct way to get there is to walk, which takes three hours. By vehicle, you'll need to head back to pretty wooded Villa Berna, and from there it's 38 km west, along a poor gravel road. See www.turismocordoba.com.ar/losreartes (in Spanish), or contact **Villa Alpina's tourist office** ① *T03547-15-595163, www.villaalpinacordoba.com.ar*.

Graf Spee

The famous *Graf Spee* was a German 'pocket' battleship, successful because she was of cruiser size and speed, but with the fire power of a battleship. Early in the Second World War, in 1939, the *Graf Spee* sank nine merchant ships in the Atlantic before being cornered outside Uruguay on 13 December by three Allied cruisers sent to find and destroy her. After the 14-hour Battle of the River Plate, in which one British ship was badly damaged, the *Graf Spee's* commander, Captain Hans Langsdorff, retreated into the neutral port of Montevideo, where he landed most of his crew, and the 36 dead German crewmen were buried. Under British pressure, the Uruguayan government, which operated the neutral harbour, granted Langsdorff just two days to repair his ship, and on 17 December the *Graf Spee* sailed out to sea. Crowds lined the shore expecting to see another battle, but watched the vessel sink within minutes. All the remaining crew and 50 captured British seamen on board were rescued. Langsdorff had been trapped into believing that a superior British force was waiting for him over the horizon, and Hitler had given him the order to scuttle the vessel rather than allow it to be captured. Two days later in Buenos Aires, Langsdorff wrapped himself in the flag of the Imperial German Navy and committed suicide.

Most of the crew were interned in Argentina and warmly welcomed by the German community of Buenos Aires, but British pressure forced the Argentine government to disperse them. In Mendoza, they were stoned by the locals and beaten up by the police. In Córdoba they were welcomed by the governor, while the German embassy tried to enforce military discipline and prevent the men from getting too friendly with local women.

In 1944, the US and British governments demanded the repatriation of all the men to Germany. Nearly 200 managed to avoid this by marrying Argentine women, and another 75 escaped: after six years in Argentina, many had no wish to return to a country shattered by defeat. German communities created a distinctive culture in many areas, none more so than Villa General Belgrano in Córdoba, with its German architecture, beer festival and superb chocolate and pastries, where many members of the *Graf Spee* crew made their homes. Meanwhile the carcass of the *Graf Spee*, once visible above the sea line, has been lying on the sea floor for some six decades.

Villa Alpina is the best base for the three-day trek to **Cerro Champaquí** (2790 m), 19 km from the village. It's possible to take a 4WD almost to the summit, but the longer walk is much more rewarding for the superb mountainous scenery and the chance to meet local inhabitants as you stop at the *puestos* on the way. You'll need an all-season sleeping bag to stay in the *puestos*, and be aware that it can snow even in summer. Take a local guide to avoid getting lost. Information is available from Villa General Belgrano tourist office (see page 167), or in La Cumbrecita (see above).

There are more picturesque hilly landscapes with streams and falls close to **Yacanto de Calamuchita**, a village in the mountains, reached via Santa Rosa de Calamuchita, the largest town in this part of the valley, and a very popular, but drab resort. From Yacanto de Calamuchita you can drive almost to the summit of Cerro Champaquí, thanks to a dirt road climbing up to Cerro de los Linderos, leaving you with only a 40-minute walk. See www.villayacanto.gov.ar for planning information or call T03546-485007 (Spanish only). For access to Champaquí from the west, see page 175.

⊙ Southern Córdoba province: Calamuchita Valley listings

For hotel and restaurant price codes and other relevant information, see pages 20-26.

● Where to stay

Alta Gracia *p164*
$$$$-$$$ El Potrerillo de Larreta, on the road to Los Paredones, 3 km from Alta Gracia, T03547-423804, www.potrerillodelarreta.com. Old-fashioned, fabulous 1918 resort and country club in gorgeous gardens with wonderful views. Tennis courts, 18-hole golf course, swimming pool. Great service.
$$$ 279 Boutique Bed + Breakfast, Giorello 279, T03547-424177, www.279altagracia.com. This small, immaculate bed and breakfast is the best place to stay in town. A short stroll to the centre of town, quiet. Recommended.
$ pp Alta Gracia Hostel, Paraguay 218, T03547-428810, www.altagraciahostel.com.ar. Family-run hostel, with dorm beds, nice bathrooms and kitchen. 3 blocks from the main street. Highly recommended.

Villa General Belgrano *p167*
Many *cabaña* complexes, chalet-style hotels, often family-oriented.Book ahead Jan-Feb, Jul and Easter.
$$ La Posada de Akasha, Los Manantiales 60, T03546-462440,

www.laposadadeakasha.com. Extremely comfortable, spotless chalet-style house, with small pool, welcoming.
$ pp El Rincón, Fleming 347, T03546-461323, www.hostelelrincon.com.ar. The only hostel in town is beautifully set in dense forests and green clearings 10-min walk from bus terminal. Dorms (US$13-14), doubles or singles with bath ($ pp) and camping (US$8-9 pp). US$3.50 for superb breakfasts. HI discounts, half price for children under 16. In high season rates are higher and the hostel is usually full. 10-min walk from terminal. Recommended.

La Cumbrecita and the sierra villages *p168*
Various hotels and *cabañas*, prices **$$$-$$**.
$$ El Ceibo, T03546-481060, www.hosteriaelceibo.com. Neat rooms for 2-4, near the entrance to the town, great views, access to the river.

⊘ Restaurants

Alta Gracia *p164*
$$ Alta Gracia Golf Club, Av Carlos Pellegrini 1000, T03547-422922, www.altagraciagolf.com.ar. Superb food in elegant surroundings in this charming neighbourhood golf club, with the added advantage that you can watch the machinations of small town upper

echelons social life unfold around you. Recommended.

$ Betos, Av del Libertador 917, T03547-430996. Great value *parrilla*, plus pizzas, *empanadas* and snacks, as-much-as-you-can-eat deals including drinks and dessert.

$ Hispania, Urquiza y Mateo Beres. Excellent restaurant serving fish and seafood, including paella and *fidebua*, with sangría and occasionally gazpacho. Desserts such as *crema catalana* are fabulous.

$ Leyendas, Blvd Pellegrini 797, T03547-429 086. This American-style, sport-inspired bar has cosy nooks to sit in, and really good hamburgers and snacks. A buzzing atmosphere and friendly, welcoming staff. Recommended.

Villa General Belgrano *p167*

$$ Bierkeller, Av Las Magnolias and R5, T03546-461425. Look for the giant beer bottle outside. A chalet-style building with a welcoming family feel. Goulash and *spatzle* recommended, trout too. Slow service but the staff wear jolly Tyrolean outfits. Recommended.

$$ Blumenhaus, Roca and Bolivia, where Roca divides, T03546-462568. Touristy but with nice gardens. Pretty place to sit outside.

$ El Viejo Munich, Av San Martín 362, T03546-463122, www.cervezaartesanal. com. The first brewery in the town, serving superb beer. There are 9 different kinds of the stuff on draft (ask for 'Chopp') and legendary cold cuts of meat (*fiambres*), superb smoked meats, hams and trout, in a charming rustic Bavarian-style interior. Recommended.

$ La Casa de Dina, Los Incas 463, T03546-461040, www.lacasadedina.com. Superb cakes and fondues in this cheery and welcoming place.

$ La Posta del Arroyo, Ojo de Agua 174, T03546-461767. Smart *parrilla* that also serves such delicacies as kid and frogs. Good pastas, welcoming atmosphere.

$ Ottilia, Av San Martín y Strauss. A traditional cosy Austrian tea room. Delicious *apfelstrudel* and *kirschtorte*.

⊛ Festivals

Alta Gracia *p164*
Dec Festival de Falla.

Villa General Belgrano *p167*
Easter week Viennese Pastry Festival.
Jul Alpine Chocolate Festival.
Oct Oktoberfest, www.elsitiodelavilla. com/oktoberfest.

◑ What to do

Alta Gracia *p164*
Golf
Alta Gracia Golf Club, T03547-422922, www.altagraciagolf.com.ar. Beautifully landscaped 9-hole golf course, with a fine restaurant (see Restaurants, above).

Sky diving
Paracaidismo, Aero Club de Alta Gracia, Route C45, T0351-15-348 7628, www. paracaidismo-ag.com. Sky diving in tandem and courses

Villa General Belgrano *p167*
Cycling
Fly Machine, Av Roca 50, T03546-462425. Bike hire.

Tour operators
Alto Rumbo, www.champaqui.com.ar. Often recommended tour company that specializes in alternative tours. They run trips for beginners and also experienced climbers.

DAPA, Av Roca 74, T03546-463417, www.dapaturismo.com.ar. Day trips to La Cumbrecita and guided walks in the surroundings: Cerro Champaquí in 4WD and a 40-min walk to the summit; El Durazno or San Miguel de los Ríos.
Diego Caliari, T03546-461510, T03546-15-431046, www.champaquiadventure.com. An excellent, trained, friendly young guide who has worked extensively in Traslasierra, and who can take you hiking up Champaquí or on other walks, or arrange horse-riding trips in the area.
Friedrich, Av Roca 224, T03546-461372, www.dusseldorf.com.ar. Reliable company offering adventure tourism, 4WD hire and day trips to La Cumbrecita or Yacanto de Calamuchita. Also a 10-hr walk across Sierras Chicas along Camino de los Chilenos.
Peperinatur, Av Roca 235, T03546-461800, peperinatur@vgb.org.ar. Great company organizing treks to Champaquí and Traslasierra and trips in 4WD.

Villa Alpina and Cerro Champaquí *p168*
Climbing
For **Cerro Champaquí** (2790 m), near Villa General Belgrano, see operators like **Alto Rumbo** in Córdoba (see above), or ask at the information offices in Villa Alpina, or Villa Yacanto. **Club Andino Córdoba**, 27 de Abril 2050, Barrio Alto Alberdi, Córdoba, T0351-480 5126, www.clubandinocordoba.com.ar. Information on climbing and trekking throughout the region. It has *refugios* in the Tanti area, northwest of Villa Carlos Paz.

⊝ Transport

Alta Gracia *p164*
Bus
For **Villa General Belgrano** and other towns in Calamuchita valley, buses stop at the bus terminal and at the El Crucero roundabout, a 30-min walk from centre. To **Córdoba**, buses leave every 15 mins, 1 hr, US$2, **Empresa La Serranita** T03547-432588; **Sarmiento** T03547-432588; **Sierras de Calamuchita** T0351-422 904 (from El Crucero). To **Villa Carlos Paz**, 1 hr, US$2, **Sarmiento**. To **Villa General Belgrano**, 1 hr, US$2, **Sierras de Calamuchita**. To **Buenos Aires**, 10-11 hrs, US$52-70, **Chevallier**, T03547-425585; **Sierras Cordobesas**; **TUS**, T03547-429370; **Valle de Calamuchita**.

Car hire
Rodar Rent a Car, T03547-427164, www.autosrodar.com.ar.

Villa General Belgrano *p167*
Bus
To **Córdoba**, 1½-2hrs, US$2.50, **La Villa**; **Lep**; **Pájaro Blanco**; **Sierras de Calamuchita**. To **Buenos Aires**, 10-11 hrs, US$50-57, **Chevallier**, **Sierras Cordobesas**, **TUS**, **Valle de Calamuchita**; to **La Cumbrecita**, every 2-4 hrs, 1 hr 20 mins, US$10 return **Pájaro Blanco**, Av San Martín 105, T03546-461709; also goes to the nearby villages of **Los Reartes**, **Villa Berna**, **Villa Alpina** and **Yacanto de Calamuchita**.

Remise taxi
Central de Remises, Ojo de Agua 33, T03546-462000.

La Cumbrecita and the sierra villages *p168*
Bus
Reliable daily bus service to **Córdoba city**, 2½ hrs, US$5; from **Villa General Belgrano**, 1½ hrs, US$3).

Traslasierra Valley

Situated west of the Sierra Grande, Traslasierra (literally, 'across the mountains') is far less developed for tourism than neighbouring valleys, but ideal for those looking for an adventure. With its drier climate and generally slower pace of life, it's also a perfect place to relax for a few days. It can be accessed from Córdoba city by the Camino de las Altas Cumbres ('Route of the high peaks'; see below); from the north, via the long but not uninteresting Route 15 across the Pampa de Pocho; or from San Luis province in the south, via Villa Dolores. See www.valledetraslasierra.com.ar and www.turismotraslasierra.com.ar (in Spanish).

Camino de las Altas Cumbres → *For listings, see pages 175-178. Phone code 03544.*

The main road (Route 20) to the Traslasierra Valley from Córdoba is the most spectacular route in the sierras. Running southwest from Villa Carlos Paz, the road passes Villa Icho Cruz before climbing into the Sierra Grande and crossing the Pampa de Achala, a huge granite plateau at 2000 m, and descending into the Traslasierra valley near Mina Clavero. This road provides access to the Parque Nacional Quebrada del Condorito, where condors can be seen circling in a spectacular gorge (see box, page 176).

Mina Clavero, is probably too busy if you've come to escape the crowds, but it is really picturesque. Further south lie Nono, Los Hornillos and San Javier which are quieter and just as pretty. They all make great bases for hiking.

Mina Clavero → *Colour map 4, A2. Phone code 03544. Population 6800.*

Mina Clavero (915 m) has the best nightlife and most raucous atmosphere in the entire valley (during school holidays), with nightclubs, theatres, a casino and dozens of hotels, restaurants and small shops. It's a good base for trips into the surrounding natural beauty. It lies at the foot of the **Camino de las Altas Cumbres** and at the confluence of the Río Panaholma and Río Mina Clavero, which form many small falls among impressive rocks right in the town centre, and there are attractive views along the riverside. The large **tourist office** ⓘ *next to the intersection of Av San Martín and Av Mitre at Plazoleta Merlo, T03544-470171, www.minaclavero.gov.ar, daily 0800-2200,* has an ATM. The bus terminal can be found in the centre at Avenida Mitre 1191.

On the other side of the rivers is the quieter **Villa Cura Brochero**, named after Father Brochero who built schools, roads and aqueducts here at the end of the 19th century. Every March, around the 20th, he is remembered with the *Cabalgatas brocherianas*, a gaucho procession on horses and mules that follows a section of the former road he helped to build across the mountains.

Around Mina Clavero

Nearby rivers offer several attractive places for swimming among huge rocks and waterfalls, all busy in high season. About 5 km north of Villa Cura Brochero, a dirt road passing San Lorenzo branches east to the **Cascada de Toro Muerto**, where icy water falls into a 7-m-deep pool. The *balneario* (bathing area) serves very good meals.

Las Maravillas, a *balneario* set in a deep ravine, is 4 km north of San Lorenzo, and it's another 7 km to the hamlet of Panaholma with its old chapel. The **Camino de los Artesanos** is an 18-km stretch of road from Mina Clavero to Villa Benegas along which a dozen families offer hand-woven handicrafts and distinctive black ceramics.

North of Villa Cura Brochero, Route 15 crosses the vast **Pampa de Pocho**, a strange landscape covered by palm trees, with small inactive volcanoes in the background. At Taninga, Route 28 branches off east across the Sierra Grande and the northern edge of Reserva Hídrica Pampa de Achala to Villa Carlos Paz.

Nono and around → *Colour map 4, A2. Phone code 03544. Altitude 900 m.*

Nono, 8 km south of Mina Clavero, is an attractive little town. On the plaza there is a handicraft market in summer and a lovely little church. Among other well-conserved houses is the historic **Casa Uez**, which serves as a shop, café and basic hotel, and has been the lively meeting point for locals since 1931. For information on the town and surroundings, visit the **tourist office** ① *T03544-498332, www.nonoturismo.gob. ar, daily 0900-1500, 1600-2200, and* see www.traslasierra.com/nono and www.nono-cordoba.com (in Spanish) for planning advice.

The most visited sight is the extraordinary **Museo Rocsen** ① *5 km east, following Av Los Porteños, T03544-498065, www.museorocsen.org, daily 0900 till sunset, US$5*. This eclectic selection of fabulously bizarre objects spanning archaeology, anthropology and human history is the personal vision of Frenchman Juan Santiago Bouchon. Not to be missed.

A network of minor roads east and southeast link the town with the foot of the mountains across a pretty landscape of rivers and hamlets, such as **Paso de las Tropas** and and **El Huayco**. To the west, a dusty road leads from the church to the sandy beaches of **Río Los Sauces** and 11 km beyond to the village of **Piedras Blancas**. Cerro Champaquí is accessible from Nono (via San Javier) but you need to take a guide.

Nono to Villa Dolores

South of Nono, the road skirts the base of some imposing mountains amid lush vegetation and there are scattered villages offering some accommodation. At Los Hornillos (15 km from Nono) there are good walks 500 m east of the road (left of campsite), along Río Los Hornillos. From there, footpaths lead to the nearby summits, such as the five-hour trek to **La Ventana** (2300 m) passing a 50-m fall halfway. A 1½-hour walk upstream along the riverbed takes you to **Piedra Encajada**, a huge rock with waterfalls. Ten kilometres northwest is **Dique La Viña** with a large reservoir and an impressive 106-m-high dam, not recommended for vertigo sufferers.

West of the sierras the main town is **Villa Dolores**, a useful transport hub, with a couple of banks and a few hotels, though there's no reason to stop here, unless you're keen to see the potato festival in January. There's an informative **tourist office** ① *T03544-499019*, at the bus station. For more, see www.villadolores.gov.ar.

San Javier and Yacanto → *Phone code 03544.*

These neighbouring villages lie at the foot of the **Cerro Champaquí** (2790 m), the highest peak in the sierras. They are both very pleasant, peaceful places to stay, with old houses under mature trees, and even if you're not keen to climb the peak itself, you could relax by the streams or stroll around the picturesque area. The ascent of Champaquí takes about seven hours from San Javier along the Quebrada del Tigre, but take a guide, as many people get lost. For more information, contact the **Municipalidad** ① *T03544-482041, www.sanjavieronline.com.ar.* For access to Champaquí from the east, see page 170.

Further south there are more small resort towns where tourism is developing, such as **La Población**, **Luyaba**, **La Paz**, **Luyaba**, **La Paz** and nearby **Loma Bola**, which lie along the road to Merlo, 42 km of San Javier.

ⓦ Traslasierra Valley listings

For hotel and restaurant price codes and other relevant information, see pages 20-26.

● Where to stay

Mina Clavero *p173*
Several close in low season.

$ pp Hostel Andamundos, San Martín 554, T03544-470249, www.andamundos hostel.com.ar. Doubles **$$**, dorms US$13-17. Centrally located, well-maintained and bright, great atmosphere, HI discount. They can organize local excursions.

$ pp Oh La La!! Hostel, Villanueva 1192, T03544-472634, www.ohlalahostel. com.ar. Youth hostel (double rooms **$$**), shared bathrooms, tourist information, pool and gardens.

Nono and around *p174*
Several family houses next to the plaza have signs offering rooms for rent by the day. See www.traslasierra-nono.com.ar for a full list.

$$$ Gran Hotel Nono, Vicente Castro 289, T03544-498022, www.granhotel

nono.com.ar. On the riverside with views of the sierras and surrounded by a large and leafy park with a pool and tennis courts, this is a comfortable and welcoming place with rustic decor. It has a restaurant, and breakfast is included (lots of fruit). Rates are for half-board in high season (**$$$$**).

$$$ La Lejanía, T03544-15585476, www.lalejania.com. Lovely little house surrounded by 1000 ha of wilderness. Great swimming pool, tennis courts and a fantastic breakfast.

$$$-$$ La Gloria, on the way to Museo Rocsen, 800 m from Calle Sarmiento, T03544-498231, www.hostal-lagloria. com.ar. On the rural outskirts set in 5 ha of park, this old house has comfortable though not luxurious rooms in a relaxed atmosphere. It also has *cabañas*, a pool and access to the river. Delicious breakfast included.

Camping
A road to the left of the church goes west to the river where there are

Parque Nacional Quebrada del Condorito

Covering 37,000 ha of the Pampa de Achala and the surrounding slopes at altitudes of between 1900 and 2300 m, the park was created in 1996 to protect the central section of Córdoba's sierras, including the spectacular Quebrada del Condorito. This 800-m-deep gorge is the easternmost habitat of the condor. Since you're at the same level as the top of the gorge, it's possible to see fledgling birds taking their first flying lessons. Though condors are elusive and sightings are not guaranteed, you may be lucky enough to see them take a bath under the waterfalls. There's great trekking on the *pastizal de altura* (high-altitude grassland), which is the most southerly habitat of rare tabaquillo trees. The landscapes are superb and the climate is subtropical but you should take a warm jacket.

The only accessible section of the park is its northeast corner, reached by a short walk from La Pampilla (well signposted), on Route 34, 55 km southwest of Villa Carlos Paz. It takes about three hours to get to the first vantage point (Balcón Norte) and two more hours to the Balcón Sur, by crossing the Río de los Condoritos. Tours are available from Villa Carlos Paz.

Accommodation La Posta del Qenti, 19 km west of La Pampilla, T03541 495 715, www.qenti.com.ar. This is a pricey but comfortable resort at 2300 m offering rooms and dorms together with spa packages and outdoor activities. Book in advance, and ask about full-board promotional offers.

There are three camping areas with no facilities, along the path to Balcón Norte and Balcón Sur.

Transport Ciudad de Córdoba and TAC buses will both stop at La Pampilla on their way from Villa Carlos Paz to Mina Clavero (one hour). If you go with your own vehicle, you can park in front of the Visitors' Centre.

Park information There's a national park administration office in Villa Carlos Paz at Resistencia 30 Sabattini 33, office 2, T3541-433371/486287. For an excellent guide for trekking and horse riding, contact Diego Caliari T03546-461510/15475576, dfcaliari@yahoo.com.ar. For further information, see www.condoritoapn.com.ar (in Spanish).

3 sites. Next to the *cabañas* of **Los Canadienses**, T03544-498861, www.loscanadienses.com.ar, is **La Rueda**, www.campinglarueda.com.ar, a shady place with bathrooms and electricity supply. Open high season only.

Nono to Villa Dolores *p174*
$$$ **Alta Montaña**, Los Hornillos, 300 m east of road to the mountains (signposted), T03544-499009, www.hosteriaaltamontania.com. The Von Ledebur family has run this lovely hotel on 8 ha of virgin land by the river since 1947. Neat, comfortable rooms have splendid views of the grounds and the sierras. Pool and restaurant; rates are for half board in high season. Recommended.

San Javier and Yacanto *p175*
$$$-$$ **Yacanto**, T03544-482002, www.hotelyacanto.com.ar. A traditional 1920s hotel with comfortable rooms

and a beautifully situated 9-hole golf course. Price depends on season; only half-board offered.

🍴 Restaurants

Mina Clavero *p173*
$$ Rincón Suizo, down by the river, on Calle Recalde, 1 block off Av San Martín, www.rinconsuizo.com.ar. This is an unmissable treat. It's basically a cosy tea room serving rich strudel or chocolate cakes.

Nono and around *p174*
$$ La Casona de Nono, Sarmiento 302. Not very attractive, but offers *pollo al disco* (grilled chicken) and *humita* as its specialities.
$$ La Pulpería de Gonzalo, on the plaza, opposite the church. Alfresco dining in the wonderful, romantically lit patio. *Parrilla* dishes are the speciality, but fish is also recommended.

⏰ What to do

Nono and around *p174*
Traslahuella, Sarmiento 392, T03544-498084, traslahuella@yahoo.com.ar. Local guide Martín Zalazar runs ½-day guided treks and mountain-bike tours along the river and to the nearby mountains. Also available is a day walk to the summit of Cerro Champaquí. Mountain bikes can be hired.

🚌 Transport

Mina Clavero *p173*
Bus
To **Córdoba**, **Ciudad de Córdoba** via Altas Cumbres, 3 hrs, US$4, or via Cruz del Eje, 6 hrs, US$6; and **TAC** (stopping at villages in **Pampa de Pocho**), 6 hrs, US$6. To **Buenos Aires**, 12 hrs, US$80-95, **Chevallier**, **Expreso del Oeste**, **TAC**; to **Mendoza**, 9 hrs, US$40-50, **Andesmar**; to **Merlo**, 2 hrs, US$8.50, **Expreso del Oeste**, **Monticas**. Minibuses go to **Villa Cura Brochero** and south to **Nono** and **Villa Dolores**, calling at villages in between, including Los Hornillos. **Panaholma** and **Sierra Bus** go direct to **Villa Dolores**, 45 mins, US$2.50; and **Córdoba**, 3 hrs, US$3. **TAC** buses go to **Panaholma** and some villages in the **Pampa de Pocho**. Other nearby places are only accessible with own vehicle or with a *remise* taxi. No buses go along the Camino de los Túneles, only tour operators.

Nono and around *p174*
Bus
Expreso del Oeste to **Villa Dolores**, 50 mins, US$2; or up to **Villa Cura Brochero**, 15 mins, US$2.

Remise taxis
Tele Taxi, Sarmiento 94, T03544-498115.

San Luis province

The province of San Luis has always been considered Córdoba's poorer sister: it's further from Buenos Aires; its provincial capital lacks the grandeur of its neighbour, and it's not popular with tourists, apart from the overvisited resort town of Merlo on the border. However, it has a spectacular national park, Sierra de las Quijadas, with a great red sandstone canyon and fossil-strewn lunar landscape, and you can still find remote places where rural life is sleepy and traditional.

San Luis city → *For listings, see pages 182-185. Colour map 4, B2.*

The city of San Luis was founded in 1594, but it wasn't until the late 19th century that it really started to grow, with a flood of European immigration. There was further development in the 1980s when tax incentives encouraged industry to the area. The result is a modern city with a few colonial buildings, but little to attract visitors. However, it is a friendly place with decent accommodation and food, and is a good starting point for exploring the Sierras de San Luis and the Parque Nacional Sierra de las Quijadas.

Arriving in San Luis city → *Phone code 02652. Population 169,947.*
The **airport** ① *T0266-442 2427*, is 3 km northwest from town. Access the airport via Colón, Avenida Justo Daract and Sargento Baigorria. Ordinary and *remise* taxis charge about US$3 to the centre. The **bus terminal** ① *Av España 990, T02652-424021*, is a triangular-shaped building with offices and bus stops on all sides. To reach the city centre, take Rivadavia. There is left luggage at Kiosko Portos (facing the University), which is open 24 hours. At the corner of Avenida Illia and Junín, the large **tourist office** ① *T02652-4423957*, has little information; see www.sanluisturismo.com.ar and www.infosanluis.com.ar for more information.

Places in San Luis city
The centre of the city is the attractive, leafy **Plaza Pringles**, filled with beautiful jacarandas and palm trees and thronging with young crowds after sunset. It's worth popping into the **cathedral** ① *daily 0730-1300, 1830-2130*, with its slender towers and sumptuous interior, to see replicas of famous Murillo paintings and an extraordinary *pesebre electrónico* – a personal vision of the birth of Christ, with moving figures to the accompaniment of Beethoven's *Ninth Symphony* and Scottish pipes: kitsch and marvellous. Northwest of the plaza, there's a magnificent, decaying former railway station.

For hotels and bars, stroll along Avenida Illia, which becomes very lively at night. There's a tiny **Museo de Historia Natural** ①*university campus, Italia y Ejército de los Andes, T02652-426744 (ext 290), museo.unsl.edu.ar; Tue-Sun 0900-1300, US$0.10*, which traces the evolution of San Luis, including the fossil of an alarming giant spider and a dinosaur footprint. The main commercial heart of the city is on Rivadavia, and three blocks away there's the quieter Plaza Independencia, with its extraordinary Moorish Dominican temple, with a Moorish façade. There is a handicraft market: **Centro Artesanal San Martín de Porres** ①*25 de Mayo 955, T02652-424222, Mon-Fri 0800-1300.*

Sierras de San Luis → *For listings, see pages 182-185.*

Northeast of the city, the Sierras de San Luis are a beautiful range of hills that remain little known to travellers, with just two frequently visited resorts, the small town of El Trapiche and the reservoir in La Florida. The rest of this vast hilly region is sparsely inhabited, with quiet villages that maintain old rural traditions and a simple way of life. The eastern edge of the sierras and the upper valleys and high Pampas around Carolina can be visited by taking Route 9 north from San Luis. Regular buses go up to Carolina and Intihuasi.

El Trapiche → *Phone code 02651.*
At Km 40, El Trapiche is an attractive village set on the Río Trapiche in wooded hills. There are summer homes, hotels and picnic sites, and some good easy walks to **Los Siete Cajones**, on the sparkling waters of Río Grande, and 6 km west, to the pleasant surroundings of the rivers **Virorco** and **Virorco** and **De las Aguilas**.

Carolina → *Colour map 4, A2. Phone code 02651. Population 200.*
Carolina is a former gold-mining town founded in 1792 at the foot of Cerro Tomolasta (2018 m), which offers great views from its summit. It's a picturesque village with stone houses and a gold mine, which can be visited through San Luis tour operators (see page 184). The local **Huellas agency** ① *16 de Julio and El Minero, T02651-490224, www.huellasturismo.com.ar*, dresses you up as a miner and guides you along a 300-m tunnel for about 1½ hours (English spoken), and provides tools in case you suddenly feel the desire to dig. From Carolina a rough track leads north over the Cuesta Larga to San Francisco del Monte de Oro, on Route 146. Two other roads in better condition cross attractive scenery of undulating Pampas and volcanic peaks to Libertador General San Martín or to La Toma. **Tourist information** is available in the **Municipalidad** ① *16 de Julio s/n, T02651-490214, www.slcarolina.com.ar.*

Eastern San Luis → *For listings, see pages 182-185.*

Villa Mercedes → *Colour map 4, B2. Phone code 02657. Population 90,000.*
Founded in 1856 as a fortress, Villa Mercedes is an important intersection and alternative transport hub, though it's of little of interest to the tourist. It lies on

Parque Nacional Sierra de Las Quijadas → *Phone code: 02652*

Situated 125 km northwest of San Luis in the northwestern corner of the province, the park covers 150,000 ha of wonderful scenery in one of the hottest and most arid areas of Argentina. Its only accessible area, **Potrero de la Aguada**, is an immense natural amphitheatre of nearly 4000 ha, surrounded by steep red sandstone walls, eroded into strange shapes. There's a small archaeological site next to the access road, and the fossil-rich field of Loma del Pterodaustro shows intriguing evidence of dinosaurs and pterosaurs (winged reptiles). The vegetation is largely scrub; *jarillas* are very common, though there are also trees, such as the *quebracho blanco*. Wildlife includes guanaco, collared peccaries, pumas, tortoises, crowned eagles, peregrine falcons and condors.

Near the park warden's office is **Mirador de Elda**, the first of the two vantage points on the Potrero. From here two optional footpaths go to **Mirador Superior** (an easy 45-minute return) or down to the *huella* (a more demanding two-hour return walk to a dinosaur footprint). This path also leads to the impressive cliffs of **Farallones**, reached by a five-hour return walk and only advisable well after midday.

Tours and access Open from dawn till dusk. Visit early in the morning or late afternoon for the best views and to avoid the heat. To get there, take the 8-km unpaved road that turns off from Route 147 (San Luis to San Juan) at Hualtarán. There are a few companies with daily services that link San Luis and San Juan, the two main ones are **Autotransportes San Juan** and **Del Sur y Media Agua** both stop at Hualtarán.

Tour operators in San Luis and Merlo run half- or full-day tours to the park. Entry costs US$10.

Accommodation Luxury cottages at **Complejo La Aguada**, T02652-15-650245, www.laaguada.com. Price ($$$$) includes all meals and activities. The only site for camping (free) is 100 m from the park warden's office, next to a basic canteen.

Further information T02652-490182, www.parquesnacionales.gov.ar (in Spanish).

Route 7, 100 km southeast of San Luis. Accommodation is mainly found along Avenida Mitre (six blocks east of the bus terminal). The **bus terminal** ⓘ *T02657-428035*, and **tourist office** are both at Avenida 25 de Mayo 1500. Villa Mercedes is also the gateway to the southern plains, which are dotted with dozens of small lakes that are attractive for anglers. *Pejerrey* is the main catch and the fishing season runs from November to August. Accommodation is available at local *estancias* (ask at the tourist office). For more, see www.villamercedes.gov.ar (in Spanish).

Conlara Valley → *Phone code 02656. Population 90,000.*

Lying east of the Sierra de San Luis and west of the Sierra de Comechingones, this broad valley runs into the Traslasierra Valley to the north, with a number of attractive places to visit and stay. **San José del Morro** has an 18th-century chapel in its blissfully traditional village. Nearby, the **Sierra del Morro** (1639 m) is the remains of a collapsed volcano; inside its crater are small volcanic cones, and lots of rose quartz can be found here (access through Estancia La Morena). On 3 May, at tiny **Renca**, one of the most popular religious festivities in the region, El Señor de Renca, is celebrated. **Santa Rosa del Conlara** is a pleasant small town by a river, a good alternative for accommodation when Merlo is packed (reached by bus or *combi* from San Luis). A more scenic journey is via Provincial Route 1, which runs parallel to the east of Route 148 along the base of the Sierra de Comechingones through a string of pretty villages: **Papagayos**, surrounded by natural palm tree groves of *Trithrinax campestris*; **Villa Larca**, where the waterfall **Chorro de San Ignacio** and upper natural pools offer lovely walks; **Cortaderas; Carpintería,** and up to the well-promoted Merlo.

Merlo → *Colour map 4, A2. Phone code 02656. Population 11,000.*

Situated almost at the San Luis-Córdoba border, Merlo is a popular holiday centre on the steep western slopes of the Sierra de Comechingones. It has lost much of its charm in recent years, due to mass tourism, which has made it busy and overpriced. It claims to have a special microclimate, and sunny days can certainly be enjoyed throughout the year. The town was founded in 1797, but the **church** on the plaza, said to be of Jesuit origin, dates from the early 18th century, and is soon to be replaced by the huge new red-brick church behind. There's a modern airport ① *T02656-481180*, on Route 148, 23 km west of Merlo and a **bus terminal** on Route 1, next to the roundabout (10-minutes' walk from the plaza) and two **tourist offices** ① *at the roundabout on R5 and R1; and next to the plaza at Coronel Mercau 605, T02656-476079, www.lavillademerlo.com.ar, www.turismo-merlo.com.ar.*

Merlo's surroundings at the foot of the mountains are pleasant for walking or you can hike to their summits (the **Circuito de Damiana Vega** takes three to four hours). The slopes are covered with woods and scrub and there are numerous refreshing streams with falls. Higher up there are some excellent sites for paragliding; an experienced pilot recently reached heights of 5000 m. A paved road (15 km long) leads to the top of the sierras at **Mirador del Sol**, where there are wonderful panoramic views, best at sunrise or sunset. The mirador is accessible by bus and is the starting point for a rough track leading across 82 km of Pampas and Sierras de Córdoba to Embalse del Río Tercero.

Quieter places to stay are spread in the neighbouring small settlements of **Piedra Blanca** (4 km north) or **Rincón del Este** (4 km east), but book ahead in high season.

San Luis province listings

For hotel and restaurant price codes and other relevant information, see pages 20-26.

Where to stay

San Luis city *p178*
For more listings, see www.sanluisturistico.com.ar.
$$$ Vista Suites & Spa, Av Pte Illia 526, T0266-444 6380, www.vistasuites. com.ar. Stunning hotel with a lovely view from the rooftop pool. Stylish, modern rooms (suites cost up to **$$$$**). Great bar and restaurant.
$$$ Hotel Quitana, Av Pte Illia 546, T0266-443 8400, www.hotelquintana. com.ar. 6 floors and 84 rooms make this hotel one of San Luis' biggest. The rooms are a little dated but the staff are friendly and the location is great.
$$ Belgrano, Belgrano 1440, T0266-443 5923. This is probably the best budget hotel, with welcoming staff, renovated rooms with fan and bath, and breakfast included.

Hostel
$ pp San Luis Hostel, Falucho 646, T0266-442 4188, www.sanluishostel.com.ar. Large, welcoming gardens, basic dorms and slightly old-fashioned furniture, new double and family rooms. Central, but take a taxi from the bus station.

Around San Luis *p179*
$$$$-$$$ Hotel Potrero de los Funes, R18, Km 16, T0266-444 0038, www. hotelpotrero.sanluis.gov.ar. Set in a mountainous area, this impressive lakeside resort offers affordable rooms, some with splendid views (slightly pricier). A pool and sport facilities are included (also ATM), as well as a large breakfast.

$$$-$$ Campo La Sierra, 19 km east of San Luis (access via R20), T0266-449 4171, www.campolasierra.com.ar. A warm welcome at this 70-ha farm with native flora (cacti experts visit annually). Self-contained units, German-style cooking, breakfast, pool, archery, German and Spanish lessons, English also spoken.
$$$-$$ Los Tamarindos, Balde, T0266-444 2220, www.jardinesdetamarindos. com. Rates at this attractive spa resort include breakfast and rooms with a/c in small flats for up to 6; there are both indoor and outdoor pools accessible to non-guests for US$6.25 per person.

El Trapiche *p179*
$$$ Villa Alinor, T02692-493038. Price is per house. A group of small houses at a most attractive location on a natural rocky balcony next to the river. Each house sleeps 4-6 with kitchen, fridge and phone; bedlinen and towels extra.
$ pp Hosteria El Parque, Av San Martin s/n, T02652-493076. A family-orientated hotel with full- or half-board accommodation; children under 5 free.

Estancias
$$$ Estancia Altos del Durazno, 10 km west of El Trapiche, Ruta Provincial 18, El Durazno Alto, Estancia Grande, T0266-15-426 5151, http://altosdeldurazno. tripod.com. Individual stone cottages with wooden furniture and kitchen, sleep 2-5, breakfast is brought to your cottage, airport or bus station transfer available. Horse-riding tours, trekking, a peaceful place in lovely countryside.

Carolina *p179*
$$$ Hostería Las Verbenas, 10 km south of Carolina, T0266-4430918,

www.lasverbenas.com.ar. Situated in the beautiful Pancanta Valley, this is an ideal base for walking and horse riding or for enjoying a relaxing stay. Price is for full board.
$$ La Posta del Caminante, R9, Km 0.83, T0266-445 2000, www.lapostadel caminante.com. Housed in a former residence for mining engineers. Offers comfortable rooms with bath and breakfast (cheaper with shared bath), pool in natural setting, and has a small restaurant next door. Walks to the mines and horse-riding excursions are also arranged.

Conlara Valley *p180*
$$ Hotel Río Conlara, Rivadavia and San José, T02656-492012, www.hotelrio conlara.com.ar. Next to a nicely maintained *balneario*, where the river was dammed, this place has clean, comfortable rooms. Breakfast included.

Merlo *p181*
Book in advance for high season: Jan and Feb, Easter, Jul and Aug. See www.turismo-merlo.com.ar and www. lavillademerlo.com.ar for more listings.
$$$$-$$$ Altos del Sol, Andrada and Borges, T02656-478399, www.altosdelsol. com. Charming *cabañas* set above town with endless views. For 2-7 people, nice rooms and a pool.
$$$ La Quinta Resorts, Román Gonzáles s/n, Piedra Blanca, T02656-479598, www.laquintaresort.net. Huge complex with a jacuzzi, pool and tennis courts just outside town. Lovely cabins, stylishly decorated.
$$$ Rincón de los Troncos, Av José Percau 164, T02656-476768, www. rincondelostroncos.com.ar. Huge rustic but comfortable cabins for 2-6 people. Wonderful alpine wood and stone building within tranquil grounds and

2 large pools, only a short distance to the centre of town. Often recommended.
$$$ Colonial Villa de Merlo, Pedernera and Av del Sol, T02656-475335, www. hotelvillademerlo.com.ar. Comfortable rooms with splendid views of the sierras and a large garden with pool. There are sport facilities, though the quiet atmosphere of this rather exclusive 3-star hotel is more appealing for a relaxing holiday. Moderately priced restaurant.
$$$-$$ Colonial, Av Dos Venados y P Tisera, T02656-475751, www.hchosteria colonial.com.ar. Probably the best value, in a quiet residential area not far from the centre. This attractive, neocolonial building has simple rooms on a patio with an incredibly small pool. Breakfast is included, internet access available for a fee.

Camping
Las Violetas, Chumamaya and Av Dos Venados, T02656-475730, lasvioletas@ merlo-sl.com.ar. The closest site to the centre has a small shady area for tents, a pool, canteen, grocery shop and clean but not spotless bathrooms, US$12.50

⑦ Restaurants

San Luis city *p178*
Chivito (kid) is the main local dish. Its usual accompaniment is *chanfaina* (a stew whose main ingredients are the goat's entrails).
$$ La Porteña, Junín y General Paz, T02652-443 1722. Simple meals such as the *plato del día*. Prepare for enormous portions in the enjoyable atmosphere of this popular place.
$ Crocantes, San Martín 630. A bakery where cheap and superb sandwiches are prepared at your request and with your chosen bread.

$ Grand Palace, Illia 470. At the hotel of the same name, the experienced chef Pedro Pardo offers a selection of very good dishes based on grilled meats, fish or pork, with scrumptious home-made desserts.

$ La Pulpería del Arriero, 9 de Julio 753, T0266-443 2446. With tasty regional specialities and live folk music in the evenings, this is the place for trying *empanadas* or *asado* during a lively night out. The set menus are good value.

$ Los Robles, Colón 684, T0266-443 6767. Formal atmosphere and very good food, you can eat at moderate prices at this smart *parrilla*. There is a wide choice of dishes (*bife de chorizo* is great), including *chivito* and trout. Recommended.

Cafés and bars

There's a cluster spread along Av Illia and Rivadavia between blocks 0800 and 1000. During the day, 2 enjoyable cafés on the plaza are **Aranjuez** and **Ocean**.

Merlo *p181*

$$ El Ciprés, Av del Ciprés 114. Popular with the locals. Good, filling meals are guaranteed though the menu is pretty standard.

$$ El Establo, Av del Sol 450. Handsome *parrilla*, where the grill or *asador* is strangely trapped in a glass enclosure. Try *chivito* here.

$$ La Vieja Posada, Av del Sol 2. A simple place with more than 30 different pizzas and a folk music show on Sat evenings.

$ La Estrella de Merlo, Becerra y Av del Sol. Locals come here for tasty home-made pastas.

⊛ Festivals

San Luis province *p178*

1-3 May Cristo de la Quebrada. This popular religious festival takes place at Villa de la Quebrada.

⊙ What to do

San Luis city *p178*

All agencies offer similar tours at standard rates (rates in leaflets usually do not include fees to national parks). A ½-day tour to Sierra de las Quijadas is the most popular and includes a walk to Los Miradores (1-1½ hrs) and to La Huella (2-2½ hrs). Weather permitting (usually not in summer), a more demanding walk to Los Farallones (4-5 hrs) is organized. The Circuito Serrano Chico is a short walk around El Volcán, Potrero de los Funes and the town itself, while the Circuito Serrano Grande adds El Trapiche and La Florida. Circuito de Oro goes up to Carolina and Intihuasi and may include the Circuitos Serranos. There are also tours to religious sites in Suyuque and Villa de la Quebrada, and to the hot springs of Balde and the salt flats in Salinas del Bebedero. A day trip to Merlo via La Toma is also available.

Bruno Aliberti, T02652-426021, T02652-15-502971, Bruno_aliberti@hotmail.com, guide only, for those with their own vehicle. **Dasso**, Rivadavia 540, T02652-421017, T02652-15-645410. **Gimatur**, Av Illia y Caseros, T02652-435751, gimatursl@hotmail.com, English spoken. **Luciano Franchi**, Chile 1430, T02652-420345, T02652-15-657441.

Merlo *p181*
Tour operators

Excursions to local sights and provincial attractions are provided, including full-day tours to Sierra de las Quijadas. Closer destinations include ½-day trips to Mina Los Cóndores and to Bajo de Véliz, an over-promoted palaeontological site, where giant spiders used to live millions of years ago. Surrounding villages may also be explored for a few hours.

More unusual activities such as visiting a remote ghost mining town, sleeping in caves or crossing rivers are offered by **Cimarrón Incursiones**, Av del Sol 300, T02656-478934, and **Los Tabaquillos**, Av de los Césares 2100, T02656-474010.

☉ Transport

San Luis city *p178*
Air
For airport information, see page 178. Flights to **Buenos Aires**, 1¼ hrs, **CATA** (from Merlo), Av España 950, T02652-439156.

Bus
For bus terminal information, see page 178. Check at office where your bus leaves from.

To **Buenos Aires**, 10-11 hrs, US$55-65, several companies. To **Mendoza**, 3-4 hrs, US$21, several companies. To **Córdoba**, 6-7 hrs, US$35, several companies. To **San Juan**, 4 hrs, US$14, several companies. To **Santa Rosa** (La Pampa), 10 hrs, US$35, **Dumas**; also to destinations in southern San Luis. To **Merlo**, 3 hrs, US$7, **Automotores Merlo** (packed minibuses); **Expreso Uspallata**; **SENA**; **TAC**. To **Balde** and **Salinas del Bebedero**, 2 daily Mon-Fri, 45 mins, US$0.50; and 1 hr, US$1, with **Dasso**. To **El Trapiche**, US$1, **María del Rosario**, **San José**; same services go to La Florida and Río Grande. To **Carolina** and **Intihuasi**, **Polos**, 3 daily (unreliable timetable), US$2 and US$2.50.

Car hire
Budget, Belgrano 1440, T02652-440288; **Travel**, Chacabuco 649, T02652-438500, www.travelrentacar.com.ar.

Remise taxis
Cosmos, Chacabuco 1151, T02652-440000; **Zoo**, Bolívar y Falucho, T02652-421000.

Merlo *p181*
Air
To **Buenos Aires via San Luis**, 1 hr 50 mins, **CATA**, desk at tourist office (at Merlo roundabout), T02656-478460.

Bus
Frequent services to **San Luis**, 3 hrs, US$7, **several companies**. To **Buenos Aires**, US$63-84, 10-12 hrs, **several companies**. To **Córdoba**, 5 hrs, US$19, **Andesmar**; **Expreso Uspallata**; **Monticas**. To **Mina Clavero**, 2 hrs, US$5, **Expreso del Oeste**; **Monticas**. To **Villa Dolores**, 2 hrs, US$2 (via San Javier); or 1 hr, US$3 (via R148), **Sierras Cordobesas**. **La Costa** goes daily along R1 to Cortaderas, Villa Larca and Papagayos. **STU** runs frequent services to **Mirador del Sol**, stopping there for 10 mins, US$2.50 return.

Remise taxis
Avenida, Becerra 575, T02656-476031; **Unión**, Videla 114, T02656-478444.

☉ Directory

San Luis city *p178*
Banks Banex, Rivadavia and Pringles. **Currency exchange** Banco de Galicia, Colón and Pringles; **Montemar**, Belgrano 980. **Post office** San Martín y Av Illia, offers Western Union services.

Contents

Footprint features

Border crossings

Mendoza & the West

At a glance

☺ **Getting around** The local buses are the best way to get around, but a bicycle can be a great way to see the wineries.

⏱ **Time required** At least 4-5 days to explore the city and wineries.

☁ **Weather** Mild summers (Dec-Mar), but winters (May-Aug) can be cold and windy.

✖ **When not to go** From May-Aug it can be particularly cold, with harsh winds coming down off the Andes. Some hotels and tour operators close during this time.

★ **Don't miss ...**
1 Mendoza's fine wineries, page 196.
2 Aconcagua Provincial Park, page 210.
3 Las Leñas, page 221.
4 La Payunia Reserve, page 222.
5 Parque Provincial Ischigualasto, page 230.

Argentina's west is wild and largely unvisited, despite having one of the country's most stylish and vibrant cities at its heart. Mendoza is the centre of the biggest wine-producing region in Argentina, and with plenty of fine restaurants and a beautiful setting at the foothills of the Andes, it's a great base for exploring the surrounding vineyards for a few days. The secret to Argentina's successful wine industry is the climate: hot days and cool nights, and a consistent supply of pure snow-melt from the Andes. You could happily spend a week visiting bodegas, before heading west to climb Mount Aconcagua, South America's highest mountain. If this is too daunting, there are many other dramatic peaks to hike up in summer, or ski down in winter, with the country's most famous ski and snowboarding resort, Las Leñas, in the south of the province.

South of Mendoza, find sparkling wine producers in San Rafael, or set off for adventures in the wild landscapes beyond. Go rafting in the eerie ravine of Cañón del Atuel; find yourself seduced by the quieter charms of Llancanelo where thousands of flamingos rise from the Prussian-blue waters; or ride a horse through the starkly beautiful volcanic landscape of La Payunia, where *guanacos* roam unhindered. A spirit of adventure is definitely needed to explore the quieter provinces of San Juan and La Rioja, but the intrepid will be rewarded with forgotten valleys offering perfect peace and natural beauty.

The undoubted stars of the region are two national parks; each likely to make you feel dwarfed by both time and space. The 'Valley of the Moon' at Ischigualasto is an other-worldly landscape: a 200-million-year-old lake-bed, strewn with fossils from first life forms to dinosaurs. And Talampaya's vast canyons of terracotta rock, eroded by wind into gigantic sculptures, are magnificent at sunset when they turn a vivid red.

Mendoza city

Mendoza is undoubtedly the tourism hub of the west of Argentina, and is a good place to spend a few days, with its pretty plazas, wide boulevards and sophisticated nightlife. Its flourishing economy is based entirely around wine, as it is the centre of Argentina's wine industry. Any trip to the city should include a tour of some of the vineyards at Maipú and Luján de Cuyo to the south. There are large flashy commercial bodegas and smaller family wineries, and after seeing the process of winemaking, you'll be treated to a generous tasting to appreciate why Argentina's wine is receiving such worldwide acclaim. Wine is part of the city's culture too: there's a profusion of wonderful *vinotecas* where you can taste fine wines, and a spectacular festival held to celebrate the wine harvest every March in Mendoza's splendid Parque San Martín.

The city has some small interesting museums and a lively nightlife, with sophisticated restaurants serving all kinds of fine food. It's also a good place to plan a trip into the mountains to the west; the snow-capped peaks form a dramatic backdrop to the city. You can hire ski gear, get expert advice on climbing Aconcagua or find specialist adventure tour operators for climbing or rafting elsewhere in the region. The city is well set up for tourism, with a huge range of comfortable hotels, and plentiful bilingual tour operators.

Arriving in Mendoza city → *Colour map 3, A2. Phone code 0261.*
Population: city 115,000; greater Mendoza 1 million (estimated).

Getting there
Mendoza is 1060 km west of Buenos Aires. **El Plumerillo Airport** ① *T0261-520 6000*,
is 8 km northeast of the city. It has money exchange, tourist information, shops,
restaurant and *locutorio*, but no left luggage. To get to Plaza Independencia in the
centre catch bus 6 (line 63 'Mosconi'), hourly, 50 mins journey. Remise taxi to/from
centre US$9.

Buses arrive at Mendoza from almost everywhere in the country, with several
services daily from Buenos Aires, Salta and Bariloche, as well as the nearby cities
of San Rafael and San Juan. Mendoza is a good stopping point for routes in and
out of Chile with frequent services to Santiago, and at least one bus a day stopping
at Uspallata and the mountainous region on the way to the Chilean border for
those wanting to trek or ski. The long-distance bus terminal is on Avenida Videla,
15 minutes' walk from the centre (go via Av Alem, which has pedestrian tunnel to
gates opposite platforms 38-39). It has shops, *locutorio*, tourist information, ATMs, a
good café, left luggage (opposite platform 53) and toilets. Beware of thieves at all
times in the bus station and note that it's not a place to linger at night. Taxi to/from
centre US$2.50; prepare for long queues. ▸▸ *See Transport, page 206.*

Getting around
Mendoza's city centre is easy to find your way around on foot, with the large leafy
Plaza Independencia occupying four blocks at its centre. Pedestrianized Sarmiento
runs between the plaza and the main shopping street, San Martín, which runs north
to south.

You're unlikely to need transport in the centre, but if you do, there are plentiful
buses (single fares from US$0.45), six trolley bus routes, a streetcar 'Metrotranvía'
that runs along Avenida Belgrano in the centre from Mendoza station to Gutiérrez
station in Maipú (30 minutes, US$0.45) and a tourist bus decorated as a streetcar that
runs along the main commercial avenues (US$0.40). In addition, taxis are plentiful
and safe. The bodegas (wineries) in the nearby towns of Luján de Cuyo and Maipú,
just to the south, can be reached by bus, but if you're keen to see more than one, it's
better to hire a car. ▸▸ *See Transport, page 206.*

Best time to visit
The biggest festival of the year, **Fiesta de la Vendimia**, is held from mid-February to
mid-March to celebrate the start of the wine harvest. The festival includes a carnival
queen, a procession of floats and outdoor extravaganzas in the park – but little wine
tasting. A parallel event is the less-promoted but equally entertaining **Gay Vendimia
Festival** with parties, shows and the crowning of the Festival Queen. Bodegas can be
visited all year round, and at harvest time (March and April) you'll see the machinery in
action. If you're heading beyond Mendoza to explore the landscape, note that trekking
in the mountains is only possible from November to April, when the snow has melted.
The most pleasant time for trekking is December to February, which is also the only

feasible season for trekking at higher altitudes. Skiing at Los Penitentes (on the road to Chile) is from July to October, though Las Leñas further south is open from mid-June.

Tourist information

Mendoza has a well-developed tourism infrastructure, with tourist offices all over the city. The city's **main office** ① *Garibaldi y San Martín, T0261-420 1333, www. ciudaddemendoza.gov.ar, daily 0900-2100*, provides tourist and cultural information for the city. There's a useful booth on the street outside. There are also tourist offices at **Las Heras y Perú** ① *T0261-429 6298, Mon-Sat 0900-2000*; and at the **Municipalidad** ① *9 de Julio 500*, 7th floor, T0261-449 5185, Mon-Fri 0900-1300. There are two small but very helpful kiosks at the airport and at the bus terminal, and another extremely helpful office at the entrance to **Parque San Martín** ① *daily 0800-1800*. All hand out maps and accommodation lists, lists of private lodgings in high season, information on bodegas and advice on buses. The city also runs free walking tours and the Bus Turístico (see What to do, page 204). For regional information, try the **provincial tourist office** ① *Av San Martín 1143, T0261-413 2101, www.turismo.mendoza.gov.ar*, or visit www.mendoza.com.ar and www.welcometomendoza.com.ar (in English).

Background

Mendoza was founded by Pedro del Castillo in 1561, who was sent from the Spanish colony in Chile by Captain General García Hurtado de Mendoza to cross the 4000-m pass over the Andes and start a new city. Mediterranean fruits were introduced to the region soon afterwards and thrived in its sunny climate, aided by pre-Hispanic irrigation channels that are still used today to water the dry lands with abundant snow-melt from the Andes. The city's wealth grew, although it remained largely isolated throughout the colonial period, being governed from Chile and having little contact with modern-day Argentina. The city's greatest blow came on Easter Saturday in 1861 when it was completely destroyed in a devastating earthquake which killed some 4000 of its 12,000 inhabitants. Very quickly, a new centre was built by the French architect Ballofet, several blocks to the southwest of the original. This modern city was designed with low, quake-proof buildings, broad avenues and many plazas to aid evacuation in case of further tremors. Plane trees were planted on all the streets, watered by a network of irrigation channels which still gush with water every spring. Nowadays, Mendoza's main industry is wine, though a busy university and, increasingly, tourism help to sustain its wealth and lively character.

Places in Mendoza city → *For listings, see pages 201-207.*

Plaza Independencia and around

The large **Plaza Independencia** is a popular meeting place for *mendocinos*, with its shady acacia and plane trees and pretty fountains. In the middle is the small **Museo de Arte Moderno** ① *T0261-425 7279, Tue-Fri 0900-2000, Sat, Sun and hols*

San Martín El Libertador

If you learn about only one Argentine hero on your trip, make it San Martín, one of the greatest independence heroes of South America. Celebrated by statues in every town in the country, José Francisco de San Martín hoped to unite Spanish America after independence, and though he failed to achieve this aim, his military genius played a major role in securing independence. He possessed a tremendous organizational ability, even when leading troops scattered over large distances and mountainous terrain, and his epic crossing of the Andes in 1817 was a turning point in the Wars of Independence, and the bloody campaigns that followed in Chile and Peru ended Spanish rule in South America.

Born in Yapeyú, Corrientes, in 1778 and educated in Spain, San Martín served in the Spanish army in North Africa, Spain and France from the age of 15. In 1811 he resigned from the army and made contact with Francisco de Miranda and other supporters of South American independence, returning to Buenos Aires in 1812 to train the new cavalry regiment. The following year, he replaced Belgrano as commander of the northern armies and, once appointed governor of Cuyo province, spent the next two years preparing to capture Peru from his base in Mendoza by means of a giant flanking movement through Chile and up through the coast to Lima. His 'Army of the Andes' was drawn from regular troops sent by Buenos Aires, but San Martín personally reconnoitred the mountain passes to plan the crossing to Chile himself. He also planned a brilliant deception, calling a meeting of Pehuenche chiefs to ask their permission to cross their territory to invade Chile via mountain passes south of Mendoza. As he'd expected, spies carried this news across the Andes, leaving San Martín free to use a more northerly route, with the main force crossing by Los Patos and Uspallata passes. Some 3778 men set out on 19 January 1817, with equipment and 10,791 horses and mules, and they crossed the Andes in 21 days, arriving on time at their intended destinations. Within days, the army defeated the Spanish at Chacabuco and entered Santiago, Chile, in triumph, though the conclusive victory was at the Battle of Maipú in April 1818.

With Chilean independence secure, San Martín led his forces by sea to Peru in 1820. Avoiding battle against the larger Spanish forces, he negotiated a truce. Finally entering Lima in triumph in July 1821, he assumed political and military command of the new republic of Peru. Afterwards, San Martín resigned his post and returned to his small farm in Mendoza, before travelling to Europe in 1824 to settle in Brussels and then Grand Bourg, France. He died in Boulogne-sur-Mer in 1850, and his remains now lie in the Buenos Aires cathedral. Symbolizing to many Argentines the virtues of sacrifice, bravery and the lack of personal gain, he's remembered by street names in even the smallest towns.

1400-2000, US$2 (valid also 24 hrs for Museo del Area Fundacional and Aquarium).
Originally designed to be an emergency bunker for victims of earthquakes, it now houses temporary exhibitions. On the western side is the new and luxurious **Park Hyatt Hotel** ⓘ *www.mendoza.park.hyatt.com*, which was once a splendid 1920s palace where Juan Perón and Evita stayed. The eastern side of the plaza is filled with a handicrafts market at weekends, where Sarmiento runs to San Martín.

One block out from the four corners of Plaza Independencia are four smaller plazas. The most attractive is the **Plaza España**, to the southeast. Its floor and benches are

Mendoza

N

200 metres
200 yards

Where to stay
1 Alamo Hostel & Suites *B1*
2 Campo Base *B1*
3 Chimbas Hostel *C3*
4 Confluencia *A2*
5 Damajuana *C1*
6 Hostel Internacional Mendoza *C2*
7 Hostel Suites Mendoza *A2*
8 InterContinental *C3*
9 Mendoza Backpackers *C2*
10 Mendoza Inn *C1*
11 NH *B1*
12 Nutibara *C1*
13 Park Hyatt *B1*
14 Sheraton *B2*

Restaurants 🍴
1 Anna Bistro *A1*
2 Azafrán *B1*
3 Facundo *B1*
4 Ferruccio Soppelsa *A2*
5 Francesco Barbera *B1*
7 La Marchigiana *A2*
9 Las Tinajas *B2*
10 Liverpool *B2*
11 Mesón Español *C2*
13 Montecatini *A1*

15 Por Acá & Tres con Noventa *C1*
16 Quinta Norte *B1*
17 Vía Civit *B1*

Bars & clubs 🍸
18 Gio Bar *B1*

➡ **Mendoza maps**
1 Mendoza, page 194
2 Mendoza wineries, page 197

beautifully tiled and it's a lovely place to sit under the trees and gaze at the rather sentimental mural displaying historical episodes as well as scenes from *Don Quijote* and the famous gaucho poem, *Martín Fierro*. Four blocks west along Montevideo, with its pretty Italianate and colonial-style buildings, is **Plaza Italia**, with wonderful mature tipa trees. Nearby it's worth visiting the small **Museo del Pasado Cuyano** ① *Montevideo 544, T0261-423 6031, Tue-Sat 1000-1400 (0900-1300 in summer), US$1.25*, housed in a beautiful 1873 mansion owned by the Civit family. There's a lot of of San Martín memorabilia, and an exquisite Spanish 15th-century carved altarpiece. The director will give you an excellent tour and insights into the city's history.

Area Fundacional
① *Getting there: buses 5 (line 54) and 3 (line 112) from C Chile; the Bus Turístico also stops here.*
The original city centre, destroyed by the earthquake in 1861, was located 12 blocks to the northeast of today's Plaza Independencia and is now known as the **Area Fundacional**. Here there is a broad tranquil plaza and a beautifully designed **Museo del Area Fundacional** ① *Beltrán and Videla Castillo, T0261-425 6927, Tue-Sat 0800-2000 (Jun-Aug 0900-1900), Sun 1500-2000, hols 1000-1900, US$2 (valid also 24 hrs for Museo Municipal de Arte Moderno and Aquarium)*, whose glass floor reveals the continuing excavation of the foundations of the old Cabildo and the buildings that followed, with an array of objects salvaged from the rubble. The informative free tour is highly recommended to give you a picture of Mendoza's history. Under the plaza you can see the first fountain to bring running water to the city, and nearby, at the corner of Ituzaingó and Beltrán, are the ruins of the Jesuit **Iglesia de San Francisco**. **Plaza Pellegrini** is another attractive little plaza, at Avenida Alem and Avenida San Juan, where wedding photos are taken on Friday and Saturday nights, and there's a small antiques market on Friday at lunchtime.

Not far from the Area Fundacional, at the southern end of Parque O'Higgins, kids might enjoy the small aquarium **Acuario Municipal** ① *Ituzaingó and Buenos Aires, daily 0900-1930, US$2.25*. Across the street is a small **Serpentario** ① *daily 0930-1300, 1500-1930, US$2.25*, with plenty of snakes and lizards.

Parque General San Martín and around
Ten blocks west of Plaza Independencia, wrought-iron gates mark the entrance to the great **Parque General San Martín**, 350 ha of lavishly planted parkland designed by famous Argentine landscape architect Charles Thays, with sports facilities, a big lake where regattas are held, a sports stadium and an amphitheatre. There's also a helpful **tourist information office** next to the main gates. Within the park is the **Cerro de la Gloria**, popular with paragliders, which gives splendid views of the Andes to the west. There's a monument here to San Martín, showing him leading his army across the Andes to liberate Argentina and Chile from the Spanish. Bus Turístico and El Oro Negro tourist buses run to the top of the Cerro de la Gloria from the city centre, otherwise it's a 45-minute walk from park's gates.

On the side of the Cerro is the **Jardín Zoológico** ① *T0261-427 1559, www.zoo. mendoza.gov.ar, Tue-Sun 0900-1700 (0900-1800 in summer), US$3.75*, one of the country's best zoos. At the south end of the lake is the **Museo de Ciencias Naturales y Antropológicas** ⓘ T0261-428 7666 (temporarily closed in 2014), with an ancient female mummy and stuffed animals among its collections.

The city's best art gallery is in the nearby suburb of **Luján de Cuyo**, in the house where Fernando Fader painted his beautiful murals. The **Museo Provincial de Bellas Artes** ⓘ *Casa de Fader, Carril San Martín 3651, Mayor Drummond, T0261-496 0224, Tue-Fri 0830-1300, Sat-Sun 1400-1800, US$1.25*, has a small, charming collection of Argentine paintings. There are also sculptures in the lovely gardens. To get there catch bus 1 (line 19) from Calle La Rioja, between Catamarca and Garibaldi (40 minutes).

Zona Alta del Rio Mendoza → *For listings, see pages 201-207.*

There are three main wine-producing areas in Mendoza province. The **High zone of Río Mendoza**, the oldest wine-producing area, is immediately to the south of Mendoza city with bodegas sprinkled among two towns, Maipú and Luján de Cuyo. Wineries in this region are described in more detail below. The second region is the **Uco Valley**, to the south of the small town of Tupungato which lies southwest of Mendoza in the foothills of the Andes. And the third region is around **San Rafael** (286 km south of Mendoza city). Both Tupungato and San Rafael are described in the Southern Mendoza section (see page 217).

Argentina's wine industry has grown considerably in recent years (see box, page 198). Now it's being shaken up by the arrival of foreign investors who have bought extensive vineyards in the region. As well as wine growers, other enthusiasts have settled here and started up related businesses, running bodega tours, wine clubs, wine magazines and opening restaurants. This area of tourism is bound to change dramatically in the next few years, so check for new information if you're serious about your wine. For more information on the Mendoza wine-growing region in general, see the following websites: www.turismo.mendoza.gov.ar (has maps and information on the Camino del Vino); www.mendoza.com.ar (in Spanish with lots of information); www.vendimia.mendoza.gov.ar (covers the annual wine harvest festival in Mendoza); www.welcometomendoza.com.ar (another very useful site, designed in English by expats with a good general overview). For tips on visiting bodegas, see box, page 205.

The area immediately to the south of Mendoza city, around the sprawling centres of Maipú and Luján de Cuyo, contains the oldest and some of the most famous vineyards in the province, producing wines with a high concentration of fruit. Malbec, particularly, thrives here, in altitudes between 650 m and 1050 m. Although the grape was brought from France, many experts argue that it is in Argentina that Malbec has found its real home, and in Zona Alta del Río Mendoza that it is at its best. Winegrowing styles are eclectic in the various vineyards here, but this area produces premium wines, thanks to the unique combination of soil and climate. Other grape varieties grown here are Cabernet Sauvignon, Merlot, Chardonnay, Syrah and Tempranillo.

This is the closest region to the city of Mendoza and easily visited in a few hours. But since the wineries are spread out along pretty country roads, with few signs to guide you, it's worth taking a map, and contacting the bodegas ahead of your visit.

Escorihuela
① *Belgrano 1188, Godoy Cruz, T0261-424 2698, www.escorihuela.com.ar. Getting there: the winery is easily reached by all buses going south along Av San Martín (Belgrano runs parallel to San Martín, one block east) or by 5-min taxi ride.*

② Mendoza wineries

➡ **Mendoza maps**
1 Mendoza, page 194
2 Mendoza wineries, page 197

Argentine wine

Wine is grown in Argentina along the length of the Andean foothills, from Cafayate in Salta to the Río Negro valley in Neuquén, with the oldest and most famous wine-producing areas in Mendoza and San Juan provinces, where the climate is ideal: warm, almost consistently sunny days, and cold nights, with a 'thermal amplitude' of 15C which gives grapes such a rich flavour. Water is the other magical ingredient: wine was made in Argentina long before the Jesuits planted their first vines here in the 1550s, and irrigation canals made by pre-Incan cultures still carry pure, mineral-rich snow-melt from the Andes today, compensating for the low rainfall, less than 200 mm a year.

When Argentina was flooded with Spanish and Italian immigrants in the late 19th century, wine-growing became an imperative, and modern grapes were introduced, so that today the main grapes grown are Cabernet Sauvignon, Merlot, Malbec and Syrrah; Chardonnay, Chenin and Sauvignon Blanc. 'High-altitude wine' is a tiny, but fast-growing industry in Salta's Calchaquí Valley, with superb boutique wineries Colomé and El Estecco producing wines of extraordinary intensity. Cafayate is the only place on earth where the white Torrontés grape thrives, producing a deliciously dry, fruity wine with an aromatic bouquet.

Argentina was among the five biggest wine producers of the world in the early 20th century, but exported very little, since home consumption used up all that was produced. However, in the 1970s, after the local market became glutted with cheap wine – much of it of inferior quality – wine drinking slumped, Argentines preferring beer and soft drinks with their steaks. In the 1990s, Chile's vigorous marketing campaign secured their wines a place on every European supermarket shelf, but Argentina failed to compete, despite the fact that their wines, particularly their reds, are generally superior. But in the last five years the Argentine wine industry has been revolutionized, producing far more sophisticated premium wines, and resulting in a renaissance of wine drinking within the country, and a boom in exporting wine. Try a bottle or two at home before you visit the bodegas of Mendoza or Salta, and look out for the famous names in Argentine restaurants: Valentín Bianchi, Trapiche, Flichman, Navarro Correas, Senetiner and Norton. In Argentine supermarkets, wines can be bought for US$1.50-10 a bottle, but better by far to go to a *Vinoteca* (specialist wine shop) where US$15 will buy you a superb bottle, you'll get expert advice, and can try smaller labels.

Fur further information go to: www.argentinewines.com/ing/; www. vinosdeargentina.com; www.turismo.mendoza.gov.ar; www.welcomeargentina.com/vino; and magazine *El Conocedor*, www.el conocedor.com.ar, as well as the wonderful free English-language magazine *Wine Republic* distributed in cafés and shops. Learn about Argentine wines and improve your Spanish at AEAV Spanish & Wine School, http://cable modem. fibertel.com.ar/aeav, or email aeav@ fibertel.com.ar.

Before you reach Maipú or Luján de Cuyo, it's worth stopping to visit one of the most famous bodegas in the country, in the suburb of Godoy Cruz. This is the closest winery to the city and was founded in 1884 by Spanish immigrants; it retains its traditional atmosphere in the original buildings. Escorihuela exports wine to the UK under the Gascón label and still produces Pont L'Eveque, which was Perón's favourite brand. The stunning centrepiece of your tour is in the cellars, where there's an ornately carved barrel from Nancy, France. If your Spanish isn't strong, you might like to visit this bodega before the others for its helpful brochure explaining the whole wine production process in pictures. Escorihuela also has an excellent and expensive restaurant, 1884 **Francis Mallman** (see Restaurants, page 203) with a superb menu – the perfect complement to the bodegas' fine wines.

Maipú
ⓘ *From Mendoza take bus No 10 (173), at Rioja y Garibaldi.*
The satellite town of Maipú sprawls immediately southeast of Mendoza. You may find it useful to collect information from the local **tourist office** ⓘ *Pablo Pescara 190, T0261-497 2448*, where bus No 10 (173) stops. There are many famous brands in this area, and some more intimate bodegas described here.

If you've only time for one bodega, make it **La Rural** ⓘ *Montecaseros 2625, Coquimbito, T0261-497 2013, www.bodegalarural.com.ar*; bus No 10 (173) stops nearby. This is a large traditional bodega founded in 1885 by Felipe Rutini, which has been modernized recently with the latest technology, allowing it to bottle 6000 units per hour. This bodega is renowned not only for its excellent wines but also for the marvellous **Museo Nacional del Vino** ⓘ *T0261-497 5255, Mon-Sat 0900-1300, 1400-1700, closed Sun*, where you can see the history of winemaking through an amazing display of implements dating back to the pre-Colombian skin of an entire cow; grapes were trodden in the belly so that juice flowed out of its neck. Felipe Rutini and Trumpeter labels are exported worldwide: look out for the San Felipe bottles in the UK.

Quite a long way east of Maipú town centre, and 35 km east of Mendoza, is the large and highly developed **Familia Zuccardi winery** ⓘ *R33, Las Margaritas, Km 7.5, San Roque, T0261-441 0000, www.familiazuccardi.com, Mon-Sat 0900-1700, Sun 1000-1600*. This is an exceptionally welcoming winery with a good restaurant, extensive wine tasting, a tea room, and occasional music concerts on offer. Anyone wanting to pick grapes during the harvest is always welcome, and cookery lessons are available with the restaurant's chef. Their wines are easily found abroad, where they're known as Q and Santa Julia.

There are also several wineries in Coquimbito district, immediately east of Maipú. Two smaller family-owned wineries, both delightful for a visit, lie very close to each other. **Tempus Alba** ⓘ *Perito Moreno 572, Coquimbito, T0261-481 3501, www.tempusalba.com*, is a modern bodega where the Biondolillo family takes great pride in their attention to detail and are happy to share it with you. **Viña El Cerno** ⓘ *Perito Moreno 631, Coquimbito, T0261-496 4018, www.elcerno-wines.com.ar*, has a lovely country house, a restaurant and olive groves. Founded in 1887, the historic bodega of **Inti Huaco** ⓘ *Carril Gómez 3602, Coquimbito, T0261-155 652630, bodegaintihuac@infovia.com.ar*, has elegant mid-range rooms coming off a central courtyard in beautiful surroundings.

Another charming, small and welcoming winery is the French-owned **Carinae** ① *Videla Aranda 2899, Cruz de Piedra, south of Maipú town centre, T0261-499 0470, www.carinaevinos.com, daily 1000-1800*. As the name might suggest, wines aren't the only passion of Philippe and Brigitte, but astronomy too. They have an interesting collection of telescopes, which you can use. They produce Malbec, Syrah and Cabernet Sauvignon under the Carinae name (for export), and Octans and El Galgo labels (within Argentina).

Luján de Cuyo

Southwest of Maipú, Luján de Cuyo is another wine-producing area, with restaurants and small hotels in the leafy suburb of Chacras de Coria. For information, contact the local **tourist office** ① *Roque Sáenz Peña 1000, T0261-498 1912, www.lujandecuyo.gov.ar*.

The large and impressively modern pyramid-like bodega, **Catena Zapata** ① *Cobos, Agrelo, T0261-413 1100, www.catenawines.com*, is in one of the most beautiful settings in the region. It's owned by a traditional family who produce outstanding wines that are exported under the names Catena Alta, Alamos, Nicolás Catena Zapata and Catena. There is a restaurant too. A smaller winery, but also highly developed, **Carlos Pulenta-Vistalba** ① *Roque Sáenz Peña 3135, Vistalba (west of Luján de Cuyo town centre), T0261-498 9400, www.carlospulentawines.com*, is renowned for its marvellous Vistalba wines and for having an exclusive lodge, La Posada, on its ultra-modern premises. Further west, **Séptima** ① *R7, Km 6.5, Agrelo, T0261-498 9558, www.bodegaseptima.com, Mon-Fri 1000-1*800, Sat 1000-1400, with *sunset tastings* on Thu in summer, is another large, modern bodega with fantastic mountain views.

There are now several wineries that offer accommodation, but the most famous and deservedly popular is the exquisite **Tapiz** ① *Pedro Molina, Russell, T0261-490 0202, www.tapiz.com.ar*, a small winery that owns a *finca* in Luján de Cuyo. The restored 1890s house is the region's most exclusive hotel (Club Tapiz, www.tapiz.com) and has one of the finest restaurants in Mendoza (El Terruño, see page 202).

The Malbec grape flourishes wonderfully at **Renacer** ① *Brandsen 1863, Perdriel (south of Luján de Cuyo town centre), T0261-524 4416, www.bodegarenacer.com.ar*, which produces Punto Final Reserva, one of the top Argentine Malbec wines. Quite close to here, you'll find **Achával Ferrer** ① *C Cobos 2601, by the Mendoza river, Perdriel (southwest of Luján de Cuyo town centre), T0261-15-553 5565, www.achaval-ferrer.com*, a young, modern and repeatedly prize-winning boutique bodega which produces the finest quality red wines, including the great Finca Altamira. **El Lagar de Carmelo Patti** ① *Av San Martín 2614, Mayor Drummond (north of Luján de Cuyo town centre), T0261-498 1379*, is highly recommended for its welcoming owner, who personally leads the tours, and takes pride in serving his excellent Cabernet Sauvignon or his Gran Assemblage for tasting, even straight from the barrel (Spanish only).

◉ Mendoza city listings

For hotel and restaurant price codes and other relevant information, see pages 20-26.

◉ Where to stay

Mendoza city *p190, map p194*
Breakfast is included, unless specified otherwise. Hostels advertise themselves outside the tourist office in town, offering free transfers and lots of extras; don't be pressurized into something you don't want. Hostels cost about US$12-18 pp.

The **Hyatt** (www.mendoza.park. hyatt. com), **InterContinental** (www. intercontinental.com), **Sheraton** (www. starwoodhotels.com) and **NH** (www.nh-hotels.com) chains have good hotels in the city; for something more unique stay at one of the bodegas (see below).

$$$ Nutibara, Mitre 867, T0261-429 5428, www.nutibara.com.ar. Its small rooms are in need of renovation, but it's still a good choice due to its central and quiet location and its pool.

$ pp Alamo Hostel & Suites, Necochea 740, T0261-429 5565, www.hostelalamo. com. Beautiful hostel in a very well-kept 1940s residence with dorms for 4 to 8 and doubles with or without bath (**$$**). Bike rental and tiny pool in a pleasant patio. Recommended for a quiet, yet sociable stay.

$ pp Campo Base, Mitre 946, T0261-429 0707, www.hostelcampobase.com.ar. A lively place, discounts for HI members, cramped rooms and private doubles (**$$**), lots of parties and barbecues, popular with mountain climbers, excursions run by YTA agency.

$ pp Chimbas Hostel, Cobos 92 y Acceso Este, T0261-431 4191, www. chimbashostel.com.ar. Cheaper without bath and in triples, also private doubles

with bath (**$$**), close to bus station (phone in advance for pick-up), 20 mins walk to centre, swimming pool, gym, pleasant, quiet atmosphere.

$ pp Confluencia, España 1512, T0261-429 0430, www.hostalconfluencia.com.ar. Slightly more expensive than rest of hostels, it is a convenient choice though for groups who care for tidiness and a central location. Rooms for 2 to 4 (private doubles (**$$**), all with bath, some ensuite. In the same group as Cordón del Plata tour agency, which offers lots of adventure activities as well as wine tours, cycling and riding, www.cordondelplata.com.

$ pp Damajuana, Arístides Villanueva 282, T0261-425 5858, www.damajuanahostel. com.ar. A great hostel, comfortable stylish dorms with bath, also double rooms (**$$**), pool and garden.Recommended.

$ pp Hostel Internacional Mendoza, España 343, T0261-424 0018, www.hostel mendoza.net. A comfortable hostel, HI discount, 15 min walk south of Plaza Independencia, small rooms for 4 and 6 with bath (cheaper without a/c), doubles with bath (**$$**), warm atmosphere, good value dinners on offer, barbecues on Fri, bike rental, huge range of excursions run by YTA agency. Warmly recommended.

$ pp Hostel Suites Mendoza, Patricias Mendocinas 1532 (at Av Heras), T0261-423 7018, www.hostelsuites.com.

$ pp Mendoza Backpackers, San Lorenzo 19, T0261-429 4941, www. mendozabackpackers.com Well-run central hostel with an attractive lounge and terrace bar, dorms for 4 and 6, some with bath. HI discounts. Excursions run by YTA agency.

$ pp Mendoza Inn, Arístides Villanueva 470, T0261-420 2486, www.mendoza hostel.com. In the lively bar area, small dorms for 4 to 8, some with bath, and a private double (**$$**), large garden with a tiny pool, dinners offered extra, HI discounts. Excursions run by YTA agency.

Camping
Camping Suizo, Av Champagnat, El Challao, 8 km from city, www. campingsuizo.com.ar. Modern, shady, with pool, barbecues, hot showers and *cabañas* for 4 and 6. Recommended.

Zona Alta del Río Mendoza *p196, map p197*
$$$$ Cavas Wine Lodge, Costaflores, Alto Agrelo, Luján de Cuyo, T0261-410 6927, www.cavaswinelodge.com. A pricey but heavenly experience, ideal for a romantic and wonderfully relaxing stay. Spacious rooms in a beautifully restored rural mansion, surrounded by vineyards, with restaurant and spa. Each room has a fireplace and terrace, swimming pool, wonderful views. Highly recommended.
$$$ Club Tapiz, C Pedro Molina, Russell, Maipú, T0261-496 3233, www.tapiz.com. Surrounded by vineyards, Tapiz is a small, beautifully restored Italianate villa, where the minimalist style helps you unwind in comfort. A spa and the superb cuisine in its **Terruño** restaurant make this unquestionably one of the top hotels in Mendoza, see page 200.
$$$ Parador del Angel, 100 m from main plaza, Chacras de Coria, Luján de Cuyo, T0261-496 2201, www.parador delangel.com.ar. Restored 100-year-old house, tastefully decorated, very relaxing, gardens, pool. Owner is an experienced mountain climber.
$$$ Tikay Killa Lodge & Wines, Montecaseros 3543, Coquimbito, Maipú, T0261-542 3232, www.tikaykilla.com.ar. Small lodge in the Ruta del Vino, white rooms, parking, garden, wine tours

and other activities organized, helpful English-speaking manager.

🍴 Restaurants

Mendoza city *p190, map p194*
There are many open-air cafés for lunch on Peatonal Sarmiento and restaurants around Las Heras. The atmospheric indoor market on Las Heras, Mon-Sat 0830-1300, 1700-2100; Sun 0930-1300, has cheap pizza, *parrilla* and pasta. A few food stalls remain open 0830-2300. Calle Arístides Villanueva, the extension of Colón heading west, has good restaurants (as well as hostels). See also Bars and clubs, below.
$$$ Anna Bistró, Av Juan B Justo 161, T0261-425 1818. One of the most attractive restaurants in town, informal, French-owned, very welcoming, good food and drink, French and Italian flavours, open from breakfast to a late dinner, excellent value. Recommended
$$$ Azafrán, Sarmiento 765, T0261-429 4200. A fine-wine lover's heaven, with an extensive range from all the best bodegas, expert advice on wines and a fabulous delicatessen where you can enjoy superb *picadas*. Its menu changes with the season. Recommended.
$$$ El Mesón Español, Montevideo 244, T0261-429 6175. Spanish food, including great paella, live music Wed-Sat.
$$$ Facundo, Sarmiento 641, T0261-420 2866. Good modern *parrilla*, lots of other choices including Italian, good salad bar.
$$$ Francesco Barbera, Chile 1268, T0261-425 3912. Smart old town house with a wonderful garden, excellent Italian food, choose from over 350 different wines.
$$$ La Marchigiana, Patricias Mendocinas 1550, T0261-423 0751. One of Mendoza's best restaurants

and great value. Italian food served in spacious surroundings with charming old-fashioned service.

\$\$\$ Montecatini, Gral Paz 370, T0261-425 2111, Good Italian food, seafood and *parrilla*, more tourist oriented, popular with families.

\$\$\$-\$\$ 3 90 (Tres con Noventa), Arístides Villanueva 451, T0261-429 8686. Delicious pastas, good value, studenty, warm cosy atmosphere. Highly recommended.

\$\$ Gio Bar, Chile 1288. Attractively set and casual, a good choice for Italian-style sandwiches, pizzas and salads.

\$\$ Las Tinajas, Lavalle 38, T0261-429 1174, www.lastinajas.com. Large buffet-style/all-you-can-eat at very reasonable prices, wide selection of pastas, grills, Chinese, desserts and so on. Cheap wine, too.

\$\$ Por Acá, Arístides Villanueva 557. Open 2100 till late. Bar for pizzas and drinks, popular, noisy.

\$\$ Quinta Norte, Mitre 1206. Cheap deals and generous portions in an elegant mansion on Plaza Independencia.

\$\$ Vía Civit, Emilio Civit 277. Open from breakfast onwards. For first-class sandwiches, tarts and pastries in a relaxed, elegant traditional bakery.

Ferruccio Soppelsa, Espejo y Patricias Mendocinas, with several branches. The best place for ice cream (even wine flavours!). Recommended.

Zona Alta del Río Mendoza *p196*
\$\$\$ 1884 Francis Mallman, Bodega Escorihuela, Belgrano 1188, Godoy Cruz, T0261-424 2698. Open for dinner only, reservation advisable. The place to go for a really special dinner. Mallman is one of the country's great chefs, exotic and imaginative menu. Highly recommended.
\$\$\$ Terruño, Bodega Tapiz, Pedro Molina Russell, Maipú, T0261-496 0131,

www.club-tapiz.com. Refined minimalist decor in the beautifully restored rooms of an Italianate residence. Exquisite dishes made from local produce match Mediterranean flavours with a dash of Asian style. Recommended.

🍸 Bars and clubs

Mendoza city *p190, map p194*
Av Arístedes Villanueva, just 10 mins' walk southwest of the main plaza, is the area for an evening stroll and has exciting bars and restaurants that are popular with a younger crowd. (Note that this street changes its name to Colón at Belgrano.) You'll find it quiet if you're heading out for an early dinner, but it livens up after 2400 when the bars are full. La Alameda (Av San Martín, north of C Córdoba) is another pleasant bar area with some basic restaurants that are also open at lunchtime. For other suggestions, see www.mendozanoduerme.com.ar (in Spanish).
Antares, Av Villanueva 153. Popular place to hang out Fri nights, try the microbrewery beer.
Iskra, Av San Martín Sur 905, www.iskradiscopub.com.ar. Late-night club, with live music.
Liverpool, San Martín y Rivadavia. Pub food, sandwiches, burgers, Beatles memorabilia and European football matches on the screen.

🎉 Festivals

Mendoza city *p190, map p194*
The riotous wine harvesting festival, **Fiesta de la Vendimia**, www.vendimia.mendoza.gov.ar, is held in the amphitheatre of the Parque San Martín in early Mar. Local wine festivals start in Dec. A parallel event is the less-promoted

but equally entertaining **Gay Vendimia Festival**, featuring parties, shows and the crowning of the Festival Queen. Much more modest is the Vendimia Obrera in mid-Mar, when vineyard workers, many of whom are of Bolivian origin, recover the roots of the original celebration with live music, wine and food in Cordón del Plata, a village in the Uco valley. Hotels fill up fast and prices rise; also at Easter, Jul (the ski season) and around mid-Sep (Chilean holidays).

O Shopping

Mendoza city *p190, map p194*
The main shopping area is along San Martín and Las Heras, with good clothes, souvenir, leather and handicraft shops as well as vast sports emporia. There's a **Mercado Artesanal**, San Martín 1133, Mon-Fri 0900-1900 (Jan mornings only), Sat 0900-1300, for traditional leather, baskets, weaving; also weekend market on Plaza Independencia. Cheap shops include: **El Turista**, Las Heras 351, and **Las Viñas**, Las Heras 399. For higher quality head to Raíces, Peatonal Sarmiento 162, or Alpataco, next door. *Vinotecas* offer a good choice of wines; try **Winery,** Chile 898, T0261-420 2840 and The **Vines of Mendoza**, Belgrano 1194, T0261-438 1031, www.vinesofmendoza.com, Mon-Sat 1500-2200, a tasteful but pricey wine-tasting and shopping experience, presenting the best of the region's boutique bodegas, international orders only.

O What to do

Mendoza city *p190, map p194*
The sight of distant purple mountains is bound to draw you from the city up into the dramatic Andes to the west.

This area, known as Alta Montaña (see page 207), is the undoubted highlight of the region and shouldn't be missed, but if you're thinking of taking a day trip from Mendoza city, bear in mind that you'll get very little chance to explore; you're better off hiring a car and spending a few days staying up in the mountains. For water sports, **Embalse El Carrizal**, an artificial lake 60 km south of Mendoza, has yachting and fishing, campsites and picnic areas.

Bus tours
Bus Turístico, www.mendozacitytour.com Open-top sightseeing bus with 15 stops, including Cerro de la Gloria. Hourly departures from Peatonal Sarmiento y Av San Martín, Tickets (US$10, hop on/hop off) sold at city's tourist offices.
Bus Vitivinícola, www.busvitivinicola.com. Four departures each week from top hotels and Av San Martín y Garibaldi to Luján de Cuyo's main wineries in 2 alternative circuits, half- or full-day tours, hop on/hop off, US$20.
El Oro Negro, T0261-498 0510, www.bateatour.com.ar. Open-top bus offering 2½-hr bilingual city tours (US$8) including Cerro de la Gloria, 3 daily departures from Plaza Independencia (on C Chile); also 90-min bilingual tours of Parque San Martín and Cerro de la Gloria (US$5), 3 to 4 daily departures from same point.

Climbing
Club Andinista Mendoza, FL Beltrán 357, Guaymallén, T0261-431 9870, www.clubandinista.com.ar. Treks and climbs are also organized by the famous climber Sr Fernando Grajales, T1-800-516 6962 (US toll free), www.grajales.net.

Visiting bodegas

Transport

There are plenty of tours on offer from agencies in Mendoza city, allowing you to visit a couple of bodegas in an afternoon. These are fine if you haven't got a car, but it's much more interesting to go independently, so that you can choose where you'd like to visit, and take your time over the visits. Touring wineries by bus really isn't an option, since almost all the bodegas are some way out of any town, it's easy to get lost in labyrinthine rural roads with little signposting, and you might waste a lot of time waiting for buses. Cycle tours are an appealing alternative to exploring one limited area, such as Mapiú, with a couple of specialized agencies based in the wine regions, and reasonable distances to cover: you could put together a tour of bodegas that are a five- to 20-minute ride from each other.

Reserve in advance

If you choose to visit the bodegas, remember always to ring and book your tour first, and if you don't speak Spanish, ask if they have an English-speaking guide. You'll be able to get a vague idea of the process but it will be far more interesting if you understand the detail.

Map

Get hold of a map of the wine region: there are lots of maps available in free tourist brochures, but the best is the *Winemap Turístico*, www.winemap turistico.com, sold in some restaurants and wine stores: very good and informative. There is also a good free wine magazine in English called *Wine Republic*, pick one up if you can.

Variety

Limit yourself to four or five bodegas in a day, especially if you're driving. It's worth trying to see both a big modern winery and smaller and more intimate places, since their processes are quite different, and often a smaller winery will take even more time and trouble to share their produce with you.

Try it at home

One of the great things about visiting these bodegas is that often you'll be trying wines that are available in your own country, so that even if you can't carry a crate home with you, you can buy the same wine from your home wine supplier, and share it with friends as you show them the photos of where the wine was grown.

Cycling

For bike tours and rentals, try **Internacional Mendoza**, Pedro Molina 63, T0261-423 2103, www.intermza.com. See also **YTA** below for bike tours and rentals, or shop around the handful of agencies along C Urquiza in the wine region of Coquimbito, Maipú, such as **Mr Hugo**, Urquiza 2288, Coquimbito, Maipú, T0261-497 4067, www.mrhugobikes.com. Good.

Skiing

There are three resorts within striking distance of Mendoza: Los Penitentes, Los Puquios and Vallecitos; for all, see the Alta Montana section.

Whitewater rafting

Popular on the Río Mendoza; ask agencies for details. **Argentina Rafting**, Amigorena 86, T0261-429 6325, www.argentinarafting.com. Offers varied activities from its base camp in Potrerillos (see page 204).

Tour operators

Many agencies, especially on Peatonal Sarmiento, run trekking, riding and rafting expeditions, as well as traditional tours to Alta Montaña and the bodegas.
Aconcagua Spirit, Rivadavia 345, Maipú, T0261-559 2819, www.aconcaguaspirit. com.ar. Recommended for their 11-day horsebackexpeditions across the Andes.
The Grapevine, T0261-429 7522, www. thegrapevine-winetours.com. British owned and run, it organizes personalized tours in the wine region, including flights combined with visits and lunch and summer full-moon wine tours, among a great diversity of choices.
Huentata, Las Heras 529, T0261-425 7444, www.huentata.com.ar. Conventional tours including Villavicencio and Cañón del Atuel. Recommended.
Inka Expediciones, Juan B Justo 345, T0261-425 0871, www.inka.com.ar. Climbing expeditions, including Aconcagua, highly professional, fixed departure dates, mules for hire.
Kahuak, Rivadavia 234, T0261-423 8409, www.kahuak.com.ar. Mainly focused on a wide range of wine tours. Recommended.
Mendoza Viajes, Peatonal Sarmiento 129, T0261-461 0210, www.mendoza viajes.com. Imaginative tours in comfortable coaches, professional, cheap deals available.
Trekking Travel, Adolfo Calle 4171, Villa Nueva, Guaymallén, T0261-421 0450, www.trekking-travel.com.ar. From easy horseback riding to the Andes crossing; trekking in the Aconcagua and Cordón del Plata.

YTA, Peatonal Sarmiento 231, T0261-425 5511, www.youthtravelargentina. com. All bilingual excursions starting from half-day wine tours (US$20 pp) to full-day Alta Montaña circuit (US$38 pp), offering also varied activities such as paragliding, trekking, horseback riding, rafting, delightful bike rides through vineyards (US$35 pp) and exclusive Harley-Davidson wine tours in Uco valley. Occasional treks in Aconcagua area. Discounts for HI members and own hostel network guests. Make sure about extra costs.

☉ Transport

Mendoza city *p190, map p194*
Air
El Plumerillo airport has daily flights to **Buenos Aires** and **Santiago de Chile**. Also to **Córdoba**, **Bariloche**, **Iguazú** and a few other national destinations.

Bus
Local Most local buses have 2 numbers: the big number painted onto the bus in the top front corner is the bus company or *grupo*, while the smaller number (*subnúmero*) shown on a card propped in the window is the actual route (*recorrido* or *línea*). For example, if you're going to the bodega La Rural in Maipú, you'll need bus No 10, *subnúmero* 173; don't be tempted to get on all the other 10s that go past. Bus fares within and near the city start from US$0.45 and are paid with *Red Bus* magnetic cards (US$1.25), which are sold and topped up at designated outlets.
Long distance Buses depart from the huge terminal on the east side of Av Videla. To **Buenos Aires**, 13-17 hrs, US$76-108, many companies. To **Bariloche**, 17 hrs, US$90-102, with Cata. To **Córdoba**, 9-12 hrs, US$54-72, several

companies. To **San Juan**, US$13-14, 2-2½ hrs. To **La Rioja**, US$42-60, 8-9½ hrs. To **Catamarca** 10-11½ hrs, US$52-74. To **Tucumán**, 1 3-20 hrs, US$68-96. To **Salta**, 18 hrs, US$109-124, with **Andesmar**. To **Potrerillos**, 1 hr, US$2.25 with Buttini (opposite platform 56), which goes on to **Uspallata**, US$5.75, 2¼ hrs, and up to **Las Cuevas** (Chilean border), twice a day, US$7, 4 hrs. To **Tupungato**, US$4.50-5.50, 1½-2 hrs, with TBMitre/Cata. To **San Rafael**, US$7.50-9.50, 3-3½ hrs, with Buttini, Cata and Iselin. To **Malargüe**, direct with Viento Sur minibuses, US$15, 5 hrs, or with Cata, 6½ hrs, US$15; alternatively with Buttini, Cata or Iselin, for connection in San Rafael. **International buses** To **Santiago**, Chile, minibuses (US$32, 6-7 hrs) run by **Chi-Ar**, **Nevada** and **Radio Móvil** daily; also daily buses with **Cata Internacional** (US$42-57, 8 hrs, from *semi-cama* without service to Royal Suite), **Andesmar** and **El Rápido Internacional**. Most buses and minibuses are comfortable enough, but it's worth paying for a good service as waiting time at the border can be several hours. Buses also go daily to **Viña del Mar** and **Valparaíso**; enquire at Mendoza bus terminal and shop around. For all services to Chile, book at least 1 day ahead; passport required, tourist cards given on bus. The ride is spectacular.

There are also direct services, though not daily, to **Lima** (Perú) with **Ormeño**

and **El Rápido Internacional**; to **Santa Cruz de la Sierra** (Bolivia) with Quirquincho, and to **Montevideo** (Uruguay), with **El Rápido Internacional**.

Car hire
Most companies have their offices along C P de la Reta (900 block), next to Plaza Pellegrini.

ⓘ Directory

Mendoza city *p190, map p194*
Banks Open 0800-1245. Many ATMs on and around Plaza San Martín taking all cards. Many *casas de cambio* along San Martín, corner of Espejo/Catamarca; most open till 2000 Mon-Fri (closed for siesta) and some open Sat morning.
Consulates Chile, Belgrano 1080, T0261-425 5024, cgchilmen@itcsa.net.
Language schools Intercultural , República de Siria 241, T0261-429 0269, www.spanishcourses.com.ar. **Medical services** Central hospital near bus terminal at Alem y Salta, T0261-420 0600; **Lagomaggiore**, public general hospital (with good reputation) at Timoteo Gordillo s/n, T0261-425 9700; Children's **Hospital Notti**, Bandera de los Andes 2603 (Guaymallén), T0261-445 0045.
Useful addresses Migraciones, San Juan 211, T0261-424 3512. Unidad Policial de Asistencia al Turista, Av San Martín 1143, T0261-413 2135, 24 hrs.

Alta Montaña

The high Andes to the west of Mendoza city are the world's highest mountains outside the Himalayas and offer some of the country's most amazing scenery. This spectacular landscape is the setting for hiking, mountain climbing and adventures of all kinds, and is easily accessible from the Route Nacional 7 to Chile; simply driving west along Route 7 is an unforgettable experience. Alta Montaña is an essential part of any trip to the province, even if you're not crossing the border, or planning to climb Aconcagua. From the pretty oasis town of Uspallata, the road to Chile climbs up between the jagged snow-capped mountains, with staggering views of Volcán Tupungato in the distance to the south and Aconcagua closer at hand to the north. In winter, you'll quickly reach the snowline and the charming small ski resort of Los Penitentes; beyond it is the natural wonder of the bridge at Puente del Inca, near the base for climbing Aconcagua. The road climbs finally to the border, crossing at Túnel Cristo Redentor, and if you continue to Chile, the steep descent on the other side offers yet more superb views. In the mountains, the road may blocked by snow and ice from June to October; if travelling by car at these times, enquire about road conditions and requirements for snow chains and a shovel in Mendoza before setting out (www.vialidad. mendoza.gov.ar and www.gendarmeria.gov.ar). Snow can lie as late as September and October, so bring appropriate clothing, even if you're just going for a day trip.

There are two ways to reach Uspallata from Mendoza, both offering great views. Most dramatic is the climb north via many hairpin bends past the (abandoned) spa resort of Villavicencio (104 km, of which 52 km is on unpaved roads); alternatively, you can head south from Mendoza to pleasant Potrerillos (102 km, all paved roads) and take a short detour to the thermal springs at Cacheuta.

Villavicencio → *Colour map 3, A2. Phone code 0261.*

Famous to all Argentines from the image of its Alpine-style 1940s hotel seen on bottles of ubiquitous mineral water, Villavicencio (1800 m, Km 47) is reached by a wonderful drive. From Mendoza, head north along Route 52, across flat plains growing nothing but scrubby *jarilla* bushes, following the *pre-cordillera* mountains on your left. The road rises steeply to climb through thickly forested mountains to the beautiful old spa resort, closed for many years but under renovation (2014) and now the centre of its own little nature reserve – a good place for a picnic and a stroll. The reserve protects the sources of mineral water and the whole area is owned by the French company **Danone**, who run a smart information centre on the local wildlife and employ *guardaparques* who can direct you to nearby walks (see www.rnvillavicencio.com.ar). You can also stroll around the splendid grounds of the hotel, visit its chapel and eat at the **Hostería Villavicencio** ① *T0261-424 6482*, run by a friendly local family who offer good value lunches and teas with fine local produce such as *jamón crudo* (prosciutto) and *chivo* (goat), which you can enjoy at tables outside.

Beyond Villavicencio the *ripio* road climbs up over the spectacular **Cruz de Paramillo**, via the ridiculously twisting hairpin bends of the Caracoles de Villavicencio. In total, there are allegedly 365 hairpin bends along the route, which give the road its name *La Ruta del Año* (Route of the Year). At an altitude of 3050 m, there are breathtaking views all around, and this is a marvellous introduction to the vast peaks of Aconcagua, Tupungato and Mercedario. Descending to the fertile valley of Uspallata, there are rocks popping up like jagged teeth through the earth, in extraordinary colours from aubergine through to oxidized copper green, orange and creamy white. There are no bus services, but many tour operators include this trip. With your own transport, this makes for a great route to Uspallata. Cyclists should carry plenty of water and be warned of the dangers of altitude and lack of shade. Take your time.

Cacheuta

An alternative route to Uspallata and into the Andes is via the pretty villages of Cacheuta and Portrerillos, offering thermal spa and watersports respectively. If you're driving, note that since the river has been dammed there is no direct road between Cacheuta (1245 m) and Potrerillos, so you need to take a detour to get to Cacheuta. From Mendoza, head south out of the city by Avenida J Vicente Zapata, access Route 7, leading to Ruta 40. Follow signs to Cacheuta, passing the area's biggest petrochemical plant, before you climb up into the hills. Cacheuta's

Parque Provincial Aconcagua

The Aconcagua Provincial Park is 190 km west of Mendoza city, and apart from Aconcagua itself – the highest peak in the world outside the Himalayas, at 6959 m – it includes 30 other peaks over 4000 m, nine of them over 5000 m, making it a great centre for hiking and climbing. Mount Aconcagua gets its name from the Quechua for 'stone sentry', and it is indeed a majestic peak with five great glaciers hanging from its slopes. It's a demanding climb even for the experienced, and it's absolutely essential to take at least eight to 10 days just to adapt to the altitude before you ascend. Pulmonary and cerebral oedema are serious risks and the dangers should not be underestimated: climbers die on the mountain every year. If you're planning to climb Aconcagua, it's essential to seek expert advice and plan your trip carefully. See the official website, www.aconcagua. mendoza.gov.ar, for more details.

Access

Valle de los Horcones (2950 m), 2 km west of Puente del Inca and another 2 km off R7: *guardaparque* and free camping, open in the climbing season. This is the last accessible point for vehicles. No permits are required, but there is an entrance fee of US$1.50 for the short walk to the mirador on Laguna Horcones, where you have excellent views of Aconcagua's southern face.

Advice

Climbers are advised to make use of the medical services where they're available (some base camps) to check for early symptoms of altitude sickness and oedema. See www.aconcagua.org. ar and www.aconcagua.com.ar. Tents must be able to withstand 160-kph winds. Clothing and sleeping gear for temperatures below -40°C. Always carry plenty of water, as there are very few sources. Take all your rubbish out with you: no litter is to be thrown away in the park, and bags are handed out at the park entrance to be collected when you leave. Bring a stove and sufficient fuel; no wood is to be used for lighting fires. For emergencies only, use the *guardaparques* radio frequency 142.8 Mhz.

Permits

It's essential to obtain a permit for trekking or climbing at any time of year: pay a fee (much cheaper for Argentine nationals) and fill in a form. You'll need to submit certain other documents for some specific activities. The rules and prices vary according to time of year and activity. For climbing in the high season (15 December-31 January) you must obtain a permit in person in Mendoza, at the Subsecretaría de Turismo, Avenida San Martín 1143. In the winter season (1 April-14 November) permits to climb Aconcagua are sold at Dirección de Recursos Naturales Renovables, next to the gates of Parque General San Martín in Mendoza. An ascent permit lasts for 20 consecutive days from the moment it is stamped at the park entrance, and prices vary from US$384 (US$520 via Plaza Guanacos) in high season to US$512 (for any route) in winter. Be warned that places selling the permits, and fees, may change, so it's vital to check the official website (www. aconcagua.mendoza.gov.ar). Trekking permits are needed for all walks up to any of the base camps (excluding Plaza

Guanacos camp, at the end of the only ascent trek) and are sold near the park itself at Horcones ranger station. These cost: US$153 for seven consecutive days; US$66 for three consecutive days in high season; US$46 the rest of the year. Day permits are US$20.

Trekking and climbing routes

There are two access routes to Aconcagua's summit, Río Horcones and Río de las Vacas, which lead to the two main base camps, Plaza de Mulas and Plaza Argentina respectively. For climbing Aconcagua, allow two weeks for the complete trip. Getting to the summit is not technically difficult: the problem is in taking sufficient time for your body to adjust to the high altitude. Most people fail simply because they take it too fast. All climbers should allow at least one week for acclimatization at lower altitudes before attempting the summit. Allow another few days for the weather. The best time is from the end of December to end of February.

Day permits allow you to walk from Horcones four hours up to Confluencia Base Camp (3390 m) and then two hours back, all along the Quebrada del Río Horcones. The walk presents no difficulties, except for the high altitude – don't be surprised that some people in your group will be affected more than others. Altitude sickness affects everyone differently.

Confluencia Base Camp can get horribly crowded in summer with dozens of climbers and many more mules. There is a ranger station, public showers and medical services (in high season). From here you can either take the North Face route, used by 80% of climbers, to Plaza de Mulas (4365 m), in eight hours, or the South Face route to Plaza Francia (4250 m), in five hours. It's a tiring, rather monotonous walk up to Plaza de Mulas, another busy camp, with a ranger station, medical services and the highest hotel in the world another 20-minute walk away.

South Face route leads from Confluencia to Plaza Francia base camp (five hours), with a mirador after about four hours looking over the lower Horcones glacier, with an outstanding view of the 3000-m high rock and ice walls of Aconcagua's south face. Plaza Francia Camp is less crowded, but has no services at all.

Route via the Polish Glacier: This little-used route starts at Punta de Vacas (2400 m), 16 km east of Puente del Inca. Plaza Argentina (4200 m) is the base camp with intermediate camps at Pampa de Leñas (2900 m), with ranger station, reached after four hours of easy walking from Punta de Vacas, and Casa de Piedra (3240 m), reached after a further moderate six-hour walk along the same Quebrada del río de las Vacas, also with ranger station. From here, it's a steep seven-hour walk to Plaza Argentina (ranger station and medical services).

Facilities and services

Mules are available from Puente del Inca: about US$140 for 60 kg of gear one way to Plaza de Mulas or US$260 for 60 kg one way to Plaza Argentina; arrange return before setting out for a reduced two-way price. Organized trekking expeditions and tours can be booked in Mendoza (see Tour operators, Mendoza, page 206; and the official website).

pretty setting in a narrow valley merits the extra journey to reach it. There's a huge complex of several thermal pools where you can spend a day, and next to this, a fine hotel in attractive gardens with a good restaurant. It's better to stay at least a night to really enjoy the mountain scenery. ►► *See Where to stay, page 215.*

Potrerillos → *Colour map 3, B1. Phone code 02624.*

Potrerillos (1354 m, Km 68), just 10 km further on from Cacheuta, is a charming, laid-back village sprawling among the foothills of the Cordón del Plata mountains. In the summer it's a popular retreat among *Mendocinos*, but it's excellent for a weekend's walking or horse riding at any time of year, though particularly lovely in spring, or in autumn, when the avenues of *álamo* (poplar) trees are a rich yellow against the mauve haze of mountains beyond. From December to February, you can go rafting and kayaking on Río Mendoza, which runs through the valley below the village. The water level depends on the time of year and the amount of snow melt swelling the river, so that the high season varies from year to year. In summer you can hike from Potrerillos to Vallecitos over two days. There's also a lovely walk to Cascada del Salto, but the path isn't marked, so take a guide (see What to do, page 216).

From Potrerillos' centre – where there's little more than a hotel, campsite and YPF station on a crossroads – you could take the road south up to Vallecitos via the little hamlets of El Salto, Las Vegas and San Jorge, with its small *cervecería* (microbrewery). There are *parrilla* restaurants, tea rooms and lots of *cabañas* for hire around these areas, and the views are wonderful.

Vallecitos → *Phone code 02622.*

This tiny hamlet (2900 m) is 27 km west of Potrerillos along a madly winding *ripio* road, certainly not to be attempted in poor weather conditions. There's little here apart from a couple of *refugios* with hostel accommodation and a rather basic family ski resort, but it's popular as a day trip from Mendoza. The **ski centre**, Valles del Plata Centro de Esqui, has 4.7 km of pistes, mostly intermediate standard, seven ski lifts and a ski school. Vallecitos is used as a base camp by climbers for training in the nearby peaks, before attempting Aconcagua. Contact **Expediciones Cordón Del Plata** ① *T0261-423 7423, www.cordondelplata.com*, to take part in a climbing expedition to the beautiful summits of the Cordón del Plata range. They're less well known than Aconcagua, but also spectacular.

Uspallata → *Colour map 3, A2. Phone code 02624. Population 3400.*

The picturesque village of Uspallata (1751 m, 120 km from Mendoza and 52 km from Potrerillos) lies in its own wide valley, very close to the high Andes, and so it's become a popular stopping point on the road to Chile. All routes pass through it, and yet it has retained a rather charming unspoilt atmosphere – out of peak season at least. With distant mountains glimpsed through a frame of *álamo* (poplar) trees, it is reminiscent of the Himalayas and was the setting for *Seven Years in Tibet*. Stay for a day at least to explore the mysterious white egg-shaped domes of **Las Bóvedas** ① *2 km on RN 149 north, US$2*, built in the early 19th century by the indigenous Huarpes people, under instruction by the Jesuits, to melt silver. There is a small, interesting museum.

From Uspallata, the Route Provincial 39 leads north to **Calingasta** and **Barreal** (see pages 231 and 232), unpaved for its first part and tricky when the snow-melt floods it in summer. Here you'll find the remains of the Inca road, one of the most important archaeological sites in the region, with foundations of an Inca Tambo (post house) too; look for signs on the left-hand side of the road. Uspallata has a few hotels, a hostel, food shops, bakeries, a post office and a YPF station with restaurant, shop and *locutorios*. The tourist office in Upsallata keeps unreliable hours. For information, see www.turismo.lasheras.gov.ar.

Uspallata to Chile via Parque Provincial Aconcagua → *For listings, see pages 215-216.*

This dramatic road, which runs past the foothills of Aconcagua, is one of Mendoza's most memorable sights and not to be missed. From Uspallata, a good paved road to Chile crosses a broad plain, with maroon and chalk-white rocks sticking up from the rolling land. The road winds alongside a ravine with a thread of turquoise water below, before climbing up into a mountain pass with amazing terracotta rock formations and a heart-stopping glimpse of Volcán Tupungato – one of the giants of the Andes, rising to 6600 m. The first tiny village you come to, **Punta de Vacas**, has a large *gendarmería* (police station) but little accommodation.

Ski resorts
The road continues, climbing quickly beyond the snowline in winter, to the charming small ski resort of **Los Penitentes** (2580 m) ⓘ *Km 183, T02624-420356, www. penitentesweb.com, May-Sep, daily ski hire US$35-47.* The resort is named after the mass of pinnacled rocks on its mountainside, which you might think looks vaguely like a group of cowled monks climbing upwards. It is a low-key family resort and is surprisingly quiet. There is good skiing on the 28 pistes (total length of 25 km, with 10 lifts); most of them are graded difficult but there are a couple of long descents of medium difficulty and three beginners' slopes. It's good value and uncrowded.

Another low-key ski resort in the area is **Los Puquios** ⓘ *www.lospuquios.com.ar,* 5 km west. It's small, ideal for beginners and good value. It's also used as a base camp for climbers for acclimatization to the high altitudes, and as a departure point for mule caravans to higher base camps closer to Aconcagua. On the southern side of Route 7, opposite, you'll find a cemetery for climbers who have died on Aconcagua's slopes; a reminder that this summit is not to be undertaken lightly.

Puente del Inca → *Colour map 3, B1.*
Puente del Inca (2718 m, Km 190), 7 km further on, is set among breathtaking mountains and is a great base for exploring the peaks on foot or on horseback, with access to the Parque Provincial Aconcagua. The naturally formed bridge, after which the village is named, is said to be one of the Great Wonders of South America. Crossing a tributary of the Río Mendoza at a height of 19 m, the natural bridge is 21 m long and 27 m wide and seems to have been formed by sulphur-bearing hot springs below which have stained the whole ravine an incredible ochre yellow, and

Border crossing: Argentina–Chile

Las Cuevas

The paved road to the border goes through the 3.2-km **Cristo Redentor tunnel**, 0930-2030 in winter and 24 hours in summer, US$4 for cars (no cyclists), into Chile. The last settlement before the tunnel is tiny forlorn Las Cuevas, 16 km from Puente del Inca, offering only a *kiosko*, café and hostel accommodation. In summer you can take the old road over La Cumbre pass to **El Cristo Redentor** (Christ the Redeemer), an 8-m-high statue erected jointly by Chile and Argentina in 1904 to celebrate the settlement of their boundary dispute. If you want to see this, take an all-day excursion from Mendoza, or drive up in a 4WD, after the snow has melted, or walk from Las Cuevas (4½ hours up, two hours down – only to be attempted by the fit, in good weather). Expreso Uspallata runs buses to here from Mendoza.

Accommodation Arco de las Cuevas ($ pp, doubles $$), T0261-426 5273, www.arcodelascuevas.com.ar. Set right above the old road to Cristo Redentor on a picturesque old Alpine-like stone and wooden arch, this has very spartan though comfortable dorms, a restaurant and a bar that mostly attracts climbers, some skiers and mountain guides. They can organize adventure trips into Chile. Transfer for access to Aconcagua Provincial Park for an extra US$4.

Precautions There are many dangerous bends on this route so drive slowly, and at Km 1097 the 13-m bridge over Río Blanco is only 4.70 m wide, so there is only one car allowed past at any one time. Due to fog, snow, mud or falling rocks, this route is sometimes closed. For up-to-date information **Escuadrón 27 Punta de Vacas**, T0261-4205 275, esc27p_vacas@fullzero.com.ar. For information on the curves and look outs see, www.gendarmería.gov.ar/pasos/ficheris.htm (in Spanish).

Chilean customs The Chilean border is beyond Las Cuevas, but customs is back near Los Horcones, 2 km west of Puente del Inca.

Note No fresh food can be taken into Chile. Hire cars need special papers, and the number plate engraved in the window: tell your hire company if you plan to take the car into Chile.

left the bridge an eerie orange colour. Underneath the bridge are the ruins of a 1940s spa hotel, destroyed by a snow avalanche and now mostly washed away by the river, but a torrent of hot sulphurous water still gushes from its walls. (Watch your footing on the steps as they are extremely slippery.) The old baths, to the side of the river, between the bridge and the small church, have basic facilities and are good for a soak amidst magnificent scenery.

West of the village is the access road for Laguna Horcones in the Parque Provincial Aconcagua, see page 210. Route 7 continues west, with fine views of Aconcagua sharply silhouetted against the sky, to the customs post at Los Horcones, the settlement of Las Cuevas (16 km beyond Puente del Inca) and on through the Cristo Redentro tunnel to Chile (see box, above).

☉ Alta Montaña listings

For hotel and restaurant price codes and other relevant information, see pages 20-26.

☉ Where to stay

Cacheuta *p209*

$$$$-$$$ Hotel & Spa Termas Cacheuta, R82, Km 38, T02624-490152, www.termas cacheuta.com. A warm and inviting place with comfortable rustic-style rooms and thermal water piped into the private bathrooms. There's a large swimming pool, a good restaurant and access to the lovely spa included. Prices are full board and are cheaper Sun-Thu. Entry into the **Thermal Spa Park** is US$46 for a full day. Recommended.

Potrerillos *p212*

$$$ Silver Cord B&B, Valle del Sol, T02624-481083, www.silvercordbb.com. ar. With breakfast, internet, laundry service, lots of outdoor activities and 4WD trips, guides speak English.

Camping

Excellent **ACA site**, T02624-482013. Shady, hot water after 1800, pool, clean.

Uspallata *p212*

$$$ Gran Hotel Uspallata, on RN 7, Km 1149, towards Chile, T02624-420449, www.granhoteluspallata.com.ar. Lovely location, spacious and modern in big gardens away from the centre, pool, good value, restaurant.

$$$ Los Cóndores, Las Heras s/nº, T02624-420002, www.loscondoreshotel. com.ar. Low season prices, bright, neat rooms, good restaurant (dinners only), heated pool.

$$$ Valle Andino, Ruta 7, T02624-420095, www.hotelvalleandino.com.

Modern airy place, good rooms, heated pool, restaurant, breakfast included.

$ pp Mountain Chill Out Hostel (officially Hostel Internacional Uspallata), RN 7, Km 1141.5, T0261-575 9204, www. hosteluspallata.com.ar. Dorms for 4 to 6 with or without bath, private rooms sleep 1-6, with bath ($$$-$$), also comfortable cabins for up to 5, discounts for HI members, bar, restaurant, tours arranged, bike and ski rental, attractive surroundings.

Route to Chile via Parque Provincial Aconcagua *p213*

$$$ Hostería Puente del Inca, RN7, Km 175, T0261-423 4848, http://hosteria puentedelinca.onlinetravel.com.ar. Next to the small ski centre at Los Puquios. Full-board available, huge cosy dining room, advice on Aconcagua, helpful owners, great atmosphere.

$$ pp Hostería Penitentes, Villa Los Penitentes, T0261-524 4708, www. hosteriapenitentes.com. Cheery place near ski slopes, with breakfast, good café, cheaper for several nights. Recommended.

$ pp Campo Base Penitentes, T0261-425 5511, www.penitentes.com.ar. A cheap ski resort option, lively, slightly cramped dorms, shared bath, restaurant, bar, minibus service to Mendoza. Hostel is open all year, offers ski programmes in season. HI discounts.

There is also camping at Los Puquios.

Parque Provincial Aconcagua *p210*

$$$ Hotel Plaza de Mulas, book through www.aconcaguaspirit.com. ar/pmulas.htm. Full-board or cheaper without meals. Good food, information, medical treatment, also camping area, open high season only. Recommended.

🍴 Restaurants

Potrerillos *p212*
$$$-$$ Tomillo, Av Los Cóndores,
El Salto, T02624-483072, www.tomillo
restaurant.com.ar. Open all day (closed
Tue and Wed in low season). Excellent
home-made cooking, including trout.
Also simple and warm accommodation
in private doubles (**$$**).

Uspallata *p212*
$$$ La Estancia de Elías, Km 1146.
Opposite petrol station, a good and
crowded *parrilla*.
$$$-$$ Lo de Pato, RN7 Km 1148.
A popular *parrilla*; also pasta;
take-away food and bakery.

⛏ What to do

Potrerillos *p212*
Argentina Rafting, base camp at
Ruta Perilago, T02624-482037, www.
argentinarafting.com. Reliable company,
organizes good trips with climbing,
hiking, kayaking and other adventure
sports. Office in Mendoza city at
Amigorena 86, T0261-429 6325.
Ríos Andinos, 5 km north of Potrerillos,
T0261-517 4184, www.riosandinos.com.
Rafting, horse riding, trekking
and combinations.

Uspallata *p212*
Desnivel Aventura, RN 7 by the YPF
petrol station, T0261-15-589 2935,
www.desnivelaventura.com. Offers
rafting, riding, mountain biking,
trekking, climbing, skiing.

🚌 Transport

Mendoza to Uspallata *p208*
Bus
Expreso Uspallata, T0261-432 5055,
and **Buttini**, T0261-431 5932, have daily
services to and from **Mendoza** with
stops at all towns along RN 7; there are
fewer services in winter, when roads can
be blocked by snow, west of **Uspallata**.
To **Mendoza**: from **Uspallata**, several
services daily, 2-2½ hrs, US$5.75; from
Cacheuta, daily; from **Potrerillos**, 1 hr,
US$2.25; Uspallata to **Puente del Inca**,
US$3.75. Buttini continues twice a day
from Puente del Inca to Las Cuevas, US$9
return. Note that buses going to Chile do
not pick up passengers on their way.

Puente del Inca *p213*
Bus
To **Mendoza**, 3 a day, 4 hrs, US$7, with
Expreso Uspallata and Buttini (see
above). **Buttini** continues twice a day
from Puente del Inca to Las Cuevas.

Southern Mendoza province

The southern half of the province is wilder and less visited by tourists than the area around Mendoza city. There are two main centres, the closest of which, and most appealing, is the charming town of San Rafael, the centre of its own wine-growing region, with tree-lined streets and excellent bodegas. Near here, there's rafting heaven in the extraordinary Cañón del Atuel, a canyon of weird rock formations with a wonderful fast-flowing river running through it. The other centre, much further south, is the fledgling tourist town of Malargüe, which you could use as a base for skiing at Las Leñas, or for visiting remote areas of natural beauty at La Payunia and Llancanelo. There are two possible routes to the south of the province: you can take the fast Ruta 40 directly to San Rafael or the picturesque route from Potrerillos along the Cordón del Plata to Tupungato, a sleepy place with superb wineries and the starting point for long excursions into Tupungato Provincial Park. An appealing detour here is to scenic Manzano Histórico, right in the foothills of the Andes.

Tupungato and around → *For listings, see pages 223-226. Colour map 3, B2. Phone code 02622. Population 11,700.*

To reach the quiet little town of Tupungato (1050 m), take the picturesque road (Route 89) from Potrerillos, descending along the Cordón del Plata mountain range, with splendid views of the mountains, and through the fertile fruit- and vine-growing Uco Valley. (Otherwise, take Route 86 from Route Nacional 40, south of Mendoza.) Nearby are the stunningly wild mountain landscapes of Tupungato Provincial Park, named after the imposing peak of its volcano, 6600 m, which is inaccessible to the public unless you go with an approved guide; Rómulo Nieto's company (see Tour operators, page 225) is recommended. There are also superb wild landscapes on the upper Río de Las Tunas, to the west of town; contact the tourist office at Tupungato to stay overnight at the nearby Refugio Santa Clara (they'll direct you to the army for the key). **Tourist information** on Tupungato and the surrounding area is available from the foyer of **Hotel Turismo** ① *Belgrano 348, T02622-488007, www.tupungato. gov.ar.* Ask them about nearby bodegas and *estancia* visits for horse riding.

There are many vineyards around Tupungato; one of the most famous is **Bodega Salentein** ① *Los Arboles, 15 km south, T02622-429500, www.bodegasalentein. com, tours of the bodega daily,* whose fine wines you may have noticed in many restaurants. With a beautiful setting against the foothills of the Andes, the bodega produces some of the country's finest wine (the Malbec is exquisite) and you can stay in **Posada Salentein**, which has comfortable rooms, extremely welcoming hosts; there's perfect peace in which to walk, ride and relax. Recommended.

A much newer winery also worth visiting is the Spanish-owned **O Fournier** ① *Los Indios, La Consulta, west of San Carlos, T02622-451579, www.ofournier.com*. Its output is dedicated mainly to Tempranillo grapes, and here you can admire both the vines and the avant-garde architecture of the winery building, which is strictly functional and state of the art.

Continue south from Salentein to **Manzano Histórico**, a tiny hamlet in fabulous scenery, where a statue of San Martín marks his victorious return via this route from Chile. A *hostería* and campsite make this a good base for trekking, and there's a little shop and bar for provisions.

San Rafael → *For listings, see pages 223-226. Colour map 3, B2. Phone code 0260. Population 191,323.*

San Rafael (688 m, 236 km south of Mendoza) is a charming, quiet, airy town in the heart of fertile land that produces wine, fruit and olives in abundance. It's a relaxed place, smaller and less sophisticated than Mendoza but trim and well-maintained, with a good range of accommodation. It makes an ideal base for exploring the vineyards and for trying adventure sports at nearby Cañón del Atuel or more challenging activities further west.

Arriving in San Rafael

The airport is at Las Paredes, seven kilometres west of town, with access from Route 143. A bus to the centre costs US$1.20 with Buttini bus; remise taxis charge US$7. The central bus terminal is at General Paz y Paunero, a 10-minute walk to the centre. Most people cycle around the city, so you'll see more bikes than cars on the streets. The main thoroughfare, Avenida Hipólito Yrigoyen, runs northwest to southeast through the city, changing names at Avenida San Martín/El Libertador to become Avenida Mitre. There are ATMs and *locutorios* all along Yrigoyen, and a friendly and helpful **tourist office** ① *Av H Yrigoyen 775 y Balloffet, T0260-443 7860, www.sanrafaelturismo. gov.ar*; also in the bus terminal (mornings only). For online information see www.sanrafael.gov.ar, and www.sanrafael-tour.com (both in Spanish).

Places in San Rafael

There are lovely, leafy boulevards of French-influenced buildings in the city centre, thanks to the arrival of a significant French community here in the early 1900s. Río Diamante runs just south of the town, with a lovely park, **Parque Mariano Moreno**, situated on on an island in the middle of the stream. Among its attractions are a zoo and a small museum, the **Museo Municipal de Historia Natural** ① *6 km southwest of town, daily 0800-1900, US$0.70; Iselin bus along Av JA Balloffet*.

San Rafael is at the heart of an important wine-producing region, whose wines are at least as excellent as those around Mendoza. One of the country's most important wineries is **Bianchi** ① *Ruta 143, 9 km west of the centre, T0260-444 9600, www.casabianchi.com*, whose vineyard and champagne house can be visited on a commercialized tour. It's worth seeing for the fascinating process and rather over-the-top pseudo-classical building (take a taxi as buses are infrequent). They also have a traditional bodega in town, at the corner of Comandante Torres and Ortiz de Rosas, which offers an excellent and detailed tour, and sells the top wines at reduced prices after a generous tasting. (Look for their exported wines abroad under the names Elsa, Elsa's vineyard or Valentín Bianchi Premium.) **Jean Rivier** ① *H Yrigoyen 2385, T0260-443 2675, www.jeanrivier.com*, is a smaller, more intimate bodega in town which also produces excellent wine.

At a walking distance from town is San Rafael's oldest winery, **La Abeja** ① *Av H Yrigoyen 1900, T02627-439804, www.bodegalaabeja.com.ar*, while on the way to Malargüe, around 20 km southwest of San Rafael, is **Algodón Wine Estates** ① *Ruta 144, Cuadro Benegas, T0260-442 9020, www.algodonwineestates.com*. A state-of-the-art winery with pricey accommodation, restaurant, tennis courts and a golf course.

Around San Rafael → *For listings, see pages 223-226.*

San Rafael is a great centre for all kinds of activities, including rafting, horse riding, trekking, climbing and fishing.

Valle Grande and Cañón del Atuel
The most spectacular place for adventure is the nearby **Cañón del Atuel**, 35 km southwest. The gorge lies between two lakes 46 km apart, Valle Grande (508 ha) and El Nihuil (9600 ha). It's an atmospheric drive along the *ripio* road, which winds through the 20-km-long ravine of extraordinary rock formations in vibrant hues of cream, pink, metallic green and vivid terracotta. There are constantly changing views and an eerie atmosphere in the darker recesses of the canyon, where birds of prey wheel overhead. The best place for rafting is near **Valle Grande**, 2 km down the river from the Valle Grande Dam (about 40 km from San Rafael). On the south side of the river, near the bridge, you'll see plenty of adventure tour operators (see page 225 for the most reliable ones). Many offer river rafting (Grade II for beginners), horse riding and excursions for more challenging rafting, such as the upper Atuel or Diamante river (up to Grade V, experience required). There are plenty of hotels and campsites lining the pretty riverbanks on the north side of the river, in a 13-km stretch from this bridge back in the direction of San Rafael.

From San Rafael, Iselin runs daily buses to the Valle Grande dam at the near end of the canyon, returning in the evening, US$2.50. Remise taxis from San Rafael to Valle Grande charge about US$20. The only public transport through the entire gorge up to El Nihuil is the Iselin bus at weekends in summer.

Other excursions
Lago Los Reyunos is another popular excursion, 35 km west of San Rafael, a lake set in a barren rocky landscape, which can only be reached on a tour, as there are no

buses. But far more spectacular is the **Laguna Diamante**, 200 km northwest of San Rafael, an ultramarine blue expanse of water, whipped by perpetual winds, set against the craggy backdrop of the Andes and the perfectly conical Volcán Maipo. Only 4WD vehicles will make it over the last 60 km or so of track, and it's best to go on an excursion from San Rafael with **Taiel Viajes**, www.sierrapintada.com (see page 225).

There is some superb horse riding in the region into the Andes. You could take an excursion from El Sosneado (see below) or Tupungato (see above) to the place where the Uruguayan plane crashed into the mountains, subject of the book and film *Alive!*. This is less gruesome than you might think, since the landscapes are amazing: stark and very beautiful. **Laguna del Atuel**, 200 km west of San Rafael, has incredible turquoise water lapping against ochre mountains, and makes for another fabulous five-day horse-riding trip.

San Rafael to Las Leñas → *For listings, see pages 223-226.*

The greatest attraction west of San Rafael is the superb ski resort of Las Leñas. A good paved road (Ruta 144 and then Ruta 40) leads west from San Rafael across the vast plain of the Río Atuel, passing saltflats and marshland as you head towards stark snow-dusted mountains rising steeply out of the ochre-coloured land. If you're heading southwest this way to ski or hike, or south to explore the area around Malargüe, you might like to stop off at **El Sosneado**, at Km 138.

El Sosneado
El Sosneado is the only settlement in this area, with a service station and a small shop for fine home-cured hams and olives, where you can also take away delicious sandwiches. The YPF station sells snacks and hot drinks. El Sosneado is also the starting point for good rafting and treks into the mountains, but there is little infrastructure in the village itself, and most visitors prefer to arrange their trips before coming here, in San Rafael or Malargüe.

Nearby there's a good lake for trout fishing, **Laguna El Sosneado**, 42 km away, reached by a *ripio* side road following the valley of the Río Atuel northwest. Some 13 km or so beyond the lake are natural thermal pools, the **Termas el Sosneado**, where you can bathe in the sulphurous waters for free, since there's no organization here, and the Hotel Termas El Sosneado is in ruins. Ahead, you'll see the Overo volcano (4619 m).

Los Molles → *Colour map 3, B1. Phone code 02627.*
Twenty-one kilometres southwest of El Sosneado and 156 km southwest of San Rafael a road branches off RN 40 towards Las Leñas, following the Río Salado west into the Andes. After 30 km, the road passes through the tiny hamlet of Los Molles, a small, faded old thermal resort, now little more than a cluster of hotels, the oldest of which has access to thermal springs. None of these establishments is luxurious but they offer an alternative to expensive Las Leñas hotels, plus some adventure tourism trips in the summer that mainly include horse riding to nearby sites. Opposite Los Molles a *ripio* road leads to the *refugio* of the **Club Andino Pehuenche** and, 8 km further on,

to the **Laguna de la Niña Encantada**, a beautiful little lake and shrine to the Virgin. Continuing towards Las Leñas, there are the strange **Pozo de las Animas** (Well of the Spirits), two natural circular pits filled with water (the larger is 80 m deep), where wind blowing across the holes makes a ghostly wail, hence the name. They're a curious sight if you happen to be passing, but don't quite merit a special excursion.

Las Leñas → *Colour map 3, B1. Altitude: 2240 m.*
ⓘ *Ski season: mid-Jun to end-Oct. T011-4819 6060, or T0800-222 5362, www.laslenas. com, lift pass in high season US$73 per day, equipment hire from US$29.50 daily, 13 ski lifts.*
Las Leñas (2250 m), 49 km off the San Rafael–Malargüe road, is internationally renowned for its excellent skiing and snowboarding. As a result, it's one of the most expensive resorts in the country, full of wealthy Argentine families and beautiful people in trendy bars. Set at the end of a spectacular valley, in the middle of five snow-capped peaks, it has powder snow throughout the season on 29 pistes with a total length of 64 km, and, despite the frequent bad weather and lack of tree cover, it's the best resort in South America, thanks to its steep slopes, with a vertical drop of some 1230 m, and the fact that you can walk straight out of your hotel onto the pistes. A constantly circulating free bus service picks up guests from further-flung hotels in the resort. The season runs from mid-June to early October but the busiest and most expensive time is July and August, when prices are at least 50% higher. The resort also has a ski school, a special snowboard park, many cafés, bars and restaurants (several right on the pistes), a useful information point where there are lockers, banks, doctors and tourist information. There are also ski patrol units all over the pistes, so you are in safe hands here. In summer, Las Leñas operates as a resort for adventure sports, such as trekking and climbing. Beyond Las Leñas the road continues into **Valle Hermoso**, a beautiful valley accessible only from December to March.

Malargüe and around → *For listings, see pages 223-226. Colour map 3, B2. Phone code 0260. Population 27,660.*

Situated 186 km southwest of San Rafael in reach of really spectacular unspoilt landscapes, Malargüe (1426 m) is slowly developing as a centre for hiking and horse riding, although its self-promotion as the national centre for adventure tourism is probably over-blown. In ski season it serves as a cheap alternative to Las Leñas, with frequent minibus services between the two and a 50% reduction on your ski pass if you stay in a hotel in Malargüe. However the best time to come is from spring to autumn, when you can make the most of the landscape for walking and riding. The **Fiesta Nacional del Chivo** (locally produced kid, a local delicacy) is held in the first fortnight of January, with live music and partying, attracting national *folclore* stars, as well as Chilean performers and public from across the Andes.

Arriving in Malargue
The **bus terminal** is at Aldao and Beltrán. The **airport** ⓘ *T0260-447 1600*, is on the southern edge of town. Malargüe has a broad main street, San Martín, with an assortment of small shops, *locutorios*, cafés and the odd run-down hotel, but the

Border crossing: Argentina–Chile

Paso Pehuenche

Paso Pehuenche (2553 m) is reached by a *ripio* road that branches off Ruta 40, 66 km south of Malargüe. On the Chilean side the road continues down the valley of the Río Maule to Talca.

Opening hours The border is open from 0800-1700. See http://www.gendarmeria. gov.ar/pasos/fichpehuenche.htm for detailed information (in Spanish).

best accommodation is in the outskirts, north of the centre. The helpful **tourist office** ① *Ruta 40 Norte, T0260-447 1659, www.malargue.gov.ar, daily 0800-2130, also at the bus station*, can arrange visits to the nearby provincial parks.

Places in Malargüe

Malargüe has gained the interest of astrophysicists by hosting the world's largest **Pierre Auger Cosmic Ray Observatory** ① *Av San Martín (Norte) 304, T0260-447 1562, www.auger.org, free lectures Mon-Fri 1700 (ask in advance for English presentations)*. A visit here should be combined with the excellent **Planetarium** ① *Comandante Rodríguez (Oeste) 207, T0260-447 2116, www.planetariomalargue.com.ar, free guided visits and daily shows (US$4)*.

Around Malargüe

The wild untouched landscape around Malargüe is surprising and extraordinarily beautiful. There are three main places to visit, all pretty remote and with little or no public transport, so unless you have your own vehicle, they can only be visited on a tour. Even if you do have your own transport, you must be accompanied by an authorized guide, which must be arranged in advance and requires a certain amount of planning.

La Payunia Reserve, 208 km south, is the most remarkable of the three, and dominated by the majestic peaks of several snow-capped volcanoes. The vast expanse of seductive altiplano grasslands is studded with volcanic peaks and deep red and black crags of extraordinary sculpted lava. The appearance of hundreds of guanaco running wild across your path adds to the magic. The entrance is 100 km south of Malargüe on sandy *ripio* roads. You can bring your own vehicle here and the *guardaparques* will show you around in their 4WD. Ask at the tourist office in Malargüe for directions; they will also radio the *guardaparques* and tell them to expect you. The best way to enjoy the reserve is on horseback, on a three-day expedition, or you can take a tour from Malargüe with **Karen Travel** ① *www.karentravel.com.ar*.

The **Laguna Llancanelo** (pronounced *shancannello*), 65 km southeast, is filled with hugely varied birdlife in spring, when 150 species come to nest on its lakes. At any time of year you'll see Chilean flamingos, rising in a pink cloud from pale turquoise waters where volcanic peaks are perfectly reflected. You may also see tern, curlews, grebes, teal and black-necked swans, among others. To get there, contact the Llancanelo *guardaparques* via the tourist office, or go on a trip from Malargüe.

At **Caverna de las Brujas** ① *1 hr's drive away, 2-hr guided tours, lights and helmets provided, children over 7 welcome*, there are 5 km of underground caves to explore, taking you through the Earth's development from the Jurassic period onwards; enjoy the fantastic variety of elaborate stalactites and stalagmites. There is no independent access to the caves and all visits must be arranged with one of the authorized tour operators in Malargüe; the tourist office in Malargüe can make recommendations (see What to do, page 225).

⦿ Southern Mendoza province listings

For hotel and restaurant price codes and other relevant information, see pages 20-26.

⦿ Where to stay

Tupungato *p217*

$$$$ Chateau d'Ancon, R89, San José, Tupungato, T0261-4235843, www.estanciancon.com.ar. Open mid-Oct to Apr. At the foot of the mighty Tupungato volcano, a 1933 French-style rural mansion is at the heart of a traditional *estancia* owned by the Bombal family, who were originally French, but have been living in Mendoza since 1760. The magnificent park was designed by famous Argentine landscape architect Charles Thays, and all the fruit and vegetables used for meals here are grown in nearby orchards and kitchen gardens. A wonderfully comfortable place to stay, with elegant decor inside the house, and excellent service.

$$$-$$ Hostería Don Romulo, Almirante Brown 1200, T02622-489020, www.donromulo.com.ar. This *hostería* is owned by Rómulo Nieto, who runs his own tour company (see Tour operators, page 225). There are simple rooms with TV and bath for 2-4 with a cosy lounge to relax in and decent, very inexpensive food from the restaurant.

$$ Hotel Turismo, Belgrano 1060, T02622-488007. A slightly modernized 1940s place, basic but comfortable rooms with wonderful kingfisher-blue tiles in the bathrooms, some family rooms, a pool and a good restaurant. Tourist information in the foyer.

Camping

Camping San Antonio, R94, Km 27.5, T0261-15-535 4888, www.campingsanantonio.com.ar. There are various attractive spots in the Manzano Histórico, but this one is particularly recommended for its good, well-kept facilities, including a large pool. They also rent out small *cabañas*.

Patios de Correa, Calle La Costa, El Peral, 4.3 km northwest of Tupungato. A good site in woods of willow and walnut trees, on the riverbank, also a good picnic spot.

San Rafael *p218*

$$$ Nuevo Mundo, Av Balloffet 725, T0260-444 5666, www.hnmsanrafael.com. Small business hotel, a little out of town, with pool, restaurant and spa.

$$ San Rafael, C Day 30, T0260-443 0127, www.hotelsanrafael.com.ar. A decent and reasonably priced option with plain rooms in need of some renovation.

$$ Francia, Francia 248, T0260-442 9351, www.alojamientofrancia.com.ar. A lovely place on a quiet street in town with simple, functional rooms on a manicured garden; excellent value.

$$ Regine, Independencia 623, T0260-442 1470, www.hotelregine.com.ar. Some 8 blocks away from centre, it is a comfortable choice with good rooms, a restaurant and a large pool in an attractive garden. Very good value.

$ pp Tierrasoles Hostel, Alsina 245, T0260-443 3449, www.tierrasoles. com.ar. 5 blocks from bus station, it has small dorms for 6 to 8 and doubles (**$$**) in a quite nice residence with a backyard. HI discounts.

$ pp Trotamundos Hostel, Barcala 298, T0260-443 2795, www.trotamundos hostel.com.ar. In a quiet area next to the main streets. A lively hostel with a nice patio, small dorms for 3 to 6 and a private double (**$$**).

Around San Rafael p219

$$$-$$ Valle Grande Hotel & Resort, T0260-15-458 0660, www.hotelvalle grande.com. Well situated on the banks of the river in the Cañón del Atuel, with a big terrace and good views from its restaurant, this has smart rooms, a pool and friendly service. There are lots of activities laid on for guests. Also *cabañas* for hire (**$$$**), popular with families and very lively in summer.

$$$-$$ Finca El Maitén, Mercado 1405, T0260-15-434 3948, www.fincaelmaiten. com.ar. Charming B&B, 10 km from town in the wine-growing region. Spacious, rustic-style double bedroom and a lovely garden to relax in.

Los Molles p220

Cheaper options than Las Leñas.

$$$ Complejo Los Molles, T0260-15-459 1654, www.complejolosmolles.com. Wood and stone detached houses, plain

and comfortable, for 4-8 people with breakfast. Restaurant and ski rental.

$$$ Hotel Termas Lahuen-Có, T0260-449 9700, www.hotellahuenco.com. Dating from 1930s and now rather kitsch, with thermal baths, meals.

$$$ La Valtellina, T0260-15-440 2761, www.lavaltellina.com.ar. Attractively rustic Alpine cottages, Italian owned and run, with an excellent restaurant and tea house.

Las Leñas p221

There are several plush hotels, all **$$$$-$$$**, most with pool, plus a disco, ski rental shop and several restaurants (see www. laslenas.com). For cheaper accommodation stay in Los Molles or Malargüe.

Malargüe p221

$$$ Malargüe, Av San Martín (Norte) 1230, T0260-447 2300, www. hotelmalarguesuite.com. On the northern access to town, this comfortable 4-star hotel has a new wing with slightly bigger rooms, an indoor pool, restaurant, spa and a casino to be opened in 2015.

$$ Rioma, Fray Inalicán (Oeste) 127, T0260-447 1065, www.hotelrioma. com.ar. Small, family-run and spotless place with basic facilities and a pool. Convenient for the bus station.

$ pp Eco Hostel Malargüe, Prolongación Constitución Nacional (Finca No 65), Colonia Pehuenche, 5 km from centre, T0260-447 0391, www.hostelmalargue. com. Eco-hostel built with an enhanced traditional *quincha* method, in rural surroundings, on dairy farm with organic fruit and veg, good meals, basic, comfortable dorms and rooms (**$$**), cheaper without bath and HI discount, Choique travel agency.

🍴 Restaurants

Tupungato *p217*
Apart from the hotels' restaurants, there are a few pizzerias and cafés to choose from on the main street, Belgrano.
$$ La Posada del Jamón, R92, Km 14, Vista Flores, Tunuyán, T02622-492053, www.laposadadeljamon.com.ar. Pork rules on the menu here, in this charmingly rustic and very popular roadside restaurant. There are other tasty dishes on offer though, and excellent local wines.

San Rafael *p218*
An area of attractive open-air cafés and small restaurants lies along C Pellegrini between Chile and Day in town.
$$$ El Rey del Chivo, Av H Yrigoyen 651. A good and basic place for trying the regional speciality, *chivito*, or kid.
$$$ Pettra, Av H Yrigoyen 1750. Very good choice for a great range of meals in an area full of restaurants.
$$ Las Duelas, Pellegrini 190. For tasty sandwiches and salads.
$$ Nina, Av San Martín y Olascoaga. A casual, open-airplace on a central corner, good for a light meal, including fine salads, open till late.
La Delicia del Boulevard, Av H Yrigoyen 1 594. Very good ice cream on the way to wineries.

Malargüe *p221*
$$$ La Cima, Av San Martín (Norte) 886. *Parrilla* and more elaborate meals, including fish. Good value.
$$$-$$ El Chuma, Illescas (Oeste) 155. The place for trying kid, the local speciality.
$$ Bonafide, Av San Martín (Sur) 364. Very good café open till late, serving simple meals, including good pizza.
$$ La Posta, Av Roca (Este) 174. Popular *parrilla*, offering pastas and pizza too.

🎯 What to do

Tupungato *p217*
Tour operators
A highly recommended guide is **Rómulo Nieto**, www.donromulo.com.ar. He organizes trekking and horse-riding excursions into the provincial park, where he also runs the base camp **Refugio El Cóndor**. In summer, Rómulo offers trekking to the summit and horse riding along the old path to Chile from Manzano Histórico to Portezuelo de los Piuquenes.
Tupungato Expedición, Liniers 1139, T02622-489791, www.tupungato expedicion.com.ar. Run by 2 professional guides, 1- and 2-day treks or 18-day adventures.

San Rafael *p218*
Tour operators charge similar prices for standard excursions, including the most popular day tour to Cañón del Atuel for about US$35 pp (lunch and extra activities are not included). Ask in advance for tours in English.
Atuel Travel, Buenos Aires 31, T0260-442 9282, www.atueltravel.com.ar. A recommended agency.
Raffeish, Valle Grande, T0260-443 6996, www.raffeish.com.ar. Recommended as the most professional rafting company.
Renta Bike, Day 487, T0260-15-440 1236, www.renta-bike.com.ar. Bike rental, wine tours and excursions along Cañón del Atuel.

Malargüe *p221*
Tour operators charge similar rates for standard excursions (eg Payunia for about US$70 pp), which take a full day in most cases and may include a light meal. Two-day treks in Payunia, fly-fishing, rafting and several-day horse rides in

the Andes, including the approach to the remains of the crashed Uruguayan airplane (described in the film *Alive!*) are also available, though some activities are in summer only. Ask in advance for tours in English.

A recommended range of tours is offered by **Choique**, Av San Martín (Sur) 33, T0260-447 0391, www.choique. com, and **Karen Travel**, Av San Martín (Sur) 54, T0260-447 2226, www.karen travel.com.ar.

Some 30 km south of Malargüe, in the Cuesta del Chihuido area on route 40, are Manqui Malal, T0260-447 2567 and Turcará, T0260-15-453 5908, where trekking, zip lining, camping and meals are offered.

⊖ Transport

Tupungato *p217*
Bus
To **Mendoza** and Las Heras, daily, 1½-2 hrs, US$3.50.

San Rafael *p218*
Air
To/from Buenos Aires with **Aerolíneas Argentinas**/Austral.

Bus
To/from **Mendoza**, 3-3½ hrs, many daily, US$7.50-9.50; **Neuquén**, US$37-48, 7-9½ hrs. To **Buenos Aires**, 12½-14 hrs, US$74-98. To **Valle Grande**, US$2.50, with Iselin. To **Las Leñas**, 3 hrs, US$8.50, 3 weekly services (daily in winter holidays), with Iselin. To **Malargüe**,

2½-3 hrs, US$7.50. To **Talca** (Chile), via Paso Pehuenche or Maule, once weekly (snow may occasionally block the road), 9 hrs, US$37.50, with **Cata**.

For wineries west of town, take Buttini bus (destination 25 de Mayo) along C Avellaneda and then Av H Yrigoyen, and tell the driver which bodega you want to visit.

El Sosneado and around *p220*
Bus
Daily buses to/from **Malargüe**, Las Leñas and **San Rafael** all stop at El Sosneado.

Malargüe *p221*
Air
Chartered flights from **Buenos Aires** and **São Paulo** (Brazil) in the skiing season.

Bus
Terminal at Aldao y Beltrán. To **Mendoza**, direct daily with **Viento Sur** minibuses, 5 hrs, US$15, or with **Cata**, 6½ hrs, US$15; alternatively change buses in San Rafael. To **San Rafael**, 2½-3 hrs, US$7.50, with **Buttini**, **Cata** or **Iselin**. There are **Cata** buses and several transfer services to **Las Leñas** in ski season. **Cata** leaves twice weekly across La Payunia to **Agua Escondida** on the border with La Pampa province, and also heads south along route 40 to Barrancas, on the border with Neuquén province. Otherwise, to **Neuquén** (via route 40 and Rincón de los Sauces), Sun-Fri 2115, with **Leader/ Rincón** from Los Amigos bar, Av San Martín (Sur) 765, by the clock tower.

San Juan province

The province of San Juan extends north and west from the capital, San Juan city, which lies in the broad valley of the Río San Juan, and is the centre of a wine-producing area as big as Mendoza's but not of the same quality. The city itself is sleepy and not wildly interesting for visitors, but there are two areas in the province that might lure you here. San Juan's jewel is the little-visited west of the province, where the foothills of the Andes rise in ranges separated by beautiful, lush valleys such as the lovely Calingasta. There is great climbing and trekking here, with several Andean peaks to explore, including the mighty Mercedario (6770 m), and incredibly peaceful ancient hamlets provide charming places to completely unwind. The northeast of the province, near the border with La Rioja, is the site of the Ischigualasto Provincial Park, often known as the Valle de la Luna (Valley of the Moon), where millions of years of the planet's history and dinosaur fossils are on display in dried-out lagoons, Talampaya National Park, just over the border in La Rioja, has fabulous dramatic canyons and eroded rocks. This northern region is inhospitably hot and dry almost all year round, but the landscapes are impressive: empty and starkly beautiful.

San Juan city → For listings, see pages 233-236. Colour map 3, A2.

The provincial city, 177 km north of Mendoza, is much less inviting than the marvellous landscapes all around and you're most likely to arrive here on the way to the Calingasta Valley or the parks further north. However, it's a good base for organizing those trips as there are several good places to stay and eat, and some good bodegas for wine tasting. There's also one sight of fascinating cultural interest in the shrine to pagan saint La Difunta Correa. Although the city was founded on its present site in 1593, little of the original settlement remains, since the most powerful earthquake in Argentine history struck in 1944, killing over 10,000 inhabitants. Though it's been rebuilt in modern style, San Juan has not yet recovered, unlike Mendoza. It was at a fundraising event at Luna Park in Buenos Aires for the victims of the tragedy that Juan Perón met Eva Duarte, the radio actress who became his second wife.

Arriving in San Juan city → *Phone code 0264. Population: city 109,123; greater San Juan 480,000 (estimated). Altitude: 650 m.*

Chacritas Airport is 11 km southeast of the city on Route 20. There are no regular buses, but there are *remise* taxis to the centre, about US$10. The **bus terminal** ① *Estados Unidos 492, terminal information T0264-422 1604,* is nine blocks east of the city centre (with almost all buses going through the centre). A taxi to the centre costs US$3. » *For further information see Transport, page 236.*

There is a basic **tourist office** ① *Sarmiento Sur 24 and San Martín, T0264-421 0004, www.turismo.sanjuan.gov.ar or www.ischigualasto.com (both in Spanish), Mon-Fri 0700-2030, Sat-Sun and holidays 0900-2000, and at bus station.* See also www. sanjuanlaestrelladelosandes.com. Note that the main street, Avenida San Martín, is often called Libertador.

Places in San Juan city

This is an important wine-producing area and there are lots of bodegas to visit, if you haven't seen those in Mendoza. See www.travelsanjuan.com.ar/vino.html for some suggestions of bodegas to visit. Those offering tours include **Santiago Graffigna** ① *Colón 1342 N, Desamparados, northwest of centre, T0264-421 4227, www. graffignawines.com, Mon-Sat 0915-1715, Sun 1015-1515,* the oldest in San Juan, with an interesting museum displaying winemaking machinery and old photos, and a wine bar. **Fabril Alto Verde** ① *R40, between Calle 13 and 14, Pocito, south of centre, T0264-421 2683, www.fabril-altoverde.com.ar. Mon-Sat,* is an organic winery with a smart showroom and small bar. **Antigua Bodega** ① *Salta 782 N, near the ring road, northwest of centre, T0264-421 2722, www.antiguabodega.com,* has a museum, below which the sparkling wine is made. **Viñas de Segisa** ① *Aberastain and Calle 15, La Rinconada, Pocito, south of centre, T0264-492 2000, www.saxsegisa.com.ar,* is a small boutique bodega with attractively renovated buildings. Not far from here is the charming, family-run bodega **Las Marianas** ① *Nueva, La Rinconada, Pocito, south of centre, T0264-15-463 9136, www.bodegalasmarianas.com.ar.* **Cavas de Zonda** ① *R12 Km 15, Rivadavia, west of centre, T0264-494 5144,* has an interesting setting right inside a mountain and a champagne house at the end of a tunnel carved into the rocky hills, where wines are made following traditional Spanish and French methods.

Opposite Plaza 25 de Mayo, take the lift 53 m up to the top of cathedral's **campanile** ① *daily 0930-1300, 1830-2130, US$1.25,* for city views. San Juan's museums are mostly rather dry, but if you're interested in Argentine history, pop into **Museo Casa Natal de Sarmiento** ① *Sarmiento 21 Sur, T0264-422 4603, www.casanatalsarmiento.com. ar, Tue-Fri and Sun 0900-1900, Mon and Sat 0900-1500, US$2.50 (free Sun),* dedicated to the important Argentine President and educator, Domingo Sarmiento. **Museo Histórico Celda de San Martín** ① *Laprida 57 Este, daily 1000-1300, 1600-1900, US$2,* includes the restored cloisters and two cells of the Convent of Santo Domingo. San Martín slept in one of these cells on his way to lead the crossing of the Andes. The **Museo de Ciencias Naturales** ① *Predio Ferial, España and Maipú, T0264-421 6774, temporarily closed in 2014,* has some of the fossils from Ischigualasto Provincial Park, which you won't see at the site itself. There's a wonderful collection of pre-Hispanic indigenous artefacts including several well-preserved mummies, at the **Museo Arqueológico** ⓘ *University of San Juan, Acceso Sur entre Calle 5 and Progreso, Rawson, a few kilometres south of centre, T0264-424 1424, www.ffha.unsj.edu.ar/gambier.htm, Mon-Fri 0800-1400, US$2, buses 15, 49, 50 run from the centre.* The museum offers fascinating insights into the culture of the indigenous Huarpe peoples and into the Inca practice of mountain-top sacrifices.

San Juan to Valle de la Luna → *See page 230, for Parque Provincial Ischigualasto.*

The Parque Provincial Ischigualasto (or Valle de la Luna) is one of the highlights of San Juan province. From San Juan it can be reached by taking Route 20 and Route 141 east via Vallecito, then turning north onto Route 510 via **San Agustín del Valle Fértil**.

La Difunta Correa
At **Vallecito**, 64 km east of San Juan city, the famous shrine to Argentina's most beloved pagan saint, **La Difunta Correa** has to be seen to be believed and will give you far more insight into the Argentine character than any cathedral. By now, you'll have noticed piles of bottles at roadside shrines all over Argentina. The legend goes that the beautiful young Correa was making the long walk to reclaim the body of her young husband, killed in the wars of independence, when she fell by the roadside dying of thirst. No one would help her, but, by some miracle, the baby she was carrying suckled at her breast and survived, and thus La Difunta Correa became the pagan patron saint of all travellers. People leave bottles of water by her shrine to quench her thirst and to thank her for her protection on their journey. During Holy Week, 100,000 pilgrims visit this extraordinary series of shrines at Vallecito, to make offerings to splendidly florid effigies of Difunta and her child. Testimony to their faith is a remarkable collection of personal items left in tribute, filling several buildings, including cars, number plates from all over the world, photographs, stuffed animals, tea sets, hair (in plaits), plastic flowers, trophies, tennis rackets and guitars – and vast numbers of bottles of water (which are used for the plants, and the plastic recycled). There are cafés, toilets, a hotel and souvenir stalls. Bizarre and fascinating. Buses from San Juan to La Rioja stop here for five minutes, or Vallecito runs a couple of services a day.

San Agustín del Valle Fértil → *Phone code 02646. Population 3900.*
San Agustín is a charming little town, 250 km northeast of San Juan, and is definitely the best base for exploring the Ischigualasto park, with several good places to stay and eat. You could also fish in the Dique San Agustín, and buy ponchos and blankets from the local weavers here. There's a very helpful **tourist information office** ⓘ *Municipalidad, General Acha 52, T02646-420104, www.vallefertilsanjuan.gob.ar, daily 0700-2200*, who can give you a map and advice on accommodation.

Parque Provincial Ischigualasto → *Colour map 3, A2.*

Popularly known as the Valle de la Luna (Valley of the Moon), this protected area covers 62,000 ha of spectacular desert landforms, and is the site of important palaeontological discoveries. Named after a Huarpe chief, the site occupies an immense basin, which was once filled by a lake, lying, at an average altitude of 1200 m, between the scarlet red Barrancas Coloradas to the east and the green, black and grey rocks of Los Rastros to the west. The vegetation is arid scrub and bushes; you may be lucky enough to see guanacos, vizcachas, Patagonian hares or red foxes and rheas. For many visitors, the attraction lies in the bizarre shapes of massive hunks of rock eroded into fantastical shapes, dotted throughout the park's other-worldly terrain. With the Argentines' charming penchant for naming all natural structures after things that they resemble, these are signposted accordingly: 'The Submarine', 'The Kiosk', '*Gusanos*' (Worms), and '*La Cancha de Bochas*' (the Bowling Green) – extraordinary spheres of fine compacted sand.

Sadly, '*El Hongo*' (the Mushroom) has fallen over. However, the park's real fascination lies in the 250 million years of strata that you can see in the eroded cliffs of the rocks where fossils from all the geological periods have been found, among them fossils of the oldest dinosaurs known, including *Eoraptor*, 225 million years old and discovered in 1993. Your tour guide will show you the extraordinary strata, but you'll be disappointed to discover that there's no evidence of the dinosaur fossils here: you'll have to go to the **Museo de Ciencias Naturales** in San Juan (see page 228). The views throughout the park are impressive though, and the span of time you can witness here is mind-blowing. Highly recommended.

Tours and access
Entrance costs US$17, including a tour. The tour route is about 40 km long, lasting three hours, visiting only a part of the park but encompassing the most interesting sites. If you're in your own vehicle, you'll be accompanied by one of the rangers, whose knowledge and interest vary greatly: with luck

Calingasta Valley → *For listings, see pages 233-236.*

The most beautiful part of the province, this long fertile valley lies 100 km west of San Juan between the jagged peaks of the snow-capped Andes and the stark crinkled range of the Sierra del Tontal, west of San Juan city. Inhabited since at least 10,000 BC, the Calingasta Valley was once the route of the Camino del Inca, and though little of this history remains today, it still carries a compelling attraction. Its few oasis villages are charming places to stay to explore the hills, utterly tranquil and unspoilt.

The valley is reached from San Juan by the scenic paved Route Provincial 12. About halfway between Calingasta and Barreal, this passes the Cerros Pintados, to the east, a range of red, white and grey stratified hills, striped like toothpaste.

you'll get a knowledgeable one. There's no fee but a tip is appreciated. It can be crowded at holiday times, January, Easter and July. There are no regular buses that reach the park, so your only alternative is to take an excursion, either from San Juan, La Rioja or San Agustín. From San Juan, tours cost around US$70 (including breakfast and lunch) and take 14 hours. In San Agustín, there are a couple of small agencies (Paula Tour, T02646-420096; you'll see them at bus terminal) charging US$30, and giving you less time in the bus (ask at tourist office); they also offer a useful day trip combining Ischigualasto with Talampaya Park. Talampaya Park (in La Rioja province) lies only 94 km away from Ischigualasto, and some agencies organize a combined visit to both parks in one intense day: explore this option before you set off, and plan accordingly. For around five days every full moon, the park runs Full Moon tours, US$20 plus entrance fee.

A taxi to the park costs US$38 from San Agustín (recommended if there are four or five people), more expensive out of season. If you are travelling in your own transport, plan to overnight at San Agustín or the less lovely Villa Unión, as the drive is long, hot and tiring. From San Juan, both Ischigualasto and Talampaya can be reached by taking Route 20 east through Caucete and joining Route 141, via Difunta Correa to Marayes, then turning north onto Route 510 for 174 km northwest up to Los Baldecitos, from where it's 17 km to the entrance to Ischigualasto. If you're driving, beware of the donkeys and goats wandering across the roads.

Accommodation
You can camp opposite the ranger station in the park (US$2.50), which has a small museum, but bring all food and water as there's only an expensive *confitería* here, and nothing else for miles.

Further information
Visit www.ischigualasto.org, excellent website full of interesting research and articles about the park, well worth a look before you come; www.ischigualasto.com for tourism in San Juan (both in Spanish).

There are beautiful views of the whole valley here, with its meandering river, a ribbon of green running through the dusty plain between the *cordillera* and Sierra del Tigre. Cyclists should note that there is no shade on these roads; fill up with water at every opportunity and consult the police before cycling between Calingasta and San Juan.

Calingasta → *Phone code 02648. Population 2100.*
The road from Pachaco to Calingasta follows the winding course of the Río San Juan through a steep-sided gorge of astonishingly coloured and stratified rock. After Pachaco the landscape opens out, and Calingasta village lies at the confluence of the Ríos de los Patos and Calingasta, a vivid green splash on the otherwise arid landscape. This idyllic, secluded little village (1430 m, 135 km west of San Juan) is a

delightful place to rest for a few days or plan a trek into the mountains. The Jesuit chapel, **Capilla de Nuestra Señora del Carmen**, is worth seeing: a simple adobe building dating from the 1600s, with the original bells. There is a **tourist information office** ① *Av Argentina s/n, T02648-421066, www.calingastaturismo.gob.ar*, or at the Municipalidad in Tamberías, Lavalle and Sarmiento, T02648-492005.

Barreal and around → *Colour map 3, A2. Phone code 02648. Population 2400.*

Another peaceful oasis, Barreal (1650 m) offers more accommodation and services than Calingasta and is the best base if you plan to trek into the Andes. However, it's still small and quiet enough to feel like a village and offers spectacular views of the peaks all around. From here you can explore the mountains of **Sierra del Tontal**, which rise to 4000 m and give superb views over San Juan, Mercedario and Aconcagua, or climb the mighty **Cerro Mercedario** (6770 m) itself, one of the Andes' greatest peaks. For information, contact the **tourist office** ① *Calle Las Heras s/n, T02648-441066*, in Barreal.

Barreal is famous for *carrovelismo* (wind-car racing), thanks to its vast expanse of flat land known as Barreal del Leoncito, parallel to the main road, south of town. A more tranquil attraction are the two observatories at nearby **Parque Nacional El Leoncito** (2348 m), 26 km from Barreal: CESCO ① *T02648-441087, centrohugomira@yahoo.com.ar, daily visits 1000-1200, 1600-1800 (US$2.50)* and nocturnal visits with small telescopes from sunset (US$6.25); and **CASLEO** ① *T02648-441088, www.casleo.gov.ar, mid-Sep to mid-Mar daily 1000-1200, 1500-1730, mid-Mar to mid-Sep daily 1000-1200, 1430-1700, US$1.25*; phone in advance for night visits with small telescopes, US$13, also with dinner and accommodation (US$65 pp). There's a ranger post at the observatory entrance but no facilities, so if you if you want to camp, take all supplies. The observatories were built here because of the climate, with 320 clear nights a year, making it a perfect place for observing the stars and planets. The observatories are set within an immense **nature reserve** ① *office: Cordillera de Ansilta s/n, Barreal, T02648-441240, www.elleoncito.gob.ar, free,* covering 76,000 ha of the western slopes of the Sierra del Tontal and rising to over 4000 m. To the west there are fine views of Mercedario and other peaks in the *cordillera* with the flat plain and lush valley between. But hiking in the reserve is limited to one short walk to a small waterfall, near the entrance. Fauna includes suris (rheas), guanacos, red and grey foxes and peregrine falcons.

There's no public transport to the park except *remise* taxis from Barreal; take the partly paved road (17 km) that turns off Route 412, 22 km south of Barreal or take a tour from Barreal or San Juan.

Cerro Mercedario

Known in Chile as El Ligua and rising to 6770 m, the mighty peak of Mercedario, southwest of Calingasta, is considered by many mountaineers to be a more interesting climb than Aconcagua. It was first climbed in 1934 by a Polish expedition, which went on to climb the nearby peaks of Pico Polaco (6050 m), La Mesa (6200 m), Alma Negra (6120 m) and Ramada (6410 m). This is a serious climb and requires the same time to adjust to the altitude and the careful preparation as Aconcagua. You must not consider this expedition without hiring an experienced mountain guide (*baqueano*), who can provide mules if necessary, as there are no facilities and no rescue service. The best time to climb is from mid-December to the end of February. No authorization is required to climb, but it is advisable to inform the Gendarmería Nacional at Barreal. Note that the mountain passes to Chile here are not officially open, making the crossing illegal.

⊙ San Juan province listings

For hotel and restaurant price codes and other relevant information, see pages 20-26.

⊜ Where to stay

San Juan city *p227*
$$$ Alkázar, Laprida 82 Este, T0264-421 4965, www.alkazarhotel.com.ar. Comfortable rooms, sauna, pool, gym, well run, central, excellent restaurant.
$$$ América, 9 de Julio 1052 Este, T0264-427 2701, www.hotel-america. com.ar. A good, quite comfortable choice if you need to be next to bus station.
$$$ Gran Hotel Provincial, Av J I de la Roza 132 Este, T0264-430 9999, www. granhotelprovincial.com. Large, central, good rooms, pool, gym, restaurant.
$$$-$$ Albertina, Mitre 31 Este, T0264-421 4222, www.hotelalbertina.com. Next to cinema on plaza, a small hotel with comfortable rooms, restaurant and jacuzzi in the junior suites, no parking. Very good value.
$ pp San Juan Hostel, Av Córdoba 317 Este, T0264-420 1835, www.sanjuan hostel.com. Kind owner, central, with dorms for 4 to 10, and private rooms with and without bath (**$$-$**), barbecues on rooftop, bike rental, tours arranged.
$ pp Zonda, Caseros 486 Sur, T0264-420 1009, www.zondahostel.com.ar. Simple, light rooms for 2-6, shared bath, room for 4 with bath (**$$**). Trips and Spanish lessons arranged. HI member discount.

San Agustín del Valle Fértil *p233*
At Easter all accommodation is fully booked. There are a couple of good hotels and lots of *cabañas*; the following are recommended:
$$$-$$ Cabañas Valle Pintado, Tucumán y Mitre, T0264-434 5737, www.vallepintado.com.ar. Incredibly good-value option with cabins for up to 6 people also available. Basic, clean rooms, with a large swimming pool surrounded by trees.
$$$-$$ Finca La Media Luna, La Majadita, T0264-420 1950, www. fincalamedialuna.com.ar. Only 12 km from the centre of San Agustín, each room in this hotel has a private outdoor area, with views over the trees to the mountains. A lovely good-sized pool adds to the attraction. Cabins for up to 4 (**$$$**) available.
$$ Hostería Valle Fértil, Rivadavia s/n, T02646-420015, www.hosteriavallefertil. com. Smart, comfortable hotel with fine views from its elevated position above town (though it's an ugly building), also has *cabañas* and a good restaurant open to non-residents.

Hostels
$ pp Campo Base, Tucumán between San Luis and Libertador, T02646-420063, www.hostelvalledelaluna.com.ar. Lively, cheerful hostel with basic dorms, shared bath and small kitchen. Discounts to HI

members. Tours arranged to Ischigualasto.
$ pp Los Olivos, Santa Fe and Tucumán, T02646-420115, posada_losolivos@hotmail.com. Welcoming and simple, with hostel accommodation and a good restaurant.

Camping
There are several campsites, of which the most highly recommended is **La Majadita** in a lovely spot on the river 8 km to the west of town with hot showers and great views. There's a municipal campsite in the town on Calle Rivadavia, 5 blocks from the plaza, T02646-420104 (municipal office for information on both sites).

Calingasta *p231*
$$ Hotel de Campo Calingasta, take the left fork from the *gendarmería*, cross the river and continue 2 km, hotel is up a hill on your right, T02648-421220. A restored colonial-style building with airy rooms off a colonnaded patio, with open views to the mountains and a pool in the garden. Very tranquil. Meals also available. Recommended.

Barreal *p232*
$$$ Eco Posada El Mercedario, Av Roca y C de los Enamorados (Las Tres Esquinas), T0264-15-509 0907 or T02648-441167, www.elmercedario.com.ar. Built in 1928 on the northern edge of town, this lovely adobe building preserves a traditional atmosphere with renovated comfort in its good rooms; solar-heated water, good-value restaurant, a tiny pool in a large garden, bicycles and excursions arranged through their own agency Ruta Sur. Recommended.
$$$ El Alemán, Los Huarpes s/n, T02648-441193, elalemanbarreal@gmail.com. Run by Perla, Bernhard and their daugher, very functional apartments for 2 to 4 (with

solar-heated water) facing a neat garden in a rural area next to the river. Restaurant with some German specialities.
$$$ Posada de Campo La Querencia, T0264-15-436 4699, www.laquerenciaposada.com. A few spotless comfortable rooms in a homely place south of town run by very attentive owners. Delicious breakfast, manicured park with a pool and magnificent views of the Andes.
$$$ Posada Paso de los Patos, Patricias Mendocinas y Gualino, T0264-463 4727, www.posadapasolospatos.com.ar. In a lovely location south of town with grand views, a stylish building with 10 well-equipped rooms facing the Andes, restaurant, pool, bikes and half-day bike rides to the nearby mountains.
$$$-$$ Posada San Eduardo, Av San Martín s/n, T02648-441046, saneduardobarreal@yahoo.com.ar. Charming colonial-style house, simple rooms around a courtyard, superior rooms with fireplace, relaxing, beautiful park with a large pool, restaurant, horseback rides.
$ pp Hostel Barreal, Av San Martín s/n, T02648-441144, www.hostelbarreal.com. A neat place with rooms with bath and a lovely garden. Rafting and kayaks and excursions organized.
$ pp Hostel Don Lisandro, Av San Martín s/n, T0264-15-505 9122, www.donlisandro.com.ar. In a house built in 1908, a few dorms in rustic style for 3 and 4 and doubles with or without bath (**$$-$**). Its table football is a gem. Trekking and excursions organized, including fabulous blokarting.

Camping
Municipal site at C Belgrano, T0264-15-672 3914, shady, well-maintained, pool, open all year.

🍴 Restaurants

San Juan city *p227*
A lively area of bars and restaurants lies along Av San Martín Oeste (west of 1500 block).
$$$ Club Sirio Libanés 'Restaurant Palito', Entre Ríos 33 Sur. Pleasant and long-established, serving tasty food, some Middle-Eastern dishes, including an 'arab potpourri', buffet. Recommended.
$$$ Las Leñas, Av San Martín 1670 Oeste. Huge, popular *parrilla*.
$$ Remolacha, Av de la Roza y Sarmiento, T0264-422 7070. Stylish, warm atmosphere, great terrace on C Sarmiento, superb Italian-inspired menu, delicious steaks and pastas. Recommended.
$$ Soychú, Av de la Roza 223 Oeste, T0264-422 1939. Great-value vegetarian food. Highly recommended.
$$ Tagore, Av San Martín 1556. Vegetarian meals to take away.

San Agustín del Valle Fértil *p233*
$ El Astiqueño, Tucumán next to the Dique. Good regional specialities.
$ Noche Azul, General Acha s/n, off the plaza. *Parrilla* offering local *chivito* (kid).

🛍 Shopping

San Juan *p227*
San Juan is known for its fine bedspreads, blankets, saddle cloths and other items made from sheep and llama wool, fine leather, wooden plates and mortars and, of course, its wines. The **Mercado Artesanal Tradicional**, España and San Luis, T0264-421 4189, sells woven blankets/saddlebags, knives and ponchos. If you haven't time for a bodega tour, there are a few wine stores where you can buy the local produce, such

as **La Bodega**, 25 de Mayo 957 Este, or **La Reja**, Jujuy 424 Sur.

🎯 What to do

San Juan city *p227*
Tour operators
CH Travel, General Acha 714 Sur, T0264-427 4160, www.chtraveltur.com. Recommended for its tours to Barreal, Valle de la Luna and 4-day expeditions to Parque Nacional San Guillermo, in the remote north of San Juan's high plateau. All great experiences.
Nerja Tours, Mendoza 353 Sur, T0264-421 5214, www.nerja-tours.com.ar. Good for local day trips and adventure tourism inside the national parks.

San Agustín del Valle Fértil *p233*
Paula Tour, Tucumán s/n, T02646-420096, www.paula-tour.com.ar. Worthwhile tours to Ischigualasto, plus a day trip combining Ischigualasto with Talampaya Park.

Barreal *p232*
Tour operators
Don Lisandro Expediciones, Av San Martín s/n, T0264-15-505 9122, www.donlisandro.com.ar. Full-day to several-day high-altitude treks in the Andes, including Laguna Blanca and Balcón de los Seis Mil. Combined visit to astronomical observatories and blokarting on Pampa del Leoncito. Check available activities in winter. Recommended.
Fortuna, Viajes, Av Roca s/n (at Posada Don Ramón, northern outskirts), T0264-15-404 0913. 1-week horseback crossing of the Andes led by expert Ramón Ossa. Also trekking in the Andes and 4WD excursions in Precordillera.
Ruta Sur, Av Roca y C de los Enamorados (at Eco Posada El Mercedario), T0264-444

1167 or 0264-15-661 9057. Bike tours and rental, and 4WD excursions to the Andes foothills and Precordillera.

🚍 Transport

San Juan city *p227*
Air
Daily flights to/from Buenos Aires with **Aerolíneas Argentinas/Austral**.

Bus
La Rioja, 5½-7 hrs, US$30-43, many daily. **Chilecito**, 8 hrs, US$26, daily with **Vallecito**. **Tucumán**, many daily, 11-14 hrs, US$55-80. **Córdoba**, many daily, 8-14 hrs, US$40-49. **Buenos Aires**, 14-17 hrs, US$79-113 (**Autotransportes San Juan**, **Mar del Plata**). **San Agustín**, with **Vallecito**, 3 a day (2 on Sun), 4 hrs, US$12. To **Mendoza**, US$13-14, 2-2½ hrs. Also to **Barreal**, 3½ hrs, US$13, and **Calingasta**, 3 hrs, US$12, 2 a day with **El Triunfo**, T0265-421 4532 (tell the driver your accommodation is in Barreal, as the bus stops en route).

Car hire
Trébol, Laprida 82 Este, T0264-422 5935, trebolrentacar@live.com.ar.

San Agustín del Valle Fértil *p233*
Bus
Empresa Vallecito runs daily to **San Juan**, 4 hrs, US$12; there are also 3 buses a week to **La Rioja**, 3 hrs, US$9.

Barreal *p232*
Bus
To **San Juan**, **El Triunfo** departs Mon-Fri 0300, 1600, 1700, Sat 0300, 1600, Sun 1600, 3½ hrs, US$13; bus stops en route along main road (Av Roca); tickets sold at YPF station.

ⓘ Directory

San Juan *p227*
Banks Open 0800-1300. **Banelco** and **Link** ATMs accept international credit cards. **Currency exchange** Cambio **Santiago**, General Acha 52 Sur, T0264-421 2232, closed Sat afternoon and Sun.

La Rioja and Catamarca

La Rioja is usually visited for the wonderful Parque Nacional Talampaya, a vast canyon of rock sculpted by wind and water into fantastic shapes, declared a World Heritage Site by UNESCO. However, there's also stunning scenery beyond the national park and places where you can find perfect tranquility, since the area is sparsely populated and little visited. Between the mountain ranges of the west are the extended Famatina and Vinchina valleys with verdant oasis villages at the foot of colourful eroded hills. The city of La Rioja itself has two fine museums of indigenous art.

Most of the population of Catamarca province live in the hot, sleepy capital, leaving the stunning countryside to the north and west virtually empty of people. The province has one really impressive archaeological find: the ruined Inca town of El Shincal, close to Londres, but accessible on a tour from Belén. West of here are remote outposts on the road to Chile, while to the north, a lonely road leads across the *puna* to Antofagasta de la Sierra, surrounded by a vast expanse of salt flats. Catamarca's most appealing place to stay is the charming hilltop town of El Rodeo; a popular weekend retreat for Catamarqueños, with its refreshing microclimate and good walks.

Beyond the main towns, the infrastructure in La Rioja and Catamarca provinces can be frustratingly basic, but you'll be warmly welcomed in the remotest reaches; and you'll want to stuff olives, walnuts and superb woven textiles in your bag to bring home. For more information, see www.lariojaturismo.com (in English) and www.catamarcaguia.com.ar (in Spanish).

La Rioja city → *For listings, see pages 247-252. Colour map 1, C2.*

Though not obviously touristy, the capital of the province does offer decent accommodation and is a good starting point for a trip to more remote parts. Founded in 1591 at the edge of the plains, with views of Sierra de Velasco, La Rioja has a few interesting museums, some neocolonial houses and the oldest building in the country. Sleepy and oppressively hot from November to March, the town becomes very lively every day after siesta time and during the local carnivals, such as 'chaya' and the 'Tinkunaco'.

Arriving in La Rioja city → *Phone code 0380. Population: department 180,995. Altitude 498 m.* Airport VA Almonacid ① *T0380-446 2160*, is 5 km northeast of La Rioja city, and taxis charge US$4 to the centre. The **bus terminal** ① *information T0380-442 5453*, is a few kilometres out of town at Avenida Circunvalación and Ortiz de Ocampo. To get into town, take bus No 2, US$0.50, 15 minutes, taxi US$4, or you could walk, 45 minutes to one hour. Minibuses are useful for journeys within *the* province; they have their own terminal at Artigas y España. **Tourist information** for the city is available from the Municipalidad ① *Av Perón 401, T0380-447 0000 ext 337, Mon-Fri 0800-1300, 1600-2100*, and on the **plaza opposite the cathedral** ① *Mon-Fri 0800-1300, 1600-2100; Sat, Sun and holidays 0800-2100*. Both offices are friendly, helpful and hand out a map of the city. Ask here about accommodation, including rooms with families (*casas de familia*). There's also a **provincial tourist office** ① *Av Ortiz de Ocampo y Av Félix de la Colina (opposite bus terminal), T0380-442 6345, daily 0800-2100, www.turismolarioja.gov.ar.*

Places in La Rioja city

The centre of the city is **Plaza 25 de Mayo** with its shady tipas, sycamores, araucarias and pine trees. Here, in 1637, the head of the native leader of an insurrection was exhibited as a trophy by the Spaniards. On the plaza is the early 20th-century **cathedral** with the image of San Nicolás de Bari and a room full of silver offerings. Other interesting sights on the plaza are the neocolonial government buildings, **Casa de Gobierno** and **Poder Judicial**, together with the pink building of the **Club Social**. The oldest surviving church in Argentina is one block northeast, the **Church of Santo Domingo** ① *Pelagio B Luna y Lamadrid*. It's a quaint stone temple, sparsely decorated inside but with magnificent carved wooden doors, dating from 1623 and renovated in later centuries. There is a lovely patio in the adjacent convent.

The **Church and Convent of San Francisco** ① *25 de Mayo y Bazán y Bustos, Tue-Sun 0900-1200, 1830-2100, free*, contains the Niño Alcalde, a remarkable image of the infant Jesus. You can also see the cell (celda) in which San Francisco Solano lived and the orange tree, now dead, which he planted in 1592 (25 de Mayo 218). San Francisco helped to bring peace between the Spaniards and the indigenous people in 1593, an event celebrated at the Tinkunaco festival.

By far the most interesting sight in the town is the **Museo Arqueológico Inca Huasi** ① *JB Alberdi 650, Tue-Fri 0900-1230, 1600-2000, Sat 0900-1300, US$1*, which houses one of the most important collections of pre-Hispanic ceramics in Argentina. These beautiful pieces were made by the ancient cultures that originally inhabited the region and include a remarkable funerary urn from the Aguada culture which existed 1500 years ago.

The **Mercado Artesanal** ① *Luna 782, Tue-Sat 0900-1230, 1600-2000*, has expensive handicrafts. In a beautiful and well kept house, the **Museo Folklórico** ① *Luna 802, T0380-442 8500, Tue-Sat 0900-1230, 1600-2000, US$1.25, free guided visits*, gives a fascinating insight into traditional La Rioja life, with a superb collection of native deities, rustic wine-making machinery and delicate silver *mates*. It's well worth a visit for its leafy patio.

Around La Rioja city

Seven kilometres west of La Rioja is **Las Padercitas**, where there is a large stone temple protecting the adobe remains of what is supposed to have been a Spanish fortress in the 16th century. Route 75 passes Las Padercitas before following the **Quebrada del Rio Los Sauce**s for 4 km to the reservoir of Dique Los Sauces. Just 10 km west of La Rioja, this is the fastest escape from the heat of the city. There's a shaded river with campsites and a reservoir amidst lovely mountain scenery. From the reservoir, a 13-km dirt track (no shade) leads to the summit of the **Cerro de la Cruz** (1648 m) with great panoramic views; it's popular with hang gliders.

Regular minibuses or *diferenciales*, as they're called here, depart from Rivadavia 519 to Villa Sanagasta via the Quebrada and **Dique Los Sauces**, US$1.50. *Remise* taxis charge US$10. Some tour operators also run excursions.

La Rioja to Catamarca → *For listings, see pages 247-252.*

Two roads head north from La Rioja: Route 75 to Aimogasta (see page 242) and Route 38 to Catamarca. From Route 38, you could take a detour to visit thermal baths at **Termas Santa Teresita** ① *Km 33 take R9 (later 10) to Villa Mazán, Km 99*. The *termas* are some 7 km north and there's a budget **Hostería Termas Santa Teresita** ① *T03827-420445*, which has an open-air thermal pool, thermal baths in all rooms and breakfast included.

Catamarca city → *Colour map 1, C3. Phone code 03833. Population 172,000.*

The provincial capital's real name is the rather lengthy San Fernando del Valle de Catamarca, and it is sleepy and traditional. Unless you're here for the Poncho festival in mid-July, there's little to draw you to the city. The summers are unbearably hot with temperatures up to 45°C; very sensibly, the siesta is strictly observed here and everything closes down between 1230 and 1700. El Rodeo, an hour away by regular minibus, makes a far more appealing alternative base.

Arriving in Catamarca city Catamarca's airport, **Aeropuerto Felipe Varela** ① *20 km south, T0383-445 3684*, has a daily flight from Buenos Aires. The **bus terminal** ① *Av Güemes 881 and Tucumán T0383-443 7578*, is seven blocks southeast of the main plaza. It has shops, a café, an ATM and a *locutorio*. The entrance is through a car park. Buses link the city to outlying areas of the province, and there are many minibuses a day to Villa

Parque Nacional Talampaya → *Phone code: 03825*

Extending over 215,000 ha at an altitude of 1200 m, Talampaya is remarkable for its impressive rock formations, of which the main feature is the 4-km canyon surrounding the River Talampaya. A stroll through this vast chasm gives you the unforgettable experience of being entirely dwarfed by the landscape. Though some sections of the park are only accessible by vehicle, guided walks and cycle rides are possible.

The park and circuits

The park itself occupies a basin between the Sierra Morada to the west and the Sierras de Sañogasta to the east. This is the site of an ancient lake, where piled-up sediments have since been eroded by water and wind for the last 200 million years, forming a dramatic landscape of pale red hills named **Sierra de los Tarjados**. Numerous fossils have been found, and some 600-year-old petroglyphs can be seen not far from the access to the gorge. As in Ischigualasto, along the canyon there are extraordinarily shaped structures which have been given names such as 'the balconies', 'the lift', 'the crib' or 'the owl'. At one point, the gorge narrows to 80 m wide and rises to 143 m deep. A refreshing leafy spot in the centre of the gorge has been named 'the botanical garden' due to the amazing diversity of plants and tree specimens living here. The end of the canyon is marked by the imposing cliffs of 'the Cathedral' and the curious 'King on a camel'. 'The chessboard' and 'the monk', 53 m high, lie not far beyond the gorge, marking the end of the so-called **El Monje** circuit. Only accessible with 4WD vehicles, another circuit, **Circuito Los Cajones**, continues in the same direction up to 'los pizarrones', an enormous wall of rock covered with petroglyphs, and then to 'los cajones', a narrow pass between rock walls. Two additional circuits in other areas within the park are organized from an entrance on Route 76, Km 134. **Ciudad Perdida**, southeast of the gorge, accessible only with 4WD vehicles, leads to an area of high cliffs and a large number of breathtaking rock formations, and the **Arco Iris circuit** leads to a multi-coloured canyon.

Access and information

The park is reached by Route 76: turn off at Km 134 (217 km from La Rioja), 61 km north of the police checkpoint at Los Baldecitos and 55 km south of Villa Unión, onto a paved road, 14 km

El Rodeo. The **tourist office** ① *Rivadavia 598, T0810-777 4321, www.turismocatamarca. gov.ar, daily 0900-2100*, is helpful. There's also a **provincial tourist office** ① *Roca and Virgen del Valle, T0383-455 5308*, and an information point at the airport.

Places in Catamarca city The central, leafy **Plaza 25 de Mayo** was designed by the illustrious architect Charles Thays and contains tall trees that provide much-needed shade from the scorching summer heat. Around the plaza are the white stuccoed **Casa de Gobierno** (1891), designed by Caravati, and the faded red bulk of his neoclassical **cathedral** (1878). In a chapel high above and behind the altar, you long. Independent access is possible, since buses or *combis* (minibuses) linking La Rioja and Villa Unión stop at the park entrance, but note that it's a long (14 km), lonely and unshaded walk to the administration building. No private vehicles are allowed beyond the administration building, where you have to park, and arrange alternative transport around the park: either a park vehicle, walking or bicycle.

Accommodation
The only option inside the park is a basic campsite, next to the administration office (US$1.50 per person). The closest base for visiting the park is the small town of Villa Unión, 67 km north, see under Western La Rioja, page 246, see www.turismovillaunion.gov.ar.

Tour operators
Tour operators in La Rioja and Chilecito organize tours into the park, sometimes combining a visit with Ischigualasto, which is otherwise difficult to access. Check when you book that both the entrance fee and guides' fees are included in the cost of your tour.

Tours of the park along the **El Monje**, and **Circuito Los Cajones** circuits can be arranged at the administration office, but not for the **Ciudad Perdida** and **Arco Iris** circuits. These both take 4½ hours and cost US$22 per person each; tours start from Route 76, Km 133.5. For more information, call T03822-1568 1114.

Guided walks, cycle rides and tours
Guides speak English.
Guided walks to Quebrada Don Eduardo, a secondary gorge, next to the canyon (about three hours, US$17 per person).
Guided bike rides (three hours, US$17 per person, cycle and helmet provided) follow the whole length of the *cañón* up to *'la catedral'*. A shorter journey is also on offer up to 'the botanical garden'.
Guided visits in a park vehicle for El Monje circuit (two hours, US$22 per person), Circuito Los Cajones circuit (four hours, US$24 per person).

Best time to visit
The best time to visit is in the morning, when the natural light is best, avoiding the strong winds in the afternoon.

Entry cost
US$6.50, September to April 0800-1800, May to August 0830-1730.

Further information
Call the park administration T0351-570 9909, or see www.talampaya.com (in English) or www.talampaya.gov.ar (in Spanish), for more information on excursions and for advance bookings.

can visit the much-worshipped Virgen del Valle, surrounded by plaques and cases crammed with thousands of offerings. One block north of the plaza, the **Iglesia de San Francisco** (1882) has an impressive colonial-style façade.

The must-see of the city is the incredible **Museo Arqueológico 'Adán Quiroga'** ⓘ *Sarmiento 450, T0383-443 7413, Mon-Fri 0700-1300, 1430-2030, Sat-Sun 0830-1230, 1530-1830, free*, containing an enormous collection of artefacts from the sophisticated pre-Hispanic cultures who inhabited the area from around 1000 BC. There are carved stone vessels with animal figures leaping off their sides, beautifully painted funerary urns, deliberately flattened skulls (compressed by the owners by wearing wooden boards), and quite a shocking mummified baby, naturally conserved above 5000 m. Allow at least an hour to discover the many fascinating finds. Highly recommended.

Around Catamarca city

Some 25 km north of Catamarca, the **Dique Las Pirquitas** has good fishing and water sports, as well as trekking and mountain biking. To get to the lake, take bus No 1A from the bus terminal to the **Hostería de Turismo** at Villa Pirquitas, from where it is about 45-minute walk. An alternative excursion is to visit a series of attractive churches in the **Valle de Catamarca**. The oldest of these is **La Señora del Rosario**, 2 km east of the city, a simple white building dating from 1715. Others are at **San Isidro**, 5 km east; **Villa Dolores**, 1 km further north, and at **San José**, a further 4 km north, which dates from 1780.

Northeast of Catamarca, there are fine panoramic views over the Valle de Catamarca and the city at the **Cuesta del Portezuelo**, along the road snaking up the Sierra de Ancasti. Over 20 km, the Cuesta rises through 13 hairpin bends to 1680 m then descends via El Alto (950 m). There's a reservoir nearby, **Dique Ipizca**, that's good for *pejerrey* fishing.

The best place to head to escape from the city is the pretty weekend retreat of **El Rodeo**, some 37 km north of Catamarca in a lovely mountain setting with a cool microclimate and lots of good walks and horse riding. There's a great two-day hike to Cerro el Manchao 4550 m, and trout fishing in the Río Ambato. Ask for advice at the **tourist information** ① *T0383-449 0043*. It's easy to get here by bus or hire car, and there are plenty of delightful *hosterías*, but if you plan to stay overnight, make sure you book beforehand, especially at weekends. **Las Juntas**, 20 km away on the same road, is another attractive mountain retreat from the city.

North of La Rioja → *For listings, see pages 247-252.*

La Costa

If you have time and want a tranquil place to hang out or retreat to for a few days, with no distractions, head north from La Rioja for the long narrow strip of land known as La Costa, lying at the edge of the plains at the foot of the Sierra de Velasco mountains. There are delightful small villages with old chapels dotted all along Route 75, surrounded by vineyards, orchards and olive groves.

The first town you'll come across on Route 75 to La Costa is **Villa Sanagasta**, nicely set among orchards. On the last Friday in September a big religious procession takes place from here to La Rioja. At Santa Vera Cruz, near Anillaco, look out for the **Castillo de Dionisio**, a house built on a rock and surrounded by cacti that looks like something from a fairy tale or horror story (depending on your mood). In the desert 30 km east of Anillaco is the massive **Señor de la Peña**, a naturally shaped rock and very popular religious sanctuary during Holy Week. Also near Anillaco is the 18th-century **chapel of Udpinango**.

The largest town in the area and centre of olive production is **Aimogasta**, which serves as a good transport hub, with links to several towns in the province of Catamarca.

Londres → *Population 2100.*

From Aimogasta, Ruta 60 goes 41 km north to the provincial border, where it joins Ruta 40. The latter continues north for 70 km to Londres (1300 m), a pretty and quiet village with a remote feel. Founded in 1558, it is the second oldest town in Argentina (though its site was moved several times) and was named in honour of the marriage of Mary Tudor and Philip II. The Municipalidad displays a glass coat-of-arms of the city of London and a copy of the marriage proposal. There are important Inca ruins at **El Shincal** (see below), signposted from the second plaza you come to after entering the village from Belén. Londres celebrates its walnut festival in January. There are no hotels here, but several *hospedajes*, an *estancia* (**Estancia La Casona**) and a campsite (T03835-491019) on the route to Shincal. Food can be bought from the few shops around the plaza.

El Shincal

ⓘ *7 km from Londres, daily 0700-1900. Cóndor buses between Belén and Londres stop 100 m from the ruins, US$2.50. Taxi from Belén about US$30 with wait. The site is quite small and you will only need around 2 hrs there.*

This ruined town is one of the most astonishing remains of the Incas' occupation of Argentina from the 1470s to their demise in 1532. The setting is superb, in a flat area between a crown of mountains and the river – a place the Incas clearly recognized as having sacred significance. Their religious beliefs were deeply entwined with their worship of mountains and their modification of natural forms – the most extreme example of which is Machu Picchu in Peru. Cuzco, too, follows strict conventions that ensure the town lines up auspiciously with sacred hills, water sources and the home of the ancestors. According to expert Ian Farrington, El Shincal is a 'little Cuzco', following precisely the same rules of orientation to mountains and water sources. There are large *kallankas* (thought to be either grain stores or military barracks), sleeping areas and a central plaza, lined up between two artificially shaped hills and perfectly aligned with the rising and setting sun at the solstice. In the middle of the plaza is a sacred platform with a specially designed trough for sacrifices.

It's best to visit El Shincal with a guide, but you'll be lucky to find one in Londres so take a tour from Belén. It's a remarkable site, well worth visiting.

Belén → *Colour map 1, B2. Phone code 03835. Population 8224.*

From whichever direction you approach Belén (1240 m) – whether west from Andagalá on Route 46, north along Ruta 40 from La Rioja or south from Santa María – you'll be very relieved to arrive. Ruta 40 is a better road than Route 46, but still should not be attempted in the rainy season (February to March) when the rivers crossing the roads are high. Both roads are easier and safer in a 4WD.

Belén is an intimate little town, famous for its ponchos, saddlebags and rugs, which you can see being woven. The museum, **Cóndor Huasi** ⓘ *San Martín y Belgrano, 1st floor, daily*, contains fascinating Diaguita artefacts. There are good views from the **Cerro de Nuestra Señora de Belén**, a hill above the town, where a relatively new statue of the Virgin (the last one was struck by lightning) watches over the place. Information is available from the small **Dirección de Turismo** ⓘ *at the bus* terminal, a block from the plaza on Rivadavia and Lavalle, T03835-461304, daily 0900-1300, 1600-2000. For excursions by 4WD, go to the friendly and extremely helpful **Ampujaco Tur** ① *General Roca 190, T3835-461189*, or ask at **Hotel Belén** ① *Belgrano and Cubas, T03835-461501, www.belencat.com.ar*, in town.

North of Belén

There are two routes north from Belén. Ruta 40 runs northeast across vast open plains fringed with chocolate-coloured flaking mountains and through the desolate little village of **Hualfin. (There are** thermal baths in summer at **Pozo Verde**, to the north.) The road continues to Santa María (176 km, see page 262) and Cafayate (page 270). The alternative is Ruta 43, which branches west off Ruta 40 at a point 52 km north of Belén and runs across the high *puna* to Antofagasta de la Sierra and San Antonio de los Cobres (see page 300). This route is challenging at the best of times and impassable for ordinary cars after heavy rains. The stretch just after the junction with Ruta 40 is very difficult, with 37 km of fords. At Km 87 is Cerro Compo (3125 m), from which the descent is magnificent. At Km 99 the road turns right to Laguna Blanca, where there is a museum and a small vicuña farm (don't go straight ahead at the junction). There are thermal springs along this road at **Villavil**, 13 km further north, open from January to April. Drivers should note that you'll need enough fuel for 600 km on unmaintained roads, with fuel consumption being double at high altitudes. Fill up at Hualfín and San Antonio de los Cobres, and possibly carry extra.

Antofagasta de la Sierra → *Colour map 1, B2. Phone code 03835. Population 1000. Altitude 3365 m.*

① *Buses from Belén and Catamarca arrive Mon, Wed and Fri evening, or hire a car.*

Antofagasta de la Sierra is the main settlement in the sparsely populated northwest corner of Catamarca province, situated on the Río Punilla, 260 km north of Belén and 557 km northwest of the provincial capital. With its low pinkish adobe buildings, surrounded by vast empty lunar landscapes and massive volcanoes, it's a wonderfully remote place. To the west are the salt flats of the **Salar de Antofalla**, though these are pretty much inaccessible. The **Salar del Hombre Muerto** on Ruta 43 can be visited, but it's best to hire a guide. It's a wonderful journey. There's nothing at all to do here and that's just the point. There are few places on earth that remain so wild and untouched, and these other-worldly landscapes are a paradise for photographers. If you're attracted to wild, immense open spaces and long roads leading apparently to nowhere, you'll love it.

Within reach of Antofagasta de la Sierra are several interesting archaeological sites including the ruins at **Campo Alumbreras**, in the shadow of the volcano of the same name. There's a pre-Columbian *pucará* (fort) and some nearby petroglyphs. Guides can be found at the small but wonderful museum **Museo del Hombre** ① *Fiambalá Abaucán s/n, T03835-471001, Mon-Fri 0900-1200, 1500-1900*, which contains incredibly well preserved pre-Hispanic textiles and a 2000-year-old mummified baby. There's no petrol station, but fuel can be bought from the *intendencia*.

Chilecito → *Colour map 1, C2. Phone code 03825. Population: department 49,432. Altitude 1074 m.*

The second biggest town in La Rioja province and certainly the most attractive, Chilecito lies at the foot of the snow-capped Famatina Mountains in an area of vineyards and olive groves, and is the best base for exploring the hills and nearby villages. Founded in 1715, its name derives from the influx of Chilean miners in the 19th century. The town centre, with lots of cafés and a modern church, is centred around Plaza de los Caudillos, beautifully shaded with mature pine and red gum trees, and two pergolas covered with grapevines. Each February the plaza is the focus of the *chaya* celebrations (see Festivals, page 250) and the anniversary of the town's foundation. The bus station can be found on Avenida Perón (on the south access to town).

There is good local wine to sample at the **Cooperativa La Riojana** ① *La Plata 646, T03825-423150, www.lariojana.com.ar, free 45-min guided visits and a smart wine shop open in the morning*, where you can watch local grapes being processed to make a wide variety of red and white wines, including organic products, many of which are exported to Europe under the labels Inti, 7 Days, Pircas Negras or Santa Florentina. For an easy five-minute walk from the plaza, head along El Maestro, past the pleasant Parque Municipal and up to the **Mirador El Portezuelo** where there are splendid panoramic views of the town and the Velasco and Famatina mountains. Another delightful nearby attraction is the botanical garden at **Chirau Mita** ① *Av Primera Junta, Km 0.25, take Arturo Marasso northwards, turning right at Primera Junta; it's on the way to La Puntilla*. The beautiful private garden has a rich collection of over 1500 cacti and succulent plants (native and non-native species) growing on terraces on the rocky slopes, and using the same techniques ancient Andes people used for cultivation. Not to be missed. For further information contact the **tourist office** ① *Castro and Bazán 52, T03825-422688, www.emutur.com.ar, daily 0800-1230, 1530-2100*, also at the bus station. A useful website is www.chilecitotour.com.

Finca Samay Huasi ① *San Miguel, 3 km southeast of town, T03825-422629, Mon-Fri 0800-1900, Sat-Sun 0800-1200, 1400-1800 (closed 22 Dec-6 Jan), US$1.25*, is an attractive place to come and relax for a day, or stay overnight. The estate was once the summer residence of Joaquín V González, founder of La Plata University, who designed the gardens using native trees and strange stone monoliths expressing his love of ancient cultures. There's also a small natural history museum here.

Around Chilecito: the Famatina Valley

One of the richest areas of the province and only a few hours west of the capital, the immense Famatina valley is attractively flanked to the west by the magnificent Famatina Mountains, 6000 m high, and to the east by the Sierra de Velasco, rising to 4000 m. Once an important mining area, it's now famous for its tasty wines, olives and walnuts. You can combine the most challenging treks in the region with a relaxing stay in a calm, rural *finca*. While the mountains are best explored on a guided tour, you can amble to the villages around Chilecito, with their old adobe houses and historical chapels, quite easily on your own. In **Famatina**, Good Friday

Border crossing: Argentina–Chile

Paso San Francisco

In summer the border is open 24 hours, T03837-498001. On the Chilean side roads run to El Salvador and Copiapó. This route is closed by snow June to October; take enough fuel for at least 400 km as there are no service stations from Fiambalá to just before Copiapó.

and Christmas Day are celebrated with fabulous processions, and there's also a good site for paragliding. At **Santa Florentina** (8 km northwest of Chilecito), the impressive remains of a huge early-20th-century foundry can be reached by cable car.

Western Catamarca

From Chilecito it's 126 km to the junction with Ruta 60 at the Catamarca/La Rioja border. The desert here is spectacular, with a distinct culture and remote untouristy towns. In this region the *Zonda*, a strong, dry mountain wind, can cause dramatic temperature increases.

The small settlement of **Tinogasta** (phone code: 03837) is set in an oasis of vineyards, olive groves and poplars. It is the starting point for expeditions to Ojos del Salado (6891 m) and **Pissis** (6795 m), the second and third highest mountains in the Western hemisphere. Ruta 3 goes northeast from Tinogasta to Londres (see above).

Fiambalá lies 49 km north of Tinogasta, a peaceful place in a vine-filled valley, with the **Termas de Fiambalá** hot springs situated 16 km east (take a taxi; make sure fare includes wait and return). 4WD vehicles may be hired for approaching the Pissis-Ojos del Salado region; ask at the Intendencia. **Fiambalá** is also the starting-point for the crossing to Chile via Paso San Francisco (4726 m), 203 km northwest along a paved road.

Western La Rioja → *For listings, see pages 247-252.*

Western La Rioja is remote and undiscovered, but you might want to base yourself in the town of Villa Unión for Talampaya Park (see box, page 230), or to visit the strange otherworldly landscapes of the Reserva Natural Laguna Brava. The westernmost inhabited valley in La Rioja (also known as Valle del Bermejo) follows the **Río Vinchina,** which flows along the western side of the Sierra de Famatina. The valley can be reached from La Rioja city along Route 26 via the Parque Nacional Talampaya, or from Chilecito by Ruta 40, via Sañogasta and the spectacular **Cuesta de Miranda**. Winding its way between Sierra de Famatina and Sierra de Sañogasta, through eroded red sandstone rocks, the road rises to 2020 m and drops again, passing through 320 bends in 11,500 m.

Villa Unión and around → *Colour map 1, C1. Phone code 03825. Population 4700.*

Some 92 km west of Nonogasta, Villa Unión (1240 m; www.turismovillaunion. gov.ar) is the largest settlement in the valley and is another base for visits to the Parque Nacional Talampaya, 67 km south. North of Villa Unión, paved Route

76 heads along the arid valley to **Villa Castelli** and **Vinchina** (70 km north of Villa Unión) offering the last comfortable accommodation option before the high mountains (**$$**), Corona del Inca ① *T0380-442 2142, www.coronadelinca.com.ar.*

On the west side of Route 76, on the northern outskirts of town is the **Estrella de Vinchina**, the only surviving star-shaped stone mosaic made by ancient settlers centuries ago. Immediately north of Vinchina, Route 76 enters the spectacular **Quebrada de la Troya,** and 36 km northwest of Vinchina it reaches **Jagüe** (1900 m), with food and basic facilities; here you will be approached by park wardens of the nearby Reserva Natural Laguna Brava (see below). This is the starting point for a 154-km route to Chile through the Andean mountain pass of **Pircas Negras** (4165 m). About every 20-30 km you'll see stone huts, built in the 19th century to shelter cattle wranglers on their way across the Andes.

Reserva Natural Laguna Brava → *Colour map 1, C1.*
① *Route 76, 170 km northwest of Villa Union. Entry US$2.25 per person.*
This reserve protects Laguna Brava, a salt lake at 4271 m, that's 16 km long, 3 km wide, plus some 405,000 ha of mountains and high plateau, rising from 3800 m to 4360 m. The lake lies beyond the Portezuelo del Peñón, with superb views and some of the mightiest volcanoes on Earth in the background. From the left, these are: the perfect cone **Veladero** (6436 m), **Reclus** (6335 m), **Los Gemelos** (6130 m), **Pissis** (6882 m) the highest volcano in the world, though inactive, and **Bonete** (6759 m) which is also visible from Villa Unión and Talampaya. The park is home to thousands of flamingos and *vicuñas*, the more elegant cousins of the llama. There are many organized 4WD tours on offer here, which take you to the high plateau, the Laguna Brava itself and, occasionally, the small lagoon Corona del Inca lying at the crater of a volcano at 5300 m (see What to do, page 250). The nearest settlement is Jagüe, at the western end of Route 76, and from here, 4WD vehicles or mountain bikes are essential to enter the park. The nearest accommodation is at Villa Unión. Tours are run by agencies in Villa Unión, La Rioja and Chilecito. Access is limited by summer rainfall and winter snow, so the best times for a visit are April and early May.

⚇ La Rioja and Catamarca listings

For hotel and restaurant price codes and other relevant information, see pages 20-26.

⚉ Where to stay

La Rioja city *p238*
A/c or fan are essential for summer nights. High season is during Jul winter holidays.
$$$ King's, Av Quiroga 1070, T0380-442 2122. 4-star in the need of renovation, buffet breakfast included, a/c, gym, pool.

$$$ Plaza, San Nicolás de Bari y 9 de Julio (on Plaza 25 de Mayo), T0380-443 6290, www.plazahotel-larioja.com. Functional 4-star, pool on top floor, breakfast included, a/c. Superior rooms have balconies on plaza.
$$$ Vincent Apart Hotel, Santiago del Estero 10, T0380-443 2326, www. vincentaparthotel.com.ar. Spotless flats for up to 4, a/c, dining room, kitchen and fridge, breakfast included, excellent value.

$$ Savoy, San Nicolás de Bari y Roque A Luna, T0380-442 6894, www.hotelsavoy larioja.com.ar. In a quiet residential area, tidy, comfortable, a/c, 2nd floor is best.
$ pp Apacheta Hostel, San Nicolás de Bari 669, T0380-15-444 5445, www.apacheta hostel.com.ar. Cheerfully decorated, it is a well-run central hostel with dorms for 5 to 8 and a private double (**$$**).

Catamarca city *p239*
See also www.turismocatamarca.gov.ar.
$$$ Amerian Park, República 347, T0383-442 5444, www.amerian.com. A modern but expensive business hotel, with spacious, attractively decorated and very comfortable rooms. Large restaurant and pool.
$$$ Ancasti, Sarmiento 520, T0383-443 5951, www.hotelancasti.com.ar. Aspiring to be a business hotel. The rooms are comfortable but the bathrooms are tiny. Deals include dinner in the pleasant airy restaurant.
$$$ Hostel Casino Catamarca, Esquiú 151, corner Ayachuco, T0383-443 2928, www.hotelcasinocatamarca.com. Large and surprisingly inviting hotel with comfy beds, a nice pool and a day spa.
$$$ La Aguada, 16 km from the city along Ruta 38, T0383-15-436 5723, www.la-aguada.com. This wonderful boutique hotel has 5 beautifully decorated rooms. The friendly owners also offer trekking, horse riding and abseiling. Breakfast, local phone calls, laundry and bicycle hire are included in the price.
$$$-$$ Arenales, Sarmiento 542, T0383-443 1329, www.hotel-arenales.com.ar. Welcoming, but slightly institutional in feel. Plain rooms with well-equipped bathrooms, minimalist though not exactly stylish. The most comfy in this price range.
$$ Grand Hotel, Camilo Melet 41, T0383-4426715, www.grandhotelcatamarca.

com.ar. You'll get the friendliest welcome here and they have spacious and comfortable rooms, all with bath, TV and a/c.

Hostels
$ pp Hostel San Pedro, Sarmiento 341, T0383-445 4708, www.hostelsanpedro. com.ar. Cheapest option in town, this new hostel offers brightly coloured dorms, a large garden, small pool and lively bar.

Around Catamarca city *p242*
$$$-$$ Hostería El Rodeo, R4, El Rodeo, T0383-449044. Lovely spacious rooms, pool, good restaurant and great views. Climbing, 4WD trips and excursions for children. Highly recommended.
$$ La Casa de Chicha, Los Gladiolos s/n, T0384-4490082. With fewer facilities than **El Rodeo**, but with a more idyllic setting right in the mountains, and rooms with antique furniture. Try the excellent restaurant for lunch and dinner, or have tea in the beautiful garden filled with pear trees.
$ pp Hostel El Rodeo, Las Maravillas and Las Aljabas, T0383-449 0380. Although the dorms are basic and the double is small, this hostel has a nice, relaxed atmosphere. Bicycles for hire.

La Costa *p239*
$ Hostería Anillaco (ACA), T03827-494064. The best place to stay in the area. Breakfast included, a pool and also a decent restaurant.

Londres *p243*
$$$-$$ Estancia La Casona, Ruta 38, T03835-4911061. With a capacity of 10 people, this *estancia* has basic rooms and can organize an excursion to El Shincal. In your free time you can help harvest nuts and herbs.

Belén p243

$$$ Belén, Belgrano y Cubas, T03835-461501, www.belen cat.com.ar. Comfortable, with restaurant. Prices depend on day of arrival and excursions taken.

$$ Samai, Urquiza 349, T03835-461320. Old fashioned but welcoming, homely little rooms with bath and fan.

Antofagasta de la Sierra p244

Several family houses have cheap, basic but very welcoming accommodation, including private bath and breakfast. Ask the tourist office for details, T03833-422300.

$$-$ Hostería Municipal de Antofagasta, T0351-226 9966, www. facebook.com/HosteriaMunicipal Antofagasta. This is the only really comfortable accommodation, and though its 23 rooms are simple, they're perfectly decent, and the owners also have a restaurant and offer travel advice.

Chilecito p246

$$$ Chilecito (ACA), TGordillo y A G Ocampo, T03825-422201, acachilecito@ hotmail.com. Comfortable, renovated rooms, parking, pool, cheap set menus.

$$$ Hotel Ruta 40, Libertad 68, T03825-422804, www.hotelruta40.com. ar. Family-run hotel with all services, including kitchen and laundry, bicycles, local produce for breakfast.

$$$ Posada del Sendero, Pasaje Spilimbergo, San Miguel, T03825-15-414041, www.posadadelsendero.com.ar. In peaceful Chilecito's rural suburbs, a pleasant family-run place with simple rooms with a/c on a lovely park with pool. Excursions with own Salir del cráter agency.

$$ Hostal Mary Pérez, Florencio Dávila 280, T03825-423156, hostal_mp@ hotmail.com. Good value, comfortable, welcoming atmosphere, good breakfast.

Western Catamarca p246

$$$ Hotel de Adobe Casagrande, Moreno 801, Tinogasta, T0387-421140, www.casagrandetour.com. Individually designed rooms, bar, restaurant, pool, jacuzzi, can arrange tours and activities.

$$ Hostería Municipal, Almagro s/n, Fiambalá, T03837-496291. Good value, also restaurant.

$$ Hotel Nicolás, Perón 231, Tinogasta, T0387-420028, www.nicolastinogasta. com.ar. Small hotel with breakfast, a/c, Wi-Fi, laundry service and parking.

$ pp Complejo Turístico, at the Termas, Fiambalá, bookings at tourist office T03837-496250. With cabins, restaurant, also camping.

Villa Unión and around p246

$$$ Cañón de Talampaya, on Ruta 76 Km 202 (southern access), T03825-470753, www.hotelcanontalampaya. com. Comfortable rooms in rustic style with a/c, restaurant serving some organic products, and a pool.

$$$ Hotel Pircas Negras, on Ruta 76 (southern access), T03825-470611, www. hotelpircasnegras.com. Large modern building, comfortable rooms, restaurant and pool, excursions organized.

$$ Chakana, in Banda Florida, T03825-15-51 0168, www.chakanahospedajeruralblog spot.com.ar. In rural surroundings across the river from Villa Unión, this charming little hotel is carefully run by Natalia and Martín, who also prepare very good meals.

$$ Hotel Noryanepat, JV González 150, T03825-470133, www.hotelnoryanepat. com.ar. Small rooms with a/c, good.

$$ Hostel Laguna Brava by Runacay, T03825-470368 or 03865-15-417531, www.runacay.com. A short walk from the main plaza. Doubles, triples, quads with a/c and private bathrooms. Runacay is a recommended tour agency.

🍽 Restaurants

La Rioja city p238
$$$ El Nuevo Corral, Av Quiroga y Rivadavia. Traditional rustic *comidas de campo* and good local wines.
$$$ La Vieja Casona, Rivadavia 425. Smart *parrilla*, offering chivito (kid).
$$ La Aldea de la Virgen de Luján, Rivadavia 756. Lively atmosphere, cheap and popular small place, including some Middle Eastern dishes.

Catamarca city p239
There are many cheap restaurants around the Plaza 25 de Agosto, and also at the bus terminal but this area is not safe at night.
$$$-$$ La Tinaja, Sarmiento 533, T0383-443 5853. The best eating choice by far, this delicious *parrilla* does excellent pasta. Slightly pricey, but worth it. Deservedly popular.
$$ Salsa Criolla, República 546, on the plaza, T0383-443 3584. Traditional and popular *parrilla*. Sloppy service, but the beef is recommended. The same owner runs **Trattoria Montecarlo** next door.
$$ Sociedad Española, Av Virgen del Valle 725, T0383-443 1896. Recommended for its quality and variety, serving paella, seafood and other Spanish specialities, with friendly service. Worth the 5-block walk from the main plaza.

Belén p243
$$ 1900, Belgrano 391. Laid-back restaurant with affordable food. Popular with locals.
$$ El Unico, corner of General Roca and Sarmiento. Great *parilla* for a light meal.

Chilecito p246
$$$-$$ El Rancho de Ferrito, PB Luna 647, T03825-422481. Popular *parrilla*, with local wines.

$$ La Rosa, Ocampo 149, T03825-424693. Relaxing atmosphere, huge variety of pizzas, more extensive menu Fri and Sat.

🎉 Festivals

La Rioja city p238
It's worth planning your visit to coincide with one of La Rioja's 2 lively festivals.
Jan Tinkunaco. Beginning on New Year's Eve and lasting 4 days, this festival is a vestige of the peacemaking efforts of San Francisco Solano. A colourful procession accompanies the meeting of the images of San Nicolás de Bari and the Niño Alcalde in front of the cathedral.
Feb Chaya. At this very popular festival, flour and basil are thrown, and percussion music is played for 4 nights at the Estadio del Centro.

Catamarca city p239
Mar-Apr Virgen del Valle pilgrimage. In the week following Easter, there are pilgrimages to the Virgen del Valle. Hotel rooms are hard to find.
Jul Festival Nacional del Poncho. The city's major festival. It includes a huge *feria artesanal* with the best of the province's handicrafts, as well as those from other parts of the country, and 10 nights of excellent *folclore* music.
29 Nov-8 Dec Virgen del Valle pilgrimage. A crowded pilgrimage in which thousands of people show their devotion to the Virgin. Hotel rooms are hard to find.

Belén p243
20 Dec-6 Jan Fiesta de Nuestra Señora de Belén. The town's most important fiesta.
Feb Carnival. Celebrated in style.
Mar/Apr Easter. There are processions for the Virgin.

O Shopping

Catamarca city *p239*
Catamarca specialities are available from
Cuesta del Portezuelo, Sarmiento 571,
T0383-445 2675; and **Fábrica Valdez**,
Sarmiento 578, T0383-445 2675. There's
a range of handicrafts and you can see
carpets being woven at the **Mercado
Artesanal**, Av Virgen del Valle 945, www.
artesaniascatamarca.com, Mon-Fri 0800-
1300, 1500-2100, Sat-Sun 0800-2000.

O What to do

La Rioja city *p238*
The most common destination, Talampaya,
is usually offered together with Valle de
la Luna (see box, page 230) in a long day
tour, plus occasionally Cuesta de Miranda
in 1 or 2 days. Check if park entry, IVA
(VAT) and meals are included. Trips to the
high mountains and plateaux in the west
are restricted to good weather, Sep-Apr.
Corona del Inca, PB Luna 914, T0380-445
0054, www.coronadelinca.com.ar. Wide
range of tours to Talampaya, Valle de
la Luna, Laguna Brava, Corona del Inca
crater, horse riding in Velasco mountains
and further afield, English spoken.

Catamarca city *p239*
Tours are offered to El Rodeo, and there
are opportunities for adventure sports.
Alta Catamarca, Sarmiento 569, T0383-
443 0333, www.altacatamarca.tur.ar.
Adventure-style trips into the mountains,
visits to local villages and spa packages.
Catamarca Viajes y Turismo, Sarmiento
589, T0383-442 9450, www.catamarca
viajesytur.com.ar. Conventional tours to
main sights in eastern Catamarca.
La Lunita, T011-4776 7821, www.lalunita.
com.ar. Great trekking company that runs
tours throughout the region.

Belén *p243*
Ampujaco Tur, General Roca 190, T03835-
461189, organizes interesting Spanish-only
tours to El Shincal for US$18 per person
for 4, with tour guides and possibly an
archaeologist (if requested in advance).

Chilecito *p246*
This is an excellent base for amazing treks
in the Famatina mountains and 1-day
trips to Talampaya and Valle de la Luna.
Inka Ñan, 25 de Mayo 37, T03825-422418,
www.inkananturismo.tur.ar.
Salir del cráter, T03825-423854, www.
salirdelcrater.com.ar. Trekking and 4WD
trips around Chilecito, plus excursions to
neighbouring provinces.

Villa Unión and around *p245*
Runaca, T03825-470368, www.runacay.
com. Tours to Laguna Brava.

O Transport

La Rioja city *p238*
Air
To **Buenos Aires** daily with **Austral**.

Bus
To **Buenos Aires**, **Urquiza** and **Chevallier**
US$81-108, 13½-17 hrs. To **Mendoza**,
US$42-60, 8-9½ hrs, many companies.
To **San Juan**, 5½-7 hrs, US$30-43, many
daily. To **Tucumán**, US$26-31, 5-7 hrs.
To **Villa Unión**, 4 companies daily, 4 hrs,
US$12. To **Chilecito**, several daily, 3 hrs,
US$8. Minibuses run provincial services;
they are faster and more frequent than
buses but cost a little more.

Catamarca city *p239*
Air
Aerolíneas Argentinas, Sarmiento 589,
T0383-442 4460, fly to **Buenos Aires**
and **La Rioja**.

Bus

To **Tucumán**, 4 hrs, US$16.50, several companies. To **Buenos Aires**, daily, 16-18 hrs, US$80-95, 4 companies. To **Córdoba**, daily, 5 hrs, US$87, 6 companies. To **Santiago del Estero**, 2 buses a day, 4½-6 hrs, US$18-27. To **Mendoza**, daily, 10 hrs, US$52, several companies. To **La Rioja**, daily, 2 hrs, US$10.75, several companies. To **Tinogasta**, 5 hrs, US$16, **Gutiérrez** or **Robledo**. To **Belén,** via Aimogasta and Londres, 4-6 hrs, US$14, 3 companies. To **Andagalá**, 4½-6 hrs, US$18, 4 companies including **Marín** (via Aconquija). **Los Hermanos Vergara** (T0383-442 7005) run buses to Las Juntas, Mon-Sat. **El Rodeo Bus** runs several *combis* (minibuses) a day to El Rodeo from the car park half a block east of the plaza on San Martín, returning the same day.

Belén *p243*
Bus

To **Santa María**, **San Cayetano** and **Parra** (connection there with other companies to Cafayate and Salta), daily, 5 hrs, US$11. To **Tinogasta**, 4 weekly, 2-3 hrs, US$8, with **Robledo**. To **Antofagasta de la Sierra**, **El Antofagasteño**, T03837-461152, Mon,Tue and Sun, return Mon, Fri, 8-9 hrs, US$19. Buses to **Catamarca** leave at 1200 and late at night, US$11, 4-6 hrs; check with **Gutiérrez, El Antofagasteño** and **Robledo** bus companies. For more frequent services to **Catamarca** or **La Rioja**, take bus to **Aimogasta**, 2½ hrs, US$5.

Antofagasta de la Sierra *p244*
Bus

Buses to **Belén**, Mon and Fri 1000, with **El Antofagasteño**.

Chilecito *p246*
Bus

Terminal on Av Perón, on southern access road to town. To **San Juan** with **Vallecito**, 8 hrs, US$26; to **La Rioja**, several times daily, US$8, 3 hrs. To **Córdoba**, US$35-39, 7-8 hrs, and **Buenos Aires**, US$84-92, 17 hrs, **with Urquiza** (T03825-423279). There are many daily minibus services (*combis*) from **Chilecito** to villages in the valley.

Western Catamarca *p246*
Bus

Empresa Gutiérrez runs buses from Fiambalá, via Tinogasta, to **Catamarca** (connection to Buenos Aires); also Tinogasta to Catamarca with **Robledo**, 4-5 hrs, US$16. For Belén, change at Aimogasta.

● Directory

La Rioja city *p238*
Currency exchange US$ cash can be changed at **Banco de Galicia**, Buenos Aires and San Nicolás de Bari. More ATMs along San Nicolás de Bari. **Post office** Av Perón 258, Western Union branch.

Catamarca city *p239*
Banks and currency exchange Many ATMs for all major cards along Rivadavia and at bus terminal; **Banco de la Nación**, San Martín 632. TCs can only be cashed at **BBVA Banco Francés**, Rivadavia 520. **Post office** San Martín 751, slow, Mon-Fri 0900-1800.

Chilecito *p246*
Currency exchange US$ cash can be changed at **Banco Macro**, Castro Barros 50 (on plaza). **Post office** Joaquín V González and Pelagio B Luna, Western Union branch.

Contents

Footprint features

Border crossings

The Northwest

At a glance

⊕ Getting around The cheap local buses, although slow and hardly modern, connect even the smallest towns in the region.

↻ Time required A minimum of 5-7 days will allow you to see both Jujuy and Salta, with a stop in Cafayate and the Quebrada de Humahuaca.

❀ Weather Mostly warm days and cool nights year round with temperatures rising to 47°C in summer.

✕ When not to go Jan-Feb can be extremely hot and Easter can be very busy – accommodation books up and tour companies sell out.

N

50 km
50 miles

BOLIVIA

CHILE

Villazón
La Quiaca   Pocitos
Yavi
Reserva
Nacional Laguna
de los Pozuelos   Parque
Nacional Baritú   Tartagal
Abra
Pampa   Aguas
Iruya   Blancas
Casabindo   Tres   Coctaca   Orán
Cruces   Embarcación
JUJUY   Humahuaca   34
Salinas
Grandes   Uquía
Paso de Jama   Susques   Tilcara   Parque
Nacional
Huacalera   Calilegua
Maimará   Libertador
Catua   Purmamarca   General
Paso de Sico   San   San Martín
Pedro
Cauchari   San Antonio
de los Cobres   Finca El Bordo
Paso de   Salar de   Jujuy   de las Lanzas
Socompa   Pocitos   Parque Nacional
Socompa   Paso Abra   Santa Rosa   El Rey
de Acay   de Tastil
La Poma   Güemes
Salar de   Embalse
Arizaro   Cabra Corral   16
Cachi   SALTA   Salta
Campo de
Quijano   Parque Nacional
Seclantás   los Cardones
Salar de   Molinos   La Viña   Metán
Antofalla   Angastaco   68   9
Rosario de
la Frontera
San Carlos   Antilla   La
Cafayate   Fragua
Antofagasta   Trancas
de la Sierra   40
Quilmes   Amaichá
Santa María   TUCUMÁN   Santos
Tafí del   Lugares
Valle   Tucumán
Paso de   307
San Francisco   CATAMARCA   38   Pozo
Ojos de   Monteros   Hondo
Salado   Embalse   Termas de
(6882m)   Río Hondo   Río Hondo
Pissis   Palo Blanco   34
(6882m)   Hualfín   Santiago
Bonete   Fiambalá   Belén   Andalgalá   del Estero
(6759m)   La Madrid   Villa San
Reserva Natural   Londres   Martín
Laguna Brava   Tinogasta   El Rodeo   Lavalle
60   Catamarca

The northwest of the country is a different Argentina. The Andes here are wilder and less travelled, and ancient civilizations have left ruined cities sprawling over rugged mountainsides in the vast canyons at Quilmes, Purmamarca and Santa Rosa de Tastil. Traditional Andean culture is thriving, with lively celebrations of the ancient *Pachamama* (Mother Earth) festivities throughout the indigenous communities. The poorer province of Jujuy has even more spectacular riches in the stunning Quebrada de Humahuaca, a vast gorge of stratified rock where tiny white churches are filled with treasures, and Easter draws thousands of musicians in a moving procession.

Landscapes of the northwest are among Argentina's most breathtaking: winding roads snake up the Quebrada del Toro, steep gorges clad with cloudforest, through terracotta canyons dotted with giant cacti and then streak across the endless expanse of the high-altitude *puna*, with its shimmering salt flats and vast skies. Set off up the dramatic Cuesta del Obispo to the magical Valles Calchaquíes to find giant cacti set against snow-capped mountains, and tranquil villages at Cachi and Molinos, or sophisticated wineries at Colomé and the charming village of Cafayate – a wine-growing region to rival Mendoza.

Salta is the splendid colonial city at the heart of the region, with fine hotels in its plazas of crumbling buildings and waving palm trees, vibrant *peñas* where passionate *folclore* music is sung live, luxurious *fincas* all around for great hospitality and unforgettable horse riding up into the cloudforest. For more information on the area, see www.norteargentino.gov.ar (in Spanish).

Tucumán and Santiago del Estero provinces

Two of the oldest cities in Argentina, Santiago del Estero and
Tucumán, are at the start of the route to the fascinating Northwest.
Both have some good museums and other sites of interest, and the
subtropical climate is ideal for growing sugar, tobacco and lemons,
but the summer heat may urge you to press on to the mountains.
Of the two routes north to the atmospheric city of Salta, the more
beautiful is via Tafí del Valle and the wine-producing town of
Cafayate at the foot of the enchanting Valles Calchaquíes. Pretty
towns in arid landscapes, archaeological remains and the Andes
in the distance make for a memorable journey.

Santiago del Estero and around → *For listings, see pages 263-268.*
Colour map 1, B3. Phone code 0385. Population 328,000.

This quiet, provincial town makes a handy stopping point if you're heading from
the flat landscape of the Chaco to explore the northwest corner of Argentina but
little of the architectural heritage of Argentina's oldest city remains. There are,
however, some comfortable places to stay, a couple of museums worth seeing, and
the people are among Argentina's most friendly and welcoming.

Santiago was founded in 1553 and was an important base for establishing
other major cities in the northwest. As the other cities grew, Santiago was left
behind and the town is now a rather impoverished older neighbour. In 1993, a
demonstration over unpaid wages to government employees turned into a riot in
which several public buildings were destroyed. However, the city has a warm, laid-
back atmosphere and the siesta here is legendary.

Arriving in Santiago del Estero

Mal Paso airport is on the northwestern outskirts of town, T0385-434 3654. The **bus
terminal** ① *Perú y Chacabuco, bus information T0385-422 7091, www.tosde.com.ar*,
has toilets, a *locutorio*, basic café and kioskos, as well as stalls selling food. A taxi
into town from the bus terminal costs US$2, and this will save you a 12-block walk.
However, if you find a taxi a little further from the terminal you'll avoid being
surcharged by some taxi drivers. There's a **tourist office** ① *Plaza Libertad 417, T0385-
421 4243*, in the town centre. See also www.sde.gov.ar.

Quilmes: not just a lager

Of all the indigenous peoples of Argentina, perhaps the most tragic were the inhabitants of Quilmes. This ancient city, now an intricate lacework of terraces climbing high up the mountainside, housed around 5000 people from 5000 years ago until AD 117, with a well-developed social structure and its own language, *kakán*, now extinct. The Quilmes people lived on the plains, but built the site as a defensive stronghold to retreat to in times of attack, since the whole Calchaquí valley was the site of frequent warfare between rival clans. Added to this excellent strategic position, they were hard to dominate thanks to their sophisticated weaponry: with *boleadoras* made from stones tied with llama hide thongs, and slings of plaited lamb's wool, they hurled egg-shaped stones with great accuracy over long distances. Their houses consisted of adjacent dwellings buried some way into the earth, and lined with stone walls, which also served as walkways between houses. Posts of sturdy algarrobo wood were used to support pitched roofs (now vanished), and they lived in clans or family groups. The higher social orders and those who held shamanic or religious positions in the community occupied dwellings highest up the mountainside, closest to the gods.

They cultivated fruit, beans, potato, pumpkins and maize in the valley, using irrigation canals to redirect snow-melt from the mountain tops. Chicha was the popular, mildly alcoholic drink made from ground and fermented algarrobo seeds, and their shamans cured people using local herbs and plants, as they do today.

The Incas were the first to dominate the Quilmes clan in the late 15th century, but the Quilmes adapted and survived. It was the arrival of the Spanish in the 17th century that proved fatal. After many years of failed attacks on the Quilmes, the Spanish finally besieged them and cut off all their supplies. Their hillside position proved to be their downfall and, in 1668, the Quilmes surrendered. The community was broken up, and the largest group was made to walk for weeks to an area now known as Quilmes, near Buenos Aires. In 1812, the last descendent died, and Argentina's most popular lager brewery was later built in the town. Few Argentines are aware that its namesake was this sophisticated civilization. The next time you have a sip of Quilmes, take a moment to think of this forgotten people.

Places in Santiago del Estero

On the Plaza Libertad stand the **Municipalidad** and **Jefatura de Policia**, built in 1868 in the style of a colonial *cabildo*. On the west side is the **cathedral**, the fifth on the site, dating from 1877. Two blocks southeast of the plaza is the **Convento de Santo Domingo** ① *Urquiza and 25 de Mayo*, containing one of two copies of the 'Turin Shroud', but otherwise unremarkable. Six blocks east of the plaza is the welcome greenery of the **Parque Francisco de Aguirre**, which stretches to the river and incorporates the town's campsite.

The best museum is the **Museo de Ciencias, Antropológicas y Naturales** ① *Avellaneda 355, T0385-421 1380, www.wagnermuseo.gov.ar, Mon-Fri 0700-1300, 1730-2130, free*, with a wonderfully eclectic collection of pre-Hispanic artefacts gathered by brothers Emilio and Duncan Wagner, now sadly haphazardly presented and badly conserved. Amongst the stuffed armadillos, bone flutes, delicate spindles and board-flattened skulls is a breathtaking quantity of beautifully decorated funerary urns, some rare bronze ceremonial *hachas*, and anthropomorphic pieces. Also interesting is the **Museo Histórico Provincial** ① *Urquiza 354, T0385-421 2893, Mon-Fri 0700-1300, 1730-2100, Sat-Sun 1000-1200, free*. In a 200-year old mansion, it has 18th- and 19th-century artefacts from wealthy local families. **Centro Cultural del Bicentenario de Santiago del Estero** ① *Libertad 439, T0385-422 4858, contacto@ ccbsantiago.gov.ar, Tue-Sun 0900-1400, 1700-2100*, acts as an umbrella organization for all cultural activities in the city.

Termas de Río Hondo → *Colour map 1, B3. Phone code 03858. Population 28,000. Altitude 265 m.*

Argentina's most popular spa town, 65 km northwest of Santiago del Estero, is also its most dreary. It was very popular in the 1950s, but much of it remains unmodernized from that era, and the only real reason to visit is if you want to take advantage of the warm mineral-laden waters, which are piped into every hotel in the city. Older Argentines hold it in fond regard and it's a mecca for visitors with arthritic or skin conditions in July and August, when you'll need to book in advance. Out of season, it's a depressing place. The **bus terminal** ① *Av 12 de Octubre y 25 de Mayo*, is eight blocks north of centre near Route 9, but buses will drop you at the plaza, on Alberdi, opposite the casino. With the casino dominating the scruffy triangular plaza, the resort consists of 160 hotels interspersed with *alfajores* shops (the much-loved chocolate and flour biscuit), mostly in run-down and flaking buildings. Even in high season, there's little to make you feel better here, and another biscuit isn't likely to help.

Tucumán city → *For listings, see pages 263-268. Phone code 0381. Population 1,242,300 (province).*

The city of San Miguel de Tucumán, known simply as Tucumán, lies almost equidistant from Catamarca and Salta on a broad plain, just east of the massive Sierra de Aconquija. It's the largest and most important city in the province, though it has suffered economically during the recession. Visually, the city lacks Salta's style or architectural splendour, despite being one of the first cities to be founded by the Spanish, and few of its colonial buildings remain. There are few attractions for visitors, and it's overwhelmingly hot in summer – the siesta is strictly observed from 1230 to 1630 – but it does have a couple of good museums and lively nightlife. It's a busy city with plenty of restaurants and a huge park designed by architect Charles Thays.

Arriving in Tucumán city → *Colour map 1, B3. Phone code 0381. Population 472,000.*

Getting there There are daily flights from Buenos Aires (via Córdoba) to Aeropuerto Benjamín Matienzo, 10 km east of town. The airport is linked to the city by bus No 120, taxi (US$10) or minibus transfer either to Plaza Independencia (US$2) or to a hotel (US$7). There's a huge **bus terminal** ① *Av Brígido Terán, T0381-400 2000/5000, www.terminaltuc.com,* seven blocks east of Plaza Independencia, with long-distance services to and from all parts of the country. The terminal has a shopping complex, left luggage lockers (US$1.50), **tourist information office** ① *by boletería 1, Mon-Fri 0800-2200, Sat-Sun 0900-2100, locutorios,* toilets and banks (with ATM). Bus No 4 goes from outside the terminal to San Lorenzo y 9 de Julio in the centre. A taxi to the centre costs US$3.75. Tucumán is one of the few places that can also be reached by long-distance train from Buenos Aires. ➤➤ *For more details, see Transport, page 267.*

Getting around **Plaza Independencia** is the city's heart, with busy pedestrianized shopping streets to the north and west. Tucumán is an easy place to get around on foot, but taxis are cheap and reliable. Note that local buses require rechargeable *Ciudadana* cards, sold in kiosks for US$1.85 or US$3. There are several good accommodation options, but if this is a strategic stopover for you, it would be better to retreat to the cooler mountains of Tafí del Valle, as the *Tucumanos* do at weekends.

Best time to visit The city's big festivals include **Independence Day** on 9 July, when Tucumán becomes capital of the country for the day. On 24 September, the city celebrates Belgrano's victory at the Battle of Tucumán with a huge procession. September also sees the **Tucumán Empanada Festival**. Summer is best avoided because of the heat, especially January and February.

Tourist information There's a very helpful **tourist office** ① *on the plaza, 24 de Septiembre 484, T0381-422 2199/430 3644, www.tucumanturismo.gov.ar, Mon-Fri 0800-2200, Sat-Sun 0900-2100.* There are also offices in the bus terminal and airport – the bus station office is particularly good at finding accommodation. The municipal website is www.sanmigueldetucuman.gov.ar.

Background

Tucumán was an important city in Spanish colonial times. Founded in 1565 and transferred to its present site in 1685, it was a strategic stop for mule trains on the routes from Bolivia to Buenos Aires and Mendoza. With a colonial economy based on sugar, citrus fruit and tobacco, it developed an aristocracy distinct from those in Buenos Aires and Córdoba. The city was the site of an important battle during the Wars of Independence. Belgrano's victory here in 1812 over a royalist army ended the Spanish threat to restore colonial rule over the River Plate area. Tucumán's wealth was derived from sugar, and this remains the biggest industry, though lemons have also become vital exports in recent decades.

Places in Tucumán

Plaza Independencia in the city's commercial centre has many tall palms and mature trees that give welcome shade in the sweltering heat. At night the plaza is full of *Tucumanos* eating ice cream from one of the many *heladerías*. Among its attractive buildings are the ornate **Casa de Gobierno** (1910), with tall palms outside and art-nouveau balconies. Next door is a typical *casa chorizo* (sausage house), **Museo Casa Padilla** ① *25 de Mayo 36, Mon-Sat 0900-1230, 1600-1900, US$0.50*, a series of skinny rooms off open patios, whose collection of china and paintings belonging to a wealthy Tucumán family gives you a flavour of 19th-century life. Across the road, the **Iglesia San Francisco** (1891) has a rather gloomy interior, but a picturesque façade and tiled cupola. On the south side of the plaza, the neoclassical **cathedral** (1852) has a distinctive cupola, but a disappointingly bland modern interior, the ceiling painted with rainbows and whales.

South of the plaza, on Calle Congreso 151, is the **Casa Histórica** ① *T0381-431 0826, daily 1000-1800, US$1.20; son et lumière show in garden Fri-Wed at 2030 when fine, US$2.50, tickets also from tourist office on Plaza Independencia, no seats*. Rooms are set around two attractive patios, filled with old furniture, historical documents and some fine Cuzqueño-school paintings. The highlight is the room where the Declaration of Independence was drafted, with portraits of the Congressmen lining the walls. Next to it is a room full of interesting religious artefacts. The **Museo Folklórico General Manuel Belgrano** ① *24 de Septiembre 565, Tue-Fri 0900-1300,1700-2100, Sat-Sun 1700-2100*, has an impressive collection of silverwork from Peru and musical instruments in an old colonial house. To see local art and sculpture, try the **Museo de Bellas Artes Timoteo Navarro** ① *9 de Julio 36, T0381-422 7300*, which has over 680 works of art set in a wonderfully restored building.

Tucumán's enormous park, **Parque Nueve de Julio**, east of the centre, is a much-used green space with many subtropical trees, designed by French landscape architect Charles Thays, who also designed the Parque Tres de Febrero in Buenos Aires. It was once the property of Bishop Colombres who played an important role in the development of the local sugar industry, and whose handsome house is now the **Museo de la Industria Azucarera** ① *daily 0830-1800, free*, with a display on sugar-making. The park also has a lake and lots of sports facilities.

Northwest Tucumán province → *For listings, see pages 263-268.*

Tucumán has stunning mountain scenery in the west and north of the province, along the Nevados de Aconquija, where there are several attractive small towns to visit on the way to Salta. Of the two possible routes, Route 9, via Rosario de la Frontera and Güemes, is far quicker, but it would be a shame to miss one of the most spectacular routes in the whole area: along Ruta 307 and Ruta 40 towards Cafayate. The road rises up though verdant Tafí del Valle, over the massive Infiermillo pass and then runs through spectacular landscapes all the way to the archaeological site of Quilmes, with the added small town charms of Amaichá del Valle and Santa María on the way.

Tafí del Valle → *Colour map 1, B3. Phone code 03867. Population 11,483.*

The journey from Tucumán to Tafí is very satisfying. Route 307 leads northwest towards Cafayate, climbing through sugar and citrus fruit plantations, and then jungle subtropical forest, before entering the wide Valle de Tafí, surrounded by mountains densely covered in velvety vegetation. At Km 69 there is a statue to 'El Indio', with good views from the picnic area.

Tafí (2000 m) has a cool microclimate and is a popular weekend retreat from the heat of the city for *Tucumanos*. It makes a good base for walking, with several peaks of the Sierra de Aconquija providing challenging day-hikes. For hikes into the mountains, it's best to go with a guide, available from **La Cumbre Hostel**, see What to do, page 267. There's some excellent accommodation, especially at the upper end of the market, making this an appealing alternative to staying in Tucumán. Most shops are on the main streets, Avenida Gobernador Critto (becoming Los Faroles to the west near the plaza) and Avenida Perón. At the junction you can buy good locally made cheese and delicious bread.

Arriving in Tafí del Valle There is a small but welcoming Aconquija bus station two blocks from the centre on Avenida Gobernador Critto, which you might mistake for another hotel, with café, public phones, toilets and helpful information, T0381-421025. There's also a basic **tourist office** ① *Peotonal Los Farores, T0381-156 438337,* opposite the park, which has a good map of the town and the surrounding areas (US$1.40), and listings of accommodation options. For more, see www.tafidelvalle. com (in Spanish).

Places in Tafí del Valle Tafí's most historic building is the attractive **Capilla Jesuítica y Museo de La Banda** ① *T03867-421685, Mon-Sat 0900-1900, Sun 0900-1600 (closes early off season), US$1 including guided tour.* This 18th-century chapel and 19th-century *estancia* has a small museum with interesting finds from the valley and 18th-century religious art. Cross the bridge over Río Tafí southwest of town, and the museum is on your left after 500 m.

Within the sprawling town, you can stroll by the ríos El Churqui and Blanquito or walk 10 km south to the Parque de los Menhires, which lies in an attractive spot at the south of a reservoir, the Dique la Angostura. The *menhires* are 129 granite stones, engraved with designs of unknown significance, said by some to symbolize fertility. They are undeniably intriguing, but not quite the mystical sight the tourist brochures claim, since the stones were unearthed in various places in the valley and put here in 1977. There's a decent campsite nearby and windsurfing and sailing are available on the reservoir in summer. Five kilometres further west, **El Mollar** is another weekend village with campsites and *cabañas*, and is popular with teenage and student crowds.

Northwest of Tafí del Valle

One of Argentina's most memorable journeys is along Route 307 northwest from Tafí, climbing out of the valley up to the **Abra del Infiernillo** mountain pass (3042 m) at Km 130, on the way to Amaichá del Valle and Cafayate. There are panoramic views south over the **Cumbres de Mala Mala**, the steeply sided deep green valley below, then breathtaking vistas as you emerge over the pass, looking north over the **Cumbres Calchaquíes**, veiled purple in the distance, and finally over the dramatic Valles Calchaquíes. The road descends along hairy zig-zags to the beautiful rocky valley of the **Río de Amaichá**.

Amaichá del Valle → *Colour map 1, B2. Phone code 03892. Population 1100.*

Claiming rather grandly to have the best climate in the world, Amaichá (1997 m) is a lovely, tranquil little place that does indeed always seem to be sunny. There's a splendid museum, the **Complejo Museo Pachamama** ① *T03892-421004, daily 0830-1230, 1400-1830 (closed Sun in low season), US$2.50, explanations in English, guided tour in Spanish*, also known also as Casa de Piedra. The museum was designed by the Argentine sculptor Héctor Cruz, who uses the iconography of the region's pre-Columbian art with bold flair in his own ceramics and weavings. It's part gallery, part archaeological museum, and is a great place to relax for a couple of hours, with wonderful views from the mosaic cactus gardens. The shop sells an extensive range of handicrafts, and bold rugs and hangings, designed by Cruz and made by local weavers.

The road forks at Amaichá: take Route 357 north for 14 km to the junction with Ruta 40, then follow it north towards Cafayate for the turn-off to Quilmes. For Santa María and western Catamarca, head south to join Ruta 40.

Santa María → *Colour map 1, B2. Phone code 03838. Population 10,800.*

With its lively village feel, still untainted by tourism, Santa María (1880 m) makes a very attractive place for a stopover on the road between Cafayate, Tucumán and western Catamarca. There's a lovely plaza full of mature trees, several friendly places to stay and to eat, and a wonderful small museum. **Centro Cultural Yokavil** ① *corner of plaza, daily 0830-1300, 1700-2100, donation requested*, houses a fine collection of sophisticated ceramics tracing the development of the various indigenous cultures who lived in the Calchaquí valleys. Ask the well-informed staff to show you around. In the same building is a handicrafts gallery selling weavings, wooden objects and the delicious local *patero* wine. There is a helpful but small **tourist office** ① *on the plaza, Belgrano and Sarmiento, T03838-421083*, which can provide a map and a list of places to stay.

In January the town has handicrafts fairs and a live music festival, with the crowning of *La Reina de Yokavil* (the old indigenous name for Santa María). For the **Fiesta de San Roque** on 16 August, thousands of pilgrims descend on the town, and accommodation fills up fast. There's a *locutorio* on the plaza, the only ATM for miles around on Mitre and Sarmiento, taking Visa and MasterCard, a post office and several service stations. Buses arrive at Avenida 9 de Julio and Maestro Argentino, eight blocks south of the plaza.

Quilmes → *Colour map 1, B2.*

① *17 km northeast of Amaichá or 32 km north of Santa María, 5 km along a dirt road off R40 (no shade, tiring walk up hill). Normally the site is open daily 0800-1800, but owing to an administrative dispute it was closed to tourists in 2014. The hostería with restaurant, gift shop and good café were also closed in 2014.*

Quilmes is one of the most important archaeological sites in Argentina, sadly little known by most Argentines, who are more likely to associate the name with the country's most popular lager, see box, page 257. Located on the slopes of the Sierra de Quilmes, at an altitude of 1850 m, it has commanding views over the entire valley. The city was home to 5000 Diaguitan people, who lived here peacefully for hundreds of years until the Incas and then the Spanish arrived. What remains today is an extensive network of thousands of roofless rooms bordered with low walls, mostly heavily reconstructed. Walk up to the top of the mountain and you'll see a beautiful and elaborate lacework that continues right up from the valley to the higher slopes. It's a spectacular site, especially early or late in the day, when the silvery walls are picked out against the pale green of the enormous cacti.

For a day trip to the site, take the 0600 Aconquija bus from Cafayate to Santa María, and after an hour get off at the stop on Ruta 40, 5 km from the site. Alternatively, take the 0700 El Indio bus from Santa María, which runs Friday to Wednesday. Take the 1130 bus back to Cafayate for US$3. You can also take a tour from Cafayate. Check that the site is open before going.

⦿ Tucumán and Santiago del Estero listings

For hotel and restaurant price codes and other relevant information, see pages 20-26.

⦿ Where to stay

Santiago del Estero *p256*
$$$ Carlos V, Independencia 110, T0385-424 0303, www.carlosvhotel.com. Corner of the plaza, the city's most luxurious hotel, elegant rooms, pool, good restaurant, still good value for its range.
$$$ Centro, 9 de Julio 131, T0385-421 9502, www.hotelcentro.com.ar. Nice decor, very comfortable, airy restaurant.
$$$ Libertador, Catamarca 47, T0385-421 9252, www.hotellibertadorsrl.com. ar. Smart and relaxing, spacious lounge, plain rooms, patio with pool (summer only), elegant restaurant, 5 blocks south of plaza in the better part of town.
$$$ Savoy, Peatonal Tucumán 39, T0385-421 1234, www.savoysantiago.com.ar. Good option, characterful, art nouveau grandeur, swirling stairwell, large airy rooms, small pool.

$ pp Res Emaus, Av Moreno Sur 675, T0385-421 5893. Good cheap choice, with bath and TV, helpful.

Camping
Las Casuarinas, Parque Aguirre, T0385-421 1390. Insect repellent essential.

Termas de Río Hondo *p258*
Ask the helpful tourist office for accommodation advice, at Caseros 268, T03858-421969, or at Av Alberdi 245, T03858-421571.
$$$$ Hotel de los Pinos, Maipú 201, T03858-421043, www.lospinoshotel.com.ar. The best option in an attractive Spanish-style building a little removed from the centre in a huge park, with fantastic pools and rooms with private thermal baths. Rates are for minimum 3-night all-inclusive stays.
$$$ El Hostal del Abuelo, Francisco Solano 168, T03858-421489, www.el hostaldelabuelo.com.ar. Most central in town, this spa hotel has a huge range of facilities, comfortable rooms but pricey.

Tucumán city *p258*

$$$$ Catalinas Park, Av Soldati 380, T0381-450 2250, www.catalinaspark. com. The city's most comfortable and luxurious hotel, overlooking Parque 9 de Julio, outstanding food and service, pool (open to non-residents), sauna, gym. Highly recommended.

$$$ Carlos V, 25 de Mayo 330, T0381-431 1666, www.hotelcarlosv.com.ar. Central, good service, with elegant restaurant.

$$$ Dallas, Corrientes 985, T0381-421 8500, www.dallashotel.com.ar. Welcoming, nicely furnished large rooms, good bathrooms. Recommended, though far from centre.

$$$ Mediterráneo, 24 de Septiembre 364, T0381-431 0025, www.hotel mediterraneo.com.ar. Good rooms, TV, a/c. 20-30% discount for *Footprint* owners.

$$$ Suites Garden Park, Av Soldati 330, T0381-431 0700, www.gardenparkhotel. com.ar. Smart, welcoming 4-star, views over Parque 9 de Julio, pool, gym, sauna, restaurant. Also apartments.

$$$-$$ Miami, Junín 580, 8 blocks from plaza, T0381-431 0265, www. hotelmiamitucuman.com.ar. Good modern hotel, refurbished rooms, pool.

$$$-$$ Versailles, Crisóstomo Alvarez 481, T0381-422 9760, www.hotelversailles tuc.com.ar. Comfortable beds though rooms a bit small, good service, price depends on season. Recommended.

$ pp Backpacker's Tucumán, Laprida 456, T0381-430 2716, www. backpackerstucuman.com. Youth hostel with HI discounts in restored house with quiet atmosphere, lovely patio, basic dorms (US$12-15), English spoken, good. Plus **$$-$** double room with bath.

$ pp Hostel OH!, Santa Fé 930, T0381-430 8849, www.hosteloh.com.ar. Neat, modern hostel with shared (US$15-18 pp)

or private rooms (**$$**), quiet, *parrilla*, pool, games, garden.

$ pp Tucumán Hostel, Buenos Aires 669, T0381-420 1584, www.tucumanhostel. com. HI hostel in a refurbished building. Large, high-ceiling dorms (US$15-16), double room with bath **$$**, **$** without. Slightly unkempt but chilled garden. Recommended.

Tafí del Valle *p261*

Many places, including hotels, close out of season.

$$$ Hostería Tafí del Valle, Av San Martín y Gdor Campero, T03867-421027, www.soldelvalle.com.ar. Right at the top of the town, with splendid views, good restaurant, luxurious small rooms, pool.

$$$ La Rosada, Belgrano 322, T03867-421323, http://larosadatafi.com. Spacious rooms, well decorated, plenty of hot water, comfortable, excellent breakfast included, helpful staff, lots of expeditions on offer and free use of cycles.

$$$ Lunahuana, Av Critto 540, T03867-421330, www.lunahuana.com.ar. Stylish comfortable rooms with good views, spacious duplexes for families.

$$$ Mirador del Tafí, R 307, Km 61.2, T03867-421219, www.miradordeltafi. com.ar. Warm attractive rooms and spacious lounge, superb restaurant, excellent views, look for midweek offers. Highly recommended.

$ pp La Cumbre, Av Perón 120, T03867-421768, www.lacumbretafidelvalle. com. Basic, cramped rooms, but central, helpful owner is a tour operator with wide range of activities (see What to do).

Estancias

$$$ Estancia Las Carreras, R 325, 13 km southwest of Tafí, T03867-421473, www. estancialascarreras.com. A fine working *estancia* with lodging and a restaurant serving its own produce (including cheeses). It offers many activities, such as riding, trekking, mountain biking and farm visits.

$$ Los Cuartos, Av Gob Critto y Av Juan Calchaquí s/n, T0381-15-587 4230, www.estancialoscuartos.com. Old *estancia* in town, rooms full of character, charming hosts. Recommended. Also offer a day at the *estancia*, with lunch. Delicious *té criollo*, US$7-9, lunch, US$16, and farm cheese can be bought here.

Amaichá del Valle *p262*

$$$ Altos de Amaicha Posada, Ruta 307 at Km 117, just outside town, T0381-15-445 0191, www.amaichadelvalle.com/hotel-altos-de-amaicha.html. Wonderful boutique hotel with 7 well-decorated rooms, an amazing pool and a notable restaurant. Ask for a room with a view of the mountains. Recommended.

$$ pp El Portal de Amaichá, on the main road, next to the petrol station, T0381-15-464 5904, www.elportaldeamaicha.blogspot.com. Quiet and comfortable accommodation with great views either in simple rooms, dorms or in *cabañas*.

$ pp La Rocca Camping, Ruta 337 La Puntilla, T011-15-6249 1964, www.laroccacamping.com.ar. Fantastic new camping facility from the team behind the popular La Rocca hostels. They offer rented tents, mountain bikes and also can organize trekking trips. The facilities are modern and comfortable.

Santa María *p262*

$$ Hotel de Turismo Cielos del Oeste, San Martín 450, corner 1 de Mayo, T03838-420240. Occupying a block of its own, 2 blocks east of the plaza, this large institutional place is the best option, with several new-ish and very comfortable rooms. Free internet, a restaurant and a pool surrounded by a large garden.

$ Inti-Huaico, Belgrano 146, T03838-422060. A bargain, with nice clean rooms with bath, friendly owners and lovely gardens.

$ Plaza, San Martín 258, on the plaza, T03838-420240. Small, simple and rather dark but comfy rooms all with bath and TV, breakfast included.

Camping

Municipal campsite, at end of Sarmiento, about 6 blocks east of the plaza, T03838-421 083, with *albergue* ($) and restaurant.

🍴 Restaurants

Santiago del Estero *p256*

$$ Mia Mamma, on the main plaza at 24 de Septiembre 15. A cheery place for *parrilla* and tasty pastas, with good salad for starters.

Termas de Río Hondo *p258*

San Cayetano ($$) or homely **Renacimiento ($$)**, both on the main drag Sarmiento, are reasonably priced for *parrilla*. **El Chorizo Loco ($)**, Alberdi and Sarmiento, is a very cheap and lively pizzeria.

Tucumán city *p258*

Many popular restaurants and cafés along 25 de Mayo, north from Plaza Independencia, and on Plaza Hipólito Yrigoyen.

$$$-$$ El Fondo, San Martín 848, T0381-422 2161. Superb renowned steak house.

$$$-$$ La Leñita, 25 de Mayo 377. Recommended for *parrilla*, superb salads, live folk music at weekends.

$$ Il Postino, 25 de Mayo y Córdoba. Attractive buzzing pizza place, plus tapas and tortillas too, stylish decor. Recommended.
$ Sir Harris, Laprida y Mendoza. A Tucumán institution, cosy with good quality *tenedor libre*, some veggie dishes. Recommended.

Cafés
Café de París, Santiago del Estero 502 y 25 de Mayo. Tapas bar and stylish little restaurant.
Cosas del Campo, Lavalle 857 (south of centre, next to Plaza San Martín), T0381-420 1758. Renowned for its *empanadas*, also for take-away.
Panadería Villecco, Corrientes 749. Exceptional bread, also wholemeal (*integral*) and pastries.

Tafí del Valle *p261*
Many places along Av Perón.
$$ Parrilla Don Pepito, Av Perón 193. Very good food, excellent *empanadas*.

Santa María *p262*
There are some good and lively places on the plaza, including:
$ El Colonial del Valle. Serves *empanadas* and other meals, and it is also a nice *confitería*.

🍷 Bars and clubs

Tucumán city *p258*
Costumbres Argentinos, San Juan 666 y Maipú. An intimate place with a good atmosphere for late drinks.
Plaza de Almas, Santa Fe and Maipú, north of centre. This bar attracts young crowds in the late evenings.

☺ Festivals

Tucumán city *p258*
9 Jul Independence Day
24 Sep Battle of Tucumán. Both are celebrated with huge processions and parties.
Sep Fiesta Nacional de la Empanada 3 days of baking, eating and folk music in Famaillá, 35 km from Tucumán, usually in 1st half of the month.

⊙ Shopping

Tucumán city *p258*
Handicrafts
Mercado Artesanal, 24 de Septiembre 565, daily 0800-1300, 1700-2200 (mornings only in summer). Small, but nice selection of lace, wood and leatherwork.
Mercado del Norte, Maipú between Mendoza and Córdoba, Mon-Sat 0900-1400, 1630-2100. Indoor market and bazaar featuring cheap regional foods, meat and local produce.
Regionales del Jardín, Congreso 18. Good selection of local jams, *alfajores*, etc.

⚙ What to do

Tucumán city *p258*
Tour operators
Duport Turismo, Congreso 160, T0381-422 0000, www.duport-turismo.com.ar. Local tours, plus a circuit of the local valleys, 6 hrs.
Montañas Tucumanas, Laprida 196, 1st floor, T0381-467 1860, www.montanas tucumanas.com. Great company that organizes trekking, rappelling, horse riding, canyoning and paragliding.

Tafí del Valle p261
Tour operators
La Cumbre, see Where to stay, above. Energetic and helpful company, offering full day walks to nearby peaks, waterfalls and ruins, or to Cerro Muñoz, with an *asado* at the summit (4437 m), has open-sided truck.

⊖ Transport

Santiago del Estero p256
Air
Flights to Buenos Aires and **Tucumán**, with **Aerolíneas Argentinas/Austral**, 24 de Septiembre 547, T0385-422 4333.

Bus
To Córdoba, 6 hrs, US$28-35; to **Salta**, 6-6½ hrs, US$30-45; to **Tucumán**, 2 hrs, US$10-13; to **Catamarca,** go via Tucumán.

Termas de Río Hondo p258
Bus
To **Santiago del Estero**, 1 hr, US$3, and to **Tucumán**, 2 hrs, US$5; also several to **Buenos Aires**, 13-14 hrs, US$45.

Tucumán city p258
Air
To **Buenos Aires** via **Córdoba**, with AR, 9 de Julio 110, T0810-222 86527.

Bus
Long-distance buses to all parts of the country depart from the huge **bus terminal** on Av Brígido Terán. To **Buenos Aires**, many companies, 14-16 hrs, US$75-100. To **Salta** direct (not via Cafayate), 4-4½ hrs, several companies US$19-25. To **Tafí del Valle**, **Aconquija** (http://transporteaconquija.com.ar), 10 daily (6 on Sun), 2½ hrs, US$6. To **Cafayate**, 5½ hrs (6½ hrs if via Santa María),

US$17.50, with **Aconquija**. To **Mendoza**, 13-14 hrs, US$68-96, via Catamarca, La Rioja and San Juan. To **Córdoba**, 8 hrs, US$60-643-498. To **Santiago del Estero**, 2 hrs, US$10-13. To **Posadas**, 16 hrs, US$93, with **Vosa**. To **Catamarca**, 4 hrs, US$16.50, with **Aconquija** and others. To **La Quiaca (Bolivian border)**, 10-11 hrs, US$39, with **Andesmar** and **Balut**.

Car hire
Movil Renta, San Lorenzo 370, T0381-431 0550, www.movilrenta.com.ar, and at airport. 20% discount for **Footprint** book owners.

Train
To **Buenos Aires** via **Rosario**, with **Ferrocentral**, T0381-430 9220, www.sateliteferroviario.com.ar. For more information see Buenos Aires Mitre line, page 85.

Tafí del Valle p261
Bus
To **Tucumán**, 10 daily (6 on Sun), 2½ hrs, US$6, with **Aconquija**. To **Cafayate**, 4 a day, 2½ hrs, US$11.

Amaichá del Valle p262
Bus
To **Tucumán**, 6 daily, 5 hrs, US$8, sit on the right for best views. To **Santa María**, 15 mins, US$1, with **Gutiérrez**.

Santa María p262
Bus
To **Tucumán**, 5 daily, 4½-5 hrs, US$8, with **Aconquija**. To **Cafayate**, daily, 2 hrs, US$5, with **Aconquija** and **El Indio**. To **Salta**, daily, 5-6 hrs, US$16.50, with **El Indio**. To **Belén**, 4 hrs, US$11, check with tourist office for current times, with **Cayetano** and **Parra**. To **Amaichá del Valle**, 15 mins, US$3, with **Gutiérrez**.

To **Catamarca**, Sun-Fri, US$16.50, with **Gutiérrez**.

ℹ Directory

Santiago del Estero *p256*
Banks Banco Francés, 9 de Julio and 24 de Septiembre.

Tucumán city *p258*
Banks Most along San Martín, especially the 700 block between Junín and Maipú. **Bicycle shop**

Bike Shop, San Juan 984, T0381-431 3121. **Currency exchange** Maguitur, San Martín 765, T0381-431 0032, accepts TCs; **Maxicambio**, San Martín 779, T0381-422 5399. **Post office** Córdoba and 25 de Mayo, Mon-Fri 0800-1400, 1700-2000, Sat 0900-1300.

Tafí del Valle *p261*
Banks Banco de Tucumán, Miguel Critto 311, T03867-421033. ATM for all major cards.

Los Valles Calchaquíes

Dramatic, constantly changing and stunningly beautiful, the Valles Calchaquíes are perhaps the most captivating part of Salta province. The river Calchaquí springs 5000 m up on the slopes of the Nevado de Acay, just south of San Antonio de los Cobres, and flows – via a series of timeless oasis villages – through a spectacularly long and broad valley to Cafayate and beyond.

Driving north on Ruta 40, the first destination in the valley is the established wine-growing centre of Cafayate, with extraordinary rock formations just to the north at Quebrada de las Flechas. Beyond, there are unspoilt villages dotted along the valley: San Carlos; Angastaco; Molinos, with its lovely church, and Seclantás, with its poncho weavers, all reached by the rough *ripio* Ruta 40. The pretty town of Cachi is set against the massive Nevado de Cachi mountain range, with its hidden valley, Cachi Adentro, irrigated since pre-Inca times to produce the bright red peppers you'll see drying in the sun in April. From Cachi, a breathtaking drive up the Cuesta del Obispo and through the giant cactus park, Parque Nacional los Cardones, will take you east to Salta. Ruta 40, meanwhile, continues north to La Poma, set in wide open red rocky land, and on to San Antonio de los Cobres.

Arriving in the Calchaquí valleys

It's possible to reach both Cachi and Cafayate using public transport. To reach Cafayate quickly, there are several buses daily along the fast, paved Ruta Nacional 68 from Salta. There are also buses to Cafayate from Santa María (Catamarca) and Tucumán to the south. If you're short of time, there are one or two day tours from Salta to the Cafayate and Calchaquíes valleys, but they are frustratingly brief, with many hours spent cooped up in a minibus. Only a few buses each day go from Salta to Cachi and Molinos along the nail-biting Cuesta del Obispo (see page 277) – quite an experience in itself. And, from Molinos there's only one bus a week south to Angastaco, leaving you stranded for days. All things considered, the best way to see this region is to hire a car – note there is a rough stretch between Cachi and Cafayate and a 4WD is essential in summer, when rains swell the rivers.

Background

The whole vast Calchaquí Valley was densely populated in pre-Hispanic times by sophisticated people, often referred to as 'Diaguitan', who built stone dwellings in large organized 'cities', the impressive remains of which you can see still at Las Pailas, near Cachi, and at Quilmes, further south. Much archaeological work has yet to be done to establish more detail about their daily lives and there are currently digs at Las Pailas and La Borgata, near Cachi Adentro. The Diaguita were just one of several tribes in the valley. They left a rich legacy of ceramics, which you can see today in all the small museums throughout the region. From beautifully painted urns made to contain the bodies of their dead, to simple cooking pots and glazed black polished vessels, these artefacts speak of a population with a high degree of social organization.

After the defeat of the indigenous population in the Calchaquí Wars, the Spanish established missions and haciendas in the valley, which were run along feudal principles – some until as recently as the 1980s. During the colonial period the valley prospered, providing pasturage for mules and herds of cattle en route to the mountain passes into Chile and Alto Perú (Bolivia). After independence, lower parts of the valley became the primary wheat-growing and wine-producing area for Salta city, but the local economy declined in the late 19th century when the railway brought cheap wheat from the Pampas and wine from Mendoza. Salta's endemic racism and the feudal legacy have meant that the indigenous people in the valley are only recently coming to value their own cultural inheritance. Rather than taking a commercial group tour from Salta, seek out local guides who will tell you about their fascinating history.

Cafayate and around → For listings, see pages 278-283.

Cafayate (1660 m) is beautifully situated in a broad stretch of valley at the confluence of the Santa María and Calchaquí rivers. There are mountains on all sides, and the valley is filled with vineyards, which produce wine to rival Mendoza in quality, if not in quantity. Cafayate has long been a popular excursion destination for visits to the bodegas, which open their doors to tourists with free tours and wine tastings. There are superb red grapes grown at high altitude here, and it's worth asking specifically to try the white Torrontés grape, which is grown in few places other than Argentina and flourishes in the annual 350 days of sunshine, and the cool nights.

There's lots of accommodation and one exquisite place to stay, **Patios de Cafayate** ① www.patiosdecafayate.com, making this a good base for exploring the dramatic scenery all around or just relaxing for a couple of days.

Arriving in Cafayate → Colour map 1, B2. Phone code 03868. Population 11,785.

Getting there and around Cafayate has two separate bus terminals: **El Indio** bus terminal on Belgrano, half a block from the plaza, T03868-421002; and the **Aconquija** terminal at Güemes Norte and Alvarado, T03868-421052 (open only when buses are due). There are buses from Tucumán and Santa María, and several

Cafayate

To Cachi & Molinos (RN40)

N

80 metres
80 yards

To Cerro San Isidro & Bodega
San Pedro de Yacochuya

Río Chuscha

Bodega
Vasija Secreta

Bodega
El Esteco

To Salta (RN68)

Lamadrid

Sevilla

Buenos Aires

Bartolomé Mitre

Pedraza

Brachieri

ACA

Alvarado

Aconquija

Córdoba

Gral Güemes Norte

Salta

To ⑨

Rivadavia

Pharmacy ⑧

D de Almagro

ATM ⑦

Q de Niño

San Martín

Municipalidad

To Cerro
Santa Teresita

Cathedral

Mercado
Municipal de
Artesanía

El Indio

Belgrano

Toscano

Banco de
la Nación

Museo
Arqueológico
Rodolfo I Bravo

Bodega
Nanni

Nuestra Señora del Rosario

Colón

Hurtado

S Chavarría

Gral Güemes Sur

Museo
de la Vid
y el Vino

To Camino al Divisadero, Bodega
Finca de las Nubes & ⑥

Calchaquí

Chacabuco

Bodega
Domingo
Hermanos

25 de Mayo

To ⑧, Bodega
Etchart, Quilmes
& Tucumán

Where to stay 🛏

Camping Luz y Fuerza **8**
El Balcón **7**
El Hospedaje **2**
Hostal del Valle **12**
Hostel Ruta 40 **4**
Killa **1**
Patios de Cafayate **3**
Portal del Santo **11**
Rusty K Hostal **9**
Villa Vicuña **5**

Viñas de Cafayate **6**

Restaurants 🍴

Baco **8**
El Rancho **1**
El Terruño **2**
Helados Miranda **5**
La Carreta de
Don Olegario **6**
La Casa de Las
Empenadas **3**

buses daily from Salta along the fast Ruta Nacional 68; this is an easy drive in a hire car, though the road is winding for the last 30 km as you enter the amazing rock formations of the Quebrada de las Conchas (see below). The alternative and even more scenic route from Salta is the Ruta 40 via Cachi and the Valles Calchaquíes (see below) but the road is rough *ripio* and there are very few buses between Molinos and Angastaco. There are many excursions on offer from Salta to Cafayate (US$45, including lunch and visit to a bodega), with brief stops in the Quebrada de las Conchas. But these make for a long day, and you'll miss the chance to walk around the region.

Cafayate is easy to get around on foot, with restaurants and shops located around the main plaza, but you'll need transport to reach many of the bodegas further out. Take a taxi or hire a bike, available from shops on the plaza.

Tourist information There's a tiny but informative **tourist centre** ① *20 de febrero, T03868-422442/422223, www. cafayate.todowebsalta.com.ar, daily 0800-2200*, in a hut on the northeast corner of the plaza. They have a basic map with the bodegas marked, and an accommodation list. Tour operators can be found along Calle General Güemes (this street changes names from Norte to Sur across the plaza, and, confusingly, identical numbers can be found on both sides).

Places in Cafayate

Conventional sights aren't Cafayate's strong point; it's much more interesting to explore the landscape and the bodegas. The **Museo de la Vid y El Vino** ① *Güemes Sur y F Perdiguero, www.museodelavidyelvino.gov.ar, Tue-Sun 1000-1930, US$4*, in a new building, contains old winemaking equipment and a display on the history of wine. The **Museo Arqueológico Rodolfo I Bravo** ⓘ *Calchaquí y Colón 191, T03868-421054, Mon-Fri 1130-2100, Sat 1130-1500, free,* is tiny but has some beautiful funerary urns, black ceramics from the fifth century, and Inca pieces too – well worth seeing if you haven't come across them elsewhere.

Bodegas

Cafayate's wines are sophisticated and generally of very high quality, with intense high-altitude reds (Malbec and Cabernet Sauvignon predominate) and the famous white Torrontés. This superbly fruity dry wine with delicious floral aromas is grown only in the Valles Calchaquíes and makes an excellent aperitif. There are several bodegas that can be visited and all are shown on the tourist office's map; the best are described below. Tours usually take around 45 minutes, most are free, and are followed by a free tasting. Ask if the guides speak English.

The most highly recommended bodega, with an informative tour, is **El Esteco** ⓘ *at the junction of R68 and R40, T011-5198 8000, www.elesteco.com.ar, Mon-Fri 8 tours daily 1000-1830, Sat-Sun 1000, 1100, 1200.* Visitors can learn more about the process of winemaking and tasting on one of the courses on offer. Next door is Cafayate's best accommodation: the sumptuous **Patios de Cafayate** (see Where to stay, page 278), formerly part of the bodega and now with luxury spa. It's also a great place for lunch.

Another excellent bodega is **Etchart** ⓘ *2 km south on R40, Km 1047, T03868-421310, www.bodegasetchart.com, tours daily on demand, open Jan, Feb, Jul, closed for lunch, book in advance,* which produces high-quality wines, some of which are exported to Europe.

The diminutive **San Pedro de Yacochuya** ⓘ *7 km behind Cafayate, T03868-431 9439, www.sanpedrodeyacochuya.com.ar, phone to arrange a tour, Mon-Fri 1000-1700, Sat-Sun 1000-1300,* is a boutique bodega, beautifully situated high up into the hills, making exquisite wines. To get there, take Ruta 40 in the direction of Cachí; after 2 km turn left on Ruta 2, then follow this for 6 km until you reach the bodega.

Once you've visited the best three, you could go to **Finca de las Nubes** ⓘ *3 km above Cafayate, on the Camino al Divisadero, beyond Hotel Viñas de Cafayate, T03868-422129, www.bodegamounier.com, guided visits are available Mon-Sat 1000-1700, Sat 1000-1300,* dramatically set against the mountains. This is a small family bodega, which produces fine wines and offers simple meals so you can sit and enjoy a bottle of wine on the terrace.

Then there are two interesting mass-production bodegas that can also be visited: **Domingo Hermanos** ⓘ *Nuestra Sra Del Rosario s/n, T03868-421225, www. domingohermanos.com,* and **Vasija Secreta** ⓘ *outskirts of Cafayete, next to ACA hostería, T03868-421296, www.aca.tur.ar.*

If you only have an hour spare and don't want to wander far from the centre of town, head to **Nanni** ⓘ *Chavarría 151, T03868-421527, www.bodegananni.com, US2.50,* also recommended. It's only one block from the plaza, but once you're inside, you feel you're in the outskirts of town with only vineyards and the mountains in sight. The bodega is very traditional and has been family-owned for over 100 years.

They grow Malbec, Torrontés, Tannat and Cabernet Sauvignon grapes, and produce organic wines.

Around Cafayate

In addition to the Quebrada de las Conchas to the east (see below) and the Quebrada de las Flechas to the north (see below), there are lots of places to walk, cycle or drive to from the Cafayate itself. **Cerro San Isidro**, 5 km west, has cave paintings and views across the Aconquija mountains in the south and to the Nevado de Cachi in the north. Behind it, the waterfalls of **Río Colorado** are a pretty place for bathing in summer. For a stroll and a good view, take Vía Toscano west out of the centre up to **Cerro Santa Teresita**, 2 km each way.

Quebrada de las Conchas

Heading north from Cafayate towards Salta, the Ruta Nacional 68 enters the Quebrada de las Conchas (Gorge of Shells). Though no one seems to know why it has this name, it's a truly magnificent stretch of road, with huge ochre, burgundy and terracotta rocks carved into extraordinary forms by wind and rain. These formations have been helpfully named after the things they most resemble: *El Anfiteatro* (the amphitheatre), Km 48; the *Garganta del Diablo* (devil's throat), Km 49; *El Sapo* (the toad), Km 35; and *El Fraile* (looks vaguely like a praying friar), Km 29. Take a few minutes to walk inside the Garganta del Diablo and to stop to photograph *Los Castillos* (the castles), Km 20. The best light for photography is in the early morning or late afternoon. The valley floor beside the Río de las Conchas is richly green with tipa and algarrobo trees, contrasting beautifully with the chocolate-coloured mountains and raspberry ripple strata. There's lots of birdlife to be spotted, including *ñandúes* (rheas). If you haven't got a car but want to experience the Quebrada, take a bus from Cafayate towards Salta and get off at Los Loros, Km 32, or at the Garganta del Diablo; walk back, and catch a return bus from Salta. Or, hire a bike, take it on an El Indio bus and cycle back.

Cafayate to Cachi

San Carlos and the Quebrada de las Flechas → *Colour map 1, B2.*

San Carlos (1710 m, Km 24) is a pleasant place and was the most important village in the valley until the growth of Cafayate. The main buildings are on the pretty plaza, including the church, the largest in the valley, which was built between 1801 and 1860. Nearby, there's a small **archaeological museum** ① *daily 1000-1400*, which contains superb archaeological finds from the region, including fine funerary urns. Also on the plaza are artisans' shops and workshops, and a craft market.

The highlight of your trip on this fabulous route will probably be the next stretch of road through the **Quebrada de las Flechas** (the gorge of arrows) from San Carlos. You'll find yourself surrounded by massive rocks, eroded into complex forms and massive sharp peaks, towering above you into the blue sky – all very photogenic.

Angastaco → *Colour map 1, B2. Population 881.*

Angastaco (1900 m) is a modern village, 2 km off Ruta 40, at Km 77, less picturesque than Cachi, but it does have an **archaeological museum** in the Centro Cívico. The church is modern, so it's worth the trek to the much older one, the **Iglesia del Carmen de Angastaco** (1800) about 8 km further north on the **Finca El Carmen**. Stop in Angastaco to try the *vino patero*, for which the town is famous. This sweet red or white wine is traditionally made by treading the grapes in the traditional manner – hence the name (*pata* is the informal word for leg). The **Fiesta Patronal Virgen del Valle** is held on the second weekend of December, with processions, music, dancing, gauchos and rodeos. Information is available from the **tourist office** ① *in the municipalidad on the plaza, Mon-Fri 0900-1400.*

Molinos

From Angastaco, Ruta 40 weaves its way through some of the most exquisite scenery in the region, but the road is rough *ripio* and only manageable in a hire car as long as it hasn't rained; consider hiring a 4WD for safety. The landscape is beautiful: tiny settlements with green fields and orchards, against the constant backdrop of the rugged Andes. Some 52 km before Cachi, you come to the village of **Molinos** (2220 m), hidden away 1 km off Ruta 40 at Km 118. Set in a bowl of craggy mountains with a wide plaza and neat adobe houses, it's a peaceful place and an idyllic retreat for relaxing and doing very little. Founded in 1659, it has a fine church dating from 1692, with a simple gold *retablo*, containing the mummified body of the last Royalist governor of Salta, Don Nicolás Severo Isasmendi. The house he built, opposite the church, is now the **Hostal Provincial de Molinos**. There are a couple of satisfying two-hour walks: either across the river bed (usually dry) and then up the hill opposite; or up to the Cross above the town. Both offer fine views of Molinos and the surrounding country.

Accommodation is limited in Molinos, but the nuns opposite the church have pristine little rooms to rent, and there are several families that rent rooms in the village. There are a few simple places to eat near where the bus to Cachi stops – ask around, or at the basic **tourist office** ① *municipalidad, on the plaza at Belgrano s/n, daily 0800-2200, low season daily 0900-1300, 1600-2100.* No one speaks English here but they are kind and want to help. Molinos celebrates **La Virgen de la Candelaria** in February, with processions, music and handicrafts.

Just 20 km from Molinos along a road running west into the mountains, is the extraordinary and fabulous winery, **Colomé** ① *4 hrs from Salta, 2½ hrs from Cafayate via a short cut, 20 km west of Molinos, T0387-421 9132, www.bodegacolome.com.* Owned by charming art collector Donald Hess and his wife, Ursula, this remote retreat is more than just a swish place to stay (see page 279). As well as having a stunningly lovely setting, the bodega produces the highest-altitude wines in the world, at 2300 m. In an arid valley of red and grey rock, surrounded by mountains, there are hundreds of hectares of rare pre-Phylloxera vines, producing Malbec-heavy wines of exquisite intensity – and all grown on organic and biodynamic principles. A Spanish-style house with nine rooms provides ultra-luxurious accommodation and delicious meals, and there is great walking and riding in the extensive *finca*. It's impressive in terms of social responsibility too, since the Hesses have built a church, clinic and community centre for the 400 families living on their land, and take great care of their well-being.

Seclantás → *Colour map 1, B2. Phone code 03868. Population 900.*

The road continues north to Cachi on the west side of the river, via the *hostería* Casa de Campo La Paya (see Where to stay, page 280), 9 km from Cachi, where there are interesting archaeological ruins of an important pre-Inca town and administrative centre. For a pretty detour to the hamlet of **Seclantás**, cross the river and follow signs. This is a quaint tranquil village with simple colonial-style houses and an interesting church dating from 1835. Seclantás' weavers are among the finest in the country, and they sell ponchos directly from their workshops on the side of the road; look for the looms strung up between the pillars on a porch. The quality is higher and prices are much lower than in the Cachi tourist office shop, and you have the satisfaction of knowing that the profits go directly to the weavers. Wander down the main street and ask around for *telares* (weavers), as there are few signs. There's currently nowhere great to stay in Seclantás, but a couple of places sell food and snacks and there is a camping ground.

Cachi → *Colour map 1, B2. Phone code 03868. Population 7000. Altitude 1228 m.*

Cachi is a beautiful, tranquil town (180 km from Salta) in a wide green valley at the foot of the majestic Nevado del Cachi, whose nine peaks are snow-covered for much of the year and whose highest summit is **San Martín** (6380 m). Founded in 1694, it had been a Diaguita settlement long before the Incas arrived in 1450, and the extensive irrigation channels they built to channel the Nevado's snow-melt are still used today to make the valley green and to grow huge fields of peppers. These are an amazing sight when harvested in April and laid out to dry in huge scarlet squares, which stand out against the arid mountains beyond.

The **tourist office** ① *on the plaza, opposite side to the church, Av Gral, Güemes s/n, T03868-491902, www.cachi.todowebsalta.com.ar, Mon-Fri 0900-2100, Sat-Sun 0900-1300, 1700-2100,* can provide a basic leaflet and map. No one speaks English, but they are well meaning and will give advice if you're patient. Also on the plaza you'll find an ATM, restaurants and cafés. A private tourist office has opened, **Casa de Turismo de Cachi** ① *by the entrance to the town on the left.* Local guides can be found here, and they sell crafts.

Cachi has a pleasingly simple church, the **Iglesia de San José**, whose roof and lecterns are made of cactus wood. Next door, there's a fascinating survey of pre-colonial Calchaquí culture in the **Museo Arqueológico** ① *T03868-491080, Mon-Fri 1000-1900, Sat 1000-1800, Sun 1000-1300, US$1.50,* with impressive painted funerary urns and an intriguing cat/man petroglyph. There are panoramic views from Cachi's spectacularly sited hilltop cemetery, just 20 minutes' walk from the plaza.

The town feels more like a small village and has a lively community life with fiestas throughout the year, where you can hear traditional *folclore* music as well as the *bagualas* and *coplas* from the indigenous traditions. The **Fiesta de la Tradición Calchaquí**, held in the third week in January, and the **Carnaval** in February are particularly worth experiencing. **Pachamama** is celebrated in August.

Around Cachi

With its sunny climate, Cachi is the perfect place for a few days' rest, but there are satisfying walks into the mountains all around. A pleasant walk will take you to **La Aguada**, 6 km southwest along the lush valley fringed with *álamo* trees and dotted with adobe farmhouses. Leave town by Calle Benjamín Zorrilla at the southwest of the plaza, and walk along the *ripio* track. There's also wonderful accommodation here at *finca* El Molino (see Where to stay, page 279), with its tiny bodega and charming hospitality.

Don't miss the ancient ruins at **Las Pailas**, 16 km northwest of Cachi (via Cachi Adentro), with intriguingly complex circular dwellings, long irrigation channels and worked stone cultivation terraces. The views are breathtaking, with huge cacti set against the snow-topped Nevado de Cachi behind. To get there you can take a bus to Las Arcas from where it's a two-hour walk. The bus leaves Cachi early in the morning (check the current timetable with the tourist office) and returns in the afternoon. However, it's better to go with a guide, since Cachi has the special advantage of being one of the few original towns in the region with trained local guides.

Cerro de la Virgen is another rewarding day hike near Cachi, up through a pretty hanging valley and slopes strewn with giant boulders to a peak with wonderful views over the Calchaquí Valley beyond. The hamlet **Cachi Adentro**, on the opposite side of the valley from La Aguada, has more fine views, a school, church and dairy farm, **El Tambo**.

Serious climbers should plan to spend a week or so climbing the spectacular peaks of the Nevado de Cachi. To climb any of the peaks, you must take a mountain guide who is trained and familiar with the route; do not attempt these peaks alone.
➤➤ *For further information, see What to do, page 282.*

Beyond Cachi → *For listings, see pages 278-283.*

La Poma to San Antonio de los Cobres

From Cachi it is 61 km north to Poma (3015 m), whose modern adobe houses and population of 600 sit beneath the massive Cumbre del Libertador General San Martín (6380 m). It's the most northerly village in the Calchaquí valley but not the original one, which was destroyed by an earthquake in 1930; its ruins lie 2 km north at La Poma Vieja.

North of La Poma, Ruta 40 heads towards **San Antonio de los Cobres** (see page 300) via the **Paso Abra del Acay** (4900 m, Km 282), the highest pass in South America negotiable by car. Road conditions vary depending on the weather and whether the roads have been recently cleared, so a 4WD vehicle is strongly advised. The critical part of the route is south of the pass at **Mal Paso** (Km 257), where summer rains can wash the road away. Buses do not travel on this road and anyone tempted to try it on a bicycle should think twice: there is no shade; night temperatures are several degrees below freezing, and you need to be well adapted to the altitude. Take plenty of water and an arctic sleeping bag.

Cachi to Salta

Cachi is 170 km west of Salta, along one of the most unforgettable routes in Argentina. About 11 km beyond Cachi is the small village of **Payogasta**, where you can find the **Hostería de Payogasta** ① *T03868-496034*, and the **administrative office for the Parque Nacional Los Cardones** ① *T03868-496005, loscardones@apn.gov. ar*. The road runs east through the national park at altitudes between 2700 m and 5000 m, along a dead-straight stretch known as **La Recta del Tin-Tin**, surrounded by an astonishing landscape of huge candelabra cacti. Walking amongst these giant sentinels, their arms thrust up to the cloudless sky, with a backdrop of stratified bright pink rock, is an extraordinary experience. There are occasionally *guardaparques* at Recta del Tin-Tin, but no services. Camping is officially not allowed.

Beyond the arid **Piedra del Molino Pass** (3347 m), where you'll want to stop for photos, the road (mostly *ripio*) snakes along the hairpins of the breathtaking **Cuesta del Obispo**. Take great care if you drive the Cuesta del Obispo in fog, which often hangs in the valley in the early mornings, or in rain. It is not advisable at all at night. Throughout the journey, you'll pass tiny hamlets of adobe houses shrouded in low cloud. As the cloud clears, you'll glimpse dramatic views of the vast bronze, green-velvety mountains. There are two places to stop for tea roughly halfway to Salta: Café **Margarita** serves coffee and layered *tortillas* for bus passengers, and at **El Maray** (70 km from Salta), there's a nice *confitería* in a yellow building; delicious jams and walnuts are sold opposite. You might also like to take the turn-off down to the **Valle Encantado**, an eerie, fascinating place for a picnic amongst bizarre wind-sculpted terracotta rocks.

The road enters the fertile **Quebrada de Escoipe and heads towards** the quaint little town of **Chicoana**, where you could stay the night. After Chicoana, turn left at El Carril onto Ruta Nacional 68 and head north to Salta city.

Chicoana

There's not much to do in Chicoana, but it's an interesting example of a colonial-style town, sitting amidst some of the finest tobacco-producing land in the world, and with lots of buildings dating from the 1900s. Religious festivals are celebrated with much enthusiasm, and the **Carnaval** (February) and the **Fiesta Patronal** (16 July) are particularly recommended for a fun day out. Easter celebrations are impressive too, with the Passion re-enacted throughout the town. The weekend afterwards (around 23 July) is the town's famous **Fiesta de Tamales** when regional delicacies (meat and corn tied up in corn-husk bundles) are traditionally made on a massive scale, famous *folclore* musicians come to sing, and gauchos compete in Doma contests – roughly equivalent to rodeo and very impressive.

⊚ Los Valles Calchaquíes listings

*For hotel and restaurant price codes and
other relevant information, see pages 20-26.*

● Where to stay

Cafayate and around *p270, map p271*
Accommodation is hard to find during
holiday periods (Jan, Easter, late Jul),
but there are many places to stay.
Off season, prices are much lower.
All those listed are recommended.
See also www.munayhotel.com.ar.
$$$$ Patios de Cafayate, Routes 68
and 40, T0387-422 229, www.patiosde
cafayate.com. A stunning hotel, in the
converted building of the old winery
(now **El Esteco**, see page 272 for visits to
the bodega), with beautifully designed
rooms, sumptuous lounges, and set in
gorgeous gardens with a lovely pool.
There are interesting wine-oriented
treatments in the spa and the restaurant
serves fine food, has a lovely terrace and
excellent wines. Highly recommended.
$$$$-$$$ Viñas de Cafayate,
R21, Camino al Divisadero, T03868-
422272/282, www.cafayatewineresort.
com. On a hillside above Cafayate,
colonial style, calm, welcoming with
pretty, spacious bedrooms, some with
views. Excellent restaurant with local
delicacies, open to non-residents with
reservation, full buffet breakfast.
$$$ Killa, Colón 47, T03868-422254,
www.killacafayate.com.ar. A delightfully
restored colonial house with pleasing
views. Delightful owner, who has a
fascinating garden, tranquil, comfortable,
good breakfasts.
$$$ Portal del Santo, Silvero Chavarria
250, T03868-422400, www.portaldel
santo.todowebsalta.com.ar. Family-run

hotel with lovely large rooms overlooking
a beautiful pool and garden.
$$$ Villa Vicuña, Belgrano 76, T03868-
422145, www.villavicuna.com.ar. Half a
block from the main plaza, 2 colourful
patios, bright rooms, pleasant and calm.
Afternoon tea with home-made pastries
served on demand.
$$ Hostal del Valle, San Martín 243,
T03868-421039. Well-kept big rooms
around leafy patio, charming owner. New
living room at the top has superb views
over the valley (as do upper floor rooms).
$ El Balcón, Pasaje 20 de Febrero,
T03868-421739, www.hosteltrail.com/
hostels/elbalcon. The cheapest option.
Basic rooms, very central, the views from
the roof are wonderful.
$ pp El Hospedaje, Quintana de Niño y
Salta, T03868-421680, www.elhospedaje.
todowebsalta.com.ar. Simple but
pleasant rooms in colonial-style house,
wonderful pool, good value, heater in
room, HI discount.
$ Hostel Ruta 40, Güermes Sur 178,
T03868-421689, www.hostel-ruta40.com.
Very sociable place to stay, dorms US$18,
private room **$$**. Discount for HI members.
$ Rusty K Hostal, Rivadavia 281, T03868-
422031, www.rustykhostal.todowebsalta.
com.ar. Neat, basic rooms and a great
garden with barbecue. 2 blocks from
the main plaza. Lots of activities to enjoy
by bike.

Camping
Camping Luz y Fuerza, on R40, south
of the town, T03868-421568. More
appealing than the municipal site and
quieter, with pool, games, grills, showers
and a buffet.

San Carlos and the Quebrada de las Flechas p273

$$ La Casa de Los Vientos, Las Alfareras s/n, San Carlos, T03868-495075, www.casadelosvientos.com.ar. Comfortable accommodation in a colonial-style house built almost entirely of adobe, recreating a traditional Calchaquí residence. Just 8 rooms, and it's rustic but very welcoming with the friendly Swiss owner on hand to make your stay enjoyable. Excellent value, with breakfast included.

Camping
Municipal campsite, Rivadavia and San Martín, T03868-491123. Well tended with plenty of shade.

Angastaco p274

$$-$ Hostería de Angastaco, Av Libertador s/n, T03868-491123. Breakfast included, and prices negotiable in low season. Rooms are basic but comfortable, and this place is especially recommended for its warm welcome from reception staff who are very helpful and can provide information on the region. Pool, meals on request.

Molinos p274

$$$$ Colomé, 20 km west of Molinos, T0387-421 9132, www.bodegacolome.com. Leave town via the vicuña farm and follow signs, or phone for directions from Cafayate. Recommended as one of the best places to stay in Argentina, winery in a beautiful setting with delightful rooms, horse riding, tastings of excellent wines, all food is organic, power is hydroelectric.

$$$$-$$$ Hacienda de Molinos, A Cornejo (by the river), T03868-494094, www.haciendademolinos.com.ar. Open all year round. Stunning 18th-century hacienda, with rooms around a courtyard. Great attention to detail, the

rooms are an oasis of calm. Swimming pool with a view of the Cachi mountains.

$ pp Hostal San Agustín, Sarmiento y A Cornejo at the Colegio Infantil, T03868-494015. Small but spotless rooms, some with private bath, run by nuns (who don't like to advertize the place, ask around discretely for 'las monjas' and someone will come and give you a key).

Camping
Municipal campsite, in the sports complex, Alvarado and Mitre, T03868-494037. Hot showers, electricity, also has cabins for rent.

Seclantás p275

$$ Hostería El Capricho, Abrahan Cornejo s/n, T0387-421 6322, www.elcaprichosalta.com.ar. With 4 nicely decorated double rooms set around a well-kept courtyard, this *hostería* is the best choice in town. Rooms are **$** with shared bath. Includes breakfast.

$ Hostería La Rueda, Abrahan Cornejo and Pedro Ferreyra, T03868-498041. The small, basic rooms in this clean *hostería* are the cheapest option. Welcoming staff make up for the lack of luxuries.

Cachi and around p275

$$$$ El Molino de Cachi, 4 km on the road to La Aguada, T03868-491094, www.bodegaelmolino.com.ar. In restored 300-year-old mill, only 5 rooms, pool, superb food, exquisite in every way; has its own bodega.

$$$$-$$$ Finca Santana, take the road to Cachi Adentro, and ask for camino to Finca San Miguel, on right at top, T0387-432 1141, fincasantana@fibertel.com.ar. 2 rooms in boutique B&B in the heart of the valley, spectacular views, and complete sense of privacy and silence. Welcoming, spacious living room, terrace and garden, gourmet breakfast, trekking can be arranged. Wonderful.

$$$ ACA Hostería Cachi, at the top of Juan Manuel Castilla, T0387-491904. Smart modern rooms (with wheelchair access), great views, pool, good restaurant, non-residents can use the pool if they eat lunch.

$$$ Casa de Campo La Paya, 12 km south of Cachi at La Paya, clearly signposted from the road, T0387-491139 A restored 18th-century house, pool, elegant rooms, excellent dinners, hospitable, Recommended.

$$$ El Cortijo, opposite the ACA hotel, on Av Automóvil Club s/n, T0387-491034, www.elcortijohotel.com. Lovely peaceful rooms, each with its own style, warm hospitality, original art works. Recommended.

$$$ Llaqta Mawk'a, Ruiz de Los Llanos s/n, up from plaza, T0387-491016. Traditional frontage hides modern block, garden/terrace, view of the Nevado de Cachi, pool. Comfy rooms, ample breakfast, good value, popular with tourists (street parking). Horse riding with Ariel Villar arranged.

$$ Hospedaje Don Arturo, Bustamante s/n, T0387-491087, hospedajedonarturo. blogspot.com. Homely, small rooms, quiet street, charming owners.

$ Hospedaje El Nevado de Cachi, Ruiz de los Llanos y F Suárez, T0387-491912. Impeccable small rooms around a central courtyard, hot water, *comedor*.

$ Viracocha Art Hostel, Ruiz de los Llanos s/n, T03868 491713, www.hostel cachi.com.ar. Good central option offering bike hire, cable TV, private and shared rooms.

Camping
Municipal campsite at Av Automóvil Club Argentina s/n, T0387-491902, with pool and sports complex, also *cabañas* and *albergue*.

La Poma to San Antonio de los Cobres *p276*
$$ Hostería La Poma, Sarmiento and Belgrano 40, La Poma, T03868-491003. Welcoming place, breakfast included, also serves meals.

Chicoana *p277*
$$$$-$$$ Finca Los Los, T0387-683 3121, www.redsalta.com/loslos. Mar-Dec. Most welcoming and highly recommended, beautifully situated on a hilltop with fabulous views from the colonial-style galleried veranda. Spacious rooms, decorated with old furniture, and beautiful gardens with a pool. Includes unforgettable horse riding into the forested mountains of the huge *finca*, where you will be cooked lunch in a remote rustic lodge. Reserve in advance.

$$$-$$ Hostería de Chicoana, on the plaza at España 45, T0387-490 7009, www.new sendas.com. A pretty colonial building, now slightly faded, but with the added advantage of expert guide Martín Pekarek (see New Sendas, under What to do, below).

🍴 Restaurants

Cafayate and around *p270, map p271*
Cafayate has lots of lovely choices around the plaza, most of them huge and prepared for coach parties. In summer many provide live music. The following are recommended:

$$$ Viñas de Cafayate, R21, Camino al Divisadero, T03868-422272, www. cafayatewineresort.com. Elegant food, simple surroundings, but lovely views from this hotel. Book ahead.

$$ Baco, Güemes Norte y Rivadavia. *Parrilla*, *pasta casera*, pizzas, regional dishes, *empanadas* and *picadas*. Seating inside and on attractive street corner, lively atmosphere. Good selection of local wines and beers.

$$ El Rancho, Toscano 4, T03868-421256. A traditional restaurant on the plaza serving *parrilla* and good regional dishes (try the *tamales*).

$$ El Terruño, Güemes Sur 28, T03868-422460, www.terruno.todowebsalta.com. ar. Meat and fish dishes, including local specialities, good service.

$$ La Carreta de Don Olegario, Güemes Sur 20 and Quintana de Niño, T03868-421004. Huge, but does good set menus for the usual meat dishes and pastas. Good wine menu.

$$-$ La Casa de Las Empanadas, Mitre 24, T03868-15-454111, www. casadelaempanada.com.ar. Cosy place with exposed brick and wooden tables featuring local specialities, such as *humitas* and the titular *empanadas*.

Ice cream parlours
Helados Miranda, Güemes Norte 170. Cafayate's unmissable treat is this fabulous home-made ice cream. The creative owner makes wine-flavoured ice cream as well as many other delicious flavours.

Molinos p274
$$$-$$ Bodega Colomé, 20 km west of Molinos, T0387-421 9132, www.bodega colome.com. Good local specialities. After eating world-class delicacies on the terrace, stay around and try out the inviting spa. Pure luxury. See also Where to stay.

Cachi p275
$$$-$$ La Merced del Alto, Fuerte Alto, T03868-490030, www.lamerceddelalto. com. Set in luscious surroundings, this is a treat to your taste buds and your eyes. Make sure you try a local wine.

$$-$ Ashpamanta, Bustamante – Cachi 4417, T03868-15-578 2244. Just off the main plaza, this little restaurant serves universal favourites, such as pizza and pasta, plus some regional gems such as quinoa risotto.

$ Oliver Café, Ruiz de Los Llanos 160, on the plaza. Tiny café for ice creams, coffee, breakfasts, fruit juices, sandwiches and pizza.

O Shopping

Cafayate and around p270, map p271
Lots of fairly trashy souvenir shops have opened on the plaza, but there are some fine handicrafts shops to be found if you dig around. There's the **Calchaquí tapestry exhibition** of Miguel Nanni on the main plaza (Güemes 65), silver work at **Jorge Barraco**, Colón 157, T03868-421244. Local pottery, woollen goods, and more are sold in the **Mercado de Artesanos Cafayetanos** on the plaza (small, pricey).

Cachi p275
Cachi has a great tradition in weaving, and you can buy beautiful handmade ponchos, shawls, rugs and wall hangings at the government-run **handicrafts shop** in the same room as the tourist office on the plaza. But these are more expensive than if bought directly from weavers, and they receive hardly any of the profit. Instead, go up the street to find the workshop of **Oscar Cardozo**, Juan Calchaquí, opposite the monument, T03868-491037. Oscar teaches weaving

and can direct you to other weavers in his association.

☼ What to do

Cafayate and around *p270, map p271*
Cycling
There are many places to hire a bike around the main plaza; compare rates before renting.

Tour operators
Turismo Cordillerano, Güemes Sur 178, T03868-421689, www.turismocordillerano.com. Tours, trekking, horses, bike hire.
Wichay Turismo Aventura, 9 de Julio 64, T03868-421333. Guided trips on mountain bikes, or high-mountain trekking and mountaineering.

Cachi *p275*
Horse riding
Hostería Llaqta Mawk'a, T03868-491016, www.hotelllaqtamawka.todowebsalta.com.ar, see Where to stay, above. Ask for Ariel Villar.

Tour operators and guides
Fernando Gamarra, corner of Benjamín Zorrilla and Güemes, T0387-431 7305, fg_serviciosturisticos@yahoo.com.ar. More conventional trips around Cachi with genial Fernando, who is good company: to Las Pailas, La Poma and Seclantás, including the beautiful Laguna de Brealito. Knowledgeable, reasonably priced, especially if divided amongst a group.
Santiago Casimiro, T03868-15-638545, santiagocasimiro@hotmail.com. Particularly recommended for all mountain hikes; he's a nurse trained in mountain rescue and has lived in the valley all his life. He'll take you to La Poma, Cerro de la Virgen and up the Nevado peaks, all very reasonable. Highly recommended.
Tourism Urkupiña, Benjamin Zorrilla s/n, T03868-491317, uk_cachi@hotmail.com. Local agency that can book tours and bus tickets.

Chicoana *p277*
New Sendas, T0387-490 7009, www.newsendas.com. Expert guide Martín Pekarek offers wine tours, adventure excursions and horses for hire, English and German spoken. Also with lodging at **Hostería de Chicoana** (see above).
Sayta, T0387-15-683 6565, www.saltacabalgatas.com.ar. An *estancia* specializing in horse riding, for all levels of experience, good horses and attention, great *asados*, also has lodging for overnight stays, adventure and rural tourism. Recommended.

◉ Transport

Cafayate and around *p270, map p271*
Bus
El Indio (T03868-421002) to **Santa María** (for Quilmes) 4 daily, US$5; also to **Salta** (via the Quebrada de las Conchas), 3 a day, 3 hrs, US$11, travel in daylight to see the rock formations; to **Angastaco**, 1 daily Mon-Fri, US$5, 1½ hrs (note this bus does not continue to Molinos and Cachi). **Aconquija** to **Tucumán**, 4 daily, 5½ hrs, US$17.50; to **Tafí del Valle**, 4 daily, US$11, 3 hrs (more services via **Santa María**, 5½ hrs); and to **Salta**, US$29-32.50.

San Carlos and the Quebrada de las Flechas *p273*
Bus
El Indio has 5 services a day to **Cafayate**, 30 mins, US$5.

Angastaco *p274*
Bus
To **Salta**, Mon-Fri, US$11. To **Cafayate** via San Carlos, Mon-Fri, US$8, with **El Indio**.

Remise taxi
Alto Valle Remis, 12 de Octubre 233, Cachi, T03871-5502 0981.

Molinos *p274*
Bus
To **Salta** (via Cachi), **Ale** (as above), Mon, Tue, Thu, Sat 0700, Sun 1355, 2 hrs to **Cachi**, 7 hrs to **Salta**, US$11.50.

Cachi *p275*
Bus
To **Salta**, **Ale**, T0387-423 1811, www.alehnos.com.ar, 2 to 3 times daily, 4 hrs,

US$8.25. Also to **Molinos**, Mon, Wed, Fri, Sun at 1130 and Sat at 1945, 2 hrs.

Remise taxis
Los Calchaquíes, T03868-491071; **San José**, T03868-491907.

O Directory

Cafayate and around *p270, map p271*
Banks Banco de la Nación, Toscano and NS del Rosario, ATM; **Banco Salta**, Mitre and San Martín, ATM, open all year, good service. **Medical services** Pharmacy, F Pastor, Rivadavia 35. **Post office** Güemes 197.

Salta city and around

Salta is one of Argentina's most charismatic and historical cities; its colourful past is tangible in palm-filled plazas lined with crumbling 17th-century buildings, such as the plum-coloured Iglesia San Francisco and the handsome colonial Cabildo. Its fine museums chart the city's fascinating past, including the amazing finds from an Inca burial site on remote Mount Llullaillaco. Salta's tourist infrastructure is well established, and agencies offer trips south to the beautiful Calchaquí Valley and to the splendid wineries around Cafayate. You could take the 'train to the clouds' into the dramatic Quebrada del Toro, or take your time to explore the ancient archaeological site of Santa Rosa de Tastil. Head further west into the shimmering salt flats, and discover the ancient way of life on the *puna* (high-altitude desert).

Salta city is worth at least a couple of days of your trip. It buzzes with life in the mornings, grinds to a complete halt at lunchtime and comes alive again at night. Balmy evenings are perfect for wandering the streets to find live music played with passion in the local *peñas* of calle Balcarce. Or sample the superb food, such as *locro*, *tamales* and *humitas*, for which Salta is famous, accompanied by a glass or two of the region's fine 'high-altitude' wine. This region is rich in indigenous culture, and you can buy the characteristic blood-red Güemes ponchos, as well as other handicrafts, in smart shops around the main plaza, or in the Mercado Artesenal. The city is particularly lively in the second week of September, when the Fiesta del Milagro is celebrated with a huge procession uniting the population in an ancient communal act of superstition: parading the Christian figures that keep Salta safe from earthquakes. The countryside is on your doorstep, with lush jungle to explore on horseback in nearby San Lorenzo – also a good place for a relaxing evening. For more information, see www.turismoensalta.com (in English).

Getting there

There are daily flights from Buenos Aires to Salta's **airport** ① *T0387-424 7356, www.aa2000.com.ar*, 12 km southwest of the city. It has a café, *locutorio* with internet, ATM and car rental companies. There's also a **Movitrack** stand, useful for information on tours as you wait for your luggage. **Tourist information** is in the main hall, next to Avis, but isn't always open. **Transfer del Pino** buses meet all flights, US$4 to the centre, or take a *remise* taxi, US$8, 15 minutes. Bus on Corredor 8A to airport from San Martín, US$0.30.

The **bus terminal** ① *T0387-421 4716, information T0387-431 5022*, is eight blocks east of the main plaza; walk along Avenida Yrigoyen and then Caseros, or take a taxi to the centre for US$2. There is a *confitería*, toilets, *locutorio*, café, *panadería*, kiosks, ATM and left luggage, but no internet. The **train station** ① *20 de Febrero and Ameghino*, is nine blocks north of Plaza 9 de Julio; a taxi costs US$2. ➤➤ *For further details, see Transport, page 295.*

Getting around

The best way to get around Salta is on foot, allowing you to soak up the atmosphere and see the main examples of its splendid architecture, all within four blocks of the main plaza, 9 de Julio. The main area for nightlife (Thursday to Saturday) and site of a weekend handicraft market is Calle Balcarce, 10 blocks north and west of the main plaza. This is five minutes in a taxi (US$2), but it's a pleasant stroll, past attractive Plaza Güemes. There is also a hop-on, hop-off bus called the BTS (Bus Turístico Salta) which does a circuit of the town. City buses charge US$0.30 (www.saetasalta.com.ar). To get a grand overview of the whole city, take the cable car from central Parque San Martín to the top of Cerro San Bernardo (or it's a 45-minute walk if you have the energy). At the top there are impeccably manicured gardens, waterfalls and a café with an amazing view.

Tourist information

The **provincial tourist office** ① *Buenos Aires 93 (1 block from main plaza), T0387-431 0950, www.turismosalta.gov.ar, Mon-Fri 0800-2100, Sat and Sun 0900-2000*, is helpful and provides free maps, both of the city and the province, gives advice on tours and arranges accommodation in private houses in high season (July), when hotels are fully booked. Staff speak English. The **municipal tourist office** ① *Caseros 711, T0800-777 0300, Mon-Fri 0800-2100, Sat and Sun 0900-2100*, is for Salta city only and is small but helpful. There is also a **national parks office** ① *España 366, 3rd floor, T0387-431 2683, Mon-Fri 0800-1430, elrey@apn.gov.ar*. Useful websites include www.turismoensalta.com of the **Cámara de Turismo** ① *Gral Güemes 15 y Av Virrey Toledo, T0387-480 0719; www.saltalalinda.gov.ar and www.saltaciudad.com.ar.*

The first Spanish expedition, led by Diego de Almagro from Cuzco (Peru), entered Argentina in 1536 and soon a busy trade route was established through the Quebrada de Humahuaca (now in Jujuy). Along this route the Spanish founded a group of towns: Santiago del Estero, Tucumán, Salta and Jujuy. Throughout the colonial period these were the centres of white settlement, and *encomiendas* were established to subdue the indigenous population. Jesuit and Franciscan missions were also attempted, but resistance was fierce, especially in the Calchaquí and Humahuaca valleys and, as a result, this is one of the few areas in Argentina that retains a rich indigenous culture.

The city of Salta was founded in 1582 and became one of the viceroyalty's most important administrative centres, governing a wide area and gaining considerable wealth from the fertile outlying land. The city also had an important role in the Wars of Independence between 1810 and 1821, when General Güemes led gaucho anti-Royalist forces to victory, utilizing their detailed knowledge of the terrain and inventing the now-famous red poncho which his men wore. Through the 19th century, Salta suffered a decline, since trade went directly to the country's new capital, Buenos Aires. Relatively little immigration and expansion allowed the city's colonial buildings to survive, boosted by neocolonial architecture in the 1930s when there was a large influx of newcomers. Today, Salta retains its old, aristocratic population but has a more affluent middle class than its neighbour, Jujuy. Tourism has taken off since devaluation in 2002 and is now the province's main source of income.

Plaza 9 de Julio and around

In just a few hours you can get a feel for the city. At its heart is the pleasant Plaza 9 de Julio, richly planted with wonderful tall palm trees and orange trees and surrounded by colonial-style buildings. The whole area has been spruced up and three sides of it are now pedestrianized with cafés where you can sit and watch teenagers hanging out on the plaza and smart businessmen having their shoes shined. There's an impressive **Cabildo** built in 1783, one of the few that remains intact in the whole country, and behind its pleasingly uneven arches is an impressive museum, the **Museo Histórico del Norte** ① *Caseros 549, Tue-Fri 0900-1900, Sat-Sun 0900-1330, US$2, free Wed.* In a series of rooms around two open courtyards, the collection charts the region's history from pre-Hispanic times, with particularly good displays on the Wars of Independence and on Güemes leading the gauchos to victory. Upstairs, among some lovely religious art, is a fine golden 18th-century pulpit and some Cuzco school paintings, while outside are carriages and an ancient wine press. Fascinating and informative.

Opposite the museum, on the north side of the plaza, is the lovely **cathedral**, built 1858-1878, now strangely painted pastel pink, and open mornings and evenings so that you can admire a huge baroque altar (1807) and the images of the Cristo del Milagro and of the Virgin Mary. These are central to Salta's beliefs and psyche, and the focus of Salta's biggest mass ritual. In 1692 Jesuit priests were amazed to discover that two statues, of Christ and the Virgin of Rosario, had survived a severe earthquake intact. During a series of tremors they paraded them through the

Salta

Where to stay		
1	Apart Ilusión D3	
2	Ayres de Salta B1	
4	Backpackers Home D2	
3	Backpackers Suites D1	
6	Bloomers Bed & Brunch C2	
7	Carpe Diem D2	
8	Correcaminos Hostel B2	

9	Del Antiguo Convento C2
10	El Lagar A1
11	Hostal Quara B2
13	Las Marías D2
14	Las Rejas B1
15	Legado Mítico B1
16	Munay D1
18	Posada de las Nubes A1
19	Salta C1

20	Solar de la Plaza B1
Restaurants 🍴	
1	Doña Salta C2
2	El Churrúa C2
3	El Corredor de las Empanadas C2
4	El Solar del Convento C1
6	La Casa de Güemes C1

7	La Criollita B1
9	Mama Paca B2
Bars & clubs 🍸	
11	Gauchos de Güemes A3
12	La Casona del Molino C1
13	La Vieja Estación A1

streets in procession, and the following day, 14 September, the tremors stopped. The **Milagro** (miracle) is now the biggest event of Salta's year, when thousands of pilgrims walk to the city from hundreds of kilometres away.

Next to the cathedral is the **Museo de Arqueología de Alta Montaña** (MAAM) ① *Plaza 9 de Julio at Mitre 77, T0387-437 0592, www.maam.gob.ar, Tue-Sun 1100-1930, US$5, shop and café*, which houses the *Niños de Llullaillaco*. Like the Christian statues next door, these Inca deities were intended to avert earthquakes and volcanic eruptions. They were unearthed from a sacred burial site by a National Geographic expedition in 1999. Controversially, MAAM has on show the mummified remains of sacrificial children as well as many of the other fabulous objects found in the burial, with texts in English. A guided tour is included in the entry price; the guides are trained by resident archaeologist Christian Vitry. There's a fine library too. Opposite MAAM on the other side of the plaza is the interesting **Museo de Arte Contemporáneo** ① *Zuviria 90, T0387-437 3036, www.macsaltamuseo.org, Tue-Sat 0900-2000, Sun 1000-1400*, which is also worth a look.

Near the plaza, there are also a couple of historical houses worth visiting for a glimpse of wealthy domestic life, of which the best is **Casa de los Uriburu** ① *Caseros 417, T0387-421 8174, www.museonor.gov.ar, Tue-Fri 0900-1900, Sat 1600-2000, Sun 0900-1330*, situated in the former mansion of the Uriburu family, the most distinguished of *Salteño* families, containing furniture, clothes and paintings.

A block west of the Cabildo, on one of the main pedestrian streets, are a couple of interesting museums housed in colonial mansions. The **Casa Leguizamón**, Caseros and Florida, has interesting architecture and the **Casa Arias Rengel**, next door, now houses the **Museo de Bellas Artes** ① *Belgrano 992, T0387-422 1745, Mon-Fri 0900-1900, Sat 1100-1900, free*, which has the city's finest collection of paintings, including superb Cuzqueño school works and small exhibitions of Salteño painters and sculptors.

Across the street is the **Museo de la Ciudad 'Casa de Hernández'** ① *Florida 97 and Alvarado, T0387-437 3352, www.museociudadsalta.gov.ar, Mon-Fri 0900-1300, 1600-1800, Sat 1700-1300, free*, in a fine 18th-century mansion with a collection of old furniture, musical instruments and dull portraits, but a marvellous painting of writer Güemes.

East of Plaza 9 de Julio
Walk east from the plaza, along Caseros, an appealing street of slightly crumbling buildings. After a block, you'll come to the **Iglesia San Francisco** (1796) ① *Caseros and Córdoba, daily 0800-1200, 1700-2100*, one of the city's landmarks, with its magnificent plum-coloured façade ornately decorated with white and golden stucco scrolls, and its elegant tower (1882) rising above the low city skyline. The interior is relatively plain, but there are some remarkable statues to admire, such as the rather too realistic San Sebastián. Two blocks further east is the **Convento de San Bernardo** ① *Caseros and Santa Fe*, built in colonial style in 1846, with an exquisitely carved wooden door dating from 1762. You can't enter the convent as it's still home to nuns, but they'll open up the little shop for you, with its collection of quaint handicrafts.

Continuing along Caseros for two blocks and turning right at Avenida Yrigoyen, you come to the wide open green space of **Parque San Martín**, where you'll find the **Museo de Ciencias Naturales** ① *Mendoza 2, T0387-431 8086, Tue-Sun 1530-1930*, with various stuffed animals. It's not a particularly elaborate park, but there's a boating lake, and from here you can take the *teleférico* (cable car) up to **Cerro San Bernardo** (1458 m) ① *daily 1000-1900, www.telefericosanbernardo.com, US$8.75 return, children US$4.50*, whose forested ridge looms over the east of the city centre. The top of the hill can be climbed in 45 minutes by a steep path (which starts beside the Museo Antropológico, see below). At the top there are lovely gardens and a great café with deck chairs and fabulous views. Recommended.

At the base of the hill is an impressive **statue** of General Güemes by Victor Gariño. His gaucho troops repelled seven powerful Spanish invasions from Bolivia between 1814 and 1821. The nearby **Museo Antropológico Juan M Leguizamón** ① *follow Paseo Güemes behind the statue and up Av Ejército del Norte, T0387-422 2960, www.antropologico.gov.ar, Mon-Fri 0830-1900, Sat 0900-1300, 1500-1900, closed Sun, US$1.50*, makes a good introduction to the pre-Hispanic cultures of the region. It has a superb collection of anthropomorphic ceramics and beautifully painted funerary urns. There's also an exhibition on high-altitude burial grounds, complete with mummies, objects found at the ancient ruins of Tastil (see page 299) and, most mysteriously, skulls flattened during the owner's life by wearing boards to squash the head (thought to confer higher intelligence). It's all very accessible and well laid out.

Around Salta city → *For listings, see pages 290-296.*

There are many lovely places close to Salta where *Salteños* go to relax: the smart leafy suburbs of **San Lorenzo**, 11 km to the west; jungly **Campo Quijano** on the way to Quebrada del Toro (see page 299), Chicoana en route to Cachi (see page 277) or the **Dique Cabra Corral** for fishing and water sports.

Dique Cabra Corral
Salta makes a big deal of its only big lagoon – one of the largest artificial lakes in Argentina, the Dique Cabra Corral. It's popular with locals for fishing *pejerrey*, the tasty local delicacy, and for enjoying a bit of beach life, with water-skiing, fishing, camping and restaurants also on offer. The best place to stay is the **Hotel del Dique**, on the banks of the lake; the **Finca Santa Anita** (see Where to stay below) is nearby and also gives you ready access to the water. The nearest town is the quaint gaucho town of **Coronel Moldes**, which, though not perhaps worth a special trip, has a quiet charm all of its own. There's a strong sense of community with wonderful local processions of gauchos on the celebration days of the Patron saints, **Fiesta Patronal** (1 August).

For hotel and restaurant price codes and other relevant information, see pages 20-26.

⊜ Where to stay

Salta city *p286, map p287*
All hotels and hostels listed are recommended. Book ahead in Jul holidays and around 10-16 Sep during celebrations of Cristo del Milagro.
$$$$ Legado Mítico, Mitre 647, T0387-422 8786, www.legadomitico.com. This small, welcoming hotel is absolutely lovely: luxurious rooms each with its own personality. The personalized pre-ordered breakfasts are a fantastic way to start the day.
$$$$ Solar de la Plaza, Juan M Leguizamon 669, T0387-431 5111, www.solardelaplaza.com.ar. Elegant old former Salteño family home, faultless service, sumptuous rooms, great restaurant and a pool.
$$$$-$$$ Ayres de Salta, Gral Güemes 650, T0387-422 1616, www.ayresdesalta.com.ar. Spacious, central 4-star hotel near Plaza Belgrano. Everything you would expect in this price range: spacious rooms, heated pool, great views from roof terrace.
$$$ Apart Ilusión (Sweet Dreams), José Luis Fuentes 743, Portezuelo Norte, T0387-432 1081, www.aparthotelilusion.com.ar. On the slopes of Cerro San Bernardo, well-equipped self-catering apartments for 2-4, decorated with local handicrafts, beautiful views. English-speaking owner, Sonia Alvarez, is welcoming. Breakfast and parking available, good value.
$$$ Bloomers Bed & Brunch, Vicente López 129, T0387-422 7449, www.bloomers-salta.com.ar. Closed mid-May to mid-Jun. In a refurbished colonial house, 5 spacious non-smoking rooms individually decorated, and one apartment. Use of kitchen and library. The brunch menu, different each day, is their speciality.
$$$ Carpe Diem, Urquiza 329, T0387-421 8736, www.bedandbreakfastsalta.com. Welcoming B&B, beautifully furnished, convenient, comfortable public areas, German/Italian-owned, no children under 14.
$$$ El Lagar, 20 de Febrero 877, T0387-431 9439, www.ellagarhotel.com.ar. An intimate boutique hotel owned by wine-making Etchart family. Beautifully furnished rooms full of fine paintings, excellent restaurant, gardens.
$$$ Salta, Buenos Aires 1, on main plaza, T0387-426 7500, www.hotelsalta.com. A Salta institution with neocolonial public rooms, refurbished bedrooms, marvellous suites overlooking plaza, *confitería* and honorary membership of the Polo and Golf Club.
$$ Del Antiguo Convento, Caseros 113, T0387-422 7267, www.hoteldelconvento.com.ar. Small, convenient, with old-fashioned rooms around a neat patio, very helpful, a good choice.
$$ Las Marías, Lerma 255, T0387-422 4193, www.saltaguia.com/lasmarias. Central hostel, **$** pp in shared rooms, close to Parque San Martín.
$$ Las Rejas, General Güemes 569, T0387-421 5971, www.lasrejashostel.com.ar. 2 houses converted into a small B&B and a hostel (US$15-17 pp), comfortable, central, helpful owners.
$$ Munay, San Martín 656, T0387-422 4936, www.munayhotel.com.ar. Good choice, smart rooms for 2-5 with good

bathrooms, warm welcome. Also have hotels of the same standard in Cafayate, Humahuaca, Jujuy and La Quiaca.

$$ Posada de las Nubes, Balcarce 639, T0387-432 1776, www.posadadelas nubes.com.ar. Charming, small, with simply decorated rooms around a central patio. Great location for Balcare nightlife; might be a little too loud at weekends.

$ Backpackers Home, Buenos Aires 930, T0387-423 5910; **Backpackers Suites**, Urquiza 1045, T0387-431 8944, www. backpackerssalta.com. HI-affiliated hostels, well run, with dorms and private rooms (**$$**, cheaper for HI members), with laundry and budget travel information. Crowded and popular.

$ Correcaminos Hostel, Vicente López 353, 4 blocks from plaza, T0387-422 0731. Modern dorms and 2 doubles, shared bath, laundry, pleasant garden, good, lively.

$ Hostal Quara, Santiago del Estero 125, T0387-422 0392, www.hostalquara. com.ar. Dorms US$13-14, also doubles with and without bath, with heating, TV room, drinks for sale. The helpful staff can organize tours.

Around Salta city *p289*

It's worth considering staying outside Salta if you're in search of more tranquillity: at San Lorenzo (11 km); at the Dique Cabra Corral; at Campo Quijano in the Quebrada del Toro (see page 299); or at one of the many *fincas* within an hour of the city. See www. turismosalta.gov.ar for more information.

$$$ El Castillo, Juan Carlos Dávalos 1985, San Lorenzo, T0387-492 1052, www.hotelelcastillo.com.ar. Stunning building in an amazing location with lots of places to hike to. High ceilings, antique furniture, a lovely pool and a nice garden to enjoy. There is a good

restaurant which is open to non-guests (see below).

$$$ Hotel del Dique, Dique Cabra Corral, R47, Km 12, T0387-490 5111, www.hoteldeldique.com. Extremely comfortable, great lakeside position, with a pool and good food.

Estancias/fincas

To experience the beautiful landscape of this region and to meet the people, stay at an *estancia*, or *finca* to use the local term. Most owners speak English, are extremely hospitable and are delighted to have guests from abroad. Stay for at least a couple of days to make the most of the facilities, which usually include horse riding, a pool and lovely places to walk. There are many *fincas* throughout the region, but the following are some of the most distinctive within easy access of the city. All are in the **$$$$-$$$** price range, mostly per person.

Finca El Bordo de las Lanzas, El Bordo, 45 km east of Salta, in department of General Güemes, T0387-684 1176, www.turismoelbordo.com.ar. Formal and luxurious, a taste of aristocratic life, with splendid accommodation, horse riding on the immense tobacco plantation, dining with the charming hosts. Highly recommended.

Finca El Manantial del Milagro, La Silleta, 25 km from Salta, T0387-490 8080, www.hotelmanantial.com. ar. Beautiful views from the superbly decorated rooms in this historical *estancia*, offering swimming, walking and riding on the estate. Gorgeous.

Finca Santa Anita, Coronel Moldes, 60 km from Salta, on the way to Cafayate, T0387-490 5050, www.santaanita.com.ar. The whole family makes you welcome on this prize-winning organic farm with superb goat's cheese, which has twice

won 'Slow Food' prizes: great organic food and all activities included in the price. A traditional, colonial-style *finca*, beautiful views, swimming, guided walks to prehistoric rock paintings and horse riding in wonderful landscapes.
Finca Valentina, Ruta 51, Km 6, La Merced Chica, T0387-15-415 3490, www.finca-valentina.com.ar. Italian-owned, excellent accommodation, only 5 rooms, activities include horse riding, cookery classes, massage, day visits arranged. Associated with recommended tour operator **Socompa**, below.
La Casa de los Jazmines, R51, Km 6 south towards La Silleta, T0387-497 2002, www.houseofjasmines.com. Not exactly an *estancia*, but a beautiful place to unwind: old *finca* building redesigned to the height of luxury and good taste, perfumed with roses and jasmine, with a pool and superb spa offering a great range of treatments. Recommended.
Selva Montana, C Alfonsina Storni 2315, San Lorenzo, T0387-492 1184, www.hostal-selvamontana.com.ar. Nestling high up in the lush leafy hills of San Lorenzo, just 15 mins by car from Salta. Complete comfort, and peace and quiet in stylish rooms, with a pool, horses, walking and birdwatching on offer. Take a taxi or bus **El Indio interurbano** from terminal.

🍴 Restaurants

Salta city *p286, map p287*
There are lots of great *peñas* for live music, serving good regional food at night along the north end of C Balcarce. Salta has delicious and distinctive cuisine: try the *locro*, *humitas* and *tamales*, served in the municipal market at San Martín y Florida.

$$$ El Solar del Convento, Caseros 444, half a block from plaza, T0387-421 5124. Elegant and not expensive, champagne when you arrive, delicious steaks. Recommended.
$$ El Charrúa, Caseros 221, T0387-432 1859, www.parrillaelcharrua.com.ar. A good, brightly lit family place with a reasonably priced and simple menu; the *parrilla* is particularly recommended.
$$ Doña Salta, Córdoba 46 (opposite San Francisco convent library), T0387-432 1921. Excellent regional dishes and pleasant, rustic atmosphere, good value.
$$ Chirimoya, España 211, T0387-431 2857. Those looking to get away from the *carne* can opt for this café located a few blocks off the main plaza. It offers veggie twists on pastas, sandwiches and milanesas. There's even a 'raw ravioli'.
$$ La Casa de Güemes, España 730. Popular, local dishes and *parrilla*, traditionally cooked in the house where General Güemes lived.
$ El Corredor de las Empanadas, Caseros 117 and Zuviría 913. Delicious *empanadas* and tasty local dishes in airy surroundings.
$ La Criollita, Zuviría 306. Small and unpretentious, a traditional place for tasty *empanadas*.
$ Mama Paca, Gral Güemes 118. Recommended by locals, traditional restaurant for seafood from Chile and home-made pastas.

Cafés
There are lots of cafés on Plaza 9 de Julio; it's a great place to sit now that it's largely pedestrianized, although the 2 cafés outside MAAM, Havana and El Palacio, are very touristy.
Don Blas, Balcarce 401. A lovely old corner of Balcarce serving good coffee.

Fili, corner of Güemes and Sarmiento 299. The best ice cream in Salta, try the *dulce de leche* with almonds or cinnamon. Heaven.

MAAM, inside the museum, Plaza 9 de Julio. Lovely airy café for meals and drinks.

New Time, Plaza 9 de Julio, corner with Alberdi. Avoid the tourist cafés and go where the *Salteños* go. Great juice, salads and light meals.

Plaza Café, next to **Hotel Salta**. This elegant café is popular with *Salteños* late morning, when the centre is buzzing. A nice spot for breakfast.

Around Salta city *p289*

See www.sanlorenzosalta.org.ar for more information.

$$$ Castillo de San Lorenzo, Juan Carlos Dávalos 1985, San Lorenzo, T0387-492 1052, www.hotelelcastillo.com.ar. Fabulous interior in this castellated building, delicious meals, stylish setting. Recommended.

$$ Lo de Andrés, Juan Carlos Dávalos y Gorritti, San Lorenzo, T0387-492 1600. Fabulous restaurant. Great steaks and pasta.

☺ Entertainment

Salta city *p286, map p287*

No trip to the northwest is complete without sampling its stirring *folclore* music. You can eat *empanadas* while watching great musicians playing live in Salta's *peñas* or listening to spontaneous performers in the crowd. Most are concentrated at the north end of C Balcarce, where you will find many *peñas* within 3 blocks, including **Los Cardones** (No 885, T0387-432 0909, www.cardonessalta.com.ar), which has good food and a good nightly

show, and **La Vieja Estación** (No 877, T0387-421 7727, www.la-viejaestacion. com.ar), great atmosphere, good food. This area also has a number of popular rock and jazz bars, such as **Macondo** or **Café del Tiempo**, as well as intimate restaurants and nightclubs. The result is an entertaining and noisy mix, though there are quieter bars here too. This area is most alive Thu, Fri and Sat nights from 1900 (taxi US$1.50). **La Casa de Güemes**, España 730, close to Plaza 9 de Julio, is recommended for shows and frequented by *Salteños*. West of the centre (reached by taxi), **La Casona del Molino**, Luis Burela 1, T0387-434 2835, is the most authentic place for spontaneous *peña*, in a crumbling old colonial house, serving good food and drink.

☺ Festivals

Salta city and around *p286, map p287*

Feb/Mar Carnival. Salta celebrates with processions on the 4 weekends before Ash Wed at the *corsódromo*, located on Av Gato Mancha near the convention center (US$4). On **Mardi Gras** (Shrove Tue) there is a procession of decorated floats and dancers with intricate masks of feathers and mirrors. It is the custom to squirt water at passers-by and *bombas de agua* (small balloons to be filled with water) are on sale for dropping from balconies.

16-17 Jun Commemoration of the death of Martín Güemes. There's folk music in the afternoon and a gaucho parade in the morning around his statue.

6-15 Sep Cristo del Milagro. Salta's biggest event (see page 286). All accommodation is heavily booked ahead, so reserve at least a month in advance.

24 Sep Battles of Tucumán and Salta.

○ Shopping

Salta city *p286, map p287*

The best places for shopping are the parallel pedestrianized streets of Alberdi, off Plaza 9 de Julio, and Florida, a block to the west. There are pricey but high-quality local goods on C Buenos Aires near the plaza, and in the shopping centre next to MAAM on the plaza.

Mercado Artesanal, in the Casa El Alto Molino, San Martín 2555, on the western outskirts, T0387-434 2808, daily 0900-2100. If you're short of time, head straight for this lovely 18th-century mansion, selling beautiful handicrafts made by craftsmen in the surrounding areas. Perhaps a little more expensive than if you buy them from a tiny village, but superb quality and all under one roof. Look out for soft and warm llama wool socks, wonderful hand-woven ponchos, delicately carved wood and weavings. Opposite is a cheaper tourist market for similar items, but factory-made. To get there, take bus 2, 3, or 7 from Av San Martín in centre and get off where the bus crosses the railway line.

Mercado Municipal, San Martín and Florida. Closed 1300-1700 and Sun. Wonderful place for cheap food; great fruit and vegetables and some handicrafts.

○ What to do

Salta city and around *p286, map p287*

There are many tour operators, mostly on Buenos Aires, offering adventure trips and excursions; staff give out flyers on the street. Out of season, tours often run only if there is sufficient demand; check carefully that the tour will run on the day you want. All agencies charge similar prices for tours (though some

charge extra for credit card payments): city tour, US$20; Valles Calchaquíes, US$115 (2 days); Cachi, US$46; Puna and salt lakes, US$83. The tourist office gives reports on agencies and their service.

Clark Expediciones, Mariano Moreno 1950, T0387-497 1024, www.clarkexpediciones.com. Specialist birding tours, eco-safaris and treks. English spoken.

Movitrack, Caseros 468, T0387-431 6749, www.movitrack.com.ar. Entertaining safaris in a 4WD truck to San Antonio de los Cobres, Humahuaca, Cafayate. German and English spoken. Expensive. They also have an **OxyBus** for high-altitude journeys.

Norte Trekking, Gral Güemes 265, T0387-431 6616, www.nortetrekking. com. Mon-Fri 0900-1400, 1500-1900. Excellent tours in 4WDs and minivans all over Salta and Jujuy, including small group tours to Iruya, over Jama Pass to San Pedro de Atacama, hiking, horse riding and excursions to El Rey national park with a highly experienced guide, Federico Norte, who speaks English. Tailors tours to your interest and budget. Highly recommended.

Puna Expediciones, Agustín Usandivaras 230, T0387-416 9313, www.puna expeditions.com.ar. Qualified and experienced guide Luis H Aguilar organizes treks in remote areas of Salta and Jujuy and safaris further afield. Recommended.

Socompa, Balcarce 998, p 1, T0387-577 0444, www.socompa.com. Excellent company specializing in trips to salt flats and volcanoes in the *puna*, 3 days to the beautiful, remote hamlet of Tolar Grande; can be extended to 12 days to include Atacama and Puna of Catamarca; 4 days to Puna of Catamarca. English and Italian spoken, knowledgeable guides. Highly recommended.

☻ Transport

Salta city and around *p286, map p287*

Air

Aerolíneas Argentinas/Austral, Caseros 475, T0387-431 1331, flies to **Buenos Aires**, 2¼ hrs, also **Andes**, Caseros 459, T0387-437 3514, 3 times a week.

Bus

Local Buses to local destinations, such as **Coronel Moldes** and Cabra Corral can be caught next to the *teleférico* office on the corner of San Martín and Yrigoyen. There are hourly buses to Silleta and **Campo Quijano** (at the head of the Quebrada del Toro).

Long distance To **Buenos Aires**, several companies daily, US$75-90, 20-22 hrs. To **Córdoba**, several companies daily, 12 hrs, US$50-65. To **Santiago del Estero**, 6-7 hrs, US$30-45. To **Tucumán**, 4 hrs, several companies, US$19-25. To **Mendoza** via Tucumán, 2 companies daily, US$85-105, 18-20 hrs. To **La Rioja**, US$50, 10-11 hrs. To **Jujuy**, frequent service, US$6.50, 2-2½ hrs.

To **Cachi**, 0700, 1330, US$6.50, 4-4½ hrs, with **Ale Hnos**, T0387-421 1588/423 1811, www.alehnos.com.ar, US$8.25; also **Marcus Rueda**, T0387-421 4447, spectacular journey. **Ale** buses continue to **Molinos**, Mon, Wed, Fri, Sat, Sun, 6½ hrs from Salta, US$11.30. To **Cafayate**, US$13-14, with **El Indio**, T0387-422 9393, and **Aconquija**. To **Santa María**, daily, 5½ hrs, US$16.50. To **Rosario de la Frontera**, 2½-3 hrs, US$13. To **San Antonio de Los Cobres**, 5 hrs, **El Quebradeño**, daily, US$7, and **Ale**, US$5.65.

International To **Paraguay**: travel to **Resistencia**, daily, 12 hrs, US$57, with **La Veloz del Norte** or **Flecha Bus,** or to **Formosa**, US$64-73, 16 hrs, then change

to a direct bus to Asunción. To **Chile**: There are services to **Calama** and **San Pedro de Atacama**, via Jujuy and the Jama Pass, with **Andesmar**, T0387-431 0263, **Géminis**, T0387-431 7778, and **Pullman**, T0387-422 1366, 3 each a week, but check days as they change, US$60-70, 11 hrs. Géminis and Pullman offices are at booths 15 and 16 in the terminal. To **Bolivia**: To **La Quiaca**, on Bolivian border, **Balut, Andesmar, Flecha**, 7½ hrs, US$25. To **Aguas Blancas** US$21, 5 hrs, or **Pocitos** (both on the Bolivian border, see pages 324 and 325), US$26, 8 hrs, 2 companies daily.

Car hire

Avis, Caseros 420 and, T0387-421 2181 and at the airport, Ruta 51, T0387-424 2289, salta@avis.com.ar. Efficient and very helpful, recommended. **NOA**, Buenos Aires 1, T0387-431 7080, www.noarentacar.com, in **Hotel Salta**, helpful, also mountain bike, US$13 per day. Many others.

Train

The only train service is the **Tren a las Nubes**, which usually runs end Mar to early Dec on Sat, with extra trains in high season (Semana Santa and July) between Salta and La Polvorilla viaduct, departing 0705, arriving back in Salta 2348, weather permitting. The regular route is train to La Polvorilla and back to San Antonio de los Cobres, where passengers change to a bus arriving back in Salta by 2300. There are also several multi-day tours to the region which include the train (see website). The basic fare (train up, bus back) is US$182, 50% discount for minors and seniors. Contact T0387-422 3033, or Buenos Aires T011-5258 3000, www.trenalasnubes.com.ar. For more information, see box, page 298.

● Directory

Salta city *p286, map p287*

Banks Banks, open 0900-1400, all have ATMs (many on España, also *casas de cambio*). **Consulates** Bolivia, Mariano Boedo 34, T0387-421 1040, coliviansalta@ yahoo.com.ar, Mon-Fri 0900-1400. **Chile**, Santiago del Estero 965, T0387-431 1857, Mon-Fri 0830-1330. **Immigration office** Maipú 35, T0387-422 0438, daily 0730-1230. **Medical services** Hospital San Bernardo, Tobias 69, T0387-432 0300, www.hospitalsanbernardo.com.ar.

Northwest Salta and the Quebrada del Toro

The landscapes of northwestern Salta province are utterly spectacular. In one unforgettable journey up the Quebrada del Toro from Salta city to the town of San Antonio de los Cobres, you'll travel through an extraordinary spectrum from dense forest, through gorges of brightly coloured rock strewn with cactus, to the silent expanses of high-altitude desert in the *puna*. This is the route of Argentina's famous narrow-gauge railway, Tren a las Nubes (Train to the Clouds), but it's a long, frustrating and very touristy experience. Far better to take a minibus tour or hire a car and take time to pause and explore on the way. You might stay a night in the forested weekend resort of Campo Quijano, and don't miss the superb ruined city of Santa Rosa de Tastil, one of Argentina's archaeological gems. Set in stunning rocky landscapes there's fascinating evidence of ancient pre-Inca and Inca civilizations here, and a local guide will bring it all alive. At the top of the gorge, the quiet mining town of San Antonio de los Cobres is at its best for the Fiesta de la Pachamama in August; it's a good stopping point before setting off into the *puna*. To offset altitude sickness, stop off for coca tea with typical *puna* family Sandro Yampa at el Mojón, and then be dazzled by the shimmering white expanse of the Salinas Grandes salt flats. From here you could drop to Purmamarca in the Quebrada de Humahuaca down the thrilling Cuesta de Lipán road. Or head west, further into the *puna* to discover tranquil isolation at Tolar Grande.

Train to the Clouds

The famous narrow-gauge Tren a las Nubes is an extraordinary feat of engineering, and a good way to experience the dramatic landscape up to the *puna*.

Built to enable commerce over the Andes to Chile, the track, which runs 570 km from Salta to Socompa on the Chilean border, was the outstanding achievement of Richard Maury, an engineer from Pennsylvania. Work started in 1921 and took 20 years. The track starts in Salta at 1200 m above sea level, rising to 4200 m, up through the impossibly rocky terrain of the steep Quebrada del Toro gorge, with several switchbacks and 360° loops to allow diesel engines to gain height over a short distance with a gentler gradient. One thousand men worked with only the most basic tools through inhospitable conditions, detonating rock and carving away at steep mountainsides through howling winds and snow. Many died in the attempt. The destination of the tourist train (passengers no longer being allowed on the weekly cargo trains) is La Polvorilla viaduct, near San Antonio de los Cobres, a delicate bridge across a mighty gorge, spanning 224 m. At 63 m high, it feels like you're travelling on air: both scary and exhilarating.

The tourist train is a comfortable ride, though a long day out. Leaving Salta at 0705 (cold and dark in winter)

to the cheerful accompaniment of *folclore* singers on the platform, the train edges to the entrance of Quebrada de Toro, steep forested mountains tinged with pink as the sun rises, and a light breakfast is served. The landscape, dotted with farms and adobe houses, changes to arid red rock as you climb through the gorge, where giant cacti perch, past multicoloured sculptural mountains to the staggeringly beautiful *puna*. The seven hours of the ascent are kept lively by chats from bilingual guides (English spoken; French and Portuguese too on request). Altitude sickness hits many people, and oxygen is on hand. At La Polvorilla viaduct, you can get out briefly to admire the construction and to buy locally made llama wool goods from the people of San Antonio. Don't bother haggling: these shawls and hats are beautifully made and are these people's only source of income. At San Antonio, the Argentine flag is raised to commemorate those who worked on the railway, and the national anthem is sung in a rather surreal ceremony. The descent, however, is slightly tedious, despite the constant stream of entertainment from *folclore* singers and Andean bands. Consider returning by road instead to see the ruins at Santa Rosa de Tastil. For more information, see www.trenalasnubes.com.ar.

Arriving in northwest Salta

This part of Salta has traditionally been the sole preserve of the Tren a las Nubes, but in the last few years another tour operator, **Movitrack** ① *www.movitrack.com. ar*, has run very successful tours along the same route which actually allow you to see far more of the impressive engineering of the train track and absorb more of the landscape. Inevitably, other tour operators followed, and along Salta's Calle Buenos Aires, you'll find plenty of tours on offer, though Movitrack is the only company to have pressurized oxygen-pumped vehicles to counter the inevitable effects of altitude. Hiring a car will give you more time to explore the Quebrada del Toro and to visit Santa Rosa de Tastil, which few agencies include in any detail. Ask the tourist office for latest information on local guides at the site, since there is a new project to put trained locals in place. There is comfortable accommodation at San Antonio de los Cobres, but very little on the way. If cycling, note that much of the road is *ripio*, that there is no shade, and it's extremely cold at night. However you travel, the effects of altitude are not to be underestimated, since you'll be climbing to nearly 4000 m. You must take time for your body to adjust if you're going to exert yourself beyond a gentle stroll. Drink plenty of water, avoid alcohol and don't overeat. Take it easy and you should feel fine.

Quebrada del Toro and Tren a las Nubes → *For listings, see page 302.*

The route for the Train to the Clouds is the same as the road through the Quebrada del Toro. The only difference is that travelling by road gives you the chance to get out and walk around – and to examine the spectacular feat of engineering of the train track – which of course you can't see from the train itself.

You'll leave Salta's subtropical valleys via the jungle weekend retreat of **Campo Quijano**, at Km 30, which lies in a beautiful, thickly vegetated valley at the entrance to the gorge and is an attractive place for a stop. The road and track then climb along the floor of the Quebrada del Toro, fording the river repeatedly amidst densely growing Pampas grass and *ceibo*, Argentina's national flower, with its striking fringed red blossoms. At **Chorrillos**, you'll see one of several identical wooden 1920s train stations along the route, with outside ovens built to heat steel fixings during the building of the track. From here the train track zigzags as it climbs past tiny farmsteads lined with *álamo* trees, up into the dramatic **Quebrada Colorada** – so called because of its bright red, pink and green stratified rock – to Ingeniero Maury (2350 m, Km 65), where there is a police control point. From Km 96, now paved, the road climbs the **Quebrada de Tastil**, parting company from the railway which continues through the **Quebrada del Toro**. The road passes through the tiny hamlet of Santa Rosa de Tastil, where there are marvellous pre-Inca ruins, and the only accommodation before San Antonio de los Cobres.

Santa Rosa de Tastil → *Colour map 1, A2. Phone code 0387.*
This picturesque little hamlet (3080 m, Km 103) lies near the site of one of Argentina's most important pre-Hispanic settlements, which once contained well over 400 houses and over 2000 people. It is believed to have been inhabited from AD 1336 to 1439. There is a small worthwhile **museum** ① *at the side of the road, Mon 0900-1500, Tue-Sun 0900-1900, free,* which has some of the finds from this intriguing culture, among them a well-preserved mummy, delicate jewellery and a xylophone of sonorous rocks. The remains of this ancient city are extraordinarily beautiful:

Santa Rosa de Tastil

Spread out over 12 ha and looming 60 m over the Valle de Lerma in Salta's dry centre are the ruins of a complex pre-Inca civilization founded around AD 1336. The site is one of the most complete archaeological sites in the country, and the intricate houses (not built to any recognizable grid) sprawl haphazardly on the slope. As it hardly ever rains in this area, walls are still standing, pottery and arrow tips can still be found on the ground and erosion to the structures has been kept to a minimum (although some walls have been rebuilt). Abandoned around AD 1439 and rediscovered in 1903 by anthropologist Eric Boman, the site was once home to over 2000 people who traded with the neighbouring Andean towns and farmed at the foot of the mountains. They were excellent weavers, bred llamas and guanacos, and made stone and rustic pottery. No one is quite sure why the highly developed site was abandoned, but we can learn about their religion and beliefs from the rock paintings they left behind. If you are in the area, consider a trip to these remote and well-preserved ruins. They are a great example of the civilizations that lived peacefully up and down the Andes until the Incas arrived.

a vast expanse of regular walls and roads, stretching out on an exposed hillside with views along the entire gorge. The ruins themselves are well worth visiting, but be sure to ask for a local guide, since the site is extensive and you'll get more out of it with a little interpretation. Guides are unpaid so appreciate a tip.

San Antonio de los Cobres → *Colour map 1, B2. Phone code 0387. 3774 m, 168 km northwest of Salta.*

Beyond Tastil the road climbs through green hanging valleys where cattle roam, and then up over the **Abra Blanca Pass** (4050 m) where the landscape changes dramatically, suddenly becoming vast, open and eerily empty. At the top of the pass, the road drops and runs across the *puna*, offering views of Mount Chañi (5896 m) to the right, Acay (5716 m) to the left, and Quewar (6102 m) in the far distance.

San Antonio de los Cobres is a simple, remote mining town of low adobe houses situated in a shallow hollow. There's nothing much to do here but it's a good introduction to the reclusive life of the *puna*, and it does have its subtle charms. It's also one of the few places that retains authentic indigenous culture and where the **Pachamama festival** is celebrated in style every August. This is a wonderful tradition of the indigenous peoples of the entire Andean region, in which they give thanks to mother earth, *La Pachamama*, with offerings of drinks and food, in a fascinating ceremony that binds the whole community. Tourists are welcome at this great event, which is not to be missed. People are friendly and the handicrafts on offer are of high quality and incredibly cheap. However, altitude sickness can strike heavily here, so avoid eating too much or drinking alcohol until you've acclimatized.

From San Antonio you can continue west into Chile (see below) or head south along Ruta 40 to La Poma and Cachi over the mighty Paso Abra del Acay (4900 m),

Border crossings: Argentina–Chile

Paso de Sico

The border should be open 24 hours, but you should check in San Antonio de los Cobres before setting out, T0387-498 2001. Note that no fresh food may be taken into Chile (there is a search 20 km west of Paso de Sico).

Argentine immigration The offices are at the pass itself and in San Antonio de los Cobres at the other end of town from the *aduana* (customs house). There is a police checkpoint at Catúa, 26 km east of Paso de Sico and in Toconao.

Chilean customs and immigration San Pedro de Atacama.

Note This is a very high-altitude pass, with the road reaching up to 4080 m above sea level. From Salta the road is tarmac for the first 110 km of the Ruta Nacional 51, after that it is sealed road. On the Chilean side it continues via Mina Laco and Socaire to Toconao; it may be in bad condition between these two points). For more detailed information, see www.gendarmeria.gov. ar/pasos/fichsico.htm.

Paso de Socompa

The border is open 24 hours. From Paso de Socompa a poor road runs to Pan de Azúcar, with roads west to the Pan-American Highway, or north via the Salar de Atacama to San Pedro de Atacama. No fuel is available until San Pedro or Calama.

Note This is another very high-altitude pass, with the road reaching up to 4080 m above sea level. Snow in this area is common from May to August and can reach as high as 2 m. In winter temperatures can drop to -15°C. This route is rocky, with lots of bends and uneven roads, and as such it is not recommended.

see page 276. This road should only be attempted in a 4WD as it is very rough in places. Alternatively, you could head north to the fabulous salt flats at Salinas Grandes and on to Purmamarca in the Quebrada de Humahuaca – a spectacular journey, see below. Ask at the Municipalidad, Belgrano s/n, T0387-490 9045, about minibus tours to the salt flats and Purmamarca.

San Antonio to Chile

From San Antonio there are two possible crossings to Chile. The best, closest, and most used, is the **Paso de Sico** (see box, above), due west on Route Nacional 51. (About 14 km west of San Antonio de los Cobres, there is a road that runs below the famous **La Polvorilla** railway viaduct, giving you the chance to photograph it.) Alternatively, at Caucharí, take Route Provincial 27 southwest across the giant Salar de Arizaro to the Chilean border at the **Paso de Socompa**. The road runs through very beautiful scenery including salt flats and desert, but be warned that it is extremely isolated and only for the very intrepid. There are no services whatsoever, so make sure you stock up on drinking water and fuel before setting out from San Antonio.

San Antonio to Purmamarca

The Ruta 40 continues north from San Antonio and is recommended for a taste of the extraordinary landscapes of the northwest. The road runs dead flat across the scrubby yellow *puna* – its horizons edged with pinkish mauve or bronze mountains, with the occasional flock of llamas or cows grazing. It's either wonderfully meditative or unbearably monotonous, depending on your point of view, but the salt flats, **Salinas Grandes**, which you'll reach in two hours from San Antonio, are certainly worth seeing. The huge expanses of dazzling white salt, crazy paved with crusted lines, are silent and other-worldly. There are crossroads some 20 north of the salt flats, where you could head west to Susques (in Jujuy, see page 314), up to Abra Pampa or follow the spectacular road to Purmamarca in the Quebrada de Humahuaca (see page 307), down the broad slalom bends of **Cuesta de Lipán** with breathtaking views of the valley below.

⦿ Northwest Salta and the Quebrada del Toro listings

For hotel and restaurant price codes and other relevant information, see pages 20-26.

● Where to stay

Quebrada del Toro *p299*
$$$ Hostería Punta Callejas, in Campo Quijano, R51, 30 km west of Salta, T0387-490 4086, www.puntacallejas.com.ar. Very clean and comfortable, with a/c, pool, tennis, horse riding, excursions and meals. Breakfast included.

Camping

There's a municipal campsite at the entrance to Quebrada del Toro: lovely spot with good facilities, hot showers, bungalows.

Santa Rosa de Tastil *p299*
Basic accommodation in shared dorms is available in the village, ask at the museum.

San Antonio de los Cobres *p300*
Ask at the Municipalidad, Belgrano s/n, T0387-490 9045, about other lodgings ($).
$$$ Hostería de las Nubes, edge of San Antonio on Salta rd, T0387-490 9059, www.hoteldelasnubes.com. Smart, comfortable, modern and spacious. Recommended.
$$-$ Hospedaje Belgrano, Belgrano s/n, T0387-490 9025. Welcoming, basic, hot showers, evening meals.

⊖ Transport

San Antonio de los Cobres *p300*
Bus
To **Salta city,** via Santa Rosa de Tastil, **El Quebradeño**, daily, 5 hrs, US$7. Also **Ale**, daily, US$5.65.

Jujuy province → *Colour map 1, A3. Phone code 0388. Population 611,888.*

The beautiful province of Jujuy lives slightly under wealthier Salta's shadow, but it has some of the richest culture of the whole country thanks to its large population of indigenous people, who most Argentines refer to as 'los indios'. Absorb the lively street life in Jujuy city, take part in a Pachamama (Mother Earth) ceremony, or witness the vibrant festival in remotest Casabindo, and you'll feel the palpable energy of the authentic Andean culture that has survived over 300 years of colonial rule. So, although Jujuy is less developed in terms of tourist infrastructure, it's definitely worth making the effort to explore, and as tourism brings more income to the region, bus services and hotels are opening up fast in response.

Jujuy's great attraction is the Quebrada de Humahuaca, made a World Heritage Site by UNESCO in 2003 for its spectacular beauty. Easter and Carnival are celebrated here in exuberant style, combining Christian traditions with pre-existing Andean religious beliefs. Dotted along the Quebrada are pleasant towns where you can hang out for a few days' walking and exploring. Further north, there are beautifully situated, remote villages to discover along the Bolivian border.

East and west of the province are two contrasting landscapes: in Jujuy's expanse of *puna* in the west, you'll find the fascinating small villages of Susques and Casabindo, Jesuit gold mines and Laguna de los Pozuelos with its wealth of birdlife. To the east, explore the cloudforest in Calilegua National Park, accessible from Libertador General San Martín. For more information on travelling in and around Jujuy, see www.norteargentino.gov.ar (in English).

Often overlooked by tourists, the capital of Jujuy province (pronounced whoo-whooey) may be Salta's poorer sister but it has plenty of life and culture to make it a good starting point for the Quebrada de Humahuaca which stretches northwest from here. Properly referred to by locals by its full name, San Salvador de Jujuy, it sits at 1260 m in a bowl of lushly wooded mountains, 100 km north of Salta. Jujuy was founded in 1593, between two rivers, the Río Grande and Chico, or Xibi Xibi, but it has sprawled south supporting a growing population on dwindling industry. Wars and earthquakes have left the city with few colonial buildings, but there's

Jujuy

N

100 metres
100 yards

Where to stay 🛏
Club Hostel **12**
El Arribo **3**
Gregorio I **4**
Hostal Casa de Barro **5**

Munay Tierra de Colores **7**
Sumay **1**
Yok Wahi **11**

Restaurants 🍴
Chung King **1**
Krysys **4**
Madre Tierra **5**
Manos Jujeñas **2**

some fine architecture around its plaza and from the bridge over the Río Xibi Xibi, with its brightly coloured market stalls, you have wonderful views of the dramatic purple mountains, contrasting with the thick green vegetation that fills the river bed. Although more chaotic than Salta, Jujuy has some lively bars where you can hear the region's wonderful *folclore* music, and its history is worth exploring, with two fine churches, a packed archaeological museum and a fabulous market. All this makes a good introduction to the province's rich indigenous culture and a handy base for exploring a variety of landscapes within easy reach. The region's most accessible cloudforest park, Calilegua, is just 125 km east of here.

Ruta 9 **3**
Sociedad Española **6**
Tío Bigote **11**

Arriving in Jujuy city → *Colour map 1, A3.*
Phone code 0388. Population 238,000.

Getting there Jujuy's airport, El Cadillal ① *T0388-491 1505*, is 32 km southeast of the capital. Minibuses run between the airport and the Aerolíneas Argentinas office in town (US3.75, 25 minutes); a taxi costs US$10. The **bus terminal** ① *information T0388-422 1373*, is six blocks south of the main street, Belgrano, over the river at Dorrego e Iguazú. The terminal serves the whole province, including all destinations north of the city and border towns with Bolivia, as well as south to Salta (two hours) and from there to most major destinations. There are direct overnight buses to Buenos Aires taking at least 21 hours. ▶▶ *For further details, see Transport, page 321.*

Getting around The city is pleasant to walk around and is particularly interesting around the plaza, the market opposite the bus terminal, and on the bridges. The most interesting sights are within six blocks and could comfortably be visited in a day.

Tourist information The city tourist office ① *on the plaza at Gorriti 295 and Belgrano, T0388-422 1325, www.turismo. jujuy.gov.ar (also in English), Mon-Fri 0700-2200, Sat-Sun 0900-2100*, has a helpful accommodation leaflet and a map, but little information about the rest of the province or transport. There is another smaller and more limited office at the **bus terminal** ① *T0388-422 1343, daily 0700-2100*, offering helpful advice on accommodation, though few staff speak English. A provincial government's website, with lots of information, is www.jujuy.gov.ar (in Spanish).

Background

Jujuy has an extraordinary history. The Spanish wanted to found a city to link the chain of settlements connecting Alto Perú with Córdoba but met extreme resistance from the indigenous people, who destroyed their first two attempts in 1561 and 1575. The city was finally established in 1593 and prospered until the 18th century, but the province of Jujuy bore the brunt of fighting during the Wars of Independence when the Spanish launched 11 invasions down the Quebrada de Humahuaca from Bolivia between 1810 and 1822. Then, in August 1812, General Belgrano, who was commander of the Republican troops, demanded an incredible sacrifice from Jujuy's people when he ordered the city to be evacuated and destroyed before the advancing Royalist army. The people obeyed his orders and left the city, which was razed to the ground. The citizens of Jujuy remain proud of this event, which is marked on 22-23 August by festivities known as **El Exodo Jujeño**, with gaucho processions and military parades. As a tribute to the city for obeying his orders, Belgrano donated the flag which is displayed in the lavish Casa de Gobierno in Plaza Belgrano.

Jujuy has experienced growing poverty in recent years; its traditional industries – sugar and tobacco – suffered in the economic crisis, resulting in widespread unemployment. It's one of the few Argentine cities where the population is largely indigenous, boosted in the last 20 years by considerable immigration from Bolivia. You may well find bus journeys in the region delayed en route by peaceful demonstrations of *piqueteros* blocking the road, protesting about job and benefit cuts. Tourism is the main growth industry in the area as the city is slowly waking up to its huge natural asset: the extraordinary beauty on its doorstep.

Places in Jujuy city

If you arrive in the city by bus, you will be greeted by a perfectly typical example of the usual mayhem of *boleterías* (ticket offices) for 20 different bus companies, crowds waiting with huge packages to be carried to remote parts of the *puna* and people selling balloon-like plastic bags of pink popped corn. To get into town from the bus station, walk along Dorrego/Lavalle, crossing the bridge across the thickly vegetated river bed where the city teems cheerfully with life, and you'll pass the fabulous fruit and vegetable market with delicious *empanadas* and stalls selling razors and peaches, tights and herbal cures, pan pipes and plimsols.

In the eastern part of the city is the tranquil **Plaza Belgrano**, a wide square planted with tall palms and lined with orange trees, with a striking equestrian statue of Belgrano at its centre. On the south side stands the **Casa de Gobierno** ① *daily 0800-2100*, a cream French-style neoclassical building built in 1927. Inside, you can see the very flag that Belgrano gave the city in recognition of their great sacrifice in a sumptuously decorated long hall with pleasing art nouveau statues representing Justice, Liberty, Peace and Progress, by the Argentine sculptor, Lola Mora.

On the west side of the plaza is the **cathedral**, whose neoclassical façade was built in the late 19th century to replace the early 17th-century original, which was destroyed by an earthquake. It contains an exquisite gold-plated wooden pulpit, carved by indigenous tribes in the Jesuit missions. Its elegant biblical illustrations are very moving and the delicate modelling of the dove overhead and of the angels' faces is stunning. It's one of Argentina's finest colonial treasures. There are also several fine 18th-century paintings. On the north side of the plaza is the **Cabildo**, built in 1867 and now occupied by the police, with a rather dull police museum inside.

The **Iglesia de San Francisco** ① *Belgrano and Lavalle, 2 blocks west of the plaza, daily 0730-1200, 1700-2100,* is modern but has a calm interior and contains another fine gilded colonial pulpit, with ceramic angels around it, like that at Yavi (see page 311). There are well informed guides on hand. The **Iglesia de San Bárbara** (1777), San Martín and Lamadrid, is similar in style to the colonial churches in the Quebrada de Humahuaca.

The **Museo Arqueológico Provincial** ① *Lavalle 434, T0388-422315, Mon-Fri 0800-2000, US$1,* has some superb ceramics from the pre-Inca Yavi and Humahuaca cultures, and beautifully painted funerary urns, some containing the tiny bones of children. The museum may be underfunded and poorly displayed, but it's definitely worth visiting – particularly for a fabulous 2500-year-old sculpture of a goddess giving birth and the rather gruesomely displayed mummified infant.

If you like military portraits, you could visit the **Museo Histórico Provincial Juan Galo Lavalle** ① *Lavalle 256, T0388-4221355, Mon-Fri 0800-2000, Sat-Sun 0900-1300, 1600-2000, US$0.50,* though it's pretty dry. A whole room is dedicated to the death of General Lavalle which occurred in this house, a turning point in the civil war between Federalists and Unitarists. There are also a couple of fine Cuzco-school paintings dating from 1650.

Around Jujuy city

Termas de Reyes ① *T0388-492 2522, www.termasdereyes.com, 1 hr by bus Etap (línea 1C) from bus terminal or corner of Gorriti and Urquiza, US$0.75,* is a thermal resort set among magnificent mountains. It has baths and a pool (US$3.25) plus cabins with thermal water. Day use costs US$63, plus various treatments; there are also packages from one to seven nights. See also Where to stay, page 316.

Quebrada de Humahuaca → *For listings, see pages 315-322.*

Since it was declared a World Heritage Site by UNESCO in 2003, the Quebrada de Humahuaca has attracted a deluge of visitors. However, while a couple of its main towns are being transformed beyond recognition by tourism, much of the area retains its ancient authentic indigenous culture.

The main route north from Jujuy city to the Bolivian border is one of the most dramatic areas of natural beauty in the country, passing through a long gorge of intensely coloured rock strata and arid mountains speckled with giant cacti. In the fertile valley floor of the Quebrada are several small historic towns, some with their neat adobe houses now mingled with modern new developments, but all centred around the characteristic squat, white 18th-century churches of the region. Tilcara is probably the best base for exploring the area, with lots of good accommodation, a lively market, a museum and the Pucará, a ruined pre-Incan fortress. Further north, Humahuaca is popular and friendly, and provides access to remote border region in the far north of the province. For more tourist information, see www.turismo.jujuy.gov.ar and www.norteargentino.gov.ar (both in English).

Arriving in the Quebrada de Humahuaca

Getting around Starting at the city of Jujuy, Route 9 heads north through the Quebrada to the Bolivian border. Public transport is easy to use. A number of bus companies go up and down the Quebrada from Jujuy to Humahuaca, stopping at Purmamarca, Tilcara, Maimará and Uquía. **El Quiaqueño**, **Panamericano** and **Balut** go all the way to La Quiaca on the Bolivian border. If driving, fuel is available at Jujuy, Tilcara, Humahuaca, Abra Pampa and La Quiaca, so you might need to take a spare can if you're heading far into rural areas. It's a good area for cycling, preferably away from the Ruta Nacional 9 where there can be a lot of traffic through the valley and there's not much shade. ▶ *For further details, see Transport, page 321.*

Purmamarca → *Colour map 1, A3. Phone code 0388. Population 2100. Altitude 2200 m.*

The first village you come to in the Quebrada, just off Ruta Nacional 9 at Km 61, is Purmamarca, a perfect place to rest and acclimatize to the altitude. It's a tiny, peaceful, slightly expensive village with a choice of comfortable places to stay (no hostels) and a stunning setting at the foot of the Cerro de los Siete Colores – a mountain striped with at least seven colours, from creamy pink to burgundy and copper to green. Once the steady trickle of tour buses has left, Purmamarca resumes its own quiet rhythm of life. There's a good market on the plaza, selling a mixture of locally made llama wool goods, but lots of alpaca spoons and weavings are imported from Bolivia. At the top of the plaza, there's a beautiful church, **Iglesia de Santa Rosa** (1648, rebuilt in 1778), typical of those you'll see elsewhere in the Quebrada, with its squat tower, whitewashed adobe walls and simple, well-balanced construction. Inside there's a splendid time-darkened cactus roof and pulpit, and a series of exquisite paintings depicting the life of Santa Rosa. Next to the church is an algarrobo tree thought to be 500 years old. There's a tiny, helpful tourist office on the plaza, open 0700-1800, which can provide maps, information on accommodation and bus tickets.

Maimará → *Phone code 0388. Population 2200. Altitude 2383 m.*

About 12 km from Purmamarca at Km 75, Maimará is a lovely, tranquil oasis village. Its green fields of onion and garlic are set in contrast with the backdrop of richly coloured marbled rock, known as La Paleta Del Pintor, to the east of the village. For an enjoyable walk in the low evening light, when the colours of the rock are at their warmest, walk along the old road to the east of Maimará; take your camera. Just off the road, 3 km south, is **La Posta de Hornillos** ① *open, in theory, Wed-Mon*

0830-1800, free, one of the chain of colonial posting houses that used to extend from Buenos Aires to Lima. It was the scene of several battles and is where Belgrano stayed. Now restored, the building houses a historical **museum** with a collection of 18th- and 19th-century furniture, as well as weapons and historical documents. North of Maimará there's a huge cemetery on the hillside, brightly decorated with paper flowers at Easter.

Tilcara → *Colour map 1, A3. Phone code 0388. Population 5600. Altitude 2461 m.*

Tilcara lies 22 km north of Purmamarca at Km 84. It's the liveliest Quebrada village and the best base for exploring the area, with plenty of places to stay and to eat. There's an excellent handicrafts market around its pleasant plaza, though be discerning as lots of the goods are mass produced in Bolivia. For fine local weavings, visit the women's weaving co-operative, **La Flor del Cardón**, next to the **tourist office** ① *Belgrano 590, T0388-495 5720, www.tilcara.com.ar, daily 0800-2100*, which has very helpful staff. Useful websites include www.tilcarajujuy.com.ar (in Spanish).

Tilcara was the site of an important pre-Hispanic settlement, and you can visit the **Pucará** ① *daily 0900-1800, US$1 including entry to the museum (below)*, a restored hilltop fortress above the town. There are panoramic views of the gorge from its complex web of low-walled dwellings, made more splendid by mighty cacti. To get there, turn right off Belgrano where signposted; head up the hill and across the metal bridge over the Río Huasamayo. At the entrance to the Pucará, there's also a small handicrafts shop where you can get helpful information, and a small botanical garden with many species of cactus. On the plaza is a superb **Museo Arqueológico** ① *Belgrano 445, daily 0900-1230, 1400-1800, US$1 including entry to Pucará and the Jardín Botánico*, with a fine collection of pre-Columbian ceramics, masks and mummies. There are four art museums in town, of which **Museo Regional de Pintura** ① *Rivadavia 459, closed Mon, US$0.50*, is worth a look, with paintings on the customs and traditions of Tilcara.

There are fiestas in Tilcara throughout the extended Carnival period, but the Easter celebrations are justifiably famous: on Holy Thursday night a gathering of thousands of pan pipe musicians follow the procession of the Virgin de Copacabana down the mountain into the town. It's an extraordinary, noisy and moving event. Book accommodation well in advance.

Huacalera and Uquía

Huacalera lies 2 km north of the Tropic of Capricorn; a sundial 20 m west of the road marks the exact location. The church, several times restored, has a roof made of cactus wood and a small museum. **Uquía** is one of the smaller villages along the Quebrada and is totally un-touristy with a tranquil atmosphere and a narrow main street of adobe houses. However, it also has one of the valley's finest churches, whose beautifully proportioned white tower is very striking against the deep red rock of the mountain behind. Built in 1691, **Iglesia San Francisco de Paula** contains an extraordinary collection of Cuzqueño-style paintings of angels in 17th-century battle dress, the *ángeles arcabuceros*. Painted by local indigenous artists under the tuition of Jesuits, the combination of tenderness and swagger in these winged figures, brandishing their weapons, is astonishing.

Humahuaca and around → *Colour map 1, A3. Phone code 03887. Population 11,300.*
Although Humahuaca (2940 m) was founded in 1591 on the site of a pre-Hispanic settlement, it was almost entirely rebuilt in the mid-19th century. It is a labyrinth of narrow streets, with low adobe houses around a small central plaza. Despite being the most popular tourist destination for Argentines along the Quebrada, it retains its own culture. Accommodation here is more limited than at Tilcara, but once the coach trips have left, it's quiet and is a useful stopping point for travelling north up to the *puna*, or to Iruya. The bus terminal has toilets and a *confitería*, and there are fruit and sandwich sellers outside.

La Candelaria festival is celebrated on 2 February, and the beginning of carnival here is famously lively with **Jueves de Comadres**, and **Festival de las Coplas y de la Chicha**, when everyone throws flour and water at each other and gets very drunk. Book accommodation ahead.

On the tiny plaza is the church, **La Candelaria**, originally constructed in 1631, rebuilt 1873-1880, containing wonderfully gaudy gold *retablos* and 12 fine Cuzqueño-school paintings. Every day at 1200, tourists gather outside **El Cabildo**, the neocolonial town hall on the plaza, to watch a large mechanical figure of San Francisco Solano emerge to bless the town from his alcove high in the wall. You may find this kitsch rather than spiritually uplifting, but it's quite a sight. Overlooking the town and surrounded by fantastically large cacti is the **Monumento a la Independencia Argentina**, commemorating the scene of the heaviest fighting in the country during the Wars of Independence. There is a good *feria artesanal* on Avenida San Martín (on the far side of the railway line) and a fruit market at Tucumán and Belgrano. The small but helpful **tourist office** ① *Tucumán and Jujuy*, can be found on the plaza in the lovely white Cabildo building. Ask for a map of the area; as they are underfunded and have no resources they will ask you to make a small donation, but it is worth it as the map can be very helpful.

About 10 km northeast of Humahuaca, near **Coctaca**, there's an impressive and extensive (40 ha) series of pre-colonial agricultural terraces – the largest archaeological site in Jujuy, though you'll have to go with a guide to find them. Contact **Ser Andino** ① *Jujuy 21, Humahuaca, T03887-421659, www.serandino.com.ar*, who offers two- to three-hour tours to Coctaca from Humahuaca, US$18.75 per person. Ask the tourist office about trips over the mountains to enter **Parque Nacional Calilegua** (see page 323), via the beautifully situated little hamlet of Abra Zenta.

Iruya → *Colour map 1, A3. Population 5500.*
Highly recommended is a night or two at least in the peaceful hamlet of **Iruya**, reached by a breathtaking (or hair-raising) three-hour bus ride. Twenty-five kilometres north of Humahuaca, a rough *ripio* road turns northeast off the Ruta Nacional 9, 8 km to Iturbe (also called Hipólito Irigoyen). The bus stops here for five minutes, giving you a chance to glimpse captivating rural life and perhaps buy a woven hat from women waiting by the bus stop. There are no facilities. The

road then crosses the broad river (manageable in an ordinary car only if it hasn't rained heavily) and climbs up over the 4000-m pass, Abra del Cóndor, where you have panoramic views, before dropping steeply, around an amazing slalom of many hairpin bends, into the Quebrada de Iruya.

Iruya is an idyllic small town tucked into a steep hillside, remote and hidden away, but full of warm and friendly inhabitants. In recent years, its character has started to change due to the influx of wealthier tourists staying at the *hostería* at the top of the town.

The town still retains its festivals, with a colourful **Rosario** festival on the first Sunday in October, and lively Easter festivities, when accommodation is booked up in advance. It's worth spending a few days here to lap up the tranquil atmosphere, and to go horse riding or walking in the beautiful valleys nearby. The hike to the even more remote hamlet of **San Isidro** (seven hours return) is unforgettable. At **Titiconte**, 4 km away, there are some unrestored pre-Inca ruins, though you'll need to take a guide to find them. Iruya has a tourist office on Calle San Martín but the hours are irregular; there is also a *locutorio* and food shops. Wander up the tiny narrow main street to find a post office, a shop selling wonderful herbal teas of all kinds and dried peaches from a local co-operative, and another selling superb woven and knitted goods. Not to be missed. For more information see www.iruyaonline.com (in Spanish).

La Quiaca and into Bolivia → *Colour map 1, A2. Phone code 03885. Population 14,000.*

La Quiaca (3442 m) lies on the border with Bolivia, linked by a concrete bridge to **Villazón** on the Bolivian side. Neither town is appealing, but if you have to stay the night, La Quiaca is definitely preferable: there are a few decent places to stay, and if you're around here on the third weekend in October, you can see the three-day **Fiesta de la Olla** when villagers from the far reaches of the remote *puna* arrive on donkeys and in pickups to sell their ceramic pots, sheepskins and vegetables during a colourful festival that involves a lot of dancing and drinking *chicha*. The bus terminal at España y Belgrano has luggage storage. If your bus arrives in the early morning when no restaurants are open and it is freezing cold outside, wrap up warm and stay in the terminal until daylight as the streets are unsafe in the dark.
➤➤ *For more information on the border crossing, see box, page 312.*

Yavi and around

ⓘ *Yavi is 16 km from La Quiaca but no buses go there. A remise taxi from La Quiaca costs US$17 return, including ½-hr stay.*

By far the best place to stay around here is actually in Yavi, 16 km east, which has a couple of good *hosterías*. Yavi is an intriguing *puna* village, consisting of little more than a few streets of uniformly brown adobe dwellings, most often deserted, but it has a beguiling, hidden quality. It was founded in 1667 and was the crossing point to Bolivia until rail and road connections were built through La Quiaca. The surrounding landscape is wide open, with the distinctive swooping stratified hills of the Siete Hermanos to the east. These have long been an important landmark and their stark beauty immediately catches your attention, even before you stumble

Border crossings: Argentina–Bolivia

La Quiaca

The border bridge is 10 blocks from La Quiaca bus terminal (15 minutes' walk, taxi US$2).

Argentine customs and immigration The office is open 0700-2400. If leaving Argentina for a short stroll into Villazón (not really advised), show your passport, but do not let it be stamped by Migración, otherwise you will have to wait 24 hours before being allowed back into Argentina. Formalities on entering Argentina are usually very brief at the border but thorough customs searches are made 100 km south at Tres Cruces. Leaving Argentina is very straightforward, but travellers who need a visa to enter Bolivia (check with your embassy) are advised to get it before arriving in La Quiaca. The Bolivian consulate in La Quiaca is at 9 de Julio 100 y República Arabe Siria, T03885-422283, colivianlaquiaca@yahoo.com.ar, Monday-Friday 0700-1830 (in theory).

Transport There are at least nine buses a day from Jujuy to La Quiaca (stopping at most bigger villages in the Quebrada de Humahuaca), five to six hours, US$11, three hours from Tilcara. The bus terminal in La Quiaca at España and Belgrano and there is luggage storage available.

Villazón

This is a grim place, little more than the centre of commercial activity in an otherwise remote and uninhabited area. The road from the border bridge, Avenida República de Argentina, is lined with shops and stalls selling sandals, toys, sunglasses, paper flowers, sacks of pink puffed corn and armfuls of coca leaves. Women in traditional Bolivian dress, with their enormous skirts (*cholitas*), spin wool and weave vividly coloured textiles on the pavement, and there's plenty of fresh orange juice and cheap ice cream for sale. However, there's nowhere decent to stay and no tourist information. The bus station has toilets, but they aren't pretty.

Note Argentina time is one hour ahead of Bolivia, two hours when Buenos Aires adopts daylight saving. Remember not to photograph the border area. For more detailed information, see www.gengarmeria.gov.ar/pasos/fichquiaca.htm (in Spanish).

across the prehistoric petroglyphs on the rocks at the foot of the hills. Ask at **Hostal de Yavi** for a tour, see page 318.

Yavi also has perhaps the finest church in the northwest, well worth the detour from La Quiaca. The **Iglesia de Nuestra Señora del Rosario y San Francisco** ① *Mon 1500-1800, Tue-Fri 0900-1200, 1500-1800, Sat-Sun 0900-1200*, was built in 1676-1690, a sturdy, white construction with buttresses and a single tower. Inside are the most magnificent gold *retablo* and pulpit, made by artisans who were brought, like the gold, from Peru. The *retablo* is adorned with a gold sculpture of an angel in 18th-century battle dress (like a three dimensional version of the paintings of Uquía) and the tabernacle is lined with mirrors to make candlelight within glow like the sun. Above the exquisite pulpit, decorated with ceramic cherubs, flies a golden dove. All this splendour is seen in the yellowy light from windows made of transparent onyx, giving the beautiful Cuzqueño paintings even more power. It's an impressive and moving sight.

Opposite the church is the 18th-century **Casa del Marqués Campero y Tojo** ① *Mon-Fri 0900-1200, 1400-1700, Sat-Sun 0900-1800*, the austere former mansion of the family that was were granted large parts of the *puna* by Philip V of Spain. It's an imposing building with empty courtyards, whose one-room museum houses a strange and eclectic collection of 18th-century bedsprings, arrowheads and candelabras. There's a small but excellent selection of handicrafts for sale inside, and some nicely carved local slate with petroglyphs on a stall outside. There is a colourful evening procession during Easter week.

For a really marvellous experience of the wild beauty and isolation of this region, make time to visit the remote town of **Nazareno**, a four-hour drive east of La Quiaca. The road crosses astonishingly bold rolling hills, before climbing and then dropping thousands of metres to find Nazareno nestled in a crown of vermillion mountains. There are some wonderful walks along old Inca roads to Cuesta Azul and to Milagro. Accommodation is with local families; the hospitality is warm and the landscapes are unforgettable. If you speak Spanish and can chat to the people living here, you'll be able to get a real taste of fascinating Andean culture.

Puna Jujeña → *For listings, see pages 315-322.*

The Puna Jujeña (3700 m, Km 213) covers all the area to the west of the Quebrada de Humahuaca. It's a specially remote and bleak place with few settlements, but extraordinary salt flats, lakes full of birdlife and plenty of history to be explored. If you have time it's definitely worth spending a few days in the area. The *puna* is high altitude (between 3000 and 4000 m) and it's an inhospitable area to travel alone, so although you could hire a 4WD vehicle and be independent, consider trips with adventure travel company **Socompa** ① *www.socompa.com*, which enable you to explore the *puna* in the company of expert guides without having to worry about the many practicalities.

There are two main areas to explore. **Salinas Grandes** and **Susques** can be reached either from San Antonio de los Cobres in Salta, or from Purmamarca in the Quebrada de Humahuaca. The second area, in the far north, is the **Monumento Natural Laguna de los Pozuelos**, reached by turning west from Abra Pampa. You could do one round trip (now offered by **Movitrack** and other tour companies), setting off from Salta, climbing the Quebrada del Toro to San Antonio de los Cobres, and reaching the Salinas Grandes (Ruta 40), before descending via the spectacular **Cuesta de Lipán** (Route 52) to Purmamarca in the Quebrada de Humahuaca.
➤ *For further information, see Salta, What to do, page 294.*

Susques and Salinas Grandes → *Colour map 1, A2. Phone code 03887.*
The main crossing to Chile is via Route 52 which links Purmamarca and the Salinas with the little village of **Susques**, and on to the **Paso de Jama** (see box, opposite) over the awesome Abra Potrerillos pass (4170 m). Susques is the only settlement between Purmamarca and the border, lying in a hollow at the meeting of the Río Susques and Río Pastos Chicos. It has a stunning little church, dating from 1598 – one of the outstanding examples of colonial architecture in the region, with a roof of cactus-wood and thatch. Inside is an old bellows-organ. There are regular buses from Jujuy, with Andes Bus and Purmamarca (four to six hours), but it's best to hire a car or join a tour. There are a few basic places to stay and eat in Susques, see listings page 318.

The salt flats of Salinas Grandes are astonishing – a seemingly endless, perfectly flat expanse of white, patterned with eruptions of salt around regular shapes, like some kind of crazy paving. Against the perfectly blue sky, the light is dazzling. It's safe to walk or drive onto the surface, and you'll find men mining salt, creating neat oblong pools of turquoise water where salt has been cut away, and stacking up piles of white and brown salt blocks, ready for refining.

Casabindo → *Colour map 1, A3.*
Heading north from Susques on Route 11, you'll reach the tiny hamlet of Casabindo (3500 m), founded in 1602. It can also be approached by travelling 63 km southwest from Abra Pampa – quite a trip over the *puna*. There's a magnificent church, one of the finest in the whole region, with twin towers dating from 1772. It's beautifully proportioned and contains a superb series of 16th-century paintings of *ángeles arcabuceros* (archangels in military uniforms) like those at Uquía. It's worth trying to visit on 15 August, when there's a lively celebration of **La Ascensión de la Virgen**, accompanied by the last remaining *corrida de toros* (running with bulls) in Argentina. El Toreo de la Vincha takes place in front of the church, where a bull defies onlookers to take the ribbon and medal it carries: a symbolic offering to the virgin rather than a gory spectacle. Most visitors come on a day trip from Tilcara and return there to sleep at night. If you wish to stay in the village, ask at the village school where you may be able to stay.

Monumento Natural Laguna de los Pozuelos → *Colour map 1, A3. Phone 03887.*
ⓘ *Park office: Rivadavia 339, Abra Pampa, T03887-491349, www.parquesnacionales.gov.ar.*
Monumento Natural Laguna de los Pozuelos (3650 m) is a nature reserve 50 km northwest of Abra Pampa and centred around the lake. Laguna de los Pozuelos hosts 44 species of bird and is visited by huge colonies of up to 25,000 flamingos. It's a stunning landscape, well worth exploring if you have a few days. Be warned, however, that this is high-altitude *puna*, and temperatures can drop to -25°C at night in winter; don't attempt camping unless you have high-mountain gear and all the food, warm clothing and drinking water you're likely to need, plus spare supplies. There is a ranger station at the southern end of the Laguna with a campsite nearby. At **Lagunillas**, further west, there is a smaller lagoon, which also has flamingos. There are no visitor services and no public transport. Unless you have your own car, the only real option is to go with a guide. Try **Socompa** (see page 294).

Border crossing: Argentina–Chile

Paso de Jama
The border (4200 m) is open 0700-2000 and is 360 km west of Jujuy, reached by a 60-km road that branches off Route 70. This is the route taken by most passenger and truck traffic from Salta or Jujuy to San Pedro de Atacama. There is a car park, toilets and phone services but no money exchange. **Note** Even in summer it can drop to -5°C at night. For more detailed information, see www.gendarmeria.gov.ar/pasos/fichjam.htm.

Argentine customs and immigration At Susques. On the Chilean side the road continues (unpaved) to San Pedro de Atacama (Km 514), where fuel and accommodation are available, and Calama.

Chilean immigration At San Pedro de Atacama.

If you're keen to explore the wild *puna* further, you could head for the tiny village of **Santa Catalina**, 67 km west of La Quiaca, along *ripio* Route 5. There's a *centro artesanal*, La Negra, and a 19th-century church with a dazzling gold and red interior, and a small museum of artefacts from local history housed in the oldest building in the village.

◉ Jujuy province listings

For hotel and restaurant price codes and other relevant information, see pages 20-26.

◉ Where to stay

Jujuy city *p304, map p304*
All hotels will be fully booked for the festival of **El Exodo Jujeño**, 22-23 Aug: book ahead. For a complete listing with prices, see www.turismo.jujuy.gov.ar and www.welcomeargentina.com. See also www.munayhotel.com.ar.

\$\$\$ El Arribo, Belgrano 1263, T0388-422 2539, www.elarribo.com. Attractive, well located *posada* set in a restored colonial house with swimming pool, smiling staff. Highly recommended.

\$\$\$ Gregorio I, Independencia 829, T0388-424 4747, www.gregoriohotel.com. Wonderful, small boutique hotel with 20 rooms. Smart, modern style, with local art scattered throughout. Recommended.

\$\$ Sumay, Otero 232, T0388-423 5065, www.sumayhotel.com.ar. Rather dark, but clean, very central, helpful staff.

\$ pp Club Hostel, San Martín 134, 2½ blocks from plaza, T0388-423 7565, www.clubhosteljujuy.com.ar. Dorms and doubles **\$\$**; with jacuzzi, patio, lots of information, welcoming, has a good travel agency.

\$ pp Hostal Casa de Barro, Otero 294, T0388-422 9578, www.hostalcasade barro.com.ar. Lovely double, triple and quadruple rooms from US\$11.50 pp, whitewashed with simple decorations, shared bathrooms and a fantastic area for eating and relaxing. The wonderful staff provide dinner on demand. Highly recommended.

$ pp Yok Wahi/Dublin Hostel and Bar, Independencia 946, T0388-422 9608, www.yokwahi.com. Hostel and Irish pub 6 blocks from bus station, with dorms (US$12 pp) and doubles with and without bath (**$$**), heating, *parrilla*, book exchange, information.

Around Jujuy city *p307*

Although there's plenty of accommodation in Jujuy itself, you might want to head out to Termas de Reyes or Yala for a more relaxing experience within easy reach of the city.

$$$$-$$$ Hotel Termas de Reyes, Termas de Reyes, 19 km northwest of Jujuy, T0388-492 2522, www.termasdereyes.com. 1 hr by bus from Jujuy bus terminal, US$0.75. This sumptuous thermal spa resort with a grand neoclassical hotel is set among magnificent mountains at an altitude of 1800 m. Rates include the use of the thermal pools. No children allowed.

$$$ La Escondida, Ejército del Norte s/n, T0388-15-682 2141, www.laescondidadeyala.com.ar. This homestead is actually in the village of Yala, which is a great alternative (if you have car) to the bustle of Jujuy as it is only 14 km away. Minimum 2-night stay, lovely doubles, and also main homestead for rent (for up to 8), and 2 bungalows (for 2-5). Impressive swimming pool set in luscious gardens.

$ pp Aldea Luna, Tilquiza, 20 km (1 hr) from Jujuy, 3 hrs from Salta, T0388-15-509 4602, www.aldealuna.com.ar. A new concept in hostelling, set in 900 ha of lush rainforest, with native trees, rivers and mountains in a natural reserve. The accommodation (dorms US$9 pp, private room US$13 pp) is in solar-powered stone cottages with bathrooms (yes, there's hot water!). Call to arrange a pick up from Jujuy US$41 for up to 4 people, or from Salta US$150 for up to 4. In summer, the 4WD can't make it all the way to the hostel, so you will have to walk the remaining 1 km. All the food served is vegetarian and is not included in the price.

Camping

$ pp El Refugio, R9, Km 14, Av Libertador 2327, Yala, T0388-490 9344, www.elrefugiodeyala.com.ar. This is the nearest campsite to the city in a pretty spot on the banks of the river. There's also a hostel, pool, restaurant, and trekking and horse-riding excursions are on offer. Highly recommended, a great place to relax.

Purmamarca *p308*

$$$$ El Manantial del Silencio, Ruta 52 Km 3.5, T0388-490 8081, www.hotelmanantial.com.ar. Signposted from the road into Purmamarca. Luxurious rooms, modern building, wonderful views, spacious living rooms with huge fire, charming hosts, includes breakfast, heating, riding, pool, superb restaurant (guests only).

$$$ Casa de Piedra, Pantaleon Cruz 6, T0388-490 8092, www.postadelsol.com. Well-situated new hotel made of stone and adobe with very comfortable rooms.

$$$ La Posta, C Santa Rosa de Lima 4 blocks up from plaza, T0388-490 8029, www.postadepurmamarca.com.ar. Beautiful setting by the mountain, comfortable rooms, helpful owner. Highly recommended.

$$ El Viejo Algarrobo, C Salta behind the church, T0388-490 8286, www.hotelviejoalgarrobo.com.ar. Small but pleasant rooms, cheaper with shared bath, helpful, good value and quality regional dishes in its restaurant (**$**).

$ El Pequeño Inti, C Florida 10
m from plaza, T0388-490 8089,
elintidepurmamarca@hotmail.com.
Small, modern rooms around a little
courtyard, breakfast, hot water, good
value. Recommended.

Maimará *p308*
$$$ La Casa del Tata, Belgrano s/n,
T0388-499 7389, www.lacasadeltata.
com.ar. Nicely decorated and welcoming
hostería serving great breakfasts which
include home-baked pastries. Rooms have
cable TV and good bathrooms with hot
water. They also serve a fantastic afternoon
tea with several varieties of cakes.
$$$ Posta del Sol, Martín Rodríguez
y San Martín, T0388-499 7156, www.
postadelsol.com. Comfortable *hostería*
with a good restaurant. The owner, a
tourist guide, can take you on a tour of
the area and has helpful information.

Tilcara *p309*
Book ahead during carnival and around
Easter when Tilcara is very busy. All those
listed are recommended.
$$$ Alas de Alma, Dr Padilla 437,
T0388-495 5572, www.alas.travel.
Central, relaxed atmosphere, spacious
doubles, and *cabañas* for up to 4 people.
2 mins from the main street.
$$$ Posada con los Angeles, Gorriti 156
(signposted from access to town), T0388-
495 5153, www.posadaconlosangeles.
com.ar. A much-recommended favourite
with charming rooms, each in a different
colour, all with fireplace and door to the
garden with beautiful views.
$$$ Quinta La Paceña, Padilla 660
at Ambrosetti, T0388-495 5098, www.
quintalapacena.com.ar. This architect-
designed traditional adobe house is a
peaceful haven. The garden is gorgeous
and wonderfully kept.

$ Casa los Molles, Belgrano 155, T0388-
495 5410, www.casalosmolles.com.ar.
Not really a hostel, this affordable
casa de campo offers simple dorms
in a friendly atmosphere (US$12-13 pp),
as well as a charming double (**$$-$**)
and 2 comfortable *cabañas* (**$$$** for
up to 4 people). Small and central,
book in advance.
$ pp Malka, San Martín s/n, 5 blocks
from plaza up steep hill, T0388-495
5197, www.malkahostel.com.ar.
A superb youth hostel, one of the
country's best. It has beautifully
situated rustic *cabañas* (**$$$** up to 8),
dorms for 5 people, US$18 pp, and
doubles with bath (**$$$**). Catch a taxi
from town or walk for 20 mins.
$ Tilcara Hostel, Bolívar 166, T0388-
15-507 4372, www.tilcarahostel.com.
This hostel is welcoming with dorms
at US$9 pp. Also offer doubles and
comfortable cabins (**$$**).

Camping
Camping El Jardín, access on Belgrano
700, T0388-495 5128, www.eljardintilcara.
com.ar. Hot showers, also hotel and
basic hostel.

Huacalera and Uquía *p309*
$$$ Solar del Trópico, T0388-154 785021,
www.solardeltropico.com. 2 km from
Huacalera, Argentine/French-owned
B&B offering fusion food on request.
Rustic, spacious bedrooms, organic
gardens, artist's studio; workshops
are run regularly. Tours offered.
Call to arrange a pickup beforehand.

Humahuaca and around *p310*
See also www.munayhotel.com.ar.
$$$$-$$$ Hotel Huacalera, Ruta 9 km
1790, T0388-54388, T0388-15-581 3417,
www.hotelhuacalera.com. Upscale resort

in the *puna* offering colourful rooms with terraces, spa, swimming pool and nature excursions.
$$ Hostal Azul, B Medalla Milagrosa, La Banda, T0388-421107. Across the river, smart, welcoming, pleasant, simple rooms, good restaurant and wine list, parking. Recommended.
$ pp Posada El Sol, Medalla milagrosa s/n over bridge from terminal, then 520 m, follow signs, T0388-421466, www.posadaelsol.com.ar. Quiet rural area, shared rooms or private (**$$**) in a warm welcoming place, laundry, horse riding, owner will collect from bus station if called in advance. HI affiliated. Recommended.

Iruya *p310*
$$$ Hostería de Iruya, San Martín 641, T03887-482002, www.hoteliruya.com. A special place, extremely comfortable, with good food, and great views from the top of the village. Highly recommended.
$$$-$$ Mirador de Iruya, La Banda s/n, T03887-421463, www.elmiradordeiruya. com.ar. Cross the river and climb a little to this hostal. Doubles, triples and quads available. Fantastic views from the terrace.
$ Hospedaje Asunta, Belgrano s/n (up the hill), T0387-154 045113. Friendly hostel with 28 beds. Fantastic views. Recommended.

La Quiaca and into Bolivia *p311*
$$ Munay, Belgrano 51-61, T03885-423924, www.munayhotel.com.ar. In same group as Munay in Salta, rooms with heating and fan, parking.
$ Hostel Copacabana, Pellegrini 141, T03885-423875, www.hostelcopacabana. com.ar. Only a few blocks from the bus terminal and the plaza. Clean dorms and doubles and comfortable living areas.

Camping
Camping Municipal, R5, on the route to Yavi, T03885-422645. Very basic facilities and quite a way out of town.

Yavi and around *p311*
$$ Hostal de Yavi, Güemes 222, T03541-15-633522, www.hostaldeyavi. blogspot.com. Simple bedrooms with bath, and some hostel space. Cosy sitting room, good food. Tours also arranged: to see cave paintings; moonlight walks; trekking; and trips to the Laguna de los Pozuelos. Recommended.
$ La Casona, Senador Pérez y San Martín, T03887-422316. Welcoming, with and without bath, breakfast.

Susques and Salinas Grandes *p314*
$$ El Unquillar, R52, Km 219 (1 km west of Susques), T03887-490201,www. hotelelunquillar.com.ar. Attractive, with local weavings, good rooms. Restaurant open to public. Phone for pick-up.
$$ Pastos Chicos, R52, Km 220 (at Casas Quemadas, 3 km west of Susques), T0388-423 5387/0388-15-487 4709, www.pastoschicos.com.ar. A rustic building providing comfortable accommodation. Good value. Its restaurant serves delicious regional specialities and is open to non-residents. Wi-Fi available. Phone for pickup.
$ Res La Vicuñita, San Martín 221, Susques, T03887-490207, opposite the church. Without bath, hot water, breakfast available, simple and welcoming.

⊙ Restaurants

Jujuy city *p304, map p304*
There are lots of great places to eat in Jujuy. Following Lavalle across the bridge to the bus terminal (where it changes

names to Dorrego) there are lots of cheap places selling *empanadas*.

$$$ Krysys, Balcarce 272. Popular bistro-style *parrilla*, excellent steaks.

$$ Chung King, Alvear 627. Closed Sun. Atmospheric, serving regional food for over 60 years; with pizzería at No 631.

$$ Manos Jujeñas, Senador Pérez 381. Tue-Sun 1200-1500, 2000-2400. Regional specialities, the best *humitas*, charming, good for the *peña* at weekends.

$$ Ruta 9, Belgrano 743 and Costa Rica 968. Great places for regional dishes such as *locro* and *tamales*, also a few Bolivian dishes.

$ Madre Tierra, Belgrano 619. Mon-Sat 1130-1430. Vegetarian café, behind a wholemeal bakery, delicious food.

$ Sociedad Española, Belgrano y Senador Pérez. Closed Sun. Good cheap set menus with a Spanish flavour.

$ Tío Bigote, Senador Pérez y Belgrano. Closed Mon and Sun evening. Very popular café and pizzería.

Purmamarca *p308*

$$ El Rincón de Claudia Vilte, Libertad s/n, T0388-490 8088. *Folclore* music and regional dishes served at this pretty restaurant 1 block from the main plaza.

$ La Posta, Rivadavia s/n, on the plaza. Excellent local dishes – *humitas* and *tamales* especially recommended. Touristy, but the service and the food are good. A small handicrafts shop next door sells high-quality goods.

Cafés

$ Arte y Té, C Sarmiento. Ideal for tea, or for regional *picadas* with a drink, in the informal atmosphere of an artist's home.

Tilcara *p320*

$$ El Patio, Lavalle 352, T0388-495 5044. Great range, lovely patio at the back, popular, very good.

$$ Pucará, up the hill towards the Pucará, T0388-495 5721. Imaginative, posh Andean food and hearty puddings, intimate, rustic atmosphere.

$ Música Esperanza (Bar del Centro), Belgrano 547, T0388-495 5462. Small restaurant/café serving local dishes in the patio. Not always open. Both the restaurant and crafts shop next door sustain an NGO that organizes free art and music workshops for local children.

Humahuaca and around *p310*

$$-$ El Portillo, Tucumán 69, T0387-424 9000. A simply decorated room, serves slightly more elaborate regional meals than the usual, such as llama with a fine plum sauce.

$$-$ La Cacharpaya, Jujuy 317, T0387-421 016. This brightly lit, large place lacks sophistication, but it's central and the food is good. Attracts an interesting mix of clientele.

Iruya *p310*

All hotels have their own restaurant, see Where to stay, above. They all serve regional meals (*locro, empanadas, humita, tamales*). **Hostal Federico Tercero** (on the plaza at the bottom of the hill) is the most welcoming place to hang out, but the most sophisticated and elegant place to eat is the pricey **Hostería de Iruya** (at the top of the town).

$ Comedor Margarita, near the plaza, T0388-15-497 0926. Good home-made food and a menu that changes daily. The *menú del día* is always good.

$ Comedor Iruya, Lavalle and San Martín. Basic but tasty menu serving local cuisine.

La Quiaca and into Bolivia *p311*
$ Frontera, Belgrano and Siria, T03885-422269. An atmospheric place, with a generous set menu.

⊙ Entertainment

Jujuy city *p304, map p304*
Head for a *peña* to hear the region's passionate *folclore* music played live. **La Casa de Jeremías**, Horacio Guzmán 306, T0388-424 3531; **La Yapa**, Mejias 426; and **Savoy**, Alvear and Urquiza, all have live music and dancing at weekends, and during the week in busy holiday periods. **Salamanka**, San Martín 889, has resident and guest DJs, and good cocktails.

Tilcara *p309*
El Cafecito de Tukuta, Rivadavia s/n, on the plaza. Serves good coffee and wonderful locally grown herbal teas during the day, and has superb live *folclore* and jazz music at weekends from celebrated local musicians.
Lapeña de Carlitos, Lavalle 397, on the plaza, www.lapeniadecarlitos.com.ar. Regional music from the charismatic and delightful Carlitos, also cheap meal-of-the-day, *empanadas* and drinks. A selection of all the typical music of the area, with bits of history and culture thrown in. Recommended.

⊙ Shopping

Jujuy city *p304, map p304*
Food
You can't beat the colourful **Municipal market**, Dorrego y Alem, near the bus terminal. Outside it, women sell home-baked *empanadas* and *tamales*, and delicious goat's cheese, as well as all kinds of herbal cures. There is a **Norte**

supermarket, Belgrano 823, and a bigger branch at 19 de Abril y Necochea.

Handicrafts
Handicrafts are sold from stalls on Plaza Belgrano near the cathedral and from **Paseo de las Artesanías**, on the west side of the plaza. Try also **Centro de Arte y Artesanías**, Balcarce 427.

⊙ What to do

Jujuy city *p304, map p304*
Tour operators offer full-day excursions from Jujuy into the *puna* and the Quebrada de Humahuaca, but if you have the time it's far better to take at least a couple of days to explore both areas properly. Jujuy is also the starting point for the cloudforest park of **Calilegua**, by bus via Libertador General San Martín (see Transport, below).
Noroeste, San Martín 155, T0388-423 7565, www.noroestevirtual.com.ar. Excursions to Quebrada de Humahuaca, salt flats, the *puna*. Also offer adventure tourism. Located at Club Hostel (see Where to stay, above). Recommended.

Tilcara *p309*
Caravana de Llamas, Alverro and Ambrosetti, T0388-15-408 8000, www.caravanadellamas.com.ar. Hiking into the mountains while llamas carry your belongings, reviving the ancient tradition. Explore magnificent mountain landscapes, ½- to 3-day excursions departing daily.
Cerro Morado, T0388-495 5117, branchesi_guia@yahoo.com.ar. Oscar Branchesi will take you to meet locals, giving you great insight into indigenous culture. Recommended.

Humahuaca and around *p310*
Ser Andino, Jujuy 21, T03887-421659,
http://ser-andino.com.ar. Really nice
people offering an attractive range of
trips along the Quebrada, plus tours to
Coctacta (2- to 3-hrs, from US$18.75 per
person), Iruya and the *puna*, including
Laguna de los Pozuelos.

Iruya *p310*
For local guides (walking and mules) in
the surrounding area, ask at the tourist
office in Iruya, T03887-482001, www.
iruyaonline.com. If you're short of time,
however, it's probably a good idea to
contract a guide in Humahuaca or Salta:
Norte Trekking, T0387-15-509 3299,
www.nortetrekking.com, based in Salta,
is highly recommended.

⊖ Transport

Jujuy city *p304, map p304*
Air
Flights to **Buenos Aires, Salta** and
Córdoba with **Aerolíneas Argentinas**,
Belgrano 1053, T0388-422 7198.

Bus
Long distance Several companies run
buses almost hourly up the Quebrada
de Humahuaca. To **Humahuaca**, US$5,
2½ hrs, several daily with **Balut**, via
Tilcara 1½ hrs, US$3.50. To **Purmamarca**,
take buses to Susques or to Humahuaca
but check they call at Purmamarca
village, off the main road. To **Susques**,
Purmamarca and **Andes Bus**, US$11,
4-6½ hrs, Tue-Sun. To the Bolivian border
at **La Quiaca**, 5-6 hrs, US$11, with **Balut**;
several rigorous luggage checks en route
for drugs, including coca leaves.
  To **Salta,** hourly, 2 hrs, US$6.50.
Vía Tucumán, Panamericano and
La Veloz del Norte to **Tucumán**, 6 hrs,

US$25, and **Córdoba**, 15-16 hrs, US$65.
To **Buenos Aires**, several daily, 21-24 hrs,
US$90-150, with **Flecha Bus**; **La Veloz del
Norte**; **Panamericano**.
  To **Orán** and **Aguas Blancas** (border
with Bolivia), US$22, daily with **Balut**,
via San Pedro. To **Calilegua**: various
companies to Libertador Gral San Martín
almost every hour (eg **Balut**, US$4.50);
from there take **Empresa 23 de Agosto** or
Empresa 24 de Setiembre, leaving 0830,
to **Valle Grande**, across Parque Nacional
Calilegua. All **Pocitos** or **Orán** buses pass
through **Libertador Gral San Martín**.
  To Chile: the route via the **Jama** pass
(4400 m) is taken by most traffic crossing
to northern Chile, including trucks; hours
0800-2200. **Géminis** bus tickets sold at
Paisajes del Noroeste, San Martín 134,
www.paisajesdelnoroeste.tur.ar.

Car hire
At the airport: **Earth Rent a Car**, T0388-
491 2734; **Hertz**, T0387-424 0113,
www.hertzargentina.com.ar
  In town: **Sudamerics**, Belgrano 601,
T0388-422 9034/15-436 5502,
www.sudamerics.com.

Purmamarca *p308*
Buses to Jujuy, 1½ hours, US$6; to Tilcara,
US$1. Buses between Salta and San Pedro
de Atacama can also be boarded here.

Tilcara *p309*
El Quiaqueño and **Andesmar/Brown**
buses pass Tilcara en route to **Jujuy**
4 times a day from 1340, 1½-2 hrs, and
en route to **La Quiaca** 6 times a day
from 1110. **Jama Bus** runs between
Tilcara, Humahuaca and La Quiaca.

Humahuaca and around *p310*
Buses to all places along the Quebrada
depart from the terminal. To **Iruya**,

Iruya SA, daily 0820, 1030 and Sun-Fri also 1600, 3-3½ hrs, US$5 one way, also **Panamericano de Jujuy**, daily 0830. To **La Quiaca**, with **Balut** and **La Quiaqueña** (more comfortable), several daily, 2½ hrs, US$6.

Iruya *p310*
Tickets are available from the bus station and from the food shop round the corner from the church. Buses stop outside Hostal de Gloria.

To **Humahuaca**, **Iruya SA**, Mon-Sat 0600, daily 1300, 1515, 1600, 1800, 3-3½ hrs, US$5; also **Panamericano de Jujuy**, daily 1400, US$5.

La Quiaca and into Bolivia *p311*
Bus
There are several buses a day to **Salta**, US$24, 7½ hrs, with **Balut** and others. To **Humahuaca**, with **Balut** and **La Quiaqueña** (more comfortable), several daily, 2½ hrs, US$6. To **Jujuy**, with **Balut**, 5-6 hrs, US$11. Take your own food, as there are sometimes long delays. Buses

are stopped for routine border police controls and rigorous searches for drugs. To **Buenos Aires** (via Jujuy), 26-28 hrs with **Balut**, US$127, including meals. **Andes Norte** links several villages west of R9, including **Santa Catalina**, Mon-Fri.

Remise taxis
Remiseria Acuario, España y 25 de Mayo, s/n, T03885-423333. You can take a *remise* taxi to Yavi for US$17 return, including ½-hr stay.

⊙ Directory

Jujuy city *p304, map p304*
Banks There are banks with ATMs on Alvear. **Embassies and consulates** Bolivia, Independencia 1098, T0388-424 0501, Mon-Fri 0830-1300. **Immigration** 19 de Abril 1057, T0388-423 5658. **Medical services** Farmacia Del Pueblo, Guemes 301, T0387-490 2783. **Post office** Independencia and Lamadrid.

Las Yungas

In complete contrast to the *puna* and the Quebradas, the Yungas
(pronounced 'shungas') are areas of cloudforest lying along the
eastern edges of Salta and Jujuy provinces. These forests receive
heavy rainfall and support an incredible wealth of wildlife and
vegetation, together with fragile indigenous communities. Three
national parks were created to protect them: Baritú and El Rey in
Salta, and Calilegua in Jujuy. All three are very much worth visiting,
but you'll need to be determined. Access is restricted, and planning
is required as infrastructure is still limited. If you don't have a 4WD
vehicle, contact one of the few adventure tourism agencies who
are allowed to operate in the parks. All three parks are difficult
to access during the rainy season, January to March, when the
roads are mostly impassable. There are lots of mosquitoes all year
round, so take plenty of repellent. The prevalence of malaria varies
from year to year, so check with your doctor about medication,
especially in mid-summer. For more information, see www.
redyaguarete.org.ar/yungas and www.welcomeargentina.com/
parques (both in English).

Parque Nacional Calilegua → *For listings, see pages 327-328.*

Parque Nacional Calilegua is 125 km northeast of Jujuy and the most accessible of
the three cloudforest parks in the region. The park protects an area of mountains,
sub-tropical valleys and cloudforest on the eastern slopes of the Serranía de
Calilegua. There are some surprisingly high peaks, including **Cerro Amarillo**
(3720 m), which you can climb in a three-day trek round trip, starting from the
park entrance, and **Cerro Hermoso** (3200 m), which lies closer to the road, but is
attempted by few visitors as you must go with a guide. The climate is subtropical
with average temperatures ranging from 17°C in winter to 28°C in summer. Mean
annual rainfall is 2000 mm, falling mainly in summer (November to March). Several
rivers flow southeast across the park into the Río Ledesma. The wildlife is wonderful
with at least 300 species of bird, including the red-faced guan and the condor, and
over 60 species of mammal. You're likely to see tapirs, otters, taruca (Andean deer)
and perhaps even pumas. The unpaved Route 83 runs through the park climbing
from southeast to northwest and affording splendid views, before reaching Valle

Grande beyond the park's borders. From Valle Grande there is a basic road leading, via Aparzo, to the Quebrada de Humahuaca. Or you could hike west from the park to Humahuaca and Tilcara (allow at least four days); you'll need to take a guide.

Arriving in the Parque Nacional Calilegua

The park entrance and ranger station is at Aguas Negras, 12 km along unpaved Ruta 83, a dirt road (4WD essential when wet) that turns off Ruta 34 just north of Libertador General San Martín. From the entrance, Ruta 83 climbs through the park for 13 km to another guardaparque at Mesada de las Colmenas and continues to Valle Grande, 90 km from Libertador, where there's basic accommodation and shops. There are frequent buses, including **Balut** ⓘ *T03886-422 2134, US4.50*, from Jujuy's terminal to Libertador General San Martín (also called Ledesma). From there, buses run to the park, where you'll be met by the *guardaparque* guides. Hitching is also possible. For further information contact the **park administration office** ⓘ *San Lorenzo 4514, T03886-422046, calilegua@apn.gov.ar, www.calilegua.com*, in the village of Calilegua, 4 km northeast of Libertador.

Walks

Within the park, there are 22 km of trails for trekking, most of which are close to the Aguas Negras ranger station. There are also some roads crossing the park for cars and bikes, and horse riding is allowed. A good tourist circuit is to **Calilegua** and then on to **Aguas Calientes**, a very rural place, where there are *hosterías* and a covered pool. You can do this in a day, if it hasn't rained, and it is accessible in an ordinary vehicle.

Cerro Amarillo ⓘ *3720 m*. A three-day trek starting from the entrance. Ask the *guardaparques* for advice on directions.

Alto Calilegua You could walk to an interesting shepherds' hamlet at 2700 m, starting near the base of Cerro Amarillo. It's actually outside Calilegua park but close to its northern border and only accessible on foot (eight to 10 hours each way) or on horseback (three hours each way). Mules can be hired from San Francisco (contact Luis Cruz). There are some small pre-Hispanic ruins near the hamlet, but the main point of visiting is to witness a culture that has remained isolated for centuries, in a picturesque mountainous setting. Locals will tell you they're tired of transporting everything by mules, and long for a road to be built. Visit now, before the road comes.

Routes to Bolivia → *For listings, see pages 327-328.*

From Libertador, Ruta 34 runs northeast for 244 km to the Bolivian border at **Pocitos** (also called **Salvador Mazza**) and Yacuiba in southeastern Bolivia. It passes through **Embarcación** and **Tartagal**, which has a good regional museum. In Pocitos, the border town, is **Hotel Buen Gusto**, just tolerable. There are no *casas de cambio* here.

The border is open 24 hours. From Yacuiba, across the border, buses go to Santa Cruz de la Sierra and Tarija. **Bolivian consulate** ① *Av San Martín 446, T03873-471336, Mon-Fri 0900-1400*. Several bus companies have services from the border to Salta and Tucumán.

An alternative route is via Aguas Blancas. At Pichanal, 85 km northeast of Libertador, Ruta 50 heads north via **Orán** (full name San Ramón de la Nueva Orán), an uninteresting place where you can re-fuel. The **Bolivian consulate** is also here at ① *Av San Martín 134, Orán, T03878-421969, Mon-Fri 0830-1300, 1600-1900*. **Aguas Blancas** is 53 km beyond **Orán** on the border (open 24 hours). There are restaurants, shops and fuel here but no accommodation. Nor is there anywhere to change money; note that Bolivianos are not accepted south of Aguas Blancas. Buses run from Bermejo, across the river by bridge, to Tarija, three to four hours, US$3 (US$6 by shared taxi).

Parque Nacional Baritú → *For listings, see pages 327-328.*

Baritú is Argentina's only tropical park, lying north of the Tropic of Capricorn. It's spectacularly beautiful, covering 72,439 ha of the eastern slopes of the Andean foothills, with peaks rising to around 2000 m, mostly covered by cloudforest. Fauna is abundant and varied, including many of the same birds and animals as Calilegua but also several species that are close to extinction, such as the yaguarete which lives only in a few eco-regions of this kind and whose only rival carnivore is the puma. There are also rare plant and tree species here, making the park a great destination for serious nature lovers. Baritú is the hottest of the three parks, with average temperatures of 21°C in winter and 30°C in summer. Summer also brings between 900 and 1300 mm of rain, making roads completely impassable in January and February. This makes Baritú one of the most inaccessible parks in the country, and you'll have to be determined to make a visit. There are no facilities apart from ranger posts, campsites at the entrances and rustic *cabañas*.

Arriving in Parque Nacional Baritú
Although the park lies entirely within Salta province, to reach it you'll have to go into Bolivia first. Start in Orán and travel up Route 50 to Aguas Blancas. Then drive 110 km through Bolivian territory – a beautiful winding road through hills – to reach the international bridge El Condado–La Mamora. Take Route 19 south (now back in Argentina). After 14 km you'll reach the region known as Los Toldos; keep heading south for a further 26 km until you reach the northern boundary of the park.

Remember to bring your passport (with a Bolivian visa if necessary) and, if hiring a car in Argentina, warn the hire company that you plan to take it into Bolivia. Fill up with fuel in Orán or Aguas Blancas, and check the state of the roads before setting off at Salta's **tourist office** (see page 285), or by contacting the **park's officers** ① *T0387-15-507 4432/4433, baritu@apn.gov.ar, www.parquesnacionales.gov.ar (follow links under 'Areas protegidas').*

Walks

There are many walks in the northeast area of the park, affording you close contact with the many species of bird in the park. A recommended walk is to **Termas de Cayotal**, two hours' walk from the *guardaparque's* office in El Lipeo. Another is to the settlement of **Campo Grande**, where you can meet local indigenous peoples living in the park and get a glimpse of their rich culture. From here, you could also walk the seven hours to **Angosto del Río Lipeo**.

Parque Nacional El Rey

Parque Nacional El Rey is the closest of the three cloudforest parks to Salta city (196 km), though it's still not easily accessible unless you go with a special expedition, since visitors to the park are few and far between, and there's little vehicular access. Covering 44,000 ha, it was once a privateestate, 'El Rey' (the king), on the eastern border of the Spanish territory, owned by Coronel Fernández Cornejo, who carried out the expulsion of the Jesuits. The remains of his 18th-century house can still be found in the park. The park has a warm climate and relatively high average rainfall. Its landscapes stretch from arid steppe in the east, at 750 m above sea level, to mountainous regions at over 2000 m, resulting in extremely varied vegetation. In the east, you can find Chaqueño-serrano forest, then transition jungle in the middle and high mountain forest at the most western extreme. The natural amphitheatre formation of the park's terrain is created by the horseshoe-shaped ridge of the Sierra de la Cresta del Gallo, northwest of the park, which reacges heights of around 1700 m. Rivers descend from here through lush jungle to the Río Popayán flowing below. There's abundant wildlife, much of it easily spotted. Toucans and other birdlife abound, and you might be lucky enough to spot wild cats and tapirs.

Arriving in Parque Nacional El Rey

Getting there The park entrance is 46 km off Route 5, but no public transport reaches the park so it's best to take a tour from Salta city with one of the three operators licensed to take groups into the park: **Norte Trekking** ① *T0387-431 6616, www.nortetrekking.com,* **Clark Expediciones** ① *T0387-497 1024, www. clarkexpediciones.com),* and **Movitrack** ① *www.movitrack.com.ar.* These are highly recommended, with expert guides to the interesting flora and fauna in the park, offering one- and two-day trips in 4WD vehicles with walks in the park, and camping. No other accommodation is possible in the park.

Park information The best time to visit is May to November, avoiding the very rainy season of January to March. There is a rangers' office near the entrance with a clearing where you can camp. This is a simple campsite with drinking water and bathrooms. There is a **park office** ① *España 366, 3rd floor (4400), T03487-431 2683,* in Salta. More information is available on the Parques Nacionales website, www. parquesnacionales.gov.ar.

Walks

There are several good paths you can take to explore the park's varied landscape and accompanying wildlife. **Los Patitos** is a small lake, 1.5 km from the *guardaparques* centre and a great one-hour walk for spotting aquatic birds and mammals. **Popayán River** is 10 km (a two-hour walk) from the *guardaparques* centre. **Pozo Verde** path is 12 km from the *guardaparques* centre and challenging for the first 3 km. Part of the way there is a footpath with interpretation information called 'Los Ocultos'. **Santa Elena Field and Los Lobitos waterfall** is a challenging hike but good for seeing transition jungle; 4 km from the *guardaparques*, two hours each way; you'll need a guide. **Chorro de los Loros** is a pedestrian path of medium-high difficulty. It is 10 km long and crosses the transition jungle. It starts at the *guardaparques* centre.

⊛ Las Yungas listings

For hotel and restaurant price codes and other relevant information, see pages 20-26.

⊜ Where to stay

There is no accommodation inside the parks themselves, except for very basic campsites with few facilities. However, there are some recommended places to stay nearby that can arrange trips into the parks.

Parque Nacional Calilegua *p323*
$$$ Finca Portal de Piedra, Villa Monte, Santa Bárbara, T03886-15-682 0564, www.ecoportaldepiedra.com. 17 km north of Libertador General San Martín. Fabulous eco-run *finca* in its own reserve (Las Lancitas), convenient for PNs Calilegua and El Rey. Guesthouse accommodation and self-contained cabin available, with simple food, horse riding, trekking, birdwatching and other excursions. To get there from Jujuy take a bus via San Pedro and Palma Sola (which is 12 km north of the *finca*).
$$$ Posada del Sol, Los Ceibos 747 at Pucará, Libertador General San Martín, T03886-424900, www.posadadelsoljujuy. com.ar. Comfortable, functional hotel,

with gardens and pool, has advice on local trips.
$$ Termas de Caimancito, Aguas Calientes, east of Libertador General San Martín, T03886-15-650699, www.termasdecaimancito.com.ar. A beautiful and tranquil place in tropical surroundings, owned by a welcoming, English-speaking family. Simple rooms with bath, a campsite, thermal pools and a small restaurant. The owner, Tony Strelkov, runs bilingual excursions and trekking into the park, just a 30-min drive from here.

Camping

There is a campsite at Aguas Negras, near the 1st rangers' station; you'll find it when entering Calilegua park from the R34. There is drinking water from the river nearby, and some cooking facilities and tables. To camp at Mesada de las Colmenas, ask permission at Aguas Negras.

⊙ What to do

Parque Nacional Baritú *p325*
Movitrack and **Clark Expediciones**, both in Salta, are authorized to take visitors

into the park. Both are recommended for specializing in natural history, with 1- to 2-day trips in 4WD vehicles, camping and walking inside the park.

⊖ Transport

Parque Nacional Calilegua *p323*
From Libertador San Martín **Empresa 23 de Agosto** or **Empresa 24 de Setiembre** leave 0830 to **Valle Grande**, across Parque Nacional Calilegua (US$4, 5 hrs), returning

the same day. *Remise* charges about US$7-10 from Libertador to park entrance.

Routes to Bolivia *p324*
All Pocitos or Orán buses pass through Libertador San Martín. Between Aguas Blancas and **Orán** buses run every 45 mins, US$1, luggage checks on bus. Some services from Salta and Jujuy call at **Orán** en route to **Tartagal** and **Pocitos**. Note that buses are subject to slow searches for drugs and contraband.

Contents

Footprint features

Border crossings

At a glance

⊜ **Getting around** Local buses and minibuses are the best option.

⟳ **Time required** With 5 days you can visit both sides of the falls, and the mission ruins of San Ignacio. Add at least 3-4 more if you intend to visit the Esteros del Iberá.

❀ **Weather** Dec-Feb is hot and humid. Temperatures average 25°C in summer, 15°C in winter.

✖ **When not to go** Jan-Feb can be hot and humid, and Easter is very busy. There is more rain in Mar and Jun.

The Northeast

BRAZIL

PARAGUAY

Espinillo

PN Pilcomayo

Ibarreta

Clorinda

FORMOSA

Foz do Iguaçu

Iguazú Falls

PN Foz do Iguaçu

Ciudad del Este

Puerto Iguazú

PN Iguazú

Wanda

Esperanza

Formosa

CHACO

Avia Terai

PN Chaco

Resistencia

Corrientes

Paso de la Patria

Empedrado

Las Toscas

Reconquista

Vera

SANTA FE

San Javier

Santa Elena

Santa Fé

Paraná

Vialle

Diamante

Victoria

San Lorenzo

Rosario

Villa Constitución

San Nicolás

San Pedro

Pergamino

Zárate

Itatí

Ita Ibaté

Posadas

Encarnación

Santa Ana

Mburucuyá

Reserva Natural del Iberá

Parque Nacional Mburucuyá

Concepción

San Miguel

Apóstoles

Salsas

Bella Vista

Santa Lucía

Goya

Rio Corrientes

Curuzú

Monte Caseros

La Paz

ENTRE RÍOS

Embalse Salto Grande

Concordia

San Salvador

Ubajay

PN El Palmar

Villaguay

Colón

Paysandú

Concepción del Uruguay

Gualeguaychú

Fray Bentos

Ibicuy

Delta del Paraná

Puerto Rico

Capiovi

Jesús

Trinidad

San Ignacio

San Ignacio Mini

Campo Viera

Oberá

LN Alem

MISIONES

Eldorado

Mocona Falls

Rio Uruguay

CORRIENTES

Mercedes

Yapeyú

Paso de los Libres

Santo Tomé

Garruchos

Colonia Carlos Pellegrini

BRAZIL

URUGUAY

N

50 km

50 miles

★ Don't miss ...
1 Carnaval in Gualeguaychú, page 339.
2 El Monumento de la Bandera, Rosario, page 342.
3 Reserva Natural del Iberá, page 363.
4 San Ignacio, page 374.
5 Boat ride under the Iguazú Falls, page 393.

Of all Argentina's many natural wonders, there is nothing quite as spectacular as the Iguazú Falls. With a magical setting in subtropical rainforest, alive with birdsong and the constant dancing of butterflies, the colossal Garganta del Diablo waterfall at their centre is an unforgettable sight. Take a boat underneath and get drenched in the spray, or stroll along nature trails at first light. Misiones province holds other delights: Jesuit missions unearthed from the jungle at San Ignacio, and the extraordinary Saltos de Moconá, 3000 m of falls more horizontal than vertical.

El Litoral's wealth of wildlife is astounding. In the vast wetlands of Esteros del Iberá, giant storks and caiman nestle between floating islands and water lilies. In Mburucuyá, tall palms wave in grasslands and passion flowers thrive in abundance. In the Chaco, watch out for pumas and monkeys, while the palm forests of Entre Ríos are centuries old. Stop on the lazy Paraná river either at relaxed, pretty Colón with its port and sandy beaches or amid the faded splendour of Paraná. For more stimulation, historical Corrientes is a riot at Carnival time, and lively Rosario produces the country's finest musicians.

The northeast's rich culture stems from its indigenous peoples, the Guaraní and Wichí, who produce beautiful art. The gently meandering rivers set the pace, giving the land its lush vegetation and generating in its people a charming, laid-back warmth. *Yerba mate* is the nation's favourite drink, and everywhere you'll encounter friends gathered on riverbanks on balmy afternoons sipping from their *mate* gourd. For more details on the *mate* ritual, see the box on page 25.

Along the Río Uruguay

The mighty Río Uruguay, which forms Argentina's eastern boundary with Uruguay and Brazil, is over 1600 km long, and a staggering 10 km wide in places. It. Unless you're in a rush to reach Iguazu, you could meander northeast from Buenos Aires along the river, stopping off at some interesting towns on the Argentine side. Gualeguaychú is so keen to party, it celebrates its carnival every weekend for two months, but you can calm down in Concepción del Uruguay, with its attractive old buildings, or Colón, with its historic port area and sandy beaches. There's a national park protecting splendid palm forests, though the reserve La Aurora del Palmar is more accessible. You can stay on colonial *estancias*, jungle islands, and with small communities at Irazusta and Arroyo Barú.

Gualeguaychú and around → *For listings, see pages 338-339. Colour map 4, A5.*

The first town of any size on the Ruta 12/14 north from Buenos Aires, Gualeguaychú is famous for its extended carnival. En route to Gualeguaychú, you may want to stop at **Villa Paranacito,** a village set in the delta islands, accessible only via a 22-km dirt road, branching off Route 12, 10 km south of Ceibas. (There are daily buses to Villa Paranacito **with Nuevo Expreso from Gualeguaychú, Zárate** and **Buenos Aires.**) Houses here are built on tall stilts and boats are the essential means of transport. It's popular with anglers in the waters of the nearby Río Uruguay (half an hour further east by boat) and anyone looking for a quiet place to stay, immersed in the islander culture. There are campsites, a hostel and *cabañas* offering boat excursions, and delicious local fish at **Villa Paranacito Annemarie**.

Estancia La Azotea ① *10 km north of Villa Parancito, on Route 12 in Ceibas, T03446-4794 8964, gesino@fibertel.com.ar,* is a 19th-century house popular for day visits, with cattle ranching, horse riding, an *asado* lunch and the use of a pool in summer. Very good value.

Arriving in Gualeguaychú → *Phone code 03446. Population 109,461 (department).*
The **bus terminal** ① *Blvd Artigas and Blvd Jurado, T03446-440688,* is a 30-minute walk from the centre (*remise* taxi US$3). The terminal has tourist information, a post office, phones, a small restaurant and 24-hour left luggage.

A thatched hut houses the **tourist office** ① *Paseo del Puerto, T03446-422900, daily 0800-2000 (2200 in summer, 2400 Fri-Sat); also at 25 de Mayo 718 in the centre, T03446-437062, Mon-Sat 0800-1400, www.gualeguaychuturismo.com.*

Border crossing: Argentina–Uruguay

Puente Libertador General San Martín

Situated 33 km southeast of Gualeguaychú, the Libertador General San Martín Bridge (5.4 km long) provides the most southerly route across the Río Uruguay, to Fray Bentos. Open 24 hours.

Customs and immigration These are at opposite ends of the bridge and it's an uncomplicated crossing; formalities take about 10 minutes. Passport details are noted when booking bus tickets and passed to officials at the border, and passports are inspected on the bus. **Note** Pedestrians and cyclists can only cross in motor vehicles, though officials may arrange lifts. Vehicle toll is US$6. Don't carry any dairy products, meat, fruit and vegetables, flowers, plants and seeds, or animals.

Argentine consulate in Fray Bentos at 18 de Julio 1031, T+598-4562 3510.

Uruguayan consulate in Gualeguaychú at Rivadavia 510, T03446-426168, conurugale@entrerios.net, Monday-Friday 0800-1400.

Transport From Gualeguaychú to Fray Bentos, there are two daily buses (one on Sunday) with Ciudad de Gualeguay, T03446-440555, also ETA CUT (not Sunday), 1½ hours, US$5. To Montevideo, from US$35, 6½ hours, Plus Ultra. Arrive 30 minutes before departure to do the border paperwork.

Note Due to ongoing demonstrations regarding the building of a paper mill on the Uruguayan side, the bridge and border are sometimes closed.

Places in Gualeguaychú

Gualeguaychú is lively throughout the summer, with an attractive *costanera* on the Río Gualeguaychú, where there are several *balnearios* and restaurants; it's a pleasant place for a stroll with views of the picturesque port. Carnival is celebrated at the local *corsódromo* (arena), a hugely popular event lasting well beyond the usual fortnight to fill every weekend for a couple of months. The port and *balneario municipal* (town bathing spot) are the departure points for short boat excursions and city tours. About 200 m south of the port in Plazoleta de los Artesanos, local handicrafts are sold at weekends in summer.

On the *costanera* at Gervasio Méndez is **El Patio del Mate** ⓘ *T03446-424371, www.elpatiodelmate.com.ar, daily 0800-2100 (2200 in summer),* a workshop where dedicated craftsmen make the cups from which *mate* is drunk, varying widely from simple dyed gourds to ornate silver goblets.

On the outskirts are thermal pools at **Termas del Guaychú** ⓘ *Ruta 14 Km 63.5, www.termasdelguaychu.com.ar,* and **Termas del Gualeguaychú** ⓘ *Ruta 42 Km 2.5, T03446-499167.*

Into Uruguay: Fray Bentos → *Colour map 4, A6. Phone code +598-(0)562. Population 25,047.*

Fray Bentos is the main port on the east bank of Río Uruguay, a friendly little town with an attractive *costanera*. The main reason to visit is to see the meat-packing factory. The name Fray Bentos was synonymous with corned beef in Britain throughout the 20th century, and the factory (*frigorífico*) known as El Anglo, which produced Oxo for many years, has been beautifully restored as the **Museo de La Revolución Industrial** ① *T+598 4562-2918, Mon-Fri 0930-1730, US$2.20 including a 1½-hr guided tour in Spanish at 1000 and 1500, leaflet in English, Tue free*. The office block in the factory has been preserved and some of the old machinery can be seen; there's also a restaurant on site. The **tourist office** ① *T+598-4562 2233*, is at 25 de Mayo 3400.

Concepción del Uruguay and around → *For listings, see pages 338-339.*
Colour map 2, C1.

Concepción del Uruguay lies on the western shore of the Río Uruguay, 74 km north of Gualeguaychú, with views of islands in the river opposite. Founded in 1783, it was capital of Entre Ríos province between 1813-1821 and 1860-1883, and retains some fine architecture in its public buildings. It has a distinctively lively character, thanks to a young student population.

Arriving in Concepción del Uruguay → *Phone code 03442.*
Population: 100,728 (department).
The **bus terminal** ① *Rocamora y Los Constituyentes, T03442-4562 2737*, is 11 blocks from Plaza Ramírez (remise to centre, US$2). Luggage can be left at the information desk.
  Tourist office ① *Galarza y Supremo Entrerriano, T03442-425820, and Galarza y Daniel Elías, T03442-440812, www.concepcionentrerios.tur.ar, daily 0800-2000 (0700-2200 in high season).*

Places in Concepción del Uruguay
The old town is centred on beautiful **Plaza Ramírez**, with the Italian neoclassical-style **Basílica de la Inmaculada Concepción**, containing the remains of General Urquiza on its western side. Next to it is the **Colegio Superior Justo José de Urquiza**, the first secular school in the country, although its 19th-century buildings were largely replaced in 1935. One block northeast of the plaza is **Museo Casa de Delio Panizza** ① *Galarza and Supremo Entrerriano 58, daily 0900-1200, 1600-1900, US$0.25*, in a mansion dating from 1793 and containing 19th-century furnishings and artefacts.

West of Concepción del Uruguay
① *Buses going to Paraná or Rosario del Tala will stop at El Cruce or Caseros, and from here, the palacios are 4 km and 8 km away, respectively (take a remise taxi from Caseros; Palacio San José's website recommends 2 companies). Tour operators run combis (minibuses) only in high season (check companies at tourist office, since they change every year). Basavilbaso has regular buses which link Concepción del Uruguay and Paraná or Rosario del Tala.*
Palacio San José ① *32 km west of the town, www.palaciosanjose.com.ar, Mon-Fri 0800-1900, Sat-Sun 0900-1800, US$2.50, information in Spanish, French and English,*

free guided visits throughout the day, and night visits at Easter, Jan-Feb (on Fri) and Oct-Dec (1 Sat a month), is the former mansion of General Urquiza and dates from 1848. Built in Italian style with 38 rooms and a chapel, it was once the country's most luxurious residence. Now a museum with artefacts from Urquiza's life, the palace stands in a beautiful park with an artificial lake. It can be reached by taking Route 39 west and turning right after Caseros train station.

There is also a second *palacio*, **Palacio Santa Cándida** ⓘ *www.santacandida. com*, which is another wonderfully old *estancia* that can be visited and which offers accommodation and lots of outdoor activities.

Basavilbaso, 68 km west, is a historical small town which in the early 20th century was an urban centre for Lucienville, inhabited by Jewish immigrants from Russia. There's a **tourist office** ⓘ *Lagocen and Hipólito Yrigoyen, T03445-481015, www. turismoentrerios.com/basavilbaso*, and information is available at **Asociación Israelita** ⓘ *T03445-481908*. There are three well-preserved synagogues, of which the **Tefila L Moises** has a beautifully painted wooden ceiling. It's also worth visiting the **Navibuco synagogue**, 2.5 km out of town, dating from 1895, and two Jewish cemeteries nearby. Basavilbaso used to be a busy transport hub until the last passenger train left in 1992. The station now houses a museum where the rich history of the local railway can be explored.

Colón → *For listings, see pages 338-339. Colour map 2, C1.*

One of the prettiest towns on the river, Colón was founded in 1863 as a port for the Swiss colony of San José, 9 km west, and it's an excellent base for visiting several interesting places nearby, including the **Parque Nacional El Palmar** ⓘ *www. colonentrerios.com.ar/elpalmar*. It is also linked by a bridge to the Uruguayan city of Paysandú. Colón itself has many well-preserved early 19th-century houses and a beautiful riverbank with long sandy beaches and shady streets.

Arriving in Colón
The **bus terminal** ⓘ *Paysandú and Sourigues, T03447-421716*, is 10 blocks from the main plaza. Left luggage storage is available at **Remises Base** (opposite the terminal) on 9 de Julio. Not all long-distance buses enter Colón: buses going north from Colón will stop at Ubajay. The former passenger boat terminal in the port area now houses the **tourist information office** ⓘ *Av Costanera Quirós y Gouchón, T03447-421233, www.colonturismo.gov.ar, daily 0600-2000 (until 2200 in high season)*.

Places in Colón → *Phone code 03447. Population: 62,160 (department)*.
The most attractive part of town is the port district, next to the Plaza San Martín, with fine old houses on the plaza and nearby streets leading down to the riverside. At the corner of Avenida 12 de Abril and Paso is **La Casona** (1868), where there's a handicrafts exhibition and shop. North of the port, Calle Alejo Peyret gives access to the *balnearios* and their sandy beaches on the river and Calle Belgrano leads to the **Complejo Termal** ⓘ *T03447-424717, daily 0900-2100, US$7.50*, where there

are 10 thermal pools (34-40°C) in an attractive setting, very popular for treating a variety of ailments. Most shops and banks can be found on Avenida 12 de Abril, with the old **Teatro Centenario**, opened in 1925.

Arroyo Barú
Some 40 km north of Villa Elisa (east of Colón) is **Arroyo Barú**, a village whose inhabitants have opened their houses to visitors who want to enjoy the tranquillity of this small rural community. This place, together with Irazusta (west of Gualeguaychú), are both study cases for NGO research. The village is reached via a 35-km-long dirt road, branching off Route 130, 5 km west of Villa Elisa.

Parque Nacional El Palmar → Colour map 2, C1.
ⓘ Entrance on Ruta 14, 58 km north of Colón, 6 km south of Ubajay, T03447-493049, www.pnelpalmar.com.ar. US$10. Buses from Colón, 1 hr, US$2, will drop you at the entrance; it may be possible to hitch the 12 km to the park administration, otherwise you have to walk. Local JoviBus services run to Ubajay, from where a remise taxi to the park administration costs about US$10; ask at Parador Gastiazoro where buses stop. Remises also go from Colón and Concordia. Otherwise take a tour.

On the west bank of the Río Uruguay km north of Colón, this park covers 8500 ha of gently undulating grassland and mature palm forest, including *Yatay* palms that are hundreds of years old. These graceful trees were once found all over the Pampas, until the introduction of cattle, who found the young seedlings irresistible. Growing in *palmares*, or groves, mature trees may reach 12 m in height, with fronds some 2 m in length. Along the Río Uruguay, and the *arroyos* streams that flow into it, there are gallery forests of subtropical trees and shrubs. You'll find indigenous tombs hidden away on the edge of the Río Uruguay where there are **beaches** and the remains of an 18th-century quarry and port. Look out for capybaras, foxes, lizards and vizcachas as well as rheas, monk parakeets and several species of woodpecker.

At the entrance gates on Route 14, you are given a map and information on walks. From here, a *ripio* road leads to the administration centre, in the east of the park, near the Río Uruguay, with access to several viewpoints: **Mirador de La Glorieta**, **Mirador del Arroyo El Palmar**, **Mirador del Arroyo Los Loros** and to the coast of the Río Uruguay. There are walks between 300 m and 1000 m and you are free to walk around the main roads, though there's little shade. The administration centre is the departure point for guided walks and cycle tours run by **Capybara Aventura** (English spoken). Nearby there's camping (www.campingelpalmar.*com.ar*, US$3.75 plus US$5.75 per person) with electricity, hot water, a restaurant opposite and a small shop. Visit at any time of year, but note that the park is very popular at weekends in summer and during Easter week. In summer there are more chances of thunderstorms and very hot weather.

Border crossing: Argentina–Uruguay

Puente General José Artigas

Open 24 hours. 7 km southeast of Colón, the General José Artigas Bridge gives access to the Uruguayan city of Paysandú. Toll US$6.

Argentine consulate in Paysandú at Gómez 1034, T+598-4722 22253, Monday-Friday 1300-1800.

Uruguayan consulate in Colón at San Martín 417, T03447-421999, crou@ciudad. com.ar.

Immigration Argentine and Uruguayan formalities are both dealt with at the Uruguayan end of the bridge. *Migraciones* officials board the bus, but non-Argentines or Uruguayans should get off the bus to have their passports stamped. When driving you don't need to get out of your car, just present your passport and car registration details when asked.

Transport From Colón to Paysandú, take a **Copay** bus, 45 minutes, US$4.

Refugio de Vida Silvestre La Aurora del Palmar

ⓘ *Opposite the Parque Nacional El Palmar, 3 km south of Ubajay, on Route 14, Km 202, T0345-490 5725, www.auroradelpalmar.com.ar, free. There are buses from Colón; ask for Ruta 14 Kilómetro 202 and tell the driver you are going to La Aurora del Palmar to avoid confusion with the national park. For transport from Ubajay, see Parque Nacional el Palmar, above.*

More accessible than the national park, the wildlife reserve of La Aurora del Palmar was created to protect a similar environment. It covers 1150 ha, of which 200 are covered with a mature palm forest. There are also gallery forests and patches of *espinal*, or scrub. There's lots of birdlife, and capybaras can also be spotted along the streams. You can reach the vantage point of the *quincho panorámico* for a drink (try the *yatay* spirit), while enjoying the view of the palm forest. The administration centre is only 500 m from Route 14, and offers well-organized services for visitors. Guided excursions include horse riding into the palm forest and the Arroyo de los Pájaros (one hour, US$12.50 per person); canoe journeys along Arroyo El Palmar (two hours, US$12.50 per person); and walks to the Mirador del Cerro de Piedra. All recommended. There's accommodation and camping available too (see Where to stay, page 338), but you should book in advance for lodging and to check the availability of excursions.

For hotel and restaurant price codes and other relevant information, see pages 20-26.

⊙ Where to stay

Gualeguaychú *p332*
Accommodation is scarce during carnival. Prices 25% higher Dec-Mar, Easter and long weekends. The tourist office can contact estate agents for short stays in private flats.
$$$ Puerto Sol, San Lorenzo 477, T03446-434017, www.hotelpuertosol. com.ar. Good rooms next to the port, plus a small resort on a nearby island (transfer included) for a relaxing drink.
$$$ Tykuá, Luis N Palma 150, T03446-422625, www.tykuahotel.com.ar. 3 blocks from the bridge, with all services including safe.

Camping
There are several sites on the riverside, others next to the bridge and north of it. **El Ñandubaysal**, on the Río Uruguay, 15 km southeast, T03446-423298, is the smartest.

Concepción del Uruguay and around *p334*
$$$$-$$ Grand Hotel Casino, Eva Perón 114, T03442-425586, www.grand hotelcasino.com.ar. Originally a French-style mansion with adjacent theatre. Superior rooms have a/c and TV; VIP rooms have new bathrooms.
$$$ Antigua Posta del Torreón, España y Almafuerte, T03442-432618, www.postadeltorreon.com.ar. 9 comfortable rooms in a stylish boutique hotel with a pool.
$$ Nuevo Residencial Centro, Moreno 130, 1½ blocks from the plaza, T03442-

427429, www.nuevorescentro.com.ar. One of the cheapest options in town. Basic rooms, some with a/c, in a traditional 19th-century building with a lovely patio. No breakfast.

Colón *p335*
$$$ Holimasú, Belgrano 28, T03447-421305, www.hotelholimasu.com.ar. Nice patio, a/c extra, **$$** in low season.
$$$ Hostería Restaurant del Puerto, Alejo Peyret 158, T03447-422698, www.hosteriadecolon.com.ar. Great value, lovely atmosphere in old house, pool, no credit cards.
$$ La Posada de David, Alejo Peyret 97, T03447-423930, www.colonentrerios. com.ar/posadadedavid. Welcoming family house, garden, good double rooms, great value.

Camping
There are several sites, some with cabins, on the river bank, from US$7 daily.

Refugio de Vida Silvestre La Aurora del Palmar *p337*
$$$ Casona La Estación, T0345-490 5725/T03447-15-431689, www. auroradelpalmar.com.ar. Rooms for up to 6 people and apartments for up to 8, with breakfast, bath, a/c, well-suited to families. Also offers one of the most extraordinary places to stay: train carriages (**$$$-$$**) converted intoin double rooms or dormitories. Camping is also permitted in the park's own site.

⊙ Restaurants

Gualeguaychú *p332*
$$ Campo Alto, San Lorenzo and Concordia, T03446-429593. A large

quincho (rustic place to eat) at the end of the *costanera*, lots of local fish such as *surubí, boga, dorado* and *patí* on the menu.
$ Dacal, Av Costanera and Andrade, T03446-427602. A traditional restaurant, serving good food; the *surubí* is recommended.

Concepción del Uruguay *p334*
$$$ El Conventillo de Baco, España 193, T03442-433809. A refined choice with some outside tables and a chance to try fish from the river.

Colón *p335*
$$$ Chiva Chiva, Gral Urquiza y Brown. An artist's refuge; her creativity is in evidence in the meals, drinks and pottery on display.
$$$ La Cosquilla del Angel, Alejo Peyret 180. The smartest place in town, with fish dishes, set menu and live piano music in evenings.
$$$ Viejo Almacén, Gral Urquiza y Paso. Cosy, very good cooking and excellent service.

⊛ Festivals

Gualeguaychú *p332*
Jan/Feb Carnival, www.grancarnaval. com.ar and www.carnavaldelpais.net (in Spanish). Carnival is celebrated every weekend throughout Jan and Feb at the *corsódromo*, a purpose-built parade ground with grandstand, at the back of the former railway station on Piccini y Maipú. Local teams or *comparsas* compete in colourful parades to the powerful drumbeats of the *batucada*, with *carrozas* and dancers dressed in brightly coloured costumes and feathers. Tickets for adults in 2014 cost from

US$7.50 to US$22 depending on the night; details of how to buy can be found on the websites.

Colón *p335*
Feb Fiesta Nacional de la Artesanía. Held over 9 evenings in Parque Quirós, where craftspeople display a wide variety of handicrafts. There are also *folcore* and pop music concerts.

⊖ Transport

Gualeguaychú *p332*
Bus
To **Concepción del Uruguay**, 1 hr, US$3. To **Buenos Aires**, US$18, 3½ hrs, several daily. Buses to **Zárate** or **Buenos Aires** stop at **Ceibas**, not far from Estancia La Azotea, and there are also regular buses to **Larroque** and **Urdinarrain**, where *remise* taxis will take you to **Irazusta** and **Aldea San Antonio**. There are daily buses to **Villa Paranacito** with **Nuevo Expreso**.

Concepción del Uruguay *p334*
Bus
To **Buenos Aires**, frequent, 4-4½ hrs, US$20. To **Colón**, 1 hr, US$3.

Colón *p335*
Bus
To **Buenos Aires**, US$21-26, 5-6 hrs. To **Mercedes** (for Iberá), several companies, 7-8 hrs, US$18. To **Paraná**, 4-6 hrs, US$10. To **Paysandú (Uruguay)**, Copay and **Río Uruguay**, US$4, 1 hr.

⊕ Directory

Gualeguaychú *p332*
Banks Banco de la Nación, 25 de Mayo and Alberdi; Credicoop, 25 de Mayo 860.

Río Paraná

Running parallel to the Río Uruguay, the Río Paraná weaves its lazy course right across the northeast of Argentina, from Misiones to Buenos Aires where it forms a vast delta. If you have time for a road trip from Buenos Aires to Corrientes, there are two main routes north: the more major route north along the western banks, through the cities of Rosario and Santa Fe to Reconquista and Resistencia; or an interesting journey along the eastern banks of the river, through Paraná via small towns for wildlife spotting and fishing and onwards to Goya and Corrientes.

Rosario → *For listings, see pages 349-354. Colour map 4, A5.*

Rosario is Argentina's third largest city, renowned for its rich cultural life, since it is home to many famous artists and pop musicians. Although little visited by travellers, it has some fine buildings in its attractive centre and a well-kept *costanera* along the Paraná River. The nightlife is lively, with plenty of cafés, restaurants and nightclubs, and there are daily theatre and live music shows at venues all around the city. To recover from all that entertainment, visit the nearby islands in the river, just minutes away from the centre, where you can relax on sandy beaches. It is a fantastic place to spend the weekend.

Arriving in Rosario → *Phone code 0341. Population 1,159,000.*

Fisherton Airport ① *T0341-451 3220*, is located 15 km west of the centre. *Remise* taxis charge US$25 for the journey to town. Transfers are also arranged by airline companies. The **bus terminal** ① *Santa Fe and Cafferata, T0341-437 3030, www.terminalrosario.gov.ar*, is about 30 blocks west of the Monumento de la Bandera. The terminal has an information point, post office, shops, restaurants and left luggage (open 24 hours). There are several bus lines to the centre with stops on Córdoba (eg 101, 115); from the centre to the bus terminal, catch a bus on Plaza 25 de Mayo, via C Santa Fe. *Remise* taxis charge US$8. Note that to use local buses you must buy a rechargeable magnetic card sold at kiosks in the centre or near bus stops (US$1.50 for card and first journey), There is also the **Rosario Norte railway station** ① *Av del Valle 2750 and Av Ovidio Lagos, operated by Ferrocentral, T0341-436 1661, www.ferrocentralsa.com.ar, ticket office Thu-Tue.* ▶▶ *For further details, see Transport, page 353.*

The main **tourist office** ① *Av Belgrano y Buenos Aires, on the riverside park down from the Monumento a la Bandera, T0341-480 2230, www.rosarioturismo.com*, has very efficient staff and hands out a free tourist card for discounts at several hotels, restaurants and other services around the city. See also www.viarosario.com (in Spanish) for the latest events information.

Background

Unlike most Spanish American cities, Rosario was never officially founded. Though a fort was established in 1689 by Luis Romero de Pineda, it was just a place to export mules and tobacco throughout the 18th century. However, it grew rapidly in the late 19th century, with the opening of a railway line to Córdoba in 1870 and the increase of shipping along the Paraná: its port became a major exporter of grain and beef, while new industries were established, including breweries, grain mills and leather industries. In the late 20th century, Rosario attracted thousands of immigrants from the northern provinces of Argentina who settled on the outskirts, later forming one of the largest deprived communities in the country.

Rosario

Where to stay
Boulevard 8
Esplendor Savoy 3
La Lechuza 1
Passers Hostel 6
Hostel Point 15
Merit Majestic 7

Punto Clave Hostel 10

Restaurants
Amarra 1
Antares 2
El Born 3
Kaffa 11

La Estancia 5
La Maltería del Siglo 4
New Taipei 6
Rock&Feller's 14
Verde Que Te Quiero
Verde 9

¡Che!

Ernesto 'Che' Guevara is one of the most recognized faces in the word, and his image can be seen on T-shirts, posters, mugs and key rings virtually everywhere you go. His is an enduring image of youthful revolutionary zeal, something he would have never predicted when he set off on his now legendary travels around South America with a friend and a beaten-up motocycle called *El Poderoso*, the powerful one.

The future revolutionary was born into a middle-class family in Rosario in 1928, but his parents soon moved with their asthmatic son to the healthier climate of the Sierras of Córdoba. The large white house at Entre Ríos y Urquiza where he lived the first two years of his life is now an insurance company. You can visit the house where the family lived in Alta Gracia (see page 164). After growing up in a small town, his eyes were soon opened to the plight of South America's poor during his famous journey around the continent documented in his book *The Motorcycle Diaries*, which is a recommended and entertaining read. Rather than pursue a career in medicine, he decided mid-trip to dedicate the rest of his life to the fight for the 'liberation of the American continent'.

In 1956 he met Fidel Castro in Mexico and together they planned to create the ideal Socialist model in Cuba, as well as establish links with other sympathetic nations. His overriding ambition had always been to spread the revolutionary word, and take the armed struggle to other parts. So he began his fight in Bolivia. After spending a little time in La Paz, he then travelled to a guerrilla base at Nanchuazú. However, the constant movements of the group aroused the suspicion of neighbours and the army were alerted. The group fled and spent several months wandering the steep valleys of eastern Bolivia. In August 1967, the small group was ambushed by Bolivian troops and Ernesto Guevara was executed, photographed and buried in an unmarked grave, aged just 39. In 1997 his body was exhumed and taken to Cuba. The name 'Che' was given to him as a form of reverence. Che in Argentina roughly translates as 'mate' or 'buddy', and is used by friends and family.

Places in Rosario

The old city centre is on the Plaza 25 de Mayo, just a block south of the Parque a la Bandera which lies along the riverside. Around it are the cathedral, in somewhat eclectic style and containing the *Virgen del Rosario*, and the Palacio Municipal. On the north side is the **Museo de Arte Decorativo** ① *Santa Fe 748, T0341-480 2547, museo@ museoestevez.gov.ar, Wed-Sun 0900-1400, in winter to 1700, US$0.50,* a sumptuous former family residence housing a valuable private collection of paintings, furniture, tapestries, sculptures, and silver, brought mainly from Europe. To the left of the cathedral, the **Pasaje Juramento** is the pedestrian access to the imposing **Monumento a la Bandera** ① *T0341-480 2238, www.monumentoalabandera.gov.ar, Mon 1400-1800, Tue-Fri 0900-1800, Sat-Sun 0900-1230, 1400-1800, US$0.65 (tower),* *free (Salón de las Banderas)*, an impressively large monument built on the site where General Belgrano raised the Argentine flag for the first time in 1812. The tower has a vantage point 70 m high with excellent panoramic views over the city and the river.

From Plaza 25 de Mayo, Calle Córdoba leads west towards Plaza San Martín and the **Paseo del Siglo**, the largest concentration of late 19th- and early 20th-century buildings in the city. The palm-lined **Boulevard Oroño** leads north to the riverside parks, the Rosario Norte railway station and south to the **Pichincha district**, popular for nightlife, and to **Parque Independencia** at the south end. This beautiful 126-ha park was designed by the landscape architect Charles Thays. It has a large lake, gardens with fountains and fine statues, shady avenues and the Newell's Old Boys football club stadium. There are also three museums in the area.

Just outside the park, the **Museo de Bellas Artes J B Castagnino** ① *Av Pellegrini 2202, T0341-480 2542, www.museocastagnino.org.ar, Wed-Mon 1400-2000, US$1*, is considered one of the best fine arts museums in the country, with a large collection of European paintings, particularly French Impressionist, Italian Baroque and Flemish works, and one of the best collections of paintings and sculpture by renowned Argentine artists.

Next to the stadium is the **Museo Histórico Provincial** ① *Av Pellegrini and Oroño, T0341-472 1457, www.museomarc.gob.ar, Tue-Fri 0900-1800, Sat 1400-1900, free*, which has a very well displayed collection of Latin American aboriginal artefacts and valuable pieces of religious art including Cuzco-school paintings and a magnificent altar covered with silver plaques, which was used by Pope John Paul II in 1987.

The riverside is lined with several parks, making it a very attractive place to walk. Eight blocks south of the Monumento a la Bandera is an open-air theatre, **Parque Urquiza** ① *T0341-480 2533, shows on Sun 2000, museum open Sat-Sun 1730-2030, US$0.40*, and the **Complejo Astronómico Municipal** with an observatory, a planetarium and a small science museum.

Further north is the **Estación Fluvial** where boats leave for excursions around the islands and where you'll find the **Museo del Paraná y las Islas** ① *T0341-440 0751, Wed-Sun 1600-1930, US$1*, which gives an insight into islander culture through local art and artefacts. At the foot of the monument is the **Parque a la Bandera**, one of the most appealing parks, and the tourist office, beyond which is the **Parque de España**, a modern red-brick development which incorporates the old railway arches as an exhibition centre and offers fine views over the Río Paraná. Further up the river is the fantastic **Museo de Arte Contemporáneo** (MACRO) ① *Blvd Ortoño on the river shore, T0341-480 4981, www.macromuseo.org.ar, Thu-Tue 1400-2000, US$1*. Located inside a massive old silo, this remarkable museum is 10 levels high with one small gallery on each level, and at the top is a viewing deck. Highly recommended.

On Sunday afternoons there is a great craft, antiques and vintage-clothing market along the river starting at Boulevard Ortoño. It's great fun and less crowded than Buenos Aires' markets.

The most popular destinations for locals as well as visitors are the dozens of riverside resorts on the islands and sandy banks opposite Rosario. These have restaurants and bars, and most have comfortable facilities for an enjoyable day's stay, with woods, beaches and lagoons. There are campsites and *cabañas* for rent on some of them. Boats depart daily in summer from *La Fluvial* or from *Costa Alta* to the island resorts, each with its own transfer service. Weekend services run throughout the rest of the year.

Santa Fe → *For listings, see pages 349-354. Colour map 4, A5.*

Santa Fe is capital of its province and one of the oldest cities in the country, though there's little architectural evidence and this is not really a tourist destination. It lies near the confluence of the Santa Fe and Salado rivers in a low-lying area with lagoons and islands just west of the Río Paraná and was severely flooded in May 2003, one of Argentina's most shocking disasters. It is connected to the smaller city of Paraná, on the east bank of the river, by road bridges and a tunnel.

Arriving in Santa Fe → *Phone code 0342. Population 525,093.*

The airport, **Sauce Viejo** ① *T0342-499 5064*, is located 17 km south of the centre; a taxi to the bus terminal costs US$6. The **bus terminal** ① *Belgrano 2910, T0342-457 4124*, is near to the centre. It has luggage lockers and a **tourist office** ① *T0342-457 4124, 0700-2000 (0800 at weekends)*. There are additional information offices opposite the **Teatro Municipal** ① *San Martín 2020; also at Bulevar Gálvez 1150 and Santiago del Estero 3100, T0800-777 5000, www.santafeturismo.gov.ar*, all good. **Provincial office** ① *San Martín 1399, T0342-458 9475, www.turismosantafe.com.ar*.

Places in Santa Fe

The city's **commercial centre** lies a few blocks southwest of the bus terminal, along the partially pedestrianized San Martín. This street leads southwards to the historic centre, around Plaza 25 de Mayo, with the oldest buildings and a few museums.

On the plaza itself is the majestic **Casa de Gobierno**, built in 1911-1917 in French style on the site of the historic cabildo, in which the 1853 constitution was drafted. Opposite is the **cathedral**, dating from 1751 but remodelled in 1834, its twin towers capped by blue-tiled cupolas.

Across San Martín, southeast of the plaza, is the extensive Parque General Belgrano. The **Museo Histórico Provincial** ① *San Martín 1490, T0342-457 3529, all year 0830-1230, afternoon hours change frequently, closed Mon, free*, is in a former family house dating from 1690 (one of the oldest surviving civil buildings in the country). It's worth visiting for the house itself rather than the exhibition of two 17th-century Cuzco-school paintings. About 100 m south is the **Iglesia y Convento de San Francisco** built between 1673 and 1695. The church has walls nearly 2 m thick and fine wooden ceilings, built from timber floated down the river from Paraguay, carved by indigenous craftsmen and fitted without the use of nails. The pulpit and altar are 17th-century baroque.

On the opposite side of the park is the superb **Museo Etnográfico y Colonial** ① *25 de Mayo 1470, Tue-Fri 0830-1200, 1530-2030, Sat-Sun from 1530, 1600 or 1730 depending on season, US$0.50*, with a chronologically ordered exhibition of artefacts from aboriginal inhabitants from 2000 BC to the first Spanish settlers who lived in

Santa Fe la Vieja, the town's original site. The most remarkable objects are delicate zoomorphic ceramic pots, Spanish amulets and board games, and a model of both Santa Fe towns, showing that the distribution of the main buildings remained unchanged after the move.

Paraná → *For listings, see pages 349-354. Colour map 4, A5.*

Capital of Entre Ríos province, Paraná stands on the eastern bank of a bend in the Río Paraná, opposite Santa Fe. Its centre lies on a hill offering fine views over the river, and if you're travelling up the Paraná river, it is a good place to stop on a journey north. It was founded in 1649, when Santa Fe was moved from its original spot and settlers crossed the river in search of higher ground for cultivation, and a suitable port. In the mid-19th century it gained importance as capital of the Argentine Confederation and a subsequent period of growth left some sumptuous public buildings. The city's faded splendour creates a quiet, rather melancholic atmosphere but there is an appealingly calm pace of life here. For more information, see www.turismoparana.com.ar.

Arriving in Paraná → *Phone code 0343. Population: 339,930 (department).*
Getting there and around From Santa Fe, the road goes under the Río Paraná by the Hernandarias tunnel (toll) and then crosses a number of bridges to reach Paraná (bus service, US$3, 50 minutes). The bus terminal ⓘ *Av Ramírez 2598, T0343-422 1282,* is 10 blocks southeast of Plaza Primero de Mayo. Leave the small plaza on your right and take Avenida Echagüe right to the centre, or buses No 1, 6, US$1. A remise taxi will cost US$8. Left-luggage facilities are available Monday to Saturday 0700-2300, and Sunday 0800-1200, 1730-2300.

The city can easily be visited on foot, since the most interesting sights lie around the two main plazas, Plaza 1 de Mayo and, three blocks north, Plaza Alvear.

Tourist information Paraná has four city tourist offices (all open daily 0800-2000): in the centre at ⓘ *Buenos Aires 132, T0343-423 0183;* at the bus terminal ⓘ *T0343-420 1862;* at Parque Urquiza ⓘ *Av Laurencena and Juan de San Martín, on the east side, T0343-420 1837;* and at the Hernandarias tunnel. There is also a provincial tourist office ⓘ *Laprida 5, T0810-444 8874,* www.unatierradiferente.com.

Places in Paraná
From Plaza Alvear, Avenida Rivadavia leads to the beautiful **Parque Urquiza** and the riverside. Though nothing remains from the colonial period, the city retains many fine 19th- and 20th-century public buildings, centred around Plaza Primero de Mayo. On the east side is the impressive **cathedral**, built in 1883 in Italianate neoclassical style, with a fine dome and colonnaded portico, though the interior is plain. Also on the plaza are the **Municipalidad** (1890), with its distinctive tower, and the **Club Social** (1906), for years the elite social centre of the city. Take pedestrianized San Martín half a block west of the corner with 25 de Junio to see

the fine **Teatro 3 de Febrero** (1908). Two blocks north is the **Plaza Alvear**, and opposite one of its corners, the provincial tourist office (see above). On the same block is the mildly engaging **Museo Histórico Martiniano Leguizamón** ⓘ *Laprida and Buenos Aires, T0343-420 7869, Tue-Fri 0800-1200, 1600-2000, Sat 0930-1200, 1630-1900, Sun 0930-1200, US$1.*

On the west side of the plaza is the **Museo de Bellas Artes** ⓘ *Buenos Aires 355, T0343-420 7868, Tue-Fri 0700-1300, 1500-1900, Sat 1000-1400, 1700-2000, Sun 1000-1300, US$0.75*, housing a vast collection of Argentine artists, with many works by painter Cesáreo Bernaldo de Quirós. On the north side of the plaza is the **Museo de Ciencias Naturales y Antropológicas** ⓘ *Carlos Gardel 62, T0343-420 8894, Tue-Sat 0830-1230, 1500-1900, Sun 0930-1230, US$1*, particularly appealing for kids, with an insect collection (see the 25-cm-wide moth), and lots of stuffed animals. Among fascinating artefacts by Guaraní people are a rare ornate urn, with red geometrical paintings, and small utensils made by groups of indigenous peoples to the north, and a rather alarming display of jars containing human foetuses, from five weeks to six months old.

From the northwestern corner of the plaza, it's a pleasant stroll along tree-lined Avenida Rivadavia, with the monumental **Escuela del Centenario** (1910) ⓘ *Av Rivadavia 168*, to reach the city's pride and joy, the **Parque Urquiza**. Extending along the low cliffs of the Paraná River, with wonderful views and many fine statues, the park is well planted with *lapachos*, *palos borrachos* and pines. There's an open-air theatre, and steps to the Avenida Costanera. The cobbled street **Bajada de los Vascos**, which in the 19th century gave access to the port area, is now known as Puerto Viejo and retains some original buildings. The Avenida Costanera is lively, with restaurants, sports clubs and sandy beaches on the river.

North of Paraná → *For listings, see pages 349-354.*

Heading north from Paraná along the Río Paraná, you can take monotonous Route 11 to Resistencia on the western bank, or Route 12 north to Corrientes, which closely follows the eastern banks of the river through varied landscapes giving access to two attractive small towns on the coast with good fishing: Santa Elena and La Paz, and a marvellous traditional *estancia*, **Vizcacheras** ⓘ *www.vizcacheras.com.ar*.

Santa Elena → *Phone code 03437. Population 18,000.*

Santa Elena lies on the Río Paraná about 150 km north of the provincial capital. It is a small port whose fishing attracts many anglers. Its history is closely associated with its meat-packing factory, which was run by British firms from the late 19th century until it closed down in 1993. The red-brick buildings of the *frigorífico* can still be seen in town. At the end of the *costanera* is the Paseo La Olla, with beautiful views over the river. There is a tourist office ⓘ *Eva Perón y 9 de Julio, T03437-481223.*

La Paz → *Colour map 4, A5. Phone code 03437. Population 22,700.*

La Paz, 168 km north of Paraná, is a small port in an area popular for fishing, where the fishing festivals **Fiesta Provincial del Surubí** and **Fiesta Provincial del Dorado** are held respectively every April and September. The undulating terrain and the cliffs above the river make a picturesque setting for the old houses still standing in the town. The tourist office ① *Vieytes and España, T03437-422389*, can provide information on accommodation at a few nearby *estancias*.

There is a a small history museum at the Parque Berón de Astrada, from where there are fine views, while another park, the **Parque de la Aventura**, has trails along the riverside for walking or cycling. Access is on the way to La Armonía, reached by Bulevar 25 de Mayo and then Yrigoyen.

Corrientes → *For listings, see pages 349-354. Colour map 1, B6.*

Capital of its province, Corrientes lies some 30 km southwest of the meeting of the rivers Paraná and Paraguay. The city is mainly a service centre for its agricultural hinterland, which produces beef, cotton, tobacco, rice and *yerba mate*. Although Corrientes is a less important transport hub than Resistencia, it is a pleasant place for a stopover. The city centre, with its peaceful traditional streets and squares, is well preserved and its *costanera* is one of the most attractive in the country. The national capital of Carnival, the city is also famous as the location of Graham Greene's novel *The Honorary Consul*. In summer the air can be oppressively hot and humid, but in winter the climate is pleasant.

Arriving in Corrientes → *Phone code 0379. Population 356,310.*

Dr Fernando Piragine Niveyro (Cambá Punta) Airport ① *T0379-445 8684*, is 10 km east of the city and is reached by Route 12 (remise US$5.) The bus terminal ① *Av Maipú 2700, T0379-447 7600*, is 5 km southeast of the centre. Bus No 103 goes to the centre (but check with the driver as the same line has many different routes), 20 mins, US$1. A left-luggage facility is available at the Crucero del Norte office. See Transport, below, for details.

The city tourist office ① *Carlos Pellegrini 542, T0379-442 3779, daily 0700-2100, www.ciudaddecorrientes.gov.ar*, provides a good map. There is also a provincial office ① *25 de Mayo 1330, T0379-442 7200, Mon-Fri 0700-1300, and in the bus station, T0379-441 4839, 0700-2200, www.corrientes.gov.ar*.

Background

Corrientes was founded in 1588 on the Paraná river, next to seven relatively high *puntas*, or promontories, by an expedition from Asunción, led by Juan Torres de Vera y Aragón. It became important as a port on the route between Buenos Aires and Asunción. Numerous shipyards led to the development of a naval industry that endured for centuries. The Guaraní population that inhabited the region were mainly absorbed into the Jesuit missions or became workers for the *estancias*. They progressively mixed with the Spanish newcomers giving the local society a distinctive character, still evident today in the faces of the inhabitants, and also in the daily use of Guaraní words and a particular accent in spoken Spanish.

Places in Corrientes

The main Plaza 25 de Mayo, one block inland from the *costanera*, is a beautiful shady space. You could take a pleasant stroll from here around the surrounding blocks, with their fine old houses and river views, and to the Avenida Costanera. On the north side of the plaza is the **Jefatura de Policía**, built in 19th-century French style. The **Museo de Artesanías** ① *Quintana 905, Mon-Fri 0800-1200, 1600-2000, free*, is a large old house with an exhibition of handicrafts made from the most diverse materials imaginable, by indigenous groups, as well as by contemporary urban and rural artisans. Tiny skeleton-shaped images represent San La Muerte, a popular devotion that ensures the bearer a painless death. A large room at the front is a workshop where you can watch the patient work of the local craftspeople. On the east side of the plaza are the Italianate **Casa de Gobierno** (1881-1886) and the **Ministerio de Gobierno**. On the south side is the church **La Merced**, where there are confessionals carved by the indigenous inhabitants of Misiones in the mid-18th century, and a colonial-style altar. The **Casa Lagraña**, a huge building with three interior patios, built in 1860 for the governor, lies one block south. At 9 de Julio 1044 is the **Museo Histórico** ① *Tue-Fri 0800-1200, 1600-2000, free*, displaying, among other pieces, a collection of religious objects dating from the 18th and 19th centuries. Only two blocks north is the **Teatro Juan de Vera** ① *San Juan 637, T03783-4427743*, a lively cultural centre and a beautiful building itself (1913). Across the road is the **Museo de Bellas Artes** ① *San Juan 634, www.museovidalctes.es.tl, Mon-Fri 0800-2030, free*, a small arts museum with temporary exhibitions and a permanent collection including valuable works by the painters Petorutti, Fader and Quinquela Martín. The quite impressive **Iglesia y Convento de San Francisco** ① *Mendoza 468*, was rebuilt in 1861 on the site of the original which dated from 1608. Six blocks south of the Plaza 25 de Mayo is the leafy Plaza de la Cruz and opposite, the church of **La Cruz de los Milagros**, whichhouses the Santo Madero. This miraculous cross was placed by the founder of the city, and when the indigenous residents tried to burn it, they were allegedly killed by lightning from a cloudless sky. Near the plaza, the **Museo de Ciencias Naturales 'Amadeo Bonpland'** ① *San Martín 850, Mon-Sat 0900-1200, 1600-2000*, has a large archaeology collection and plants with a remarkable display of 5800 insects including a huge wasp nest.

The attractive Avenida Costanera, lined with *lapachos* and *palos borrachos*, leads along the Río Paraná from its southwestern end, next to the bridge, to **Parque Mitre**, from where there are good views of sunsets over the river.

For hotel and restaurant price codes and other relevant information, see pages 20-26.

● Where to stay

Rosario *p340, map p341*
Rosario has a good range of business hotels (including 4 in the Solans group, www.solans.com) and a number of hostels at the budget end.

$$$ Esplendor Savoy Rosario, San Lorenzo 1022, T0341-448 0071, www.esplendorsavoyrosario.com. Early 20th-century mansion, once Rosario's best, now completely remodelled as a luxury hotel with all modern services. Gym, business centre, Wi-Fi, etc.

$$$ Merit Majestic, San Lorenzo 980, T0341-440 5872, www.amerian.com. Modern, inviting 3-star, well designed rooms in an ornate turn-of-the-century building, stylish.

$$$-$$ Boulevard, San Lorenzo 2194, T0341-447 5795, www.hotelboulevard.com.ar. Small 1920s house, tastefully renovated as a charming B&B with doubles and triples. Recommended.

$ Hostel Point, Catamarca 1837, T0341-440 9337, www.hostelpoint.com.ar. Central, nicely designed, brightly coloured dorms (US$10.55-11.25) and a lovely double. Recommended.

$ pp La Lechuza, San Lorenzo 1786, T0341-424 1040, www.lalechuzahostel.com.ar. Welcoming, sociable hostel with helpful owner, dorms from US$10.55, private rooms **$$**, with bar, central.

$ pp Passers Hostel, 1 Mayo 1117, T0341-440 4590, www.passershostel.com.ar. Funky wallpaper and furniture, spacious dorms. Only a few metres from the Monumento a la Bandera.

$ pp Punto Clave, Ituzaingó 246, T0341-481 9569, www.puntoclavehostel.com.ar. A fun, cheerful hostel with helpful owner. Large dorms and, a comfortable common area with big bean bags. Recommended.

Sante Fe *p344*
$$$-$$ Hostal Santa Fe de la Veracruz, San Martín 2954, T0342-455 1740, www.hostalsf.com. Traditional favourite, 2 types of room, both good value, large breakfast, restaurant, sauna (extra).

$$ Castelar, 25 de Mayo 2349, T0342-456 0999, www.castelarsantafe.com.ar. On a small plaza, 1930's hotel, good value, comfortable, breakfast included, restaurant.

Paraná *p345*
$$$ Gran Hotel Paraná, Urquiza 976, T0343-422 3900, www.hotelesparana.com.ar. Overlooking Plaza Primero de Mayo, 3 room categories, smart restaurant **La Fourchette**, gym.

$$ San Jorge, Belgrano 368, T0343-422 1685, www.sanjorgehotel.com.ar. Renovated rooms, helpful staff, older rooms are cheaper than the modern ones at the back.

$$-$ Paraná Hostel, Andrés Pazos 159, T0343-422 8233, www.paranahostel.com.ar. Small, central, nice living room with cable TV and comfy sofas. Smart dorms and private rooms available. Best budget option in the area.

Santa Elena *p346*
$$$$ Estancia Vizcacheras, R12, Km 554.5, T011-4719 5613 (in Buenos Aires), www.vizcacheras.com.ar. South of Santa Elena, the *estancia* was built in the early 1900s by the Bovril company in British colonial-style with Argentine

touches. The owners are extremely hospitable, making guests feel at home in luxuriously furnished bedrooms, all with their own bathroom (some with old fashioned baths) and private verandas. Have drinks on the terrace with splendid views of the gardens and the grasslands beyond, and delicious dinner served under the stars. You'll be invited to see the daily routines of the working cattle ranch, with walking and horse riding, fishing and birdwatching also arranged. Highly recommended.

La Paz p347
$$ Milton, Italia 1029, T03437-422232, www. miltonhotel.com.ar. Central, with comfortable-enough rooms. A/c and breakfast extra.
$$ Posta Surubí, España 180, T03437-421128,www.postasurubi.com.ar. Nicely located by the river with good rooms and fine views. Has a restaurant. Breakfast included.

Corrientes p347
$$$ La Alondra, 2 de Abril 827, T03783-443 0555, www.laalondra.com.ar. The best place to stay in town. 7 beautiful rooms and a wonderful communal area. Antique furniture throughout, exquisite styling and a homely feel. Lovely patio and 12-m pool.
$ pp Bienvenida Golondrina, La Rioja 455, T03783-443 5316, http:// bvngolondrina.blogspot.com. The only hostel in the city. Half a block from the port, in a carefully remodelled old building. Bright dorms, cheaper with fan, private rooms (**$$**), a roof-top terrace and lots of internal patios to relax in.

⊕ Restaurants

Rosario p340, map p341
$$$ Escauriza, Bajada Escauriza y Paseo Ribereño, La Florida, 30 mins' drive from centre, near bridge over the Paraná, T0341-454 1777. Said to be the "oldest and best" fish restaurant, with terrace overlooking the river.
$$ Amarra, Av Belgrano y Buenos Aires, T0341-447 7550. Good food, including fish and seafood, quite formal, cheap set menus Mon-Fri noon.
$$ La Estancia, Av Pellegrini 1510 y Paraguay. Typical good *parrilla* that's popular with locals, a few blocks east of Parque Independencia.
$$ Rock & Feller's, Blvd N Oroño 106, T0341-423 4002, http://rockandfellers. com.ar. Popular American-style restobar serving upmarket international fare including Tex-Mex options. Rock 'n' roll theme. Popular at night.
$ New Taipei, Laprida 1121. Decent Chinese food for a change from the usual Argentine fare.

Cafés
Kaffa, Córdoba 1473. Good coffee served inside the large bookshop **El Ateneo Yenny**.
La Maltería del Siglo, Santa Fe 1601. Daily for food, drinks and background music. Livens up when major football matches are on.
Verde que te quiero Verde, Córdoba 1358. Open 0800-2100, closed Sun. Great vegetarian café, serving a fantastic brunch and lots of good veggie options. Recommended.
Victoria, Jujuy and Blvd Oroño. One of the oldest cafés in town and the most traditional.

Sante Fe *p344*
Many places in the centre close on Sun.
$$ El Quincho de Chiquito, Av Almirante
Brown y Obispo Príncipe (Costanera
Oeste). Classic fish restaurant, excellent
food, generous helpings and good value.
$$ España, San Martín 2644. An elegant
place, specializing in seafood and fish.
$ El Brigadier, San Martín 1670. This
colonial-style place next to the Plaza 25
de Mayo serves superb *surubí al paquete*
(stuffed fish) and many *parrilla* dishes.
$ Club Sirio Libanés, 25 de Mayo 2740.
Very good Middle Eastern food, popular
Sun lunch for families.

Cafés
Las Delicias, Hipólito Yrigoyen and San
Martín. A well-preserved, early 20th-
century café and bakery, with beautiful
decor, serving a wide variety of coffees
and sweet pastries. Try their speciality,
the *alfajorsantafesino*.
Tokio, Rivadavia y Crespo (on Plaza
España). Another café with a rich history
in Santa Fe.

Paraná *p345*
$$ Giovani, Urquiza 1047. A popular
place in the centre, good for pasta.
$$ La Fourchette, Urquiza 976 (at
Gran Hotel Paraná). The finest
restaurant in town is a small, stylish
place. Choose from a small menu
of really fine dishes. Perfect for a
sophisticated, intimate dinner.
$ Club de Pescadores, access from
Av Estrada at Puerto Viejo. Another
good traditional fish restaurant in the
old and picturesque section of the port.
$ Coscoino, Corrientes 373. A relaxed
family establishment serving good
and very filling home-made pastas,
tenedor libre, except Sat evenings
and Sun lunchtime.

$ El Viejo Marino, Av Laurencena 339,
the opposite end of Av Costanera.
Well-prepared fish dishes.
$ Playa, Av Costanera (at **Club Atlético
Estudiantes**). Nicely situated on a sandy
beach with fine views of the river. A good
place for fish such as *surubí*, *boga* or
pejerrey (caught upstream in Corrientes
or Misiones).

Corrientes *p347*
$ Martha de Bianchetti, 9 de Julio y
Mendoza. Smart café and bakery.
Panambí, Junín near Córdoba.
A traditional, central *confitería*, serving
good pastries and regional breads.

Bars and clubs

Rosario *p340, map p341*
Bars
Antares, Callao 286, T0341-437 0945.
Daily 1830. A good choice of own label
beers, happy hour, serves food.
El Born, Pellegrini 1574. Daily 0800-0300,
from 1800 Sat-Sun. Tapas bar, also has a
clothes shop.
Piluso, Catamarca and Alvear. A lively
meeting point at night, also open during
the day.
Roots Reggae Bar, Pte Roca 1051. This
lively place is owned by the people who
run the HI hostel in town. Good music,
always busy.

Sante Fe *p344*
Santa Fe has a long tradition of brewing
and is one of the few places where local
lagers can compete with the big national
monopoly, Quilmes. Beer is usually sold in
a *liso* (not a very large glass). There are lively
areas of bars and nightclubs, popular with
young crowds, all along the Costanera Este;
beyond the bridge on Laguna Setúbal;
in the Recoleta district, north of centre;

🎭 Entertainment

Rosario *p340, map p341*
A good listings guide can be found in
a section of the daily paper *Pagina 12*:
Rosario 12, as well as www.viarosario.com.

Cinema
In the centre there are cinemas in the
shopping malls, **Del Siglo**, Córdoba y
Presidente Roca, www.shoppingdelsiglo.
com, and **Alto Rosario**, Caning y Junín,
www.alto-rosario.com.ar; also **El Cairo**,
Santa Fe 1120.

Cultural centres
Centro Cultural Bernardino Rivadavia,
San Martín 1080, T0341-480 2401. A large
centre holding year-round art exhibitions,
video screenings, plays, music shows,
seminars and puppet shows.
Centro Cultural Parque de España,
on Parque de España, T0341-426 0941,
www.ccpe.org.ar. Shows temporary art
exhibitions, photography and plays at the
Teatro Príncipe de Asturias.
**Centro de Expresiones
Contemporáneas**, Sargento Cabral
y El Río (on the riverside, opposite
Ex Aduana building), T0341-480 2245,
www.cecrosario.org.ar. A large
warehouse with almost daily music,
theatre and cinema events.

Theatre
De la Comedia, Cortada Ricardone
y Mitre, T0341-480 2597, www.
teatrolacomedia.com.ar; **El Círculo**,
Laprida 1235, T0341-424 5349, www.
teatro-elcirculo.com.ar; **Lavarden**,
Mendoza and Sarmiento, T0341-472
1462, www.plataformalavarden.com.ar.

⚜ Festivals

Rosario *p340, map p341*
20 Jun Día de la Bandera Nacional.
It is worth going to the Monumento
a la Bandera for the swearing-in
ceremony made by hundreds of
school pupils to the country's flag.
Nov Fiesta de las Colectividades.
Every year during Nov at the Parque
a la Bandera (opposite the monument)
the town celebrates the diverse origins
of the inhabitants, offering food, folk
music and dancing.

Corrientes *p347*
Feb Carnival, www.carnaval.com/
argentina/corrientes/. This has been
one of the most popular celebrations for
decades in Argentina and is celebrated
on Fri and Sat evenings throughout Feb
at the Corsódromo. This stadium lies a
little distance from the centre reached by
bus No 105 along 9 de Julio. The colourful
parade opens the competition among
the different *comparsas*, passionately
supported by the audience as football
teams. Tickets are not sold in the stadium,
but in many shops in the centre.
Dec/Jan Chamamé Festival,
www.corrienteschamame.com.ar.
The regional music *chamamé* has
its own festival in Corrientes at
Anfiteatro Tránsito Cocomarola, Barrio
1000 Viviendas, 10 blocks south of Av 3
de Abril. This cheerful music is danced
in couples with the upper body close,
legs far apart. Join in!

🛍 Shopping

Rosario *p340, map p341*
The main shopping street is the
pedestrianized Córdoba.

Books

Balcarce, San Nicolas 650, a massive place for second-hand books and vinyl records; **El Ateneo**, Córdoba 1473; **Stratford**, Santa Fe 1340, sells English books.

Markets

Feria del Boulevard, Blvd Oroño and Rivadavia. A weekend handicraft market.
Mercado de Pulgas, next to the tourist office on the riverside. Flea market at weekends,
Mercado Retro La Huella, Av del Valle and Callao (next to Rosario Norte railway station in Pichincha district). Every Sun and bank holiday there is a large flea market.

Outdoor gear

Central de Pesca, San Juan 1089; **El Combatiente**, San Martín 816.

Shopping malls

Alto Rosario, Caning and Junín, www.alto-rosario.com.ar, an impressive mall; **Del Siglo**, Córdoba and Presidente Roca; **Palace Garden**, Córdoba 1358.

⏰ What to do

Rosario *p340, map p341*
Swimming
On Laguna Setúbal, from El Espigón; at the **Club de Regatas**, next to the bridge; or from Piedras Blancas on Costanera Este.

Tour operators
For city tours check agencies at **Asociación Rosarina de Agencias de Viaje**, T0341-421 3554, www.arav.org.ar. **Barco Ciudad de Rosario**, T0341-449 8688, www.barcocr1.com. A large passenger boat leaves from the pier next to Estación Fluvial for 2-hr excursions on the river on weekend afternoons.

Paraná *p345*
Tour operators
Costanera 241, Buenos Aires 212, T0343-423 4385, www.costanera241.com. City tours and boat excursions on the Paraná river.

🚌 Transport

Rosario *p340, map p341*
Air
Daily flights to **Buenos Aires**.

Bus
To **Buenos Aires**, 4 hrs, US$22-26.
To **Córdoba**, 6 hrs, US$30-33.50.
To **Santa Fe**, 2½ hrs, US$10-11.

Train
To **Buenos Aires**, Wed 1115 and Sat 1408, US$2.75, US$3.75 and US$6.75; to **Tucumán**, Mon and Fri 1455.

Sante Fe *p344*
Air
Daily flights to and from **Buenos Aires**.

Bus
To **Córdoba**, US$25-32, 5 hrs. Many buses to **Buenos Aires**, US$31-36, 6 hrs; to **Paraná**, frequent service, US$4.50, 50 mins.

Paraná *p345*
Bus
To **Colón** on Río Uruguay, 4-5 hrs, US$10. To **Buenos Aires**, 7-8 hrs, US$34.50-40.

Corrientes *p347*
Air
Flights to/from Buenos Aires.

Bus
To **Resistencia**, 1 hr, US$3-5. To **Posadas** US$16-27, 3½-4 hrs, several companies. To **Buenos Aires**, several companies,

11-12 hrs, US$63-71. **Sol**, **NS de la Asunción** and **El Pulqui** run Corrientes–Resistencia–**Asunción** (Paraguay), US$25.

❶ Directory

Rosario *p340, map p341*
Banks Many banks along C Córdoba, east of plaza San Martín. **Bike hire and repair** Bike House, San Juan 973, T0341-424 5280, info@bikehouse.com.ar. **Bike Rosario**, Zeballos 327, T0341-15-5713812, www.bikerosario.com.ar, Sebastián Clérico. Bike rental (US$11.50 per day), bike tours, also kayak trips. **Speedway Bike Center**, Roca 1269, T0341-426 8415, info@speedwaybikecenter.com.ar.

Sante Fe *p344*
Banks Banking district around San Martín and Tucumán. **Currency exchange** Columbia, San Martín 2601;

Tourfe, San Martín 2500. **Post office** Mendoza 2430, Western Union branch.

Paraná *p345*
Banks Banco de la Nación, San Martín 1000; Banco Francés, San Martín 763; Banco Río, Pellegrini 29. **Medical services** Hospital San Martín, Perón 450, T0343-4234545. **Post office** 25 de Mayo and Monte Caseros, Western Union branch.

Corrientes *p347*
Banks Bank Boston, San Juan y Carlos Pellegrini; Banco de la Nación, 9 de Julio y Córdoba. **Currency exchange** El Dorado, 9 de Julio 1343, Western Union branch. **Emergencies** Medical emergencies: T107; Police T101. **Medical services** Hospital Escuela General San Martín, Rivadavia 1250, T03783-430113; Sanatorio del Norte, Carlos Pellegrini 1354, T0370-441 0410.

The Argentine Chaco

Little visited by travellers, the Argentine Chaco is just part of an immense sprawling lowland some 900 km wide, covering half of Paraguay and huge areas of Bolivia and Brazil. Rising gently from east to west, it's crossed by meandering rivers, and filled in central parts with cattle and cotton fields, soya and sunflowers. Though much of the Chaco is inaccessible, with little public transport, and rough roads that become almost impassable after heavy rains, two national parks can easily be reached all year round, both hosting a rich diversity of wildlife largely uninterrupted by human activity: Parque Nacional Chaco reached from Resistencia, and Parque Nacional Río Pilcomayo reached from Formosa. These are the region's two main cities, both close to Río Paraguay; the only other settlement is Presidencia Roque Sáenz Peña, 170 km northwest of Resistencia, it's an uninspiring place though its thermal waters are among the country's finest.

The most fascinating aspect of the Chaco is its pure and extensive indigenous population. Two of the largest groups are the Qom/Toba, mainly settled in towns next to the Paraná River, and the semi-nomadic Wichí in the west, who maintain their traditions of fine weaving, woodwork and ancient fishing techniques. For more information, see www.chacoturismo.com. For introductory articles see http://pueblos-originarios-argetnina.wikispaces.com/, http://pocnolec.blogspot.co.uk/ and www.chacolinks.org.uk.

Arriving in the Argentine Chaco

Getting there From Resistencia and Formosa, parallel Routes 16 and 81 head dead straight northwest across the plains until they encounter the first hills of eastern Salta, which mark the border of this vast territory. Buses to Salta take Route 16; Route 81 has long unpaved sections west of the small town of Las Lomitas, making the journey tough going after heavy rains.

Background

The Chaco falls into two distinct zones along a line south of the boundary between Chaco and Formosa provinces: the Wet Chaco and the Dry Chaco. The **Wet Chaco** spreads south from the Río Pilcomayo (the border with Paraguay) and west of the Río Paraguay, and consists of fertile wetlands supporting rich farming and abundant vegetation, and marshlands with savanna and groves of *Caranday* palms, hosting many species of bird. Further west, as rainfall diminishes, the **Dry Chaco** is arid and wild, with little plant or, indeed, human life. The scrub vegetation is dotted with the algarrobo trees, white quebracho, the spiny bloated trunks of palo borracho and various types of cacti. This is one of the hottest places in South America and is sometimes known as 'El Impenetrable'.

Resistencia and around → *For listings, see pages 360-361. Colour map 1, B6.*

The hot and energetic capital of the Province of Chaco, Resistencia – together with the port of Barranqueras, just to the south on the Río Paraná – is the commercial centre for the Chaco region. It's a modern city, not architecturally rich, but boasting an impressive number of sculptures by renowned artists, earning it the title of 'city of statues'. There's also a splendid central plaza, a nature reserve and the lovely **Isla del Cerrito** within easy reach, making it an appealing alternative stopover to neighbouring Corrientes on the journey between Iguazú and Salta.

Arriving in Resistencia → *Phone code 0362. Population 386,390.*
The **airport** ① *T0362-444 6009*, is 8 km west of town (taxi US$3. The modern **bus terminal** ① *Av Malvinas Argentinas and Av MacLean, T0362-446 1098*, is on the western outskirts; bus 3 or 10 runs to/from Oro y Perón, one block west of plaza (20 minutes, US$1); *remise* US$5. Left luggage is open 24 hours.

The main Plaza 25 de Mayo is where you'll find the **city tourist office** ① *T0362-445 8289, Mon-Fri 0800-2000*. If they can't give you a map try the **provincial tourist office** ① *Av Sarmiento 1675, T0362-443 8880, www.chaco.travel, Mon-Fri 0800-1300, 1400-2000, Sat 0800-1200*, where you can also get information on other destinations.

Places in Resistencia

The large Plaza 25 de Mayo occupies four blocks in the centre of the city, with a variety of indigenous plants and palms turning it into a mini botanical garden.
Five blocks from here, there's an informal cultural centre, **Fogón de los Arrieros** (literally, 'the hearth of the muleteers') ① *Brown 350 (between López and Planes and*

French), T0362-442 6418, open to non-members Mon-Fri 0900-1200, 2100-2300, Sat 0900-1200, US$2. This rather wonderful institution was formed in the late 1960s by artists who decided to make the city an open-air gallery, with public spaces filled with sculpture and murals. The centre itself still operates as a meeting place and exhibition space: inspiring, and highly recommended. In the surrounding streets, you'll find more than 175 pieces of art by the country's finest artists.

Take López and Planes (later Sáenz Peña) and turn right at Juan B Justo to reach the **Museo del Hombre Chaqueño** ① *Juan B Justo 280, Mon-Fri 0800-1200, 1600-2000, free.* This small anthropological museum covers the story of colonization in the region, with a fine exhibition of handicrafts by native Wichi, Toba and Mocoví peoples, together with a fascinating mythology section in which small statues represent the Guaraní peoples' beliefs. Many of the rituals detailed are still practised in rural areas today and are characterized by creatures of the marsh and woodland.

Isla del Cerrito

The **Isla del Cerrito**, a beautiful island northeast of Resistencia at the confluence of the Paraná and Paraguay rivers, has a provincial nature reserve of 12,000 ha, covered mainly with grassland and palm trees. At the eastern end of the island (51 km from Resistencia), on the Río Paraná, in Cerrito, there's an attractive tourist complex with white sand beaches, a history museum, accommodation and restaurants. It all gets very busy during the **Fiesta Nacional del Dorado**, which is held on the opposite shores in Paso de la Patria.

To get to Cerrito, follow Route 16 east and turn north 3 km before the bridge to Corrientes; from here a road, the last 20 km of which are dirt (difficult after heavy rain), leads to a bridge, from where it is 17 km further to Cerrito. **Combi Arco Iris** ① *3 daily, 1 hr's journey, stopping 30 mins there, US$2,* leaves for Cerrito from bus stop at Juan B Justo and Avenida Alberdi (off Banco Hipotecario).

Parque Nacional Chaco → *Colour map 1, B6.*

The Chaco National Park, 115 km northwest of Resistencia, extends over 15,000 ha and protects one of the last remaining untouched areas of the Wet Chaco. There are exceptional *quebracho colorado* trees, *Caranday* palms and dense riverine forests, with orchids growing along the banks of the Río Negro. It is a very good place for birdwatching, with 340 species having been sighted in the park, including the parrot *loro hablador*. You're certain to be woken in the morning by the loud screams of *Carayá* monkeys, though other mammals living in the park may be less obtrusive, like the collared *peccary*, the *corzuela parda*, the puma and the *yaguarundí cat* (*Felis jaguamindi*).

Arriving in the park Access to the park is free and open 24 hours. It's best visited between April and October to avoid intense summer heat and voracious mosquitoes To get to the park from Resistencia, follow paved Route 16 northwest; after about 60 km take Route 9 north to Colonia Elisa and Capitán Solari, which lies 5 km east of the park entrance via a dirt road. La Estrella runs daily buses between Resistencia and Capitán Solari, from where *remise* taxis make the short journey to the park, which can also be done on foot. Or, if there's a group of you, call the park in advance to be picked up at Capitán Solari. For more information contact T03725-499161, chaco@apn.gov.ar.

Exploring the park At 300 m from the park's entrance there's a visitor centre and a free campsite with hot showers and electricity. Two short footpaths, *sendero del puente colgante* and *sendero del abuelo* respectively, lead to the banks of the Río Negro and to an 800-year-old specimen of the *quebracho* tree. A vehicle road goes north 6 km up to two high *mangrullos* or viewpoints, overlooking the two lakes, Laguna Carpincho and Laguna Yacaré, where, with a bit of patience, you'll see *yacarés* (alligators). Another track, suitable only for 4WD vehicles, goes south through a forest of *quebracho* trees and, after 9 km, reaches the peaceful Laguna Panza de Cabra. There is a campsite by the lake, without facilities, where you'll often hear the rare maned wolf *(aguará guazú)* at night. Tour operators run day-long excursions to the park from Resistencia.

North of Resistencia → *For listings, see pages 360-361.*

Route 11 runs north to Formosa and then onwards to the Paraguayan border near **Clorinda**, with the city of Asunción just over the border. Crossing low-lying pastures with streams and *Caranday* palms, this route offers views of the diverse birdlife of the Wet Chaco, and is beautiful in the evening.

Formosa → *Colour map 2, A1. Phone code 0370. Population 233,028.*
Formosa is the capital of its province and the only Argentine port of any note on the Río Paraguay. Oppressively hot from November to March, the city is the base for boat trips along the rivers in the eastern part of the province during the winter, when the weather is mild. It's also a possible stopover on the way to the **Parque Nacional Río Pilcomayo** or the **Bañado La Estrella**, and it's close to the Paraguayan capital, Asunción. From the town's small port, boats cross the river to Alberdi (only if you have a multiple entry visa).

Arriving in Formosa El Pucu Airport ① *T0370-445 2490*, is 5 km southwest (*remise*, US$3). The **bus terminal** ① *Av Gutnisky 2615, T0370-445 1766, www.terminalformosa. com.ar*, is 15 blocks west of plaza San Martín (*remise* US$3). See Transport, below, for details.

Tourism is not well developed here yet, but increasingly activities are offered: guided excursions and accommodation at *estancias*; ask at the **tourist office** ① *José M Uriburu 820 (on Plaza San Martín), T0370-442 5192, www.formosa.gob.ar/turismo, daily 0800-1300, 1600-2100.*

Parque Nacional Río Pilcomayo → *Best visited in winter.*
This park, 162 km north of Formosa, covers 48,000 ha of Wet Chaco environment bordering Paraguay on the southern bank of the Río Pilcomayo. The lower parts may be flooded during the rainy season and the resulting lakes and *esteros*, or marshlands, create the park's most beguiling landscapes. The rest is grassland with *Caranday* palm

Border crossing: Argentina–Paraguay

Puente Loyola

The easiest crossing into Paraguay is by road via the Puente Loyola, 4 km north of Clorinda. From Puerto Falcón, at the Paraguayan end of the bridge, the road runs 40 km northeast, crossing the Río Paraguay at Puente Remanso (US$1.25 toll, pedestrian walkway on upstream side, 20 minutes to cross) to reach Asunción.

Immigration The border is open 24 hours. Formalities for entering Argentina are dealt with at the Argentine end, at Puerto Pilcomayo, and for those leaving Argentina at the Paraguayan end at Itá Enramada, easy crossing.

Transport Several companies run buses from Corrientes to Asunción via Resistencia, between five and seven hours, US$17 from Corrientes or Resistencia. Alternatively take the bus from Clorinda to Asunción (one a day), or to Puerto Falcón, US$1, then **Empresa** Falcón, US$1.50, every hour from the border, last bus to the centre of Asunción 1830. **Note** Buses don't wait for you to go through formalities: if you cannot process in time, wait for the same company's next bus and present ticket, or buy a new ticket.

forests, where rheas can be seen, with some Chaco forest in the upper lands, habitat of three monkey species and several types of woodpecker. Due to its significance as a natural wetland, the park is a Ramsar site with diverse birdlife, including herons and three different species of stork. Anteaters, capybaras, coatis, two species of *yacaré* and *aguará guazu* are on the list of animals protected within the park.

Arriving in the park From Formosa, take R11 to Clorinda, and from there take R86 going west. After 47 km, a 5-km dirt road leads north to the Laguna Blanca entrance; follow R86 for a few kilometres further for the 5-km access dirt road to the Estero Poí entrance. **Godoy** buses run from Formosa or Resistencia to the small towns of Laguna Naineck, 5 km from the park (for Laguna Blanca) and Laguna Blanca, 8 km from the park (for Estero Poí). **Remise** taxis from both towns should charge no more than US$5 for these short journeys. There are police controls on the way to the park. Access to the park is free and open 24 hours. The administration centre is in the town of **Laguna Blanca** ⓘ *Av Pueyrredón and R86, T03718-470045, riopilcomayo@ apn.gov.ar, Mon-Fri 0700-1430.*

Exploring the park The park has two entrances leading to different areas. The most visited and easier to reach if you are on foot is Laguna Blanca, where there's an information point and a free campsite with electricity and cold water. From there, a footpath leads to the **Laguna Blanca**, the biggest lake in the park where you'll spot alligators among the rich aquatic plant life. The lake is not recommended for swimming, since the resident piranhas have a penchant for human toes. The second entrance leads to **Estero Poí**, another information point and a campsite without facilities. Here take the 1200-m footpath, which has informative signs on the botany of the upper areas of the park. A vehicle road goes into the park up the Río Pilcomayo and the international border, but can only be used with special permission.

For hotel and restaurant price codes and other relevant information, see pages 20-26.

🛏 Where to stay

Resistencia *p356*

$$$ Covadonga, Güemes 200, T0362-444 4444, www.hotelcovadonga.com.ar. Comfortable, swimming pool, sauna and gym.

$$$-$$ Niyat Urban Hotel, Hipólito Yrigoyen 83, T0362-444 8451, www.niyat urban.com.ar. The newest and best hotel in town. Modern, spacious and stylish rooms overlooking the park, efficient staff.

$$-$ Bariloche, Obligado 239, T0362-442 1412, jag@cpsarg.com. Good budget choice, welcoming owner, decent rooms with a/c. No breakfast, but there's a nearby café at **Gran Hotel Royal**.

Formosa *p358*

$$ Colón, Belgrano 1068, T0370-442 6547, www.hotelcolonformosa.com. Central, comfortable rooms, all usual services.

$$ Plaza, José M Uriburu 920, T0370-442 6767, plaza_formosa@hotmail.com. On plaza, pool, very helpful, some English spoken, secure parking.

$ El Extranjero, Av Gutnisky 2660, T0370-452276. Opposite bus terminal, OK, with a/c.

🍴 Restaurants

Resistencia *p356*

There is a lack of choice when it comes to good-value restaurants but these are recommended:

$$ Kebon, Don Bosco and Güemes, T0362-444 4111.

$ San José, Roca and Av Alberdi, Plaza 25 de Mayo. A popular café and *confitería* with excellent pastries (try the *medialunas*) and ice creams.

Formosa *p358*

$$ El Fortín, Mitre 602. A traditional place, good varied local fish dishes.

$ Yayita, Belgrano 926. Regional dishes such as *soyo*, or *sopa paraguaya* are offered in this central restaurant.

⊛ Festivals

Resistencia *p356*

10-12 Oct Fiesta Nacional de Pescado de los Grandes. Celebrated every Oct in the Río Antequeros, 14 km from Resistencia.

Formosa *p358*

Mar/Apr The world's longest **Via Crucis** pilgrimage with 14 stops all the way along R81 (already registered in the *Guinness Book of Records*) takes place every **Easter** week, starting in Formosa and ending at the border with the province of Salta, 501 km northwest.

31 Jul Festival de la Caña Con Ruda. On the night of the last day of Jul, when a drink of the Paraguayan *caña* flavoured by the ruda plant is taken as a protection for the mid-winter blues. The celebration is very popular and organized annually by the local authorities (ask at tourist office about the venue). It's also a good chance to try regional dishes.

Nov Festival Provincial de Folclore. Held at Pirané (115 km northwest), the major music festival in the northeast, attracting national stars of stirring *folclore* music.

O Shopping

Resistencia *p356*
Fundación Chaco Artesanal, Carlos
Pellegrini 272. A charity selling fine
handicrafts made by Toba, Wichi and
Mocoví native groups in varied materials,
whose profits return to those communities.

○ Transport

Resistencia *p356*
Air
Flights to/from **Buenos Aires**, 1¼ hrs.

Bus
To **Buenos Aires** 12-13 hrs, US$63-71
several companies. To **Formosa** 2-2½ hrs,
US$9-12. To **Iguazú**, 8-10½ hrs, US$47-57,
several companies, some require change
of bus in **Posadas**, 5½ hrs, US$26-33.
To **Salta**, **FlechaBus** and **La Veloz del
Norte**, 12½ hrs, US$57. To **Asunción**
3 companies, 6 hrs, US$15.

Formosa *p358*
Air
Flights to/from **Buenos Aires** 1½ hrs.

Bus
To **Asunción**, 3 hrs, US$14. To **Buenos
Aires** 15-17 hrs, US$74-80.

❶ Directory

Resistencia *p356*
Banks Banco de Galicia, Mitre 153;
Banco de la Nación, Güemes and Av 9 de
Julio. **Currency exchange** El Dorado,
J M Paz 50, Western Union branch.
Medical services Hospital Pediátrico
(Children's Hospital), Juan B Justo 1136,
T0362-442 2171; **Hospital Perrando**,
Av 9 de Julio 1101, T0362-444 0743.
Post office Av Sarmiento and Hipólito
Yrigoyen on Plaza 25 de Mayo.

Formosa *p358*
Banks Banco de Galicia, Av 25 de
Mayo 160; **Banco de la Nación**, Av 25 de
Mayo 614. **Medical services** Hospital
Central, Salta 550, T0370-42 6194;
Hospital de la Madre y el Niño (for
children), Ayacucho 1150, T0370-442 6519.

Esteros del Iberá

The immense and beautiful Esteros del Iberá wetlands are among the largest expanse of virgin lagoons in South America, bettered only by the far more famous Pantanal in Brazil. Fed by an expanse of freshwater the size of Belgium, the Esteros (marshes) del Iberá host an incredible diversity of bird and animal life in one of Argentina's most exquisite landscapes. The area has been loved by ornithologists for some time, and they still come here in great numbers to tick off rare species, which can't be seen elsewhere, and certainly not at such close quarters. However, the great appeal of a stay here is that you don't have to be an expert to find the varied wildlife fascinating. Stay in one of the *estancias* at Colonia Carlos Pellegrini, or further south at Rincón del Socorro, and your accommodation includes at least one boat trip on the lagoons, with a guide who can tell you all about the flora and fauna. In this country of so many natural wonders, it's one of the most unforgettable experiences. Come here soon before everyone else does. For more information, see www.esterosdelibera.com (mostly in Spanish).

On the western side of the region, in an area of lowlands and higher woodlands, is the Parque Nacional Mburucuyá, where natural conditions are ideal for a close view of the local wildlife.

The Esteros del Iberá – 'shining water' in the Guaraní language – are fed exclusively by fresh water from rain: no rivers flow into them. The marshes extend 250 km northeast to Ituzaingó on the Alto Paraná, and are some 70 km wide at their broadest. Clear waters cover 20-30% of the protected area, and there are over 60 *lagunas*, or small lakes, astonishingly no more than a few metres deep, the largest being the **Laguna Iberá** and **Laguna de la Luna**. The area is rich in aquatic plants, including the beautiful purple *camelote*, tiny cream-coloured star-shaped flowers, *irupé* (*Victoriana cruziana*) which forms a kind of floating plate supporting animal and birdlife; when it stretches along the shoreline, it's hard to differentiate the land from the lake. The area owes its rich animal life to the profusion of *embalsados*, which sit like islands in the *lagunas*, but are just floating vegetation, dense enough to support large animals, such as the marsh deer, and sizeable trees and bushes. *Carpinchos* (capybaras) make their homes along the edges, and alligators can be seen basking on any protruding clump of mud. Watch out for the ghastly but ingenious colonial spiders, weaving enormous horizontal nets for unsuspecting insects in the late afternoon. Prolific birdlife is all around. Among the 370 species of bird, herons and egrets soar elegantly from bush to bush, swifts and kingfishers swoop low on the water, giant storks nest on the many floating islands, rich with plant life, and there are tiny bright red-headed federal birds, long-tailed flycatchers, families of southern screamers – *chajá* – with their fluffy heads and rasping cry, amongst many others

This beautiful area at the heart of Corrientes province became a nature reserve in 1983 and has only recently opened to tourism. Previously it was a rich territory for hunters and grazing land for cattle ranchers. Several local *estancias* are now open to guests, keen to enjoy the perfect tranquillity here as much as the birdlife. The Esteros have yet to gain national park status, however, which would ensure their greater protection. North American conservationist Douglas Tompkins and the Conservation Land Trust is campaigning for this and has been buying up huge sections of the land from private owners, in order to rescue it from cattle farming and rice growing which pollute the pristine waters. Though he's a controversial figure, his aims are sincere: he plans to give all the land to Argentina if it can be guaranteed national park status.

Reserva Natural del Iberá

ⓘ *T03773-15-459110, www.ibera.gov.ar.*
This reserve protects nearly 13,000 sq km of the Esteros del Iberá wetlands and is really only accessible to visitors from the small village of Colonia Carlos Pellegrini, from where excursions depart.

Arriving in Esteros del Iberá

Getting there and around Part of the magic of the Esteros del Iberá is that they are isolated. It's best not to hire a car, but rather to allow your accommodation to arrange transport from Posadas or Mercedes. The quickest way to get to the region is to fly from Buenos Aires to Posadas (daily, 1½ hours), from where the 200-km journey to Colonia Carlos Pelegrini takes four to five hours. Note, that the roads are earth and gravel after the first 60 km and negotiable only in a 4WD vehicle; they are impassable after heavy rain. Another option is to take the overnight bus (*coche-cama*, 10 hours) from Buenos Aires to **Mercedes**, and ask your *estancia* or hotel to arrange a 4WD *remise* transfer from there. Mercedes is 120 km from Pellegrini, but note that this journey takes two hours on the gravel roads. There is a bus from Mercedes to Colonia Carlos Pelegrini but it takes forever and leaves at inconvenient times (see Transport, below).

Esteros del Iberá

The hotels are all near the Iberá Lagoon, the easiest lagoon to access in the Esteros, reached by boat from the sleepy little village of **Colonia Carlos Pellegrini**. **Estancia Rincón del Socorro** ① www.rincondelsocorro.com, 30 km south of Pellegrini, is slightly closer to Mercedes. ▶▶ *See Transport, page 369.*

Best time to visit Autumn, winter or spring are the best times to visit to avoid the intense heat of midsummer. There is less chance of rain and thunderstorms during these months.

Mercedes → *For listings, see pages 367-369.*
Colour map 2, B1. Phone code 03773.
Population 47,425.

Mercedes, 250 km southeast of Corrientes, is the most convenient access point for Colonia Carlos Pellegrini and the Esteros del Iberá, with regular overnight buses from Buenos Aires. and. A chirpy little town, with some quaint 1900s buildings, it has a couple of decent places to stay and a few restaurants, internet facilities and ATMs around the plaza, where there is also a small **tourist office** ① *Sarmiento 650, T03773-420100.* Both Calle Pujol and Calle San Martín lead from the bus station to the plaza, and you're likely to see *gauchos* hanging around here wearing the distinctive red berets of Corrientes province. A few kilometres west of town, on the road to Corrientes, is a shrine to **pagan saint Gauchito Gil** at the place where it's said he was killed. Shrines to Gil can be seen all over the country, decorated with red flags.

Colonia Carlos Pellegrini → *For listings, see pages 367-369. Colour map 2, B2.*
Phone code 03773. Population 900.

With a remote setting on the beautiful Laguna Iberá 120 km northeast of Mercedes, the sprawling village of Pellegrini is the only base for visiting the Esteros del Iberá. A quiet, very laid-back place with only 900 inhabitants, it has just a few blocks of earth roads, and all the hotels are a few hundred metres away from each other. There are not many restaurants or shops and no ATMs, so bring everything you may need, including extra money as few places accept credit cards. There are few streetlights in the village, so carry a torch at night. Bring a hat, mosquito repellent, plenty of sunblock, and binoculars too, if you're keen to spot the more distant birds as well as those right by your boat.

The rangers' office and reserve visitor centre, **Aguas Brillantes** ① *Mbigua and Yacare, daily 0730-1200, 1400-1800,* is just by the bridge as you come into town on the right. Here, you can chat to the *guardaparques*, study a map of the natural reserve, and get more information on the flora and fauna. They also sell an excellent guide to all the plants, birds and animals you'll find here – *Iberá, Vida y Colour*, in Spanish and English with the Latin names noted as well – which is indispensable if your guide on the boat trip doesn't speak English. From the visitor centre you can walk to see the howler monkeys in a patch of lovely jungle nearby. (Most accommodation will include or charge extra for this walk, but you can actually do it yourself.) It is

Colonia Carlos Pellegrini

To Cementario

To Galarza

Laguna Iberá

To 9 & Mercedes

Bridge

N

Not to scale

Where to stay 🛏
Ecoposada del Estero **2**
Hostería Ñandé Retá **4**
Irupé Lodge **3**
Posada Aguapé **1**
Posada de la Laguna **6**

Posada Yacaré **10**
Posada Ypa Sapukai **5**
Rancho Iberá **7**
Rancho Inambú **8**
Rincón del Socorro **9**

Restaurants 🍴
Don Marcos **1**
Santa Rita **4**
Yacarú Porá **5**

clearly marked, each new species of tree is labelled and it takes about 20 minutes to complete. See www.coloniapellegrini.gov.ar for more information.

There are several hotels and *estancias* around Pellergini, most very comfortable and all offering full board, or a picnic if you're out during the day. They also provide boat trips on the lake as part of your accommodation, and some *estancias* offer walking and horse riding too. A one-day visit allows for a three-hour boat excursion (US$22.50 per person if not included in hotel rates), but you may want to plan to stay for three or four nights to really unwind and lap up the tranquil atmosphere.

Boat trips and walks in the Reserve

Your hotel or *estancia* will offer at least one boat trip included in your accommodation into Laguna Iberá to visit areas where there are lots of birds, alligators and capybaras. Depending on the time of day, these usually take two to three hours, and in summer it's best to go out in the early morning or later evening, to avoid the intense heat and to stand a better chance of seeing more birds. If you're lucky, your trip will be timed to return as the sun sinks on the water – sunsets here are really spectacular, when the whole world of water and sky is tinted vivid vermillion, an unforgettable sight. The boat trip is at its most exciting when you travel down narrow creeks between the *embalsados*, and when you're invited to walk on them – they are amazingly stable, but yield subtly to your feet with a pleasing springiness. In case you don't understand your guide's instructions in Spanish: if you suddenly start sinking, you're advised to spread out your arms before the *embalsado* closes in over you. But don't worry – this is very unlikely to happen. Do ask your hotel or *estancia* at the time of booking if there are guides who speak your language: many of the local guides are excellent and know the *lagunas* like the back of their hands, complete with all the resident wildlife, but speak little English. You can be guaranteed English-speaking guides at **Posada de la Laguna, Irupé Lodge** and **Rincón del Socorro** (see Where to stay, below).

Some *estancias* also offer walks to the jungle to see and hear howler monkeys swinging off the trees and roaring, especially when rain is approaching. Night safaris are fun too: mammals, vizcachas, owls and lots of capybaras running around by the light of your guide's lamp.

Western Iberá

The western side of Iberá, some two hours from Corrientes by road, has several access points, including Portal San Nicolás, which is on a reserve owned by **The Conservation Land Trust** (CLT) ⓘ *www.proyectoibera.org*. The Trust's aim is integrate its lands into the publicly-owned national reserve. San Nicolás, reached from San Miguel (160 km from Corrientes) has a *guardaparques* post and a campsite. From the jetty it's 45 minutes by boat or a two-day, one-night ride to CLT's San Alonso lodge (see Where to stay below). Another access point is Portal Yahaveré, southwest of San Nicolás. Between here and Corrientes is **Parque Nacional Mburucuyá.**

Parque Nacional Mburucuyá

ⓘ *12 km east of the town of Mburucuyá, national park office T03782-498907, www. pnmburucuya.gob.ar, free. See also www.parquesnacionales.gov.ar. Buses go from San Antonio Corrientes daily to Mburucuyá, the journey takes 2½ hrs and costs US$4. A remise taxi from there to the park is US$15.*

If you can't make it over to the Esteros del Iberá and are in Corrientes city, you might like to visit this park, which stretches north from the marshlands of the Río Santa Lucía. It's 180 km southeast of Corrientes, 12 km east of the small town of Mburucuyá (where there are several places to stay overnight), accessible by a 47-km-long road branching off at Saladas. Unpaved Route 86 (later Route 13) links Mburucuyá with the park and this sandy road leads northeast to Itá Ibaté, on Route 12, 160 km east of the provincial capital.

The land was donated by Danish botanist Troels Pedersen, whose long research had identified 1300 different plants, including some newly discovered species. There's a variety of natural environments, ranging from savanna with *yatay* palms and 'islands' of Wet Chaco forest, with *lapacho* trees (which have purple blossom in late winter) and *timbó* trees, to the aquatic vegetation of the *esteros*. You'll also see the *mburucuyá* (passion flower) that gives its name to the park. There's lots of interesting wildlife too: capybaras, the rare *aguará guazu* (maned wolf) and the *aguará pope*, similar to the North American raccoon (though these are both nocturnal animals), deer, such as *corzuela parda (Mazama gouazoubira)* and *ciervo de los pantanos*, foxes *aguará-í*, monkeys and many bird species, such as the lovely *yetapá de collar* (*Alectrurus risora*) or strange-tailed tyrant, with its beautiful double tail.

Provincial Route 86 (unpaved) crosses the park for 18 km, to the **information centre** and free **campsite** (hot water and electricity) at the centre of the park. From there, two footpaths branch off the access road. The **Sendero Yatay** goes south to a vantage point on Estero Santa Lucía, winding 2.5 km through gallery forests and grassland with mature palms. The Sendero Aguará Pópé goes north 1.2 km, through thick vegetation and Wet Chaco forests, and near the western access to the park, the road crosses the *arroyo Portillo*, where 2-m-long *yacarés negros* alligators are often spotted.

◉ Esteros del Iberá listings

For hotel and restaurant price codes and other relevant information, see pages 20-26.

◉ Where to stay

Mercedes *p364*

$$ Sol, San Martín 519 (entre Batalla de Salta y B Mitre), T03773-420283, www. corrientes.com.ar/hotelsolmercedes/.

Comfortable rooms around a wonderful patio with black and white tiles and lots of plants. Lovely.

$$ La Casa de China, Mitre y Fray L Beltrán, call for directions, T03773-15-627269, lacasadechina@hotmail.com. A delightful historical old house with clean rooms and a lovely patio. Recommended.

Colonia Carlos Pellegrini *p365,*
map p365
Rates are generally full board and include
water- and/or land-based excursions.
$$$$ pp Posada Aguapé, T03773-
499412, www.iberawetlands.com.
On a lagoon with a garden and pool,
comfortable rooms, attractive dining
room. Recommended.
$$$$ pp Posada de la Laguna, T03773-
499413, www.posadadelalaguna.com.
A beautiful place run by Elsa Güiraldes
(grand-daughter of famous Argentine
novelist, Ricardo Güiraldes) and set on
the lake, very comfortable, large neat
garden and a swimming pool, English
and some French spoken, excellent
country cooking. Highly recommended.
$$$$ pp Rincón del Socorro, T03773-
475114, www.rincondel socorro.com
(Conservation Land Trust). Incredibly
luxurious, beautifully set in its own
12,000 ha 35 km south of Carlos
Pellegrini, with 6 spacious bedrooms,
each with a little sitting room, 1 double
bungalow, and elegant sitting rooms and
dining rooms. Delicious home-produced
organic food, bilingual guides, *asados* at
lunchtime, night safaris and horse riding.
Gorgeous gardens, pool with superb
views all around. Highly recommended.
$$$$-$$$ Ecoposada del Estero,
T03773-15-443602, www.ecoposada
delestero.com.ar. 2-room bungalows
and restaurant, associated with Iberá
Expediciones, Yaguarete y Pindó,
www.iberaexpediciones.com, who run
guided treks, horse riding, 4WD trips,
birdwatching, lots of information.
$$$$-$$$ Irupé Lodge, T03752-438312
or T03773-402193, www.ibera-argentina.
com. Rustic, simple rooms, great views
of the *laguna* from dining room, offers
conventional and alternative trips,
camping on islands, diving, fishing,

several languages spoken. Offers
combined Iberá and Iguazú tours.
$$$ pp Hostería Ñandé Retá, T03773-
499411, www.nandereta.com. Large old
wooden house in a shady grove, play
room, full board, home cooking.
$$$ pp Posada Ypa Sapukai, Sarmiento
212, T03773-15-514212, www.ypasapukai.
com.ar. Private rooms and shared single
rates **$** pp. Good value, nice atmosphere,
excellent staff.
$$$ Rancho Iberá, Caraguatá y Aguará,
T03783-15-318594, www.posadarancho
ibera.com.ar. Designed like an old
Argentine country house, *posada* with
double and triple bedrooms and a well-
maintained garden. Also has a cottage
for 5.
$$$ Rancho Inambú, T03773-15-436159,
Yeruti, entre Aguapé y Pehuajó, www.
ranchoinambu.com.ar. Nice rustic rooms
set in lush garden, lovely common area
and a great bar (open to non-guests).
$$$ pp San Lorenzo, at Galarza, T03756-
487084, www.rincontreslagunas.com.
Next to 2 lakes on the northeast edge of
the region, splendid for wildlife watching,
only 3 rooms. Access from Gobernador
Virasoro (90 km), via Rutas 37 and
41. Transfer can be arranged to/from
Virasoro or Posadas for an extra charge.
Closed Jan-Feb. See also associated
tour company, Rincón Tres Lagunas,
T03756-15-511931, same website, for
birdwatching, nighttime boat excursions,
tours to Misiones and more.
$$$-$$ Posada Yacaré, Curupi y
Yaguareté, T03773-15-499415. Small
hostel 4 blocks from the lake, 1 from
the plaza, with restaurant and garden.

Camping
Municipal campsite, T03773-15-629656,
with hot showers, jetty for boat trips,
also riding and other guided tours.

Western Ibera *p366*

$$$$ San Alonso Lodge, 45 mins by boat from San Nicolás, T03773-475114. Owned and managed by the Conservation Land Trust. A 2-night programme includes rustic rooms, criollo food and all excursions.

🍴 Restaurants

Colonia Carlos Pellegrini *p365, map p365*
There aren't many restaurants here since all hotels and *estancias* offer full board. There are a couple of *kioskos* selling cold drinks and snacks on the road leading to the bridge; these have unreliable opening times. The following are all within walking distance of the main plaza:
$ Don Marcos, RP 40 and Guasuvirá, T03773-457697. Offering a variety of *empanadas* and *milanesas*, but also regional dishes such as *chastaca*, *bai pui*, *carbonada* and *locro*.
$ Santa Rita, Curupí and Tuyuyú, T03773-15-411053. Pizza, pastries and delicious home-made desserts.
$ Yacarú Porá, Yaguarte y Cara Huata, T03773-15-413750. Tasty barbecue, pasta, pizzas and *empanadas*. Vegetarians catered for.

🎯 What to do

Colonia Carlos Pellegrini *p365, map p365*
As part of your stay at most lodges you will have at least a few activities included but local enterprises also offer several tours, such as boat trips, horse riding and kayaking. Ask at the visitor centre for details.

Iberá Expediciones, Yaguarete and Pindo, T03773-15-5020 4031, www.ibera expediciones.com. Small but professional tour agency run by the informative José Martín, who can organize boat trips, birdwatching tours, horse riding and treks. He can also help you find accommodation and is happy to help with information on the area. Recommended.

🚐 Transport

Mercedes *p364*
Bus
To **Colonia Carlos Pellegrini**, Itatí II provides a combi service Mon-Sat 1230 (but check as times change), from Pujol 1166, T03773-420184, T03773-15-629598, 4-5 hrs, US$11. Note that it spends 1 hr picking up passengers from the whole of Mercedes after leaving the office.

To **Buenos Aires**, 9-10 hrs, US$50-64, several companies. To **Corrientes**, 3 hrs, US$12, several companies. To Posadas 6 hrs, US$20 with **Crucero del Norte**. To **Puerto Iguazú**, go via Corrientes or via any important town along Ruta 14, such as Paso de los Libres, 130 km southeast.

Colonia Carlos Pellegrini *p365, map p365*
Bus
To **Mercedes**, Itatí II combi, daily at 0430, 3-5 hrs, US$11. Booking is required before 2200 the night before, at the office in a local grocery (ask for directions). To **Posadas**, enquire if there is a direct bus, or catch a bus back to Mercedes and on to Posadas.

Misiones province and the Jesuit missions

There are wonderfully evocative remains of several Jesuit missions in the south of picturesque Misiones province. Testimony to the Jesuits' great organization and extensive expansion in the early 17th century, they make a worthwhile stop on your way to or from Iguazú Falls. And if you're interested in seeing more, there are the ruins of San Ignacio Mini, Santa Ana, and Loreto, all within reach of the small pleasant town of San Ignacio. Misiones' lush landscapes of red earth roads cutting through fecund green jungle and forest plantations are matched by a rich culture, generated by the mix of indigenous Guaraní and European immigrants, particularly from Eastern Europe, together with a constant flow of Paraguayans and Brazilians from over the borders. The fertile land produces pine forests for wood, huge plantations of tea, and most important of all, the *yerba* for *mate*, the Argentine drink without which the country would grind to a halt (see box, page 26). It's a fairly wet region: the annual rainfall exceeds 2000 mm, generating hundreds of rivers and waterfalls, the most magnificent of which are the overwhelming Iguazú Falls, at the province's northernmost tip. But there are more falls, the Saltos de Moconá, almost as spectacular and staggeringly wide, on the southeasternmost edge of the province and accessible for those adventurous enough to make the trip. With time to spare, you could head inland to Oberá, whose 35 churches represent immigrants from an amazing 15 countries. Misiones' climate might be uncomfortably hot for much walking in summer, but it's pleasantly warm in winter, while flowers and birdlife are most abundant in spring. For more information, see www.turismo.misiones.gov.ar (in Spanish), or www.misionesvive. com.ar (in Spanish and English).

Arriving in Misiones province

Getting there and around From the region's capital, the unattractive business-hub of Posadas, two parallel roads run northeast to the Iguazú Falls, but only Route 12, the northernmost one is tarmacked and negotiable in an ordinary vehicle. The Jesuit ruins at San Ignacio are 60 km north of Posadas and the road continues, via a series of small towns such as Eldorado, to Wanda, famous for its open mines of semi-precious stones, to Puerto Iguazú, the best base for visiting the falls. The other road, Route 14, runs parallel and south along the interior of the province, via Oberá to Bernardo de Irigoyen. It's paved but there are no buses. To visit the Saltos de Moconá in the southeast, you'll need to take an even rougher road further south, Route 2, which is unpaved from Alba Posse onwards (about halfway), so you'll need a 4WD vehicle. ►► *See Transport, page 381.*

Best time to visit Summers are incredibly hot here, with temperatures reaching 40°C from November to March, but winters are warm and sunny.

Posadas and around → *For listings, see pages 379-382. Colour map 2, B2.*

Posadas is the lively but unattractive capital of Misiones, set on a bend on the southern bank of the Río Paraná, with views over the river from its *costanera* (riverbanks). It was founded in 1814 and developed after the War of Triple Alliance as a useful strategic post. It's a modern city and there aren't any particularly remarkable sights; if you are looking for a place to stop on your way from the Esteros del Iberá to Iguazú, head up to the small town of San Ignacio instead.

Arriving in Posadas → *Phone code: 0376. Population: 324,756 (department).*
General San Martín Airport ① *T0376-445 7413*, is on Route 12, 12 km west of town, which can be reached by *remise*, US$10. The **bus terminal** ① *Av Santa Catalina and Av Luis Quaranta, T0376-445 4888*, is 3 km south of the centre on the road to Corrientes. A *remise* to town costs US$8. For a bus into town, cross the street from the terminal and look for Nos 15, 21 or 8 to the centre, US$1.50. For more details, see Transport, below.

Tourist information The **tourist office** ① *2 blocks south of the Plaza 9 de Julio at Colón 1985, T0376-444 7539 www.turismo.misiones.gov.ar, daily 0800-2000*, can provide a basic map but not much else. There is a small tourist office in the bus station (T0376-445 6106) but it isn't often open.

Places in Posadas
The centre of the city is the Plaza 9 de Julio, with its French-style cathedral and government building, and several hotels. Banks and ATMs can be found one block west on San Martín, or one block south on Félix de Azara. Two blocks southeast, there's a peaceful spot at Paseo Bosetti, a quiet plaza with mural paintings. There are a couple of rather old-fashioned museums near the Plaza, the **Museo de Ciencias Naturales e Historia 'Andrés Guaçurarí'** and the **Museo Regional de Posadas**

The Jesuit mission

Jesuits were the religious force that accompanied the Spanish conquest of much of northern Argentina, and though their impact on indigenous culture was far more positive, their rule remains controversial. Were they pioneers of a primitive socialism or merely exploiting the local Guaraní in the name of religious enlightenment?

Between 1609, when they built their first *redacción* or mission, in present-day Brazil, and 1767 when they were expelled by the Spanish King, the Jesuits founded about 50 missions around the upper reaches of the rivers Paraná, Paraguay and Uruguay. In 1627, they were forced to flee southwards, when their northern missions were attacked by slave-hunting *bandeirantes*. The priests led some 1000 converts down the Parapanema River into the Paraná on 700 rafts, only to find their route blocked by the Guaíra Falls. They pushed on for eight long days through dense virgin forest, built new boats below the falls and continued their journey. Some 725 km from their old homes, they re-established their missions, and trained militias to protect them from further attacks.

The missions prospered on agricultural produce, which raised profits to fund religious teaching. The Guaraní grew traditional crops such as manioc (the local root vegetable), sweet potatoes and maize, plants imported from Europe, such as wheat and oranges, and they also kept horses and herds of cattle and sheep. The missions became major producers of *yerba mate* (see page 26), favoured by the Jesuits as an alternative to alcohol. Apart from common lands the Guaraní also farmed their own individual plots. Due to their

with the obligatory collection of stuffed animals. There's also a cultural centre and arts exhibition hall at **Museo de Arte Juan Yaparí** ① *Sarmiento 319, www.museojuanyapari.misiones.gov.ar, Mon-Fri 0800-1230, 1600-2030, Sat-Sun 0900-1230, 1730-2130 free*, a block north of the plaza, and next door is **Mercado de Artesanías**, where Guaraní handicrafts are for sale, and the **Museo Arqueológico** ① *General Paz 1865, Mon-Fri 0900-1230, 1700-2030, Sat-Sun, 0900-1230 free*.

Posadas' main feature is the long Costanera, extending northeast of the centre alongside the broad river Paraná and a good place for a stroll. In the afternoon you'll see residents sitting on folding chairs sipping *mate* as the sun goes down. **Avenida Andrés Guaçurarí** (referred to also as Avenida Roque Pérez) is a pretty boulevard which becomes livelier by night with several popular bars. A few blocks northwest is the small **Parque Paraguayo** and the **Museo Regional Aníbal Cambas** ① *Alberdi 600, T0376-444 7539, Mon-Fri 0700-1900, free*. This is Posadas' most interesting museum with a permanent exhibition of Guaraní artefacts and pieces collected from the nearby Jesuit missions, including the façade of the temple at San Ignacio Mini.

Around Posadas

There is a marvellous traditional *estancia* nearby, **Estancia Santa Inés** ① *R105, Km 8.5, 20 km south of Posadas, T0376-443 5771, www.estancia-santaines.com.ar,* growing wealth, they became a powerful force in the Americas and in time they were considered a threat to Spanish rule in the area.

The decision by Carlos III to expel the Jesuits from South America in 1767 was made under the conditions of highest secrecy: sealed orders were sent out to the colonies with strict instructions that they should not be opened in advance. On the appointed date, over 2000 members of the order were removed by force and put on ships for Italy. Jesuit property was auctioned, schools and colleges were taken over by the Franciscans and Dominicans, and many missions fell into disuse, or were destroyed.

The Jesuits had attracted many enemies since their wealth and economic power angered landowners and traders, and their control over the Guaraní irritated farmers short of labour. Rumours circulated that the missions contained mines and hoards of precious metals, which gold diggers still look for today. In fact, when building the new bridge just outside of San Ignacio government workers found 60 kg of Jesuit gold! The Jesuits may have exploited their manpower of the Guaraní, but they certainly defended the Guaraní from enslavement by the Spanish and Portuguese, and many feel their societies were a vanished arcadia.

Only four of the missions retain their former splendour: San Ignacio Mini in Argentina, Jesús and Trinidad in Paraguay, and São Miguel in Brazil. The first three can be visited with ease from San Ignacio, along with several others, including Santa Ana and Loreto, which are a short bus ride away.

which covers 2000 ha and grows *yerba mate*. Activities include walking, horse riding and, between February and October, helping with *mate* cultivation. Half-day activities, US$50; taxi from Posadas, US$18.75. If you're here in July, you might also like to visit the **Fiesta Nacional de la Yerba Mate** (*mate* festival) in **Apóstoles**, a prosperous town 65 km south of Posadas, founded in 1897 by Ukrainian and Polish immigrants on the site of a Jesuit mission dating from 1633. The town is set in the heart of *yerba mate* plantations in a picturesque hilly region, reached by regular buses and the festival attracts *folclore* singers to the region.

The **Museo Histórico Juan Szychowski** ① *13 km further at La Cachuera, follow the 6-km dirt road, branching off R1, 7 km south of Apóstoles*, is worth a trip if you have a car. It displays tools and machinery invented by a young Polish immigrant: mills for processing rice, corn and *yerba mate*, and hydraulic works, which can be seen in the grounds, that still amaze engineers. He was the founder of a *yerba mate* processing plant, **La Cachuera** ① *T0376-442 2077, www.yerbamanda.com.ar*, still operating, now under the brand name of *Amanda*.

You could also cross the border to Encarnación in Paraguay to visit more Jesuit missions at Trinidad and Jesús. For access to Esteros del Iberá, see page 363.

San Ignacio and the Miní Jesuit Mission → *For listings, see pages 379-382.*
Colour map 2, B2.

The pleasant town of San Ignacio, 63 km northeast of Posadas, is the site of the most impressive Jesuit mission in Misiones province. The site, together with the nearby Jesuit missions of Loreto and Santa Ana, was declared a World Heritage Site by UNESCO in 1984. It's a very sleepy area, but is a rural and welcoming place to recharge for a few days if you have just been in, or are heading to, busy Puerto Iguazú. Only a few of the streets are paved, the rest have red dirt.

Arriving in San Ignacio → *Phone code 0376. Population 6300.*
Getting there Buses from Posadas and further south stop in San Ignacio on their way to the falls. Most come into town, but a few stop at the terminal on Avenida Roca/RN 12, near the junction with Avenida Sarmiento, leaving a 15-minute walk into town. San Ignacio Miní Jesuit Mission is located six blocks from Avenida Sarmiento on the northwest side of town. Walk straight ahead down Sarmiento, and you'll see signposts 'To the Ruins'. Keep walking and you'll find the ruins on your right. Note that the entrance on Calle Alberdi is 200 m beyond the exit, which is on Calle Rivadavia. There are plenty of restaurants and cafés along this road near the ruins.

Tourist information There is a municipal **tourist office** ① *Independencia 605, T0376-447 0130.* There is another office on RN12 at the entrance to town. See What to do page 381.

Background San Ignacio Miní ('small' in comparison with San Ignacio Guazú – 'large' – on the Paraguayan side of the Río Paraná) was originally founded in 1610 near the river Paranapanema in the present Brazilian state of Paraná, but frequent attacks from the *bandeirantes* (hunting for slaves as workers) forced the San Ignacio Jesuits to lead a massive exodus south, together with the neighbouring Loreto mission. Taking their Guaraní population down the river by a series of rafts, they established San Ignacio on the river Yabebiry, not far from its present site, which was settled by 1696.

At the height of its prosperity in 1731, the mission housed 4356 people. Only two priests ran the mission: a feat of astounding organization. Latin, Spanish and Guaraní were taught in the school, and nearly 40,000 head of cattle grazed in the surrounding land, where *yerba mate* and cotton, maize and tobacco were also cultivated. The mission itself once covered around 14 ha: today you can see remains of only 6 ha, but these are still an impressive sight with the immense central plaza lined with buildings in dramatic red sandstone. For almost a hundred years, the Jesuit *reducciones* operated successfully, growing in size from a population of 28,000 in 1647 to 141,000 in 1732. But after the expulsion of the Jesuits in 1767 by the Spanish king, the mission rapidly declined. By 1784 there were only 176 Guaraní, and by 1810 none remained. In 1817, by order of the Paraguayan dictator, Rodriguez de Francia, San Ignacio was set on fire. The ruins, like those of nearby Santa Ana and Loreto, were lost in the jungle until the late 19th century when attempts at colonization forced the founding of new towns; San Ignacio was founded near the

Border crossing: Argentina–Paraguay

Puente San Roque

A bridge, the Puente San Roque, links Posadas with Encarnación. Pedestrians and cyclists are not allowed to cross the bridge; cyclists must ask officials for assistance. Argentine pesos are accepted in Encarnación, so there is no need to change them. Paraguay is one hour behind Argentina, except during Paraguayan summer time (October-April).

Immigration and customs The border is open 24 hours. Formalities are conducted at respective ends of the bridge. The Argentine side has different offices for locals and foreigners; Paraguay has one for both. Formalities for boat crossing are carried out at both ports.

Argentine consulate in Encarnación Artigas 960, T+595-(0)71-201066, cenca@mrecic.gov.ar. Monday-Friday 0800-1300.

Paraguayan consulate in Posadas San Lorenzo 1561, T0376-442 3858. Monday-Friday 0800-1400.

Transport To Encarnación (Paraguay), Servicio Internacional, 50 minutes, US$1.25, leaving at least every 30 minutes from platforms 11 and 12 (lower level) of the bus station, tickets are available on the bus. Boats cross to Encarnación, 15 minutes, hourly Monday to Friday 0800-1800, US$2.50. Formalities and ticket office are in the main building. Port access is from Avenida Costanera y Avenida Andrés Guaçurarí.

site of the former mission. It wasn't until the 1980s that there was some attempt to give official protection to the ruins.

The mission

ⓘ *Daily 0700-1900. US$9 with leaflet and tour (ask for English version), which leaves from the entrance every 20 mins (tips are appreciated). You can reliably leave your luggage by the ticket office. Ticket also valid for the Jesuit ruins at Santa Ana, Santa María La Mayor and Loreto, within a 15-day period. Son et lumière show, T0376-447 0186, daily 1900 or 2000 (weather permitting), US$9.*

Like other Jesuit missions, San Ignacio Miní was constructed around a central plaza: to the north, east and west were about 30 parallel one-storey buildings, each with a wide veranda in front and each divided into four to 10 small, one-room dwellings for slaves. Guaraní communities lived in the surrounding areas. The roofs of these buildings have gone, but the massive 1-m-thick walls are still standing except where they have been destroyed by the *ibapoi* trees. The public buildings, some still 10 m high, are on the south side of the plaza; in the centre are the ruins of the church, 74 m by 24 m, finished in about 1724. To the right is the cemetery, which was divided for men and women, priests and children; to the left are the cloisters, the priests' quarters, guest rooms and the workshops for wood and metal work, gold and silver. Sculpture was of particular significance in San Ignacio, and some of the most pleasing details are to be found in the red sandstone masonry.

While the architecture is the traditional colonial baroque style found in all Jesuit public buildings, the influence of the Guaraní culture can be seen in the many natural details in bas-relief on walls and lintels: elegantly entwined grapes, fruit and flowers, together with naïve human forms and angels, so that even the buildings reveal a harmony between the Jesuit priests and their Guaraní workers. The chapel was designed by two Italian *sacerdotes*, and it took 36 years to build. Along the same stretch of terrace, you will see the remains of the music conservatory, library and kitchen. Many of the porticos and windows are elaborately carved, testimony to the highly trained workforce and high standards of aesthetics. The whole area is excellently maintained and is a most impressive sight.

Just 40 m inside the entrance to the ruins is the **Centro de Interpretación Jesuítico-Guaraní**, with a fine model of the mission in its heyday and an exhibition that includes representations of the lives of the Guaraní before the arrival of the Spanish, displays on the work of the Jesuits and the consequences of their expulsion.

You are advised to visit San Ignacio early in the day to avoid the crowds and to have the best light for pictures.

Other sights

Follow Avenida Sarmiento to its very end and turn right for a picturesque view of a row of wooden houses on a reddish road amidst lush vegetation. An interesting art collection is at the **Museo Provincial Miguel Nadasdy** ① *Sarmiento 557, Sat 0700-1900, Sun 0900-1200, 1500-1800*, which contains a collection of artefacts from the Guaraní and Jesuits of the missions, some beautiful examples of stone carving and a bas-relief of San Ignacio de Loyola, founder of the Jesuit order.

On the other side of the town, in the opposite direction to the ruins, there's a really delightful 20-minute walk (with little shade) along San Martín to the house of celebrated Uruguayan writer Quiroga. Walk to the end of the street, past the *Gendarmería* and two attractive wooden and stone houses. After 200 m the road turns left and 300 m later, a signposted narrow road branches off leading to the **Casa de Horacio Quiroga** ① *daily 0700-1900, US$0.50 including a 40-min guided tour; ask for an English guide; phone the tourist office for details*. Quiroga (1878-1937) lived here for part of his tragic life as a farmer and carpenter between 1910 and 1916, and again in the 1930s. Many of his fantastical short stories were inspired by this subtropical region and its inhabitants. The scenery is beautiful, with river views, a garden with palms and an amazing bamboo forest planted by him. There's a replica of his first house, made for a movie set in the 1990s, while his second house is still standing, and contains an exhibition of a few of his belongings. Return to the main road, follow it down the slope amongst thick vegetation for a gorgeous riverside (25-minute) walk.

Other missions: Loreto and Santa Ana

If you have time, it's interesting to complement your visit to San Ignacio with a trip to see the ruins of two other Jesuit missions nearby. The mission of **Loreto** ① *access via a 3-km dirt road (signposted) off Route 12, 10 km south of San Ignacio, daily 0700-1830, on same ticket as San Ignacio within 15 days*, has far fewer visitors than San Ignacio, and under thick shady trees, the silence of the still air and the refreshing darkness add an attractive touch of mystery. The mission was moved to its present site in 1631, after the exodus from the former Jesuit province of Guayrá, and more than 6000 people were living here by 1733. It's thought that this was the site of the first printing press in the Americas and of an extensive library. It was also impressively productive: cattle and *yerba mate* were grown here, and ceramics were made. Little remains of this once-large establishment other than a few walls, though excavations are in progress. Note the number of old trees growing entwined with stone buttresses. No public transport enters Loreto, but take a tour from San Ignacio with Misiones Excursions or catch one of the minibuses which leave every 15 minutes from outside the church on the square; ask the driver to drop you outside the mission. You can ask for help at the tourist office if your Spanish isn't up to it.

Some 16 km south of San Ignacio at **Santa Ana** ⓘ *700 m along a path from Route 12 (signposted), daily 0730-1930 (1830 in winter), on same ticket as San Ignacio within 15 days*, are the ruins of another Jesuit mission, not as extensive as San Ignacio, but revealing interesting architectural adaptation to the terrain and founded much earlier, in 1633. Moved to its present site in 1663, Santa Ana housed the Jesuit iron foundry. In 1744 the mission was inhabited by 4331 people and covered an area of 37 ha, of which only 10 remain. The impressively high walls are still standing and there are beautiful steps leading from the church to the wide-open plaza. Regular buses stop on Route 12 near the ruins.

You could also explore the ruins of **Santa María la Mayor**, 76 km southwest, on paved Route 2 linking San Javier and Concepción de la Sierra, 9 km west of Itacaruare. They date from 1637 and were never restored. Remains of the church and a jail are still standing, and a printing press operated there in the early 18th century.

Oberá → *For listings, see pages 379-382. Colour map 2, B3. Phone code 03755. Population 51,400.*

Oberá is the second largest town in Misiones, located amongst tea and *yerba mate* plantations, with factories open for visits. It's one of the province's biggest centres of 20th-century European immigration, and there are around 15 different nationalities here, including Japanese, Brazilian, Paraguayan and Middle Eastern communities, represented every September in the annual Fiesta Nacional del Inmigrante, held in the Parque de las Naciones. The town has over 35 churches and temples, but there's little reason to make a special trip. Oberá's **tourist office** ⓘ *Plazoleta Güemes, Av Libertad 90, T03755-401808, Mon-Fri 0700-1900, Sat-Sun 0800-1200, 1500-1900, www.obera.gov.ar*, has information on local *estancias* open to visitors. There is a **zoo** ⓘ *Italia y Venezuela*, with the **Jardín de los Pájaros** ⓘ *T03755-427023, Mon-Fri 0700-1800, Sat-Sun, 0900-1200, 1400-1800 US$1*, which houses native birds.

If you're interested in tea, you could head for **Campo Viera**, 21 km north of Oberá on Route 14. The 'national capital of tea', it has about 8000 ha of tea fields and 25 processing plants. The Fiesta Nacional del Té is held here every September with the Queen of Tea coronation (for more information, go to the **Casita del Té**).

San Ignacio to Puerto Iguazú

From San Ignacio Route 12 continues northeast, running parallel to Río Alto Paraná, towards Puerto Iguazú, through appealing landscapes of bright red soil and green vegetation; plantations of *yerba mate*, manioc and citrus fruits can be seen as well as timber yards and *yerba mate* factories. The road passes through several small, modern, uninteresting towns, including Jardín America, Puerto Rico, Montecarlo and Eldorado. If you're driving and feel like an extra stop you could consider the **Salto Capioví**. Just 100 m from Route 12 in Capioví, 60 km from San Ignacio, this 7-m waterfall is immersed in a patch of jungle, with a campsite. Nearby, there's the **Parque Natural Las Camelias**.

One hundred kilometres south of Puerto Iguazú is **Eldorado**, a quaint, friendly and typical little Misiones town with an interesting archaeological collection at the **Museo Municipal** ① *T03751-430788, Thu-Sun 1600-1800, free.* The bus stops here between Puerto Iguazú and San Ignacio. For information visit the **tourist office** ① *Av San Martín 2060, 2nd floor, T03751-421787.*

If you're interested in seeing how amethyst and quartz are mined, you might like to stop off at **Wanda**, 50 km north, a famous open-cast mine, which also sells precious gems. There are daily guided tours to two mines, Tierra Colorada and Compañía Minera Wanda; consult tour operators in Eldorado or Puerto Iguazú.

Saltos del Moconá → For listings, see pages 379-382.

While the main tourist route through Misiones runs along Route 12, if you have time, a 4WD and a spirit of adventure, you might well want to get off the beaten track and explore Misiones' hilly interior. Beautiful waterfalls are hidden away in the dense subtropical forests, and, at the furthest end of the track, you'll find the remote Saltos de Moconá. Tourist services are less well developed here, but you can stay next to the falls or in San Pedro or El Soberbio.

For a staggering 3 km, on the Argentine side of the Río Uruguay, water falls over a vast shelf of rock from 18 m up to 120 m, creating one of the most magnificent sights in the region. The rocky edge is quite easily reached on foot from the bank of the river, in an area surrounded by dense woodland, and protected by the Parque Estadual do Turvo (Brazil) and the Parque Provincial Moconá, the Reserva Provincial Esmeralda and the Reserva de la Biósfera Yabotí (Argentina). The Reserva de la Biósfera Yabotí protects one of the last major areas of Paraná forest in South America – the Selva Paranaense is more endangered than the Amazon rainforest – and tucked deep within the reserve, two tiny communities (around 40 families in 2006) of Mbya Guaraní people survive on ancestral grounds, seriously threatened by timber exploitation.

The **Parque Provincial Moconá** covers 1000 ha, with vehicle roads and footpaths, and there's accommodation nearby where activities and excursions to the falls are arranged. Note that, if the river is high (May-October), the falls may be underwater. In all three natural reserves the hilly forested landscape offers tremendous trekking, kayaking, birdwatching and exploring in 4WD vehicles. Alternative bases for exploring the area are the small towns of **El Soberbio** (70 km southwest) or **San Pedro** (92 km northwest). From the former a paved road runs to the park entrance; from the latter the road is impassable after heavy rain.

There is a regular bus service from Posadas to El Soberbio or San Pedro, and from Puerto Iguazú to San Pedro. Eldorado bus company runs a direct Puerto Iguazú to Moconá service, once a day, leaving Iguazú at 0700, returning 1800, taking three hours 40 minutes.

ⓔ Misiones province and the Jesuit missions listings

For hotel and restaurant price codes and other relevant information, see pages 20-26.

ⓔ Where to stay

Posadas *p371*
$$$ Julio César, Entre Ríos 1951, T0376-442 7930, www.juliocesarhotel.com.ar. 4-star hotel, pool and gym, spacious reasonably priced rooms, some with river views. Recommended.
$$ City, Colón 1754, T0376-433901, citysa@arnet.com.ar. Good rooms, some overlooking plaza, restaurant on 1st floor, parking.
$$ Le Petit, Santiago del Estero 1630, T0376-443 6031, www.hotellepetit. com.ar. Good value, small, a short walk from centre on a quiet street.
$$ Residencial Colón, Colón 2169, T0376-442 5085, www.residencialcolon.blogspot. com. Small but affordable rooms, parking. Also apartments for up to 6 people.
$ pp Hostel Posadeña Linda, Bolívar 1439, T0376-443 9238, www.hostel posadasmisiones.com. Central, good value, very pleasant, with all hostel facilities and tourist information.

San Ignacio *p374*
$$ La Toscana, H Irigoyen y Uruguay, T0376-447 0777, www.hotellatoscana.

com.ar. Family-run, 12-bedroom hotel with rustic, inviting rooms and a wonderful pool with a terrace. It's an easy 10-min walk from the tourist office and main plaza. Highly recommended.
$$ San Ignacio, San Martín 823, T0376-447 0047, www.hotelsanignacio.com.ar. Good if dated rooms with a/c, plus self-catering apartments for 4-5 people. Breakfast extra. An interesting view of town from the reception.
$ pp Adventure Hostel, Independencia 469, T0376-447 0955. Large hostel with a fantastic pool and a games area. Spacious communal areas, comfortable double rooms (**$$**). Camping available. Short walk to centre of town.
$ pp Hostel El Jesuita, San Martín 1291, T0376-447 0542, http://eljesuitahostely camping.blogspot.co.uk. Welcoming owners, spacious double rooms with their own exit to the garden, small comfortable dorm (US\$10), 1½ blocks from the ruins. Call when you arrive to be picked up. Lots of travel advice. Camping, US\$4.50. Recommended.

Camping
Complejo Los Jesuitas, C Emilia Mayer, T0376-446 0847, www.complejolos jesuitas.com.ar. Campsite and cabins for 4 people.

Oberá p377

Ask the tourist office for details of farms run by host families of different nationalities.

$$$ Cabañas del Parque, Ucrania y Tronador, T03755-426000, www.hotel cabanas.com.ar. Situated next to the Parque de las Naciones, this is a tourist complex of several houses or rooms for 2 to 8 people. Kitchen, a/c and breakfast included. Also has a large swimming pool and a restaurant.

$$$-$$ Premier, 9 de Julio 1114, T03755-407400, www.hotelpremierobera.com. A good central option, with a/c but no breakfast.

$ Cuatro Pinos, Sarmiento 853, T03755-429808. A well-located hotel.

Saltos del Moconá p378

$$$ pp El Refugio Moconá, 3 km from access to the reserve, 8 km from the falls (or contact at Bolívar 1495, Posadas), T0376-442 1829, www.refugiomocona. com.ar. Price for 3-day package. Rustic rooms for 4-5 with shared bath, campsite, tents for rent, meals available. Many activities, boat trips and excursions. Transfer with sightseeing to and from San Pedro, 2 hrs.

$$ Hostería Puesta del Sol, C Suipacha s/n, El Soberbio, T03755-495161 (T011-4300 1377 in Buenos Aires). A splendid vantage point overlooking town, with a swimming pool and restaurant. Comfortable rooms, full board available. They also run boat excursions to the falls, 7-8 hrs, landing and meal included (minimum 4 people), via Brazil or on the Argentine side.

There are other lodges in the vicinity, for example: www.donenriquelodge. com.ar, www.lodgelamision.com.ar, www.posadalabonita.net.

🍴 Restaurants

Posadas p371

Most places offer *espeto corrido*, eat as much as you can *parrilla* with meat brought to the table.

$$ El Mensú, Fleming y Cnel Reguera (in the Bajada Vieja district). Closed Mon. Attractive house with a varied menu of fish and pasta, large selection of wines.

$$ La Querencia, Bolívar 1849 (on Plaza 9 de Julio). A large traditional restaurant offering *parrilla*, *surubí* and pastas.

$$ Plaza Café, Bolívar 1979 just outside the shopping centre. Great salads and large mains. Busy during the day and busier at night. Highly recommended.

$ Bar Español, Bolívar 2085. Open since 1958, this restaurant has tasty Spanish-influenced food. Have an ice cream for dessert next door at **Duomo**.

$ La Nouvelle Vitrage, Colón y Bolívar. Good pizzas, sandwiches and coffee, nice view of the plaza.

San Ignacio p374

There are several restaurants catering for tourists on the streets by the Jesuit ruins.

$$ La Carpa Azul, Rivadavia 1295. Large restaurant near the ruins serving quality meals but you will be surrounded by tour buses.

$ La Misionera, Rivadavia 1105. Offers a tourist meal. Nicely decorated.

$ Pizzería La Aldea, San Martin 1240, Friendly place serving good cheap pizzas, *empanadas* and other simple meals. Will make sandwiches to take away. Recommended.

Oberá p377

$$ Del Monte, Costa Rica 334. Great modern fare.

$$ Engüete, Cabeza de Vaca 340. Good food and a varied menu is available.

⊛ Festivals

Oberá *p377*
Sep Fiesta Nacional del Inmigrante.
Vibrant festival that lasts a week around
Sep 4 (Immigrants' Day). In the Parque
de las Naciones, houses built in various
national styles are the attractive setting
for folk dances, parades, tasting national
dishes and the election of a queen.
Very popular.

◐ What to do

Posadas *p371*
Abra, Salta 1848, T0376-442 2221,
www.abratours.com.ar. Tours to San
Ignacio, including Santa Ana Jesuit ruins,
also those in Paraguay and in Brazil, plus
tours to waterfalls.
Guayrá, San Lorenzo 2208, T0376-443
3415, www.guayra.com.ar. Tours to Iberá,
to Saltos del Moconá, to both sites in
a 5-day excursion, and to other sites in
Misiones, also car rental and transfers to
Carlos Pellegrini (for Iberá).

San Ignacio *p374*
Misiones Excursions, Rivadavia and
Sarmiento, T03752-15373448, www.
misionesexcursions.blogspot.com.
Excellent, small company with its
office in the tourist information centre.
Personalized tours around San Ignacio,
including visits to the other ruins of Santa
Ana and Loreto, local Guaraní villages
and a *yerba estancia*. All cost US$31.25 per
person. They also organize kayaking trips,
cycling excursions and can organize a full
day trip into Paraguay to see the famous
mission ruins of Trinidad (US$62.50).
If you contact then in advance they
can organize 2-night excursions to
the Esteros de Iberá, including luxury
accommodation, breakfast, a boat trip

on the wetlands and personal 4WD
transfers, for US$250 for two people.
Recommended.

San Ignacio to Puerto Iguazú *p378*
Eldorado
Delmonte, Av San Martín 1734, Km 9,
T03751-422113, cebrera@ceel.com.ar.
Transfers from Iguazú to San Ignacio,
and to *estancias*.

Saltos del Moconá *p386*
Hostería Puesta del Sol, www.h-puesta
delsol.com.ar (see Where to stay, above).
Boat excursions arranged to the falls,
7-8 hrs, landing and meal included. The
journey to the falls is by a boat crossing
to Brazil, then by vehicle to Parque do
Turvo, 7 hrs, meal included. Otherwise, a
4WD journey on the Argentine side with
more chances for trekking takes 7 hrs,
with a meal included.

⊜ Transport

Posadas *p371*
Air
To **Buenos Aires**, direct or via Corrientes
or Formosa, 1 hr 50 mins.

Bus
Travel agencies in the centre can book
bus tickets in advance. To **Buenos Aires**,
12-13 hrs, US$77-88. Frequent services to
San Ignacio Miní, 1 hr, US$4.75-6, and
Puerto Iguazú, US$18-20, 5-6 hrs.
    To reach **Brazil** and the Jesuit Missions
in Rio Grande do Sul, take an **Aguila
Dorada** or **Horianski** bus from Posadas
to **San Javier**, 124 km, then a ferry, US$5,
to Porto Xavier, from where buses run
to Santo Ângelo, 4 hrs. Immigration is
at either end of the ferry crossing.

San Ignacio p374
Bus
Frequent service to **Posadas** or to **Puerto Iguazú** (US$17).

To **Paraguay**, a ferry crosses the Río Paraná at **Corpus** to **Bella Vista**, foot passengers US$2 (cars weekdays only), which is a good route to the Paraguayan Jesuit missions. There are immigration and customs facilities.

Oberá p377
Bus
To **Posadas**, 1½ hrs, US$6, with **Capital del Monte, Don Tito, Expreso Singer** and **Horiansky. Don Tito** also goes to **El Soberbio**.

ⓘ Directory

Posadas p371
Banks Banco de La Nación, Bolívar 1799; **Banco Río**, Félix de Azara; **Citibank**, San Martín and Colón; **HSBC**, Félix de Azara. **Currency exchange** Mazza, Bolívar 1932. **Immigration** Dirección **Nacional de Migraciones**, Buenos Aires 1633, T0376-442 7414. **Medical services** Hospital Dr Ramón **Madariaga**, Av Marconi 3736, T0376-444 3700. **Post office** Bolívar and Ayacucho, Western Union branch.

Iguazú Falls

Any trip to Argentina should include the Iguazú Falls. They're the biggest falls in South America – half as high again as Niagara – and a spectacular experience. In 2012 they were confirmed as one of the New7Wonders of Nature. In all, there are 275 falls stretching over 2.7 km but the main attraction is the Garganta del Diablo (devil's throat), where walkways take you right above the falls to see the smooth river transformed in an instant into a seething torrent as the water crashes 74 m over a horseshoe-shaped precipice onto basalt rocks below, filling the air with bright spray and a deafening roar. The whole chasm is filled with billowing clouds of mist in which great dusky swifts miraculously wheel and dart, and an occasional rainbow hovers. Then you can walk close to the bottom of the immensely wide Saltos Bossetti and Dos Hermanos, or take a boat trip, which speeds you beneath the falling water to get a total drenching. Viewed from below, the rush of water is unforgettably beautiful, falling through jungle filled with begonias, orchids, ferns, palms and toucans, flocks of parrots, cacique birds and myriad butterflies. There are some longer trails enabling you to enjoy the diverse flora and fauna in this national park, and several excellent guides on hand whose expertise will considerably add to your enjoyment.

Argentina shares the falls with Brazil and you can visit them from either side for two quite different experiences. The Brazilian side has a smaller, more restricted park and offers a panoramic view from its limited trails but you're kept at a distance from the falls themselves. If you have to choose just one, go for the Argentine side, where you can get closer to the falls, walk in the jungle and explore the rainforest. The most pleasant place to stay is undoubtedly the laid-back Argentine town of Puerto Iguazú, where hotels are cheaper and the streets are far safer than in the Brazilian city of Foz do Iguaçu, where there is a serious crime problem. On either side, most establishments will accept Brazilian reais, Argentine pesos or dollars.

Arriving at Iguazú Falls

Getting there and around The falls on both sides are contained within national parks, both of which charge entry fees (see below) and have well-organized free transport to take you to the waterfalls. **On the Argentine side** you should allow at least a day and start early; the park opens at 0800 and it takes six hours to see the main attractions if you do it quickly. If you find a brisk pace exhausting in the heat of summer, you can revisit the park the next day at half the price – make sure you keep your ticket. Just opposite the entrance, a free mini-train takes you from the visitor centre to Estación Garganta, where a 1-km-long walkway leads to the Garganta del Diablo falls and then to Estación Cataratas, where two trails, taking at least an hour each, offer great views of the falls and a free boat crossing to Isla San Martín for even closer views. There are optional extra boat trips right up to the falls themselves run by **Jungle Explorer** (www.iguazujungle.com), including a great trip that takes you rushing right underneath the falls. You will get wet. In the rainy season, when water levels are high, waterproof coats or swimming costumes are advisable for some of the lower catwalks and for all boat trips. Cameras should be carried in a plastic bag. See www.iguazuargentina.com.

On the Brazilian side, the park opens at 0900 and a visit takes around two hours. Free buses take you to the start of a walkway with steps down to the falls. See also www.cataratasdoiguacu.com.br (in Portuguese and English). Both parks have visitor centres, cafés and restaurants.

When to visit The falls can be visited all year round. There's officially no rainy season, though it tends to rain more in March and June and there can be heavy downfalls in summer. The average temperatures are 25°C in summer and 15°C in winter. The busiest times are the Argentine holiday periods – January, Easter week and July – when you must book accommodation in advance, and on Sundays when helicopter tours over the falls from the Brazilian side are particularly popular (and noisy). Remember that between October and March Argentina is one hour behind Brazil (daylight saving dates change each year) and, from December to March, one hour behind Paraguay.

Background

Iguazú means 'big water' in the local Guaraní language (i = water, guazú = big). The first recorded European visitor to the falls was the Spaniard Alvar Núñez Cabeza de Vaca in 1542, on his search for a connection between the Brazilian coast and the Río de la Plata: he named them the *Saltos de Santa María*. Though the falls were well known to the Jesuit missionaries, they were unexplored until the area was covered by a Brazilian expedition sent out by the Paraguayan president, Solano López, in 1863.

Parque Nacional Iguazú (Argentina) → *For listings, see pages 391-394.*

Created in 1934, the park extends over an area of 67,000 ha of dense subtropical rainforest. There is excellent access to the falls themselves from various angles and

Dos and don'ts

- Get to the park as early as you can to spot wildlife and avoid queues.
- Wear a hat, good sunscreen and sunglasses: the sun is fierce here.
- In the rainy season, when water levels are high, wear waterproof coats or swimming costumes for some of the lower catwalks and for boat trips.
- Bring insect repellent, bottled water and some snacks.

- Wear shoes with good soles, as the walkways can be very slippery.
- Protect cameras and binoculars from the spray with a plastic bag.
- Take all rubbish out of the park with you, or use the bins.
- Don't feed animals or birds, don't damage the flora, and walk quietly so as not to disturb wildlife.
- Get your ticket stamped on entry; your next day visit will be half price.

along two further trails that wind through the forest to give you an experience of the wildlife.

Arriving in Parque Nacional Iguazú

Getting there and around The park lies 20 km east of the town of Puerto Iguazú along Route 12. A public **Cataratas/Waterfalls** bus runs every 30 minutes 0730-1830 from Hito Tres Fronteras. It stops at Puerto Iguazú bus terminal 10 minutes after departure, at the park entrance for the purchase of entry tickets, then continues to the Visitor Centre, US$4, journey time 45 minutes; return buses from the park run 0815-1915. You can get on or off the bus at any point en route. For transport between the Argentine and Brazilian sides, see Foz do Iguaçu, page 395, and the border box, page 389.»*See also Transport, page 394.*

From Estación Central, just beyond the visitor centre, a natural-gas-powered mini-train (free), the *Tren de la Selva*, whisks visitors on a 25-minute trip (2.3 km) through the jungle to Estacíon Cataratas, from where you can walk to the Sendero Verde, the Circuito Inferior and the Circuito Superior. The train continues to Estación Garganta, for the Garganta del Diablo falls. Allow at least two hours for the whole trip: train, walking, watching the falls and photos.

Park information The park is open daily 0800-1800. Entry is US$27 (children US$18.75) for all foreign visitors (payable in pesos only). Entry next day is half price with the same ticket, which you must get stamped at the end of the first day.

There's an excellent **visitor centre (Centro de Interpretación)** on the right after you enter, with information and photographs of the flora and fauna, and details of the history of the area from the earliest settlers. Opposite, you'll find plenty of places to eat in the **Patio de Comidas**, including a pizzeria, *parrilla* and snack bar. As you walk towards the barriers where you pay the entry fee, there are excellent souvenir shops selling both commercial souvenirs and local Guaraní handicrafts (note that these are cheaper when bought from the Guaraní people themselves, just inside the entrance). These shops will also download digital photos to CD. Opposite are clean toilets, *locutorio* (a public phone centre) and ATMs. Further along the 'Sendero Verde' at the Estacíon Cataratas, towards the start of the 'Circuitos Inferior' and 'Superior' there's a great open-air café, *parrilla, locutorio* and toilets At the **Estación Garganta** there's another little café, toilets and shop selling postcards and water.

The **guardería** (ranger station) is next to the Estación Cataratas, on the way to the Circuitos Inferior and Superior. The *guardaparques* are hugely knowledgeable about the park and will give you detailed information on wildlife and where to spot it, and will even accompany you if they're not too busy. They also hand out a helpful leaflet with a clear map of the park, and another in English, *Birds of Iguazú*.

Every month on the five nights of full moon, there are 1½-hour guided walks (bilingual) that may include a dinner before or after the walk at the Restaurant La Selva, depending on the time of departure. See www.iguazuargentina.com for dates, times and email booking form; reservations also in person at the park, T03757-491469, or through agencies: US$68 with dinner; US$50 without.

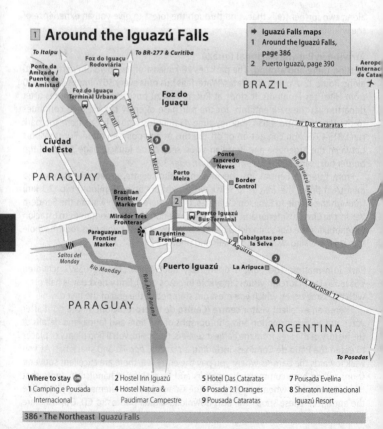

1 Around the Iguazú Falls

➡ Iguazú Falls maps
1 Around the Iguazú Falls, page 386
2 Puerto Iguazú, page 390

To Itaipu
To BR-277 & Curitiba
Aeropo
Internac
de Cata

Ponte da Amizade / Puente de la Amistad
Foz do Iguaçu Rodoviária

BRAZIL

Foz do Iguaçu Terminal Urbana

Foz do Iguaçu

Ciudad del Este

Av Das Cataratas

PARAGUAY

Ponte Tancredo Neves

Porto Meira

Border Control

Rio Iguazú Inferior

Brazilian Frontier Marker

Mirador Tres Fronteras

Puerto Iguazú Bus Terminal

Paraguayan Frontier Marker

Argentine Frontier

Cabalgatas por la Selva

Saltos del Monday

Rio Monday

V Aguirre

Rio Alto Paraná

Puerto Iguazú

La Aripuca

Ruta Nacional 12

PARAGUAY

ARGENTINA

To Posadas

Where to stay 🛏
1 Camping e Pousada Internacional
2 Hostel Inn Iguazú
4 Hostel Natura & Paudimar Campestre
5 Hotel Das Cataratas
6 Posada 21 Oranges
7 Pousada Evelina
8 Sheraton Internacional Iguazú Resort
9 Pousada Cataratas

Recommended books *The Laws of the Jungle,* by Santiago G de la Vega, and *Iguazu Life and Colour* are both available in English from visitor centres throughout Puerto Iguazú. Also useful is *Birds of Southern South America and Antarctica*, by De la Peña and Rumboll, published by Harper Collins, 1998.

Wildlife

You'll see amazingly rich wildlife whatever time you visit the park: there are more than 430 species of bird, 70 species of mammal and over a hundred species of butterfly. But you'll need to come in the early morning or late afternoon to stand a good chance of seeing the more elusive species: pumas and tapirs. Look out for restless and curious brown capuchin monkeys, seen in groups of around 20, howler monkeys and friendly coati with their striped tails. Toucans are ubiquitous, with their huge orange cartoon beaks, and also the curious plush crested jays, black with pale yellow breasts, which can be seen perched inquisitively around the park's restaurants. You'll also see two kinds of vultures wheeling above the falls themselves, both with fringed wing tips: the red-headed turkey vulture, and the black vulture whose wing tips are white. You should spot blue-winged parakeets, the red-rumped cacique, which builds hanging nests on *pindo* palms, and fruit-eaters like the magpie tanager and the colourful purple-throated euphonia. The butterflies are stunning: look out for electric blue *morpho* butterflies, as big as your hand, the poisonous red and black *heliconius*, and species of *Papilionidae* and *Pieridae*, with striking black and white designs.

Trails

Garganta del Diablo From Estación Garganta, it's a 1-km easy walk along boardwalks (fine for wheelchairs) across the wide River Iguazú to the park's centrepiece, the Garganta del Diablo falls.

Circuito Inferior and Circuito Superior There are excellent views of the wider range of falls, from Salto San Martín to Salto Dos Hermanos, from the two well-organized trails along sturdy walkways: the **Circuito Superior** (650 m) and **Circuito Inferior** (1400 m), both taking around 1½ to two hours to complete. To reach them, get off the train at the Estación Cataratas (after a 10-minute journey) and follow signs a short distance to where the trails begin. Alternatively, you can walk from the visitor centre along the Sendero Verde to the Estación Cataratas, which takes 10-15 minutes and avoids the crowds waiting for the next train.

Start with the **Circuito Superior**, a level path that takes you along the westernmost line of falls – Saltos Dos Hermanos, Bossetti, Bernabé Mendez, Mbigua (Guaraní for cormorant) and San Martín – allowing you to see these falls from above. This path is safe for those with walking difficulties, wheelchairs and pushchairs, but you should wear supportive, non-slippery shoes.

The **Circuito Inferior** takes you down to the water's edge via a series of steep stairs and walkways with superb views of both San Martín falls and the Garganta del Diablo from a distance, and then up close to Salto Bossetti. Wheelchair users, pram pushers, and those who aren't good with steps should go down by the exit route for a smooth and easy descent. There's a café on the way down and plenty of shade. You could then return to the **Estación Cataratas** to take the train to Estación Garganta, at 10 minutes and 40 minutes past the hour, and see the falls close up from above.

Isla San Martín An optional extra hour-long circuit is to take the free two-minute ferry ride (leaves every 10 minutes 0930-1530, or on demand) at the very bottom of the Circuito Inferior, which crosses to the small hilly island of Isla San Martín where two trails lead to *miradores* (viewpoints): take the right-hand path for good close views of the San Martín Falls and straight ahead to Salto Rivadavia, or left for a longer walk to the same place. Bathing on the beach here is strictly speaking not allowed, but there are usually a few Argentines sunning themselves. Note that the paths down to the ferry and up to the *miradores* on the island are very steep and uneven. Take water to drink, as there are no services. The ferry ride may be suspended due to high waters at times; ask at the entrance.

Alternative trails The park offers two more trails through the forest which allow you to get closer to the wildlife. The **Macuco Nature Trail** (7 km return; allow six hours) allows you to see particularly superb birdlife. It starts from the path leading from the visitor centre to the Sheraton Hotel, and is a magnificent walk down to the river via a natural pool (El Pozón) fed by a slender, ice-cold, 20-m-high waterfall, **Salto Arrechea**. This is a good place for bathing (and the only permitted place in the park), and the walk is highly recommended. See the helpful leaflet in English produced by the Iguazú National Park: *Macuco Nature Trail*. The first 3 km are easy but the next 150 m are more challenging, as the path descends steeply, before the final easy 200 m; the elderly and children may find this route tough. The path is open 0800-1500, but leaving in the early morning is recommended. There are no services, so bring water and lunch and contact tour agencies for guides. The **Sendero Yacaratía** trail starts from nearer the visitor centre and reaches the river by a different route, ending at **Puerto Macuco**, where you can take the *Jungle Explorer* boat to see the falls themselves. This trail is really for vehicles and less pleasant for walkers, so it's best visited on an organized safari. ▶▶ *See What to do, page 393.*

Border crossing: Argentina–Brazil

Puente Tancredo Neves

This crossing is straightforward.

Argentine immigration When leaving Argentina, Argentine immigration is at the Brazilian end of the bridge. Before setting off, check if you need a visa for Brazil. The border is open 0700-2300. Both Argentine and Brazilian officials stamp you in and out, even if only for a day visit. Whether you are entering Brazil for the first time, or leaving and returning after a day in Argentina, you must insist on getting off the bus to get the required stamp and entry card. Buses also stop at the Duty Free mall. The bus does not wait for those who need stamps, just catch the next one, of whatever company.

Brazilian consulate in Puerto Iguazú: Avenida Córdoba 278, T03757-420192, info.piguazu@itamaraty.gov.br. Open Monday-Friday 0800-1400.

Transport Buses leave Puerto Iguazú terminal for Foz do Iguaçu every 15 minutes, 0730-1830, US$4. Taxis between the border and Puerto Iguazú cost US$30.

Puerto Iguazú → *For listings, see pages 391-394. Colour map 2, A3.*

Puerto Iguazú (210 m) is a friendly, atmospheric place, its low white buildings splashed with the red dust from roads, and with bright green vegetation growing abundantly everywhere. Its houses are neat, decorated with flowers, and although the centre is slightly chaotic, the town has an appealing authentic life of its own, despite the massive daily influx of tourists on whom the economy depends. It's a pleasant place to walk around, and with several comfortable and economical places to stay, it's a much more appealing base than Foz on the Brazilian side.

Arriving in Puerto Iguazú → *Phone code 03757. Population 31,000.*

The **airport** is some 20 km southeast of Puerto Iguazú near the falls. The Four Tourist Travel bus service between the airport and the bus terminal, US$4, will also drop off/collect you from your hotel. A taxi to town costs US$15. The **bus terminal** ① *Av Córdoba and Av Misiones, T03757-423006,* has a phone office, restaurant, various tour company desks and bus offices. ▶▶ *See Transport, page 394, for more details.*

The **tourist office** ① *Aguirre 311, Puerto Iguazú, T03757-420800,* and **Municipal office** ① *Av Victoria Aguirre y Balbino Brañas, T03757-422938/T0800-266 4482, daily 0900-2200, www.iguazuturismo.gov.ar,* are useful only for the very patient and those who speak good Spanish. They are not always friendly but they do have a basic map with useful phone numbers and bus timetables. Also try www.misiones.gov. ar. There is also a **national park office** ① *Victoria Aguirre 66, T03757-420722, daily 0900-2200, www.iguazuargentina.com; in park T03757-420180.*

Places in Puerto Iguazú and around

The town's main street is Avenida Victoria Aguirre where, at No 66, you will find the Iguazú national park information office (see above). This avenue runs northwest from the entrance to the town to the little plaza at its hub, and changes names to Avenida Tres Fronteras as it turns east and heads to the spectacular viewpoint high above the meeting of rivers Paraná and Iguazú, known as the **Hito Tres Fronteras** (three borders landmark). You can also reach this point via an attractive *costanera*, running above the Río Iguazú, past the small port where boats leave for cruises along the Paraná and to Paraguay. At the Hito, there's a string of touristy souvenir stands, where children will press you to buy orchid plants and little rolls of the local *chipita* bread, made from mandioc root (very tasty). The views over the rivers and neighbouring Paraguay and Brazil are impressive.

There are a couple of interesting projects worth visiting. **La Aripuca** ① *T03757-423488, www.aripuca.com.ar, daily 0900-1800, US$3; turn off Ruta 12 at Km 4.5 just after Hotel Cataratas; or get off the bus here and walk 250 m*, is a charming centre for appreciation of the native trees of the forest – a good option for families if it's

2 Puerto Iguazú

→ **Iguazú Falls maps**
1 Around the Iguazú Falls, page 386
2 Puerto Iguazú, page 390

Where to stay
1 Garden Stone
2 Hostería Casa Blanca
3 Iguazú Jungle Lodge
4 Marco Polo Inn
8 Noelia
5 Panoramic
6 Peter Pan
10 Secret Garden

Restaurants
1 Aqva
2 El Quincho del Tío Querido
5 La Rueda
6 Pizza Color
8 Tango Bar Iguazú

raining. An Aripuca is a traditional Guaraní trap for birds, and a giant version of the pyramidic structure that they use has been made from the fallen logs of 30 ancient trees of different species. A 30-minute guided tour (English, Spanish or German) explains all about the tree life, and then you can clamber up their trunks, or enjoy the sculpture from enormous chairs made from tree roots. Sponsor a living tree in the forest to protect it. Recommended. Nearby, **Güira Oga** ① *Casa de los Pájaros, T03757-423980, www.guiraoga.com.ar, daily 0830-1830 (0900-1645 in winter), US$2*, is a sanctuary for birds that have been injured or rescued from traffickers. Here, they are treated and reintroduced to the wild; there are exquisite parrots and magnificent birds of prey. Endangered species are bred here, and eagles and hawks are taught to hunt. It is an entirely self-funded family enterprise. A 1-km-long trail from the road winds through the forest and through the large aviaries, with families of monkeys in trees overhead. A guided visit in English or Spanish takes 40 minutes, after which you can wander around at your leisure, and enjoy the peace. It is inspiring and informative. To get there, turn off Ruta 12 at Hotel Orquídeas Palace, and the entrance is 800 m further along the road from Aripuca.

⦿ Iguazú Falls listings

For hotel and restaurant price codes and other relevant information, see pages 20-26.

⦿ Where to stay

Parque Nacional Iguazú *p384, map p386*
$$$$ Sheraton Internacional Iguazú Resort, T491800, www.sheraton.com/iguazu. Fine position overlooking the falls, excellent, good restaurant and

breakfast, sports facilities and spa. Taxi to airport available. Recommended.

Puerto Iguazú *p389, map p390*
$$$$ Panoramic, Paraguay 372, T0800-999 4726, www.panoramic-hoteliguazu.com. On a hill overlooking the river, this hotel is stunning. Serene outdoor pool with great views, large well-designed rooms and all 5-star inclusions.
$$$$ Posada Puerto Bemberg, Fundadores Bemberg s/n, Puerto

Libertad (some 35 km south of Iguazú), T03757-496500, www.puertobemberg. com. Wonderful luxury accommodation and gourmet cuisine in **Casa Bemberg**, dating from 1940s, surrounded by lush gardens. Huge living areas, beautifully decorated rooms and helpful staff. Good birdwatching with resident naturalist. Highly recommended.

$$$$ Yacutinga Lodge, 30 km from town, pick up by jeep, www.yacutinga. com. A beautiful lodge in the middle of the rainforest, with 2- to 4-night packages, learning about the bird and plant life and Guaraní culture. Accommodation is in rustic adobe houses in tropical gardens, superb food and drinks included, as well as boat trips and walks.

$$$ Iguazú Jungle Lodge, Hipólito Iyrigoyen y San Lorenzo, T03757-420600, www.iguazujunglelodge.com. A well-designed complex of lofts and family suites, 7 blocks from the centre, by a river, with lovely pool. Comfortable and stylish, DVDs, great service, restaurant. Warmly recommended.

$$$ Posada 21 Oranges, C Montecarlo y Av los Inmigrantes, T03757-15-571403, www.21oranges.com. 10 simple but comfortable rooms set around a pool, lovely garden, welcoming. US$7 taxi ride or 20-min walk to town.

$$$ Secret Garden, Los Lapachos 623, T03757-423099, www.secretgarden iguazu.com. Small B&B with attentive owner, fern garden surrounding the house. Spacious rooms, good breakfast and cocktails, relaxing atmosphere.

$$$-$$ Hostería Casa Blanca, Guaraní 121, near bus station, T03757-421320, www.casablancaiguazu.com.ar. Family-run, large rooms, good showers, beautifully maintained.

$$ Petit Hotel Sí Mi Capitán, Las Guayabas 228, http://petithotelsimi capitan.com. 3 blocks from the town centre, with 2 standards of room and bungalows, safe in room, can arrange transfers, packed lunches, tourist information, parking, swimming pool, bar

$ pp Garden Stone, Av Córdoba 441, T03757-420425, www.gardenstonehostel. com. Lovely hostel with a homely feel set in nice gardens, with a large outdoor eating area, swimming pool. Recommended for a tranquil stay.

$ pp Hostel Inn Iguazú, R 12, Km 5, T03757-421823, http://hiiguazu.com. 20% discount to HI members and 10% discount on long-distance buses, dormitories US$13, a/c doubles **$$**. Large, well-organized hostel which used to be a casino. Huge pool, games and a range of free DVDs to watch. They also organize package tours to the falls, which include accommodation. No guests under 18.

$ pp Marco Polo Inn, Av Córdoba 158, T03757-425559, www.hostel-inn.com. The biggest and most central hostel in town, right in front of the bus station, a/c doubles **$$**. Nice pool, fun bar at night (open to non-residents). It gets busy so reserve in advance. Recommended.

$ pp Noelia, Fray Luis Beltrán 119, T03757-420729, www.hostelnoelia.com. Cheap, well-kept and helpful, good breakfast, family-run, good value.

$ pp Peter Pan, Av Córdoba 267, T03757-423616, www.peterpanhostel.com. Just down the hill from the bus station, spotless, central pool and large open kitchen. The doubles (**$$**) are lovely. Helpful staff.

● Restaurants

Puerto Iguazú *p389, map p390*
$$ Aqva, Av Córdoba y Carlos Thays, T03757-422064. Just down from the bus station, this lovely restaurant serves

dishes made with ingredients from the area.

$$ El Quincho del Tío Querido, Bompland 110, T03757-420151. Recommended for *parrilla* and local fish, very popular, great value.

$$ La Rueda, Córdoba 28, T03757-422531. Good food and prices, fish, steaks and pastas, often with mellow live music. Highly recommended.

$$ Tango Bar Iguazú, Av Brasil 1, T03757-422008. Bar which serves pizzas and pastas. It turns into a *milonga* with tango classes and dancing at night.

$$ Pizza Color, Córdoba 135. Popular for pizza and *parrilla*.

⊙ Bars and clubs

Puerto Iguazú *p389, map p390*
Cuba Libre, Av Brasil and Paraguay, T03757 528984. Just a block from the newly popular area of town for eating out, this is a fun place for a drink, or if you fancy dancing salsa. Owned by a Cuban, the music is great and the atmosphere lively at weekends.

La Tribu, Av Brasil 149. A pub/club which has good, cheap live shows.

⊙ What to do

Parque Nacional Iguazú *p384, map p386*
Agencies arrange day trips from Puerto Iguazú to the Argentine side of the falls, including transfer from your hotel and guide (request English speakers), and to the Brazilian side with lunch in Foz, but neither includes the park entrance fee. The tour to the Brazilian side of the falls may include a stop at the **Duty Free Shop**, a large, flash indoor mall between the 2 customs points selling perfumes

and cosmetics, electrical goods, spirits and cigarettes at reduced prices
There are also **Full Moon Walks**: night-time walking tours to the falls when the moon is full (see above).

Boat trips
Jungle Explorer, T03757-421696, www.iguazujungle.com. Run a series of boat trips, all highly recommended, including **Aventura Náutica**, an exhilarating journey by launch along the lower Río Iguazú, from opposite Isla San Martín right up to the San Martín falls and then into the Garganta del Diablo, completely drenching passengers in the mighty spray. Great fun; not for the faint-hearted, 12 mins. On **Paseo Ecológico** you float silently for 2.5 km from Estación Garganta to appreciate the wildlife on the river banks: basking tortoises, caiman, monkeys and birdlife. A wonderful and gentle introduction to the river, 30 mins, US$17.50.

Gran Aventura combines the Aventura Náutica with a longer boat trip along rapids in the lower Río Iguazú to Puerto Macuco, followed by a jeep trip along the Yacaratiá trail, 1 hr, US$63. Other combinations at reduced prices and tailor-made tours. Tickets available at all embarkation points.

Tour operators
Argecam Turismo, T03757-423085, www.argecamturismo.com. Can arrange tours to the mines and San Ignacio from Puerto Iguazú.

Iguazú Forest, T03757-421140, www.iguazuforest.com. Runs a ½- or full-day's adventure in the jungle offering the chance to try canopying, climbing waterfalls, repelling and mountain biking. Great for kids and teenagers.

Wildlife safaris

Explorador Expediciones, Perito Moreno 217, T03757-491469, www. rainforestevt.com.ar. Offers small-group safaris (Safari a la Cascada and Safari en la Selva), 3-day packages, birdwatching trips, adventure tours, trips to Moconá. Expert guides will bring the natural world alive and provide fantastic insights into the jungle. Recommended.

Puerto Iguazú *p389, map p390*
Tour operators

Aguas Grandes, Entre Ríos 66, T425500, www.aguasgrandes.com. Tours to both sides of the falls and further afield, activities in the forest, abseiling down waterfalls, good fun.

Agroturismo Sombra de Toro, Ruta Nacional 101, Bernardo de Yrigoyen, T03757-15-449425. By the Parque Provincial Urugua-í, which adjoins the Iguazú national park, this farm owned by the Mackoviak family offers tours and accommodation on their private reserve, which contains Selva Paranaense and examples of the rare *sombra de toro* tree.

Cabalgatas Ecológicas, T03757-15-50942, www.cabalgatasecologicas.com. Good personalized horse-riding tours around Iguazú.

Hostel Inn and Marco Polo Inn (for details see Where to stay, above) run friendly and efficient travel agencies where you can arrange trips to the falls and surrounding area.

⊙ Transport

Puerto Iguazú *p389, map p390*
Air
Direct flights to **Buenos Aires**, 1½ hrs.

Bus
To **Buenos Aires**, 16-18 hrs, US$99-115, 6 companies. To **Posadas**, stopping at San Ignacio Miní, frequent, 5-6 hrs, US$18-20; to **San Ignacio Miní**, US$17.

Taxi
T03757-420973/421707. Fares in town, US$2.50-4.

⊙ Directory

Puerto Iguazú *p389, map p390*
Banks Banks are generally open 1000-1500. Many ATMs in town, including at **Banco de la Nación**, Av Aguirre 179, and **Macro Misiones,** Misiones y Bonpland, which is just down from the bus station. The *Sheraton* also has an ATM. **Currency exchange** Cambios Links, Av Victoria Aguirre 228, T03757-423200; **Libres Cambios** in the Hito Tres Fronteras, T03757-422354. Good exchange rates at the Brazilian border. **Embassies and consulates** Brazil, Av Córdoba 264, T03757-420192. **Medical services** Hospital SAMIC, T03757-420288.

Parque Nacional Foz do Iguaçu (Brazil)

The Brazilian National Park was founded in 1939 and declared a World Heritage Site in 1986. The park covers 170,086 ha, extending along the north bank of the Rio Iguaçu, sweeping northwards to Santa Tereza do Oeste on the BR-277. The experience is less impressive than on the Argentine side since you are not immersed in the jungle, but it's fascinating to see the whole panorama of the falls from a distance and, because there are fewer crowds, it is more tranquil and you will see more wildlife. For more information on the park, see www.cataratasdoiguacu.com.br (in English).

Arriving in Parque Nacional Foz do Iguaçu

Getting there
It is 17 km from the city of Foz do Iguaçu to the park entrance. Buses leave Foz do Iguaçu, from the Terminal Urbana on Avenida Juscelino Kubitschek and República Argentina every 40 minutes starting at 0730-1800, and are clearly marked 'Parque Nacional'. You can get on or off at any point on the route past the airport and **Hotel das Cataratas**, 40 minutes US$1.50 one way, payable only in reais or pesos. The bus route ends at the park entrance where you purchase entry tickets (see below) and change to a park bus.

Getting around
From the entrance, shuttle buses leave every 10-15 minutes for Porto Canoas, stopping at the start of the trails mentioned below. There are Portuguese, Spanish and English announcements of the five stops.

Park information
Entry is US$21, payable in reais, Argentine pesos, dollars, euros or by credit card, also online by credit card, and the park is open daily 0900-1700. At the entrance is a smart modern visitor centre, with toilets, ATMs, a small café, a large souvenir shop and a Banco Itaú *câmbio* (1000-1500). An Exposição Ecológica has information about the natural history of the falls and surrounding park (included in entry fee; English texts poor). Nature lovers are advised to visit first thing in the morning or late in the afternoon, preferably in low season, as crowds can significantly detract from the experience of the falls and surrounding park (at peak times, such as Semana Santa, the park receives up to 10,000 visitors a day).

Border crossing: Brazil–Paraguay

Ponte de Amizade/Puente de Amistad (Friendship Bridge)

The Ponte de Amizade/Puente de Amistad (Friendship Bridge) over the Río Paraná, 12 km north of Foz, leads straight into the heart of Ciudad del Este.

The border crossing over the Friendship Bridge to Foz do Iguaçu is very informal, but is jammed with vehicles and pedestrians all day long. No passport stamps are required to visit Ciudad del Este for the day. Motorcycle taxis (helmet provided, hang on tight) are a good option if you have no luggage. There are lots of minibuses, too. On international buses, eg from Florianópolis to Ciudad del Este and Asunción, or from Foz to Asunción, the procedure is: non-Brazilians get out at immigration for an exit stamp, then take the bus across the bridge to Paraguayan immigration where everyone gets out for an entry stamp. On buses from Asunción to Foz and beyond, non-Paraguayans get out at Paraguayan immigration for an exit stamp, then the bus takes all passengers across the river to Brazilian immigration for the entry stamp. Make sure you get all entry and exit stamps.

Transport Two bus companies cross the international bridge between Ciudad del Este and Foz's bus terminals: Pluma, T+595 (0)61-510434, www.pluma. com.br. Buses (marked Cidade-Ponte) leave from the Terminal Urbana, Avenida Juscelino Kubitschek, Foz do Iguaçu, for the Ponte de Amizade (Friendship Bridge). From Ciudad del Este: daily 0700-1830 each way every 10 minutes, 30-40 minutes, US$2, and Rafagnin, T+55 (0)45-3523 1986 (Brazil; no office in Paraguay) 0800-1900, US$3. Speak to the driver about waiting at the immigration posts at either end of the bridge. Most buses will not wait at immigration, so disembark to get your exit stamp, walk across the bridge (10 minutes) and obtain your entry stamp; keep

---

Exploring the national park

Wildlife

Most frequently encountered are the little and red brocket deer, South American coati, white-eared opossum and brown capuchin monkey. Much harder to see are the jaguar, ocelot, puma, white-lipped peccary, bush dog and southern river otter. The endangered tegu lizard can also been seen. Over 100 species of butterfly have been identified, among them the electric blue *morpho* and the poisonous red and black *heliconius*, and the birdlife is especially rewarding for the birdwatcher. Five members of the toucan family can be seen including toco and red-breasted toucans. Never feed wild animals and keep your distance when taking photos; coatis have been known to attack visitors with food.

Trails

The shuttle bus stops first at Park Administration. Next is the start of the Poço Preto trail (9 km through the forest to the river, walking or by bicycle), then the Bananeiras trail and Macuco Safari (see What to do, below). After 10 km the bus stops at the your ticket and continue to Foz on the next bus free. Paraguayan taxis cross freely to Brazil (US$30), but it is cheaper and easier to walk across the bridge and then take a taxi, bargain hard. You can pay in either currency (and often in Argentine pesos). Obtain all necessary exit and entry stamps.

To Argentina Direct buses to Puerto Iguazú, leave frequently from outside the Ciudad del Este bus terminal, US$2.50. If continuing into Argentina, you need to get Argentine and Paraguayan stamps (not Brazilian), but the bus usually does not stop, so ask driver if he will. Also check what stamps you need, if any, if making a day visit to Puerto Iguazú.

There is a friendly tourist office in the customs building on the Paraguayan side, open 24 hours. You can get out of the bus here, rather than going to the bus terminal. Taxis wait just beyond immigration, US$4.50-5.50 to most places in Ciudad del Este, but settle price before getting in as there are reports of exorbitant fares. Remember to adjust your watch to local time (Brazil is one hour ahead). Although Paraguay observes daylight saving throughout the country, only some states in Brazil (including Paraná) do so. Brazilian consulate in Ciudad del Este Ciudad del Este, Pampliega 205 y Pa'í Pérez, T+595 (0)61-500985, consulado.deleste@itamaraty.gov.br, Monday-Friday 0800-1400, issues visas. Argentine Consulate in Ciudad del Este, Avenida Boquerón y Adrián Jara, Edificio China p 7, T+595 (0)61-500945, www.embajada-argentina.org.py/V2/consulados/consulado-gral-en-cde, Monday-Friday 0800-1300.

Argentine consulate in Foz do Iguaçu, Travessa Eduardo Bianchi 26, T+55 (0)45-9113 8167, Monday-Friday 1000-1600. Paraguayan consulate in Foz do Iguaçu, R Marechal Deodoro 901, T+55 (0)45-3523 2898.

start of the Cascadas Trail and the Hotel das Cataratas, and finally at the end of the road, Porta Canoas.

The 1200-m paved walk from **Hotel das Cataratas** to the falls is an easy stroll, taking you high above the Río Iguazú, giving splendid views of all the falls on the Argentine side from a series of galleries. At the end of the path, you can walk down to a viewing point almost right under the powerful **Floriano Falls**, a dramatic view, since you're in the middle of the river. A catwalk at the foot of the Floriano Falls goes almost to the middle of the river to give a good view of the **Garganta del Diablo**. From here, there are 150 steps up to the **Porto Canoas complex**, a quick and easy walk, but for those who find stairs difficult, you can take a lift, or return the way you came, and walk a little further along the road. The Porto Canoas complex consists of a big souvenir shop, toilets, a smart buffet restaurant, a café and *lanchonete*. All have a fantastic view of the river above the falls. Return to the visitor centre and entrance by the free shuttle bus. The visit will take you around two hours; allow extra time for lunch.

Foz do Iguaçu (Brazil) → *For listings, see pages 399-402. Colour map 2, A3.*

A small modern city, Foz lies 28 km from the falls, with a wide range of accommodation and good communications by air and road with the main cities of southern Brazil and Asunción in Paraguay. It's not a particularly attractive town, and Argentina's Puerto Iguazú makes a better base, with cheaper hotels and better access to the falls. Street crime has increased in Foz in recent years, but the inhabitants are friendly and welcoming, and there are some good places to eat.

Arriving in Foz do Iguaçu → *Phone code +55-(0)45. Population 232,000.*

Getting there Iguaçu international Airport ⓘ *T+55-(0)45-3521 4200*, is 19.5 km south of town near the falls. In arrivals there is a Banco do Brasil and Caribe Tours e Câmbio, car rental offices, a tourist office and an official taxi stand. Taxis charge US$25 for a trip into town. All buses marked Parque Nacional pass the airport in each direction daily 0525-0040 and cost US$1.50 to anywhere around town; they allow backpacks but not lots of luggage. Many hotels run minibus services for a small charge.

The bus terminal ⓘ *Av Costa e Silva, T+55-(0)45-3522 2590*, is 4 km from the centre on the road to Curitiba; take any bus that says 'Rodoviária', US$1.50, or a taxi for US$10. There's a tourist office open 0630-1800, **Cetreme** desk for tourists who have lost their documents, *guarda municipal* (police), ATM and luggage store. For transport to the falls, see page 402.

Tourist information The municipal tourist office ⓘ *T+55(0)45-2105 8100, or 0800-451516 (freephone 0700-2300), www.pmfi.pr.gov.br*, is at Avenida das Cataratas 2330, midway between town and the turn-off to Ponte Tancredo Neves. The staff are extremely helpful and well organized, and speak English. There are also tourist offices at the **bus terminal** (open 0700-1800), the Terminal de Transporte Urbano (open 0730-1800) and at the **airport** (open 0830-2200), with map and bus information. If you arrive without a place to stay, there are plenty of agencies to help you find a hotel and transfer you there.

Tourists are warned not to stray from the main roads in town and to leave all valuables and documents in the safe in the hotel. Avenida Kubitschek and the streets south of it, towards the river, have a reputation for being unsafe at night as there is a *favela* or shanty town, nearby. Having said that there are some nice places to stay here with their own restaurants, so you shouldn't need to be out in town at night too much.

Around Foz do Iguaçu

Apart from the Parque Nacional do Iguaçu there are a couple of other attractions. The **Parque das Aves** ⓘ *next to the visitor centre at Rodovia das Cataratas, Km 18, just before the falls, www.parquedasaves.com.br (in English), daily 0830-1700, US$15*, contains Brazilian and foreign birds, many species of parrot and beautiful toucans, in huge aviaries through which you can walk, with the birds flying and hopping around you. There are other birds in cages and a butterfly and hummingbird house.

The world's largest hydroelectric dam is at **Lago Itaipu** ① *12 km north, T0800-645 4645, www.itaipu.gov.br, www.turismoitaipu.com.br, daily 0800-1600, short bus tours, US$12, full tours US$30, night views Fri and Sat 2000, US$7; take buses Conjunto C Norte or Conjunto C Sul from Terminal Urbano, Av JK and República Argentina, US$1.50*. It's a major feat of human achievement, an interesting contrast to the natural wonder of the falls. It was built jointly by Brazil and Paraguay. The main dam is 8 km long, creating a lake of 1400 sq km. A short film is shown at the visitor centre 10 minutes before each guided visit. Wear long trousers and sensible shoes. Check times with the tourist office and take your passport.

Several beaches can be visited around the lake. A large reforestation project is underway and six biological refuges have been created on the lakeshore in both countries. There is also the **Ecomuseu de Itaipu** ① *Av Tancredo Neves, Km 11, T0800-645 4645, Tue-Sun 0830-1730, US$5*, and **Refúgio Bela Vista** ① *closed Tue, 4 visits a day from the visitor centre, US$10*, animal rescue centre and home to the fauna displaced by the dam, both geared to educate about the preservation of the local culture and environment. Recommended. In addition there is the **Polo Astronômico** ① *Wed-Sun at 0930 and 1530, Fri-Sat also 1900, US$9*, a planetarium and astronomical observatory.

◉ Parque Nacional Foz do Iguaçu (Brazil) listings

For hotel and restaurant price codes and other relevant information, see pages 20-26.

◉ Where to stay

Parque Nacional Foz do Iguaçu *p395*
Good selection of hotels and many also offer excursions to the falls. The tourist office has a full list. Taxis are only good value for short distances when you have your luggage.

$$$$ Hotel das Cataratas, directly overlooking the falls, 28 km from Foz, T+55 (0)45-2102 7000, www.hoteldas cataratas.com. Elegant, pale pink colonial-style building with a pool in luxuriant gardens, where you might spot wildlife at night and early morning. Generally recommended, caters for lots of groups, The restaurant is open to non-residents for midday and evening buffets, also à la carte dishes and dinner with show. Member of the Belmond group (www.

belmond.com). An environmental fee of about US$10 is added to the room rate.
On the road to the falls (Rodovia das Cataratas) are several expensive modern hotels with good facilities (eg **Bristol Viale Cataratas**, www.vialecataratas. com.br, **Carimã**, www.hotelcarima. com.br, **San Martin**, www.hotelsan martin.com.br), but for budget travellers, check out:

$$ Hostel Natura, Rodovia das Cataratas Km 12.5, Remanso Grande, T+55 (0)45-3529 6949, www.hostelnatura.com (near the Paudimar). Rustic hostel with a small pool set in fields. Rooms with fan, **$** pp in dorm, camping, pool table, TV lounge, small kitchen, arrange visits to the falls; website has detailed instructions for how to reach them.

$$-$ Paudimar Campestre, Av das Cataratas Km 12.5, Remanso Grande, near airport, T+55 (0)45-3529 6061, www.paudimar.com.br. In high season HI members only. From airport or town take Parque Nacional bus (0525-0040) and get out at Remanso Grande bus stop, by **Hotel San Juan Eco**, then take the free alimentador shuttle (0700-1900) to the hostel, or walk 1.2 km from main road. Camping as well (**$**), pool, soccer pitch, quiet, kitchen and communal meals, breakfast. Highly recommended. Tours run to either side of the falls (good value). Paudimar desk at *rodoviária*.

Foz do Iguaçu *p398*
Note Check hotels' websites for internet prices and special offers. Av Juscelino Kubitschek and the streets south of it, towards the river, are unsafe at night. Many prostitutes around R Rebouças and Almirante Barroso. Taxis are only good value for short distances when you are carrying all your luggage.
$$$$ Suíça, Av Felipe Wandscheer 3580, T+55 (0)45-3025 3232, www.hotelsuica. com.br. Some way out of the city, rooms, suites and lodges, comfortable, Swiss manager, helpful with tourist information, attractive pools, gym.
$$$$-$$$ Luz, Av Gustavo Dobrandino da Silva 145, near *rodoviária*, T+55 (0)45-3522 3535, www.luzhotel.com.br. Buffet restaurant, pool. Recommended.
$$$ Baviera, Av Jorge Schimmelpfeng 697, T+55 (0)45-3523 5995, www. hotelbavieraiguassu.com.br. Chalet-style exterior, on main road, central for bars and restaurants, comfortable, renovated.
$$$ Del Rey, R Tarobá 1020, T+55 (0)45-2105 7500, www.hoteldelreyfoz.com.br. Nothing fancy, but perennially popular, little pool, great breakfasts.
$$$ Foz Plaza, R Marechal Deodoro 1819, T+55 (0)45-3521 5500, www.foz plazahotel.com.br. Serene and very nice, restaurant, pool. Also has a new annex.
$$$ Foz Presidente I, R Xavier da Silva 1000 and II at R Mcal Floriano Peixoto

1851, T+55 (0)45-3572 4450, www.foz presidentehoteis.com.br. Good value, decent rooms, restaurant, pool, No 1 is convenient for buses.
$$$ San Juan Tour, R Marechal Deodoro 1349, T+55 (0)45-2105 9100, www.sanjuanhoteis.com.br. Cheaper if booked on-line. Comfortable, excellent buffet breakfast, popular, good value. Recommended. The more expensive **San Juan Eco** is on the road to the falls.
$$$ Tarobá, R Tarobá 1048, T+55 (0)45-2102 7770, www.hoteltaroba. com.br. In Best Western chain, bright and welcoming, small pool, nice rooms, helpful, good breakfast (extra), good value. Recommended.
$$ Pousada Cataratas, R Parigot de Sousa 180, T+55 (0)45-3523 7841, www. pousadacataratas.com.br. Well-maintained modern rooms with decent hot showers, small pool, good value with regular discounts and promotions through the website. Can organize tours and transfers to and from the airport and *rodoviária*.
$$ Pousada da Laura, R Naipi 671, T+55 (0)45-3572 3374. **$** pp in shared dorm with good breakfast. Secure, kitchen, laundry facilities, a popular place to meet other travellers.
$$ Pousada El Shaddai, R Rebouças 306, near Terminal Urbana, T+55 (0)45-3025 4493, www.pousadaelshaddai.com.br. Rooms are cheaper with fan and shared bath, **$** pp in dorm, pool.
$$ Pousada Evelina, R Irlan Kalichewski 171, Vila Yolanda, T+55 (0)45-3574 3817, www.pousadaevelina.com.br. Lots of tourist information, English, French, Italian, Polish and Spanish spoken, good breakfast and location, near Muffato Supermarket, near Av Cataratas on the way to the falls. Warmly recommended.
$$-$ Arterial, Av José Maria de Brito 2661, T+55 (0)45-3573 1859,

hotelarterial@hotmail.com. Near *rodoviária*. Good value, huge breakfast, opposite is a 24-hr buffet restaurant.

Camping
Camping e Pousada Internacional, R Manêncio Martins 21, 1.5 km from town, T+55 (0)45-3529 8183, www. campinginternacional.com.br. For vehicles and tents, half price with International Camping Card, also basic cabins (**$**), helpful staff, English, German and Spanish spoken, pool, restaurant. **Note** Camping is not permitted by the **Hotel das Cataratas** and falls.

⑦ Restaurants

Foz do Iguaçu *p398*
$$$ Búfalo Branco, R Rebouças 530, T+55 (0)45-3523 9744. Superb all-you-can-eat *churrasco*, includes filet mignon, bull's testicles, salad bar and desert. Sophisticated surroundings and attentive service. Highly recommended.
$$$ Rafain, Av das Cataratas 1749, T+55 (0)45-3523 1177, www.rafainchurrascaria. com.br. Closed Sun evening. Out of town, take a taxi or arrange with travel agency. Set price for excellent buffet with folkloric music and dancing (2100-2300), touristy but very entertaining. Recommended.
$$$ Zaragoza, R Quintino Bocaiúva 882, T+55 (0)45-3574 3084. Large and upmarket, for Spanish dishes and seafood. Recommended.
$$ Atos, Av Juscelino Kubitschek 865, T+55 (0)45-3572 2785. Per kilo buffet with various meats, salads, sushi and puddings. Lunch only.
$$ Bier Garten, Av Jorge Schimmelpfeng 550, T+55 (0)45-3523 3700. Bustling pizzeria, *churrascaria* and *choperia*.

Cafés
Marias e Maria, Av Brasil 505. Good *confeitaria*.
Oficina do Sorvete, Av Jorge Schimmel-pfeng 244. Daily 1100-0100. Excellent ice creams, a popular local hang-out.

⑦ Bars and clubs

Foz do Iguaçu *p398*
Bars, all doubling as restaurants, concentrated on Av Jorge Schimmelpfeng for 2 blocks from Av Brasil to R Mal Floriano Peixoto. Wed to Sun are best nights; crowd tends to be young.
Armazém, R Edmundo de Barros 446, T+55 (0)45-3572 7422. Intimate and sophisticated, attracts discerning locals, good atmosphere, mellow live music. Recommended.
Capitão Bar, Av Jorge Schimmelpfeng 288 and Almte Barroso, T+55 (0)45-3572 1512. Large, loud and popular, nightclub attached.
Oba! Oba!, Av Mercosul 400, T+55 (0)45-3529 9070, www.obaobasambashow. com.br. At **Churrascaria Bottega**. Daily 1200-1530 for lunch, Mon-Sat 2000-2200, with live samba show at 2200.
Pizza Park Bar, R Almirante Barroso 993. Specializes in vodka and whisky brands. Wi-Fi zone.

⑦ What to do

Parque Nacional Foz do Iguaçu *p395*
Tour operators
Macuco Safari, T+55-(0)45-3529 6040, www.macucosafari.com.br. Run the Macuco Safari Tour, 2 hrs, US$70, which leaves from the 1st stop on the free shuttle bus service. Ride down a 3-km-long path through the forest in open electric jeeps, and then a motor boat takes you close to the falls themselves,

similar to **Jungle Explorer** on the Argentine side. Portuguese, English and Spanish spoken. Take insect repellent and a waterproof camera bag.

Foz do Iguaçu *p398*
Tour operators
Lots of companies organize conventional tours to the falls – convenient as they collect you from your hotel, ½-day, price does not include park entrance.
Cânion Iguaçu, T+55-(0)45-3529 6040, www.campodedesafios.com.br. Local adventure company that can organize abseiling, rafting and rock climbing in the area.
Caribe Tur, at the international airport, and at **Hotel das Cataratas** and **Hotel Bourbon**, T+55-(0)45-3521 3900, www. grupocaribe.com.br. Run tours from the airport to the Argentine side, and **Hotel das Cataratas**.
Conveniotur, Rua Rui Barbosa 820, T+55-(0)45-3523 3500, www.conveniotur.com.br.
Guayi Travel, R Irian Kalichewiski 265, Vila Yolanda, T+55-(0)45-3027 0043, www.guayitravel.com. Excellent tours to both sides of the falls, Ciudad del Este, Itaipu and around, including options for birders and wildlife enthusiasts. English and Spanish spoken.

⊖ Transport

Foz do Iguaçu *p398*
Air
There are daily flights to **Rio de Janeiro**, **São Paulo**, **Curitiba** and other Brazilian cities.

Bus
To Brazil To **Curitiba**, 9-11 hrs, paved road, US$62, with **Pluma and Sulamericana**. To **Guaíra** via Cascavel only, 5 hrs, US$20. To **Florianópolis**, 16 hrs, US$72-76; to **Porto Alegre**, US$65-74. To **São Paulo**, 16 hrs, US$85.

   To Paraguay To **Asunción**, direct, US$20-22, with **Pluma** and **Nuestra Señora de la Asunción**. Buses are cheaper from Ciudad del Este.

⊕ Directory

Foz do Iguaçu *p398*
Banks It is difficult to change money on Sun, but quite possible in Ciudad del Este (Paraguay), where US dollars can be obtained on credit cards. There are plenty of banks with ATMs, *câmbios* and travel agencies on Av Brasil. **Post office** Praça Getúlio Vargas 72.

Contents

Footprint features

Border crossings

At a glance

☺ **Getting around** Minibuses connect even the smallest towns and some campsites. A car or bicycle gives more freedom.
⏱ **Time required** At least 4-7 days for Bariloche, 1-2 for towns and hikes or skiing.
☂ **Weather** Rainy and cold from May-Aug, and high temperatures from Nov-Mar.
✖ **When not to go** May-Jul, unless skiing. In Aug Bariloche can be busy with students.

N

50 km
50 miles

Tromen
(3978m) ▲

Reserva
Provincial
Copahue ◆

Gdor
Ayala

Rincón de
los Sauces

Copahue
Caviahue ◆

Loncopué

Río Neuquén

Catriel

NEUQUEN

Bajado
del Agrio

Añelo

Paso Pino
Hachado

Las
Lajas

Paso de
Icalma

Villa Pehuenia

Moquehue

1

Lago
Aluminé

Norquinco

Parque
Nacional
Laguna
Blanca ◆

Zapala

Plaza
Huincal

Neuquén

Cipolletti

22

Cutral-Có

Gral Roca

Villa El Chocón

Quillén
Rahue

Aluminé

40

Picún Leufú

Embalse Ezequiel
Ramos Mexía

Paso
Mamuil Malal
(Tromen)

Lanín
(3768m) ▲

Lago
Huechulafquen

Parque
Nacional
Lanín ◆

Piedra del
Aguila

237

Trica-Có

El Cuy

Paso Hua Hum

Junín de
los Andes

San Martín
de los Andes

RIO NEGRO

Lago
Lácar

234

Confluencia

Río Limay

CHILE

Villa Traful

237

Sierra Colorado

Los Menucos

Paso Samoré
(Puyehue)

Villa La Angostura

Parque Nacional
Nahuel Huapi ◆

Lago
Nahuel
Huapi

Llao Llao

2

Bariloche

23

Paso Pérez Rosales

3

Pampa Linda

Catedral
(2388m) ▲

Ingeniéro
Jacobacci

Tronador
(3478m) ▲

4

Villa Mascardi

Lago
Mascardi

40

258

5

El Bolsón

El Maitén

CHUBUT

Parque Nacional
Lago Puelo ◆

Epuyén
Cholila

Leleque

★ Don't miss ...

Lago
Menéndez

6

Parque Nacional
Los Alerces ◆

Lago
Futulaufquen

Esquel

40

1 Villa Pehuenia, page 416.
2 Bariloche, page 451.
3 Estancia Peuma Hue, page 466.
4 Mount Tronador, page 472.
5 Jauja ice cream, page 484.
6 Parque Nacional Los Alerces,
   page 491.

Trevelin

Paso Futaleufú

40

Tecka

Paso Palena

Trek amongst craggy snow-capped peaks flanked by glaciers and crystalline rivers running through virgin Valdivian rainforest to lakes of peppermint green and Prussian blue. Ski down long pistes with panoramic views of lagoons below, or hike for days among the mountain tops without seeing any signs of civilization. Take a slow boat across fjords or a hair-raising whitewater rafting trip. Or simply step onto the terrace of your lakeside hotel and sip a Malbec as the sun sinks over the mountains. Whatever you choose to do, Argentina's Lake District is spectacular and unforgettable.

Bariloche is the main tourist centre, a friendly but large town in alpine style with chocolate shops, lakeside hotels and chalet-style restaurants selling wild boar and smoked trout. Towering above is a range of peaks where you can hike, ski or cycle. Or take a cable car and admire the incredible views. Bariloche could easily entertain you for a week. A magical road winds north from here through seven lakes and three national parks to the pretty tourist towns of Villa La Angostura and San Martín de los Andes. Retreat to Lago Huechulafquen, where perfectly conical Volcán Lanín is reflected in cobalt blue waters. North of here, it's wilder and less visited. Pehuenia is a quiet haven with forests of prehistoric monkey puzzle trees, broad lagoons and the rich culture of the native Mapuche people.

At the southern end of the lakes, El Bolsón and Esquel are wonderfully relaxed places for a few days' hiking, where the mountains are magnificent, and the local *cerveza* is excellent. Take the *Old Patagonian Express*, try a Welsh tea in quaint Trevelin, and then explore the region's most unspoilt national park, Los Alerces. A jade-green river flows between the cinnamon trunks of *arrayán* trees and 1000-year-old *alerce* trees tower above you.

Arriving in the Lake District

Getting there

Air There are several flights daily from Buenos Aires to Neuquén, Chapelco (for Junín and San Martín de los Andes), Bariloche and Esquel (for the southern lakes), as well as flights from Santiago in Chile to Bariloche. In addition, the army airline **LADE** runs weekly flights connecting Bariloche with other Patagonian towns. If you're short on time, flying is preferable to long bus journeys, and it's relatively inexpensive. Consider buying two singles (same price as a return), flying to San Martín de los Andes in the north and leaving from Esquel in the south, allowing you to see the whole area by hired car or bus. Book well in advance from December to March.

Bus Long-distance buses connect busy Neuquén and Bariloche with Buenos Aires and all major cities in Argentina, as well as over the Chilean border. But distances are huge and these long journeys will probably take a day or more out of your holiday – Bariloche to Buenos Aires is 22 hours; to Mendoza, 19 hours; and to Puerto Madryn, 14 hours. Unless your budget is really tight, it's better to fly.

Train One of the country's few long-distance railways, the Tren Patagónico, runs to Bariloche from Viedma on the east coast, a comfortable overnight service that also carries cars. Trains were cancelled in December 2013, but services were restarted in May 2014 only for a train to be derailed a month later. It is best check in advance if the service is running; the company's website is www.trenpatagonico-sa.com.ar. The current service starts in Viedma, but there is talk of running the service from Buenos Aires via Bahía Blanca.

Getting around

Bicycle The area is fabulous for cycling with unparalleled views, lots of hills, but generally good roads, even where they are *ripio* (gravel). Avoid cycling in January and early February when there is lots of car traffic around the lakes. During the rest of the year there are few cars and you'll have some superb rides. There are good bike shops in Bariloche and San Martín that carry a wide range of spares and can also do repairs. You can also rent bikes, although they're not of the highest standard. Carry plenty of food and water, as services are few and far between, though there are plenty of campsites. There is almost no shade on the stretch from Bariloche to Esquel.

Boat There are lots of boat trips around Lago Nahuel Huapi which can be used as a means of transport, as well as a day out. The Three Lakes Crossing to Chile from Bariloche is a good way of getting to Puerto Montt in Chile, but the bus is cheaper.
➤➤ *For more information on the Three Lakes Crossing, see box, page 462.*

Bus and car Hiring a car is the most appealing option as it allows you to stop where you like and explore places off the beaten track. However, if you're travelling alone, you might find the distances tedious. There are excellent bus services around

Bariloche, making it possible to do long hikes in more remote areas. There are also regular bus services running north/south between Junín de los Andes, San Martín de los Andes, Bariloche and El Bolsón, and on to Esquel, with less frequent services via Cholila, Lagos Puelo and Epuyen. Many big buses will take bicycles, but always arrange this beforehand. The national parks are less easy to access by bus, although there is a daily bus into and out of Los Alerces from Esquel. Reaching both Pehuenia and the dinosaur region near Neuquén is almost impossible by bus. These places largely cater for Argentine tourists, who mostly bring their own cars. Unless you have a lot of spare time to wait for buses, hiring a car or arranging a tour is the best way to get the most out of the northern lakes.

Car hire is easiest in Bariloche, but is also possible in San Martín de los Andes, El Bolsón, and Esquel. If you plan to take a hire car over the border into Chile, let the car-hire company know ahead of time as by law the vehicle must have its registration number etched on the windows.

Walking There are plenty of *refugios* in the mountains behind Bariloche making it possible to plan four- or five-day hikes. They vary in quality but most will provide hot meals and advice on routes. There are more *refugios* near Pampa Linda, in the hills around El Bolsón, and a couple in both Los Alerces and Lanín national parks. Get advice from park offices or **Club Andino offices** (see page 448). Bus services around Bariloche are well set up to help hikers get about, but are more limited elsewhere (see above).

Best time to visit
Summer (December to February) is the obvious time to come, but be aware that January is impossibly busy throughout the region as this is when Argentines take their holidays en masse and accommodation is hard to find. In summer, *tábanos* (horseflies) are common on the lake shores and at lower altitudes; their bites are very annoying but not harmful, and the only solution is to climb higher. Come in March and early April instead, when days are still likely to be clear and there are far fewer visitors, making it much easier to get flights and be spontaneous with accommodation. Late spring and early summer (October to November) can be lovely, though cool, and also busy. Autumn is the most beautiful time of year to visit, with brilliant displays of autumn leaves in late April and early May. The ski season runs from late June to September and is busiest in July, when prices rise and Bariloche is inundated. Outside the peak season, transport services are fewer, requiring more flexible schedules, but well worth it to enjoy greater tranquillity. Hotels are all more expensive in peak periods, with the highest prices in January and July.

Tourist information
The best information centre is in Bariloche. It is well set up for tourism with good tour operators and well-organized boat and cable-car services to make the most of the stunning mountain landscape nearby. Tourist offices can be found in each town, but to plan your trip and for more information before you come, check out these sites: www.neuquentur.gob.ar (in English); www.barilochepatagonia.info (a

great multilingual site); www.visitchile.org; www.interpatagonia.com (excellent site for general information on the area in English); www.clubandino.org (for walks and mountain climbing); www.activepatagonia.com.ar (hiking and trekking expeditions); and www.revistapatagonia.com.ar (a useful magazine).

National parks

There are five national parks covering enormous swathes of the Lake District, and these areas are generally where you'll find the best hiking, rafting and horse riding, in the most unspoilt forests and mountain landscapes you can imagine. The area's main centre, **Bariloche**, is inside **Parque Nacional Nahuel Huapi** and has a well-developed infrastructure for activities in the park, see page 467. Inside this park is another tiny park, **Parque Nacional Los Arrayanes**, accessed from **Villa La Angostura**. Immediately to the north of Nahuel Huapi is **Parque Nacional Lanín**, which contains the town of **San Martín de los Andes**, and also has superb hiking, especially around **Volcán Lanín** (see page 428). South of Bariloche there is the tiny but beautiful **Parque Nacional Lago Puelo**, just south of **El Bolsón**. Finally, **Los Alerces** is the most pristine of all the parks, with just one road running through it, and most areas accessible only on foot. The nearest towns are **Esquel** and **Trevelin**, see pages 488 and 490. Each park has a ranger's station, where *guardaparques* will give you a map and advise on walks in the park, as well as on accommodation and the state of the paths.

Eastern and central Neuquén

The northern half of the Lake District falls into the province of Neuquén, encompassing an enormous region that stretches from the border with Mendoza, beyond Copahue and Caviahue in the north, to just north of Bariloche in the south. The provincial capital is the pleasant modern city of Neuquén, centre of an important fruit-growing area, providing most of Argentina's apples, pears and grapes. You're likely to stop off only briefly here on the way to greater adventures in the mountains further west, but it's worth making time for a brief encounter with dinosaurs at several sites easily reached from Neuquén city. There are incredibly huge dinosaur footprints and a good museum at Villa El Chocón, where you can see proof that the largest carnivores ever known actually stomped around these lands 100 million years ago. You could try a spot of excavation yourself at Valle Cretacico or see the skeleton of the largest herbivorous dinosaur on earth in Plaza Huincul. For more information, see www.neuquen.com.

Neuquén city and around → *For listings, see pages 414-415. Colour map 5, A3.*

The *provincial* capital is at the eastern tip of the province and is an attractive industrial town, founded in 1904, just after the arrival of the railway. It's on the opposite side of the Río Neuquén from Cipolletti, a prosperous centre of the Río Negro fruit-growing region. While it has no major tourist attractions, it's a useful stopping point for the lakes and also a good base for exploring the dinosaur finds in the area to the immediate southwest.

Arriving in Neuquén city → *Phone code 0299. Population of Greater Neuquén: 362,673.*
Getting there There are daily flights from Buenos Aires to the **airport** ① *T0299-440 0245*, 7 km west of town. A taxi costs US$11, or take city buses No 10 or 11. There are frequent long-distance services to the **bus terminal** ① *Ruta 22 y Solalique, 4 km west of town, T0299-445 2300*, from Buenos Aires and towns throughout the Lake District as well as north to Mendoza and west to Chile. The bus terminal is huge and modern, with lots of services and clean toilets. A taxi to the centre costs US$7.

Getting around The town can easily be explored on foot in a few hours, with most hotels and restaurants around the main street Avenida Argentina, which runs north from the disused railway track running east–west across the town, just south of General San Martín. Don't get confused with the street Félix San Martín, three blocks further south. Note that city buses, **Indalo**, take rechargeable magnetic cards, sold at the bus terminal and elsewhere, from US$1.

Tourist information The **tourist office** ① *Félix San Martín 182, T0299-442 4089, and at El Ceibo 438, Barrio Alta Barda, T0299-449 1200, www.neuquentur.gob.ar, www.neuquen.com, daily 0700-2100*, provides helpful lists of accommodation and a map. There's also a **municipal office** ① *Av Argentina y Roca, T0299-449 1200, www.ciudaddeneuquen.gob.ar/turismo/,* and further tourist offices at the airport and the bus terminal, T0299-15-576 4264.

Places in Neuquén city

At the northern end of Avenida Argentina at the Parque Centenario is the **Mirador Balcón del Valle** with panoramic views over the city and the confluence of the rivers (be sure not to take the bus to Centenario industrial suburb). The city is home to the **Museo Paleontológico de la Universidad Nacional del Comahue**, but this is currently closed indefinitely. Consult the tourist office regarding the possible reopening of the museum as well as exhibitions of dinosaur fossils found in the region. The **former railway station**, at Olascoaga and Pasaje Obligado, has been converted into a cultural centre and exhibition centre. South of the centre there is a pleasant walk along the Río Limay. There's also a bodega you can visit, **Bodega del Fin del Mundo** ① *R8, Km 9, near San Patricio de Chañar, T0299-15-580 0414, www.bodegadelfindelmundo.com, daily 1000-1630.* Free tours take an hour and include a tasting.

Centro Paleontológico at Lago Barreales

① *Ruta 51, Km 65, northwest of Neuquén, T0299-15-549 0784, www.proyectodino.com.ar.* If you're really into dinosaurs, you should consider visiting the **Centro Paleontológico at Lago Barreales**, where you can get hands-on experience of a dinosaur excavation. A team of palaeontologists is currently working on a large site, where some 30 fossils of dinosaur vertebrates have already been found, some of them belonging to a small dinosaur so far unnamed. Leave Neuquén on Route 7 and then take Route 51 towards Añelo. Before reaching this district, and after having passed Lake Mari Menuco, you'll find Lake Barreales. The entrance to the paleontological centre is located in the detour towards the lake.

Routes to the lakes

From Neuquén, there are various ways to approach the lakes. An attractive route involves continuing due west to Zapala on Ruta 22, and then south to Junín de los Andes on Ruta 40. Or from Zapala, you could continue west to Villa Pehuenia, or north to Caviahue and Copahue. For the direct route to Bariloche, take Ruta 237, via **Piedra del Aguila** and Confluencia and the astounding scenery of the **Valle Encantado**, with mountains whipped into jaggy peaks. The road continues to Lago Nahuel Huapi where there are fine views over Cerros Catedral and Tronador.

To the southwest of Neuquén lies the huge lake **Embalse Ezequiel Ramos Mexía** in an area that has become famous in recent years for the wealth of dinosaur fossils found here from the Cretaceous period (100 million years ago). There are a number of places where you can see the finds and even walk close to the footsteps of dinosaurs. The towns themselves are not appealing, but they make convenient stopping points along the road from Neuquén to the lakes, with a good museum at Villa El Chocón.

Villa El Chocón → *Colour map 5, A3. Phone code 0299.*
ⓘ *For information on reaching the footprints and how they were formed, see www.interpatagonia.com/paseos/huellas (in English).*

Your only reason to visit Villa El Chocón at the northern end of Lago Ezequiel Ramos Mexía, 72 km from Neuquén, is to see the remains of dinosaurs. It's a neat, rather uninspiring town, a strictly functional place built for workers on the hydroelectric dam. To see the amazing evidence of **dinosaurs**, take Route 237 towards Piedra del Aguila and turn left at Barrio Llanquén, where indicated, to the lake shore. Red sedimentary rocks have preserved, in relatively good condition, bones and even footprints of the creatures that lived in this region during the Cretaceous period about 100 million years ago. Some of the fossils can be seen in the **Museo Paleontológico Ernesto Bachmann** ⓘ *Civic Centre, El Chocón, T0299-490 1223, www.interpatagonia.com/paseos/ernestobachmann, daily 0700-2100, US$4*, where there's a well laid out and informative display and guides give very good tours. Exhibits include fossils of the mighty 10-ton, 15-m-long *Gigantosaurus carolinii*, a carnivorous dinosaur larger than the famous *Tyrannosaurus rex*. Alejandro París of **Aventura Jurásica** ⓘ *El Chocón, T0299-490 1243*, offers guided two- to three-hour visits to the museum and surroundings from US$3 per person not including transfers. The **tourist office** is at ⓘ *Ruta 237, T0299-15-633 7761, www.chocon.gov.ar.*

Excavation at Valle Cretácico
ⓘ *www.interpatagonia.com/paseos/valle_cretacico2, has information in English.*

The lunar landscape around Villa El Chocón is rather amazing and contains a surprising number of dinosaur remains. So much so that an area has been named 'Cretaceous Valley'. The valley lies 18 km south of Villa El Chocón, near the Dique and has improbably shaped pedestals of eroded pink rock coming out of the blue water. There are two walks beside the lake to see the dinosaur footprints, which are amazingly well preserved.

Plaza Huincul → *Colour map 5, A2. Population 11,000.*
There are more dinosaur remains at a quite impressive little museum in the otherwise rather dull town of Plaza Huincul. The road to Zapala, Route 22, leaves Neuquén and passes through the fruit-growing region of the Río Limay and the much duller oil-producing zone. Situated 107 km west of Neuquén, Plaza Huincul was the site of the country's first oil find in 1918. The **Museo Municipal Carmen Funes** ⓘ *on the way*

Walking with dinosaurs

Few countries are as important as Argentina for palaeontologists. The relative abundance of fossils near the surface has made the country a centre for the study of dinosaur evolution. The Ischigualasto and Talampaya parks (in San Juan and La Rioja respectively) have yielded rich evidence of dinosaurs from the Triassic period (225-180 million years ago), among them, the small *Eoraptor lunensis*, 220 million years old.

Patagonia was home to Jurassic dinosaurs (180-135 million years old), with some outstanding examples found here: Cerro Cóndor in Chubut is the only site of Middle Jurassic period dinosaurs found in the Americas, and has given palaeontologists an important breakthrough in understanding the evolutionary stages of the period. The five examples of *patagosaurus* found here indicated that these dinosaurs were social creatures, perhaps uniting for mutual defence. In Santa Cruz, traces of dinosaurs from the Upper Jurassic period have been found in rocks, surprising palaeontologists with the news that dinosaurs could live and breed in arid and desert-like conditions.

The most important discoveries of dinosaurs from the Cretaceous period (135-70 million years ago) have been made in Neuquén and Chubut. Dating from the period of separation of the continents of South America and Africa, these provide evidence of the way dinosaurs began to evolve differently due to geographic isolation. The *Carnotaurus sastrei* found in Chubut has horns and small hands, for example, whereas the Patagonian dinosaurs are huge. The carnivorous *Gigantosaurus carolinii*, found near Neuquén city, was larger even than the better known *Tyranosaurus rex*, discovered in North America. You'll find dinosaur footprints, eerily well preserved, near Villa Chocón, southwest of Neuquén city, and more finds in the local museum. You can even take part in excavation at a site in Cretaceous Valley, and there are remains of the largest herbivorous dinosaur on earth at Plaza Huincul's famous museum.

Trelew on the Atlantic coast has the country's finest dinosaur museum, the Museo Paleontológico Egidio Feruglio (www.mef.org.ar). There's an associated site with 40 million years of history near the Welsh village of Gaiman (see page 518). The museum announced in May 2014 the discovery of the largest dinosaur found to date: a 40-m-long, 80,000-kg herbivorous Titanosaur found near Trelew.

into Plaza Huicul, at the crossing of R22 and RP17, T0299-496 5486, Mon-Fri 0900-1900, Sat-Sun 1030-2030, US$1.75, includes the vertebrae of *Argentinossaurus huinclulensis*, believed to have weighed over 100 tons and to have been one of the largest herbivorous dinosaurs ever to have lived, as well as a nest of fossilized dinosaur eggs. It's mainly a centre for research, and you can see the results of the fieldwork in fossils, photographs and videos, as well as the skeletons themselves. For more information, see www.plazahuincul.com.ar and www.plazahuincul.gov.ar (in Spanish).

Zapala → *Colour map 5, A2. Phone code 02942. Population 36,550.*
Zapala (1012 m) lies in a vast dry plain with views of snow-capped mountains to the west. It's a modern and rather unappealing place, but you'll need to stop here at the **bus terminal** ⓘ *Etcheluz y Uriburu, T02942-423191,* if you want to take buses to Pehuenia, Copahue and Caviahue, or to cross the border into Chile at the Icalma Pass. There is a **tourist office** ⓘ *RN 22, Km 1392, T02942-424296, Mon-Fri 0700-1930, Sat-Sun 0800-1300, 1600-1900 in summer, closes earlier off season.*

The **Museo Mineralógico Dr Juan Olsacher** ⓘ *Etcheluz 52 (by bus terminal), T02942-422928, Mon-Fri 0900-1930, free,* is one of the best fossil museums in South America; it contains over 2000 types of mineral and has the finest collection of fossils of marine reptiles and marine fauna in the country. On display is the largest turtle shell from the Jurassic period ever found and an ophthalmosaur, as well as photos of an extensive cave system being excavated nearby.

Parque Nacional Laguna Blanca → *Colour map 5, A2.*
Covering 11,250 ha at altitudes of between 1200 m and 1800 m, this park is one of only two reserves in the Americas created to protect swans and lies 35 km southwest of Zapala. This is a rare example of high arid steppe, and its 1700-ha lagoon is one of the most important nesting areas of the black-necked swan in Argentina. Other birdlife includes several duck species, plovers, sandpipers, grebes and Chilean flamingos, with birds of prey such as the red-backed hawk and the peregrine falcon nesting on the steep slopes of the *laguna*. It's best visited in spring, when young can be watched at many sites around the *laguna*. The landscape is indeed very dry, and rather bleak, with fierce winds, encouraging only the lowest and most tenacious plant life. A rough track runs round the lake, suitable for 4WD vehicles only.

Nearby, the **Arroyo Ñireco** has eroded the volcanic rock to form a deep gorge, and it's worth seeking out a small cave, inhabited in prehistoric times and decorated with cave paintings. Southwest of the park Route 46 continues through the spectacular Bajada de Rahue, dropping 800 m in under 20 km before reaching the town of Rahue, 120 km southwest of Zapala.

Park information The park entrance is 10 km from the junction of Route 46 (which runs across the park) with Ruta 40. The *laguna* itself lies 5 km beyond this. There's no public transport, so without your own vehicle the only option is a tour from Zapala. There's a *guardería* post near the southeast corner of the *laguna*, with a **visitors' centre** ⓘ *Mon-Thu 0900-1600, Fri-Sun 0900-1900, free.* Take drinking water and a hat for the heat. There's a hiking trail which takes in 10 lagoons in all. There's free camping by the *guardaparque*; otherwise Zapala has the nearest accommodation, see www.pnlagunablanca.com.ar or www.parquesnacionales.gov.ar.

Eastern and central Neuquén listings

For hotel and restaurant price codes and other relevant information, see pages 20-26.

Where to stay

Neuquén city and around *p409*
$$$$ Del Comahue, Av Argentina 377, T0299-443 2040, www.hoteldelcomahue.com. 4-star, extremely comfortable, spa, pool, good service, wine bar and excellent restaurant, **1900 Cuatro**, specializing in Patagonian fare.
$$$ Hostal del Caminante, JJ Lastra (Ruta 22, Km 1227), 13 km west of Neuquén, towards Zapala, T0299-444 0118, www.hostaldelcaminante.com. A comfortable suburban place set among fruit plantations with garden, swimming pool and restaurant.
$$$ Royal, Av Argentina 143, T0299-448 8902, http://www.royalhotel.com.ar. Central hotel with all services, free continental breakfast, parking.
$ Hostel Punto Patagónico, Periodistas Neuquinos 94, T0299-447 9940, www.puntopatagonico.com. A bit out of the centre, good hostel, reductions for HI members, breakfast, rustic furniture. Recommended.

Villa El Chocón *p411*
$$$ La Posada del Dinosaurio, Costa del Lago, Barrio 1, Villa El Chocón, T0299-490 1201, www.posadadinosaurio.com.ar. Comfortable, modern, all rooms have lake view.

Plaza Huincul *p411*
$$ Hotel Tortorici, Av Olascoaga and Di Paolo, Cutral-Co, 3 km west, T0299-496 3730, www.hoteltortorici.com.ar. The most comfortable option is this basic but slightly run-down hotel with neat rooms and a restaurant. Can arrange golf on a nearby course.

Zapala *p413*
$$$ Hue Melén, Brown 929, T02942-422407, www.hotelhuemelen.com. Good value, decent rooms and restaurant with the best food in town. Try your luck in the downstairs casino.
$$ Coliqueo, Etcheluz 159, opposite bus terminal, T02942-421308. Convenient and fair.
$$ Pehuén, Elena de la Vega y Etcheluz, 1 block from bus terminal, T02942-423135. Comfortable and recommended.

Restaurants

Neuquén city and around *p409*
$$ El Ciervo, Argentina 219. Good central option featuring an abundance of fresh seafood dishes.
$ La Birra, Santa Fe 19. Lots of choice, welcoming, chic, modern.

Zapala *p413*
See Where to stay, above, for hotel restaurants.
$$ Del Hotel Hue Melen, Brown 929. Great value for money and has a varied menu.
$ Don Quijote, Etcheluz 162. Rustic furniture and friendly staff, home-cooked meals.
$ El Chancho Rengo, Av San Martín and Etcheluz, T02942-30956. Where all the locals hang out.

Festivals

All the towns in the valley celebrate the **Fiesta Nacional de la Manzana** (apples are the main local crop) in the 2nd half of Mar.

● What to do

Neuquén city and around *p409*
Arauquen, H Yrigoyen 720, T0299-442 5101, www.arauquen.com. Great local agency that can organize day tours and trips further afield.

Zapala *p413*
Mali Viajes, Alte Brown 760, T02942-432251.
Monserrat Viajes y Turismo, Etcheluz 101, T02942-422497. Both offer traditional day tours to the surrounding area. Can help with bus and plane tickets.

● Transport

Neuquén city and around *p409*
Air
Flights to **Buenos Aires** and **Comodoro Rivadavia**; LADE also flies to **Bariloche**. Schedules change frequently.

Bus
Many companies to **Buenos Aires**, daily, 15-19 hrs, US$88-100. To **Zapala**, daily, 3 hrs, US$12-15. To **Junín de los Andes**, 5-6 hrs, US$28-39, with **Albus**, T0299-443 6876/445 2265, www.albus.

com.ar. To **San Martín de los Andes**, 7 hrs, US$28-39, **Albus**. Also Albus daily to Villa Pehuenia, 7 hrs, US$30, and **Aluminé**, 6 hrs, US$23.50 (less predictable in winter, when the roads are covered in snow. To **Bariloche**, many companies, 5-6 hrs, US$43-50, sit on left. To **Mendoza**, with **Andesmar, Cata**, and others, daily, 12-13 hrs, US$51-63. To **Chile**: several companies, eg Albus, run to **Temuco**, 12-14 hrs, US$37, also from Zapala. Buy Chilean pesos before leaving. See box, page 419.

Zapala *p413*
Bus
To **San Martín de los Andes**, 4 hrs, US$17-23, via Junín de los Andes. To **Bariloche**, change at San Martín.

● Directory

Neuquén city and around *p409*
Banks Lots of ATMs along Av Argentina.
Currency exchange Exterior, San Martín 23; **Pullman**, Alcorta 144.
Embassies and consulates Chile, La Rioja 241, T0299-442 2447. **Post office** Rivadavia and Santa Fe.

Zapala *p413*
Banks Bansud, Etcheluz 108; **Banco de la Nación Argentina**, San Martín 401.

Pehuenia and northwest Neuquén

Pehuenia is the area due west of Zapala, running along the border with Chile. It is a wonderful expanse of unspoilt wilderness, which is only now opening up to visitors, around the picturesque villages of Villa Pehuenia and Moquehue. Pehuenia is quite different from the southern lakes, thanks to its large forests of ancient *pehuén* or *araucaria* – monkey puzzle trees. These magnificent silent forests exert a mysterious force and give a prehistoric feel to the landscape, while sleepy backwater feel of the villages makes them appealing for a few days' rest or gentle walking. Further north there are two little-visited tourist centres, useful stopping points if you're heading to Mendoza: Caviahue is good for walking in rugged and unspoilt landscapes or skiing in winter, while bleaker Copahue is known for its high-quality thermal waters. See www.villa pehuenia.org and www.caviahue.com.

Pehuenia → *For listings, see pages 421-424. Phone code 02942.*

The magical and unspoilt region of Pehuenia is named after the unique forests of *pehuén* trees, which grow here in vast numbers. Covering a marvellous open mountainous landscape, these ancient, silent trees create a mystical atmosphere, especially around the lakes of Aluminé and Moquehue, where a pair of small villages provides good accommodation. Villa Pehuenia is the best set up for tourism, with its picturesque setting on the lakeside, a cluster of upmarket *cabañas* and one exceptionally lovely boutique hotel, La Escondida ⓘ *www.posadalaescondida.com.ar*. Moquehue is quite different in style: more sprawling and relaxed. There are more *cabañas* here, excellent hiking up La Bella Durmiente and good fly fishing. You can approach Pehuenia from Neuquén city, or, even closer, from Temuco over the border in Chile.

Villa Pehuenia

This pretty village on sprawling Lago Aluminé's northern shore is picturesquely set amongst steep wooded hills, and makes a lovely base for a few days' relaxation or gentle walks in the hills and forests around. This is Mapuche land and was chosen for a settlement when the Mapuche were forcefully flushed out of Buenos Aires province in the late 19th century. It has special significance because seven volcanoes in a chain are visible from here, and because the area abounds with *pehuén* (monkey puzzle) trees, which are sacred to the Mapuche (see box, opposite). With the rapid building of *cabaña* complexes, tourism is slowly taking off here, and at the moment

Monkey puzzle trees

The stunningly beautiful area of Pehuenia is remarkable for its forests of araucaria, or monkey puzzle trees (*Araucaria araucana*). Growing slowly to a mighty 40 m high, the trees exert a powerful presence when seen en masse, perhaps because their forests are silent, moving little in the breeze. A true conifer, the araucaria is a descendent of the petrified pines found in Argentina's *bosques petrificados*. For centuries the *pehuén* or *araucaria* have been revered by indigenous peoples, and the local Mapuche still eat its pine nuts, rich in vitamins and fats. The custom of collecting their nuts, around which a whole array of foods and a celebratory harvest festival are based, has been the source of a bitter territory dispute in parts of the northern Lake District. The Mapuche feel that they have a natural right to harvest the fruits of their trees, and local landowners, backed by local government, clearly don't agree.

There's a growing respect for the Mapuche in the area, and they are beginning to get involved in the provision of basic tourist services with great success. You'll see *pan casero* (home-made bread), *tortas fritas* (fried pastries) and handicrafts for sale on roadsides, as well as the winter sports centre near Villa Pehuenia, all run by the local Mapuche. These small enterprises enable them to survive financially, while retaining their traditions and customs, and with luck, access to the magnificent araucarias which they hold so sacred.

you have the best of both worlds: an unspoilt feel but enough tourist infrastructure to stay in comfort, with good restaurants. Walk onto the peninsula stretching out into the lake from the village for wonderful walks along the araucaria-fringed shore, and up to the **Mirador del Cipres** with fabulous views.

Arriving in Villa Pehuenia To reach Villa Pehuenia, you could take one of the daily buses from Neuquén city via Zapala, but these take a long time, and once you're here you may want to explore the area in your own transport so car rental is the best option. Hire a car in Neuquén (3½-hour drive) and drop it off in San Martín de los Andes or Bariloche afterwards. Route 13 continues to the Paso de Icalma crossing to Chile, just a few kilometres from Villa Pehuenia, with easy access to Temuco, 130 km further, on the other side. See box, page 419.

The centre of the village is just off the main road, Route 13, where you'll find a service station, *locutorios*, food and handicrafts shops, and a pharmacy. There are two tour operators who can arrange trekking, boat trips on the lake and bike hire, and there is another area of restaurants and tea rooms by the lake side.

There is a **tourist kiosk** ① *off the main road, by the turning for Villa Pehuenia, T02942-498044, www.villapehuenia.gov.ar*, which, along with most hotels, has the excellent free leaflet showing a detailed map of Villa Pehuenia with all the hotels and restaurants marked. In March, the harvest of the *piñones* is celebrated during the **Fiesta del Pehuén** with horse-riding displays and live music.

Parque de Nieve Batea Mahuida

ⓘ *www.interpatagonia.com/bateamahuida.*

Just off the main road, a few kilometres west of town, this reserve was created to protect an area of *pehuén* trees and the majestic volcano Mahuida (1900 m), which is regarded as sacred by the Mapuche people. The skiing and winter sports area here is one of the few businesses in the area run by Mapuche people, and is good for limited skiing in winter, with snowmobile and snowshoe walking. It's also a lovely place for walking in summer, with tremendous views of all seven volcanoes around. Delicious home-cooked food is served; contact the Mapuche Puel community at the entrance. It takes three hours to walk up here or one hour by bike.

Walk to Lago Moquehue

For walks through the *araucaria* forests, drive west from Villa Pehuenia towards Chile for 4 km, until you reach the end of the lake, where you turn left at the *gendarmería*, following a dirt road across the bridge over a narrow strip of water, La Angostura. Follow the arrow to a campsite 50 m further on, **El Puente** (a delightful place, recommended). Continue past it and, when you come to a little hut and a sign to Lago Redonda, take the right fork and follow the track. Park or leave your bike at the largest of the three small *lagunas*, and take the path due south when the track comes to an end at a farmstead by a large lagoon. Climb from here to a ridge with great views, and then take the path which drops and skirts around **Lago Moquehue** – the view is awe-inspiring. You could walk to Moquehue from here, but you need a map; ask for the *Sendas y Bosques* map of Norte Neuquino, which shows the Pehuenia-Moquehue area, and some paths.

This whole area is the heart of the Mapuche community: many houses offer *pan casero* (home-made bread), horse riding or walking guides.

Moquehue → *Phone code 0299. Population 600.*

Another 10 km on Route 13 brings you to the sprawling village of Moquehue. It's a wilder, more remote place than Villa Pehuenia, spreading out on the shores of its lake, with a lovely wide river. Famous for fishing, this is a beautiful and utterly peaceful place to relax and walk, and it has a less cultivated feel, inspiring adventurous treks. A short stroll through araucaria forests brings you to a lovely waterfall; a longer hike to the top of Cerro Bandera (four hours return) gives wonderful views over the area, and to Volcán Llaima. There are fine camping spots and a couple of comfortable places to stay. For more information, see www.villapehuenia.org (in English).

Aluminé → *Colour map 5, A2. Population 4000. Phone code 02942.*

In the splendid Aluminé Valley, on Route 23 between Pehuenia and Junín de los Andes, lies the area's self-proclaimed rafting capital, the small town of Aluminé. There is indeed superb rafting (Grades II or IV to VI, depending on rainfall) nearby on Río Aluminé. There are places to stay, but despite the lovely setting, it's a drab place. There's a very friendly **tourist office** ⓘ *C Christian Joubert 321, T02942-496001, www.alumine.gov.ar, daily 0800-2100.* There's a service station too, the last between Villa Pehuenia and Junín de los Andes. ⏭ *See What to do, page 424.*

Border crossings: Argentina–Chile

Paso Pino Hachado

Paso Pino Hachado (1864 m) lies 115 km west of Zapala via Route 22, which is almost completely paved. Buses from Zapala and Neuquén to Temuco use this crossing. On the Chilean side a paved road runs northwest to Lonquimay, 63 km west of the border. Temuco lies 145 km southwest of Lonquimay.

Argentine immigration and customs 9 km east of the border, daily 0900-2000. There are toilets and a kiosk. For more information, see www.gendarmeria.gov.ar/pasos/chile/fichpihacha.html.

Chilean immigration and customs Liucura, 22 km west of the border, daily 0800-1900. Very thorough searches and two- to three-hour delays reported.

Paso de Icalma

Paso de Icalma (1303 m) lies 132 km west of Zapala and is reached by Route 13 (*ripio*). It is used as an alternative border crossing when other crossings at higher altitude are closed due to snow. On the Chilean side this road continues unpaved to Melipeuco, 53 km west of the border, and then to Temuco. See www.gendarmeria.gov.ar/pasos/chile/fichicalma.html.

Argentine immigration and customs 9 km east of the border, daily 0800-1900. All paperwork is carried out at the customs office, clearly signposted.

Chilean immigration and customs Daily 0800-1900.

Rucachoroi

From Aluminé there is access to Lago Rucachoroi, 23 km west, inside Lanín national park. The biggest Mapuche community in the park live here, in gentle farmland surrounded by ancient *pehuén* forests. Access is by a rough *ripio* road, best in a 4WD in winter, and spectacular in autumn when the deciduous trees are a splash of orange against the bottle-green araucarias. The only accommodation is in two campsites, both offering Mapuche food and horse riding. Here too, there's a *guardería* where you can ask about a possible trek to Lago Quillén. The landscape is very beautiful and you will want to linger, but bring provisions and camping gear. Private transport is essential.

Lago Quillén

At the junction by the small town of Rahue, 16 km south of Aluminé, a road leads west to the valley of the Río Quillén and the exquisite Lago Quillén, from where there are fine views of Volcán Lanín peeping above the mountains. The lake itself is one of the region's most lovely, jade green in colour, with beaches along its low-lying northern coast. Further west, where annual rainfall is among the heaviest in the country, the slopes are thickly covered with superb Andean Patagonian forest. There's no transport, and the only accommodation (with food shop and hot showers) is at **Camping Quillén** ① *T02942-496599, camping.quillen@gmail.com*, on the lake shore. Here you can get advice about walks, and register with *guardaparques* if you plan to hike to Rucachoroi. There's another walk to the remote **Lago Hui Hui**, 6 km north from the second campsite (3½ hours return). For fishing, contact **Estancia Quillén** (see Where to stay, page 422).

Copahue and Caviahue → *For listings, see pages 421-424. Colour map 3, C1.*

About 150 km north of Zapala, the **Reserva Provincial Copahue** covers an arid, dramatic and other-worldly landscape at whose heart is a giant volcanic crater surrounded by mountains. The park was created to protect the araucaria trees that grow on the slopes, and there are some wonderful walks that take you to unexpectedly stunning landscapes.

Arriving in Copahue and Caviahue → *Phone code 02948. Population 700.*
Both towns are easily reached by public transport from Zapala, 150 km southeast, or by flying to Neuquén, 300 km southeast. In Caviahue, there is a **tourist office** ① *8 de Abril, bungalows 5 and 6, T02948-495036, www.caviahue-copahue.gov.ar.* For information on the thermal waters, check out www.caviahuetours.com. To find out about the ski centre, contact **Caviahue Base**, www.caviahue.com. There's an ATM at the *municipalidad*, several restaurants and a tea room, as well as some decent accommodation. In Copahue, the **tourist office** is on the approach road into town, Route 26.

Caviahue and around
Caviahue is by far the most attractive of the two towns in this area, with an appealing lakeside setting and opportunities for walking and horse riding; it converts into a skiing and winter sports centre from July to September and swells to a winter population of over 10,000. There are three ski lifts, excellent areas for cross-country skiing, snow-shoeing and snowmobiling, all with tremendous views, and it's one of cheaper resorts in the Lake District.

Volcán Copahue on the Chilean-Argentine border is an active volcano, with recent eruptions in 2012 and 2013. In 2000 an eruption destroyed the bright blue lake in its crater, but it's still a popular destination for horse riding, and the views of the prehistoric landscape are astounding. The most highly recommended excursion, however, is to **El Salto del Agrio**, 15 km northeast of Caviahue along Route 27. This is the climax in a series of delightful falls, approached by a road passing between tall, ancient araucaria trees poised on basalt cliffs.

Copahue and around
Copahue (1980 m) is a thermal spa resort enclosed in a gigantic amphitheatre formed by mountain walls and boasting the best thermal waters in South America, though it's decidedly the bleaker of the two towns. Fantastic walks in the area are to the extraordinary **Las Máquinas**, 4 km south, where sulphurous steam puffs through air holes against a panoramic backdrop, making the weirdest noises. At **El Anfiteatro**, there are thermal waters reaching 150°C, in a semicircle of rock

edged with araucaria trees. Just above Copahue, a steep climb takes you to **Cascada Escondida**, a torrent of water falling 15 m over a shelf of basalt into a pool surrounded by a forest of araucaria trees; above it Lago Escondida is a magical spot.

⊙ Pehuenia and northwest Neuquén listings

For hotel and restaurant price codes and other relevant information, see pages 20-26.

⊙ Where to stay

Villa Pehuenia *p416*
You'll find 1 superb boutique hotel, and plenty of *cabañas*, many with good views over the lake and set in idyllic woodland. Email or ring first for directions, since there are no road names or numbers here. For more listings, see www.villapehuenia.org (in English).

$$$$-$$$ La Escondida, western shore of the península, T02942-15-691166, www.posadalaescondida.com.ar. By far the best place to stay in the whole area, this is a really special boutique hotel with just 9 rooms in an imaginatively designed building on the rocky lakeside. Each room is spacious and beautifully considered, with smart bathrooms (all with jacuzzi), and private decks, all with gorgeous views over the lake. The restaurant is superb and non-residents can dine here with a reservation. The whole place is relaxing and welcoming. Highly recommended.

$$$ Altos de Pehuén, T02942-15-5383 6300, www.altosdelpehuen.com.ar. Comfortable *cabañas* with lovely views, and a *hostería*.

$$$ Cabañas Caren, T02942-15-400615, www.cabanascaren.com.ar. Simple A-frame *cabañas*, but with open views and balconies, and made especially welcoming by the warm friendly owner Walter.

$$$ Complejo Patagonia, T02942-15-548787 (T011-15-5011 4470 in Buenos Aires), www.complejopatagonia.com. ar. Very comfortable indeed, these lovely *cabañas* are traditionally designed and the service is excellent. Recommended.

$$$ Complejos del Lago Aluminé, T02942-15-665068, www.villa-pehuenia. com.ar. Complejo La Serena has beautifully equipped and designed *cabañas* for 2-6 people with lovely uninterrupted view, gardens going down to beach, sheltered from the wind and furnished with rustic-style, handmade cypress furniture, and wood stoves, all very attractive. Also has Complejo Culle Lafquen.

$$$ Cabañas Bahía Radal, T02942-498057, www.bahiaradal.com.ar, on the peninsula (ask the tourist office for directions). Luxurious *cabañas*, with clear lake views from its elevated position.

$$$-$$ Las Terrazas, T02942-498036, www.lasterrazaspehuenia.com.ar. Recommended: the owner is an architect, who has retained Mapuche style in his beautiful design of these comfortable *cabañas*, tasteful, warm and with perfect views over the lake. Also with bed and breakfast. He can direct you to magical places for walking, and to Mapuche communities to visit.

$$ Puerto Malén Club de Montaña, T02942-498007 (T011-4226 8190 in Buenos Aires), www.puertomalen.com. Well-built wooden *cabañas* with lake views from their balconies, and the highest-quality interiors. Also a luxurious *hostería* **$$$**). Recommended.

Moquehue *p418*

$$ La Bella Durmiente, T0299-496172, www.bdurmientemoquehue.com.ar/home.html. In a rustic building, rooms heated by wood fires, also camping, summer only, the welcoming owner offers good food and also trekking, horse riding, diving in the lake and mountain biking. Call for directions.

Cabañas

$$$ Cabañas Los Maitenes, T0299-4242 1681, T02942-15-665621, www.complejolosmaitenes.com.ar. Right on the lake, well-equipped *cabañas*, with breakfast included and friendly owners. Recommended.

$$$ La Busqueda, T02942-15-660377, www.labusquedamoquehue.com.ar. Just north of the lake, before you reach the head of Lago Moquehue. Interesting design in these well-equipped *cabañas* with TV, including breakfast. Recommended

$$$-$$ Cabañas Melipal, T02948-495556, www.melipalcopahue.com.ar. Very attractive, rustic, stone-built *cabañas* in secluded sites on the lake. Lovely old-fashioned style, well equipped and warm, fabulous views from balcony, use of boats. Highly recommended.

Camping

Along R13, 11 km to Lago Ñorquinco, past mighty basalt cliffs with *pehuenes* all around, there's idyllic camping. **Camping Trenel**, www.trenel.alojar.com.ar. In a fabulous site elevated on the southern shore of Lago Moquehue, just beyond the **Hostería Moquehue**. Beautiful, well-kept sites in the thick of little *nirre* trees, with seats and *parrillas* overlooking the lake. Smart, hot showers, good restaurant, food shop, information and excursions. Recommended.

Ecocamping Ñorquinco, T02942-496155, www.ecocampingnorquinco.alojar.com.ar. There is 1 amazing rustic *cabaña* right on the lake, with a café by the roadside, US$8 per person per night, US$3 for under 12s, Dec or Mar, Apr to Easter. Great fishing, hot showers and a *proveduría*. Lovely place to eat if it rains.
Los Caprichosos, on Lago Ñorquinco. Open Nov-Apr only, with water and food shop.

Aluminé *p418*

$$$ Piedra Pintada, T011-4328 0145, www.piedrapintada.com.ar. Only 35 km from town, this is the best option. 12 rooms, stylishly fitted out, with a sauna, fantastic views over the lake and impressive restaurant.

$$ Aluminé, C Joubert 312, T02942-496174, www.hosteriaalumine.com.ar. In the middle of town, opposite tourist information, this is a drab 1960s place, with clean, functional rooms. There's an excellent little restaurant next door, **La Posta del Rey**.

Rucachoroi *p419*
Camping

There are 2 sites, **Rucachoroi 1** and **Rucachoroi 2**, located before and after the lake (www.campingruka.blogspot.com). Open all year, but ideal only Dec-Feb. The 1st has more facilities, with toilets, but no hot water, some food supplies, including Mapuche home-made bread and sausages, and horse riding.

Lago Quillén *p419*

$$$ Estancia Quillén, R46 near Rahue, near the bridge crossing Río Aluminé, T02942-496196, www.interpatagonia.com/quillen. A comfortable, traditionally furnished house, with spacious rooms and a restaurant, where you'll be welcomed by the *estancia* owners. Great for fishing and hunting. Open Dec-Apr.

Caviahue *p420*

$$$ Lago Caviahue, Costanera Quimey-Co, T02948-495110, www. hotellagocaviahue.com. Better value than the Nevado; comfortable but dated lakeside apartments with kitchen, also a good restaurant and great views. 2 km from the ski centre.

$$$ Nevado Caviahue, 8 de Abril s/n, T02948-495053, www.hotelnevado.com. ar. Plain, modern rooms, and there's a restaurant and cosy lounge with wood fire. Also 6 *cabañas*, well-equipped but not luxurious.

$$ Farallón, Caviahue Base, T02948-495085, www.hotelfarallon.com.ar. Neat apartments, some with kitchens.

$$ La Casona de Tito, Puesta del Sol s/n, T02948-495093, www.lacasonadetito. com.ar. *Cabañas*, excellent meals.

Hostels

$ pp Hebe's House, Mapuche y Puesta del Sol, T02948-495138, www. hebeshouse.com.ar. Lovely chalet-style building with great communal areas and only 2 blocks from the centre of town. Doubles (**$$**) available.

Camping

Copahue, T02948-495111, Hueney Municipal. Open summer only. Basic but well maintained.

Copahue *p420*

$$$ Aldea Termal, T0299-442 5605, www.aldeatermal.com. Attractively decorated chalet-style apartments. Recommended.

$$$ Hotel Copahue, Olascoaga y Bercovich, T0236-442 3390, www. copahuejunin.com.ar. This lovely old

place, where you'll be warmly welcomed by Pocho and Moriconi, is the most recommended place in Copahue. There are well-built wood and stone *cabañas*.

🍴 Restaurants

Villa Pehuenia *p416*

$$$ La Escondida, on the western shore of the peninsula, T02942-15-691166, www.posadalaescondida.com. ar. By far the best in town. Only open to non-residents with a reservation, this is really special cuisine. All local ingredients, imaginatively prepared and served. Highly recommended.

$$ Anhedonia, on the lakeside, T02942-15-469454. Fondue, beef and pasta.

$$ Gnaien Chocolatería and tea room, on the lakeside, T02942-498082. Good for tea, with lovely views of the lake, chocolate delicacies, *picadas* and range of wines.

$$ La Cantina del Pescador, on the lakeside, T02942-498086. Fresh trout.

$ Costa Azul, on the lakeside, T02942-498 035. Tasty local dishes and pasta; *chivito* (kid) *al asado* is the speciality of the house.

Aluminé *p418*

$ La Posta del Rey, next to the service station, opposite the plaza, Cristian Joubert, T02942-15-695138. The best place by far, with friendly service, great trout, local kid, delicious pastas and sandwiches. Recommended.

Copahue and Caviahue *p420*

$ Copahue Club Hotel, Valle del Volcán. Serves good *chivito al asado* and local trout.

$ Hotel Lago Caviahue. The most stylish place to eat with an inspired *chivo a la cerveza* (kid cooked in beer), along with more traditional favourites and local specialities.

⊛ Festivals

Villa Pehuenia *p416*
Mar Fiesta del Pehuén, www. villapehuenia.org (in Spanish). The harvest of the *piñones*, celebrated with riding displays and live music.

◑ What to do

Villa Pehuenia *p416*
Los Pehuenes, T02942-15-566 4827, www. pehuenes.com.ar. Excellent company offering wide range of excursions and adventures: trekking in the mountains; rafting (US$65 for full day, Grade IV); horse riding; visits to the local Mapuche communities, with kid *asado*, and local history and culture; and fishing and boat trips. Professional, helpful and friendly. Ask for Fernando. Can also arrange transfers to Pehuenia from San Martín and Neuquén.

Aluminé *p418*
Aluminé Rafting, Villegas 610, T02942-496322, www.interpatagonia.com/alumineerafting. Price for 3 hrs' rafting depends on difficulty, Grades II-VI, all equipment included. Options are: Circuito Abra Ancha, 2½ hrs, Grade II,

6 km, very entertaining, suitable for everyone; Circuito Aluminé Superior, 12 or 15 km run, 5-6 hrs, Grade III-IV, very technical river leaving Lago Alumine, for those who like a thrill, passing little woods of araucarias and *ñirres*; family trips Grades I and II. Also offers trekking, kayaking and biking.

Caviahue *p420*
Caviahue Tours, Maipu 42, Buenos Aires, T011-3326 1631, www.caviahuetours.com. Good information.

⊖ Transport

Villa Pehuenia *p416*
Albus (www.albus.com.ar) has daily buses to **Neuquén** (less predictable in winter, when the roads are covered in snow), 7 hrs, US$30. Also to Aluminé, 1 hr.

Aluminé *p418*
Buses daily to **Neuquén via Zapala**, 3 hrs, with **Albus** (T02942-496672) and **Campana Dos**, (T02942-496666). **Albus** also daily to **Villa Pehuenia**, 1 hr.

Caviahue *p420*
Bus
To **Neuquén**, 6 hrs via Zapala, 4 daily, with **Conosur**; tickets can be booked through **Caviahue Tours**, see above.

Parque Nacional Lanín

Some of the most beautiful sights in the Lake District are to be found in one of the country's largest national parks, Lanín, which stretches north from Nahuel Huapi National Park all the way to Lago Norquinco and along the border with Chile for some 200 km.

The park's centrepiece, and its most climbed peak, is the magnificent, extinct, snow-capped Volcán Lanín. The ascent takes two days and starts from close to the border at Paso Tromen (also known as Paso Mamuil Malal). Lanín is especially superb seen from the two connected lakes in the centre of the park: Lago Huechulafquen and Lago Paimún. These lakes are the easiest part of the park to visit, with a good road leading west from Junín de los Andes. They have shores of volcanic black sand with opportunities for great hiking, fishing and camping.

Quiet Lago Lolog further south also offers good fishing, and it's worth the drive to find two more tranquil and very pretty lakes hidden away in the mountains: Lago Curruhué Grande and Lago Chico. Further along the same road, there are thermal waters at Lahuen-Co, at the western end of Lago Epulafquen, which you could also reach in a spectacular two-day hike from Lago Paimún.

The southern park can be visited easily from San Martín de los Andes, which sits at the head of picturesque Lago Lacar (well set up for tourism). Northernmost areas of the park are harder to access, and infrastructure here is building only slowly. But there are several Mapuche communities living in the park who organize campsites and horse riding, and sell home-made bread and other provisions, making this area interesting to visit.

The whole park is definitely more rewarding if you visit in your own transport, as bus services are sporadic at best, and there is a great deal of unspoilt landscape to explore, varying from lowland hills in the east to steep craggy mountains in the west, all heavily clad in native beech trees, *coihue*, *lenga* and *ñire*.

Getting there

Bus transport into the park is tricky. There are some high season services from Junín de los Andes to Lago Paimún, and KoKo Bus usually runs a service to Lago Huechulafquen from San Martín de los Andes, although the timetable varies from year to year. To explore the park, you will need to join a tour or have your own transport.

The park has two official entrances. **Lago Huechulafquen** provides the easiest access to the beautifully situated lakes in the centre of the park. To get there, travel west on Route 61 from Junín de los Andes, a good dirt road, as far as the *guardaparque* office at the eastern end of the lake, where you can get free maps and information on hikes. The other entrance to the park is at **San Martín de los Andes**, which is the main tourist centre and gives easy access to Lago Lacar and the River Hua Hum on its western end. It is also the access point for Lago Lolog further north.

The very north of the park is hard to access, since the roads are poor, but it's possible to reach Quillén from Rahue by heading west along Route 46, which is signposted off Route 23. There's little infrastructure when you reach Quillén, but there are Mapuche communities to visit and some rural campsites. For details of this area, see page 419.

Park information

Park entry is US$9 (paid at the entry point). You're supposed to register at the **park administration** ① *Perito Moreno 1006 y Elordi, San Martín de los Andes, T02972-427233, servicioslanin@apn.gov.ar, Mon-Fri 0800-1300*, before setting out on any major treks. If you don't manage this, then be sure to notify the *guardaparque* office at the Huechulafquen entrance to the park instead. Ask them about your route and if paths are open. They have two really good free leaflets: one on the park itself and another on climbing Lanín, both with sections in English. You should also check out www. parquesnacionales.gov.ar (Areas Protegidas section) or www.tresparques.com.ar/lanin. Having a good map is essential: look out for the *Sendas y Bosques* (Walks and Forests) map for Parque Nacional Lanín, 1:200,000, which is laminated and easy to read, with a book containing English summaries of the walks, www.guiasendasybosques. com.ar. Wherever you are in the park, fires are a serious hazard: always put out campfires with lots of water, not just earth and take all rubbish away with you.

Around the park

Lago Huechulafquen and around

From Lago Huechulafquen there are fabulous walks up into the hills and along the shore, and along beautiful Lago Paimún further west. Three *hosterías* and great campsites offer accommodation, and there are simple food shops and places to eat. Trips on the comfortable catamaran **José Julián** ① *T02972-429264, www.catamaranjosejulian.com.ar, US$30*, start at Puerto Canoa, on the northern shore of Lago Huechulafquen. This is a fantastic boat trip, offering the chance to

Parque Nacional Lanín

Climbing Volcán Lanín

One of the world's most beautiful mountains, Lanín (3776 m), is geologically one of the youngest volcanoes (though now extinct) in the Andes. It is a challenging three-day return climb to the summit, with two *refugios* at 2400 m (both without charge), sleeping 14 to 20 people. The normal departure point for the climb lies some 3 km east of the Mamuil Mamal pass. This is a beautiful spot, with a good campsite and some lovely walks: from the guardaparque centre, footpaths lead to a mirador (1½ hours round trip), or across a grassy prairie with magnificent clear views of Lanín and other jagged peaks, through ñirre woodland and some great araucaria trees to the point where Lago Tromen drains into Río Malleo (4 km).

Access The ascent of Lanín starts from the Argentine customs post, 3 km east of the Mamuil Malal Pass (see box, page 430), where you must register with *guardaparques* and obtain a free permit. They will check that you are physically fit and experienced enough, and also check that you have the equipment listed below. If they judge that you are not suitably prepared for the climb, they will insist that you hire the services of a trained and licensed guide. Access is usually possible only between November and May. Outside this period, climbing is subject to conditions and guides are not always available. Set off between 0800 and 1400; to start climbing before 0800, obtain clearance the previous day before 2100. The number of climbers is limited to 60 per day; no bookings can be made. It's vital to get detailed descriptions of the ascent from the *guardaparques*, and take a detailed map.

Preparation and cautions Because of its relative accessibility, the risks of climbing Lanín are often

see Lanín and the beautiful surrounding mountains from the water, and to reach the relatively inaccessible Lago Epulafquen with its impressive 6-km lava deposit.

Termas de Lahuen-Co

It's well worth getting to beautiful Lago Curruhué and the thermal pools at **Lahuen-Co** in the far west of the park. You can hike there in two days from Lago Paimún (see below), but if that's too much, they can also be accessed on Route 62, a good dirt road, starting either south of Junín, or from Lago Lolog. Route 62 heads west past Lago Curruhué Chico and Lago Grande, through ancient *pehuén* forests along the southern shores, and then passes the impressive lava field at Laguna Escorial. At the thermal baths there is a fantastic spa and eco lodge (www.lahuenco.com), which organizes tours in the area.

Trekking routes

There are some delightful walks near Lago Huechulafquen, indicated by yellow arrows; allow plenty of time to return before dark. Guides are only needed for the underestimated. An authorized guide is absolutely necessary for anyone other than the very experienced, and crampons and ice-axe are essential. Other equipment you will be required to show includes: good walking boots, an all-season sleeping bag, stove and fuel, sunglasses, torch, first-aid kit, walking sticks, helmet and VHF radio (frequency is VHF 155675). Start hydrating 24 hours before setting off and continue doing so as you climb. Take at least two litres of water with you. Eat light and frequent snacks, including bananas, raisins, cereal bars and chocolate. Bring all rubbish down with you. You will be given numbered waste bags for this purpose. On your return, it is essential to check in with the *guardaparques*, so that they can log your safe return.

Route To climb the north face, follow the path through *lenga* forest to the base of the volcano, over Arroyo Turbio and up the Espina de Pescado (fish bone), following red and yellow marks. From here the path becomes steeper. Follow the signs to the Camino de Mulas (mule track), and then follow the red markers to reach the Nuevo Refugio Militar (new military shelter). From here keep right to the Viejo Refugio Militar (old military shelter) and the CAJA Refugio. From then on, the ascent is steep and requires ice-climbing techniques. The section to the *refugios* may be done in one day if you set out early and are mentally and physically prepared. See the excellent free leaflet produced by the Parque Nacional Lanín on the ascent, with all GPS references provided and English translation.

Mountain guiding agency
Alquimia Viajes, O'Higgins 603, Junín de los Andes, T02972-491355, www.alquimiaturismo.com.ar.

longer treks where paths are not marked. (For these, ask in the Junín park office or at San Martín de los Andes.) Ask *guardaparques* for advice on routes before setting off.

El Saltillo Falls ① *2 hrs return, fabulous views*. Start from campsite **Piedra Mala** (where you can stock up on provisions) at Lago Paimún, and head west towards the Paimún *guardaparque* office. From here you can also walk on to Río Paimún, three to four hours one way, from Piedra Mala campsite.

Termas de Lahuen-Co ① *Best done over 2 days*. Start from beautiful **La Unión**, where Lago Huechulafquen meets Lago Paimún. (To cross to the other side of Lago Paimún at La Unión, there's a boat operated by the local **Mapuche** community; just ring the bell.) From here, it is an eight-hour walk along the northern shore to reach the western end of Lago Paimún, then four more to reach the Termas. You must consult the book of walks *Sendas y Bosques* for Parque Nacional Lanín, and notify *guardaparques* and the San Martín administration office before setting off It's a beautiful walk, and you'll be rewarded by a soak in the pools at the end.

Border crossing: Argentina–Chile

Paso Mamuil Malal (formerly Tromen)

Paso Mamuil Malal, is 64 km northwest of Junín de los Andes and reached by *ripio* Route 60 which runs from Tropezón on Route 23, through Parque Nacional Lanín. Parts of the road are narrow and steep, so it is unsuitable for bicycles. On the Chilean side the road continues through glorious scenery, with views of the volcanoes of Villarrica and Quetrupillán to the south, to Pucón, 76 km west of the pass, on Lago Villarrica.

The border is open all year, but is closed during heavy rain or snow (phone the gendarmerie to check, T02972-427339). For more detailed information, see www.gendarmeria.gov.ar/pasos/chile/fichmamal.html.

Argentine immigration and customs Puesto Tromen, 3 km east of the pass, daily 0900-2000, co-ordinated with the Chilean side.

Chilean immigration and customs Puesco, 8 km west of the pass, daily 0900-2000.

Transport San Martín buses run from San Martín de los Andes and Junín de los Andes to Pucón in Chile (4¾ hours from San Martín, four hours from Junín), US$22. Hire cars will need special documents (ask when you rent), and the car's number plate must be etched into all windows. **Note** No fresh fruit or vegetables may be taken into Chile.

Base of Volcán Lanín ① *8 hrs return.* A satisfying walk. Start from Puerto Canoa. For other walks and the ascent of Lanín, see box, page 428.

Cerro El Chivo ① *2064 m, 8-9 hrs return.* Set off early, and register in campsite at Bahía Cañicul. This is a more challenging walk through forest. Note that heavy snow can lie till January. Potentially dangerous without a guide. Consult *Sendas y Bosques* book for Parque Nacional Lanín, and notify *guardaparques.*

Junín de los Andes → For listings, see pages 435-440. Colour map 5, A2.

Phone code 02972. Population 10,300.

Situated on the Río Chimehuin, the quiet town of Junín de los Andes (773 m) is justifiably known as the trout-fishing capital of Argentina. It offers some of the best fly fishing in the country during the season from mid-November to May. Junín is also an excellent base for exploring the wonderful Parque Nacional Lanín to the west and for climbing its extinct volcano, as well as for rafting on Río Aluminé further north.

Founded in 1883, Junín is a real town, not as picturesque or tourist-orientated as its neighbour, San Martín: there are far fewer chalet-style buildings and few chocolate shops here. But it's a quiet, neat place with genuinely friendly people. The hotels are not as upmarket as San Martín, but **Estancia Huechahue** nearby (see Where to stay, page 435) is superb, and there are some decent family-run hotels here, plus one excellent restaurant, making it worth an overnight stop. Don't forget to try the celebrated local trout.

Arriving in Junín de los Andes

Chapelco Airport is 19 km southwest of town on the road to San Martín de los Andes, and can be reached by taking any bus towards San Martín. A taxi to the centre will cost US$12. The **bus terminal** ① *Olavarría and Félix San Martín (do not confuse with General San Martín), information T02972-492038*, has a public phone but no other facilities.

There is a fantastic **tourist office** ① *Domingo/Padre Milanesio and C Suárez, T02972-491160, daily 0800-2200 in summer, 0800-2100 in winter*, on the main plaza, which has friendly staff who can advise on accommodation, and who hand out

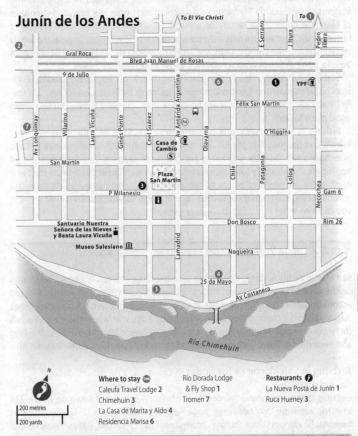

Junín de los Andes

To El Via Christi
To ①

Where to stay
Caleufa Travel Lodge **2**
Chimehuin **3**
La Casa de Marita y Aldo **4**
Residencia Marisa **6**

Río Dorada Lodge
& Fly Shop **1**
Tromen **7**

Restaurants
La Nueva Posta de Junín **1**
Ruca Hueney **3**

200 metres
200 yards

maps. The **Parque Nacional Lanín** office ① *T02972-491160*, is in the same building and is very helpful. See also http://junindelosandes.com.

Places in Junín de los Andes

Most of what you need can be found within a couple of blocks of the central Plaza San Martín with its fine araucaria trees among mature *alerces* and cedars. The small **Museo Salesiano** ① *Ginés Ponte and Nogueira, Mon-Fri 0900-1400, 1600-1930*, has a fine collection of Mapuche weavings, instruments and arrowheads, and you can buy a whole range of excellent Mapuche handicrafts in the **Feria Artesanal** behind the tourist office. There's an impressive religious sculpture park, **El Vía Christi** ① *www.neuquentur.gob.ar/turismo-religioso/1311/via-christi-en-junin-de-los-andes*, situated among pine forest on a hillside just west of town. To get there from the plaza, walk up Avenida Antárida Argentina across the main road, Route 234, to the end. The Stations of the Cross are illustrated with touching and beautifully executed sculptures of Mapuche figures, ingeniously depicting scenes from Jesus's life together with a history of the town and the Mapuche community. It's a lovely place to walk and highly recommended. The church, **Santuario Nuestra Señora de las Nieves y Beata Laura Vicuña**, also has fine Mapuche weavings, and is a pleasing calm space.

Some 7 km away, clearly signposted, at Km 7 on Route 61 towards Lago Huechuflafquen, is the **Centro Ecológico Aplicado de Neuquén** (CEAN) ① *Mon-Fri 0900-1300, US$1*, where trout are farmed, and ñandus and llamas can be seen; a good place for kids.

Fishing is undoubtedly one of the great attractions of Junín, and the best fishing is at the mouth of the Río Chimehuin, 22 km from town on the road to Lago Huechulafquen. On your way to the national park, stop off here for a moment to appreciate the heavenly turquoise water edged by a black sandy shore. In the town itself, there are pleasant places to fish and picnic along the river, and there are several fishing lodges in the area that cater for experts, with guides whose services you can hire. ➤➤ *See also What to do, page 438.*

San Martín de los Andes and around → *For listings, see pages 435-440.*

San Martín de los Andes is a charming upmarket tourist town in a beautiful setting on the edge of Lago Lacar, with attractive chalet-style architecture and lots of good accommodation. It's an excellent centre for exploring southern parts of the Parque Nacional Lanín including the nearby lakes Lolog and Lacar, where there are beaches for relaxing and good opportunities for rafting, canoeing, mountain biking, trekking and even diving. There is also excellent skiing at the Chapelco resort, 10 km south.

Arriving in San Martín de los Andes → *Colour map 5, A2. Phone code 02972. Population 25,000.*

Getting there The nearest **airport** is Chapelco, northeast of town on Route 234 towards Junín de los Andes (see page 431); a transfer costs US$25-30. The **bus terminal** ① *Villegas y Juez del Valle, information T02972-427044*, is reasonably central and has all the usual services, including luggage store, toilets, *locutorio* and a tiny tourist office ⓘ *daily 1130-1730.* ▸▸ *See What to do, page 439.*

Getting around It's easy to orientate yourself here as the town nestles in a valley surrounded by steep mountains at the eastern end of Lago Lacar. Beware of confusing street names: Perito Moreno runs east–west, crossing Mariano Moreno, which runs north–south, and Rudecindo Roca which is two blocks north of General Roca.

Tourist information The large and helpful **tourist office** ⓘ *San Martín y J M de Rosas 790, on the main plaza, T02972-427347, www.sanmartindelosandes.gov.ar/turismo, www.sanmartindelosandes.com (in English), daily 0800-2100*, hands out maps and has lists of accommodation, with prices up on a big board. The staff speak English and French, but are very busy in summer, when it's advisable to go early in the day before they get stressed. Also check out www.chapelco.com.ar.

Places in San Martín de los Andes

The main street, San Martín, runs perpendicular to the *costanera*, and here you'll find most shops and plenty of places to eat. Of the two plazas, the more interesting is Plaza San Martín, which has a sporadic crafts market. It's a pleasant 1½-hour walk north and west up the hill to **Mirador Bandurrias**, with great views and a *quincho*-like restaurant, **Lola Mora**, run by the local Mapuche community. Start at the far northernmost end of the *costanera*, passing the fish trap and walk along the shore before ascending the path, 40 minutes up. Even lovelier, set off from the *costanera* up to **Mirador Arrayán**, where there's a gorgeous tea room, **La Casa de Té Arrayán**, and restaurant with spectacular views over the lake.

The town is surrounded by lakes and mountains that are ripe for exploration. In addition to trips around Lago Lacar, the most popular excursions are south along the **Seven Lakes Drive** to Lagos Traful, Meliquina, Filo Hua Hum, Hermoso, Falkner and Villarino (see page 442) and north to the thermal baths at **Termas de Lahuen-Co** (see above). Trips to the *termas* via **Lago Curruhué** are offered by tour operators, but you could also cycle or drive there along *ripio* roads from Lago Lolog. There's no public transport to these places at present.

Lago Lacar

The north shore of Lago Lacar can be explored by car along much of its length, following *ripio* Route 48 towards the Chilean border at **Paso Hua Hum**, 41 km. **Río Hua Hum** has become a popular place for rafting, with some good stretches of rapids, as the river flows west towards the Pacific; take a tour from an agency in town. You can cycle or walk all the way around the lake on a rough track and also to **Lago Escondido** to the south. There are beaches at **Catrite**, 4 km south of San Martín, at **Hua Hum** and at **Quila Quina** on the southern shore, 18 km from San Martín. This is a quieter beach, with a walk to a lovely waterfall along a guided nature trail. There's also a two-hour walk from here that takes you to a tranquil Mapuche community in the hills above the lake. Both Quila Quina and Hua Hum can be reached by boat from the pier in San Martín, T02972-428427: to

Border crossing: Argentina–Chile

Paso Hua Hum

Paso Hua Hum (659 m) lies 47 km west of San Martín de los Andes along Route 48 (*ripio*), which runs along the north shore of Lago Lacar and crosses the border to Puerto Pirehueico (very tough going for cyclists). From here, a boat crosses Lago Pirihueico, a long, narrow and deep lake, to Puerto Fuy at its northern end. The border is usually open all year 0800-2000 and is an alternative to the route via Paso Mamuil Malal (Tromen), see page 430. For more information, see www.gendarmeria.gov.ar/pasos/chile/fichhuahum.html.

Immigration Argentine and Chilean immigration is open daily 0800-1900 (Chile open till 2000 in summer).

Transport Ko Ko/Lafit (T02972-427422) run buses from San Martín to Puerto Pirehueico, two hours, leaving San Martín early in the morning; check terminal for schedule. They connect with Somarco ferries across the lake to Puerto Fuy (T+56 (0)63-228 2742/T+56 (0)2-2322 3900, www.barcazas.cl). These run three times a day in January to February, but at 1600 only the rest of the year (1300 from Puerto Fuy to Puerto Pirehueico). Fares are US$1.50 for foot passengers, US$9 for motorbikes and US$30 for cars; bicycles are also taken. Buses connect Puerto Pirehueico with Panguipulli, US$7, from where transport is available to other destinations in the Chilean Lake District. For further information, contact the tourist office in Panguipulli, T+56 (0)63-231 0436, or see www.sietelagos.cl and www.municipalidadpanguipulli.cl.

Quila Quina hourly, 30 minutes each way, US$24 return; to Hua Hum, US$72 return, three daily in season.

Chapelco ski and summer resort

ⓘ *2394 m, 19 km south of San Martín, www.chapelco.com.ar.*

Cerro Chapelco (www.cerrochapelco.com) offers superb views over Lanín and many Chilean peaks. The ski resort is well organized, with 29 km of pistes for skiing and snowboarding, many of them challenging, including several black runs and a lovely long easy piste for beginners. With an overall drop of 730 m and very good slopes and snow conditions, this is a popular resort for wealthier Argentines and, increasingly, foreigners. There's also a ski school and snowboards for hire. The price of a day pass varies from US$73 in high season (15 July to 2 August). There is a daily bus in high season from San Martín to the slopes, US$12 return, with **Transportes Chapelco** ⓘ *T0294-15-461 8875*. Details of the resort, passes and equipment hire are available in season from the **Chapelco office** ⓘ *Moreno 859, T02972-427845, www.sanmartindelosandes.gov.ar.* At the foot of the mountain is a restaurant and base lodge, with three more restaurants on the mountain and a small café at the top. In summer this is a good place for cycling (take your bike up on the cable car then cycle down), trekking, archery or horse riding.

For hotel and restaurant price codes and other relevant information, see pages 20-26.

● Where to stay

Parque Nacional Lanín *p426, map p427*
$$$ Hostería Paimún, Ruta 61, Lago Paimún, T02972-491758, www.hosteria paimun.com.ar. Basic, comfortable rooms, private beach, fly fishing guide, lake excursions, cosy restaurant, stunning views all around
$$$ Huechulafquen, Ruta 61, Km 55, Lago Huechulafquen, T02972-427598, www.hosteriahuechulafquen.com. Nov-May. Half board, comfortable cabin-like rooms, gardens, expert fly fishing guide, restaurant open to non-residents in high season.

Camping
Several sites in beautiful surroundings on Lagos Huechulafquen and Paimún. The most recommended are: **Bahía Cañicul** (48 km from Junín), **Camping Lafquen-co** (53 km from Junín) and **Piedra Mala** (65 km from Junín); US$7 pp. Also try **Mawizache**, beyond **Hostería Paimún** and the picturesque little chapel, Lago Paimún. Run by Raúl and Carmen Hernández, who are both very knowledgeable and offer fishing trips. Good restaurant. Open all year.

Junín de los Andes *p430, map p431*
$$$$ Río Dorado Lodge & Fly shop, Pedro Illera 378, T02972-492451, www. riodorado.com.ar. Comfortable rooms in log cabin-style fishing lodge, big American breakfast, good fly shop, fishing excursions to many rivers and lakes, lovely gardens, attentive service.

$$$ Caleufu Travel Lodge, JA Roca 1323 (on Ruta 234), T02972-492757, http://www.caleufutravellodge.com. ar. Excellent value, welcoming, very good, homey rooms, neat garden, also comfortable apartments for up to 5 people, 3- to 6-night packages and fly fishing. Owner Jorge speaks English. Recommended.
$$ Hostería Chimehuin, Col Suárez y 25 de Mayo, T02972-491132, http:// www.hosteriachimehuin.com.ar. Closed May. Cosy, quaint fishing lodge by the river, fishing and mountain guides. Recommended.
$$ Res Marisa, JM de Rosas 360 (on Ruta 234), T02972-491175, residencialmarisa@ hotmail.com. A simple place with helpful owners, breakfast extra, very good value.
$ pp La Casa de Marita y Aldo, 25 de Mayo 371, T02972-491042, casademarita yaldo@hotmail.com. A cheery and popular family house with basic accommodation. Very helpful owners.
$ pp Tromen, Lonquimay 195, T02972-491498, www.hosteltromen.com.ar. Small house with dorms and private rooms for up to 4 people. At night take a taxi from the bus station as the streets in the area have no signs or lights.

Estancias
$$$$ Estancia Huechahue, 30 km east of town off R234, near Río Collon Curá and junction with Ruta 40, www. huechahue.com. The best riding in the Lake District can be experienced at this marvelous self-sufficient, traditional Patagonian *estancia*, where they breed horses and cattle and welcome guests to stay in very comfortable rooms in the main house and in cabins. Other activities on offer include fishing, rafting and

walking. Sauna and jacuzzi, great *asados* in the open air. Highly recommended.

San Martín de los Andes and around *p432*

There are 2 high seasons, when rates are much higher: Jan/Feb and Jul/Aug. Single rooms are expensive all year. *Cabañas* are available in 2 main areas: up Perito Moreno on the hill to the north of town, and down by the lakeside; prices for these increase in high season but they are good value for families or groups. When everywhere else is full, the tourist office will provide a list of private addresses in high season. See www.sanmartindelosandes.gov.ar for a full list of places to stay. All those listed here are recommended.

$$$$ La Casa de Eugenia, Coronel Díaz 1186, T02972-427206, www.lacasade eugenia.com.ar. B&B in a beautifully renovated 1900s house, very welcoming and relaxing, cosy rooms, huge breakfast, charming hosts.

$$$$ Le Châtelet, Villegas 650, T02972-428294, www.lechatelethotel.com. Chic and luxurious, beautiful chalet-style hotel with excellent service to pamper you. Wood-panelled living room, gorgeous bedrooms and suites, buffet breakfast, spa and pool with massage and facial treatments. Also, welcome glass of wine.

$$$ Arco Iris, Los Cipreses 1850, T02972-428450, www.arcoirisar.com. Comfortable, well-equipped *cabañas* with Wi-Fi and cable TV in a quiet area of town, each has a cosy living room and spacious kitchen. Own access to the river, so you can fish before breakfast or enjoy a drink on the water side in the evening.

$$$ Hostería Bärenhaus, Los Alamos 156, Barrio Chapelco (8370), T02972-422775, www.baerenhaus.com.ar. 5 km outside town, pick-up from bus terminal

and airport arranged. Welcoming young owners, very comfortable rooms with heating, English and German spoken.

$$$ Hostería Walkirias, Villegas 815, T02972-428307, www.laswalkirias.com. A lovely place, smart, tasteful rooms with big bathrooms. Sauna and pool room. Buffet breakfast. Great value off season and for longer stays, open all year.

$$$ Plaza Mayor, Cnel Pérez 1199, T02972-427302, www.hosteriaplaza mayor.com.ar. A chic and homely hostería in a quiet residential area, with traditional touches in the simple elegant rooms, excellent home-made breakfast, heated pool with solarium, barbecue, parking.

$$ Crismalú, Rudecindo Roca 975, T02972-427283, www.interpatagonia. com/crismalu. Simple rooms in attractive chalet-style converted home, good value.

$$ Hostería Las Lucarnas, Cnel Pérez 632, T02972-427085, www.hosterialas lucarnas.com.ar. Great value, centrally located, pretty place with simple comfortable rooms, English-speaking owner, breakfast included. Discounts for more than 5 nights, open all year.

$ pp Bike Hostel, Av Koessler 1531, T02972-424117, www.hosteltrail.com/bikehostel. Rooms for 4-6 in a split-level alpine house, US$12-15, well-cared-for, good, includes bike rental.

$ pp Puma, A Fosbery 535 (north along Rivadavia, 2 blocks beyond bridge), T02972-422443, www.pumahostel.com.ar. Discount for HI and ISIC members, small dorms with bath and a double room with view, laundry, bikes for hire, very well run by mountain guide owner, good value.

$ pp Rukalhue, Juez del Valle 682 (3 blocks from terminal), T02972-427431, www.rukalhue.com.ar. Large camp-style accommodation with 1 section full of dorm rooms (US$13-22) and 1 section with doubles, triples and apartments

($$$-$$). Also has apartments with private bath and kitchenette.

Camping
ACA Camping, Av Koessler 2175, T02972-429430, www.interpatagonia.com/aca. With hot water and laundry facilities, also *cabañas*.
Camping Quila Quina, T02972-411919. Lovely site on a stream near Lago Lácar, 18 km from San Martín, with beaches, immaculate toilet blocks, restaurant and shop, access to boats and treks. Open only in summer and Easter.

🍴 Restaurants

Parque Nacional Lanín *p426, map p427*
There are lots of places to eat on Lago Huechulafquen, with *provedurías* selling good *pan casero* at **Bahía** and **Piedra Mala**. **Mawizache Campsite** (see page 435) has a great restaurant serving fabulous local dishes very inexpensively, plus hot chocolate and cakes.

Junín de los Andes *p430, map p431*
$$$ Ruca Hueney, Col Suárez y Milanesio, T02972-491113. Good steak, trout and pasta dishes, popular, great atmosphere.
$ La Nueva Posta de Junín, JM de Rosas 160 (on Ruta 234), T02972-492080. *Parrilla* with good service and wine list; also trout, pizza and pastas.

San Martín de los Andes *p432*
$$$ 54 La Vaca, Rivadavia y San Martín, T02972-422564. A traditional Argentine *parilla*, great atmosphere.
$$ El Regional, Mascardi 822, T02972-425326. Popular for regional specialties – smoked trout, venison, wild boar, pâtés and hams, El Bolsón's home-made beer, cheerful German-style decor.

$$ La Costa del Pueblo, Costanera opposite pier, T02972-429289. Overlooking the lake, huge range of pastas, chicken and trout dishes, generous portions, good service, cheerful.
$$ La Tasca, Mariano Moreno 866, T02972-428663. Good for venison, trout and home-made pastas, varied wine list.

Cafés
Beigier, Av Costanera 815. Hidden cottage with views of the bay serving a fantastic afternoon tea with home-made goodies.
Deli, Villegas y Juez del Valle, T02972-428631. Affordable place with views of the bay and nice salads, pastas and pizzas.

🍸 Bars and clubs

San Martín de los Andes *p432*
Down Town Matias, Coronel Díaz y Calderón, www.matiaspub.com.ar/v01/. Fantastic, welcoming building, good for a late night drink with snacks.
Dublin South Bar, Av San Martín 599. Huge pub (with no reference to Ireland at all) with comfy seats, great food – try the home-made pasta – and a good atmosphere.

🎉 Festivals

Junín de los Andes *p430, map p431*
Jan Agricultural show and **exhibition of flowers** and **local crafts**, at the end of the month.
Feb Fiesta Provincial de Puestero. Mid-Feb sees the election of the queen, handicrafts, *asados* with local foods and fabulous gaucho riding. This is the most important country fiesta in the south of Argentina.
Mar Carnival.

Jul Festival of Aboriginal Arts, mid-month.
Nov Opening of the fishing season, 2nd Sat.
Dec Inauguration of the church of **Laura Vicuña**, with a special Mass on the 8th and singing to celebrate the life of Laura Vicuña.

○ Shopping

Junín de los Andes *p430, map p431*
Patagonia Rodeo, Padre Milanesio 562, 1st floor, T01972-492839. A traditional shop selling what real gauchos wear in the field, plus quality leather work: belts, wallets, saddlery. Look like the real thing before you turn up at the *estancias*.

San Martín de los Andes *p432*
A great place for shopping, with chic little shops selling clothes and handmade jumpers; try **La Oveja Negra**, San Martín 1025, T02972-428039, for wonderful handmade scarves and jumpers, plus esoteric crafts and interesting souvenirs. There's also a handicraft market in summer in Plaza San Martín. There are 2 recommended places for chocolates: **Abuela Goye**, San Martín 807, T02972-429409, www.abuelagoye.com, which serves excellent ice creams and a killer hot chocolate, and **Mamusia**, San Martín 601, T02972-427560, which also sells home-made jams. Lots of outdoor shops on San Martín sell clothes for walking and skiing, including **Nomade**, San Martín 881.

○ What to do

Parque Nacional Lanín *p426, map p427*
Lahuen Co, T02972-424 709, www.lahuenco.com. This thermal spa resort can organize trekking, kayaking, biking and fishing excursions in the area, and afterwards you can relax in their thermal water pool.

Horse riding
You can explore much of the area on horseback, including the trek to the base of Volcán Lanín. 5 places along the lake hire horses: ask *guardaparques* for advice, or ask at the local Mapuche community where you see the signs, *cabalgatas* (horse rides).

Junín de los Andes *p430, map p431*
Fishing
The season runs from 2nd Sat in Nov to May. For fly casting and trolling the best places are lakes Huechulafquen, Paimún, Epulaufken, Tromen and Currehue, and the rivers Chuimehuin, Malleo, Alumine and Quilquihué. Ask the helpful tourist office for more information and also see Tour operators, below.
Río Dorado Lodge, Pedro Illera 448, T02972-492451, www.riodorado.com.ar. The luxury fishing lodge at the end of town has a good fly shop, and organizes trips, run by experts and passionate fishermen.

Horse riding
Estancia Huechahue, www.huechahue.com. Located northeast of Junín, this *estancia* offers unbeatable riding and hospitality. Rides into the national park enable you to reach areas that are otherwise completely inaccessible. Recommended.

Tour operators
Alquimia Viajes and Turismo, O'Higgins 603, T02972-491355, www.alquimiaturismo.com.ar. Offers fishing excursions with expert local guides among a range of adventure tourism options, including

climbing Lanín, climbing in rock and ice, rafting, and transfers.
Tromen, Lonquimay 195, T02972-491498. Trips up Volcano Lanín, horse riding, mountain biking, car rental and bicycle rental.

San Martín de los Andes *p432*
Canopying
Canopy, 8 km from town, T0294-15-459 6215, www.canopyensmandes.com.ar. 1400 m of course, spread over 10 different resting-stations with a height that varies from 8 to 20 m off the ground. Recommended.

Cycling
Many places in the centre rent mountain and normal bikes, US$10-20 per day, maps provided.
HG Rodados, San Martín 1061, T02972-427345, hgrodados@smandes.com.ar. Arranges trips, rents mountain bikes, also spare parts and expertise.

Fishing
For guides contact the tourist office or the park office. A licence costs US$30 for a day, US$120 for a season, with extra charges for trolling.
Jorge Cardillo Pesca, Villegas 1061, T02972-428372, www.jorgecardillo.com. Sells equipment and fishing licences and offers excursions.
Jorge Trucco, based in **Patagonia Outfitters**, Pérez 662, T02972-427561, www.jorgetrucco.com. Expert and professional trips, good advice and many years of experience.

Skiing
For details of the Chapelco resort, see page 434.

Tour operators
Prices for conventional tours, such as the Seven Lakes Drive, are similar with most agencies. Most tours operate from 2 Jan. 1 day's rafting at Hua Hum costs US$60-70.
El Claro, Col Díaz 751, T02972-428876, www.elclaroturismo.com.ar. For conventional tours, horse riding, mountain biking and trekking.
El Refugio, Pérez 830, just off San Martín, upstairs, T02972-425140, www.elrefugioturismo.com.ar. Bilingual guides, conventional tours, boat trips, also mountain bike hire, rafting, horse riding and trekking. Recommended.
Lanín Expediciones, San Martín 851, oficina 5, T02972-429799, www.lanin expediciones.com. Adventure tourism for beginners or experts, from a 3-hr walk near San Martín, winter night walks in the forest, rafting in Aluminé, trekking in Lanín area, a 3-day ascent of the volcano, and climbs to 4700-m Domuyo peak.

☉ Transport

Junín de los Andes *p430, map p431*
Air
Chapelco airport is served by **AR** from Buenos Aires.

Bus
To **San Martín**, with **Centenario**, **Castelli** and others, 50 mins, US$1.75-3. **Castelli** also goes daily in Jan-Feb (Sun, Mon, Wed, Fri in Dec) to **Lago Paimún**, 2 hrs, US$8. To **Buenos Aires**, 20-21 hrs, US$160-175. To **Chile** (via Paso Mamuil Malal), see box, page 430.

San Martín de los Andes *p432*
Air
See under Junín de los Andes above. **LADE** office in bus terminal, T02972-427672.

Bus

To **Buenos Aires**, 21-22 hrs, US$120-150, daily, 4 companies. To **Villa La Angostura**, **Albus** 4 a day, US$9. To **Bariloche** (not via 7 Lagos), 3½-4 hrs, US$16, **Vía Bariloche** and **Ko Ko**. To Chile: **Pucón, Villarrica** and **Valdivia** via Junín de los Andes and Paso Mamuil Malal, US$23, 5 hrs to Pucón with **San Martín,** heavily booked in summer (see box, page 430). Alternatively, **Ko Ko/Lafit** (T02972-427422) run buses to Puerto Pirehueico, via Paso Hua Hum, 2 hrs; check terminal for schedule (see also box, page 434).

⊙ Directory

Junín de los Andes *p430, map p431*
Currency exchange Banco Provincial Neuquén, San Martín and Lamadrid. TCs can be cashed at **Western Union**, Crl. Suarez 1, Mon-Fri 0800-1900. **Post office** Suárez and Don Bosco.

San Martín de los Andes *p432*
Banks and currency exchange Many ATMs along San Martín: **Andina Internacional Cambio and Turismo**, Cap Drury 876; **Banelco**, at the tourist office, San Martín 1093 y Rosas; **Banco Nación**, San Martín 687; **Banco de la Provincia de Neuquén**, Obeid and Belgrano, also has ATM, T02972-427243. **Laundry** Laverap, Drury 880; **Marva**, Perito Moreno 980, fast, efficient and cheap. **Medical services** Hospital Ramón Carrillo, San Martín y Coronel Rodhe, T02972-427211. **Post office** General Roca and Pérez, Mon-Fri 0800-1300, 1600-1900.

San Martín to Bariloche

The journey south to Bariloche along the celebrated Seven Lakes Drive is the most famous tourist route in the Argentine Lake District. It follows Route 234 through the Lanín and Nahuel Huapi national parks and passes seven magnificent lakes, all flanked by mixed natural forest; it is particularly attractive in autumn (April to May) when the forested slopes turn red and yellow.

The seven lakes are (from north to south): Lácar, Machónico, Falkner, Villarino, Espejo, Correntoso and Nahuel Huapi. The road is only partially paved, but mostly decent, apart from a very potholed stretch in the middle, not recommended after heavy rain or snowfall.

On the way from picturesque San Martín de los Andes, there are two good bases for further adventures. Remote Villa Traful is tucked into a deep fold between dramatic, spired mountains, on the side of a navy blue sliver of lake. It's a peaceful place for a few days' rest, with a couple of good walks and some appealing places to stay. Further south, on the northern side of Lake Nahuel Huapi, is the pretty, upmarket town of Villa la Angostura. Much loved by wealthier Argentines, there's no shortage of smart places to stay and eat here, such as famous and blissful boutique hotel, Las Balsas (www.lasbalsas.com). From Villa la Angostura you can visit the tiny national park, Los Arrayanes, by boat or on foot, created to protect a rare forest of *arrayán* trees with their cinnamon-coloured bark and twisting trunks. For more information, see www.interpatagonia.com/loslagos (in Spanish and English).

Leaving San Martín, Route 234 is paved for the first section south past Lago Machónico. The first lake you reach in the Nahuel Huapi national park is Lago Falkner, which is popular with fishermen. It's a wide and open lake, with thickly forested fjord-like mountains descending steeply into it. There's a long narrow sandy beach on the roadside, a good place for a picnic stop, and wild camping; **Camping Lago Falkner** nearby has facilities. To the south, there's another pretty, if exposed, free campsite (with no facilities) by the deep green Río Villarino, near Lago Villarino, and a campsite and picnic ground amidst little beech trees at Pichi Traful, at the northern tip of Lago Traful. This is a beautiful spot by the wide green banks of a river, with steeply rising mountains on all sides.

At Km 77, Route 65 branches off to the east, running along the south shore of Lago Traful through Villa Traful to meet the main Neuquén–Bariloche highway (Route 237) at Confluencia. If you have a couple of days to spare, this makes a lovely detour (see below). Continuing south, however, the drive (now unpaved) passes gorgeous, secluded Lago Espejo ('lake mirror'), which has lovely beaches on its shore. Opposite, you'll be treated to a superb view of Lago Correntoso on the final stretch towards Villa la Angostura on Lago Nahuel Huapi.

You can see the route from the windows of a bus on a round trip excursion from Bariloche, Villa la Angostura or San Martín, which will take about five hours, but you may prefer your own transport, so you can stop and explore. Buses will stop at campsites on the route. It's a good route for cycling, as you can really appreciate the beauty of the ever-changing landscape, though note that there's more traffic in January and February.

The alternative route to Bariloche

There's a quicker route from San Martín to Bariloche, via **Confluencia**, further east. Head south from San Martín on Route 234, but at Lago Machónico, instead of continuing southwest, take Route 63 along the tranquil shore of Lago Meliquina. Further south, you could turn off to isolated Lago Filo-Hua-Hum at Km 54 (unpaved track). A little further on the road climbs to the **Paso de Córdoba**, Km 77 (1300 m), with fabulous views, from where it descends to the valley of the Río Traful, following it east to Confluencia. From Confluencia, you can head west along Route 65 to Villa Traful and rejoin the Seven Lakes Drive, or continue south to Bariloche on Route 237 through the astounding **Valle Encantado**, where there are weird rock formations including El Dedo de Dios (The Finger of God) and El Centinela del Valle (The Sentinel of the Valley).

Villa Traful → *Phone code 0294. Population 503.*

If you want to get off the beaten track, Villa Traful is ideal. It was created after the Nahuel Huapi National Park was set up, with the aim of giving visitors the greatest possible contact with nature. Approaching from the west, along the southern shore of Lago Traful, the winding road passes through forests of lenga and tall *coihue* trees, their elegant trunks creating a woody cathedral, with idyllic spots to camp all along the shore.

The quiet pretty village sprawls alongside the narrow deep-blue sliver of Lago Traful, enclosed on both sides by stunning sharp-peaked mountains. There's not much to do here, but it's popular with fishermen, and there are a couple of wonderful walks and waterfalls to see, it's a pleasant place to unwind. At the heart of the village opposite the main pier is a pay phone, a kiosk selling basic supplies and bus tickets, and the best restaurant. There's a small but very helpful **tourist office** ① *Ruta Provincial 65, T0294-447 9099, see www.villatraful.gov.ar or www.interpatagonia.com/villatraful*, which has information on walks, riding and fishing. The national park *guardería* is opposite the pier, open only in high season, with advice on walks.

The best time to visit Villa Traful is December or late February to March when the few restaurants aren't full of tourists. Traful is prone to mercurial winds, so check the forecast if you're coming for a few days as it's miserable being stuck here in bad weather and the buses are infrequent.

Walks around Villa Traful

A 1½-hour walk from the village centre takes you to the lovely **Cascadas del Arroyo Coa Có y Blanco** waterfalls thundering down through beech forest and *cañas colihues* bamboo. Walk up the hill from the Ñancu Lahuen restaurant and take the left-hand path to the mirador over Cascada Coa Có, and from here take the right-hand path through *coihue* forest. Better still, there's a satisfying hike up to **Cerro Negro** (2000 m) five hours up, following uncertain yellow markers. Ask at the national park office to get the best advice on the route. It's a stiff climb to start with, through gorgeous *coihue* and *lenga* forest, and the views as you clear the tree line are unbelievable, with the dramatic spired peaks visible on the northern side of Lago Traful. There's a lot of scree near the summit, but the views of Lanín, Tronador and the others make it all worthwhile. Alternatively, cross the lake (15 minutes) by boat, leaving from the main pier, to reach a sand beach from where you can walk up a steep path to twin lagoons and some superbly well conserved prehistoric cave paintings nearby. Ask in the tourist office to see which companies are currently running trips.

Villa La Angostura and around → *For listings, see pages 446-450.*

This is a delightful little town which, apart from in January when it is packed out, is an appealing place to stay, especially for those who like their nature seen from the comfort of a luxurious hotel. There are some superb restaurants here and some seriously chic hotels. *Cabaña* complexes and great hostels have mushroomed up everywhere, so there's no shortage of places to stay. And there are some good walks nearby, excellent fly fishing, and a golf course, as well as skiing in winter.

Arriving in Villa La Angostura → *Colour map 5, B2. Phone code 0294. Population 13,000.*

The small **bus terminal** ① *at the junction of Av 7 Lagos and Av Arrayanes*, is opposite the ACA service station. You can leave your baggage at the small café below for

US$2. Urban buses, run by **15 de Mayo**, US$1, link El Cruce (main bus stop on main road, 50 m from tourist office), La Villa, Correntoso and Puerto Manzano, and go up to Lago Espejo (US$1-2) and Cerro Bayo (US$3) in high season. The **tourist office** ① *Av Arrayanes 9, T0294-449 4124, www.villalaangostura.gov.ar; also opposite the bus terminal, Av Siete Lagos 93, high season 0830-2230, low season 0900-2100*, is helpful, with lots of information. English spoken.

Places in Villa La Angostura

The town is divided into several different *barrios*: around the sprawling centre, **El Cruce**; around the lakeside area of **Puerto Manzano**, and around the picturesque port, known as **La Villa**, 3 km away at the neck of the Quetrihué Peninsula, which dips into the northern end of Lago Nahuel Huapi. From La Villa it's a short trip on foot or by boat to Villa La Angostura's great attraction, the **Parque Nacional Los Arrayanes** (see box, opposite), at the end of the peninsula. Also from La Villa, a short walk leads to lovely **Laguna Verde**, an intense emerald-green lagoon surrounded by mixed *coihue* cypress and *arrayán* forests, where there's a 1-km self-guided trail, taking about an hour. There are no services in La Villa apart from a *kiosko*, a tea room in high season, and the restaurant at **Hotel Angostura**. A bus runs from the centre at El Cruce to La Villa every couple of hours, taking 15 minutes, but it's a pleasant walk.

About halfway between the two centres is a chapel (1936), designed by Bustillo, the famous architect who gave this region's buildings their distinctive style, and nearby is **El Messidor** (1942), the summer resort of Argentine presidents, where you can visit the beautiful gardens with lake views. There's also a tiny museum, **Museo Regional** ① *Blvd Nahuel Huapi 2177, on the road to La Villa, Mon, Tue, Thu, Fri 1030-1730, Wed 1030-1430 Sat 1430-1730*, with interesting photos of the original indigenous inhabitants.

In winter, there's good skiing at Villa La Angostura's popular ski resort **Cerro Bayo** ① *9 km north of town, T0294-449 4189, www.cerrobayoweb.com*, with 24 pistes, 20 km in total, many of them fabulously long, and all with excellent views over the lakes below. It's a great area for snowboarding. This is one of Argentina's pricier resorts: a one-day ski pass costs US$70 for adults in high season.

Walks around Villa La Angostura

Parque Nacional Los Arrayanes For an easy flat walk, take the boat to the head of the Quitrihué Peninsula and walk the 13 km back. See box, opposite.

Mirador Belvedere Offers fine views of Lagos Correntoso and Nahuel Huapi. It's a 3-km drive or walk up the old road, northwest of El Cruce; and from the mirador a path to your right goes to **Cascada Inacayal**, a waterfall 50 m high, situated in an area rich in native flora and forest.

Cascada Río Bonito A delightful walk leading to a beautiful waterfall, lying 8 km east of El Cruce off Route 66. The steep path gives tremendous views, and the falls themselves are impressive, falling 35 m from a chasm in basalt cliffs to an emerald-

Parque Nacional Los Arrayanes

This park covers the Quetrihué Peninsula, which dips south from Villa La Angostura into the Lago Nahuel Huapi and lies within the Parque Nacional Nahuel Huapi. It was created to protect a rare forest of *arrayán* trees, since it's one of the few places in the world where the *arrayán* grows to full size, and some of the specimens are 300 years old. This myrtle-like tree grows near water in groves and likes to have its roots wet, since it really has no bark. The trunks are extraordinary: a smooth powdery or peeling surface, bright cinnamon in colour and cold to the touch. They have no outer bark to protect them, but the surface layer is rich in tannins that keep the tree free from disease. They have creamy white flowers in January and February, and produce blue-black fruit in March. The sight of so many of these trees together, with their twisting trunks, creates a wonderful fairy-tale *scene*. The most rewarding way to see the wood is to take the boat trip across the deep-blue lake, fringed with spectacular peaks, to the tip of the peninsula, and then take a leisurely walk along the wheelchair-friendly wooden walkways through the trees, waiting until the guided tour has left. Halfway along you'll see a small wooden café which serves tea and coffee and has great views of the forest. Stroll back to the port through the mixed forest, passing two pretty and secluded lakes, Laguna Patagua, and Laguna Hua Huan.

Arriving in Parque Nacional Los Arrayanes

The entrance to the park is a walkable 2 km south of the port area of Villa la Angostura, known as La Villa. Bus company **15 de Mayo** runs buses from El Cruce to La Villa every two hours (15 minutes). A taxi to Villa costs US$3.50. For information contact the Nahuel Huapi **park office** in Bariloche, San Martín 24, T0294-442 3121, www.parques nacionales.gob.ar. You may enter the park 0900-1400 in summer, 0900-1200 in winter, US$9.65. You must leave the park by 1700 and 1500 respectively.

Walking and cycling

There's a clear path all the way from the tip of the Quetrihué Peninsula where the boat arrives, through the prettiest part of the *arrayán* forest, and then running the length of the peninsula back to La Villa. You can walk or cycle the whole length: three hours one-way walking; two hours cycling (for cycle hire, see page 448).

Boat trips

Two companies run catamarans from the pier in La Villa to the end of the peninsula, and take passengers on a short guided tour through the forest. **Catamarán Patagonia Argentina**, T0294-449 4463, and **Greenleaf Turismo**, Avenida Arrayanes 111, Villa La Angostura, T0294-449 4004, www.bosquelosarrayanes.com.ar; tickets, US$15.50 one-way, US$30 return. Boats also run from Bariloche, via Isla Victoria, with Turisur, T0294-442 6109, www.turisur.com.ar.

green pool. Further along the same path, you can reach the summit of Cerro Bayo (1782 m). Alternatively, 1 km further along the road, a ski lift takes you to the platform at 1500 m, where there's a restaurant with great views, and from here, it's a short trek to the summit. The ski lift runs all year; cyclists can take bikes up in the lift and cycle down.

⊕ San Martín to Bariloche listings

For hotel and restaurant price codes and other relevant information, see pages 20-26.

⊖ Where to stay

The alternative route to Bariloche
p442
$$$-$$ Hostería La Gruta de las Virgenes, Confluencia, T0294-442 6138. On a hill with views over the 2 rivers, very hospitable.

Villa Traful *p442*
$$$ Hostería Villa Traful, T0294-447 9005, www.hosteriavillatraful.com. A cosy house with a tea room by the lake, also *cabañas* for 4-6 people, pretty gardens, good value. The owner's son, Andrés, organizes fishing and boat trips.
$$ Cabañas Aiken, T0294-447 9048, www.aiken.com.ar. Well-decorated *cabañas* in beautiful surroundings near the lake (close to the tourist office), each with its own *parrillada*, also has a restaurant. Recommended.
$ pp Vulcanche Hostel, Los Sorbus 67, T0294-15-469 2314, www.vulcanche.com. Chalet-style hostel in gardens with good views, with good dorms and **$$** doubles, breakfast extra, large park for camping.

Villa La Angostura and around *p443*
$$$$ La Escondida, Av Arrayanes 7014, T0294-447 5313, www.hosteriala escondida.com.ar. Wonderful setting,

right on the lake, 14 rooms, heated pool, offers mid-week, weekend and long-stay specials. Recommended.
$$$$ La Posada, R 231, Km 65, Las Balsas (no number), T0294-449 4450, www. hosterialaposada.com. In a splendid elevated position off the road with clear views over the lake, welcoming, beautifully maintained hotel in lovely gardens, with pool, spa, fine restaurant; a perfect place to relax.
$$$$ Las Balsas, on Bahía Las Balsas (signposted from Av Arrayanes), T0294-449 4308, www.lasbalsas.com. One of the best small hotels in Argentina, with fabulous cosy rooms, warm relaxed public areas, fine cuisine, impeccable service, and a wonderfully intimate atmosphere in a great lakeside location with its own secluded beach. Lakeside heated swimming pools, spa, trips and excursions arranged. Highly recommended.
$$$ Hostería ACA al Sur, Av Arrayanes 8 (behind the petrol station), T0294-448 8413, www.acavillalaangostura.com.ar. Modern, attractive single-storey hotel with well-designed rooms in the centre of town. Recommended.
$$$ Hostería Le Lac, Av de los 7 Lagos 2350, T0294-448 8029, www.hosteria lelac.com.ar. 3-star, 8 rooms, some with jacuzzi and DVD, gardens, lake view, can arrange lots of activities, several languages spoken by owner.
$$$ Hotel Angostura, Nahuel Huapi 1911, at La Villa, T0294-449 4224, www.

hotelangostura.com. Built in 1938, this traditional hotel has a lovely lakeside setting and a good restaurant and tea room, **Viejo Coihue**. Also has 3 cabins for 6 (**$$$$**). Boat excursions along the nearby shore are arranged.
$$ Bajo Cero, Av 7 Lagos al 1200, T0294-449 5454, www.bajocerohostel.com. Well-situated, rooms for 2-6, can arrange trekking, cycling and other excursions.
$ pp Hostel La Angostura, Barbagelata 157, 150 m up road behind tourist office, T0294-449 4834, www.hostella angostura.com.ar. A warm, luxurious hostel, all small dorms have bathrooms (US$18), good doubles (US$50), HI discounts, welcoming owners organize trips and rent bikes. Recommended.
$ pp Italian Hostel, Los Maquis 215 (5 blocks from terminal), T0294-449 4376, www.italianhostel.com.ar. Welcoming, small, with dorms (US$18) and doubles (US$43), rustic, functional and nice, run by a biker who closes the place in Apr-Oct. Fireplace and orchard from where you can pick berries and herbs for your meals. Recommended.

Camping
Osa Mayor, signposted off main road, close to town, T0294-449 4304, www.campingosamayor.com.ar. Well designed leafy and level site, US$8-13, all facilities, also rustic *cabañas* US$83 for 2 people, and dorms US$49 for 2 people, helpful owner.

🍴 Restaurants

Villa Traful *p442*
$$ Ñancu Lahuen, T0294-447 9017. A chocolate shop, tea room and restaurant serving local trout. Delightful and cosy, with big open fire, delicious food and reasonably priced.

Villa La Angostura and around *p443*
Plenty of places are to be found on the main Av Arrayanes, lots of them chalet-style and open all day from breakfast onwards. Prices reflect the fact that this is a popular tourist town. Don't miss out on some of the really excellent places for fine cuisine here.
$$$ Cocina Waldhaus, Av Arrayanes 6330, T0294-447 5323. Highly recommended, this is 'auteur cuisine' with gorgeous local delicacies created by Chef Leo Morsea, served in a charming chalet-style building.
$$ El Esquiador, Las Retamas 146 (behind the bus terminal), T0294-449 4331. Good, popular *parrilla* has an all-you-can-eat choice of cold starters, a main meal and a dessert.
$$ Los Pioneros, Av Arrayanes 267, T0294-449 5525. Famous for fine local dishes in a chalet-style building and great Argentine steaks. Great pizza place next door run by the same owners. They also serve locally brewed beers.
$ Hora Cero, Av Arrayanes 45, T0294-449 5800. Hugely popular, this serves a big range of excellent pizzas.
$ TemaTyCo, Ruta 231 y Mirlo, T0294-447 5211. Chic tearoom with a wide range of teas and delicious cakes.

⬤ What to do

Villa Traful *p442*
Fishing
Andres Quelin, T0294-447 9005, www.hosteriavillatraful.com. A fishing guide who organizes boat trips to see a submerged cypress wood. Find him at **Hostería Villa Traful**, see Where to stay.

Mountain biking
Del Montanés, along the road running up the slope behind the centre of

the village, T0294-447 9035, www.
interpatagonia.com/delmontanes/.
Rents mountain bikes in summer.

Villa La Angostura and around *p443*
Boat trips
There are 3 companies running
catamaran trips: **Catamarán Patagonia
Argentina**, T0294-449 4463, runs trips
on a 60-passenger catamaran; **Greenleaf
Turismo**, Av Arrayanes 111, T0294-449
4004, www.bosquelosarrayanes.com.ar,
runs *Catamarán Futuleufu*; **Turisur**, T0294-
442 6109, www.turisur.com.ar, runs boats
from Bariloche, via Isla Victoria.

Velero Luz de Luna, T0294-449 4834,
www.vela-aventura.com.ar, offers trips
on sailing boats with a special meal on
board, or a drink with *picadas* of smoked
meat and fish.

Canopying
Canopy Villa la Angostura, Curruhué
and Melinquina, T0294-440 0 286, www.
canopybariloche.com. Runs a great trail
in the forest nearby, with over 1400 m of
cable to zoom along.

Climbing
Club Andino Villa La Angostura, Cerro
Bayo 295, T0294-449 4954, www.cavla.
com.ar. Excursions, maps and information.

Cycling
Expect to pay around US$15-20 per day
for bike hire.
Bayo Abajo, Av Siete Lagos 94,
bayoabajo@argentina.com. Bike hire.
Taquari Bici Shop, Av Arrayanes 259, www.
taquari.com.ar. New bikes, knowledgeable.

Fishing
The season runs from mid-Nov to May.
For permits and a list of fishing guides,
ask at the tourist office.

Anglers Home Fly Shop, Belvedere 22,
T0294-449 5222. Arranges fishing trips.
Banana Fly Shop, Av Arrayanes 282,
T0294-449 4634. Fly shop.
PatagonFly, www.patagonfly.com.
A fly shop and association of local
fishing guides, also runs trips.

Horse riding
Cabalgatas Correntoso, Cacique
Antrao 1850, T02944-15-451 0559,
www.cabalgatacorrentoso.com.ar.
Offers horseback excursions in the
surrounding area and to Villa Traful.

Skiing
Cerro Bayo (www.cerrobayoweb.com),
although smaller is more popular with
families than the famous Cerro Catedral
in Bariloche. See description, above.

Tour operators
Nómades de la Montaña, Ruca Choroy
38 y Cerro Inacayal 35, T0294-15-
455 1385, www.nomades.tur.ar.
Offering everything from trekking
and mountain biking to rappelling,
diving and fly fishing.
Rucán Turismo, Av 7 Lagos 239, T0294-
447 5263, www.rucanturismo.com.
Offers skiing, riding, mountain biking
and conventional tours.

Trekking
Alma Sur, T0294-456 4724/T0294-15-
456 4724, www.almasur.com. Great
trips in the local area and further afield,
with bilingual, knowledgeable Anthony
Hawes. A trained guide of Nahuel
Huapi National Park, he creates really
imaginative walks, which can include
boats, climbing and hiking way off the
beaten track. Recommended.

Border crossing: Argentina–Chile

Paso Samoré

Paso Samoré, formerly **Paso Puyehue** (1280 m), lies 125 km northwest of Bariloche on Route 231 at Km 122. It's a spectacular six-hour journey, with plenty of buses from Bariloche, making it a cheaper alternative to the expensive Three Lakes Crossing (see box, page 462). The road is rough *ripio* from Villa La Angostura, with the occasional paved stretch. On the Chilean side the road is paved via Entre Lagos and Lago Puyehue to Osorno. Cyclists should note that there are no supplies between Villa La Angostura and Entre Lagos. For more information, contact the gendarmería in Bariloche, T0294-442 2711 or visit www.gendarmeria.gov.ar/pasos/chile/fichsamo.html.

Argentine customs and immigration El Rincón, Route 231, Km 105. Open daily 0800-2000 but liable to be closed after snowfalls.

Chilean immigration It's 22 km from the pass to Chilean customs at Pajarito (Km 145) in the middle of a forest, over a wonderful mountain pass. Immigration is open daily 0900-2000.

Accommodation Termas Puyehue, Route 215, Km 76, T+56-600-293 6000, www.puyehue.cl. Luxurious accommodation and excellent thermal baths at a huge complex set in beautiful open parkland, framed by mountains, with an impressive spa. There are humbler places to stay in the town of Entre Lagos at the southwestern end of Lago Puyehue.

Transport For bus services from Bariloche to Osorno, Puerto Montt and Valdivia, see page 469. For vehicles entering Chile, formalities take about 30 minutes and include the spraying of tyres and wiping of shoes on a mat. Argentine hire cars must have the necessary documentation, and the car's number plate etched on the windows. Tell your car hire company 24 hours in advance that you plan to cross to Chile.

Notes You are strongly advised to get rid of all your Argentine pesos before leaving Argentina; it is useful to have some Chilean pesos before you cross into Chile from Bariloche, though you can buy them at a reasonable rate at the Chilean border post. Since the government lifted restrictions on foreign currency in 2014, it is now possible to buy Chilean pesos at official exchange houses. There is an absolute ban in Chile on importing any fresh food from Argentina.

◎ Transport

Villa Traful *p442*
Bus

In high summer, a **La Araucana** bus between **Villa la Angostura** and **San Martín** stops here daily; otherwise there are buses to Bariloche Thu-Tue. **Kiosko El Ciervo**, by the YPF service station, sells tickets and has the timetable.

Villa La Angostura and around *p443*
Bus

To **Bariloche**, 1 hr, US$6-8, several companies. Buses from Bariloche to **Osorno** in Chile will pick you up in La Angostura by arrangement.

❶ Directory

Villa La Angostura and around *p443*
Banks Andina, Arrayanes 256, T02944-495197, for cash and TCs; **Banco de** Patagonia, Av Arrayanes 275, ATM; **Banco Provincia de Neuquén**, Av Huapi 70, ATM. **Medical services** Hospital Rural Arraiz, Copello 311 (at *barrio* Pinar), T02944-494170. **Post office** Las Fucias 121.

Bariloche and around

Beautifully situated on the steep and wooded southern shore of Lago Nahuel Huapi, surrounded by high peaks, San Carlos de Bariloche (its official name) is an ideal base for exploring the Lake District. It's right in the middle of Nahuel Huapi National Park and there's so much on offer from the town itself that you'd be quite content to spend a week or so here.

The town was founded in 1902 but really took off in the 1930s when the national park was created. The chalet-style architecture was established at this time by early German and Swiss settlers. The famous Hotel Llao Llao (www.llaollao.com) and the civic centre were designed by major Argentine architect Bustillo, who set the trend for 'Bariloche Alpine style', with local stone, brightly varnished wood and carved gable ends, now ubiquitous throughout the region.

Bariloche is well set up for tourism with the main street, Mitre, bustling with tour operators, outdoor clothing shops and chocolate makers. There are also many restaurants serving fondue, as well as delicious local trout and wild boar, some of them bordering on kitsch, but appealing nevertheless. There are plenty of hotels and restaurants in the town centre, but the best places are sprinkled along the shore of Lake Nahuel Huapi, towards Llao Llao, where Argentina's most famous hotel enjoys a spectacularly beautiful setting. To the immediate south of Bariloche there are fabulous walks in the mountains, and up giant Mount Tronador, reached from Pampa Linda further west. On the way are two gorgeous lakes: Gutiérrez, with Estancia Peuma Hue on its shores for excellent horse riding and relaxing; and Mascardi, with access to rafting on the Río Manso. In summer there are good bus and boat services to reach these mountains and lakes, as well as cable cars up two of the peaks behind Bariloche. Ski resort Cerro Catedral is arguably the best in South America and makes a great base for trekking in summer.

Parque Nacional Nahuel Huapi

To San Martín de los Andes

Lago Hermoso

Lago Villarino

Parque Nacional Lanín

Lago Falkner

Falkner (2350m)

To Osorno

Lago Espejo

Lago Correntoso

Lago Traful

Villa Traful

To Confluencia & Neuquén

Paso Samore/ Puyehue 231

Villa La Angostura

Península de Quetrihué

Parque Nacional Los Arrayanes

Isla Victoria

Lago Gallardo

CHILE

Río Limay

To Peulla, Puerto Varas & Puerto Montt

Lago Ortiz Basualdo

Puerto Blest

Los Cántaros

Brazo Blest

Puerto Alegre

Península Llao-Llao

Puerto Pañuelo

Campanario (1049m)

Península San Pedro

Lago Nahuel Huapi

Bariloche

Paso Pérez Rosales

Lago Frías

Puerto Frías

Río Frías

Paso de Las Nubes

Lago Moreno

Otto (1405m)

Berghoff

To San Antonio Oeste

Otto Meiling

Negro Navidad

San Martín

Italia

Villa Catedral

Tronador (3478m)

Garganta del Diablo

Ventisquero Negro

Lago Frey

Laguna Ilón

Pampa Linda

Río Manso

Catedral (2388m)

Frey

Lago Gutiérrez

Estancia Peuma Hue

Neumeyer Laguna Verde

Lago Fonck

Isla Pluke Huapí

Lago Mascardi

Villa Mascardi

Lago Hess

Río Manso

Lago Guillermo

258

Lago Roca

Graniticco (2109m)

81

Lago Felipe

Cascada Los Alerces

Lago Martín

Lago Steffen

N

5 km
5 miles

Río Manso Inferior

Río Villegas

To El Bolsón & Esquel

Getting there

The **airport** ⓘ *access from Ruta 40, 7 km east of the centre, T0294-440 5016,* is 15 km east of town; bus service 72 runs to the town centre, as do colectivos and taxis (US$10). If you're staying on the road to Llao Llao, west of town, expect to pay more for transport to your hotel. The airport has car rental agencies, internet, exchange, ATM and café.

The **bus station** ⓘ *T0294-443 2860, http://terminaldebariloche.com.ar,* and the **train station** ⓘ *T0294-442 2450,* are both 3 km east of the centre. The bus terminal has toilets, small *confitería, kiosko, locutorio* with internet, left luggage and a tourist information desk. A taxi into town costs US$5-8. Otherwise, the following urban buses run by **3 de Mayo** (Moreno 480, http://3demayobariloche.com.ar) all travel between the bus station and the centre: 'Mascardi', 'Manso', 20, 21, 22; buses 10, 11, 72 also use the terminal. Buy a rechargeable ticket before travelling.

Getting around

Bariloche is an easy city to walk around and to orient yourself in, since the lake lies to the north and the mountains to the south. The main street is Mitre, running east to west, and unmistakable with its souvenir and chocolate shops. Here you'll find all the tour operators, *locutorios* and internet cafés, as well as banks and some food shops. The tourist information office (see below) is in the distinctive chalet-style Centro Cívico, with an open space giving good views onto the lake, and most hotels and restaurants are gathered within three or four blocks from here, with cheaper accommodation and hostels tending to be a few blocks further south on the upper slopes of town. More upmarket hotels and many restaurants are spread out along Avenida Bustillo, the road running beside the southern shore of Lago Nahuel Huapi for some 25 km, as far as the famous **Hotel Llao Llao**, and in an area known as Colonial Suiza. This is a viable place to stay even if you haven't got a car since frequent local buses, run by **3 de Mayo**, run along its length. Take No 20 to Llao Llao, for lakeside hotels and restaurants and Puerto Pañuelo; Nos 10 and 11 to Colonia Suiza and Bahía López for trekking; No 50 to Lago Gutiérrez, via the base for the cable car to Cerro Otto; and the bus labelled 'Catedral' for Cerro Cathedral.

Tourist information

The **tourist office** ⓘ *Centro Cívico, p6, T0294-442 2484, www.barilochepatagonia. info, daily 0800-2100,* has helpful staff who speak English, French and German, and have maps showing the town and whole area, with bus routes marked. They can also help with accommodation and campsites in the area. **Nahuel Huapi National Park intendencia** ⓘ *San Martín 24, T0294-442 3111, www.nahuelhuapi.gov.ar, daily 0900-1400,* is pretty unhelpful; far better to go straight to **Club Andino Bariloche** (CAB) ⓘ *just above the Centro Cívico, 20 de Febrero No 30, T0294-442 2266, www. clubandino.org, Mon-Fri 0900-1300 (also 1500-1930 in high season),* for information on walks, hikes, mountain climbs, *refugios* and buses to reach all the local areas for walking. They sell excellent maps and books for walks, including *Carta de Refugios,*

Parque Nacional Nahuel Huapi

Nahuel Huapi is the national park you're most likely to visit since Bariloche is right at its heart. It stretches along the Andes for over 130 km, from south of Lago Mascardi to north of Villa Traful, and so there are no official entry points like most of the other national parks. It was Argentina's first ever national park, created in 1934 from a donation made to the country by naturalist Francisco 'Perito' Moreno of 7500 ha of land around Puerto Blest. Extending across some of Argentina's most dramatic mountains, the park contains lakes, rivers, glaciers, waterfalls, torrents, rapids, valleys, forest, bare mountains and snow-clad peaks. Among those you can climb are Tronador (3478 m), Catedral Sur (2388 m), Falkner (2350 m), Cuyín Manzano (2220 m), López (2076 m), Otto (1405 m) and Campanario (1052 m). The outstanding feature is the splendour of the lakes and the pristine nature of the virgin forests.

Park information

To enter the park costs US$9.65. There are many centres within the park, at Villa la Angostura and at Villa Traful, for example, but Bariloche (see page 451) is the usual first port of call for park activities, and here you can equip yourself with information on transport, walks and maps. The National Park Intendencia, San Martín 24, Bariloche, T0294-442 3111, www.nahuelhuapi.gov. ar, daily 0900-1400, is fairly unhelpful, with little hard information. Much better information on walks, *refugios* and buses is available from the trained guides and mountaineers at Club Andino Bariloche (CAB), 20 de Febrero No 30, T0294-442 2266, www.club andino.org, Monday-Friday 0900-1300 (also 1500-1930 in high season). They also sell excellent maps showing walks, with average walking times, and *refugios*, and can advise on which have room. Ask for the Sendas y Bosques (walks and forests) series, which are 1:200,000, laminated and easy to read, with good books containing English summaries of the walks, www. guiasendasybosques.com.ar. Also recommended is the Active Patagonia map, with fabulous detail, and the Carta de Refugios, Senderos y Picadas for Bariloche. CAB can also tell you about transport: services: these vary from year to year and between high and low season, so it's best to check.

Flora and fauna

Vegetation varies with altitude and climate, but you're most likely to see large expanses of southern beech forest – the magnificent *coihue* trees

Senderos y Picadas maps for Bariloche and the book *Infotrekking de la Patagonia*, which gives great detail on all the possible walks, times, distances and *refugios* where you can stay, with satellite-based maps to guide you. For climbing, get hold of the booklet *Guía de Escalada [climbing] en Roca*, by Eduardo (Tato) López, with translations in English and explanations of all the areas to climb. All Club Andino staff know the mountains well and some of them speak English, French or German.

(small-leaved evergreen beeches) – many over 450 years old, and near the Chilean border where rainfall is highest, there are areas of magnificent virgin rainforest. Here you will see an alerce tree years old, with the ancient species of bamboo cane *caña colihue* growing.

Eastern parts of the park are more steppe-like with arid land, supporting only low shrubs and bushes. Wildlife includes the small pudú deer, the endangered huemul and river otter, as well as foxes, cougars and guanacos. Among the birds, scarlet-headed Magellan woodpeckers and green austral parakeets are easily spotted as well as large flocks of swans, geese and ducks.

Around the park

The centrepiece of the park is its largest lake, Lago Nahuel Huapi, which measures a huge 531 sq km and is 460 m deep in places. It is particularly magnificent to explore by boat since the lake is very irregular in shape and long fjord-like arms of water, or *brazos*, stretch far into the west towards Chile, where there is superb virgin Valdivian rainforest. There are many islands, the largest of which is Isla Victoria, which has a luxurious hotel (www.islavictoria. com). Onern shores of the lake is the Parque Nacional Los Arrayanes (see page 445), which contains a rare woodland of exquisite *arrayán* trees, with their bright cinnamon-coloured flaky bark. Access to this park within a park is from the small, upmarket village of Villa La Angostura at the southern end of the famous Seven Lakes Drive (see page 442). The northernmost stretch of this drive and three of its lakes are in Parque Nacional Lanín (see page 472), but Lagos Correntoso and Espejo near Villa Angostura are both within Nahuel Huapi and offer stunning scenery and tranquil places to stay and walk. Another tiny centre, Villa Traful (see page 465), lies on the shore of navy blue Lago Traful, with fishing, camping and walking.

The tourist town of Bariloche (see page 451) on the southern shore of Lago Nahuel Huapi is the main tourist centre the national park. It has plentiful accommodation and opportunities for hiking, rafting, tours and boat trips. West of Bariloche, there are glaciers and waterfalls near Pampa Linda, the base for climbing Mount Tronador and starting point for the trek through Paso de las Nubes to Lago Frías. South of Lago Nahuel Huapi, Lagos Mascardi, Guillelmo and Gutiérrez have even grander scenery, offering horse riding, trekking and rafting along the Río Manso.

Best time to visit

Bariloche is busiest in the school holidays (January and July), but it's also the destination for all graduating secondary school students in August, September and January, though these groups are now confined to special hotels (not listed here), and rarely stray beyond the city's bars and nightclubs for their inevitable rites of passage. Accommodation is cheaper outside the peak periods, but the weather becomes unpredictable at the end of April. For skiing, July and August are best, though hotels are packed with mass tourism from Chile and Brazil. Try June or September instead, and always book well ahead.

Places in Bariloche → *For listings, see pages 464-470.*

At the heart of the city is the **Centro Cívico**, designed in 'Bariloche Alpine style' on an attractive plaza above the lake, where there's also a small museum, **Museo de la Patagonia** ① *T0294-442 2309, www.bariloche.com.ar/museo, Tue-Fri 1000-1230, 1400-1900, Sat 1000-1700, entry by donation,* with some indigenous artefacts and material from the lives of the first white settlers. Mitre is the main commercial area, and here all the chocolate shops are clustered – a sight in themselves, and not to be missed: **Abuela Goye** and **Mamushka** are most highly recommended. The **cathedral**, built in 1946, lies south of Mitre; opposite is a huge rock left in this spot by a glacier during the last glacial period. On the lakeshore is the **Museo Paleontológico** ① *12 de Octubre and Sarmiento, T0294-15-461 1210, Mon-Sat 1600-2100, US$1.25,* which has displays of fossils mainly from Patagonia including an ichthyosaur and replicas of a giant spider and shark's jaws.

Bariloche's real sights are the mountains themselves; don't miss a cable car trip up to either **Cerro Otto** or **Cerro Campanario** to see lakes and mountains stretching out in front as far as the eye can see.

1 Bariloche

Where to stay 🛏
1 Below 41 *A1*
2 Antiguo Solar *B2*
4 Familia Arko *B1*
5 Hostel Inn Bariloche *A1*
6 Hostería Güemes *B1*
7 La Bolsa *B2*
8 Penthouse 1004 *A1*
9 Periko's *B1*
10 Premier *A2*
11 Pudu *A1*
12 Ruca Hueney *B2*
13 Tres Reyes *A2*

Restaurants 🍴
1 Chez Philippe *B1*
2 Covita *A3*
3 El Boliche de Alberto *B2*
4 Huang Ji *A2*
5 Jauja *B2*
6 Kandahar *B1*
7 La Alpina *A2*
10 Vegetariano *B1*

Bars & clubs 🍸
11 Cerebro *A1*
12 Wilkenny *A1*

Llao Llao and the Circuito Chico

To really appreciate the splendid setting of Bariloche, you need to get out of town and head 25 km west towards the area known as **Llao Llao**. Named after one of Argentina's most famous hotels, this is a charming area that offers lovely walking and gorgeous views. It's at the end of Avenida Bustillo, which runs along Lago Nahuel Huapi to the port (Puerto Pañuelo), from where boat trips depart. Frequent buses run along this road, so it's easy to explore even without your own transport. (Bus No 20 departs from the big bus stop at Moreno y Rolando for a lovely 45-minute ride, US$0.50.) There's easy access to the mountains above Avenida Bustillo and parallel **Avenida de los Pioneros**: just get off the bus at the kilometre stop you want. The free tourist office map *Circuito Chico* shows the stops clearly.

The Circuito Chico is a classic old Argentine tour: you sit in the car and gaze at the view. These days, you're more likely to want to stop, hike, take photos and find somewhere to eat, so the tour as offered by tour operators can be a frustrating experience. To really enjoy this great introduction to the area, drive or cycle instead. This is a satisfying all-day cycle ride, but beware that Avenida Bustillo is a busy road, and drivers will show you no mercy, expecting you to pull over onto the gravel verges as they pass.

Start by travelling along Avenida Bustillo. At Km 17.5, a **chairlift** ⓘ *T0294-442 7274, daily 0900-1800, 7 mins, US$3.75 return, extended opening in summer;* bus No 10, 20 or 22, goes up to Cerro Campanario (1049 m). There is a restaurant and bar at the top with fabulous views of the lake, edged with mountains, as well as of the San Pedro peninsula below and Lago Moreno.

Back on Avenida Bustillo, turn off at Km 18.3 to go around Lago Moreno Oeste, past Punto Panorámico (with really great views) and continue around **Bahía López**, through the Parque Municipal Llao Llao. Covering a small peninsula that juts into the lake, the park offers superb walks in beautiful virgin forest that is rich in wildlife. There's a small hill to climb and a little beach, **Villa Tacul**, both offering good views. Hotel Llao Llao and Puerto Pañuelo are located just east of the park.

Hotel Llao Llao (see Where to stay, page 465) is one of Argentina's finest hotels and worth the extortionate rates for its view, spa and restaurant. The hotel was designed by Bustillo and opened in 1937. Originally almost entirely a wooden construction, it burned down within a few months of opening and was rebuilt using local stone. Superbly situated on a hill with incredible views over the lake, it's a good place for tea on the terrace.

You could extend the circuit by returning via **Colonia Suiza** and the ski resort of **Cerro Catedral** (2388 m), both of which are possible starting points for longer treks (see Trekking and climbing, page 468).

Cerro Otto

A free bus service runs from Mitre y Villegas or Pagano y San Martín, daily from 1000 in high season, to Km 5 on Avenida de los Pioneros, from where a **cable car** (*teleférico*) ⓘ *T0294-444 1035, www.telefericobariloche.com.ar, daily 1000-1730 (last descent at 1900), US$8.75,* goes up to Cerro Otto (1405 m) with its revolving restaurant and really wonderful views over the lakes and mountains all around. Alternatively, 20 minutes' walk away on the summit at **Refugio Berghof** is a *confitería* belonging to Club Andino Bariloche. Highly recommended. Urban buses 50 and 51 also go to the cable car station, or by car, take Avenida de los Pioneros, then the signposted dirt track 1 km out of town.

To climb Cerro Otto on foot (two to three hours), turn off Avenida de los Pioneros at Km 4.6, then follow the trail past **Refugio Berghof**, with splendid views. This is not recommended alone, as paths can be confusing.

Cerro Catedral
ⓘ *T0294-440 9000, www.catedralaltapatagonia.com. Slopes are open from mid-Jun to end of Sep and are busiest 15 Jun-15 Aug (school holidays). Ski lifts daily 0900-1630; adult passes US$50-75 per day depending on season.*

Cerro Catedral (2338 m), 21 km southwest of Bariloche, is one of the major ski resorts in Argentina and is extremely well organized with a great range of slopes for all abilities. There are 120 km of slopes of all grades, allowing a total drop of 1010 m, starting at 2000 m, and 52 km of cross-country skiing routes, all with utterly spectacular views. There are also snowboarding areas and a well-equipped base with hotels, restaurants, equipment hire, ski schools and nursery care for children. As a summer resort, there's a cable car to take you further into the hills, useful for

② Bariloche – the road to Llao Llao

Where to stay 🛏		
1 Alaska	5 El Yeti	9 Llao-Llao
2 Aldebaran	6 Hostería Santa Rita	10 Petunia
3 Departamentos Bellevue	7 Katy	11 Selva Negra
	8 La Caleta	12 Tunquelén

starting walks to **Refugio Lynch** (from where you can walk on to Laguna Jakob) and **Refugio Frey**, or for cycling down to Lago Gutiérriez.

To get to Cerro Catedral, take the bus marked 'Catedral' from the bus terminal or the bus stop on Moreno y Palacios to the ski station base (known as Villa Catedral). The bus leaves every 90 minutes, takes 35 minutes and costs US$3; taxis cost US$25. The **cable car** ⓘ *T0294-446 0090*, from Villa Catedral is US$25 return.

Lago Gutiérrez → *Phone code 0294.*

Easily accessible by bus from Bariloche, Lago Gutiérrez feels like a fjord, with mountains dropping steeply into its western side and spectacular views all around. There are many ways to access the lake and it can be explored on foot or bike almost all the way round. There are several campsites, a hostel and fine hotels at its northern end, or a fabulous comfortable *estancia*, **Peuma Hue** ⓘ *www.peuma-hue.com*, see page 466, on the southern lakeshore, offering great trekking and horse riding.

For an adventurous approach, you could hike down from **Refugio Frey** or walk or cycle down the stony track from Cerro Catedral (see page 461). Or just get off any bus heading from Bariloche to El Bolsón to explore either end of the lake. Water sports can be practised on the lake in summer, and there's a golf course at Arelauken on the northern shore.

> ➡ **Bariloche maps**
> 1 Bariloche, page 456
> 2 Bariloche – the road to
>   Llao Llao, page 458

Lago Nahuel Huapi

Isla Huemul

To Ruta 40,
Neuquén &
Buenos Aire:

Centro
Cívico

Moreno

Av Bustillo

Belgrano Gallardo

Av de Los Pioneros

Supermarket
Todo

Onelli

Cable Car

Cerro Otto
(1405m) ▲

Refugio
Berghof

To Cerro
Catedral   ◀ To Lago Gutiérrez

To Lago Gutiérrez ▶

To Lago
Gutiérrez

Restaurants ⓐ
Butterfly
Cervecerías Berlina & Blest
Di Como

4 Il Gabbiano
5 Rincón Patagónico

Boat trips on Lago Nahuel Huapi

Isla Victoria and Bosque de Arrayanes

There are popular excursions from Puerto Pañuelo (bus No 10, 11 or 20 to get there) and other departure points to Isla Victoria and on to Parque Nacional Los Arrayanes, on the Quetrihué Peninsula (see page 443). Park entry (US$9.65) is not included in the tour price. The **national park** can also be visited by boat or on foot from **Villa La Angostura**, which allows you more time in the forest and a good 13-km hike back.

Puerto Blest

The other great boat trip in the area is the all-day excursion to Puerto Blest, **Cascada de los Cántaros**, at the western end of Lago Nahuel Huapi, and **Lago Frías**, visiting native forest and Valdivian rainforest – highly recommended. This is usually done as a nine-hour trip from Bariloche, leaving at 0900 from Puerto Pañuelo (Km 25.5), and sailing down to fjord-like Puerto Blest, where there's a good *hostería* and restaurant at the end of the lake. *Coihue*-clad mountains drop steeply into Prussian blue water, and it's usually raining, but very atmospheric. The tour then continues by short bus ride to **Puerto Alegre** on Lago Frías, and you cross the still, peppermint-green lake by launch. From Puerto Blest, the walk through beautiful forest to the **Cascada de los Cántaros** (one hour) is superb. If you set off while the rest of the party stops for lunch, you'll have time for your picnic by the splendid falls before the crowd arrives by boat. Or walk beyond them up to quiet **Lago de los Cántaros**, enclosed by vertical granite cliffs.

Boat trips run by Turisur depart Puerto Pañuelo at 1000. They cost US$46, plus an extra US$11 for a bus transfer to Puerto Pañuelo; it's cheaper to take a bus before 0800 from the centre of town. Boats are comfortable but be aware that they fill up entirely in high season; they are much more pleasant in December and March. There's a good (but expensive) *cafetería* on board and set lunch is available at Hostería Blest; cheaper sandwiches are available from the snack bar next door or you should stock up on picnic provisions before you go. The **Hotel y Restaurant Puerto Blest ($$$)** is a small cosy hotel built in 1904, with homely rather than luxurious rooms. It's worth staying a night if you want to try any of the treks from here, or fish for trout, and the only other option is camping *libre* with no facilities. The *guardaparques* at Puerto Blest can advise on the many walks from here (and their state), but the seven-hour, 15-km trek to **Lago Ortiz Basualdo** is recommended (mid-December to March only).

▶ For information on the Three Lakes Crossing into Chile, see box, page 462.

Walks around Bariloche

There are many superb walks in this area. A network of paths in the mountains and several *refugios* allow for treks over several days. *Refugios* are leased by **Club Andino Bariloche**, who charge US$10-20 per night, plus US$8-20 for food. Take a good sleeping bag. On treks to *refugios* remember to also allow for the costs of ski lifts and buses.

Below is just a small selection of walks of various grades of difficulty, recommended for the surrounding natural beauty: There's not space here to give detailed descriptions or instructions, so for all walks contact **Club Andino Bariloche** (see page 453) for advice, maps and to check paths are open before you set off: crucial in spring when snow may not have cleared the upper slopes. You could also consider contacting a trekking company to take you on guided hikes rather than setting off alone.

Around Llao Llao There are several easy and very satisfying walks from Llao Llao: a delightful easy circuit in Valdivian (temperate) rainforest in the Parque Municipal Llao Llao (turn left off the road, just past the golf course, two hours); the small hill Cerrito Llao Llao (900 m) for wonderful views (turn right off the road and follow signs – one to two hours), or a 3-km trail through to Brazo de la Tristeza (turn right off the road opposite the *guardebosque*), via tiny Lago Escondido, with magical views. Bus No 20 to Llao Llao, every 20 minutes from 0540.

Refugio López ⓘ *2076 m, 5-7 hrs return*. This is a great hike with some of the most wonderful views of the whole area. Starting from the southeastern tip of Lago Moreno, go up alongside Arroyo López, and then along a ridge to the distinctive rose-coloured **Refugio López**, with its fabulous views. Refugio López is the only *refugio* that is privately owned and not part of CAB's chain. The owners may charge you to use the paths. From Refugio López, you could do some climbing, or continue to make this a three- to four-day trek: head south to **Refugio Italia**, which is on the shores of the incredibly calm Laguna Negra at the foot of Cerro Negro. Then from here, you could hike on via Cerro Navidad to Laguna Jakob and **Refugio San Martín**. But note that this section is poorly signposted, and advisable only for very experienced walkers who are well equipped and can use a compass proficiently. Take a trekking guide if in any doubt, and always ask at CAB for the conditions of the paths. Bus No 10 or 11 to Colonia Suiza and Arroyo López (check return times).

Refugio Frey ⓘ *1700 m*. From the ski station at **Villa Catedral**, there are two ways up: 1) Walk up to Refugio Frey, or take the cable car to **Refugio Lynch** (check before you set off, as precise cable-car routes change each year) and from here walk along the ridge of Cerro Catedral to Refugio Frey, which occupies a beautiful setting on a small lake (two to four hours one-way, experience necessary); or 2) from Villa Catedral, walk south and up alongside the Arroyo Van Titter to **Refugio Piedritas**, a very basic emergency shelter with no services, to reach Refugio Frey (three to six hours to climb one-way). The area around **Refugio Frey** is the best area for climbing in the whole region, with innumerable options in the granite walls around. From Refugio Frey there are several possibilities: walk on to Refugio Piedritas (four hours each way), and then down the Arroyo Van Titter to reach Lago Gutiérrez. Once you reach the lake, you could either walk around its southern head to join the Route 258, which runs from Bariloche to El Bolsón, or ask **Estancia Peuma Hue** (see Where to stay, page 466) to collect you at the start of a few night's stay there. (The same is also possible in reverse.)

Lago Gutiérrez You can reach this grand lake southwest of Bariloche by walking 2 km downhill from the ski base at Cerro Catedral and along the northern lake shore, reaching the El Bolsón road (Route 258) where you can take a bus back to Bariloche

Border crossing: The Three Lakes to Chile

This popular route to Puerto Varas in Chile, with ferries across Lago Nahuel Huapi, Lago Frías and Lago Todos Los Santos, is outstandingly beautiful whatever the season, though the mountains are often obscured by rain and heavy cloud. It's a long journey, however, and is not recommended in really heavy rain. Book well ahead in high season (you can reserve online), and take your passport when booking in person. The journey can be done in one or two days, but the one-day crossing is only available 1 September to 30 April. No cars are carried on the boats on this route.

The route is Bariloche to Puerto Pañuelo by road (30 minutes, departure 0900), Puerto Pañuelo to Puerto Blest by boat (one hour), Puerto Blest to Puerto Alegre on Lago Frías by bus (15 minutes), cross the lake to Puerto Frías by boat (20 minutes) for Argentine immigration, then two hours by road to Peulla (lunch is not included in the price). Leave for Petrohué in the afternoon by boat (one hour 40 minutes), cross Lago Todos Los Santos, passing the Osorno volcano and other peaks, then by bus to Puerto Varas (two hours, arrive 1930).

If you take two days over the journey, you spend the first afternoon and second morning in Peulla, staying overnight in either the Hotel Peulla (T+56-(0)65-297 2288, www.hotelpeulla.cl) or the Hotel Natura Patagonia (T+56-(0)65-297 2289, www.hotelnatura.cl); breakfast is included, but supper, lodging and the second day's lunch are not. Nor are the prices of any excursions you may choose to do in Peulla, such as horse riding, canopy, boat trips or kayaking.

The mid-2014 season price was US$280 one way, 50% on return ticket; check the website before booking as prices alter with the season. Cruce Andino (www.cruceandino.com) has the monopoly on this crossing. In Bariloche bookings are handled by Turisur (Mitre 219, T0294-442 6109, www.turisur.com.ar), although tickets are sold by various operators. The trip runs every day except 1 May.

Paso Pérez Rosales
The Three Lakes Crossing enters Chile via the Paso Pérez Rosales. For more information, see www.gendarmeria.gov.ar/pasos/chile/fichperezro.html
Argentine immigration and customs At Puerto Frías, open daily.
Chilean immigration and customs At Peulla, open daily 0900-2000. Note there is a ban on importing any fresh food – meat, cheese, fruit – into Chile from Argentina, so if you take your own lunch on the crossing, eat it before you reach Chile. Chilean currency can be bought at Peulla customs at a reasonable rate.

(six hours). Or arrange with **Estancia Peuma Hue** (see Where to stay, page 466) to collect you by boat from the shore of Lake Gutiérrez and stay a couple of nights at the *estancia* for more great walks.

Refugio Neumayer ① *has an office in town: Diversidad, 20 de Junio 728, T0294-442 8995, www.eco-family.com. Some 12 km south of Bariloche, this makes a really*

Puerto Varas

This beauty spot was the southern port for shipping on Lago Llanquihue in the 19th century and now makes a good base for trips around the lake, although many places close in the off-season. North and east of the Gran Hotel Puerto Varas (1934) are German style mansions dating from the early 20th century. On the south shore, two of the best beaches are Playa Hermosa (Km 7) and Playa Niklitschek (Km 8, entry fee charged). La Poza, at Km 16, is a little lake to the south of Lago Llanquihue reached through narrow channels overhung with vegetation. Isla Loreley, an island on La Poza, is very beautiful (frequent boat trips, US$5); a concealed channel leads to yet another lake, the Laguna Encantada. Just past the village of Nueva Braunau, 9 km west of Puerto Varas, is the remarkable Museo Antonio Felmer (T+56 (0)65-233 0831, www.museoaleman.cl, summer daily 1100-2000, otherwise Sat and Sun 1100-1300, 1500-1800 or by appointment, US$4.45), a huge private collection of machinery, tools and household items used by the first Austrian immigrants to the area, some with English descriptions. There's a municipal tourist office at Del Salvador 320 (T+56 (0)65-236 1194, www.ptovaras.cl). Pullman is the only long-distance bus company to have its terminal in the town centre (Diego Portales). Other companies have ticket offices dotted around the centre but buses leave from the outskirts of town. Minibuses to Puerto Montt (Expreso Puerto Varas, Thaebus and Full Express) leave from San Bernardo y Walker Martínez every 15 minutes, US$1.70, 30 minutes.

Puerto Montt

South of Puerto Varas, Puerto Montt is a less appealing, but still popular centre for excursions to the Chilean Lake District and is the departure point for boats to Puerto Chacabuco and Puerto Natales (if operating). A paved road runs 55 km southwest to Pargua, where there is a ferry service to the island of Chiloé. The little fishing port of Angelmó, 2 km west, has become a tourist centre with many seafood restaurants and handicraft shops (reached by Costanera bus along Portales and by colectivo Nos 2, 3 or 20 from the centre). For information and town maps, the Sernatur office is just southwest of the Plaza de Armas at Antonio Varas 415 y San Martín (T+56 (0)65-222 3016, infoloslagos@sernatur.cl, Mon-Fri 0830-1300, 1500-1730). There are information desks at the airport and the bus station; see also www.puertomonttchile.cl.

charming centre for exploring the area, with eight paths to walk, information and guides on offer. Two are particularly recommended, to **Laguna Verde**, and to a mirador through Magellanic forest at **Valle de los Perdidos**. This is a cosy, friendly *refugio*, very well set up for walkers and families, and offering a wonderful range of activities. There is also superb cross-country skiing (also called Nordic skiing) around here, with bilingual guides and equipment available for hire. Great fun.

For hotel and restaurant price codes and other relevant information, see pages 20-26.

⊙ Where to stay

Bariloche *p456, map p456*
Prices rise in 2 peak seasons: Jul-Aug for skiing, and mid-Dec to Mar for summer holidays. If you arrive in the high season without a reservation, consult the listing published by the tourist office (address above). This selection gives lake-view, high-season prices where applicable. In low season you pay half of these prices in most cases. All those listed are recommended.

\$\$\$ Tres Reyes, 12 de Octubre 135, T0294-442 6121, www.hotel3reyes. com.ar. Traditional lakeside hotel with spacious rooms, splendid views, all services, gardens.

\$\$\$ Premier, Rolando 263, T0294-442 6168, www.hotelpremier.com. Good central choice (very good value in low season), small 'classic' rooms and larger superior rooms, English spoken.

\$\$ Antiguo Solar, A Gallardo 360, T0294-440 0337, www.antiguosolar.com.ar. Not far from the centre, nice simple B&B on the upper level of an attractive residential building, with parking, breakfast includes fresh biscuits and local jams.

\$\$ Hostería Güemes, Güemes 715, T0294-442 4785, www.hosteriaguemes. com.ar. Lovely, quiet, lots of space in living areas, very pleasant, big breakfast included, owner is a fishing expert and very knowledgeable about the area.

\$ pp 41 Below, Pasaje Juramento 94, T0294-443 6433, www.hostel41below. com. Central, quiet, relaxing atmosphere, good light rooms for 4-6 (US\$16-18) and an apartment (US\$50).

\$ Familia Arko, Güemes 685, T0294-442 3109, arko@eco-family.com. English and German spoken, helpful, good trekking information, beautiful garden.

\$ pp Hostel Inn Bariloche, Salta 308, T0294-442 6084, www.hostelbariloche. com. Large, well-designed hostel with great views of the lake from the communal areas and rooms. Comfortable beds, in dorm US\$15 pp); also doubles (US\$55), discount for HI members. The best feature is the great deck with a view in the garden. Neighbouring **Marco Polo Inn**, T0294-440 0105, is in the same group.

\$ pp La Bolsa, Palacios 405 y Elflein, T0294-442 3529, www. labolsadeldeporte.com.ar. Relaxed atmosphere, rustic rooms with duvets, 1 double with bath, some rooms with views, deck to sit out on.

\$ pp Penthouse 1004, San Martín 127, 10th floor, T0294-443 2228, www. penthouse1004.com.ar. Welcoming hostel at the top of a block of apartments with amazing views. Helpful staff, cosy rooms, dorms US\$18-19, doubles US\$48-50. Big communal area for chilling and watching the sunset.

\$ pp Periko's, Morales 555, T0294-452 2326, www.perikos.com. Welcoming, quiet, nice atmosphere, dorms. US\$13-17, and doubles US\$38-44 (depending on season), breakfast included, washing machine. Arranges tours, including to Ruta 40. Reserve in advance by email.

\$ pp Pudu, Salta 459, T0294-442 9738, www.hostelpudu.com. "A gem". Irish/Argentine-run, dorms US\$17 and doubles US\$50 with spectacular lake views, downstairs is a small garden and a bar. Long-term rates available.

\$ pp Ruca Hueney, Elflein 396, T0294-443 3986, www.rucahueney.com. Lovely and calm, comfortable beds with duvets, rooms for 2 to 6 people, great view, very kind owners.

The road to Llao Llao *p457, map p458*
There are lots of great places to stay along the shore of Lago Nahuel Huapi, many of them very close to the centre. All can be reached by buses which run every 20-30 mins.

$$$$ Aldebaran, on Península San Pedro, reached from Av Bustillo Km 20.4, T0294-444 8678, www.aldebaranpatagonia.com. Not in chalet style, but tasteful rooms in this modern boutique hotel on the lake shore, superb views. Rustic-style restaurant, sauna and spa with outdoor pool, so you can bask under the stars. Great service from helpful bilingual staff.

$$$$ Llao-Llao, Av Bustillo Km 25, T0294-444 5700/8530, www.llaollao.com. Deservedly famous, superb location, complete luxury, golf course, pool, spa, water sports, restaurant.

$$$$ Tunquelén, Av Bustillo, Km 24.5, T0294-444 8400/8600, www.tunquelen. com. 4-star, comfortable, splendid views, feels quite secluded, superb restaurant, attentive service.

$$$ Departamentos Bellevue, Av Bustillo, Km 24.6, T0294-444 8389, www.bellevue.com.ar. Open year-round. A famous tea room with beautiful views also offers accommodation with high-quality furnishings, very comfortable, well-equipped self-catering *cabañas*, delicious breakfast included. Access to beaches on Lake Moreno, lovely gardens.

$$$ Hostería Santa Rita, Av Bustillo, Km 7.2, T0294-446 1028, www.santarita. com.ar. Bus 10, 20/21 to Km 7.5. Peaceful lakeside views, comfortable, lovely terrace, great service.

$$$ Katy, Av Bustillo, Km 24.3, T0294-444 8023, www.gringospatagonia.com. Delightful, peaceful garden full of flowers, charming Slovenian family Kastelic (also half-board, **$$$$**). Also offers adventure tourism.

$$$ La Caleta, Av Bustillo, Km 1.95, T0294-15-460 7727, www.bungalows-bariloche.com.ar. *Cabañas* sleep 4, open fire, excellent value, minimum booking 3 nights (7 in high season). Also owns **San Isidro** *cabañas* at Km 5.7, further west.

$ pp Alaska, Lilinquen 328 (buses 10, 20, 21, get off at La Florida, Av Bustillo Km 7.5), T0294-446 1564, www.alaska-hostel.com. Well run, cosy with shared rustic rooms for 4, US$14 pp, also doubles **US44** (cheaper without bath), nice garden, washing machine, organizes horse riding and rafting, rents mountain bikes. Recommended.

Camping
A list of sites is available from the tourist office. These are recommended among the many along Bustillo: **Petunia**, Km 13.5, T0294-446 1969, www.camping petunia.com. A lovely shady site going down to lakeside with all facilities. Shops and restaurants on most sites; these are closed outside Jan-Mar.

Selva Negra, Km 2.95, T0294-444 1013, www.campinglaselvanegra.alojar.com.ar. Very good, discounts for long stay.

El Yeti, Km 5.7, T0294-444 2073, www. elyeti.alojar.com.ar. All facilities, *cabañas*.

Cerro Catedral *p458*
$$$$ Pire-Hue, Villa Catedral, T011-4782 0322 (Buenos Aires), www.pire-hue.com.ar. Exclusive 5-star hotel with beautifully decorated rooms and all the facilities. Prices rise in Jul/Aug and fall in Jun/Sep.

Lago Gutiérrez p459

$$$$ El Retorno, Villa Los Coihues, on the shore of Lago Gutiérrez, T0294-446 7333, www.hosteriaelretorno.com. Stunning lakeside position, comfortable hunting lodge style, family-run, with a beach, tennis, very comfortable rooms (**$$$** in low season) and self-catering apartments (Bus 50, follow signs off the road to El Bolsón).

$$$$ Estancia Peuma Hue, Ruta 40, Km 2014, T0294-15-450 1030, www. peuma-hue.com. Best comfort in a homely environment, on the southern shores of Lago Gutiérrez, below Cerro Catedral Sur. Charming owner Evelyn Hoter and dedicated staff make it all work perfectly: tasty home-made food, superb horse riding and other activities, health treatments, yoga, meditation, etc, candlelit concerts. All inclusive, varied accommodation. Highly recommended.

Camping

Villa los Coihues, Lago Gutiérrez, T0294-446 7481, www.campingloscoihues. com.ar. Well equipped and beautifully situated. Camping from US$7.50 and dorm rooms from US$12.50. Take bus No 50 or take the track down to Gutiérrez from Cerro Catedral (4WD advisable) or the road to El Bolsón (Ruta 258), and follow signs.

🍴 Restaurants

Bariloche p456, map p456

Bariloche is blessed with superb food, much of it locally produced, including smoked trout and salmon, wild boar and other delicacies, not least fine chocolate and, in season, delicious berries. There are many good delicatessens.

$$$ Chez Philippe, Primera Junta 1080, T0294-442 7291. Delicious local delicacies and fondue, fine French-influenced cuisine.

$$$ Jauja, Elflein 148, T0294-442 2952. www.restaurantejauja.com.ar. Recommended for delicious local dishes, quiet and welcoming, good value.

$$$ Kandahar, 20 de Febrero 698, T0294-442 4702. Atmospheric, warm and intimate, with exquisite food, run by ski champion Marta Peirono de Barber, superb wines and pisco sour. Dinner only, reserve in high season. Highly recommended.

$$ Covita, Rolando 172, T0294-442 1708. Mon-Sat for lunch, Thu-Sat for dinner. Vegetarian restaurant (also serves fish), offering curries, masalas and pastas.

$$ El Boliche de Alberto, Villegas 347, T0294-443 1433, www.elbolichede alberto.com. Very good pasta, huge portions, popular after 2000 (queues in summer). There is a 2nd location at Bustillo Km 8800 that specializes in grilled meats.

$$ Vegetariano, 20 de Febrero 730, T0294-442 1820, www.vegetarian patagonia.com.ar. Also fish, excellent food, beautifully served, warm atmosphere, take-away available. Highly recommended.

$ Huang Ji, Rolando 268, T0294-442 8168. Good Chinese, next to a bowling alley.

La Alpina, Moreno 98. Old-fashioned café serving delicious cakes, good for tea, Wi-Fi, charming.

The road to Llao Llao p457, map p458

$$$ Butterfly, Hua Huan 7831, just off Av Bustillo Km 7.9, T0294-446 1441, www. thebutterflygroup.com.ar. 2 seatings: 1945/2130. German/Argentine/Irish owned, an elite dining experience, tasting menus using only local ingredients, carefully selected wines, art exhibitions, only 6 tables. Reserve in advance and discuss the menu with the chef.

$$$ Il Gabbiano, Av Bustillo Km 24.3,
T0294-444 8346, www.gabbiano.com.ar.
Closed Wed. Delicious Italian lunches
and dinners. Booking essential (no
credit cards).
$$$ Rincón Patagónico, Av Bustillo,
Km 14, Paraje Laguna Fantasma, T0294-
446 3063, www.rinconpatagonico.com.
ar. Traditional *parrilla* with Patagonian
lamb cooked *al palo*, huge menu but
service can be minimal at busy times.
$$ Di Como, Av Bustillo, Km 0.8, T0294-
452 2118. A 10-min walk from town.
Good pizza and pasta, terrace and
great views of the lake.

Bars and clubs

Bariloche *p456, map p456*
Cerebro, JM de Rosas 406, www.cerebro.
com.ar. Jun-Dec. The party starts at 0130,
Fri best.
Cervecería Berlina, Ruta 79 y F Goye,
T0294-445 4393, www.cervezaberlina.
com. Open 1200 until last person has
left. 3 good brews. They have a diverse
menu (**$$**) at their restaurant at
Av Bustillo Km 11.750, with a deck
for watching the sunset.
Cervecería Blest, Av Bustillo Km 11.6,
T0294-446 1026, www.cervezablest.
com.ar. Wonderful brewery with
delicious beers, serving imaginative
local and German dishes and steak and
kidney pie (**$$$-$$**). Recommended.
Cerveza Artesanal Gilbert, Km 24,
Barrio Las Cartas, Circuito Chico, T0294-
445 4292. Daily 1100-2300. Popular beers
and simple meals (**$$**).
Wilkenny, San Martín 435, T0294-442
4444. Lively Irish pub with expensive
food but it really gets busy around 2400.
Great place to watch TV sport.

Shopping

Bariloche *p456, map p456*
The main shopping area is on Mitre
between the Centro Cívico and
Beschtedt, also on San Martín. Local
chocolate is excellent, and wines from
the Alto Río Negro are also good buys.

Chocolate
Several shops on Mitre.
Abuela Goye, Mitre 258 and Quaglia
219, www.abuelagoye.com. First
rate chocolatier, also with café in
the Quaglia branch (2 other
branches and outlets nationwide).
Fenoglio, Av Bustillo 1200, Mitre 76
and others. Daily 1100-1900.
Chocolate production with
tastings and a good shop.
Mamuschka, Mitre y Rolando,
www.mamuschka.com. Considered
the best chocolate here, also with café.

Handicrafts
Feria Artesanal Municipal, Moreno
y Villegas.

What to do

Bariloche *p456, map p456*
Adventure tours
Canopy, Colonia Suiza, Cerro López,
T0294-440 0286, www.canopybariloche.
com. Zip line adventure in the forest,
including 4WD ride to get there and
night descents.
Eco Family, 20 de Junio 728, T0294-442
8995, www.eco-family.com. Riding,
walking, skiing, other adventures,
bilingual guides. Highly recommended.
Senza Limiti Adventures, J Cortázar
5050, T0294-452 0597, www.slimiti.com.
Adventure travel company, including
kayaking, mountain-biking, hut-to-

hut treks and much more, licensed by National Parks Administration.

Tronador Turismo, Quaglia 283, T0294-442 5644, www.tronadorturismo.com.ar. Conventional tours, trekking and rafting. Also to Refugio Neumeyer, and to Chilean border. Great adventurous wintersports options.

Climbing

Note that at higher levels, winter snow storms can begin as early as Apr, making climbing dangerous. Contact **Club Andino Bariloche**, see, pages 453 and 454. for mountain guides and information.

Cycling

Bikes can be hired at many places in high season.

Circuito Chico, Av Bustillo 18300, T0294-459 5608, www.circuitochicobikes.com. Rents mountain bikes, with road assistance service, and kayaks.

Dirty Bikes, Lonquimay 3908, T0294-444 2743, www.dirtybikes.com.ar. Very helpful for repairs, tours and bike rentals (US$6-45 per day).

Fishing

Martín Pescador, Rolando 257, T0294-442 2275. Fishing, camping and skiing equipment.

Horse riding

Ariane Patagonia, T0294-452 3488, www.arianepatagonia.com.ar. Horse riding trips, visits to farms and *estancias*, personalized service.

Bastion del Manso, Av Bustillo 13491, T0294-445 6111, www.bastiondelmanso.com. Relaxed place with tuition and full-day's riding offered, including rafting and longer treks.

See also **Estancia Peuma Hue**, below.

Kayaking and rafting

Aguas Blancas, Morales 564, T0294-443 2799, www.aguasblancas.com.ar. Rafting on the Río Manso, all grades, with expert guides, and all equipment provided, also 'duckies' – inflatable kayaks for beginners.

Patagonia Infinita, T0294-15-455 3954, www.patagoniainfinita.com.ar. Kayaking and trekking trips in Parque Nacional Nahuel Huapi.

Pura Vida Patagonia, T0294-15-441 4053, www.puravidapatagonia.com. Informative, attentive guides, good-value trips from 1-9 days in Nahuel Huapi.

Paragliding

There are several paragliding schools. Take-offs are usually from Cerro Otto, but there are other starting points, 10- to 40-min tandem flights.

Skiing

Cerros Otto and Catedral (see pages 457 and 458).

Tours

Check what your tour includes; cable cars and chair lifts are usually extra. Tours get booked up in season. Most travel agencies will pick you up from your hotel, and charge roughly the same prices: Circuito Chico half day, US$19; Isla Victoria and Bosque de Arrayanes, full-day boat trip from Puerto Pañuelo, US$46, or US$30 from other departure points (park entry, US$9.65, not included); Tronador, Ventisquero Negro and Pampa Linda, US$40 plus National Park entry via Lago Mascardi by boat; El Bolsón US$35, full-day, including Lago Puelo; several other tours.

Turisur, Mitre 219, T0294-442 6109, www.turisur.com.ar. Boat trips to Bosque de Arrayanes, Isla Victoria on a 1937 ship and to Tronador via Lago Mascardi. Licensee for the Cruce Andino trip to Puerto Montt. Always reserve 1 day ahead.

Trekking
For further information, contact Club Andino Bariloche (see page 453).
Active Patagonia, 20 de Febrero 30, T0294-452 9875, www.active patagonia. com.ar. As well as trekking to Tronador and Refugio Frey, also offers kayaking, rafting, horse riding, mountain biking and climbing.
Andescross, T0294-15-463 3581, www. andescross.com. Expert guides, all included. Trekking to Chile across the Andes, via Pampa Linda, Lago Frías, Peulla.

Lago Gutiérrez *p459*
Horse riding
From **Estancia Peuma Hue** on the southern shore of Lago Gutiérrez (see page 466), you can ride into the mountains and over to Pampa Linda. Riding is also available from **Los Baqueanos**, signposted from R258, on the eastern shore of Lago Gutiérrez, T0294-15-4423 0556, www.complejobaqueanos.com.ar.

⊙ Transport

Bariloche *p456, map p456*
Air
Many flights a day to **Buenos Aires**. AR also flies to **El Calafate** in summer only. LADE flies to **Buenos Aires, Comodoro Rivadavia, Esquel** and several other destinations in Patagonia.

Boat
For boat trips, see page 460. For the route by boat and bus to Chile, see box, page 462.

Bus
Tickets can be bought at the bus company offices in town or at terminal: **Vía Bariloche/El Valle/Don Otto/TAC**, Mitre 321, T0294-442 9012, terminal T0294-443 2444; **Chevallier/Flechabus**, Moreno 107, T0294-442 3090. **Andesmar/ Tramat**, at terminal, T0294-443 0211; **Ko Ko**, at terminal, T0294-443 1135.
Local To **Llao Llao**, bus No 20 from Moreno y Rolando, US$0.50, journey time 45 mins. To **Villa Catedral**, bus 'Catedral' from the bus terminal or Moreno y Palacios, every 90 mins, US$3, journey time 35 mins. To **Pampa Linda**, daily 0830 in season from Club Andino Bariloche, 2¼ hrs, US$12.50, returning from Pampa Linda in the afternoon (T0294-452 9875).
Long distance To **Buenos Aires**, 7 companies daily, 19-22 hrs, US$118-131. To **Bahía Blanca**, 5 companies, 14 hrs, US$70-85. To **Mendoza**, US$90-102, with **Andesmar** and **Tramat**, 17-19 hrs. Several daily, with **Don Otto, TAC, Vía Bariloche** (T0800-333 7575, www. viabariloche.com.ar) and others to El Bolson, US$9.50-11, 2 hrs, and on to Esquel, 4-5 hrs, US$13-15, heavily, even over-booked in high season. To **San Martín de los Andes** (not via 7 Lagos), 3½-4 hrs, US$16, with **Vía Bariloche** and **Ko Ko**. To **Villa La Angostura**, 1 hr, US$6-8, several companies. To **Comodoro Rivadavia**, US$56-63, **Don Otto, Andesmar**, 14 hrs, and **Marga** who continue to **Río Gallegos**, US$55-65, 23 hrs; in Río Gallegos make other onward connections to El Calafate and Ushuaia. **Taqsa** (T0800-333-1188, www.taqsa.com. ar) run to **El Chaltén** and **El Calafate** via El Bolsón, Esquel, Perito Moreno and Los Antiguos on Ruta 40, US$108, 27 hrs. Or take **Chaltén Travel**'s 3-day trip on Ruta 40, www.chaltentravel.com (page 525),

depart 0645 on odd-numbered days from **Turacción**, Quaglia 262.
To Chile: Vía Bariloche runs daily services via Samoré pass to **Osorno**, 5 hrs, US$30, and **Puerto Montt**, 6-7½ hrs, same fare; **Andesmar** goes to **Valdivia** via Osorno, US$35, US$50 cama, not daily. Take passport when booking. Sit on left side for best views.

Car hire

Rates are from US$50-65 for a small car, up to US$130 per day for something more substantial. Larger companies may permit hiring in one town and returning to another for an extra charge (about US$40). **Lagos**, Mitre 83, T0294-442 8880, www.lagosrentacar.com.ar, among many others. To enter Chile, a permit is necessary; it's generally included in the price but you should state your intention of driving to Chile when booking the car, allow 24 hrs.

Train

See page 406 for Tren Patagónico service to Viedma, www.trenpatagonico-sa.com.ar.

ⓘ Directory

Bariloche *p456, map p456*
Banks ATMs at many banks on Mitre, Moreno and San Martín. **Cambio Sudamérica,** Mitre 63, has good rates. **Consulates** Chile, España 275, T0294-442 3050, Mon-Fri 0900-1300, 1400-1730, helpful. **Immigration office** Libertad 191, T0294-442 3043. **Language schools** ILEE, www.argentinailee.com, arranges classes and home stay. **La Montaña**, Elflein 251, T0294-452 4212, www.la montana.com. Spanish courses, family lodging, activities and volunteering. **Medical services** Emergencies: Dial 107. Hospital Zonal, Moreno 601, T0294-442 6119. **Police** T0294-442 2772, or 101.

Bariloche to El Bolsón

Some of Argentina's most spectacular and unspoilt scenery lies south of Bariloche, where tourism has developed more recently and there is a wilder, more relaxed feel to the landscape. Route 258, the road south from Bariloche to El Bolsón, is breathtaking, passing the picturesque lakes of Gutiérrez and Mascardi, lying below a massive jagged range of mountains. There are some fabulous, peaceful places to stay here and wonderful hikes and horse riding. From Villa Mascardi, a road leads west along the Lago Mascardi's southern shore to glorious Pampa Linda, where there is enough excellent trekking to entertain you for several days, including access to climb Mount Tronador. Further south, Río Manso Medio has become famous for whitewater rafting, and at Lago Hess there is a *hostería* and the lovely Cascadas Los Alerces.

El Bolsón is a pretty and relaxed town, sprawled out between two mountain ranges, with superb hikes nearby and beautiful rivers, waterfalls and mountains to explore. The town itself started as a hippy community in the 1970s. Now there are several microbreweries here converting local hops into fine handmade beers, and craftsmen supplying the local market with wood and leather work, as well as delicious jams from the abundant soft fruits in summer. Further south, Lago Puelo is a tiny national park, offering great fishing, some good walks and a boat trip to the Chilean border. As you head south, Cholila might attract Butch Cassidy fans, but though it feels authentically like the Wild West, there's little appeal here now.

Lago Mascardi → *Colour map 5, B2. Phone code 0294.*

At the southern end of Lago Mascardi (Km 35), **Villa Mascardi** is a small village from where the *ripio* Route 81 runs towards Lago Hess and Cascada Los Alerces. This road operates a one-way system: going west 1000-1400, east 1600-1800, two-way 1900-0900; times may vary, check with the Bariloche **tourist office** (see page 453). Along Lago Mascardi, there are several beautifully situated places to stay, all easily reached by car, or bus when the service is running in summer. Shortly after the lovely straight beach of Playa Negro, handy for launching boats and fishing, the road forks, with the left-hand branch following the crystalline Río Manso Medio to Lago Hess. The **Río Manso** is popular for rafting (arranged through tour operators in Bariloche, see page 468). The right fork of the road, meanwhile, follows a narrow arm of Lago Mascardi northwest, with a viewpoint in lovely woodland to see Isla Piuke Huapi in the centre of the lake. A few kilometres further on is the lakeside paradise of Hotel Tronador before reaching Pampa Linda and Mount Tronador at the end of the road.
➤ *For further information, see Where to stay, page 482.*

Pampa Linda

Pampa Linda lies 40 km west of Villa Mascardi in the most blissfully isolated location, with spectacular views of Cerro Tronador towering above. There's a *guadería* (ranger station) with very helpful *guardaparques* who can advise on walks, and whom you must consult about the state of the paths and register your name before setting out. From Pampa Linda, a lovely track (*ripio*) continues to **Ventisquero Negro** (Black Glacier), which hangs over a fantastically murky pool in which grey 'icebergs' float. The colour is due to sediment, and while not exactly attractive, the whole scene is very atmospheric. The road ends at the awesome **Garganta del Diablo**, one of the natural amphitheatres formed by the lower slopes of Mount Tronador. A beautiful walk (90 minutes' walk there and back) from the car park through beach forest takes you to a more pristine glacier, and up to the head of the gorge, where thin torrents of ice melt from the hanging glacier above and fall in columns like sifted sugar. Another pleasant walk is to tranquil **Laguna Ilon** (5½ hours each way), with bathing on the shore in summer.

A day tour to Pampa Linda from Bariloche will usually include both **Ventisquero Negro** and the falls at **Garganta del Diablo**, as well as the beautiful lakes Gutiérrez and Mascardi en route, but will not allow much time for walking. A good way to make the most of the area is to take a tour with an agency, and then stay on at Pampa Linda for trekking, returning with the minibus service run by **Transitando lo Natural** ① *20 de Febrero 25, T0294-452 7926*. Alternatively, buses to Pampa Linda run daily in season from outside **Club Andino Bariloche** ① *T0294-452 9875, US$12.50*. There's a great simple *hostería* at Pampa Linda, offering lunch.

Cerro Tronador

The highest peak around is mighty Mount Tronador ('The Thunderer', 3478 m). From Pampa Linda two other paths lead up **the mountain**: the first is 15 km long and leads to **Refugio Otto Meiling** (2000 m), in itself a wonderful walk (five hours each way), situated on the edge of the eastern glacier. Another hour from the *refugio*, a path takes you to a view over Tronador and the lakes and mountains of **Parque Nacional Nahuel Huapi**. The other path leads to a *refugio* on the south side of the mountain. Otto Meiling is a good base camp for the ascent, with lots of facilities and activities, including trekking and ice climbing; always ask the *guardaparques* in Pampa Linda if there's space (capacity 60); dinner is available (let them know in advance if you're vegetarian). The lower sections of these paths are great for mountain biking in the forest,

Paso de los Nubes
Pampa Linda is the starting point for a 22-km walk over Paso de los Nubes (1335 m) to **Laguna Frías** and **Puerto Frías** on the Chilean border. Allow at least two days; start the walk at Pampa Linda, rather than the other way around, as there's a gentler rise to the pass this way. There is camping at **Campamento Alerce** (after four hours) or **Campamento Glacier Frías** (after seven hours); from here it's another five hours to Puerto Frías. You'll see a spectacular glacial landscape, formed relatively recently (11,000 years ago), and the pass lies on the continental divide, with water flowing north to the Atlantic, and south to the Pacific. Views from the Río Frías valley are tremendous, and from Glacier Frías you enter Valdivian rainforest. Boats cross Lago Frías three times a day in summer, but check this before leaving Bariloche. From Puerto Frías a 30-km road leads to Peulla on the shore of Chilean Lago Todos Los Santos. Or you can take a boat back to Bariloche – highly recommended.

You must register with *guardaparques* at Pampa Linda before setting out, and check with them about conditions. The route is not always well marked and should only be attempted if there is no snow on the pass (it's normally passable only between December and February) or if the path is not excessively boggy. Do not cross rivers on fallen bridges or trees. Buy the map produced by Infotrekking for Mount Tronador/Paso de las Nubes before you leave Bariloche (available from **Club Andino Bariloche**, see page 453) and also consult the excellent leaflet for *Paso de las Nubes* produced by Parque Nacional Nahuel Huapi.

Río Manso Medio and Lago Hess
Some 9 km west of Villa Mascardi, a road runs 18 km through the beautiful valley of the Río Manso Medio to Lago Hess and on to the nearby **Cascada Los Alerces**. This is the starting point for trekking excursions in a more remote area of small lakes and forested mountains, including lagos Fonck, Roca, Felipe, and Cerros Granito and Fortaleza. Check with *guardaparques* at Lago Hess about the conditions of the paths. There is also wonderful rafting here, but you have to take an organized trip from Bariloche. Note that there is also rafting on the **Río Manso Inferior**, further south (see below). ►► *For further information, see What to do, page 486.*

Lago Steffen and Lago Martín → *Phone code: 02944.*
About 20 km south of Villa Mascardi, another one-way dirt road leads to Lago Steffen, where a footpath runs along both northern and southern shores (of Lago Steffen) to Lago Martín. Both lakes are quite outstandingly lovely, fringed with beech and *álamo* trees, with far-off mountains in the distance and pretty beaches

where you can sit at the water's edge. There's also great fishing here. The *guardería* is at Lago Steffen and wild camping is possible further north on the lake shore. To the south, a road leads west from Villegas along the Río Manso Inferior towards Chile. The river here is ideal for wilder rafting and for the trip to the Chilean border, run by rafting companies in Bariloche (see page 468).

El Bolsón → *For listings, see pages 482-486. Colour map 5, B2.*

El Bolsón is a very seductive little place with a laid-back atmosphere, sprawled out in a broad fertile valley 130 km south of Bariloche. It is contained within huge mountain ranges on either side (hence it's name 'the big bag'), and it makes a great base for relaxing for a few days and for hiking in the tempting peaks around. The great serrated ridge of Cerro Piltriquitrón (2284 m) dominates the town, apparently emitting healthy positive ions, which might be why you feel so relaxed while you're here. Certainly it's a magical setting, and it's not surprising that it inspired thousands of hippies to create an ideological community here in the 1970s. What remains is a young, friendly place where the locals make lots of handicrafts. With the sparkling Río Azul running close by and a warm sunny microclimate, you're likely to want to stay for a few days to try the home-brewed beers and fruit for which the town is famous.

Nearby there are many beautiful mountain walks, a couple of waterfalls and rafting on the Río Azul. The small national park of Lago Puelo is within easy reach, 18 km south, and there's a small family-orientated ski centre in the winter at **Centro de Ski Perito Moreno**.

Arriving in El Bolsón → *Phone code 0294. Population 16,000.*
Getting there Note there is not a central bus terminal. Different bus companies stop at different places. There are hourly buses from Bariloche (two hours) and buses every two hours from Esquel (2½ hours) to El Bolsón, arriving off the main street at **Via Bariloche's** offices at Sarmiento and General Roca. There are also buses to and from Parque Nacional Los Alerces, and from destinations in Chile. There are equidistant airports at Bariloche and Esquel.

Getting around El Bolsón sprawls out from the spine of Avenida San Martín which runs through the town, where you'll find places to eat. There are lots of places to stay dotted around the town, though the prettiest *cabañas* are in Villa Turismo up the hill. There are buses to Lago Puelo, but buses to other sites are infrequent and geared to locals rather than tourists. However, El Bolsón is a lovely place to walk around; you can hire bikes, and there are plenty of cheap *remises* (taxis).

Tourist information The **tourist office** ⓘ *San Martín and Roca opposite the big post office, T0294-449 2604, www.elbolson.gov.ar, daily 0900-2100, till 2400 in summer,* is on the side of the semicircular plaza. Staff are helpful and friendly (with plenty of English speakers). They'll give you an excellent map of the town and the area, and suggest places to stay. They can also give limited advice on hikes and sell useful maps, including *Sendas y Bosques El Bolsón and Los Alerces.* However, for more detailed advice on mountain walking, go to **Club Andino Piltriquitrón** ① *Sarmiento and Roca, T0294-449 2600, www.capiltriquitron.com.ar, Mon-Fri 1800-2000, where all walkers must register before setting off.* For more information, see www.elbolson.com.

El Bolsón

Where to stay 🛏

Altos del Sur **2**
El Pueblito **4**
Hostel La Casa del Viajero **1**
La Casona de Odile **6**
La Chacra **7**
La Posada de Hamelin **9**
Quem Quem **13**
Refugio Patagónico **14**

Restaurants 🍴

Amancay **5**
Arcimboldo **1**
El Rey de Sandwich **2**
Jauja **3**
Martin Sheffield **4**
Pasiones Argentinas **7**

Best time to visit Summer is obviously the best time to visit, when you can take full advantage of the blissful rivers and mountains, and there's a lively atmosphere on the plaza with music at nights. But it's very busy here in January, so try to come in February or March, or even in April, when autumn turns the trees brilliant yellow and orange, and there are sunny days but cold nights. Winter is very rainy and best avoided, though there is a basic ski resort at Cerro Perito Moreno.

Around El Bolsón

El Bolsón's great attraction – apart from the pleasure of being in the town itself – are the superb hikes up to the mountains west of the town (see opposite). These start from the other side of turquoise Río Azul, where there are lovely places to sunbathe, camp and picnic. East of town, a pleasant hour-long walk will take you to the top of **Cerro Amigo**, with lovely views. Follow Calle General Roca east until it becomes Islas Malvinas and continue up the hill. Better still are the panoramic views from **Cerro Piltriquitrón**, the jagged peak looming over El Bolsón to the east. Drive, join a tour or take a taxi 10 km up winding earth roads. Then it's an hour's walk to the **Bosque Tallado**, where sculptures have been carved from fallen trees by local craftspeople; from the mirador there are fabulous views over the valley to the Andes beyond. It's a six- to seven-hour round trip walking all the way. Food and shelter are available at the *refugio* (1400 m), and from there it's three hours' walk to the summit. You can also do paragliding from here. ▸▸ *See What to do, page 486.*

There are also good views from **Cabeza del Indio**, so called because the rock's profile resembles a face, a good 6-km drive or bike ride from the centre. Take Calle Azcuénaga west to cross the bridge over Río Quemquemtreu and follow signs to Cabeza del Indio. From here, there's a waymarked walk north to **Cascada Escondida**. This impressive sweep of waterfalls, 10 km northwest of El Bolsón, is a good place for a picnic, with a botanical garden in woods reached from winding gravel roads. This area is also worth visiting for the good rustic *parrilla* El Quincho, which serves local lamb and other great meat dishes (vegetarians: don't even think about it). There are rather less exciting falls at **Cataratas Mallín Ahogado**, a little further north, but it's still a pleasant spot for a stop. La Golondrina runs three buses daily Monday to Friday from the plaza to the loop around Mallin Ahogado, but extra walking is required to reach both falls. See the tourist office map for details.

There are many microbreweries dotted around town – Cervecería El Bolsón ⓘ *R258, Km 123.9, just north of town, www.cervezaselbolson.com*, is particularly worth a visit, with brief guided tour, restaurant and no fewer than 18 different beers on offer, including three for celiacs. You could also ask at the tourist office for the *Agroturismo* leaflet, which details the *chacras* (fruit farms) throughout El Bolsón and El Hoyo that you can visit in summer for delicious, freshly picked soft fruits and berries, jams and other delights.

The famous narrow gauge railway **La Trochita** (www.patagoniaexpress.com/el_ trochita.htm), (also known as the *Old Patagonian Express,* is a novel way of seeing the landscape and a catching a glimpse into Patagonia's past. As well as the better known route from Esquel, there's another journey from El Maitén, near El Bolsón, where you can see the fascinating steam railway workshops too. ▸▸ *See What to do, page 486.*

El Bolsón benefits from a gentle microclimate which means it's warmer than much of the Lake District, even in winter. However, there is a ski centre, **Centro de Ski Perito Moreno** (www.bolsonweb.com/aventura/ski.htm), on the upper slopes of Cerro Perito Moreno (2216 m). With good snow and no wind, its 720 skiable metres are good for families, but there are three ski lifts and ski instructors too. It's a newish centre and the only place to stay at the moment is the **Refugio Perito Moreno**, with 120 beds. Ask the tourist office for more information. Leave town by Route 258, and take the left-hand turn to Río Azul. Follow signs to Refugio Perito Moreno.

Walks → *For Parque Nacional Lago Puelo, see below.*
There are wonderful treks in the mountains west of the town. For all walks, get the *Sendas y Bosques* (Walks and Forests) map and book for El Bolsón, Lago Puelo and Los Alerces. Maps are 1:200,000, laminated and easy to read, and the book is full of great walks, with English summaries. Register for all walks before setting off at the **Club Andino Piltriquitrón** (see Tourist information, above). There are some eight shelters which offer basic accommodation (US$9.65-12 per night, sleeping bag required), some meals (US$5-7.50), hearty breakfasts (U$$3.65), basic supplies (such as home-baked bread and home-brewed beer), camping and hot showers.

Cerro Lindo Due west of town, there's a great hike up Arroyo Lali to Cerro Lindo (2105 m), in one of the most beautiful mountain landscapes of the whole area, with **Refugio Cerro Lindo** halfway up, after a five-hour walk. From here, you can reach an ancient glacier and climb onwards to several viewpoints. You'll need a map, and you should check the route before setting off. The altitude difference is pretty extreme here, so you're advised to go slowly and steadily.

Cerro Hielo Azul This is a more serious and demanding hike up to Cerro Hielo Azul (2255 m); it's steep and takes six hours one-way. You can stay at comfortable **Refugio Cerro Azul** at 1300 m, from where you can also walk to the glacier on the slopes of Cerro Hielo Azul (three hours return), or on to Cerro Barda Negra. It's often suggested that you could walk from here via **Refugio Natación** to **Refugio Cajón de Azul**, but this is really not to be recommended without a local guide. The path can be confusing in places, the area remains marshy well into the summer months, and people have got lost, with dangerous consequences. Ask in the **Club Andino Piltriquitrón** for advice (see page 475).

Cajón de Azul One of the loveliest and most accessible walks can be done in a day, although once you reach the delightful *refugio* (600 m) at Cajón de Azul, you're going to wish you could stay at least a night. It's a fabulous four-hour walk up the Río Azul which flows from a deep canyon. There's a well-marked path. It's a bit hairy crossing the two single-file wood-and-wire bridges, and there are queues in January (replacement bridges are being built), but it's worth it for a dip in the sparkling turquoise water on the way down. Set off early to allow for a leisurely lunch at the top, or spend the night in the *refugio* in the company of Atilio and friends, who make a fine dinner with produce from the lovely garden. To get to the start of the walk, take a *traffic* (minibus) from El Bolsón at 0900. You'll be collected by the *traffic* at 2000. Buses and information are availabl efrom Transportes Nehuén, at Belgrano and Perito Moreno, in the same office as Andesmar.

Refugio Los Laguitos This wonderful four-day walk takes you right into the deepest part of the Andes Cordillera, almost to the border with Chile, and through outstanding *alerce* forests. Allow four hours to **Refujio Cajón de Azul**, another three hours to the Mallín de los Chanchos, and another four hours on from there to reach the basic **Refugio Los Laguitos** in a beautiful spot on the shore of Lago Lahuán. A map and guidebook are absolutely essential; seek advice before setting out.

Parque Nacional Lago Puelo → *For listings, see pages 482-486.*

This lovely green and wooded national park is centred around the deep turquoise-coloured Lago Puelo, 15 km south of El Bolsón on the Chilean border, surrounded by southern beech forest and framed by the spiky peaks of snow-dusted far-off mountains. It's a blissful spot out of the busy holiday season. With relatively low altitude (200 m) and high rainfall, the forest is rich in tree species, particularly the cinnamon-bark *arrayán* and the *pitra*, *coihues* (evergreen beech) and cypresses. There's lots of wildlife, including the *huemul*, *pudu* and foxes, and the lake is known for its good fishing for trout and salmon. There are gentle walks on marked paths around the northern shore area, boat trips across the lake and canoes for rent. *Guardaparques* at the park entrance can advise on these and provide a basic map.

Arriving in Parque Nacional Lago Puelo
Getting there Entry fee US$6. The main entrance is along a pretty road south from El Bolsón, through *chacras* (small farms) growing walnuts, hops and fruit, to Villa Lago Puelo, 3 km north of the park, where there are shops, plenty of accommodation and fuel. From here the road is unpaved. Entry is also possible at **El Desemboque**, on the eastern side of the park: take the bus from El Bolsón to Esquel, alight at El Hoyo, then walk 14 km to El Desemboque. There are regular buses (US$1-2) from Avenida San Martín and Dorrego in El Bolsón to the lake via Villa Lago Puelo. It's best to come between November and April, though the northern shore of the lake can get crowded in January and February. The lake is glorious in April, when the trees turn a vivid yellow.

Park information The **Intendencia** ⓘ *500 m north of the lake, T0294-449 9232, lagopuelo@apn.gov.ar, Mon-Fri 0800-1500, with a booth at the pier in summer,* can provide a helpful leaflet and advice on walks. You must register here before embarking on long hikes, and register your return. In the town of Lago Puelo there's a **tourist office** ⓘ *Av 2 de Abril and Los Notros, T0294-449 9591, www.lagopuelo. gov.ar, daily 0900-2100 in summer, 0900-1900 in winter,* on the roundabout as you enter town. Staff are helpful, English-speaking and can advise on accommodation.

Walks

For all walks, get the *Sendas y Bosques* (Walks and Forests) map and book for El Bolsón, Lago Puelo and Los Alerces, www.guiasendasybosques.com.ar.

Bosque de las Sombras (Forest of the Shadows). An easy 400-m walk on wooden walkways, through delightful overgrown forest on the way to the shingle beach at 'La Playita', with guided trails and signs telling you what trees you're passing.

Senda los Hitos A 14-km (five hours each way) walk through marvellous woods to the rapids at Río Puelo on the Chilean border (passport required). There is some wild camping on the way at **Camping de Gendarmería**, after two hours.

Cerro Motoco There's a tremendous two-day hike up Cerro Motoco, with **Refugio Motoco** at the top of the path. Leave Lago Puelo heading north and cross the hanging bridge to access Río Motoco. It's 25 km altogether, and could be done in seven hours, one way, but you'll want to stay at the top. Take the walks book with you.

Cerro Plataforma From the east of the lake, you can hike to **El Turbio** and Cerro Plataforma, crossing the lake first by boat to El Desemboque (or taking the bus and walking 14 km). At Cerro Plataforma, there's a tremendous amount of marine life in evidence, as this was a beach in the ice age. It's about seven hours to Río Turbio, where there's a *guardaparque*, and then 12 hours to Cerro Plataforma; allow three days for the whole trip. There's also a three-day trek through magnificent scenery to **Glaciar y Cerro Aguaja Sur**: get advice and directions from the *guardaparques*.

Other activities

There is wonderful **fly fishing** in the park, thanks to the fact that this is the lowest crossing in the whole of the Andes region (at only 190 m). The lack of snow and the mild, warm summers mean that Pacific salmon come here in large numbers. Contact fishing guides through the park *guardería*. Also check out **Puelo Trout** for fishing trips. There are boat trips across Lago Puelo with **Juana de Arco** (T0294-449 8946, www.interpatagonia.com/juanadearco) and others, as well as kayaking.
▶▶ *For further information, see What to do, page 486.*

South of El Bolsón → *For listings, see pages 482-486.*

Epuyén → *Colour map 5, B2. Phone code 02944. Population 1500.*
Some 40 km southeast of El Bolsón on Route 258, the little settlement of Epuyén (pronounced epooSHEN) is relatively undeveloped for tourists, with nothing much to do except stroll around Lago Epuyén. Buses between El Bolsón and Esquel stop (briefly) at Lago Epuyén, though some don't enter the village itself. There's a simple *hostería*, which also has rustic *cabañas* with meals on request. Nice picnic grounds with facilities (no camping) and a Centro Cultural overlook the lake. The centre sells *artesanía* and exhibits wood carving. A fire destroyed the trees on one hillside some

years ago, making the area less attractive for walks, but there's a good trek around the lakeside and good fishing in the lake.

Cholila → *Colour map 5, B2. Phone code 02945. Population 2000.*

Cholila lies 76 km south of El Bolsón on Route 71, which branches off Route 258 at Km 179. It is a real Patagonian settlement that one day will make a great place to stay, thanks to its lovely setting in broad open landscape with superb views of Lago Cholila, crowned by ranges of mountains all around. For the moment, there's excellent fishing, canoeing and kayaking on rivers nearby, but very little tourist infrastructure; the accommodation is extremely limited, and there's little information.

You might have heard that the reason to visit Cholila is to see the wooden cabins where **Butch Cassidy**, the **Sundance Kid** and **Etta Place** lived between 1901 and 1905 (see box, opposite). You can understand why they hid out here for so long: Cholila still feels remote and untouched, and the views from their land are breathtaking. The cabins themselves were rather evocative, falling to pieces, patched up with bits of wood and with a lichen-stained slatted roof, but, in 2006, the owner of the land started to 'renovate' them, by replacing the tattered timbers with brand new bright orange beams, doors and window frames. As a result, little remains of the authentic cabins where Butch and Sundance lived, and, unless you're a true fan, it might not be worth the considerable effort required to visit them. To get there make a detour from Route 258 heading south from El Bolsón, towards Los Alerces National Park's northern entrance; 13 km north of Cholila along Route 71, look out for a sign on the right; park by the little kiosk and walk 400 m to the cabins. Entry is US$1.50, if anyone's around to charge you.

There is a good walk around **Lago Mosquito**: continue down the road from El Trébol past the lake then take a path to the left, following the river. Cross the river on the farm bridge and continue to the base of the hills to a second bridge. Follow the path to the lake and walk between the lake and the hills, crossing the river via a suspension bridge just past El Trébol – six hours.

Leleque → *Colour map 5, B2.*

Ruta 40 (paved) is a faster way to get from El Bolsón to Esquel than Route 71 via Cholila, and this is the route the bus takes. You could stop off at Leleque to see the **Museum of Patagonia (Museo Leleque)** ① *off the R40, Km 1440, 90 km from Esquel and 80 km from El Bolsón, www.benetton.com/patagonia/inglese/index-net.html, Thu-Tue 1100-1700, 1100-1900, closed May, Jun and Sep, US$1.50*, on the estate owned by Carlo and Luciano **Benetton**, of Italian knitwear fame. There's a beautifully designed exhibition on the lives of indigenous peoples, with dwellings reconstructed of animal skins, using the original techniques, a huge collection of delicate arrowheads and the *boleadoras* for catching cattle. Other moving exhibits focus on the first pioneers in Patagonia, especially the Welsh. There's an attractive café in a reconstructed *boliche* (provisions shop and bar).

Butch Cassidy and the Sundance Kid

Near Cholila, south of El Bolsón, is a wooden cabin which was home to infamous US bank robbers Butch Cassidy (Robert LeRoy Parker) and the Sundance Kid (Harry Longabaugh) immortalized by Paul Newman and Robert Redford in the 1969 film. In America in the late 1890s, the two were part of a loosely organized gang, known variously as the Train Robbers' Syndicate, the Hole in the Wall Gang and the Wild Bunch, which carried out hold-ups on railway payrolls and banks in the borders of Utah, Colorado and Wyoming. In 1900, the gang celebrated the wedding of one of their colleagues by having their photo taken: a big mistake. The photo was recognized by a Wells Fargo detective, and with their faces decorating Wanted posters across the land, Cassidy, Sundance and his girlfriend Etta Place escaped to Argentina in February 1901.

Using the names Santiago Ryan and Harry Place, the outlaws settled on government land near Cholila and applied to buy it, but Pinkerton detectives hot on their trail soon tracked them down and informed the Argentine authorities. The three lay low in their idyllic rural retreat until 1905, when, needing money to start up elsewhere, the gang raided banks in Villa Mercedes and a particularly audacious job in Río Gallegos. Posing as ranching company agents, they opened a bank account with US$7000, spent two weeks at the best hotels and socialized with the city's high society,

and then entered the bank to close their accounts and empty the safe before escaping to Chile. Then Etta returned to the United States, and disappeared from the history books.

Butch and Sundance moved to Bolivia, and worked at the Concordia tin mine, disappearing every now and then to carry out the occasional hold-up. Lack of capital to settle as respectable ranchers was, however, their undoing. In 1908, near Tupiza in southern Bolivia, they seized an Aramayo mining company payroll, but gained only a fraction of the loot they expected. With military patrols in pursuit and the Argentine and Chilean forces alerted, they rode into the village of San Vicente and were recognized. Besieged, they did not, as in the film, run into the awaiting gunfire. Their deaths were not widely reported in the United States until the 1930s, and rumours abounded: Butch was said to have become a businessman, a rancher, a trapper and a Hollywood movie extra, while Sundance had run guns in the Mexican Revolution, migrated to Europe, fought for the Arabs against the Turks in the First World War, sold mineral water, founded a religious cult, and still found time to marry Etta.

Their ramshackle wooden cabin was, until June 2006, an evocative place to visit. Now the owner has restored it with brand new bright orange wood, ruining the outlaw hideout feel. The location is still spectacular, however, and worth the trip for fans.

For hotel and restaurant price codes and other relevant information, see pages 20-26.

Where to stay

Lago Mascardi *p472*
$$$ pp **Hotel Tronador**, T0294-4449
0556, www.hoteltronador.com. 60 km
from Bariloche, on the narrow road
between Villa Mascardi and Pampa
Linda. Open Nov-Apr, full board, lakeside
paradise, lovely rooms with lake view,
beautiful gardens, charming owner,
also riding, fishing and lake excursions.

Camping
Camping La Querencia, R81 towards
Pampa Linda, Km 10, T0294-15-461 6300,
www.campinglaquerencia.com.ar.
A pretty and peaceful spot on the side
of the river and the banks of the lake,
opposite Playa Negro. Camping from
US$6.25 per person.
Camping Las Carpitas, Lago Mascardi,
at Km 33, T0294-449 0527, www.camping
lascarpitas.com.ar. Set in a great lakeside
position, summer only, with *cabañas*
and restaurant. Camping from US$6
and dorms from US$12.
Camping Los Rápidos, R258, Km 37,
T0294-15-431 7028, www.losrapidos.
com.ar. Attractive shaded site going
down to the lake, with *confitería*, food
store and all facilities, US$6 per person.
Also bunk beds in a basic *albergue* US$10
per person (sleeping bag needed).
Friendly owners organize trekking,
kayaking, fishing and mountain biking.

Pampa Linda *p472*
$$$ Hostería Pampa Linda, T0294-449
0517, www.hosteriapampalinda.com.ar.

A comfortable, peaceful base for
climbing Tronador and many other treks
(plus horse riding, trekking and climbing
courses), simple rooms, all with stunning
views, restaurant, full board optional,
packed lunches available for hikes.
Charming owners, Sebastián de la Cruz
is one of the area's most experienced
mountaineers. Highly recommended.

Camping
Los Vuriloches, Pampa Linda, T0294-
446 2131, pampalindatere@hotmail.com.
Idyllic spacious lakeside site, *confitería*
serving good meals and food shop.
Excellent service, run by the Club Andino
Bariloche (www.clubandino.org/refugios-
y-campings/refugio-pampa-linda.asp).

Río Manso Medio and Lago Hess *p473*
$$$$ Río Manso Lodge, T0294-449
0546, www.riomansolodge.com.
Spectacularly set on the bank of the
Río Manso in beautiful mountainous
scenery, this is a top-class fishing
lodge, with lovely rooms with great
views from their large windows, fine
food and great fishing. Loved by experts.
Transfers organized.

El Bolsón *p474, map p475*
Difficult to find accommodation in the
high season: book ahead.
$$$ Amancay, Av San Martín 3207,
T0294-449 2222, www.hotelamancay
elbolson.com. Good, comfortable and
light rooms, though small and a bit
old-fashioned, breakfast included.
$$$ La Posada de Hamelin, Int
Granollers 2179, T0294-449 2030,
www.posadadehamelin.com.ar.
Charming rooms, welcoming
atmosphere, huge breakfasts with

home-made jams and cakes, German spoken. Highly recommended.

$$ La Casona de Odile, Barrio Luján, T0294-449 2753, www.odile.com.ar. Private rooms and 3-6-bed dorms (US$17 pp) by stream, delicious home cooking, bicycle rental. Recommended.

$ pp Altos del Sur, Villa Turismo, T0294-449 8730, www.altosdelsur.bolsonweb. com. Peaceful hostel in a lovely setting, HI member, shared rooms and private doubles, dinner available, will collect from bus station if you call ahead. Recommended.

$ pp El Pueblito, 4 km north in Barrio Luján, 1 km off Ruta 40 (take bus from Plaza Principal, US$0.50), T0294-449 3560, www.elpueblitohostel.com.ar. Wooden building in open country, dorms (US$12-15 depending on season and if with breakfast), also has cabins (US$43-50, laundry facilities, shop, open fire. Recommended.

$ pp Hostel La Casa del Viajero, Liberdad y Las Flores, Barrio Usina, T0294-449 3092, www.lacasadelviajero.com.ar. A little out of the centre in a beautful setting, surrounded by organic gardens. Simple, comfortable rooms (dorms – US$15, and private – US$25). Call them for pick up from the centre of town.

$ pp Refugio Patagónico, Islas Malvinas y Pastorino, T0294-448 3628, www. refugiopatagonico.com. Basic hostel, with small dorms (US$12.50) and doubles (US$45), in a spacious house set in open fields, views of Piltriquitrón, 5 blocks from the plaza.

Camping

Camping La Cascada, at Mallín Ahogado, near La Cascada Escondida, north of El Bolsón, T0294-483 5304. On the edge of a botanical garden and a forest reserve. Spacious, tranquil, lovely view of the Valley of the Arroyo del Medio and the snowcapped mountains beyond. Helpful owner, Pablo Panomarenko has good contacts with the *refugios* and businesses in Bolsón. Has *cabañas*, a great club house, homegrown organic vegetables available, home-made bread and beer for sale, delicious mountain spring water from the tap, swimming in the brook that feeds the waterfall. Recommended.

La Chacra, Av Belgrano 1128, T0294-449 2111, www.campinglachacra.com.ar. 15 mins' walk from town, well shaded, good facilities, lively atmosphere in season.

Quem-Quem, on Río Quemquemtreu, T0294-449 3550, www.quem-quem.com. ar. Lovely site, hot showers, good walks, free pick-up from town.

There are many *cabañas* in picturesque settings with lovely views in the Villa Turismo, about US$60-100 for 2 people.

Parque Nacional Lago Puelo p478

Apart from wild camping, there's no accommodation in the park itself, but plenty in Villa Lago Puelo, just outside, with *cabañas*, restaurants and campsites spread out along R16 through the little village.

Cabañas

$$$ Lodge Casa Puelo, R16, km 10, T0294-449 9539, www.casapuelo.com.ar. *Cabañas* for up to 6. Beautifully designed rooms and self-catering cabins right against forested mountains where you can walk. Good service, English-speaking owner Miguel knows the local area intimately. Very comfortable, dinner offered. Recommended.

$$$-$$ La Granja, 20 m from Río Azul, T02944-499 265, www.interpatagonia. com/lagranja. Traditional chalet-style *cabañas* with simple furnishings, nothing out of this world, but there's a pool, and these are good value.

$$$-$$ La Yoica, just off R16, Km 5, T0294-449 9200, www.layoica.com.ar. Charming Scottish owners make you feel at home in these traditional *cabañas* set in lovely countryside with great views. Price for up to 4 people.

$$$ Frontera, Ruta Nacional 40, 9 km from Lago Puelo, isolated in woodland, off the main road heading for Esquel, T0294-447 3092, www.frontera-patagonia.com.ar. *Cabañas* for 4 and *hostería*, in native forest, furnished to a very high standard, delicious breakfasts and dinner if required.

$$ San Jorge, a block from the main street, on Plaza Ilia, Perito Moreno and Azcuénaga T02944-491313, www.san jorgepatagonico.com. Excellent value, neat but dated self-catering apartments in a pretty garden, with friendly, helpful owners.

$ pp La Pasarela, 2 km from town, T0294-449 9061, www.lpuelo.com.ar. Dorms (US$10 pp), cabins (us$60) and camping US$7.50, shops, fuel.

Camping

There are 2 free sites in the park itself, on Lago Puelo, of which **Camping del Lago** is most highly recommended; it offers all facilities, plus rafting, fishing and trekking.

Outside the park there are many good sites with all facilities; these are recommended: **Ailin Co**, Km 15, T02944-499078, www.ailincolagopuelo.com.ar; **Los Quinchos**, Km 13.

Epuyén *p479*

$$ El Refugio del Lago, T02945-499025, www.elrefugiodellago.com.ar. Transfers available on request. Relaxed, comfortable rooms in a lovely wooden house a short walk from the lakeshore, also cabins, dorms (US$19), with

breakfast, good meals. Camping US$6-7 pp. Recommended.

Camping

Puerto Patriada, 25 km south of El Bolsón, access through El Hoyo. Free and paying pitches on the shore of Lago Epuyén, also has *cabañas*.

Cholila *p480*

$$$-$$ Cabañas Cerro La Momia, Ruta 71, Villa Lago Rivadavia, T011-4964 2586, www.cabanascerrolamomia.com.ar. Very good *cabañas* for up to 6, picturesque setting among fruit orchards and wooded slopes. Restaurant, excursions arranged.

⦿ Restaurants

El Bolsón *p474, map p475*
$$$ Pasiones Argentinas, Av Belgrano y Berutti, T0294-448 3616, www. facebook.com/pasiones.restaurant. Traditional Argentine food in a wonderful cosy setting.
$$ Amancay, San Martín 3217, T0294-449 2222, www.hotelamancayel bolson.com. Good *parrilla* and home-made pastas.
$$ Arcimbaldo, Av San Martin 2790, T0294-449 2137. Good value *tenedor libre*, smoked fish and draft beer, open for breakfast.
$$ Jauja, Av San Martín 2867, T0294-449 2448. The best restaurant in town is a great meeting place, serving delicious fish and pasta. It also makes outstanding ice cream from organic milk and local berries: there are 11 varieties of chocolate alone. English spoken.
$$ Martin Sheffield, Av San Martín 2760, T0294-449 1920. Central, good food, Patagonian specialities, menu of the day, with or without a drink.

Cafés
Cerveza El Bolsón, RN 258, Km 123.9, T0294-449 2595, www.cervezaselbolson. com. Microbrewery where you can see how the beer is made and sample the 18 varieties. *Picadas* are served with beer, and you can sit outside in the gardens. Highly recommended.
El Rey de Sandwich, Roca 345. Good value sandwiches at this *rotisería*, next to **Via Bariloche** bus terminal.

Parque Nacional Lago Puelo *p478*
$$ Familia von Fürstenberg, R16 on the way to the national park, T0294-449 9392, www.vonfuerstenberg.com.ar. In a delightful, perfectly decorated Swiss-style chalet, try the beautifully presented traditional waffles and home-made cakes. Sumptuous. Also *cabañas* (**$$$**) to rent.

Cholila *p480*
La Casa de Piedra, R71 outside village, T02945-498056. Welsh tea room, chocolate cake recommended.

⊛ Festivals

El Bolsón *p474, map p475*
Jan Fiesta de la Fruta Fina (Berry Festival) at nearby El Hoyo.
Feb Fiesta del Lúpulo (Hop Festival), at the end of the month.
Oct Fiesta de la Cerveza Artesanal. The home-brewed beer festival, much more civilized than an Oktoberfest!
Dec Jazz festival. Attracts many famous musicians, lasts 10 days.

⊙ Shopping

El Bolsón *p474, map p475*
The handicraft and food market is on Tue, Thu and Sat 1000-1600 in season around the main plaza. Some fine leather and jewellery, carved wood and delicious organic produce.
Centro Artesanal, Av San Martín 1866, T0294-449 1150, daily 1000-2000. If the market's not open, a selection of the best crafts can be bought here: wood, leather, precious stones, ceramics and candles.
Granja Larix, R258, Km 118.5, T0294-449 8018, alejandra@bariloche.com.ar. Fabulous smoked trout and home-made jams.
La Huella, Sarmiento and Dorrego, T0294-449 1210. For tent hire and outdoor equipment.
Museo de Piedras Patagónicas, Laten K'Aike, 13 km from El Bolsón, T0294-449 1969, daily from 1100. For exquisite semi-precious stones.
Mercado Artesanal, Av San Martín 1920, Mon-Fri 0800-1300, 1400-2000, Sat 0900-1300. Wonderful Mapuche weavings can be bought in this co-operative of local weavers, and you can watch women spin and weave beautiful rugs, scarves and bags, in the traditional way. Also knitted goods, all incredibly high quality and beautifully made. Recommended.
Monte Viejo, San Martín y Hube, T0294-449 1735. Excellent selection of high quality handicrafts from all over Argentina.
Verde Menta Almacén Naturista, Av San Martín 2137, T0294-449 3576. Good supplier of dried foods, fruits and cereals.

⊙ What to do

Lago Mascardi *p472*
Boat trips
Victoria II Lago Mascardi Paseos Lacustres, T0294-444 1062, lmascardi@ bariloche.com.ar. Trips on Lago Mascardi are a wonderful way to see the mountains in summer.

Rafting

Rafting on the Río Manso is arranged through operators in Bariloche; see page 468.

El Bolsón *p474, map p475*
Tour operators

Grado 42, Av Belgrano 406, on the corner with Av San Martín, T0294-449 3124, www.grado42.com. Excellent company offering wide range of tours, including La Trochita's lesser-known trip from El Maitén, where there is a superb steam railway workshop and you can learn all about how the trains work. Also rafting on the Río Manso; horse riding in glorious countryside at Cajón de Azul; wonderful fishing in Lago Puelo; paragliding from Plitriquitron. Recommended.

⊖ Transport

Lago Mascardi *p472*
Bus

Services from Bariloche to **El Bolsón** pass through **Villa Mascardi**. Buses to **Los Rápidos** run from the terminal in Bariloche at 0900, 1300, 1800 daily in summer. Check with **Vía Bariloche/ El Valle** for times.

Pampa Linda and Mount Tronador *p472*
Bus

A bus to Bariloche leaves daily at 1700 in summer only; contact **Transitando**

lo Natural, 20 de Febrero 25, Bariloche, T0294-452 7926, transitando1@hotmail. com. From Pampa Linda you can also often get a lift with an excursion trip returning to **Bariloche**, if there's room.

El Bolsón *p474, map p475*
Bus

Several daily to **Bariloche** and **Esquel**, with **Don Otto**, **TAC** and **Vía Bariloche** (T0800-333 7575, www.viabariloche. com.ar). Heavily, even over-booked in high season; to Bariloche, US$9.50-11, 2 hrs; to Esquel, US$13.50, 2½-3 hrs. Other destinations are accessible from these towns. Buses to **Lago Puelo** with **Vía Bariloche** every 2 hrs, 4 on Sun, 45 mins, US$5. To **Parque Nacional Los Alerces** (highly recommended route), with **Transportes Esquel,** depart from ACA service station once a day, US$10, 4-5 hrs, via Cholila and Epuyen.

Parque Nacional Lago Puelo *p478*

Transportes Esquel, www.transportes esquel.com.ar, run daily buses connecting Lago Puelo with **Cholila**, **PN Los Alerces** and **Esquel**.

❶ Directory

El Bolsón *p474, map p475*

Banks Exchange cash at **Banco Patagonia**, San Martín and Roca, with ATM outside. **Post office** San Martín 2860.

Southern Lake District

This southernmost area of the lakes is the most Patagonian in feel, with pioneer towns Esquel and Trevelin caught between the wild open steppe to the east and the dramatic mountains of the Andes to the west. Esquel retains the quiet charm of an ordinary country town but has one very famous attraction: it's the starting point for the narrow-gauge railway known as 'La Trochita', an atmospheric way to see the surrounding landscape. The town also boasts a family ski resort and a few places to trek and mountain bike. Far more tranquil is the village of Trevelin, which still bears signs of its origins as a Welsh colony. Both towns make good bases for exploring the most unspoilt national park in the Lake District: Los Alerces. With just one road running through it, the park has pristine forested mountains and several stunning lakes, and is best enjoyed on foot. There are wonderful hikes, boat trips to see ancient *alerce* trees, and some unforgettable views, like Río Arrayanes and Lago Verde. Since this area is less developed for tourism than the rest of the lakes, it's best to hire a car to see it independently if you don't want to do a full-day tour.

One of the most authentic towns in the Lake District, Esquel is a pleasant, breezy place that still feels like a pioneer outpost, set where the steppe meets the mountains. It's a typical Patagonian country town, with many buildings dating from the early 1900s and battered pickups filling the streets in the late-morning bustle when local farmers come into town. There are few tourist sight, but it's all the more appealing for that. It is the starting point for the narrow-gauge railway, 'La Trochita', made famous by Paul Theroux as the *Old Patagonian Express* and is the best base for visiting the Parque Nacional Los Alerces and for skiing at La Hoya in winter. The tranquil village of Trevelin, where the Welsh heritage is more in evidence, is just 25 km away. For more information, see www.esquelonline.com (in Spanish).

Arriving in Esquel → *Phone code 02945. Population 30,000.*
Getting there and around Esquel has its own **airport** ① *T02945-451676*, 20 km east of town by paved road, US$20 by taxi, US$14 by bus. There's a smart modern **bus terminal** ① *Av Alvear 1871, T02945-451584*, six blocks from the main commercial centre (US$2.50 by taxi). It has toilets, *kiosko*, *locutorio* with internet, café, tourist information desk and left luggage. Buses arrive here from Comodoro Rivadavia on the Atlantic coast and Bariloche, with connections from those places to all other destinations in Patagonia and to the north. See Transport, below.

Tourist information The **tourist office** ① *in a little hut on the corner of Av Alvear and Sarmiento, T02945-451927, www.esquel.gov.ar, daily 0800-2200*, is friendly enough, but doesn't seem to have much information. They do hand out a useful town map, however, and another leaflet with a yellow map of Los Alerces National Park showing all access and accommodation in the park, as well as the crossing to Chile via Paso Futulaeufú. You might have to press them patiently for bus timetables. For further information on Los Alerces and the whole area, see www.comarcadelosalerces.com.ar.

Places in Esquel
The main point of visiting Esquel is to get to Los Alerces, or Trevelin, but it's a pleasant place to walk around. There aren't any sights, as such, although there is the **Museo Lituano Olgbrun** ① *Calle Los Ñires 1138, T02945-450536*, a few kilometres south of town, near the road to Trevelin. This is a Lithuanian museum with a well-stocked giftshop. All the food shops and services you need are contained within a few blocks east of Avenida Alvear, between Mitre and the wide Avenida Fontana.

La Trochita
① *Estación Viejo Expreso Patagonico, six blocks north of the town centre at the corner of Brown and Roggero, T02945-451403 in Esquel/T02945-495190 in El Maitén, www. patagoniaexpress.com/el_trochita.htm. The train runs once daily Mon-Fri and twice a day on Sat in high season (much less frequent in winter), US$36, children under 5 free; tour operators in town sell tickets.*

The famous narrow-gauge railway, **La Trochita** (*Old Patagonian Express*), also known in Spanish as *El Viejo Expreso Patagónico*, chugs off into the steppe from a pretty old station north of town. While it's obviously a tourist experience, this is a thoroughly enjoyable trip, and as the steam train rumbles across the lovely valleys and mountains of the *precordillera* on tracks just 75 cm wide, you'll find yourself wanting to know how it works. There's Spanish and English commentary along the way. The quaint carriages each have little wood stoves, and there's a small tea room on board, but it's worth waiting for the home-made cakes (and handicrafts) for sale at the wild and remote Mapuche hamlet of **Nahuel Pan**, where the train stops, and where you'll hear an interesting explanation of how the engine works. Recommended. In high season a service also runs from El Maitén at the northernmost end of the line to Desvío Thomae (55 km) three days a week (infrequently in winter), US$30.

La Hoya

ⓘ *15 km north of Esquel, information from Club Andino Esquel, Pellegrini 787, T02945-453248, www.skilahoya.com, www.cerrolahoya.com.*

There's good skiing on high quality powder snow over a long season at this low-key family resort. It is popular with Argentines, since it's one of cheapest and friendliest. There are 22 km of pistes, many of them suitable for kids or beginners, with good challenging pistes too, and seven ski lifts. There are three daily buses to La Hoya from Esquel. A skipass costs US$30 per day in high season, with reductions for a week or longer. Equipment can be rented.

Esquel

To Laguna La Zeta

La Trochita Station (Narrow Gauge)
Pte Artemio Book A Alsina

Banco de la Nación
RS Peña
Av Alvear
Norte Supermarket
9 de Julio
Patagonia Verde
Benroth
Rivadavia
San Martín
La Casona de Olgbrun
Av Ameghino
Chacabuco

Plaza San Martín
Casa de Esquel

Braese

To Laguna La Zeta

Where to stay 🛏	La Chacra 12	Restaurants 🍴
Angelina 2	La Colina 6	Don Chiquino 1
Anochecer Andino 9	La Posada 7	La Española 2
Canela 5	La Tour d'Argent 8	María Castaña 5
Casa de Pueblo 1	Millalen 10	Vascongada 9
Cumbres Blancas 4	Planeta Hostel 3	
Hospedaje Rowlands 11	Res El Cisne 13	

400 metres
400 yards

Walks around Esquel

There are some challenging walks and mountain-bike trails in the surrounding mountains. See the map *Sendas y Bosques* (Walks and Forests) for El Bolsón, Lago Puelo and Los Alerces, which has the trails clearly marked. It's an easy climb along a clear path to **Laguna La Zeta**, 5 km from the centre of town, with good views and a lake with birdlife. From there, head further north up the Río Percey or towards Cañadón Huemul. The path is signposted from the end of Avenida La Fontana. Another good hike, with spectacular view, is to **Cerro La Cruz**, five hours return; walk from the centre of town signposted from the end of the street 25 de Mayo. There are longer hikes to **Cerro Veinte Uno** (five to eight hours return) and the pointy cone of Cerro Nahual Pan (eight hours return).

Trevelin → *For listings, see pages 496-499. Colour map 5, B2.*

The pretty village of Trevelin, 25 km southwest of Esquel, was once an offshoot of the Welsh colony of Gaiman on the Atlantic coast (see box, page 517), founded when the Welsh travelled west to find further lands for growing corn. The name means Town (*tre*) of the Mill (*velin*) in Welsh. You can still hear Welsh spoken here, and there is plenty of evidence of Welsh heritage in several good little museums around the town. With a backdrop of snow-capped mountains, the village is an appealing place to rest for a few days, to go fishing and rafting on nearby Río Futuleufu, or to see the beautiful waterfalls at the reserve of Nant-y-fall.

Places in Trevelin → *Phone code 02945. Population 5000.*

Trevelin remains a quiet village with a strong sense of community, and its history is manifest in several sights. The Welsh chapel (1910), **La Capilla Bethel**, can be visited, with a guided tour to fill you in on a bit of history. A fine old flour mill (1918) houses the **Museo Histórico Regional** ⓘ *Molino Viejo 488, T02945-480545, daily 1100-2000, US$4*, which has fascinating artefacts from the Welsh colony. The **Museo Cartref Taid** ⓘ *El Malacara s/n, ask for directions in the tourist office, T02945-480108, daily 1600-2000, US$4*, is another great place for exploring the Welsh pioneer past. It's the house of John Evans, one of Trevelin's first settlers, and filled with his belongings. There's another extraordinary and touching relic of his life in **La Tumba del Caballo Malacara** ⓘ *200 m from main plaza, guided tours are available, US$4*, a private garden containing the grave of his horse, Malacara, who once saved his life. The enthusiastic and helpful staff at the **tourist office** ⓘ *central octagonal plaza, T02945-480120, www.trevelin.gob.ar, Mon-Fri from 0800, Sat and Sun from 0900*, speak English and can provide maps and advice on accommodation and fishing.

Eisteddfods are still held here every year in October, and you'll be relieved to hear that Té Galés, that other apparently traditional Welsh ritual, is alive and well in several tea rooms, which offer a ridiculous excess of delicious cakes. Extensive research has established that **Nain Maggie** is, in fact, the town's best. There are good day walks in idyllic scenery around the town; get directions on routes from the tourist office. It's also a good area for horse riding or mountain biking.

Around Trevelin

For a gentle outing with quite the best insight into the Welsh history in Patagonia, visit the rural flour mill **Molino Nant Fach** ① *Route 259, T02945-15-698058, entry US$2.50,* 22 km southwest towards the Chilean border. This beautiful flour mill was built by Merfyn Evans, descendant of the town's founder, Thomas Dalar Evans, as an exact replica of the first mill built in the town in 1899. Merfyn's fascinating tour (in Spanish, but English booklet available to read) recounts a now familiar tale of the Argentine government's persistent mismanagement of natural resources and industry, through the suppression of the Welsh prize-winning wheat industry. It's a beautiful spot, and Merfyn tells the rather tragic story in a wonderfully entertaining way. Highly recommended.

Before you reach Molino Nant Fach, look out for the **Nant-y-fall Falls** on the same road (Route 259), 17 km southwest of Trevelin, heading to the Chilean border. These are a series of spectacular waterfalls reached by an easy 1½-hour walk along a trail through lovely forest. There's an entry charge of US$4.25 per person (reductions for children and local residents). Guides will take you to all seven falls.

Route 259 continues to the Chilean border at the spectacularly beautiful Paso Futaleufú. ▸▸ *For further details, see box, page 495.*

Fishing is popular in many local rivers and lakes, most commonly in Río Futuleufú, and Corintos, and Lagos Rosario and Corcovado. The season runs from the end of November to mid-April, and the tourist office can advise on guides and where to go.

Parque Nacional Los Alerces → *For listings, see pages 496-499.*

One of the most magnificent and untouched expanses of wilderness in the whole Andes region, this national park was established to protect the stately *alerce* trees (*Fitzroya cupressoides*). The *alerce* is among the longest-living tree species in the world, and there are some specimens in the park that are over 4000 years old. They grow deep in the Valdivian rainforest that carpets these mountains a rich velvety green, beside vivid blue Lago Futalaufquen and emerald Lago Verde. There are several good hikes, plus rafting and fishing, in the park, and idyllic lakeside campsites and *hosterías*, making this a great place to spend a few days.

The park is enormous at over 200,000 ha, and it remains the most virgin park in the whole Lake District, since much of it is only accessible on foot. There are four large lakes: navy-blue **Lago Futalaufquen**, with fine fishing; **Lago Menéndez**, which can be crossed by boat to visit the ancient *alerce* trees; the exquisite green **Lago Verde**; and the almost inaccessible **Lago Amutui Quimei**. In order to protect this fragile environment, access by car is possible only to the eastern side of the park, via *ripio* Route 71, which runs between Cholila and Trevelin alongside the eastern side of Lagos Futalaufquen, Verde and Rivadavia. The western side of the park, where rainfall is highest, has areas of Valdivian forest, and can only be accessed by boat or by hiking to Lago Krügger.

Arriving in Parque Nacional Los Alerces

Park entrance costs US$9.65. There are two main entrances to the park, both off Route 71: one is at the northern end of Lago Rivadavia (south of Cholila), and the other is 12 km south of Lago Futulaufquen. Head from this entrance to the southern tip of the lake, 52 km west of Esquel, to reach the the Intendencia (park office) with a **visitor centre** ① *T02945-471015, www.parquesnacionales.gov.ar, see also http://losalercesparquenacional.blogspot.com*, offering useful information on the park. Helpful *guardaparques* give out maps and advise on walks. Right by the Intendencia, and less than 2 km from Route 71, **Villa Futulaufquen** is a little hamlet which is very useful for services. There's a petrol station, *locutorio*, two food shops

Parque Nacional Los Alerces

Where to stay 🛏
Bahía Rosales **6**
Cabañas Tejas Negras **7**

El Aura: Lago Verde
Wilderness Resort **2**
Hostería Cume Hue **8**

Hostería Quimé Quipán **1**
Los Maitenes **9**

and a restaurant, **El Abuelo Monje**. Fishing licences can be obtained either from the food shops, the *kiosko* or **Hostería Cume Hue**.

A daily bus runs along Route 71 in each direction, picking up and dropping off passengers at lakeside campsites and *hosterías*, and also at the petrol station opposite the Intendencia. Ask at the petrol station for bus times, or contact the visitor centre in Villa Futalaufquen, above.►► *See Transport, page 499.*

Walks

For all walks, get the *Sendas y Bosques* (Walks and Forests) map and book for El Bolsón, Lago Puelo and Los Alerces. Maps are 1:200,000, laminated and easy to read, and the book is full of great walks, with English summaries and detailed directions in Spanish (www.guiasendasybosques.com.ar). The park office Intendencia also has leaflets listing the walks, but these have insufficient detail.

Cave paintings There are *pinturas rupestres* to be found just 40 minutes' stroll from the park Intendencia (Km 1). You'll also pass a waterfall and a mirador with panoramic views over Lago Futulaufquen.

Cascada Arroyo This is a satisfying and easy four-hour walk south of Villa Futalaufquen to see waterfalls, passing various miradors.

Pasarella Lago Verde Signposted off Route 71 at Km 34.3. The most beautiful walk in the whole park and unmissable, no matter how little time you have, is across the suspension bridge over Río Arrayanes to heavenly Lago Verde. A self-guided trail leads around a peninsula to Puerto Chucao on Lago Menéndez, where boat trips begin (see below). Go in the early evening to see all kinds of birdlife from the beach by Lago Verde, including swifts and swallows darting all around you. While you're in the area, take a quick 20-minute stroll up to **Mirador Lago Verde** for gorgeous views up and down the whole valley. From here you can appreciate the string of lakes, running from Lago Futulaufquen in the south to Lago Rivadavia in the north.

Cerro Dedal For a great day hike, there is a longer trek up Cerro Dedal (1916 m). This is a circular walk, at least eight hours return, with a steep climb from the Intendencia and wonderful views over the lake and mountains further west. Register with *guardaparques* and get detailed instructions. You're required to start before 1000. Carry plenty of water.

Lago Krügger There is also a long but rewarding two- to three-day (12- to 14-hour) hike though *coihue* forest to the southernmost tip of **Lago Krügger**, where there is a *refugio* (open only in January and February) and campsite, as well as a *guardaparque's* office. Here you can take a boat back to Puerto Limonao on Lago Futalaufquen, but check when the boat is running before you set off and always register with the park's Intendencia. From Lago Krügger, you could walk south along the course of Río Frey, though there is no *refugio* here. For information on the boat service and the *refugio* contact **Hostería Lago Krügger** ① *T011-15-4424 7964,* *www.lagokrugger.com.ar*, a little rustic fishing lodge. Note: **Lago Krügger** was closed in the 2014 season; check in advance if it is accessible.

Boat trips

All boat trips run frequently in high season (1 December to 31 March), and all can be booked through **Safari Lacustre** ① *T02945-456359, www.brazosur.com.ar*, and **Patagonia Verde** ① *Esquel, T02945-454396, www.patagonia-verde.com.ar*, or when you get to the pier, though tickets tend to sell out in high season.

Boat trips leave from Puerto Limonao at the southwestern end of Lago Futalaufquen: follow signs up the western side of the lake, just for a few kilometres. They cross Lago Futalaufquen and travel along the pea-green Río Arrayanes, which is lined with the extraordinary cinnamon-barked *arrayán* trees (depart 0930, return 1900, US$51). Even more spectacular are the trips from Puerto Chucao, which is reached from the suspension bridge crossing Lago Verde, halfway along Route 71. These cross Lago Menéndez (1½ hours) where you land, and walk a short distance to see a majestic 2600-year-old *alerce* tree, known as 'el abuelo' (the grandfather). From here you walk to the hidden and silent jade-green Lago Cisne and then back past the rushing whitewaters of Río Cisne: an unforgettable experience (depart 1130, return 1700, US$41). Boats also go from Puerto Limonao to Lago Krügger, or you can trek there and take the boat back (see above), but check the boat times before you set off. Boats sail in summer only.

South of Esquel → *For listings, see pages 496-499.*

The iconic Ruta 40 continues (paved) south from Esquel across very deserted landscapes that give you a taste for the full experience of Patagonia. It's a tricky section for travel by public transport, since there are few settlements or services along this section of road until you reach the small town of Perito Moreno (about 14 hours' drive). At **Tecka**, Km 101, Route 62 (paved) branches off east and follows the valley of the Río Chubut to Trelew: another lonely road. (West of Tecka is the Paso Palena border with Chile, see box, opposite) Ruta 40 continues south to **Gobernador Costa**, a small service centre for the *estancias* in this area on the Río Genoa at Km 183. Buses go up and down Ruta 40 to the town of Perito Moreno, and from here you can take a daily service on to El Chaltén or El Calafate; ask in Esquel's bus terminal.

Río Pico → *Colour map 5,C2. Phone code 02945. Population 1000.*

Río Pico lies in a wide green valley close to the Andes and has become quietly known among trout-fishing circles as a very desirable place to fish. Permits are available from the *municipalidad* in Gobernador Costa. Río Pico is the site of an early 20th-century German settlement and some old houses remain from that period. Nearby are several lakes that are good for fishing and free camping; ask locals for hitching advice. The northern shore of Lago Tres, 23 km west of town, is a peaceful

Border crossings: Argentina–Chile

There are two border crossings south of Esquel, the spectacularly beautiful Paso Futaleufú and Paso Palena. On the Chilean side roads from these crossings both link up to the route to Chaitén.

Paso Futaleufú

Paso Futaleufú is 70 km southwest of Esquel via Trevelin and is reached by Route 259 (*ripio* from Trevelin). The border is crossed by a bridge over the Río Futaleufú, and formalities should take no longer than an hour. For more information, see www.gendarmeria.gov.ar.

Argentine immigration and customs On the Argentine side of the bridge, open 0900-2100. Eat all your fresh food, as no fruit or vegetables may be taken into Chile.

Chilean immigration and customs In Futaleufú, 9 km west of the border, open 0800-2000.

Transport There are regular buses to Paso Futaleufú from Esquel and Trevelin (see Transport, page 499). From the border, Futaleufú (T+56 (0)65-272 1458) runs a connecting bus service three times a week (daily in January and February) to Futuleufú and on to Chaitén. From Chaitén there are services to Coyhaique. Cars must have special papers and the number-plate number etched into all windows: advise your hire company when booking.

Paso Palena

Paso Palena, or Río Encuentro, lies 120 km southeast of Esquel and is reached by Route 17 from Trevelin, which runs to Corcovado, 75 km east of Tecka (reached by *ripio* road). From Corcovado it is 26 km west to the border.

Argentine immigration and customs At the border, open daily 0900-2100.

Chilean immigration At Palena, 11 km west of border, open 0800-2000. Frontera del Sur buses run between Palena and Futaleufú (T+56 (0)65-272 1360).

and remote place, with a rich birdlife and wild strawberries at the end of January. Some 30 km north of Río Pico lies the huge Lago Vintter, reached by Route 44. There are also smaller lakes good for trout fishing.

South of Gobernador Costa

At Km 221, Ruta 40 (poor *ripio*) forks southwest through the town of **Alto Río Senguer** from which visits can be made to the relatively unexplored Lago Fontana and Lago La Plata. Provincial Route 20 (paved) heads almost directly south for 81 km, before turning east towards Sarmiento and Comodoro Rivadavia. At La Puerta del Diablo, in the valley of the lower Río Senguer, Route 20 intersects provincial Route 22, which joins with Ruta 40 at the town of Río Mayo in Patagonia (see page 543). This latter route is completely paved and preferable to Ruta 40 for long-distance motorists.

For hotel and restaurant price codes and other relevant information, see pages 20-26.

⦿ Where to stay

Esquel *p488, map p489*
Ask at tourist office for lodgings in private houses.

$$$ Angelina, Av Alvear 758, T02945-452763, www.hosteriaangelina.com.ar. Good value, welcoming, big breakfast, English and Italian spoken, open high season only.

$$$ Canela, Los Notros y Los Radales, Villa Ayelén, on road to Trevelin, T02945-453890, www.canelaesquel.com. Bed and breakfast and tea room in a lovely, quiet residential area, English spoken, owner knowledgeable about Patagonia.

$$$ Cumbres Blancas, Av Ameghino 1683, T02945-455100, www.cumbres blancas.com.ar. Attractive modern building, a little out of centre, very comfortable, spacious rooms, sauna, gym, airy restaurant. Recommended.

$$$-$$ La Chacra, Km 5 on Ruta 259 towards Trevelin, T02945-452802, www.lachacrapatagonia.com. Relaxing, spacious rooms, huge breakfast, Welsh and English spoken.

$$ La Posada, Chacabuco 905, T02945-454095, www.laposadaesquel.blogspot. com.ar. Tasteful B&B in quiet part of town, lovely lounge, very comfortable, excellent value.

$$ La Tour D'Argent, San Martín 1063, T02945-454612, www.latourdargent. com.ar. Bright, comfortable, family-run, very good value.

$ pp Anochecer Andino, Av Ameghino 482, 4 blocks from the commercial centre and 2 from the mountains, T02945-450498. Basic, helpful, can organize ski passes and excursions. They also can provide dinner and have a bar.

$ pp Casa del Pueblo, San Martín 661, T02945-450581, www.esquelcasadel pueblo.com.ar. Smallish rooms but good atmosphere (**$$** double), laundry, HI discounts, organizes adventure activities.

$ pp Hospedaje Rowlands, behind Rivadavia 330, T02945-452578, gales01@ hotmail.com. Warm family welcome, Welsh spoken, breakfast extra, basic rooms with shared bath and a double with bath (**$**), good value.

$ pp Planeta Hostel, Roca 458, T02945-456846, www.planetahostel.com. 4- to 6-bed dorms (US$15-18), doubles **$$**, shared bath, specialize in snowboarding, climbing and mountain biking, English spoken.

$ Res El Cisne, Chacabuco 778, T02945-452256. Basic small rooms, hot water, quiet, well kept, good value, breakfast extra.

Camping
La Colina, Darwin 1400, T02945-455264, www.lacolinaesquel.com.ar. Complex a little out of the centre with cramped dorms (US$15 pp), doubles US$32 and shady camping, US$5 per tent or vehicle.
Millalen, Av Ameghino 2063 (5 blocks from bus terminal), T02945-456164, good services and cabins.

Trevelin *p490*
$$$ Casa de Piedra, Almirante Brown 244, T02945-480357, www.casadepiedra trevelin.com. Stone and wood cottage in the suburbs. King-size beds, heating and a charming common area, popular.
$$ Pezzi, Sarmiento 351, T02945-480146, hpezzi@intramed.net. Charming family

house with a beautiful garden, English spoken. Recommended.

$ pp Casa Verde Hostal, Los Alerces s/n (9203), T02945-480091, www.casa verdehostel.com.ar. Charming owners, spacious log cabin with panoramic views, comfortable dorms for 4-6 and doubles (**$$**), laundry, HI member, breakfast extra. English and Welsh spoken, excursions into Los Alerces, bikes for hire. Highly recommended.

Camping
Many sites, especially on the road to Futaleufú and Chile; also many *cabañas*; ask for full list at the tourist office.

Parque Nacional Los Alerces *p491, map p492*
$$$$ El Aura: Lago Verde Wilderness Resort, T011-4816 5348 (Buenos Aires), www.elaurapatagonia.com. Exquisite taste in these 3 stone cabins and a guest house on the shore of Lago Verde. Luxury in every respect, attention to detail, eco-friendly. Impressive place.

$$$ Hostería Quime Quipan, east side of Lago Futalaufquen, T02945-425423, www.hosteriaquimequipan.com.ar. Comfortable rooms with lake views, dinner included. Recommended.

$$ Bahía Rosales, northeast side of Lago Futalaufquen, T02945-15-403413, www.bahiarosales.com. Comfortable *cabaña* for 6 with kitchenette and bath, **$ pp** in small basic cabin without bath, and camping in open ground, hot showers, restaurant, all recommended.

$$ Cabañas Tejas Negras, east side Lago Futalaufquen, T02945-471046, www.tejasnegras.com.ar. Really comfortable *cabañas* for 4, also good camp site, and tea room.

$$ Motel Pucón Pai, next to Tejas Negras, T02945-451425. Slightly

spartan rooms, but good restaurant, recommended for fishing; basic campsite with hot showers.

Camping
Several campsites at Villa Futalaufquen and on the shores of lagos Futalaufquen, Rivadavia, Verde and Río Arrayanes.

❼ Restaurants

Esquel *p488, map p489*
$$ Don Chiquino, behind Av Ameghino 1641, T02945-450035. Delicious pastas in a fun atmosphere with plenty of games brought to the tables by magician owner Tito. Recommended.

$$ La Española, Rivadavia 740, T02945-451509. Excellent beef, salad bar and tasty pasta. Recommended.

$$ Vascongada, 9 de Julio y Mitre, T02945-452229. Traditional style, trout and other local specialities.

$ La Tour D'Argent, San Martín 1063, T02945-454612, www.latourdargent. com.ar. Delicious local specialities, good-value set meals and a warm ambience in this popular, traditional restaurant.

Cafés
María Castaña, Rivadavia y 25 de Mayo. Popular, good coffee.

Trevelin *p490*
$$ Parrilla Oregon, Av San Martín y JM Thomas, T02945-480408, www.oregon trevelin.com.ar/restaurante.html. Large meals (particularly breakfasts), set menus based on *parrilla* and pastas.

$ Nain Maggie, Perito Moreno 179, T02945-480232, nainmaggieguia patagonia.net. Tea room, offering *té galés* and *torta negra*, expensive but good.

Shopping

Esquel *p488, map p489*
Benroth, 9 de Julio 1027. Chocolates.
Braese, 9 de Julio 1540. Home-made
chocolates and other regional specialities.
Casa de Esquel, 25 de Mayo 415.
A range of rare books on Patagonia,
also souvenirs.
La Casona de Olgbrun, Los Nires s/n.
A variety of handicrafts and souvenirs.

What to do

Esquel *p488, map p489*
Tourist office has a list of fishing guides
and companies hiring out equipment.
For details of skiing at **La Hoya**, 15 km
north, see above.

Tour operators
Brazo Sur, Rivadavia 891, T02945-
456359, www.brazosur.com.ar. For **Safari
Lacustre** boat trips, adventure activities
and regional tours.
Frontera Sur, Sarmiento 784, T02945-
450505, www.fronterasur.net. Good
company offering adventure tourism
of all sorts, as well as more traditional
excursions, ski equipment and trekking.
Patagonia Verde, 9 de Julio 926,
T02945-454396, www.patagonia-verde.
com.ar. Boat trips to El Alerzal on Lago
Menéndez, rafting on Río Corcovado,
tickets for 'La Trochita' and for Ruta 40
to El Calafate. Also range of adventure
activities, horse riding, short local
excursions and ski passes. Ask about
lodging at **Lago Verde**. English spoken.
Excellent company, very professional.

Trevelin *p490*
Gales al Sur, Alvear 1871, in the same
building as the *locutorio*, T02945-
480550, www.galesalsur.com.ar. Tours

to Chilean border; Los Alerces National
Park and Futaleufú dam; La Trochita.
Recommended for their rafting, trekking,
biking, 4WD and horse-riding excursions.
Friendly and English spoken.

Parque Nacional Los Alerces *p491,
map p492*
Agencies in Esquel or Trevelin run tours
including the boat trip across Lago
Menéndez to the *alerce* trees. For short
guided excursions, ask at the Intendencia
in Villa Futalaufquen. Lago Futalaufquen
has some of the best fishing in this part
of Argentina (the season runs end Nov
to mid-Apr); local guides offer fishing
trips and boat transport. Ask in the
Intendencia or at **Hostería Cume Hue**.

Transport

Esquel *p488, map p489*
Air
To **Buenos Aires, Comodora Rivadavia**
and **Trelew**. LADE (Av Alvear 1085,
T02945-452124) to **Bariloche, Comodoro
Rivadavia, El Calafate, Mar del Plata**
and several other destinations in
Patagonia; weekly departures.

Bus
To Buenos Aires with **Andesmar**, T02945-
450143, or **Vía Bariloche**, T02945-454676,
change in Bariloche. To **Bariloche** (via
El Bolsón, 2½ hrs), 4-5 hrs, US$13-15,
with **Don Otto** (T02945-453012), **Vía
Bariloche, TAC** and others. To **Puerto
Madryn**, 9 hrs, US$54, with **Ejecutivo de
Chubut**. To **Trelew,** US$50-60, 8-9 hrs
overnight, with **Don Otto** and **Ejecutivo
de Chubut**. To **Río Gallegos** (for
connections to El Calafate or Ushuaia),
take a bus to Trelew and change there.
To **Trevelin**, **Vía Trevelin** (T02945-
455222) and **Jacobsen** (T02945-454676,

www.transportejacobsen.com.ar), Mon-Fri hourly 0600-2300, Sat and Sun every 2½ hrs, US$1. To **Paso Futaleufú** (Chilean border) via Trevelin, with **Jacobsen**, Jan and Feb daily at 1000, Mar-Dec Mon, Wed and Fri 0800 and 1800, return 0930 and 1930, US$4. To **Río Pico**, via Tecka and Gobernador Costa, Mon, Wed and Fri at 0900, 4½ hrs, with **Jacobsen**. To **Alto Río Senguer**, Mon and Thu, with **ETAP**.

Car hire
Los Alerces, Sarmiento 763, T02945-456008, www.losalercesrentacar.com.ar. Good value, good cars, top service.

Train
See page 488.

Trevelin *p490*
Bus
To **Esquel**, **Vía Trevelin** (T02945-455222) and **Jacobsen** (T02945-454676, www.transportejacobsen.com.ar), Mon-Fri hourly, Sat and Sun every 2½ hrs, US$1. To **Paso Futaleufú** (Chilean border) with **Jacobsen**, Jan and Feb daily, Mar-Dec Mon, Wed and Fri. To **Villa Futalaufquen** (**Los Alerces**), with **Martín** Mon, Wed, Fri 0830, Sat and Sun 0830, 1430, US$3 one way.

Parque Nacional Los Alerces *p491, map p492*
Bus
Transporte Esquel, T02945-471015, runs from Esquel bus terminal daily at 0800 and 1400 along the east side of Lago Futalaufquen; the first bus goes to Lago Puelo, the second to Lago Rivadavia, both pass through Villa Futalaufquen, US$5. From **Trevelin**, **Martín** runs to Villa Futalaufquen daily except Tue and Thu at 0830, plus 1430 Sat-Sun, return 2100, plus 1230 Sat-Sun, US$3 one way.

South of Esquel *p494*
Bus
To Esquel via Gobernador Costa and Tecka, Mon, Wed and Fri 1400, 4½ hrs, with **Jacobsen**, contact as above.

❶ Directory

Esquel *p488, map p489*
Banks Banco de la Nación, Alvear and Roca, ATM accepts all cards; **Banco Patagonia**, 25 de Mayo 739, ATM; **Bansud**, 25 de Mayo 752, ATM. **Post office** Alvear 1192 and Fontana, Mon-Fri 0830-1300 and 1600-1900.

Contents

Border crossings

At a glance

⬤ **Getting around** Long distances dictate many hours on buses. Car hire is preferred, as are local flights if your budget allows.
🕐 **Time required** 7-9 days is enough to see El Calafate, do a short hike near El Chaltén and see the whales in Puerto Madryn.
☁ **Weather** May-Jul is extremely cold and the months either side can bring low temperatures. It warms up from Dec-Mar/Apr, but the winds never really stop.
✖ **When not to go** Accessible all year round, but from May-Oct the weather is cold and windy, some places close down and transport is less frequent.

Punta Norte

Península Valdés

Punta Delgada

★ Don't miss ...
1 Península Valdés, page 513.
2 Staying at a Patagonian *estancia*, pages 537 and 570.
3 Travelling along Ruta 40, page 543.
4 Perito Moreno and Upsala glaciers, pages 545 and 560.
5 Trekking around Cerro Fitz Roy, page 564.

Atlantic Ocean

N

50 km
50 miles

Patagonia has become the stuff of legends, and for good reason. It's more immense than you can possibly imagine, more empty, more windswept and more beautiful. No wonder it has attracted pioneers and runaways from the modern world. From Welsh settlers to Butch and Sundance; from Bruce Chatwin to Ernesto 'Che' Guevara riding the Ruta 40, Patagonia invites adventure.

East of the Andes, Patagonia makes up the whole southernmost cone of the Americas: a vast expanse of treeless steppe, dotted with the occasional sheep *estancia*. But at its edges are extraordinary extremes: whales bask and thousands of sea lions cavort at Península Valdés, and descendants of the Welsh still hold Eisteddfods (Welsh Festival of Arts) at Gaiman. Thousands of handprints are testimony to Stone Age life at Cueva de las Manos, and there are two petrified forests of mighty fallen monkey puzzle trees.

Take the Ruta 40 south, and you'll travel hundreds of kilometres without seeing a soul, until the magnificent granite towers of Mount Fitz Roy rise up from the flat plains: this trekking mecca is far less crowded than Torres del Paine, and on the southern ice field there are no beaten tracks whatsoever. El Calafate is the base for boat trips to the Perito Moreno Glacier: put on your crampons to walk its sculpted turquoise curves, or escape to splendidly isolated Estancia Cristina. Once you've seen Upsala Glacier stretching out into a milky Prussian-blue lake, silent and pristine, you'll be addicted. Allow plenty of time, bring walking boots and don't forget your camera.

Patagonia is vast, and it's no surprise that getting around takes some organization. Strictly speaking, Patagonia is the whole southern cone of South America, combining all parts of Argentina and Chile, south of the Río Colorado, which runs from west to east, just north of Viedma. It includes the Andes, running north–south (marking the Chilean border) and therefore the Lake District, which has been given its own chapter in this book, see pages 403-499. The Patagonia chapter includes all of Argentine Patagonia apart from the Lake District and Tierra del Fuego, the island at the very bottom, which also has its own chapter, see pages 611-643.

The main centres, with good accommodation and services, are Puerto Madryn for the northern Atlantic Coast, El Calafate on the edge of Parque Nacional Los Glaciares, Río Gallegos for the southern Atlantic Coast (these all have airports) and El Chaltén for Cerro (Mount) Fitz Roy.

Getting there

Fortunately Patagonia is served by good public transport. There are daily flights from Buenos Aires to Viedma, Puerto Madryn (in high season), Trelew, Comodoro Rivadavia, Río Gallegos, El Calafate's airport Lago Argentino and also to Ushuaia. **Aerolíneas Argentinas** ① *freecall from within Argentina T0810-222 86527, www.aerolineas.com.ar*, and **LADE** ① *freecall from within Argentina T0810-810 5233, www.lade.com.ar*, fly these routes, and flights fill up very quickly, so it's vital that you book in advance in the summer (December to March) and during the winter ski season for Ushuaia (July and August). At other times of the year, flights can be booked with just a few days' warning. The Chilean airline, **Lan Chile** ① *freephone from within Chile T0600-526 2000, freecall from within Argentina T0810-999 9526, www.lan.com*, also flies to Ushuaia from Argentine destinations as well as from Punta Arenas, Puerto Montt and Santiago in Chile.

Getting around

Air Flying between the main towns in Patagonia is complicated and may involve flying all the way back to Buenos Aires, since connecting flights within Patagonia are only provided by the army airline **LADE**. Instead, to get between Puerto Madryn and Ushuaia or El Calafate, for example, your best bet is an overnight bus.

Road Long-distance buses cover the whole of Argentina, are very comfortable – if you choose *coche-cama* (bed seat) – and reasonably cheap. There are several daily services between all the towns in Patagonia, though tourist routes book up quickly. There are two main routes south: Ruta 3 along the Atlantic coast and Ruta 40 (made famous by Ernesto 'Che' Guevara on his motorcycle) running along the Argentine side of the Andes. This road is fabulously bleak and empty, mostly unsurfaced, and there is very little traffic, but a number of bus companies run daily services in summer for tourists between the lovely oasis of Los Antiguos on Lago Buenos Aires and El Chaltén. From Los Antiguos you can reach Chile and the Lago General Carrera, and from El Chaltén there are frequent services to El Calafate. Some buses stop over at Cueva de las Manos, and if you have the time (14 hours) it's a great way to get a feel for Patagonia, with fine views of the Andes and plenty of wildlife to be spotted.

Hiring a car gives you great flexibility if you want to be independent, but isn't recommended if you're travelling alone – not that you're at risk from people, since Patagonia's rural inhabitants are among the world's most friendly and helpful – but the elements are harsh, distances are enormous and if you run out of petrol or get a stone through your windscreen, it's not a place to be stranded alone. However, hire companies will now let you rent a car in one place and drop it off in another for a rather large but worthwhile fee, so you could consider combining flying with driving.

Driving and cycling in Patagonia require care and patience. Most of the roads are *ripio* (gravel) limiting driving speeds to 60 kph, or slower where surfaces are poor, and it's worth driving your hire car very carefully, as there are huge fines for dents or turning them over. Carry spare fuel, as service stations may be as much as 300 km apart, carry warm clothing in case of breakdown at night, and make sure your car has anti-freeze. There are lots of cattle grids (watch out for signs saying *guardaganados*) to be crossed with care. Hitchhiking is difficult, even on Ruta 3 in the tourist season, and hitching along Ruta 40 is only possible with a lot of luck and a little assistance from locals; it helps to speak good Spanish.

The Ruta 40 has become a long-distance favourite among hardy cyclists, and it is an amazing experience. But do your research first: winds are fierce; there are few places to get food and water and a complete absence of shade. A tent is essential, with camping allowed pretty much everywhere, but very few *hosterías* or places to stay.

Train One of the country's few long-distance railways, the Tren Patagónico (www.trenpatagonico-sa.com.ar), runs between Bariloche in the Lake District and Viedma on the east coast, a comfortable overnight service that also carries cars. Trains were cancelled in December 2013, but services were restarted in May 2014 only for a train to be derailed a month later. It is best check in advance if the service is running. While current service starts in Viedma, there is talk of extending it from Buenos Aires via Bahía Blanca.

Best time to visit
The summer months from December to mid-April are best for trekking. However, January should be avoided everywhere but the most remote places if possible, as this is when most Argentines go on holiday, and transport and accommodation are both heavily booked. Most hotels close from mid-April until mid-November, and many bus services don't operate. This is because temperatures in the south plummet to -20°C, making it very inhospitable. For Península Valdés, the season for spotting whales is between September and November, when all services are open.

Practicalities
Traveller's cheques are hard to change throughout Patagonia; it's easier and safer to use credit or debit cards to withdraw cash. There are ATMs in all the main towns in Patagonia (even in El Chaltén, which recently got its first).

Tourist information

There are tourist offices in even the smallest towns that have any tourist potential, although the best ones are inevitably in El Calafate and El Chaltén, with excellent information centres in Puerto Madryn, Trelew and Río Gallegos. Many have good websites, worth a look before you set off, some with links to hotels for booking accommodation: **Puerto Madryn** and **Península Valdés**, www.madryn.gov.ar; **Chubut province** (northern half of Patagonia), www.chubutur.gov.ar; **Santa Cruz province** (southern half of Patagonia), www.santacruz.gov.ar; **El Chaltén**, www.elchalten.com; **El Calafate**, www.turismo.elcalafate.gov.ar. Also worth visiting is the national parks site, www.parquesnacionales.gov.ar. For further information on towns and tourist services, try the site www.interpatagonia.com.

National parks and nature reserves

Parque Nacional Los Glaciares is the most famous park in Patagonia. At the northern end the main centre is El Chaltén for trekking around **Mount Fitz Roy** and at the southern end are the glaciers, reached from El Calafate. Both have *guardaparques* offices where staff speak English and other languages, hand out maps and can advise on where to walk and camp. See www.parquesnacionales.gov.ar (in Spanish) for more information.

Parque Nacional Perito Moreno is also spectacular, and well worth the considerable effort involved in reaching its remote lakes and mountains. Access is via the Ruta 40, but there is almost no infrastructure whatsoever and little information for visitors. The best way to see the park is to stay at an *estancia*, such as La Maipú, and ride horses into the park.

Marine life abounds on the Atlantic Coast in Península Valdés, reached by organized tour or hire car from Puerto Madryn. Although it's not a national park, this is a well-organized area for visits, with several *estancias* on the peninsula where you can stay in great comfort. Further south, **Parque Nacional Monte León** is reached by Ruta 3, you'll need your own transport, but there is a comfortable *hostería*. There are many other colonies of penguins and other sea life reserves along the Atlantic Coast. Unless you have your own transport it's best to take an organized tour to reach these, as services are few at the sites themselves.

Background

Patagonia was inhabited by various groups of indigenous peoples from thousands of years ago until colonization by the Europeans. The region gets its name from early Spanish settlers' first impressions of these native people: big feet (*pata* being the informal word for leg). The first European visitor to the coast of Patagonia was the Portuguese explorer Fernão Magalhães in 1519, who gave his name to the Magellan straits. This sea passage afforded ships a safer route through the southern extreme of the continent, going north of the island of Tierra del Fuego, rather than heading south on the perilous route around Cape Horn. The first to traverse Patagonia from south to north was the English sailor, Carder, who survived a shipwreck in 1578 in the Strait of Magellan, walked north to the Río de la Plata and arrived in London nine years later.

For several centuries European attempts to settle along the coast were deterred by isolation, lack of food and water, and the harsh climate, as well as understandable resistance from the indigenous peoples. Sadly, the indigenous population was almost wiped out in the bloody war known as the Conquest of the Desert in 1879-1883 (see box, page 100). Before this there had been a European colony at Carmen de Patagones, which shipped salt to Buenos Aires, and a Welsh settlement in the Chubut Valley from 1865. After the Conquest of the Desert, colonization was rapid. Welsh, Scots and English farmers were among the biggest groups of immigrants; others included sheep farmers from Las Malvinas/Falkland Islands and Chilean sheep farmers from Punta Arenas moving eastwards into Santa Cruz. The discovery of large oil reserves in many areas of southern Patagonia brought wealth to Chubut and Santa Cruz provinces in the 1900s. However, when President Menem privatized the national oil company YPF in the 1990s, much of that wealth immediately diminished. One of the few people to gain from it all was the former president, Néstor Kirchner (husband of Argentina's current president, Christina Kirchner), who had been governor of Santa Cruz province while it was rich and influential within the country.

Northern Atlantic Coast and Puerto Madryn

The sight of a mother and baby whale basking in quiet waters just a few metres from your boat is an unforgettably moving sight. Not, perhaps, what you expected to see after travelling for days through the wild, unpopulated, open plains of Patagonia. But the whole Atlantic coast hosts huge colonies of marine life, and there is no region quite as spectacular as Península Valdés. This wide splay of land stretching into the Atlantic from a narrow isthmus enclosing a gulf of protected water attracts an astonishing array of animals which come to breed here each spring, most famously the southern right whales, who can be seen from September to November. The small breezy town of Puerto Madryn is the best base for exploring the peninsula, though there are *estancias* on Valdés itself. Just to the south, Trelew is worth a visit for its superb palaeontological museum, and as a base to reach the old Welsh pioneer villages of Gaiman and Dolavon further west. If you're heading south by road, consider stopping off at historic Carmen de Patagones, a quaint Patagonian town. Patagonia's fine *estancias* start here, with riding and sheep mustering at La Luisa.

Viedma and Carmen de Patagones → *For listings, see pages 519-527.*
Colour map 5, A5.

These two towns straddle the broad sweep of the Río Negro, about 250 km south of Bahía Blanca, and while neither has any real tourist attractions, you could stop off here on the way south and find warm hospitality and a couple of decent places to stay. The two towns face each other and share a river, but little else. Capital of Río Negro province, Viedma, on the south bank, was founded as Mercedes de Patagonia in 1779 but was destroyed almost immediately by floods, after which Carmen de Patagones was founded on higher ground on the north bank later that same year. The little town prospered for many years by shipping salt to Buenos Aires. However, in 1827, it was the site of an extraordinary battle and was destroyed. Poor old Viedma was rebuilt, but destroyed again by floods in 1899. Now, it's a rather dull place, rather less attractive than Patagones, and serves as the administrative centre for the province of Río Negro. Patagones (as it's called by the locals) has more tangible history, with the towers of a handsome church thrusting above charming streets of 19th-century adobe houses near the river, where the tiny ferry takes you across to Viedma, and there's a fabulous little museum.

Viedma → *Phone code 02920. Population 80,000.*

Viedma is quite different in character from Carmen de Patagones: it's the provincial administrative centre, rather than the home of farmers and landowners. An attractive *costanera* runs by the river, with large grassy banks shaded by willow trees, and the river water is pleasantly warm in summer and clean, good for swimming. On a calm summer's evening, when groups gather to sip *mate*, the scene resembles Seurat's painting of bathers.

There are two plazas. The cathedral, built by the Salesians (1912), is on the west of Plaza Alsina, with a former convent next door. This was the first chapel built by the Salesians (1887) in the area and is now a cultural centre housing the **Museo del Agua y del Suelo** and the **Museo Cardenal Cagliero**, which has ecclesiastical artefacts. Two blocks east, on Plaza San Martín, is the French-style **Casa de Gobierno** (1926). Most diverting, though, is the **Museo Gardeliano** ① *Rivadavia y Colón (1st floor)*, a fabulous collection of biographical artefacts of tango singer Carlos Gardel. It also has a space for cultural events. The entire Manzana Histórica (historical centre), including the Museo Gardeliano, was under review in 2013-2014 and many of the buildings were closed or abandoned. Along the attractive *costanera*, the **Centro Cultural**, opposite Calle 7 de Marzo, houses a small **Mercado Artesanal** selling beautifully made Mapuche weavings and woodwork. The **Municipal tourist office** ① *Av Francisco de Viedma 51, T02920-427171, www.viedma.gov.ar, daily 0900-2100*, is helpful. There is also a **provincial tourist office** ① *Av Caseros 1425, T02920-422150, www.rionegrotur.gob.ar (Spanish only), Mon-Fri 0700-1400, 1800-2000*. The bus terminal ① *Av Pte Perón and Guido, www.terminalpatagonia.com.ar*, is 15 blocks from the plaza; a taxi to town costs US$3.50.

Carmen de Patagones → *Population 18,189.*

This is the more dynamic of the two towns (which isn't saying much), with a feeling of bustle on the main street on weekday mornings. The town centre, just east of the river, lies around the Plaza 7 de Mayo, and just west is the **Iglesia del Carmen**, built by the Salesians in 1880. Take a stroll down the pretty streets winding down to the river to find many early pioneer buildings along the riverside: the **Torre del Fuerte**, tower of the stone fortress built in 1780 against indigenous attacks; the **Casa de la Tahona**, a disused 18th-century flour mill now housing the **Casa de la Cultura**; and another late-colonial building, **La Carlota**, one block east. Nearby there's the fascinating **Museo Histórico Regional 'Emma Nozzi'** ① *JJ Biedma 64, T02920-462729, Mon-Fri 1000-1200, 1500-1700, Sat-Sun and bank holidays 1700-1900*, which gives a great insight into early pioneer life. There are Tehuelche arrowheads, stone *boleadoras*, silver gaucho stirrups and great early photos (one of a baptism by Salesians of a 100-year-old Tehuelche man in a field), next to delicate tea cups. There are guided tours too. The **Museo de la Prefectura Naval** ① *Mitre s/n y Costanera, T02920-461742, Mon-Fri 0800-1230*, is also worth a look if you're into ships – it's housed in a building dating from 1886 and contains a marine history of the area.

Patagones is linked to Viedma by two bridges and a very small ferry which takes four minutes and leaves every 15 minutes, US$1. There's a helpful and dynamic **tourist office** ① *Mitre 84, T02920-464819, www.patagones.gov.ar*. The town is packed out for the **Fiesta de 7 de Marzo**, which celebrates the victory at the Battle of Patagones. It's great fun but make sure you book accommodation in advance. ▸ *For more information, see Festivals, page 524.*

South of Viedma and Carmen de Patagones

This whole stretch of coast is great for shore fishing, with *pejerrey*, variada and even shark among the many other species. Equipment is available in Viedma (see Shopping, page 524). There's a well-established little fishing resort at **Bahía San Blas**, 100 km east of Patagones, an area renowned for its shark fishing, with plentiful accommodation. For more information, see www.bahiasanblas.com.

At **El Cóndor**, 30 km south of Viedma (three buses daily in summer), there is a beautiful beach (also known as La Boca), with the oldest lighthouse in the country, dating from 1887. Facilities include a hotel, restaurants and shops (open January and February only) and a tourist office, open daily 0900-2200. There's free camping on a beach 2 km south. **Playa Bonita**, 12 km further southwest is known as a good fishing spot, and offers more good beaches. Ask the tourist office for their leaflet about the *Lobería Punta Bermeja*, 60 km west of Viedma. This sea lion colony is visited by some 2500 sea lions in summer, which you can see at close range (daily bus in summer; but hitching is easy). There's also an impressive visitor centre (with toilets).

Puerto Madryn → *For listings, see pages 519-527. Colour map 5, B5.*

The undoubted highlight of the whole Atlantic Coast in Patagonia is the splendid array of marine wildlife on Península Valdés, best visited from Puerto Madryn. This seaside town has a grand setting on the wide bay of Golfo Nuevo and is the perfect base for setting off to Valdés to the east, as there are plenty of hotels and reliable tour operators running excursions to the peninsula, including boat trips to see the whales. Puerto Madryn itself is a good place to enjoy the sea for a couple of days, with lots of beachfront restaurants selling superb locally caught seafood.

Arriving in Puerto Madryn → *Phone code 02965. Population 74,000.*

Getting there **El Tehuelche Airport** ① *T02965-445 6774*, is 8 km west of the centre and can be reached by taxi, US$17. More frequent flights serve Trelew airport (see page 515), some 60 km south, with buses to Puerto Madryn that meet all flights, US$4; the journey takes one hour. The **bus terminal** ① *Av Dr Ávila, entre Necochea e Independencia, T02965-445 1789*, has a café, toilets, *locutorio* and a small but helpful tourist office.

Getting around The city centre is easy to get around on foot, with many restaurants and hotels lined up along the seafront at Avenida Roca, and most shops and excursion companies on the streets around 28 de Julio, which runs perpendicular to the sea and past the town's neat little plaza, all contained within four or five blocks.

Tourist information Efficient and friendly, the **tourist information centre** ① *Av Roca 223, just off 28 de Julio, T02965-445 3504, www.madryn.travel, Mar-Nov daily 0700-2100, Dec-Feb daily 0700-2200*, is found on the seafront, next to the shopping complex; there's another branch at the **bus station** ① *daily 0700-2100*. The staff are extremely well organized and speak English and French. They have leaflets on Península Valdés and accommodation, and can advise on tours.

Background
Puerto Madryn was the site of the first Welsh landing in 1865 and is named after the Welsh home of the colonist, Jones Parry. However, it wasn't officially founded until 1889, when the railway was built connecting the town with Trelew to enable

Puerto Madryn

Where to stay 🏨		
1 ACA Camping		
2 Australis Yene Hue	9 Hostería Viajeros	**Restaurants** 🍴
Hotel and Spa	10 La Tosca Hostel	2 Several food
3 Bahía Nueva	11 Marina	& drink places
5 Chepatagonia	12 Muelle Viejo	3 Bomke
6 El Gualicho	13 Península Valdés	5 Lizard Café
7 El Retorno	15 Tolosa	6 Los Colonos
8 Hostería Las Maras	16 Yiliana Hostel	8 Placido
		9 Rosendo
		10 Taska Beltza

the Welsh living in the Chubut Valley to export their produce. The town is a modern, relaxed and friendly place, and hasn't been ruined by its popularity as a tourist resort, with a large workforce occupied by its other main industry: a huge aluminium plant (which you can visit by arrangement through the tourist office). Accommodation is generally of a high standard, but can be pricey. This is one of several tourist centres in Argentina where higher rates apply for foreigners than Argentines for hotel rooms and some entrance fees; it's hopeless to argue.

Places in Puerto Madryn

You're most likely to be visiting the town to take an excursion to Península Valdés (see below), but there are other tourist sights closer to hand. In the town itself, the real pleasure is the sea, and it's a pleasant first day's stroll along the long stretch of beach to **El Indio**, a statue on the road at the southeastern end of the bay, marking the gratitude of the Welsh to the native Tehuelche people whose shared expertise ensured their survival. As the road curves up the cliff here, don't miss the a splendid **EcoCentro** ① *Julio Verne 3784, T02965-445 7470, www.ecocentro.org.ar, Wed-Mon 1500-2000 (2100 high season), US$9*. This interactive sea-life information centre combines an art gallery, café and fabulous reading room with comfy sofas at the top of a turret. The whole place has fantastic views of the bay.

Just a little closer to town, perched on the cliff, is the tiny **Centro de Exposición de Punta Cuevas** ① *daily 1700-2100, www.puntacuevas.org.ar, US$2.50*, of interest if you're tracing the history of the Welsh in Patagonia. It's little more than a couple of rooms of relics near the caves and basic huts on the cliffs where the settlers first lived, but enthusiastic guides make the visit worthwhile. A more conventional museum, with displays on local flora and fauna, is the **Museo de Ciencias Naturales y Oceanográfico** ① *Domecq García y J Menéndez, T02965-445 1139, Mon-Fri 0900-2000, Sat 1600-2000, US$1.50*, which is informative and worth a visit.

Around Puerto Madryn

During the right season, you can spot whales at the long beach of **Playa El Doradillo**, 16 km northeast of town, along the *ripio* road closest to the coast. There are also sea lions at the **Punta Loma Reserve** ① *daily 0900-1700, US$8, child US$4, many companies offer tours*, 15 km southeast of Puerto Madryn and best visited at low tide in December and January. Access is via the coastal road from town and, like the road to the north, makes a great bike ride; allow 1½ hours to get there. Puerto Madryn is Patagonia's **diving** capital, with dives to see wildlife and many off-shore wrecked ships, together with all kinds of courses from beginners' dives to the week-long PADI course on offer from tour operators, such as **Puerto Madryn Buceo**. You can also hire mountain bikes and windsurfing boards here, from many places along the beachfront. ⏩ *For more information, see What to do, page 524.*

Whatever time of year you visit Península Valdés you'll find a wonderful array of marine life, birds and a profusion of Patagonian wildlife such as guanacos, rheas, Patagonian hares and armadillos. But in spring (September-November), this treeless splay of land is host to a quite spectacular numbers of whales, penguins and seals, who come to breed in the sheltered waters south of the narrow Ameghino isthmus and on beaches at the foot of the peninsula's chalky cliffs. The land is almost flat, though greener than much of Patagonia, and at the heart of the peninsula are large salt flats, one of which, **Salina Grande**, is 42 m below sea level. The peninsula is privately owned – many of its *estancias* offering comfortable and wonderfully remote places to stay in the middle of the wild beauty – but it is also a nature reserve and was declared a World Heritage Site by UNESCO in 1999. The beach along the entire coast is out of bounds and this is strictly enforced. The main tourist centre on the peninsula is **Puerto Pirámides**, on the southern side, which has a few good hotels and hostels, places to camp and a handful of restaurants.

Arriving on Península Valdés

Getting there and around Península Valdés can most easily be visited by taking one of the many well-organized full-day excursions from Puerto Madryn (see Tour operators, page 525). These usually include a whale-watching boat trip, which departs from Puerto Pirámides (see below), together with a stop or two on the eastern coastline to see sea lions, penguins and other wildlife at close hand. Minibus travel, the boat trip and transfers to your hotel are included, but not lunch or entrance to the peninsula.

If you'd rather see the peninsula independently, you can hire a car relatively inexpensively for a group of four, and then take a boat trip to see the whales (September to November) from Puerto Pirámides. Note that distances are long on the peninsula, and roads beyond Puerto Pirámides are *ripio*, so take your time – hire companies charge a heavy excess if you damage the car. A cheaper option is the daily bus to Puerto Pirámides with **Mar y Valle**, leaving Puerto Madryn's terminal daily at 0855, returning at 1900, 1½ hours, US$8 each way. This would only allow you to see the whales though, since there is no public transport to other areas of the peninsula. To explore the peninsula in more detail and gain closer contact with nature, a stay one of the peninsula's *estancias* is recommended.

Tourist information Information is available from the tourist office in Puerto Madryn (see above) and from the interpretation centre on the peninsula (see below). There is also a **tourist office** ① *1ra Bajada al Mar, near the beach, T02965-449 5084, www.puertopiramides.gov.ar*, in Puerto Pirámides, offering useful information for hikes and driving tours.

Best time to visit Much of Península Valdés' wildlife can be enjoyed throughout the year, with sea lions, elephant seals, dolphins and many species of bird permanently resident. The bull elephant seals can be seen fighting for females from September to early November, and killer whales can sometimes be sighted off the coast at this time too, staying until April. Penguins can be seen from September to March, and the stars of the show, the southern right whales, come to these waters to breed in spring (September to November).

Around the Peninsula → *The following are the main marine wildlife colonies.*
The entrance to the reserve is about 45 km northeast of Puerto Madryn, where you buy the **ticket** ① *administration T02965-445 0489, www.peninsulavaldes.org.ar, daily 0800-2100 (2000 in low season), US$21 for foreigners, children US$10.50*, for visiting all the sites on the peninsula. Twenty kilometres beyond, on the isthmus, there's an interesting **interpretation centre** with stuffed examples of the local fauna, many fossils and a wonderful whale skeleton, which makes a great complement to seeing the real thing gracefully soaring through the water. Ask for the informative bilingual leaflet on southern right whales.

Isla de los Pájaros, is in the Golfo San José, 5 km from the interpretation centre. Its seabirds can be viewed through fixed telescopes (at 400 m distance), since only recognized ornithologists can get permission to visit the island itself. Between September and April you can spot wading birds, herons, cormorants and terns.

Caleta Valdés, 45 km south of Punta Norte in the middle of the eastern shore, has huge colonies of elephant seals which can be seen at close quarters. In the breeding season, from September to October, you'll see the rather unappealing blubbery masses of bull seals hauling themselves up the beach to make advances to one of the many females in their harem. During the first half of August the bull seals arrive to claim their territory, and can be seen at low tide engaging in bloody battles over the females. At **Punta Cantor**, just south of here, you'll find a good café and clean toilets. There are also three marked walks, ranging from 45 minutes to two hours. **Estancia La Elvira** is a short distance inland from here, and is clearly signposted.

Punta Delgada, at the southeastern end of the peninsula, 110 km from the entrance, is where elephant seals and sea lions can be seen from the high cliffs in such large numbers that they seem to stretch out like a velvety bronze tide line on the beautiful beach below. It's mesmerizing to watch as the young frolic in the shallow water and the bulls lever themselves around the females. There's a hotel nearby, **Faro Punta Delgada** (see Where to stay, page 521), which is a good base for exploring this beautiful area further.

Punta Norte, at the northern end of the peninsula, 97 km from the entrance, is not often visited by the excursion companies, but it has colonies of elephant seals and sea lions. Killer whales (orca) have also been seen here, feeding on sea lion pups at low tide in March and April. **Estancia San Lorenzo** is nearby.

There are several *estancias* on the peninsula which allow you to really appreciate the space and natural beauty of the land, and give you much more access to some of the most remote places, with great wildlife to observe. Ask the tourist office for advice. Day trips to the *estancias* can also be arranged, which might include wildlife trips, an *asado* and perhaps horse riding. For further details, see Where to stay, page 521.

Whale watching from Puerto Pirámides → *Colour map 5, B5. Population 429.*
Puerto Pirámides, 107 km east of Puerto Madryn, is the departure point for whale-watching boat trips, which leave from its broad sandy beach. Every year, between June and December, 400 to 500 southern right whales migrate to the Golfo Nuevo to mate and give birth. It is without doubt one of the best places in the world to watch these beautiful animals, since in many cases the whales come within just a few metres of the coast. From Puerto Pirámides, boat trips take you gently close to basking whales; if you're lucky, you may find yourself next to a mother and baby. Sailings are controlled by the Prefectura (Naval Police), according to weather and sea conditions; if you're very prone to sea sickness, think twice before setting off on a windy day.

On land, a 3-km track (beware of the incoming tide), or a 15-km ripio road go to a *mirador* at Punta Pardelas where you can see the whales. The prevailing currents may throw smelly carcasses of the young whales who didn't make it onto the beach. Camping is allowed, but there are no services nor drinking water.

Trelew and the Chubut Valley → *For listings, see pages 519-527.*

The Río Chubut is one of the most important rivers in Patagonia, flowing a massive 820 km from the eastern foothills of the Andes into the Atlantic at Bahía Engaño. It's thanks to the Río Chubut that the Welsh pioneers came to this part of the world in 1865, and their irrigation of the arid land around it enabled them to survive and prosper. You can trace their history west along the valley from the pleasant airy town of Trelew to the quiet little village of Gaiman, which has a wonderful museum and cafés serving traditional Welsh afternoon tea. Further west, past little brick chapels sitting amidst lush green fields, is the quieter settlement of Dolavon. If you're keen to investigate further into the past, there's a marvellous museum full of dinosaurs in Trelew and some ancient fossils in the Parque Palaeontológico Bryn-Gwyn near Gaiman. From Trelew you could also visit South America's largest single colony of Magellanic penguins on the coast at Punta Tombo.

Trelew → *Colour map 5, B5. Phone code 02965. Population 90,000.*
Some 70 km south of Puerto Madryn, Trelew is the largest town in the Chubut Valley. Founded in 1884, it was named in honour of Lewis Jones, an early settler, and the Welsh colonization is still evident in a few remaining chapels in the town's modern centre. It's a cheerful place with a quietly busy street life, certainly more appealing than the industrial town of Rawson, 20 km east on the coast. Trelew boasts a splendid paleontological museum, a great tourist office and a couple of fabulous cafés.

Arriving in Trelew The airport is 5 km north of centre. A taxi costs US$7 and local buses to/from Puerto Madryn will stop at the airport entrance if asked. The **bus terminal** is on the east side of Plaza Centenario at Urquiza y Lewis Jones, T02965-442 0121. On the main plaza you'll find the very helpful **tourist office** ① *Mitre 387, T02965-422 0139, Mon-Fri 0800-2000, Sat-Sun 0900-2100*; also at bus station (same opening times) and at the airport when flights arrive. They'll give you an excellent map, directing you to the town's older buildings. Useful websites include www. trelewturismo.wordpress.com (in Spanish only) and www.trelewpatagonia.gov.ar.

Places in Trelew There's the lovely shady **Plaza Independencia** in the town centre, packed with mature trees, and hosting a small handicraft market at weekends. Nearby is the **Capilla Tabernacle**, on Belgrano between San Martín and 25 de Mayo, a red-brick Welsh chapel dating from 1889. Heading east, rather more impressive is the **Salon San David** ⓘ *Mon-Fri 0900-1300, extended hours during Sep-Oct*, a Welsh meeting hall first used for the Eisteddfod of 1913. It has a mini-museum of objects donated by descendants of the Welsh settlers and also organizes Welsh language and dance classes. On the road to Rawson, 3 km south, you'll find one of the oldest standing Welsh chapels, **Capilla Moriah**. Built in 1880, it has a simple interior and a cemetery with the graves of many original settlers, including the first white woman born in the Welsh colony.

Back in Trelew itself, not the oldest but quite the most wonderful building is the 1920s **Hotel Touring Club** ⓘ *Fontana 240, www.touringpatagonia.com.ar*. This was the town's grandest hotel in its heyday. Politicians and travellers met in its glorious high-ceilinged mirrored bar, which is now full of old photographs and relics. You can eat lunch here and there's simple accommodation available; you should also ask the friendly owner if you can see the elegant 1920s meeting room at the back: almost perfectly preserved.

The town's best museum – and indeed one of the finest in Argentina – is the **Museo Paleontológico Egidio Feruglio** ⓘ *Fontana 140, T02965-442 0012, www.mef.org.ar, Sep-Mar daily 0900-1900, Apr-Aug Mon-Fri 1000-1800, Sat-Sun 1000-1900, US$8, full disabled access, guides for the blind*. Imaginatively designed and beautifully presented, the museum traces the origins of life through the geological ages, displaying dynamically poised dinosaur skeletons, with plentiful information in Spanish. Tours are free and are available in English, German and Italian. There's also a reasonably cheap café and a shop. It's highly recommended and great for kids. For details of the **Geoparque Bryn Gwyn** near Gaiman, see below.

The **Museo Regional Pueblo de Luis** ⓘ *Fontana and Lewis Jones 9100, T02965-442 4062, Mon-Fri 0800-2000, Sat-Sun 1400-2000, US$2*, is appropriately housed in the old railway station, built in 1889, since it was Lewis Jones who founded the town and started the railways that exported Welsh produce so successfully. It has interesting displays on indigenous societies, on failed Spanish attempts at settlement, and on Welsh colonization. Next to the tourist office is the **Museo Municipal de Artes Visuales** ⓘ *MMAV, Mitre 350, T02965-443 3774, Mon-Fri 0800-2000, Sat-Sun 1400-1900, free*, located in an attractive wooden building. Recommended.

South of Trelew

There is a lovely rock and sand beach at **Playa Isla Escondida**, 55 km south of Trelew along unpaved Ruta 1, which is a possible route to Punta Tombo. It's a favourite spot for sports fishermen, and you can see sea elephants, sea lions and birds here. There's secluded camping but no facilities. The main destination to the

Welsh Patagonia

Among the tales of early pioneers to Argentina, the story of Welsh emigration, in search of religious freedom, is one of the most impressive. The first 165 settlers arrived in Patagonia in July 1865. Landing on the bay where Puerto Madryn now stands, they went south in search of drinking water to the valley of the Chubut river, where they found cultivatable land and settled.

The settlement was partly inspired by Michael D Jones, a non-conformist minister whose aim was to create a 'little Wales beyond Wales', far from the intruding influence of the English restrictions on Welsh religious beliefs. He provided much of the early finance and took particular care to gather people with useful skills, such as farmers and craftsmen, recruiting settlers through the Welsh language press and through the chapels. Between 1865 and 1915, the colony was reinforced by another 3000 settlers from Wales. The early years brought persistent drought, and the Welsh only survived through creating a network of irrigation channels. Early settlers were allocated 100 ha of land

and when, by 1885, all irrigable land had been allocated, the settlement expanded westwards along the valley to the town of Trevelin in the foothills of the Andes.

The Welsh colony was tremendously successful, partly due to the creation of *its* own cooperative society, which sold their excellent produce and bought necessities in Buenos Aires. Early settlers were organized into chapel-based communities of 200 to 300 people, which were largely self-governing and organized social and cultural activities. The colony thrived after 1880, producing wheat from the arid Chubut Valley which won prizes all over the world. However, the depression of the 1930s drove wheat prices down, and poor management by the Argentine government resulted in the downfall of the Welsh wheat business. Many of the Welsh stayed, however; most of the owners of Gaiman's extraordinary Welsh tea rooms are descendants of the original settlers. The Welsh language is kept alive in both Gaiman and Trevelin, and Gaiman's festival of the arts – Eisteddfod – is held every October.

south, however is the **Reserva Natural Punta Tombo** ⓘ *www.puntatombo.com, daily 0800-1800 in high season, US$9.50, children US$5*, which is the largest breeding ground for Magallenic penguins in Patagonia and the largest single penguin colony on the South American continent. The nature reserve is best visited from September to March, when huge numbers of Magallenic penguins come here to breed. Chicks can be seen from mid-November and they waddle to the water in January or February. It's fascinating to see these creatures up close, but noisy colonies of tourists dominate the place in the morning; it's quieter in the afternoon. You'll see guanacos, hares and rheas on the way.

To reach the reserve follow Ruta 1 for 100 km south towards Camarones; this is a ripio road best attempted in a high clearance vehicles. Alternatively, take paved

Ruta 3 south, then turn onto Ruta Provincial 75 until it reaches Ruta 1, 122 km in total. Tours from Trelew and Puerto Madryn cost US$70, allow 45 minutes at the site and usually include a stop at Gaiman.

Gaiman → *Colour map 5, B4. Phone code 02965.*

The quaint village of Gaiman lies west of Trelew, in the floodplain of the Río Chubut, and was made beautifully green and fertile thanks to careful irrigation of these lands by Welsh settlers. After travelling for a few days (or even hours) on the arid Patagonian steppe, it will strike you as a lush green oasis, testimony to the tireless hard work of those hardy Welsh emigrants. Gaiman is the first village you come to on Route 25, which heads west past Dolavon before continuing through attractive scenery to Esquel and the other Welsh colony of Trevelin in the Andes (see page 490). On the way, you'll find old Welsh chapels tucked away amongst the poplars in this green valley.

Gaiman is a pretty little place with old brick houses, which retains the Welsh pioneer feel despite the constant influx of tourists, and it hosts the annual Eisteddfod (Welsh Festival of Arts) in October. Around its pretty plaza you'll find the **tourist office** ① *Av Belgrano 574, T02965-449 1571, www.gaiman.gov.ar, Mon-Sat 0900-2000, Sun 1100-1800 (shorter hours in low season)*, and several tea rooms, many of them run by descendants of the original pioneers, serving delicious Welsh teas and cakes. Before you fill up on those, gain an insight into the spartan lives of those idealistic pioneers by visiting the **old railway station** (1909), which now houses the wonderful, tiny **Museo Histórico Regional Galés** ① *Sarmiento and 28 de Julio, T02965-449 1007, Tue-Sun 1500-1900, US$0.65*. This has an impressive collection of Welsh artefacts, objects and photographs that serve as an evocative and moving testimony to extraordinary lives in harsh conditions. It is a great resource if you're looking for books on the subject or trying to trace your emigrant relatives.

Many other older buildings remain, among them the low stone first house, **Primera Casa** (1874) ① *corner of main street, Av Tello y Evans, daily 1400-1900, US$1*; the old hotel (1899), at Tello and 9 de Julio; and the **Ty Nain tea room** (1890), on the Plaza at Yrigoyen 283. Cross the bridge to the south side of the river, and then take the first right to find two old chapels: pretty **Capilla Bethel** (1913) and the **Capilla Vieja**.

Some 8 km south of town, there are fossil beds dating back 40 million years at the **Geoparque Bryn Gwyn** ① *T02965-443 2100, www.mef.org.ar, Tue-Sun 1000-1600 US$2.50, taxi from Gaiman US$7*. This is a mind-boggling expanse of time brought to life by a good guided tour. It takes two hours to do the circuit, with fossils to see, as well as a visitor centre where you can try some fieldwork in palaeontology.

Dolavon → *Colour map 5, B4. Phone code 02965. Population 2700.*

Founded in 1919, Dolavon is the most westerly Welsh settlement in the valley and not quite as inviting as Gaiman, though its quiet streets are rather atmospheric, and on a short stroll you can find a few buildings reminiscent of the Welsh past. The main street, Avenida Roca, runs parallel to the irrigation canal built by the settlers, where willow trees now trail into the swiftly flowing water; there's a Welsh chapel, **Capilla Carmel**, at its quieter end. The old **flourmill** ① *T080-15-468 1212 (mobile phone,*

Mirna), Tue-Sun 1100-1600, US$2, at Maipú and Roca dates from 1927 and can be visited. There's **Autoservicio Belgrano** at the far end of San Martín for food supplies, but there is only one tea room, **El Molienda** ① *Maipú 61, T02804-492290, US$10*, and nowhere really to stay apart from the municipal campsite two blocks north of the river which is free and has good facilities.

If you're in your own transport, it's worth driving from Dolavon back towards Gaiman via the neat squared fields in this beautiful irrigated valley, where you'll see more Welsh chapels tucked away among poplar trees and silver birches. Follow the main road that leads south through Dolavon, and then turn left and take the next right, signposted to Iglesia Anglicana. The **San David Chapel** (1917) is a beautifully preserved brick construction, with an elegant bell tower and sturdy oak-studded door, in a quiet spot surrounded by birches. Further on you'll cross the raised irrigation canals the Welsh built, next to small orchards of apple trees and tidy fields bordered by *álamo* trees.

West of Dolavon
West from Dolavon, paved Ruta 25 runs to the upper Chubut Valley, passing near the **Florentino Ameghino** dam, 120 km west of Trelew, a leafy spot for a picnic. The road from Ameghino to Tecka (on the junction with Ruta 40 south of Trevelín) is one of the most beautiful routes across Patagonia to the Andes, with lots of wildlife to see. It goes through Las Plumas (mind the bridge if driving), reaching Los Altares at Km 321, which has an ACA motel (**$$**) with restaurant and bar, a basic campsite 400 m behind the service station, fuel and some shops. Beyond, Route 25 continues via Paso de Indios.

⦿ Northern Atlantic Coast and Puerto Madryn listings

For hotel and restaurant price codes and other relevant information, see pages 20-26.

⦿ Where to stay

Viedma and Carmen de Patagones
p508
The best places to stay are in Viedma.
$$$ Nijar, Mitre 490, T02920-422833, www.hotelnijar.com. Most comfortable, smart, modern, good service.
$$$ Peumayen, Buenos Aires 334, T02920-425222, www.hotelpeumayen.com.ar. Old-fashioned friendly place on the plaza.
$$ Res Roca, Roca 347, T431241. A cheap option with comfortable beds, helpful staff, breakfast included.

Camping
At the sea lion colony, **La Lobería**, T02920-428883, and **Trenitos**, T02920-497098; both have good facilities.

Puerto Madryn *p510, map p511*
Book ahead in summer and during whale-watching season.
$$$$ Australis Yene Hue Hotel and Spa, Roca 33, T02965-447 1214, www.hotelesaustralis.com.ar. Luxury hotel on the beachfront with a small spa, modern rooms, and nice buffet breakfast. Ask for a room with a view.
$$$$-$$$ Península Valdés, Av Roca 155, T02965-447 1292, www.hotel peninsula.com.ar. Luxurious seafront hotel with great views. Spa, sauna, gym.

$$$ Bahía Nueva, Av Roca 67, T02965-445 1677, www.bahianueva.com.ar. One of the best seafront hotels, quite small but comfortable rooms, professional staff, cheaper in low season.

$$$ Hostería Las Maras, Marcos A Zar 64, T02965-445 3215, www.hosteria lasmaras.com.ar. Nice modern place, well decorated rooms with large beds, cheaper with fan, parking.

$$$ Tolosa, Roque Sáenz Peña 253, T02965-447 1850, www.hoteltolosa. com.ar. Extremely comfortable, modern, great breakfasts. Disabled access. Recommended.

$$ Hostería Viajeros, Gob Maíz 545, T02965-445 6457, www.hostelviajeros. com.ar. Rooms for 2, 3 and 4 people, big kitchen/dining room, lawn, parking, new superior rooms on 2nd floor (**$$$**), helpful, family-run.

$$ Marina, Roca 7, T02965-447 1429, marina19852011@hotmail.com. Good value seafront apartments for up to 6 people, book ahead.

$$ Muelle Viejo, H Yrigoyen 38, T02965-447 1284, www.muelleviejo.com. Ask for the comfortable modernized rooms in this funny old place. Rooms for 4 are excellent value.

$ pp Chepatagonia, Alfonsina Storni 16, T02965-445 5783, www.chepatagonia hostel.com.ar. Good view of the beach (and whales in season), helpful owners, mixed and single dorms, doubles with shared bath (**$$**), lockers, bicycle hire and many other services. A good choice.

$ pp El Gualicho, Marcos A Zar 480, T02965-445 4163, www.elgualicho. com.ar. Best budget option, some double rooms (**$$**), HI discounts, nicely designed, enthusiastic owner, English-speaking staff, heating, free pick up from bus terminal, *parrilla*, garden, bikes for hire, runs tours with good

guides and value, parking, pool table. Highly recommended.

$ El Retorno, Bartomolmé Mitre 798, T02965-445 6044, www.elretornohostel. com.ar. 3 blocks from beach, hot water, lockers, cosy common area, free bus terminal pick-up. Double rooms available (**$$**). Also rents apartments with seaview (**$$$**).

$ pp La Tosca Hostel, Sarmiento 437, T02965-445 6133, www.latoscahostel. com. Dorms have bathrooms, free pick-up from bus station if you call them, helpful. Also has small but cosy doubles (**$$**). Organizes tours. Friendly and welcoming. Recommended.

$ pp Yiliana Hostel, Av Gales 268, T02965-447 5956, www.yilianahostel. com.ar. Family-run, dorms and private rooms (**$$** with bath), nice patio area, hot showers, laundry arranged, bike hire.

Camping

ACA, Blvd Brown 3860, 4 km south of town centre (at Punta Cuevas), T02965-445 2952, www.acamadryn.com.ar. Open year-round, hot showers, café, shop, also duplexes for 4-6, no kitchen facilities, shady trees, close to the sea. Cheaper rates Apr-Nov.

Península Valdés *p513*

The following are all in Puerto Pirámides; hotels are packed out in Jan and Feb.

$$$$-$$$ Las Restingas, 1ra Bajada al Mar, T02965-449 5101, www.lasrestingas. com. Exclusive, 8 rooms with sea views, very comfortable, with sophisticated regional restaurant. Good deals available in low season.

$$$ ACA Motel, Julio A Roca s/n, T02965-449 5004, www.motelacapir amides.com. Welcoming, handy for the beach, with good seafood restaurant (you might spot whales from its terrace).

There is also an ACA service station (daily) with good café and shop.

$$$ Cabañas en el Mar, Av de las Ballenas y 1ra Bajada al Mar, T02965-449 5049, www.piramides.net. Comfortable, well-equipped 2-6 bed *cabañas* with sea view.

$$$ Del Nómade, Av de las Ballenas s/n, T02965-449 5044, www.ecohosteria. com.ar. Eco lodge using solar power and water recycling, buffet breakfast, heating, café, specializes in wildlife watching, nature and underwater photography, kayaking, scuba diving, adventure sports, courses offered.

$$$ The Paradise, 2da Bajada al Mar, T02965-449 5030, www.hosteriaparadise. com.ar. Large comfortable rooms, suites with jacuzzis, fine seafood restaurant.

$$ La Nube del Angel, 2da Bajada al Mar, T02965-449 5070. Open all year. Lovely owners, small *cabañas* for 2-6 people, quiet, 5 mins' walk from the beach.

Camping

Municipal campsite by the black sand beach, T02965-449 5084. Hot showers in evening, good, get there early to secure a place. Do not camp on the beach: people have been swept away by the incoming tide.

Estancias

For more *estancias* in Patagonia, see www.interpatagonia.com/estancias.

$$$$ El Pedral, Punta Ninfas, T011-5272 0342, www.elpedral.com. By a pebble beach, with lots of wildlife-watching opportunities, farm activities, horse riding, zodiac trips (extra), guesthouse with en-suite rooms, restaurant and bar, swimming pool.

$$$$ Faro Punta Delgada, Punta Delgada, T02965-445 8444, www.punta delgada.com. Next to a lighthouse, amazing setting, half and full board, excellent food, very helpful. Recommended; book in advance, no credit cards.

$$$ La Elvira, Caleta Valdés, near Punta Cantor, T02965-420 1482 (office in Puerto Madryn Av Roca 835, local 3, T02965-445 8820), www.laelvira.com.ar. Traditional Patagonian dishes and comfortable accommodation (B&B, half and full board available).

$$$ San Lorenzo, on RP3, 20 km southwest of Punta Norte, T02965-445 8444 (contact through **Argentina Visión** in Puerto Madryn, see Tour operators). Great for day excursions to a beautiful stretch of coast to see penguins, fossils, birdwatching and horse treks.

Trelew *p515*

$$$$-$$$ La Casona del Río, Chacra 105, Capitán Murga, T02965-443 8343, www.lacasonadelrio.com.ar. 5 km from town, pick-up arranged, attractive, family-run B&B with heating, TV, meals available, bicycles, massage, laundry, tennis and bowls, English and French spoken. Higher prices Feb-Jul.

$$$ Galicia, 9 de Julio 214, T02965-443 3802, www.hotelgalicia.com.ar. Central, grand entrance, comfortable rooms, excellent value. Recommended.

$$$ Libertador, Rivadavia 31, T02965-442 0220, www.hotellibertadortw.com. Modern hotel, highly recommended for service and comfortable bedrooms.

$$$ Rayentray, Belgrano 397, cnr San Martín, T02965-443 4702, www.cadena rayentray.com.ar. Large, modern, comfortable rooms, professional staff, pool, Wi-Fi.

$$ Rivadavia, Rivadavia 55, T02965-443 4472, www.rivadaviahotel. com.ar. Simple, comfortable rooms, breakfast extra.

$$ Touring Club, Fontana 240, Peatonal Luis Gazín, T02965-443 3997, www.touringpatagonia.com.ar. Gorgeous 1920s bar, faded elegance, simple rooms, great value, breakfast included. Open from breakfast to the small hours for sandwiches and drinks. Wi-Fi in rooms and bar. Recommended.

Camping

Camping Patagonia, R7 and Rawson, 11 km from town, T0280-1544 6907, leave Trelew on R7 in the direction of Rawson, pass a roundabout, the road bends sharply to the right, take right fork, a *ripio* road, and the campsite is after 3 blocks on the right. Pretty site with *parrilla*, hot showers, football pitch and *proveduría* (food shop). US$5 per person.

Gaiman *p518*

$$$$-$$$ Posada Los Mimbres, Chacra 211, 6 km west of Gaiman, T02965-449 1299, www.posadalosmimbres.com.ar. Rooms in the old farmhouse or in modern building, good food, very relaxing, cheaper Apr-Aug.

$$$-$$ Ty Gwyn, 9 de Julio 111, T02965-449 1009, tygwyn@tygwyn.com.ar. Neat, comfortable, above the tea rooms, excellent value.

$$ Hostería Ty'r Haul, Sarmiento 121, T02965-449 1880, www.hosteriatyrhaul.com.ar. Historic building, rooms are comfortable and well-lit. Recommended.

$$ Plas y Coed, Yrigoyen 320, T02965-449 1133, www.plasycoed.com.ar. Marta Rees' delightful tea shop has double and twin rooms in an annex next door. Highly recommended.

Camping

Camping de los Bomberos is the municipal site.

● Restaurants

Viedma and Carmen de Patagones *p508*

$$ La Balsa, on the river at Colón and Villarino. By far the best restaurant, inexpensive with a pleasant atmosphere. Delicious seafood accompanied a bottle of superb Río Negro wine, Humberto Canale Merlot, is highly recommended.

Puerto Madryn *p510, map p511*

One of the unmissable pleasures of Puerto Madryn is its great seafood. While you're here, try at least one plate of *arroz con mariscos* (rice with a whole selection of squid, prawns, mussels and clams). Most restaurants are mid-range and charge around the same price, but differ widely in quality. The block of 9 de Julio between 25 de Mayo and Mitre has an interesting mix of food and drink places, including a winebar, a craft beer pub and several restaurants.

$$$ Placido, Av Roca 506, T02965-445 5991, www.placido.com.ar. On the beach, great location and service, but food can be hit and miss. Seafood and vegetarian options, also cheaper pasta dishes.

$$$ Taska Beltza, 9 de Julio 461, T02965-447 4003, closed Mon. Excellent food with a Basque influence – book ahead. Highly recommended.

$$ Los Colonos, Av Roca y A Storni, T02965-445 8486. Quirky, cosy restaurant built into the wooden hull of a boat, plenty of maritime heritage, *parrilla*, seafood and pastas.

$ Rosendo, Av Roca 549, 1st floor. Open lunchtime and evenings in high season, from 1700 in low season. Snack bar/café overlooking the main street. Excellent home-made *empanadas*, snacks, cocktails and wines. Reading and games room. Recommended.

Cafés
Bomke, Av Roca 542. Popular ice cream place with outdoor seating at the back. Excellent ice creams. Recommended.

Península Valdés *p513*
There are many restaurants on the main street in Puerto Pirámides and reasonably priced ones at Punta Norte, Punta Cantor and the Faro in Punta Delgada. These recommendations are on the beach:

$$$ Las Restingas, Primera Bajada on the beach, Puerto Pirámides, T0280-4495101, www.lasrestingas.com/eng/hotel/hotel.php. Perfect for a romantic dinner, sea views and tranquillity. An imaginative menu combines quality local produce with a touch of sophistication.

$$ The Paradise, Av De los Bellenas y Segunda Bajada, T0280-4495030,www.hosteriatheparadise.com.ar/inicio_i.html. Just off the beach, good atmosphere and great seafood. Also offers lamb and a few vegetarian choices.

$$ Quimey Quipan, Primera Bajada opposite Las Restingas, Puerto Pirámides, T02965-458 609. By the beach and next to **Tito Bottazzi**, this family-run place specializes in delicious seafood with rice and has a cheap set menu. Always open for lunch, ring to reserve for dinner. Recommended.

$ Margarita Resto Bar, Av R Sáenz Peña 27, Puerto Pirámides, T0280 447 5871, open from 2100. Midway along the main street, small and intimate bar serving light meals.

$ Towanda, 1ra Bajada al Mar s/n, Puerto Pirámides, T02965-447 3806. Quirky café and snack bar with outside seating overlooking the main street and beach. Friendly staff, recommended.

Trelew *p515*
$$ La Bodeguita, Belgrano 374, T02965-443 7777. Delicious pastas and pizzas. Reasonable wine list. Recommended.

$$ La Casona, Pasaje Jujuy and Lewis Jones, near Plaza Centenario. Patagonian lamb, *parrilla*, good lunctime venue.

$$ Miguel Angel, next door to Touring Club (see Where to stay), in Peatonal Luis Gazín, Av Fontana. Good standard fare of meat and pasta dishes.

Cafés
Café de mi Ciudad, Belgrano 394. Smart café serving great coffee; read the papers here. Also has Wi-Fi.

Café Verdi, attached to Teatro Verdi, San Martín 130. Home-made waffles, pizzas and pasta, drinks.

Gaiman *p518*
Welsh teas
You're unlikely to be able to resist the Welsh teas for which Gaiman has become famous, though quite how the tradition sprung up remains a mystery. It's hard to imagine the residents' abstemious ancestors tucking into vast plates filled with 7 kinds of cake and scones at one sitting. Tea is served from 1500; all the tea rooms charge about the same – US$16 – and include the most well known of the 'Welsh' cakes, *torta negra* – a delicious dense fruit cake.

Plas Y Coed (see Where to stay, above). The best, and oldest; Marta Rees is a wonderful raconteur and fabulous cook.

Ty Gwyn, 9 de Julio 111. Opens 1400. Large tea room, more modern than some, welcoming; generous teas.

Ty Nain, Yrigoyen 283. The prettiest house and full of history (mini museum inside), owned by the charming Mirna Jones, whose grandmother was the first woman to be born in Gaiman.

🎵 Bars and clubs

Puerto Madryn *p510, map p511*
La Frontera, 9 de Julio 254. Popular with locals, this nightclub only really gets busy in the small hours and closes at 0500.
Lizard Café, Av Roca y Av Galés, near the seafront. Lively funky place with friendly people. Good for generous pizzas or late-night drinks.
Margarita, RS Peña 15, T0280-4472659, next to Ambigu on RS Peña and Av Roca. Late-night bar for drinks and live music, serves expensive but tasty food.
Mr Jones, 9 de Julio 116, T02695-475368. With over 45 Argentine and imported beers, this pub is a popular hang-out. The pub food is good value and there is a great atmosphere.

🎉 Festivals

Viedma and Carmen de Patagones *p508*
Mar Fiesta de 7 de Marzo, www. maragato.com.ar. Celebrates victory at the Battle of Patagones with a week of music and handicrafts, fine food, a huge procession, gaucho horse-riding displays and lots of meat on the *asados*.

🛍 Shopping

Viedma *p508*
Patagonia Out Doors Life, 25 de Mayo 340, and **Tiburón**, Zatti 250, both stock fishing equipment.

Puerto Madryn *p510, map p511*
You'll find clothes, T-shirts, high-quality Patagonian handicrafts and leather goods, and artesanal *alfajores* and cakes for sale on 28 de Julio and Av Roca. For fishing tackle, guns and camping gear, try **Nayfer**, 25 de Mayo 366. For

diving gear, there's **Pino Sub**, Yrigoyen 200, www.pinosub.com.
Cardon, Shopping El Portal de Madryn, Av JA Roca and 28 de Julio. Recommended for regional goods and leather bags.
Portal de Madryn, 28 de Julio and Av Roca, www.portaldemadryn.com. The indoor shopping centre has all the smart clothes shops, a café on the ground floor, and a kids' games area with a fast-food place, **Mostaza**, on the top floor (not cheap).

Trelew *p515*
The main shopping area is around San Martín and from the plaza to Belgrano. Though Trelew can't compare with Puerto Madryn for souvenirs, it has a good little handicrafts market on the plaza. There is a **Norte** supermarket, Rivadavia y 9 de Julio.

🌊 What to do

Viedma and Carmen de Patagones *p508*
Tour operators
Mona Tour, San Martín 225, Viedma, T02920-422933, www.monatour. com.ar. Sells flights as well as tickets for the train to Bariloche, www. trenpatagonico-sa.com.ar.

Puerto Madryn *p510, map p511*
Diving
Puerto Madryn is a diving centre, with several shipwrecked boats in the Golfo Nuevo. A 1st dive ('bautismo') for beginners costs about US$60-70 pp.
Aquatours, Av Roca 550, T02965-445 1954, www.aquatours.com.ar. A variety of options, including PADI courses, good value.
Lobo Larsen, Roca 885, loc 2 (also Blvd Brown 860), T02965-447 0277,

www.lobolarsen.com. Friendly company that specializes in diving with the sea lion colony at Punta Lomas. Wide variety of courses offered.

Scuba Duba, Blvd Brown 893, T02965-445 2699, www.scubaduba.com.ar. Professional and good fun, diving with sealions at Punta Loma, pick-up from hotel, offer a hot drink and warm clothes after the dive, good equipment, instructor Javier A Crespi is very responsible.

Horse riding
Huellas y Costas, Blvd Brown 1900, T080-447 0143, www.huellasycostas.com. Also whale watching.

Mountain bike hire
El Gualicho, Marcos A Zar 480, T02965-445 4163, from US$10.

Tour operators
Many agencies do similar 7- and 9-hr tours to the Península Valdés, about US$55-70 pp, plus the entrance to the Peninsula. They include the interpretation centre, Puerto Pirámides (the boat trip is US$65 extra), Punta Delgada and Caleta Valdés. Most tour companies stay about 1 hr on location. Shop around to find out how long you'll spend at each place, how big the group is and whether your guide speaks English. On all excursions take binoculars. Tours do not run after heavy rain in the low season. Tours to see the penguins at Punta Tombo and the Welsh villages are better from Trelew (see below). Many of the agencies below now also have offices at the bus terminal (Dr Ávila 350); all are recommended for Península Valdés:
Alora Viaggio, Av Roca 27, T02965-445 5106, www.aloraviaggio.com. Helpful company, also has an office in Buenos Aires (T011-4827 1591, daily 0800-1300).

Argentina Visión, Av Roca 536, T02965-445 5888, www.argentinavision.com. Also 4WD adventure trips and *estancia* accommodation, English and French spoken.

Chaltén Travel, Av Roca 115, T02965-445 4906, www.chaltentravel.com. Runs a tourist bus service to Perito Moreno on Ruta 40 every other day, for connections north to Bariloche and south to El Chaltén and El Calafate.

Cuyun Có, Av Roca 165, T02965-445 1845, www.cuyunco.com.ar. Offers a friendly, personal service and a huge range of conventional and more imaginative tours: guided walks with biologists, 4WD expeditions, and can arrange *estancia* accommodation. Bilingual guides.

Tito Botazzi, Blvd Brown y Martín Fierro, T02965-447 4110, www.titobottazzi.com, and at Puerto Pirámides (T02965-449 5050). Particularly recommended for its small groups and well-informed bilingual guides; very popular for whale watching.

Puerto Pirámides p515
Hydrosport,1ra Bajada,al Mar, T02965-449 5065, www.hydrosport.com.ar. Rents scuba equipment and boats, and organizes land and sea wildlife tours to see whales and dolphins.
Whales Argentina, 1ra Bajada al Mar, T02965-449 5015, www.whales argentina.com.ar. Recommended for whale watching.

Trelew p515
Tour operators
Agencies run tours to Punta Tombo, Chubut Valley (half- and full-day). Tours to Península Valdés are best done from Puerto Madryn.
Nieve Mar, Italia 20, T02965-443 4114, www.nievemartours.com.ar. Trips to

Punta Tombo and Valdés, bilingual guides (reserve ahead), organized and efficient. Has a branch in Puerto Madryn (Av Roca 493).

⊙ Transport

Viedma and Carmen de Patagones
p508
Air
LADE (Saavedra 576, T02920-424420, www.lade.com.ar) flies to **Buenos Aires**, **Mar del Plata**, **Bahía Blanca**, **Comodoro Rivadavia** and other Patagonian destinations.

Bus
To **Buenos Aires,** 13 hrs, daily, US$100-125, with **Don Otto** and others. To **Bahía Blanca**, 4 hrs, many daily, US$25-35. To **Puerto Madryn**, 6½ hrs, several daily, US$46-53, with **Don Otto** and others.

Train
A comfortable sleeper train, which also carries cars, normally goes from Viedma to **Bariloche** overnight once a week. For information on the current state of the service, T02920-422130, www.trenpatagonico-sa.com.ar.

Puerto Madryn *p510, map p511*
Air
Daily flights to **Buenos Aires** in high season. Also limited **LADE** (Roca 119, T02965-451256) flights to **Buenos Aires**, **Bahía Blanca**, **Viedma**, **Trelew**, **Comodoro Rivadavia** and other Patagonian airports (in low season Mon and Fri departures only). More frequent flights from **Bariloche**, Buenos Aires, Ushuaia and El Calafate serve Trelew airport (see below), with buses to Puerto Madryn that meet all flights.

Bus
To **Buenos Aires**, 18-19 hrs, several companies, US$98-115. To **Bahía Blanca**, 9½ hrs with **Don Otto** and others, US$50-57. To **Comodoro Rivadavia**, 6 hrs, US$35-42 with **Don Otto** and **Transportadora Patagónica**. To **Río Gallegos**, 18 hrs; US$98-112, with **Andesmar**. To **Trelew**, 1 hr, every hr, US$4 with **28 de Julio/Mar y Valle**. To Puerto Pirámides, Mar y Valle, daily 0855, returns 1800, US$8 each way, 1½ hrs.

Car hire
Expensive, US$75 per day, and note large excess for turning car over. Drive slowly on unpaved *ripio* roads; best to hire 4WD. Many agencies on Av Roca, including **Dubrovnik**, Av Roca 19 (head office Moreno 941, Comodoro Rivadavia), T0297-444 1844, http://rentacardubrovnik.com. Reliable company with offices in El Calafate and Bariloche. **Wild Skies**, Morgan 2274, p 1, Depto 6 B Sur, T02965-15-467 6233, www.wildskies.com.ar. Efficient service, English spoken, recommended.

Taxi
Taxis can be found outside the bus terminal, T02965-445 2966/447 4177, and on the main plaza.

Trelew *p515*
Air
Aerolíneas Argentinas (Rivadavia 548, T0810-222 86527)_ has flights to/from **Buenos Aires**, **Bariloche**, **El Calafate** and **Ushuaia**. **LADE** (Italia 170, T02965-443 5740) flies to Patagonian airports and Buenos Aires once a week.

Bus
Local 28 de Julio/Mar y Valle go frequently to **Gaiman**, 30-45 mins, US$1,

US$2 return; to **Dolavon** 1 hr, US$4; to **Puerto Madryn** (via Trelew airport), 1hr, US$4; to **Puerto Pirámides**, 2½ hrs, US$11, daily.

Long distance To **Buenos Aires**, daily, 19-20 hrs, US$110-150, several companies; to **Comodoro Rivadavia**, 5 hrs, US$30-37, many departures; to **Río Gallegos**, 17 hrs; US$91-121 (with connections to El Calafate, Puerto Natales, Punta Arenas), many companies. To **Esquel**, 9-10 hrs, US$50-60, 2 companies.

Car hire
Car hire desks at the airport are staffed only at flight arrival times and cars are taken quickly. All have offices in town: **AVIS**, Italia 98, T0280-4436060; **Hertz**, at the airport, T02965-424421, T02965-1540 5495; **Fiorasi**, Urquiza 310, T02965-443 5344, www.fiorasirentacar.com.

Gaiman *p518*
Bus
To **Trelew**, several a day, with 28 de Julio, 30-45 mins, US$1, US$2 return; buy tickets from Mar y Valle, as buses take different routes, some on unpaved roads.

Dolavon *p518*
Bus
To **Trelew**, several a day, 1 hr, US$4, with 28 de Julio.

ⓘ Directory

Viedma and Carmen de Patagones *p508*
Banks ATMs at Colón y San Martín in Viedma; and at Bynon y Alsina or Bynon and Paraguay in Carmen de Patagones.

Puerto Madryn *p510, map p511*
Banks Lots of ATMs at banks. **Medical services** For emergencies call 107 or SEP, Sarmiento 125, T02965-445 4445. **Post office** Maíz 293, daily 0800-1300, 1600-1900.

Trelew *p515*
Banks Mon-Fri 0800-1300. **Banco de la Nación**, 25 de Mayo y Fontana; **Banco del Sud**, 9 de Julio 320, cash advance on Visa. **Currency exchange** Patagonia Grandes Espacios, Belgrano 338. **Post office** 25 de Mayo and Mitre.

Southern Atlantic Coast

Quieter, and much less visited by tourists than Puerto Madryn and Península Valdés, the southern stretch of the Atlantic coastline from Camarones to Río Gallegos is extremely rich in marine life of all kinds. There are several wonderful reserves protecting a wide variety of species of bird and mammal, and a few good bases for exploring them at the coastal towns of Camarones, Puerto Deseado and Puerto San Julián, with decent services and accommodation. If you have your own transport, you could head out to the only national park on the coast, Monte León, where you can walk the shore for miles and stay in a remote but comfortable *hostería*. And on the last spit of land before Tierra del Fuego, there's ancient history to explore near the coast at Cabo Vírgenes.

There are two cities in this huge region, of which the most appealing is the southernmost town on the Argentine mainland, Río Gallegos. It's a small, pleasant place, with fair accommodation and tours offered to penguin colonies, though there's little else to draw you here unless you're changing buses. The other city, Comodoro Rivadavia, is probably best avoided if possible, unless you're keen to see the petroleum museum. Aside from coastal attractions, this region also boasts the country's finest petrified forest, the Monumento Natural Bosques Petrificados, difficult to reach on public transport, 250 km west of Puerto Deseado.

Camarones and around → *Colour map 5, B5. Phone code 0297. Population 1100.*
Camarones is a quiet fishing port on Bahía Camarones, south of Trelew, whose main industry is harvesting seaweed. This is also prime sheep-rearing land, and Camarones wool is world-renowned for its quality. Aside from the salmon festival in early February, the only real attraction is a penguin colony, which you can walk to from the town.

There's another well-known penguin colony with lots more species of marine life, 35 km southeast at **Reserva Natural Cabo Dos Bahías** ① *open daily, US$6 per person; there are buses to the reserve from Trelew, see page 515.* This is a small reserve at the southern end of the bay, reached by a dirt road. It protects a large penguin colony of some 12,000 couples, which you can see close up; there are also seals and sea lions all year round, and whales from March to November; killer whales might be spotted from October to April.

Bahía Bustamante
Some 90 km south of Camarones along the coast is **Bahía Bustamante**, a settlement of seaweed harvesters and sheep ranchers on Golfo San Jorge (180 km north of Comodoro Rivadavia). Its main attractions are the coastal and steppe landscapes of the surrounding Patagonia Austral Marine national park, which offers exceptional opportunities to see birds (including 100,000 penguins), marine and land mammals. An award-winning resort (T011-4778 0125/T0297-480 1000, www.bahiabustamante. com, electricity dusk to 2300, closed April to August) offers full-board and self-catering accommodation, plus hiking, cycling, riding and kayaking; guides are on hand. If you don't have your own transport, you can phone or email in advance for a pick-up from the ACA station in Garayalde, or there are regular buses from Trelew.

Comodoro Rivadavia and around → *Colour map 5, C4. Phone code 0297. Population 145,000.*
The largest city in the province of Chubut was established primarily as a sheep-exporting port, and early settlers included Boer immigrants fleeing British rule in southern Africa. The city began to flourish suddenly when oil was discovered here in 1907, bringing in many international companies. However, since the petrol industry was privatized by President Menem in the 1990s, there's been consequent unemployment and now the town has a slightly sad, rather unkempt feel. You're most likely to end up here if you need to change buses, and there's little to make you want to stay.

Arriving in Comodoro Rivadavia Situated at the end of the Bioceanic Corridor, a fast road to Chile, Comodoro is the hub for terrestrial transport and a bus nexus from all areas of Patagonia. The **airport** is 13 km north of town and bus No 6 leaves hourly for the bus terminal, 45 minutes, US$0.75. A taxi from the airport costs US$6. The **bus terminal** ① *Pellegrini 730, T0297-446 7305*, is convenient for the town centre. It has a luggage store, good *confitería* upstairs, toilets, tourist information office (open from 0800 to 2100) and a few kiosks. There's another tourist office, **CEPTur** ① *Av H Yrigoyen* *y Moreno, T0297-444 0664, www.comodoroturismo.gob.ar, Mon-Fri 0900-1400; also in bus terminal daily 0800-2100*, which is very helpful and English is spoken.

Places around Comodoro Rivadavia There's a good view of the city from **Cerro Chenque**, 212 m high, a dun-coloured hill, unattractively adorned with radar masts, whose cliffs give the town its drab backdrop. It's interesting to take a taxi up there, if you don't feel like the walk, to see the first pioneers' homes, now dilapidated, but with panoramic views of the bay. If you're really stuck for something to do, you could also visit the **Museo Nacional del Petróleo** ① *San Lorenzo 250, 3 km north of the centre, T0297-455 9558, Tue-Fri 0900-2000, Sat-Sun 1500-2000, taxi US$4,* for a good history of local oil exploitation. Some 20 km north is **Museo Paleontológico de Astra** ① *Sat-Sun 1500-1800,* which has fossils and reconstructions of dinosaurs.

There's a good beach at the resort of **Rada Tilly,** 8 km south, where you can walk along the beach at low tide to see sea lions. **Expreso Rada Tilly** runs buses every 30 minutes, US$0.75; they're packed in summer. You could use Comodoro Rivadavia as a base for exploring a second petrified forest, the Bosque Petrificado Héctor Szlápelis (see page 544), but the little town of **Sarmiento**, some 140 km west, is far more pleasant. ▸▸ *For information on getting to Sarmiento, see Transport, page 539.*

South of Comodoro Rivadavia → *For listings, see pages 536-541.*

Caleta Olivia → *Colour map 5, C4. Phone code 0297. Population 40,000.*
Caleta Olivia lies on the Bahía San Jorge, 74 km south of Comodoro Rivadavia. Founded in 1901, it became the centre for exporting wool from the *estancias* of Santa Cruz. It boomed with the discovery of oil in 1944 but has suffered since the petroleum industry was privatized in the 1990s and is now a rather sad place with high unemployment. However, there's a lovely 70-km stretch of pebbly beach, popular with locals for bathing, and lots of fishing nearby. There's a **tourist information office** ① *San Martín y Güemes, T0297-485 0988, turismocaletaolivia on Facebook.* Municipal website is www.caletaolivia.gov.ar.

At **Pico Truncado**, some 50 km southwest, there's the gas field that feeds the pipeline to Buenos Aires and an enterprising art project, **Ciudad Sonora** ① *www. ciudadsonora.net,* in a spectacular open setting; the wind sings through structures made of metal and marble, producing strange and eerie sounds. There's a daily bus service from Caleta Oliva, and nearby Pico Truncado has a few simple hotels, a campsite, and **tourist information** ① *T0297-499 2202.*

Monumento Natural Bosques Petrificados
① *256 km west of Puerto Deseado; access is via Route 49 which branches off the R3 at Km 2063, 86 km south of Fitz Roy. Daily 1000-2000, donations welcome.*
Extending over 10,000 ha in a bizarre, wind-wracked lunar landscape surrounding the **Laguna Grande**, this park contains much older petrified trees than the forests further north around Sarmiento. The trunks, mainly of giant araucaria trees, are up to 35 m long and 150 cm in diameter. They were petrified in the Jurassic period

140 million years ago by intense volcanic activity in the Andes cordillera which blew ash over the entire area. It was the silicates in this volcanic ash that petrified the trunks of fallen trees and created these strange jasper-like hulks, which were only revealed when other organic matter around them eroded. The place is more eerie than beautiful, but it does exert a strange fascination, especially when you consider that the fossils of marine animals that you see on the site are a mere 40 million years old, belonging to a sea that covered the land long after the trees had turned to stone. There is a small visitor centre and museum, and a well-documented 1-km trail that takes you past the most impressive specimens. You may be very tempted to take away your own personal souvenir: don't.

Note that there are no facilities in the park and no accommodation. Camping is not allowed, and you're advised to bring your own food and drink. The nearest campsite is at **Estancia La Paloma** ① *Ruta 49, 24 km before the entrance, T0297-444 3503*. The only way to visit the park, unless you have your own transport, is with a tour: try Los Vikingos based in Puerto Deseado. ▸▸ *For further information, see What to do, page 539.*

Puerto Deseado and around → *For listings, see pages 536-541. Colour map 6, A4. Phone code 0297. Population 10,200.*

Puerto Deseado is a pleasant fishing port on the estuary of the Río Deseado, which drains, curiously, into Lago Buenos Aires in the west. It's a stunning stretch of coastline, rich in wildlife: the estuary encompasses a wonderful reserve, and there are more reserves within reach, protecting sea lions and penguins. The **Museo Regional Mario Brozoski** ① *Belgrano (9050) and Colón, Mon-Fri 0800-2000, Sat-Sun 1500-1900*, has remains of an 18th-century ship that sank off the coast here in 1770, as well as some evocative photos. Outside the former railway station, a rather fine old building in vaguely English medieval style, is the **Vagón Histórico** ① *San Martín 1525, T0297-487 0220, www.deseado.gov.ar*, an 1898 carriage now used as the tourist office. The **Gruta de Lourdes**, 24 km west, is a cave that attracts pilgrims to see the Virgen de Lourdes. Further south along the same road is the **Cañadón del Puerto**, a mirador offering fine views over the estuary.

Reserva Natural Ría Deseado

The submerged estuary (*ría*) of the Río Deseado, 42 km long, is an important nature reserve and a stunning area to visit. The crumbling chalky cliffs in mauve and ochre are splattered with *guano* (droppings) from many varieties of seabird. There's a colony of Magellanic penguins and four species of cormorant, including the unique red-legged cormorant, most appealing with their smart dinner-jacketed appearance. These birds nest from October to April on four islands offshore. The reserve is also a breeding ground for Commerson's dolphins, beautiful creatures that frolic playfully around your boat. Excellent tours run from the pier in Puerto Deseado; they last about two hours and are best in early morning or late evening (see Tour operators, page 539).

Other reserves round Puerto Deseado

There are several other nature reserves within easy reach if you have transport, and all offer good places to walk. North of Puerto Deseado, some 90 km on the northern shore of the peninsula, is **Cabo Blanco**, the site of the largest fur seal colony in Patagonia. It's another magnificent area, a rocky peninsula bursting out from flat lands, with one of the oldest lighthouses on the coast perched on top and thousands of seals on the rocks below. The breeding season is December to January. A little further west, you should also visit **Cañadón de Duraznillo** and Monte Loayza, which combine to form the Reserva Natural Provincial Monte Loayza ① www.monteloaza.com.ar. **Cañadón de Duraznillo** is an area of Patagonian steppe, while Monte Loayza is a strip of coastal and marine habitat. Here you'll see lots of guanacos, ñandues, foxes and birds, as well as the largest seal colony in the province on spectacular unspoilt beaches. The visitors centre is at Estancia La Madrugada, which is 83 km from Puerto Deseado; the reserve is 18 km further west, towards Jaramillo. Visits are limited to groups of 10 or less from November to March and must be accompanied by a specialist guide; if you arrive without a guide you will only be allowed in to the visitors centre.

South of Puerto Deseado are two more reserves: **Isla Pingüino**, an offshore island with a colony of Magellanic penguins, as well as cormorants and steamer ducks, and the **Reserva Natural Bahía Laura**, an uninhabited bay where black-necked cormorants, ducks and other seabirds can be found in abundance. Isla Pingüino can be reached by boat, and Bahía Laura by *ripio* and dirt roads. ⇥ *For further information, see What to do, page 539.*

The **Gruta de Lourdes**, 24 km west, is a cave which attracts pilgrims to see the Virgen de Lourdes. Further south along the same road is the **Cañadón del Puerto**, a mirador offering fine views over the estuary.

Puerto San Julián and further south → *For listings, see pages 536-541.* Colour map 6, A4.

Puerto San Julián → *Phone code 02962. Population 6200.*

The quiet port town of Puerto San Julián, lying on a peninsula overlooking the Bahía San Julián 268 km south of Fitz Roy, is the best place for breaking the 834-km run from Comodoro Rivadavia to Río Gallegos. It has a fascinating history, although little of it is in evidence today. The first Mass in Argentina was held here in 1520 after the Portuguese explorer Magellan had executed a member of his mutinous crew. Then, in 1578, Francis Drake also put in here to behead Thomas Doughty, after amiably dining with him. In 1780, Antonio Viedma attempted to found a colony here, but it failed due to scurvy. (You can visit the ruins of the site at **Florida Blanca**, 10 km west.) The current town was founded in 1901 as a port to serve the sheep *estancias* of this part of Santa Cruz.

The small **Museo Regional at Rivadavia and Vieytes** houses the amazingly well-preserved dinosaur footprint found in the town. There's plenty of wildlife to be seen in the area, especially in the coastal Reserva Natural San Julián, which is very accessible; ask about the superb tours at the **tourist office** ① *Av San Martín entre*

Rivadavia y M Moreno, T02962-452009, www.sanjulian.gov.ar, and in the bus station. The reserve, on the shores of Bahía San Julián, includes the islands **Banco Cormorán** and **Banco Justicia**, thought to be the site of the 16th-century executions; there is a colony of Magellanic penguins and nesting areas for several species of cormorant and other birds. You're also very likely to spot Commerson's dolphins. It's a lovely location and the concentration of marine life is stunning. The best time to visit is in December to see dolphins and cormorants, though there's plenty to see from December to April.

There are 30 km of spectacular coastline north of San Julián, including **Cabo Curiosa**, 15 km north, which has fine beaches; it's a popular bathing place for the whole of the region. It's also worth visiting **Estancia La María**, 150 km west, which has one of the main archaeological sites in Patagonia: a huge canyon with 87 caves full of paintings including human hands and guanacos, 4000-12,000 years old. The *estancia* offers transport and accommodation (see Where to stay, page 537).

Piedrabuena → *Colour map 6, B3. Phone code 02962. Population 4900.*
Known officially as Comandante Luis Piedrabuena, this quiet town is named after the famous Argentine explorer and sailor, Piedra Buena, who built his home on Isla Pavón, an island in the river Santa Cruz, in 1859. On this small mound in the deep emerald green fast-flowing river you can visit the **Casa Histórica Luis Piedra Buena**, a reconstruction of the original building where he carried on a peaceful trade with local indigenous groups. However, the island has become most popular as a weekend resort for those fishing steelhead trout. It's a world-renowned fishing spot, and there's a smart four-star *hostería* as well as an attractive campsite to cater for anglers and their families on weekend breaks (see Where to stay, page 537). In March there's a national trout festival. For further information contact the **tourist office** ⓘ *Av G Ibáñez 157 (bus station), T02962-1557 3065.* Piedrabuena is a good base for exploring the Parque Nacional Monte León, which protects 40 km of coastline and steppe, 30 km south.

Parque Nacional Monte León and around
The only national park on Argentina's long Atlantic coastline, Monte León is a beautiful stretch of steppe and shore, south of Piedrabuena. It includes 40 km of coastline, with many caves and little bays, as well as the tiny island Monte León, an important breeding area for cormorants and terns. In addition, there's the world's fourth largest colony of penguins and several colonies of sea lions. It was acquired for the Argentine nation by North American millionaire Douglas Tompkins (who also owns Parque Pumalín in Chile, and Rincón del Socorro in Los Esteros del Iberá, see page 368), and was looked after by the organization **Vida Silvestre**, before being made a national park in 2004.

It's not easy to access the park, but your efforts to get here will be rewarded by wonderful walks along wide isolated beaches with their extraordinary rock formations, and cliffs dotted with vast caverns, fabulous at low tide. The park also protects an important habitat of sea-shore steppe, which is home to pumas and wolves as well as guanacos and choiques. The old house at the heart of the park has been converted into a *hostería*; staying here is by far the best way to enjoy the surroundings in comfort (see Where to stay, page 537). Plans for the national park include improving access and turning the old shearing shed into a visitor centre.

Arriving in Parque Nacional Monte León It's difficult to reach the park unless you have a 4WD; access is along 23 km of poor *ripio* road which branches off Route 3, 36 km south of Piedrabuena. Or fly from Buenos Aires to Río Gallegos and take a taxi from the airport (two hours, US$130 for up to four passengers). Further information is available from the **park office** ① *Belgrano y 9 de Julio, Puerto de Santa Cruz, T02962-489184, monteleon@apn.gov.ar, www.parquenacionales.gov.ar, www.viasilvestre.org.ar.*

Río Gallegos → *For listings, see pages 536-541. Colour map 6, B3.*

The capital of Santa Cruz province lies on the estuary of the Río Gallegos (pronounced rio ga-shay-gos), which is famous for its excellent brown trout fishing. It's a pleasant, airy town, founded in 1885 as a centre for the trade in wool and sheepskins, and is by far the most appealing of the main centres on Patagonia's southern Atlantic Coast (which isn't saying a great deal). It has always been a major transport hub, but receives fewer visitors since the airport opened at El Calafate. However, if you come here to change buses, you could visit the penguin reserve at **Cabo Vírgenes** some 130 km south, or Monte León National Park 210 km north. The town itself has a couple of museums and boasts a few smart shops and restaurants.

Arriving in Río Gallegos → *Phone code 02966. Population 75,000.*
Getting there Flights arrive at the airport from Buenos Aires, Ushuaia and Río Grande, as well as LADE flights connecting all major Patagonian towns. The **airport** is 10 km from the centre; a *remise* taxi should cost US$8. The bus terminal is inconveniently 3 km from the centre, at the corner of Route 3 and Avenida Eva Perón, T02966-442159. Bus Nos 1 and 12 will take you into town, or take a taxi for US$4. The **terminal** is small and crowded; there's no left luggage, but there is a *confitería*, toilets and some kiosks.

Tourist information There's a provincial **tourist office** ① *Av Pres Kirchner 863, T02966-437412, http://santacruzpatagonia.gob.ar, Mon-Fri 0900-1600.* At Kirchner y San Martín is the **Carretón Municipal**, an information caravan open till 2100 in summer. The staff are helpful and speak English; they have a list of *estancias* and will phone round hotels for you. There's another **municipal office** ① *Av Beccar 126, T02966-436920, www.turismo.mrg.gov.ar,* an information desk at the airport in high season and a small desk at the **bus terminal** ① *T02966-442159, daily till 2030.*

Places in Río Gallegos
The tidy, leafy Plaza San Martín, two blocks south of the main street, Avenida Roca, has an interesting collection of trees, many planted by the early pioneers, and a diminutive corrugated iron **cathedral**, with a wood-panelled ceiling in the chancel and stained-glass windows. The best of the town's museums is the small **Museo de**

los Pioneros ① *Elcano y Alberdi, T02966-437763, daily 1000-1900, free.* Set in a house built in England and shipped here in 1890, there are interesting photographs and artefacts telling the story of the first Scottish settlers, who came here in 1884 from the Falklands/Malvinas Islands enticed by government grants of land. There's an interesting tour given by the English-speaking owner, a descendent of the Scottish pioneers, and great photos of those first sheep-farming settlers. There's work by local artists at **Museo de Arte Eduardo Minichelli** ① *Maipú 13, Mar-Dec Mon-Fri 0800-1900, Sat-Sun and holidays 1400-1700.* **Museo Regional Provincial Padre Jesús Molina** ① *Complejo Cultural Santa Cruz, Av San Martín y Ramón and Cajal 51, Mon-Fri 0900-2000, Sat 1500-2000,* has some dull rocks and fossils and a couple of dusty dinosaur skeletons. **Museo Malvinas Argentinas** ① *Pasteur 74, Mon and Thu 0800-1300, Tue and Fri 1300-1730, 3rd Sun of month 1530-1830,* is quite stimulating. It aims to inform visitors why the Malvinas are Argentine.

Around Río Gallegos **Laguna Azul**, 62 km south near the Monte Aymond border crossing, is nothing more than a perfect royal-blue lagoon in the crater of an extinct volcano, but it does have a certain atmosphere, set in an arid lunar landscape, and

Río Gallegos

Where to stay ⬤
2 Comercio
3 Covadonga
4 Nevada
5 Oviedo
6 París

7 Punta Arenas
8 Santa Cruz
9 Sehuen

Restaurants ⬤
1 El Chino

2 El Club Británico &
   Café Central
4 La Ría
7 RoCo

it's a good place for a walk. Take a tour, or get off the bus along Route 3, which stops on the main road.

Reserva Provincial Cabo Vírgenes ① *134 km south of Río Gallegos via Ruta 3 and Ruta 1 (*ripio*), 3½ hrs, entry US$3; tours with tour operators US$60*, is a nature reserve protecting the second largest colony of Magellanic penguins in Patagonia. There's an informative self-guided walk to see their nests amongst the *calafate* and fragrant *mata verde* bushes. It's good to visit from November to January, when chicks are born and there are nests under every bush: fascinating for anyone and wonderful for children. You can climb the **Cabo Vírgenes lighthouse** (owned by the Argentine Navy) for wonderful views. There's a *confitería* close by for snacks and souvenirs. Both the reserve and the lighthouse are usually included in tours from Río Gallegos or you could stay at **Estancia Monte Dinero** (see Where to stay, below,) 13 km north of Cabo Vírgenes, which is a wonderful base for visiting the reserve. It is a working sheep farm, where the English-speaking Fenton family offers accommodation, food and excursions (US$90 for a day visit); all excellent.

South of Cabo Vírgenes are the ruins of **Nombre de Jesús**, one of the two settlements founded by Pedro Sarmiento de Gamboa in 1584 and where, tragically, all its settlers died.

◉ Southern Atlantic Coast listings

For hotel and restaurant price codes and other relevant information, see pages 20-26.

● Where to stay

Camarones *p529*
For other lodgings see www.
interpatagonia.com/camarones/
$$$-$$ Complejo Indalo Inn,
Sarmiento and Roca, T0297-496 3004,
www.indaloinn.com.ar. Simple but clean,
doubles and singles with en suite. Good
food, and the owner runs trips to the
penguin colony. Recommended.

Comodoro Rivadavia *p529*
$$$ Lucania Palazzo, Moreno 676,
T0297-449 9300, www.lucania-palazzo.
com. Most luxurious business hotel,
superb rooms, sea views, good value,
huge American breakfast, sauna and
gym included. Recommended.

$$ Azul, Sarmiento 724, T0297-446 7539,
info@hotelazul.com.ar. Breakfast extra,
quiet old place with lovely bright rooms,
kind, great views from the *confitería*.
$$ Hospedaje Cari Hue, Belgrano 563,
T0297-447 2946, www.hospedajecarihue.
com.ar. Sweet rooms, with separate
bathrooms, very nice owners, breakfast
extra. The best budget choice.

Camping
Camping Municipal, Rada Tilly, reached
by **Expreso Rada Tilly** bus from town.
Hot showers.
San Carlos, 37 km north on R3, T0297-
456 0425. Covers 20 ha, open all year.

Caleta Olivia *p530*
$$$ Patagonia Hotel, Av Eva
Perón 1873, T0297-483 0517, www.
patagoniahotelco.com.ar. Welcoming,
slightly dated hotel with clean bright
rooms and views of the ocean.

$$ pp Hotel Robert, San Martín 2152, T0297-485 1452, www.hotelrobert.com.ar. Comfortable option. All rooms have bathroom, and breakfast is included.
$ Grand Hotel, Mosconi and Chubut, T0297-485 1393. Reasonably comfortable rooms.

Camping
Municipal campsite, T0297-485 0999, ext 476. Hot showers and near the beach.

Monumento Natural Bosques Petrificados *p530*
There are no services, no water source anywhere close by, and no accommodation in the area, apart from camping at **Estancia la Paloma**, on Ruta 49, 25 km away, T0297-444 3503. Note that camping is not allowed in the park.

Puerto Deseado *p531*
$$ Isla Chaffers, San Martín y Mariano Moreno, T0297-487 2246, administracion@hotelislachaffers.com.ar. Modern, central.
$$ Los Acantilados, Pueyrredón y España, T0297-487 2167, www.hotelosacantilados.com.ar. Beautifully located, good breakfast.

Camping
Camping Cañadón de Giménez, 4 km away on R281, T0297-487 2135; **Camping Municipal**, Av Lotufo, on the seafront, T0297-487 2728. Lovely locations but the sites are a bit run-down.

Puerto San Julián *p532*
$$$ Bahía, San Martín 1075, T02962-453144, hotelbahia@yahoo.com.ar. Modern, comfortable, good value. Recommended.
$$ Municipal Costanera, 25 de Mayo y Urquiza, T02962-452300,

www.costanerahotel.com. Very nice, well run, good value, no restaurant.
$$ Sada, San Martín 1112, T02962-452013, www.hotelsada.com.ar. Fine but on busy main road.

Estancias
$$$ Estancia La María, 150 km northwest of Puerto San Julián; office in San Julián, Saavedra 1163, T02962-452328. Offers transport, lodging, meals and trips to cave paintings that are less visited than Cueva de las Manos (see page 545).

Camping
Good municipal campsite, Magallanes 650, T02962-454506. Repeatedly recommended, all facilities.

Piedrabuena *p533*
$$$ Hostería El Alamo, Lavalle 8 y España, T02962-497166/497249, www.hosteriaelalamo.com. Quiet, breakfast extra. Recommended.
$$ Res Internacional, Ibáñez 99, T02962-497197. Recommended.

Camping
Sites south of town on R3; also on Isla Pavón.

Parque Nacional Monte León *p533*
$$$$ Hostería Estancia Monte León, R3, Km 2399, T011-4621 4780 (Buenos Aires), www.monteleon-patagonia.com. Nov-Apr. 4 tasteful rooms, all decorated with Douglas Tompkins' considerable style. There's a good library, living room and even a small museum. Fishing is good here, too. It's a fantastic place to stay.

Río Gallegos *p534, map p535*
Most hotels are situated within a few blocks of the main street, Av Roca,

running northwest to southeast. Do not confuse the street Comodoro Rivadavia with (nearby) Bernardino Rivadavia.

$$$ Santa Cruz, Kirchner 701, T02966-420601, www.hotelsantacruzrgl.com.ar. Good value, spacious rooms with good beds, full buffet breakfast. Recommended.

$$$ Sehuen, Rawson 160, T02966-425683, www.hotel sehuen.com. Good, cosy, helpful.

$$ Comercio, Kirchner 1302, T02966-422782, www.hotelcomerciorg.com. Good value, including breakfast, nice design, comfortable, cheap *confitería*.

$$ Covadonga, Kirchner 1244, T02966-420190, hotelcovadongargl@hotmail.com. Small rooms, attractive old building, breakfast extra.

$$ Nevada, Zapiola 480, T02966-425990. Good budget option, nice simple rooms, no breakfast.

$$ París, Kirchner 1040, T02966-420111, elhotelparis@yahoo.com.ar. Simple rooms, shared bath, good value.

$$ Punta Arenas, F Sphur 55, T02966-427743, www.hotelpuntaarenas.com. Rooms with shared bath cheaper. Smart, rooms in new wing cost more. **Something Café** attached.

$ Oviedo, Libertad 746, T02966-420118. A cheaper budget option, breakfast extra, laundry facilities, café, parking.

Around Río Gallegos *p536*
Estancias

$$$$ Monte Dinero, near Cabo Vírgenes, T02966-428922, www.montedinero.com.ar. Comfortable accommodation on a working sheep farm. The house is lined with wood rescued from ships wrecked off the coast, and the food is delicious and home-grown. Highly recommended.

$$$ Hill Station, 63 km north of Río Gallegos on R58, T02966-423897 (in Río Gallegos). An *estancia* with 120 years of history, run by descendants of the founder, William Halliday. A sheep farm, also breeding *criollo* horses, this offers wonderful horse riding to see flora and fauna of the coast, and also simple accommodation.

Camping

Club Pescazaike, Paraje Guer Aike, Ruta 3, 30 km west, T02966-423442, info@pescazaike.com.ar. Also *quincho* and restaurant.

🍴 Restaurant

Comodoro Rivadavia *p529*
$$ Cayo Coco, Rivadavia 102. Bistro with excellent pizzas, good service. Also Cayo Coco del Mar, Av Costanera 1051.
$$ Maldito Peperoni, Sarmiento 581. Cheerful, modern, pastas.

Puerto Deseado *p531*
$$ Puerto Cristal, España 1698, T0297-487 0387. Panoramic views of the port, a great place for Patagonian lamb, *parrilla* and seafood.

Puerto San Julián *p532*
$$ La Rural, Ameghino 811. Good, but not before 2100.

Río Gallegos *p534, map p535*
$$ El Club Británico, Kirchner 935, T02966-432668. Good value, excellent steaks.
$$ La Ría, Sarmiento y Gob Lista, T2966-444114, near the river, looking across Plaza de la República. Patagonian dishes.
$$ RoCo, Kirchner 1157. Large, smart restaurant, popular, with a varied menu of meat, fish, pasta and other dishes.
$ El Chino, 9 de Julio 27. Varied *tenedor libre*.

Café Central, Kirchner 923. Smart and popular.

ⓞ What to do

Caleta Olivia *p530*
Zoyen Turismo, Güemes 2121, T0297-485 1632, www.zoyenturismo.com.ar. Tour operator that can help with R40 connections and *estancia* visits. They also have an office in Perito Moreno.

Puerto Deseado *p531*
Darwin Expediciones, España 2551, T0297-15-624 7554, www.darwin-expeditions.com. Excursions by boat to Ría Deseado reserve and trips to the Monumento Natural Bosques Petrificados.
Los Vikingos, Estrada 1275, T0297-15-624 5141/0297-487 0020, www.losvikingos.com.ar. Excursions by boat to Ría Deseado reserve and Reserva Provincial Isla Pingüino, bilingual guides, customized tours.

Puerto San Julián *p532*
Excursiones Pinocho, Av Costanera between San Martín and Mitre, T02962-454600, www.pinochoexcursiones.com.ar. Excellent Zodiac boat trips, lasting 90 mins, into Reserva Natural San Julián.
Tur Aike Turismo, Av San Martín 446, T02962-452086.

Río Gallegos *p534, map p535*
Fishing
The southern fishing zone includes rivers Gallegos, Grande, Fuego, Ewan, San Pablo and Lago Fagnano, near Ushuaia. It is famous for runs of sea trout. Ask the tourist office for fishing guides and information on permits, or visit www.pescaenlapatagonia.com.ar (in Spanish).

Tour operators
Macatobiano Turismo, Av San Martín 1093, T02966-422466, macatobiano@macatobiano.com. Air tickets and tours to Pingüinero Cabo Vírgenes and to Estancia Monte León, as well as tickets to El Calafate and Ushuaia. Recommended.

⊖ Transport

Camarones *p529*
Bus
To **Trelew**, Mon-Fri 1600, 2½ hrs, with **Don Otto**.

Comodoro Rivadavia *p529*
Air
Aerolíneas Argentinas (Rivadavia 156, T0297-447 3302) has regular flights to **Buenos Aires**. **LADE** (Rivadavia 360, T0297-447 0585) flies to all Patagonian destinations once or twice a week, plus **Bariloche**, **El Bolsón** and **Esquel**.

Bus
In summer buses usually arrive full, so book ahead. To **Buenos Aires,** several daily, 24-28 hrs, US$121-136. To **Bariloche**, 14½ hrs, US$56-63, with **Don Otto** (T0297-447 0450), **Marga and Andesmar**. To **Esquel** (paved road), 9 hrs direct with **EETAP**, T0297-447 4841, **Marga** and **Don Otto**, US$44-50. To **Río Gallegos**, daily, 10-12 hrs, US$63-73. To **Puerto Madryn**, US$35-42. To **Trelew,** 3 daily, 5 hrs, US$30-37, several companies including **Don Otto**. To **Caleta Olivia**, 1 hr, US$9. To **Sarmiento**, 3 daily, 2½ hrs, US$11. To **Puerto Deseado**, **Sportman**, 2 a day, US$27.

Car rental
Avis, Moreno 725 (in the Hotel Austral lobby), T0297-4464828; **Patagonia Sur Car**, Rawson 1190, T0297-446 6768.

Caleta Olivia p530
Bus
To **Río Gallegos**, with **Andesmar**, **Sportman** and others, US$57-66, 9½ hrs. Many buses to/from **Comodoro Rivadavia**, 1 hr, US$9, and 2 daily to **Puerto Deseado**, 2½-3 hrs, US$20, with Sportman. To **Perito Moreno** and **Los Antiguos**, 5-6 hrs, US$24-26, **Sportman**, 2 a day.

Puerto Deseado p531
Air
LADE (Don Bosco 1519, T0297-487 2674) flies weekly to **Comodoro Rivadavia**, **El Calafate**, **Río Gallegos** and **Ushuaia**.

Bus
To **Caleta Olivia**, daily, US$20, with **Sportman**.

Puerto San Julián p532
Air
Weekly services (Mon) with **LADE**, Martín 1552, T02962-452137, to **Santa Cruz**, **Río Gallegos**, **El Calafate**, **Puerto Deseado**, **Gobernador Gregores**, **Comodoro Rivadavia** and **Río Turbio**.

Bus
Many companies to both **Comodoro Rivadavia**, US$34-39, and **Río Gallegos**, 6 hrs, US$28-32.

Río Gallegos p534, map p535
Air
Aerolíneas Argentinas (San Martín 545, T02966-420181) have regular flights to/from **Buenos Aires**, **Ushuaia** and **Río Grande** direct. **LADE** (Fagnano 53, T02966-422326, closed in low season) flies to many Patagonian destinations between **Buenos Aires** and **Ushuaia**, including **El Calafate** and **Comodoro**

Rivadavia, but not daily. Book as far in advance as possible.

Bus
For all long distance trips, turn up with ticket 30 mins before departure. Take passport when buying ticket; for buses to Chile some companies give out immigration and customs forms.
To **El Calafate**, 4-5 hrs, US$19-25, with **Sportman** and **Taqsa** (T02966-442194, and at airport, www.taqsa.com.ar). To **Comodoro Rivadavia**, with **Andesmar**, **Don Otto/Transportadora Patagónica**, **Sportman** and others, 10-12 hrs, US$63-73. To **Bariloche**, with **Marga**, daily, 24 hrs, US$55-65, change in Comodoro Rivadavia.

To **Buenos Aires**, 36 hrs, several daily with **Andesmar**, US$184-241. To **Río Grande** US$55, 9 hrs, with **Marga** and Tecni Austral; also to **Ushuaia,** US$72.

To Chile: Puerto Natales, with **Pacheco** (T02966-442765, www.busespacheco.com) and **Bus Sur** (T02966-457047, www.bus-sur.cl), 2 weekly each, 4½ hrs, US$28. To **Punta Arenas**, with **Pacheco**, 4 a week, and **Ghisoni** (T02966-457047, www.busesbarria.cl), 5 a week, 5½ hrs, US$24.

Car
To Chile Make sure your car papers are in order: go first to tourist office for necessary documents, then to the customs office at the port, at the end of San Martín, very uncomplicated.

Localiza, Sarmiento 245, T02966-436717. **Cristina**, Libertad 123, T02966-425709. **Hertz** at the airport. Essential to book rental in advance in season.

Taxis
Hiring a taxi for group excursions may be the same price as a tour bus. Taxi ranks

are plentiful; rates are controlled, *remises* are slightly cheaper. **Note:** *Remise* meters show metres travelled, refer to card for price; taxi meters show cost in pesos. Also consider hiring a car with driver from **Todo Transfer Patagonia** (www. interpatagonia.com/todotransfer/).

ℹ Directory

Comodoro Rivadavia *p529*
Banks Many ATMs and major banks along San Martín. Change money at **Thaler**, Mitre 943, Mon-Fri 0900-1300, or at weekends at **ETAP** in the bus terminal. **Consulates** Chile, Almte Brown 456, entrepiso, of 3, T0297-446 2414.

Puerto San Julián *p532*
Banks Banco de la Nación, Mitre and Belgrano; **Banco de la Provincia de Santa Cruz**, San Martín and Moreno. **Post office** Belgrano and San Martín.

Río Gallegos *p534, map p535*
Banks 24-hr ATMs for all major international credit and debit cards all over town. Change TCs here if going to El Calafate, where it is even more difficult. **Cambio El Pingüino**, Zapiola 469, and **Thaler**, San Martín 484. Both will change Chilean pesos as well as US$. **Consulates** Chile, Mariano Moreno 148, T02966-422364. Mon-Fri 0900-1300, 1400-1730.

Ruta 40

The Ruta 40 – known in Argentina, with affection and awe, simply as *'La Cuarenta'* – is one of the wildest and least travelled roads on the planet. It runs the whole length of Argentina, from La Quiaca on the border with Bolivia in the north, all the way down to El Chaltén and Río Gallegos in the south. Ernesto 'Che' Guevara travelled along much of it on his famous motorcycle jaunts and his experience helped form his revolutionary spirit. You can get a flavour of the toughest parts by travelling this stretch through Patagonia. In the 14 hours it takes to go from Los Antiguos to El Chaltén, you're likely to see no more than a few cars; you'll also spot condors wheeling high above the Andes, the occasional Patagonian fox, and not much else apart from the clouds, whipped into amazing shapes by the ubiquitous winds.

Along the way you could veer off the battered track to hide out at a number of isolated *estancias*, visible from miles away where you see a fringe of tall poplars protecting a cluster of buildings. Many welcome guests, and you can enjoy horse riding, walking and the warm hospitality of their owners. Estancia La Oriental is the best base for exploring the stark and beautiful landscapes of Parque Nacional Perito Moreno (not to be confused with Glaciar Perito Moreno), many of which are inaccessible by car. To the north of this stretch is the Cueva de las Manos, a cave containing thousands of human handprints, made more than 8000 years ago. Just to the north, near Sarmiento, there's a petrified forest, with huge trunks of monkey puzzle trees turned to stone 140 million years ago.

Mount Fitz Roy, whose great turrets of granite can be seen rising up from the flat steppe from 100 km away, is one of the most magnificent sights in the whole country, made all the more spectacular by hours or days travelling across the relentless flat lands. For travel information on the Ruta 40, see www.rutanacional40.com (in Spanish with good maps).

Getting around

Travelling along the Ruta 40 is quite an experience, and unless you're taking the bus, it's one that requires careful planning. Travelling south, the road is paved as far as Perito Moreno, and then is good *ripio*, improving greatly after Las Horquetas. From Río Mayo to El Calafate, the wide stony *ripio* track of the Ruta 40 zigzags its way across windswept desolate land. Every few hundred kilometres or so, there will be a small, improbable signpost to an *estancia*, somewhere off the road unseen; many are just ordinary sheep farms and do no accept paying guests. The best time to go is between October and April. Outside these months travel is still possible, but accommodation and transport is harder to find, and the winter is deadly cold. There are several logical places to start your journey along the Ruta 40 through Patagonia. Travelling from the Atlantic Coast, you can reach Río Mayo from Comodoro Rivadavia, with regular buses along the Route 26. There are also daily buses from Esquel, at the southernmost end of the Lake District. Those travelling south along the Carretera Austral in Chile can take the ferry across Lago General Carrera/Lago Buenos Aires, from south of Coyhaique to Chile Chico, and cross the border into Argentina at Los Antiguos before continuing the journey south along the Ruta 40.

Bus The most efficient way to travel this stretch is by making use of the bus services offered by two companies. **Chaltén Travel** (www.chaltentravel.com) runs a service every other day in each direction between Bariloche and El Calafate, via Los Antiguos and El Chaltén. This service operates from November to Semana Santa. Alternatively a year-round no-frills service is run by **Taqsa** (www.taqsa.com.ar), departing daily in summer and twice a week for the rest of the year between El Calafate and Bariloche.

Car/motorbike/bike Hiring a car in one town and dropping it off in another is possible and allows great flexibility. But it can be expensive and is only fun if you're not travelling alone. Make sure you know exactly where the next petrol station is, as they can easily be 300 km apart, carry spare fuel and allow more time than you think to reach your destination before nightfall. There are only a few service stations for fuel along the whole stretch and few places offering accommodation (see below). It's not advisable to travel faster than 60 kph on *ripio* roads. Take warm clothes, liquids and a blanket, in case you become stranded at night. If cycling, note that food and water stops are scarce, the wind is fierce, and there is no shade whatsoever. Hitching along this road is virtually impossible and isn't recommended, as you could be stranded for days.

Accommodation

Be warned that there are few decent places to stay along this entire route. The best bases for accommodation after Esquel in the north are the pretty little town of Los Antiguos, near the border with Chile, and Perito Moreno. After that, there are only remote rural *estancias* and some very bleak one-horse towns until you reach the tourist haven of El Chaltén. Take a tent if you're on a bike. To get to the *estancias*, you'll need to have booked in advance and to have your own transport. Various companies organize tours along the route, with *estancia* stays and travel included.

Along Ruta 26 → *For listings, see pages 550-553.*

The vital east–west road link between Chile and the Atlantic is Route 26, also known as the Bioceanic Corridor, which runs east from the Chilean towns of Coyhaique and Puerto Aisén, over the Chilean border in the Andes and across the steppe, dotted with oil wells, to Comodoro Rivadavia. Mainly used by lorries, it gives access to two petrified araucaria forests at José Ormachea and Héctor Szlapelis, both within easy reach of the small town of Sarmiento.

Sarmiento and the petrified forests → *Colour map 5, C3. Phone code 0297. Population 10,000.*

Sarmiento is reached by Ruta 20, which brances off Ruta 26 110 km west of Comodoro Rivadavia. (Beyond Sarmiento Ruta 20 joins Ruta 22 towards Río Mayo.) Just to the north of town are two great lakes, **Lago Musters** and **Lago Colhué Huapi**, both of which offer good fishing in summer. Founded in 1897 and formally known as Colonia Sarmiento, it was first settled by Welsh, Lithuanians and Boers. It's a quiet and relaxed place, sitting in fertile, well irrigated land on the Río Senguer, and it's little visited by tourists. The **tourist offices** ① *Av Regimiento de Infantería 25 y Pietrobelli, T0297-489 2105, and Av San Martín y 12 de Octubre, T0297-489 3401, www.sarmientochubut.gov.ar,* are helpful and have a map of the town. They can also provide information about transport to the petrified forests. Most accessible is the **Bosque Petrificado José Ormachea** ① *32 km south of Sarmiento on a good ripio road, warden T0297-489 8282/8047, Apr-Sep daily 1000-1800, Oct-Mar daily 0800-2000, US$7.* Less easy to reach is the rather bleaker **Bosque Petrificado Héctor Szlápelis**, some 40 km further southwest along the same road (follow signposts). These forests of fallen araucaria trees, nearly 3 m in circumference and 15-20 m long, are 60 million years old and are a remarkable sight, best visited in summer as the winters are very cold. There are *guardaparques* (rangers) at both sites, who can give tours and information.

Río Mayo → *Colour map 5, C2. Phone code 02903. Population 2900.*

Set in beautifully bleak landscape by the meandering Río Mayo, this very rural little town has little of tourist interest, but it's an important junction at the intersection of routes 40 and 26, so you're likely to find yourself here to change buses or pick up fuel. Every November, it is the site for an extraordinary display of dexterity at the **Fiesta Nacional de la Esquila** (national sheep-shearing competition). Teams of five or six *esquiladores*, who travel around Patagonia from farm to farm in shearing season, compete to shear as many sheep as possible: a good shearer might get through 20 in an hour. There's a little **tourist office** ① *Av Argentino s/n, T02903-420058, www.turismoriomayo.gob.ar.*

From Río Mayo, Ruta 26 runs west 140 km to the Chilean border at Coyhaique Alto (see box, page 546). South of Río Mayo Ruta 40 is unpaved as far as Perito Moreno (124 km, high-clearance advised).

Perito Moreno and around → *For listings, see pages 550-553. Colour map 5, C2. Phone code 02963. Population 6000.*

Not to be confused with the famous glacier of the same name near El Calafate, nor with Parque Nacional Perito Moreno (see page 548), this Perito Moreno is a spruce little town, 25 km west of Lago Buenos Aires. It's the nearest but not the most attractive base for exploring the mysterious cave paintings at the **Cueva de las Manos** to the south.

Arriving in Perito Moreno
The airport is 7 km east of town and the only way to get there is by taxi. The bus terminal, T02963-432072, is on the edge of town next to the EG3 service station. It is open only when buses arrive or depart. The friendly **tourist office** ① *Av San Martín 2005, http://peritomoreno.tur.ar, low season Mon-Fri 0700-2400, Sat-Sun1000-2000, high season daily 0700-2400,* can advise on tours to the cave and *estancias*.

Places around Perito Moreno
The town has no sights as such, apart from the pleasure of watching a rural community go about its business. But southwest of the town is **Parque Laguna**, where you can see varied birdlife, including flamingos and black-necked swans, and go fishing. You could also walk to the crater of **Volcán Cerro**, from a path 12 km outside Perito Moreno: ask at the tourist office for directions.

Cueva de las Manos → *Colour map 6, A2. Phone code 02962.*
① *Access is via a new, 28-km road which branches east off Ruta 40, 88 km south of Perito Moreno; another 46-km access road, branches off Ruta 40 at Km 124, 3 km north of Bazjo Caracoles. The road can be difficult after rain. Compulsory guided tours with rangers Nov-Apr 0900-1900, Mar-Oct 1000-1800, US$10, under-12s free.*
Situated 47 km northeast of Bajo Caracoles, the stunning canyon of the **Río Pinturas** contains outstanding examples of handprints and cave paintings, estimated to be between 9500 and 13,000 years' old. It is one of the major cultural and archaeological sites in South America, declared a World Heritage Site by UNESCO in 1999, and definitely one of the highlights of any trip to Patagonia. In the cave's four galleries are over 800 paintings by the Toldense peoples of human hands, all but 31 of which are of left hands, as well as images of guanacos and rheas, and various geometrical designs. The red, orange, black, white and green pigments were derived from earth and calafate berries, and fixed with a varnish of guanaco fat and urine. They are mysterious and rather beautiful, albeit indecipherable. The canyon itself is also worth seeing: 270 m deep and 480 m wide, it has strata of vivid red and green rocks that are especially beautiful in the early morning or evening light. *Guardaparques* living at the site give helpful information and a tour.▶ *See Transport, page 552.*

Border crossings: Argentina–Chile

Paso Huemules

From Río Mayo, there are two roads crossing the border into Chile to take you to Coyhaique, the main town for visiting the southern part of the Carretera Austral. The more southerly of the two, via Paso Huemules, has better roads and is the crossing used by buses between Comodoro Rivadavia and Coyhaique. It is reached by a road that branches off Ruta 40 some 31 km south of Río Mayo and runs west 105 km via Lago Blanco (small petrol station), where there is an *estancia* community, 30 km from the border. There's no hotel here but the police are friendly and may permit camping at the police post. The border is open 0800-2200 in summer, 0900-2000 in winter. The road continues from Balmaceda on the Chilean side of the border to Coyhaique. See www.gendarmeria.gov.ar for further information.

Coyhaique Alto

This border crossing is reached by a 133-km road (87 km *ripio*, then dirt) that branches off Ruta 40 about 7 km north of Río Mayo. On the Chilean side this road continues to Coyhaique, 50 km west of the border. **Chilean immigration** is 6 km west of the border, April to November daily 0800-2000, December to April daily 0800-2200.

Los Antiguos

The main reason to enter Chile here is either to explore the beautiful southern shore of Lago General Carrera, or to take the ferry over the lake north to Puerto Ibáñez which has minibus connections on to Coyhaique.
Transport Four bus companies cross the border by the bridge to the village of Chile Chico, 8 km west, US$4, 45 minutes. If crossing from Chile Chico to Los Antiguos, there are buses daily in summer, taking one hour, US$4; company offices are at B O'Higgins 426, and at Santiago Ericksen 150.

Paso Roballos

From Bajo Caracoles Route 41 (unpaved) goes 99 km northwest to the Paso Roballos border with Chile. On the Chilean side this road continues 201 km to Cochrane, Km 177. Though passable in summer, it is often flooded in spring (September to November). There's no public transport available here.

Los Antiguos and border with Chile → *Colour map 6, A2. Phone code: 02963. Population 3000.*

Though there are two crossings to Chile west of Perito Moreno, the easiest and most commonly used is via the pretty little village of Los Antiguos, which lies just 2 km east of the border. The town lies on the southern shore of Lago Buenos Aires, the second largest lake in South America, extending into Chile as Lago General Carrera, where the landscape is very beautiful and unspoilt. The Río Baker, which flows from the lake, is world-renowned for excellent trout fishing.» *For further information on crossing the border here, see box, opposite.*

Los Antiguos is a sleepy little place, but it has a pleasant atmosphere, thanks largely to its warm microclimate, and it's a nicer place to stay than Chile Chico or Perito Moreno. New hotels are being built and there are countless new services, including restaurants, internet cafés and a new bus terminal on Avenida Tehuelches with a large café/restaurant and free Wi-Fi. Minibuses from Chile arrive at this terminal. It is a good place to stay for two days or longer and to stock up on basics before continuing the journey. The **parque municipal** at the east end of the town is a pleasant place to walk, along the bank of the river, with birdlife to look at, and two blocks down, there's a superb campsite. There is a small **tourist office** ① *Av 11 de Julio 446, T02963-491261, www.losantiguoshabla.com, Dec-Easter daily 0800-2400, Easter-Nov daily 0800-2000.*

This is a rich fruit-growing area with a popular **cherry festival** in early January (**Fiesta Nacional de la Cereza**) that attracts national *folclore* stars. While you're here, there are two local *chacras* (small farms) worth visiting. You can walk from the main street to **Chacra Don Neno**, where there are strawberries growing and jam for sale. You'd have to drive, or take a taxi, though, to the idyllic **Chacra el Paraíso**, where the charming owners make delicious jams and chutney.

Bajo Caracoles and south to Tres Lagos → *Colour map 6, A2. Phone code 0297. Population 100.*

After hours of spectacular emptiness, even tiny Bajo Caracoles is a relief. It's nothing more than a few houses with an expensive grocery store and very expensive fuel. From Bajo Caracoles Route 41 (unpaved) goes 99 km northwest to the **Paso Roballos** border with Chile (see box, opposite), passing Lago Ghio and Lago Columna. Route 39, meanwhile, heads southwest from Bajo Caracoles, reaching **Lago Posadas** and **Lago Pueyrredón** after 72 km. These two beautiful lakes with contrasting blue and turquoise waters are separated by a narrow isthmus. Guanacos and rheas can be seen and there are sites of archaeological interest.

South to Tres Lagos
South of Bajo Caracoles Ruta 40 crosses the Pampa del Asador and then, near Las Horquetas, Km 371, swings southeast to follow the Río Chico. Some 92 km south of Bajo Caracoles is the turn-off west to Lago Belgrano and Parque Nacional Perito Moreno (see below). From the Parque Moreno junction to Tres Lagos, Ruta 40 improves considerably. About 23 km east of the turn-off, along Route 521 is **Tamel Aike**, Km 393, where there is a police station and water but little else. At Km 464, Route 25 branches off to **San Julián** via **Gobernador Gregores**, 72 km southeast, where there is fuel and a good mechanic. (This is the only place with fuel before Tres Lagos, so carry extra if you want to avoid the 72-km detour.) The Ruta 40, meanwhile, continues southwest towards Tres Lagos. At Km 531, a road heads west to Lago Cardiel, a very saline lake with no outlet and good salmon fishing.

Tres Lagos, at Km 645, is a solitary village with a supermarket and fuel at the junction with Route 288. A road also turns off northwest here to Lago San Martín, which straddles the Chilean border (the Chilean part is Lago O'Higgins). From Tres Lagos, Ruta 40 deteriorates rapidly and remains very rugged until after the turn-off to the Fitz Roy sector of Parque Nacional Los Glaciares (see page 554). Twenty-one kilometres beyond this turn-off is the bridge over Río La Leona, where delightful **Hotel La Leona** serves good cakes.

Parque Nacional Perito Moreno → For listings, see pages 550-553.

Situated southwest of Bajo Caracoles on the Chilean border, this is one of the wildest and most remote parks in Argentina. It encompasses a large, interconnected system of lakes, lying between glaciated peaks of astonishing beauty, and boasts good trekking and abundant wildlife. However, since much of the park is dedicated to scientific study, it's largely inaccessible.

Arriving in Parque Nacional Perito Moreno

The **park office** ① *Av San Martín 883, T02962-491477, www.parquesnacionales.gov.ar or www.turismoruta40.com.ar/pnperitomoreno.html*, is 220 km away in Gobernador Gregores; get information here before reaching the park itself. Access to the park is via a turning off the paved Ruta 40, 100 km south of Bajo Caracoles, onto 90 km of unpaved road (see above). There is no public transport into the park. There is nowhere to buy fuel inside the park, unless you're staying at one of the *estancias*, and cyclists should bring water, as there is no source along the 90 km branch road. The *guardaparques* office is 10 km beyond the park entrance and has maps and leaflets on walks and wildlife. It's essential to get detailed maps here and to ask advice about hikes and paths. Bring an all-season sleeping bag and plenty of warm clothing, as the climate here is mercurial. The best time to visit is in summer (December to February). The access road may be blocked by snow at other times.

There are two *estancias* inside the park boundaries: Estancia La Oriental and Estancia Menelik. There are also several good sites for camping (free) – although much of the park is closed to visitors. The most accessible part is around Lago Belgrano, 12 km from the entrance. ▸▸ *For more information, see Where to stay, page 550.*

Around the park

Lago Belgrano, in the park's centre, is the biggest in the chain of lakes; its vivid turquoise waters contrast with the surrounding mountains which are streaked with a mass of differing colours, and you might find ammonite fossils on its shores. Just outside the park, but towering over it to the north, is **Cerro San Lorenzo** (3706 m), the highest peak in southern Patagonia. Between the lakes are other peaks, permanently snow-covered, the highest of which is Cerro Herros (2770 m). The vivid hues of Sierra Colorada run across the northeast of the park: the erosion of these coloured rocks has given the lakes their differing colours. At the foot of Cerro Casa de Piedra is a network of caves containing cave paintings, accessible only with a guide. Wildlife in the park

Exploring Argentina

Francisco 'Perito' Moreno was one of Argentina's most prolific explorers. He played a leading role in defending Argentine rights in Patagonia and was pivotal in creating Argentina's first national park. Born in Buenos Aires in 1852, he showed an interest in flora and fauna early on, and by the age of 14 he had created his first collection of specimens – a collection that would go on to form the basis of the famous La Plata History Museum. When he was 20 he embarked on a series of expeditions for the Argentine Scientific Society, and it was through these that he became a household name throughout the fledgling nation. He began with a survey of the uncharted Río Negro territory, which had just opened up thanks to Roja's Conquest of the Desert campaign (see box, page 100), and by 1876 he had reached Lake Nahuel Huapi in the Lake District.

On the same trip, he 'discovered' El Chaltén in the south and named Cerro Fitz Roy. His second expedition was, however, decidedly more dangerous as he was captured by an unfriendly Tehuelche tribe and taken prisoner. He managed to escape down a river, with an injured leg the day before his execution. After several more expeditions, namely to claim Patagonian land for Argentina, he was given the name 'Perito' (expert) in 1902. For his exploring efforts the government gave him land in the Lake District, which he subsequently donated in order to create the country's first national park, Parque Nacional Nahuel Huapi. Ironically, Perito Moreno never set eyes on the famed Perito Moreno Glacier; it was simply named after him because he had extensively explored the surrounding lakes and mountains.

includes guanacos, foxes and one of the most important surviving populations of the rare huemul deer. Birds include flamingos, ñandus, steamer ducks, grebes, black-necked swans, Patagonian woodpeckers, eagles and condors. The lakes and rivers are unusual for Argentina in that only native species of fish are found here, whereas in the rest of the country, trout and salmon have been introduced for fishing.

Hiking

Several good hikes are possible from here. There are also longer walks of up to five days. Ask the *guardaparques* for details, and see the website. You should always inform *guardaparques* before setting out on a hike.

Lago Belgrano ① *1-2 hrs.* Follow the Senda Natural Península Belgrano to the peninsula of the lake, 8 km, where there are fine views of Cerro Herros and an experience of transition landscape from steppe to forest.

Lago Burmeister ① *Via Cerro Casa de Piedra, 16 km.* The trail follows the northern shore and offers nice views of the lake. There is free camping (no fires permitted). It is hard to find the official trail in parts, but if in doubt, follow the shore.

Cerro León ① *4 hrs*. Start at **Estancia La Oriental**. This walk has fabulous panoramic views over the park and offers the chance to see condors in flight.

◉ Ruta 40 listings

For hotel and restaurant price codes and other relevant information, see pages 20-26.

● Where to stay

There are some superb *estancias* in this region. They are tricky to get to without your own transport but offer an unforgettable experience of Patagonian life.

Sarmiento and the petrified forests *p544*

$$$ Chacra Labrador, 10 km from Sarmiento, T0297-489 3329, agna@ coopsar.com.ar. Excellent small *estancia*, breakfast included, other meals extra and available for non-residents, English and Dutch spoken, runs tours to petrified forests at good prices, will collect guests from Sarmiento (same price as taxi).
$ Colón, Perito Moreno 645, T0297-489 4212. One of the better cheap places in town.
$ Los Lagos, Roca y Alberdi, T0297-489 3046. Good, heating, restaurant.

Camping
Club Deportivo Sarmiento, 25 de Mayo y Ruta 20, T0297-489 3101. **Río Senguer**, RP 24, 1 km from centre, T0297-489 8482.

Río Mayo *p544*
$$$$ Estancia Don José, 3 km west of Río Mayo, T02963-420015 or T0297-15-624 9155, www.turismoguenguel.com.ar. Excellent *estancia*, with superb food, 2 rooms and 1 cabin. The family business involves sustainable production of guanaco fibre.

Camping
There is a free campsite on the northern outskirts, near the river.

Perito Moreno and around *p545*
$$ Americano, San Martín 1327, T02963-432074, www.hotelamericanoweb.com. ar. 12 pleasant rooms, some superior, decent restaurant.
$$ Hotel El Austral, San Martín 1381, T02963-432605, hotelaustral@speedy. com.ar. Similar to others on the main street, but clean.
$$ Belgrano, San Martín 1001, T02963-432019. This hotel is often booked by Ruta 40 long-distance bus companies, basic, not always clean, 1 key fits all rooms, helpful owner, breakfast extra, excellent restaurant.
$ Alojamiento Dona María, 9 de Julio 1544, T02963-432452. Basic but well-kept.
$ pp Santa Cruz, Belgrano 1565, T02963-432133. Simple rooms.

Camping
Municipal site 2 km at Paseo Roca y Mariano Moreno, near Laguna de los Cisnes, T02963-432072. Also 2 *cabaña* places.

Estancias
$$$$ pp Telken, sheep station of the Nauta family, T02963-432079, telkenpatagonia@argentina.com or jarinauta@yahoo.com.ar. Oct-Apr. Comfortable rooms, all meals shared with family, English and Dutch spoken, horse treks and excursions (Cueva de las Manos US$80). Highly recommended.

$$$ Hostería Cueva de Las Manos, 20 km from the cave at Estancia Los Toldos, 60 km south, 7 km off the road to Perito Moreno, T02963-432207 or T0297-15-623 8811 (mobile), www.cuevadelasmanos.net. 1 Nov-5 Apr, closed Christmas and New Year. Private rooms and dorms, runs tours to the caves, horse riding, meals extra and expensive.

$$ Estancia Turística Casa de Piedra, 80 km south of Perito Moreno on Ruta 40, in Perito Moreno ask for Sr Sabella, Av Perón 941, T02963-432199. Price is for rooms, camping, hot showers, home-made bread, use of kitchen, excursions to Cueva de las Manos and volcanoes by car or horse.

Los Antiguos p546

$$$ Antigua Patagonia, Ruta 43, T02963-491038, www.antiguapatagonia.com.ar. Luxurious rooms with beautiful views, excellent restaurant. Tours to Cueva de las Manos and nearby Monte Zevallos.

$$$-$ Mora, Av Costanera 1064, T02963-15-420 7472, www.hotelmorapatagonia.com. Rooms range from dorms to 1st class with private bath. Parking, lake views, corporate rates, multi-purpose room.

$$ Sol de Mayo, Av 11 de Julio, Chacra 133 'A', T02963-491232, chacrasoldemayo@hotmail.com. Basic rooms with shared bath, kitchen, central, also has cabins for rent.

$ pp Albergue Padilla, San Martín 44 (just off main street), T02963-491140. Comfortable dorms, doubles (**$$**); *quincho* and garden. Also camping. El Chaltén travel tickets.

Camping

An outstanding **Camping Municipal**, 2 km from centre on Ruta Provincial 43, T02963-491387, with hot showers, US$4 pp, also has cabins for 4 (no linen).

Bajo Caracoles and south to Tres Lagos p547

$$$$ Hostería Lagos del Furioso, Lago Posadas, on the peninsula between the lakes, reached along R39, T02963-490253 (Buenos Aires, T011-5237 4043), www.lagosdelfurioso.com.ar. Open mid-Oct to Easter. Extremely comfortable accommodation in cabins in a really incredible setting by the lake. Offers superb Patagonian cooking with home-grown produce and good wines. Also offers horse riding, trekking and excursions in a 4WD. 2 nights minimum – you'll want to stay longer.

$$ Hotel Bajo Caracoles, Bajo Caracloes, T02963-490100. Old-fashioned but hospitable, meals.

$ Restaurant Ahoniken, Av San Martín, Tres Lagos. Has rooms.

Estancias

$$$ pp La Angostura, 55 km from Gobernador Gregores, T02962-491501, www.estancialaangostura.com.ar. Offers horse riding, trekking and fishing. Recommended.

Camping

The campsite is in the middle of Bajo Caracoles. Rooms (**$ pp**) are also available. A simple and welcoming place, also runs excursions to Cueva de las Manos, 10 km by vehicle then 1½-2 hrs' walk, and to nearby volcanoes by car or horse. Ask for **Señor Sabella**, Av Perón 941, Perito Moreno, T02963-432199.

Estancia La Lucia, Tres Lagos, US$2.50, water, barbecue, 'a little green paradise'; supermarket, fuel.

Parque Nacional Perito Moreno p548

$$$ full board Estancia La Oriental, T02962-452196, laorientalpatagonia@yahoo.com.ar. Splendid setting, with comfortable rooms. Nov-Mar, with horse riding, trekking.

🍴 Restaurant

Perito Moreno *p545*
There's good food at **Pipach**, next to Hotel Austral.

Los Antiguos *p546*
Viva El Viento, 11 de Julio 477, T02963-491109, www.vivaelviento.com. Daily 0900-2100 in high season. Dutch-owned, good atmosphere, food and coffee, also has Wi-Fi internet, lots of information, boats on the lake arranged, horse riding, trips to Cueva de Las Manos. Live music Tue. Recommended.
Several other places in town.

⏰ What to do

Sarmiento and the petrified forests *p544*
Aonikenk Viajes, Rawson 1190, T0297-446 6768, www.aonikenk.com.ar. Tours to the petrified forest.

Perito Moreno *p545*
Tour operators
Las Loicas, Transporte Lago Posadas, T02963-490272, www.lasloicas.com, offers an all-day tour with the option of collecting passengers from Bajo Caracoles. Also does the Circuito Grande Comarca Noroeste, one of the highlights of Santa Cruz, taking in some of the province's scenery.
Zoyen Turismo, San Martín near Saavedra, T02963-432207, www.zoyen turismo.com.ar. The friendly staff can help with R40 connections and *estancia* visits.

Los Antiguos *p546*
Tour operators
Turismo Toscas Bayas, 11 de Julio 797, T02963-491016, toscasbayas@yahoo.com. ar. Can arrange trips to the Cueva de las Manos, Monte Zeballos, Lago Posadas and more. They also run city tours, 4 hrs. Friendly.

🚌 Transport

Sarmiento and the petrified forests *p544*
Bus
Overnight services to **Esquel**, Sun-Fri, with **Etap**, T0297-454756, US$32-37; take food for the journey, as cafés are expensive. Frequent buses to **Comodoro Rivadavia**, US$11.

Río Mayo *p544*
Bus
To **Sarmiento** once a day (2115) with **Etap**, US$13, 2 hrs.

Perito Moreno *p545*
Air
LADE (Av San Martín 1059, T02963-432055) flies to **Perito Moreno** from **Río Gallegos**, **Río Grande**, **Ushuaia**, **El Calafate** and **Gobernador Gregores**.

Bus
Road distances: Bariloche 823 km, El Chaltén 582 km, El Calafate 619 km; it is nearly impossible to hitchhike between Perito Moreno and El Calafate as there's hardly any traffic and few services.To **Los Antiguos border** crossing, 2 buses daily in summer, 1 hr, US$3.35, with **La Unión** T02963-432133. To **El Chaltén** and **El Calafate**, **Chaltén Travel** (www.chaltentravel.com) at 1015.

Chaltén Travel also runs a tourist service to **Puerto Madryn** at 0630 every other day from **Hotel Belgrano**.

Car
Several mechanics on C Rivadavia and Av San Martín, good for repairs.

Taxi
Parada El Turista, Av San Martín y Rivadavia, T02963-432592.

Los Antiguos *p546*
Bus
To **Comodoro Rivadavia**, with **Sportman** (at Terminal, T0297-15-405 3769) 2 daily, US$37. **Chaltén Travel** (open only in high season, at Hotel Belgrano, www.chaltentravel.com) runs to **El Chaltén** (10 hrs, US$80) and **El Calafate** (12 hrs, US$106), via Perito Moreno, every other (even) day at 0800; also north to **Bariloche**, every even day, mid-Nov to

Apr, US$80. Also **Marga** to El Calafate, all year round at 0700, US$90, 16½ hrs, and **Cal-Tur** (www.caltur.com.ar). To **Chile**: La Unión to **Chile Chico**, 8 km west, US$4, 45 mins including border crossing.

🅘 Directory

Perito Moreno *p545*
Banks and currency exchange
There are 2 ATMs at **Banco de la Provincia de Santa Cruz** and **Banco de la Nación**. TCs can be cashed at Banco Santa Cruz SA, Av San Martín 1385, T02963-432028, where they also change US$, € and Chilean pesos.

Los Antiguos *p546*
Banks ATM on Av 11 de Julio.
Medical services Hospital Patagonia, Argentina 68, T02963-491303. **Farmacia Rossi Abatedaga**, Av 11 Julio 231, T02963-491204.

Parque Nacional Los Glaciares

Of all Argentina's impressive landscapes, the sight of these immense glaciers stretching out infinitely and silently before you may stay with you longest. This is the second largest national park in Argentina, extending along the Chilean border for over 170 km, almost half of it covered by the 370-km-long Southern Ice Cap. From it, 13 major glaciers descend into two great lakes: Lago Argentino in the southeast and Lago Viedma to the northeast. Two quite different areas of the park are centres for tourism. At the southern end, the spectacular glaciers themselves can be visited from El Calafate, with bus and boat trips to Glaciares Moreno, Upsala and Spegazzini. At the northern end, reached from El Chaltén, 217 km northwest of El Calafate, there is superb trekking around the dramatic Fitz Roy massif and ice climbing on glaciers near its summit. The central section, between Lago Argentino and Lago Viedma, is composed of the ice cap on the western side, with a couple of *estancias* open to tourists. East of the ice fields, there's plentiful southern beech forest, but further east still, the land flattens to the typical wind-blasted Patagonian steppe, with sparse vegetation. Birdlife is surprisingly prolific, and you'll spot the scarlet-headed Magallenic woodpecker, black-necked swans, and perhaps even the torrent duck, diving for food in the streams and rivers. Guanacos, grey foxes, skunks and rheas can be seen on the steppe, while the rare huemul inhabits the forest. The entire national park is a UNESCO World Heritage Site. For more information, see www.losglaciares.com.

Arriving at Parque Nacional Los Glaciares

Getting there
Access to the park is very straightforward at both El Calafate and El Chaltén, although all transport gets heavily booked in the summer months of January and February. There are flights to El Calafate from Buenos Aires, Ushuaia, Río Gallegos, Esquel, Comodoro Rivadavia, Bariloche and Puerto Natales in Chile. There are regular bus services into the park from El Calafate, as well as many tourist excursions, combining bus access with boat trips, walking and even ice trekking on Glaciar Perito Moreno. From El Chaltén you can hike directly into the park, with a well-established network of trails leading to summits, lakes and glaciers around Mount Fitz Roy, with many campsites. There are several buses daily to El Chaltén from El Calafate.

Best time to visit
Although this part of Patagonia is generally cold, there is a milder microclimate around Lago Viedma and Lago Argentino, which means that summers can be reasonably pleasant, with average summer temperatures between 5°C and 22°C, though strong winds blow constantly at the foot of the Cordillera. Precipitation on the Hielo Sur, up to 5000 mm annually, falls mainly as snow. In the forested area, rainfall is heavier and falls mainly between March and late May. In winter, the whole area is inhospitably cold, and most tourist facilities are closed, although El Calafate and the Perito Moreno Glaciar are open all year round. The best time to visit is between November and April, avoiding January and early February, when Argentines take their holidays, campsites are crowded and accommodation is hard to find.

Park information
The park is open 0800-2100 daily in January and February and 0800-1600 for the rest of the year. Entrance costs US$27.50, to be paid at the gates of the park, 50 km west of El Calafate. There is a **park office** ① *Av del Libertador 1302, T02901-491005, www. losglaciares.com, Oct-Apr daily 0800-1900, May-Oct daily 0800-1800,* in El Calafate. The **El Chaltén park office** ① *T02962-493004, same opening hours,* is across the bridge at the entrance to town. Both hand out helpful trekking maps of the area, with paths and campsites marked, distances and walking times. Note that the hotel, restaurant and transport situation in this region changes greatly between high and low season.

El Calafate → *For listings, see pages 568-576. Colour map 6, B2.*

El Calafate sits on the south shore of Lago Argentino and exists almost entirely as a tourist centre for visiting Parque Nacional los Glaciares, 50 km west. Though the town was founded in 1927, it grew very slowly until the opening of the road to the Perito Moreno Glacier in the 1960s, since which time it has expanded rapidly as a tourist town. Almost all of El Calafate's inhabitants, as is the case with El Chaltén, came from Buenos Aires or other large provincial capitals. Over the last few years, the global economic recession and a decline in tourism has seen many people

Parque Nacional Los Glaciares

Perito Moreno
Cerro Torre (3102m)
Fitz Roy (3405m)
Laguna Torre
El Chaltén
Río de las Vueltas
Glaciar Viedma
Gemelos Blancos (3127m)
Lago Viedma
23
To Route 40
Canal Viedma
Estancia Helsingfors
Glaciar Upsala
Murallón (3158m)
Lago Pascale
Lago Azul
69
To Route 40
Estancia Cristina
Agassiz (3180m)
Bolados (2544m)
Lago Tannhäusser
Brazo Upsala
Brazo Onelli
Lago Onelli
Glaciar Agassiz
Onelli (2620m)
Glaciar Spegazzini
Canal Spegazzini
Brazo Norte
19
To Route 40
Inmaculado (2343m)
Lago Escondido
Lago Argentino
Estancia Alice
Isla Solitaria
Punta Gualicho
Canal de los Témpanos
Punta Bandera
El Calafate
11
Seno 44 Mayo
Paredon (2165m)
Glaciar Ameghino
Península Magallanes
Los Notros
Brazo Rico
Estancia Alta Vista
15
Pietrobelli (2950m)
Glaciar Perito Moreno
Lago Roca
Estancia Nibepo Aike
CHILE
Brazo Sur
Lago Frías
N
10 km
10 miles
Comandante Piedrabuena (2464m)

returning back north, and the population of El Calafate has dropped by a couple of thousand. The town itself can be expensive, and sometimes in January and February the hotels, hostels and *cabañas* can't quite accommodate the hordes, so it's essential to book ahead. The town is empty and quiet all winter, when it can be extremely cold, and most tourist services close down; it's best to come in March or April if you can, although, if you can brave the weather, you can visit the Perito Moreno Glacier all year round. For more information on El Calafate, see www. losglaciares.com and www.todocalafate.com.

Arriving in El Calafate → *Phone code 02902. Population 8000.*
Getting there The airport, Lago Argentino ① *T02902-491220*, is 23 km east of town. A minibus service run by **Transpatagonia Expeditions**, T02902-493766, runs from town to meet flights, US$10 open return. A taxi (T02902-491655/491745) costs US$13. Bus travel to El Calafate is convenient, with buses from Río Gallegos (where you can connect with buses to Ushuaia) arriving in the centre of town. There are also buses to Puerto Natales, via Cerro Castillo, if you want to come directly from Torres del Paine. The bus terminal ① *Julio A Roca 1004, T02902-491090, daily 0800-2200*, is centrally located up a steep flight of steps from the main street, Avenida del Libertador. A terminal fee of US$0.65 is always included in the bus ticket price. Some bus companies will store luggage for a fee.

Getting around El Calafate's shops, restaurants and tour operators can mostly be found along its main street, Avenida del Libertador, running east to west, with hotels lying within two blocks north and south and smaller *hosterías* scattered through the residential areas sprawling up the hill and north of centre, across the river. There are many *estancias* on the way to the national park, and also campsites. A small local public transport system carries people from one end of the city to the other, which is useful if you are staying at some of the hotels on the edge of town. Bus travel and tour trips to the Perito Moreno glaciers are well organized, although they can be more difficult to arrange out of season. The cheapest method is with a regular bus service, but tours can be informative and some include a boat trip.

Tourist information There is a helpful **tourist office** ① *in the bus station, T02902-491476, www.elcalafate.tur.ar, and at Rosales y Av del Libertador, T02902-491090, both daily 0800-2000*. They have folders of helpful information that you can browse.

Places in El Calafate
Just west of the town centre is **Bahía Redonda**, a shallow part of Lago Argentino that freezes in winter, when ice-skating and skiing are possible. At the eastern edge of the bay, **Laguna Nímez** ① *high season daily 0900-2000, low season 1000-1700, US$6*, is a bird reserve where there are flamingos, black-necked swans and ducks; the 2.5-km self-guided trail with multilingual leaflets is recommended for an hour's stroll either early morning or late afternoon. To get there from the **Intendencia del Parque** ① *Av del Libertador 1302*, follow Calle Bustillo up the road to cross the bridge. Keep heading north across a pleasant new residential area: the *laguna* is signposted.

On the way back, you can stop by the **Centro de Interpretación Histórica** ① *Av Brown and Bonarelli, T02902-492799, US$8*, a small well-run centre housing a very educative exhibition created by an anthropologist and a historian with pictures and bilingual texts about the region. There's also a very relaxing café and library. The **Glaciarium** ① *6 km from town on R11, http://glaciarium.com, daily 0900-2000, US$18, US$10 (6-12s), free bus from provincial tourist office hourly*, is a modern museum dedicated to Patagonian ice and glaciers, with an ice-bar (daily 1100-2000, US$15 for 25 mins, includes drink), café and shop.

Around El Calafate

From El Calafate you can visit Glaciar Perito Moreno by bus and boat, and even go trekking on its surface. Alternatively, travel by boat along the western arms of Lago Argentino, between stately floating icebergs, to see the glaciers of Spegazzini and Upsala. Best of all, take the long-day excursion by boat to **Estancia Cristina**, which

El Calafate

To ②⑧, Punta Gualicho, Laguna Nimez & Centro de Interpretación Histórica

200 metres
200 yards

Where to stay 🛏
1 Albergue y Hostal Lago Argentino
2 Alto Verde
3 América del Sur
4 Ariel
5 Cabañas Nevis
6 Calafate Hostel & Hostería
7 Camping AMSA
8 Casa de Grillos B&B
10 El Quijote
11 Hostel Buenos Aires
12 Hostel del Glaciar 'Libertador'
13 Hostel del Glaciar 'Pioneros'
14 i Keu Ken Hostel
15 Kau Yatún
16 Kosten Aike
17 Los Alamos
18 Marcopolo Inn Calafate
19 Michelangelo
20 Patagonia Rebelde
21 Sir Thomas
22 Vientos del Sur

Restaurants 🍴
1 Borges y Alvarez
2 Casablanca
4 Heladería Aquarela
5 La Lechuza
6 La Tablita
7 La Vaca Atada
9 Pura Vida
10 Rick's Restaurante
11 Viva la Pepa

gives you the chance to trek or ride horses up to a spectacular viewpoint above the Upsala glacier. All these trips are breathtakingly beautiful and an unforgettable part of your visit to Patagonia. For details, see page 573. However, El Calafate has a number of other attractions, worth considering if you're here for a few days, including some good places for trekking, horse riding and exploring by 4WD.

At **Punta Gualicho** (or Walichu) on the shores of Lago Argentino, 7 km east of town, there are cave paintings. Though they're rather badly deteriorated, the six-hour horse ride (US$50 per person) is worthwhile. Some tour operators run excursions to the top of nearby hills for views of the southern end of the Andes, **Bahía Redonda** and Isla Solitaria on Lago Argentino. An easy five-hour walk (or horse ride) is possible to the top of Cerro Calafate for panoramic views too; ask for directions at the **Hostel del Glaciar Pioneros**. Trekking, 4WD or horse-riding trips to the top of Cerro Frías (1030 m) for fantastic views of Mount Fitz Roy, Paine and Lago Argentino are organized by **Cerro Frías** ① *Libertador 1857, T02902-492808, www. cerrofrias.com*, for around US$63 per person, including lunch (US$43 without lunch).

Several *estancias* are within reach, offering a day on a working farm, a lunch of Patagonian lamb, cooked *asado al palo* (speared on a metal structure over an open fire), and activities such as trekking, birdwatching and horse riding. **Estancia Alice** ① *T02902-497503 (T011-5217 6719 in Buenos Aires), www.elgalpondelglaciar.com.ar*, also known as 'El Galpón del Glaciar', 21 km west, is a lovely house with views of Lago Argentino. It offers 'El Día de Campo', including tea with home-made cakes, walks through a bird sanctuary where 43 species of bird have been identified, displays of sheep shearing, *asado* and music shows, all for US$64 per person (including transfer to and from hotels); English spoken. See also Where to stay, page 568.

Lago Roca, 40 km southwest of El Calafate, is set in beautiful open landscape, with hills above offering panoramic views, perfect for lots of activities, such as trout and salmon fishing, climbing, walking. There are *estancias* here too, such as the beautifully set **Estancia Nibepo Aike** ① *on Brazo Sur of Lago Argentino in the national park, 55 km southwest (book at Av Libertador 1215 p 1A, T02902-492797, Buenos Aires T011-5272 0341, www.nibepoaike.com.ar)*, where you can watch typical farm activities, such as the branding of cattle in summer. There is good camping in a wooded area and a restaurant. At **Estancia Quien Sabe**, strawberries and walnuts are grown, and you can see beehives and sheep shearing, and eat an *asado* lunch; contact **Turismo Leutz**, www.leutzturismo.com.ar.

Lago Argentino → *For listings, see pages 568-576.*

Glaciar Perito Moreno

The sight of this expanse of ice, like a frozen sea, its waves sculpted by wind and time into beautiful turquoise folds and crevices, is unforgettable. You'll watch in awed silence, until suddenly a mighty roar announces the fall of another hunk of ice into the milky turquoise water below. Glaciar Moreno is one of the few accessible glaciers in the world that you can see visibly advancing. Some 30 km long, it reaches the water at a narrow point in one of the fjords, **Brazo Rico**, opposite Península

Magallanes. At this point the glacier is 5 km across and 60 m high. It occasionally advances across Brazo Rico, blocking the fjord, but, in recent decades, as the water pressure builds up behind it, the ice has broken, reopening the channel and sending giant icebergs (*témpanos*) rushing down the appropriately named **Canal de los Témpanos**. This happened in February 1988, March 2004, March 2006, in winter 2008 and January 2013. The frequency is raising concern that global warming is causing a marked change in the glacier's behaviour. Walking on the ice itself is a wonderful way to experience the glacier: what appear from a distance to be vertical fish scales, turn out to be huge peaks; climb their steep curves and look down into mysterious chasms below, lit by refracted bluish light.

Access There are various ways to approach the glacier. Tour companies in El Calafate offer all of these or some in combination. The regular bus service and all excursions not involving boat trips will take you straight to the car park that is situated 77 km west of El Calafate (around 30 km beyond the gates of the park). From here you begin the descent along a series of extensive wooden walkways (*pasarelas*) to see the glacier slightly from above, and then, as you get lower, directly head-on. There are several wide viewing areas, where crowds wait expectantly in summer, cameras poised, for another hunk of ice to fall with a mighty roar from the vertical blue walls at the glacier's front into the milky turquoise lake below. There is a large and fairly inexpensive café at the site with clean bathrooms.

You could also approach the glacier on a boat trip from two different piers. To survey the glacier from the south (and for trekking on the glacier), boats leave from Bajo de las Sombras pier (7 km east of the glacier). To approach from the north, boats leave regularly from Perito Moreno pier (1 km north of the glacier, where there is a restaurant). This latter service is offered as an extra (US$18) when you book your standard excursion to the glacier or it can be booked directly at the pier.

To get closer still, there are guided treks on the ice itself, known as Big Ice and Minitrekking, which allow you to walk along the crevices and frozen wave crests in crampons (provided). The latter is not technically demanding and is possible for anyone with a reasonable level of fitness. The glacier is approached by a lovely walk through lenga forest, and there's a place to eat your lunch outside, with wonderful views; but bring your own food and drink. ➤➤ *See What to do, page 573.*

Glaciar Upsala

The fjords at the northwestern end of Lago Argentino are fed by four other glaciers. The largest is the Upsala Glacier, named after the Swedish university that commissioned the first survey of this area in 1908. It's a stunning expanse of untouched beauty, three times the area of the Perito Moreno Glacier and the longest glacier flowing off the Southern Patagonian icefield. However, Upsala is suffering tremendously from the effects of global warming. Unusually, it ends in two separate frontages, each about 4 km wide and 60 m high, although only one frontage can be seen on the lake excursion by motorboat from Punta Bandera on Lago Argentino, 50 km west of Calafate. The trip also goes to other, much smaller, glaciers: **Spegazzini**, which has a frontage 1.5 km wide and 130 m high, and **Agassiz** and **Onelli** glaciers, both of which feed into **Lago Onelli**. This is a quiet and very beautiful lake, full of icebergs of every size and sculpted shape, surrounded by beech forests on one side and ice-covered mountains on the other.

The best way to see Upsala Glacier is to visit the remote **Estancia Cristina** ⓘ *9 de Julio 69, El Calafate, T02902-491133 (T011-4218 2333 in Buenos Aires), www. estanciacristina.com*, which lies in a lonely spot on the northern shores of Lago Argentina, not far from the glacier. It's beautiful, utterly wild and yet is an unbeatably comfortable base for exploring the region. Accommodation is available (see Where to stay), or you can come on a full-day visit that includes lunch and the option to go hiking for five hours, horse riding or driving in sturdy 4WD vehicles to a vantage point high above the lake. You'll walk through incredible ancient landscapes, alongside massive rocks polished smooth by the path of glaciers, to see Upsala Glacier from above. This is an overwhelmingly beautiful sight, stretching apparently endlessly away from you, with the deep, still Prussian-blue lake below, and rocks the colour of fire all around. Boat trips and day visits to **Estancia Cristina** are run by the *estancia* itself; see the website for details.

Cerro Fitz Roy and around → *For listings, see pages 568-576.*

The soaring granite towers of Mount Fitz Roy rise up from the smooth baize of the flat steppe, more like a ziggurat than a mountain, surrounded by a consort of jagged snow-clad spires, with a stack of spun-cotton clouds hanging constantly above them. **Cerro Fitz Roy** (3405 m) is one of the most magnificent mountains in the world, and it towers above the nearby peaks, its polished granite sides too steep for snow to settle. Its Tehuelche name was El Chaltén ('smoking mountain' or 'volcano'), perhaps because occasionally at sunrise the pink towers are briefly lit up bright red for a few seconds, the *amanecer de fuego* ('sunrise of fire'). Perito Moreno named the peak after the captain of the *Beagle*, who saw it from afar in 1833, and it was first climbed by a French expedition in 1952. It stands in the northern section of Parque Nacional Los Glaciares, at the western end of Lago Viedma, 230 km north of El Calafate. Around it are other high peaks, lakes and glaciers that combine to make marvellous trekking country, every bit as satisfying as Torres del Paine across the border.

Arriving in the Fitz Roy area

Getting to Cerro Fitz Roy The base for walking and climbing around Fitz Roy is the tiny town of El Chaltén. The quickest way to reach the town is by flying to El Calafate's airport, 220 km away. There are frequent bus connections from El Calafate (four hours), and regular bus services in summer from Ruta 40 in the north, useful if you've come from the Lake District in either Argentina or Chile.

Getting around Most paths are very clear and well worn, but a map is essential, even on short walks. The park information centre provides helpful maps of treks, but the best are published by *Zagier and Urruty*, www.patagoniashop.net, regularly updated and available in various scales (1:50,000; 1:250,000; 1:350,000), US$6-15. They are sold in shops in El Calafate and El Chaltén. Do not stray from the paths. Always wear sunscreen (factor 30 at least) and be prepared for bad weather. See below for minibus services to Lago del Desierto.

The Fitz Roy area

Camping Δ
Capri **4**
De Agostini **5**

Laguna Toro **6**
Piedra del Fraile **1**
Poincenot **3**

Río Blanco
(Climbers only) **2**

Trekking advice and information

• There are campsites at Poincenot, Capri, De Agostini and Laguna Toro. (Note Rio Blanco is only for climbers with prior permission arranged.) Campsites have no services, but all have toilets, apart from Laguna Toro.
• Access is free. There's no need to register before you leave on walks, and the paths are well marked. But stick to the centre of the path so as not to make it any bigger and walk in single file (at times that means you'll be walking in a rut).
• The park information centre will give you a good map which recommends lots of walks, times for walking and tells you where campsites are. Times given on their sheet are for walking one way only.
• As you leave El Chaltén, don't let the dogs follow you, as they frighten the huemules (rare wild deer, an endangered species).
• Don't bathe in rivers and lakes, and take water away from source to wash.
• Don't go to the toilet near water sources, and take all rubbish down the mountain with you.
• A gas/alcohol stove is essential for camping as fires are prohibited everywhere in the park.
• Take plenty of warm clothes and a good sleeping bag. It is possible to rent equipment in El Chaltén; ask at the park office or Rancho Grande hostel.

Tourist information The **tourist information office** ① *Güemes 21, T02962-493011, www.elchalten.com, Mon-Fri 0900-2000, Sat-Sun 1300-2000*, has an excellent website with accommodation listed. The staff hand out trekking maps of the area that show paths, campsites, distances and walking times. There's another tourist office at the bus station. The national park office is across the bridge, right at the entrance to the town, T02962-493004, www.parquesnacionales.gov.ar, see above for opening hours. Visitors are met by the friendly *guardaparques* (some speak English), who you should ask for advice on trekking and climbing.

Best time to visit Walking here is only really viable from mid-October to April, with the best months usually March to early April when the weather is generally stable and not very cold, and the autumn colours of the beech forest are stunning. Midsummer (December and January) and spring (September to October) are generally very windy. In December and January the campsites can be full to bursting, with many walkers on the paths. Outside of these months most accommodation and many services close.

El Chaltén → *Phone code 02962. Colour map 6, B2.*
The small modern town of El Chaltén is set in a wonderful position at the foot of Cerro Fitz Roy and at the mouth of the valley of the Río de las Vueltas. The village was founded very recently, in 1985, in order to settle the area and pre-empt Chilean territorial claims. However, it has grown very rapidly, along with its popularity as a centre for trekking and climbing in summer, and for cross-country skiing in winter. It

El Chaltén

can be an expensive and not particularly attractive place, especially when the harsh wind blows. But its visitors create a cheerful atmosphere, there are some great bars, and from its concrete and tin dwellings you can walk directly into breathtaking landscapes. There is a small chapel, the **Capilla Tomás Egger**, named after an Austrian climber killed on Fitz Roy and built entirely from materials brought from Austria. Tourist infrastructure is still developing, and so far there is only one ATM (right next to the gas station at the entrance to town); consider taking extra cash in case it isn't working. Luckily credit cards are accepted in all major hotels and most restaurants. Accommodation is available and ranges from camping and hostels to not-quite-luxurious *hosterías* and some top hotels, all overpriced in high season. Food is expensive too, though there is an increasing amount of choice.
�»» *For listings, see pages 568-576.*

Trekking

The main attraction here is the trekking around the Fitz Roy or Torre cordons. Always ask at your accommodation, at the tourist office or with the *guardaparques* for up-to-date information on trails and weather conditions. The best day walks are Laguna Capri and Mirador Laguna Torre, both of which have great views.

Laguna Torre For a dramatic approach to Cerro Torre, take the path to Laguna Torre (three hours each way). After 1½ hours you'll come to Mirador Laguna Torre, with views of Cerro Torre and Cerro Fitz Roy, and after another 1¼ hours, to busy Camping De Agostini (formerly Bridwell), next to the lake, with fantastic views of the Cordón Torre.

Laguna de los Tres For closer views of Cerro Fitz Roy, take the path to Laguna de los Tres (four hours each way). Walk up to **Camping Capri** (just under two hours), with great views of Fitz Roy, then another hour to **Camping Poincenot**. Just beyond it is **Camping Río Blanco** (only for climbers, previous registration at park office required). From Río Blanco you can walk another hour, though it's very steep, to Laguna de los Tres where you'll get a spectacular view (although not if it's cloudy). In bad weather, you're better off walking an hour to Piedras Blancas (four hours total from El Chaltén). You can connect the two walks (to Laguna Torre and Laguna de los Tres) by taking a transverse path (two hours) from a point northwest of Laguna Capri to east of **Camping De Agostini**, passing two lakes, Laguna Madre and then Laguna Hija; but note that this alternative can take more than one day.

Loma del Pliegue Tumbado A recommended day walk is to the Loma del Pliegue Tumbado viewpoint (four hours each way) where you can see both *cordones* and Lago Viedma. There's a marked path from the *guardería* with excellent panoramic views, best in clear weather. The onward trek to **Laguna Toro**, a glacial lake on the route across the ice cap (seven hours each way) is for more experienced trekkers.

Piedra del Fraile The trek up Río Blanco to Piedra del Fraile (seven hours each way) is beautiful. It starts at Campamento Río Blanco running north along the Río Blanco and west along the Río Eléctrico via Piedra del Fraile (four hours) to Lago Eléctrico. Piedra del Fraile can be reached more easily from the road to Lago del Desierto in about two hours. At Piedra del Fraile, just outside the park, there are *cabañas* (**$** per person, hot showers) and a campsite. From here a path leads south, up Cerro Eléctrico Oeste (1882 m) towards the north face of Fitz Roy (two hours); it's tough going but offers spectacular views. You should take a guide for this last bit.

Climbing
Base camp for Fitz Roy (3405 m) is Campamento Río Blanco. Other peaks include Cerro Torre (3102 m), Torre Egger (2900 m), Cerro Solo (2121 m), Poincenot (3002 m), Guillaumet (2579 m), Saint-Exupery (2558 m), Aguja Bífida (2394 m) and Cordón Adela (2938 m): most of these are for very experienced climbers. The best time to climb is generally mid-February to end March; November and December are very windy; January is fair; winter (May to July) is extremely cold, but the weather is unpredictable and it all depends on the specific route being climbed. Permits for climbing are available at the national park information office in El Chaltén. Guides are also available in El Chaltén, see What to do, page 574. **Fitz Roy Expediciones**, www.fitzroyexpediciones.com.ar, are recommended.

Lago Viedma
Lago Viedma to the south of El Chaltén can be explored by boat. The trips usually pass Glaciar Viedma, with the possibility of ice trekking too. Contact **Fitz Roy Expediciones** (see What to do, page 574) for trekking circuits that connect Lago Viedma and Lago San Martín.

Border crossings: Argentina–Chile

All crossings may have different hours in winter; see www.gendarmeria.gov.ar.
For the crossing from Lago del Desierto to Villa O'Higgins (on foot, on horseback
or by bike only), see page 567.

Paso Río Don Guillermo/Cancha Carrera
The Paso Río Don Guillermo or Cancha Carrera, 129 km west of La Esperanza and
48 km north of Río Turbio is open all year, and is the most convenient crossing
to reach Parque Nacional Torres del Paine in Chile. On the Chilean side the road
continues to Cerro Castillo, where it meets the road between Puerto Natales,
65 km south, and the national park.
Argentine customs and immigration Cancha Carrera, 2 km east of the border,
fast and friendly, daily 0900-2300.
Chilean immigration West of the border at Cerro Castillo, daily 0800-2200.

Paso Mina Uno/Dorotea
Paso Mina Uno/Dorotea is 5 km south of Río Turbio and is open all year, daily
0900-2300. On the Chilean side this road runs south to join the main Puerto
Natales–Punta Arenas road. This is the crossing used by buses from Río Turbio
to Puerto Natales.

Paso Casas Viejas
Paso Casas Viejas is 33 km south of Río Turbio via 28 de Noviembre and is open all
year, daily 0900-0100. It runs west on the Chilean side to join the Puerto Natales–
Punta Arenas road.

Lago del Desierto and around
There is stunning virgin landscape to explore around **Lago del Desierto**, 37 km
north of El Chaltén. The long skinny lake is fjord-like and surrounded by forests. It's
reached by unpaved Route 23, which leads north along the Río de las Vueltas. After
about 30 minutes' drive, there is a one-hour hike along a marked path to Chorillo del
Salto, a small but pristine waterfall. Route 23 continues via **Laguna Cóndor**, where
flamingos can be seen, to Lago del Desierto. A short walk to a mirador at the end of
the road gives fine views. There is a campsite at the southern end of the lake (usually
no food, although there is a kiosk that advertizes *choripán*), and a path runs along
the east side of the lake to its northern tip (4½ hours), where there are *refugios*. From
here a trail leads west along the valley of the Río Diablo to Laguna Diablo.

Estancia El Pilar is the best place to stay on the way to Lago del Desierto; it's in a
stunning position and has views of Fitz Roy. Visit for tea and use it as an excellent base
for trekking up Río Blanco or Río Eléctrico, with a multi-activity adventure circuit. In
summer **Transporte Las Lengas** in El Chaltén (www.transportelaslengas.com; see
also page 574) runs a minibus twice daily to Lago del Desierto, stopping at **El Pilar**
(US$11.50), and three times a day to **Río Eléctrico** (US$14). Highly recommended.

There are also excursions with Chaltén Travel daily in summer to connect with boats across the lake (see What to do, page 525).

From December to April, it is possible to travel on foot, horseback and boat from Lago del Desierto to **Villa O'Higgins** in Chile, the southernmost town on the Carretera Austral. Take the Las Lengas minibus to Lago del Desierto, then either take a boat (45 minutes) to the northern end, or walk up the eastern shore (4½ hours). From there you can trek or go on horseback (19 km, seven hours with guide, US$36) across the border to Puerto Candelario Mancilla on Lago O'Higgins. Hans Silva in Villa O'Higgins (T+56 (0)67-243 1821) offers horses and a 4WD service from the Chilean border to Candelario Mancilla (14 km, US$18, US$9 for luggage only, reserve in advance). Spend the night at Estancia Candelario Mancilla and then, the next day, take a boat to Bahía Bahamóndez (three hours, US$76.50), followed by a bus to Villa O'Higgins, 7 km, US$4. For further information on dates, tours and boat availability, see www.villaohiggins.com. Note that the border is closed from May to November.

El Calafate to Chile → *For listings, see pages 568-576.*

If travelling from El Calafate to Torres del Paine in Chile by car or bike, you can take the paved combination of Route 11, Route 40 and Route 5 to **La Esperanza** (165 km), where there's fuel, a campsite and a large but expensive *confitería* (accommodation **$$** with bath). From La Esperanza, paved Route 7 heads west along the valley of the Río Coyle. A shorter but rougher route (closed in winter), missing Esperanza, goes via El Cerrito and joins Route 7 at Estancia Tapi Aike. Route 7 continues to the border, crossing at Cancha Carrera (see box, opposite) and then meets the good *ripio* road between Torres del Paine and Puerto Natales (63 km). For bus services along this route, see Transport, page 575.

Río Turbio → *Colour map 6, B2. Phone code 02902. Population 6650.*
Located near the border, 250 km south of El Calafate, Río Turbio is a charmless place you're most likely to visit en route to or from Torres del Paine in Chile. It has a cargo railway connecting it with Punta Loyola, and visitors can see Mina 1, where the first mine was opened, but the site of Argentina's largest coalfield hasn't really recovered from the depression that hit the industry in the 1990s. There's a small ski centre nearby, **Valdelén**, which has six pistes and is ideal for beginners; there is also scope for cross-country skiing between early June and late September. For more information, visit the **tourist information** office on Plazoleta Agustín del Castillo, T02902-421950, or see www.welcomeargentina.com/rioturbio.

For hotel and restaurant price codes and other relevant information, see pages 20-26.

🛏 Where to stay

El Calafate *p555, maps p556 and p558*
Prepare to pay more for accommodation here than elsewhere in Argentina. El Calafate is very popular in Jan-Feb, so book all transport and accommodation in advance. Many hotels are open only from Sep/Oct to Apr/May.

$$$$ El Quijote, Gob Gregores 1191, T02902-491017, www.quijotehotel. com.ar. A very good hotel, spacious, well designed with traditional touches, tasteful rooms with TV, restaurant, stylish lobby bar, English and Italian spoken.

$$$$ Kau Yatún, Estancia 25 de Mayo (10 blocks from centre, east of arroyo Calafate), T02902-491059, www.kauyatun. com. Renovated main house of a former *estancia*, well-kept grounds, 2 excellent restaurants, half board or all-inclusive packages that include excursions in the National Park. Sometimes closed in low season.

$$$$ Kosten Aike, Gob Moyano 1243, T02902-492424, www.kostenaike.com.ar. Open year-round. Relaxed yet stylish, elegant spacious rooms (some superior), jacuzzi, gym, excellent restaurant, **Ariskaiken** (open to non residents), cosy bar, garden, English spoken. Recommended.

$$$$ Los Alamos, Gob Moyano y Bustillo, T02902-491144, www.posadalos alamos.com. Cheaper in low season. Very comfortable, charming rooms, good service, lovely gardens, good bar and without doubt the best restaurant in town, **La Posta**.

$$$ Alto Verde, Zupic 138, T02902-491326, www.welcomeargentina.com/ altoverde. Top quality, **$$** in low season, spotless, spacious, helpful, also with apartments for 4.

$$$ Cabañas Nevis, Av del Libertador 1696, T02902-493180, www.cabanas nevis.com.ar. Owner Mr Patterson offers very nice cabins for 5 and 8 (price quoted is for 5), some with lake view, great value.

$$$ Casa de Grillos B&B, Los Cóndores 1215, T02902-491160, www.casadegrillos. com.ar. Welcoming B&B in the calm green area, next to Nímez nature reserve. It has all the comfort and charm of a family house, **$$** low season.

$$$ Michelangelo, Espora y Gob Moyano, T02902-491045, www. michelangelohotel.com.ar. Lovely, quiet, welcoming, restaurant. Recommended.

$$$ Patagonia Rebelde, José Haro 442, T02902-494495 (in Bs As T015-5890 1276), www.patagoniarebelde.com. Charming new building in traditional Patagonian style, like an old inn with rustic decor, good comfort with well-heated bedrooms and comfy sitting-rooms.

$$$ Vientos del Sur, up the hill at Río Santa Cruz 2317, T02902-493563, www.vientosdelsur.com. Very hospitable, calm, comfortable, good views, kind family attention.

$$$-$$ Ariel, Av Libertador 1693, T493131, www.hotelariel.com.ar. Modern, functional, well maintained. Breakfast included.

$$ Hostel Buenos Aires, Buenos Aires 296, 200 m from terminal, T02902-491147, www.glaciarescalafate.com. Quiet, kind owner, helpful, comfortable with doubles, cheaper without bath, good hot showers, laundry service, luggage store, bikes for hire.

$$ Sir Thomas, Espora 257, T02902-492220, www.sirthomas.com.ar. Modern, comfortable wood-lined rooms, breakfast included.

$$-$ pp Albergue y Hostal Lago Argentino, Campaña del Desierto 1050-61 (near bus terminal), T02902-491423, www.hostallagoargentino.com.ar. **$ pp** shared dorms, too few showers when full, nice atmosphere, good flats, *cabañas* and **$$** doubles on a neat garden and also in building on opposite side of road.

$$-$ pp Calafate Hostel & Hostería, Gob Moyano 1226, T02902-492450, www.calafatehostels.com. A huge log cabin with good rooms: dorms with or without bath, breakfast extra, **$$** doubles with bath and breakfast. Book a month ahead for Jan-Feb, HI discounts, travel agency, **Always Glacier** and restaurant **Isabel** on premises.

$$-$ pp Marcopolo Inn Calafate, Calle 405, T02902-493899, www.marcopoloinncalafate.com. Part of Hostelling International. **$ pp** in dorms. Laundry facilities, various activities and tours on offer.

$ pp América del Sur, Puerto Deseado 153, T02902-493525, www.americahostel.com.ar. Panoramic views from this comfortable, relaxed hostel, welcoming, well-heated rooms (dorms for 4, **$$** doubles with views, 1 room adapted for wheelchair users, chill-out area, fireplace. Warmly recommended, but can be noisy.

$ pp Hostel del Glaciar 'Libertador', Av del Libertador 587 (next to the bridge), T02902-492492, www.glaciar.com. HI discounts, open Sep-May. Smaller and pricier than 'Pioneros', rooms are good and well-heated, all with own bath (US$20 pp dorms for 4 and **$$$-$$** doubles), breakfast included. Free transfer from bus terminal, laundry service. Owners run **Patagonia**

Backpackers (see below under What to do). Recommended.

$ pp Hostel del Glaciar 'Pioneros', Los Pioneros 255, T02902-491243, www.glaciar.com. Discount for HI members, open mid-Sep to mid-Mar. Accommodation for all budgets: standard **$$** doubles (also for 3 and 4) with bath, superior **$$$** doubles with bath, shared dorms up to 4 beds, US$16.50 pp. Many languages spoken, lots of bathrooms, no breakfast in dorms, only for guests in private rooms, free shuttle from bus terminal, laundry service, Wi-Fi, movie rental. Very popular, so book well in advance and double-check.

$ pp i Keu Ken Hostel, F M Pontoriero 171, T02902-495175, www.patagonia ikeuken.com.ar. On a hill, very helpful, flexible staff, hot water, heating, luggage store, good.

Camping

Ferretería Chuar, 1 block from bus terminal, sells camping gas.
AMSA, Olavarría 65 (50 m off the main road, turning south at the fire station), T02902-492247. Hot water, open in summer, US$6.50 pp.

Around El Calafate *p558*
$$$$ Hostería Alta Vista, 35 km west of El Calafate, on R15 towards Lago Roca, T02902-499902, www.hosteriaaltavista.com.ar. Set within the land of **Estancia Anita**, the largest *estancia* in the area (74,000 ha), Alta Vista is a famous *estancia* with all facilities you could possibly need, and only 15 guests. Favoured by celebrities and politicians, the lovely house was built in the 1930s and mostly retains its original style. Full-board is possible, with excellent cuisine and wines included. There are attractive walks and a great range of excursions

all within the vast expanse of the ranch. Recommended.

\$\$\$ El Galpón del Glaciar (aka **Estancia Alice**), 21 km west of El Calafate, T02902-491793 (T011-4312 7206 in Buenos Aires), www.estanciaalice.com.ar. A lovely house with views of Lago Argentino. Day trips also available.

\$\$\$ Estancia Nibepo Aike, in the far south of the park on the shores of Brazo Sur of Lago Argentino (T02966-436010 in Río Gallegos), www.nibepoaike.com.ar, www.lagosanmartin.com. Open Oct-Apr. In a spectacular setting inside the national park, near the shores of the lake. The house has 15 simple rooms, decorated with lovely old furniture, and there's a cosy sitting room. Lots of activities are possible in the park, or the surrounding 12,800 ha. The premises are open for day visits too.

Camping
El Huala, 42 km from El Calafate, on the road to Lago Roca. Free with basic facilities, open all year round.
Lago Roca, 50 km from El Calafate, T02902-499500, www. losglaciares.com/campinglagoroca. Oct-Apr. Beautifully situated, US\$6pp, bike hire, fishing licences, restaurant/*confitería*.

Lago Argentina *p559*
\$\$\$\$ Estancia Cristina, office at 9 de Julio 69, El Calafate, T02902-491133 (T011-4218 2333 in Buenos Aires), www.estanciacristina.com. Located at the northern tip of Lago Argentina, this remote *estancia* offers unrivalled access to the Upsala glacier and its surroundings. 20 comfortable rooms available in 5 lodges. Boat transfers from El Calafate are included.
\$\$\$\$ Los Notros, 70 km west of Calafate on the road to the Moreno glacier,

T02902-499510/T011-4813 7285 (Buenos Aires), www.losnotros.com. Exclusive retreat with wonderful views of the glacier, spacious rooms. You can walk, hike, trek and ride horses here. Expensive, but there are all-inclusive packages with free transfers to the glacier pasarelas included. Triple rooms available.

Fitz Roy area *p561, maps p556 and p562*
Camping
A gas/alcohol stove is essential for camping as open fires are prohibited in the National Park. Take plenty of warm clothes and a good sleeping bag. It is possible to rent equipment in El Chaltén; ask at the park office or Rancho Grande. There are campsites at Poincenot, Capri, Laguna Toro, Laguna Torre. None has services. all river water is drinkable, so do not wash within 70 m of rivers. Pack up all rubbish and take it back to town. **Camping Los Troncos/Piedra del Fraile** on Río Eléctrico is beyond the park boundary. It is privately owned and has facilities.

El Chaltén *p563, maps p562 and p564*
In high season places are full: you must book ahead. Most places close in low season.
\$\$\$\$ Hostería El Puma, Lionel Terray 212, T02962-493095, www.hosteria elpuma.com.ar. A little apart, splendid views, lounge with log fire, tasteful stylish furnishings, comfortable, transfers and big American breakfast included. Recommended.
\$\$\$\$ Los Cerros, Av San Martín 260, T02962-493182, www.loscerrosdel chalten.com. Stylish and sophisticated, in a stunning setting with mountain views, sauna, whirlpool and massage. Half-board and all-inclusive packages with excursions available.

$$$$ Senderos, Perito Moreno 35, T02962-493336, www.senderoshosteria.com.ar. 4 types of room and suite in a new, wood-framed structure, comfortable, warm, can arrange excursions, excellent restaurant.

$$$ Estancia La Quinta, on R23, 2 km south of El Chaltén, T02962-493012, www.estancialaquinta.com.ar. Oct-Apr. A spacious pioneer house with renovated rooms surrounded by beautiful gardens, very comfortable. A superb breakfast is included and the restaurant is also open for lunch and dinner. Transfer to and from El Chaltén bus terminals is included.

$$$ Lunajuim, Trevisán 45, T02962-493047, www.lunajuim.com. Stylish yet relaxed, comfortable (duvets on the beds), lounge with wood fire. Recommended.

$$$ Nothofagus, Hensen y Riquelme, T02962-493087, www.nothofagusbb.com.ar. Oct and Apr (**$$**). Cosy bed and breakfast, simple rooms, cheaper without bath and in low season, good value. Recommended.

$$ Hospedaje La Base, Av Lago del Desierto 97, T02962-493031. Good rooms for 2, 3 and 4, tiny kitchen, self service breakfast, great video lounge. Recommended.

$$-$ Ahonikenk Chaltén, Av Martín M de Güemes 23, T02962-493070. Nice simple rooms, some dorms, restaurant/pizzería attached, good pastas.

$ pp Albergue Patagonia, Av San Martín 493, T02962-493019, www.patagoniahostel.com.ar. Closed Jun-Sep. HI-affiliated, cheaper for members, small and cosy with rooms for 2 with own bath (**$$**) or for 2 (**$$**), 4, 5 or 6 with shared bath, also has cabins, video room, bike hire, laundry, luggage store and lockers, restaurant, very welcoming. Helpful information on Chaltén, also run excursions to Lago del Desierto.

$ pp Albergue Rancho Grande, San Martín 724, T02962-493005, www.ranchograndehostel.com. HI-affiliated, in a great position at the end of town with good open views and attractive restaurant and lounge, rooms for 4, with shared bath, breakfast extra. Also **$$** doubles, breakfast extra. Helpful, English spoken. Recommended. Reservations in Calafate at **Hostel/Chaltén Travel**.

$ pp Cóndor de los Andes, Av Río de las Vueltas y Halvorsen, T02962-493101, www.condordelosandes.com. Nice little rooms for up to 6 with bath, sheets included, breakfast extra, also doubles with bath (**$$$-$$**), laundry service, library, quiet, HI affiliated.

Camping
Camping del Lago, Lago del Desierto 135, T02962-493010, centrally located with hot showers. Several others.

Lago Viedma *p565*
$$$$ Estancia Helsingfors, 73 km northwest of La Leona, on Lago Viedma, T011-5277 0195 (Buenos Aires), reservations T02966-675753, www.helsingfors.com.ar. Nov-Apr. Fabulous place in a splendid position on Lago Viedma, stylish rooms, welcoming lounge, delicious food (full board), and excursions directly to glaciers and to Laguna Azul, by horse or trekking, plus boat trips.

Lago del Desierto and around *p566*
$$$ Aguas Arriba Lodge, RP23, Km 130, T011-4152 5697, www.aguasarribalodge.com. Comfortable wooden lodge on the eastern shore, reached only by boat or by a 2- to 3-hr walk (luggage goes by boat). Great views and trekking opportunities.

$$$ El Pilar, RP23, Km 17, T02962-493002, www.hosteriaelpilar.com.ar. Country house in a spectacular setting at the meeting of Ríos Blanco and de las Vueltas, with clear views of Fitz Roy. A chance to sample the simple life with access to the less-visited northern part of the park. Simple comfortable rooms, great food, breakfast and return transfers included.

Río Turbio *p567*
Hotels here are almost always full.
$$ Nazó, Gob Moyano 464, T02906-421800. Modern building, rooms for 2-4, laundry service, restaurant and bar.
$ Hostería Capipe, Paraje Julia Dufour, 9 km from town, T482935. Simple, with restaurant.

🍴 Restaurants

El Calafate *p555, map p556*
$$ La Lechuza, Av del Libertador 1301, www.lalechuzapizzas.com.ar. Good quality pizzas, pasta, salad and meat dishes. Excellent wine list. Has another branch up the road at No935.
$$ La Tablita, Cnel Rosales 28 (near the bridge). Typical *parrilla*, generous portions and quality beef. Recommended.
$$ La Vaca Atada, Av del Libertador 1176. Good home-made pastas and more elaborate and expensive dishes based on salmon and king crab.
$$ Mi Viejo, Av del Libertador 1111. Closed Tue. Popular *parrilla*.
$$ Pura Vida, Av Libertador 1876, near C 17. Open 1930-2330 only, closed Wed. Comfortable sofas, home-made Argentine food, vegetarian options, lovely atmosphere, lake view (reserve table). Recommended.
$$ Rick's Restaurante, Av del Libertador 1091. Lively *parrilla* with good atmosphere.

$$ Viva la Pepa, Emilio Amado 833. Mon-Sat 1100-2300. A mainly vegetarian café with great sandwiches and crêpes filled with special toppings. Wi-Fi, craft beers. Child-friendly.

Cafés
Borges y Alvarez, Av del Libertador 1015, 1st floor, Galería de los Gnomos, T02902-491 464. Daily till 0400. Cosy, wooden cafe-bar with huge windows looking out over the shopping street below. Affordable, with delicious lunch and dinner options, as well as live music and books for sale. Excellent place to hang out. Recommended.
Casablanca, 25 de Mayo y Av del Libertador. Jolly place for omelettes, burgers, vegetarian, 30 varieties of pizza.
Heladería Aquarela, Av del Libertador 1197. The best ice cream – try the *calafate*. Also home-made chocolates and local produce.

El Chaltén *p563, map p564*
$$ Estepa, Cerro Solo y Antonio Rojo. Small, intimate place with good, varied meals, friendly staff.
$$ Fuegia, San Martín 342. Dinner only. Pastas, trout, meat and vegetarian dishes.
$$ Josh Aike, Lago de Desierto 105. Excellent *confitería*, home-made food, beautiful building. Recommended.
$$ Pangea, Lago del Desierto 330 y San Martín. Open for lunch and dinner, drinks and coffee, calm, good music, varied menu. Recommended.
$$ Patagonicus, Güemes y Madsen. Midday to midnight. Lovely warm place with salads, *pastas caseras* and fabulous pizzas for 2, US$3-8. Recommended.
$$ Ruca Mahuida, Lionel Terray 55, T02962-493018. Widely regarded as the best restaurant with imaginative and well-prepared food.

$$ Zaffarancho (behind Rancho Grande), music bar-restaurant, good range and reasonably priced. Film nights 3 times a week.
$ Domo Blanco, San Martín 164. Delicious ice cream.
$ Las Lengas, Viedma 95, opposite tourist office, T02962-493023, laslengaselchalten@yahoo.com.ar. Cheaper than most. Plentiful meals, basic pastas and meat dishes. US$3 for meal of the day. Lots of information. Transporte Las Lengas operates from here (see What to do, page 574).

🍸 Bars and clubs

El Calafate *p555, map p556*
Borges y Alvarez, see Cafés, above.
Elba'r, 9 de Julio 57, T02902-493594. Just off the main street, this café/bar serves hard to find waffles and juices, as well as home-made beer and sandwiches.
Shackleton Lounge, Av del Libertador 3287, T02902-493516, on the outskirts of town (take a taxi). A great place to relax, with lovely views of the lake, old photos of Shackleton, a great atmosphere and good music. Highly recommended for a late drink or some good regional dishes. Also serves afternoon tea.

El Chaltén *p563, map p564*
Cervecería Bodegón El Chaltén, San Martín 564, T 02962-493109. Brews its own excellent beer, also local dishes and pizzas, coffee and cakes, English spoken. Recommended.

🎉 Festivals

El Calafate *p555, map p556*
15 Feb Lago Argentino Day. Live music, dancing and *asados*.
10 Nov Día de la Tradición. Displays of horsemanship and *asados*.

🛍 Shopping

El Calafate *p555, map p556*
Plenty of touristy shops along the main street, Av del Libertador.
Estancia El Tranquilo, Av del Libertador 935, www.eltranquilo.com.ar. Recommended for home-made local produce, especially Patagonian fruit teas, sweets and liqueurs.

El Chaltén *p563, map p564*
Several outdoor shops. Also supermarkets, although these are all expensive, with little fresh food available: **El Gringuito**, Av Antonio Rojo, has the best choice. Fuel is available next to the bridge.

🎯 What to do

El Calafate *p555, map p556*
Most agencies charge the same rates for similar excursions: minibus tours to the Perito Moreno glacier (park entry not included), US$36; minitrekking tours (transport plus a 2½-hr walk on the glacier), US$128. Note that in winter boat trips can be limited or cancelled due to bad weather.
Calafate Mountain Park, Av del Libertador 1037, T02902-491446, www.calafatemountainpark.com. Excursions in 4WD to panoramic views, 3-6 hrs. Summer and winter experiences including kayaking, quad biking, skiing and more.
Chaltén Travel, Av del Libertador 1174, T02902-492212, also Av Güemes 7, T493092, El Chaltén, www.chaltentravel. com. Huge range of tours (has a monopoly on some): glaciers, *estancias*, trekking and bus to El Chaltén. English spoken. Also sells tickets along the Ruta 40 to Perito Moreno, Los Antiguos and Bariloche (see Transport, below).

Hielo y Aventura, Av del Libertador 935, T02902-492205, www.hieloyaventura. com. Mini-trekking includes walk through forests and 2½-hr trek on Moreno glacier (crampons included); Big Ice full-day tour includes a 4-hr trek on the glacier. Also half-day boat excursion to Brazo Sur for a view of stunning glaciers, including Moreno. Recommended.

Lago San Martín, Av del Libertador 1215, p 1, T02902-492858, www.lagosanmartin. com. Operates with **Estancias Turísticas de Santa Cruz**, specializing in arranging *estancia* visits, helpful.

Mar Patag, 9 de Julio 57, of 4, T02902-492118, www.crucerosmarpatag.com. Exclusive 2-day boat excursion to Upsala, Spegazzini and Moreno glaciers, with full board. Also does a shorter full-day cruise with gourmet lunch included.

Mundo Austral, 9 de Julio 2427, T02902-492365, www.mundoaustral.com.ar. For all bus travel and cheaper trips to the glaciers, helpful bilingual guides.

Patagonia Backpackers, at Hosteles del Glaciar, T02902-491792, www. patagonia-backpackers.com. Alternative Glacier tour, entertaining, informative, includes walking, US$45. Recommended constantly.

Solo Patagonia, Av del Libertador 867, T02902-491155, www.solopatagonia.com. This company runs 2 7-hr trips taking in Upsala, Onelli and Spegazzini glaciers, US$92.

El Chaltén *p563, map p564*
Casa De Guías, Av San Martín s/n, T02962-493118, www.casadeguias. com.ar. Experienced climbers who lead groups to nearby peaks, to the Campo de Hielo Continental and on easier treks.

Chaltén Travel, Av Güemes 7, T02962-493092, www.chaltentravel.com.

Huge range of tours (see under El Calafate, above).

El Relincho, T02962-493007, www. elrelinchopatagonia.com.ar. For trekking on horseback with guides, also trekking, accommodation and rural activities.

Fitz Roy Expediciones, San Martín 56, T02962-436424, www. fitzroyexpediciones.com.ar. Organizes trekking and adventure trips including on the Campo de Hielo Continental, ice climbing schools, and fabulous longer trips. Climbers must be fit, but no technical experience required; equipment provided. Email with lots of notice to reserve. Ecocamp with 8 wilderness cabins recently opened. Highly recommended.

Patagonia Aventura, T02962-493110, www.patagonia-aventura.com. Has various ice trekking and other tours to Lago and Glaciar Viedma, also to Lago del Desierto.

Transporte Las Lengas, Viedma 95, T02962-493023; also at the bus station, T02962-493227, www.transportelas lengas.com. Transfers from El Calafate airport, plus minibuses to Lago del Desierto and Río Electrico.

⊖ Transport

El Calafate *p555, map p556*
Air
Daily flights to/from **Buenos Aires**. Many more flights in summer to **Bariloche**, **Ushuaia** and **Trelew**. LADE (J Mermoz 160, T02902-491262) flies to **Ushuaia**, **Comodoro Rivadavia**, **Río Gallegos**, **Esquel** and other Patagonian airports). Note that a boarding fee of US$21, not included in the airline ticket price, has to be paid at El Calafate.

Bus

To **Perito Moreno** glacier, with **Taqsa** and **Interlagos**, US$25 return; also guided excursions. Many agencies in El Calafate also run minibus tours (see What to do, above). Out of season trips to the glacier may be difficult to arrange.

To **Río Gallegos** daily, 4-5 hrs, US$19-25, with **Sportman** (T02966-15-464841) and **Taqsa** (T02902-491843). To **El Chaltén** daily with **Taqsa**, US$26, **Chaltén Travel** (T02902-492212, at 0800, 1300, 1830), **Los Glaciares** and **Cal-Tur** (T02902-491368, www.caltur.com. ar, who run many other services and tours), 3 hrs, US$30. To **Bariloche**, via Los Antiguos and Perito Moreno, 36 hrs, with Chaltén Travel, departs mid-Nov-Apr 0800 on odd-numbered days (0900 from El Chaltén) with an overnight stop in Perito Moreno (cheaper to book your own accommodation); also **Cal-Tur** and Taqsa to Bariloche via Los Antiguos, US$108 (frequency depends on demand). To **Ushuaia**, take a bus to Río Gallegos for connections.

To **Puerto Natales (Chile)**, daily in summer with **Cootra** (T02902-491444), via Río Turbio, 7 hrs; also with **Pacheco**, Mon, Wed, Fri 1100, or with **Turismo Zaahj** (T02902-491631), 3-9 a week depending on season, 5 hrs, US$25 (advance booking recommended, take your passport when booking, tedious customs check at border). **Note** Argentine pesos cannot be exchanged in Torres del Paine.

Car hire

Average price under US$100 per day for small car with insurance but usually only 200 free kilometres.
ON Rent a Car, Av del Libertador 1831, T02902-493788 or T02966-15-629985, onrentacar@cotecal.com.ar.

All vehicles have a permit for crossing to Chile included in the fee, but cars are poor. **Bikes for hire**, US$17 per day. Other companies include: **Localiza**, Av del Libertador 687, T02902-491398, localizacalafate@hotmail.com, and **Nunatak**, Gob Gregores 1075, T02902-491987, www.nunatakrentacar.com.ar.

Taxi

Taxis charge about US$75 for 4 passengers round trip to Perito Moreno glacier including wait of 3-4 hrs. A reliable driver is Ruben, T02902-498707. There is small taxi stand outside the bus terminal

El Chaltén *p563, map p564*
Bus

Tax of US$1.15 is charged at the terminal. In summer, buses fill quickly, so book ahead; there are fewer services off season. Daily buses to **El Calafate**, 4-5 hrs (most also stop at El Calafate airport), with **Taqsa**, US$26, **Chaltén Travel** (T02962-493092), **Los Glaciares** and **Cal-Tur** (T02962-493079). Chaltén Travel also go to Los Antiguos and Bariloche, mid-Nov to Apr 0900 on odd-numbered days. To **Piedrabuena** on Ruta 3 (for connections to Los Antiguos, Puerto Madryn, etc), Transporte **Las Lengas** (www.transportelaslengas.com.ar), 6 hrs, once a day, US$37. **Las Lengas** also has a service to El Calafate airport 3 times a day, 3 hrs, US$28, reserve in advance.

Taxi

Servicio de Remís El Chaltén, Av San Martén 430, T02962-493042, reliable.

Río Turbio *p567*
Bus

To **Puerto Natales**, 2 hrs, US$8, hourly with **Cootra** (Tte del Castillo 01, T02902-

421448), and other companies. To **El Calafate**, with **Cootra**, 4 hrs, US$20. To **Río Gallegos**, 5 hrs, US$23, **with Taqsa/Marga** (T02902-421422).

❶ Directory

El Calafate *p555, map p556*
Banks Best to take cash as high commission is charged on exchange, but there are ATMs at airport and banks. **Thaler**, Av del Libertador 963, loc 2, changes money and TCs.

El Chaltén *p563, map p564*
Banks 24-hr ATM next to the gas station at the entrance to town. Credit cards are accepted in all major hotels and restaurants.

Contents

Chilean Patagonia

At a glance

⊖ **Getting around** Local buses are
expensive and time-consuming but
reliable. If you can afford it, a hire car
is invaluable.

↻ **Time required** 3-5 days will allow
you to hike in the Torres del Paine
National Park and relax in Puerto
Natales for a day afterwards.

❀ **Weather** Dec-Mar is usually
warm and dry. The rest of the year
can be cold and windy, or humid.

✖ **When not to go** May-Jun is cold
and most places close down. Jan
can be busy, with campsites overcrowded and hiking trails packed.

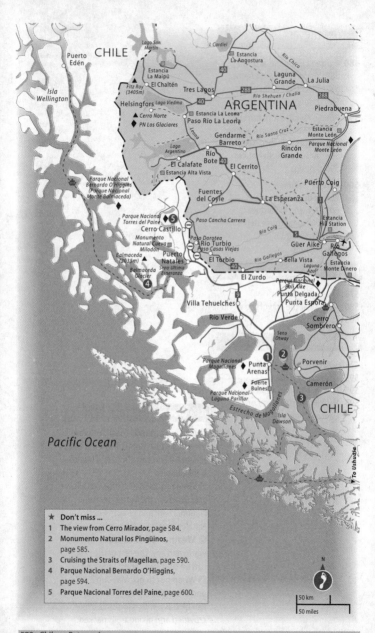

This remote land of silent fjords, hanging glaciers, pristine lakes and jagged mountains is the most visited part of Chile. Yet much of it remains a vast wilderness, with areas of staggering beauty. In the Parque Nacional Torres del Paine you can trek around the mighty towers of granite that thrust up like fingers from a mass of basalt buttresses, passing minty-green and icy-blue glacial lakes in which icebergs float. In summer, you'll share the awe-inspiring landscape with a steady stream of walkers, but start out at dawn, and you'll find solitude and silence amid some of the most dramatic landscapes on earth.

The quaint port of Puerto Natales is the nearest town, with views over the Ultima Esperanza Sound, fringed by lofty far-off peaks. Take a boat from here into Parque Nacional Bernardo O'Higgins, where glaciers descend steeply into the water, and you can even trek on the ice.

Punta Arenas is Chile's southernmost city, a complete contrast to the endless windswept sheep farms all around. Here you'll find superb fish restaurants and classy hotels in grand 1900s stone buildings, relics from the city's heyday of sheep-farming millionaires. Sail from here through the Straits of Magellan to the Argentine city of Ushuaia, or head for adventure nearby in the Parque Nacional Pali Aike to get a sense of how precarious civilization is in this wildest part of Patagonia. For general travel information on Chilean Patagonia, see www.interpatagonia.com.

Punta Arenas and around

After hours of travelling through the barren steppe of Patagonia, Punta Arenas comes as a surprise. With a grand plaza surrounded by neoclassical mansions and several fine monuments, Chile's most southerly city has an affluent history. Its strategic position on the eastern shore of the Brunswick Peninsula made it a thriving port of call when trading ships sailed through the Strait of Magellan. Landowners Braun and Menéndez made their fortunes from sheep and built a sumptuous palace filled with treasures that now forms one of the city's two fascinating museums. The other recounts the more sombre history of the ousted indigenous peoples and their own rich culture. The cemetery, an oddly beautiful place, also deserves a visit.

Although no longer as wealthy, Punta Arenas remains an upbeat, breezy place, with traditional bright tin houses away from the handsome architecture of the centre. It's a good place to spend a couple of days, with plenty of decent accommodation and some excellent fish and seafood restaurants. It's also the starting point for visiting the Magellanic penguins at Isla Magdalena and the mysterious landscape of Pali Aike, as well as for more challenging expeditions into the wilderness of Tierra del Fuego. For more information on Punta Arenas, see www.welcomechile.com.

Arriving in Punta Arenas → *Colour map 7, B1. Phone code +56 (0)61. Population 123,000.*

Getting there

Punta Arenas is cut off from the rest of Chile. If you're coming from Argentina, the only road connections are via Río Gallegos (see page 534) or via the border crossings near Río Turbio (see box, page 567) to Puerto Natales, 247 km north of Punta Arenas (many buses daily). If you're travelling down the Carretera Austral in Chile, you will need to cross into Argentina at Paso Huemules, Coyhaique Alto or Chile Chico/Los Antiguos (see box, page 546), from where roads go east to Caleta Olivia and Comodoro Rivadavia for onward transport to Río Gallegos and Punta Arenas. The alternative is to travel east from Puerto Varas and Puerto Montt to cross into Argentina near Bariloche, then take Ruta 40 south to El Calafate and cross back into Chile via the border crossings near Río Turbio to Puerto Natales. It is quicker, and often cheaper, therefore, to take one of the many daily flights from Puerto Montt or Santiago instead. There are also direct flights to/from Porvenir, Puerto Williams and Ushuaia.

Carlos Ibáñez del Campo Airport is 20 km north of town. A minibus service by **Transfer Austral** ① *Av Independencia 595-B, T061-272 3358, www.transferaustral.com, costs US$6.* Taxis charge US$14 to the city, and US$10 in the other direction. Note that in most taxis much of the luggage space is taken up by natural gas fuel tanks. Buses from Punta Arenas to Puerto Natales will only stop at the airport if they are scheduled to pick up passengers there. The bus terminal is at the northern edge of town by the Zona Franca. Ferries to/from Tierra del Fuego use the port at Tres Puentes, 5 km north of Punta Arenas or, at Punta Delgada, 170 km north (see Arriving in Tierra del Fuego, page 614, for details). ▶▶ *See Transport, page 590, for further details.*

Getting around

Calle Pedro Montt runs east to west, while Jorge Montt runs north to south. Buses and *colectivos* in Punta Arenas tend to go either north along the 21 de Mayo–Magallanes–Bulnes axis, south down Chiloe, or east to west up Independencia. In any case, Punta Arenas is not a huge city and walking about is a pleasant way of getting to know it. Buses and *taxi-colectivos* are plentiful and cheap (US$2 flat fee from taxi stands) but is only really necessary for some hostels and for out-of-town excursions.

Tourist information

Sernatur ① *Lautaro Navarro 999 y Pedro Montt, T061-222 5385, infomagallanes@sernatur.cl, Mon-Fri 0830-2000, Sat-Sun 0900-1300 and 1400-1800,* is helpful and has lots of information, English spoken. There is also the **municipal tourist information** ① *opposite Centro Español, T061-220 0610, www.puntaarenas.cl (Spanish only) Mon-Fri 0800-2000, Sat-Sun 0900-1800,* kiosk on the plaza, which has experienced English-speaking staff and can provide a good town map with all hotels marked. **CONAF** ① *Av Bulnes 0309, p 4, opposite the shepherd monument, between the racetrack and the cemetery, T061-223 8554, magallanes.oirs@conaf.cl,* doesn't have much useful information. See also www.patagonia-chile.com (Spanish only).

Background

After its foundation in 1848, Punta Arenas became a penal colony modelled on Australia. In 1867, it was opened to foreign settlers and given free port status. From the 1880s, it prospered as a refuelling and provisioning centre for steam ships and whaling vessels. It also became a centre for the new sheep *estancias* in Tierra del Fuego, since it afforded the best harbour facilities. The city's importance was reduced overnight by the opening of the Panama Canal in 1914. Most of those who came to work on the *estancias* were from the island of Chiloé; many people in the city still have relatives there and feel an affinity with the island. (The *barrios* on either side of the upper reaches of Independencia are known as Chilote areas.) In turn, the Chilotes who returned north took Patagonian customs with them, hence the number of *mate* drinkers on Chiloé.

Places in Punta Arenas → *For listings, see pages 587-591.*

Around the attractive **Plaza Muñoz Gamero** are a number of mansions that once belonged to the great sheep-ranching families of the late 19th century. A good example is the **Palacio Sara Braun** ① *www.hotelnogueira.com, Mon-Sat 1000-1300, 1700-2030, US$2*, built between 1894 and 1905 with materials from Europe. The Palacio has several elegantly decorated rooms open to the public and also houses the **Hotel José Nogueira**. In the centre of the plaza is a statue of Magellan with a mermaid and two Fuegian Indians at his feet. According to local wisdom, those who rub or kiss the big toe of one of the Indians will return to Punta Arenas.

Just north of the plaza is the **Museo Regional de Magallanes** ① *Palacio Braun Menéndez, Magallanes 949, T061-224 4216, www.museodemagallanes.cl, Wed-Mon 1030-1700 (closes 1400 May-Sep), US$2*, the opulent former mansion of Mauricio Braun, built in 1905. A visit is recommended. Part of the museum is set out as a room-by-room regional history; the rest of the house has been left with its original furniture. Guided tours are in Spanish only, but a somewhat confusing information sheet in English is also available. In the basement there is a café. One block further north is the **Teatro Cervantes**, now a cinema with an ornate interior.

Three blocks east of the plaza, the **Museo Naval y Marítimo** ① *Pedro Montt 981, T061-220 5479, www.museonaval.cl/en/museo-de-p-arenas.html, Tue-Sat, 0930-1230, 1400-1700, US$2*, houses an exhibition of local and national maritime history, with sections on naval instruments, cartography, meteorology, as well as shipwrecks. There is a video in Spanish and an information sheet in English. Further east, the city's waterfront has been given an extensive face-lift, with public boardwalks and outdoor spaces under special shelters giving protection from the sun's strong ultraviolet rays.

West of Plaza Muñoz Gamero on Waldo Seguel are two reminders of British influence in the city: the **British School** and **St James's Anglican Church** next door. Nearby on Calle Fagnano is the **Mirador Cerro de La Cruz** offering a view over the city and the Straits of Magellan, including its various shipwrecks. Three blocks further west is the **Museo Militar** ① *Regimiento Pudeto, Zenteno and Balmaceda, Tue-Fri 0900-1700, Sat-Sun 0900-1200, 1400-1700, free*, with lots of knives, guns,

Punta Arenas

To Instituto de la Patagonia, Bus Terminal,
Free Port, Airport, Puerto Natales
& Ferry to Porvenir

Carrera

Cemetery

Carrera

To ❷ 2

To & Hostels on Calles Caupolicán & Maipú

Señoret

Angamos

Av Bulnes

Jorge Montt

To ❷ 12

❶⓱

Ⓐ

Museo Regional
Salesiano Maggiorino
Borgatello 🏛

❶⓲

Maipú

Chiloé

Bories

Magallanes

❶⓳

❸❹

Sarmiento

Armando Sanhueza

Croacia

Mejicana

Ⓑ

❶13

Mejicana

Lautaro Navarro

❷❾

❶❶

Quillota

Unimarc
Supermarket

Fernández,
Cruz del Sur,
Turibus 🚌

Carrera Pinto

Central de
Pasajeros 🚌

Pacheco

⓵0 ⓵2 ⓵6

Almte Señoret

Arauco

❶23

Bus Sur 🚌

❶⓲

J Menéndez

Payne Turismo
& Rent a Car

Av Colón

O'Higgins

J Montt

To ❺ ❼

To ❺ ❼

Ⓒ

British School

❶❹

Museo de
Historia
Regional 🏛

Ghisoni

❶❷❷

Aerovías
DAP

Mirador Cerro
de la Cruz

Waldo Seguel

Turismo
Comapa

❷⓶0 ⓵6

Cathedral ✝

Plaza Muñoz
Gamero ℹ

❷❷

Museo Naval
y Marítimo 🏛

❷❻ ❷❾ ❷❽

J Nogueira

Fagnano

Av España

Roca

⓵0

❷❺

21 de Mayo

Turismo
Yamana

Av Costanera

Ⓓ

❶ 1

Balmaceda

Errázuriz

❶⓳

Estrecho de
Magallanes

To ⓵2 ⓵3 & Parque
María Behety

To Fuerte Bulnes &
Puerto del Hambre

To ❽
(½ block)

N

200 metres
200 yards

flags and other military memorabilia plus many items brought from Fuerte Bulnes. There are explanatory notes in excruciating English. Expect to be watched over by a young private.

North of the centre along Bulnes is the **Museo Regional Salesiano Mayorino Borgatello** ⓘ *Colegio Salesiano, Av Bulnes 336, entrance next to church, T061-222 1001, www.museomaggiorinoborgatello.cl, Tue-Sun 1000-1230, 1500-1730, US$5,* an excellent introduction to Patagonia with a large collection of stuffed birds and animals from the region, exhibits on local history, geology, anthropology, aviation and industry. It covers the fascinating history of the indigenous peoples and their education by the Salesian missions. The Italian priest, Alberto D'Agostini, who arrived in 1909 and presided over the missions, took wonderful photographs of the region and his 70-minute film can be seen on video (ask). This is easily the most complete and fascinating regional museum in Chile.

Three blocks further on, the **Cementerio Municipal Sara Braun** ⓘ *Av Bulnes 929, daily 0800-1800, 0730-2000 in summer, US$4,* is one of the most interesting places in the city, with cypress avenues and many mausolea and memorials to pioneer families and victims of shipping disasters. The gravestones in many languages bear testimony to the cosmopolitan provenance of Patagonian pioneers. Look out for the statue of Indicito, the little Indian, on the northwest side, which is now an object of reverence, bedecked with flowers. Further north still, the Instituto de la Patagonia houses the **Museo del Recuerdo** ⓘ *Av Bulnes 1890, Km 4 north (opposite the university and zona franca), outdoor exhibits Mon-Fri 0830-1130, 1430-1830, Sat 0830-1230, US$4,* an open-air museum with 3000 artefacts used by the early settlers, pioneer homes, research library and botanical gardens.

Around Punta Arenas Reserva Nacional Magallanes
ⓘ *7 km west of town, US$3, taxi US$7.50.*

Known locally as the Parque Japonés, Reserva Nacional Magallanes extends over 13,500 ha and rises to 600 m. **Viento Sur** offers a scheduled transport service to the reserve, but it can also be reached on foot or by bike: follow Independencia up the hill and take a right turning for Río de las Minas, about 3 km from the edge of town; the entrance to the reserve is 2 km beyond. Here you will find a self-guided nature trail through lenga and coigue trees. The road continues through the woods for 14 km passing several picnic sites. From the top end of the road a short path leads to a lookout over the **Garganta del Diablo** (Devil's Throat), a gorge with views over Punta Arenas and Tierra del Fuego. From here a slippery path leads down to the Río de las Minas Valley and then back to Punta Arenas.

Cerro Mirador is 8 km west of town in the Reserva Nacional Magallanes. It is one of the few places in the world where you can ski with a sea view. The ski season is June to September, weather permitting. Transfer buses leave at weekends from the main plaza; taxi US$8. A daily lift-pass is US$21 and equipment rental is US$34.50. There's a mid-way lodge with food, drink and equipment. Note that the ski centre is often closed due to lack of snow. There's also a good two-hour hike here in summer; the trail is clearly marked and flora are labelled. Skiing is also available at Tres Morros.

Fuerte Bulnes and Puerto del Hambre

Some 56 km south, **Fuerte Bulnes** (US$24) is a replica of the wooden fort erected in 1843 by the crew of the Chilean vessel *Ancud* to secure Chile's southernmost territories after Independence. It's an interesting story, but there's not that much to see. Nearby is **Puerto del Hambre**, a beautiful, panoramic spot where there are ruins of the church built in 1584 by Sarmiento de Gamboa's colonists. Tours are run by several agencies.

Isla Magdalena

A small island, 30 km northeast, Isla Magdalena is the location of the **Monumento Natural Los Pingüinos**, a colony of 150,000 penguins, administered by CONAF. Deserted apart from during the breeding season from November to early February, Magdalena is one of a group of three islands visited by Drake (the others are Marta and Isabel), whose men killed 3000 penguins for food. A small lighthouse on the island gives the best views of the surroundings, and the half-hour walk up there gets you close to the all the penguin action. Tread carefully and don't get too close to the nests: protective parent penguins sometimes get a bit fierce. Boat trips to the island are run by Turismo **Comapa** and **Solo Expediciones**, and the Australis cruise ships also call here. ▸▸ *See What to do and Transport, below.*

Seno Otway (Otway Sound)

Seventy kilometres north of Punta Arenas, Seno Otway is the site of a colony of around 11,000 Magellanic penguins, which can be visited from October to mid-March, for US$11. There are beautiful views across the sound to the mountains to the north, and rheas, skunks and foxes can also be seen. It is best to go early in the day. Try to avoid going at the same time as the large cruise ship tours; it is not much fun having to wait behind 200 people for your turn at the viewing stations. **Fernández** (see Transport) runs buses at 1500, return 1900, US$13.50; there are also tours by several agencies, US$20 (plus entry fee); taxis charge US$50 return.

Parque Nacional Pali Aike

ⓘ *US$2, half price in low season. For more details, ask at CONAF (address above), who manage the park, www.conaf.cl/parques/parque-nacional-pali-aike/.*

Route 255 heads north from Punta Arenas, reaching the Argentine border at Monte Aymond/Integración Austral and continuing beyond the border as Argentine Route 3 to Río Gallegos (see box, page 615). Thirty kilometres before the border at Kimiri Aike, a road heads east to Punta Delgada for the ferry crossing to Tierra del Fuego (see Arriving in Tierra del Fuego, page 614).

Some 210 km northeast of Punta Arenas, near the border, is **Parque Nacional Pali Aike** (Pali Aike means 'desolate place of bad spirits' in Tehuelche). This is one of the oldest archaeological sites in Patagonia, with evidence of aborigines from 10,000-12,000 years ago, in an extraordinary volcanic landscape pockmarked with countless tiny craters, rocks of different colours and several caves. Tour operators offer full day trips, US$70-80.

A cruise at the end of the world

From September to April, Australis Expedition Cruises have two vessels running cruises between Punta Arenas and Ushuaia, the *Vía Australis* and the newer *Stella Australis*. Vía Australis has capacity for 136 passengers, while Stella Australis can accommodate 210. Passengers sail in comfort, treated to fine food and expert service, through the Straits of Magellan and the channels and fjords between Tierra del Fuego and the islands that cling to its southern shore. These were the waters fished by the Yámana and Kawéskar people and surveyed by Robert Fitzroy and his crew.

The cruise takes four nights each way. Each includes a visit to Cape Horn where, sea conditions permitting, you can land to see the monuments and to sign the visitors' book in the lighthouse, manned by a Chilean naval officer and his family. The landing follows a rigorous procedure: everyone is togged up in waterproofs and lifejackets, and is transferred from ship to Zodiac, before disembarking with the aid of crew standing in the surf. From the shore, 160 wooden steps lead up the cliff to wooden walkways. On a relatively benign day – sunny, with an icy breeze – it's hard to imagine the tragedies of so many mariners lost, to remember the many souls that, according to legend, have become albatrosses, and to accept that this is the last piece of terra firma before Antarctica.

Other shore trips are followed by a whisky or hot chocolate. You need the sustenance, especially after a visit to Piloto and Nena glaciers in the Chico fjord. The blue ice of Piloto calves into the water, while Nena is scarred by rocky debris. All around water pours off the mountains; sleet and rain drive into your face as the Zodiac powers away.

En route from Ushuaia to Punta Arenas (the itinerary varies according to the route and the weather), there are other landings. At Wulaia Bay on Isla Navarino two walks are available, up a hill or along the shore to look for birds and flora. A museum, in an old radio station, tells the history of the place. It was here that one of Fitzroy's Fuegians, Jemmy Button, who was briefly a celebrity in England in the 1830s, was reportedly present at the massacre of missionaries in 1859. Another visit is to Isla Magdalena, just off Punta Arenas. Here, between November and January, 60,000 pairs of Magellanic penguins breed in burrows.

At all times the ship is accompanied by giant petrels, black-browed albatross and king cormorants. Occasionally, dolphins ride the wake. If it is too cold on deck, you can go onto the bridge and be entertained by the navigator. The bar is open almost all the time; stewards and guides are on hand at any hour; and there are lectures and films, visits to the engine room and cookery lessons to fill the hours at sea. Everything runs like clockwork thanks to clear instructions for safety and fine-tuned organization: when the captain says you'll dock at 1100, dock at 1100 you will.

For more information on these cruises, see www.australis.com, and What to do, page 589.

For hotel and restaurant price codes and other relevant information, see pages 20-26.

⊙ Where to stay

Punta Arenas *p580, map p583*
Hotel prices are lower during winter months (Apr-Sep). A few streets, in particular Caupolicán and Maipú, some 10-15 mins' walk from the centre have become a "hotbed of hostels", most of them with similar facilities and similar prices (**$$**). These include Ely House, The Pink House, Shangri-la, Maipú Street and Hostal Dinka's House, the latter painted bright-red and run by the indomitable Dinka herself. The area is also full of car repair places, which can make it noisy during the day and occasionally at night. For accommodation in private houses, usually **$** pp, ask at the tourist office. There are no campsites in or near the city. Remember to dial the international code for Chile (+56) and drop the initial 0, if calling from Argentina or abroad.

$$$$-$$$ Cabo de Hornos, Plaza Muñoz Gamero 1025, T061-271 5000, www.hoteles-australis.com. 4-star, comfy, bright and spacious rooms, with good views from 4th floor up.

$$$$-$$$ Diego de Almagro, Av Colón 1290, T061-220 8800, www.dahoteles puntaarenas.com. Very modern, good international standard, on waterfront, many rooms with view, heated pool, sauna, small gym, big bright rooms, good value.

$$$$-$$$ José Nogueira, Plaza de Armas, Bories 959 y P Montt, in former Palacio Sara Braun, T061-271 1000, www.hotelnogueira.com. Best in town, stylish rooms, warm atmosphere,

excellent service. Smart restaurant in the beautiful loggia. A few original rooms now a 'small museum'.

$$$ Chalet Chapital, Sanhueza 974, T061-273 0100, www.hotelchalet chapital.cl. Small well-run hotel, smallish rooms, helpful staff, a good choice in this price range.

$$$ Patagonia Pionera, Arauco 786, T061-222 2045, www.hotelpatagonia pionera.cl. Beautiful 1930s wooden *casona* now a comfortable high-end B&B. Helpful staff, onsite parking.

$$$ Hostal de la Patagonia, O'Higgins 730, T061-224 9970, www. ecotourpatagonia.com. Rooms with heating, good services, dining room, 10 mins' walk from centre. Organizes a variety of tours, including fly fishing.

$$ Hostal Al Fin del Mundo, O'Higgins 1026, T061-271 0185, www. alfindelmundo.hostel.com. Rooms and dorms, bright, cosy, shared baths, central, helpful, pool table, English spoken.

$$ Hostal Ayelen, Lautarro Navarro 763, T061-224 2413 www.ayelenresidencial. com. 120-year-old house with some new rooms at the back, bathroom a bit small but super clean, comfy.

$$ Hostal del Sur, Mejicana 151, T061-222 7249, www.hostaldelsurmag.com. Impeccable old house with modern rooms in residential area, welcoming, with charming reception areas.

$$ Hostel Keoken, Magallanes 209, T061-224 4086/6376, www.hostelkeoken.cl. Light, wooden, spacious building on 3 floors each with its own entrance up rickety outside staircases. Some rooms with small bath. Good value, some info. Top-floor rooms with shared bathroom have paper-thin walls. Currently expanding into an even bigger, rambling place.

$$ Hostal La Estancia, O'Higgins 765, T061-224 9130, www.estancia.cl. Simple but comfortable rooms, some with bath. **$** pp in dorms. English spoken, small shop attached, music and games room recently opened.

$$ Hostal Sonia Kuscevic, Pasaje Darwin 175, T061-224 8543, www.hostalsk.cl. One of the city's oldest guesthouses, with heating and parking. Better value for longer stays, good discount if you have a Hostelling International card.

$$ Hostal Taty's House, Maipu 1070, T061-224 1525, www.hostaltatyshouse.cl. Nice rooms with good beds, decent choice in this price bracket, basic English spoken.

$$-$ Backpackers' Paradise, Carrera Pinto 1022, T061-224 0104, backpackersparadise@hotmail.com. Popular good kitchen, 1 private and 5 shared rooms. Facilities much improved in recent years.

$ Hostal Independencia, Independencia 374, T061-222 7572, www.chileaustral.com/independencia. Rooms, dorms and camping with use of kitchen and bathroom. Trekking equipment rental, parking, fishing and other tours, lots of information.

🍴 Restaurants

Punta Arenas *p580, map p583*
Many eating places close on Sun.
Note *Centolla* (king crab) is caught illegally by some fishermen using dolphin, porpoise and penguin as live bait. There are seasonal bans on *centolla* fishing to protect dwindling stocks; out of season *centolla* served in restaurants will probably be frozen. If there is an infestation of red tide (*marea roja*), a disease which is fatal to humans, bivalve shellfish must not be eaten. Mussels should not be picked along the shore because of pollution and the marea roja. Sernatur and the Centros de Salud have leaflets.

$$$ Remezón, 21 de Mayo 1469, T061-224 1029. Regional specialities such as krill. Very good, but should be, given the prices.

$$$-$$ Damiana Elena, Magallanes 341, T061-222 2818. Stylish restaurant serving Mediterranean food with a Patagonian touch, popular with locals, book ahead at weekends, Mon-Sat from 2000.

$$$-$$ Sotitos, O'Higgins 1138. An institution, famous for seafood in elegant surroundings, excellent. Book ahead in season. New 2nd floor serving local specialties and Italian food. Daily (Sun 1200-1500 only).

$$$-$$ La Tasca, Plaza Muñoz Gamero 771, above Teatro Cervantes in Casa Español. Large helpings, limited selection, decent set lunch, views over the plaza.

$$ La Luna, O'Higgins 1017, T061-222 8555. Fish, shellfish and local specialities, huge pisco sours, popular, reasonable. Quirky decor, friendly staff. Recommended.

$$ La Marmita, Plaza Sampaio 678, www.marmitamaga.cl. Regional dishes with international twist, vegetarian options, good-sized portions, prettily presented, chatty owner, Mon-Sat 1230-1500, 1830-2330, generally very good.

$$-$ La Piedra, Lautaro Navarro 1087. Meat dishes, fish, soups, salads, good burgers and sandwiches, daily lunch specials, housed over 2 floors. Mon-Sat 1200-0100.

$ Lomit's/Lomito's, Menéndez 722. A fast-food institution with bar attached, cheap snacks and drinks (local beers are good), open when the others are closed, good food.

$ Mercado Municipal, 21 de Mayo 1465. Wide range of *cocinerías* offering cheap *empanadas* and seafood on the upper floor of the municipal market.

$ Kiosco Roca, Roca 875, unassuming sandwich bar, voted best in Punta Arenas. Mon-Fri 0800-1900, Sat 0800-1300, always packed. Takeaway or a few seats available at the counter.

Cafés

Café Inmigrante, Quillota 599 (esq Mejicana), T061-222 2205, www.inmigrante.cl. Hugely popular cafe run by 3rd generation Croatian expats. Beautifully prepared sandwiches, daily changing cake menu, huge portions, family history on menus. Quirky and popular. Book in advance if possible. Open daily afternoons and evenings. Highly recommended.
Café Montt, Pedro Montt 976. Coffees, teas, cakes, pastries and snacks, Wi-Fi. Cosy, friendly, recommended.
Imago Café, Costanera y Colón. Tiny, laid-back café hidden away in a beachfront bunker overlooking the straits.

🍸 Bars and clubs

Punta Arenas *p580, map p583*
La Taberna del Club de la Unión, on the plaza in the basement of the Hotel Nogueira. Atmospheric bar, good for evening drinks, open Mon-Sat from 1830.
Santino, Colón 657, www.santino.cl. Also serves pizzas and other snacks, large bar, good service, open 1800-0300, live music Sat.
Sky Bar, O'Higgins 1235. Bar with panoramic views on the top floor of the luxury **Dreams** hotel and spa. Open from 1830.

⊛ Festivals

Punta Arenas *p580, map p583*
Late Jan/Feb Muestra custumbrista de Chiloé. The Chilote community celebrates its culture.
Jun Carnaval de invierno. The winter solstice is marked by a carnival on the weekend closest to 21 Jun.

⦿ Shopping

Punta Arenas *p580, map p583*
Punta Arenas has certain free-port facilities. Zona Franca, 3.5 km north of the centre, opposite Museo del Recuerdo, Instituto de la Patagonia, is cheaper than elsewhere. The complex now has over 100 shops and is open daily from 1000 (www.zonaustral.cl), bus E or A from Plaza Muñoz Gamero; many colectivos; taxi US$3.

Handicrafts
Chile Típico, Carrera Pinto 1015, T061-222 5827. Beautiful knitwear and woollen ponchos.
Mercado Municipal (see Restaurants, above). Excellent handicrafts and souvenirs on the lower floors, recently enlarged.

⦿ What to do

Punta Arenas *p580, map p583*
Skiing
For information on **Cerro Mirador**, see above and contact **Club Andino**, T061-224 1479, www.clubandino.cl.

Tour operators
Most tour operators organize trips to Torres del Paine, Fuerte Bulnes, the *pingüineras* on Isla Magdalena and Otway Sound and Tierra del Fuego; shop around.

Arka Patagonia, Manuel Señoret 1597, T061-224 8167, www.arkapatagonia. com. All types of tours, whale watching, trekking etc.

Australis Expedition Cruises, at Comapa, Magallanes 990, T061-220 0200, www.australis.com (also Av El Bosque Norte 0440, p 11, Santiago, T02-2442 3115, and Buenos Aires, T011-5199 6697). Runs expedition cruises on the *Vía Australis* and the larger *Stella Australis* between Punta Arenas and **Ushuaia**, through the Magellan Straits and the 'avenue of glaciers', with stops at Cape Horn and Isla Navarino, glaciers and Isla Magdalena (the itinerary varies according to route). There are plenty of opportunities to disembark and see wildlife. Round trips are 3-7 nights, one-way is 3-4 nights, service from Sep-Apr, check website for promotions. Very safe and comfortable, first-class service, fine dining, daily lectures, an unforgettable experience. Advance booking is essential; check-in is at **Comapa**. Highly recommended.

Solo Expediciones, Nogueira 1255, T061-224 3354, www.soloexpediciones. com, operate their own service to **Monumento Natural Los Pingüinos**, on a faster, smaller boat, also passing by Isla Marta, half-day tour, mornings only.

Turismo Aventour, Patagonia 779, T061-222 0174, http://aventourpatagonia.cl. Specializes in fishing trips, organizes tours to Tierra del Fuego, helpful, English spoken.

Turismo Comapa, Magallanes 990, T061-220 0200, www.comapa.com. Tours to Torres del Paine (responsible, well-informed guides), Tierra del Fuego and to see penguins at Isla Magdalena. Agents for **Australis Expedition Cruises** (see above).

Turismo Laguna Azul, Menéndez 786, T061-222 5200, www.turismolagunaazul. com. Full-day trips to a colony of king penguins on Tierra del Fuego. Trips run all year round. Also city tours, trips to glaciers and others.

Turismo Yamana, Errázuriz 932, T061-222 2061, www.yamana.cl. Conventional and deluxe tours, trekking in Torres del Paine, kayaking the fjords of Parque Nacional De Agostini (Tierra del Fuego), multilingual guides.

Whale Sound, Lautaro Navarro 1191, T09-9887 9814, www.whalesound.com. Whale-watching trips in the Magellan Straits.

🚌 Transport

Punta Arenas *p580, map p583*
Most transport is heavily booked from Christmas to Mar: advance booking strongly advised.

Air
To **Santiago**, with LAN, via **Puerto Montt**, and **Sky** (several stops) daily. To **Porvenir**, Aerovías DAP (O'Higgins 891, T061-261 6100, www.aeroviasdap.cl) 3 daily Mon-Fri, 2 on Sat, 9 passengers, 12 mins. To **Puerto Williams**, daily Mon-Sat, 1¼ hrs. (Book a week in advance for Porvenir, 2 weeks in advance for Puerto Williams.) To **Ushuaia**, 1 hr, LAN, 3 a week in summer (schedules change frequently); take passport when booking tickets to Argentina.

Bus
At the time of writing bus companies were maintaining their own offices in the city centre: **Cruz del Sur**, **Fernández** and **Turibus**, Sanhueza 745, T061-224 2313/ 222 1429, www.buses fernandez.com.

Pacheco, Colón 900, T061-224 2174, www.busespacheco.com; **Pullman**, Colón 568, T061-222 3359, www.pullman.cl, tickets to destinations throughout Chile. **Central de Pasajeros**, Colón y Magallanes, T061-224 5811, for booking all tickets, also *cambio* and tour operator. **Bus Sur**, Menéndez 552, T061-222 2938, www.bus-sur.cl. **Ghisoni** and **Tecni Austral**, Lautaro Navarro 975, T061-261 3422.

To **Puerto Natales**, 3-3½ hrs, with **Fernández**, **Bus Sur** and **Pacheco**, up to 8 daily, last departure 2015, US$10; look out for special offers and connections to Torres del Paine; buses may pick up at the airport with advance booking and payment. To **Río Grande** and **Ushuaia** via **Punta Delgada** (route is described in Arriving in Tierra del Fuego, see page 614; no buses via Porvenir) with **Pacheco**, **Sur**, **Tecni-Austral** and others, 8-10 hrs, US$42, heavily booked, US$70-85 to Ushuaia, 12 hrs. Some services have to change in Río Grande for Ushuaia, others are direct. Check companies for frequencies. Book well in advance in Jan-Feb. To **Río Gallegos**, Argentina, via Punta Delgada, US$24, 5-8 hrs depending on customs (15 mins on Chilean side, up to 2 hrs on Argentine side), with **Pacheco**, Sun, Mon, Tue, Fri; with **Ghisoni**, Mon, Wed, Thu, Fri, Sat.

Car hire
EMSA, Kuzma Slavic 706, T061-261 4378, www.emsarentacar.cl. **Payne**, Menéndez 631, T061-224 0852, www.payne.cl, also tours, treks, birdwatching, etc. Also multinational companies. **Note** You need a hire company's authorization to take a car into Argentina. This takes 24 hrs (not Sat or Sun) and involves mandatory international insurance at US$30 per week, plus notary fees.

Ferry
For services to **Porvenir** (Tierra del Fuego), see Arriving in Tierra del Fuego, page 614. For **Australis Expedition Cruises** to Cape Horn and Ushuaia, see above.

Taxi
Ordinary taxis have yellow roofs. *Colectivos* (all black) run on fixed routes and pick up from taxi stands around town, US$2 flat fee.

❶ Directory

Punta Arenas *p580, map p583*
Banks Most banks and some supermarkets have ATMs; many on the Plaza. **Casas de cambio** on Lautaro Navarro 1000 block. **Consulates Argentina**, 21 de Mayo 1878, T061-226 1532, cparenas@embargentina.cl, Mon-Fri 0900-1800, visas take 24 hrs. **Medical services** Hospital Regional Lautaro Navarro, Av Los Flamencos 01364, T061-229 3000. Public hospital with dental services; for emergency room ask for 'la posta'. **Clínica Magallanes**, Bulnes 01448, T061-221 1527. Private clinic. **Hospital Naval**, Av Bulnes 200, esq Capitán Guillermos. Open 24 hrs, good, friendly staff.

Puerto Natales and around

Beautifully situated on the calm waters of Canal Señoret fjord, an arm of the Ultima Esperanza Sound edged with spectacular mountains, Puerto Natales is a pretty, quiet town of brightly painted corrugated-tin houses. It's the base for exploring the magnificent Balmaceda and Torres del Paine national parks, and although it's inundated with visitors in the summer, it retains a quiet unhurried feel and is a recommended place to relax for a few days.

Arriving in Puerto Natales → *Colour map 6, B3. Phone code 061. Population 17,000.*

Getting there

Puerto Natales is easily reached by many daily buses from Punta Arenas, as well as by daily buses from Río Turbio and El Calafate in Argentina. There are also two buses weekly from Río Gallegos. All buses use the new bus terminal, 20 minutes outside town at Avenida España 1455, but tickets can be bought at the individual company offices (see Transport, page 599). Aerodromo Teniente Julio Gallardo, 7 km north of town, has summer services from Santiago via Puerto Montt and charter services. The town is the terminus of the **Navimag** ship to Puerto Montt (for further details, see page 599). If driving between Punta Arenas and Puerto Natales make sure you have enough fuel. From Puerto Natales, the Argentine frontier can be crossed at three points, all of which meet Ruta 40, which runs north to El Calafate. For further information, see box, page 595.

Getting around

Puerto Natales is not a large place. *Colectivos* leave regularly from the centre, US$0.60 (US$0.70 Sunday); taxis charge US$2 flat fee throughout Puerto Natales but are only really needed for journeys out of town.

Tourist information

There is a municipal **tourist office** ① *at the bus station, Av España 1455, www.muninatales.cl*, and information is also available at **Sernatur** ① *on the waterfront, Av Pedro Montt 19, T061-241 2125, infonatales@sernatur.cl, Oct-Mar Mon-Fri 0830-1900, Sat-Sun 1000-1300, 1430-1800, Apr-Sep Mon-Fri 0830-1800, Sat 1000-1300, 1400-1800*, which has good leaflets on Puerto Natales and Torres del Paine in English, and information on bus and boat transport in the park. A website that includes Puerto Natales, as well as the rest of Chile, is www.welcomechile.com.

Places in Puerto Natales → *For listings, see pages 596-599.*

In town is the **Museo Histórico Municipal** ⓘ *Bulnes 285, T061-241 1263, Mon 0800-1700, Tue-Fri, 0800-1900, Sat 1000-1300, 1500-1900, US$2*, which has displays and photos of early colonizers, as well as a small collection of archaeological and natural history exhibits. The colourful old steam train in the main square was once used to take workers to the meatpacking factory at Puerto Bories, 5 km north of town, which was converted into the **Museo Frigorífico Puerto Bories** and is now joined to The Singular Hotel (see Where to stay, below). In its heyday the plant was the biggest of its kind in Chile, with a capacity for 250,000 sheep. Bankrupted in the early 1990s, much of the plant was dismantled in 1993. Belatedly the plant was given National Monument status and is slowly being restored. It is a pleasant hour-long walk along the shore to Bories, with glimpses of the Balmaceda Glacier across the sound.

Puerto Natales

To 21 24 , Punta Arenas & Parque Nacional Torres del Paine

Seno Ultima Esperanza

Estero Natales

Plaza de Armas

Pier for Balmaceda Glacier

Pier for Puerto Montt

Museo Municipal

To 9 23

N

200 metres
200 yards

Where to stay 🛏
1 Aquaterra *C2*
4 Casa Cecilia *B2*
5 Casa Teresa *C2*
6 Costaustralis *C1*
7 Hosp Casa Lili *B1*
8 Hosp Nancy *C3*
9 Hostal Las Carretas *C3*
10 Hostal Sir Francis Drake *A2*
11 Hostel Natales *B1*
12 Indigo Patagonia *B1*
13 Josmar 2 Camping *C2*
14 Keoken *B1*

16 Lili Patagónico's *C3*
17 Martín Gusinde *B2*
20 Patagonia Adventure *B2*
21 Remota *A2*
23 The Singing Lamb *C3*
24 Weskar Patagonian Lodge *A2*

Restaurants 🍴
1 Afrigonia *B2*
3 Angelica's *B2*
4 Cormorán de las Rocas *A2*
5 El Asador Patagónico *B2*

6 El Living *B2*
7 La Mesita Grande *B2*
8 La Picada de Carlitos *C3*
9 Parrilla Don Jorge *B2*
10 Patagonia Dulce *B1*
11 Ultima Esperanza *B2*

Bars & clubs 🍸
12 Baguales Brewery *B2*
13 El Bar de Ruperto *B2*

There are lovely walks along the waterfront or up to the slab-like **Cerro Dorotea**, which dominates the town and offers superb views of the whole Seno Ultima Esperanza (Ultima Esperanza Sound). It can be reached on foot or by any Río Turbio bus (take any bus going east and alight at Km 9.5 for the summit) or taxi (recommended, as the hill is further off than it seems). The trail entrance is marked by a sign 'Mirador Cerro Dorotea'. Expect to be charged a small amount in one of the local houses, where you will be given a broomstick handle, which makes a surprisingly good walking stick. It is a 1½-hour trek up to the 600-m lookout along a well-marked trail. In theory you can continue along the top of the hill to get better views to the north, but the incredibly strong winds often make this dangerous.

Around Puerto Natales

Monumento Nacional Cueva Milodón
ⓘ *25 km north of Puerto Natales, daily 0800-2000, US$8 (US$4 low season). To get there, bus from Prat 517 (T061-241 2540), daily 0945 and 1500 (returns 1200 and 1700), US$8; taxi US$30 return, or check if you can get a ride with a tour bus to Torres del Paine – some stop at the cave.*
This massive cave, 70 m wide, 220 m deep and 30 m high, was formed by the lapping of glacial lakes in the ice age, whose waters were then 300 m above current levels. Remains have been found here of a prehistoric ground sloth, together with evidence of occupation by early Patagonian humans some 11,000 years ago. The ceiling of the cave is dimpled with mineral deposits, and inside the eerie depths it's as silent as a library, with marvellous views through the letterbox slit of the cave's mouth. There's a small visitor centre with summaries in English, toilets and a restaurant. This was the end point of Bruce Chatwin's famous travelogue *In Patagonia*.

Parque Nacional Bernardo O'Higgins
Often referred to as the **Parque Nacional Monte Balmaceda**, Bernardo O'Higgins covers much of the Campo de Hielo Sur, plus the fjords and offshore islands further west, and is only accessible by boat from Puerto Natales. A three-hour trip up the Seno de Ultima Esperanza takes you to the southernmost section of the park, passing the Balmaceda Glacier, which drops from the eastern slopes of **Monte Balmaceda** (2035 m). The glacier is retreating; in 1986 its foot was at sea level. The boat docks further north at **Puerto Toro**, from where it is a 1-km walk to the base of the Serrano Glacier on the north slope of Monte Balmaceda. On the trip, dolphins, sea lions (in season), black-necked swans, flightless steamer ducks and cormorants can be seen. There is a route from Puerto Toro along the **Río Serrano** for 35 km to the Torres del Paine administration centre; guided tours are available on foot or on horseback. **Punta Alta** and 21 de Mayo also offer the opportunity to continue along the river by zodiac to Camping Serrano at the southern edge of Torres del Paine (from US$180-215 one way). The views are better going towards Torres del Paine, as the landscape suddenly opens up and then just gets better and better.

Border crossing: Chile–Argentina

From Puerto Natales, the Argentine frontier can be crossed at three points, all of which meet Ruta 40, which runs north to El Calafate. These crossings are open, subject to weather conditions, 24 hours a day from September to May and daily 0700 to 2300 between June and August.

Paso Casas Viejas
This crossing, 16 km east of Puerto Natales, is reached by turning off Route 9 (the Punta Arenas road) at Km 14. On the Argentine side, the road (*ripio*) runs east to meet Ruta 40, en route to Río Gallegos (or north to El Calafate). This crossing is open all year.

Paso Mina Uno/Dorotea
This crossing is reached by branching off Route 9, 9 km east of Puerto Natales and continuing north a further 11 km. On the Argentine side, the road (*ripio*) continues north to Ruta 40 via **Río Turbio**, see page 567.

Paso Rio Don Guillermo/Cancha Carrera
The most northerly of the three crossings is reached by turning off the road north to Torres del Paine at Km 65.
Customs and immigration Chilean formalities are at Cerro Castillo; Argentine formalities are at Cancha Carrera, 2 km further east.
Transport On the Argentine side of the frontier, the road meets Route 40 in a very desolate spot – hitching may be possible, but this route is more feasible if you have your own transport.

Arriving in Parque Nacional Bernardo O'Higgins There are sailings from Puerto Natales daily at 0800 in summer, returning at 1730 (Sunday only in winter) for a minimum of 10 passengers. Take warm clothes, hat and gloves. Boats get heavily booked in high season. All agencies can arrange the boat trips, which are run by **Punta Alta** and **Turismo 21 de Mayo** (see Tour operators, page 599). Both take the same route, but the former uses a faster boat. Although the park is uninhabited, guest accommodation is available at **Hostería Montes Balmaceda** (see Where to stay, below); book through **Turismo 21 de Mayo**.

For hotel and restaurant price codes and other relevant information, see pages 20-26.

⦿ Where to stay

Note that more information on where to stay, and tour companies, can be found at www.torresdelpaine.com (in English).

Puerto Natales *p592, map p593*
In season cheaper accommodation fills up quickly. Hotels in the countryside open only in summer months: dates vary. Good deals in upper range hotels may be available out of season and prices may be 50% lower.
$$$$ Costaustralis, Pedro Montt 262, T061-241 2000, www.hoteles-australis.com. Very comfortable, tranquil, lovely views (but not from inland-facing rooms), lift, English spoken, waterfront restaurant Paine serves international and local seafood.
$$$$ Indigo Patagonia, Ladrilleros 105, T061-243 26800, www.indigopatagonia.cl. Relaxed atmosphere, on the water front, great views, a boutique hotel with roof-top spa, rooms and suites, café/restaurant serves good seafood and vegetarian dishes. Tours organized.
$$$$ Remota, Ruta 9 Norte, Km 1.5, Huerto 279, T061-241 4040, www. remota.cl. Modernist design with big windows, lots of trips, activities and treks offered, spa, all-inclusive packages, good food, first-class.
$$$$ The Singular, Km 5 Norte, Puerto Bories, T061-272 2030, www.thesingular. com. Recent converted warehouses, outside the town centre, in a scenic spot overlooking the Ultima Esperanza Sound. Spa, gourmet restaurant and varied excursions offered.
$$$$-$$$ Martín Gusinde, Bories 278, T061-271 2180, www.hotelmartin

gusinde.com. Modern 3-star standard, smart, parking, laundry service, excursions organized.
$$$$-$$$ Weskar Patagonian Lodge, Ruta 9, Km 05, T061-241 4168, www. weskar.cl. Quiet lodge overlooking the fjord, standard or deluxe rooms with good views, 3-course dinners served, lunch boxes prepared for excursions, many activities offered, helpful.
$$$ Aquaterra, Bulnes 299, T061-241 2239, www.aquaterrapatagonia.com. Good restaurant with vegetarian options, 'resto-bar' downstairs, spa, warm and comfortable but not cheap, very helpful staff. Excursions and tours.
$$$ Cabañas Kotenk Aike, 2 km north of town, T061-241 2581. Sleeps 4, modern, very comfortable, great location.
$$$ Hostal Sir Francis Drake, Phillipi 383, T061-241 1553, www.hostalfrancisdrake. com. Calm and welcoming, tastefully decorated, smallish rooms, good views.
$$$ Keoken, Señoret 267, T061-241 3670, www.keokenpatagonia.com. Cosy, upmarket B&B, spacious living room, some rooms with views. All rooms have bathroom but not all are en suite, English spoken, helpful staff, tours.
$$$-$$ Hostel Natales, Ladrilleros 209, T061-241 4731, www.hostelnatales.cl. Private rooms or dorms in this high-end hostel, comfortable, cash only (pesos, dollars or euros).
$$ Casa Cecilia, Tomás Rogers 60, T061-241 2698, www.casaceciliahostal.com. Welcoming, popular, with small simple rooms, private or shared bath. English, French and German spoken, rents camping and trekking gear, tour agency and information for Torres del Paine.
$$ Hosp Nancy, Ramírez 540, T061-241 0022, www.nataleslodge.cl.

Warm and hospitable, information, tours, equipment rental.

$$ Hostal Las Carretas, Galvarino 745, T061-241 4584. Tastefully decorated and spotless B&B 15 mins' walk to the centre, comfortable rooms, some with bath, good beds, English spoken.

$$ Lili Patagónico's, Prat 479, T061-241 4063, www.lilipatagonicos.com. **$** pp in dorms. Small but pleasant heated rooms, helpful staff. Lots of information, good quality equipment rented. Tours offered. Indoor climbing wall.

$$ Patagonia Adventure, Tomás Rogers 179, T061-241 1028, www.apatagonia. com. Lovely old house, bohemian feel, shared bath, **$** pp in dorms, equipment hire, bike and kayak tours and tour arrangements for Torres del Paine.

$$-$ pp **The Singing Lamb**, Arauco 779, T061-241 0958, www.thesinginglamb. com. Very hospitable New Zealand-run backpackers, dorm accommodation only but no bunks. Home-from-home feel. Good information.

$ Casa Teresa, Esmeralda 463, T061-241 0472, freepatagonia@hotmail.com. Good value, but thin walls and no heating in rooms, tours to Torres del Paine arranged.

$ Hosp Casa Lili, Bories153, T061-241 4063, lilinatales@latinmail.com. Dorms or private rooms, small, family-run, rents equipment and can arrange tickets to Paine.

Camping

Josmar 2, Esmeralda 517, in centre, T061-241 1685, www.josmar.cl. Family-run, convenient, hot showers, parking, barbecues, electricity, café, tent site or double room.

Around Puerto Natales *p594*

$$$$ Hostería Montes Balmaceda, book through **Turismo 21 de Mayo**, Eberhard 560, T061-261 4420, www.

turismo21demayo.cl. Beautifully situated on Ultima Esperanza Sound, close to the Río Serrano. Comfortable rooms, restaurant. Also organize tours. Handy for boat trip up Río Serrano. Recommended.

$$$ Posada Río Verde, Ruta I-50, Km 97, on Seno Skyring, T061-311131, www.estanciarioverde.cl. Private bath, heating. Recommended.

🍽 Restaurants

Puerto Natales *p592, map p593*
More suggestions for restaurants can be found at www.interpatagonia.com/ puertonatales (in English).

$$$ Afrigonia, Eberhard 343, T061-241 2232. An unexpected mixture of Patagonia meets East Africa in this Kenyan/Chilean-owned fusion restaurant, considered by many to be the best, and certainly the most innovative, in town.

$$$ Angelica's, Bulnes 501, T061-241 0007, www.angelicas.cl. Elegant Mediterranean style, well-prepared pricey food with quality ingredients.

$$$-$$ Cormorán de las Rocas, Miguel Sánchez 72, T061-261 5131-3, www. cormorandelasrocas.com. Patagonian specialities with an innovative twist, wide variety of well-prepared dishes, *pisco sours*, good service and attention to detail, incomparable views.

$$$-$$ El Asador Patagónico, Prat 158 on the Plaza. Spit-roast lamb, salads, home-made puddings.

$$$-$$ Parrilla Don Jorge, Bories 430, on Plaza, T061-241 0999, www.parrilla donjorge.cl. Also specializes in spit-roast lamb, but serves fish too, good service.

$$ La Mesita Grande, Prat 196 on the Plaza, T061-241 1571, www.mesita grande.cl. Fresh pizzas from the wood-burning oven, also pasta and good desserts.

$$ Ultima Esperanza, Eberhard 354, T061-241 1391. One of the town's classic seafood restaurants.

$$-$ El Living, Prat 156, Plaza de Armas, www.el-living.com. Comfy sofas, good tea, magazines in all languages, book exchange, good music, delicious vegetarian food, British-run, popular. Wi-Fi, recommended.

$$-$ La Picada de Carlitos, Blanco Encalada y Esmeralda. Good, cheap traditional Chilean food, popular with locals at lunchtime, when service can be slow.

Cafés

Patagonia Dulce, Barros Arana 233, T061-241 5285, www.patagoniadulce.cl. Mon-Sat 1400-2030. For the best hot chocolate in town, good coffee and chocolates.

🍸 Bars and clubs

Puerto Natales *p592, map p593*
Baguales Brewery, Bories 430, on the plaza, www.cervezabaguales.cl. Pub with microbrewery attached. Also serves hamburgers and other snacks. Sep-Mar Mon-Sat 1800-0300.

El Bar de Ruperto, Bulnes 371, T061-9218 9535. Lively place with DJs, live music, lots of drinks and some food. 2130-0330.

Murciélagos, Bulnes 731. Popular bar with late-night music and dancing.

🛍 Shopping

Puerto Natales *p592, map p593*
Camping equipment
See under Where to stay and What to do for places that rent out equipment, eg **Casa Cecilia**, **Lili Patagónico's**, **Sendero Aventura**, **Erratic Rock**. Check all camping equipment and prices carefully. Deposits are required. Camping gas is widely available in hardware stores.

Supermarkets
Several in town. The town markets are also good.

⚫ What to do

Puerto Natales *p592, map p593*
Many agencies along Eberhard. It is better to book tours direct with operators in Puerto Natales than through agents in Punta Arenas or Santiago. Several agencies offer tours to the Perito Moreno glacier in Argentina, 1 day, 14-hr trip, 2 hrs at the glacier, US$80-100 not including food or park entry fee. You can then leave the tour in Calafate to continue into Argentina.

Baguales Group, Barros Araña 66, T061-241 2654, www.baqualesgroup.com. Specialists in the route from Torres del Paine back to Puerto Natales. Tailor made multi-activity tours that can incorporate zodiacs, horse riding, kayaking and trekking, mostly off the beaten track.

Blue Green Adventures, M Bulnes 1200, T061-241 1800, www.bluegreen adventures.com. Adventure tour specialist and travel agent, with trekking, riding, kayaking, fishing and multi-activity options, *estancia*, whale-watching, wine and yoga programmes. Also caters for families.

Comapa, Bulnes 541, T061-241 4300, www.comapa.com. Large regional operator offering decent day tours to Torres del Paine.

Encuentro Gourmet, Bories 349, T061-6720 3725, www.encuentrogourmet. com. Patagonian cookery workshops at lunch and dinner-time, US$44 pp, book at least 24 hrs in advance,

Erratic Rock, Baquedano 719 and Zamora 732, T061-241 4317, www.erraticrock. com. Trekking experts offering interesting expeditions from half a day to 2 weeks.

Also B&B lodge, good-quality equipment hire, daily trekking seminar at 1500.
Estancia Travel, Casa 13-b, Puerto Bories, T061-241 2221, www.estanciatravel.com. Based at the Estancia Puerto Consuelo, 5 km north of Puerto Natales, offers horse riding trips from 1 to 10 days around southern Patagonia and Torres del Paine, with accommodation at traditional *estancias*. Also kayaking trips, British/Chilean-run, bilingual, professional guides, at the top end of the price range.
Punta Alta, Blanco Encalada 244, T061-241 0115, www.puntaalta.cl. Boat trips to PN Bernardo O'Higgins, also car hire.
Sendero Aventura, Carlos Bories 349, T061-6171 3080, www.senderoaventura.com. Adventure tours by land rover, bike or kayak.
Skorpios, www.skorpios.cl. 2- to 3-day cruises up the southern fjords to Puerto Edén and the Pío XI Glacier. No office in Puerto Natales; book online or through an agency.
Turismo 21 de Mayo, Eberhard 560, T061-261 4420, www.turismo21demayo.cl. Boat trips to PN Bernardo O'Higgins.

⊝ Transport

Puerto Natales *p592, map p593*
Air
To **Santiago** via Puerto Montt, with **Sky** airline, summer only. Also charter services to **Punta Arenas** and onward connections to Argentina with **Aerovías DAP**.

Bus
In summer book ahead at the company offices in town: **Bus Fernández**, E Ramírez 399, T061-241 1111, www.busesfernandez.com; **Pacheco**, Ramírez 224, T061-241 4800, www.busespacheco.com; **Bus Sur**, Baquedano 668, T061-261 4220, www.bussur.com; **Zaahj**, Prat 236, T061-241 2260, www.turismozaahj.co.cl.

For buses to Torres del Paine, see page 601. To **Punta Arenas**, several daily, 3-3½ hrs, US$9.50, Fernández, Pacheco, Bus Sur and others, comfortable Pullman service with Zaahj, US$24. To Argentina: to **Río Gallegos,** direct with **Bus Sur** and **Pacheco**, 2-3 weekly each, US$28, 4-5 hrs; to **Río Turbio**, hourly, with **Cootra** and other companies, US$8, 2 hrs (depending on customs – change bus at border); to **El Calafate**, US$35, with **Cootra** via Río Turbio, daily, 4 hrs, or with **Pacheco**, 3 weekly, or with **Zaahj**, 3 weekly, 4½ hrs, via Cerro Castillo. Otherwise travel agencies run several times a week to Parque Nacional Los Glaciares depending on demand, 12-hr trip, shop around and reserve 1 day ahead; tickets do not include Perito Moreno glacier entry fee.
Bus Sur also runs 4 buses a week to **Ushuaia**, Oct-Apr, 15 hrs, US$70.

Car hire
Car hire agents can arrange permission to drive into Argentina; this takes 24 hrs to arrange and extra insurance is required.
EMSA, Eberhard 577, T061-261 4388, www.emsarentacar.cl. **Punta Alta**, Blanco Encalada 244, T061-241 0115, www.puntaalta.cl.

Ferry
The weekly Navimag ferry service between Puerto Natales and Puerto Montt resumed in 2014 after several months' hiatus. Contact **Navimag**, Pedro Montt 308, T061-241 1642, www.navimag.com, for up to date information.

❶ Directory

Puerto Natales *p592, map p593*
Banks There are several ATMs. *Casas de cambio* on Blanco Encalada, Bulnes and Prat. **Bicycle repairs** El Rey de la Bicicleta, Ramírez 540. Good, helpful.

Parque Nacional Torres del Paine

Parque Nacional Torres del Paine is spectacular. World-renowned for its challenging trekking, the park contains 15 peaks above 2000 m. At its centre is the glacier-topped granite massif Macizo Paine from which rise the vertical pink granite Torres (towers) de Paine and below them the strange Cuernos (horns) de Paine, swooping buttresses of lighter granite under caps of darker sedimentary rock. From the vast Campo de Hielo Sur ice cap on its western edge, four main glaciers (ventisqueros) – Grey, Dickson, Zapata and Tyndall – drop into vividly coloured lakes formed by their meltwater: turquoise, ultramarine and pistachio expanses, some filled with wind-sculpted royal blue icebergs. Wherever you explore, there are constantly changing views of dramatic peaks and ice fields. Allow five to seven days to see the park properly. The park is also one of the best places on the continent for viewing rheas and *guanacos*. Apart from the 3500 *guanacos*, 24 other species of mammal can be seen here, including hares, foxes, skunks, *huemules* and pumas (the last two only very rarely). For helpful information on the park see www.torresdelpaine.com (in English).

Getting there

The most practical way to get to Torres del Paine is with one of the many bus or tour companies that leave Puerto Natales daily from early November to mid-March or April (details are given in the Transport section, below). At other times, services by travel agencies are subject to demand; arrange your return date with the driver and try to coincide with other groups to keep costs down. The park administration is 147 km northwest of Puerto Natales via the old road, which runs through the eastern side of the park and is used by public buses. The administration can also be reached via a shorter, quicker paved road, 85 km, which enters the park to the south via a bridge over the Río Serrano. It takes about 1½ hours to travel from Puerto Natales to the park administration by this route, but if you're driving there yourself, bear in mind that this road is narrow with lots of blind corners and sudden gusts of wind and can be rough in patches: use your horn a lot. If you want to drive, hiring a pickup from Punta Arenas or Puerto Natales is an economical proposition for a group (up to nine people). Always fill up with fuel in Puerto Natales. ▶ *See Transport, page 608.*

Getting around

Allow a week or 10 days to see the park properly. Most visitors will find that they can get around on foot. However, in season there are frequent minibus connections within the park: from Laguna Amarga to **Hotel Las Torres**, US$5, and from the administration centre to **Hostería Lago Grey**, US$15. There are also boats across Lago Pehoé. Other than these routes getting around the park without your own transport is difficult and expensive. Roads inside the park are narrow and winding with blind corners.

Tourist information

The park is administered by **CONAF**: the **Administration Centre** ① *T061-223 8959/269 1931, www.parquetorresdelpaine.cl, daily 0830-2030 in summer, daily 0830-1230, 1400-1830 off season*, is in the south of the park at the northwest end of Lago del Toro. It puts on a good slideshow at 2000 on Saturday and Sunday and there are also excellent exhibitions on the flora and fauna of the park in Spanish and English. There are park entrances at Laguna Amarga, Lago Sarmiento, Laguna Azul and the Puente Serrano, and you are required to register and show your passport when entering the park, since rangers (*guardaparques*) keep a check on the whereabouts of all visitors. There are 13 ranger stations (*guarderías*) staffed by rangers, who give help and advice. Entry for foreigners coss US$32 (low season US$18), payable in Chilean pesos only; there are reduced prices for children and Chileans, and proceeds are shared between all Chilean national parks. The fee includes a reasonable trail map to take with you (not waterproof). If you are based outside the park and plan on entering and leaving several times explain this when you are paying your entrance to be given a multiple entry stamp valid for three consecutive days.

Climbing the peaks requires two permits, first from **DIFROL** (can be obtained free online, www.difrol.cl), then from **CONAF** in the park itself (take passports, **DIFROL** permit, insurance and route plan).

Accommodation is available on three levels: there are hotels (expensive, over US$300 for a double room per night), privately run *refugios* (well equipped and staffed, offering meals and free hot water for tea, soup, etc) and campsites with amenities and basic *campamentos*. All options fill up quickly in peak summer months, January and February, so plan your trip and book hotels and *refugios* in advance. Pay in dollars to avoid IVA (VAT). See Where to stay for more details.

Best time to visit

The weather in the park can change in a few minutes. The warmest time is from December to March, although it can be wet and windy. January and February are the busiest months, when the impact of huge numbers of visitors to the park (over 100,000 a year) is often visible in litter around the *refugios* and camping areas. The spring months of October and November are recommended for wild flowers. Rain and snowfall are heavier the further west you go and bad weather sweeps off the Campo de Hielo Sur without warning. Snow may prevent access in winter, but well-equipped hikers can do some good walking when conditions are stable. For information on weather conditions, in Spanish, phone the administration centre. The park is open all year round.

Trekking → *For listings, see pages 606-609.*

There are about 250 km of well-marked trails. Visitors must keep to the trails: cross-country trekking is not permitted. It is vital not to underestimate the unpredictability of the weather, nor the arduousness of some of the long hikes. Some paths are confusingly marked and it is all too easy to end up on precipices with glaciers or churning rivers below; be particularly careful to follow the path at the Paso John Garner on El Circuito (see below). The only means of rescue are on horseback or by boat; the nearest helicopter is in Punta Arenas and high winds usually prevent its operation in the park. Always report your route to staff. Mobile phone coverage is erratic. An Argentine visitor disappeared as recently as Christmas 2013 and was not found, despite extensive searches.

Equipment

It is essential to be properly equipped against cold, wind and rain. A strong, streamlined, waterproof tent is essential if doing El Circuito (although you can hire camping equipment for a single night at most *refugios*). Also essential are protective clothing, strong waterproof footwear, compass, good sleeping bag and sleeping mat. In summer also take shorts and sunscreen. You are strongly advised to bring all necessary equipment and your own food from Puerto Natales and not to rely on availability at the *refugios* within the park; the small shops at the *refugios* (see below) and at the **Posada Río Serrano** are expensive and have a limited selection. See the

Torres tips

• The summer months (January and February) should be avoided due to overcrowding, especially at *refugios* and campsites. Try to visit the park either side of the peak season: late November/early December or mid-April are best.
• Litter has become a problem, especially around *refugios* and camping areas; take all your rubbish out of the park, including toilet paper.
• Forest fires are a serious hazard. Make sure you follow all instructions about lighting fires to the letter. Most importantly, if you are using your own cooking stove, only cook in designated areas.

• Try to leave early in the morning in order to catch the sunrise and also to arrive at the next camping ground in time to choose a nice spot.
• Most campsites are riddled with field mice. These guys eat everything, so it's best to string up all your food, including toothpaste and chewing gum, in a couple of plastic bags and hang it from a tree, so they aren't tempted to nibble through your tent.
• Search for campsites that are less popular; it may mean extending your trek by a day, but it will be worth it.

box, above, for advice on how to protect consumables from rats and mice, which are a real problem around camping sites and the free *refugios*. It is worth repeating here that you are not allowed to build fires in the park. Unauthorized campfires in 2005 and 2011 led to the destruction of 160 sq km and 110 sq km respectively.

A decent map is provided with your park entrance ticket; other maps are obtainable in many places in Puerto Natales but most have one or two mistakes. The map produced by **Cartografía Digital** has been recommended as more accurate, as is the one produced by **Patagonia Interactiva**.

Treks
There are also plenty of shorter walks in the park, see park website www.torres delpaine.com.

El Circuito ⓘ *in theory, lone walkers are not allowed on this route*. The park's emblematic trek is a circuit round the Torres and Cuernos del Paine. It is usually done anticlockwise starting from the *guardería* at **Laguna Amarga** and, although some people complete the route in less time, it normally takes five to six days. The circuit is often closed in winter because of snow; major rivers are crossed by footbridges, but these are occasionally washed away. From Laguna Amarga the route is north along the western side of the Río Paine to **Lago Paine**, before turning west to follow the lush pastures of the valley of the Río Paine to the southern end of **Lago Dickson** (it is possible to add a journey to the *campamento* by the Torres on day one of this route); the *refugio* at Lago Dickson lies in a breathtaking position in front of the icy white lake with mountains beyond. From Lago Dickson the path runs along the wooded valley of the **Río de los Perros**, past the Glaciar de los Perros, before climbing through bogs and up scree to **Paso John Garner** (1241 m, the highest point on the route), then dropping steeply through forest to follow the Grey Glacier southeast to **Lago Grey**, continuing to **Lago Pehoé** and then joining up with the 'W' (see below)

Parque Nacional Torres del Paine

Where to stay 🏠	2 Dickson Shelter (Vértice)	B Dickson	K Japonés
1 El Chileno	3 Grey (Vértice)	C Grey	L Lago Pehoé
2 Explora	4 Las Torres (Fantástico Sur)	D Las Torres	M Las Carretas
4 Hostería Mirador del Payne	5 Los Cuernos	E Los Perros	N Los Guardas
5 Hostería Pehoé	(Fantástico Sur)	F Paine Grande	O Paso
6 Hotel Lago Grey	6 Lodge Paine Grande	G Serón	P Pingo
7 Hotel Las Torres	(Vértice)	H Serrano	Q Torres
8 Tierra Patagonia			R Zapata
	Campamentos with	**Basic campamentos** 🔺	
Refugios 🏠	**facilities** 🔺	I Británico	
1 Chileno (Fantástico Sur)	A Chileno	J Italiano	Ranger stations 🏠

back to the Hostería Las Torres or Laguna Amarga. There are superb views en route, particularly from the top of Paso John Garner.

Walking times between campsites are four to six hours. The most difficult section is the very steep, slippery slope from Paso John Garner down to the Campamento Paso; the path is not well signed at the top of the pass, and some people have got dangerously lost and ended up on the Grey Glacier itself. Camping gear must be carried, as some *campamentos* (including Campamento Paso and Campamento Torres) do not have *refugios*.

The 'W' The 'W' is a popular alternative to El Circuito. This four- to five-day route can be completed without camping equipment if preferred, as there is accommodation in *refugios* en route. It combines several of the hikes described separately below. From Refugio Laguna Amarga the first stage runs west via **Hostería Las Torres** and up the valley of the **Río Ascensio** via Refugio Chileno to the base of the **Torres del Paine** (see below). From here return to the Hostería Las Torres and then walk along the northern shore of **Lago Nordenskjold** via Refugio Los Cuernos to Campamento Italiano. Next climb the Valley of the **Río del Francés** (see below) before continuing to Refugio Pehoé. From here you can complete the third part of the 'W' by walking west along the northern shore of **Lago Grey** to Refugio Grey and the Grey Glacier before returning to Refugio Pehoé and the boat back across the lake to the Refugio Pudeto. To do the hike from west to east take the scheduled catamaran service across Lago Pehoé to Lodge Paine Grande and start from there.

Valley of the Río del Francés From Refugio Pehoé this route leads northeast across undulating country along the western edge of **Lago Skottberg** to Campamento Italiano and then follows the valley of the Río del Francés, which climbs between Cerro Paine Grande and the Ventisquero del Francés (to the west) and the Cuernos del Paine (to the east) to Campamento Británico; the views from the mirador, an hour's walk above Campamento Británico, are superb. Allow 2½ hours from Refugio Pehoé to Campamento Italiano, 2½ hours further to Campamento Británico.

To the base of the Torres del Paine From Refugio Laguna Amarga, this six-hour route follows the road west to Hotel Las Torres (1½ hours), before climbing along the western side of the **Río Ascensio** via Refugio Chileno (two hours) and Campamento Chileno to Campamento Las Torres (two hours), close to the base of the **Torres del Paine** (be careful when crossing the suspension bridge over the Río Ascensio near Hotel Las Torres, as the path is poorly marked and you can end up on the wrong side of the ravine). The path alongside the Río Ascensio is well marked, and the Campamento Las Torres is in an attractive wood (no *refugio*). Here there is a fork: the path to the base of the towers is well-marked but these 30 minutes are up the moraine. The towers seem so close that you almost feel you could touch them. To see the Torres lit by sunrise (spectacular but you must have good weather), it's well worth carrying your camping gear up to Campamento Torres and spending the night. One hour beyond Campamento Torres is Campamento Japonés, another good campsite for climbers only.

Treks from Guardería Grey Guardería Grey, 18 km west by road from the administration centre, is the starting point for a five-hour trek to Lago Pingo, recommended if you want to get away from the crowds, and one of the best routes in the park for birdwatching (this trek can only be undertaken with a certified CONAF guide). From the *guardería* follow the **Río Pingo**, via Refugio Pingo and Refugio Zapata (four hours), with views south over Ventisquero Zapata (look out for plenty of wildlife and for icebergs in the lake) to reach the lake. **Ventisquero Pingo** can be seen 3 km away over the lake. Note there is a bridge over a river here, marked on many maps, which has been washed away. The river can be forded when it is low, however, allowing access to the glacier. Two short signposted walks from Guardería Grey have also been suggested: one is a steep climb up the hill behind the ranger post to **Mirador Ferrier**, from where there are fine views; the other is via a suspension bridge across the Río Pingo to the peninsula at the southern end of **Lago Grey**, from where there are good views of the icebergs on the lakes.

Laguna Verde From the administration centre follow the road north 2 km, before taking the path east over the **Sierra del Toro** and then along the southern side of **Laguna Verde** to the Guardería Laguna Verde. Allow four hours. This is one of the easiest walks in the park and may be a good first hike.

Laguna Azul and Lago Paine This route runs north from Laguna Amarga to the western tip of **Laguna Azul**, from where it continues across the sheltered **Río Paine** valley past Laguna Cebolla to the Refugio Lago Paine at the western end of the lake. Allow 8½ hours. Good birdwatching opportunities.

⊕ Parque Nacional Torres del Paine listings

For hotel and restaurant price codes and other relevant information, see pages 20-26.

● Where to stay

Parque Nacional Torres del Paine
p600, map p604
All the park's hotels are expensive, many feel overpriced. Agencies in Puerto Natales offer accommodation and transfers or car hire.
$$$$ Explora (Hotel Salto Chico Lodge), T061-241 1247 (reservations: Av Américo Vespucci Sur 80, p 5, Santiago, T02-2395 2800, www.explora. com). The park's priciest and most

exclusive place is nestled into a nook at Salto Chico on edge of Lago Pehoé, superb views. It's all included: pool, gym, horse riding, boat trips, tours. Arrange packages from Punta Arenas.
$$$$ Hotel Lago Grey, head office Lautaro Navarro 1077, Punta Arenas, T061-271 2100, www.turismolagogrey.com. Great views over Lago Grey, superior rooms worth the extra, glacier walks.
$$$$ Hostería Mirador del Payne, Estancia Lazo, lovely location on Laguna Verde on east edge of the park, 52 km from Sarmiento entrance, reservations from Fagnano 585, Punta Arenas, T061-222 8712, www.miradordelpayne.com.

Comfortable, meals extra, but inconvenient for park itself, riding, hiking, birdwatching. Private transport essential, or hike there from the park.

$$$$ Hostería Pehoé, T061-296 1238, www.pehoe.cl, 5 km south of Pehoé ranger station, 11 km north of park administration. Beautifully situated on an island with spectacular view across Lago Pehoé, restaurant.

$$$$ Hotel Las Torres, T061-261 7450, www.lastorres.com. Comfortable rooms, beautiful lounge with wood fire and great views of the Macizo, excellent evening buffet, good service, horse riding, transport from Laguna Amarga ranger station, spa, disabled access. Visitor centre and *confitería* open to non-residents.

$$$$ Tierra Patagonia, T02-2207 8861, www.tierrapatagonia.com. Excellent, environmentally sensitive luxury hotel with spa, pool and outdoor jacuzzi on the edge of the national park overlooking Lago Sarmiento. Full- and half-day guided trips by minibus, on foot or on horseback. Gourmet dining in panorama restaurant overlooking the lake and mountains. Highly recommended.

Refugios

2 companies, **Vértice Refugios** and **Fantástico Sur**, between them run the *refugios* in the park, which consist of comfortable dormitory or *cabaña* accommodation (bring your own sleeping bag, or hire sheets for US$8-10 per night). Prices start from US$46pp bed only and go up to US$200pp in a *cabaña* with full board. Meals can be bought individually (US$11, US$15 and US$21), restaurants are open to non-residents. *Refugios* have good hot showers and space for camping, US$8-16. All *refugios* hire tents for US$13-15 per night, plus US$3 per sleeping mat (book in advance for Vértice Refugios as they have

very few tents available). Kitchen facilities are available in some Vértice Refugios. Fantástico Sur will not let you prepare your own hot food unless you are camping. Most close in winter, although 1 or 2 may stay open, depending on the weather. Advance booking essential in high season.

Fantástico Sur, Esmeralda 661, Puerto Natales, T061-261 4184, www.fslodges. com (or through agencies in Puerto Natales): **Refugio El Chileno**, in the Valley of Río Ascencio, at the foot of the Torres; **Refugios Las Torres (Torre Central, Torre Norte)**, 2 *refugios* next to the Hotel Las Torres (see above), good facilities, especially in the newer Torre Central; **Refugio Los Cuernos**, on the northern shore of Lago Nordenskjold, also has 8 cabins (US$155 double occupancy without board, US$251 full board).

Vértice Refugios, Bulnes 1200, Puerto Natales, T061-241 2742, www.vertice patagonia.com (or through agencies in Puerto Natales): **Mountain Lodges Paine Grande**, on the northwest tip of Lago Pehoé (kitchen facilities, internet) and **Vértice Grey**; also the basic **Vértice Dickson Shelter**.

Camping

Free camping is permitted in 10 locations in the park: these sites are known as *campamentos* and are generally extremely basic. Fires may only be lit at organized campsites, not at *campamentos*. The wind tends to rise in the evening so pitch your tent early. Mice can be a problem around campsites, so do not leave food in packs on the ground. The *guardaparques* expect people to have a stove if camping; equipment hire is available in Puerto Natales (see Shopping).

In addition to sites at the *refugios*, there are the following sites:

Camping Lago Pehoé, www.camping pehoe.com. US$16 pp, tent rental US$24 for 2 including sleeping mat, also pre-pitched dome tents, hot showers, shop, restaurant.

Camping Serón and **Camping Las Torres** (by the Refugio Las Torres) are both run by **Fantástico Sur** (see above), US$9-11, hot showers.

Vértice Patagonia runs **Camping Los Perros**, **Paine Grande**, **Dickson** and **Grey** (from US$8pp).

Other campsites in or near the park: **Camping Río Serrano**, just outside the park's southern entrance on a working *estancia*, www.campingchile.com. Campsite, also has horse rides and hikes.

Ecocamp Patagonia, bookings from Don Carlos 3227C, Las Condes, Santiago, T02-2923 5950, www.eco camp.travel. The only ISO14001, environmental sustainability-certified hotel in Chile offers indigenous Kaweskar-influenced domes.

Patagonia Camp, at Lago Toro, www.patagoniacamp.com. Luxury yurts.

⚙ What to do

Parque Nacional Torres del Paine
p600, map p604
Before booking a tour, check all the details carefully and get a copy in writing, as there have been increasingly mixed reports of the quality of some tours. Many companies who claim to visit the Grey Glacier, for example, only visit Lago Grey (you see the glacier in the distance). Note that after mid-Mar there is less public transport and trucks are irregular.

Several agencies in Puerto Natales offer many variations of tours to the national park, some including other sites, some with one or more overnight stops. One-day tours by minibus (park entry

not included) give a good impression of the lower parts of the park, although you spend most of the day in the vehicle and many travellers would argue that you need to stay several days, or at least overnight, in the park to appreciate it fully. Cheaper tours are also available, but both guide and vehicle may not be as good as the established operators. There are many more operators based in Puerto Natales offering trekking, kayaking, ice-hiking, boat trips and other tours (see page 598).

Experience Chile, T02-2570 9436, www. torresdelpaine.org, www.experience chile.org. Specializes in tailor-made itineraries for individuals, couples and small groups.

☉ Transport

Parque Nacional Torres del Paine
p600, map p604
After mid-Mar/Apr there is little public transport and trucks are irregular.

Boat
Catamarán Hielos Patagónicos, Los Arrieros 1517, Puerto Natales, T061-241 1380, info@hielospatagonicos.cl. Boats between Refugio Paine Grande and Refugio Pudeto, US$24 one way with 1 backpack (US$8 for extra backpacks), US$38 return. Departs from Pudeto high season daily 0930, 1200, 1800, returns from Paine Grande 1000, 1230, 1830, journey time 30 mins; low season 1200 only. Reserve in advance in Puerto Natales or at the *refugios* at either end, and always check that boats are running.

Other boats run from **Hostería Grey** to the glacier, 2-4 daily, 3½ hrs, US$90 return, and from **Hostería Grey** to **Refugio Grey** via the glacier for US$60 one-way. See page 594 for details of the 3-hr zodiac trip up the Río Serrano to Torres del Paine from the Balmaceda glacier.

Bus

There are several companies running daily services into the park, leaving Puerto Natales between 0630 and 0800, and again (Dec-Feb) at 1430, using the old road, with a 20-min stop at Cerro Castillo (3 cafés and some shops), 2½ hrs to **Laguna Amarga**, 3½ hrs to **Guardería Pudeto** and 4½ hrs to the administration centre. All charge US$17 one way, US$32 open return to the administration centre (return tickets are not interchangeable between different companies). Buses will stop anywhere en route, but all stop at the Laguna Amarga entrance, Salto Grande del Paine and the administration centre. Buses also wait at Refugio Pudeto until the 1200 boat from Refugio Paine Grande arrives. Return buses to Puerto Natales stop at Laguna Amarga from 1430 to 2000 but in high season they fill quickly so it is best to board at the administration centre for the return to Puerto Natales.

Services are provided by **Bus Gómez**, Prat 234, T061-241 1971; **JBA**, Prat 258, T061-241 0242; and **Trans Vía Paine**, Bulnes 518, T061-241 3672.

To **El Calafate** (Argentina), take a bus from Puerto Natales (see above) or, alternatively, take a bus directly from the park to Cerro Castillo (106 km south of administration centre), then catch a direct service to Calafate (see border box, page 595). **Zaahj** has a very comfortable *Super Pullman* service, US$28, between Cerro Castillo and El Calafate. Beware that border crossings can take up to several hours in peak season.

Car hire

Hiring a pick-up in Punta Arenas is an economical proposition for a group (up to 9 people): US$400-420 for 4 days. A more economical car can cope with the roads if you go carefully; ask the rental agency's advice.

Contents

Footprint features

Border crossings

Argentina–Chile

At a glance

◉ **Getting around** Local buses will take you to the local attractions, but not much further afield. Some short-distance flights.

◑ **Time required** 3-4 days will allow you to visit Ushuaia and the surrounding area.

✿ **Weather** Mar-Nov brings harsh winds and cold temperatures, with snow in Jun and Jul.

✖ **When not to go** The height of winter (May-Jul) can be unpleasantly cold, unless you want to ski.

★ **Don't miss ...**
1 Dientes de Navarino, page 619.
2 Fishing around Río Grande, page 625.
3 Museums in Ushuaia, page 629.
4 Estancia Harberton, page 630.
5 A boat trip on the Beagle Channel, page 631.
6 Parque Nacional Tierra del Fuego, page 611.

The island of Tierra del Fuego is the most mysterious and captivating part of all Patagonia. At the very foot of the South American continent and separated from the mainland by the intricate waterways of the Straits of Magellan, this is America's last remaining wilderness and an indispensable part of any trip to the south. The island is divided between Argentina and Chile by a north–south line that grants Argentina the Atlantic and southern coasts and gives Chile an expanse of wilderness to the west, where the tail of the Andes sweeps east in the form of the mighty Darwin range.

The Chilean side is largely inaccessible, apart from the small town of Porvenir, though expeditions can be organized from Punta Arenas to take you hiking and trout fishing. On the Argentine side, glaciers and jagged peaks give a dramatic backdrop to the city of Ushuaia, the island's main centre, set in a serene natural harbour on the Beagle Channel, with views of the Dientes de Navarino mountains on the Chilean island of Navarino opposite. Sail from Ushuaia along the channel to the pioneer home of Harberton; to Cape Horn; or even to Antarctica. Head into the small but picturesque Parque Nacional Tierra del Fuego for strolls around Bahía Lapataia and for steep climbs with magnificent views out along the channel. The mountain slopes are covered in lenga forest, and if you visit in autumn you might think the name 'Land of Fire' derives from the blaze of scarlet and orange leaves. Elsewhere on the island, lakes and valleys can be explored on foot or on horseback, and in winter the valleys are perfect for cross-country skiing, while the slopes at Cerro Castor offer good powder snow and skiing with spectacular views of the end of the world.

Arriving in Tierra del Fuego

Getting there

Note that accommodation is sparse, and planes and buses fill up quickly from November to March. It's essential to book ahead.

Air **Argentine Tierra del Fuego** is easy to reach with several flights daily from Buenos Aires to Río Grande and Ushuaia, and less frequent flights from El Calafate, and some other towns in Patagonia. Flights are heavily booked in advance throughout the summer months (December to February). **Chilean Tierra del Fuego** is only reached by plane from Punta Arenas to Porvenir, daily, and to Puerto Williams on Isla Navarino, Monday to Saturday (but always check for seasonal variations).

Ferry and bus There are no road or ferry crossings between the Argentine mainland and Argentine Tierra del Fuego. You have to go through Chilean territory.

From Río Gallegos, Route 3 reaches the Integración Austral border at Monte Aymond, after 67 km, passing Laguna Azul (see box, opposite.) The road continues beyond the border as Chilean Route 255, reaching Kamiri Aike after 30 km. Take Route 257 for 16 km east of here to reach the dock at Punta Delgada for the 20-minute Straits of Magellan ferry crossing over the Primera Angostura (First Narrows) to Bahía Azul in Chilean Tierra del Fuego. At Punta Delgada is the Hostería El Faro where you can get food and drink. There are three boats working continuously, each with a café, lounge and toilets on board. Buses can wait up to 90 minutes to board and the boats run every 40 minutes from 0830 to 0100, US$25 per vehicle, foot passengers US$3. See www.tabsa.cl for more information. From Bahía Azul, the road is paved to Cerro Sombrero, from where *ripio* roads run southeast to Chilean San Sebastián (130-140 km from ferry, depending on the route taken). It's 15 km east, across the border (see box, opposite), to Argentine San Sebastián. From here the road is paved to Río Grande (see below) and Ushuaia.

The second main ferry crossing is Punta Arenas to Porvenir. Route 255 from Kamiri Aike goes southwest 116 km to the intersection with the Punta Arenas–Puerto Natales road, from where it is 53 km to Punta Arenas. The ferry dock is 5 km north of Punta Arenas centre, at Tres Puentes. The ferry crosses to Bahía Chilota, 5 km west of Porvenir, Tuesday to Sunday taking two hours 20 minutes, US$67 per vehicle, motorcycles US$19, foot passengers US$10. **Transportadora Austral Broom** ⓘ *www.tabsa.cl*, publishes a timetable a month in advance but this is dependent on tides and subject to change, so check in advance. Reservations are essential, especially in summer. From Porvenir a 234-km *ripio* road runs east to Río Grande (six hours, no public transport) via San Sebastián. Note that fruit and meat may not be taken onto the island, nor between Argentina and Chile.

There is also a weekly ferry service on the **Yaghan** (also www.tabsa.cl) from Punta Arenas to Puerto Williams on Isla Navarino. It takes 24 passengers, US$165 for chair, US$230 for Pullman, a 30-34-hour trip through beautiful channels. It will not take passengers if it is carrying petrol, so ask in advance.

Border crossing: Argentina-Chile

Integración Austral

The border is located at Monte Aymond, 67 km southwest of Río Gallegos via Route 3, and is open 24 hours in summer and 0900-2300 from 1 April to 3 October. On the Chilean side the road continues as Route 255 to Punta Arenas (two hours by bus). At Kamiri Aike, 30 km south of the border, there is a turn-off to the ferry crossing at Punta Delgada. For bus passengers the border crossing is easy, although you have about a 30-minute wait at each border post as luggage is checked and documents are stamped. Hire cars need special documents in order to cross the border. For more information see www.gendarmeria.gov.ar/pasos/chile/fichaust.html.

San Sebastián

This is the border between the Chilean and Argentine sides of Tierra del Fuego and is open daily 0900 to 2300. Chilean San Sebastián is located 130 km southeast of the ferry dock at Bahía Azul, via Cerro Sombrero. It consists of just a few houses with Hostería La Frontera (see page 621) 500 m from the border. Argentine San Sebastián is 15 km further east, across the border. It has a seven-room ACA hostería (T02961-15-405834) and a service station, open 0700-2300. For further details, see www.gendarmeria.gov.ar/pasos/chile/fichssebas.html.

Getting around

There are good bus links from Punta Arenas to Río Grande in Argentina, with an option of going via Porvenir, along the decent loop of road on the Chilean side. From Porvenir your options are limited to a *ripio* road around Bahía Inútil to near Lago Blanco, though there's no public transport here. Argentine Tierra del Fuego is much easier to get around, via Route 3 between Río Grande and Ushuaia with several buses a day. A fan of roads spreads out south and west from Río Grande to the *estancias* on the Argentine side, but these are unpaved and best attempted in a 4WD vehicle. A good *ripio* road leads east of Ushuaia along the south coast, and another goes part of the way along the north coast to Estancia San Pablo; there is no public transport here either.

Background

Tierra del Fuego's narrated history began with the early 16th-century explorers, but the island had been inhabited by indigenous groups for some 10,000 years. The most populous of these groups, the Onas (also known as the Selk'nam), were hunter-gatherers in the north, living mainly on guanaco which they shot with bow and arrow. The south eastern corner of the island was inhabited by the Haus or Hausch, also hunter-gatherers. The Yaganes or Yámana lived along the Beagle Channel and on the islands further south and were seafaring people who survived mainly on seafood, fish and birds. They were physically smaller than the Onas but with a strongly developed upper body for rowing long distances. The fourth group, the Alacalufe, lived in the west of Tierra del Fuego as well as on the Chonos Archipelago, surviving by fishing and hunting seals.

The first Europeans to visit the island came with the Portuguese navigator Fernão Magalhães (Magellan), who, in 1520, sailed through the channel that now bears his name. It was Magellan who named the island 'Land of Fire' when he saw the smoke from many fires lit along the shoreline by local inhabitants. As a result of numerous maritime disasters and the failure of Sarmiento de Gamboa's attempt to colonize the Straits in 1584, the indigenous population were left undisturbed for three centuries.

Fitzroy and Darwin's scientific visits in 1832 and 1833 recorded some fascinating interaction with the indigenous peoples, four of whom Fitzroy had earlier brought to London to see if they could be 'civilized'; he now returned the surviving three to the island. Fitzroy and Darwin's visits were a precursor to attempts to convert the indigenous groups to Christianity so that the island could be used by white settlers without fear of attack. Several disastrous missions followed, encountering stiff resistance from the inhabitants. In 1884, Reverend Thomas Bridges founded a mission at Ushuaia. He was the first European to learn the Yámana language, and he compiled a Yámana-English dictionary. He soon realized that his original task was a destructive one. The purpose of the missionary work had been to facilitate lucrative sheep farming on the island, but the Ona were attracted to the 'white guanacos' on their land and took to hunting sheep, which proved far easier than catching the fast-footed guanaco. In response, the colonists offered two sheep for each Ona that was killed (proof was provided by a pair of Ona ears). The indigenous groups were further ravaged by epidemics of European diseases. In a desperate attempt to save the Ona, Salesian missionaries founded three missions in the Straits of Magellan in the early 20th century, but, stripped of their land, the Ona lost the will to live, and the last Ona died in 1999. The Hausch also died out. The last of the Yámana, a woman called Cristina Calderón, presently survives near Puerto Williams. She is 86 years old.

Imprecision in the original colonial land division and the greed of the rush southwards led to border disputes between Argentina and Chile, which still rumble on today. The initial settlement of the dispute in 1883 was followed by a desire by both governments to populate the area by allocating large expanses of land for sheep farming. The main beneficiaries of this policy on Tierra del Fuego were the Menéndez and Braun families, already established in Punta Arenas.

For many years, the main economic activity of the northern part of the island was sheep farming, but Argentine government tax incentives to companies in the 1970s led to the establishment of new industries in Río Grande and Ushuaia and a rapid growth in the population of both cities; the subsequent withdrawal of incentives has produced increasing unemployment and migration. Tourism is increasingly important in Ushuaia.

For a detailed narrative account of Tierra del Fuego, the best book is the classic by Lucas Bridges, *Uttermost Part of the Earth*, out of print but easily obtained second-hand on www.abebooks.co.uk. Also fascinating is *Patagonia, Natural history, prehistory and ethnography at the uttermost part of the earth* (British Museum press). *Savage – The Life and Times of Jemmy Button* by Nick Hazelwood (Hodder & Stoughton) is also recommended.

Chilean Tierra del Fuego

The Chilean half of Tierra del Fuego is in two sections: the western half of Isla Grande (the main island) and the whole of Isla Navarino, to the south of the main island. Much less developed than the Argentine side of Tierra del Fuego, it has just two small towns where Chile's Fuegians are mostly concentrated: Porvenir on Isla Grande, easily reached by ferry from Punta Arenas; and Puerto Williams on Isla Navarino, which can be reached by a flight from Punta Arenas, a weekly ferry also from Punta Arenas and by boat from Ushuaia. The northern part of Isla Grande is flat steppe, but the south is dominated by the Darwin range of mountains, which provide a dramatic visual backdrop, even if you can't easily get to them. Tourism on Chilean territory is limited, but it's possible to organize trekking tours from Punta Arenas, and there are fishing lodges offering magnificent trout fishing, particularly on the Río Grande.

Puerto Porvenir → *For listings, see pages 621-623. Colour map 6, C3. Phone code: +56 (0)61. Population 5100.*

Chilean Tierra del Fuego has a population of 7000, most of whom live in the small town of Porvenir – the only town on the Chilean half of the main island. Founded in 1894 during the gold boom, when many people came seeking fortunes from Croatia and Chiloe, Porvenir is a quiet place with a wide open pioneer feel, streets of neat, brightly painted houses of corrugated zinc and quaint tall domed trees lining the main avenue. There is a small museum, the **Museo Fernando Cordero Rusque** ① *Zavattaro 402, on the plaza, T061-581800, www.museoporvenir.cl, Mon-Thu 0900-1700, Fri 0900-1600, Sat-Sun 1030-1330, 1500-1700, US$0.85*, with archaeological and photographic displays on the Onas, and good displays on natural history and the early gold diggers and sheep farmers. There's little else to do here, but you could stroll around the plaza, with its **Iglesia San Francisco de Sales**, and down to the shoreside promenade, where there's a strange collection of 19th-century farm machinery and a striking wooden monument to the Selk'nam.

Tourist information is available at the museum (the best option), on notice boards outside the Municipalidad, on the seafront and elsewhere, and from a handicrafts stall in a kiosk on the seafront (opposite Comercial Tuto, No 588). See also www.patagonia-chile.com.

Beyond Porvenir

Beyond Porvenir there is wonderfully wild virgin territory to explore. However, if you want an adventure, your best bet is to arrange a trip through tour operators in Punta Arenas, since there's still very little infrastructure on the Chilean side of the island. All roads are good *ripio* except a paved section from Bahía Chilota to Porvenir and in Porvenir itself. ▶ *For suitable tour operators in Punta Arenas and Porvenir, see What to do, page 589 and page 622.*

North of Porvenir, 6 km, is the **Monumento Natural Laguna de los Cisnes**. Access is across private land; the owner will give permission. Another place to see wildfowl, including black-necked swans from December is **Laguna Santa María**, not far from Porvenir on the road to **Bahía Inútil**, a wonderful windswept bay. Cabo Boquerón, the headland at the start of Bahía Inútil, has great views on a clear day, as far as Cabo Froward, Isla Dawson and the distant Cordillera Darwin's snow peaks. Driving east along the bay you pass Los Canelos, with trees, a rare sight, and then the junction for the Cordón Baquedano, on the **Circuito de Oro**. This is a recommended tour, on which you can see gold panning using the same techniques that have been employed since mining began in 1881; it's a four-hour, 115-km round trip. Miner Sr Jorge Gesell Díaz is happy to show tourists his workings (very enthusiastic), in summer only; write in his visitors' book and leave a tip.

Camerón and further south

About 90 km east of Porvenir, roads head east to San Sebastián and south to Camerón via Onaisin (99 km from Porvenir). Camerón is a large farm settlement and the only other community of any size on the Chilean part of the island. It is 149 km from Porvenir on the opposite shore of Bahía Inútil. This wonderful windswept bay, with views of distant hills and the snow-capped Darwin range all along the southern horizon, was named 'useless' by British engineers making a hydrographic survey here in 1827 because it has no useful port. Nevertheless, as you near Camerón, the road passes secluded canyons and bays, interspersed with a few farms, and the whole feel is dramatic, isolated and somehow rather magical.

Other options are sailing from Porvenir to **Río Cóndor** across Bahía Inútil, south of Camerón, and trekking or riding from Camerón to **Seno Almirantazgo**, a beautiful, wild and treeless place, where mountains sink into blue fjords with icebergs.

A large part of the peninsula between Bahía Inútil and Seno Almirantazgo is covered by the **Karukinka** nature reserve (www.karukinkanatural.cl). From Camerón a road runs southeast past an airfield and into the hills, through woods where guanacos hoot and run off into glades, and the banks are covered with red and purple moss. The north shores of **Lago Blanco** can be reached by cutting east through the woods from Sección Río Grande, with superb views of the mountains surrounding the lake and the snows in the south.

Meanwhile, the rough road continues as far south as Estancia Lago Fagnano on Lago Fagnano, four hours from Onaisin. The government is hoping to complete the road to **Yendegaia** on the Beagle Channel with a view to having a summer route, including ferry, to Puerto Navarino. This would traverse the new Parque Nacional Yendegaia, which was created in December 2013 (www.theconservationlandtrust.

org) and which adjoins the Parque Nacional Tierra del Fuego in Argentina. It's essential to organize any trip to this area through a reliable tour operator with solid infrastructure.

Isla Navarino → *For listings, see pages 621-623.*

Situated on the southern shore of the Beagle Channel, Isla Navarino is totally unspoilt and beautiful, offering great geographical diversity, thanks to the **Dientes de Navarino** range of mountains, with peaks over 1000 m, covered with southern beech forest up to 500 m, and south of that, great plains covered with peat bogs, with many lagoons abundant in flora. The island was the centre of the indigenous Yaganes (Yámana) culture, and there are 500 archaeological sites, the oldest dated as 3000 years old. Guanacos and condors can be seen inland, as well as large numbers of beavers, which were introduced to the island and have done considerable damage. The flight from Punta Arenas is beautiful, with superb views of Tierra del Fuego, the Cordillera Darwin, the Beagle Channel and the islands stretching south to Cape Horn.

Arriving on Isla Navarino

Ushuaia Boating (www.ushuaiaboating.com.ar) travel from Ushuia to Puerto Williams, US$120 each way, which includes a 40-minute crossing in a semi-rigid boat to Puerto Navarino. Despite Ushuaia Boating dealing with documents when you buy the ticket, there is a lot of hanging around at Puerto Navarino, but the setting is nice and they sometimes offer coffee and pastries for impatient passengers. Then it's a one-hour ride in a combi on a lovely, *ripio* road to Williams; make sure you are clear about transport arrangements for your return. **Fernández Campbell** has a 1½-hour crossing from **Ushuaia**, on Friday, Saturday and Sunday at 1000, returning at 1500. Tickets (US$125 for foreigners) are sold at **Naviera RFC** in Puerto Williams and **Zenit Explorer**, Juana Fadul 126, in Ushuaia, T02901-433232.

Puerto Williams → *Colour map 7, C2. Phone code 061. Population 2500.*

The only settlement of any size on the island is Puerto Williams, a Chilean naval base situated about 50 km east of Ushuaia on Argentine seas across the Beagle Channel. Puerto Williams is the southernmost permanently inhabited town in the world; 50 km east-southeast is Puerto Toro, the southernmost permanently inhabited settlement on earth. Some maps mistakenly mark a road from Puerto Williams to Puerto Toro, but it doesn't exist; access is only by sea. Due to the long-running border dispute with Argentina here, Puerto Williams is controlled by the Chilean navy. Outside the naval headquarters, you can see the bow section of the *Yelcho*, the tug chartered by Shackleton to rescue men stranded on Elephant Island.

Your main purpose for visiting the island is likely to be the trekking on the Dientes de Navarino, but you should take time to explore the indigenous heritage here too. It's beautifully documented in the **Museo Martín Gusinde** ⓘ *www. museoantropologicomartingusinde.cl, Nov-Mar Tue-Fri 0930-1300, 1500-1800, Sat-Sun 1430-1830; Apr-Oct Tue-Fri 0930-1330, 1430-1730, Sat 1430-1830, US$1,* known as the

Museo del Fin del Mundo (End of the World Museum), which is full of information about vanished indigenous tribes, local wildlife and the famous voyages by Charles Darwin and Fitzroy of the *Beagle*. A visit is highly recommended. One kilometre west of the town is the yacht club (one of Puerto Williams' two nightspots), whose wharf is made from a sunken 1930s Chilean warship. The town has a **tourist information office** ① *Municipalidad de Cabos de Hornos, O'Higgins 293, T061-262 1011, www.ptowilliams.cl/turismo.html, closed in winter*, where you can ask for maps and details on hiking; there's also a bank, supermarkets and a hospital.

Exploring the island

For superb views, climb **Cerro Bandera**, which is reached by a path from the dam 4 km west of the town (it's a steep, three- to four-hour round trip, take warm clothes). There is excellent trekking around the **Dientes de Navarino** range, the southernmost trail in the world, through impressive mountain landscape, frozen lagoons and snowy peaks, giving superb views over the Beagle Channel. It's a challenging hike, over a distance of 53 km in five days, possible only from December to March, and a good level of fitness is needed. There is no equipment rental on the island. Ask for information in the tourist office at Puerto Williams, but it's best to go with an organized expedition from Punta Arenas.

Beyond Cerro Bandera, a road leads 56 km west of Puerto Williams to Puerto Navarino, where there is a jetty, the Alcaldía del Mar and four more houses, plus a few horses and cows. There is little or no traffic on this route and it is very beautiful, with forests of lengas stretching right down to the water's edge. You can also visit Villa Ukika, 2 km east of town, the place where the last descendants of the Yámana people live, relocated from their original homes at Caleta Mejillones, which was the last indigenous reservation in the province, inhabited by hundreds of Yámana descendants. At **Mejillones**, 32 km from Puerto Williams, is a graveyard and memorial to the Yámana people. Just before Estancia Santa Rosa (10 km further on), a path is said to cross the forest, lakes and beaver dams to Wulaia (four to six hours), where the *Beagle* anchored in 1833; however, even the farmer at Wulaia gets lost following this track.

Cape Horn

It is possible to catch a boat south from Isla Navarino to Cape Horn (the most southerly piece of land on earth apart from Antarctica). There is one pebbly beach on the north side of the island; boats anchor in the bay and passengers are taken ashore by motorized dinghy. A stairway climbs the cliff above the beach, up to the building which houses the naval post. A path leads from here to the impressive monument of an albatross overlooking the wild, churning waters of the Drake Passage below. See also A cruise to the end of the world, page 586.

For hotel and restaurant price codes and other relevant information, see pages 20-26.

⊙ Where to stay

Puerto Porvenir *p617*
$$$ Hostería Yendegaia, Croacia 702, T061-258 1919, www.hosteriayendegaia. com. Comfortable, family-run inn with good facilities and helpful staff. English-speaking owner runs birdwatching tours and to the king penguins.
$$ Central, Phillipi 298, T061-258 0077, opposite **Rosas**. All rooms with bath.
$$ España, Croacia 698, T061-258 0540, www.hotelespana.cl. Comfortable, well equipped, light and spacious rooms, helpful and friendly. Good restaurant with food all day.
$$ Rosas, Phillippi 296, T061-258 0088, hotelrosas@chile.com. Heating, restaurant and bar.
$ pp Hostal Kawi, Pedro Silva 144, T061-258 1638, hostalkawi@yahoo.com. Comfortable, rooms for 3, meals available, offers fly-fishing trips.

Beyond Porvenir *p618*
If you get stuck in the wilds, note that it is almost always possible to camp or bed down in a barn at an *estancia*.
$$$-$$ Hostería Tunkelen, Arturo Prat Chacón 101, Cerro Sombrero, T061-221 2757, www.hosteriatunkelen.cl. 3 buildings with rooms of different standards: with private bathrooms, shared bathrooms or backpacker dorms. Restaurant. Good for groups.
$$-$ Hostería de la Frontera, San Sebastián, T061-269 6004, frontera@ entelchile.net. Where some buses stop

for meals and cakes, cosy, with bath (the annex is much more basic), good food.

Puerto Williams *p619*
$$$$ Lakutaia, 2 km west of town, T061-8429 6630 (Santiago: T02-946 2703), www.lakutaia.cl. A 'base camp' for a range of activities and packages (riding, trekking, birdwatching, sailing, flights), 24 double rooms in simple but attractive style, lovely views from spacious public areas, bikes for hire, 3 golf 'holes' – most southerly in world!
$$$-$$ Hostal Bella Vista B&B, bookings through Victory Adventures, T061-222 7089, www.victory-cruises.com. Rooms and suites sleep 1-4, internet services and a minimarket.
$$ Forjadores de Cabo de Hornos, Uspashun 58, Plaza B O'Higgins, T061-262 1140, www.hostalforjadoresdelcabode hornos.cl. Simple place to stay, meals, agency for tours and transport, welcoming.
$$ Hostal Akainij, Austral 22, T061-262 1173, www.turismoakainij.cl. Comfortable rooms, very helpful, excellent, filling meals, basic English spoken, adventure tours and transfers.
$$ Hostal Coirón, Ricardo Maragaño 168, T061-262 1227, or through **Ushaia Boating** or **Sim Ltda** (see What to do). Double rooms or dorms, shared bath, helpful, good food, relaxed, quite basic, but OK.
$$ Hostal Pusaki, Piloto Pardo 222, T061-262 1116. Double room or dorms, good meals available, owner Patty is helpful and fun.
$$ Hostal Yagan, Piloto Pardo 260, T061-262 1118, hostalyagan@hotmail. com. Comfortable, some rooms with bath, meals available, run by Daniel

Yevenes, who offers tours and transport to Ushuaia.

$$ Refugio El Padrino, Costanera 276, T061-262 1136/8438 0843, ceciliamancillao@yahoo.com.ar. The vivacious Cecilia Mancilla is great fun, good food.

🍴 Restaurants

Puerto Porvenir *p617*
There are many lobster fishing camps nearby, where fishermen prepare lobster on the spot.

$$ Club Croata, Señoret entre Phillippi y Muñoz Gamero, next to the bus stop on the waterfront. A lively place with good food.

$$-$ El Chispa, Señoret 202, T061-258 0054. Good restaurant for seafood and other Chilean dishes.

$$-$ La Picá de Pechuga, Bahía Chilote s/n, by ferry dock. Good fresh seafood and fish. Owner Juan Bahamonde runs **Cordillero de Darwin** tours (see below):

$ Panadería El Paine, Sampaio 368. Shop and tea room, very friendly.

Puerto Williams *p619*
There are several grocery stores; prices are very high because of the remoteness. **Simón & Simón** and **Temuco** are opposite each other on Piloto Pardo, junction Condell. The former seems to be centre of reference in town. Most hotels and hostels will offer food.

$$-$ Café Angelus, Centro Comercial Norte 151, T061-262 1080. Also travel agent and transport. Run by Loreto Camino, friendly cheerful atmosphere, small, good simple cooking, coffee (including Irish), beer.

$ Los Dientes de Navarino, Centro Comercial Sur. Popular with locals, limited fare.

⚙ What to do

Puerto Porvenir *p617*
For adventure tourism and trekking activities contact tour operators in Punta Arenas (see What to do, page 589).
Turismo Cordillera de Darwin, run by Juan 'Pechuga' Bahamonde, T09-9888 6380, or T061-258 0167, gerencia@ cordilleradarwin.com or jebr_darwin@ hotmail.com (cordilleradarwin on Facebook). Runs land, fishing and boating tours. Oro circuit, 4 hrs without lunch, or 0800-1700 with lunch, including Laguna Santa María. Costs of tours to far south vary according to circumstances. Boat and fishing trips, 6 days allowing a day for unforeseen delays.

Puerto Williams *p619*
Boat trips
Australis Expedition Cruises, Av El Bosque Norte 0440, p 11, Las Condes, Santiago, T02-2442 3115, www.australis. com (see page 586), call at Wulaia Bay on the west side of Isla Navarino after visiting Cape Horn; you can disembark to visit the museum and take a short trek.
Victory Adventures, Tte Muñoz 118, Casilla 70, T061-222 7089, www.victory-cruises.com. Captain Ben Garrett and his family run this online travel agency for many tours and expeditions around Tierra del Fuego, Patagonia and the southern oceans to Antarctica.

Trekking
You must register first with *carabineros* on C Piloto Pardo, near Brito. Tell them when you get back, too. Sometimes they will not allow lone trekking.

Tour operators
Akainij, see Where to stay.
Sea, Ice and Mountains, Ricardo Maragaño 168, T061-262 1150, www. simltd.com. Sailing trips, trekking tours and many other adventure activities, including kayaking and wildlife spotting.
Shila, O'Higgins 322 (a hut at entrance to Centro Comercial), T061-7897 2005, www.turismoshila.cl. Luis Tiznado Gonzales is an adventure guide offering trekking and fishing, plus equipment hire (bikes, tents, sleeping bags, stoves, and more). Lots of trekking information, sells photocopied maps.

⊖ Transport

For details of how to get to Tierra del Fuego, see Arriving in Tierra del Fuego, above.

Puerto Porvenir p617
Air
To **Punta Arenas** (weather and bookings permitting), with **Aerovías DAP**, Señoret s/n, T061-258 0089, www.aeroviasdap.cl. Heavily booked so make sure you have your return reservation confirmed (see also page 590).

Bus
The only public transport on Chilean Tierra del Fuego is Jorge Bastian's minibus Porvenir–Cerro Sombrero, T061-234 5406/8503-3662, jorgebastian@hotmail.com, or axelvig20@hotmail.com, which leaves Sombrero 0700 on Mon, 0830 on Wed and Fri; returns from Porvenir Municipalidad, 2 hrs, US$4.50.

Puerto Williams p619
Air
To **Punta Arenas** with **DAP** (details under Punta Arenas). Book well in advance; long waiting lists (be persistent). The flight is beautiful (sit on right from Punta Arenas) with superb views of Tierra del Fuego, the Cordillera Darwin, the Beagle Channel, and the islands stretching south to Cape Horn. Also army flights available (they are cheaper), but the ticket has to be bought through DAP. Airport is in town.

Boat
See Arriving in Tierra del Fuego, above, for details of the **Yaghan** ferry of Broom, www.tabsa.cl. For boats services between Puerto Navarino and Ushuaia, see Arriving on Isla Navarino, above.

❶ Directory

Puerto Porvenir p617
Banks There is a bank with an ATM on the plaza (not all cards accepted, best to take cash from the mainland).

Argentine Tierra del Fuego

The Argentine half of Tierra del Fuego is much easier to visit than the Chilean half and more rewarding. The northern half of the island is windswept steppe, and its only town, Río Grande, once rich in oil, is now very faded. But pause before you head straight for Ushuaia to visit two splendid *estancias*. Viamonte (www.estanciaviamonte.com) was built by Lucas Bridges to protect the indigenous Ona people and is an evocative place to stay, while Estancia María Behety (see www.maribety.com.ar) is world famous for its brown trout fishing. The landscape turns to hills as you head south, and there's a lovely silent lake, Lago Fagnano, ideal for a picnic.

Ushuaia is the island's centre, beautifully set on the Beagle Channel, with a backdrop of steep mountains. With a picturesque national park on its doorstep, boat trips up the Beagle Channel to the Bridges' other superb *estancia*, Harberton, and a ski centre at Cerro Castor, there's plenty to keep you here. Huskies will draw your sledge in winter, and in summer you can walk around Bahía Lapataia and contemplate the serenity of the end of the world.

Río Grande → *For listings, see pages 634-643. Colour map 6, C4. Phone code: 02964. Population 67,000.*

Río Grande is a sprawling modern coastal town, the centre for a rural sheep-farming community that grew rapidly in the 1970s, with government tax incentives. The new population was stranded when incentives were withdrawn, but revival came with expansion into mobile phone and white goods assembly. This in turn declined when Argentina relaxed import restrictions and currently the town is benefitting from the exploitation of oil and gas in the vicinity. It's a friendly place which you are most likely to visit in order to change buses. There are a couple of good places to stay, however, and a small museum worth seeing.

Arriving in Río Grande

There is an **airport** ① *T02964-420600*, 4 km west of town. A taxi to the centre costs US$3. The **tourist office** ① *Rosales 350, T02964-431324, www.tierradelfuego.org.ar, Mon-Fri 0900-1700*, in the blue-roofed hut on the plaza is small but helpful. There's also a **provincial office** ① *Av Belgrano 319, T02964-422887, infuerg1@tierradelfuego.org.ar.*

Places in Río Grande

The city's architecture is a chaotic mix of smart nouveau-riche houses and humble wooden and tin constructions. It was founded by Fagnano's Salesian mission in 1893, and you can visit the original building, **La Candelaria** ⓘ *11 km north, T02964-421642, Mon-Sat 1000-1230, 1500-1900, US$2, afternoon tea US$3, getting there: taxi US$8 with wait*, whose museum has displays of natural history and indigenous artefacts, with strawberry plantations, piglets and an aviary. The **Museo Virginia Choquintel** ⓘ *Alberdi 555, T02964-430647, Mon-Fri 0900-1700, Sat 1500-1900,* is recommended for its history of the Selk'nam, the pioneers, missions and oil. Next door is a handicraft shop called **Kren** ('sun' in Selk'nam), which sells good local products.

Around Río Grande

The **fly fishing** in this area is becoming world-renowned and it's now possible to stay in several comfortable lodges in Río Grande and at Lago Escondido. This area is rich in brown trout, sea run brook trout and steelheads, weighing 2-14 kg; you could expect to catch an average of eight trout a day in season. Contact specialist fly-fishing tour operators. The season runs from 15 October to 14 April, with the best fishing from January to April.

Estancia María Behety, 15 km from town, built by the millionaire José Menéndez, has a vast sheep-shearing shed and is heaven for brown trout fishing. **Estancia Viamonte**, on the coast, 40 km south of town, is a working sheep farm with a fascinating history. Here, Lucas Bridges, son of Tierra del Fuego's first settler, built a home to protect the large tribe of indigenous Onas, who were fast dying out. The *estancia* is still inhabited by his descendants, who will take you riding and show you life on the farm. There is also a house to rent and superb accommodation, highly recommended.

Río Grande to Ushuaia → *For listings, see pages 634-643.*

From Río Grande, several roads fan out southwest to the heart of the island, though this area is little inhabited. The paved road south, Route 3, continues across wonderfully open land, more forested than the expanses of Patagonian steppe further north and increasingly hilly as you near Ushuaia. After around 160 km, you could turn left along a track to the coast to Cabo San Pablo. There is an *estancia* here, in a beautiful position with native woodland, although in 2014 indications were that it was not open to the public. There are also other trips to places of interest within reach. Route 3 then climbs up above Lago Fagnano and Tolhuin.

Tolhuin and around → *Phone code 02964.*

This is a friendly, small settlement close to the shore of Lago Fagnano, a large expanse of water, right at the heart of Tierra del Fuego. The village has a stretch of beach nearby and is a favourite Sunday afternoon destination for day-trippers from Ushuaia. There's a YPF service station just off the main road, but it's worth driving into the village itself for the famous bakery **La Unión** (see Restaurants, page 637), where you can buy delicious bread, *empanadas* and fresh *facturas* (pastries). It's also a good source of information. There's a tiny, friendly **tourist office** ① *Av de los Shelknam 80, T02901-492125, tolhuinturismo@tierradelfuego.org.ar, daily 0900-1500*, with very helpful staff. Handicrafts, including fine leather goods, are available at El Encuentro half a block from the tourist information office. From the village a road leads down to the tranquil lake shore, where there are a couple of good places to stay.

Further along Route 3, 50 km from Ushuaia, a road to the right swoops down to **Lago Escondido**, a fjord-like lake with steep, deep-green mountains descending into the water. After Lago Escondido, the road crosses the cordillera at Paso Garibaldi. It then descends to the Cerro Castor winter-sports complex and the Tierra Mayor Recreation area (see What to do, page 641). There is a police control just as you enter Ushuaia city limits; passports may be checked.

Ushuaia → *For listings, see pages 634-643. Colour map 6, C4. Phone code 02901. Population 57,000.*

The most southerly town in the world, Ushuaia's setting is spectacular. Its brightly coloured houses look like toys against the dramatic backdrop of vast jagged mountains. Opposite are the forbidding peaks of Isla Navarino, and between flows the serene green Beagle Channel. Sailing those waters you can just imagine how it was for Darwin, arriving here in 1832, and for those early settlers, the Bridges, in 1871.

Ushuaia

Where to stay 📍
1 Albergue Cruz del Sur
2 Antarctica
3 Canal Beagle
4 Cap Polonio
5 Familia Velásquez
7 Galeazzi-Basily
9 Hostería Posada Fin del Mundo
10 La Casa de Tere
11 Lennox
12 Los Cormoranes
13 Mil810
14 Nahuel
15 Paisaje del Beagle
16 Tzion
17 Yakush

Though the town has expanded in recent years, sprawling untidily along the coast, Ushuaia still retains the feel of a pioneer town, isolated and expectant. There are lots of places to stay, which fill up entirely in January, a fine museum and some great fish restaurants. There is spectacular landscape to be explored in all directions, with good treks in the accessible **Parque Nacional Tierra del Fuego** ① *www.tierradelfuego. org.ar*, just to the west of the city, and more adventurous expeditions offered into the wild heart of the island, trekking, climbing or riding. There's splendid cross-country skiing and downhill skiing nearby at **Cerro Castor** ① *www.cerrocastor. com*. And to the east, along a beautiful stretch of coastline is the historic *estancia* of Harberton, which you can reach by a boat trip along the Beagle Channel. Ushuaia is also the starting point for expeditions to Antarctica; for more information, see www.dna.gov.ar. For more about Ushuaia, see www.e-ushuaia.com.

Arriving in Ushuaia

Getting there The airport, **Aeropuerto Internacional Malvinas Argentinas** ① *T02901-461232 for information*, is 4 km from town on a peninsula in the Beagle Channel. A taxi to or from the airport costs US$5-7 (there is no bus). There are daily flights from Buenos Aires and Río Gallegos, and frequent flights from El Calafate and Punta Arenas, as well as weekly flights from other Patagonian towns. Schedules tend to change from season to season. Buses and minibuses from Río Grande arrive at their respective offices around town. ►► *See Transport, page 642.*

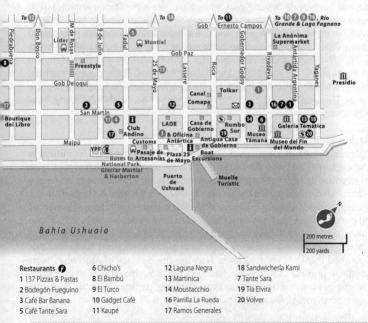

Restaurants 🍴	6 Chicho's	12 Laguna Negra	18 Sandwichería Kami
1 137 Pizzas & Pastas	8 El Bambú	13 Martinica	7 Tante Sara
2 Bodegón Fueguino	9 El Turco	14 Moustacchio	19 Tía Elvira
3 Café Bar Banana	10 Gadget Café	16 Parrilla La Rueda	20 Volver
4 Café Tante Sara	11 Kaupé	17 Ramos Generales	

Getting around It's easy to walk around the town in a morning, since all its sights are close together. You'll find banks, restaurants, hotels and shops along San Martín, which runs parallel to the shore, a block north of the coast road, Avenida Maipú. Ushuaia is very well organized for tourism, and there are good local buses to the national park and other sights, as well as many boat trips. Urban buses run from west to east across town; most stop along Maipú, US$0.50. The tourist office provides a list of minibus companies that run daily to nearby attractions; most of these use the bus stop at the junction of Maipú and Fadul (see map). Boat trips leave from the Muelle Turístico (tourist pier) by a small plaza, 25 de Mayo on the seafront.

Best time to visit Ushuaia is at its most beautiful in autumn (March to May), when the dense forests all around are turned a rich red and yellow, and there are many bright clear days. Summer (December to February) is best for trekking, when maximum temperatures are around 15°C, but try to avoid January, when the city is swamped with tourists. Late February is much better. The ski season is mid-June to October, when temperatures are around zero, but the wind drops.

Tourist information The **tourist information office** ① *San Martín 674, corner with Fadul, T02901-424550, www.turismoushuaia.com, Oct-Mar daily 1700-2100, Apr-Sep daily 0900-2000*, is one of the best in Argentina. The helpful staff speak several languages. They have a map and a series of leaflets about all the things to see and do, and can provide bus and boat times. Next door is the **Oficina Antártica** ① *at entrance to the port, T02901-430015, antartida@tierradelfuego.org.ar, Mon-Fri 0900-1700*, which has information on Antarctica and a small library with navigational charts. Other branches of the tourist office can be found at the **Pier (Muelle Turístico)** ① *T02901-437666, Oct-Mar daily, closed Apr-Sep, which has free Wi-Fi and toilets*, and at the **Airport** ① *T02901-423970, open only at flight times*. There is also a **Provincial tourist office** ① *Maipú 505, T02901-423423, info@tierradelfuego.org.ar*, and an office for the **Tierra del Fuego National Park** ① *San Martín 1395, T02901-421315*, which has a basic map of the park.

Background

Founded in 1884 after missionary Thomas Bridges had established his mission in these inhospitable lands, Ushuaia attracted many pioneers in search of gold. Keen to populate its new territory, the government set up a penal colony on nearby Staten Island, which moved to the town in 1902, and the town developed rapidly. Immigration was largely Croatian and Spanish, together with those shipwrecked on the shores, but the town remained isolated until planes arrived in 1935. As the prison closed, a naval base opened and in the 1970s there was a further influx, attracted by job opportunities in assemblage plants of electronic equipment that flourished thanks to reduced taxes. Now the city is capital of Argentina's most southerly province, and though fishing is still a traditional economic activity, Ushuaia has become an important tourist centre, particularly as the departure point for voyages to Antarctica.

Places in Ushuaia

There are several museums worth visiting if bad weather forces you indoors, and the most fascinating is **Museo del Fin del Mundo** ① *along the seafront at Maipú y Rivadavia, T02901-421863, Mon-Fri 1000-1900, Sat, Sun and bank holidays 1400-2000, US$9, guided tours 1100, 1400, 1700, fewer in winter*. Located in the 1912 bank building, it tells the history of the town through a small collection of carefully chosen exhibits on the indigenous groups, missionaries, pioneers and shipwrecks, together with nearly all the birds of Tierra del Fuego (stuffed), and you can get an 'end of the world museum' stamp in your passport. There are helpful and informed staff, and also an extensive reference library. Recommended. Further east, the old prison, Presidio, at the back of the naval base, houses the **Museo Marítimo** ① *Yaganes y Gobernador Paz, www.museomaritimo.com, daily 0900-2000, US$14, ticket valid 24 hrs*, with models and artefacts from seafaring days. The cells of most of the five wings of the huge building also house the **Museo Penitenciario**, which details the history of the prison. Excellent guided visits (1130, 1630, 1730 in Spanish; 1400 in English) also include a tour of the lighthouse (a life-size replica of the original) that inspired Jules Verne's novel, *Around the World in Eighty Days*. Recommended. Much smaller but also interesting is **Museo Yámana** ① *Rivadavia 56, T02901-422874, www.tierradelfuego.org.ar/mundoyamana, daily 0900-2000, US$7.50*, which has interesting scale models showing scenes of everyday life of Yámana people and the geological evolution of the island.

The most recently opened museum is the **Galería Temática** ① *San Martín 152, PB, 1er y 2do pisos, T02901-422245, www.historiafueguina.com, Mon-Sat 1100-2100, Sun 1700-2100, US$10*, where numerous life-sized displays take you through an informative history of Tierra del Fuego with a useful audioguide in different languages. There is also a themed garden at the back, reached through a huge souvenir shop with good knitwear and other goods.

Around Ushuaia → *For listings, see pages 634-643.*

Whatever you do, unless it's absolutely pouring with rain, take the chairlift (*aerosilla*) up to **Cerro Martial** ① *7 km from town, daily 1000-1730 (last ascent 1615), US$10*, for exhilarating views along the Beagle Channel and to Isla Navarino opposite. To reach the chairlift, follow Magallanes out of town; allow 1½ hours. Several companies run frequent minibus services in summer from the corner of Maipú and Fadul, US$4. Taxis charge US$7.50-9 to the base, from where you can walk all the way back. There are several marked trails, ranging from 600 m to 1 km (a leaflet is given out at the lower platform), including to a viewpoint and to Glaciar Martial itself. There is a splendid tea shop at the Cumbres de Martial *cabañas* at the base, and a basic *refugio* with no electricity up at the Cerro. Also by the lower platform is the **Canopy** ① *T02901-15-510307, www.canopyushuaia.com.ar, US$35, US$25 for a shorter run, US$28 and US$20 under 12s*, a series of zip lines and bridges in the trees. All visitors are accompanied by staff; it's safe and good fun. The café at the entrance, Refugio de Montaña, serves hot chocolate, coffee, cakes, pizzas and has a warm stove.

Estancia Harberton

In a land of extremes and superlatives, Harberton stands out as special. The oldest *estancia* in Tierra del Fuego, it was built in 1886 on a narrow peninsula overlooking the Beagle Channel. Its founder, the missionary Thomas Bridges (see box, page 633, for information on his life), was granted land by President Roca for his work amongst the indigenous people and for his help in rescuing victims of numerous shipwrecks in the channels. Harberton is named after the Devonshire village where his wife Mary was born, and the farmhouse was prefabricated by her carpenter father and assembled on a spot chosen by the Yámana people as the most sheltered. The English connection is evident in the neat lawns, shrubs and trees between the jetty and the farmhouse. Behind the buildings is a large vegetable garden, a real rarity on the island, and there's noticeably more wildlife here than in the Tierra del Fuego National Park, probably owing to its remoteness.

Still operating as a working farm, mainly with cattle and sheep, Harberton is run by Thomas Goodall, great-grandson of the founder, whose wife Natalie has created an impressive museum of the area's rich marine life with a thriving research centre. Visitors receive a guided tour of the museum, or of farm buildings and grounds with reconstructions of the Yámana dwellings. Tea or lunch (if you reserve ahead) are served in the tea room overlooking the bay, and you may well be tempted to rent one of the two simple cottages on the shore. There are wonderful walks along the coast, and nowhere in Argentina has quite the feeling of peace you'll find here. For more information, see www.estanciaharberton.com (in Spanish and English).

Parque Nacional Tierra del Fuego (see below), just outside Ushuaia, is easily accessible by bus and offers superb walks for all levels of fitness. Another way to get to the park is on the **Tren del Fin del Mundo** ① *T02901-431600, www.trendelfindelmundo. com.ar, 4-5 departures daily, US$36.50 tourist, US$60 1st class return, US$82 premium and US$126 special (cheaper in winter), plus US$17.20 park entrance.* This is the world's southernmost steam train, running new locomotives and carriages on track first laid by prisoners to carry wood to Ushuaia. It's a totally touristy experience with commentary in English and Spanish. Sit on the left side on the outbound journey to get the views. See Transport, below, for buses to the train station.

The **Estancia Harberton** ① *T02901-422742, www.estanciaharberton.com, 15 Oct-15 Apr daily 1000-1900, except 25 Dec, 1 Jan and Easter, US$7.50, (see box, above),* 85 km from Ushuaia, is the oldest *estancia* on the island and is still run by descendants of the British missionary Thomas Bridges, whose family protected the indigenous peoples here. It's a beautiful place, with the attractive wood-framed house that Thomas built sitting in quiet contemplation on a tranquil bay. You'll get an excellent guided walk (bilingual guides) around the *estancia*, through protected forest, and delicious teas or lunches are served in the Manacatush tea room overlooking the water. Highly recommended. The impressive **Museo Akatushún** ⓘ *phone as above, www.acatushun.org, 15 Oct to 15 Apr daily 1000-1900, except 25 Dec, 1 Jan and Easter, US$2.25,* has skeletons of South American sea mammals, the result of 25 years' scientific investigation in Tierra del Fuego, with excellent tours in English. You can camp for free with permission from the owners, or stay in cottages. Access is along a good unpaved road (Route 33, ex 'J') that branches off Route 3 40 km east of Ushuaia and runs 25 km through forest and then through the open country around Harberton with marvellous views; it takes about two hours, and there's no petrol outside Ushuaia and Tolhuin. See What to do and Transport, below, for trips to Harberton with Pira-Tur and bus services (irregular). For boat trips to Harberton, see below.

Excursions can be made to Lagos Fagnano and Escondido: agencies run seven-hour tours for US$70 per person without lunch; or check the list of cheaper but rather unreliable minibuses that go there, which is available at the tourist office. Tour agencies offer many good packages, which include trekking, canoeing, birdwatching and horse riding in landscape accessible only by 4WDs. See the tourist office's list of excursions, indicating which companies go where.

Boat trips

All these trips are highly recommended, but note that the Beagle Channel can be very rough. Food and drink on all boats is pricey. Excursions can be booked through most agencies, or at the Muelle Turístico where boat companies have their ticket offices; most boats leave from the Muelle Turístico, with a few excursions leaving from Muelle AFASYN (next to the old airport). All passengers must pay US$1.25 port tax; this is not included in tickets.

Most popular excursions visit the small islands southeast of Ushuaia in 2½ to three hours, all year round, passing next to the sea lion colony at Isla de los Lobos, Isla de los Pájaros and Les Eclaireurs lighthouse. Alternatively, they add an hour or so for a landing on Bridges Island. Prices vary depending on whether trips are made on big catamarans or on more exclusive sailing boats. A few pricier services include lunch onboard; otherwise a light snack or a coffee is served. Summer options add more to the itinerary, with some trips going further east past the Isla Martillo penguin colony and on to Estancia Harberton. Note that Harberton is included only on a few trips, and you should check that your tour actually visits the *estancia* and not just the bay, as some do. A few excursions also go west to the national park in about 5½ hours. See What to do, page 639, for companies and prices.

Parque Nacional Tierra del Fuego → *For listings, see pages 634-643.*

Covering 63,000 ha of mountains, lakes, rivers and deep valleys, this small but beautiful park stretches west to the Chilean border and north to **Lago Fagnano**, though large areas have been closed to tourists to protect the environment. All walks are best attempted in the early morning or afternoon to avoid the tour buses. You'll see lots of geese, the beautiful torrent duck, Magellanic woodpeckers and austral parakeets.

Arriving in Parque Nacional Tierra del Fuego

Access and information The park entrance is 12 km west of Ushuaia, on the main road west signposted from the town centre, where you'll be given a basic map with marked walks. Entry is US$17.20. The **park administration** ① *San Martín 1395, T02901-421315, tierradelfuego@apn.gov.ar, Mon-Fri 0900-1600*, is in Ushuaia. Ask at the tourist office for bus details (see also Transport, below) and a map of the park, with walks. There are no legal crossing points from the park to Chile. Wear warm, waterproof clothing: in winter the temperature drops to as low as -12°C, and although it can reach 25°C in summer, evenings can be chilly. There's a helpful *guardaparque* (ranger) at Lago Acigami (formerly known as Roca) and good camping here too in a picturesque spot, with a *confitería*.

For a really rich experience, go with guides who know the territory well and can tell you about the wildlife. Inexpensive trips for all levels are available with the highly recommended **Compañía de Guías de Patagonia** ① *www.companiadeguias.com.ar.*

Walks

The leaflets provided at the entrance show various walks, but these are recommended:

Senda Costera ① *8 km, 3 hrs each way* This lovely easy walk along the shore gives you the essence of the park, its rocky coastline, edged with a rich forest of beech trees and glorious views of the low islands with a backdrop of steep mountains. Start at Bahía Ensenada (where boat trips can be taken around the bay, and where the bus can drop you off). Walk along a well-marked path along the shoreline, and

Parque Nacional Tierra del Fuego

🏴 Bus stop

1 km
1 miles

Uttermost Part of the Earth

If you read one book about Patagonia, make it *Uttermost Part of the Earth*. The story of the first successful missionary to Tierra del Fuego, Thomas Bridges, and his son Lucas, is one of the most stirring in the whole history of pioneers in Argentina. An orphan from Bristol, Thomas Bridges was so called because he was found as a child under a bridge with a letter T on his clothing. Adopted by Rev Despard, he was taken as a young man to start a Christian mission in wild, uncharted Tierra del Fuego where no white man had survived. He brought his young wife and daughter after Despard had left following the massacre of the last lot of Christians by the indigenous inhabitants. Until his death in 1898, Bridges lived near the shores of the Beagle Channel, first creating the new settlement of Ushuaia and then at Harberton. He devoted his life to his work with the Yámanas (Yaghanes)

and soon gave up converting them, in favour of compiling a dictionary of their language, and – ultimately – protecting them from persecution. His son Lucas (1874-1949), one of six children, spent his early life among the Yámanas and Onas, living and hunting as one of them, learning their languages, and even, almost fatally, becoming involved in their blood feuds and magic rituals. Lucas became both defender and protector of the indigenous people whose culture he loved and was fascinated by, creating a haven for them at Harberton and Estancia Viamonte when most sheep farmers were more interested in having them shot. Lucas's memoirs, *Uttermost Part of the Earth* (1947), trace the tragic fate of the native population with whom he grew up. A compelling account of 20th-century man colliding with an ancient culture (out of print, but easily obtained from www.abebooks.co.uk).

then rejoin the road briefly to cross Río Lapataia (ignoring signs to Lago Acigami to your right). After crossing the broad green river and a second stretch of water (where there's a small camping spot and the *gendarmería*), it's a pleasant stroll inland to the beautifully tranquil **Bahía Lapataia**, an idyllic spot, with views across the sound.

Senda Hito XXIV ⓘ *Along Lago Acigami (Roca), 3.5 km, 90 mins one way.* Another easy walk beside this peaceful lake, with lovely pebble beaches, and through dense forest at times, with lots of birdlife. This is especially recommended in the evening, when most visitors have left. Get off the bus at the junction for Lago Acigami, turn right along the road to the car park (passing the *guardaparque*'s house) and follow the lake side.

Cerro Guanaco ⓘ *4 km, 4 hrs one way.* A challenging hike up through the very steep forest to a mirador at the top of a hill (970 m) with splendid views over Lago Acigami, the Beagle Channel and far-off mountains. The ground is slippery after rain: take care and don't rush. Allow plenty of time to return while it's light, especially in winter. The path branches off Senda Hito XXIV (see above) after crossing Arroyo Guanaco.

For hotel and restaurant price codes and other relevant information, see pages 20-26.

● Where to stay

Río Grande *p624*

Book ahead, as there are few decent choices. Several *estancias* offer full board and some, mainly on the northern rivers, have expensive fishing lodges; others offer horse riding.

$$$ Posada de los Sauces, Elcano 839, T02964-430868, www.laposadadelos sauces.com.ar. Best by far, with breakfast, beautifully decorated, comfortable, good restaurant (trout recommended), cosy bar, very helpful staff.

$$$ Villa, Av San Martín 281, T02964-424998, hotelvilla@live.com. Central, modern, restaurant/*confitería*, parking, discount given for cash.

Estancias

$$$$ Estancia María Behety, 15 km from Río Grande, reservations at **The Fly Shop**, www.maribety.com.ar. Established in 1897 on a 40-km stretch of the river that has become legendary for brown trout fishing, this *estancia* has accommodation for 18 anglers, and good food. It is one of the country's priciest fishing lodges, deservedly so. Guides and equipment included.

$$$$ pp Estancia Viamonte, 40 km southeast on the coast, T02964-430861, www.estanciaviamonte.com. For an authentic experience of Tierra del Fuego, built in 1902 by pioneer Lucas Bridges, writer of *Uttermost Part of the Earth*, to protect the Selk'nam/Ona people, this working *estancia* has simple and beautifully furnished rooms in a spacious cottage. Price is for full board and all

activities: riding and trekking; cheaper for dinner, bed and breakfast only. Delicious meals. Book a week ahead.

Camping

Club Naútico Ioshlelk-Oten, Montilla 1047, T02964-420536, www.nautico-rg. blogspot.com. Situated 2 km from town on the river. Clean, cooking facilities, heated building available in cold weather. YPF petrol station has hot showers.

Tolhuin and around *p625*

$$$ Cabañas Khami, on Lago Fagnano, 8 km from Tolhuin, T02964-15-611243, www.cabaniaskhami.com.ar. Well-equipped, rustic cabins, good value with linen. Price given for 6 people, 3-night weekend rates available.

$$ Terrazas del Lago, R3, Km 2938, T02964-432300, www.lasterrazasdellago. com.ar. A little way from the shore, smart wooden *cabañas*, well decorated, and also a *confitería* and *parrilla*.

$ pp Refugio Solar del Bosque, Lago Escondido, R3, Km 3020, 19 km from Ushuaia, T02901-444743. Basic hostel for walkers, with shared bathrooms, dorms for 4. Breakfast.

Camping

Camping Hain del Lago, T02964-1560 3606, robertoberbel@hotmail.com. Lovely views, fireplaces, hot showers, and a *quincho* for when it rains.

Camping La Correntina, T02964-492 137, 17 km from Tolhuin. In woodland, with bathrooms, and horses for hire.

Ushuaia *p626, map p626*

The tourist office has a comprehensive list of all officially registered accommodation and will help with rooms in private homes, campsites, etc. An excellent choice is to stay with Ushuaia families on a B&B basis. The range of lodging is growing at all budget levels, from the very chic, to *cabañas*, to basic B&Bs in the centre and the suburbs. There are too many to list here. Despite the expansion, you must book in advance in high season.

$$$$ Canal Beagle, Maipú y 25 de Mayo, T02901-432303, www.hotelcanal beagle.com.ar. ACA hotel (discounts for members), **$$$** Apr-Oct, comfortable and well-attended, with a small pool, gym, spa, business centre, some rooms with channel views (others overlook the container dock), good restaurant.

$$$$ Cap Polonio, San Martín 746, T02901-422140, www.hotelcappolonio. com.ar. Smart, central, modern, comfortable, popular restaurant/café **Marcopolo**.

$$$$ Lennox, San Martín 776, T02901-436430, www.lennoxhotels.com. Boutique hotel on the main street, with breakfast, services include hydromassage, minibar, restaurant and confitería on 4th floor. Laundry service.

$$$$ Mil810, 25 de Mayo 245, T02901-437714, www.hotel1810.com. City hotel with 30 standard rooms, one with disabled access, no restaurant but breakfast and *confitería*, all rooms with minibar, safe, quite small but cosy, calm colours, good views, business centre and multiple use room where you can hang out while waiting for flight.

$$$ Galeazzi-Basily, G Gob Valdez 323, T02901-423213, www.avesdelsur.com. ar. Among the best, beautiful family home, incredible welcome, in pleasant area 5 blocks from centre, 4 rooms with shared bath. Also excellent *cabañas* (**$$$**) in the garden. Highly recommended.

$$$ Hostería Posada Fin del Mundo, Rivadavia 610, T02901-437345, www. posadafindelmundo.com.ar. Family atmosphere, comfortable rooms, good value, has character.

$$$ Paisaje del Beagle, Gob Paz 1347, T421214, www.paisajedelbeagle.com.ar. Family-run, quiet, with a cosy dining area for good breakfast, laundry service. Recommended.

$$ pp La Casa de Tere, Rivadavia 620, T02901-422312, www.lacasadetere. com.ar. Shared or private bath, use of kitchen facilities, freshly baked bread, open fire, singles, doubles and triples, hot water, helpful owner.

$$ Nahuel, 25 de Mayo 440, T02901-423068, www.bybnahuel.com.ar. Charming Sra Navarrete has a comfortable B&B with channel views from the upper rooms and the terrace, good value, but noisy street.

$$$ Tzion, Gob Valdez 468, T02901-432290, tzion_byb@hotmail.com. B&B with 3 rooms, 1 with bath, high above town, 10 mins' walk from centre, nice family atmosphere, cheaper low season, laundry service, English and French spoken, great views. Highly recommended.

$$-$ Familia Velásquez, Juana Fadul 361, T02901-421719,losnokis_figueroa@ hotmail.com. Cosy, welcoming house of a pioneer, with basic rooms, breakfast, cooking and laundry facilities, good.

$ pp Albergue Cruz del Sur, Deloqui 242, T02901-434099, xdelsur@yahoo.com. Cosy, free tea, coffee and *mate*, book in advance.

$ pp Antártica, Antártida Argentina 270, T02901-435774, www.antarctica hostel.com. Central, welcoming, spacious chill-out room, excellent 24-hr bar, dorms for 6 and large doubles, breakfast included, game night Thu with good prizes. Recommended.

$ pp **Los Cormoranes**, Kamshén 788 y Alem, T02901-423459, www.loscormoranes.com. Large hostel, with good views, cosy rooms with lockers, OK bathrooms. Doubles (**$$**) available. They can book tours. HI member discount.

$ pp **Yakush**, Piedrabuena 118 y San Martín, T02901-435807, www.hostelyakush.com.ar. Very well run, central with spacious dorms, also doubles (**$$**, cheaper without bath), book exchange and library, dining room, steep garden with views. In-house tour operator organizes excursions. Recommended.

Camping

La Pista del Andino, Leandro N Alem 2873, T02901-435890. Set in the Club Andino ski premises in a woodland area, it has wonderful views over the channel. Electricity, hot showers, tea room and grocery store, very helpful. Recommended.

Around Ushuaia *p629*

$$$$ **Cabañas del Beagle**, Las Aljabas 375, T02901-432785, www.cabanasdelbeagle.com. 3 rustic-style cabins 1.3 km above the city, fully equipped with kitchen, hydromassage, fireplace, heating, phone, self-service breakfast, very comfortable, personal attention.

$$$$ **Cumbres del Martial**, Luis F Martial 3560, 7 km from town, T02901-424779, www.cumbresdelmartial.com.ar. At the foot of the *aerosilla* to Glaciar Martial, 4 *cabañas* and 6 rooms, beautifully set in the woods, charming, very comfortable, cabins have whirlpool baths. Small spa (massage extra) with saunas and gym. The tearoom, with disabled access, is open all year, restaurant with traditional fondues.

$$$$ **Finisterris Lodge Relax**, Monte Susana, Ladera Este, 7 km from city, T02901-15-612121, www.finisterrislodge.com. In 17 ha of forest, 5-star luxury in individual cabins, with top-of-the-range fittings, hydromassage and private spa (massage arranged, extra), rustic style but spacious, 'home-from-home' atmosphere, 24-hr attention from owner, given mobile phone on arrival. Meals can be ordered in, or private chef and sommelier can be booked for you.

$$$$ **Las Hayas**, Luis Martial 1650 (road to Glaciar Martial), T02901-430710, www.lashayashotel.com. 4 standards of room, all very good with TV, safe, 3 types of view, channel, mountains or forest. 2 restaurants: **Martial** for lunch and dinner, **Drake** for breakfast. Everything is included in room price except massages and hairdresser. A fine hotel. Just beyond and run by the same family company is:

$$$$ **Los Acebos**, Luis F Martial 1911, T02901-442200, www.losacebos.com.ar. All rooms with channel view, safe, games room, **Rêve d'Orange** restaurant independent of hotel. Golf days organized. Very comfy, as expected, but less characterful than **Las Hayas**.

$$$$ **Los Cauquenes**, at Bahía Cauquen, De La Ermita 3462, T02901-441300, www.loscauquenes.com. High quality 5-star hotel overlooking Beagle Channel, price varies according to size and view, spa, very tastefully decorated, prize-winning restaurant, regional food on dinner menu, wine bar with over 100 Argentine wines.

$$$$ **Los Yámanas**, Costa de los Yámanas 2850, western suburbs, T02901-446809, www.hotelyamanas.com.ar. In the same group as Canoero tour operator, all rooms with Channel view, spacious, well-decorated, hydromassage,

fitness centre, spa and conference centre outside in wooded grounds, shuttle to town. Very pleasant.

$$$$ Tierra de Leyendas, Tierra de Vientos 2448, T02901-446565, www.tierradeleyendas.com.ar. In the western suburbs. 5 very comfortable rooms with views of the Beagle Channel, or the mountains at the back, 1 room with jacuzzi, all others with shower, excellent restaurant serving regional specialties, open only for guests for breakfast and dinner. No cable TV, but DVDs, living room with games, library, deck overlooking Río Pipo's outflow. Only for non-smokers. Recommended and award-winning.

$$$ pp Estancia Harberton, T02901-422742, www.estanciaharberton.com. Mid-Oct to mid-Apr. 2 restored buildings on the *estancia* (see above), very simple rooms, wonderful views, heating. Price includes walking tour and entry to museum; 2 rooms with bath, 1 room with 2 beds, shared bath, 1 room with bunks, shared bath. Kitchenette for tea and coffee. Lunch and dinner extra. No credit cards.

Parque Nacional Tierra del Fuego
p631, map p632

Camping
Camping Lago Roca, T02901-433313, 21 km from Ushuaia, by forested shore of Lago Acigami (Roca), a beautiful site with good facilities, reached by bus Jan-Feb. It has a backpackers' *refugio*, toilets, showers, restaurant and *confitería*, expensive small shop; camping equipment for hire with deposit.

There are also campsites with facilities at **Río Pipo**, 16 km from Ushuaia, and at **Laguna Verde**, 20 km, near Lapataia, and at **Bahía Ensenada**, with no facilities.

● Restaurants

Río Grande *p624*
$$ El Rincón de Julio, next to **Posada de los Sauces**, Elcano 800 block. For excellent *parrilla*.
$$ La Nueva Colonial, Av Belgrano 489. Delicious pasta, warm family atmosphere.

Cafés
El Roca (sic), Espora 643, ½ block from Plaza. **Confitería** and bar in historic premises (the original cinema), good and popular.
Tío Willy, Alberdi 279. Serves *cerveza artesanal* (micro brewery).

Tolhuin and around *p625*
La Posada de los Ramírez, Av de los Shelknam 411. A cosy restaurant and *rotisería*, open weekends only, lunch and dinner.
La Unión bakery, Jeujepen 450, www.panaderialaunion.com. Daily 24 hrs, except Mon 2400-Tue 0600. Deservedly famous.

Ushuaia *p626, map p626*
Lots of restaurants along San Martín and Maipú. Most are open 1200-1500 and again from 1900 at the earliest. Several cafés are open all the time. Ask around for currently available seafood, especially *centolla* (king crab) and *cholga* (giant mussels). Much cheaper if you prepare your own meal. **Note** *centolla* may not be fished Nov-Dec. Beer drinkers should try the handcrafted brews of the **Cape Horn** brewery: Pilsen, Pale Ale and Stout.
$$$ Bodegón Fueguino, San Martín 859. Tue-Sun 1230-1500, 2000-2400. Snacks, home-made pastas and good roast lamb with varied sauces in a renovated 1896 *casa de pioneros*.

$$$ Tía Elvira, Maipú 349. Mon-Sat 1200-1500, 1900-2300. Excellent seafood.

$$$ Volver, Maipú 37. Delicious seafood and fish in atmospheric 1896 house, with ancient newspaper all over the walls. Recommended.

$$$-$$ Moustacchio, San Martín 298. Long established, good for seafood and meat, all-you-can-eat brunch US$13.

$$$-$$ Parrilla La Rueda, San Martín y Rivadavia. Good *tenedor libre* (US$24 with dessert) for beef, lamb and great salads. Recommended for freshness.

$$ 137 Pizzas and Pastas, San Martín 137. Tasty filling versions of exactly what the name says, plus excellent *empanadas*, elegant decor.

$$ Chicho's, Rivadavia 72, T02901-423469. Bright, cheerful place just off the main street, friendly staff, kitchen open to view. Fish, meat and chicken dishes, pastas, wide range of *entradas*.

$$ El Turco, San Martín 1410. A very popular place, serving generous *milanesas*, pastas, pizzas, seafood and meat. Very tasty *empanadas*.

$$-$ Martinica, San Martín entre Antártida Argentina y Yaganes. Cheap, small, busy, sit at the bar facing the *parrilla* and point to your favourite beef cut. Takeaway (T02901-432134) and good meals of the day, also pizzas and *empanadas*.

Cafés

El Bambú, Piedrabuena 276. Daily 1100-1700. One of few purely vegetarian places in town, take-away only, home-made food, delicious and good value.

Café Bar Banana, San Martín 273, T02901-424021. Quite small, always busy, pool table, offers good fast food, such as burgers, small pizzas, puddings, breakfasts and an all-day *menú* for US$7.50.

Café Tante Sara, San Martin 701, opposite the tourist office. Very good, smart, good coffee, tasty sandwiches, always busy. Also has restaurant and *panadería* at San Martín 175, selling breads, sandwiches, chocolates, *empanadas* and snacks, coffee, lots of choice.

Gadget Café, Av San Martín 1256, www.gadgettugelateria.com.ar. The best ice cream parlour in town, multiple flavours, friendly, recommended.

Laguna Negra, San Martín 513. Mainly a shop selling chocolate and other fine produce, catering to the cruise ship passengers, but has a good little café at the back for hot chocolate and coffee. Also has a bigger branch at Libertador 1250, El Calafate. Sells postcards and stamps, too.

Ramos Generales, Maipú 749, T02901-424317. Daily 0900-2400 in high season. An old warehouse with wooden floors and a collection of historic objects. Sells breads, pastries, wines and drinks, also cold cuts, sandwiches, salads, ice cream, Argentine *mate* and coffee. Not cheap but atmospheric. Recommended.

Sandwichería Kami, San Martín 54. Daily 0800-2100. Friendly, simple sandwich shop, selling rolls, baguettes and *pan de miga*.

Bars and clubs

Ushuaia *p626, map p626*

Dublin Bar Irlandés, 9 de Julio 168. A favourite with locals and tourists.

Küar, Av Perito Moreno 2232, east of town, T02901-437396. Daily from 1800. Great setting by the sea, restaurant, bar and brewery.

Lennon Pub, Maipú 263. Friendly atmosphere and live music.

⊗ Festivals

Río Grande *p624*
Jan Sheep Shearing Festival. Definitely worth seeing if you're in the area.
Feb Rural Exhibition. Exhibition with handicrafts in 2nd week.
Mar Shepherd's Day. An impressive sheep-dog display during the 1st week.
21-22 Jun Winter Solstice. The longest night. Fireworks and ice-skating contests; this is a very inhospitable time of year.

Ushuaia *p626, map p626*
Apr Classical Music Festival, www.festivaldeushuaia.com.
21-22 Jun Winter solstice. The longest night. Torch-lit procession and fireworks.
Aug Dog Sled Race. Held annually.
Aug Marcha Blanca. A ski trek from Lago Escondido to Tierra Mayor valley.

⊘ Shopping

Ushuaia *p626, map p626*
Ushuaia's tax-free status doesn't produce as many bargains as you might hope. Lots of souvenir shops on San Martín offer good-quality leather and silver ware. The **Pasaje de Artesanías**, by the Muelle Turístico, sells local arts and crafts.
Atlántico Sur, San Martín 627. The (not especially cheap) duty free shop. Boutique del Libro, San Martín 1120, T02901-424750, www.boutiquedellibro. com.ar. Mon-Sat 1000-1300 and 1530-2030. An excellent selection of books, including several in English and other languages on Tierra del Fuego. CDs and DVDs upstairs. (Branches throughout Argentina, see website for details.)

◓ What to do

Tolhuin and around *p625*
Sendero del Indio, T02901-1547 6803, http://senderoindio.com.ar. For horse riding.

Ushuaia *p626, map p626*
Boat trips and sea cruises
Sightseeing trips All short boat trips leave from the Muelle Turístico. Take your time to choose the size and style of boat you want. Representatives from the offices are polite and helpful. All have a morning and afternoon sailing and include **Isla de los Lobos**, **Isla de los Pájaros** and **Les Eclaireurs lighthouse**, with guides and some form of refreshment. Note that weather conditions may affect sailings, prices can change and that port tax is not included. See also **Rumbo Sur** and **Tolkeyen** under Tour operators, below.
Canoero, T02901-433893, www. catamaranescanoero.com.ar. Catamarans for 130 passengers (Ushuaia's biggest fleet), 2½ to 3-hr trips to the 3 main sites and Isla Bridges, US$54. They also have a 4½-hr trip almost daily to the Pingüinera on Isla Martillo near Estancia Harberton (Oct-Mar only), boats stay for 1 hr, but you cannot land on Martillo, US$80 (US$90 including Harberton – entry extra). Also longer tours to Estancia Harberton and Lapataia Bay.
Patagonia Adventure Explorer, T02901-15-465842, www.patagoniaadvent. com.ar. Has a sailing boat (US$60) and motor boats for the standard trip, plus Isla Bridges. Good guides.
Pira-Tour, T02901-435557, www.piratour. com.ar and www.piratour.net. Runs 2-3 buses a day to Harberton, from where a boat goes to the Pingüinera on Isla Martillo: 15 people allowed to

land (maximum 45 per day – the only company licensed to do this). US$110 including entrance to Harberton.

Tres Marías, T02901-436416, www.tresmariasweb.com. The only company licensed to visit Isla H, which has archaeological sites, cormorants, other birds and plants. 2 departures 1000 and 1500, 4 hrs. Also has sailing boat for no more than 10 passengers; specialist guide, café on board. Trip costs US$60 on *Tres Marías*, US$80 on sailing boat. Highly recommended.

To Antarctica From Oct to Mar, Ushuaia is the starting point, or the last stop en route, for cruises to Antarctica. These usually sail for 9 to 21 days along the western shores of the Antarctic peninsula and the South Shetland Islands. Other trips include stops at Falkland/Malvinas archipelago and at South Georgia. Go to the **Oficina Antártica** for advice (see page 628). Agencies sell 'last-minute tickets', but the price is entirely dependent on demand. Coordinator for trips is **Turismo Ushuaia**, Gob Paz 865, T02901-436003, www.ushuaiaturismoevt.com.ar, which operates with IAATO members only. See the website for prices for the upcoming season. Port tax is US$15 per passenger and an exit tax of US$10 is also charged.

Freestyle Adventure Travel, Gob Paz 866, T02901-15-609792, www.freestyle adventuretravel.com. Organizes 7- to 22-day cruises to Antarctica, particularly good for last-minute deals. Wide variety of itineraries. Cape Horn expeditions also available.

Polar Latitudes, sales@polar-latitudes. com, www.polar-latitudes.com. Antarctic cruises aboard small expedition vessels, some itineraries take in the Falklands/Malvinas and South Georgia. All-suite accommodation onboard.

To Chile You can ask at **Muelle AFASYN**, near the old airport, T02901-435805, about possible crossings with a club member to Puerto Williams, about 4 hrs; from Puerto Williams a ferry goes once a week to Punta Arenas. There may also be foreign sailing boats going to Cabo de Hornos or Antarctica.

Australis Expedition Cruises, www.australis.com, operates 2 luxury cruise ships between Ushuaia and **Punta Arenas**, with a visit to Cape Horn, highly recommended. Full details are given under Punta Arenas, Tour operators (see page 589). Check-in at **Comapa** (see below).

Fernández Campbell has a 1½-hr crossing to **Puerto Williams**, Fri-Sun 1000, return 1500, US$125 for foreigners, tickets sold at **Zenit Explorer**, Juana Fadul 126, Ushuaia, T02901-433232, and **Naviera RFC** in Puerto Williams.

Ushuaia Boating, Gob Paz 233, T02901-436193 (or at the Muelle Turístico), www.ushuaiaboating.com.ar. Operates a channel crossing to Puerto Navarino (Isla Navarino) all year round, 30-90 mins depending on weather, and then bus to Puerto Williams, 1 hr, US$120 one way, not including taxes.

Fishing

Trout season is Nov to mid-Apr, licences US$21 per day (an extra fee is charged for some rivers and lakes).

Asociación de Caza y Pesca, Maipú 822, T02901-423168, cazaypescaushuaia@speedy.com.ar. Mon-Fri 1600-2000. Sells licences and has a list on the door of other places that sell them.

Hiking and climbing

The winter sports resorts along Ruta 3 (see below) are an excellent base for summer trekking and many arrange excursions.

Club Andino, Fadul 50, T02901-422335, Mon-Fri 0930-1230, 1600-2000. Sells maps and trekking guidebooks; free guided walks once a month in summer; also offers classes in yoga, dancing, karate-do and has exercise bikes.
Nunatak, 25 de Mayo 296, T02901-430329, www.antartur.com.ar. Organizes treks, canoeing, mountain biking and 4WD trips to Lagos Escondido and Fagnano. Good winter excursions.

Horse riding

Centro Hípico, Ruta 3, Km 3021, T02901-15-569099, www.horseridingtierradel fuego.com. Rides through woods, on Monte Susana, along coast and through river, 2 hrs, US$40; 4-hr ride with light lunch, US$80; 7-hr ride with *asado*, US$105. Gentle horses, well-cared for, all guides have first-aid training. Very friendly and helpful. All rides include transfer from town and insurance. Hats provided for children; works with disabled children. They can arrange long-distance rides of several days, eg on Península Mitre.

Winter sports

Ushuaia is becoming popular as a winter resort with 11 centres for skiing, snowboarding and husky sledging. Cerro Castor is the only centre for Alpine skiing, but the other centres along Ruta 3, 18-36 km east of Ushuaia, offer excellent cross-country skiing and alternative activities in summer.
Cerro Castor, Ruta 3, Km 26, T02901-499301, www.cerrocastor.com. 24 km of pistes, a vertical drop of 800 m and powder snow. It's an attractive centre with complete equipment rental, also for snowboarding and snowshoeing.
Kawi Shiken, Las Cotorras, Ruta 3, Km 26, T02901-444152, T02901-15-519497,

www.tierradelfuego.org.ar/hugoflores. Specializes in sled dogs, with 100 Alaskan and Siberian huskies, with winter rides on snow and summer rides in a dog cart.
Tierra Mayor, 20 km from town, T02901-437454. The largest and most recommended. Lies in a beautiful wide valley between steep-sided mountains. It offers half and full day excursions on sledges with huskies, as well as cross country skiing and snowshoeing. Equipment hire and restaurant.

Tours operators

Lots of companies offer imaginative adventure tourism expeditions. All agencies charge the same fees for excursions; ask tourist office for a complete list: Tierra del Fuego National Park, 4 hrs, US$50 (entry fee US$14 extra, valid for 48 hrs); Lagos Escondido and Fagnano, 7 hrs, US$70 without lunch. With 3 or 4 people it might be worth hiring a *remise* taxi.
All Patagonia, Juana Fadul 58, T02901-433622, www.allpatagonia.com. Trekking, ice climbing, and tours; trips to Cabo de Hornos and Antarctica.
Canal, Roca 136, T02901-435777, www.canalfun.com. Huge range of activities, trekking, canoeing, riding, 4WD excursions. Recommended.
Comapa, San Martín 409, T02901-430727, www.comapa.tur.ar. Conventional tours and adventure tourism, bus tickets to Punta Arenas and Puerto Natales, trips to Antarctica, agents for Australis Expedition Cruises. Recommended.
Compañía de Guías de Patagonia, San Martín 628, T02901-437753, www.companiadeguias.com.ar. The best agency for walking guides, expeditions for all levels, rock and ice climbing (training provided), also diving, sailing, riding, 7-day crossing of Tierra del

Fuego on foot and conventional tours. Recommended.

Rumbo Sur, San Martín 350, T02901-421139, www.rumbosur.com.ar. Flights, buses, conventional tours on land and sea, including to Harberton, plus Antarctic expeditions, mid-Nov to mid-Mar, English spoken.

Tolkar, Roca 157, T02901-431412, www.tolkarturismo.com.ar. Flights, bus tickets to Argentina and Punta Arenas/Puerto Natales, conventional and adventure tourism, canoeing and mountain biking to Lago Fagnano.

Tolkeyen, San Martín 1267, T02901-437073, www.tolkeyenpatagonia.com. Bus and flight tickets, catamaran trips (50-300 passengers), including to Harberton (Tue, Thu, Sat-Sun, US$94) and Parque Nacional, large company.

Travel Lab, San Martín 1444, T02901-436555, www.travellab.com.ar. Conventional and unconventional tours, mountain biking, trekking etc, English and French spoken, helpful.

<hr>

⊙ Transport

Río Grande p624
Book ahead in summer as buses and planes fill up fast. Take passport when buying ticket.

Air
To **Buenos Aires**, daily, 3½ hrs direct. LADE flies to **Río Gallegos**.

Bus
To **Punta Arenas**, Chile, via Punta Delgada, 7-9 hrs, with **Pacheco** (Finocchio 1194, T02964-425611, Mon-Sat) and **Tecni Austral** (Moyano 516, T02964-430610), US$42. To **Río Gallegos**, with **Tecni Austral**, Mon-Sat, 8 hrs; with **Marga/Taqsa** (Mackinley 545, T02964-

434316), daily 0815, US$55, connection to El Calafate and Comodoro Rivadavia. To **Ushuaia**, 3½-4 hrs, with **Montiel** (25 de Mayo 712, T02964-420997) and **Líder** (Perito Moreno 635, T02964-420003, www.lidertdf.com.ar), US$25; both use small buses and have frequent departures; they stop en route at **Tolhuin**, US$15; also with **Tecni Austral**, about 1600 (bus has come from Punta Arenas), **Marga** and **Pacheco**, US$18-20.

Ushuaia p626, map p626
Air
Book ahead in summer; flights fill up fast. In winter flights are often delayed.

To **Buenos Aires** (Aeroparque or Ezeiza), 3½ hrs. To **El Calafate**, 1 hr, and **Río Gallegos**, 1 hr; also to **Río Grande**, 1 hr, several a week (but check with agents). In summer **LAN** flies to **Punta Arenas** twice a week. The **Aeroclub de Ushuaia** flies to **Puerto Williams** and organizes flight tours of Tierra del Fuego from the downtown airport, www.aeroclubushuaia.com.

Boat
See What to do, above.

Bus
Local To Parque **Nacional Tierra del Fuego,** in summer buses and minibuses leave hourly from 0900 from the bus stop on Maipú at the bottom of Fadul, including **Transporte Lautaro** and **Transporte Santa Lucía**, 3 a day each, last return 1900, US$12.50 single, US$19 return. From same bus stop, many *colectivos* go to the Tren del Fin del Mundo (0900 and 1400, return 1200, 1700 and 1745), Lago Escondido, Lago Fagnano (1000 and 1100, return 1400 and 2200) and Glaciar Martial (1000 and 1200, return 1400 and 1600). For **Harberton,**

check the notice boards at Maipú y Fadul. The only regular bus is run by **Pira-Tur**, see What to do, above.

Long distance Passport needed when booking international bus tickets. Buses always booked up Nov-Mar; buy your ticket to leave as soon as you arrive. To **Río Grande**, 3½-4 hrs, combis run by **Líder** (Gob Paz 921, T02901-436421), and **Montiel** (Gob Paz 605, T02901-421366), US$25, also buses en route to Río Gallegos and Punta Arenas. To **Río Gallegos**, with **Tecni Austral**, 0500, 13 hrs, US$72 (book through Tolkar; see Tour operators), and **Marga/Taqsa** (Gob Godoy 41), daily 0500. To **Punta Arenas**, US$68-81, with **Tecni Austral**, Mon, Wed, Fri, 0500, 11-12 hrs (book through Tolkar); with **Pacheco**, 0700 Mon, Wed, Fri, 12-13 hrs (book through Tolkeyen, see above), with **Bus Sur** (at Comapa) Tue, Thu, Sat, Sun 0800; Bus Sur also goes to **Puerto Natales**, US$70, Tue, Sat 0800.

Car hire
Most companies charge minimum US$60-70 per day, including insurance and 200 km per day, special promotions available. **Localiza**, Sarmiento 81, T02901-437780, www.localizadietrich. com. Cars can be hired in Ushuaia to be driven through Chile and then left in any Localiza office in Argentina, but you must buy a one-off customs document for US$50 to use as many times as you like to cross borders. Must reserve well in advance and pay a drop-off fee. **Budget**, Godoy 49, T02901-437373.

Taxi
Cheaper than *remises*, T02901-422007, T02901-422400. Taxi stand by the Muelle Turístico.
Remises Carlitos y Bahía Hermosa, San Martín y Rosas, T02901-422222.

❶ Directory

Río Grande *p624*
Banks ATMs at several banks on San Martín by junction with Av 9 de Julio. **Link** ATM at YPF station at river end of Belgrano. **Thaler** *cambio*, Espora 631, Mon-Fri 1000-1500.
Consulates Chile, Belgrano 369, T02964-430523, Mon-Fri 0830-1330.

Ushuaia *p626, map p626*
Banks Open 1000-1500 in summer. ATMs are plentiful all along San Martín, using credit cards is easiest (but machines can be empty on Sat, Sun and holidays). **Agencia de Cambio Thaler**, San Martín 209, T02901-421911, www. cambio-thaler.com, Mon-Fri 1000-1500 (extended hours in high season). **Consulates** Chile, Jainén 50, T02901-430909, Mon-Fri 0900-1300. **Useful addresses** Dirección Nacional de Migraciones, Fuegia Basket 187, T02901-422334. Biblioteca Popular Sarmiento, San Martín 1589, T02901-423103. Mon-Fri 1000-2000, library with a good range of books about the area.

Contents

Background

History

Much of Argentina's fascinating history is visible on a visit to the country today, not only in colonial architecture and the 19th-century artefacts which fill the museums but in the culture and customs of everyday life. Many towns in the Pampas of Buenos Aires province are just as they were in the 19th century, such as San Antonio de Areco and Chascomús, where the traditions of a lively gaucho culture are still maintained. The lives of early pioneers can be explored in the Welsh towns of Gaiman and Trevelin in Patagonia and in the more remote *estancias* throughout the country. Córdoba's history of Jesuit occupation is visible in many buildings in the city itself and *estancias* in the province. And in the northwest of Argentina you'll find the richest evidence of the country's history. This is where the Spanish first arrived in the 16th century and before them the Incas in the early 15th century, and both have left their mark in colonial architecture and intriguing archaeological evidence. Long before these invasions, the present day provinces of Salta, Catamarca, Tucumán and Jujuy were inhabited by many sophisticated indigenous cultures whose ruined cities can be visited at Santa Rosa de Tastil, Tilcara and Quilmes, and whose beautiful ceramics fill the area's many museums. This is the most rewarding part of the country to visit if you're interested in exploring Argentina's past.

Archaeology and prehistory

Earliest origins

It used to be generally accepted that the earliest settlers in South America were related to people who had crossed the Bering Straits from Asia and drifted through the Americas from about 13,000 years ago (the Clovis model). In recent years, however, a growing number of discoveries from earlier dates in North and South America have raised doubts about this. In South America these include: a coastal site in southern Chile called Monte Verde from 14,800 years ago; stone tools from the Serra da Capivara in northeastern Brazil from some 22,000 years ago, and paleontological evidence from Uruguay from earlier still. If nothing else, these finds question the theory of a single migration into South America from the north. Other early evidence of human presence has been found at various sites: in the Central Andes (with a radiocarbon date between 12,000 and 9000 BC), in northern Venezuela (11,000 BC), in southeast Brazil, and in south-central Chile and Argentine Patagonia (from at least 10,000 BC). After the Pleistocene Ice Age (8000-7000 BC), rising sea levels and climatic changes introduced new conditions, as many mammal species became extinct and coastlands were drowned. A wide range of crops were brought into cultivation, and camelids and guinea pigs were domesticated. It seems that people lived nomadically in small groups, mainly hunting and gathering but also cultivating some plants seasonally, until villages with effective agriculture began to appear, it was orignally thought, between 2500 and 1500 BC. The earliest ceramic-making in the western hemisphere was thought to have come from what is now Colombia and Ecuador, around 4000 BC, but fragments of painted pottery were found near Santarém, Brazil, in 1991, dating from 6000-5000 BC.

Northwest Argentina

Argentina has a rich history of pre-Hispanic indigenous civilizations, with the most important archaeological sites situated in the northwest and west areas of the most highly developed cultures south of the central Andes. Along a migratory path which followed the Andes, this region became a meeting place for established settlers from northern Chile, the central Andes, the Chaco and the hunter-gatherers of the south. Cave paintings and petroglyphs engraved on rocks remain from 13,000 to 10,000 years ago, made by cave dwellers who lived by hunting vizcacha, guanaco, vicuña and birds, some painted with pigments derived from minerals mixed with gesso. Their lines, dots and geometrical forms belong to a symbolic system impossible to interpret today. The extraordinary quantity of handprints visible in the Cueva de las Manos in Patagonia were made as long ago as 10,000 years, and again, their purpose and origin remains a mystery.

By about 1000 to 500 BC, the nomadic groups had grown in size and were too large to subsist on hunting alone. So they started early attempts at agriculture, growing potatoes and maize, among other staples. A mummy found from this period (displayed in Cachi's archaeological museum) with a few artefacts and belongings suggests that these peoples had a developed system of beliefs. By 2000 years ago, small communities had started to gather on the alluvial plains, living on agriculture and herding llamas. In many of the area's museums, you'll see large grinding stones made of granite used to grind maize, as well as arrowheads and pipes used for smoking tobacco. Weaving began around this time, and there are some fine fabrics found at Santa Rosa Tastil.

There were three distinct periods in the cultural development of the northwest. The Early Period (500 BC to AD 650) witnessed the beginnings of agriculture, as well as pottery and metalworking, with the remains of terraces near Humahuaca in Jujuy. The Middle Period (AD 650-850) was marked by the influence of the great culture of Tiahuanaco in present-day Bolivia. Fine metal objects, some of them of gold and silver, were made and new plant varieties were introduced. You'll find stone vessels, anthropomorphic clay pieces, and ornate ceramics from this period all over the Northwest.

In the Later Period (AD 850-1480), known as the Period of Regional Development, small groups of settlers formed communities with individual dwellings, usually based on circular stone walls, next to water sources. Both ritual and functional ceramics were made by people known as the Santamariana or Diaguita culture. Although there was no system of writing, their language, Kakán, survived until the Inca invasion in the late 15th century. These cultures made large, beautifully painted funerary urns, thought to bury the bones of children, since the infant mortality rate was high. The predominant religious beliefs centred around worship of the mother earth goddess, the *Pachamama*, and she's still worshipped in rural communities all over the Northwest today, with lively festivals on 1 August.

The Incas first arrived in the Calchaquíes valleys area between 1410 and 1430, incorporating the area into the part of their empire known as Kollasuyo. They built two parallel roads along the length of the Andes and along the Pacific shore:

busy trade routes linking their communities with the rest of the Inca Empire. The Incas made Quechua the official language, punished the chiefs of any groups whose members transgressed, and absorbed the local cult of the earth goddess *Pachamama* into their own system of worship of the sun. The Incas also brought with them their own sacrificial burial customs. The bodies of three children found at the summit of Cerro Llullaillaco on the Salta/Chile border indicate young humans were killed as offerings. These three, aged between four and 13, were taken to the summit, dressed in special garments, adorned with feather headdresses and jewellery, and put to sleep forever. Latest evidence suggests that they were given alcohol and drugs for a long period before their sacrifice. It's thought that they were offered as a sacrifice to the gods in the belief that to gain life, life has also to be sacrificed. It's also possible that their death sealed some kind of political alliance between the Inca and the chief of a new colony. The teenager's peaceful face shows no sign of distress so it's likely that she died painlessly within minutes. The fate of the younger girl and boy is less clear, but it appears that they were not as well treated. Salta's MAAM museum (see page 288) has a fascinating display of photographs and an extraordinary array of the artefacts buried with the children. The Calchaquíes valleys were the site of bloody battles when the Spanish attempted to dominate in the 16th century and many indigenous groups were wiped out, but fortunately, in the northwest of Argentina, there are living descendants from many of the original inhabitants, keeping their customs and beliefs alive.

Central and southern Argentina

The Comechingones, who inhabited what are now the provinces of Córdoba and San Luis, lived in settlements of pit-dwellings and used irrigation to produce a range of crops. In the far northeast on the eastern edge of the Chaco were the Guaraní; organized into loose confederations, they lived in rudimentary villages and practised slash-and-burn agriculture to grow maize, sweet potatoes, manioc and beans. They also produced textiles and ceramics.

Further south, the Pampas and Patagonia were much more sparsely populated than the northwest and most groups were nomadic long after the arrival of the Spanish. One of the most important groups were the Querandí, who eked out a living by hunting guanaco and rheas with *boleadoras*, three balls of stone tied with thong and hurled at the legs of a running animal. Patagonia was inhabited by scattered nomadic groups, including the Pampa, the Chonik and the Kaingang, who managed to avoid contact with white settlers until the 19th century. In the steppes of Patagonia, the Tehuelche and Puelche lived as nomadic hunters living off guanaco, foxes and game. In the far south, in southern Patagonia and Tierra del Fuego, there were four indigenous groups: the land-based Selk'nam (or Ona) and Haush (Manekenk), who hunted foxes and guanaco, wearing their hides and constructing temporary dwellings of branches covered loosely with skins; and the sea-based Yáman (Yaghan) and Alacaluf (Kaweskar), who made canoes, paddles, bailers and mooring rope, catching fish with spears or by hand, though seals were their main source of food. These peoples survived until the late 19th century and were befriended and protected by the son of Tierra del Fuego's first settler and missionary. Lucas Bridges' account in the book *Uttermost Part of the Earth* gives an extraordinary insight into the customs and hunting practices of the Selk'nam/Ona and Yámana. Within 50 years of the arrival of white sheep-farmers, many had been shot or coerced into religious missions where they could be controlled. President Roca's genocidal Conquest of the Wilderness (1879-1880) exterminated any indigenous tribes who resisted the influence of the new settlers in the Pampas and Patagonia. Today no single descendant remains of these tribes, which is why you may see that every statue of Roca is permanently disfigured and has graffiti.

European exploration and settlement

At the time of the arrival of the first Europeans, the land that is now Argentina was sparsely populated with about two-thirds of the indigenous population living in the northwest. European exploration began in the Río de la Plata estuary when in 1516 Juan de Solís, a Portuguese navigator employed by the Spanish crown, landed on the shore – though his men were soon killed by indigenous Querandí. Four years later he was followed by Fernão de Magalhães (Ferdinand Magellan) who explored the Río de la Plata, before turning south to make his way into the Pacific via the straits north of Tierra del Fuego, now named after him. In 1527 both Sebastián Cabot and his rival Diego García sailed into the estuary and up the Río Paraná and the Río Paraguay. Cabot founded a small fort, Sancti Spiritus, not far from the modern city of Rosario, but it was wiped out by indigenous inhabitants about two years later. Despite these difficulties Cabot took back to Spain stories of a great Indian kingdom beyond the Plata estuary, rich in precious metals, giving the Río de la Plata its misleading name: a translation would be 'river of silver'. A Portuguese expedition to the estuary, led by Affonso de Souza, returned with similar tales, and this led to a race between the two Iberian powers. In 1535, Pedro de Mendoza set out with 16 ships and a well-equipped force of 1600 men and founded a settlement at Buenos Aires (actually he settled closer to San Isidro along the coast), which he gave its present name, originally Puerto Nuestra Señora Santa María de Buen Ayre. The indigenous inhabitants soon made life too difficult; the settlement was abandoned and Mendoza returned home, but not before sending Juan de Ayolas with a small force up the Río Paraná in search of the Indian kingdom. In 1537 this force founded Asunción, in Paraguay, where the locals were friendly.

After 1535 the attention of the Spanish crown switched to Peru, where Pizarro was engaged in the successful conquest of the Inca Empire, where there was instant wealth in gold and silver and a malleable workforce in the enormous indigenous population. The small settlement at Asunción remained an isolated outpost until 1573, when a force from there travelled south to establish the city of Santa Fe. Seven years later Juan de Garay refounded Buenos Aires (the city's first ever street bears his name, it is in San Telmo), but it was only under his successor, Hernando Arias de Saavedra (1592-1614), that the new settlement became secure, benefiting both from back-up in Asunción and from the many cattle brought over by Mendoza which had increased and multiplied meanwhile.

However, before the time of Mendoza's expedition to the Plata estuary, Spanish expeditions were already exploring northern parts of present-day Argentina. In 1535 Diego de Almagro led a party from Peru, which crossed northwest into Argentina, and in 1543 the Spanish Viceroyalty of Peru was made administrative capital of southern South America. There was greatly increased motivation for exploring the region, however, when silver deposits were found in Potosí (now in Bolivia), and the Governorship of Tucumán was set up as an administrative centre as a halfway point between Bolivia and the port of Buenos Aires. Explorations set forth from Chile and Peru to find trade routes and a source of cheap labour to work the mines, and so the oldest towns in Argentina were founded: Santiago del Estero (1553), Mendoza (1561), San Juan (1562), Córdoba (1573), Salta (1582), La Rioja (1591), and Jujuy (1593). A total of 25 cities were founded in present-day Argentina in the 16th century, 15 of which survived, at a time when the total Spanish population was under 2000.

Colonial rule

Throughout the colonial period the Argentine territories were an outlying part of the Spanish Empire and of minor importance since Spanish colonial settlement and government was based in Peru, busy exploiting the vast mineral wealth of Potosí in Alto Perú (and large supplies of forced indigenous labour). Argentine lands offered only sparse population and little mineral wealth by comparison. Also, the nomadic nature of many indigenous groups made any attempt at control difficult, whereas in Peru, Spanish rule was more readily superimposed on the centralized administration of the defeated Incas.

Buenos Aires failed to become an important port because apart from the fact that the port wasn't deep enough to welcome large ships, from 1543 all the Spanish territories in South America were governed from Lima, the Vice-Regal capital, and trade with Spain was routed via Lima, Panama and the Caribbean. Trading through Buenos Aires was prohibited. However, the Paraná delta north of the city near Tigre provided ample opportunity for smuggling British and Portuguese goods into the city, and it rapidly expanded as a centre for contraband. By 1776 the city's population was 24,000, double the size of any of the cities of the interior. However, the Governorship of Tucumán was more important as a centre, due to the success of the *encomienda* system, in which lands belonging to indigenous peoples were seized and redistributed to Spanish settlers. The idea was that the *encomenderos* in charge would exchange work done for religious education, but in reality the majority of these men were ruthless exploiters of slave labour and offered little in the way of spiritual enlightenment or even food. In the Valles Calchaquíes the substantial indigenous population resisted conversion by Jesuit missionaries, and was effectively almost wiped out when they rose up against the Spanish landowners. Settlers in the northeast of the country also had their conflicts with the indigenous population. The Pampas and Buenos Aires province were dangerous areas for white settlement, since in these lands wild cattle had long been hunted for their hides by Tehuelches and Mapuches. They drove cattle to Chile over the Andes for trade, and their violent armies, or *malones*, clashed regularly with newly arrived settlers. Around the early 18th century, the figure of the gaucho emerged, nomadic men of mixed *criollo* (early Argentine settlers) and indigenous origin, who roamed free on horseback, living off cattle. Once the Argentine state started to control land boundaries, these characters became emblematic of freedom and were romanticized in important fictional works, *Martín Fierro* and *Don Segundo Sombra*. The gaucho is still a much admired figure all over Argentina today, though less wild and certainly no longer an outcast.

Jesuits came to 'civilize' the indigenous population under the protection of the Spanish crown in the late 16th century. They quickly set up missions, which employed the reasonably pliant Guaraní residents of the upper Paraná in highly organized societies, with a militant component, equipped to resist the frequent raids by Portuguese in search of slaves. The Guaraní were compelled to comply with their educators since this exempted them from working in the silver mines, and as many as 4000 Guaraní lived in some missions, also producing *yerba mate* and tobacco as successful Jesuit businesses. The Jesuits and their faith were, however, expelled from Argentina by King Charles III of Spain in 1767, as they had grown rich and powerful. The remains of their handsome architecture can be admired in Córdoba city and province, as well as at San Ignacio Mini and neighbouring sites in Misiones.

Buenos Aires at last gained some considerable power when the new viceroyalty of the River Plate was created in 1776, with the rapidly growing city as head of the large area and now able to trade with Spain and her other ports. However, as the trade of contraband into the city increased, flooding the market with cheaper European-produced goods, conflict increased between those advocating free trade, such as Manuel Belgrano, and those who wanted to retain a monopoly. The population of Buenos Aires increased enormously with the viceroyalty, along with its economy, as *estancias* sprang up to farm and export cattle, instead of rounding up the wild beasts, with great success.

The Wars of Independence

The drive for independence in Argentina was partly a response to events in Europe, where Spain was initially allied to Napoleonic France. In 1806 and 1807 the British, at war with Napoleon and attracted by what they thought were revolutionary tensions in Buenos Aires, made two attempts to seize the city but were defeated. In 1808 Napoleon invaded Spain, deposing King Ferdinand VII, and provoking widespread resistance from Spanish guerrilla armies. Throughout Spanish America the colonial elites debated where their loyalties lay: with Napoleon's brother Joseph, now officially king; with Ferdinand, now in a French prison; with the Viceroy; or with the Spanish resistance parliament in Cadiz.

On 25 May 1810, the *cabildo* of Buenos Aires deposed the viceroy and established a *junta* to govern on behalf of King Ferdinand VII, when the city's people gathered in front of the *cabildo* (which you can still see today) wearing pale blue and white ribbons, soon to become the colours of the Argentine flag. This move provoked resistance in outlying areas of the viceroyalty, Paraguay, Uruguay and Upper Peru (Bolivia) breaking away from the rule of Buenos Aires. Factional rivalry within the junta between supporters of independence and their opponents added to the confusion and instability. Six years later in July 1816, when Buenos Aires was threatened by invasion from Peru and blockaded by a Spanish fleet in the Río de la Plata, a national congress held at Tucumán declared independence. The declaration was given reality by the genius and devotion of José de San Martín, who boldly marched an Argentine army across the Andes to free Chile, and embarked his forces for Peru, where he captured Lima, the first step towards liberation. San Martín was aided by an extraordinary feat from a local *caudillo* in the north, Martín Miguel de Güemes, whose army of gauchos was later to liberate Salta. *Caudillos* were local warlords who governed areas far larger than today's provinces, organizing their own armies of local indigenous groups and gauchos. The *caudillos* did not recognize the Tucumán declaration, but so it was on 9 July 1816 that the United Provinces of the River Plate came into being.

Since independence

The 19th century

Much of the current rift between Buenos Aires and the rest of Argentina has its roots in a long-standing conflict, which emerged in the early 19th century. The achievement of independence brought neither stability nor unity, since the new junta was divided between Federalists and Unitarists, a conflict that was to rage for over 40 years. The Unitarists, found mainly in the city of Buenos Aires, advocated strong central government, free trade, education and white immigration, looking to Europe for their inspiration. The Federalists, backed by the provincial elites and many of the great *estancieros* of Buenos Aires province, resisted, defending local autonomy and traditional values. Behind the struggle were also economic interests: Buenos Aires and the coastal areas benefited from trade with Europe; the interior provinces did not. As the conflict raged, the territory, known officially as the United Provinces of the Río de la Plata, had none of the features of a modern state: there was no central government, nor an army, capital city or constitution.

Order, of a sort, was established after 1829 by Juan Manuel de Rosas, a powerful *caudillo* and governor of Buenos Aires. In 1833, he attempted to gain widespread support from local *caudillos* with his Campaign of the Desert, which claimed vast areas of land from indigenous groups, granted to Rosas' allies. However, his overthrow in 1852 unleashed another round of battles between Unitarists and Federalists and between Buenos Aires and the provinces. In 1853 a constitution establishing a federal system of government was finally drafted but the Buenos Aires province refused to join the new Argentine Confederation, which had its capital at Paraná, and set up its own separate republic. Conflict between the two states erupted over the attempt by Buenos Aires to control and tax commerce on the Río Paraná but the victory of Buenos Aires at Pavón (1861) opened the way to a solution: the city became the seat of the federal government. Bartolomé Mitre, former governor of Buenos Aires became the first president of Argentina. There was another political flare-up of the old quarrel in 1880, ending in the humiliation of the city of Buenos Aires, which was separated from its province and made into a special federal territory.

Although there was resistance to the new constitution from some of the western provinces, the institutions of a modern state were created in the two decades after 1861 by Mitre's important period of government. He set up a national bank, bureaucracy, a postal service and an army. The building of railways across the Pampas did most to create national unity, breaking the power of the *caudillos* by enabling the federal government to send in troops quickly. The new army was quickly employed to defeat Francisco Solano López of Paraguay in the War of the Triple Alliance (1865-1870). They were used again in President Roca's genocidal Conquest of the Wilderness (1879-1880), which exterminated the indigenous tribes of the Pampas and Patagonia.

In the last quarter of the 19th century Argentina was transformed: the newly acquired stability encouraged foreign investment; the Pampas were fenced, ploughed up and turned over to commercial export agriculture; railways and port facilities were built. The presidency of Domingo Sarmiento had been keen on widespread immigration from Europe, which transformed the character of Buenos Aires and other cities around the Plata estuary, where the population grew from 200,000 in 1870 to two million in 1920. Sarmiento also sought to Europeanize the country, and his impressive educational policy included the importing of teachers from North America. Political power, however, remained in the hands of a small group of large landowners, who had been granted territories after the Conquest of the Desert, and their urban allies. Few Argentines had the vote, and the opposition Unión Cívica Radical, excluded from power, conspired with dissidents in the army in attempts to overthrow the government.

The 20th century

As the British-built railways stretched across the country, the sheep industry flourished, making Argentina's fortune through exporting both wool and meat. Refrigerator ships were invented in the 1870s, enabling meat to be shipped in bulk to the expanding industrial countries of Britain and Europe. One of the landmarks of modern Argentine history was the 1912 Sáenz Peña law, which established universal manhood suffrage, since until then power had been centralized in the hands of the elite, with no votes for the working classes. Sáenz Peña, president between 1910 and 1916, sought to bring the middle and working classes into politics, gambling that the Conservatives could reorganize themselves and attract their votes. The gamble failed: the Conservatives failed to gain a mass following and the Radicals came to power. The Unión Cívica Radical was created in 1890, but Radical presidents Hipólito Yrigoyen (1916-1922 and 1928-1930) and Marcelo T de Alvear (1922-1928) found themselves trapped between the demands of an increasingly militant urban labour movement and the opposition of the Conservatives, still powerful in the provinces and with allies in the armed forces. Through the 1920s, Argentina was the 'breadbasket of the world' and its sixth richest nation. Fifty years later, the country had become practically Third World, a fall from grace that still haunts the Argentine consciousness. The world depression following the Wall Street Crash of 1929 devastated export markets, but the military coup that overthrew Yrigoyen in 1930 was a significant turning point: the armed forces returned to government for the first time in over 50 years and were to continue to play a major political role until 1983. Through the 1930s a series of military backed governments, dominated

Dirty War

The 'Dirty War', unleashed by the armed forces after 1976, is one of the most violent incidents in modern South American history, and hardly a month goes by without this grim episode provoking further controversy in the Argentine press.

Guerrilla groups started emerging in Argentina after 1969, in angry response to military rule, among them the Monteneros and the People Revolutionary Army (*Ejército Revolucionario del Pueblo* or ERP). The middle-class educated Monteneros, inspired by a mixture of Peronism, Catholicism and Marxism, proclaimed allegiance to the exiled Perón, and wanted to liberate the working classes from the evils of capitalism. The ERP, by contrast drawing their inspiration from Trotsky and Ernesto 'Guevara, argued that political violence would push the military government towards increased repression which would ignite working-class opposition and lead to civil war and socialist revolution.

If Peronists and non-Peronists disagreed over their aims, their methods were similar: kidnappings and bank robberies raised money and gained publicity; army and police officers were assassinated along with right-wing Peronists; and wealthy Argentine families and multinational companies were forced to distribute food and other goods to the poor to obtain the release of kidnap victims. Head of the Argentine military, General Jorge Videla retaliated by quashing any uprising before it had a chance to establish: pop concerts were banned, as was any gathering of *the* young. Far more terrifying, Videla initiated a plan called The Process of National Reorganization, *El Proceso*. The military carried out their own kidnappings of anyone they deemed likely to be dangerous. Anyone with left-wing tendencies might be taken without warning, tortured in one of over

by the Conservatives, held power. The Radicals were outlawed and elections were so fraudulent that frequently more people voted than were on the register. Yet the armed forces themselves were disunited: while most officers supported the Conservatives and the landholding elites, a minority of ultra-nationalist officers, inspired by developments in Europe, supported industrialization and the creation of a one-party dictatorship along Fascist lines. The outbreak of war in Europe increased these tensions and a series of military coups in 1943-1944 led to the rise of Colonel Juan Domingo Perón. When the military allowed a return to civilian rule in 1946, Perón swept into power winning the presidential elections. His government is chiefly remembered by many Argentines for improving the living conditions of the workers through the introduction of paid holidays and welfare measures in his *justicialismo*: social justice. Perón was an authoritarian and charismatic leader, and especially in its early years the government was strongly nationalistic, taking control over the British-owned railways in 1948 by buying them back at a staggering £150 million. Opposition parties were harassed and independent newspapers taken over since Perón wasn't at all interested in free press. Perón is also well known for his

340 detention centres, and then, mysteriously, 'disappeared'. All three armed services operated their own death squads and camps in a campaign of indiscriminate violence. By 1978-1979 both the ERP and the Monteneros had ceased to function, and in the process, tens of thousands of people disappeared: although an official report produced after the return to civilian rule put their number at 8960, some 15,000 cases have been documented and human rights groups now estimate the total at some 30,000. They are still remembered by the *Madres de la Plaza de Mayo* (Mothers of the Plaza de Mayo), a human-rights group made up of relatives, who march anti-clockwise around the Plaza de Mayo in central Buenos Aires every Thursday at 1530, with photos of their 'disappeared' loved ones pinned to their chests, demanding information.

On 24 March 2006, the 30th anniversary of the military junta was marked with a national day of awareness and demonstrations in Buenos Aires, suggesting that the scars of the Dirty War have yet to heal. Videla, along with other military leaders, was charged with human rights abuse. After serving only five years in prison, he was pardoned by President Carlos Menem in 1990, but was arrested again in 1998 and transferred to house arrest. In 2010 Videla was sentenced to life imprisonment for the torture and death of 31 dissidents. He and eight other defendants were sentenced to further prison terms in 2012 for the theft of babies from political prisoners. Videla died in May 2013. He was by no means the sole recipient of justice for human rights abuses and crimes, a process which continues to this day. For more information see www.madres.org, http://madresfundadoras.blogspot.co.uk and www.abuelas.org.ar. For a clear explanation in English, see www.yendor.com/vanished.

famous second-wife, Eva (Evita) Perón, who became the darling of the country, helping her husband's popularity no-end. Although Perón was easily re-elected in 1951, his government soon ran into trouble when economic problems led to the introduction of a wage freeze which upset the labour unions which were the heart of Peronist support. The early and tragic death of Evita in 1952 was another blow; and a dispute with the church in 1954-1955 also added to Perón's problems. In September 1955 a military coup unseated Perón who went into exile, in Paraguay, Panama, Venezuela, the Dominican Republic and, from 1961 to 1973, in Spain.

Perón's legacy dominated Argentina for the next two decades. No attempt was made to destroy his social and economic reforms but the armed forces determined to exclude the Peronists from power. Argentine society was bitterly divided between Peronists and anti-Peronists and the economy struggled, partly as a result of Perón's measures against the economic elite and in favour of the workers. Between 1955 and 1966 there was an uneasy alternation of military and civilian regimes. The military officers who seized power in 1966 announced their intention to carry out a Nationalist Revolution, with austerity measures to try to gain control of a spiralling economy, but they were quickly discredited by a deteriorating economic situation. The Cordobazo, a left-wing student and workers uprising in Córdoba in 1969, was followed by the emergence of several guerrilla groups such as the Montoneros and the People's Revolutionary Army (ERP), as well as the growth of political violence. As Argentina became more ungovernable, Perón, from his exile, refused to denounce those guerrilla groups, which called themselves Peronist.

In 1971 General Alejandro Lanusse seized power, promising a return to civilian rule and calculating that the only way to control the situation was to allow Perón to return. When the military bowed out in 1973, elections were won by the Peronist candidate, Hector Campora. Perón returned from exile in Madrid to resume as president in October 1973, but died on 1 July 1974, leaving the presidency to his widow, Vice-President María Estela Martínez de Perón, his third wife, known as 'Isabelita'. Perón's death unleashed chaos: hyperinflation, resumed guerrilla warfare and the operation of right-wing death squads who abducted people suspected of left-wing sympathies. In March 1976, to nobody's surprise, the military overthrew Isabelita and replaced her with a junta led by General Jorge Videla.

The new government closed Congress, outlawed political parties, placed trade unions and universities under military control and unleashed the so-called 'Dirty War', a brutal assault on the guerrilla groups and anyone else who manifested opposition. The military leaders were not at all interested in trying to convict those they suspected of being dissidents. They started a campaign of violence against anyone remotely troublesome as well as anyone Jewish or Marxist, and journalists, intellectuals, psychologists and anyone, according to President General Videla, who was 'spreading ideas contrary to Western Christian civilization'. As many as 30,000 people are thought to have 'disappeared' during this period, removed by violent squads who would take them to clandestine detention centres to be raped, tortured or brutally killed. This is one of Argentina's bleakest memories. In order that the disappeared should never be forgotten, the *Madres de la Plaza de Mayo* still parade around the plaza in Buenos Aires with photographs of their lost children pinned to their chests (see box, page 654) looking for answers.

Videla's nominated successor, General Roberto Viola, took over for three years in March 1981 but was overthrown by General Leopoldo Galtieri in December 1981, who failed to keep a grasp on a plummeting economy and an increasingly discontent public. Attempting to win the crowds, Galtieri's decision to invade the Falkland/Malvinas Islands in April 1982 backfired when the British retaliated by sending a fleet to the south Atlantic, subsequently forcing the Argentines to flee. This loss is still felt in every town in Argentina today. There are monuments to the dead and parades every year commemorating the battles. Many Argentines still consider the Malvinas as Argentine property. After the war was lost in June 1982 General Reynaldo Bignone took over, and promptly created a law giving amnesty to all human-rights abusers in the military (see box, page 658).

Elections in October 1983 were won by Raúl Alfonsín and his Unión Cívica Radical (UCR) and during 1985 Generals Videla, Viola and Galtieri were sentenced to long terms of imprisonment for their parts in the dictatorship. While Alfonsín's government struggled to deal with the legacy of the past, it was overwhelmed by continuing economic problems, the most obvious of which was hyperinflation. Workers rushed to the shops once they'd been paid to spend their earnings before prices rose, and supermarkets announced price increases over the loudspeaker since they were so unstable. When the Radicals were defeated by Carlos Menem, the Peronist (*Justicialist*) presidential candidate, Alfonsín, stepped down early because of economic instability. Strained relations between the Peronist government and the military led to several rebellions, which Menem attempted to appease by pardoning the imprisoned generals. His popularity among civilians declined, but from 1991 to 1992 the economy minister, Domingo Cavallo, succeeded in restoring economic confidence and the government as a whole with his *Plan de Convertabilidad*. This, the symbol of his stability, was the introduction of a new currency pegged to the United States dollar. The central bank was prevented from printing money that could not be backed up by the cash in reserve. After triumphing in the October 1993 congressional elections at the expense of the UCR, the Peronists themselves lost some ground in the April 1994 elections to a constituent assembly. The party to gain most, especially in Buenos Aires, was Frente Grande, a broad coalition of left-wing groups and disaffected Peronists. Behind the loss of confidence of these dissident Peronists was unrestrained corruption and a pact in December 1993 between Menem and Alfonsín pledging UCR support for constitutional changes, which included re-election of the president for a second term of four years.

By the 1995 elections, the majority of the electorate favoured stability over constitutional concerns and returned President Menem.

In November 1998 Alianza Democrática chose the Radical Fernando de la Rúa as its candidate for the October 1999 presidential election. Moves from Menem supporters to put forward Menem for a further (constitutionally dubious) term of office helped delay the Peronist choice of candidate until July 1999 when Eduardo Duhalde received the backing of Menem. Although Alianza Democrática offered little change in economic policy, the Peronists were harmed by the corruption scandals surrounding the Menem administration and the continuing rivalry between Menem and Duhalde, enabling De La Rúa to win the presidency and take office in December 1999.

The 21st century

Facing recession and impossible debts with the IMF, President De La Rúa implemented austerity measures, but these were not enough to save the peso, nor the many jobs which were lost in late 2000. Young people started to leave the country in massive numbers, looking for work elsewhere, taking their savings with them. In an attempt to keep these reserves of cash within the country, De la Rúa started the *corralito* (meaning 'little pen'), a law determining that individuals could only withdraw 250 pesos from their accounts per week, and converting savings to government bonds. People literally lost their savings. In December 2001, the people of Buenos Aires and other large cities took to the streets in an unprecedented display both of violent rioting, and peaceful pot bashing by furious middle-class housewives, the *cacerolazos*. The country went through five presidents in a period of a couple of months, but nothing could prevent devaluation, and in January 2002

The Falklands/Malvinas conflict

The dispute between Britain and Argentina over the Falkland Islands/ Islas Malvinas has a long history. Dutch sailor Sebald de Weert made the first generally acknowledged sighting of the islands in 1598. In 1764, France established a small colony there, while the British built an outpost on the northern tip. But when the French government sold Port Louis to Spain in 1766, the British were expelled. In 1811, following the outbreak of the Wars of Independence, Spain withdrew her forces from the islands. And after British warships expelled a force from Buenos Aires in 1833, the islands came under British rule, an act that has angered Argentines ever since.

A hundred years or so later, President Juan Perón was quick to exploit the disputed status of the islands as part of an appeal to Argentine nationalism during his first administration (1946-1955). In 1965, the United Nations called on Britain and Argentina to resolve their differences peacefully, and talks took place but were complicated by the hostility of the islanders themselves towards any change in their status.

In 1982, when the British government reduced its forces in the area, the Argentine military regime seized its chance. President General Galtieri had huge economic problems and thought a successful invasion would unite the population behind him. An Argentine force of 5000 men landed in South Georgia on 2 April 1982, quickly overwhelming the small British garrison without loss of life. The British military and civilian authorities were expelled from the Falklands/Malvinas and the islands' inhabitants placed under an Argentine military governor. Though most Latin American states sympathized with Argentina over the sovereignty issue, many were unhappy with the use of force. Backed by a United Nations resolution and the crucial logistical support of the United States, the British government launched a naval force to regain the islands.

The British reoccupation of the

the peso lost its parity with the dollar. Suddenly Argentina plummeted from being a first world nation on a par with the United States, to being a third world state, with a weak currency, and little hope of bolstering the economy. Huge numbers of Argentines lost their jobs, and many were forced into poverty and homelessness. The blow to the Argentine psyche has been severe. Duhalde was the last of the quick succession of presidents, and he attempted to impose some order, appeasing the IMF by sacking a large number of public employees who were a considerable drain on public spending. However, corruption remained and street crime increased, with an alarming fashion for express kidnappings of members of the wealthier Buenos Aires families. Elections held in May 2003 threatened to return Menem to power, in a brief rush of nostalgia for the days of apparent prosperity. But fearing defeat, before a second election could be held Menem stepped down, and ex-governor of Santa Cruz province, Néstor Kirchner, came to power with a meagre 24% of the country's votes. He was not much liked throughout the country, particularly by islands began on 21 May. They met stiff resistance from Argentine defensive positions around Stanley (Puerto Argentino), but most of the Argentine troops were conscripts, poorly trained, ill-equipped and in the end no match for British forces. On 14 June Argentine forces surrendered. Argentines to this day have never forgotten the fierceness of the fighting. One event is particularly sensitive: the sinking of the *General Belgrano*. The Argentine cruiser had apparently drifted accidently into enemy waters and, while retreating, British forces attacked and sank the cruiser with a huge loss of life. It resulted in nearly a third of the deaths of the entire conflict: over 300 personnel, out of total Argentine casualties of 746 and compared with 256 British soldiers.

The consequences of the war for Argentina were that the military government was discredited: perhaps less by defeat than by its obvious misjudgement, and by the accounts given by returning troops of incompetent leadership and lack of supplies. General Galtieri was replaced as president, and in 1983, Argentina returned to civilian rule. It was such a traumatic event in Argentina's recent history that almost every town and village has a monument to the war, and every year in Rosario the war is remembered in a large parade of veterans. In Buenos Aires the Malvinas monument is located at the base of Parque San Martín, almost at Retiro. In 2010, President Cristina Kirchner spoke of reclaiming the Malvinas, even going as far as seeking 'support' from China and other nations. In her second term in office, President Kirchner raised the issue on several occasions, including writing to Prime Minister David Cameron in January 2013, calling on Britain to relinquish the islands. She also asked Pope Francis to mediate in the dispute in March that year. In the same month, the islanders voted in a referendum on whether to stay a British overseas territory. Almost 100% of those eligible to vote chose to remain so.

landowners and farmers, since he raised taxes on exports to an absurd degree. While unemployment remained rife in Argentina, many criticized Kirchner for maintaining a dependency on Plan Trabajar, the government handout to the unemployed, which some feared was eroding the culture of work.

By October 2005, Kirchner had gained sufficient popular support to win a substantial majority in mid-term congressional elections. At the same time, the economy recovered from a decline of 11% in 2002 to growth of over 8% between 2003 and 2007. Kirchner decided not to run for the presidency in 2007, but his wife, Cristina Fernández de Kirchner, was nominated as a candidate. Her landslide victory may have indicated a desire for continuity among the electorate, but many people saw the move as a way of extending Néstor's chance of holding on to power. In certain media outlets Cristina was labelled a puppet, offering only a continuation of her husband's presidency. At any rate, she was the first elected female president in Argentina, and she has her own webpage, www.cristina.com.ar. Her first years in office were confrontational. An increase in taxes on agricultural exports, for instance, in order to redistribute income from high soya, wheat and corn prices, led to strikes and blockades which caused food shortages, adding to problems of energy shortages and general price rises. In mid-term elections in June 2009 Fernández de Kirchner's party lost its majorities in both houses of Congress. By 2011, though, the picture had changed significantly. Néstor Kirchner died of a heart attack in October 2010, but his widow was not prepared to relinquish power. With the opposition fragmented, she won a big majority in presidential elections in October 2011. Her victory was helped greatly by a thriving economy, which was registering growth of just under 10% a year on the back of healthy commodity prices, with high government spending, falling rates of poverty and unemployment, a significant rise in the minimum wage and a consumer boom. Inflation remained a problem, though (10.6% officially in 2013, unofficially put at three times that) while investment from abroad remained low, deterred by the nationalization of key industries. Other economic factors in 2012, such as a fall in GDP growth to 1.9%, began to accentuate the deep polarization of Argentine society, between those who supported the ruling party's policies and those who did not. Many low income and rural workers were in favour, but the middle classes, for example, grew more antagonistic over rising prices, the severe restriction of the sale of dollars at the official exchange rate in order to limit the use of international reserves to pay off national debts, and levels of crime. Government disputes with the media, especially the Clarín group, intensified.

Following the 30th anniversary of the 1982 Falklands/Malvinas conflict, diplomatic relations with the UK were very strained and remained so into 2013. Soon after Jorge Bergoglio, former archbishop of Buenos Aires, was elected Pope Francis I in March 2013, President Fernández asked him to mediate in the dispute. Francis, the first Latin American pope, had previously had a difficult relationship with the governments of Fernández de Kirchner and her husband, partly because of his dealings with opposition politicians, but also because of disagreements over policy towards abortion and homosexuality (gay marriage, for instance, was legalized in 2010, but the Pope remains opposed).

Mid-term congressional elections in October 2013 highlighted the divisions as Fernández' Frente para la Victoria (FPV) party struggled to maintain its majority in both houses of congress. In key Buenos Aires province polling, FPV lost to Frente Renovador, a dissident Peronist movement led by Sergio Massa, formerly Fernández' cabinet chief. FPV also lost in five other large voting districts and in Fernández's home province of Santa Cruz. Fernández herself was forced to abandon campaigning in October when she was admitted to hospital for brain surgery, from which she had recovered by the end of the year.

Confidence in the economy continued at a low ebb into 2014. Pressure on the peso from inflation, declining international reserves and savers seeking to buy dollars on the unofficial 'blue market' rather than keep their funds in the national currency, forced a devaluation of 15% in January 2014. Less than a year previously the president had vowed that this would never happen. Likewise, restrictions on buying foreign currency were lifted. In May 2014, the government renegotiated its debt to the Paris Club group of creditor countries, an issue dating back to the

2001-2002 crisis, which should allow the country to raise new loans on international markets. Nevertheless, it is clear that economic uncertainty and its political and social ramifications will dominate the final months of Cristina Fernández's presidential term until the next elections in 2015.

Population

With an estimated population of 42,600,000 (2013), the third largest in South America after Brazil and Colombia, Argentina is one of the least densely populated countries on the continent. Forty five per cent of the population lives in the Federal Capital and Province of Buenos Aires, leaving most of Patagonia, for example, with 2 sq km per inhabitant. In the province of Buenos Aires, people are mainly of European origin and the classic Argentine background is of Spanish and Italian immigrants. In Patagonia and the Lake District there's a considerable number of Scottish, Welsh, French, German and Swiss inhabitants, with Eastern Europeans to be found in the northeast of the country. In the northwestern provinces, at least half the population are indigenous, or of indigenous descent, mixed with a long line of *criollo* stock. Although *mestizos* (of mixed Spanish and indigenous origin) form about 15% of the population of the whole country, the existence of different ethnic groups wasn't recognized until the mid-1990s. There are 13 indigenous groups, totalling between 300,000 and 500,000 people, many living in communities in the northwest, and scattered throughout the country. The largest minorities are the *Toba* (20%), the *Wichí* (10%), the *Mapuche* (10%) and the *Guaraní* (10%). Several of the smaller groups are in danger of extinction: in 1987 the Minority Rights Group reported the death of the last Selk'nam/*Ona* in Tierra del Fuego and noted that the 100 remaining *Tehuelches* were living on a reservation in southern Patagonia.

Immigration

The city of Buenos Aires and the surrounding province was transformed through immigration in the 19th century into a society of predominantly European origin. White immigration was encouraged by the 1853 Constitution and the new political stability after 1862 encouraged a great wave of settlers from Europe. Between 1857 and 1930 total immigration was over 6,000,000, almost all from Europe. About 55% of these were Italians, followed by Spaniards (26%), and then, far behind, groups of other Europeans and Latin Americans. British and North Americans generally came as stockbreeders, technicians and business executives. By 1895, 25% of the population of 4,000,000 were immigrants. Over 1,300,000 Italians settled in Argentina between 1876 and 1914. Their influence can be seen in the country's food, its urban architecture and its language, especially in Buenos Aires where the local vocabulary has incorporated *lunfardo*, a colourful slang of largely Italian origin, which started out as the language of thieves. Today it is estimated that 12.8% of the population are foreign born. The large influence on immigration nowadays comes from Bolivia, Peru and Paraguay.

Culture

Religion

Throughout Spanish America the Catholic Church played an important role in the conquest. From the start of the colonial period, Spanish control in South America was authorized by the Papacy; in return the colonial powers were to support the conversion of the indigenous population to Catholicism. This close identification of Church and state helps to explain why the main centres of Church power and activity were usually (though not always) close to the main centres of Spanish settlement. While present-day Argentina, a border territory on the outskirts of empire, was therefore of relatively minor importance to the Church hierarchy, it became a focus for work by missionary orders, particularly the Jesuits. Jesuit activity in Argentina was centred in two areas: around Córdoba, where they established a training college for the priesthood, and in Misiones and adjoining areas of present-day Paraguay and Brazil, where an extensive network of *reducciones* was set up to convert and 'protect' the indigenous population.

As in much of Spanish America, the Church lost most of its formal political power at independence. Although today over 90% of Argentines are officially Roman Catholics, the Church's political and social influence is much less significant than in neighbouring Chile or in most other South American countries. One reason for this is the introduction of a system of non-religious state schools in the 19th century. The great waves of immigration in the late 19th and early 20th centuries also affected the position of the Church; while the majority of immigrants were Catholics, significant minorities were not, including the large numbers of East European Jews and the Arab immigrants from Lebanon and Syria. Both of these communities have a strong presence especially in Buenos Aires; the largest mosque in South America was opened in the capital in September 2000 and there are estimated to be 800,000 Muslims in the country. Buenos Aires also has the eighth largest Jewish population in the world.

Yet the Catholic Church's power and influence should not be underestimated. The support of the Church hierarchy was important in bringing Perón to power in 1946 and the rift with the Church played a key role in the overthrow of the latter in 1955. The strongly conservative nature of the Catholic hierarchy became particularly apparent during the 1976-1983 military dictatorship; unlike its Chilean counterpart, the Argentine hierarchy was silent on the issue of human-rights violations and gave little support to relatives of the disappeared. According to *Nunca Más*, the official report on the disappeared, military chaplains attended some torture sessions and even assisted in the torture.

The lingering influence of the Church can be seen in several ways: the continuing legal ban on abortion (divorce was finally legalized in 1986) and gay marriage, and in the constitutional provision (removed in the 1994 amendments) that required the president to be a Catholic (and which necessitated President Carlos Menem's conversion).

As in some other parts of Latin America, this close identification of the Catholic Church with the state has, in recent years, provided opportunities for evangelical churches, including the Baptists and Mormons, to recruit followers, particularly among newcomers to the large cities.

Arts and crafts

All over Argentina you'll find fine handicrafts made by local indigenous groups, which vary widely all over the country, or by the continuing tradition of gaucho craftsmen, who make fine pieces associated with rural life.

Gaucho crafts
There's a strong tradition of working precious metals, such as silver, into fine belts and buckles, since the gaucho's way of carrying his wealth with him was originally in the ornate silver *rastras* and buckles which are still used today over leather belts, or to tie *fajas* (woven cloth belts). Silver spurs, stirrups and the fine silver decoration on saddles are all extraordinary examples of traditions dating from the early 18th century. The gaucho *facón*, an all-purpose knife used especially for cutting his *asado*, is made with an elaborately wrought silver handle, and the *mate* (the vessel itself, rather than the drink) which is often just a hollowed-out gourd, can also be an exquisitely worked piece of silver which you'd probably rather display than use. Associated objects with the same fine silverwork today include earrings, belt buckles and scarf rings. Leather was always important for making all the items associated with horses, and obviously widely available, and the complexity of the traditional bridles, belts and straps is impressive. Long thin strips of leather are woven into wide plaits, or *trensas*, and used still for all parts of horse bridlery, as well as more decorative pieces. The *mate* itself is made most traditionally from the gourd, but also from wood, tin, llama (a type of material that looks like silver) or silver, with attractive examples made by artisans in the Lake District at El Bolsón, for example.

Indigenous crafts
Argentina's many indigenous groups produce fine handicrafts, and in the northeast, the Guaraní produce woodwork, much of it inspired by the rich animal and bird life all around them. Delicate fabric for bags is woven from the tough fibrous strands of tree creepers, and there are necklaces made from seeds.

Handicrafts are richest in the northwest, particularly the Valles Calchaquíes, near the *puna* and along the Quebrada de Humahuaca, where there is abundant llama wool and vicuña, which is woven into *ponchos*, or knitted into jumpers, socks, scarves and hats. Brightly coloured woven textiles from Bolivia can also be found at many markets. The ubiquitous pan pipes are the most available examples of instruments from the rich Andean musical tradition, and can be found in abundance at Tilcara and Purmamarca markets. Ponchos are woven throughout the northwest but particularly fine examples can be found in the Valles Calchaquíes and around Salta, where the red ponchos of Güemes are made, and in western Catamarca province, where the finest ponchos of woven vicuña are made. You can also find beautiful woven wall hangings in the Valles Calchaquíes, often depicting scenes of churches in the valleys, and the local symbol, the ostrich-like *suri*. Wood from the giant *cardón* cactus is used for carving distinctive small objects and furniture, with the spines of the cactus leaving attractive slits in the wood.

In the Chaco region, bags are made from textile woven from *chaguar* fibre by Wichí, Toba, and other indigenous groups of the area, as they have done for hundreds of years. The Wichí also make fine wooden objects, animals mainly, from *palo santo*, a greenish scented wood, also used extensively in wood carving by communities that live along the Río Pilcomayo, which forms the border with Paraguay. In northeastern Salta, painted wooden masks are made by the Chané culture for use in traditional agricultural ceremonies. Isolated indigenous groups of Toba, Chané and Mataco in the lowlands to the east of the province produce exquisite carvings of birds and animals, using a variety of local woods. Cow bones are used to make the beaks and feet, as well as an inlay to decorate spoons and other utilitarian items. And *Palo santo* is also used for *mate* vessels, replacing the traditional gourd. Throughout the south, there are superb Mapuche weavings in natural wool colours with bold geometric designs.

Fine art and sculpture

Colonial art

Argentina (along with neighbouring Uruguay) is arguably the most European of Latin American cultures. Mass immigration and the 19th-century extermination of the few remaining indigenous people have created a mainstream culture, which defines itself largely in relation to Europe. The exception to this is in the northwest of the country, where Andean civilizations struggle to retain their identity against the irresistible tide of westernization and the tourist industry.

As the region, which is now Argentina, was initially of little importance to the Spanish, there is relatively little colonial art or architecture in most of the country. However, in the northern regions of Salta, Jujuy and Misiones, there are some impressive colonial buildings and some good examples of colonial painting, especially the remarkable portraits of archangels in military uniform in the churches at Uquía and Casabindo, as well as some exquisite golden retables and pulpits in the churches of the Quebrada de Humahuaca. Yavi, at the very north, is the most remarkable of all these, with a golden sculpture of an angel in military uniform, and beautiful ceramic cherubs on the golden pulpit. Fine colonial art can be seen at the Museo de Arte Hispanoamericano Isaac Fernández Blanco in Buenos Aires. In Misiones, there are several sites with remains of Jesuits missions – particularly impressive is that at San Ignacio. Córdoba province too has remains of Jesuit churches and residences at Santa Catalina and Jesús María.

The 19th century

In the 19th century, as Argentina gained independence and consolidated itself as a modern nation, the ruling elite of the country were determined to make

Argentine culture as close to European as possible, against what they saw as the 'barbarism' of indigenous customs. The prosperous Buenos Aires bourgeoisie commissioned European architects to build their mansions and collected European fine and decorative arts to decorate them. Rich Argentines travelled to Europe to buy paintings, and gradually began to demand that European painters come to Argentina to depict the wealth and elegance of the ruling class through portraits and landscapes. The most famous foreign artist was Carlos Enrique Pellegrini, whose fine society portraits can be seen in the Museo Nacional de Bellas Artes in Buenos Aires.

By the middle of the century, as Argentina became more politically stable, a new generation of Argentine-trained artists appeared in Buenos Aires. They absorbed some of the techniques and interests of the European artists who were the first to depict their country, but they also discovered a new interest in Romanticism and Realism. Most famous in this period was Prilidiano Pueyrredón (1823-1870), whom many Argentines consider to be their first national painter. Of more obvious appeal is the rather eccentric Cándido López (1839-1902) whose work has only recently been re-evaluated. López followed the Argentine army to the north of the country during the wars with Paraguay and Uruguay, where he depicted the great battles in a characteristic naïve style. López left behind a remarkable series of paintings, which are often displayed in the Museo Nacional de Bellas Artes in Buenos Aires. By the end of the century, many artists who had been through the National Art School were working in Argentina. Generally speaking, they absorbed European movements decades after they appeared in their original forms. Benito Quinquela Martín's work celebrated the workers in the dockyards of La Boca, in a colourful naïve style, and his paintings can be seen in the gallery bearing his name in La Boca.

The 20th century to the present
In the 20th century, Argentina really found its artistic expression; the dynamism, size and mix of nationalities in the capital created a complex urban society in which artists and intellectuals have prospered. Some of the Bohemian attraction of Buenos Aires can still be felt in its more intellectual cafés and districts. This cultural effervescence has been at the expense of the regions; the capital totally dominates the country, and most artists are forced to move there to have any chance of success.

The first avant-garde artistic movement in Buenos Aires emerged in 1924 with the formation of a group which called itself 'Martín Fierro', in homage to the national epic poem of the same name. This group brought together a small number of upper-class intellectuals, the most famous of which was the writer Jorge Luis Borges. The most important visual artist was Xul Solar (1887-1963), who illustrated many of Borges' texts. Solar was one of the 20th century's most eccentric and engaging artists. He had a great interest in mysticism and the occult, and tried to create an artistic system to express his complex beliefs, mostly small-scale watercolours in which a sometimes-bizarre visionary world is depicted. Many of them are covered in inscriptions in one of the languages he himself created: Neo-Creole or Pan-Lengua. During the final decades of his life Solar lived in a house on the Paraná Delta near Tigre, where he created a total environment in accordance with his fantastic world, even inventing a new game of chess with rules based on astrology. There is now a

Xul Solar Museum in the house where he was born in Buenos Aires and where many of his watercolours and objects are displayed.

Intellectual life in the 1920s was divided into two factions, each named after districts in the city. The elegant Calle Florida gave its name to the Martín Fierro set, which belonged to the elite. Several blocks away, the working-class Boedo district gave its name to a school of working-class socialist artists who rejected the rarefied atmosphere of Florida in favour of socially critical paintings in a grim realistic style. Possibly the most important artist associated with this group was Antonio Berni (1905-1981), whose colourful paintings give a vivid impression of Buenos Aires working-class life, and are in the Museo de Bellas Artes and MALBA in Buenos Aires.

In the 1940s, with the political crisis provoked by the Second World War, a new avant-garde movement emerged to overtake the Martín Fierro group. In the mid-1940s, a group of young artists founded an abstract art movement called 'Madí' which attempted to combine sophisticated abstract art inspired by Russian Constructivism with a more chaotic sense of fun. Madí works are characterized by blocks of bright colours within an irregular frame often incorporating physical movement within the structure of the work. As such, they are somewhere between painting and sculpture. For the first time in Argentina, Madí developed artistic principles (such as the irregular frame, or the use of neon gas) before the rest of the world.

Madí was a short-lived adventure plagued by infighting amongst its members and political divisions. The cultural climate under Perón (1946-1955) rejected this type of 'decadent' art in favour of a form of watered-down populism. It was not until the 1960s that cultural life regained its momentum.

The 1960s were a golden age for the arts in Argentina. As in many countries, the decade brought new freedom to young people, and the art scene responded vigorously. Artistic activity was focused around the centre of Buenos Aires between Plaza San Martín and Avenida Córdoba, an area known as the 'manzana loca' (crazy block). This area contained a huge number of galleries and cafés, and most importantly the Di Tella Institute, a privately funded art centre that was at the cutting edge of visual arts. Artistic movements of the time ranged from a raw expressionism called 'Nueva Figuración' to very sophisticated conceptual art. The most provocative form of art during this period took the form of 'happenings', one of the most famous of which (by Marta Minujin) consisted of a replica of the Buenos Aires obelisk made in sweet bread, which was then eaten by passers-by.

After the military coup of 1966 the authorities began to question the activities of these young artists and even tried to censor some exhibitions. The Di Tella Institute closed, leaving the 'manzana loca' without a heart, and making it more dangerous for alternative young artists to live without harassment (often for little more than having long hair). During the 'leaden years' of the military government during the 1970s, there was little space for alternative art and many left-wing artists abandoned art in favour of direct political action. However, one space in Buenos Aires continued to show politically challenging art: the Centro de Arte y Comunicación (or CAYC), often through works that were so heavily coded that the authorities would not pick up the message.

Since the restoration of democracy in 1983, Argentina has been coming to terms with the destruction or inefficiency of many of its cultural institutions over recent decades. The last few years have seen a rebirth of activity, with improvements in the National Museum of Fine Arts and the creation of the important Centro Cultural Recoleta and more recently the Centro Cultural Jorge Luis Borges and many others. There are important alternative art centres, especially the Ricardo Rojas Centre and the Klemm Foundation, which show some of the most interesting young artists. The art scene in Buenos Aires is very vibrant, with myriad conflicting and apparently contradictory styles and tendencies. For information on exhibitions and local artists see http://artistasdebuenosaires.blogspot.com, an arts blog which started in 2004 (in Spanish) and www.whatsupbuenosaires.com (in English).

Literature

Modern Argentina has an extremely high literacy rate, around 95%, and even in small country towns there are good bookshops, and some really splendid *librerías* in Buenos Aires. Correspondingly, the country has produced some great writers, quite apart from the wonderful Borges, and it is well worth reading some of their work before you come, or seeking out a few novels to bring on your travels.

With an urban culture derived almost entirely from European immigrants, Argentina's literary development was heavily influenced by European writers in the 19th century, the works of Smith, Locke, Voltaire and Rousseau among others being inspiration for the small literate elite of young intellectuals, such as Mariano Moreno (1778-1811), one of the architects of the independence movement. The great theme was how to adapt European forms to American realities, first in the form of political tracts and later in early nationalist poetry. Outside the cities, popular culture thrived on storytelling and the music of the gauchos, whose famous *payadores* are superbly evocative. They recount lively and dramatic stories of love, death and the land, in poetic couplets to a musical background, with an ornate and inventive use of words (see Music, below). Gaucho poets, like medieval *troubadours*, would travel from settlement to settlement, to country fairs and cattle round-ups, singing of the events of the day and of the encroaching political constraints that would soon bring restrictions to their traditional way of life.

The theme of Argentine identity has been a constant through the country's development and remains a burning issue today. While many writers looked to Europe for inspiration, others were keen to distance themselves from the lands they had come from and to create a new literature, reflecting Argentina's own concerns. The extremes within the country further challenge attempts at creating a single unified identity: the vast stretches of inhospitable and uninhabited land, the vast variety of landscapes and peoples, and the huge concentration of population in a capital that little resembles any other part of the country. These conflicts were clearly expressed in 1845 by politician Domingo Faustino Sarmiento (1811-1888): *Facundo: Civilization and Barbarism*. This was the most important tract of the generation, and became one of the key texts of Argentine cultural history. Strongly opposed to the

Federalist Rosas, Sarmiento's allegorical biography of gaucho *Facundo* laments the ungovernably large size of the country which allows *caudillos* like Quiroga and Rosas to dominate. For Sarmiento, the only solution was education and he looked to what he perceived to be the democracy of North America for inspiration.

With the attempt to consolidate the nation state in the aftermath of independence Esteban Echeverría (1805-1851) played a leading role in these debates through literary salons, in poetry and in short fiction. Other memorable protest literature against the Rosas regime included Echeverría's *El Matadero* (The Slaughterhouse, published posthumously in 1871) and José Mármol's melodramatic novel of star-crossed lovers battling against the cut-throat hordes of Rosas, *Amalia* (1855).

The consolidation of Argentina along the lines advocated by Sarmiento and the growth of the export economy in alliance with British capital and technology may have benefited the great landowners of the Littoral provinces. But those who did not fit into this dream of modernity – in particular the gaucho groups turned off the land and forced to work as rural labourers – found their protest articulated by a provincial landowner, José Hernández (1834-1886). He wrote the famous gaucho epic poems *El Gaucho Martín Fierro* (1872) and its sequel, *La Vuelta de Martín Fierro* (The Return of Martín Fierro, 1879). The first part of *Martín Fierro* is most definitely the most famous Argentine literary work and is a genuine shout of rage against the despotic *caudillos* and corrupt authorities, which disrupt local communities and traditional ways of life. Framed as a gauchesque song, chanted by the appealing hero and dispossessed outlaw, it became one of the most popular works of literature, and *Martín Fierro* came to symbolize the spirit of the Argentine nation.

As a small group of families led the great export boom, the 'gentleman' politicians of the 'Generation of 1880' wrote their memoirs, none better than Sarmiento's *Recuerdos de Provincia* (Memoirs of Provincial Life, 1850). As Buenos Aires grew into a dynamic modern city, the gentleman memorialist soon gave way to the professional writer. The key poet in this respect was the Nicaraguan Rubén Darío (1867-1916), who lived for an important period of his creative life in Buenos Aires and led a movement called *modernismo* which asserted the separateness of poetry as a craft, removed from the dictates of national panegyric or political necessity. It was Darío who would give inspiration to the poet Leopoldo Lugones (1874-1938), famous also for his prose writings on nationalist gauchesque themes. Lugones's evocation of the gaucho as a national symbol would be developed in the novel *Don Segundo Sombra* by Ricardo Güiraldes (1886-1927), the story of a boy taught the skills for life by a gaucho mentor.

The early 20th century

The complex urban societies evolving in Argentina by the turn of the century created a rich cultural life. In the 1920s a strong vanguard movement developed which questioned the dominant literary orthodoxies of the day. Little magazines such as *Martín Fierro* (another appropriation of the ubiquitous national symbol) proclaimed novelty in poetry and attacked the dull social-realist writings of their rivals the Boedo group. Argentina's most famous writer, Jorge Luis Borges (1899-1986) began his literary life as an avant-garde poet in the company of writers such as Oliverio Girondo (1891-1967) and Norah Lange (1906-1972). Many of these poets were interested in expressing the dynamism and changing shape of their urban landscape, Buenos Aires, this Paris on the periphery. You can explore Borges' haunts in Buenos Aires with a free tour organized by the tourist office: ask in their information centres for dates and times. Roberto Arlt also caught the dreams and nightmares of the urban underclasses in novels such as *El Juguete Rabioso* (The Rabid Toy, 1926) and *Los Siete Locos* (The Seven Madmen, 1929).

Much of the most interesting literature of the 1930s and 1940s was first published in the literary journal *Sur*, founded by the aristocratic writer, Victoria Ocampo. By far the most important group to publish in its pages were Borges and his close friends Silvina Ocampo (1903-1993), Victoria's sister, and Silvina's husband, Adolfo Bioy Casares (1914-1999) who, from the late 1930s, in a series of short fictions and essays, transformed the literary world. They had recurrent concerns: an indirect style, a rejection of realism and nationalist symbols, the use of the purified motifs and techniques of detective fiction and fantastic literature, the quest for knowledge to be found in elusive books, the acknowledgement of literary criticism as the purest form of detective fiction and the emphasis on the importance of the reader rather than the writer.

Peronism and literature

In the 10-year period of Perón's first two presidencies, 1946-1955, there was a deliberate assault on the aristocratic, liberal values that had guided Argentina since 1880. Claiming to be a new synthesis of democracy, nationalism, anti-imperialism and industrial development, Peronism attacked the undemocratic, dependent Argentine elite (personified in such literary figures as Victoria Ocampo or Adolfo Bioy Casares). This period was seen by most intellectuals and writers as an era of cultural darkness. Some writers such as Julio Cortázar (1914-1984) – a writer of elegant fantastic and realist stories – chose voluntary exile rather than remain in Perón's Argentina. The much-loved novelist, Ernesto Sábato (1911-2011) who later confronted the *Proceso,* set his best novel *Sobre Héroes y Tumbas* (On Heroes and Tombs, 1961) partly in the final moments of the Peronist regime, when the tensions of the populist alliance were beginning to become manifest. (His novella *El Túnel* is also an interesting read). But Perón was not much interested in the small circulation of literature and concentrated his attention on mass forms of communication such as radio and cinema. This period saw further mature work from the poets Enrique Molina (1910-1997), Olga Orozco (1922-1999) and Alberto Girri (1919-1991), whose austere, introspective verse was an antidote to the populist abuse of language in the public sphere. The literary field was to be further stimulated after the downfall of Perón with the development of publishing houses and the 'boom' of Latin American literature of the 1960s.

The 1960s

In Argentina the 1960s was a decade of great literary and cultural effervescence. The novel to capture this mood was Cortázar's *Rayuela* (Hopscotch, 1963), which served as a Baedeker of the new, with its comments on literature, philosophy, new sexual freedoms and its open, experimental structure. It was promoted in a weekly journal *Primera Plana*, which also acted as a guide to expansive modernity. Thousands of copies of *Rayuela* were sold to an expanded middle-class readership in Argentina and throughout Latin America. Other novelists and writers benefited from these conditions, the most significant being the Colombian Gabriel García Márquez (1928-2014), who published what would later become one of the best-selling novels of the 20th century, *Cien Años de Soledad* (One Hundred Years of Solitude, 1967), with an Argentine publishing house. Significant numbers of women writers helped to break the male monopoly of literary production, including the novelists Beatriz Guido (1922-1988) and Marta Lynch (1925-1985) and the poet Alejandra Pizarnik (1936-1972).

Literature and dictatorship

The 'swinging' sixties were curtailed by a military coup in 1966. In the years that followed, Argentine political life descended into anarchy, violence and repression. As a result, virtually all forms of cultural activity were silenced and well known writers, including Haroldo Conti (1925-1976) and Rodolfo Walsh (1927-1977), 'disappeared'. Many more had to seek exile including the poet Juan Gelman, whose son and daughter-in-law counted among the disappeared.

Understandably this nightmare world provided the dominant themes of the literary output of these years. The return in old age of Perón, acclaimed by all shades of the political spectrum, was savagely lampooned in Osvaldo Soriano's (1943-1998) novel *No Habrá Más Penas ni Olvido* (A Funny, Dirty Little War, completed in 1975 but only published in 1982). The world of the sombre designs of the ultra right-wing López Rega, Isabel Perón's Minister of Social Welfare, is portrayed in Luisa Valenzuela's (1938-) terrifying, grotesque novel *Cola de lagartija* (The Lizard's Tail, 1983). Of the narrative accounts of those black years, none is more harrowing than Miguel Bonasso's (1940-) fictional documentary of the treatment of the Montoneros guerrilla group in prison and in exile: *Recuerdo de la Muerte* (Memory of Death, 1984). Other writers in exile chose more indirect ways of dealing with the terror and dislocation of those years. Daniel Moyano (1928-1992), in exile for many years in Spain, wrote elegant allegories such as *El Vuelo del Tigre* (The Flight of the Tiger, 1981), which tells of the military-style takeover of an Andean village by a group of percussionists who bring cacophony.

Within Argentina, critical discussion was kept alive in literary journals such as *Punto de Vista* (1978) and certain novels alluded to the current political climate within densely structured narratives. Ricardo Piglia's (1941-) *Respiración Artificial* (Artificial Respiration, 1980) has disappearance and exile as central themes, alongside bravura discussions of the links between fiction and history and between Argentina and Europe.

The return to civilian rule

Following Alfonsín's election victory in 1983, the whole intellectual and cultural field responded to the new freedoms. Certain narratives depicted in harsh realism the brutalities of the 'Dirty War' waged by the military and it was the novelist, Ernesto

Sábato, who headed the Commission set up to investigate the disappearances. He wrote in the prologue to the Commission's report *Nunca más* (Never Again, 1984): "We are convinced that the recent military dictatorship brought about the greatest and most savage tragedy in the history of Argentina".

Current literature echoes the famous lines by Borges in the essay *The Argentine Writer and Tradition* (1951): "I believe that we Argentines ... can handle all European themes, handle them without superstition, with an irreverence which can have, and already does have, fortunate consequences." While many of the writers that first brought modernity to Argentine letters have died – Borges, Victoria and Silvina Ocampo, Girri, Cortázar, Puig – the later generations have assimilated their lessons. Juan Carlos Martini (1944-) wrote stylish thrillers, blending high and low culture. Juan José Saer (1937-2005), from his self-imposed exile in Paris, recreated his fictional world, Colastiné, in the city of Santa Fe, in narratives that are complex, poetic discussions on memory and language. The most successful novel of recent years is Tomás Eloy Martínez's (1934-2010) *Santa Evita* (1995) which tells/reinvents the macabre story of what happened to Evita's embalmed body between 1952 and the mid-1970s. The narrative skilfully discusses themes that are at the heart of all writing and critical activity. The critic, like the embalmer of Evita's body, "seeks to fix a life or a body in the pose that eternity should remember it by". But what this critic, like the narrator of Eloy Martínez's novel, realizes is that a corpus of literature cannot be fixed in that way, for literature escapes such neat pigeonholes. Instead, glossing Oscar Wilde, the narrator states "that the only duty that we have to history is to rewrite it". The ending of the novel makes the point about the impossibility of endings: "Since then, I have rowed with words, carrying Santa Evita in my boat, from one shore of the blind world to the other. I don't know where in the story I am. In the middle, I believe. I've been here in the middle for a long time. Now I must write again". (*Santa Evita*, New York and London, 1996, page 369.) See Books, page 686, for recommended reading.

Music

Tango is the country's most prominent and most exported musical form, but by no means its only means of musical expression. The traditional music which binds almost the whole country is *folclore* (pronounced *folc-LAW-ray*), whose stirring rhythms and passionate singing can be found in varying forms throughout the northern half of the country. Superb music is produced in the north, in the Andean region of Salta and Jujuy. And home-grown Rock Nacional is the country's main strand of pop music, successfully fending off North American and European competition throughout the 1980s and 1990s to form a distinctive sound.

Tango
If your trip to Argentina includes any time in Buenos Aires, you'll undoubtedly see some tango – probably danced on the streets of Florida or San Telmo, though it's much more than a tourist attraction. Testimony to the enduring success of the music

among Argentines are the radio stations that only play tango, and the *milongas* (dance clubs) filled with young people learning the old steps.

Although also sung and played, the tango was born as a dance just before the turn of the 20th century. The exact moment of birth was not recorded by any contemporary observer and continues to be a matter of debate, though the roots can be traced. The name 'Tango' predates the dance and was given to the carnivals (and dances) of the local inhabitants of the Río de la Plata in the early 19th century, elements of this tradition being taken over by settlers as the local population declined. However, the name 'Tango Americano' was also given to the Habanera (a Cuban descendant of the English country dance) which became all the rage in Spain and bounced back into the Río de la Plata in the middle of the 19th century, not only as a fashionable dance together with the polka, mazurka, waltz and cuadrille but also as a song form in the very popular '*Zarzuelas*', or Spanish operettas. However, the Habanera led not a double, but a triple life, by also infiltrating the lowest levels of society directly from Cuba via sailors who arrived in the ports of Montevideo and Buenos Aires. Here it encountered the Milonga, originally a gaucho song style, but by 1880 a dance, especially popular with the so-called '*Compadritos*' and '*Orilleros*', who frequented the port area and its brothels, whence the Argentine Tango emerged around the turn of the century to dazzle the populace with its brilliant, personalized footwork, which could not be accomplished without the partners staying glued together.

As a dance tango became exceedingly popular and, as the infant recording industry grew in leaps and bounds, it also became popular as a song and an instrumental genre, with the original violins and flutes being eclipsed by the *bandoneón* button accordion, then being imported from Germany. In 1911 the new dance took Paris by storm, thanks to the performance of the dance in a Paris salon by Argentine writer Ricardo Güiraldes, one of a group of aristocrats who enjoyed frequenting the dives where tango was popular. As soon as it was the fashion in Paris, it returned triumphant to Buenos Aires, achieving both respectability and notoriety, and becoming a global phenomenon after the First World War. Actor Rudolph Valentino helped the image of the dance, when his 1926 movie *The Four Horsemen of the Apocalypse* included a tango scene.

But it was Carlos Gardel (1887-1935), Argentina's most loved tango legend, whose mellifluous voice brought popularity to the music of tango, and whose poor background made him a hero for the working classes too. Tango has always been an expression of the poor and of social and political developments in the country. Incredibly, Gardel recorded over 900 songs and was a huge success in many movies. *The Tango on Broadway* (1934) was his biggest success. Today you will still see his image on everything from posters to ice-cream shops, and people still dance to his voice. After Gardel's tragic death in 1935, tango slumped a little, frowned upon by the military regime who considered it subversive. Its resurgence in the 1940s was assisted by Perón's decree that 50% of all music played on the radio must be Argentine. Great stars of this era include the brilliant *bandoneón* player Aníbal Troilo, whose passionate and tender playing made him much loved among a wide audience. In the 1950s, tango again declined, replaced in popularity by rock'n'roll. It had become increasingly the preserve of middle class and intellectual circles, with the emphasis on nostalgia in its themes. But its next innovator and star was Astor Piazzolla (1921-1992), who had played with Troilo's orchestra, and who went on to fuse tango with jazz to create a tango for listening, as well as dancing. Threatened by the military government in the 1970s Piazzollla escaped to Paris, but his success was already international, and his experimental arrangements opened up the possibilities for other fusions. However, in the past thirty years it has made a resurgence and is once again popular with young people in Argentine bars and cafés and it has become a popular dance throughout the rest of the world. A new genre of tango music has arisen which mixes traditional themes with electronica, and groups like The Gotan Project are now world-renowned. All over Buenos Aires, and all over the province, you can find dance classes where the classic moves are taught, followed by a dance or *milonga* where couples, young and old, breathe life into the steps. Part of its attraction, perhaps, is that in the world of tango, men are allowed to be macho and seductive, while their women are required to be sensitive to the subtlety of their next move. Unlike salsa, for example, tango is a dance of repressed passion. Try a class, at least once, while you're in Argentina, to get a feel for the dance from the inside. And then, if you can afford it, see the expert dancers' dextrous footwork at a show such as *El Viejo Almácen* in San Telmo.

Folclore

Beyond Buenos Aires, the dominant musical traditions can be broadly described as *folclore*. This takes various forms over the north of the country, with the finest examples in Salta, but all the northern provinces have a very rich and attractive heritage of folk dances, mainly for couples, with arms held out and fingers clicked or handkerchiefs waved, with the '*Paso Valseado*' as the basic step. The slow and stately Zamba is descended from the Zamacueca, and therefore a cousin of the Chilean Cueca and Peruvian Marinera, where the handkerchief is used to greatest effect. Equally popular throughout most of the country are the faster Gato, Chacarera and Escondido. These are the dances of the gaucho and their rhythm evokes that of a cantering horse with wonderfully stirring syncopation. Guitar and the *bombo* drum provide the accompaniment. Particularly spectacular is the Malambo, where the gaucho shows off his dextrous footwork, creating a complex rhythm using the heels of his boots, alternating with percussion created by whirling the hard balls of the *boleadoras* into the ground, with the spurs of his boots adding a steely note to the rhythm.

Different regions of the country have their own specialities. The music of Cuyo in the west is sentimental and very similar to that of neighbouring Chile, with its Cuecas for dance and Tonadas for song. The northwest on the other hand is Andean, with its musical culture closer to that of Bolivia, particularly on the *puna*, where the indigenous groups play haunting wind instruments, the *quena*, and sound mournful notes on the great long *erke*, evocative of huge mountain landscapes. Here the dances are Bailecitos and Carnavalitos, depending on the time of year. Exquisitely beautiful and mournful songs – the extraordinary high-pitched *Bagualas* – are sung to the banging of a simple drum. And everyone, from children to grandmothers, can quote you a *copla*: two lines of rhymed verse expressing love or a witty joke. Tomás Lipan's music is worth seeking out, especially his *Cautivo de Amor*. Andean bands use the *sikus* (pan pipes) and *charango* (miniature guitar) to create ethereal and festive music which reflects the seasons of the rural calendar. In the northeast provinces of Corrientes and Misiones, the music shares cultural similarities with Paraguay. The *Polca* and *Galopa* are danced and the local *Chamamé* is sung, to the accordion or the harp, in sentimental style. Santiago del Estero has exerted the strongest influence on Argentine folk music as a result of the work of Andres Chazarreta: it is the heartland of the Chacarera and the lyrics are often part-Spanish and part-Quichua, a local dialect of the Andean Quechua language. Listen, too, to Los Caravajal, and Los Hermanos Abalos. Down in the province of Buenos Aires you are more likely to hear the gauchos singing their Milongas, Estilos and Cifras and challenging each other to a Payada or rhymed duel – protest songs and wonderfully romantic and witty stories to guitar accompaniment. Seek out Atahualpa Yupangui's *El Payador Persguido*. Argentina experienced a great *folclore* revival in the 1950s and 1960s and some of the most celebrated groups are still drawing enthusiastic audiences today. These groups include Los Chalchaleros and Los Fronterizos, the perennial virtuoso singer and guitarist, Eduardo Falú and, more recently, León Gieco from Santa Fe. Most famous of all, though, is the superb Mercedes Sosa, whose rich voice articulated much of the sorrow and joy of the last 30 years in a brilliant series of albums, which also include the most popular *folclore* songs. Start with *The Best of Mercedes Sosa*. Also listen to Ariel Ramírez, a famous singer and pianist whose moving *Misa Criolla* is among his best known work. The *cuartetos* of Córdoba, popular since the 1940s with the characteristic dance in a huge circle, can best be sampled in the much-loved records of Carlos 'La Mona' Jiménez.

Rock Nacional

The great stars of Rock Nacional are still much listened to. The movement started in the 1960s with successful bands Los Gatos and Almendra, whose songwriter Luis Alberto Spinetta later became a successful solo artist. But the Rock Nacional found its real strength in expressing unspeakable protests during the military dictatorship from 1976-1983. Charly García, who was a member of the enormously successful band Sui Generis, captured popular feeling with his song *No Te Dejes Desanimar* (Don't be Discouraged), which roused mass opposition amongst young people against the atrocities of the *Proceso*. Inevitably, the military regime cottoned on to this form of subversive behaviour and stopped rock concerts, so that many bands had given up performing by the end of the 1970s. However, the rock movement survived, and the cynical lyrics of Fito Páez in *Tiempos Difíciles* and Charly García in *Dinosaurios* remain as testimonies to that time, and guaranteed them subsequent success. Once democracy had returned, lightweight music became more popular, with likeable output from Los Abuelos de la Nada and Patricio Rey y sus Redonditos de Ricota, Soda Stereo (one of the most significant bands of the 1980s and they are still popular today) and also the work of Fito Páez who has continued to record and whose album *El Amor Después del Amor* was a success across Latin America.

Los Fabulosis Cadillacs and Andrés Calamaro also made some great records, and Charly García continues, undiminished in popularity. The 1980s also saw the rise of punk music in Argentina, with notable acts, such as Los Violadores and Sumo, spearheading a musical scene that continues to this day.

Cinema

Argentina's cinema is one of its liveliest art forms and it has enjoyed a recent renaissance with some brilliant films being made, more in the European or *auteur* tradition, than in Hollywood style. With a couple of worldwide successes and an Oscar for Best Foreign Film with *El Secreto de Tus Ojos* (The Secret of Your Eyes, 2009), Argentine cinema has made its mark on the world stage.

In 1922, Buenos Aires had some 27,000,000 film-goers each year and 128 movie theatres, the largest being the Grand Splendid which seated 1350 people. By 1933 there were 1608 cinemas throughout Argentina, with 199 in the capital. However, the taste of the cinema-going public was for Hollywood movies. Hollywood has dominated the screens in Latin America for the first hundred years of film history, averaging some 90% of viewing time in Argentina.

However, in the 1950s, New Argentine Cinema started as a movement of independent films which offered a far more honest and accurate reflection of life in the country. Film clubs and journals created a climate of awareness of film as an art form and the tenets of Italian neo-realism and the *'politique des auteurs'* of *Cahiers du Cinéma* provided alternatives to the studio-based Hollywood system. In Argentina, Leopoldo Torre Nilsson (1924-1978) explored aristocratic decadence and his early film *La Casa del Angel* (The House of the Angel, 1957) was greeted with praise all over the world. Fernando Birri (1925-) used neo-realist principles to explore the hidden realities of Argentina. His film school in Santa Fe made an important documentary about young shanty town children, *Tire Dié* (Throw us a Dime, 1957) and helped pioneer a more flexible, socially committed, cinema.

Younger film makers of the 1960s like Manuel Antín (1926-), David Kohon (1929-2004) and Leonardo Favio (1938-2012) explored themes such as middle-class alienation or the sexual rites of the youth, set in the cafés and streets of Buenos Aires. Meanwhile, the growing climate of revolutionary sentiment of the late 1960s was reflected in Solanas's *La Hora de los Hornos* (The Hour of the Furnaces, 1966-1968), a key work of populist radicalism.

After a brief spell of radical optimism in the late 1960s and early 1970s, reflected in a number of other nationalist-populist movies, the dream of the second coming of Perón turned into the nightmare that led to the brutal military takeover in March 1976. The spiralling violence affected film-makers as much as artists in any other sector and saw key industry figures threatened and, in some cases, forced into exile. Heavily censored imports, limp comedies and musicals became the norm, the only beneficiaries being foreign producers and distributors. Film-makers such as Solanas, who went into exile, found it difficult to adapt to the new conditions and remained in a cultural wilderness. Within Argentina, the tight military control began to slacken in the early 1980s and some important films were made, including María Luisa Bemberg's (1922-1995) *Señora de Nadie* (Nobody's Woman, 1982) which premiered the day before the invasion of the Falklands/Malvinas.

With the return to civilian rule in 1983, the Radical government abolished censorship and put two well known film-makers in charge of the National Film Institute, Manuel Antín and Ricardo Wullicher (1948-). Antín's granting of credits to young and established directors and his internationalist strategy had an immediate effect. For several years there was a great flowering of talent, a development that would only be halted temporarily by the economic difficulties of the late 1980s. The trade paper *Variety* (25 March 1987) commented on this new effervescence: "Never before has there been such a mass of tangible approval as in the years since democratic rule returned at the end of 1983". In 1986, the Hollywood Academy granted the first Oscar for an Argentine picture, *La Historia Oficial* (The Official History) directed by Luis Puenzo (1946-), which dealt with the recent traumas of the disappearances of the 'Dirty War', but in rather sentimental Hollywood terms. This followed the massive box office success of Bemberg's *Camila,* which commented by analogy on the same subject. Solanas' two films about exile and the return to democracy, *Tangos, el Exilio de Gardel* (Tangos: the Exile of Gardel, 1985) and *Sur* (South, 1988), both offer interesting insights in Solanas' idiosyncratic poetic style. Puenzo, Bemberg and Solanas remained the most visible directors in the 1980s and 1990s, but dozens of other directors made movies in a range of different styles. Lita Stantic made perhaps the most complex film about the 'Dirty War' of the military regime, the superb *Un Muro de Silencio* (A Wall of Silence, 1993). This was a success with the critics, but was ignored by the public who preferred to view politics and repression through a gauze of melodrama and rock music, as in Marcelo Piñeyro's *Tango Feroz* (1993).

Argentine cinema has undergone a revival in recent years, but the hard economic fact remains that by far the vast majority of screens in the country show Hollywood films, and home-grown movies have to compete in very commercial terms. However, prior to *El Secreto de Tus Ojos* (see above), the Oscar nomination of Argentine film *El Hijo de la Novia* (Son of the Bride) in 2002 had boosted national self-confidence, and was a big success within Argentina. Its anti-hero Ricardo Darín also starred in Fabiano Belinski's sophisticated heist movie *Neuve Reinas* (Nine Queens, 2000), which through a labyrinth of tricks and scams neatly articulates a Buenos Aires where no one can trust anyone. It was a huge success worldwide as well as in the country, and the death of Bielinsky following his second film, *El Aura*, was a tragic loss to Argentine cinema.

Successes of the new Argentine cinema included a return to cinema with a social conscience in Adrián Gaetano's *Bolivia*, addressing the sorry plight of an illegal Bolivian worker in urban Argentina, and his *Un Oso Rojo* (Red Bear, 2002) charting the fate of a newly released prisoner trying to reclaim the affection of his daughter from his wife's new boyfriend. Pablo Trapero's *Mundo Grúa* (1999) is a stark but touching portrayal of the life of a crane driver, while his more recent *Elefante Blanco* (2012), confronts the issues of life in a deprived barrio of Buenos Aires, and Lisandro Alonso's astonishing *Libertad* shows with utter honesty the life of a peon on an *estancia*. In Luis Ortega's charming *Caja Negra* (2004) a young woman's relationship with her outcast father and eccentric ancient grandmother is explored with great humour and compassion, while Carlos Sorin's *Bonbón El Perro* (2004), set in Patagonia, introduces a mechanic who dreams of a different life after his adopted puppy wins first prize at a local dog show.

Two other striking films are *Pizza, Birra, Faso* (Pizza, Beer, Cigarettes, 1998) by Stagnaro and Gaetano, and *No Quiero Volver a Casa* (I Don't Want to Return Home, 2001) by Albertina Carri. Lucrecia Martel showed an original voice in her disturbing *La Cienaga* (The Swamp, 2001), a vivid portrayal of a divided family's unhappy summer in their country house. Highly allegorical and rich in atmospheric detail, it's a wonderful contemporary portrait. Her *La Niña Santa* (Holy Girl, 2004) was less successful.

Although most cinemas in the country show Hollywood movies, the larger cities have an art house cinema, and if you happen to be around during any of the film festivals, you can usually catch a few recent Argentine releases: Mar del Plata Film Festival in mid-March; Buenos Aires film festival in mid-April; and Salta's film festival in the first week of December.

Spectator sports

It is said that sport came to Argentina through the port of Buenos Aires, brought first by British sailors, who played football on vacant lots near the port watched by curious locals who would later make it their national passion.

Football is out on its own, both in terms of participation and as a spectator sport, with the country being passionately divided between fans of River Plate and Boca Juniors and reaching fever pitch when the national team reached the 2014 FIFA World Cup final. In second place comes motor racing. The legend of Juan Manuel Fangio in the 1950s is still very much alive and well. Tennis is increasingly popular, especially since there are several successful Argentine tennis players, headed up by Cordobian David Nalbandian and Juan del Potro, both from Tandil. Basketball and volleyball are both popular participation sports among young people, with strong teams in many sizeable towns, and basketball attracts fans since Argentine players play for the NBA in the States.

Although the best **polo** in the world is played in Argentina, it's only accessible to an elite class, due to its cost (although you can watch it without it costing you an arm and a leg). Despite being played throughout the country and all year round, the top Argentine players, who now play all over the world, return only for the high handicap season between September and November. This consists of tournaments, played on the outskirts of Buenos Aires, followed by the Argentine Open, which takes place on Palermo's polo field, known as the 'cathedral of polo'.

Rugby was brought to Argentina by the British over a hundred years ago and is played throughout the country. The national team, Los Pumas, reached the semi-finals of the 2007 Rugby World Cup, and in 2012 they became the fourth team in the Rugby Championship (formerly Tri Nations). Locally, the most popular teams both come from San Isidro, north of the capital.

The Greatest Gardener in Buenos Aires

Next time you look up at the trees along Buenos Aires' streets, or the next time you enjoy the parks in some of Argentina's most important towns, spare a thought for French architect and landscaper Jean Charles Thays. Known as the 'greatest gardener in Buenos Aires', Thays played a large role in 'greening' Argentina by designing botanical gardens, parks and the odd *estancia* all around the country. Born in France in 1849, he had a successful career as principal assistant to leading landscape architect Édouard André until, on his master's advice, he set sail for Argentina for a short visit at the age of 40. He never left and spent the rest of his life designing and remodelling most of Argentina's green spaces, including the botanical gardens and most of the parks. He also built stylized gardens in local hospitals and other public buildings, and planted over 150,000 trees in the streets of Buenos Aires. Not satisfied with just the capital, Thays worked throughout Argentina, and you will see his name all over the place. He is remembered for combining romantic English informality with the French formal garden, as well as his use of open and closed curved roads, lakes with islands, ornamental buildings, sculptures and monuments. He received several awards, including the Légion d'Honneur in France, and when he died in 1934 he was revered for his life's work throughout Argentina and Europe.

Argentina's native sports include the squash-like *pelota paleta* and *pato*, a cross between polo and basketball. Originally played between large bands of gauchos, today, it is played by teams of four horsemen and a football with handles, and is one sport which is unique to Argentina.

Land and environment

Argentina is the second largest country in South America in area, extending across the continent some 1580 km from east to west and 3460 km from north to south. Its northern-most point is at latitude 22°S (just within the tropics); at Tierra del Fuego and Isla de los Estados it extends south of 54°S (the latitude of Scotland or Labrador). The coast of this territory, which extends over 2000 km, runs wholly along the Atlantic apart from the north coast of the Beagle Channel linking the Atlantic and the Pacific. The western border with Chile follows the crest of the Andes, but below 46°S, the drainage is complex and border disputes have arisen ever since the Treaty of 1881 when the principle that the border should follow the watershed was established.

Geology and landscape

Together with Brazil, Paraguay and Uruguay, Argentina is the visible part of the South American Plate which has been moving for the past 125 million years away from its former union with Africa. The submerged part of this plate forms a broad continental shelf under the Atlantic Ocean; in the south this extends over 1000 km east and includes the Falkland Islands/Islas Malvinas. Since the 'break' between the plates, there have been numerous invasions and withdrawals of the sea over this part of the South American continent, but the Andean mountain building from the end of the Cretaceous period (65 million years ago) to the present day dominates the surface geology. Of the many climatic fluctuations, the Pleistocene Ice Age up to 10,000 BC has done most to mould the current landscape. At its maximum, ice covered all the land over 2000 m and most of Patagonia. In the mountains, ice created virtually all the present-day lakes and glaciers, and moraine deposits can be found everywhere. However, the special feature of the heartland of Argentina is the fine soil of the Pampas, the result of ice and water erosion and the unique wind systems of the southern cone of the continent.

The Northwest

Northern and western Argentina are dominated by the satellite ranges of the Andes. Between the mountains of the far northwest is the *puna*, a high plateau rising to 3400-4000 m, on which are situated salt flats or *salares*, some of which are of interest for their wildlife. East of this is the *prepuna*, the gorges and slopes ranging in altitude from 1700 m to 3400 m which connect the *puna* with the plains. On the fringe of the Andes are a string of important settlements including Salta, Tucumán and Mendoza. Though the climate of this region is hot and dry, there is sufficient water to support maize and pasture and a thriving wine industry, mostly relying on irrigation. East of the Andes lies several ranges of hills, the most important of which are the Sierras de Córdoba and the Sierras de San Luis. These are mostly of ancient Precambrian rocks.

The Paraná Basin

The vast Paraná Basin stretches from the borders with Brazil and Paraguay to the Atlantic at Buenos Aires. In the northeast it mainly consists of geologically recent deposits. The easternmost part of this basin, between the Ríos Paraná and Uruguay, is the wettest part of the country. Known as Mesopotamia and consisting of the provinces of Entre Ríos, Corrientes and Misiones, it is structurally part of the Brazilian plateau of old crystalline rocks, the 'heart' of the South American Plate. Here there are undulating grassy hills and marshy or forested lowlands, among them the Esteros del Iberá, an extensive area of flooded forest similar to the Pantanal in Brazil. The horizontal stratum of the rocks in this area is dramatically evident in the river gorges to the north and the spectacular Iguazú Falls shared with Brazil.

The Chaco

Northwest of Mesopotamia and stretching from the Paraná and Paraguay rivers west to the Andean foothills and north into Paraguay and Bolivia lies the Gran Chaco, a vast plain that covers the provinces of Formosa, Chaco and Santiago del Estero, as well as parts of Santa Fe and Córdoba. It is crossed from west to east by three rivers, the Teuco-Bermejo, the Salado and the Pilcomayo. Annual rainfall ranges from 400 mm in the western or Dry Chaco, a semi-desert mainly used for cattle ranching, to 800-1200 mm in the eastern or Wet Chaco, where periodic floods alternate with long periods of drought.

The Pampas

South of 33°S, the latitude of Mendoza and Rosario, is a great flat plain known as the Pampas. Extending almost 1000 km from north to south and a similar distance from east to west, the Pampas cover some 650,000 sq km, including most of Buenos Aires province, southern Córdoba, Santa Fe and Entre Ríos, north eastern La Pampa and a small part of San Luís. This area is crossed by meandering rivers and streams, and there are many lakes, lagoons and marshes. Geologically the Pampas are similar to the Chaco, basic crystalline and granite rocks almost completely overlain with recent deposits, often hundreds of metres thick. Prevailing winds from the southeast and southwest help to create the fine loess-type soils which make this one of the richest farming areas in the world, ideal for grasslands and cattle ranching. Being comparatively close to the ocean, extremes of temperature are rare, another favourable feature.

A distinction is often made between the 'wet' Pampa and the 'dry' Pampa. The former, inland from Rosario and Buenos Aires, is the centre of wheat, maize and other cereal production; the latter, west of 64°W, is where cattle ranching predominates.

The Patagonian steppe

Patagonia extends from the Río Colorado (39°S) south to the Straits of Magellan and covers some 780,000 sq km. Most of this area consists of a series of tablelands and terraces, which drop in altitude from west to east. The basic rocks are ancient, some classified as Precambrian, but the surface has been subjected to endless erosion. Rainfall is lighter and the winds stronger than in the Pampas frequently stripping the surface of cover and filling the air with dust. Only where rivers have scored deep valleys in the rock base can soil accumulate, allowing more than extensive sheep farming.

From the Straits of Magellan north to Lago Argentino (46°S) and beyond, a geological depression separates the edge of the South American Plate from the Andes. Most of Patagonia was under ice during the Quaternary Ice Age and has been rising since the ice receded. This area was presumably the last to be uncovered. However, considerable volcanic activity associated with the uplift of the Andes has taken place along the depression which is transversely divided into basins by lava flows. Alluvial and glacial deposits have created relatively fertile soils in some areas, useful for sheep and producing attractive wooded landscapes in the lake regions in contrast to the general desolation of Patagonia.

The Andes

Geographically the Isla de los Estados forms the southernmost extent of the Andes, which then swing north to become the border between Chile and Argentina just north of the Paine mountains. The 350-km section north of Paine is one of the most dramatic stretches of the Andes. The crest lies under the Southern Patagonian ice cap, with glaciers reaching down to the valleys on both the Argentine and Chilean sides. On the Argentine side this has created the spectacular range of glaciers found in the Parque Nacional Los Glaciares, the most famous of which, the Perito Moreno Glacier, is one of the highlights for many travellers to Argentina. The northern end of this section is Cerro Fitz Roy, which, along with the Torres del Paine (in Chile) at the southern end, is among the most spectacular hiking and climbing centres in South America.

Further north between 46°S and 47°S there is another ice cap, the North Patagonian ice cap, centred on Monte San Valentín on the Chilean side of the border. North of this lies 1500 km of mountain ranges rarely exceeding 4000 m; on the east side of these are a series of attractive lakes, formed by a mixture of glacial and volcanic activity. The high section of the Andes begins at 35°S and includes Aconcagua (6960 m), the highest peak outside the Himalayas. For a further 1000 km northwards, the ranges continue to the border with Bolivia with many peaks over 6000 m, the Argentine side becoming progressively drier and more inhospitable.

Climate

Climate ranges from subtropical in the northeast to cold temperate in Tierra del Fuego, but is temperate and quite healthy for much of the year in the densely populated central zone. Between December and the end of February, Buenos Aires can be oppressively hot and humid. The Andes have a dramatic effect on the climate of the south: although on the Chilean side of the mountains there is adequate rainfall from Santiago southwards, very little of this moisture reaches the Argentine side. Furthermore, the prevailing winds in Patagonia are southwest to northeast from the Pacific. The result is a temperate climate with some mist and fog near the coast, but not much rain. Further inland, the westerlies, having deposited their moisture on the Andes, add strength to the southerly airstream, creating the strong dry wind (*El Pampero*) characteristic of the Pampas. Only when these systems meet humid maritime air in the northeast of the country does rainfall significantly increase, often with violent thunderstorms, and the heaviest precipitation is in Mesopotamia where the summer months are particularly wet.

The highest temperatures are found in the northeast where the distance from the sea and the continuous daytime sunshine produce the only frequently recorded air temperatures over 45°C anywhere in South America. The northwest is cooler due to the effects of altitude, rainfall here occurring largely in the summer months.

Vegetation

Few countries offer as wide a range of natural environments as Argentina; its varied vegetation supports equally diverse wildlife. The main types of vegetation are described below. Details of some of the animals to be seen are given where appropriate in the text; to avoid repetition they are not described here. There are 10 main vegetation types:

Llanura pampeana

Extensive cattle grazing and arable farming have altered the original vegetation of the Pampas, notably through the introduction of tree species such as the eucalyptus for shelter. The least altered areas of the Pampas are the coastal lowlands, the Paraná delta and the southern sierras. The sandy soils of the coastal lowlands, including marshes and estuaries, are home to Pampas grass or *cortadera*. In the marshy parts of the Paraná delta there are tall grasses with *espinillo* and *ñandubay* (*Prosopis*) woods in the higher areas. Willows and alisos grow along the riverbanks while the ceibo, the national flower of Argentina, grows in the nearby woodlands.

Espinal

These are open woodlands and savannahs which extend in an arc around the Pampas covering southern Corrientes, northern Entre Ríos, central Santa Fe, large parts of Córdoba and San Luis and the centre-west of La Pampa. In these areas xerophitic and thorny woods of prosopis and acacia predominate. The major prosopis species are the *ñandubay*; the white algarrobo; the black algarrobo and the caldén. The *ñandubay* is found in Entre Ríos and parts of Corrientes, along with the white *quebracho*, *tala*, *espinillo* and, on sandy soils, *yatay* palms. The white algarrobo and black algarrobo are found in areas of Santa Fe, Córdoba and San Luis which have been heavily affected by farming. The caldén appears across large areas of La Pampa, southern San Luis and southern Buenos Aires, along with bushes such as the alpataco and the creosote bush (*Larrea*).

Monte

Monte is a bushy steppe with a few patches of trees, in areas with rainfall from 80 mm to 250 mm. Covering large areas of San Juan, Mendoza, La Pampa and Río Negro, it can be found as far north as Salta and as far south as Chubut. Vegetation includes different species of the creosote bush, which have small resinous leaves and yellow flowers, as well as thorny bushes from the cacti family and bushes such as *brea*, *retamo* and *jume*. In the northern areas of *monte* the white algarrobo and sweet algarrobo can be found, while the native willow grows along the riverbanks as far south as the Río Chubut.

Puna and prepuna

Low rainfall, intense radiation and poor soils inhibit vegetation in the *puna*, the major species being adapted by having deep root systems and small leaves; many plants have thorny leaves to deter herbivores. These include species of cactus, which store water in their tissue, and the *yareta*, a cushion-shaped plant, which has been over-exploited for firewood, as well as the *tolilla*, the *chijua* and the *tola*. The *queñoa*, which grows to over 5 m high in the sheltered gorges and valleys of the *prepuna*, is the highest growing tree in Argentina. These valleys also support bushes from the Leguminosae family such as the *churqui*, and species of cactus, such as the cardoon and the *airampu*, with its colourful blossom.

High Andean grasslands

Extending from Jujuy to Neuquén, and then in discontinuous fashion south to Tierra del Fuego, these areas range in altitude from 4200 m in Jujuy to 500 m in Tierra del Fuego. Grasses adapted to the cold include *iros*, *poa* and *stipa* as well as some endemic species.

Subtropical cloudforest

Often known as *yungas*, this extends into Argentina from Bolivia and covers parts of the sub-Andean sierras. It is found in eastern Jujuy, central Salta and Tucumán and eastern Catamarca. Its eastern sides receive the humidity of the winds which cross the Chaco from the Atlantic. Winters are dry but temperature, rainfall and humidity vary with changes in latitude and altitude. These forests are important regulators of the water cycle, preventing erosion and floods. It is best seen in three national parks: Baritú, Calilegua and El Rey.

Vegetation changes with altitude. Along the edge of the Chaco at the foot of the hills and rising to 500 m, where there is annual rainfall up to 1000 m, is a transition zone with mainly deciduous trees such as the *palo blanco*, the *lapacho rosado* and *lapacho amarillo* (pink and yellow tabebuia); the *palo borracho* (Chorisia bottle tree), the *tipa blanca* and the huge *timbo colorado* or black eared tree. Higher and reaching from 500 to 800 m in altitude, where there is greater humidity, are montane or laurel forests. Predominant tree species here are the laurel, the jacaranda and the *tipa*; epiphytes (orchids, bromeliads, ferns, lichens, mosses) and climbers are abundant. Above 800 m and rising to 1300-1700 m annual rainfall reaches some 3000 mm, concentrated between November and March. Here myrtle forest predominates, with a great diversity of species, including great trees such as the *horco molle*, a wide range of epiphytes, and, in some areas such as Baritu, tree ferns. Higher still, the evergreen trees are replaced by deciduous species including the mountain pine (*Podocarpus*), the only conifer native to the northwest, the walnut and the alder. Above these are clumps of *queñoa* and, higher still, mountain meadow grasslands.

The Chaco

The eastern or Wet Chaco is covered by marshlands and ponds with savannah and caranday palm groves, as well as the characteristic red *quebracho,* a hardwood tree overexploited in the past for tannin. The Dry Chaco, further west, is the land of the white *quebracho* as well as cacti such as the quimil (*opuntia*) and the palo borracho (*Chorisia*). Similar climatic conditions and vegetation to those in the Dry Chaco are also found in northern San Luis, Córdoba and Santa Fe and eastern Tucumán, Catamarca, Salta, Jujuy, La Rioja and San Juan.

Subtropical rainforest

This is found mainly in Misiones, extending southwards along the banks of the Ríos Paraná and Uruguay. The wet climate, with annual rainfall of up to 2000 mm, and high temperatures produce rapid decomposition of organic material. The red soils of this area contain a thin fertile soil layer which is easily eroded.

This area offers the widest variety of flora in Argentina. There of over 2000 known species of vascular plants, about 10% of which are trees. Forest vegetation rises to different strata: the giant trees such as the *palo rosa*, the Misiones cedar, *incienso* and the *guatambú* rise to over 30 m high. The forest canopy includes species such as strangler figs and the pindo palm, while the intermediate strata includes the fast growing *ambay* (*Cecropia*), tree-ferns, the *yerba mate* and bamboos. Llianas, vines and epiphytes such as orchids and bromeliads as well as ferns and even cacti compete in the struggle for sunlight.

In the hills of northwestern Misiones there are remnants of forests of Paraná pine (*Araucaria angustifolia*).

Sub-Antarctic forest

This grows along the eastern edges of the southern Andes, from Neuquén in the north to Tierra del Fuego and Isla de los Estados in the south. These are cool temperate forests including evergreen and deciduous trees. Species of *nothofagus* predominate, the most common being *lenga* (low deciduous beech), *ñire* (high deciduous beech), *coihue* and *guindo*. The *pehuén* or monkey puzzle tree (*Araucaria araucana*), is found in northwestern and north-central Neuquén. The fungus *llao llao* and the hemiparasitic *Misodendron* are also frequent. Flowering bushes include the *notro* (firebush), the *calafate* (*Burberis boxifolis*) and the *chaura* (prickly heath).

Areas of the Lake District with annual rainfall of over 1500 mm are covered by Valdivian forest and a wider range of species. The *coihue* (southern beech) is the predominant species of *nothofagus*, reaching as far south as Lago Buenos Aires. Below colihue canes form a dense undergrowth; flowers include the *amancay* (alstromeria), mutisias, and near streams, the fuschia. *Arrayán* trees also grow near water, while the Andean Cypress and the *Maiten* grow in the transition zone with the Patagonian steppe. In areas where annual rainfall reaches over 3000 mm, there is a wider range of trees as well as epyphites, ferns, and lichens such as Old Man's Beard. The *alerce* (larch) is the giant of these forests, rising to over 60 m and, in some cases over 3000 years old.

Magallanic forest, found from Lago Buenos Aires south to Tierra del Fuego, is dominated by the *guindo* (evergreen beech) as well as the *lenga*, the *ñire* and the *canelo* (winter bark). There are also large areas of peatbog with sphagnum mosses, and even the carnivorous *Drosera uniflora*.

Patagonian steppe

Plant life in this area has adapted to severe climatic conditions: strong westerly winds, the heavy winter snowfall that occurs in some years, high evaporation in summer, low annual rainfall and sandy soils with a thin fertile layer on top. The northwest of this area is covered by bushy scrublands: species include the *quilembai, molle*, the *algarrobo patagónico*, the *colpiche*, as well as *coiron* grasses. Further south are shrubs such as the *mata negra* and species of *calafate*. Nearer the mountain ranges the climate is less severe and the soil more fertile: here there is a herbaceous steppe that includes *coiron blanco* and shrubs such as the *neneo*. Overgrazing by sheep has produced serious desertification in many parts of the Patagonian steppe.

National parks → *www.parquesnacionales.gov.ar.*

Fortunately in a country so rich in natural beauty, Argentina has an extensive network of reserves and protected areas, the most important of which are designated as national parks. The history of Argentine national parks is a long one, dating from the donation by Francisco 'Perito' Moreno of 7500 ha of land in the Lake District to the state. This grant formed the basis for the establishment of the first national park, Nahuel Huapi, in 1934.

There are 19 national parks stretching from Parque Nacional Baritú on the northern border with Bolivia to Parque Nacional Tierra del Fuego in the far south. Additional areas have been designated as natural monuments and natural reserves and there are also provincial parks and reserves. The largest national parks are all in western Argentina; these include a string of eight parks in the Andean foothills in the Lake District and Patagonia. These make ideal bases for trekking, with *guardaparque* (rangers) offices at main entrances where you can get advice and maps. Argentina has poor maps for trekking and climbing. Those available from the Instituto Geografico Militar in Buenos Aires are badly out of date and do not show all paths and refuges. Before you travel, therefore, it's a good idea to buy a good basic map of the land you want to explore and to search the national parks website for more information (sadly only available in Spanish). Access to the more remote national parks can be tricky without your own transport and you should allow a couple of extra days, especially for the cloudforest parks in the northwest, and for Parque Nacional Perito Moreno (not the one with the Glaciar Perito Moreno in it). Once you reach the parks, you'll find *guardaparques* very knowledgeable and helpful, and many are happy to take time to explain the wildlife and recommend good walks. The main national parks and other protected areas are shown on the map and further details of all of these are given in the text.

The main administration office of the Argentine National Parks authority is at Santa Fe 680, near the Plaza San Martín in central Buenos Aires. Leaflets are available on some of the parks. For more information, see Essentials A-Z, page 45.

Books

Borges, Jorge Luis, *Collected Fiction*, Penguin, UK. Strange, wonderful and sometimes a little off-the-wall, Argentina's most celebrated modern author still captivates.

Chatwin, Bruce, *In Patagonia*, Vintage/Penguin. The classic travel book. A little outdated and old fashioned but this book inspired a generation of travellers to head to Argentina.

Fernández, José, *El Gaucho Martín Fierro*, Longseller, Argentina. The ultimate gaucho poem. Long and a little difficult to read, this poem from 1872 was the first work of literature to glorify gauchos and their lives.

Guevara, Ernesto 'Che', *The Motorcycle Diaries*, Verso, UK. Funny, thoughtful and a ripping read, Guevara's diaries are great to sink into whilst travelling in Argentina.

Granado, Alberto, *Travelling with Che: The Making of a Revolutionary*, Newmarket Press, US. Ernesto Guevara's travelling partner tells his version of their journey together.

McEwan, Colin, ed, *Patagonia: Natural History, Prehistory and Ethnography at the Uttermost Part of the Earth*, British Museum Press. The indigenous cultures of Patagonia and their destruction in the early 20th century. Illustrated, well-written essays.

Palmer, Marina, *Kiss and Tell*, William Morrow, US. The story of a girl falling in love with tango and a tango dancer in the *milongas* of Buenos Aires.

Contents

Footnotes

Basic Spanish for travellers

Learning Spanish is a useful part of the preparation for a trip to Latin America and no volumes of dictionaries, phrase books or word lists will provide the same enjoyment as being able to communicate directly with the people of the country you are visiting. It is a good idea to make an effort to grasp the basics before you go. As you travel you will pick up more of the language and the more you know, the more you will benefit from your stay.

General pronunciation

Whether you have been taught the 'Castilian' pronunciation (*z* and *c* followed by *i* or *e* are pronounced as the *th* in think) or the 'American' pronunciation (they are pronounced as *s*), you will encounter little difficulty in understanding either. Regional accents and usages vary, but the basic language is essentially the same everywhere. In Argentina, the accent is distinctly different to the rest of Latin America in one crucial area. The letters *ll* in all other Spanish-speaking countries are pronounced like the *y* in yellow, in Argentina they are pronounced similar to the *sh* in she. The letter *y* in Argentina is also pronounced like the *sh* in she, instead of the *ee* in feet. Another change is that Argentines tend to use *vos* instead of *tú*.

Vowels

a	as in English *cat*
e	as in English *best*
i	as the *ee* in English *feet*
o	as in English *shop*
u	as the *oo* in English *food*
ai	as the *i* in English *ride*
ei	as *ey* in English *they*
oi	as *oy* in English *toy*

Consonants

Most consonants can be pronounced more or less as they are in English. The exceptions are:

g	before *e* or *i* is the same as *j*
h	is always silent (except in *ch* as in *chair*)
j	as the *ch* in Scottish *loch*
ll	as the *y* in *yellow*
ñ	as the *ni* in English *onion*
rr	trilled much more than in English
x	depending on its location, pronounced *x*, *s*, *sh* or *j*

Spanish words and phrases

Greetings, courtesies

hello	*hola*	I speak Spanish	*hablo español*
good morning	*buenos días*	I don't speak Spanish	*no hablo español*
good afternoon/	*buenas tardes/*	do you speak English?	*¿habla inglés?*
evening/night	*noches*	I don't understand	*no entiendo/*
goodbye	*adiós/chao*		*no comprendo*
pleased to meet you	*mucho gusto*	please speak slowly	*hable despacio*
see you later	*hasta luego*		*por favor*
how are you?	*¿cómo está?*	I am very sorry	*lo siento mucho/*
	¿cómo estás?		*disculpe*
I'm fine, thanks	*estoy muy bien,*	what do you want?	*¿qué quiere?*
	gracias		*¿qué quieres?*
I'm called...	*me llamo...*	I want	*quiero*
what is your name?	*¿cómo se llama?*	I don't want it	*no lo quiero*
	¿cómo te llamas?	leave me alone	*déjeme en paz/*
yes/no	*sí/no*		*no me moleste*
please	*por favor*	good/bad	*bueno/malo*
thank you (very much)	*(muchas) gracias*		

Questions and requests

Have you got a room for two people?
  ¿Tiene una habitación para dos personas?
How do I get to_? *¿Cómo llego a_?*
How much does it cost?
  ¿Cuánto cuesta? ¿cuánto es?
I'd like to make a long-distance phone call
  *Quisiera hacer una llamada de larga
  distancia*
Is service included?
  ¿Está incluido el servicio?

Is tax included?
  ¿Están incluidos los impuestos?
When does the bus leave (arrive)?
  ¿A qué hora sale (llega) el autobús?
When? *¿cuándo?*
Where is_? *¿dónde está_?*
Where can I buy tickets?
  ¿Dónde puedo comprar boletos?
Where is the nearest petrol station?
  ¿Dónde está la gasolinera más cercana?
Why? *¿por qué?*

Basics

bank	*el banco*	expensive	*caro/a*
bathroom/toilet	*el baño*	market	*el mercado*
bill	*la factura/*	note/coin	*le billete/*
	la cuenta		*la moneda*
cash	*el efectivo*	police (policeman)	*la policía*
cheap	*barato/a*		*(el policía)*
credit card	*la tarjeta*	post office	*el correo*
	de crédito	public telephone	*el teléfono público*
exchange house	*la casa de cambio*	supermarket	*el supermercado*
exchange rate	*el tipo de cambio*	ticket office	*la taquilla*

Getting around

aeroplane	el avión	insured person	el/la asegurado/a
airport	el aeropuerto	to insure yourself against	asegurarse contra
arrival/departure	la llegada/salida		
avenue	la avenida	luggage	el equipaje
block	la cuadra	motorway, freeway	el autopista/ la carretera
border	la frontera		
bus station	la terminal de autobuses/ camiones	north, south, east, west	norte, sur, este (oriente), oeste (occidente)
bus	el bus/el autobús/ el camión	oil	el aceite
collective/ fixed-route taxi	el colectivo	to park	estacionarse
		passport	el pasaporte
corner	la esquina	petrol/gasoline	la gasolina
customs	la aduana	puncture	el pinchazo/ la ponchadura
first/second class	primera/segunda clase	street	la calle
left/right	izquierda/derecha	that way	por allí/por allá
ticket	el boleto	this way	por aquí/por acá
empty/full	vacío/lleno	tourist card/visa	la tarjeta de turista
highway, main road	la carretera	tyre	la llanta
immigration	la inmigración	unleaded	sin plomo
insurance	el seguro	to walk	caminar/andar

Accommodation

air conditioning	el aire acondicionado	power cut	el apagón/corte
		restaurant	el restaurante
all-inclusive	todo incluido	room/bedroom	el cuarto/ la habitación
bathroom, private	el baño privado		
bed, double/single	la cama matrimonial/ sencilla	sheets	las sábanas
		shower	la ducha/regadera
		soap	el jabón
blankets	las cobijas/mantas	toilet	el sanitario/ excusado
to clean	limpiar		
dining room	el comedor	toilet paper	el papel higiénico
guesthouse	la casa de huéspedes	towels, clean/dirty	las toallas limpias/ sucias
hotel	el hotel	water, hot/cold	el agua caliente/ fría
noisy	ruidoso		
pillows	las almohadas		

Health

aspirin	la aspirina	diarrhoea	la diarrea
blood	la sangre	doctor	el médico
chemist	la farmacia	fever/sweat	la fiebre/el sudor
condoms	los preservativos, los condones	pain	el dolor
		head	la cabeza
contact lenses	los lentes de contacto	period/sanitary towels	la regla/las toallas femeninas
contraceptives	los anticonceptivos	stomach	el estómago
contraceptive pill	la píldora anti-conceptiva	altitude sickness	el soroche

Family

family	la familia	husband/wife	el esposo (marido)/la esposa
friend	el amigo/la amiga		
brother/sister	el hermano/la hermana	boyfriend/girlfriend	el novio/la novia
		married	casado/a
daughter/son	la hija/el hijo	single/unmarried	soltero/a
father/mother	el padre/la madre		

Months, days and time

January	enero	Friday	viernes
February	febrero	Saturday	sábado
March	marzo	Sunday	domingo
April	abril		
May	mayo	at one o'clock	a la una
June	junio	at half past two	a las dos y media
July	julio	at a quarter to three	a cuarto para las tres/a las tres menos quince
August	agosto		
September	septiembre		
October	octubre	it's one o'clock	es la una
November	noviembre	it's seven o'clock	son las siete
December	diciembre	it's six twenty	son las seis y veinte
		it's five to nine	son las nueve menos cinco
Monday	lunes		
Tuesday	martes	in ten minutes	en diez minutos
Wednesday	miércoles	five hours	cinco horas
Thursday	jueves	does it take long?	¿tarda mucho?

Numbers

one	uno/una	six	seis
two	dos	seven	siete
three	tres	eight	ocho
four	cuatro	nine	nueve
five	cinco	ten	diez

eleven	*once*	twenty-one	*veintiuno*
twelve	*doce*	thirty	*treinta*
thirteen	*trece*	forty	*cuarenta*
fourteen	*catorce*	fifty	*cincuenta*
fifteen	*quince*	sixty	*sesenta*
sixteen	*dieciséis*	seventy	*setenta*
seventeen	*diecisiete*	eighty	*ochenta*
eighteen	*dieciocho*	ninety	*noventa*
nineteen	*diecinueve*	hundred	*cien/ciento*
twenty	*veinte*	thousand	*mil*

Food

avocado	*la palta*	ice cream	*el helado*
baked	*al horno*	jam	*la mermelada*
bakery	*la panadería*	knife	*el cuchillo*
banana	*la banana*	lemon	*el limón*
beans	*los frijoles/*	lobster	*la langosta*
	las habichuelas	lunch	*el almuerzo/*
beef	*la carne de res*		*la comida*
beef steak	*el lomo*	meal	*la comida*
boiled rice	*el arroz blanco*	meat	*la carne*
bread	*el pan*	minced meat	*la carne picada*
breakfast	*el desayuno*	onion	*la cebolla*
butter	*la manteca*	orange	*la naranja*
cake	*la torta*	pepper	*el pimiento*
chewing gum	*el chicle*	pasty, turnover	*la empanada/*
chicken	*el pollo*		*el pastelito*
chilli or green pepper	*el ají/pimiento*	pork	*el cerdo*
clear soup, stock	*el caldo*	potato	*la papa*
cooked	*cocido*	prawns	*los camarones*
dining room	*el comedor*	raw	*crudo*
egg	*el huevo*	restaurant	*el restaurante*
fish	*el pescado*	salad	*la ensalada*
fork	*el tenedor*	salt	*la sal*
fried	*frito*	sandwich	*el bocadillo*
garlic	*el ajo*	sauce	*la salsa*
goat	*el chivo*	sausage	*la longaniza/*
grapefruit	*la toronja/*		*el chorizo*
	el pomelo	scrambled eggs	*los huevos*
grill	*la parrilla*		*revueltos*
grilled/griddled	*a la plancha*	seafood	*los mariscos*
guava	*la guayaba*	soup	*la sopa*
ham	*el jamón*	spoon	*la cuchara*
hamburger	*la hamburguesa*	squash	*la calabaza*
hot, spicy	*picante*	squid	*los calamares*

supper	la cena	vegetables	los legumbres/
sweet	dulce		vegetales
to eat	comer	without meat	sin carne
toasted	tostado	yam	el camote
turkey	el pavo		

Drink

beer	la cerveza	juice	el jugo
boiled	hervido/a	lemonade	la limonada
bottled	en botella	milk	la leche
camomile tea	la manzanilla	mint	la menta
canned	en lata	rum	el ron
coffee	el café	soft drink	el refresco
coffee, white	el café con leche	sugar	el azúcar
cold	frío	tea	el té
cup	la taza	to drink	beber/tomar
drink	la bebida	water	el agua
drunk	borracho/a	water, carbonated	el agua mineral
firewater	el aguardiente		con gas
fruit milkshake	el batido/licuado	water, still mineral	el agua mineral
glass	el vaso		sin gas
hot	caliente	wine, red	el vino tinto
ice/without ice	el hielo/sin hielo	wine, white	el vino blanco

Key verbs

to go	**ir**
I go	voy
you go (familiar)	vas
he, she, it goes,	
you (formal) go	va
we go	vamos
they, you (plural) go	van

	to be ser (permanent state) **estar**
	(positional or temporary state)	
		soy	estoy
I am	soy	estoy
you are	eres	estás
he, she, it is,		
you (formal) are	es	está
we are	somos	estamos
they, you (plural) are	son	están

to have (possess)	**tener**
I have	tengo
you (familiar) have	tienes
he, she, it,	
you (formal) have	tiene
we have	tenemos
they, you (plural) have	tienen
there is/are	hay
there isn't/aren't	no hay

This section has been assembled on the basis of glossaries compiled by André de Mendonça and David Gilmour of South American Experience, London, and the Latin American Travel Advisor, No 9, March 1996.

Menu reader

This is a list of Argentine specialities; for translations of basic food terms, see page 692.

Parrilla and asado

The most important vocabulary is for the various cuts of meat in the *asado*, or barbecue, which you can eat at any *parrilla* or steakhouse.

achuras	offal	*tamales*	corn-flour balls with meat and onion, wrapped in corn cob husks and boiled
chinchulines	entrails		
molleja	sweetbread		
chorizos	beef sausages		
morcilla	blood sausage	*locro*	stew made with corn, onions, beans, and various cuts of meat, chicken or sausage
tira de asado	ribs		
bife ancho	entrecôte steak		
bife angosto	sirloin		
bife de chorizo or cuadril	rumpsteak	*ciervo*	venison
		jabalí	wild boar
lomo	fillet steak	*bife a caballo*	steak with a fried egg on top
chivito	kid		
cerdo	pork	*guiso*	meat and vegetable stew
costilla	pork chop	*matambre*	stuffed flank steak with vegetables and hard-boiled eggs
cordero	lamb		
riñón	kidney		
pollo	chicken	*horipán*	hot dog, made with meat sausage
cocina criolla	typical Argentine food		
empanadas	small pasties, traditionally meat, but often made with cheese or other fillings	*lomito*	sandwich of thin slice of steak in a bread roll, *lomito completo* comes with tomato, cheese, ham and egg
humitas	a puree of sweetcorn, onions and cheese, wrapped in corn cob husks, steamed	*fiambre*	cold meats, hams, salami
		picada	a selection of fiambre, cheeses and olives to accompany a drink

Fish and seafood

cazuela de marisco	seafood stew	*surubí*	a kind of catfish, tender flesh
merluza	hake	*camarones*	prawns
manduví	river fish with pale flesh	*cangrejo*	crab
pejerrey	inland water fish	*centolla*	king crab
pacú	river fish with firm meaty flesh		

Puddings (postre), cakes and pastries

dulce de leche	the Argentine obsession – a sweet caramel made from boiling milk spread on toast, cakes and inside pastries	*media luna*	croissant (*dulce* or *salado* – sweet or savoury)
budín de pan	a gooey dense bread pudding, often with dried fruit	*facturas*	pastries in general, bought by the dozen
flan	crème caramel, an Argentine favourite	*tortilla*	dry crumbly layered breakfast pastry (in northwest)
helados	ice cream, served piled high in tiny cones	*torta*	cake (not to be confused with *tarte*: vegetable pie)

Index → Entries in **bold** refer to maps

Advertisers' index

Acknowledgements

Our warmest thanks go to Nicolás Kugler, who updated the Buenos Aires and the Cuyo sections. Anna Maria would also like to thank Turismo Ushuaia; Alejandro and Frances from Galeazzi-Basily B&B, Ushuaia; Daniel from Tzion B&B, Ushuaia. Thanks also to all the travellers who wrote to Footprint about their experiences in Argentina.

Credits

Footprint credits
Editor: Sophie Blacksell Jones
Editorial assistant: Leonie Drake
Production and layout: Emma Bryers
Maps: Kevin Feeney

Publisher: Patrick Dawson
Managing Editor: Felicity Laughton
Advertising: Elizabeth Taylor
Sales and marketing: Kirsty Holmes

Photography credits
Front cover: Superstock/Yadid Levy
Back cover: Kobby_dagan/
Dreamstime.com

Colour section
Page i: Shutterstock: David Thyberg
Page ii: Superstock: Roger de la Harpe
Page v: Dreamstime: Pablo Caridad/
Dreamstime.com
Page vi: Superstock: Michael Runkel/
Robert Harding Picture Library
Page vii: Superstock: age fotostock;
Hemis.fr
Page viii: Shutterstock: meunierd.
Superstock: Eduardo Dreizzen/
age fotostock
Page ix: Superstock: Hemis.fr.
Shutterstock: A Jellema
Page x: Shutterstock: Ksenia Ragozina.
Dreamstime: Javarman/Dreamstime.com

Printed in India by Thomson Press Ltd,
Faridabad, Haryana

Publishing information
Footprint Argentina
7th edition
© Footprint Handbooks Ltd
January 2015

ISBN: 978 1 910120 019
CIP DATA: A catalogue record for this
book is available from the British Library

® Footprint Handbooks and the Footprint
mark are a registered trademark of
Footprint Handbooks Ltd

Published by Footprint
6 Riverside Court
Lower Bristol Road
Bath BA2 3DZ, UK
T +44 (0)1225 469141
F +44 (0)1225 469461
footprinttravelguides.com

Distributed in the USA by
National Book Network, Inc.

Footprint Mini Atlas
Argentina

PARAGUAY

Jujuy
Salta
Cafayate
Tucumán
Santiago del Estero
Catamarca
La Rioja

Formosa
Puerto Iguazú
Resistencia
Corrientes
Posadas
Mercedes

BRAZIL

Pacific Ocean

San Juan
Córdoba
Mar Chiquito
Santa Fe
Paraná
Mendoza
San Luis
Río Cuarto
Rosario
San Rafael

URUGUAY

BUENOS AIRES
La Plata

CHILE

Santa Rosa
Tandil
Neuquén
Bahía Blanca
Mar del Plata

San Martín de los Andes
Lago Nahuel Huapi
Bariloche
El Bolsón
Esquel

Viedma

Puerto Madryn
Trelew
Península Valdés

Atlantic Ocean

Lago Buenos Aires
Perito Moreno

Comodoro Rivadavia

Puerto Deseado

Puerto San Julián

El Chaltén
Lago Viedma
Lago Argentino
El Calafate

Falkland Islands/
Islas Malvinas

Puerto Natales

Río Gallegos

West Falkland/
Gran Malvina

East Falkland/
Isla Soledad

Punta Arenas
Río Grande
Tierra del Fuego

CHILE ARGENTINA

Ushuaia

N

200 km
200 miles

Altitude in metres
4000
3000
2000
1000
500
200
0
Neighbouring Country

National highway including Pan-American Highway
Paved road
Unpaved all weather road
Seasonal unpaved road, track
Rail

Map 2

Map 5

Map 6

Index

Distance chart

Buenos Aires																		
1121	Catamarca																	
689	432	Córdoba																
939	836	894	Corrientes															
1525	565	878	873	Jujuy														
1142	156	453	992	721	La Rioja													
1042	730	675	1443	1296	580	Mendoza												
1161	1469	1167	1911	2045	1319	834	Neuquén											
1005	1158	1207	322	1175	1314	1759	2085	Posadas										
1019	820	874	19	857	970	1436	1896	341	Resistencia									
2504	3015	2583	3326	3461	3036	2728	1874	3476	3292	Río Gallegos								
1497	537	850	845	120	693	1268	2017	1147	829	3419	Salta							
1110	623	585	1435	1164	449	168	1002	1763	1419	2799	1136	San Juan						
791	685	412	1192	1229	535	255	784	1510	1185	2461	1201	323	San Luis					
485	773	342	557	1105	795	903	1357	866	537	2773	1069	927	652	Santa Fe				
1352	1863	1431	2174	2319	1884	1576	722	2338	2154	1140	2281	1647	1313	1621	Trelew			
1193	233	546	748	332	389	964	1713	1070	732	3129	304	832	918	743	1977	Tucumán		
3090	3601	3169	3912	4047	3622	3314	2460	4062	3878	586	4019	3385	3061	3359	1726	3715	Ushuaia	
911	1621	1191	1802	2069	1644	1336	567	1897	1717	1640	2041	1407	1083	1184	508	1737	2226	Viedma

Distances in kilometres   1 kilometre = 0.62 miles

Map symbols

□	Capital city	- - - -	Cable car	⑤ Bank
○	Other city, town	++++	Funicular	@ Internet
	International border	⚓	Ferry	♪ Telephone
	Regional border		Pedestrianized street	☎ Market
⊖	Customs	) (	Tunnel	✚ Medical services
	Contours (approx)	→	One way-street	P Parking
▲	Mountain, volcano	IIIIIII	Steps	Petrol
⊐	Mountain pass	≍	Bridge	⚑ Golf
	Escarpment		Fortified wall	∴ Archaeological site
	Glacier		Park, garden, stadium	♦ National park,
	Salt flat	●	Sleeping	wildlife reserve
	Rocks	❶	Eating	☀ Viewing point
	Seasonal marshland	❶	Bars & clubs	▲ Campsite
	Beach, sandbank		Building	⌂ Refuge, lodge
⊌	Waterfall	▪	Sight	Castle, fort
⌐	Reef	▪▪	Cathedral, church	Diving
	Motorway	☗	Chinese temple	Deciduous, coniferous,
	Main road	⛩	Hindu temple	palm trees
	Minor road	⚲	Meru	⇔ Hide
- - - -	Track		Mosque	Vineyard, winery
....	Footpath	⛤	Stupa	Distillery
	Railway	✡	Synagogue	Shipwreck
+∎	Railway with station	■	Tourist office	✕ Historic battlefield
✈	Airport	⛨	Museum	1 Detail map
☒	Bus station	✉	Post office	Related map
Ⓜ	Metro station	Ⓟ	Police	

Ben Box

One of the first assignments Ben Box took as a freelance writer in 1980 was subediting work on the *South American Handbook*. The plan then was to write about contemporary Iberian and Latin American affairs, but in no time at all the lands south of the Rio Grande took over, inspiring journeys to all corners of the subcontinent. Ben has contributed to newspapers, magazines and learned tomes, usually on the subject of travel, and became editor of the *South American Handbook* in 1989. He has also been involved in Footprint's Handbooks on *Central America & Mexico*, *Caribbean Islands*, *Brazil*, *Peru*, *Peru, Bolivia & Ecuador* and *Cuzco & the Inca Heartland*. Having a doctorate in Spanish and Portuguese studies from London University, Ben maintains a strong interest in Latin American literature. In the British summer he plays cricket for his local village side and year round he attempts to achieve some level of self-sufficiency in fruit and veg in a rather unruly country garden in Suffolk.

Anna Maria Espsäter

Originally from Sweden, Anna Maria Espäter first started discovering Latin America at 20, when she moved to Mexico to teach and work in an orphanage. Based in London for many years, she works as a freelance travel and food writer, specializing in Latin America and Scandinavia. Despite having visited 90 countries to date, Latin America remains one of her favourite places to roam and write. She hopes to return to Argentina for some quality steak and red wine before long. www.annamariaespsater.co.uk

Chris Wallace

Chris Wallace has been travelling through, and writing about, Central and South America since 2004. He has lived in Colombia, Argentina, Chile, Brazil and Peru. He has spent long weekends at family *fincas* in Antioquia, travelled along both ends of the Amazon river, failed at tango classes in Buenos Aires, and made frequent escapes to Valparaíso to receive the palliative benefits of coastal air and electric pink sunsets. He has tailored travel and tourism content for entrepreneurs and publishers alike, having covered events as grand and life-affirming as Barranquilla's Carnival festival on some days while dealing with tragic history by writing about Argentina's Dirty War on others. More than 10 years in, he feels he's barely scratched the surface of what this continent has to offer. Having said that, his primary goal is to see more monkeys.